CYBERNETICS AND SYSTEMS '86

CYBERNETICS AND SYSTEMS '86

Proceedings of the Eighth European Meeting on
Cybernetics and Systems Research,
organized by the Austrian Society for Cybernetic Studies,
held at the University of Vienna, Austria, 1-4 April 1986

Edited by

ROBERT TRAPPL

University of Vienna and
Austrian Society for Cybernetic Studies

D. Reidel Publishing Company

A MEMBER OF THE KLUWER ACADEMIC PUBLISHERS GROUP

Dordrecht / Boston / Lancaster / Tokyo

Library of Congress Cataloging in Publication Data

European Meeting on Cybernetics and Systems Research
    (8th : 1986 : University of Vienna)
    Cybernetics and systems '86.

    Includes index.
    1. Cybernetics–Congresses. 2. System theory–Congresses. 3.
Systems engineering-Congresses. I. Trappl, Robert. II. Österreich-
ische Studiengesellschaft für Kybernetik. III. Title.
Q300.E88 1986   001.53   86–598
ISBN-13:978-94-010-8560-1   e-ISBN-13:978-94-009-4634-7
DOI: 10.1007/978-94-009-4634-7

Published by D. Reidel Publishing Company
P.O. Box 17, 3300 AA Dordrecht, Holland

Sold and distributed in the U.S.A. and Canada
by Kluwer Academic Publishers,
190 Old Derby Street, Hingham, MA 02043, U.S.A.

In all other countries, sold and distributed
by Kluwer Academic Publishers Group,
P.O. Box 322, 3300 AH Dordrecht, Holland

To the Memory of
Professor Francis de Paula Hanika (1900-1985),
a scientist, a manager, a friend.

Patrons

Dr.Heinz Fischer,
Federal Minister of Science and Research
Dr.Helmut Zilk,
Mayor of the City of Vienna
Magn.Professor Dr.Wilhelm Holczabek,
Rektor of the University of Vienna

Chairman

Professor Dr.Robert Trappl
President, Austrian Society for Cybernetic Studies

Sponsors

Federal Ministry of Science and Research
Municipality of Vienna
Vienna Tourist Board

Programme Committee

Professor B.Banathy (USA)
Dr.R.Brachman (USA)
Professor G.Broekstra (The Netherlands)
Professor C.Carlsson (Finland)
Professor W.W.Gasparski (Poland)
Professor F.de P.Hanika (UK) +
Dr.W.Horn (Austria)
Professor N.C.Hu (China)
Professor H.Huebner (Austria)
Professor G.J.Klir (USA)
Professor C.A.Kulikowski (USA)
Professor H.Maurer (Austria)
Dr.J.G.Miller (USA)
Professor M.Nowakowska (Poland)

Professor G.Pask (UK)
Professor M.Peschel (GDR)
Professor P.K.M'Pherson (UK)
Professor F.Pichler (Austria)
Professor W.-D.Rauch (FRG)
Dr.J.Retti (Austria)
Professor L.M.Ricciardi (Italy)
Dr.N.Rozsenich (Austria)
Professor L.Troncale (USA)
Professor R.Trappl (Austria)
Acad.Ya.Tsypkin (USSR)
Professor S.A.Umpleby (USA)
Professor R.Vallee (France)
Dr.J.Warfield (USA)

Secretary General

Mag.Michael Schulte-Derne

Organizing Committee

Dipl.Ing.E.Buchberger
Dr.W.Buchstaller
Prof.F.de P.Hanika +
Dr.W.Horn
P.Hotko
P.Martin +
Prof.Dr.F.Pichler
E.Plechl

Dr.J.Retti
K.Schmid
Mag.M.Schulte-Derne
Mag.U.Stadler
Prof.Dr.R.Trappl
Dr.H.Trost
S.Wiesbauer
Mag.C.Zeller

LIST OF CONTENTS

Designing and Systems

Chairperson: W.Gasparski (Poland)

Humanity, Architecture, and Conceptualisation

Chairperson: G.Pask (UK)

Cybernetics in Biology and Medicine

Chairpersons: G.Porenta (Austria)
               L.M.Ricciardi (Italy)

Cybernetics of Socio-Economic Systems

Chairpersons: K.Balkus (U.S.A.)
                  O.Ladanyi (Austria)

Fuzzy Sets - Meeting of the EURO Working Group

Chairperson: C.Carlsson (Finland)

Systems Engineering for Design Automation

Chairpersons: K.Kellermayr (Austria)
                 F.Pichler (Austria)

Methodological Improvements and New Applications of Expert Systems

Chairpersons: W.Horn (Austria)
              C.A.Kulikowski (U.S.A.)

Knowledge Based Natural Language Processing

Chairpersons: R.Brachman (U.S.A.)
                H.Trost (Austria)

Artificial Intelligence / Symbolic Computation

Chairperson: B.Buchberger (Austria)

PREFACE

This volume contains all papers presented at the Eighth European Meeting on Cybernetics and Systems Research. 169 draft papers were submitted for evaluation. In the process of careful refereeing, 33 papers were rejected and the remaining authors were invited to submit final papers. Out of these, 119 were accepted for presentation at the conference and publication in this volume. These papers were prepared by 173 scientists, authors and co-authors, from 22 European and non-European countries, with different cultural, social, and economic structures.

Everybody tried hard to make this conference and its proceedings a true representation of state-of-the-art research worldwide: The members of the Programme Committee and the Chairmen of the Symposia were selected among the internationally leading scientists. Great care was taken not to make this conference a "European" or even "Austrian" one. We are happy and proud to hear that these "European Meetings" (the name is a purely traditional one) are recognized as <u>the</u> internationally leading conferences in cybernetics and systems research. Important scientists from all over the world carefully prepare their papers, containing their most recent research findings, and then enjoy the discussions with their colleagues.

The conference was overshadowed by the severe loss of two colleagues who had cooperated from the beginning in 1972: Professor Francis de Paula Hanika and Mr. Paul E. Martin. Prof. Hanika, just having retired in 1970 from his position as professor for management science, encouraged the Austrian Society for Cybernetic Studies to organize the first European Meeting on Cybernetics and Systems Research. Or, to be more precise, he was the driving force through all our meetings and, even though he pulled a little bit back when he reached his 80ies, he still was the grand old man behind the scene who we turned to whenever we needed advice or encouragement. It will be very difficult for us to find a replacement for him, not only in his capacity as long-term chairman of the symposia on cybernetics of organization and management of the Meetings (this Eighth Meeting was the first without it), but also as a friend and advisor. If you want to know more about Professor

Hanika and his very outstanding and unusual life, I recommend reading the obituary in "Cybernetics and Systems: An International Journal", Vol. 15, Nos. 3 - 4, 1984. You will then understand why this volume is dedicated to his memory.

Paul Martin was a great organizational help throughout all the meetings, and a very dear person, too: I remember when in 1972 we were sitting in our small office, just a few days before the conference, and we didn't know which task to tackle first, a man entered our room, just saying: My name is Paul Martin. How can I help you? I think this is the best characterization I can give of his kind personality and the assistance he always offered to people in need. -

A conference and one of its results, the proceedings, only become a reality as the result of the concerted efforts of many persons: First of all, I would like to thank the contributors who undertook so many important and interesting research projects, then were forced to condense their results to eight pages, and to submit them rapidly to make the proceedings available already at the Meeting. Second, I thank the chairmen - regretfully, there is no woman among them - of the symposia of the Meeting: they helped in the selection of the topics, often invited scientists to contribute, helped in the evaluation of the papers, and finally chaired their sessions. They joined me in the Editorial Board of this volume. Third, Ms. Steffi Wiesbauer and Mag. Michael Schulte-Derne handled all organizational tasks with diligence and care, even remaining friendly when scientists, asked to stick to the eight-page limit, sent a second - "shortened" - version, still of ten or more pages. Fourth, I am most grateful to my co-worker, Dr.Werner Horn: He not only organized the "computer-background" of the Meeting, but also was an unfailing source of help; we often burnt together the midnight-oil when preparing this conference and its proceedings. And fifth, Reidel Publishing Company and especially Mr.Ian Priestnall were very cooperative during all stages of the preparation of this volume.

I think you will enjoy studying "Cybernetics and Systems '86". Perhaps you are even persuaded to join our group at its Ninth Meeting in 1988 in charming Vienna. See you then.

Robert Trappl

IS 'CYBERNETICS AND SYSTEMS RESEARCH' A SYSTEM? A SCIENTOMETRIC ANALYSIS

Anna Lewicka-Strzalecka
Design Methodology Unit
Department of Praxiology and the Science of Science
Institute of Philosophy and Sociology
Polish Academy of Science
Nowy Swiat 72
00-330 Warsaw
Poland

ABSTRACT. This paper presents an attempt at the scientometric analysis of systems science. Science was treated as an information system in which the carriers of information are scientific publications. It was assumed that the sets of bibliographic citations listed by these publications constitute the information stream guiding this system. The material which was analyzed consisted of papers presented in Vienna at the Seventh European Meeting on Cybernetics and Systems Research (1984).

1. AN INFORMATION MODEL OF THE DEVELOPMENT OF SYSTEMS SCIENCE

This article belongs to the ever larger group of systems studies whose subject is systems science itself. These studies present and evaluate the state of research, accomplishments, its possibilities, trends and barriers in the development of this science. The nature and results of these works depend on the understanding of systems science accepted by their authors and the model assumed, e.g. historical, logical, etc. One of the possible ways of analysis in the science of science supplying important information about the discipline studied is to treat science as an information system. Such a model was accepted in this article, though the quantitative method of investigating this system is called scientometric. The basic assumption of the information model in dealing with the development of science as a process of processing and obtaining information is based on the fact that new scientific works as a rule originate on the foundation of previous accomplishments of science, that is information generated within science itself.

The main carriers of information are scientific publications, and the set of bibliographic citations which they present can be regarded as a system that can be subjected to various kinds of statistical analyses. Analysis of this system allows us to trace information flows between publications, for these are recorded in the form of bibliographic

1

R. Trappl (ed.), Cybernetics and Systems '86, 1–8.
© *1986 by D. Reidel Publishing Company.*

citations.

The material analyzed, whose results are presented below, consisted of articles presented in Vienna at the Seventh European Meeting on Cybernetics and Systems Research and published under the editorship of R. Trappl in the book 'Cybernetics and Systems Research 2' (which will be referred to henceforth with the abbreviation CSR).

2. DYNAMICS OF THE INFORMATION STREAM

If we assume that information flows are recorded by means of bibliographical citations, the information stream for a certain group of scientific works is defined as the set of all publications cited by these works. Accordingly, the CSR information stream is understood as the set of all 1660 works cited in the 134 articles published in CSR. The number of CSR bibliographical citations from successive years is presented in Fig. 1.

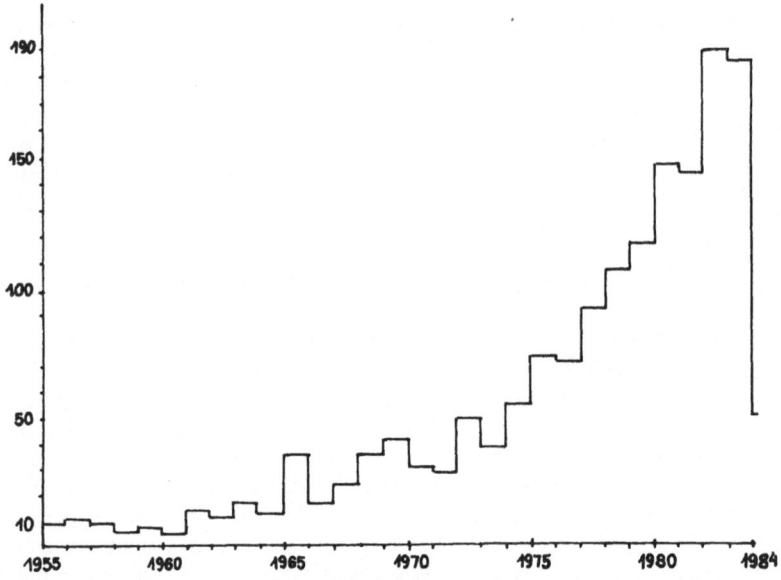

Figure 1. The number of CSR bibliographic citations from succesive years.

49 works published or to be published in 1984 is not small, considering that CSR appeared in April, 1984. Moreover, since most cited works are 1 - 2-years-old, the information stream is received with only slight delay. The average age of a cited work is 8.5 years. Figure 2. presents cumulated numbers of CSR bibliographical citations from successive years. It follows from the scientometric analyses of systems science carried out by Klir, Rogers (1977) that there was a very intensive growth in the number of systems publications in the years 1945-1976. The index of doubling was 4 years, wheras the number of all scientific publications doub-

2

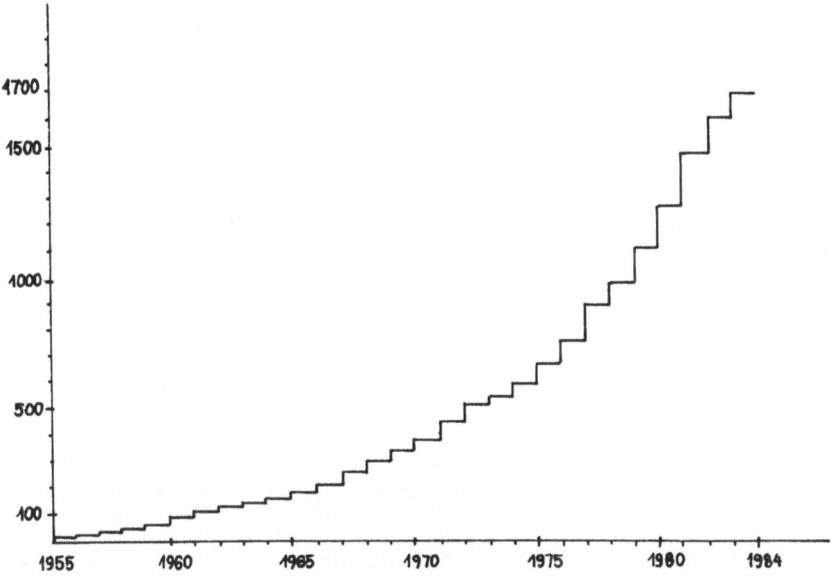

Figure 2. Cumulated numbers of CSR bibliographic citations.

les every 8 years. So on the one hand the number of new works that can be a source of information (potential candidates for citation) grows rapidly and on the other, as mentioned earlier, the information stream is received with only slight delay. Hence one can summe that the rapidity of renewal of the information stream in systems science is proportional to the size of this stream, which is expressed by the equation

$$\frac{dS}{dt} = aS \qquad a > 0 \qquad (i)$$

where a can be interpreted as a constant describing the discipline with respect to its controlability by the internal information stream. From the solution of equation (i) it follows that the information stream is described by the equation

$$S(t) = ae^{kt} \qquad (ii)$$

The graph presented in Fig. 2 suggests that the curve of the CSR information stream is indeed exponential and in that case can be described by the formula

$$S(t) = S(1955)e^{k(t-1955)} \qquad (iii)$$

The aptness of formula (iii) depends on the strenght of the linear connection between t and logS. This relation is presented in Fig. 3. The regression equation has the form: $y = 2.46 + 0.49(t-1969)$ and very closely approximates this relation (coefficient of correlation r=0.98).

3

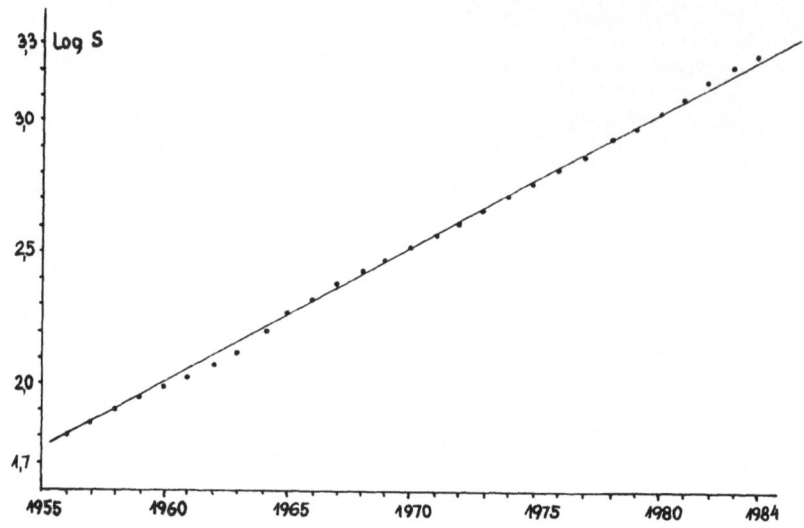

Figure 3. Dynamics of the CSR information stream.

3. DEGREE OF MUTUAL COUPLINGS OF CSR PUBLICATIONS

Evaluation of couplings between articles included in CSR was made by means of a method suggested by Kessler (1963). It was assumed that a single item of reference used by two papers was defined as a unit of coupling between them. One of the criteria formulated on such a basis is as follows:

Criterion A: "A number of papers constitute a related group G_A if each member of the group has at least one coupling unit to a given test paper P_0." (Kessler, 1963, p.10)

Using the above criterion, 134 CSR papers were analyzed. Each paper was successively taken as a test paper P_0, seeking couplings with the other 133 papers. This generated 134 G_A groups. The results of this analysis are presented in table I. The number of papers in each group varies from zero, meaning that the test paper is not coupled with any of the other articles, to eleven, which means that the test paper (in this case G. Klir's article) is coupled with 11 of the other papers.

What do these results show? In order to interpret them meaningfully they were compared with results obtain for 4 other scientific disciplines. These comparisons are presented in table II. They suggest considerable differentiation of structure in the front of scientific investigations in various disciplines. The most compact is the information stream in physics, the most scattered in mathematical statistics. Philosophical works are characterized by few couplings, while the front of scientific investigations in management science is completely scattered. The results obtained for CSR are very interesting against this background. It

4

Table I. The number of G_A groups containing N papers.

Number of papers N in group	Number of groups containing N papers	
	absolute	relative (%)
0	56	41.79
1	26	19.40
2	11	8.2
3	14	10.44
4	3	2.24
5	5	3.73
6	8	5.97
7	1	0.75
8	4	2.98
9	3	2.24
10	2	1.49
11	1	0.75

Table II. Share of G_A groups containing N papers in 5 scientific disciplines. The source of the data are: Nalimow, Mulczenko, 1969 and Langowska, 1984.

Number of papers N in group G_A	Share of G_A groups containing N papers (%)				
	Physics	Statist.	Phil.	Mang. Sci.	CSR
0	19	50	80	98.8	42
1	9	17	10	1.1	19
2,3,4	34	21	9	0	21
5 or more	38	12	0	0.1	18

turns out that the information stream is not only less scattered than in the cases of philosophy and management science but is also more compact than in mathematical statistics. Yet systems science is far-flung science, heterogeneous (owing to the subject and the method of investigation), interdisciplinary and beset with serious conceptual and terminological difficulties. The indexes obtained showing the relatively compact information stream of CSR supply grounds for hypothesizing the existence among systems researchers of certain common conceptual and methodological constructs. This would mean that of the programmatic tasks placed before systems science by SGSR - which suggests facilitating the unity of science by improvement of communication among specialists - does not seem as hopeless as is often believed. Obviously, this a tentative hypothesis whose verification requires more comprehensive investigations.

4. THE STRUCTURE OF THE CSR INFORMATION STREAM

As Troncale (1985) notes, identifying the first barrier in the development of systems science, the lack of agreement on the definitions of the basic terms of this science also concerns the terms delimiting its individual sectors. This causes certain difficulties in systematization. It seems that the method based on the criterion of bibliographic couplings could be an effective instrument making it possible to state the degree of comactness of individual sectors, the degree of their coupling with other sectors and as a result the justifiability of isolating systems science from among other sectors. Such investigations should be carried out on a sufficiently large bibliographical base. Consequently, the CSR analyses presented below are mainly methodological propositions. They can be summarized as follows. The couplings between 134 CSR papers was established on the basis of the bibliographic lists of each of them. It was assumed that the unit of internal coupling in a sector is a pair of papers included in this sector and coupled by at least one common citation. The unit of external coupling of a given sector with other sectors is a pair of papers coupled by at least one common citation, among which one belongs to this sector and the other to any one of the other sector. Table III. presents the degree of internal and external couplings for individual sectors.

Table III. The degree of internal and external couplings for individual CSR sectors.

Sector	Share of pairs of papers coupled by common citations (%)	
	internally	externally
1.General Systems Methodology	4.2	1.5
2.System and Decision Theory	4.2	1.4
3.Cybernetics in Biol. and Medic.	3.8	0.3
4.Cybernetics in Org. and Mang.	2.5	1.1
5.Economic and Social Systems	7.2	1.5
6.Health Care Systems	0.0	0.2
7.Fuzzy Sets	22.7	1.8
8.Communications and Computers	0.0	0.3
9.Humanity, Arch. and Conceptualizm	15.5	1.0
10.Artificial Intelligence	8.6	0.4

From this table it follows that sector 7 is unquestionaly the most compact sector, which means that the information stream Fuzzy Sets is the least "fuzzy". The level of external couplings in this sector is also high in comparoson with other scientific disciplines. Sectors 9, 10 and 5 have a relatively high level of compactness of information streams. No external couplings were found in sector 6 (perhaps because this was the least numerous sector) or in sector 8, which may indicate communications disturbances among specialists on communications and computers. In most of the sectors the level of internal couplings is higher than the level of external ones – which in a certain way (quantitatively) would justify the separateness of those sectors formed in a qualitative way. An exception are sectors 6 and 8, which owing to the lack of internal couplings are more (though also weakly) coupled with their "surroundings".

The structure of a set of objects can also be investigated by searching for configurations of these objects in space with a smaller number of dimensions. The configuration presented below results from the analysis of this type. The correspondence analysis (Benzecri, 1973) was used. Each of the objects (CSR papers) was described by means of a nominal scale whose classification categories respectively are bibliographical items cited at least once. From the calculations a configuration of sectors was obtained that is presented in Fig. 4. Though the explanatory

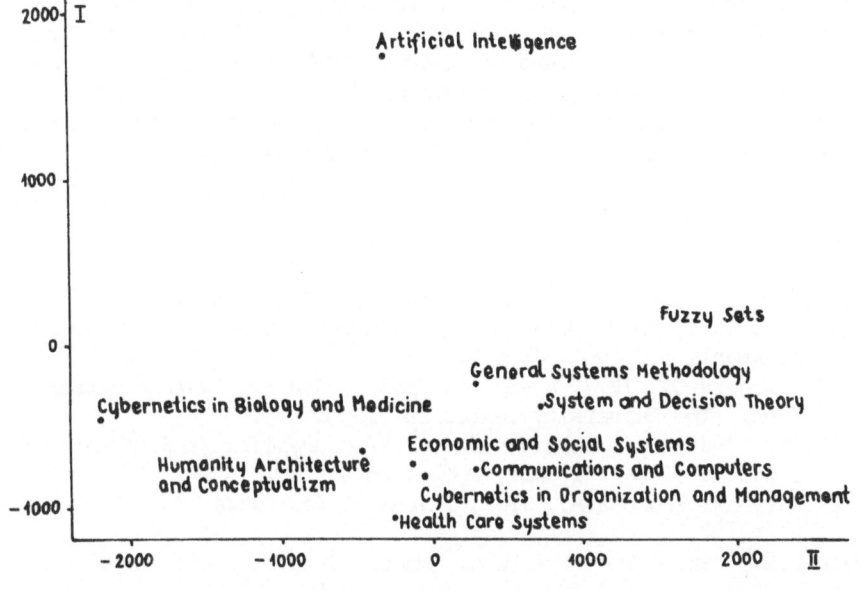

Figure 4. Configuration of CSR sectors obtained by the method of correspondence analysis.

power of the two dimensions obtained is not high (owing to the low indexes of quality of projecting the least numerous sectors), a certain qualitative interpretation suggests itself. The first dimension (horizontal) could be interpreted as closedness (separateness), i.e. the more internal couplings in a given sector in comparison with all the coup-

7

lings of that sector, the greater the coordinate of this sector in this
dimension. The second dimension can be examined as the degree of coupling with the information stream of the Fuzzy Sets sector.

5. CONCLUSION

The aim of this paper was to show what kind of new information about the
dynamics and structure of scientific discipline can be obtained through
scientometric analysis. As already mentioned, this method seems to have
special advantages in the case of systems science and should be a valuable supplement to qualitative and subjective evaluations. The results
presented above are a result of the static analysis of a small, though
seemingly rather representative, fragment of this science. Three possible directions of continuing and expanding analyses of this type come
to mind. The first would be to expand the bibliographical base to include papers published in periodicals (e.g. those which Troncale mentions,
1985, p.53) as well as book publications. Thanks to this, one could not
only investigate the structure of systems science, but also determine
the scope and character of its couplings with other disciplines. The
second trend would be to extend the temporal horizon, which would make
it possible to follow changes of various indexes of the information
stream over time. Finally, the third trend would be to introduce new indexes and improve methods of their statistical analysis.

REFERENCES

Benzecri J,P., 1973, *L'analyse des donnees* , Paris, Dunod.
Kessler M.M., 1963, 'Bibliographic Coupling Between Scientific Papers',
American Documentation, vol.14, no 1.
Klir G.J., Rogers G., 1977, *Basic and Applied General Systems Research:
A Bibliograohy*, The University Center at Binghamton.
Langowska U., 1984, *Systemowa analiza nauki o organizacji i zarządzaniu
w Polsce w latach 1963-1976*, WSP, Opole, In Polish.
Nalimow W.W., Mulczenko Z.M., 1969, *Naukomietria*, Nauka, Moskwa, In Rus-
sian.
Troncale L.R., 1985, 'The Future of General Svstems Research: Obstacles,
Potentials, Case Studies', *Systems Research*, vol.2, no 1.

General Systems Methodology

Chairperson: G.J.Klir (U.S.A.)

PHYSICAL CYBERNETICS; ITS ELEMENTARY LAWS

C. Bogdanski
Zakład Fizyki i Biofizyki W.S.R.P.
19, Novotki street - Pawilon "F"
08110 Siedlce
Poland

ABSTRACT. Instead of double description —one physical and
other cybernetic— of systems of our Universe, an integrated
approach, conceivable under the term "PHYSICAL CYBERNE-
TICS". It concerns not only one of peculiar groups of systems
—case of Biocybernetics, Psychocybernetics, Social Cybernetics
. . .— but concerns all regulatory events, called "Regulons" (R).
Modeling of the types belonging to the substantial R is based
upon the synergical activity of states being adopted in the properties called "cardinal"; states being differentiated in function
of the model's position on both: 1) scale of the metric dimensions and 2) scale of the relative time of appearence of the
first representative of each model. Spatiotemporal considerations
concerning the differenciation of systems in our Universe.

1. INTRODUCTION

The Greek term "physis" means "nature" and PHYSICAL SCIEN-
CES were devoted —at their begining— to the description of all
spontaneousely organized objects. Unfortunatly, Physics has later
restricted its epistemological range to abiotic objects exclusively.
Such a restriction resulted from two folloving factors:
    - the evolution of the approach methodologies in Physics,
consisting in the replacement of the descriptive by the mathematical formalization;
    - the increase of the number of models of newly discove-
red objects and introduction of the numerous systems constructed by Man, to the expanding nomenclature.
    The two above mentionned, factors —as well some other
ones— have inspired an idea to eliminate certain objects from
the Classical Physics nomenclature, especially those which may
involve difficulties (principles responsible to their manifestations
being not sufficiently known) as concerns their formalization procedure. We should evoke here especially the physical (We have
put here an adjective "physical" because each of the discrimina-

11

R. Trappl (ed.), Cybernetics and Systems '86, 11–18.

ted objects, such as Biotic or a Social = poli-biotic system, is composed --on its molecular level-- of the classical physical systems.) systems which have a very complex both architecture and structures and an organic origin. The rejected groups of systems are now dissipatively studied in some nonphysical disciplines, such as Biology, Sociology and Psychology.

The fact of the discrimination --from the physical nomenclature-- of a large number of models of very interesting systems, has provoked a lake of holistic points of view on the totality of the physical Universe in Classical Physics, born in the XIX-th Century. Century, during which Sciences were divided into many specialised disciplines and have manifested --in general-- a deap cleavage into two groups called "exact sciences" and "human sciences". When --in the XX-th century-- Cybernetics has introduced (see N.WIENER, ref. 6) the principles of self-organization and self-regultation $^{(+)}$, it was possible to start to formalize the totality of systems without making a discrimination according to strict limits of scientific disciplines.

Cybernetic principles have then been adopted into different classical disciplines and this fact has provoked the emergence of some new binomic developments such as Bio-cybernetics, Socio-cybernetics, Psycho-cybernetics, etc. Strangely enough, a cybernetic approach in the field of Physics, to be called for example : Physical Cybernetics, has never appeared.

The non existence of such a field has provoked a persistence of a deplorable continuation of double formalism of systems: the one conforming to the physical methodology, and the other to the cybernetic one.

Therefore, it seems now not up-to-date to propose, some foundations of a very well integrated binomic discipline called either PHYSICAL CYBERNETICS or CYBERNETIC PHYSICS.

2. METHODS

We propose to consider here in the first place:
§ 1 - a family of dynamic events --which manifest a periodicaly repetitive kinetic phenomena in conformity with the self-regulating principle-- under the common name : "Regulon". In the present paper, this family is multihierarchically subdivided according to the following taxonomy key (For the symbols explanation --and some examples-- see Table I.):

FAMILY :   R
Category :   Ru   Rs
Sub-cat :   Rue   Rum   Rsn   Rsa
Type :
Sub-type :
(+)

Systems supported by --at least-- one negative feed back (n.f.b.); the kind of the n.f.b. is a function of the architectural parameters immanent to the Event under study.

12

§ 2 – a totality of the known Regulons of our Universe under two ––fundamental in Physics–– aspects : SPACE and TIME. This in the Kartesian three-dimensional coordinate system with the axes adopted as follows :

Dm = Space occupied by the Event, corresponding to its metrical Dimension (Dm), that is:
- either : the average Event′s diameter (Dmϕ) ; case of each Rs ;
- or : the wavelength (λ) ; case of each Ru ;

T = Time corresponding to this rhythmicity period which concerns self-regulation phenomena occuring in the Event′s whole level;

t_r = relative time of the self-organization datum of the first representative of the Event′s model under study.

To be able to process the data obtained from this Kartesian approach ––without discrimination against any of those Events whose parameters have been evolutively deviated–– a Nomography technics is introduced.

§ 3 – the Rs-category of Regulons with a special attention, because the formalization of the another Regulons′category ––the Ru one–– was started yet a hundred years ago in Physics (MAXWELL and others ; from then, more recently, it was supplemented in a cybernetic language by G. SCHMIDT, ref. 5) and we have now a physical branch in Physics, devoted to the Ru-studies, called : Undulatory Physics!.

In contrast to this fact, there does not exist a physical branch devoted to the study of the representatives of Rs-category under their wholeness aspect.

Unfortunatly, principal modelable types of the Rs-category (see Table II) don′t represent a homogenous series of parameters. Fact, which contrasts with a homogenous series corresponding to the types of each of two spectra belonging to the Ru-category.

Consequently, studies on the Rs-types representatives are dissipated between different disciplines, especially between the following ones:
- PHYSICS (types "P" + "A" and poli-A = "M") ;
- CHEMISTRY (type "M") ;
- BIOLOGY (type "B") ;
- SOCIOLOGY (type poli-B = "S").

To be able to realise ––adequately–– inside the Rs-category, the inter-types comparison study, it was indispensable to search for such properties, which would be applicable to each type model belonging to this category. Finaly, we have selected ––for this purpose–– a properties group baptised by us : "cardinal properties" (see table III). Each of these properties can adopt one of its two, virtualy possible, antinomic states. A typicaly peculiar assembly of such a states constitutes a part ––the cardinal part–– of a systemogenic algorithm. Part, which ––according its typically nuanced variation– serves as support for the self-organization of each of the type-model within the Rs-category.

13

3. FAMILY OF REGULONS

Regulon constitutes a dynamical Entity, which --whithin a deter-
minated classification unity (such as Rue, Rum and Rs)-- manifests, on its global level, a positive correlationship between its
2 fundamental, spatiotemporal, properties : Dm and T.

It can be stated out that the T-value determines the Regulon's spatial expansion range, so that the Dm-value can be considered as an optimised product, issued from the systemo-urgical
processes.

Since $T = 1/N$, it seems to be interesting to remark,
here, that N --in the case of Ru-- is generaly considered as a value being directly proportional to the
energy level on which is placed the Event being studied. In an analogus way should be considered the
problem of energy level within the Rs-category.

Four common denominators, concerning a totality of the representatives of the Regulon family are presented in the Table IV.

4. PROPOSAL OF THE THEORETICAL APPROACHES
   OF THE Rs-CATEGORY OF REGULONS

While the theoretical foundations of the Ru-category of Regulons
were elaborated relatively early, the theory of the Rs-category is
still inexistant in Physics. Therefore, we are obliged to focuss
a special attention to the problem of elaboration of an adequate
theory, which will be suitable for the formalization purposes. We
propose to built it on the basis of the following three groups of
the Rs-category properties (p.) :

1^O - p. which are common to all Regulons; that are four properties belonging to this family, which were already presented in
Chapter III (see again Table IV) ;

2^O - p. whose description has emerged from a comparative
study between Rs and Ru ; eight elementary differences resulting
from this study, were published by the present author already
in 1982 (ref. 2) ;

3° - p. being specific for each type within the Rs-category.

5. MODELS OF Rs WHICH --FOLLOWING THE DOCTRINE OF
   CLASSICAL PHYSICS-- ARE INEXISTANT IN THE NOMEN-
   CLATURE OF PHYSICAL SYSTEMS

We should mention here --in the first line-- two types models :
the "B"-model and the poli-B = "S" one. These models have not
been introduced to the books of Classical Physics, in spite of the
fact that each of their representatives is built --on its molecular
level-- from systems being undoubtedly recognized as physical
systems (= representatives of the "M" model belonging to the Rs-category).

Type "B" can be distinguished, from other Rs-types, by its peculiar assembly of parameters concerning especially the following properties:
- architecture (often a multihierarchical one);
- structure patterns (very complex on many architectural levels);
- shape (often irregular);
- dynamics (growing based on the metabolism principle; self-replication $(+)$ supported by a specific matrix, etc.);
- kinetics (high number of the degrees of freedom);
- informatics (n. f. b. supported by the i_T-state channels).

The adoption of the biotic singularity, in the above mentioned properties, is deductible from the peculiar position of Biogenesis $(++)$ on the Dm-scale, namely: on its meso-physical level. There where a very peculiar assembly of states $(a_{a-c}, d_{pol-2}, k_a, i_T)$ was adopted in cardinal properties. Assembly to be considered as a cardinal part of the biogenic algorithm: this systemogenic algorithm which is responsible —within the types of the Rs-category— of the "B"-model self-organization (see Table V).

It should be underlined here that Biogenesis-point is situated, on the Dm-scale, inside the zone which corresponds to the maximal intensity of the complexification phenomena. An organization of such a zone derives from a convergence phenomenon of two forces fields (therefore "pol-2" in d_{pol-2}):
- the one concerning the micro-physics (Electrostatic field);
- the other concerning the macro-physics (Gravitational field);

The $d_{pol-2(E+G)}$ state implies appearance of a very high degree number of motion freedom (k_s) and if k_a concerns structurogenic processes: a self-organization of very complex structures. On the basis of both: very compact (a_a) and very complex (a_{a-c}) architecture: the Trans-substantial channels (i_T) have emerged to ensure the system´s n.f.b. The above mentioned states series can be expresses —under its implicative aspect— as follows:
$$Dm\phi \Longrightarrow d_{pol-2(E+G)} \Longrightarrow k_a \Longrightarrow a_{a-c} \Longrightarrow i_T \Longrightarrow \text{n.f.b. ensuring } Dm\phi$$

Living organisms are —on the Dm-band— evolutionary $(+++)$ expanded and constitute, now, a B-band of ten orders of magnitude, from 10^{-8} to 10^2m. Such extension has provoked a very high degree of diversification of parameters weights concerning many systemogenic factors and has conducted to the appearance of very large quantity of new patterns in the representatives of "B"-model. Each
$(+)$
a cell self-replication can be considerated —in a context with the Ru-category self-replication phenomena which occure within the propagaton phenomena— as an atavistic manifestation.
$(++)$
= self-organization of the first representative of the "B"-model
$(+++)$
Evolution is to consider on the t_r-scale, where we are placed ourself, now, in the Zero-point. Biogenesis is there placed in the minus 10^9 years-point.

15

of the new differentiated "B"-subtype —for example each species—
is supported simultaneousely by two parts of the systemogenic
algorithm (see again Table V):

    1 - an extinsible part (= assembly of parametric weights
which change in $f(Dm)$);

    2 - the cardinal part (remaining constant for all "B"-repre-
sentatives)

    <u>Type "S"</u>. We should insist here, at first, on the interest
which can have a "B"-representative to become fragment of
"S"-system. Interest, consisting on the fact that "B" —through
a sociogenic polimerisation phenomenon ("B" $\Longrightarrow$ poli-B = "S")—
can avoid its maximal size limitation (genetically programmed and
supported by the fact that with the $Dm\phi$ increase diminues both
surface/mass ratio and metabolic rate).

    Some preliminary conditions should be filled —by the "B" re-
presentitives— to be possible their metamorphose from "B" to the
B-fragment of "S". We should evoke, here, in the first line, a necessity to have a singular architecture a_{a-cs}, representing a sociogenic variant of the a_{a-c} state (state which is common to all
"B"-representatives). This singular architecture comprise 3 inital
sociogenic conditions concerning the following levels :

    § 1 - <u>the anatomical one</u>: self-organization of an adequate
servo mechanisms to ensure an autonomic locomotion   of each
socialised B-fragment within the poli-B = "S" system ;

    § 2 - <u>the organogenic one</u>: development —in the socialisable
"B" system— of a suitable organs, able to ensure both: emission
and interception of signals belonging to the sociogenic field (f.ade-
quate for the species being studied) ;

    § 3 - <u>the organogenic cerebral one</u>: sufficiently high deve-
lopment of the brain structure to be possible a self-constitution of
the predominance of an endodeterminative phenomena on the exo-
determinative ones, especially as concerns the behaviour of the
virtually socialisable "B"-system (to that can develop a socio-urgic
instinct).

6. CONCLUSIONS

Instead of double, physical and cybernetic, description of the
Events of our Universe, it appears preferable to make an integrated approach, notably the one called "Physical Cybernetics", based
on the uniform treatment of all self-regulatory Events, called
Regulons.

    To be able to consider the Regulons family in the global
scale, it is necessary to develop the theory of their Rs-category.

    For more details see ref. 1; 3 and 4.

7. BIBLIOGRAPHY

(1) - Bogdanski C. -1981- "Introduction to Cybernetic Physics",

Kybernetes (London), Vol. X, pp. 179-192.

(2) - Bogdanski C. -1982- "Concept cybernétique de systémo-génése pour la Théorie Générale des Systémes, Cybernetica (Namur), Vol.XXV, NO 3, pp. 167-191; see p. 186.
(3) - Bogdanski C. -1982- "Basic Elements of Cybernetic Physics" Abstracts Book of Sixth European Meeting on Cybernetic and Systems Research, Vienna, 13-15 April 1982, Proceedings edited by North Holland Publ. Co, Amsterdam, pp. 573-578.
(4) - Bogdanski C. -1985- "Théorie Générale des Systémes; Aspects dimensionnels et applications (en Physique, Chimie, Biologie et Sciences Sociales), Académie Polonaise des Sciences, Centre Scientifique à Paris; Conférences, Fascicule 134. Edité par PWN, Varsovie. 54 pp.
(5) - Schmidt G. -1971- "Kompendium der Physik", Jena, VEB Gustav Fischer Verlag.
(6) - Wiener N. -1954- "Cybernétique et Société", Union Générale d'Editions.

Table I : Taxonomy of Regulons
Categories of Regulons (R) : Ru and Rs
Ru = undulatory R (= Waves)
    Rue = Ru belonging to the electromagnetic spectrum (types
            from "cosmic rays" one to the "radio waves" one) ;
    Ruv = Ru belonging to the elastic vibration spectrum, called
            "material waves" (types: phonons, hypersounds, ultra-
            sounds, sounds, infrasounds) ;
Rs = substantial R (= natural self-regulatory systems)
    Rsn = non aggregated architecture Rs (types : "P", "A", "S";
            see Table II);
    Rsa = aggregated architecture Rs (types: "M" and "B"; see
            Table II).
Each R-type can be subdivided into subtypes, for example :
"B"-type can be subdivided into the following subtypes: Bu,Ba,Bp
    Bu = unicellular "B"
    Ba = acellular "B"
    Bp = pluricellular "B".
"Visible" - type can be subdivided into the following subtypes:
    Violet,
    Blue,
    Green,
    Yellow,
    Orange,
    Red

Table II : Principal Types of Rs-category
"P" : astro-Planetary system
"A" : Atom
"M" =poli-A : Molecule
"B"=poli-M : Biotic system
"S"=poli-B : Social system

<u>Table III</u> : Cardinal properties
and their binary antinomic states

MECHANICAL GROUP :

"d" = <u>d</u>ynamics (concerning the forces being responsible of the system's fragments interactive integration)

"k" = <u>k</u>inetics on the system's fragments trajectories inside the system's area

"a" = system's statics, manifested by its <u>a</u>rchitecture.

INFORMATIONAL GROUP :

"i" = <u>i</u>nformational channels between system's fragments

ANTINOMIC STATES VIRTUALLY POSSIBLE IN CARDINAL
PROPERTIES :

Property ;   its states :   Property ;   its states :

"a" a_a = aggregate   "k" k_s = stereotypical
        a_n = non aggregate k_a = astereotypical

"d" d_{mon} = monodynamical   "i" i_T = Trans-substantial
        d_{pol} = polydynamical i_E = Extra-substantial

<u>Table IV</u> : Common properties in the Regulons Family

Properties common to the whole Regulons'Family	The self-regulation of each Regulon is supported by --at least-- one negative feed back (n.f.b), the kind of the later is function of the R-band being studied : T=reg.period; $1/T = \nu \implies$ n.f.b. kind
Properties which are common to Regulons within the framework of the defined R-class: Rue, Rum, Rs	$$\frac{Dm/T \doteq Cte}{Cte = c \text{ or } Cte = c \cdot k_M \,;\, k_M \approx 10^{-5,7}}$$ (case of Rue) (cases of Rum+Rs)
	Existence —within the following classes: Rue; Rum; Rs— of the typical bands.

<u>Table V</u> : Rs-systemogenesis algorithm

Part :	Examples concerning the types :	
	"A"	"B"
1th: cardinal	$\Sigma(a_n, d_{mon}, k_s, i_E)$	$\Sigma(a_{a-c}, d_{pol-2}, k_a, i_T)$
2nd: parametrical	parametrical weights of all "A"-systemo-genic factors	parametrical weights of all "B"-systemo-genic factors

18

FINITE DECOMPOSABLE SEQUENTIAL SYSTEMS IN THE CATEGORY OF SEMIGROUPS

W. Jacak, I. Sierocki
Institute of Technical Cybernetics
Technical University of Wrocław
50-370 Wrocław
Poland

ABSTRACT. The notion of decomposable finite sequential system in the category of semigroups is introduced. The paper deals with the reducibility, controllability and p-definiteness properties. It is shown that many statements concerning the linear systems preserve their validity for the systems considered in this paper. For example it is proved that, under certain assumptions, the observability problem for reduced systems under considerations can be solved on the basis of a simple, single experiment.

1. INTRODUCTION

Let us recall that a finite sequential system S (finite automaton) is an ordered 5-tuple $S = (U,X,Y,f,g)$, where U is a finite input alphabet, X - a finite state-set, Y is a finite output alphabet, $f:X \times U \rightarrow X$ - a one-step transition function, $g:X \rightarrow Y$ - an output function.
In [1] using the category-theoretic approach, the notion of a decomposable dynamical (sequential) system in a category K was introduced. Remind that a decomposable finite sequential system in a category K is defined as follows: U,X,Y are finite objects of K, the function f is determined by two morphisms $a:X \rightarrow X$, $b:U \rightarrow X$, and the function g is equal to a morphism $c:X \rightarrow Y$. Therefore, a decomposable finite sequential system S can be identified with an ordered 6-tuple $S = (U,X,Y,a,b,c)$. In the case when K is the category of vector spaces over a finite field, a decomposable system is said to be linear [5]. The case when K is the category of abelian groups was investigated exhaustibely by M.A. Arbib in [6]. In turn, W. Brockett and A. Willsky [2] have introduced the notion of finite group homomorphic sequential system, i.e. they have considered the case when K is the category of groups. The theory of such systems was next developed in [4,5,9,10].
Our paper can be regarded as a further generalization of the notion of linear sequential system. Namely, we are going to deal with decomposable sequential systems determined in the category of semigroups (monoids). We shall show that many statements concerning the linear sequential systems preserve their validity for the systems considered here. For example, we will prove that, under certain assumptions, the observability problem

19

R. Trappl (ed.), Cybernetics and Systems '86, 19–25.
© *1986 by D. Reidel Publishing Company.*

for reduced decomposable systems in the category of semigroups can be solved on the basis of a single, simple experiment. Recall that "linearity" cleary implies this property.

We will also focus our attention on the exploration of the controllability and p-definiteness properties. More specifically, we shall formulate necessary and suficient conditions for a given decomposable sequential system in the category of semigroups to possess these properties.

2. BASIC NOTIONS

Begin by recalling some definitions from universal algebra. A semigroup $(A,\cdot)$ is a set together with a multiplication which is associative. An element $e_a \in A$ is the neutral element of A if for every $x \in A$; $x \cdot e_a = e_a \cdot x = x$. A semigroup with a neutral element is said to be a monoid. A semigroup $(A,\cdot)$ called a commutative semigroup if for every $x, y \in A$: $x \cdot y = y \cdot x$. We say that a semigroup $(A,\cdot)$ satisfies the right (left) cancellation law if for every $x, x', y \in A$: $x \cdot y = x' \cdot y \Rightarrow x = x'$, ($y \cdot x = y \cdot x' \Rightarrow x = x'$). Recall that a finite monoid is a group if it satisfies the cancellation law. An equivalence relation $R \subset X \times X$ is said to be a semigroup - congruence if for every $x, x', y, y' \in A$: $xRx' \wedge yRy' \Rightarrow x \cdot yRx' \cdot y'$. Let two semigroups $(A,\cdot)$, $(B,*)$ ben given. Then a mapping $h: A \rightarrow B$ is said to be a homomorphism if for every $x, y \in A$; $h(x \cdot y) = h(x) * h(y)$.

The category of semigroups and of monoids will be denoted by SGr , Mon respectively.

Definition 1
A finite sequential system $S = (U,X,Y,f,g)$ is called a finite semigroup sequential system $(S \in FSS(SGr))$ if U,X,Y are finite objects of SGr. The semigroup - operations defined on U,X,Y we will denote by $\cdot^u, \cdot^x, \cdot^y$ respectively. They will be denoted simply by $\cdot$ when its meaning is clear from context.

Definition 2
$S \in FSS(SGr)$ is said to be a decomposable system $(S \in DFSS(SGr))$ or a finite semigroup homomorphic sequential system if there are morphisms $a: X \rightarrow X$, $b: U \rightarrow X$, $c: X \rightarrow Y$ such that $g = c$ and $f(x,u) = a(x) \cdot^x b(u)$.

Let Z^* denote the free monoid over a finite set Z.

By $|\bar{z}|$ we will denote the lenght of a string $\bar{z} \in Z^*$. If Z is a semigroup with an operation $\cdot$ then one can introduce an operation $\cdot^*$ on Z defined as follows: let two strings of the same lenght $\bar{z} = z_0, \ldots, z_{n-1}$, $\bar{z}' = z'_0, \ldots, z'_{n-1}$ be given, then $\bar{z} \cdot^* \bar{z}' = z_0 \cdot z'_0, \ldots, z_{n-1} \cdot z'_{n-1}$

In the standard, inductive way one can define a transfer function

$f^*: X \times U^* \rightarrow X$, an output - generation function $g^*: X \times U^* \rightarrow Y$ and a response function $g^{**}: X \times U^* \rightarrow Y^*$.

Taking into account the associativity of the operations $\cdot^x$, $\cdot^y$, and the fact that a and c are morphisms, one can easily verify that, the transfer and the output generating functions of $S \in DFSS(SGr)$ are of the following form:

$$f^*(x,u_0,\ldots,u_{k-1}) = a^k(x) \cdot^x \prod_{i=0}^{k-1} a^{k-i-1} b(u_i) \tag{1}$$

$$g^*(x,u_0,\ldots,u_{k-1}) = c \, a^k(x) \cdot {}^{\vee}c \prod_{i=0}^{k-1} a^{k-i-1} \, b(u_i) \qquad (2)$$

PROPOSITION 1.

(i) If $S \in$ DFSS (SGr) and X,Y satisfy the commutativity law then

f^*, g^*, g^{**} are homomorphisms

(ii) If $S \in$ FSS (Mon) and f,g are homomorphisms then $S \in$ DFSS (Mon)

(iii) If $S \in$ DFSS (Mon) and X,Y satisfy the commutativity law then

$$f^*(x,\bar{u}) = f^*(x,\bar{e}_u) \cdot f^*(e_x,\bar{u})$$

$$g^*(x,\bar{u}) = g^*(x,\bar{e}_u) \cdot g^*(e_x,\bar{u})$$

$$g^{**}(x,\bar{u}) = g^{**}(x,\bar{e}_u) \cdot^* g^{**}(e_x,\bar{u})$$

and all functions on the right sides of the above equalities are appropriate homomorphisms ($\bar{e}_u \in \{e_u\}^*$ and $|\bar{e}_u| = |\bar{u}|$).
The proof is obvious and hence is omitted.

3. REDUCIBILITY

Let two finite sequential systems $S_i = (U,X_i,Y,f_i,g_i)$, $i=1,2$ be given.
Recall that a state $x_1 \in X_1$ is equivalent to a state $x_2 \in X_2$, ($x_1 \cong x_2$),
if for every input strings $\bar{u} \in U^*$; $g_1^*(x_1,\bar{u}) = g_2^*(x_2,\bar{u})$. The systems S_1
and S_2 are said to be equivalent ($S_1 \cong S_2$) if for every state $x_2 \in X_2$
there exists a state $x_1 \in X_1$ such that $x_1 \cong x_2$, and vice-versa [7].

Equivalently, $S_1 \cong S_2$ if and only if $\{g_{1x_1}^{**} \mid x_1 \in X_1\} = \{g_{2x_2}^{**} \mid x_2 \in X_2\}$.

The systems S_1 and S_2 are said to be weakly equivalent ($S_1 \sim S_2$) if for
every $x_1 \in X_1$ and for every $\bar{u} \in U^*$ there exists $x_2 \in X_2$ such that
$g_1^*(x_1,\bar{u}) = g_2^*(x_2,\bar{u})$ and vice-versa [6].

Observe, that $S_1 \sim S_2$ if and only if $\bigcup\{g_{1x_1} \mid x_1 \in X_1\} = \bigcup\{g_{2x_2} \mid x_2 \in X_2\}$,

It is well-known [7] that if any two strongly connected finite sequential
systems are weakly equivalent then they are equivalent. However, our task
is to formulate another condition under which this implication holds.
The theorem presented below can be treated as a generalization of the
appropriate theorem from [8].

THEOREM 1

Let $S_1,S_2 \in$ DFSS(SGr) and the following conditions hold:

(i) $(\exists x_1^o \in X_1)(\exists x_2^o \in X_2)(x_1^o \cong x_2^o)$,

(ii) $(\forall k \in N)(c_i \, a_i^k(x_i^o) = c_i(x_i^o))$ for $i=1,2$,

iii Y satisfies the cancellation law i.e. Y is an associative quasi-
group,

then $S_1 \sim S_2 \Rightarrow S_1 \cong S_2$. Proof is presented in [6].
Remark: If X_1, X_2 are monoids and their neutral elements are equivalent
then the condition (ii) is satisfied. In this case Y is a group.

LEMMA 1.

Let

(A) $S \in DFSS \, (Mon)$

or

(B) $S \in DFSS \, (SGr)$ and Y_k satisfy the right cancellation law,
then $x \cong x' \Leftrightarrow (\forall k \in N)(c \, a^k(x) = c \, a^k(x'))$.

Proof:

For both cases the proof of necessity is straightforward.

Now, assume that for every $\bar{u} = u_o, \ldots, u_{k-1}$

$$c \, a^k(x) \cdot c \prod_{i=0}^{k-1} a^{k-i-1} \, b(u_i) = c \, a^k(x') \cdot c \prod_{i=0}^{k-1} a^{k-i-1} \, b(u_i).$$

Using the right cancellation law or setting $\bar{u} = \bar{e}_u$, one has

$c \, a^k(x) = c \, a^k(x')$ for every $k \in N$ immediately.   Q.E.D.

Now our task is to show how one can construct a reduced realization of
a given sequential system satysfying the condition (A) or (B) from
Lemma 1. Recall that a system $\bar{S}$ is a reduced realization of S if $\bar{S}$ is
a reduced system i.e. it has no equivalent states, and $\bar{S} \cong S$ [7].
At first, one should prove that the state-equivalence relation is a semi-
group-congruence relation. Indeed, it follows directly from Lemma 1 and
from the fact that c a^k is a semigroup -homomorphism.
Let a sequential system $S = (U,X,Y,f,g)$ satisfying the conditions (A) or
(B) be given. Then, in the standard way [7], we are able to determine a
quotient sequential system $\bar{S} = (U,\bar{X},Y,\bar{a},\bar{b},\bar{c})$ where:

$$\bar{X} = X/_{\cong}$$
$$\bar{a}([x]_{\cong}) = [a(x)]_{\cong} \qquad\qquad\qquad (7)$$
$$\bar{b}(u) = [b(u)]_{\cong}$$
$$\bar{c}([x]_{\cong}) = c(x).$$

The functions $\bar{a}$, $\bar{b}$ are well-defined because the following obvious implications hold: $x \cong x' \Rightarrow c(x) = c(x')$, $x \cong x' \Rightarrow a(x) = a(x')$. Next, it is
easy to verify that the canonical mapping h: $X \rightarrow X/_{\cong}$ establishes the
epimorphism relation between $\bar{S}$ and S. For this reason $\bar{S}$ and S are equivalent. Observe that $\bar{S}$ satisfies the assumptions of Lemma 1. Assume that
$[x]_{\cong} \cong [x']_{\cong}$. Then Lemma 1 implies $(\forall k \in N)(\bar{c} \, \bar{a}^k([x]_{\cong}) = \bar{c} \, \bar{a}^k([x']_{\cong}))$.
By the definitions of $\bar{a}$ and $\bar{c}$ we can write equivalently $(\forall k \in N)(c \, a^k(x) =$
$= c \, a^k(x'))$. It means that $[x]_{\cong} = [x']_{\cong}$. So we have proved that $\bar{S}$ is a re-
duced system.
We can conclude our considerations by:

PROPOSITION 2.

The sequential system $\bar{S}$ (defined by (7)) is a reduced realization of S.
Now we are going to establish a relationship between the notions: reducibility and observability.

THEOREM 2.

Let a reduced sequential system S (satisfying the condition (A) or (B)) be
given.
The every initial state can be identified (observable) by a simple, single
experiment.

Proof:

Assume that $\bar{X} = n$. For the case when $S \in DFSS \, (Mon)$ the initial-state
identyfing experiment $\bar{u}$ is of the form $\bar{u} = \bar{e}_u$ where $|\bar{u}| \leqslant n-1$.

Now assume that $S \in$ DFSS(SGr) and Y satisfies the right cancellation law. In this case we will show that every input sequence $\bar{u} = u_0, \ldots, u_{n-2}$ can be an initial-state identyfing experiment. To do so, it suffices to verify that for every $\bar{u} = u_0, \ldots, u_{n-2}$ the function $x \mapsto g^{**}(x, \bar{u})$ is bijective. Let $x \neq x'$. Then from Lemma 1 it follows that $(\exists k \leqslant n-1)(c \ a^k(x) = c \ a^k(x'))$. Next, from the right cancellation law we get:

$$g^*(x, u_0, \ldots, u_{k-1}) \neq g^*(x', u_0, \ldots, u_{k-1}).$$

It means that $g^{**}(x, u_0, \ldots, u_{n-2}) \neq g^{**}(x', u_0, \ldots, u_{n-2})$.

This completes the proof. Q.E.D.

We would like to summarize our considerations by saying that we have just found a smaller class of reduced finite sequential systems (being at the same time a subclass of reduced linear systems) for which it is possible to identify an initial state with the help of a single, simple experiment. From experimental point of view it is one of the most important properties of sequential systems.

4. OTHER PROPERTIES OF $S \in$ DFSS (SGr)

At first, we will deal with one of the most important property, namely with the controllability (the strong connectedness).
LEMMA 2.
Assume that $S = (U,X,Y,a,b,c) \in$ DFSS(SGr), a is an automorphism and X satisfies the right cancellation law.
Then S is controllable i.e.
$(\forall x,x')(\exists \bar{u})(f^*(x,\bar{u}) = x')$ if and only if there exists $x^o \in X$ such that S is x^o-controllable i.e. $(\forall x)(\exists u)(f^*(x^o,\bar{u}) = x)$.
Proof:
The proof of sufficiency is obvious. In order to carry out the proof of necessity, we must recall that a sequential system S is reversible (in the sense of [7]) if: $(\forall x,x')(\forall u)(f(x,u) = f(x',u) \Rightarrow x = x')$.
Now we will show that $S \in$ DFSS(SGr) such that X satisfies the right cancellation law is reversible if and only if a is an automorphism.
Let $a(x) \cdot b(u) = a(x') \cdot b(u)$. From the right cancellation law we get: $a(x) = a(x')$. Next from the fact that a is bijective function it follows that $x = x'$. So we have shown that S is a reversible system. It is also easy to verify that the reversibility implies the "bijectivity" of a function a. Finally, to complete the proof of this Lemma it suffices to refer to the following theorem [7]: if a reversible sequential system is x^o-controllable then it is controllable. Q.E.D.
Using this Lemma and setting $x^o = e_x$, one can easily prove the following:
THEOREM 3.
Let $S \in$ DFSS(SGr), X be an n-element monoid satisfying the right cancellation law and a be an automorphism.
Then S is controllable if and only if $X = a^{n-1} b(U) \cdot \ldots \cdot b(U)$.
This theorem can be regarded as the generalization of Kalman's criterion for the controllability [7].
PROPOSITION 3.
Let $S \in$ DFSS(Mon) and X be a commutative monoid.

23

Then the set of states reachable from e_x i.e.

$a^{n-1} b(U) \circ \ldots \circ b(U)$ is also a commutative monoid.

Proof:

This follows from the fact that $f^*(e_x,.) : U^* \longrightarrow X$ is a homomorphism

(see Proposition 1 (iii)).

We have shown that a sequential system satisfying the assumptions of this proposition, has the following general property:

there exists a state $x^0 \in X$ such that the set of states reachable from x^0 has the same algebraic structure as a set X. It is well known that linear sequential systems and finite group homomorphic sequential systems (with an Abelian group of states) also possess this property [2,11]. We would like to stress a geometric significance this property.

Now, we shall consider the class of p-definite sequential systems. Remind that a sequential system $S = (U,X,Y,f,g)$ is called p-definite (or S has a finite memory of order p) [3] if:

$g^*(x,\bar{u}) = g^*(x',\bar{u})$ holds for every $x,x' \in X$, $\bar{u} \in U^*$ such that $|\bar{u}| \geqslant p-1$

and there exist $x,x' \in X$, $\bar{u}' \in U^*$, $|\bar{u}'| = p-1$ such that $g^*(x,\bar{u}') \neq g^*(x',\bar{u}')$.

It is known that a p-definite sequential systems can be realized without the use of feedback. For this reason, they are of great interest in systems (automata) theory. Now, we derive the necessary and sufficient condition for $S \in DFSS(SGr)$ to be a p-definite.

THEOREM 4.

Let $S \in DFSS(Mon)$ and Y satisfy the right cancellation law. Then S is p-definite if and only if ca^p is a nilpotent homomorphism i.e.

$(\forall x)(ca^p(x) = e_y)$ and $(\exists x)(ca^{p-1}(x) \neq e_y)$.

Proof:

First, we will prove the necessity. Assume that for every $x, x' \in X$, $\bar{u} = u_o,\ldots,u_{p-1} \in U^*$

$$ca^p(x) \circ c \prod_{i=0}^{p-1} a^{p-i-1} b(u_i) = ca^p(x') \circ c \prod_{i=0}^{p-1} a^{p-i-1} b(u_i).$$

Then, from the right cancellation law, one has; $ca^p(x) = ca^p(x')$.

Let us set $x' = x \circ x$. Hence $ca^p(x \cdot x) = ca^p(x) \cdot ca^p(x) = ca^p(x) \triangleq ca^p(x') = ca^p(x')$. This means that $ca^p(x) = e_y$. Now assume that there exist $\bar{u} = u_o,\ldots,u_{p-2} \in U^*$; $x, x' \in X$ such that

$$ca^{p-1}(x) \cdot c \prod_{i=0}^{p-2} a^{p-1-1} b(u_i) = ca^{p-1}(x') \cdot c \prod_{i=0}^{p-2} a^{p-i-2} b(u_i).$$

Now the right cancellation law implies that there exist $x,x' \in X$ such that $ca^{p-1}(x) \neq ca^{p-1}(x')$. Because $ca^{p-1}(x) = e_y$ or $ca^{p-1}(x) \neq e_y$, we get $(\exists x'')(ca^{p-1}(x'') \neq e_y)$.

Conversely, assume that for every $x \in X$, $ca^p(x) = e_y$.

Hence, for every $k \in N$, $ca^{p+k}(x) = e_y$. It means that for every $\bar{u}$ $(|\bar{u}| \geqslant p)$, the equality $g^*(x,\bar{u}) = g^*(x',\bar{u})$ holds.

Now, take into account the second part of the definition of a nilpotent

24

homomorphism. This yields immediately that there exist x, $x' \in X$ such that $ca^{p-1}(x) \neq ca^{p-1}(x')$. Q.E.D.

Notice: This theorem is analogous to the appropriate theorem from linear automata theory [3] but its proof is rather different.

REFERENCES

1. Arbib M.A., Manes E.G., Automatica, "Foundations of system theory: decomposable systems", 10, 1974, pp. 285-302.
2. Brockett R.W., Willsky A.S., IEEE Trans. on Automatic Control "Finite group homomorphic sequential systems", AC-17, 1972, pp. 483-490.
3. Gecseg F., Peak I., Algebraic Theory of Automata, Akademiai Kiado, Budapest 1972.
4. Jacak W., Sierocki I., Int. J. General Systems, "Levels of structural decomposition of dynamical systems", 10, 1985, pp. 177-186.
5. Jacak W., Sierocki I., Cybern. and Systems. An Int. J., "Decompositions problems of systems defined on groups", 15, 1984, pp.127-143.
6. Jacak W., Sierocki I., Cybernetics-85, Conf. Pol. Cyber., Soc. "Reducibility of finite semigroup homomorphic sequential systems", 4, Warsow 1985, pp. 63-68.
7. Kalman R.E., Falb P.L., Arbib M.A., Topics in Mathematical System Theory, Mc Graw-Hill, New York, 1969.
8. Keith D., Horward F., IEEE Trans. Circuit Theory,"Invertibility, equivalence and decomposition property of abstract systems", 16,1969.
9. Sain M.K., Introduction to Algebraic System Theory, Academic Press, New York, 1981,
10. Willsky A.S., Inform. and Control, "Invertibility of finite group homomorphic sequential systems", 27, 1975, pp. 126-147.
11. Wonham W.M., Linear Multivariable Control: a Geometric Approach, Springer Verlag, Berlin 1979.

M-D MATRIX AND M-D TRANSFORM METHODS

N. C. Hu
Shanghai University of Technology
149 Yen-chang Rd. 200070
Shanghai
CHINA

ABSTRACT. In this paper, the new concepts of multi-dimensional (M-D) spatial matrixes are proposed, the fundamental operational methods for these matrixes by the dimensional transposition are presented, then the general expressions of M-D discrete orthogonal transforms are obtained, and the recently used methods of one- and two-dimensional orthogonal transforms may be found as the particular cases of the results of this paper for the one- and two-dimensional applications.

1. INTRODUCTION

The methods of orthogonal transforms are an effective tool for the signal analysis and processing. There is a long history and wide applications of the transform analysis and processing for continuous signals. Recent years, with the developments of the digital signal processing techniques, discrete orthogonal transform processing has attracted more and more attentions and rapidly extends its application areas.

Classical matrix argebra suplies an effective tool for the one- and two-dimensional(1-D and 2-D) discrete orthogonal transforms. The 1-D transform relation may be generally expressed as

$$\{F(m)\} = \mathsf{T}\{f(n)\} \quad , \quad (m,n=0,1,\cdots,N-1) \tag{1}a$$

where $\{F\},\{f\}$ are sequences with length N; T is an $N \cdot N$-element matrix for the discrete transform. Its corresponding inverse transform is

$$\{f(n)\} = \mathsf{T}^{-1}\{F(m)\} \quad , \quad (n,m=0,1,\cdots,N-1) \tag{1}b$$

In the matrix form, we have

$$\mathsf{F} = \mathsf{T}\mathsf{f} \tag{1}c$$
$$\mathsf{f} = \mathsf{T}^{-1}\mathsf{F} \tag{1}d$$

27

R. Trappl (ed.), Cybernetics and Systems '86, 27–34.
© 1986 by D. Reidel Publishing Company.

where T^{-1} is the inverse matrix of T, F and f are N-element column matrixes, they are inverse transforms each other.

In some cases, the N-element column matrix may be understood as a matrix expression of an N-dimensional vector, but in fact, formulas in (1) represent the transforms of 1-D sequences, therefore, we will understand F and f as the 1-D matrixes.

Correspondingly, the 2-D transform relations may be expressed in the matrix form

$$F = TfT'$$ (2)a
$$f = T^{-1}F(T^{-1})'$$ (2)b

where F, f are 2-D matrixes; T' is the transposed matrix of T. In addition, if T is orthogonal, Eqs. (2) may be written in more symmetric forms.

With the developments of signal processing techniques, the processing accuracy and speed are being increased, the processing objects are not limited in the areas of 1-D data or 2-D static pictures, but also 3-D or more high dimensional information or spatial moving images; the processing methods are being progressed from non-real time to real time. Therefore, what are the transform relations in the 3-D or more high dimensional cases? are the classical matrix operations suitable for M-D analysis? which reforms or extensions of them are necessary? what are the operational rules for them? these are principal problems that necessary to solve for the M-D transform analysis and procesing. This paper proposed a new concept of M-D matrix, then the corresponding operational rules are introduced, and the general expressions of M-D discrete orthogonal transforms are obtained.

2. FUNDAMENTAL DEFINITIONS AND NOTATIONS

DEFINITION 1: The K-D array formed by a K-D discrete sequence

$$f(n_1, \cdots, n_K), \quad (n_i = 0, 1, \cdots, N_i - 1); \ i = 1, \cdots, K$$ (3)

arranged in a K-D space is called a K-D matrix; $f(n_1, \cdots, n_K)$ are its elements; the independents $n_1, \cdots, n_K$ are called the coordinates on their corresponding dimensional directions; N_i is the matrix length on i-th dimension; $n_i = 0$ is taken as the origin on the i-th dimension, and call it the initial value on this direction. The M-D matrix with the same lengths on all dimensions is called an M-D homogeneous matrix.

DEFINITION 2: The element $f(0, \cdots, 0)$ of an M-D matrix is called the original element, and its position is taken as the origin of the M-D matrix space; the element $f(N_1 - 1, \cdots, N_K - 1)$ is called the diagonal element, and its position is called the diagonal point.

DEFINITION 3: The largrst values of n_i, i.e. $N_i - 1$, $(i = 1, \cdots, K)$

28

are called the terminal values on i-th coordinates.

DEFINITION 4: The connected line between the origin and diagonal point in the M-D matrix space is called the main diagonal; other connected lines between two elements of the M-D diagonal pairs are the partial diagonals.

DEFINITION 5: In the M-D matrix space, the direction on the main diagonal from the origin to the diagonal point is called the main diagonal direction, and the counterclock direction viewed along the main diagonal direction is defined as the dimensional order direction.

DEFINITION 6: In the K-D matrix space, take the main diagonal as the axis, the $(2\pi r)/K$ angular rotation of a K-D matrix on the dimensional order direction (or the inverse dimensional order direction) is called a r-dimensional forward (or inverse) K-D matrix transposition, the transposed matrix is denoted by $F^{(r)}$ (or $F^{(-r)}$); to simplify the discussions, take the column direction from the top to bottom on the paper plane as the first dimensional direction of the K-D matrix space, and the second dimensional direction is chosen on the row direction from the left to right on the paper plane, and therefore, the other dimensional directions must be imagined along the directions from the origin into the inside of the paper plane to form an M-D directional system. The K-D matrix that its i-th dimension is accorded with the first dimensional direction of the K-D matrix space is called an i-placed K-D matrix and denoted by F_i.

PROPOSITION: There are K-1 different placed transpositions of a K-D matrix, and satisfy the relations

$$F_i = F_1^{(a)}, \quad a \equiv (i-1)(\bmod K), \quad (i=1,\cdots,K) \tag{4}$$

and

$$f_i(n_1,\cdots,n_K) = f_1(n_{K-i+2},\cdots,n_K,n_1,\cdots,n_{K-i+1}), (i=1,\cdots,K) \tag{5}$$

DEFINITION 7: If

$$T_i = \begin{vmatrix} t(0,0) & \cdots & t(0,N_i-1) \\ \vdots & & \\ t(N_i-1,0) & \cdots & t(N_i-1,N_i-1) \end{vmatrix} \tag{6}$$

is a 2-D squar matrix with the same length N_i on each dimension. And

$$\mathcal{f}_i = \begin{vmatrix} f(0,\cdots,0) & \cdots & f(0,\cdots,N_{i+1}-1,0,\cdots,0) \\ \vdots & & \vdots \\ f(0,\cdots,N_i-1,0,\cdots,0) & \cdots & f(0,\cdots,N_i-1,N_{i+1}-1,0,\cdots,0) \end{vmatrix} \tag{7}$$

successive dimensions
$(i+1)$-th dimension
i-th dimension

is an i-placed K-D matrix, then the K-D matrix

$$
A_i = \begin{vmatrix}
& & \text{successive dimensions} & \\
& & \nwarrow \longrightarrow (i+1)\text{-th dimension} & \\
A(0,\cdots,0) & \cdots & A(0,\cdots,N_{i+1}-1,0,\cdots,0) \\
\vdots & & \vdots \\
A(0,\cdots,N_i-1,0,\cdots,0) & \cdots & A(0,\cdots,N_i-1,N_{i+1}-1,0,\cdots,0) \\
\downarrow \ i\text{-th dimension} & &
\end{vmatrix}
\tag{8}
$$

is defined as the column product of the mtrixes T_i and F_i, in which

$$
A(n_1,\cdots,n_{i-1},n_i',n_{i+1},\cdots,n_K) = \sum_{n_i=0}^{N_i-1} t(n_i',n_i) f(n_1,\cdots,n_K)
\tag{9}
$$

$$
(n_i' = 0,1,\cdots,N_i-1; \ \ i=1,\cdots,K)
$$

therefore, we have

$$
A_i = T_i F_i
\tag{10}
$$

Eq. (10) represents a column processing of the 2-D matrix T_i relative to the M-D matrix F_i on the i-th dimension, this is a general expression. When K=1, we can find the 1-D transform processing relation; in the case of K=2, the column processing relation of 2-D image may be found.

3. M-D LINEAR TRANSFORMS

The M-D discrete transform relation may generally be expressed as

$$
F(m_1,\cdots,m_K) = \sum_{n_1-1}^{N_1-1} \cdots \sum_{n_K-1}^{N_K-1} f(n_1,\cdots,n_K) q(n_1,\cdots,n_K,m_1,\cdots,m_K)
\tag{11}
$$

$$
(m_i = 0,1,\cdots,M_i-1; \ \ i=1,\cdots,K)
$$

where $q(\cdot)$ is the K-D transform kernel which acted as a weighting factor. It is a 2K-D discrete sequence both connected with the input and output K-D sequences.

Clearly, if the input sequence and transform kernel all are M-D separable, the M-D transform processing may be simplified to a successive processing of 1-D transforms on every dimension. But in fact, a lot of M-D input sequences are M-D nonseparable, and the transform kernel may usually be chosen to keep the M-D separable property. In this case we have

$$F(m_1,\cdots,m_K)= \sum_{n_1=0}^{N_1-1} \cdots \sum_{n_K=0}^{N_K-1} f(n_1,\cdots,n_K) \prod_{i=1}^{K} q_i(n_i,m_i) \qquad (12)$$

$$=\left\{ \prod_{i=1}^{K} \left[\sum_{n_i=0}^{N_i-1} q_i(n_i,m_i) \right] \right\} \langle f(n_1,\cdots,n_K) \rangle \qquad (13)$$

$$(m_i=0,1,\cdots,M_i-1; \quad i=1,\cdots,K)$$

where $q_i(n_i,m_i)$ is the transform kernel on i-th dimension; and $\{\cdot\}\langle f\rangle$ represents the transform processing of $\{\cdot\}$ relative to f. By the matrix expression, Eq. (13) may be rewritten as

$$F = \mathcal{G}_K \left\{ \mathcal{G}_{K-1} \left\{ \cdots \mathcal{G}_2 \left\{ \mathcal{G}_1 f \right\}^{(1)} \cdots \right\}^{(1)} \right\}^{(1)} \qquad (14)$$

where $\mathcal{G}_i$ is the transform matrix on the i-th dimension with the elements $q_i(n_i,m_i)$.

Eq. (14) represents an M-D transform processing by the dimensional transposition of the M-D matrix. In which the M-D matrix is processed by the transform matrixes on every dimension successively.

Correspondingly, the inverse discrete M-D transform processing relation may be expressed as

$$\hat{f} = r_K \left\{ r_{K-1} \left\{ \cdots r_2 \left\{ r_1 F \right\}^{(1)} \cdots \right\}^{(1)} \right\}^{(1)} \qquad (15)$$

where r_i is the inverse transform matrix on the i-th dimension with the elements $r_i(m_i,n_i)$.

Clearly, if the errors of the forward and inverse transform processing may be neglected, we can let

$$r_i = \mathcal{G}_{K+1-i}^{-1} , \quad (i=1,\cdots,K) \qquad (16)$$

and then we can prove

$$\hat{f} = f \qquad (17)$$

That is the M-D sequence may be transformed and recovered by the forward and inverse M-D transform of dimensional transposition methods.

By means of Eqs. (9), (14) and (15), it is possible to make an M-D transform processing with different properties or requirements on different dimensions.

31

4. SEVERAL TYPICAL M-D ORTHOGONAL TRANSFORMS

To simplify the discussions, we consider the M-D homogeneous case.

4.1. M-D Discrete Fourier Transform (M-D DFT)

Its general matrix expressions of forward and inverse transforms are

$$F = \frac{1}{N^K} \cdot \mathcal{G}\{\mathcal{G}\{\cdots \mathcal{G}\{\mathcal{G}f\}^{(1)}\cdots\}^{(1)}\}^{(1)} \tag{18}$$

and

$$f = r\{r\{\cdots r\{r F\}^{(1)}\cdots\}^{(1)}\}^{(1)} \tag{19}$$

where

$$\mathcal{G} = \begin{vmatrix} W^0 & W^0 & \cdots & W^0 \\ \vdots & \vdots & & \vdots \\ W^0 & W^{(N-1)} & \cdots & W^{(N-1)^2} \end{vmatrix} \tag{20}$$

and

$$r = \begin{vmatrix} W^0 & W^0 & \cdots & W^0 \\ \vdots & \vdots & & \vdots \\ W^0 & W^{-(N-1)} & \cdots & W^{-(N-1)^2} \end{vmatrix} \tag{21}$$

with the relation

$$W = e^{-j2\pi/N} \tag{22}$$

4.2. M-D Walsh-Hadamard Transform (M-D WHT)

Let the dimensional length N to be the positive power of two, we have

$$F = H\{H\{\cdots H\{Hf\}^{(1)}\cdots\}^{(1)}\}^{(1)} \tag{23}$$

and

$$f = H^{-1}\{H^{-1}\{\cdots H^{-1}\{H^{-1}F\}^{(1)}\cdots\}^{(1)}\}^{(1)}$$
$$= \frac{1}{N^K} \cdot H\{H\{\cdots H\{HF\}^{(1)}\cdots\}^{(1)}\}^{(1)} \tag{24}$$

where

$$H = H(N) = \begin{vmatrix} 1 & 1 & \cdots & 1 \\ 1 & -1 & \cdots & -1 \\ \vdots & \vdots & & \vdots \\ 1 & -1 & \cdots & (-1)^R \end{vmatrix}, \quad (R = \log_2 N) \tag{25}$$

is an N-order Walsh-Hadamard transform matrix.

4.3. M-D Discrete Cosine Transform (M-D DCT)

we have

$$F = C_K G\{C_{K-1}G\{\cdots C_2 G\{C_1 G f\}^{(1)}\cdots\}^{(1)}\}^{(1)} \tag{26}$$

32

and

$$f = C_K^{-1} G \left\{ C_{K-1}^{-1} G \left\{ \cdots C_2^{-1} G \left\{ C_1^{-1} G F \right\}^{(1)} \cdots \right\}^{(1)} \right\}^{(1)} \tag{27}$$

where

$$G = \begin{vmatrix} G(0) & G(1) & \cdots & G(N-1) \end{vmatrix} = \begin{vmatrix} 1 & 2 & \cdots & 2 \end{vmatrix} \tag{28}$$

is an N-element row weighting matrix; and C_i is the transform matrix on i-th dimension with the elements

$$C_i(n_i, m_i) = \cos\left[\frac{2\pi m_i}{2N - a_i} \cdot (n_i + \frac{1 - a_i}{2})\right], \quad (i = 1, \cdots, K) \tag{29}$$

where

$$a_i = \begin{cases} 0, & \text{for even symmetric imaging} \\ 1, & \text{for odd symmetric imaging} \end{cases} \tag{30}$$

is the symmetric factor of the i-th dimensional transform.

5. EXAMPLE FOR APPLICATION

Let

$$f = \begin{vmatrix} \begin{array}{c} \nearrow \quad i=3(\text{third dimension}) \\ i=2(\text{second dimension}) \\ \longrightarrow \end{array} & \begin{array}{cccc} & & & \\ & 0\ 2\ 2\ 0 & \begin{array}{cccc} 2\ 0\ 0\ 2 \\ 0\ 2\ 2\ 0 \\ 0\ 2\ 2\ 0 \\ 2\ 0\ 0\ 2 \end{array} \\ 0\ 2\ 2\ 0 & 2\ 0\ 0\ 2 & 2\ 0\ 0\ 2 \\ 2\ 0\ 0\ 2 & 2\ 0\ 0\ 2 & 2\ 0\ 0\ 2 \\ 0\ 2\ 2\ 0 & 2\ 0\ 0\ 2 & 0\ 2\ 2\ 0 \\ 0\ 2\ 2\ 0 & 0\ 2\ 2\ 0 \\ 2\ 0\ 0\ 2 \end{array} \\ \downarrow i=1(\text{first dimension}) \end{vmatrix} \tag{31}$$

be a cut-layer expression of a 64-element 3-D matrix with N=4 and average value of unit, in which the inclined-up direction represents the third dimension. From Eq. (23) we can find corresponding 3-D WHT to be

$$F = H \left\{ H \left\{ H f \right\}^{(1)} \right\}^{(1)} \right\}^{(1)}$$

$$= \begin{vmatrix} & & & \begin{array}{cccc} 0\ 0\ 0\ 0 \\ 0\ 0\ 0\ 0 \\ 0\ 0\ 0\ 0\ 0 \\ 0\ 0\ 0\ 64 \end{array} \\ & 0\ 0\ 0\ 0 & 0\ 0\ 0\ 0 \\ 0\ 0\ 0\ 0 & 0\ 0\ 0\ 0 \\ 64\ 0\ 0\ 0 & 0\ 0\ 0\ 0 & 0\ 0\ 0\ 0 \\ 0\ 0\ 0\ 0 & 0\ 0\ 0\ 0 & 0\ 0\ 0\ 0 \\ 0\ 0\ 0\ 0 & 0\ 0\ 0\ 0 \\ 0\ 0\ 0\ 0 \end{array} \end{vmatrix} \tag{32}$$

Eq. (32) shows that there are two 3-D Walsh spectral bases to the 3-D sequence of Eq. (31), i. e. the constant component $f(0,0,0)$ and the alternate component $f(3,3,3)$. Keep one of them, and let the others to be zero, and then a 3-D Walsh filtering may be com-

33

pleted by the inverse transform of Eq. (24).

In the general M-D cases, similar methods may be used to obtain the ditributive properties of the base functions of an M-D sequence, and then some required processing can be realized.

6. CONCLUSIONS

When the transform kernels of the M-D Discrete transforms are M-D separable, the fundamental transform relations of Eqs. (9),(14), (15) may be used to realize the transform processing of M-D sequence, and different properties on different dimensions may also be achieved by the methods of successive dimensional transposition.

In the case of K=1 and K=2, Eqs.(14) and (15) are simplified to the widely used matrix transform relations of 1-D signal processing and 2-D image processing.

When the M-D transform kernel is nonseparable, the general M-D transform relations are very complicated, and many topics will be studied and discussed in the future.

REFERENCES

1. T. W. Hungerford, Algebra, Springer-verlag Inc. 1974.
2. A. V. Openheim and R. W. Schafer, Digital Signal Processing, Prentice-Hall Inc. Englewood Cliffs, N. J. 1975.
3. W. K. Pratt, Digital Image Processing, John Wiley and Sons, 1978.
4. N. Ahmed and K. R. Rao, Orthogonal Transforms for Digital Signal Processing, 1957.
5. A. Rosenfeld and A. C. Kak, Digital Picture Processing, Academic Press, 1976.
6. R. C. Gonzalez and P. Wintz, Digital Image Processing, 1977.
7. N. C. Hu, Frequency Sampling Design of M-D Digital Filters, Progress in Cybernetics and System Research, Hemisphere Pub. Corp. Washington, 1981.
8. N. C. Hu, Multi-dimensional FFT Computation, Cybernetics and System Research 2, Elsevier Science Pub. Corp. B. V. North-Holland, 1984.
9. R. M. Bates, Multi-dimensional BIFORE Transform, Ph. D. Dissertation, Kansas State Uni. U. S. A. 1971
10. H. Schreiber(ed), Applications of Walsh Functions and sequency Theory, 1974.
11. N. C. Hu, Multi-dimen ional Digital Windows, Advances in Communications, D. Reidel Pub. Comp. Dordrecht, Holland, 1980.
12. N.C. Hu, Frequency Response of Multi-dimensional Linear Phase FIR Digital Filters. Advances in Communications, D. Reidel Pub. Comp. Dordrecht, Holland, 1980.

SUBJECTIVE PERCEPTION OF TIME AND SYSTEMS

Robert Vallée
Université Paris-Nord
av. J.-B. Clément
F.93430 Villetaneuse
France

ABSTRACT. We modelize the subjective perception of duration by a differential model. A functional link is so established between subjective time and reference time, the subjective one being or not, depending upon cases, a good parametrization of time. The first types of perception we consider are those which do not involve memorization but only a factor of attention, depending upon time, which is a measure of the "weight" of an instant. When this factor is constant, subjective time is a linear function of reference time. When this factor is inversely proportional to reference time, subjective time is a logarithmic function of reference time, a circumstance which is to be compared with the occurence, in cosmology, of Milne's time. Then are considered the more general types where, outside from the factor of attention, a factor of oblivion is taken into account.

1. SUBJECTIVE PERCEPTION OF DURATION AND PARAMETRIZATION OF TIME

We consider a unidimensional linear differential system

$$d\theta(t)/dt = -a(t)\,\theta(t) + b(t) \qquad (1)$$

where $a(t) \geqslant 0$ and $b(t) \geqslant 0$ with $\theta(t_0) = 0$. As we have shown previously (Vallée 1977,80,84), such a system can be considered as a model representing perception and memorization of time elapsed since an initial instant t_0. Here we shall say in brief "perception", including memorization in it. We must note that the same subject has been studied along analogous but more special lines under the name of "time aberration" (Tauber 1983).

The integration of system (1) gives

$$\theta(t) = \int_{t_0}^{t} \exp(-\int_{\tau}^{t} a(\sigma)\,d\sigma)\, b(\tau)\,d\tau \qquad (2).$$

The parameter t represents <u>reference time</u>. It gives both a good parametrization of instants (two different instants are represented by two

35

R. Trappl (ed.), Cybernetics and Systems '86, 35–38.
© *1986 by D. Reidel Publishing Company.*

different values of t) and a measure of duration of time elapsed between two instants ($t-t_o$ measures time elapsed between t_o and t). Parameter θ represents <u>subjective time</u>, as perceived by the system. It is
necessay that $b(t) \geqslant 0$ in order to avoid that $\theta(t)$, which is the <u>subjec-</u>
<u>tive duration of time elapsed between t_o and t</u> (reference duration $t-t_o$),
be in some cases negative. Condition $a(t) \geqslant 0$ means that memorization
decreases in quality when instants considered are more distant in the
past. We must remark that, except in the case where $a(t) \equiv 0$, if
$t_o < t_1 < t_2$ the subjective duration between t_o and t_2 is not equal to
the sum of the subjective durations between t_o and t_1 and between t_1
and t_2.

An other important point is that θ does not necessarily give a
good parametrization of time. It can happen that we have $\theta(t_1) = \theta(t_2)$
with $t_1 \neq t_2$. This is due to the fact that $\theta(t)$ is not necessarily a
strictly increasing function. So it does not realize, in all cases, a
bijection between t and θ. Nevertheless $\theta(t)$ is continuous with the sufficient conditions : $a(t)$ and $b(t)$ piecewise continuous.

If we want θ be a <u>good parametrization of time</u>, $\theta(t)$ must be stri-
tly increasing, that is to say that $d\theta(t)/dt$ must always be strictly
positive. This condition gives

$$-a(t)\theta(t) + b(t) > 0$$

or more explicitly

$$a(t) \int_{c_o}^{t} \exp(-\int_{\tau}^{t} a(\tau)d\tau) \ b(\tau)d\tau < b(t) \qquad (3)$$

for all possible values of t_o and t, an obvious necessary condition
being that $b(t)$ is never equal to zero. Nevertheless θ can give a subjective measure of duration without giving a good parametrization of
time.

2. CASES OF PERCEPTION WITH $a(t) \equiv 0$ AND THE "WEIGHT" OF AN INSTANT

If $a(t)$ is identical to zero there is no memorization but only "pure"
perception. We have

$$\theta(t) = \int_{c_o}^{t} b(\tau)d\tau \qquad (4).$$

The factor $b(t)$ can be considered as the <u>degree of attention</u> the system gives to instant t itself so that a reference duration dt is perceived subjectively as being $d\theta = b(t)dt$. In other words $b(t)$ can be
considered as the <u>weight of instant t</u>, a terminology which could be
be used even without the connotation of subjectivity. Obviously a necessary and sufficient condition for $\theta(t)$ to be a good parametrization
of time is that $b(t)$, being supposed piecewise continuous, is never
equal to zero on an interval of length different from zero.

As a first example let us consider the case where $b(t)=b \exp(-\lambda t)$
with $b > 0$ and $\lambda > 0$. It is easy to see that

$$\theta(t) = b/\lambda \ \exp(-\lambda t_o) \ (1-\exp(-\lambda(t-t_o))) \qquad (5)$$

so that when t goes from $-\infty$ to $+\infty$, $\theta(t)$ goes from $-\infty$ to $b/\lambda \ \exp(-\lambda t_o)$. Subjective time θ is perceived as bounded on the right while reference time t is not. Nevertheless θ (t) is here a good parametrization of time.

The case where b(t)=b, can be seen as a limit case of the precedent one. Directly we have

$$\theta(t) = b(t-t_o) \qquad (6).$$

In such a case, subjective and referencetimes are the same except for a factor b, the weight of an instant is constant. On the contrary, in the precedent case, this weight was exponentially decreasing with time.

An interesting case is obtained when b(t)=b/t. We have then

$$\theta(t) = b \ (\text{Log } t - \text{Log } t_o) \qquad (7)$$

and $\theta(t)$ comes to infinity when t_o comes to zero. This is due to the fact that the weight of instants close to t=0 is preponderous and even comes to infinity when t_o comes to zero. While reference time t varies from 0 to $+\infty$, subjective time θ varies from $-\infty$ to $+\infty$. The initial instant t=0 is rejected to $-\infty$. This is to be compared with the so called Milne's cosmological time which is linked to usual time by a logarithmic law. It can be said, in our point of view, that the first instants of the universe have considerable weight, approaching infinity when we approach the "first" instant of the "big bang". If we take this weight proportional to the inverse of usual time, we obtain the Milne's time, with which there is no problem of "first" instant because there is none and of course no problem about instants "before". In all cases where the weight of instant t is b/t, analogous considerations can be done. Is it not the case, approximately, with human life where the early instants, or periods, seem to be of preponderous importance, giving the subjective feeling that our life has had no begining and seems to have lasted for an infinite duration? More generally time adapted to a phenomenon of explosive type must probably be of logarithmic nature. Anyway the subjective time given by (7) corresponds to a good parametrization.

3. CASES OF PERCEPTION WITH a(t)≢0

In such cases we have

$$\theta(t) = \int_{t_o}^{t} \exp(-\int_{\tau}^{t} a(\sigma)d\sigma) \ b(\tau)d\tau \qquad (2).$$

We must assume that b(t)≢0. If not, no subjective time would elapse at all because there would be no perception. We can write

$$d\theta(t) = (-a(t) \ \theta(t) + b(t)) \ dt \qquad (8).$$

The weight of instant t is then made up of two terms : the usual one we

37

have met before $(b(t))$ and a negative one $(-a(t)\theta(t))$. The sum of these terms gives the total weight taking into account the factor of <u>attention</u> (or importance) $b(t)$ and the negative factor due to <u>oblivion</u> $(-a(t)\theta(t))$.It can happen that the total weight be negative. This may seem paradoxical, but it is not if we consider that the only consequence is that $\theta(t)$ may, after increasing, start to decrease due to partial oblivion of instants in the very past. In such cases θ ceases to be a good parametrization of time but it still give a subjective perception of duration which can alter some usual features of the elapsing of time.

Let us consider the case where $b(t)=b\ exp(-\lambda t)$ and $a(t)=a$, with $\lambda>0$ and $a>0$. It is easy to see that

$$\theta(t) = b/\lambda-a \quad exp(-\lambda t_0)\ (exp(-a(t-t_0))- exp(-\lambda(t-t_0)))$$

if $\lambda > a.\theta(t)$ increases with t if $t-t_0 < Log(\lambda/a)\ /\lambda-a$ (9).

With that condition it is a good parametrization of time. The case where $\lambda < a$ is analogous.

If $b(t)=b$ and $a(t)=a$, with a and b strictly positive, we have

$$\theta(t) = b/a\ (1-exp(-a(t-t_0)))\quad (10).$$

Then θ is a good parametrization of time and is bounded on the right by b/a.

If we consider the rather special case where $b(t)=b/t\ exp(-at)$, which involves a factor proportional to $1/t$, we have, if $a(t)=a$,

$$\theta(t) = b\ exp(-at)\ (Log\ t - Log\ t_0)\quad (11).$$

The case, seen in paragraph 2, where $b(t)=b/t$ is a special case (take $a=0$). Here again $\theta(t)$ comes to infinity when t_0 comes to zero. The "initial" instant $t=0$ is rejected to $-\infty$ as far as subjective time is concerned. But θ is not a good parametrization of time, it is increasing with t only if we have $Log\ t < 1/at$.

REFERENCES

Vallée (R.) (1977), 'Modélisation en théorie dee systèmes, des processus de perception et d'actualisation des chroniques', in <u>Modélisation et maîtrise des systèmes techniques, économiques et sociaux</u>, p.178, Editions Hommes et Techniques,Paris.
Vallée (R.) (1980), 'Memorization in systems theory and the perception of time', in <u>Applied Systems and Cybernetics</u>, Lasker (G.E) Ed., p.697, Pergamon Press, New York.
Tauber (S.) (1983), 'Brief note : time abberation in living organisms' <u>Mathematical Modelling</u>,4,2,p.191.
Vallée (R.) (1984), 'Multidimensional subjective time and systems theory', <u>International Conference on Systems Research, Informatics and Cybernetics</u>, Baden-Baden.

BIOLOGICAL INFORMATION AS A SYSTEM DESCRIPTION

G. Kampis
Dept. of Behaviour Genetics,
L. Eötvös University
H - 2131 Göd, Jávorka S. u. 14.
Hungary

"In the beginning, there was information.
                    The word came later." (F.I. Dretske)
"Of what we don't know, doesn't exist." (Hungarian phrase)

I. INTRODUCTION

The above two conceptions surely contradict each other; and the paper is essentially about this contradiction. We cannot make statements
about a system independently of observation, and consequently, of the
observer-role (13). However, we conceive biological information as if it
were in the system, independently from us.
    What does this mean? Information is not only a quantity, but is in a
more intricate relationship to the system. I concentrate now on this relation, examining "What information?" (6) instead of "How much information?". This is meaningful only if we want to get a proper description
of the system. When speaking of information, I think of this description
now.
    Natural objects are always studied by models, but we should prefer
not their formal, semiotic properties, instead, their relationships to
the object (3,10). By now, it is clear that a careless use of information (16) is misleading in biology (25).
    A system description is giving the relations which characterize a
concrete system from some viewpoint, together with that viewpoint (or
frame, 27), which reflects the attitude of the observer to the natural
object. Such a frame is, if we consider a natural object as one instance
of all possible patterns (e.g. DNA as a sequence of letters), or we
choose a level of description (e.g. we consider molecules or organisms
as basic elements).
The general question of informational descriptions - i.e. that beyond
the actual relations of concrete systems - is the choice of the frames.
Here we need methodological reductionism, to endeavour to reduce informational descriptions to others considered more basic; otherwise there
would be no reason to prefer any viewpoint, any frame.

R. Trappl (ed.), Cybernetics and Systems '86, 39–46.
© 1986 by D. Reidel Publishing Company.

1. Background

A number of information definitions exist. The most widely known is Shannon's (26), which was formulated in relation to a special transmission problem. Usually, it is interpreted as the measure of subjective uncertainty about some message or the state of a system. Mathematically, however, it is identical with the expression of physical entropy (an objective uncertainly). This led to numerous misuses. Biological information is a describing tool of macroscopic system, and physical entropy is aspecific from the viewpoint of it. Entropy changes are not (necessarily) reflected in macroscopic objects, and changes of the latter are not always associated with entropy changes (24). Constructs, just separating entropical and non-entropical information solve the problem only partly, however, if not thinking of information as a sytem description in the above sense. Thus the status of "free information" (2, see 9) or of "structural information" (23) remains unclear. Shortly, these are contingent concepts.

Several approaches are know which seek information, more specifically, in the functioning of systems - realizing, that a microscopic description is not satisfactory and that macroscopic structures are related to the behaviour of the system. The question: What is ordinarily termed information in biology? leads also here. Polányi (14) was the first who clearly formulated that such uses of biological information are in connection with the description of boundary conditions, functioning in the system.

II. Problems

1. Boundary conditions

Polányi calls the boundary conditions of biological systems a final, irreducible form of information, saying, they are always external to the laws which they constrain, and cannot be expressed by those. Rothstein criticizes this view (22), and I share his criticism. Instead, he identifies information with a "boundary-condition-dependent", generalized entropy, and considers it a reducible concept.

But here is a problem, too, a similar thing as that criticized by Rothstein himself: endowing boundary conditions with an ontological status, i.e. thinking that they exist on their own. Boundary conditions are external in the case of a given system frame, but it what is considered a boundary condition can be described within another system which encompasses the former one; and then it disappears as such (20, 21, see also 12). The value of physical entropy, to which Rothstein builds a bridge, cannot depend on the description frame, on the system definition made by the observer.

According to Pattee - although in practice we do not doubt what to call a boundary condition - on a system theoretical basis we can be sure that "they are there" only if the system itself contains the descriptions of these constraints, in a precise sense (15). Pattee's example is the DNA in the living cell. Since, he says, all information comes from measurement, which is complementary and irreducible to the causal quantum mechanical descriptions, the inner description of boundary condi tions is an ultimate information which determines the latter.

In my view, however, the information of DNA (to stay with the example) comes not from measurements and thus the argument falls. Measurement is a choice between possible cutcomes (15,19). Its adequate system model is Rosen's autonomous state-classifier (19). Essentially, it is a dynamical system which, due to some perturbation, gets into one of its multiple stability domains. Measurement is then a relation between the direction and magnitude of the perturbation and the stability domain chosen by that. Now the premise of this is the existence of previously determined stability domains (a fixed measuring device). Information is a "choice" between alternatives, too, but these are illusory since there are no multiple possible outcomes and fixed stability domains in the processes of a natural system. In short, boundary conditions do not constitute a final information in themselves.

2. Transitive and intransitive information

Ryan distinguishes three kinds of information (23,24). Bond information (entropy) describes the exact microstate of the system, structural information corresponds to the macrostate and functional information is "necessary to specify a function identical to that performed by the system" (23). He sees a fundamental difference here: bond and structural information are transferable or transitive, while functional information is intransitive, and does not belong to the system. Later, Ryan estimates the information in the specification of the function of a watch.

I admit that this division draws attention to an important thing, but I cannot see any difference between the status of the three information. All are equally committed to frames of the observer. As far as the choice of a particular frame if necessary, information remains transferable: by another observer, the same description will be applied. It is important, however, that even functional information (what is here essentially the intricacy of a description specifying the behaviour of the system) be determined in a non-discretional frame. I think, it can be an objective system characteristic; again, in a broader system in which the outer relations of the present one become inner. The function of the watch is in its coupling to other systems.

3. Fowler's information

Fowler (9) distinguishes the information gained by an observer about a system from that what is acquisited and used by systems (machines); he intends to deal exclusively with the latter. He identifies four manifestations of this information: stored, acquisited, transferred and processed (which means some action). In his definition, information is a physical quantity which, however, guides action in the real world, and it is a choice between fixed alternatives to which it is relative (for details, see 9).

My problem is, that Fowler distinguishes sharply observer's information from the system's information without any discussion on this. However, the latter can be expressed only through the former - we determine it by observing the system. This is very important. That is, if not the same information appears for the observer, than that used by a machine, the latter <u>cannot</u> be determined. To here belongs, whether man is or is not such a <u>machine</u> - if it is, what makes the difference between the acquired information of the two types?

Further, Fowler says: the reversal of one bit in a transmitted message does not affect information, only action (processing). This statement comes from the careless use of the information-of-the-observer, I believe; information content is determined here in a discretional frame as a syntactical measure of the transferred sequence. It is similarly unsolved, that action surely does not depend on the frame which, however, appears explicitly in the definition. Whether information is related only to sequences of signs (syntax) or to their interpretation as well (semantics), whether <u>it</u> guides actions or not, is to be answered as well.

4. Information as a causal agent

Information is somehow related to the functioning, to the dynamics of systems, I propose together with others. Such a view was set forth by Fedanzo (7,8), too. His starting point is that "every system element has a nontrivial information value" (7) and that information acts towards the maintenance of the system; it is of causal nature. There is a mutual relationship between a system's construction (structure) and information: the two can be translated into each other. Struture is determined by information and information, if transmitted, can be measured by changes or modification in structure.

For me, the main question is this: For whom is this "nontrivial" information - the system, or the observer? How can we distinguish the two? Further, structure-modification of a system, caused by the outside, can appear in a larger system as the autonomous dynamics of that system and then this information disappears. What gives ground to define system boundaries in a way (seen earlier, too) on which the concept of information can depend? Finally, if we do not restrict the concept somehow, causal information either dissolves in physics or leads to an inacceptable ontological two-worlds concept. Similar problems appear with Csányi's work who gives a causal, functional definition of information (4), used but not discussed by Csányi and Kampis (5,11).

III. Information

1. Information without semantics - an illusion

According to the information theorists, the mathematical notion of information is different from the one of meaningful information in its very base (1,26). From one point of view, this is so; it is certainly true for the <u>theories</u> in their present forms.

System theoretically, however, this is not the case, in my view. Information always has a semantic, qualitative aspect. It is worth to recall the information concept of Riedl (17) here, who divided the variety (serving as the basis of determination of information) into deterministic and random parts. In this way, he solves, among others, the so-called "letter-paradox": that a letter of Einstein contains the same information as a random one. He sees the difference in that one is based on deterministic, while the other on probabilistic choices, thus the ratio of the two components is different in the total information. For me, it seems obvious that the whole thing depends on the choice of frames. If I know that the one is meaningful, this can be mirrored in the calculation. Thus semantics plays a role in the choice of proper frames. However, if the two letters have the same overall information content, they can be coded into each other. The determination of meaning depends therefore on the choice of frames, of system definitions. There is a mutual relationship between frames and the meaning of information. Precisely, the quality of information is identical to the choice-of-viewpoint and is contained in it.

The existence of such frames is inevitable in any system description. It follows, that information has a quality. If information indeed characterizes the system, this quality in manifested in the latter. What is that in a macroscopic system? I shall argue that is is the causal side of information. We know already that information is related to the functioning of systems, and has a quality or "meaning" of some kind. From this, of course, it could be a description of structural and behavioural patterns of the system, without any causal connotation. The quality of information is, however, particulate: information is linked to the individual macroscopic objects of the system and to their relations, the change of which results in changes of information. Of course, on a purely logical basis there is never enough reason to suppose causality beyond the pattern-like regularities (28), but I think, it can be thus reasonable to conceive the quality of information as causal.

2. The separation of knowledge and action

The main problem of information is the unclear relationship of the observer to the system. In the previous chapter, just one mistake appeared in a number of times, I think. The key is, that information was used in two different senses. In the cited examples, these became mixed.

"Everything said is said by an observer" (13). Any information is knowledge in this way. Still, the knowledge of observer and the information in the system are different. Knowledge belongs to the domain of interactions with the system. Action in the system falls in the oparational domain of the system. That it is possible to speak of the latter only through the former, requires a correspondance between the two - but these are in different domains.

Rothstein speaks of purely observational information but names it a specificity of the system. Pattee, on the converse, provides the system with the knowledge of information which is, however, only for the observer. Ryan does not raise the issue that what the system does and what we know about that should be related. Fowler, altough wants to distinguish these somehow, speaks of purely observer-independent information, implicitely obviously through knowledge and thus mixing the two.

What we need now is a technical tool for clearing up this relationship of <u>observer</u> to <u>system.</u>

3. Reference

Below I shall try to present a constructive solution based on the sutiable notion of reference. Varela characterized living organisms as self-referential systems in his well-known book (27). Its basic notions, originally developed by G. Spencer-Brown, are the ones of <u>distinction</u> (the separation of a domain into parts) and indication (pointing to one of the resulting domains). This forms a cognitive viewpoint, a preference which is the basis of all system descriptions. Self-reference means that a system enters its own indicational space; reference, what will be needed here, is not defined.

An indication always contains the observer in one of its sides, self-reference not. Here I see a problem, of which only one aspect is important now. Shortly, in a system description, the basis of frames cannot be distinctions of the type "I/you" but of "this/that" only, thus not containing the observer <u>immediately.</u> For example, by preferring <u>one</u> population in an ecosystem, we can examine how it effects the rest of the system; by preferring the other part, how the ecosystem influences the population. The presence of a distiction is obvious here, beyond the one which delimits the ecosystem from its environment. This is what I would call <u>reference:</u> a relation between conceptually separated phenomenal domains, one <u>of</u> which is preferred.

Two more things are important. First, when saying relation, we usually mean causal link. Second, it follows from the <u>asymmetry</u> of the viewpoint here, that the relation and, consequently, the described causal link is <u>unidirectional</u> (in order to speak of the other direction, the frame should be changed, see the example).

4. Referential/nonreferential information

Systems are delimited and this delimitation cuts some causal links. To any description, there are non-described causes which, however, have their effects in the system. Physical descriptions describe actions within systems, to which immediate, symmetric causality belongs. Here I do not see information. Instead, it is related to the effects not specified within the system, to which separated, unidirectional causality belongs. But system delimitations are never absolute. I think, in the case of information, the matter is first the separation of systems, and then their <u>partial</u> reunion, leading to the conceptual preservation of unidirectionality.

In my definition, information consists of two parts: a referential and a nonreferential one. <u>Referential information</u> is a unidirectional causal link between conceptually separated phenomenal domains. It <u>is</u> action, of a special kind. <u>Nonreferential information,</u> on the other hand, is the knowledge of the observer, corresponding to the referential part (i.e. the knowledge of actual separation and actual relations). The one has a semantical value towards the system, the other towards the observer.

44

This information is a system property, intelligible in a given natural system only. As such, it can be applied in itself, but there is one more question: does information exist as an irreducible descriptional tool? Clearly, this depends on the delimitation of systems; and in the case of biological information, the answer is yes, I think. The problem is, whether it is possible to express the examined natural object in one system frame technically, or we have some special reason to introduce distinctions (corresponding to referential information) within the object.

Biological systems consist of components, and the essence of their processes is the de novo production of new components (system theoretically, this is so even if the new components prove to be identical to the old ones). However, we do not have any tools to tell in advance the behaviour of macroscopic components getting newly in relation (21). Therefore, the separation of a natural system (e.g. an evolving eco-system) into more systems is necessary for understanding the causal aspect of system transformations; one such system consists of the actual components and their relations. Information is how the systems determine each other. It is an irreducible tool of biology, as long as it is interested in the changes of systems and not only in the characteristics of extant systems.

Applications of the present concept of information, together with discussions on its relationship to other concepts, will be found in (12).

Acknowledgment. The author wishes to thank Prof. V. Csányi for ongoing discussions and inspirations to this work. He also thanks Dr. F.J. Varela for one discussion.

References:

1. Bar-Hillel, Y. - Carnap, R.: 'Semantic Information', in: Language and Information, Massathussets, 1964.
2. Brillouin, L: Science and Information Theory, Academic Press, New York, 1962.
3. Bunge, M.: The Myth of Simplicity, Prentice-Hall, Englewood Cliffs, 1963.
4. Csányi V.: 'General Theory of Evolution', General Systems Yearbook XXVI, 1981, 73-94.
5. Csányi, V. - Kampis, G.: 'Autogenesis: The Evolution of Replicative Systems', J.theor.Biol. 114, 1985, 303-321.
6. Dretske, F.I.: 'Précis of Knowledge and the Flow of Information', Behav.Brain.Sci. 6, 1983, 55-90.
7. Fedanzo, A.J.: 'Expanding the categories of Feedback', J.Am.Soc.Inf.Sci., September 1977, 239-246.
8. Fedanzo, A.J.: 'The Origin of Information is Systems'; J.Social.Biol.Struct. 3. 1980, 17-32.
9. Fowler, T.B.: 'Brillouin and the Concept of Information', Int.J.Gen.Sys. 9. 1983, 143-155.

10. Kampis, G. - Csányi, V.: 'Simple Models Do Not Eliminate Complexity from the Real World', J.theor.Biol. 115, 1985, 467-469.
11. Kampis, G. - Csányi, V.: 'A Computer Model of Autogenesis', J.Infer.Deduct.Biol., 1985, submitted.
12. Kampis, G.: 'Problems of System Descriptions' I-II., Int.J.Gen.Syst., 1985, submitted.
13. Maturana, H.R. - Varela, F.J.: Autopoiesis and Cognition, D. Reidel, Boston, 1980.
14. Polányi, M.: 'Life's Irreducible Structure', Science 160, 1968, 1308-1312.
15. Pattee, H.H.: 'Dynamic and Linguistic Modes of Complex Systems', Int.J.Gen.Syst. 3. 1977, 259-266.
16. Quastler, H.: Information Theory in Biology, Urbana, 1953.
17. Riedl, R.: Order in Living Organisms, Wiley, New York, 1978.
18. Robinson, A.L.: 'Computing Without Dissipating Energy', Science 223, 1984, 1164-1166.
19. Rosen, R.: 'Autonomous State Classifications by Dynamical Systems', Math.Biosci. 14, 1972, 151-167.
20. Rosen, R.: a comment on Pattee's paper, in: Biogenesis, Evolution, Homeostasis, A. Locker ed., Springer, Berlin, 1973, p. 47.
21. Rosen, R.: Fundamentals of Measurement and Representation of Natural Systems, North-Holland, New York, 1978.
22. Rothstein, J.: 'Generalized Entropy, Boundary Conditions, and Biology', in: Tribus, M. - Levine, R.D. ed.: The Maximum Entropy Formalism, Plenum, New York, 1981, 423-468.
23. Ryan, J.P.: 'Information, Entropy, and Various Systems', J.theor.Biol. 36, 1972, 139-146.
24. Ryan, J.P.: 'Information-Entropy Interfaces and Different Levels of Biological Organization', J.theor.Biol. 84, 1980, 31-48.
25. Saunders, P.T. - Ho, M.W.: 'On the Increase in Complexity in Evolution' II., J.theor.Biol. 90. 1981, 515-530.
26. Shannon, C.E. - Weaver. W.: The Mathematical Theory of Communication, University of Illinois Press, Urbana, 1949.
27. Varela, F.J.: Principles of Biological Autonomy, North-Holland, Amsterdam, 1979.
28. Wartofsky, M.W.: Conceptual Foundations of Scientific Thought, Macmillan, New York, 1968.

NATURAL SYSTEMS ACCORDING TO MODERN SYSTEMS SCIENCE: THREE DUALITIES

Marc E. Carvallo
Dept. of Philosophy of Religion
State University of Groningen
Nieuwe Kijk in 't Jatstraat 104
9712 SL Groningen, The Netherlands

ABSTRACT. The aim of the paper is: a) to gain some knowledge of
the so-called 'natural systems' as interpreted or defined by modern
systemsscientists; b) to discuss these descriptions and definitions
from the viewpoint of modern philosophy of science. In the course
of both a) and b) the interwovenness of the classes of natural systems and the controversial issues connected therewith (a.o. their
interwovenness with the artificial systems) will be touched upon.

Data about 'natural systems' or respectively definitions thereof
are, to the best of my knowledge, rather scarce in modern systemsliterature. This system of scarce data ranges from literature that
from the title would comprise an explicit treatment of what 'natural
systems' exactly are, yet that on closer examination nowhere explicitly defines them, to literature that does indeed give a few explicit
definitions of them. Let us first have a closer look at this system
of scarce data. Rosen's book 'Fundamentals of Measurement and Representation of Natural Systems' (1978) for instance, chiefly (if not
exclusively) treats the fundamentals of measurement and representation
and hardly or practically not at all the natural systems themselves.
He even leaves the basic term 'system' undefined (p. 26). At a
closer look 'system' is to him identical with 'system of interest'.
This identification of 'system' with 'system of interest' is generated
by one of the basic assumptions of the phenomenological tradition
and of the non-classical reductionism under which e.g. the quantum
theory and the many current versions of General Systems Theory
may be classed. Without a further definition of what 'natural systems'
are Rosen also takes his departure from this tacit assumption ('A
system is some part of the real world which comprises our object
of study', p. 26). Under this definition that is hopelessly vague
for a metaphysician, the three basic features of natural systems,
being states, observables and interactions or dynamics, are then
successively treated. The provisional conclusion one might draw
from reading this book is that 'natural systems' means the physico-
chemical and the biological ones. It is true that he pays sufficient
attention to the controversial issues that refer to or could refer

R. Trappl (ed.), Cybernetics and Systems '86, 47–54.

to those two classes of natural systems, such as the issue of the
hidden variables. But perhaps this issue betrays his implicit division
of systems into two other categories, viz. that of the observing
systems (here thus referring to measurement and representation)
and that of the observed systems (here thus referring to the 'natural
systems'). This might suggest to us that human systems (which then
in this contxt belong to the category of observing systems) according
to him cannot be assigned to the class of 'natural systems'. An
efficient way of finding out what 'natural systems' are in modern
systemsliterature is to look for dualities of which they (i.e.
the 'natural systems') are complementary parts and so are co-consti-
tuents of the duality, deriving their definitions from this duality.
By duality I mean here a quite wide sense the concept conveying
the occurence of many forms (such as pairing, doubling, splitting,
opposing etc.) in diverse settings (physical, psychological, social,
cultural etc.). It thus stands for the two extremes, i.e. both
the unifying (such as the synthesis of opposites) and the separational
element (such as dualism).
I have so far met with seven types of duality in the descriptions
of 'natural systems' by modern systemsscientists. The first three
types will be discussed here briefly.

1. The first duality: observed system - observing system

According to Von Foerster (1984) this type of duality seems to be
present to the history of science in three distinct variants resp.
phases. The first is that of classical science according to which the
dichotomy between the 'observing system' (i.e. the observer resp. the
scientist or the subject) and the 'observed system' (i.e. the subjectless universe of the object) is one of the criteria. Science (as
process or as the product of observation) is the objective description
of this subjectless world. The second is that which, as a reaction
upon the first, is proposes by the relativity theory ('Observations
are not absolute but relative to an observer's point of view, i.e.
his coordinate-system', cf. Einstein) and the quantum theory ('Observations affect the observed so as to obliterate the observer's hope
for prediction, i.e. his uncertainty is absolute', cf. e.g. Heisen-
berg). The third posits that a description of the universe (i.e.
the observed system) implies one who describes (observes) it (i.e.
the observing system). In contradistinction to the classical problem
of scientific inquiry that postulates first a description-invariant
'objective world' and then attempts to write its description, one
is now challenged to develop a description-invariant 'subjective
world' (i.e. a world which includes the observer) and then attempts
to write its description. This is the position taken e.g. by Von
Foerster himself, Pask, Maturana and Varela.
Von Foerster's reconstruction of the development of the interpretation
of this first type of duality seems to me only partially true.
It is only true for the history of science that is predicated upon
the logical-empiristic style, but not true for the history of science
that is predicated upon the rivaling hermeneutic-dialectic style.

In this latter the third position has always been the first and prime position (cf. e.g. Radnitzky, 1970) and the development of science based on this style seems to follow just the reverse sequence! Since the tacit assumption of the first two variants concerning 'natural systems' is practically tantamount to that of Rosen, it seems to me it would be interesting to draw some possible conclusions from those of the third variant as to their tacit image of 'natural systems'. Well, if we start from the following assumptions: a) that 'observed systems' are 'natural systems' and b) that 'observing systems' (or human systems) are included in the 'observed systems', then it follows that 'natural systems' also include 'human systems'. Employing the extrapolation of the third position, the 'natural systems' would therefore consist of three classes, being that of the physico-chemical and of the biological (compare the first two positions and that of Rosen) and the human one. A problem that arises here might be formulated as follows: if the category of 'observing systems' (or: human systems) is included in the category of 'observed systems' (or: natural systems) then what could one say about artefacts in general and the scientific instruments, which are indeed artificial systems but which do constitute an essential part of the 'observing systems' (which now turn out to belong to the 'natural systems')? The third position is in principle also the position taken by the postpositivistic philosophy of science. This philosophy of science even goes a step further. It claims to be not only a theory of the 'observing systems' but also of the observations as products of the 'observing systems', i.e. of the statement sytems of the 'observing systems'. This means that it subsumes the observations of the 'observing systems' in the' category of the 'observed systems' and accordingly in the category of 'natural systems'! Naturalized epistemology belongs to one of its central themes (cf. Popper, Kuhn, Toulmin, Lakatos). Naturalized epistemology also seems to be a central theme of another group of researchers who follow the tradition represented by Piaget, Bateson, McCulloch, Maturana and Varela, where stress is laid upon the biological origins of thought (the difference between these two traditions will elsewhere be demonstrated to some extent). By analogy with the above another problem arises here which may be formulated as follows: what could be said of the class of observations as products of the 'observing systems', i.e. of the 'theories', if they also (and consequently) may (or must) be regarded as scientific instruments (for the interpretation of 'having a theory', cf. e.g. Sneed, 1979: 261-262) and therefore belong to the class of artificial systems, while it is essentially a prolongation of the class of 'observing systems', which now turns out to belong to the category of 'natural systems'?

2. The second duality: natural systems - artificial systems

The themes of that excellent periodical 'Nature and System', subtitled 'philosophical studies of natural and artificial systems', edited by Joseph L. Esposito, are concentrated around this duality. A

49

definition of 'natural system' is wisely refrained from, but reading
the articles, discussions and reviews the quarterly publishes might
lead one to question the unambiguous difference between those two
classes of systems. Other suggestions, only attendant in the present
context, which the title and subtitle of the periodical might imply
are the following: firstly that nature is not a system, secondly
that system refers only to the artificial system and finally that
natural system is consequently a contradiction in adjecto.
In the first chapter of his classic work, Monod (1979) by means
of an imaginary experiment tries to illustrate the difficulty of
defining the distinction which might seem intuitively evident,
between 'natural' and 'artificial' systems (p. 19). Reading more
closely, we find that the second and indeed the main object of
the imaginary experiment is 'to compel us to 'rediscover' the most
general properties that charactize *living beings* (my cursivation)
and distinguish them from the rest of the universe' (p. 23). Whether
these living beings should as species be included in the same higher
class of beings to which also other species belong such as mountains,
rivers, clouds, the rockformations of Apremont and quartzcristals,
as distinguishable from another higher class to which other species
belong, such as knives, handkerchiefs, cars, spaceshuttles and
the houses of Barbizon, is a matter about which he leaves us in
the dark. Apart from drawing our attention to the anthropic bias,
the arbitrariness and even the flagrant contradictions implicit
in distinguishing systems as 'natural' or 'artificial', he seems
to take it for granted that 'natural systems' are the same thing
as 'living systems', i.e. the biological systems. This seems to
be the implicit image of 'natural systems' among biologists. Varela
for one even speaks of 'living systems' and 'natural systems' inter-
changeably (cf. Varela, 1979: xi–xviii). What a 'living system'
exactly is many biologists refuse to say (cf. e.g. Waddington,
1969–1972; Hall, 1981. For an operational definition, see e.g.
Reid et al., 1983). Monod considers that he has found the three
differentiae specificae (i.e. teleonomy, autonomous morphogenesis
and reproductive invariance) that distinguish 'living systems'
from the rest of the universe. Varela thinks the specificum lies
in the autonomy which he (and Maturana) calls 'autopoiesis'. Both
with Monod and with Varela and Maturana the concept of 'living
systems' refers to all organic systems including the human systems.
About half of Monod's book is a philosophical story about the human
systems from the viewpoint of a molecular biologist. And says Varela:
'... we ourselves fall into the same class' (Varela, 1979: xvi).
Or Maturana: 'The observer is a human being, that is, a living
being, and whatever applies to living systems applies also to him'
(Maturana, 1980: 8). My first impressions when reading these authors
is that Monod now ventures to state more plainly that 'human systems'
can only be defined within the boundaries of his 'living sytems'.
That is to say that the class of 'human systems' *as a whole* falls
within the class of his 'living systems'. But from reading Maturana's
work one cannot yet conclude that his statement quoted above is
also convertible, viz. that the converse of that proposition follows

with no other variation than the transposition of terms. (For more
details about this form of scholastic modal syllogistic, see e.g.
Bochenski, 1970: 224-229). The application of the autopoiesis-idea
to human systems does not seem to be without problems for Varela
and Maturana themselves (cf. Varela, 1979: 53-55; 1980: 118). The
objective idea of the 'autopoiesis' that according to him - at
least in sensu affirmativo - is formed by three orders of autopoietic
systems (cf. Varela, 1980: 107-111) seems to me to be still too
small also to include the class of 'human systems' in its entirety.
To this and the connected problem I shall return elsewhere. This
second duality one also finds of course with Simon, best summarized
in his 'The Sciences of the Artificial' (Simon, 1975). In contrast
to e.g. Von Bertalanffy, his main concern does not regard the natural
systems (e.g. the biological systems), but the 'artificial' (sometimes
also called by him the 'artifactual' systems). But naturally he
cannot avoid telling us what his assumption is about the natural
systems. At the very outset he posits quite in general that it
is not unambiguously evident what is 'natural'. Let us take an
example from the physico-chemical level: 'To say that an astronaut,
or even an airplane pilot, is obeying the law of gravity, hence
is a perfectly natural phenomenon, is true; but its truth calls
for some sophistication in what we mean by 'obeying' a natural
law. Aristotle did not think it natural for heavy things to rise
or light ones to fall (Physics, Book IV); but presumably we have
a deeper understanding of 'natural' than he did' (p.3), he adds
ironically. The same applies to systems on the biological level:
'A forest may be a phenomenon of nature; a farm certainly is not.
The very species upon which man depends for his food - his corn
and his cattle - are artifacts of his ingenuity. A plowed field
is no more part of the nature than an asphalted street - and no
less' (p. 3). One might extend the list of examples of this ambiguous
evidence of the difference between 'natural' and 'artificial',
e.g.: a swarm of summermaking swallows in the wood certainly belongs
to the class of 'natural systems', but to what class of systems
would the same swarm of birds belong when an hour later they are
sitting in 'ordered' rows on the electric cables... Simon does
not pursue these themes which are rather central for the phenomeno-
logists and philosophers of science. For these the problematic
aspect of distiction between those two classes of systems not only
arises in the case of what Simon defines as 'outer environment',
but also in the case of the 'inner environment'. (Note: Simon's
'inner environment' corresponds to what is usually addressed as
the system's structure, i.e. the elements of the system proper
together with the relations between them. And his 'outer environment'
corresponds to what is usually adressed as the system's environment,
i.e. the environment beyond the system's boundaries (cf. Simon,
1975: 7-8).) Not only the 'hard' components (e.g. temperature in
which we spend most of our hours) and the 'soft' components (e.g.
'symbols' that we receive through eyes and ears in the form of
written and spoken language) of the 'outer environment', but also
those of the 'inner environment' are 'carpentered' (to use Heelan's

51

term): the cartesian structure of visual perception for instance
is something so familiar and so transparently evident that we regard
it as normative for ordinary observations. It is, nevertheless,
a product of scientific culture and an artifact of a technologically
reconstructed human environment. In contrast, the hyperbolic structure
of vision is not the product of scientific activity; nevertheless,
it needs a mathematical model to make the coherence of its structure
manifest (Heelan, 1983). Or from another point of view: some experiments seem to confirm the hypothesis that thinking in terms of
modules on the long run may affect the structure of the brain in
a permanent way (cf. Bohm and Welwood, 1980).
With these few examples Simon would point out that artifacts are
not apart from nature. He goes on with the characterization of
what is 'artificial', finally to conclude that 'natural systems'
are in principle artificial systems. There are four indicia that
distinguish the artificial from the natural: 1. artificial things
are synthesized by man; 2. artificial things may imitate appearances
in natural things while lacking, in one or many aspects, the reality
of the matter; 3. artificial things can be characterized in terms
of functions, goals, adaptation; 4. artificial things are often
discussed, particularly when they are being designed, in terms
of imperatives as well as descriptives (pp. 5-6). In the symmetrical
view of the artifact as 'interface' between an 'inner' environment
and an 'outer' environment he emphasizes the relations between
purpose, elements and environment of the system, and this shows
that the third indicium is the most fundamental. His conclusion
is that '... in this way of viewing artifacts applies equally well
to many things that are not man-made - to all things in fact, that
can be regarded as 'adapted' - to some situation; and in particular
to the living systems that have evolved through the forces of organic
evolution (p. 7). Mattessich rightly draws attention to the semantical
trap into which Simon might step if he identified 'adaptation'
of a system as an artificial process; then the natural sciences,
too, especially biology, become sciences of the artificial (Mattessich,
1978: 293). And if 'adaptation' is in fact the only essential criterium
of the 'natural systems' also - this is one of the basic assumptions
of the behaviorism to which Simon seems to adhere - then accordingly
'natural systems' are in fact 'artificial systems'! (Curiously
enough, this conclusion, seen from quite a different point of view,
does not sound strange at all: for those who tacitly or explicitly
adhere to classical theism, the whole universe is a great artificial
system!) To these controversial issues of the mechanistic approach
I shall return elsewhere.

3. The third duality: artificial-natural-observer-systems

The third type of duality is more or less a hybrid of the first and the
second type of duality. They are seen int.al. in the following two variants: firstly in the tripartition 'artificial-natural-observer'-sys-
tems as was recently proposed by Atlan (1983) and secondly in the triad
'observer'-'system'-'another system' of Uribe (1981). In the setting of

the first variant Atlan tries to synthesize some principles of the contemporary information theory (e.g. Von Foerster's 'order from noise'-
principle and Atlan's own 'information or complexity from noise'-prin-
ciple) with the new understanding of the physic organization as interpreted by some contemporary French philosophers and psychoanalyticians
like Ganguilhem, Serres, Foucoult and Lacan. Since for a layman in this
matter it is quite a puzzle to render this train of thought exactly, I
shall - at the risk of making mistakes - only attempt to give simple
descriptions of a few concepts that are relevant to this paragraph,
keeping strictly to the charge to find out what is meant by 'natural
systems' in this complicated context. Atlan proposes two distinctions.
The first is between the well-known artificial systems and the imperfectly known natural systems. The second is that between the observed
natural systems and the human natural systems, where the observer is
inside the system as a part (social system) or as a whole (individuals
as 'assimilating' systems, with both senses of biological and cognitive
assimilation as interpreted by Piaget) (p. 39). One of the key-concepts
upon which these distinctions pivot is 'complexity'. Let us start with
this. According to Atlan we can so far recognize three kinds of complexity in the course of the development of the information theory
which are related to the three different expressions of the H function: 'the first one, trivial (and maximum), is the variety given by
$H = \log_2 N$ (Eq. 3); the second has to do with the disorder or statistical homogeniety and is given by $H = \Sigma p(i) \log_2 p(i)$ (Eq. 1); the
third is a measure of the lack of knowledge about the internal constraints (or redundancy) of the system and is given by $H = H_{max} (1-R)$
from Eq. 4 (p. 29). The two distinctions proposed take place within
the context of the third kind of complexity. (Note: the technical
details as to the extensive use of the Shannon formulas for the H and R
functions to define what is organization, complexity, and order and the
deficiencies of these formulas, I leave here to the experts). 'A system
appears complex when we do not know how to specify it completely, although we know enough about it to recognize it and to call it a system'
(p. 27). Within this general term 'complex' we should, according to
Atlan, distinguish two concepts, being complication and complexity.
'Complication only expresses a high number of steps necessary to
describe or specify or build a system. In this sense, the complication
should be the attribute of man-made systems, and its measure could be,
for example, the minimum number of steps that a Turing machine would
need to describe it. This measure could be computed from actual blueprints. In fact, very often such measures are given by means of computer time needed to achieve some task: the more time, the more complicated the task for the same computing facilities. On the other hand,
complexity is the attribute of natural systems that we know only
partially and are unable to master and reproduce artificially. The
measure of complexity is that of our ignorance, and in this respect the
Shannon H function is very adequate' (p. 27). Following Atlan's distinction and in order to avoid the ambiguity of the adjective 'complex'
at the very outset I would propose to distinguish 'complex' from 'complicated'. 'Complex' would then be the specific attribute of the natural systems, and 'complicated' of the artificial systems. Atlan's ana-

53

lysis affords us some hints for the better understanding of the artificial and natural systems (or for a better understanding of our ignorance about these). Let me draw some conclusions from this and put them in a somewhat stronger form: (1) one of the specific criteria of the artificial systems is that they never can be 'complex', they can only be 'complicated'; (2) one of the specific criteria of the natural systems is that they can only be 'complex'. In so far as I do not misunderstand him, the natural systems may be 'complicated' too. And consequently 'complicated' resp. 'complication' and 'complex' resp. 'complexity' constitute one and the same continuum. But in fact and in principle only 'complicated' resp. 'complication' lie within the grasp of the finite computing process. Beyond this begins the realm of the 'complex' resp. 'complexity'. (3) From (1) it follows that artificial systems are well-known or well-knownable. From (2) it follows that natural systems can only be known imperfectly. (4) For those (such as cyberneticians), who like to think in terms of 'possible worlds', I point to Atlan's note that: '... the two definitions could merge if an artificial computing process were allowed to be made infinite. And, in fact, Zrinkin and Levin have shown that the Kolmogorov complexity (in the algorithmic sense, i.e. the complication) of a program n of length l(n), written by any finite-alphabet ergodic process, tends towards l(n)H(n) (i.e. Shannon's function times the length of the program viewed as message) as l(n) tends to infinity' (p. 41). This means that it is possible for the 'complication' to transcend its own boundaries and to become 'complexity'! (This conclusion turns out to contradict conclusion (1)). And what about the reverse? (5) If the term 'complexity' is attributed exclusively to natural systems, then other terms should be found for the first and the second kind of complexity, to avoid confusion.

The second distinction is that between the observed natural systems and the human natural systems, where the observer is inside the system. This second distinction thus refers (exclusively) to the domain of 'complexity'. Within this system of 'complexity' then, we would meet with the following kinds of natural systems: firstly, the natural systems in the various levels of organization, from elementary particles to societies (p. 28); these constitute the subclass of 'observed systems' including the observer resp. the class of 'observing systems'. Secondly, that particular subclass of natural systems consisting of human systems 'where the observer is inside the system'. The relation of the observer to the first kind of natural systems is in principle the classical relationship of subject-object, or at most a (tacit) combination of the first and the second variant of the duality 'observing system' - 'observed system' as meant by Von Foerster.

References: can be requested from the author.

A COMPLEXITY MEASURE FOR BINARY RELATIONAL SYSTEMS

Janusz Stokłosa
Center of Computer Science
Technical University of Poznań
60-965 Poznań
Poland

ABSTRACT. The paper describes a graph-theoretic complexity measure for binary relational systems. One-level and hierarchy systems are considered. The obtained results are the generalization of those presented in [4] and [5].

1. PRELIMINARIES

A relational system [10] is a finite sequence
$$S_q = (X, R_1, \ldots, R_q),$$
where X is a nonempty set, and $R_1, \ldots, R_q$ are relations in X. If X is finite then S_q is called finite. If $R_1, \ldots, R_q$ are binary relations, S_q is said to be a binary relational system.

A directed graph G is a pair $G = (V, A)$ such that V is a set of vertices and A is a set of arcs. A partial graph [2] G' of $G = (V, A)$ is such a graph $G' = (V, A')$ that $A' \subseteq A$. A graph is strongly connected if there is an oriented path between every two vertices. $G = (V, A)$ is connected if for every $v_1, v_2 \in V$ there is an oriented path between v_1 and v_2 or between v_2 and v_1.

A graph G is said to be planar if there exists a geometric representation of G which can be drawn on the plane (or on the sphere) in such a way that any two arcs do not cross. The plane representation of the graph devides the plane into parts called regions.

Let for the graph G m be the number of arcs, n - the number of vertices, and p - the number of connected components. By a cyclomatic number of G we mean such a number $\nu(G)$ that
$$\nu(G) = m - n + p.$$

Theorem 1 [2]. In the strongly connected graph, the cyclomatic number is equal to the maximum number of linearly independent cycles.

Definition 1. Let $G = (V, A)$ be a graph. By a minimal strongly connected extension (msce for short) of G we mean a graph $\overset{\star}{G} = (V, \overset{\star}{A})$ such that:
  (i) G is a partial graph of $\overset{\star}{G}$,

55

R. Trappl (ed.), Cybernetics and Systems '86, 55–61.
© *1986 by D. Reidel Publishing Company.*

(ii) every component of $\overset{\smallsmile}{G}$ is strongly connected,
(iii) the cardinality of $\overset{\smallsmile}{A}$-A is minimal for making every component of G strongly connected.

From Definition 1 it follows that if G is strongly connected then $\overset{\smallsmile}{G}$=G.

Example 1. Let G be such a graph as on Fig.1a. The graph presented on Fig.1b is not the msce of G because it does not fulfil the assumption (iii), and the graph on Fig.1c is such an extension.

a/

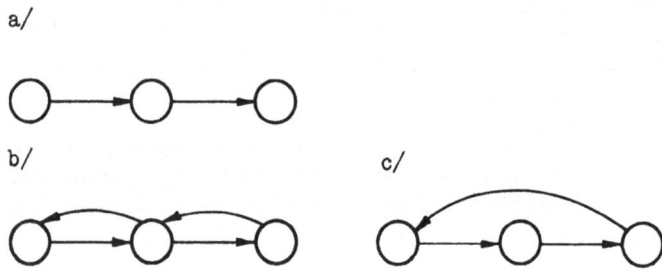

Figure 1. An example of a graph (a) and two other graphs; one of them is not a msce (b), and the other one is (c).

Let us note two facts.
i/ The msce of the graph G is not defined uniquely.

Example 2. Msce's of the graph drawn on Fig.2a are presented on Fig.2b and 2c.

a/

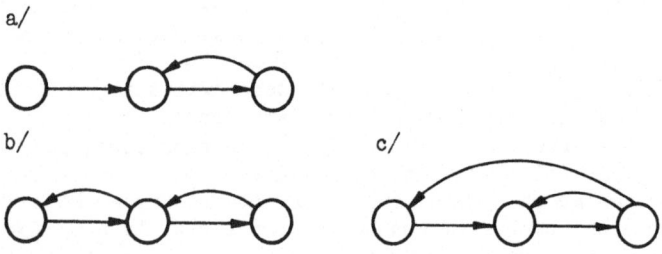

Figure 2. Two msce's (b,c) of a graph (a).

ii/ The cyclomatic numbers for different msce's of a given graph are equal.

2.   RELATIONAL SYSTEMS

The directed graph is the most natural way of presenting the binary relation. It will be used to describe the binary relational systems.

Definition 2. For a binary relational system $S_q = (X, R_1, \ldots, R_q)$ we
   define a directed graph G_q in the
   following way:
   (i) if $q=1$ then $G_1 = (V, A)$, where $V = X$ and $A = R_1$,
   (ii) if $q>1$ and G_q is the graph of S_q then G_{q+1} is constructed
   in such a way that it is equal to G_q extended by independent
   components corresponding to the graph (X, R_{q+1}).

Example 3. Let $S_3 = (\{0,1\}, \{(0,0)\}, \{(0,1),(1,0)\}, \{(1,0),(1,1)\})$. G_3 is
   presented on Fig.3.

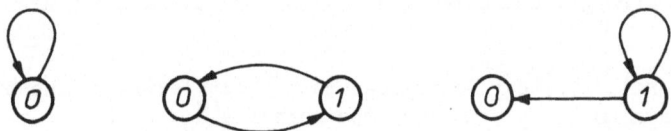

Figure 3. The graph G_3 constructed for the system S_3 from Example 3.

The two next examples serve as the basis for further consideration.

Example 4. The strongly connected graph G is presented on Fig.4. For it
   $\gamma(G) = 8-5+1 = 4$ which means that in G there exist four linearly independent cycles (the basis), e.g. (aa),(abca),(bcedb),
   (ded). With every cycle of the basis we associate a vector as
   follows:

```
              1 2 3 4 5 6 7 8
   aa :      ( 1 0 0 0 0 0 0 0 )
   abca :    ( 0 1 1 1 0 0 0 0 )
   bcedb :   ( 0 0 1 0 1 1 0 1 )
   ded :     ( 0 0 0 0 0 1 1 0 )
```

The cycle (abcabcededbca) corresponds to the vector
(0 2 3 2 1 2 1 1) which is the linear combination of the basis vectors:
(0 2 3 2 1 2 1 1) = 2(0 1 1 1 0 0 0 0) + (0 0 1 0 1 1 0 1) +
                   + (0 0 0 0 0 1 1 0).

Making use of Theorem 1 one can choose a basis set of cycles that corresponds to paths through the graph.

Example 5. Let G be the same graph as in Example 4. Let a and d be initial and finite vertices, respectively. The set of paths:
   (abced),(abceded),(aabced), and (abcabced) forms the basis.

Every path between a and d is a linear combination of the basis paths,e.g.
(aabceded)=(aabced)+(abceded)-(abced), i.e.
(2 1 1 0 0 2 1 1)=(2 1 1 0 0 1 0 1)+(0 1 1 0 0 2 1 1)-
- (0 1 1 0 0 1 0 1).

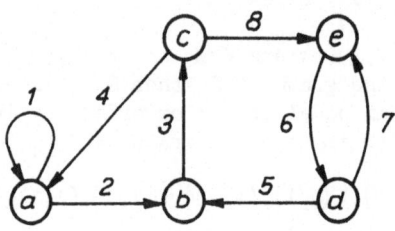

Figure 4. A strongly connected graph with 5 vertices and 8 arcs.

The overall strategy is to measure the complexity of the binary relational system S_q by computing the number $\nu(\check{G}_q)$ of linearly independent cycles of $\check{G}_q$.

Definition 3. Let $S_q =(X,R_1,\ldots,R_q)$ be a binary relational system. A cyclomatic complexity $c(S_q)$ of S_q is defined as follows:
$$c(S_q)=\nu(\check{G}_q).$$

We have the following result.

Theorem 2. For $S_q=(X,R_1,\ldots,R_q)$ by Γ_i we denote the graph (X,R_i), $i=1,2,\ldots,q.$ If X is finite and (X,R_i) is connected then
$$c(S_q)= \sum_{i=1}^{q} \nu(\Gamma_i).$$

Proof. Let n_i and m_i be the numbers of vertices and arcs of Γ_i, respectively. Then
$$\sum_{i=1}^{q} \nu(\Gamma_i)=\sum_{i=1}^{q} m_i -\sum_{i=1}^{q} n_i + q = m - n + q,$$
where m is the number of arcs, and n – the number of vertices of $\check{G}_q$.

Example 6. Let $S_4=(X,R_1,R_2,R_3,R_4)$, where $X=\{a,b,c,d,e\}$, $R_1=\{(a,b),(b,c)\}$, $R_2=\{(a,b),(a,c),(b,b)\}$, $R_3=\{(a,b),(a,c),(c,d),(c,e)\}$, $R_4=\{(b,e),(c,e),(e,b)\}$. A msce $\check{G}_4$ for S_4 is presented on Fig.5. The cyclomatic complexity $c(S_4)=\nu(\check{G}_4)= 19-14 +4 = 9.$

If $\check{G}_q$ is the planar graph the calculation of $c(S_q)$ is simplified cf.[5].

Theorem 3. If for S_q the graph $\check{G}_q$ is planar, connected, and has r regions then
$$c(S_q)=r-1.$$

58

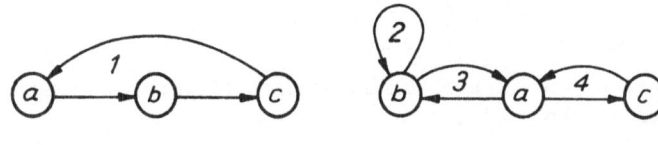

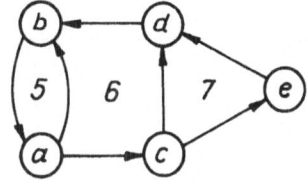

10

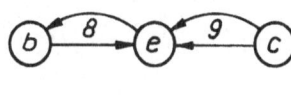

Figure 5. A msce $\overset{\lor}{G}_4$ constructed for S_4 from Example 6 (all regions are numbered).

Proof. If $\overset{\lor}{G}_q$ is a connected planar graph with n vertices, m arcs and r regions, then by Euler's formula (cf.[3], Theorem 5.6)

$$n - m + r = 2,$$

and hence

$$c(S_q) = \nu(\overset{\lor}{G}_q) = r - 1.$$

From the above theorem and Theorem 2 we have the following corollary.

Corollary 1. If $S_q = (X, R_1, \ldots, R_q)$ is finite and every Γ_i , i=1,2,...,q , is connected and planar then

$$c(S_q) = r-1.$$

Example 7. Let S_4 be the same as in Example 6. For this case r=10 (cf. Fig.5). Hence $c(S_4) = 10 - 1 = 9$.

3. HIERARCHY SYSTEMS

The binary relational system investigated in the previous section will be called here module.

Definition 4. Let $M_0, \ldots, M_t$ be modules. A hierarchy system is a binary relational system HS = (X,R), where X={$M_0, \ldots, M_t$}, and $R \subseteq X \times X$.

By analogy with [4] we define a complexity of hierarchy system as follows.

Definition 5. Let c(HS) be the hierarchy system complexity and let $c(M_i)$, i=0,1,...,t , be individual module complexities. The combined complexity is

59

$$c_H = w_1 \cdot c(HS) + w_2 \cdot \sum_{i=0}^{t} c(M_i),$$

where w_1 and w_2 are weighting factors which are assigned by the user of the system.

Example 8. (i) Let the graph of the hierarchy system be as on Fig.6 (cf. [6]). For this system

$$c_H = w_1 \cdot t + w_2 \cdot \sum_{i=0}^{t} c(M_i).$$

(ii) For the system which graph is presented on Fig.7 we have

$$c_H = w_1 + w_2 \sum_{i=0}^{2} c(M_i).$$

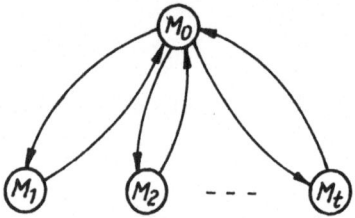

Figure 6. The graph of a hierarchy system.

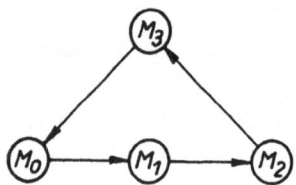

Figure 7. The graph of a pipeline-like system.

4.   CONCLUDING REMARKS

The complexity measure introduced in the paper deals with binary relational systems. This large class of systems includes iterative systems [1], k-machines [8,9], shift registers[9], computer programs [5] etc. Also networks of this kind of systems [4,7,8]. The technique can be used by the designer or the user of the system as part of a testing methodology.

5.   REFERENCES

1. Blikle A.,'Iterative systems; an algebraic approach'. Bulletin de l'Académie Polonaise des Sciences, Sér. Sci. Math., Astr. et Phys., 20 (1972), 51-53.

2. Christofides N., Graph Theory. An Algorithmic Approach. Academic Press, New York, 1975.
3. Deo N., Graph Theory with Applications to Engineering and Computer Science. Prentice-Hall, Englewood Cliffs, NJ, 1974.
4. Hall N.R., Preiser S., 'Combined network complexity measure'. IBM Journal of Research and Development, 28(1984), 15-27.
5. McCabe T., 'A complexity measure'. IEEE Transactions on Software Engineering, SE-2(1976), 308-320.
6. Mesarovic M.D., 'Mathematical theory of general systems', in: Klir J. (ed.), Trends in General Systems Theory. Wiley, New York, 1972.
7. Stokłosa J., 'Transformations of some dynamical systems - networks of (α,k)-machines generating cyclic sequences', in: Trappl R.(ed.), Cybernetics and Systems Research, North-Holland, Amsterdam, 1982, 179-183.
8. Stokłosa J., 'Computations in the network of (α,k)-machines', in: Ruschitzka M.(ed.), Parallel and Large-Scale Computers: Performance, Architecture, Applications. Elsevier, New York, 1983.
9. Stokłosa J., 'On some discrete models and relations between them'. Advances in Modelling and Simulation, 2(1985), 1-6.
10. Tarski A., 'Contributions to the theory of models, I,II'. Indagationes Mathematicae, 16(1954), 572-588.

STABILIZING PARTIALLY OBSERVABLE UNCERTAIN LINEAR SYSTEMS

Jean-Pierre Schellhorn
Department of Econometrics
University of Geneva
1211 Geneva 4
Switzerland

ABSTRACT. We consider linear systems which involve no
stochastic element,but whose state equations depend on ti-
me-varying unknown parameters. This parameter uncertainty
is not complete because we know that the parameters are
constrained to lie within known bounded intervals. The objective is to choose a dynamic observer and a feedback on
the state vector of this observer guaranteing uniform
asymptotic stability for all admissible variations of the
parameters of this control law.
After having defined fixed and mobile pairs of matrices
and presented some of their properties, we will show that
if a set of two fixed pairs are conveniently oriented,
then we can construct such an observer and a feedback
control law that we obtain the desired stabilization.
This representation with fixed pairs makes the introduction of homotopy (or: continuation) methods very natural.
Theses methods are very convenient computationnally (usable
on a pocket computer) and construct possible paths from a
known situation to the actual uncertain one.

1 Introduction

A classical way to deal with uncertain systems is to model
them with stochastic terms. This leads to stochastic or
adaptative control, whose main defect is to be practically
inappropriate if there is no so-called expectational equilibrium.
Another method is to introduce fuzzy systems and fuzzy controls; but fuzzy dynamic programming furnishes policy pres-
criptions which are not in closed form and consequently
cannot be employed to gain qualitative insights.

63

R. Trappl (ed.), Cybernetics and Systems '86, 63–70.
© *1986 by D. Reidel Publishing Company.*

A more recent trend is to postulate nothing about the system but parameter uncertainty and some boundedness of the input disturbances. This is surely more realistic if we have to deal with economic systems having some unknown and possibly even unknowable characteristics. And this encompasses also the problem of disturbed dynamical systems. For more methodological discussions, we refer the reader to the papers by Leitmann and Wan (1978,1979,1980).

2 Parameter uncertainty
THE PROPOSED MODEL

We started our investigation with the aim to generalize the special case $q=r=s=1$ analysed by Sundareshan (1977).

2.1
The evolution and observation equations are of the form:

$$\overset{\circ}{x}(t) = A(t)\ x(t) + B(t)\ u(t)$$

$$A(t) = A + f1(t)\ A1 + f2(t)\ A2 + \ldots + fq(t)\ Aq$$
$$B(t) = B + g1(t)\ B1 + g2(t)\ B2 + \ldots + gr(t)\ Br$$

$$y(t) = C(t)\ x(t)$$

$$C(t) = C + h1(t)\ C1 + h2(t)\ C2 + \ldots + hs(t)\ Cs$$

where $A,A1,\ldots,Aq$ are known $(n×n)$ matrices,
$B,B1,\ldots,Br$ are known $(n×m)$ matrices,
$C,C1,\ldots,Cs$ are known $(p×n)$ matrices,
and the uncertain parameter functions $f.(t),g.(t),h.(t)$
have values between -1 and $+1$ for $t \geqslant 0$.

Observe that $B(t)u(t) = Bu(t) + B1u1(t) + \ldots + Br\ ur(t)$, with $u.(t) = g.(t)\ u(t)$, is a special case of multiple control (Schellhorn,1981-1983).

2.2
In many cases, stabilizing such an uncertain system using state feedback is impossible because some or all states are latent (unmeasurable). Therefore we have to construct a state observer with "observer state" $z(t)$:

$$\overset{\circ}{z}(t) = A\ z(t) + B\ u(t) + J\ (\ C\ z(t) - y(t)\ )$$

and apply a feedback control of the form $u(t) = K\ z(t)$.

We will show how to construct the gain matrices J and K , under a rather general hypothesis enunciated in 4.1.
But first we have to introduce some new concepts.

3 Fixed and mobile pairs

3.1

Let $M = \left[\begin{array}{c|c} A & B \\ \hline C & D \end{array}\right]$ and $M(t) = \left[\begin{array}{c|c} A(t) & B(t) \\ \hline C(t) & D(t) \end{array}\right]$

be respectively a constant and a variable matrix.

As a generalization of the classical eigenpair (p,m) of M
(i.e. Mp=pm), we say that the pair of matrices (P , L)
is a fixed pair of M if

$$M \left[\begin{array}{c} I \\ \hline P \end{array}\right] = \left[\begin{array}{c} I \\ \hline P \end{array}\right] L \; .$$

Of course, if $\left[\begin{array}{c} X \\ \hline Y \end{array}\right]$ verifies $M \left[\begin{array}{c} X \\ \hline Y \end{array}\right] = \left[\begin{array}{c} X \\ \hline Y \end{array}\right] Z$,

and if X exists, then the pair of matrices ($P=YX^{-1}, L=XZX^{-1}$)
is a fixed pair of M. If P is positive definite, then we
say that the pair is positive.

Here are some properties of fixed pairs:

1) P is a solution of an algebraic Riccati equation (for
rectangular matrices): $\quad P A - D P + P B P - C = 0$.

   Reciprocally, every such equation defines one or more
   fixed pairs (P,L) with P a solution of the equation and
   L = A+BP.

2) $M = \left[\begin{array}{c|c} I & 0 \\ \hline P & I \end{array}\right] \left[\begin{array}{c|c} L & B \\ \hline 0 & E-PB \end{array}\right] \left[\begin{array}{c|c} I & 0 \\ \hline -P & I \end{array}\right]$,

   i.e M is similar to a block-triangular matrix with L as
   a diagonal block and

   $\left[\begin{array}{c|c} I & 0 \\ \hline P & I \end{array}\right]$ as the transformation matrix

3) If the four blocks of M are A, $-BR^{-1} B'$, $-Q(=C)$ and $-A'$
   and if (P,L) is a positive pair of M, then the linear
   system $\overset{o}{x} = Ax + Bu$ driven on the positive axis by the
   optimal Linear Quadratic (LQ) state-feedback
   $u = -R^{-1} B'Px$ is $\overset{o}{x} = L x$.

4) If Lp=pm (eigenpair) and $q = \left[\begin{array}{c} I \\ \hline P \end{array}\right] m$, then M q = q m .

65

5) To every subset of eigenvalues of M which contains complex eigenvalues in conjugate pairs corresponds a real
solution P, constructed with the associated generalized
eigenvectors. If Pk is the solution associated with
subset Sk (k=1,2,3) and if S3 is contained in the set-
union of S1 and S2, then there is a projector G such
that   P3 = (G) P1 + (I-G) P2 .

3.2
As a generalization of the eigenpairs AND of the transition
matrix of M(t), we say that the pair of matrices
(P(t),L(t)) is a mobile pair of M if

$$
M(t) \left\{ \begin{array}{c} I \\ \hline P(t) \end{array} \right\} = \left\{ \begin{array}{c} I \\ \hline P(t) \end{array} \right\} L(t) + \frac{d}{dt} \left\{ \begin{array}{c} I \\ \hline P(t) \end{array} \right\}
$$

If P(t) is positive definite, then we say that the pair is
positive.
Here are some properties of mobile pairs:

1) P is a solution of a differential Riccati equation (for
rectangular matrices): P A – D P + P B P – C = – dP/dt
Reciprocally, every such equation defines some mobile
pairs (P,L) with P a solution of the equation and
L = A+BP.

2) $$ M = \left\{ \begin{array}{c|c} I & 0 \\ \hline P & I \end{array} \right\} \left\{ \begin{array}{c|c} L & B \\ \hline P & E-PB \end{array} \right\} \left\{ \begin{array}{c|c} I & 0 \\ \hline -P & I \end{array} \right\} $$
i.e M is similar to a matrix which is near block-trian-
gular if the derivative dP/dt is near zero and which
contains L(t) as one of the diagonal blocks.

3) If the blocks of M(t) are A, –BR^{-1} B', –Q(=C) and –A',
and if (P,L) is a positive pair of M(t), then the linear
system $\dot{x}$ = Ax + Bu driven on a finite interval by the
optimal LQ state-feedback u(t) = –R^{-1} B'P x(t)
is $\dot{x}$(t) = L(t) x(t) .

4) The mobile pair (P(t), L=0) corresponds to the transition matrix T(t) , i.e.   M(t) T(t) = d T(t) /dt .

NOTE: Fixed pairs have been introduced under a different name by Eisenfeld (1976), who noticed their connection
with algebraic Riccati equations. The concept of mobile pairs and its connection with differential Riccati
equations appears in Schellhorn (1983). A new method
of computing fixed (and mobile) pairs is presented in
section 5. But first we like to explain how we can
get guaranteed stability.

4 Guaranteed stabilization
A SUFFICIENT CONDITION

Let us introduce

i) four gramians (positive-definite symmetric matrices) :
   QK and QJ (n$\times$n), RK(m$\times$m) and RJ(p$\times$p) ; these gramians
   are at the disposal of the designer;

ii) the 2(q+r+s) gramians
   A!,A^,A1!,A1^,...,Aq!,Aq^, B!,...,Br^, C!,...,Cs^
   associated to the q+r+s design matrices as follows:
   if A (or B or C) = GSD' (singular value decomposition),
   then A! (or B! or C!) = GSG'
   and A^ (or B^ or C^) = DSD' ;

iii) the six sums of gramians :
   a! = A1! +...+ Aq!   a^ = 2(A1^ +...+ Aq^)
   b! = 2(B1! +...+ Br!)   b^ = 2(B1^ +...+ Br^)
   c! = C1! +...+ Cs!   c^ = C1^ +...+ Cs^

iv) two positive fixed pairs (PK,LK) and (PJ,LJ) of the
   following Hamiltonian matrices HK , respectively HJ :

$$
HK = \left[\begin{array}{c|c} A & -BK \\ \hline -CK & -A' \end{array} \right], \qquad
HJ = \left[\begin{array}{c|c} A & -BJ \\ \hline -CJ & -A' \end{array} \right] = HJ(\ PK\ )
$$

with BK = B (RK - DK) B' + (a! + b!)
      CK = QK + (a^ + c^)
           DK = RK b^ RK   DJ = RJ c! RJ
    - BJ = QJ + (a! + b!)
      CJ = C'(RJ - DJ) C - PK (B DK B') PK

v) the gramians Q1 = PK (B RK B') PK
                 Q2 = C' RJ C + PJ (QJ) PJ

$$
\text{and the matrix} \quad W = \left[\begin{array}{c|c} QK + Q1 & -Q1 \\ \hline -Q1 & Q2 \end{array} \right] = W(PK,PJ) .
$$

Write   e(t) = x(t) - z(t) for the error and   L(x,e,t)
for the time-derivative of the positive Lyapunov function
x'(t) PK(t) x(t)   + e'(t) PJ(t) e(t) .

Using Cauchy-Schwarz's inequality , we get (e.g. for the
singular value decomposition Ak = GSD'): 2 fk x'P(Ak)x =
= 2 fk x'(GSD')x $\leqslant$ 2 $|$x'PGS$^{1/2}$ S$^{1/2}$ D'x$|$ $\leqslant$ x'PGSG'Px + x'DSD'x.
It is then possible to show that
L(x,e,t) $\leqslant$ - (x',e') W (x',e')' .
Because QK + Q3 is positive definite (p.f.), W is p.f. iff
the Schur complement   W / (QK+Q1) = Q2 - Q1 (QK+Q1)$^{-1}$ Q1
is also p.f. Let w be the least eigenvalue of W.

4.1
RESULT : If the positive fixed pairs (PK,LK) and (PJ,LJ)
        have such a mutual "orientation" that the Schur
        complement W / (QK+Q1) is positive definite, then
        $L(x,e,t) \leqslant -w (x'x + e'e)$.

4.2
RESULT: In this case, the gain matrices $J = - (PJ)^{-1} C'$ RJ
                         and   K = - RK   B' PK
        guarantee that the resulting closed-loop system will
        be uniformly asymptotic stable for all admissible
        variations of the parameters of this control law.

Actually the closed-loop system will be exponentially stable and the origin will be an attractor with "speed" w .
We can get a higher speed (and secure Result 4.1) if we
modify both Hamiltonians with two constants cK>o and cJ>o.

5 Homotopy methods
HOW THEY WORK

Over the past years the importance of homotopies has emerged as a crucial framework underlying global approaches to
systems of non-linear equations. Essentially, a homotopy is
a continuous deformation.
Suppose we are interested in some property P1 of a given
dynamical system , and suppose that a trivial system with
known properties Po is given to start. We then follow the
properties we are interested in as the trivial system is
deformed into the given system.
The continuous path created by the deformation will sometimes be proved to lead from the properties Po to the properties P1 .
Homotopy or continuation methods have been used e.g. as a
regular alternative to singular perturbations (Eitelberg,
1982) or as way to modify smoothly the coupling in a network of systems (DeCarlo&Saeks,1981). Richter and DeCarlo
(1983) have written a short tutorial. Elements of the method are illustrated by the following two examples.

5.1
Suppose that we are interested in the spectrum of a symmetric matrix A (n×n) with distinct eigenvalues. Eigenpairs
(v,m) of A , with $\|v\| = 1$, are zeros of the following
function $G (v,m) \longrightarrow \begin{bmatrix} Av - mv \\ 0.5 - 0.5 \, v'v \end{bmatrix}$

As a trivial starting point, we use any diagonal matrix F
with distinct diagonal elements fk ; if ek is the k-th column of the identity matrix , then the (ek ; fk) are the
eigenpairs of F.

If we use the homotopy
$$H(v,m;t) = \left[\begin{array}{c} [(1-t)(F-mI) + t(A-mI)]v \\ 0.5 - 0.5\,v'v \end{array} \right]$$
we are led to ask if we can join by an homotopy path any
eigenpair (v,m) of A to an eigenpair (e,f) of F .
The solution is simple (Chu,1984):

$$\frac{\partial H}{\partial(v';m;t)} = \left[\begin{array}{c|c|c} (1-t)F+tA - mI & -v & (A-F)v \\ \hline -v' & 0 & 0 \end{array} \right] \quad \text{is the jacobian}$$

matrix. Suppress the columns of $\partial H/\partial t$ to get the bordered
matrix called $T(t)$. Solving the initial value problem

$$\frac{d}{dt}\left[\begin{array}{c} v \\ m \end{array} \right] = T(t) \left[\begin{array}{c} (F-A)\,v \\ \hline 0 \end{array} \right], \quad \left[\begin{array}{c} v(0) \\ m(0) \end{array} \right] = \left[\begin{array}{c} e \\ f \end{array} \right], \quad 0 \leqslant t \leqslant 1,$$

with any canned integration scheme furnishes n trajectories,
i.e. n paths leading from the eigenpairs of F to the corresponding eigenpairs of A.

5.2
Consider the linear quadratic control problem:

$\overset{o}{x} = Ax + Bu$ (& initial conditions)

$u^\wedge = \arg\min \int_0^\infty (x'Qx + u'Ru)\ dt$

$\quad = - R^{-1} B'P\ x$, with (P,L) a positive fixed pair of M:

$$M = \left[\begin{array}{c|c} A & -BR^{-1}B' \\ \hline -Q & -A' \end{array} \right] \quad . \quad \text{Let } F = \left[\begin{array}{c|c} A & 0 \\ \hline 0 & -A' \end{array} \right] .$$

$(P=P',L)$ is a fixed pair of F iff PA is skew-symmetric.
Because every stable matrix A verifies $PA = W - Q$ with
P and Q positive definite and W skew-symmetric , the skew-
symmetricity of PA corresponds to the borderline $Q=0$,
where A is just not stable but for a small $Q= \varepsilon I$.
The (linear) homotopy

$$H(A,B;Q,P,S;t) = (1-t)F + tM = \left[\begin{array}{c|c} A & -tBR\ B' \\ \hline -tQ & - A' \end{array} \right]$$

connects the generically stable case $(t=0)$ with the case
made stable on a robust way by the optimal LQ control $(t=1)$.

5.3
Details on the coupled fixed pair problem above will appear
elsewhere. The interesting point is that any homotopy path
can be reformulated as a continuous Newton path, and any
continuous Newton method can be formulated as a homotopy.

REFERENCES.

(1) Chu,M.T.,'A simple application of the homotopy method
    to symmetric eigenvalue problems',Lin.Alg.Appl.,vol.59,
    p.85-90,1984

(2) DeCarlo,R.A.& Saeks,R.,'Interconnected Dynamical
    Systems',Dekker,New York,1981

(3) Eisenfeld,J.,'Block diagonalization and eigenvalues',
    Lin.Alg.Appl.,vol.59,p.85-90,1984

(4) Eitelberg,E.,'Model reduction and perturbation
    structures',Int.J.Control,vol.35, p.1029-50,1982

(5) Leitmann,G.& Wan,H.Y.jr.,'A stabilization policy for
    an economy with unknown characteristics',J.Franklin
    Inst.,vol.306,p.23-33,1978

(6) Leitmann,G.& Wan,H.Y.jr.,'Macro-economic stabilization
    policy for an uncertain dynamic economy',p.105-137 in
    'New Trends in Dynamic System Theory and Economics',
    M.Aoki&A.Marzollo ed.,1979

(7) Leitmann,G.& Wan,H.Y.jr.,'Performance improvement of
    uncertain macroeconomic systems',p.71-88 in 'Dynamic
    optimization and mathematical economics',P.T.Liu ed.,
    1980

(8) Richter,S.L.& DeCarlo,R.A.,'Continuation methods:
    theory and applications',IEEE TR.Autom.Control,vol.28,
    p.660-665, 1983

(9) Schellhorn,J.P.,'Multiple control with practical
    stability',p.270-273 in:"Modelling,Identification and
    Control",M.H.Hamza ed.,1981

(10) Schellhorn,J.P.,'Model following in multiple control:
     exact and approximate',p.91-96 in:'Cybernetics and
     Systems Research",R.Trappl ed.,1982

(11) Schellhorn,J.P.,'Multiple control with a cost for par-
     ticipating to the feedback',p.270-273 in:'Modelling
     and Simulation',M.H.Hamza ed.,1983

(12) Sundareshan,M.K.,'Generation of multilevel control
     and estimation schemes for large-scale systems: A per-
     turbational approach',IEEE TR.Syst.Man.Cybern,vol.7,
     p.144-152,1977

ACTIVE CONTROL OF A SYSTEM BY THE NEW GENERAL SYSTEM LOGICAL THEORY

Germano RESCONI
Università Cattolica del Sacro Cuore
Facoltà di Scienze Fisiche Matematiche e
Naturali
Via Trieste 17, I-25100 Brescia (Italy)

ABSTRACT.A new method for active control on a system is pre-sented.This new method is an application of a more general theory denoted General System Logical Theory (GSLT).The aim of the present approach is to control a system when it is impossible to foresee the future behaviour of the system for mathematical impossibility related to non-linear differential equations.The new reference point is the desired behaviour more than the future prevision of the behaviour.Applications to the control of an aircraft wing and to active noise con-trol are implemented.

1. INTRODUCTION

During the last years,considerable interest has been accor-ded ,in different fields,to control a distributed system in an active way without spatial discretization and numerical methods.The active control problem of the distributed system is formulated directly,without previous simplifications,even if the system is governed by non-linear differential equa-tions.Many approaches to active control of a distributed system in a directed way have been suggested.Reference 6 is concerned with suppressing vibration in aircraft by direct active controls.Direct active control of a sound field,by secondary sources,was implemented 4 to give effective instru-ments in the fight against noise 2.In this paper,the control problem of the distributed system is derived as a particular application of a more general theory 7 (General System Logi-Theory (GSLT)).By only one theory we can collect all the previous approaches to active control of distributed systems. The new theory will be analysed here in its fundamental parts and important applications to the active control of the air-craft wing 5 and to the active control of noise 2 will be explained.To clarify the difference between the classical active control and the new one,we will compare their flux diagrams.In the classical approach,the flux diagram is:

71

R. Trappl (ed.), Cybernetics and Systems '86, 71–78.
© 1986 by D. Reidel Publishing Company.

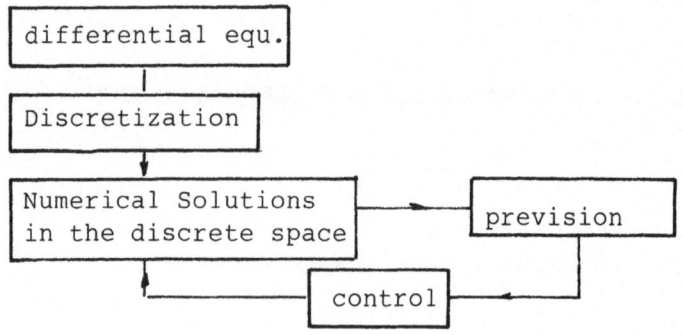

In the new active control by GSLT,will be

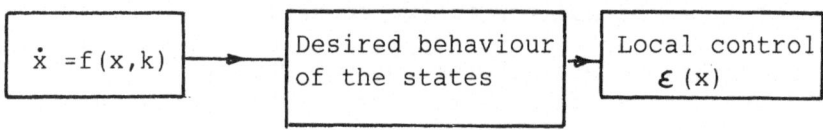

For every state x,the function $\mathcal{E}(x)$ furnishes the <u>local</u> control (without the numerical solutions or analytical solutins) needed in order to obtain the global desired behaviour of the states x in time.

2.GENERAL SYSTEM LOGICAL THEORY (GSLT)

During the last years a natural extension of the classical8 General System Theory has been proposed to solve different problems as the active control of a system.This extension is denoted General System Logical Theory (GSLT) because it is the connection of the System Theory with the Logical Mathematical Theory.

2.1 ELEMENTARY LOGICAL SYSTEM (ELS)

The GSLT is a theory with different level of refinement. At the first level the GSLT is identical to the General System Theory 8 (GSL) where a system is defined as a relation R between the input X and the output Y

$$X \xrightarrow{\ R\ } Y \qquad Y=RX \qquad [1]$$

2.1.1 DEFINITION OF AN ELS

An"Elementary Logical System" ELS is defined by the following commutative graph

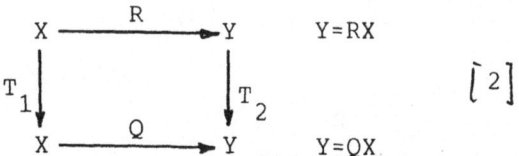

Where X is the Input set, T_1 is an operator that transforms the input vectorial space X into itself.
Where Y is the Output set, T_2 is an operator that transforms Y into itself.
Where R is an internal operator that transforms the space vector X into the space vector Y, Q is similar at R.

Definition:

T_1 and T_2 are denoted <u>external operators</u>

R and Q are denoted <u>internal operators</u>

Remark:

An Elementary Logical System ELS is similar to the classical definition of system, but in Input we have an operator T_1 and in Output an operator T_2.

$$T_1 \xrightarrow{\quad OP \quad} T_2$$

Where OP = (R , Q) internal operators.

Remark:

If R = Q then $T_2 = R^{-1}T_1R$ and T_2 is equivalent to T_1

Remark:

By T_1 and R,Q we can get T_2 with the relation

$$T_2Y = T_1Y + [R,T_1]X + T_1(Q - R)X + [(Q-R),T_1]X \qquad 1$$

Where $[a , b] = ab - ba$ is the Lie's product.

2.2 LOGICAL SYSTEM

Definition:

A Logical system is a composition of ELS

Remark:

By this property of the lie's product

73

$$\left[ab , c \right] = a \left[b , c \right] + \left[a , c \right] b$$

we get that

$$
\begin{array}{ccccc}
X_1 & \xrightarrow{R_1} & X_2 & \xrightarrow{R_2} & X_3 \\
\Big\downarrow T_1 & & \Big\downarrow & & \Big\downarrow T_3 \\
X_1 & \xrightarrow{R_1} & X_2 & \xrightarrow{R_2} & X_3
\end{array}
$$

Where $\quad T_3 X_3 = T_1 X_1 + \left[R_2 R_1 , T_1 \right] X_1 =$

$$T_1 X_1 + R_2 \left[R_1 , T_1 \right] X_1 + \left[R_2 , T_1 \right] R_1 X_1$$

is similar to

$$
\begin{array}{ccc}
X_1 & \xrightarrow{R_2 R_1} & X_3 \\
\Big\downarrow T_1 & & \Big\downarrow T_3 \\
X_1 & \xrightarrow{R_2 R_1} & X_3
\end{array}
\qquad X_3 = R_2 R_1 X_1
$$

2.2.1 LOGICAL FEEDBACK

An important example of a Logical System is the Logical feedback obtained by two ELS in this way:

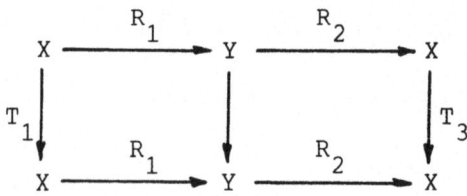

Where T_1 is an operator on X and T_3 is another operator on the same X.

2.2.2 CONVERGENT OPERATORS

The Logical System (Convergent system)

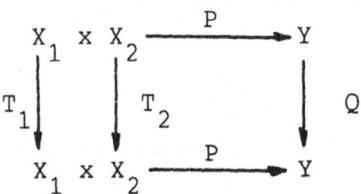

Can be represented by the ELS

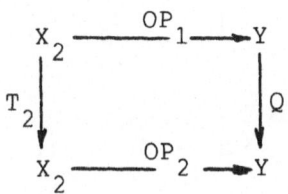

where $OP_1 = X_1 \times [\ \ ]$

$OP_2 = T_1 X_1 \times [\ \ ]$

or by

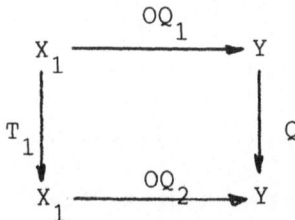

where $OQ_1 = [\ \ ] \times X_2$

$OQ_2 = [\ \ ] \times T_2 X_2$

Remark:

The internal operator OP_1, OP_2, OQ_1, OQ_2 are depended from the external operators T_1, T_2.

2.3 APPLICATIONS OF THE GSLT

2.3.1 DIFFERENTIAL EQUATIONS

If we know the differential equation

$$d\ x(t)/dt = \gamma(x(t)) \quad [2]$$

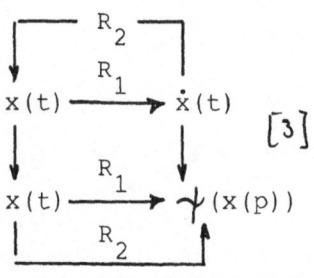

we can build the logical feedback [3]

where $R_4 = R_2 = \int_0^t$, $R_3 = d\ /dp$, p is a <u>local variable.</u>

75

By R_3 and R_4 at the first step we have

$$x(p) = \int_0^t \Upsilon(p)dt = \Upsilon(p)t + x(p)$$

After n steps in the logical loop we have

$$x(p,t) = \int_0^t \Upsilon \left[\int_0^t \Upsilon \left[\cdots \int_0^t \Upsilon(p)dt \right. \right.$$

If the previous iterative method converges,then $x(p,t)$ is a solution of [2]

In fact

$$\frac{d}{dt} \int_0^t \Upsilon \left[\int_0^t \Upsilon \cdots \left[\cdots \int_0^t \Upsilon(p)dt \right. \right. = \Upsilon \left[\int_0^t \Upsilon \left[\cdots \int_0^t \Upsilon(p)dt \right. \right.$$

Simple example:

For the differential equation $dx(t)/dt = x(t)$

we get $n=0$ $p=x(0)$

$n=1$ $\int_0^t (p)dt = x(0)t + p$

$n=2$ $\int_0^t x(0)t + p\ dt = x(0)+x(0)t+x(0)t^2/2$

....

$n=K$ $\int_0^t \Upsilon \left[t \cdots \int_0^t x(0)t+p = x(0)+x(0)t+\ldots x(0)t^k/k! \right.$

2.3.2 VOLTERRA EQUATIONS

For the differential equation (Volterra equations)

$$\frac{1}{x(t)}\frac{dx(t)}{dt} = x(t)$$

we consider in the logical loop [3] $R_4 = R_2 = e^{\int_0^t}$ and
$R_1 = R_3 = \frac{1}{x(t)}\frac{d}{dt}$ so we have the solutions

$$x(t) = e^{\int \Upsilon \cdots^{\int \Upsilon(p)dt}}$$

2.3.3 ACTIVE VIBRATION SUPPRESSION OF AIRCRAFT WING BY GSLT

During the last decade,considerable interest has been generated by the idea of suppressing vibration in aircraft by
active controls.Many approaches to flutter suppression have
been suggested.Active control of a wing is discussed in
reference 1,in which the wing is modelled as a discrete
system and the aerodynamical forces are derived by the dou-
blet-lattice method.In general it is common practice to
first discretize in state space and after to treat a continuous control system as if the system were discrete.Recently
5 a new and interesting approach treats directly the control
system without spacial discretization.

If p is the state of the wing we write the equation of the
motion in this way

$$\dot{p} = \Lambda(v)p + P$$

where v is the airstream,P the control.
If p has different modes p_c we write for every mode

$$\dot{p}_c = \lambda_c(v)p_c + P_c$$

When

$$P_c = G_c p_c \qquad G_c \text{ is a constant matrix}$$

$$P_c = S\gamma \qquad \gamma \text{ is the control surface angles on the wing}$$

$$p_c = J u \qquad u \text{ value of the sensor in the wing}$$

we have $\gamma = S^{-1}P_c = S^{-1}G_c p_c = Z p_c$ where $Z = S^{-1}G_c$ and

$$G_c = S Z$$

so we can build the ELS

$$
\begin{array}{ccc}
 & Z & \\
p_c & \longrightarrow & \gamma \\
\Lambda_c + SZ \big\downarrow & & \big\downarrow \mathcal{L} \\
\dot{p}_c & \longrightarrow & \dot{\gamma} \\
 & Z &
\end{array}
$$

$\mathcal{L}$ equiv. $\left[\Lambda_c + SZ\right]$

$\mathcal{L} Z = Z (\Lambda_c + SZ)$

$\mathcal{L}$ same eigenvalue of $\Lambda_c + SZ$

Where $\mathcal{L}$ is predetermined in such a way that the motion of
the wing is stable

aircraft wing feedback

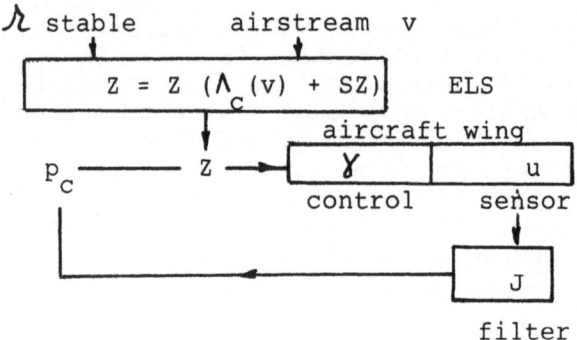

$\dot{\gamma} = \Lambda \gamma$ stable   airstream v

$$Z = Z \ (\Lambda_c(v) + SZ)$$ ELS

aircraft wing

p_c —— Z → γ | u

control   sensor

J

filter

If the solutions of $\dot{\gamma} = \Lambda \gamma$ are stable, the solution of
$\dot{p}_c = (\Lambda_c + SZ) \ p_c$ are stable because

$$\Lambda \text{ is equivalent to } \Lambda_c + SZ \text{ (same eigenvalues)}$$

2.3.4 ACTIVE CONTROL OF NOISE

In a sound field we can write, in a symbolic way, the law
source-field in this way OP F'=S' where S' is a primary
sound source and F' the field generated by S'. The problem
is to know the source S useful to obtain the predetermined
field F=MF' without solving the law source-field. For this
aim we consider the ELS

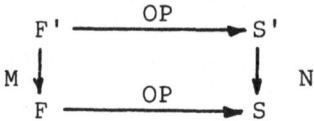

$$F' \xrightarrow{\ OP\ } S'$$
$$M \downarrow \qquad \qquad \downarrow N$$
$$F \xrightarrow{\ OP\ } S$$

where S=NS' = MS' +$[$OP , M$]$F' . When we know M,OP,S',F' we
can obtain the appropriate source S necessary to generate
the field F without solve the law source-filed.

REFERENCES:

1. I.Abel,B.Perry and H.M.Murrow,'Synthesis of active controls
   for flutter suppressions on a flight research',Nasa 77-
   1062 (1977)
2. Angevine O.L.and M.Jessel,'Active systems for global at-
   tenuation of noise'will be published on J.Acoust.Soc.Amer.
   (1985)
3. Bernard-Weil,M.Duvelleroy,and J.Droulez,'Analogical study
   of a model for regulation of ago-antagonistic couples-
   Application to adrenal-postpituitary interrelationship',
   Math.Biosci. 27

INDETERMINISM IN SYSTEM SCIENCE

C. M. Elstob
Division of Cybernetics
Brunel University
Uxbridge, Middlesex UB8 3PH
England

ABSTRACT. This paper argues for the development of a metaphysics
of indeterminism to complement the deterministic metaphysics of
current science. Deterministic ideas are analysed to show the
underlying assumptions and alternative assumptions are then proposed
which allow an indeterministic view of aspects of nature.

1. INTRODUCTION

It is my strong belief, expressed in an earlier paper (Elstob 1984),
that the assumptions of deterministic metaphysics will not yield a
full understanding of the nature of mind. I suggest that what we need
to do is develop a strong new metaphysics that places indeterminism
in a central position. I see indeterminism as a key aspect of
becoming in nature, of emergent processes, of creative evolution.
I believe that a metaphysics of indeterminism can be constructed
that will give understandings as valuable as those produced from
deterministic ideas, even though - because of the indeterminism -
we cannot get from it the same degree of predictive and manipulative
command of nature that determinism offers. I do not wish the overthrow
of determinism, but I do want to see more clearly in what contexts it
is properly applied. I want to see determinism and indeterminism both
properly understood as real aspects of the world.
  The system sciences have suffered from not having a clear metaphysics of indeterminism. They highlight the existence and nature of
complex systems which have systemic properties above those seen in
their components and which display self-organization, adaptation and
development. But the system sciences are often unable to give a satisfactory account of the emergence and becoming of such systems through
using mechanistic and reductionistic concepts. Of course, much progress
has been made, for example the notions of information, computation and
control have made many problems tractable. And ideas such as those of
autopoiesis and organizational closure (Varela 1979), and dissipative
structures (Prigogine 1980) have been a great help. But still the
dominant metaphysical ideas are those of determinism.

79

R. Trappl (ed.), Cybernetics and Systems '86, 79–86.
© *1986 by D. Reidel Publishing Company.*

I cannot give a fully argued case for indeterminism. But I can point to a perceived need, and I can ask for the investment of some effort and plea for indeterminism to be taken more seriously. My principal aim in this paper is to argue for no more than this.

2. DETERMINISM AND INDETERMINISM

In a world governed completely by determinism, the principle of universal causation operates: all events are caused and every event is a necessary consequence of existent prior events. Determinism carries with it many other concepts, such as the notion of an instantaneous present capturing all that exists, and the idea of the past and future being both fully determined, and the implication that all things are ultimately reducible to some collection of timeless and indestructable primitives or atoms. Determinism leads us to think of the universe as a closed, fixed, four-dimensional entity with one temporal and three spatial dimensions.

In contrast, an indeterministic world is seen as open with a future that is not fully determined by its past and present, and in which existences are latent and in a state of emergence as well as being fully formed. Cause and effect are seen to operate, but only locally and within the context of systemhood and not universally. The notion of indeterminism is weakly developed and receives little attention from science.

Materialistic indeterminism comes in several forms. Popper (1980) presents one interesting type through offering a refutation of what he refers to as scientific determinism:- "...the doctrine that the structure of the world is such that any event can be rationally predicted, with any desired degree of precision, if we are given a sufficiently precise description of past events, together with all the laws of nature". After considerable preparatory discussion to establish the importance of knowing precisely the initial conditions of a system in order to be able to predict its future, Popper offers a result of the mathematician Hadamard (1898) concerning the movement of a mass-point along the geodesics of an infintely curved surface with negative curvature which shows that knowledge of initial conditions within an arbitrarilly small error is still not sufficient to determine the subsequent behaviour of the mass-point even though the system operates under deterministic laws. Here Popper is showing that even within its own conceptual framework the deterministic scientific view exhibits an inherent indeterminism.

A similar argument for indeterminism is made by Prigogine and his co-workers (e.g. Prigogine and Stengers, 1984), but this starts from the directionality of time that the second law of thermodynamics implies and by examining processes in nature that are irreversible and far from equilibrium. In this treatment, the indeterminism arises from thermodynamic bifurcation points where random events are what determine the future course of a system. A consequence of this view is that structures that now exist in the world may have resulted from purely chance events, thus denying the universal operation of determinism.

Popper's and Prigogine's views both gain strength from the results of quantum theory. Their ideas require that there be some entirely chance events - i.e. events without a cause. Quantum theory proposes that this does occur at a microscopic level and Popper's and Prigogine's ideas show that such microscopic chance events can lead to large-scale macroscopic consequences.

Emergentism rests on a belief in indeterminism and gives support to the indeterministic world view. Emergent phenomena and properties arising from particular forms of organisation of matter seem widely apparent in nature. The distinctive feature of emergents is that they should not be fully explainable in terms of lower level or component features, that is that they should not be completely causally determined by the interactions of their components. Mental life and many of the characteristic aspects of living matter are often taken to be emergent features of nature. However, science has been extremely successful in providing reductionistic accounts of apparently emergentistic phenomena and so the emergentist's case can by no means be considered to have been won.

One point that is often ignored in arguing for reductionism is the fact that science has had almost no success in predicting emergents before they have come into existence. Indeed, science generally has great difficulty in providing full explanations of the causality operative between distinct integrative or phenomenal levels, as for example exists between the atomic and molecular levels, or between the non-living and living levels. To take a case in point, the propert-ies of water cannot yet be derived from the properties of the component atoms of water, even though we have both the component systems and the resultant system available for investigation. If we had knowledge only of oxygen and hydrogen as elements it is extremely unlikely that we would ever determine that they could form the molecular organisation that is water, let alone also determine from their uncombined natures the properties of this organisation. Science has its greatest success with systems that have come into being; it has had almost no success in understanding the becoming of systems. It is in the area of the becoming of new systems and existents that a metaphysics of indeter-minism has most to offer.

Although not strictly an indeterminist position, the idea of autopoiesis lends support to the indeterministic world view. The key idea of autopoiesis is of a system producing and sustaining its own being and that of its components through its own action as the system it is. We have with such systems an aspect of self-generated identity since it is the system in action that gives identity to the system and its components. Furthermore, we see the components, through their mutual interactions, finding a context of existence within the system that their collective productive processes produce. Thus we have a chicken and egg problem which is difficult for reductionism to resolve without reference to some developmental framework which is no longer in existence. It should be made clear that the processes of autopoietic systems do not themselves deny deterministic analysis. But what autopoiesis does emphasise is that we can have stable, persist-ent systems and components of these systems that only have a legitimate

81

existence taken as a whole, and not treated as separate, unrelated individuals. This fact casts doubt on the normal method of reduction-istic analysis. It also lends support to the idea of phenomena and existents that do not seem to be grounded solely in a reducible or atomic causality, but rather to have an element of system-level causality which belongs to interactions and relationships rather than merely to the components of such interactions and relationships.

3. INDETERMINISM AND FREE WILL

Determinism denies free will. We cannot be free in our conscious mental life if every mental event is determined. It also does not help if we simply have a form of indeterminism that depends purely upon chance events quite outside the domain of mental occurrences, say at the quantum level for example. Such indeterminism certainly makes the future open and can provide a spice of genuine variety in the develop-ment of mental life, but we need a good deal more than this to do justice to our common feeling and understanding of free will.

I suggest that what is required for our conscious mental life to have aspects of freedom, is for it to be open to becoming. We need to consider mental life to be operative in a domain in which the transformation, emergence and growth of systems is happening. We should accept causation within this domain, but a causation that belongs to and is characteristic of the systems existent within the domain. We should also accept an autopoietic view of the systems so that their interdependence is highlighted. On this view, then, we have determination of happening but a determination that is derived from and bounded by the systems within which it occurs. We have room for openess and freedom if there is room for the creation of new systems - systems whose emergence is not simply an unfolding of an already existing system but a genuine becoming, a genuine creation. We can see a place for free will in such a domain if our mental life can be seen to be influential in the becoming that occurs in the domain. But, to avoid falling back into the trap of determinism, we have to establish that the becoming we are talking of is not something that is deterministic. It must be indeterministic, and therefore our arguement for free will requires indeterminism. And it also requires, of course, a full understanding of indeterministic becoming.

Perhaps what I am driving at, and it is certainly a radical idea, can best be understood by briefly considering the notion of causality. Indeterminism must either deny causality or place it in a context that is narrower than that which it is normally accorded. I shall do the latter. What I suggest we do is consider seriously the proposition that causality is a context dependent aspect of the world. This means that to talk of causes and effects is to assume a context of existence in which such causes and effects are operative. This view says that the context of existence comes first and that the causes and effects appar-ent within it are merely characteristic of it and should not be thought of as prior determining primitives. Of course stable existents do have characteristic natures and we can identify these and see them manifest

82

even when the existents are buried inside systems. What I suggest we should be wary of doing is believing that we can always reduce system-level causality to the causality we recognise at the component level. We often have a firm grip on system-level causality - a causality properly belonging to the context of existence that is the system - when we have no means of reducing that level of causality to component-level causality. For example, we can identify and express causal relationships within an economic system that we cannot in the slightest capture with causal talk grounded in physics and chemistry.

Recognising the force of the point that causality is context dep-endent - that causes belong to systems and don't necessarily come before systems - gives us a way of thinking about indeterminism without having to deny causation. What we do is simply say that there are interactions that may lead to system formation and that these are not to be con-sidered in cause and effect terms. When a system comes into persistent being, then is the appropriate time to consider characterising aspects of its nature through causal accounting. Perhaps another way of saying the same thing is to say that chance may play a role in system format-ion, where by chance we mean something without assignable cause - i.e. something which occurs, or may occur, in an indefinite number of ways.

We shall return to the notion of cause towards the end of this paper. The point of this section is simply to get accross the idea that to have free will we have to have indeterminism and that further-more we want the indeterminism not to be entirely random but to offer some potential for being moulded to produce definite persistent exist-ents with their own causal consequences. On this view we see the human nervous system as having the capacity to give rise to indeterministic becomings with the becomings being open to influence from already existent becomings, but with the inflence not being fully determining. Free will is the exercise of this influence on becoming, but the will itself should be viewed as also subject to indeterministic becoming. This means that mental life has to be lived to become what it is to become - it is not pre-figured or pre-ordained. But what it becomes is influenced by aspects of itself - the conscious willing self.

The ideas presented here sound wildly speculative. They are, of course, at this stage speculative, but not, I claim, wildly so. To appreciate them more fully it is necessary to examine further the ideas of conventional science so that we may expose some of the assumptions on which it is founded. Once we have done this we can see how alternative assumptions might admit a place for indeterminism. It seems to me that a key issue to consider is the nature of existence as it is understood in conventional science.

4.   EXISTENCE UNDER DETERMINISTIC METAPHYSICS

Conventional science scores its greatest successes with systems that have strong identity, that is with systems and existents that have highly stable and reproducible natures. Or, put another way, with systems with a firm grip on being and little tendency to becoming. Such systems are highly amenable to causal analysis and a capturing of

83

their natures with statements of lawful relation. Take, for example, Newton's law of gravitational attraction. This talks about the context of existence of material objects and captures an aspect of the nature of this context through a law expressing an invariant relation of attraction. This is not a causal law because it does not relate conditions separated in time, but it is a statement about a specific class of existents - material objects - and is taken to be true at an instant in time. It is a system statement since it talks of interactions between complexes of material objects.

We can get causal statements from static laws like Newton's law of gravitation if they include state variables that actually specify change - as the variable force does in the law of gravitational attraction, remembering that the notion of force is given coherent meaning in physics by defining it in terms of rate of change of momentum. By introducing, as state variables existent within the instantaneous now, change specifying aspects of systems we can gain great support for the idea of universal causation since we can see in these infinitesimals the cause of the next instantaneous state of existence. What we have with this method is a way of capturing change within an instant - a method of freezing change so that all that is in existence can be considered to be contained within the instantaneous now. This view, universally applied, also means that the future is fully determined by the existents of the instantaneous present, that nothing new can come into being - all that can happen is simply a pre-ordained unfolding. The logical extension of this view is to see existence as a four-dimensional object of spacetime which is static and unchanging.

There is a beauty in the simplicity of the idea that everything that exists is contained within the instantaneous now, but it is a hard view to support through empirical inquiry since we cannot get hold of true instants. What happens in practice is that we select 'instants', which are actually durations, which are short enough for no appreciable change in the system we are considering to have occurred. Thus our instants are defined relative to a particular level and content of existence. What we find we can do is narrow the instant we are considering whereupon we loose sight of the existent we previously focussed upon and are able to identify lower level and shorter duration existences. The logical conclusion of this process is the identification of true atoms of existence which exist, and are the only stuff of existence, within what must then be the true instantaneous now.

5.   SOME IDEAS FOR AN INDETERMINISTIC SYSTEM METAPHYSICS

We cannot hope to build an indeterministic system metaphysics if we retain the idea of the instantaneous now containing all that is in existence. As a first step towards our new metaphysics, we will abandon this idea. We will start instead by taking systems as the fundamental stuff of existence. By a system we mean more than just a haphazard configuration. Haphazard configurations are an important part of existence (they are seen as seeds for the becoming of new systems), but they do not have the persistence and potential for causal happening that systems have. Systems have a cyclicity of change and organization that gives them persistence and definite identity. Systems have a characteristic minimum duration of identifiable existence, below which they cannot properly be said to exist. This duration is related to the nature of the cyclic processes that underlie their being.

To help clarify this idea consider some examples. An atom is an organization of components in cyclic interaction. If we consider a time interval below that of the cyclicity of the interactions we cannot be sure that we have the organization that is an atom. If we consider chemical compounds then we have systems which are made from cyclic interactions between atoms and electrons, and such interactions have a minimum duration before the cyclicity that gives identity to the compound becomes established. A living cell in an enormously more complex system of cyclic and mutually supportive interactions, and has a correspondingly longer characteristic minimum duration for the establishment of its identity. If we move to the sphere of human social phenomena then we have systems - such as friendships, work-groups, business firms, economic booms and slumps - with very much longer characteristic durations for identifiable existence.

An important consequence of the view we are developing is that we have to accept that we can never know exactly what is in existence since first, we can only discern those things with a characteristic duration lying within our range of experience, and second, we cannot know about those systems that are in a process of emergence, or are latent and which have not yet established a cyclicity of interactions that gives them systemhood and a persistent grip on existence.

It should be clear from what we are proposing that existence contains many interactions and configurations that do not form systems. These are the vast range of generally unidentified and insignificant haphazard, chaotic, structureless, chance conjunction, arrangement or interaction of things in the world. It is this non-system content of existence that I suggest is a source of indeterministic becoming in the universe. It is from here that new persistent cyclicities of interaction emerge. How this emergence occurs we do not, in general, know. Certainly we ourselves have constructive powers and can bring about, in the artifacts we create, new systems. But we have little idea how systems can emerge without the intervention of a designer/constructor.

What is important about non-guided or indeterministic becoming from non-system content of the world is that it not be causally determined. That does not mean the path of occurrences that lead to such creations should contain some uncaused individual events, but only that the path contain some events which are independent of one another and of any other system which might be orchestrating their production and interaction. Of course, we can legitimately allow,in this indeterminsitic schema, an emerging self-orchestration developing as the system comes into being. And also, of course, we should remind ourselves that once new conjunctions between systems do occur we may get the formation of a system that results in the disolution of its component systems rather than just the configuring of components without loss of their identity.

Let us return to the idea of causality so that we may obtain a better understanding of it in connection with the indeterministic metaphysics we are developing. If we adopt the deterministic metaphysical principle of universal causation in which the cause of the present instant of existence is the state of the immediately prior instant, and we also adopt the idea that all that exists is contained completely within the instantaneous now, then we cannot accept the process of indeterministic becoming that we have just sketched as being indeterministic because the determinism inherent in the instantaneous now can be seen as the orchestrator of all the events in the path of the becoming, and this was something that we disallow if the becoming is to qualify as indeterministic. What this means is simply what we have already established, that to develop a metaphysics of indeterminism we have to reject conventional ideas of causality and existence. However, as we have stated before, this does not leave us with no place for the idea of causality; it just says that it should not be taken to apply everywhere. Where we can apply it, I suggest, is within the context of systemhood. Indeed, I would claim, it is just in such a context that the idea of causality is applied in science - so we are not suggesting anthing radical here.

The stance I recommend that we take towards developing an indeterministic metaphysics is to mark out some separate territories. It seems to me that the methods of determinism work admirably whenever we have stable, identifiable, reproducible phenomena. In brief, they work well for systems with a firm grip on being. I suggest they do not work well for things that are in a condition of becoming, or for systems with a light hold on their identity and being. I think that within this context of existence we are in need of new ideas in order to increase our understanding. It is these new ideas that I am suggesting the systems community is well placed to develop.

REFERENCES

Hadamard, J. (1898) 'Les surfaces a courbures opposees', etc., Mathematiques Pures et Appliquees, 5th series, Vol. 4, 1898, pp. 27-73.

Popper, K.R. (1982) The Open Universe - an arguement for indeterminism Hutchinson & Co.

Prigogine, I. (1980) From Being to Becoming, W. H. Freeman.

Prigogine, I. and Stengers, I. (1984) Order out of Chaos, Heinemann.

Elstob, C.M. (1984) 'Emergentism and Mind', Cybernetics and Systems Research 2, R. Trappl (Ed.), Elsevier.

CHAIN MODELS FOR GROWTH PROCESSES/CODE THEORY

M. Peschel, W. Mende
Academy of Sciences GDR
1199 Berlin-Adlershof, Rudower Chaussee 5
F. Breitenecker
Technical University Vienna, Austria, Gußhausstraße

ABSTRACT. Based on the concept of Exponential Towers
(1981) $dx_i/dt = K_i x_i x_{i+1}$ a Structure Design Principle was
introduced which led to the result that a huge class of
ordinary differential equations could be represented by
the famous Lotka-Volterra Equations.
As suitable models for growth a qualitative analysis of
Exponential Towers is given and interpreted in the terms
of automata theory and interval mappings. The relation
between the socalled exponential code and the Exponential
Towers is generalised to arbitrary binary codes given by a
code generator function $z=g(s,K,z')$ and leads to a great
diversity of dynamic chains with similar properties as we
found for Exponential Towers.
Constructing by different approaches vector codes we can
imbed the generalised dynamic chains in corresponding
networks which are a generalisation of Lotka-Volterra
networks offerring new possibilities for time series analysis.

1. QUALITATIVE ANALYSIS OF EXPONENTIAL TOWERS

For studying the qualitative behaviour of arbitrary Exponential Towers we can first restrict on coefficients
$K_i = +1$ and $K_i = -1$.

For the corresponding signal $x_{0,N}(t)$ at the bottom of the
tower with normalised initial values $x_i(0) = 1$ we
introduce the notation

$$x_{0,N}(t) = e \ (s_0, s_1, \ldots, s_N) \quad \text{with } s_i = \text{sign } K_i$$

We call these functions the coordinate functions of an
Exponential Tower of order n+1.

R. Trappl (ed.), Cybernetics and Systems '86, 87–94.

By integration we get at once the first and second order coordinate functions

$$e(s_o) = \exp(s_o t) \qquad e(s_o,s_1) = \exp(s_o/s_1 \cdot (\exp(s_1 t - 1)))$$

Higher order coordinate functions cannot be expressed in a closed analytical form.
If we take into account, that $\exp(K\,I)$ is for $K > 0$ a positive monotonous and for $K < 0$ a positive antitonous operator, we get the following monotony inclusions

$$e(+) > 1 > e(-)$$
$$e(+,+) > e(+) > e(+,-) > 1 > e(-,-) > e(-) > e(-,+)$$
$$e(+,+,+) > e(+,+) > e(+,+,-) > e(+) > e(+,-,-) > e(+,-) >$$
$$> e(+,-,+) > 1 >$$
$$> e(-,-,+) > e(-,-) > e(-,-,-) > e(-) > e(-,+,-) > e(-,+) >$$
$$> e(-,+,+)$$

The study of splitting up the lower order coordinate functions into coordinate functions of the next higher order can be transparently demonstrated as it is shown in Fig. 1
We designate the corresponding linearly ordered set of binary vectors of the length l with or (W_1), and the corresponding reverse order with or (W_1).
Obviously the generation rule for the construction of or(W_{1+1}) recursively from or $W_1)$ resp. from $\underline{or}(W_1)$ is given by

$$\text{or } (W_{1+1}) = \begin{cases} + & \text{or}(W_1) \\ - & \underline{or}(W_1) \end{cases}$$

Using this linear order for binary vectors $W_1 = (s_o, s_1, \ldots, s_{1-1})$ we introduce socalled monotony classes for binary vectors of arbitrary but finite length, namely

$$> W_1 = \begin{cases} W_1 + \text{or } (W) & \text{if } \prod s_i = + 1 \\ W_1 - \text{or } (W) & \text{if } \prod s_i = - 1 \end{cases}$$

and

$$< W_1 = \begin{cases} W_1 - \underline{or} (W) & \text{if } \prod s_i = + 1 \\ W_1 + \underline{or} (W) & \text{if } \prod s_i = - 1 \end{cases}$$

Here W is an arbitrary but finite binary word.
Adjoining upper and lower monotony classes are not over-

lapping, they are always separated from each other by a
certain word of length l-1.
According to the just introduced monotony classes for
binary vectors we define now socalled monotony classes for
trajectories in regard of the coordinate functions
$e(s_0,s_1,\ldots,s_{l-1})$ by considering oneparametric families of
curves in the following way:

$$
>e(s_0,s_1,\ldots,s_{l-1}) = \begin{cases} e(s_0,s_1,\ldots,s_{l-1},+K_l) & \text{if } \pi s_i=+1 \\ e(s_0,s_1,\ldots,s_{l-1},-K_l) & \text{if } \pi s_i=-1 \end{cases}
$$

$$
<e(s_0,s_1,\ldots,s_{l-1}) = \begin{cases} e(s_0,s_1,\ldots,s_{l-1},-K_l) & \text{if } \pi s_i=+1 \\ e(s_0,s_1,\ldots,s_{l-1},+K_l) & \text{if } \pi s_i=-1 \end{cases}
$$

$> e(s_0,s_1,\ldots,s_{l-1})$ is the upper and $< e(s_0,s_1,\ldots,s_{l-1})$

the lower monotony class in reference to $e(s_0,s_1,\ldots,s_{l-1})$.

In these expressions $e(s_0,s_1,\ldots,s_{l-1},\ s_l K_l)$ ist the

solution $x_{ol}(t)$ of a chain with the parameter set
$s_0,s_1,\ldots,s_{l-1},\ s_l K_l$ and $K_l > 0$.

Obiously these classes built up bands of curves completely
covered by the corresponding curve families parametrized
by the parameter $K_l > 0$.

It can be seen easily that all these monotony classes
together are a decomposition of the whole positive qua-
drant into disjoint bands.
In the same way this construction could be repeated also
for Exponential Towers with arbitrary parameter sets
$s_i K_i$.

The monotony classes thus constructed for a given Exponential Tower with length l (as resolution power) can be also
considered from the point of view of classification or
pattern recognition as classes (of trajectories) and can
then be interpreted as signal types of the considered
Exponential Tower.
But on the other hand we are going to consider the monotony classes also as states of a corresponding finite
automaton.
We will now study how the state changes if we adjoin
another module either at the top or at the bottom of a

89

given chain with a fixed value of the chain-length l.

We get the following result:
If we adjoin another basic module at the top of the chain
the state of the automaton will not be changed.
But it is important to mention, that every module adjoined
at the top level will lead to a splitting of the given monotony classes into two being more narrow. This shows a
continuous division of given curve-formed intervals (bands)
into smaller ones thus leading necessarily to Weiter-
strass-convergence of Exponential Towers.

But if on the other hand we adjoin another basic module
at the bottom of the given chain, we get a rather transparent picture of state-transitions, that means, we pass
from a specified monotony class (as state of the automaton) to another one.
This state transition goes after the following simple rule

$$
s \gtrless e(s_0, s_1, \ldots, s_{l-1}) =
\begin{cases}
> e(s, s_0, s_1, \ldots, s_{l-2}) \\
\qquad \text{for} \quad \mathcal{T}\!\!\mathcal{T} s_i \cdot s = +1 \\
< e(s, s_0, s_1, \ldots, s_{l-2}) \\
\qquad \text{for} \quad \mathcal{T}\!\!\mathcal{T} s_i \cdot s = -1
\end{cases}
$$

Here s symbolically denotes the operator corresponding to
the chain extension by adjoining another basic module with
the sign s at the bottom level of the given chain.
Most important is the fact that we get not a splitting of
given states but really a state transition.
The result can be illustrated by graphs corresponding to
our classifying automaton.
Fig. 2 shows the corresponding state-transition graphs for
the resolution powers l = 0,1,2.
From these graphs can be seen immediately the remarkable
role of hyperbolic growth (as a monotonous class attractor)
and hyperbolic decay (as a focuslike class attractor).

2. DYNAMICAL CHAINS AND BINARY CODES

We are interested to code the coordinate functions
$e(s_0, s_1, \ldots, s_{l-1})$ in such a way that the order relation
between the corresponding binary vectors
$s_0, s_1, \ldots, s_{l-1}$ is reflected by a growing value of the
adjoined code number.
This aim can be achieved quite easily, if we introduce for
a given a, a>1, the following socalled Exponential Code

$$z = a^{s_0} a^{s_1} \cdots \cdots a^{s_{l-1}}$$

This code stimulates to study in more detail the corresponding code mapping determined by the following code generator function

$$z = a^{s\,z'}$$

This function, defined on the interval $[0,\infty)$ obviously maps for $s = +1$ the interval $[0,\infty)$ on $[1,\infty)$ and for $s = -1$ on $(0,1]$ presenting thus a dichotomy of the basic interval $[0,\infty)$ of the code.
If we iterate a finite times this code mapping, we produce apparently a dichotomy tree with smaller and smaller intervals contracting each of them to length zero as the number of iterations approaches infinity.
This is a static model for the Weierstrass-convergence we observed for the trajectories of Exponential Towers with increasing length.
This correspondence between Exponential Towers and exponential code stimulates the idea now to consider arbitrary binary code procedures and to construct for them dynamical chains. This will lead us to a huge diversity of different dynamical chains which can be used also for modelling purposes as an alternative to the use of Exponential Towers as local models.
An arbitrary binary code is uniquely determined by a code generator
$$z = g(s, z')$$
obeying the following conditions:
  . s is a binary variable with arbitrary chosen values s_1 and s_2

  . the functions $g_i = g(s_i, z')$ are monotonous functions both defined on the given base interval J of the code mapping the definition interval J of the code on intervals J_i $i = 1,2$ which define a partition of J, namely

$$J_1 \vee J_2 = J \quad \text{and} \quad J_1 \cap J_2 = \phi$$

Depending on the character of the monotonous branches of the code generator function (monotonously increasing or decreasing) we get four different types of partitions.
Fig. 3 shows these different configurations.
The concrete analytical form of the branch functions can be completely freely chosen, which opens huge possibilities to construct dynamic chains with similar properties.

If we now use the correspondence between the code generator and the basic module of a dynamic chain, we have found in the case of the Exponential Towers, we win socalled dynamic chains of type I by

$$x_i(t) = g(s_i, O(I\ x_{i+1}))$$

Here the nonlinear mapping O from the interval in which varies the integral $I\ x_{i+1}$ into the definition interval J of the code was introduced to secure always the applicability of the code mapping.
This is an advantage, because it allows us to start the construction with a normalised code and to introduce free parameters also by specifying the nonlinear mapping O (for example as a broken linear function).
The operation O can be avoided, if the code definition interval is identical with the interval in which the integral values are varying.
It is quite convenient to begin a code construction with a symmetric code on the inteval $[0,1]$ and to transform then this interval onto $[o,\infty)$ by a parametrized broken linear transformation

$$u = v\ K\ /(1-v)$$

if we want to construct a dynamic chain of type I on the interval $[0,\infty)$

3. DYNAMIC CHAINS FOR VECTOR CODES

For the construction of vector codes we use the idea to build up these codes with the help of well-studied one-dimensional codes by aggregation of them with a certain production function concept, for example by powering and multiplication.
We have two simple possibilities for the construction of higher dimensional codes, namely

1. From one-dimensional code generator functions $g_i(s^i, z^{i'})$ with the component z^i and the binary variable s^i we construct a corresponding transformed vector with the components z by

$$z^j = \prod_i g_i(s^i, z^{i'})^{k_{ji}}$$

with a certain regular matrix $K = (k_{ji})$ of exponents.

For simplicity we will assume that the code-interval of

92

all one-dimensional code generators is $[0,\infty)$.
If i=1,2,...,n, then obviously this higher dimensional
code generator has 2^n different branches.
It is quite easy to win in this case the corresponding
higher dimensional coder, because the mapping above,
defined can be easily resolved after the "rests" z^i.
We get in this case

$$z^{i'} = g_i^{-1} \left(\prod_j z^{j(l_{ij})} \right)$$

with the matrix $L = (l_{ij}) = K^{-1}$

2. From one-dimensional coders $g_i^{-1} (z^i)$ with the components z^i we can construct the corresponding binary
vector for the actual iteration tact and the corresponding vector of actual rests by the power-product
aggregation principle, namely

$$z^{i'} = \prod_j g_j^{-1} (z^j)^{l_{ij}}$$

with a certain regular matrix $L = (l_{ij})$ of exponents.

For simplicity we will also assume, that the code-
interval of all one-dimensional coders shall be the
interval $[0,\infty)$.
It is quite easy to win in this case the corresponding
higher dimensional code generator function as a function with 2 different branches.
Obviously we get the following result

$$z^j = g_j \left(s^j, \prod_i z_i^{k_{ji'}} \right)$$

with the exponent matrix $K = (k_{ij}) = L^{-1}$.

In some sense these two approaches are dual to each
other. The dynamisation for these approaches can be
done in different ways. At first we could establish
for every component a dynamic chain. In this case we
would get asresult of this step n chains coupled with
each other.
The other way is to look for dynamic networks as a
generalisation of the chains, that means for natural
networks of which chain structures can be considered
as special cases.
This is much more important because it offers us a
natural extension of the general dynamic chains of

type I into networks, thus leading to a <u>generalisation</u>
of Lotka-Volterra networks.
If we perform this dynamisation step for the first
approach, we get the following dynamic network

$$F\,x_j = \sum_{i} k_{ji}\,x_i \;/\; \prod_{r} x_r^{l_{ir}} \;/\; g_i^{-1}\,(\,\prod_{r} x_r^{l_{ir}}\,)$$

with $F = d\ln/dt$
which apparently is a generalisation of Lotka-Volterra
iteraction structures.
If we perform this dynamisation step for the second
approach we get the following dynamic network

$$dx_j/dt = \frac{g_j^{-1}(x_j)}{\overset{.}{g}_j^{-1}(x_j)} \;\sum_{i} k_{ji}x_i \;/\; \prod_{r} g_r^{-1}(x_r)^{l_{ir}}$$

representing another generalisation of Lotka-Volterra
networks.
But in this case the Lotka-Volterra equations are not
imbedded as special case.

FIGURES and REFERENCES can be obtained from the author.

GENERAL ENTITY STRUCTURES FOR SYSTEM ANALYSIS

W. Delaney, M.P. Roccotelli and E. Vaccari
Istituto di Scienze dell'Informazione
Università degli Studi,
70100 Bari,
Italy

ABSTRACT. A generalized version of Zeigler's entity structure is defined and its utility for modelling in general, and for system analysis
in particular, is illustrated.

1. INTRODUCTION

Formulation of a precise, realistic model of a complex system as a
whole can be obviated by various difficulties. An adequate theoretical
basis for a deductive approach may be lacking; on the other hand, empirical data necessary for an inductive approach may be insufficient
and the experimentation necessary to obtain more data may be very expensive.

If one is not willing to relax the objectives of the study (less
realism, less precision), the only way to overcome the above difficulties is to introduce appropriate hypotheses capable of effectuating a
consistent reduction in the complexity of the problem.

The system analysis - model synthesis approach provides a natural
framework for introducing such hypotheses. In system analysis (SA) one
conceptually decomposes a system into "parts" or subsystems; then, in
an intermediate sub-model-identification (SMI) phase, models of the
subsystems are formulated. Finally in model synthesis (MS) the submodels are combined into a model of the total system.

The rational underlying the above approach is obvious; one expects that it should be easier to identify a model for a subsystem than
for the complex system of which it is a relatively simple part.

Effectively the modeller has decomposed the original problem (directly identify a model for the total system) into three (hopefully
simpler) problems: system analysis, sub-model-identification, model
synthesis.

No methodology exists for solving these problems completely in
realistic applications, although important advances have been made in
this direction.

For example, in the context of an approach based on a hierarchy of
models (including elementary I/O relations, generative models - capable

95

R. Trappl (ed.), Cybernetics and Systems '86, 95–101.

of generating behaviours over times, and nets of sub-models) Zeigler
(1) defines criteria which must be satisified in transforming a model
into another one, it being significant that the original model could in
the limit be an ideal one, perfectly isomorfic to the real system itself. In this context Pichler (2) discusses specific transformations
which have been developed in the context of systems theory.

Klir and his collaborators (3) have developed an approach to the
solution of system problems (e.g. modelling) which is also based on a
hierarchy of models (similar to, but independent of, Zeigler's). Significant aspects include: 1) explicit recognition of an elementary
model type corresponding to a set of variables; 2) the concept of a
(user delimited) "mask" for seeking model defining patterns in data and
for characterizing such patterns in terms of probability or possibility
distributions. Methods for achieving transformations between different
types of models have been developed and a software system, GSPS, exists
for interactively helping users to solve their problems.

However, as Elzas (4) states after reviewing the approaches mentioned in the preceding: "The main obstacle to the construction of
realistic models remains untackled by the formal results outlined
above: to construct a model of a system we need to extract the main
features of that system".

Such "feature extraction" (understood to involve decomposition
into subsystems and the individuation of significant subsystem aspects,
attributes and invariant data patterns) is the essential goal of system
analysis.

Even when a system is being studied with a very precise objective
in mind, it is frequently necessary to iterate the (system analysis/-
sub-model identification/model synthesis) process many times considering, rejecting and eventually reconsidering various specific system
features until an adequate combination of features can be found. The
problem of definitively classifying a given feature as being significant or not is even more difficult in the case where an (open ended)
set of studies is foreseen for a multifacetted system.

Such considerations indicate the possible utility of a method for
uniformly representing all the different aspects of a system and for
clearly evidencing their interrelationships. In the following a method
having such finality is suggested; it is based on the entity-structure
concept of Zeigler (1).

2.   THE ENTITY STRUCTURE

A system entity structure is a labelled tree whose nodes may be of
exactly two types: entity or aspect. "Sons" of entities are aspects
and vice-versa, so that proceeding along any path from the root (an
entity) to a terminal node, there is a strict alternation between the
two node types.

In their original conceptions:
.   an entity is understood to represent a real world object which is
    independently identifyable or is postulated as a component in some
    decomposition of a real world object;

96

- an _aspect_ is intended to represent one of the possible decompositions of an entity;
- the entities of an aspect represent disjoint components of a decomposition but the aspects of an entity are not necessarily disjoint.

Some idea as to the advantages which may accrue from using an entity structure for representing the results of system analysis may be had by comparing the more traditional tree structure of Fig. 1a, where only the sub-systems obtained from a recursive decomposition of the system (a car repair shop) are shown, with the entity structure of Fig. 1b which also explicates the aspect, or point of view, underlying each decomposition.

For most modelling problems, system decompositions like those of Fig. 1 (physical objects into component physical objects, which we refer to as _structural analyses_) will contain far too little information. In fact for studying system dynamics one is particularly interested in the functional analysis of the _activity_ which a system performs into _sub-activities_. Results from this latter type of analysis can be represented in traditional system analysis by employing a second tree structure whose nodes represent activities (see Fig. 2a).

However, using an entity structure, the results of structural and functional analysis can both be accomodated in a single structure, since in fact, the distinction to be made is one of _aspect_, this is exemplified in Fig. 2b where the concise individuation of an aspect by means of verbs (contains/does) should be noted.

3.   GENERAL SYSTEM ASPECTS

In fact it is suggestive how many system aspects of potential interest in modelling can be precisely characterized by appropriate verbs.

For example, as illustrated in Fig. 3 attributes can be associated with an entity through an aspect denominated "has" and the particular subsystem performing a certain (sub) activity can be associated with that sub-activity through an aspect "done-by".

This latter example illustrates the use of a _verb-form_ (verb plus preposition "by") to denote an aspect instead of just a verb. In fact in the preceding we have glossed over cases in which verb-forms would really be necessary in order to avoid certain ambiguities. For example in the decomposition of an activity into sub-activities it is typically of essential importance whether the sub-activities are carried on simultaneously or in sequence. In order to be able to explicate such distinctions at least two aspects (e.g. "simultaneously-contains" or sequentially-contains") would be necessary.

Similarly the verb "to have" can be specialized in useful ways. Once can relate an activity to its inputs and outputs through the aspects "has-input-variables" and "has-output-variables", respectively.

Table 1 contains a partial list of system aspects/verb forms where it may be observed:

Table I
Examples of general aspects which are frequently useful
in system modelling. The slash "/" should
be read as "or".

ASPECT	DECOMPOSITION OF (MODEL OF)	INTO (AS)
contains SSS's	system S	structural sub-systems=SSS's
" simultaneous. SA's	activity A	simultaneous sub-activities
" SA sequence	activity A	sub-activities
" FSS's	functional system (FS)	functional sub-systems=FSS'S
does	system	activity it performs
done by	activity	FSS performing it
requires.FSS's	activity	necessary sub-system
influences	system (FSS)/activity	the FSS's/activities it influences
influenced by	system (FSS)/activity	the FSS's activities influencing it
has.attributes/ variables	system	attributes/variables
has.inputs/ outputs	system	inputs/outputs
has.state variables	system	state variables
uses resources	system(FSS)/ activity	the resources it consumes

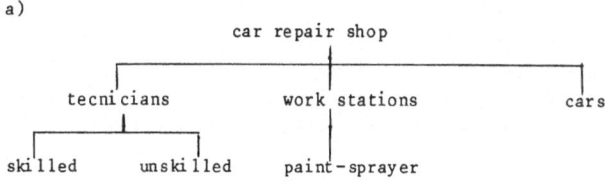

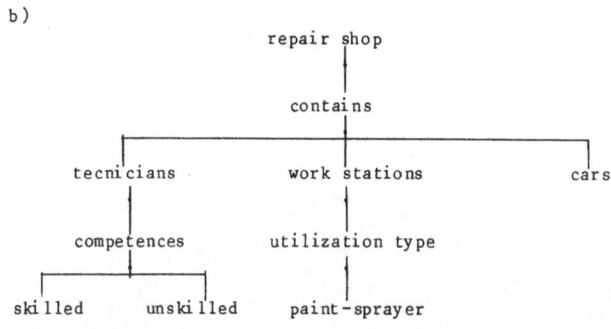

Figure 1. a) Fragment of a traditional decomposition tree representing a system (a car repair shop) analyzed into its constituent sub-systems. and b) a corresponding entity structure which also explicates the point of view, or aspect, underlying each decomposition.

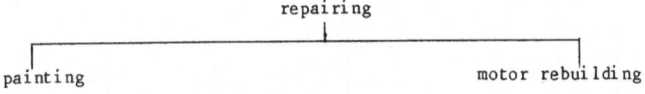

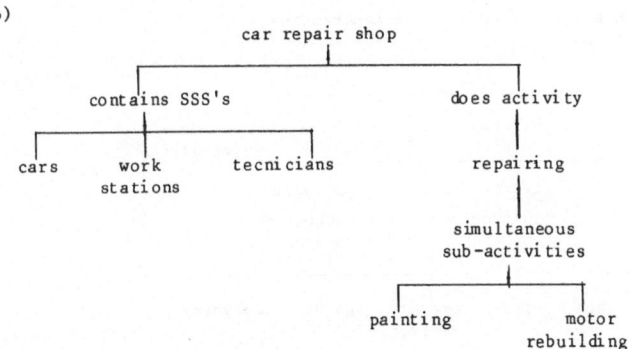

Figure 2. a) A decomposition tree representing the functional analysis of an activity into constituent sub-activities and b) an entity structure which represents the same information plus the results of structural analysis and the link between the system and its activity through the aspect "does".

99

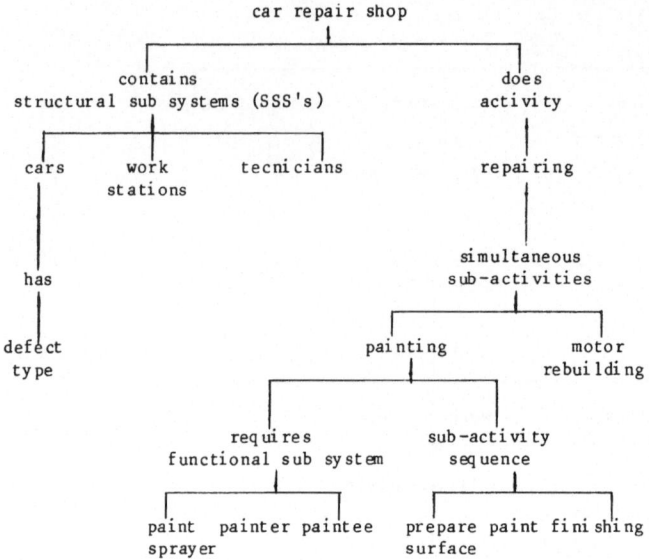

Figure 3. Use of the aspects: "has" to associate an attribute (defect-type) with an entity (car); "requires" to specify the functional subsystems needed to perform an activity (painting); and "sub-activity sequence" to represent an activity (painting) as a time sequence of sub-activities.

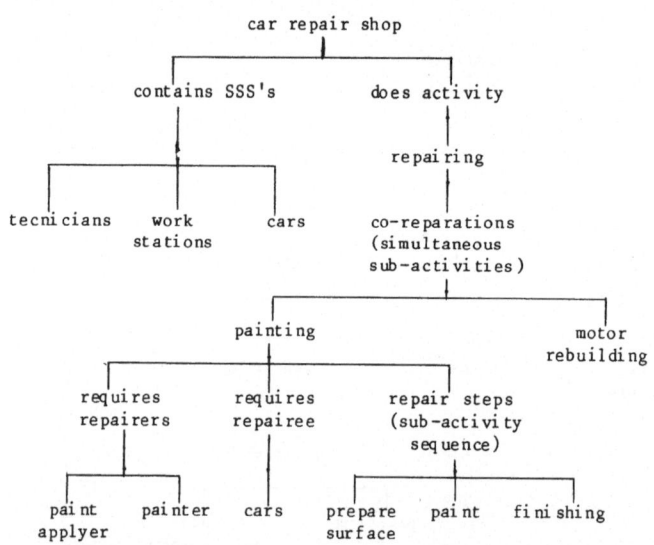

Figure 4. Fragment of an entity structure in which results of the structural and functional analyses of a car repair shop are represented using system-specific specialized aspects (here, various derivates of the verb "to repair") instead of, e.g., the more general aspects shown in parenthesis for comparision purposes.

100

- in the table heading, how aspects are characterized as "decomposition of X into Y" or, perhaps more cogently, as "model of X as Y";
- how "contains" has been further specialized as regarding either sub-systems or activities;
- that, in spite of such specializationas, the verb forms are still of a very general nature, i.e., they each have a very large set of potential subjects.

4. SYSTEM SPECIFIC ASPECTS

The above-mentioned "general aspects" would seem more useful e.g. in an environment in which a modelling expert guides a system analysis process.

Alternatively, with a more passive expert having only the task of memorizing/displaying system analysis results relative to specific systems, a user would be free to define aspects pertinent to his particular system. A possible resulting entity structure for the car repair shop is shown in Fig. 4.

The latter "system-specific" approach might be more "friendly" at least for users who are not very familiar with system theory and modelling concepts. It is immaginable however that the "general-aspects" approach might well produce less ambiguous results; also it could permit consistency checking and might even be helpful in automating some parts of the model synthesis process.

A particularly interesting possibility would be an expert capable of translating system-specific aspects into the more general ones. In general this would necessitate an expert with non-trivial natural language processing capabilities and a knowledge base like the one we use when understanding general aspects implicit in specific ones (e.g., those in Fig. 4).

REFERENCES

1. Zeigler B.P.; Multifacetted Modelling and Discret Event Simulation, Academic Press N.Y. (1984)
2. Pichler F.; Symbolic Manipulation of System Models; in Simulation and Model-Based Methodologies: An Integrative View; T.I. Oren, B.P. Zeigler, M.S. Elzas, Eds; Springer Verlag, Berlin (1984); pgs. 217, 234.
3. Klir G.; General System Framework for Inductive Modelling; in Simulation and Model-Based Methodologies: An Integrative View; T.I. Oren, B.P. Zeigler, M.S. Elzes, Eds.; Springer Verlag, Berlin (1984), pgs. 69, 90.
4. Elzas M.S.; System Paradigms as Reality Mappings; in Simulation and Model-Based Methodologies: An Integrative View; T.I. Oren, B.P. Zeigler, M.S. Elzas, Eds.; Springer Verlag, Berlin (1984); pgs. 41, 68.

LINEAR HARMONIC TRANSLATION INVARIANT SYSTEMS ON FINITE
NON - ABELIAN GROUPS

Radomir S. Stanković
Braće Taskovića 17/29
18 000 Niš
Yugoslavia

ABSTRACT. In this paper we define a class of linear harmonic translation
invariant (LHTI) systems on finite non-Abelian groups. Also, the basic
concepts of differential calculus are used for describing the introduced
LHTI systems.

1. INTRODUCTION

In the most abstract form a system is defined as a triplet (U,Y,s)where
U and Y are sets of mappings and s is a binary (input-output) relation
in U χ Y. Defined likewise, the system is much too abstract, providing
a model which is hardly tractable at all. A concrete system can be obtained by imposing certain structures on the input and output sets,as
well as on the relation s itself. In practice, it is costomary to consider the same set of functions defined on locally compact Abelian group
G for both input and output sets (a counter example is a sampling device), the normal choice being the linear spaces of (usualy complex) functions defined on the group (R,+)(continuous systems) or (Z,+)(discrete
systems) or on some of their subsets. In the case of dyadic systems [1-4]
the role of U and Y is played by the complex functions defined on a finite or infinite dyadic group. Similarly, in the case of p-adic systems
introduced in[5] we also have U=Y and this is the space of complex functions on Z_{p^n}.

In the classical context as well as in the case of dyadic or p-adic
systems, the structuring of the relation s translates as the rquirement
that the system be linear possessing certain symmetries. The example are
the systems described by linear operators wich commute with certain other operators, for instance the (arithmetic or dyadic or p-adic) translation operators.
In this paper we define a class of systems for which these classical assumptions for the operation s (linearity and translation invariance) are satisfied, but U and Y are a linear space of functions defined
on a finite non-Abelian group. We denote these systems as the linear
harmonic translation invariant (LHTI) systems on finite non-Abelian gro-

R. Trappl (ed.), Cybernetics and Systems '86, 103–110.

ups, Then we define a harmonic differential operator D on finite non-Abelian groups, and prove that this operator is a LHTI system. Finally, we use this operator to define so called the harmonic discrete differential equations. These equations can be interpreted as the input-output relations of LHTI systems.

The study of LHTI systems is warranted, in the first place, by the fact that there are real-life signals and systems which are naturally modeled as functions and, respectively, relations between functions on finite non-Abelian groups. As examples of such problems we note a problem of pattern recognition for two-colored pictures, which may be considered as a problem of realization of a function defined on the group of binary matrices, a problem of synthesis of rearrangeable switching networks whose outputs depend on the permutation of input terminals[6],[7] a problem of interconnecting telephone lines[8], etc.

In the second place, the possible applications of the proposed systems can be found in the approximation of a linear time invariant system by a system whose input and output are functions defined on non-Abelian groups. See, for example.[9]

2. NOTATIONS AND DEFINITIONS

To make this paper self-contained we shall briefly repeat some well-known definitions.

Let G be a finite non-Abelian group of order g. We denote the elements of G by $a_0, a_1, \ldots, a_{g-1}$, where a_0 is the identity and $a_1, \ldots, a_{g-1}$ are the remaining elements in some fixed order.

Let K be the number of equivalence classes of irreducible representations of G. Each such equivalence class contains just one unitary representation. We shall denote the K irreducible unitary representations of G (in some fixed order) by $R_0, R_1, \ldots R_{K-1}$. We denote by $R_w(x)$ the value of R_w at $x \varepsilon G$.

Note that $R_w(x)$ stands for a non-singular $r_w \times r_w$ matrix, with elements $R_w(i,j)(x)$, $i,j=1,2,\ldots,r_w$. It is well known that the functions $R_w(i,j)(.)$, $w=0,1,\ldots,K-1$, $i,j=1,2,\ldots,r_w$ form an orthogonal system in the space C(G) of complex functions on G.

With this notation the direct and inverse Fourier transforms of a function $f \varepsilon C(G)$ are defined respectively by

$$S_f(w) = r_w g^{-1} \sum_{u=0}^{g-1} f(a_u) R_w(a_u^{-1}),$$

$$f(x) = \sum_{w=0}^{K-1} \mathrm{Tr}(S_f(w) R_w(x)),$$

where Tr A denotes the trace of A.

Note that $\mathrm{Tr}\, R_w$ is called the character of R_w.

The convolution product $f_1 * f_2$ of two functions $f_1, f_2 \varepsilon C(G)$ is defined by

104

$$(f_1 * f_2)(x) = \sum_{u=0}^{g-1} f_1(a_u) \, f_2(xa_u^{-1}). \tag{1}$$

The convolution product has the following property:

$$r_w g^{-1} S_{f_1 * f_2}(w) = S_{f_1}(w) \, S_{f_2}(w).$$

The translation (shift) operator T on a given non-Abelian group G is defined by

$$(T^\tau f)(x) = f(x\tau), \quad x, \tau \in G, \tag{2}$$

and the following property is valid

$$S_{f(x\tau)}(w) = R_w(\tau) \, S_{f(x)}(w).$$

3. HARMONIC TRANSLATION INVARIANT LINEAR SYSTEMS ON FINITE NON-ABELIAN GROUPS

We shall now define a certain class of linear systems on finite non-Abelian groups, which have an invariant behavior against the translation described by (2) of the input functions.

<u>Definition o.</u> A scalar linear system A is defined as a triplet (U, Y, s) where U and Y are sets of complex functions defined on a finite non-Abelian group G of order g, and the input-output relation s is given by the convolution product:

$$y = h * f, \quad f \in U, \quad y \in Y$$

defined by (1), i.e.,

$$y^{(\tau)} = \sum_{x=0}^{g-1} h(x) f(\tau x^{-1}), \quad x, \tau \in G \tag{3}$$

So an ordered pair $(f, y) \in U \times Y$ is exactly then an input-output pair of A if f and y fulfill the equation (3). The function h is the impulse response of A.

It is easy to show that A is invariant against the translations given by (2) of the input functions. By that we mean that if y is the output to f, then y^τ is the output to f^τ, for all $\tau \in G$. Here f^τ and y^τ denote the translations of f and y defined by (2), i.e.,

$$f^\tau(x) = T^\tau f(x) = f(x\tau),$$

$$y^\tau(x) = T^\tau y(x) = y(x\tau).$$

105

Theorefore the so defined system A we denote as a linear harmonic translation invariant (LHTI) system. The analogy of our system A given by (3) to a linear time invariant system given by its steady-state representation is apparent.

4. HARMONIC DIFFERENTIAL CALCULUS ON FINITE NON-ABELIAN GROUPS

In this section we shall introduce some basic concepts on the differential calculus on finite non-Abelian groups. We will lather see that, a harmonic differential operator is a LHTI system.

Definition 1. The harmonic derivative Df of a function $f \in C(G)$ whose Fourier transform is S_f is defined by

$$(Df)(x) = \sum_{w=0}^{K-1} wTr(S_f(w)R_w(x)). \tag{4}$$

Notice that this definition is unique only by virtue of the fixed order adopted for the irreducible unitary representations of G, denoted by $R_0, \ldots, R_{K-1}$. If a different correspondence between the representations and the notations were adopted, then (4), though unchanged in appearance, would define a distinct differentiator. This phenomenon is nothing new: it is already present in the definition of the dyadic differentiator, which depends upon the order assumed for the Walsh functions (the characters of the dyadic group).

In what follows the harmonic derivative will be denoted by Df or, alternatively, by $f^{(1)}$.

An interesting interpretation of the harmonic derivative thus defined may be obtained by using the method applied in[2] for obtaining the corresponding interpretation of the dyadic derivative.

Define the partial sum $\hat{f}_p(x)$ $p \leq K$ by relation

$$\hat{f}_p(x) = \sum_{w=0}^{p-1} Tr(S_f(w)R_w(x)). \tag{5}$$

Also, let us define the Fejér sum as

$$\sigma_q(x) = q^{-1} \sum_{p=1}^{q} \hat{f}_p(x). \tag{6}$$

Substituting (5) into (6), we have, after simple calculation:

$$K(f(x) - \sigma_K(x)) = \sum_{w=0}^{K-1} wTr(S_f(w)R_w(x)).$$

The left hand side of this equation is the error in the approximation of $f \in C(G)$ by its Fejér sum $\sigma_K(x)$. Hence, the harmonic derivative on a finite non-Abelian group can be interpreted as this error multiplied by K.

It is easy to show that the main properties of so defined harmonic diferential operator are given by the following theorem.

Theorem 1. If $f \in C(G)$, then

a) $D(a_1 f_1 + a_2 f_2) = a_1 D f_1 + a_2 D f_2$,
    f_1, $f_2 \in C(G)$, a_1, a_2 - complex constants.

b) $Df = 0 \in C(G)$ iff f is a constant function.

c) If the Fourier transform of f is S_f, then that of $f^{(1)}$ is given by
    $S_{f^{(1)}}(w) = w S_f(w)$, $w = 0, 1, \ldots, K-1$.

    Using this property it is simple to prove that the set $\{R_w^{(i,j)}(x)\}$ is the set of eigenfunctions of the harmonic derivative, i.e.,

    $$DR_w^{(i,j)}(x) = w R_w^{(i,j)}(x).$$

    From there, due to the linearity of the harmonic derivative, we have

    $$DTrR_w(x) = wTrR_w(x). \tag{7}$$

d) From the property c) it easily follows that
    $D(f_1 * f_2) = (Df_1) * f_2 = f_1 * (Df_2)$, $f_1, f_2 \in C(G)$.

e) The operator D does not obey the product rule, i.e., it is false that, for each f_1 and f_2
    $D(f_1 f_2) = f_1(Df_2) + (Df_1)f_2$.

f) The harmonic differentiator commutes with the translation (shift) operator (2), i.e.,
    $$D(T^{\tau} f) = T^{\tau}(Df), \quad \tau \in G.$$

Proof. Proofs of the properties (a-f) are easily derived in the transform domain using properties of the Fourier transform together with some well known relations for group representations; they are therefore omitted.

The derivative D can be extended to arbitrary complex order k by way of the definition of the delta function.

$$\delta(x) = g^{-1} \sum_{w=0}^{K-1} r_w TrR_w(x).$$

The δ-function thus defined has the property

$$\delta(x) = \begin{cases} 1, & x = 0 \\ 0, & x \neq 0 \end{cases} .$$

The derivative of order k of the δ-function is obtained by a direct

107

generalization of the relation (7):

$$\delta^{(k)}(x) = g^{-1} \sum_{w=0}^{K-1} w^k r_w \, \text{Tr} R_w(x).$$

Using the property d) we have:

$$(D^k f)(x) = ((D^k \delta) * f)(x) = \sum_{w=0}^{K-1} w^k \text{Tr}(S_f(w) R_w(x)).$$

From this equation we see that the harmonic differentiator D^k is a LHTI system which has an impulse response h given by h= δ^s.

5.HARMONIC DISCRETE DIFFERENTIAL EQUATIONS AND LHTI SYSTEMS

The concept of harmonic differentation directly leads to the concept of harmonic discrete differential equations. We define an linear harmonic discrete differential equation with constant coefficients as a relation given by

$$\sum_{k=0}^{n} a_k y^{(k)} = \sum_{k=0}^{m} b_k f^{(k)} \qquad (8)$$

where a_k and b_k should be complex numbers; y denotes the general solution of (8).

The relation described by (8) can be interpreted as an input-output relation of a system A. It is clear that the system A is linear.

As in the case of ordinary differential equations we get the general solution,y,(the general output function) of equation (8) as the sum of the solution y_{zi} of the homogeneous equation (the zero-input response of the system) and the particular solution y_{zs} of the inhomogeneous equation (the zero-state response)

$$y = y_{zi} + y_{zs} .$$

In order to find y_{zi} one looks for the roots of the charasteristic equation of (8) given by

$$\sum_{k=0}^{n} a_k z^k = 0.$$

Nor, we have the following theorem.
Theorem 2. If the roots $\{z_i\}$ i=0,...,n of the charasteristic equation are distinct and belongs to the set $\{0,1,...,K-1\}$,then the homogeneous solution is

$$y_{zi}(x) = \sum_{i=0}^{n} \sum_{j,k=1}^{r_{z_i}} c_{jk}^{z_i} R_{z_i}^{(j,k)}(x)$$

108

where constant C_{jk}^{zi} depend on the boundary conditions.

Proof. Equation (8) can be considered as a special case of the general linear equation discussed in.[10] Therefore, all results presented in[10] may be applied here. Now, we have that Theorem 2 is a particular case of Theorem 6 proved in.[10]

The following statements are, in a way, often taken for granted. In fact, we could not find a proof for these statements, as it standards, anywhere.

If t of the roots of the characteristic equation are repetitions of other roots, then the number of linearly independent solutions to a linear harmonic discrete differential equation of order k is

$$\sum_{i=0}^{k-t} r_{z_i}^2 \ , \quad \text{provided that}$$

each root of the characteristic equation is in the set $\{0,1,\ldots,K-1\}$. If s of the roots are not in this set, then the number of linearly independent solutions of the given equation is $\sum_{i=0}^{k-s-t} r_{z_i}^2$.

To get the particular solution of (8) we apply the Fourier transform on both sides of (8) and get with regard to the property c) of the harmonic differentiator

$$\sum_{k=0}^{n} a_k w^k S_y(w) = \sum_{k=0}^{m} b_k w^k S_f(w) \ . \tag{9}$$

From there, providing that the equation (9) is compatible, that is $S_f(w)=0$ for all $w \in \{z_i\}_{i=0}^n$, we have

$$S_y(w) = \frac{P}{Q} S_f(w), \quad \text{where} \quad P = \sum_{k=0}^{m} b_k w^k , \quad Q = \sum_{k=0}^{n} a_k w^k \ .$$

By introducing the notation $H(w) = r_w g^{-1} \frac{P}{Q}$, we have

$$S_y(w) = r_w^{-1} gH(w) S_f(w). \tag{10}$$

The function $H(w)$ is called the transfer function of the system A. We shall see, the system A associated with (8) is a harmonic linear translation invariant system.

From (10), by using the convolution property, the inverse Fourier transform produces the particular solution

$$y_{zs}(x) = \sum_{u=0}^{g-1} h(u) f(xu^{-1}). \tag{11}$$

We see that (10) has a form identical to (3).

Now, we have that (7) has a general solution y of the form

$$y(x) = \sum_{i=0}^{n} \sum_{j,k=1}^{r_{z_i}} C_{jk}^{z_i} R_{z_i}^{(j,k)}(x) + \sum_{u=0}^{g-1} h(u) f(xu^{-1}). \tag{12}$$

For the scalar linear system A connected with the linear harmonic discrete differential equation (8), the solution (12) represents an input-output-state relation. The function h is the impulse response of A, that is the zero-state response of A to the unit impulse $\delta(x)$, and at the same time h is the inverse Fourier transform of $H(w)$, the transfer function

109

of A.

We may conclude that the system for which the input f and the output y satisfy an linear harmonic discrete differential equation with constant coefficients can be considered as a subclass of LHTI systems.

6. CONCLUSION

In this paper a class of linear harmonic translation invariant (LHTI) systems on finite non-Abelian groups is defined. Also, a harmonic differential operator for complex functions on a finite non-Abelian group is introduced. It is proved that this operator is a LHTI system. Using this operator the linear harmonic discrete differential equations are introduced. Finally it is shown that a subclass of LHTI systems consist of those systems for which the input f and the output y satisfy an linear harmonic constant coefficients discrete differential equation.

The LHTI systems defined in this paper have an analogous counterpart in the theory of linear dyadic invariant systems introduced by Picher[1] and, also, in the theory of p-adic systems described by Moraga.[5]

ACKNOWLEDGMENT. The author is grateful to Prof.C.Moraga,Dortmund University,and Dr.J.E.Gibbs,National Physical Laboratory,Teddington,Prof.M.R. Stojić,University of Belgrade, for their assistance and encouragement throughout the duration of the work reported in this paper.

REFERENCES:

1. F.R.Pichler,"Walsh functions and linear system theory', *Proc.1970.Symp. Applic.Walsh Functions,Washington,D.C.*, pp.175-182.
2. C.T.LeDinh,P.Le,R.Goulet,'An analysis of linear dyadic systems with MBL outputs',*Proc.1973.Symp.Applic.Walsh Functions,Washington,D.C.* pp.66-74.
3. D.Cheng,J.Liu,'Time domain analysis of dyadic invariant systems', *Proc.IEEE* 62, 1974, 1038-1040.
4. J.Pearl,'Optimal dyadic models of time-invariant systems', *IEEE Trans.* C-24, 1975., 598-603.
5. C.Moraga,'Introduction to linear p-adic invariant systems',*Cybernetics and System Research 2*, R.Trappl (ed.),North-Holland,1984.
6. D.C.Opferman,N.T.Tsao-Wu,'On class of rearrangeable switching networks', *Bell Systems Tech J.*, 50, 1971., pp.1579-1618.
7. K.Harada, 'Sequential permutation networks', *IEEE TRANS.*, C-21,pp. 472-479, May 1972.
8. V.Z.Benes,'Optimal rearrangeable multiusage connecting networks', *Bell Syst.Tech.J.* 43, pt.2,pp.1641-1656, July 1964.
9. M.G.Karpovsky, E.A.Trachtenberg,'Some optimization problems for convolution systems over finite groups', *Inform.Contr.* 34,1977,1-22.
10. J.D.Kečkić,'On some classes of linear equations', *Publ.Inst.Math. (Beograd)*, 24, (38),1978, 89-97.

MODELS OF DYNAMICAL MODELLING UNDER UNCERTAINTY

Rafael Pla-López
Ph.D. in Mathematics Sciences
Faculty of Mathematics, Universitat de València
C/Dr.Moliner, 50, Burjassot (València)
Spain

ABSTRACT. The objective of this work is to modelize the evolution of
a Model-System to be adapted to a Random System. This evolution is
described by means of the change of a probabilistic function, through
deterministic rules and in function of the random responses of the mode-
lized System. This probabilistic function can describe the relative
weight of distinct submodels (deterministic or random Systems, with
constant or variable stimulus), or the stimulus-response relation in the
Model-System (Adaptative Random System). We conclude that the Adaptative Random Model permits a more precise, simple and economical modelling.

1. INTRODUCTION

The elaboration of methods to evaluate the adequation of different Models at a given System (**1**) has been realized with estatical Models and
assigning the Modelling protagonism to the "human operator", which realizes the elaboration and change of the Models. From a epistemological
point of view, it is equivalent to work in the "justification context"(**2**).

On the contrary, in this work we will study processes of Dynamical
Modelling, in the style of "Expert Systems"(**3**), modelling the evolution
of a Model-System to be adapted at a given System. This Meta-Modelling
or 2nd order Modelling, from a epistemological point of view, is equivalent to work in the "discovery context"(**4**).

In this work, we will study only the Modelling of Random Systems,
but the Model-Systems will be as deterministic as random Systems. In the
line of previous works(**5**), we will study two patterns of Learning of
those Model-Systems:

A)**Learning by Selection,** through the change in the proportions of
actuation of different Models(**6**).

B)**Organized Learning** by means of Adaptative Model-Systems(**7**).

R. Trappl (ed.), Cybernetics and Systems '86, 111–116.
© *1986 by D. Reidel Publishing Company.*

2. WEIGHING OF MODELS

We will suppose, at large, that the System S_1, with a behaviour given by the probabilistic function $P_1(y_1/x,i)$, models the System S_2, with a behaviour given by the probabilistic function $P_2(y_2/x)$. Here, "x" and "y" are respectively the input and output variables, while "i" is a variable which values characterize at the different Models in the jousting field; its absolute probability, $P_t(i)$, changes through the time and determines the relative weigh of each Model. This absolute probability will change through a Learning process provoked by the comparison between the values of (x,y_1) and (x,y_2). We represent it in the Figure 1.

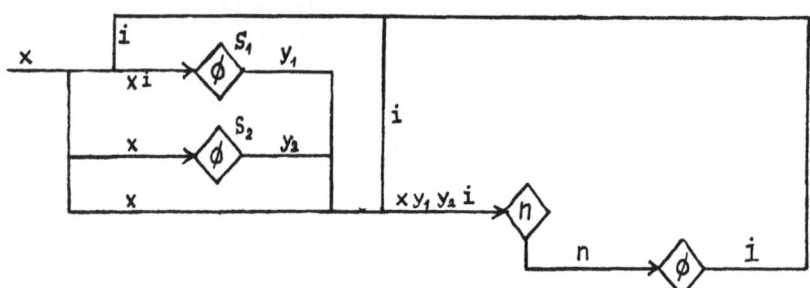

Figure 1. Model of modelling by selective weighing: the number of Models of each type change through the comparison between S_1 and S_2.

We have introduced a variable, "n", which indicates the number of Models of each type; its functional value will determine the absolute probability of each value of "i",

$$P_t(i) = \frac{n_t(i)}{\sum\limits_{i'} n_t(i')} \quad .$$

We will suppose that n changes through the time in a deterministic way according to

$$n_{t+1}(i') = n_t(i') + r(y_1, y_2)\delta_{ii'} \quad ,$$

where "δ" is the Kronecker Delta, and $r(y_1, y_2)$ will be contained between -1 and $+1$, and will concern at the probability of reproduction or destruction of one Model i' according to the concordance or discordance between the values of "y_1" and "y_2" (8).

Now, the point for point comparison between y_1 and y_2 will be relevant only if the Model-System S_1 is deterministic, that is to say,

$$P_1(y_1/x,i) = \delta_{y_1, F_1(x,i)} \quad ,$$

or, as to be the same thing, $y_1 = F_1(x,i)$.

112

So, **with x constant** and with adequate conditions for the continue approximation (9),

$$\Delta n_t(i) = n_{t+N}(i) - n_t(i) = NP_t(i) \sum_{y_2} r(F_1(x,i), y_2) P_2(y_2/x) .$$

With these conditions, we will study 3 different cases:

A) $r(y_1, y_2) = 2\delta_{y_1, y_2} - 1$ (+1 if $y_1 = y_2$, -1 if $y_1 \neq y_2$)

Then,

$$\Delta n_t(i) = NP_t(i)(2P_2(F_1(x,i)/x) - 1) ,$$

and the proportions of the different Models will evolve toward the predominance of the Models with superior values of $P_2(F_1(x,i)/x)$.

So long as, at large, the equilibrium supposes that $\Delta n_t(i)$ is proportional at $n_t(i)$, and therefore at $P_t(i)$, the equilibrium will be overtaked only when there will be only Models with the same value of $P_2(F_1(x,i)/x)$, which will be the greatest value. That is to say, the process carries to the selection of the **Modal Models** in the distribution of y_2 (10).

B) Metrized y-space,
$$r(y_1, y_2) = 1 - |y_1 - y_2|/c$$

Then,

$$\Delta n_t(i) = NP_t(i)(1 - \overline{|F_1(x,i) - y_2|}/c) ,$$

and the process will carry to the selection of the **Median Model** in the distribution of y_2 (10).

C) Metrized y-space,
$$r(y_1, y_2) = 1 - (y_1 - y_2)^2/c$$

Then,

$$\Delta n_t(i) = NP_t(i)(1 - \overline{(F_1(x,i) - y_2)^2}/c) ,$$

and the process will carry to the selection of the **Mean Model** in the distribution of y_2 (10).

On the other hand, if **x is not constant** the process will lead, in the case A, to make maximum

$$\sum_x P_2(F_1(x,i)/x)P_t(x) = \sum_x P_{2,t}(F_1(x,i),x) .$$

In the other two cases, the process will lead to make maximum, respectively,

$$\sum_{y_2 x} |F_1(x,i) - y_2| P_2(y_2/x) P_t(x)$$

and

$$\sum_{y_2 x} (F_1(x,i) - y_2)^2 P_2(y_2/x) P_t(x) .$$

113

On the other hand, if the Model-System S_1 is **Random,** we will compare the global distributions of y_1 and y_2, instead of their values point for point. For it, we will work necessarily with the continue approximation.
Particularly, we can take, with x constant

$$n_t(i) = NP_t(i)(1-\chi^2/c) = P_t(i)(Nc+1-\sum_y \frac{P_2(y/x)^2}{P_1(y/x)})/c \ ,$$

in order that the process lead to minimize the Chi-Square function (**10**).

3. ADAPTATION OF ONE MODEL

Now, we will suppose one Model-System with a variable behaviour given by the probabilistic function

$$P_1{}^t(y_1/x) = \frac{f_t(y_1/x)}{\sum_y f_t(y/x)} \ ,$$

where "f" is a **memory accumulator** variable (**11**) which will evolve according to

$$f_{t+1}(y/x') = f_t(y/x')+e(y,y_2)\delta_{xx'} \ ,$$

as it is represented in the Figure 2.

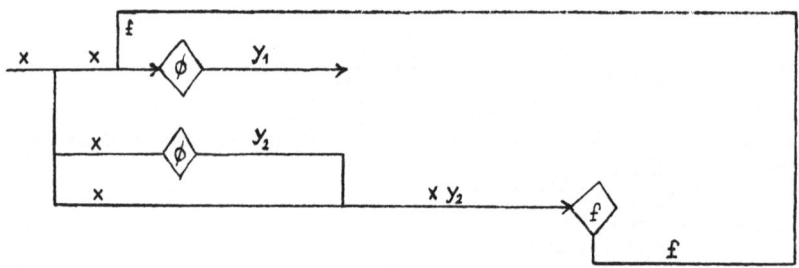

Figure 2. Model of modelling by adaptation.

With adequate conditions for the continue approximation, we will have

$$\Delta f_t(y/x) = N\sum_{y_2}e(y,y_2)P_2(y_2/x)P_t(x) \ .$$

If we will take

$$e(y,y_2) = \delta_{yy_2}$$

(thereby there will be only positive reinforcement (**12**)), then

$$\Delta f_t(y/x) = NP_2(y/x)P_t(x) \ .$$

Point out that the process of adaptation is independent for each value of "x". Particularly, the equilibrium condition will be

114

$$\frac{\Delta f_t(y/x)}{P_1{}^t(y/x)} = k(x) \text{ which lies only in "x".}$$

From this we can obtain easily, by integration, that $k(x)=NP_t(x)$, and so the equilibrium condition is reduced to

$$P_1{}^t(y/x) = P_2(y/x) \ ,$$

that is to say, to the exact reproduction by S_1 of the random behaviour of S_2.

4. CONCLUSSIONS

The adaptation of an only Model through an Organized Learning permits a more precise modelling of a random System than the weighing of different Models through a Learning by Selection. Moreover, this adaptation permits to use effectively more simple functions, and to prescind of the Models destructor negative reinforcement(13), so that the modelling economy is increased.

ACKNOWLEDGEMENT

I express my gratefullness to the Dr.Antonio Caselles-Moncho by his suggestions for the final writing of this paper.

REFERENCES

(1) A.Caselles, 'A method to compare theories in the light og General Systems Theory', Cybernetics and Systems Research 2, R.Trappl(ed), Elsevier Science Publishers BV (North-Holland), 1984, pp.27-32.

(2) H.Reichenbach, The Rise of Scientific Philosophy, Berkeley, 1951.

(3) B.Petkoff, 'A Cybernetic Model of Scientific Research and Cognition', Cybernetics and Systems Research 2, pp.721-726.

(4) T.S.Kuhn, The Structure of Scientific Revolutions, University of Chicago Press, 1962.

(5) R.Pla, 'Mathematical Foundations of a Learning General Theory", International Conference on Systems Research, Informatics and Cybernetics, Baden-Baden, RFA, 1984.

(6) R.Pla, 'Modelos de Aprendizaje por Selección', Actas XIV Congreso Nacional de Estadística, Investigación Operativa e Informática, Caja General de Ahorros de Granada, Spain, 1984.

(7) R.Pla, 'Organized Learning Models (pursuer control optimisation)', 3rd IFAC/IFIP Symposium on Software for Computer Control, Madrid, 1982, pp.251-256.

(8) R.Pla, 'Mathematical Foundations of a Learning General Theory'.

(9) R.Pla, 'Organized Learning Models (pursuer control optimisation)'.

(10) M.R.Spiegel, Statistics, McGraw-Hill Inc., USA, 1961.

(11) R.Pla, 'Mathematical Foundations of a Learning General Theory'.

(12) Ibid

(13) R.Pla, 'Systemic Transition from Ideological Learning to Scientific Learning', Cybernetics and Systems Research 2, pp.691-696.

A CELLULAR-SPACE MODEL FOR STUDYING WAVE-PARTICLE DUALISM

Dieter Gernert
Technical University
Schluderstr. 2
D-8ooo München 19
German Fed. Rep.

ABSTRACT. In the beginning, it is demonstrated by some examples that cellular-space models find an increasing attention in physics. The concept of cellular space (cellular network, cellular automaton etc.) is briefly explained. For the present model a plane square grid is presupposed, where two different zero states alternate as in a checkerboard. A set of rules is specified which allow the approximate modelling of ordinary waves propagating in space. If two such "waves" meet, two different processes may occur: the first may be regarded as the crossing of two waves which finally continue their usual propagation maintaining their original direction, whereas the second may be interpreted in analogy with the collision of two particles in classical mechanics. Finally, some limitations of the present draught and suggestions for further study are discussed.

1. CELLULAR SPACES AND PHYSICS

Cellular spaces find a steadily increasing attention as a tool for modelling various phenomena in our physical reality.

Just to quote some examples, ZELENY (1977) studies rhythms in biological systems and the formation of membranes. Another topic from biology is the analysis of cytoskeletal lattices given by S.A. SMITH et al. (1984).

Particular emphasis must be laid on the contributions by K. ZUSE (1969, 1975, with further references), who firmly advocates the concept of a discrete space structure which should be taken as a basis for modelling fundamental processes in physics; at the same time, he discusses the difficulties of such an endeavour. More recently, VICHNIAC (1984) shows how a great variety of physical phenomena can be described by cellular automata.

It is the aim of this paper to develop a first draught of a cellular-space model for wave-particle dualism; its main feature is an entity whose behaviour can be interpreted in analogy both to a wave and to a particle.

R. Trappl (ed.), Cybernetics and Systems '86, 117–122.
© *1986 by D. Reidel Publishing Company.*

2. OUTLINE OF A MODEL

2.1. Definitions

A cellular space (also called cellular network, cellular automaton, polyautomata network etc.) consists of many automata each of which is connected exactly with those automata which belong to a certain neighbourhood. As for many other purposes, it is sufficient here to presuppose a plane cellular net; in the simplest case this is given by the plane which is divided into congruent squares (called "cells"). Each square contains an automaton which can assume different states (from a finite set of possible states). The behaviour of each automation depends on its momentaneous state and on the states of its neighbour cells. All automata and all neighbourhoods are equal. An initial configuration must be specified; then the pattern of states is changed by discrete-time steps according to a set of transition rules, which must be applied simultaneously to all cells.

For the present model, two zero states Z_1, Z_2 are presupposed. The squares of the plane assume one of both zero states just in the same way as a checkerboard is coloured black and white.

In the sequel, different "states of activation" will be defined in order to describe processes occurring in the system. As soon as a single cell is no more activated (no more involved in a process), it will fall back into its previous zero state. Therefore the checkerboard-like subdivision of the plane will be maintained, although it may be partially invisible when some cells are just activated. For the sake of brevity it will be said that a certain cell is in $\underline{Z}_1$ or in $\underline{Z}_2$, where $\underline{Z}_i$ denotes the set of all cells with zero state Z_i.

A neighbourhood is given by a 5x5 square of cells which are arranged symmetrically around a certain cell (Figure 1).

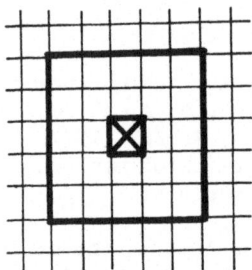

Figure 1: Neighbourhood definition

2.2 Joint features of waves and particles

A common feature of waves and particles lies in the fact that both move through space rectilinearly and at a constant speed as long as there is no disturbance. To start with, a certain process will be modelled which has the property of propagation in space. At a first glance, this process has some features of a wave, but it will be shown later that under certain conditions it can also be interpreted as a particle.

In order to describe this process on the basis of a cellular space with the definitions given above, first of all one of the two sets $\underline{Z}_1$, $\underline{Z}_2$ must be selected. The process can take place either on $\underline{Z}_1$ or on $\underline{Z}_2$, but for the moment one "half of the checkerboard" must be fixed. Under these assumptions, there are states of activation denoted by A, B, C, D, E, F (Figure 2). Now A characterizes the front-end of the process

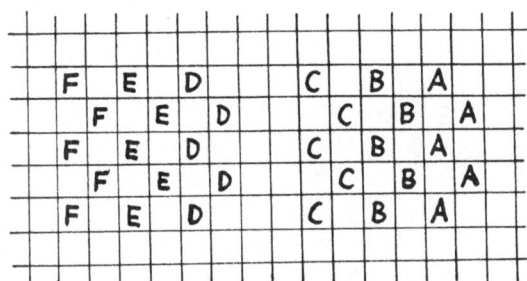

Figure 2: Momentaneous state of a process moving from left to right

moving on - at the same time it may be seen in analogy to that position within a transversal wave where the amplitude assumes approximately one half of the positive maximal value (in the usual representation $\varphi = 45°$ with $\sin \varphi = \sqrt{2}/2$ with increasing tendency). Next, B corresponds to the maximal positive amplitude, and C to a location with approximately one half of the maximum, but in the declining phase ($\varphi = 135°$ with $\sin \varphi = -\sqrt{2}/2$). Proceeding in the cellular net, the next cell belonging to the selected set $\underline{Z}_i$ is in its zero state Z_i - this corresponds to wave amplitude zero ($\sin 180° = 0$). Going on in the same direction, three cells with activation states D, E, F will follow; in a quite analogous manner they characterize locations with negative amplitude, e.g. E corresponds to $\varphi = 270°$ with $\sin \varphi = -1$.

Figure 2 gives an example for a process in a momentaneous state, whereas Figure 3 represents the transition rules in a comfortable geo-

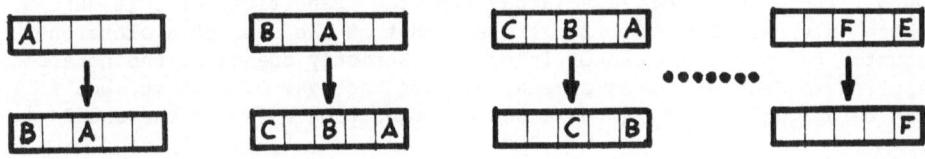

Figure 3: Transition rules for a moving process

metrical representation. With each time-step the totality of all such activation patterns will advance by two cells in the rectangular net. It can be seen from Figure 3 that the 5x5 neighbourhood as specified

119

above is sufficient.

A process is also allowed to move upward, downward, or from right to left (rotation or reflexion of the diagrams in Figure 3). In a similar manner, a motion in any diagonal direction shall be possible (Figure 4). Such processes may have different "intensities". This variable can be expressed by the different numbers of elementary sequences

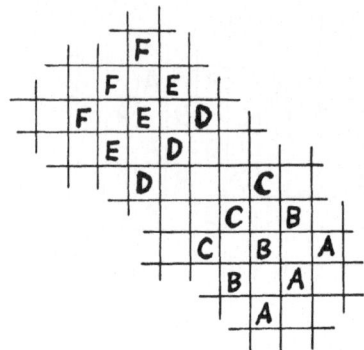

Figure 4: Process moving in a diagonal direction

(ABCDEF) moving in parallel (e.g. in Figure 2 there are five, in Figure 4 there are three such parallel sequences).

2.3. Different appearance as a wave or as a particle

Now two entities or processes as described before must be considered. If two entities move on in space, they may come closer and closer, and if elements of both are in a neighbourhood, then it will depend on the transition rules of the system which kind of interaction will take place.

First, two processes will be regarded which come in from different directions and then "meet" (in the sense of the underlying neighbourhood definition). Under certain conditions, two waves can cross without disturbing each other, and this phenomenon can be found in the model. It must be presupposed that the first "wave" moves on $\underline{z}_1$ and the second on $\underline{z}_2$. Then it follows immediately from the transition rules (Figure 3), where only one of the two $\underline{z}_i$ is used, that in the case of a close encounter two processes cannot interact. (Strictly speaking, the notation applied in Section 2.2 is a meta-rule for the sake of comfort, but it can be uniquely rewritten as a set of transition rules in the usual form.)

Hitherto, it is still undefined what will happen if two processes, both based on the same $\underline{z}_i$, will meet. The transition rules for this case are given by Figure 5 (where both processes are distinguished by low-case and capital letters, and only the first half of each is shown)

It follows from these transition rules that after the encounter both processes do still occur, and that both have altered their directions in a characteristic manner. This can be interpreted in analogy with the collision of two particles obeying the rules of classical

120

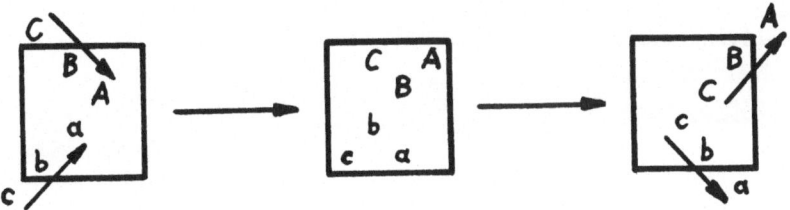

Figure 5: Transition rules for a collision-like interaction

mechanics.

3. DISCUSSION

Of course, the model presented here is only a rough sketch. It can by no means compete with the established concepts of theoretical physics; particularly, it does not yet include important phenomena, like interference between waves, nor can it supply quantitative predictions.

On the other hand, the usual formalism does not open a pathway towards an understanding of the basic underlying mechanism. (Standard textbooks, if discussing this problem at all, take refuge e.g. to the claim that there is nothing more left to be understood.)

Other phenomena can be modelled in a similar way; e.g. the picture sequence in Figure 6 indicates the diffraction of a wave front passing a narrow slot. Returning to wave-particle dualism, the present model suggests that a slight change of a parameter may suffice to switch over

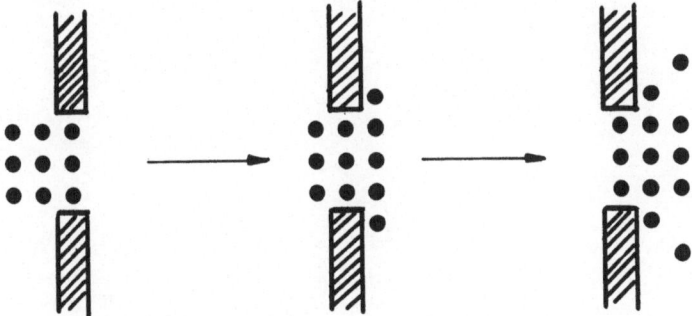

Figure 6: Model of a wave diffraction

from wave to particle behaviour or vice versa; the influence of measurement upon the result may possibly be understood as a local alteration of some parameter, which is triggered by the experimental setting.

It is the author's conviction - which has been aroused and supported mainly by ZUSE's publications - that a successive refinement of cellular-space models will finally lead to a real understanding of an underlying microstructure and its physical properties.

References

SMITH, Steven A., R.C. WATT, and S.R. HAMEROFF, 'Cellular automata in cytoskeletal lattices', *Physica D* 10 (1984) 168-174

VICHNIAC, G.Y., 'Simulating physics with cellular automata', *Physica D* 10 (1984) 96-116

ZELENY, M., 'Self-organization of living systems: a formal model of autopoiesis', *Int. J. General Systems* 4 (1977) 13-28

ZUSE, K., *Rechnender Raum*, Vieweg, Braunschweig 1969

ZUSE, K., *Ansätze einer Theorie des Netzautomaten*, Nova Acta Leopoldina, Neue Folge, Band 43, Nr. 22o, Halle/Saale 1975

A GENERAL SYSTEMS ANALYSIS OF GOAL-DIRECTED HEURISTIC COMPUTATION

Michael Weir

Department of Computational Science
St. Andrews University
United Kingdom

The paper delineates dynamic structures in heuristic computation using a general systems approach. A design for goal-directed heuristics is put forward. Distinctions begin with a discussion of the involvement of goals in computation and their differing roles in algorithmic and non-algorithmic heuristics. AI problem solving is used as a paradigm area for justifying a non-algorithmic approach, in particular a goal-directed approach using current rather than a priori control. The main distinction is between goal-directed heuristics and algorithms according to procedural criteria as well as on the guarantee of success. A general systems model of goal-directed heuristics is developed with self-alteration being a key design principle.

1. Introduction

Heuristics may be broadly defined as methods of discovery of solutions to problems. Heuristic computation is an AI methodology which is of considerable importance since heuristics together with knowledge form the main pillars of current AI techniques. As with all AI computation, heuristic computation takes place within a computer system. This has the implication that heuristic computation can be seen as a type of system behaviour. Just which type is properly the concern of Cybernetics and General Systems Theory.

The thesis of this paper is that Cybernetics and General Systems Theory, through analysis of the system behaviour, have a contribution to make in establishing features of heuristic computation which are not systematic features of current AI systems.

From the earliest days both Cybernetics and General Systems Theory have been concerned with a special type of behaviour, namely purposive behaviour. The classic papers of Rosenblueth, Wiener, and Biggelow [2], Sommerhoff [4], etc., are well known. It is intended to show how results from Cybernetics and General Systems Theory in this area especially impact on the structure of heuristic computation.

In the first part of the paper a characterisation of heuristic computation is carried out. The characterisation is done in terms which may then be used in a formal General Systems model laying out the structure of heuristic computation.

2. Computation

Computation is defined here as a system process acting on data states containing entities called symbolic expressions to produce data states containing further such expressions

123

R. Trappl (ed.), Cybernetics and Systems '86, 123–130.
© *1986 by D. Reidel Publishing Company.*

according to a well-defined procedure.

It is important to note that the definition references two types of data state. There is the *global* data state which, in conjunction with the *computation procedure*, determines the process. There is also the *local* data state of symbolic expressions contained within the global data state which is the focus of the purpose of the procedure.

Each computation procedure may contain many computations since the same computation procedure can be applied to other global data states besides the one initiating any current computation. The procedure of addition, for example, may be applied to the numbers two and three. It may also be applied to any element in a domain of number pairs to produce an element in an appropriate co-domain of numbers.

In this paper, we shall need to consider computation procedures over an interval of time. Since each computation is a process each can be seen as a path being followed which is a function of time. At any moment there will be one and only one computed data state (local or global) being produced from the current data state. A computation procedure at an instant thus may be characterised as a *transition procedure* having the mathematical form of a function. The domain and co-domain, as indicated above, may be extended to include other operable elements besides the pair involved in the current transition. The transition procedure and its function thus represent what would happen at an instant for each data state were it to be in existence at that instant.

Throughout its existence over a period of time a process may change its instantaneous form. It follows that a computation procedure may have a changing sequence of transition procedures embedded within it. The well-definedness of a computation procedure is unaffected by such change provided there is a transition function associated with each current step of the procedure.

3. Goals

Computation, like many other activities, typically has a goal. It may be done to arrive at a payroll, or provide a line of reasoning for a medical diagnosis, and so on. It is in fact on the basis of the goal (and the data) that a particular computation procedure is selected.

The sort of computation most associated in people's minds as being computation is algorithmic computation. An algorithm may be operationally defined as a fixed list of subprocedures, each of which is recursively equivalent to a fixed list of instructions, and whose process is repeated for the same inital data state and input data sequence. A goal-oriented aspect of algorithms is that the selection of the algorithm on the basis of the goal and the data means that the end data states of each algorithmic process are the desired goal states. In short, an algorithm can guarantee a correct solution with every process it generates.

In much human activity though, problems may be tackled by heuristics which are not algorithms. An algorithm may not be known or not be feasible. Games are prime examples in this respect. It is a common and interesting feature of games that the way the game should go is not certain.

The non-algorithmic heuristics used by games players have attributes which diffuse the clarity given by algorithmic structure. That is, for instance, players get beaten, so success is uncertain. Also, heuristics may prevent moves going round in circles with the conditional : "If a game position recurs, try a different move." So heuristic actions may not be fixed to the various local states involved. A more general framework than that provided by algorithms will be needed for such heuristics to bring back a focus to their characteristics.

The roles played by the goals of heuristic computation depend on the type of computation. For an algorithm, the goal plays an implicit passive role. First of all, the goal is implicit in the design of an algorithm. Also, it is not causally necessary to mention

124

any goal in an algorithm's instructions. These need only contain a priori prescribed actions and refer only to the current data state. Hence the goal is passive during computation in a reductionist sense.

In some non-algorithmic heuristics, goals are also passive and implicit. These heuristics are those which are equivalent to algorithms procedurally and only differ in that a correct solution is not always guaranteed.

This paper's positive concern is with a different type of non-algorithmic heuristic, where goals are explicit and active, namely *goal-directed heuristics*. Although goal-directedness is a technical term in Cybernetic literature, each author characterises it differently (see Weir [5(a)], Woodfield[6], for surveys of theories of goal-directedness). The present author is no exception. In our case, Sommerhoff's distinction [4] though provides a starting point at least :

> "*This contrast of the results of goal-directed activities with what is unavoidable on the one hand, and accidental on the other, is significant and illuminating.*" (p. 159)

In our case, the intention will be in particular to contrast the a priori control of an algorithm with the current ongoing control of what will be termed goal-directed heuristics. The suggestion is that goal-directed heuristics, as used for example by human games players, show current control by virtue of the goal's interaction with the current local data state. In contradistinction to algorithms, the goal will be seen to explicitly and actively play a part in steering the computation towards it.

Thus far algorithmic computation has been examined and set in the broader context of heuristic computation. Other types of heuristic, in particular goal-directed heuristics, have been put forward as intuitive alternatives. The next sections are devoted to showing in what way these intuitions are computationally relevant to current AI approaches.

4. AI Problem Solving

In this section, AI problem solving, in particular heuristic state space search techniques, are examined for their goal-directed aspects. A case example of chess-playing is used as a basis to begin from.

The features of chess that I wish to pick out are common to many pure strategy board games. The overall aim in chess for players is to achieve a win by placing their pieces on the board in a certain way relative to the opponent's pieces (i.e. checkmate). At any moment, the positions of the pieces on the board constitute a game state which is changed after every move of the players. The computational procedure considered here is a player's overall game strategy together with its embedded transition procedures for taking the game state as the local data state and computing the next move.

A common transition procedure in the AI approach to chess is firstly to take the game state to be the root node of a look-ahead tree containing the possible sequences of moves from the game state. Since for much of the game the whole tree is too large to fully explore, (Shannon [3] estimated that there were 10^{120} possible paths from the start of play), a selected portion is explored. The potential moves examined are then evaluated for their strength and the strongest is selected.

The selective and thus limited nature of the look-ahead tree is an example of a situation where complete tree-search algorithms are infeasible. This lack is not confined to chess and is a common feature of complex AI problems. A consequence of this is that, if the other option of a specific knowledge-based algorithm is also unavailable, then solution paths have to be discovered during the problem solving process by non-algorithmic heuristics. The discovery is a genuine one in the sense that there is no definite route to the goal implicitly laid down in advance. The generated paths constitute ongoing attempts rather than direct traversals of solution paths. The lack of knowledge about where the paths eventually lead to also explains why, instead of game states and paths being labelled as leading to a win, draw or loss, they may only be estimated as to their local strength.

Furthermore, environmental influence in the form of the opponent may well stop an individual winning path being repeated due to a different strategy being adopted by the opponent next time. A chess algorithm thus would have to produce sequences of moves, no matter what the opponent does, that lead to regions of the tree containing only wins.

In the absence of such an algorithm, an approach which is more like those used by human players is to use heuristics giving the opponent equal respect as far as potential for winning is concerned. Such heuristics assume that opponents have the capacity to avoid regions of losses and may instead push the game path towards a win for themselves. It is thus recognised that an opponent may throw the game path off course for a player such that the current strategy becomes invalid. In general terms, a non-algorithmic heuristic has to allow for the environment having the capacity to induce goal-failure on all paths. A countering heuristic will need to be tailored dynamically in the light of the current game path's position relative to the goal.

Present AI approaches to heuristics are many and varied. They are nevertheless unified under the common theme of heuristics being procedures which should have as much success as possible without necessarily an absolute guarantee of success every time. Such a theme has the danger of leading to the caricature of heuristics as 'possibly incomplete algorithms which may fail'. Rich's characterisation [1] is revealing in this respect (p. 35):

> " In order to solve many hard problems efficiently, it is often necessary to compromise the requirements of mobility and systematicity and to construct a control structure that is no longer guaranteed to find the best answer but that will almost always find a very good answer. Thus we introduce the idea of a heuristic. A heuristic is a technique that improves the efficiency of a search process, possibly by sacrificing claims of completeness."

Many AI designs contain aspects of current control. Heuristics using look-ahead trees in their transition procedures, for example, can be said to use current rather than a priori evaluation. There is though an acid test to be applied as to whether a heuristic rises above the level of a priori control or not. This is that a heuristic should be examined for whether it is locally state-based or not, i.e. whether the action issuing from each local data state is fixed or not. If the action from each local data state is always the same the control is equivalent to a priori control.

The use of a look-ahead tree then, even though the transition procedure may use current evaluation, in itself does not prevent the transition procedure having the same form, i.e. being a single fixed transition function, throughout the computation procedure. For a given local data state, the same evaluation, current though it may be, is always arrived at and the same path taken. A heuristic solely using a look-ahead tree in the fashion described may be reducible to an algorithm procedurally which lays down the local data state transitions a priori, the only difference being that of real-time procedural computation as against reference to a store.

Heuristics that are equivalent to algorithms in procedural terms suffer as far as the two previously mentioned features of non-algorithmic problems are concerned. Firstly, the finding of solution paths relies on predefined, albeit perhaps informed, guessing and cannot make use of current directioning towards the goal. Secondly, the attempts are undermined by environmental disturbance. No matter how directly the transitions laid down by a heuristic are pointed towards the goal, environmental disturbance may throw the actual realised path off course. The common flaw of heuristics procedurally equivalent to algorithms is that the paths of such heuristics cannot deviate back towards the goal when they are going off course. There needs to be current modification of the heuristic itself for such deviation capacity.

In espousing current control then, the concept of goal-directedness as put forward here, requires current modification as well as current evaluation to be designed into the heuristic procedure. The rest of the paper concerns itself with how such modification manifests itself in general systems and computational terms.

5. Definitions

Various points made in previous sections can now be drawn together to form part of definitions of algorithm and goal-directed heuristic. An algorithm for instance has been characterised so far as a fixed list of subprocedures and associated instructions producing state-determined processes. One aspect of algorithms relevant to all the heuristics considered here is that of sequential process. This is because a state space solution necessitates the establishment of a connecting path between an initial data state and goal data states together with a corresponding sequence of actions. Another feature of algorithms is the use of a list. A list bounds the procedure and may be taken to denote the current transition procedure. Both algorithms and goal-directed heuristics will by this token be comprised of sequential lists of subprocedures and instructions.

A recursive component of algorithms not so far mentioned is that of subgoal. A procedure can invoke various subprocedures each one having a subgoal of the procedure's goal associated with it. In the case of an algorithm for a given state a fixed sequence of instructions can always be found to carry out the subprocedure so that the subgoal is realised. An algorithm's instructions can be regarded as subgoals which are logically sufficient and always achievable.

Consider for example a typical procedure given for shampooing hair :

"*Wet hair, apply shampoo and massage into the hair. Rinse, and shampoo a second time.*"

Such a procedure is intended to be an algorithm for the human users of the shampoo. The subgoals and subprocedures of getting the hair wetted, the shampoo applied, etc., are all supposed to be automatically achievable by the user. The example also shows the logical sufficiency of an algorithm's subgoals. If the hair is wetted, shampoo applied, etc., then the hair will have been shampooed.

An algorithmic heuristic may now be defined :

A heuristic that is an *algorithm* is a computational procedure consisting of a fixed list of subprocedures with fixed lists of instructions by which subgoals are achieved in its sequential state-determined computation and which together achieve the goal.

A heuristic that is goal-directed differs from algorithmic heuristics in the various ways previously discussed. One feature to be picked out here is that such a heuristic is employed in unknown or hostile environments where the current process may at various stages be driven off course. Consequently goals and subgoals can only be attempted and not necessarily achieved.

The attempt on the goal is put into effect using current control. One impact of this is that current modification to the procedure is required. The procedure's list of instructions is variable throughout the process. Another requirement is that the procedure be goal-based rather than simply state-based. The goal in current interaction with the process, as opposed to just the process itself, determines the next action to be taken.

A goal-directed heuristic may now be defined :

A heuristic that is *goal-directed* is a computational procedure consisting of a variable list of subprocedures with variable lists of instructions by which subgoals are attempted in its sequential goal-determined computation and which together form the attempt on the goal.

The above two definitions will provide a framework for a general systems model of the two types of heuristic.

6. Formal Model

The general systems model of computational procedures developed in this section is based on earlier general systems work (see Weir [5(b)]). There is overlap with AI state space search techniques in as much as it is a phase space approach. The dynamics are however those of current rather than a priori control.

6.1. State

For the purposes of strict comparison, the algorithms contrasted with goal-directed heuristics are *local*, i.e. their global data states coincide with the local data states. The *states* in the phase space correspond to the local data states.

6.2. Path

When executed, a computational procedure enacts a process comprised of a data process and an instruction process. A process is a sequence of events. A *path* represents a process by connecting a number of states in an event sequence. The set of possible paths forms a *phase space*. The phase space in chess, for example, is the initial look-ahead tree which has the opening game state as its root node.

Paths rather than states are the causative units in goal-directed systems. This is because the attempt at the goal can only be seen to be off or on course by knowing the direction of the attempt relative to the goal. A state by itself has no direction since it is a snapshot of the process. For instance, a snapshot of a ball moving through the air cannot show us where the ball is about to go or where it has been. It is the paths in the data and instruction spaces which constitute the attempt and the direction of the process.

6.3. Field

A *field* is the phase space with all the realisable paths at an instant etched in it. The realisable paths of a chess field at some stage in the game, for example, would be the single paths branching from each of the game states possible at that stage which accord with the current pair of strategies.

A special type of field required for present modelling purposes is a *vector field*. A vector field contains the set of single next transitions that would occur for the various states in the phase space under the current conditions. An instruction executed in conjunction with a data state will produce a transition in the form of a path to the next data state. An instruction therefore has a vector field associated with it for the data states.

6.4. Goal

A computational procedure is designed to finish with the current local data path having achieved the goal. Goals or subgoals can be formed from paths as well as states, e.g. one goal might be to compute an algorithm for winning an endgame in chess, which should involve the subgoal of finding a solution path. A goal can also be satisfied by the achievement of more than a single state or path. Checkmate may be possible from a particular game state in more than one way for example. Furthermore, checkmate will be possible in different ways or not at all from other game states. A *goal* is therefore a set of states or paths.

Each procedure within a procedure, each subprocedure, has associated with it a subgoal. For an algorithm, the realised next path always achieves the subgoal. For a heuristic, environmental input or incorrect computation may take the realised path away from the subgoal.

6.5. Current Control

The model uses a basic process cycle of :
execute transition procedure, monitor generated data path, modify transition procedure.

6.5.1 Execution of transition procedure. A transition procedure has associated with it a particular instruction list which implies a particular field in the form of a vector field sequence. For a heuristic equivalent to an algorithm procedurally, the computation procedure involves a single transition procedure and so the field is fully realised. In the goal-directed case though, only some of the list is executed during each cycle, enough to give direction to the new local data path thus generated. The field in this instance is therefore changeable.

6.5.2 Monitoring of generated data path. The new local data path is evaluated for progress towards the goal. If the path is deemed to be leading away from the goal with the current transition procedure, the transition procedure requires alteration.

6.5.3 Modification of transition procedure. If the path is on course, the modification of the transition procedure is null. Otherwise the goal directs alteration of the transition procedure. The model's principle of goal-directedness is that the vector field sequence ahead of the data state is altered to guide the path back on course. This entails altering the part of the list about to be executed. As an example of such goal-directed modification consider the implications for a Turing Machine. Such a machine's actions may be determined by a state transition table. Goal-directed modification in this case would be to overwrite the cells in the table corresponding to the transitions about to be made in order to accord with the goal. That is, each overwriting changes the field ahead of the current state towards the goal.

7. Conclusion

In many AI problems, current control over the solution process is useful. This is because the control necessary for establishing a solution path may not be known or knowable a priori due to ignorance or environmental unpredictability.

The paper has analysed the implications of current control through goal-directedness for heuristic design. Algorithms, which show a priori control, and goal-directed heuristics, have been shown to be procedurally different as well as in the respect of guarantee of success. Goal-directed heuristics are of a variable kind in contrast to the fixed nature of algorithms. That is, in general systems terms, algorithms are single fixed transition functions, whereas goal-directed heuristics realise the potential of a computation procedure to be a sequence of differing transition functions.

Many AI programs explicitly incorporate goals and aspects of current control. Consider the AI heuristic of backtracking for example. Backtracking is a procedure preventing repetitions of local data state transitions from a recurring state by going back along the path to a previous state and generating a new transition. Such a heuristic is thus non-algorithmic procedurally in the local sense. The differences between heuristics such as backtracking and goal-directed heuristics as described here are subtle. They are also important. Backtracking, for example, lacks current control to the extent that it is unsuited to counter unpredictable environmental influences. The path from the new state transition is as likely to be susceptible to perturbation as the previous path. The formal model developed provides the means for establishing these differences.

The theory put forward has been exemplified by modifying standard computational models such as the Turing Machine to become self-altering. This is so that current control can be exerted over paths deviating off course from the goal. Self-altering programs may be considered poor programming practice in implementing algorithms because of the obscurity of their determinacy. However, in the case of goal-directed heuristics, there is less concern with the determinacy and more with the shaping of the process. Self-alteration in order to steer the computation towards the goal is a necessary principle.

References

[1]   Rich, E., *Artificial Intelligence*, McGraw-Hill, 1983

[2]   Rosenblueth, A., Wiener, N., and Biggelow, J., 'Behaviour, Purpose and Teleology', *Philosophy of Science*, Vol. 10, Part 1, pp 18-24, 1943

[3]   Shannon, C.E., 'Programming a Digital Computer for Playing Chess', *Philosophy Magazine*, March 4, pp 356-375, 1950

[4]   Sommerhoff, G., 'The Abstract Characteristics of Living Systems', *Systems Thinking*, ed. F. E. Emery, Penguin, 1969

[5]   (a) Weir, M. K., *Goal-Directed Behaviour*, Gordon and Breach, 1984

      (b) _____ , 'Design for a Goal-Directed System', *Cybernetics and Systems Research 1*, North Holland, 1982

[6]   Woodfield, A., *Teleology*, Cambridge University Press, 1976

TOTAL ENTROPY. A UNIFIED APPROACH TO DISCRETE ENTROPY AND CONTINUOUS ENTROPY

Guy Jumarie
Department of Mathematics and Computer Sciences
Université du Québec à Montréal
P.O. Box 8888, St. "A"
Montréal, QUE.
H3C 3P8 CANADA

ABSTRACT. This paper is made up of two parts. In the first one a brief review of discrete entropy and continuous entropy is given, which shows how, to a large extent, the latter is a more suitable measure of uncertainty than the former is in some instances. Based on this remark, the second part proposes a slight modification of the axiomatic derivation of the discrete entropy so that it exhibits properties similar to those of the continuous entropy. Some consequences of this unified approach are examined.

1. INTRODUCTION

Let $X \in \mathbb{R}^n$ denote a discrete random variable (r.v. in the following) which takes on the values $x_1, x_2, \ldots, x_m$ with the perspective probabilities $p_1, p_2, \ldots, p_m$; the informational entropy $H(X)$ of X, which measures the amount of uncertainty involved by X, is defined as

$$H(X) = - Q \sum_{i=1}^{m} p_i \ln p_i \qquad (1.1)$$

where Q denotes a constant. Likewise, when $X \in \mathbb{R}^n$ denotes a continuous r.v. with the probability density $p(x)$, the entropy $H(X)$ of X is

$$H(X) = - Q \int_{\mathbb{R}^n} p(x) \ln p(x) dx. \quad \square \qquad (1.2)$$

It is generally taken for granted that, while the discrete entropy (DE in the following) expressed by equation (1.1) may be considered as a good suitable measure of uncertainty, the continuous entropy (CE in the sequel) (1.2) on the contrary, involves many drawbacks (negativeness, dependence upon change of coordinates, lack of characterization for the deterministic event, ...) so that, it is not quite a suitable measure of information.

Our purpose herein is to show that, on the contrary, to a large

R. Trappl (ed.), Cybernetics and Systems '86, 131–138.

extent, it is the DE which is less suitable than the CE, and our arguments are of both practical and theoretical standpoints. So, after a brief review of these arguments we shall be led to suggest additional axioms in the definition of the DE so that it be the exact discrete counterpart of the CE. The result is a unified approach to discrete and continuous entropy, which may be of interest in such areas like pattern recognition problem for instance.

2. A DRAWBACK OF DISCRETE ENTROPY

2.1 Axiomatic Derivation of Discrete Entropy

One of the most popular theoretic derivation of the DE is probably the one first stated by Faddeev (1956, [1]) (see Also Aczel and Daroczy, 1975, [2]) who proposed the following prerequisite for a possible measure of uncertainty.

(A1) $H(X)$ is a function $\Phi(p_1, p_2, \ldots, p_m)$ whose the value should not be modified by any permutation on $(p_1, p_2, \ldots, p_m)$.

(A2) $\Phi(p_1, p_2, \ldots, p_m)$ should be continuous w.r.t. $p_1, p_2, \ldots, p_m$.

(A3) $\Phi(p_1, p_2, \ldots, p_m)$ should satisfy the equation

$$\Phi(p_1, p_2, \ldots, p_m) = \Phi(p_1+p_2, p_3, \ldots, p_m) + (p_1+p_2)\phi(p_1/p_1+p_2, p_2/p_1+p_2) \quad (2.1)$$

these three axioms provide $H(X)$ in the form (2.1). □

2.2 Substitution of Variables

Let $\{f: \mathbb{R}^n \rightarrow \mathbb{R}^n, Y = f(X)\}$ denotes a one-to-one mapping; the uncertainty on X and on Y are the same, namely $H(Y) = H(X)$.

Despite its likely correctness, this equality does not suitably describe the effect of the change of variables on the entropy. Indeed, assume that $f(X) = bX$, where b denotes a positive constant, we should expect to have

$$H(bX) \downarrow 0 \quad \text{as} \quad b \downarrow 0 \qquad (2.2)$$

since then $f(X) = 0$ and the uncertainty of the deterministic event is zero, but we know that this is impossible as $H(bX)$ does not depend upon b.

Nevertheless, on a practical standpoint the limiting condition (2.2) above is quite meaningful. We have of course the uncertainty contained by the finite set $(x_1, x_2, \ldots, x_m)$ irrespective of their distribution in $\mathbb{R}^n$, but we have also an uncertainty related to the range of variation of X, and the smaller the latter is, the smaller the former shoulb be.

This remark is the basic motivation of the following. □

3. REVIEW OF CONTINUOUS ENTROPY

3.1 Axiomatic Derivation

In their charge against the CE, most scientists claim that, on the contrary to the DE, the former has been defined formally, anal gously, by merely substituting an integral for the finite sum in the DE. This is partly true and partly wrong.

Indeed, in this pioneering work, Shannon defined this entropy formally, but later, Hatori (1958, [3]) discovered a set of axioms which justify this definition.

3.2 Substitution of Variables

Assume that we make the transformation of variable Y = f(X) where f(.) is differentiable, one has

$$H(Y) = H(X) + Q \int_{\mathbb{R}^n} p(x) \ln|\partial f/\partial x| dx. \tag{3.1}$$

This equation (3.1) is the main argument of those scientists who claim that H(X) as defined by equ. (1.2) is not a suitable measure of uncertainty, because such a measure should be absolute and should not depend upon the coordinate system. In this sense, following these same authors, while the DE is quite satisfactory, the CE would be considered as being faulty.

Our contention is that, on the contrary, to a large extent, it is the definition of the CE which is much more suitable and satisfactory than that of the CE. Let us examine this question.

(i) Indeed, the application f(.) by itself involves its own amount of uncertainty, and following some authors (Thom, 1972, [9]), this problem of defining the amount of information contained in a form would be one of the up-to-date question of the information theory presently. So at first glance, the entropy H(f(X)) should be somewhat considered as being equivalent to the entropy H(f,X) of the pair (f,X) which would result in a composition of H(X) with H(f), given that, of course, we have to define the latter.

(ii) Analogously with the standard theory, let us write *formally*

$$H(f(X)) = H(X) + H(f/X); \tag{3.2}$$

then, equation (3.1) clearly defines H(f/x) as

$$H(f/x) := Q \ln|\partial f/\partial x|; \tag{3.3}$$

and in effect, this expression (3.3) has been successfully used by some authors (see for instance Nicolis (1984, [6])) to measure the amount of information involved by a curved line in pattern recognition problem.

(iii) Assume that $X \in \mathbb{R}$, and $f(x) = bx$; then equation (3.1) yields

$$H(Y) = H(X) + k \, \ln|b| \, . \tag{3.4}$$

When $b = 0$, then $H(Y) = -\infty$, which is the entropy of the deterministic evett in the continuous case. The consistency is complete, and we have not the same with the DE.

(iv) Most concerned scientists claim that a good measure of uncertainty should be independent of the co-ordinate references. Our contention is that on the contrary, this dependence is of paramount importance and is a basic feature of uncertainty.

Indeed, consider $H[f(X)]$ as being the amount of uncertainty involved by the mapping $\{f: \mathbb{R} \rightarrow \mathbb{R}, \; Y = f(X)\}$ in the co-ordinate frame F. If we change the co-ordinate reference from F to F', then simultaneously we change the mapping so that f is converted into f', and the amount of uncertainty involved by f' will be generally different from that of f: basically, this question is related to the problem as to how does deforming a pattern affect the amount of information it involves.

(v) Another argument we shall provide to support the definition of the continuous entropy, and more especially equation (3.1) is the following: Linnik (1959, [6]) gave a proof of the "central limit theorem" in probability theory which is mainly based upon the latter. Explicitly speaking, if S_n^* denotes the normalized sum

$$S_n^* := S_n/b_n \tag{3.5a}$$

$$= (X_1 + X_2 + \ldots + X_n)/(\sigma_1^2 + \sigma_2^2 + \ldots + \sigma_n^2)^{\frac{1}{2}} \tag{3.5b}$$

with standard notation, then, by virtue of (3.1), one has

$$H(S_n^*) = H(S_n) - \ln s_n, \tag{3.6}$$

equation which is a milestone in the proof.

In our opinion, this proof is of importance because it exhibits the similarity between informational entropy and thermodynamic entropy, and it enlightens the analogy between the central limit theorem and the second principle of thermodynamics. (For further comments on this point see for instance Jumarie (1985, [5]).

In this way of thought, a new problem is the following. The Linnik proof applies only to continuous probability density in order to use equation (3.1); and we cannot derive a similar proof with discrete variables for the very reason that (3.1) does not hold with discrete entropy. Here is the drawback: (i) the central limit theorem applies also to discrete variables, (ii) and in this case, it should have its

134

corresponding proof in the information theoretic framework by using a suitable concept of discrete entropy.

In other words, it is of interest to modify the definition of DE in order that it fulfills equation (3.6).

(vi) Our last argument in favour of the CE is related to the so-called "maximum entropy principle".

The maximum entropy principle. Jaynes (1957, [9]) stated the following principle. Let $X \in \mathbb{R}^n$ denote a r.v. the probability distribution $\{p_i\}$ or $p(x)$ of which is unknown, and assume further that this distribution is subject to some mathematical given constraints. Then, of all the distributions which satisfy the constraints, we should choose that one which provides the largest entropy $H(X)$ for X. ☐

This principle was mainly supported by considerations relevant to thermodynamics, and it has been successfully applied to a broad range of problems outside communication theory. Recently, Shore and Johnson (1980, [8]) *proved* it in the sense that they derived it as a consequence of a set of mathematical axioms that likely should be satisfied. They did not use the properties of entropy as a measure of information, but rather they examined the consequences of requiring that a method of inference should be self-consistent.

The crucial point is that they proved the principle for the discrete entropy only, and so for the very reason that they explicitly assumed the independence of the result with respect to any co-ordinate frame.

Nevertheless, by its numerous consequences (Shore and Johnson gave and extensive list of application in the bibliography of their article) on a practical standpoint, it is likely that this principle is also valuable in the continuous case. Recall that the normal law maximized the CE with given mean and variance!

So how can we conciliate this apparent discrepancy? One way to do that is to modify the definition of the DE in such a manner that it does not affect the result of Shore and Johnson, but provides the definition of the CE in the limiting case of a discretizing span which tends to zero.

4. A NEW MEASURE OF DISCRETE UNCERTAINTY

4.1 Preliminary Definitions

Let X denote a random variable which takes on the finite values $x_1, x_2, \ldots, x_m$ with the respective probabilities $p_1, p_2, \ldots, p_m$; we shall denote by $K(X)$ the measure of the uncertainty it involves. Well obviously, $K(X)$ should depend upon the probability distribution; but according to our preceeding remark in Section 2, it is quite convenient to assume also that it depend upon the range of variation $\Delta := (\max x_i -$

min x_i). But, the use of Δ will give rise to theorecial difficulties when $\overset{i}{\Delta} = +\infty$, and to circumvent this problem, we shall rather assume that $K(X)$ should depend upon the quantity $h := \Delta/m$ referred to as the *span of definition of the r.v.* X. Of course, $K(X)$ should be increasing func function of h.

If Y, $pr(Y = y_i) = q_i$, $i \leq i \leq n$, is another random variable with the span k, then the span of the pair (X,Y) is hk.

4.2 Derivation of the Entropy K(X)

Axioms for K(X). We assume that the uncertainty functions should satisfy the following prerequisite.

(C1) $K(X)$ is a function $\chi(p_1, p_2, \ldots, p_m; h)$ whose the value should not be modified by any permutation on $(p_1, p_2, \ldots, p_m)$.

(C2) $\chi(p_1, p_2, \ldots, p_m; h)$ should be continuous w.r.t. $p_1, p_2, \ldots, p_m$ and h.

(C3) $\chi(p_1, p_2, \ldots, p_m; h)$ should satisfy the equation

$$\chi(p_1, p_2, \ldots, p_m; h) = \chi(p_1 + p_2, p_3, \ldots, p_m; h) + (p_1 + p_2) \chi(\frac{p_1}{p_1 + p_2}, \frac{p_2}{p_1 + p_2}; 1)$$

$$(4.1)$$

(C4) In addition, one should have the equation

$$\chi(p_1 q_1, \ldots, p_i q_j, \ldots, p_m q_n; hk) = \chi(p_1, p_2, \ldots, p_n; h) + \chi(q_1, q_2, \ldots, q_m, k).$$

$$(4.2)$$

Comments. Axioms C1 and C2 are standard; C3 is the counterpart of the well known Faddeev equation, and C4 expresses the additive composition law with respect to the span of definition, which pictures our remark in subsection 2.2.

We have the following result.

Proposition 4.1. A function which satisfies the axioms (C1-C5) above is

$$\chi(p_1, p_2, \ldots, p_m; h) = \phi(p_1, p_2, \ldots, p_m) + K \ln h \qquad (4.3a)$$

and on putting K = 1,

$$\chi(p_1, p_2, \ldots, p_m; h) = - \sum_{i=1} p_i \ln \frac{p_i}{h} \qquad (4.3b)$$

or else

$$K(X) = H(X) + \ln h. \quad \square \qquad (4.4)$$

5. APPLICATION OF TOTAL ENTROPY

In the framework, it is easy to show that the continuous entropy is a

136

limit of the total entropy, and to prove the maximum entropy principal
for continuous variable.

6. A BIBLIOGRAPHICAL CLEARING

6.1 Original Work by the Author

Equation (4.3b) yields

$$K = H(X) + \sum_i p_i \, {}^\ell_n h_i \tag{6.1}$$

and in this form it is nothing else but a special case of the so-called
effective entropy which we defined as

$$K(X) = H(X) + \sum_i p_i H_i \tag{6.2}$$

in 1975 [6], and which we apply to introducing a concept of negative
transinformation. In this paper, we used physical consideration to
derive (6.2). Namely we decomposed the observation of X into two ways

i) First, we assume that $X \in L(x_i)$ with the probability p_i, where
$L(x_i)$ denotes the i-th interval of the sets $\{L(x_1, L(x_2), \ldots, L(x_m)\}$ of
intervals indexed by x_i. The Shannon entropy of this experiment is
$H(X)$.

ii) Second, given that X is known to be in the i-th interval, we
determine its exact position in $L(x_i)$ and we assume that the entropy
of this experiment is H_i.

We then have the global entropy

$$H(L, x \in L) = H(L) + H(X/L) \tag{6.3}$$
$$= H(X) + \sum_i p_i H_i (x_i). \tag{6.4}$$

In other words, the Shannon modelling is quite sufficient, provided
that we refer to this physical argument.

6.2 Further Mathematical Derivation

Three years later in 1978 [2], Aczel and Daroczy, apparently
unaware of our work, derived mathematically our effective entropy, by
using the following recurrence relation

$$H_m \begin{pmatrix} x_1, x_2, \ldots, x_m \\ p_1, p_2, \ldots, p_m \end{pmatrix} = H_{m+1} \begin{pmatrix} x_1 \cup x_2, x_3, \ldots, x_m \\ p_1 + p_2, p_3, \ldots, p_m \end{pmatrix} +$$

$$+ (p_1 + p_2) H_2 \begin{pmatrix} x_1 & x_2 \\ \dfrac{p_1}{p_1 + p_2} & \dfrac{p_2}{p_1 + p_2} \end{pmatrix} \tag{6.5}$$

but in view of our physical reasonning above it is by-now clear why should this relation hold?

In addition, these authors deal with "randomized systems of events", and it is exactly a randomization technique which use to decompose our experiment into two ones!

7. CONCLUSION

In this paper, we focused on the difference of nature between the discrete entropy and the continuous entropy as defined by Shannon, and we proposed a slight modification of the former in order that it have the same practical meaning of the latter, which, in many instances, is a more suitable definition of a measure or uncertainty.

We think that, in such problems, like pattern recognition systems, for instance, $K(X)$ would be more suitable than the discrete $H(X)$.

REFERENCES

1. ACZEL, J.; DAROCZY, Z.; *On measure of Information and their Carac terizations*, Academic Press, N.Y., 1975.
2. ACZEL, J.; DAROCZY, Z.; A Mixed Theory of Information. I. Symmetric, Recursive and Measurable Entropies of Randomized Systems of Events, *RAIRO Theoretical Computer Sciences*, Vol. 12, No. 2, pp. 149-155, 1978.
3. FADDEEV, D.K.; On the Concept of Entropy of a Finite Probabilistic Scheme (Russian). *Uspehi Nat. Nauk. (N.S.)* 11, No. 1, (67), pp. 227-131, 1956.
4. HATORI, H.; A note on the Entropy of a Continuous Distribution. *Kodai Math. Sem. Rep.*, Vol. 10, pp. 172-176, 1958.
5. JAYNES, E.T.; Information Theory and Statistical Mechanics I and II. *Physical Review*, Vol. 106, pp. 620-630, Vol. 108, pp. 171-190, 1957.
6. JUMARIE, G.; Further Advances on the General Thermodynamics of Open Systems via Information Theory. Effective Entropy, Negative Information. *Int. J. Syst. Sc.*, Vol. 6, No. 3, pp. 249-268, 1975.
7. JUMARIE, G.; *Subjectivity, Information, Systems. Introduction to a Theory of Relativistic Cybernetics*. Gordon and Breach, N.Y., 1985.
8. LINNIK, V. Ya.; An Information Theoretic Proof of the Central Limit Theorem with the Lindeberg Condition. *Theory of Probability and its Applications*, Vol. 4, No. 3, pp. 288-299, 1959.
9. NICOLIS, J.S.; The Role of Chaos in Reliable Information Processing *J. of the Franklin Institute*, Vol. 317, No. 5, pp. 289-307, 1984.
10. SHORE, J.E.; JOHNSON, R.W.; Axiomatic Derivation of the Principle of Maximum Entropy and the Principle of Minimum Cross-Entropy. *IEEE Trans. Information Theory*, Vol. IT-26, No. 1, pp. 26-37, 1980.
11. THOM, R.; *Structural Stability and Morphogenesis*. Benjamin, Reading, 1972.

STRUCTURAL ENTROPY

A NEW APPROACH FOR SYSTEMS STRUCTURE'S ANALYSIS

Ivan Stantchev
University of Economics "K.Marx"
Dept.of Systems Analysis and Management
B - 1000 Sofia, Bulgaria
Bul. G.Dimitrov 53

Without entering into great details of the theory we will assume that the structure of any system can be presented quite exactly by a graph, in which the different objects (elements of the system) are represented by the nodes of the graph, while the connections between them are presented by the arcs of the graph (which may be directed). From the theory of organization the existence of extreme structures of the type "Star", "Chain","Cycle", "Full graph", is known. These structures have maximal or minimal values for some variables /1/ (parameters which determine the elements of the graph and the graph itself). On the other hand these extremal structures have the equivalent from an organizational point of view. For example the "Cycle" represents an unstable organizational management structure in which the role of the leader is greatly reduced, while the "Star" has great stability with an important role for the leader, etc./2/. Structures of the "Star" type imply a higher level of specialization and concentration of production in comparison to structures of "Full graph" or "Chain" type.

A starting point for our future studies will be the comparison between the characteristics of two of these extremal structures - "Star" and "Full graph" (see Fig.1).

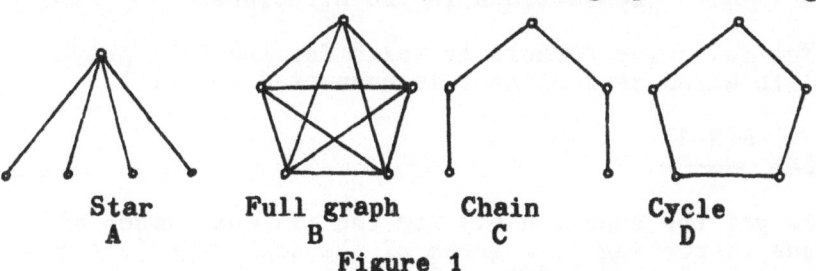

| Star | Full graph | Chain | Cycle |
| A | B | C | D |

Figure 1

In the strongly centralized system the number of

R. Trappl (ed.), Cybernetics and Systems '86, 139–146.
© *1986 by D. Reidel Publishing Company.*

connections will be minimal, while in the decentralized, maximal. At first glance this linear expression of the "degree of decentralization" by the number of connections should satisfy us; but research shows that an important part is played by the distribution in the configuration of the connections, i.e., the method of connecting the separate elements. A clear example of this is the fact that the "Chain" has also a minimum number of connections, but clearly does not correspond in its decentralization to the "Star". This leads us to the need to find some characteristics of the level of decentralization of the structure in which not only the number of connections, but their element distribution, should also participate. This last characteristic should have minimal values in the structures of "Star" type, and maximum in "Full graph". Analysis of the existing parameters used to describe the system structure shows that characteristics like these do not exist among the known ones.

We define a quantitative expression of each element called "degree" that is equal to the number of connections incidential with the respective element. In other words, the degree expresses the number of connections of a certain element with the others within the structure of the system. The degree of the I-th element – $P(I)$ is equal to the sum of the values from the I-th row of the incident matrix, respecting to the graph. It is filled with zeros and ones depending on whether there is or there is no connection between the two elements of the structure, i.e.:

$$P(I) = \sum_{Y=1}^{N} NG(I,Y) \text{ where } \|NG(I,Y)\| \text{ is the incidential matrix} \quad \begin{matrix} I=1,..,N \\ Y=1,..,N \end{matrix} \quad (1)$$

The equation (2) is valid for the sum Q of all degrees, as in the non-oriented graph the incident matrix is symmetric and each connection is assessed twice in the process of degree evaluation: once with each element incidential to the connection.

$$Q = \sum_{I=1}^{N} P(I) = 2LREAL \quad \text{where LREAL is the number of connections in the structure} \quad (2)$$

The following formula is valid for the full graph (Fig.1 B) in which each element is connected to all the rest:

$$LREAL = LMAX = \frac{N(N-1)}{2} \quad (3)$$

We get the equation (4) for the minimum number of connections respecting to a graph of the star type (a tree-like graph on one level) (Fig.1 A):

$$LREAL = LMIN = N - 1 \quad (4)$$

140

Each element from the graph is defined by a number characteristic H(I) equal to the ratio between the degree of the node and the sum of all the remaining degrees in the graph.

$$H(I) = \frac{P(I)}{2LREAL} \quad \text{where } \sum_I H(I) = 1 \text{ and } H(I) \leq \frac{1}{2} \text{ when } N \geq 2 \tag{5}$$
$$\text{as } P(I) \leq \sum_I P(I)$$

The above ratio in fact expresses the strength of connectedness of each element within the overall system structure. The smaller the value of H(I), the weaker the connection of the respective element with the rest. H(I) becomes zero when P(I)=0, in other words, when the respective element is isolated in the structure, and vice versa, H(I) grows towards 1/2 when the number of connections in the system increases.

Out of empiric considerations, piled up in the process of qualitative analysis of various types of structures, we can assume that a certain structure is most efficient when the number of connections with a definite number of elements tends to the respective one of the minimum graph. And vice versa, the structure will be less determined when more elements are connected to all the rest. The indeterminacy will then be dependent on the <u>way of connecting the separate elements within the structure.</u> The analytic expression of each unit is equation (3). On the basis of the upper reasoning we shall introduce entropy as a measure of structural indeterminacy and define it by the following equation:

$$ENTRO = -\sum_{I=1}^{N} H(I) \log_2 H(I) \tag{6}$$

This equation is known in information theory but it is applied in structural analysis for the first time.

The aim of the structural entropy's introduction is to find out qualitative characteristics respecting to the contradictory tendencies for centralization and decentralization in economic systems' structuring on the basis of a direct evaluation of the various structural variants.

A solution to the problem of defining the optimum of interaction of the abovementioned tendencies can be found by means of these characteristics.

First of all it is necessary, however, to check the formulated working hypothesis, taking into account the requirements for the properties of the particular entropies and their average meaning ENTRO. It is evident that with the structure of one element the indeterminacy disappears and ENTRO=0. When the number of connections increases some H(I) increase, others decrease, but the entropy continuously increases. This results from the properties of the function $f(pi) = -pi \log_2 pi$ in the interval $[0, 1/2]$. The value of the

141

maximum entropy for a structure with N elements for the full graph is defined by the following equation valid for each node:

$$P(I)=N-1 \tag{7}$$

We can derive the following equation out of it:

$$H(I)= \frac{N-1}{N(N-1)} = \frac{1}{N} \tag{8}$$

$$ENTRO=\log_2 N=EMAX \tag{9}$$

The result obtained shows that the full graph is characterised by a maximum indeterminacy which entropy is equal to the binary logorithm of the number of elements in the structures. The result proves the correctness of the assumption made, as entropy in information theory assumes maximum value at equal probabilities. The full graph, out of content point of view, represents <u>a structure with maximum decentralization</u> which does not contain "leading element" among the rest in the structure. This conclusion, together with the entropic property to increase with the number of structural connections, gives us grounds to accept the structural entropy as a quantitative characteristic of structural decentralization.

It is necessary, however, to check the limit case with minimum decentralization. Structures with similar property are characterized by the connection of a single element to all the other elements in the same structural position. Such a structure is interpreted by a graph of the "Star" type (Fig.1 A). Consequently, a structure of the "Star" type with N number of elements has N-1 number of elements with $P(I)=1$ degree and one element which we shall number with (1) with degree $P(1)=N-1$. Thus we get the following equation for the entropy:

$$H(I)= \frac{1}{2(N-1)} \text{ , for } I=2,\dots,N \quad H(1)= \frac{N-1}{2(N-1)} = \frac{1}{2} \tag{10}$$

$$ENTRO=1+ \frac{1}{2} \log_2(N-1)=EMIN \tag{11}$$

It becomes clear that entropy characterizes the degree of centralization in the structures, as with the "star" type with any number of elements > 2, the entropy has a minimum value as expressed by equation (11). With N=2 and one connection the entropy takes the respective maximum, which once again proves the correctness of the above reasoning.

In Fig.1 A and 1 B, N=5 and therefore we can calculate the maximal and minimal entropy by means of formulae (9) and (11).

$$EMIN=1+\frac{1}{2} \log_2 4 =2 \qquad EMAX= \log_2 5 =2,32 \tag{12}$$

The calculations of the entropy of a closed chain

(cycle) are as follows:

$$H(I) = \frac{2}{2 \times 5} = \frac{1}{5}$$

$$ENTRO = -5 \times \frac{1}{5} \log_2 \frac{1}{5} = \log_2 5 = 2,32 \tag{13}$$

The obtained result is of primary importance as the closed chain (see Fig.1 D) entropy is maximal without each unit's connection to all the others, i.e. without having the maximum possible number of structure connections. But if we create in practice a similar closed chain structure, it will be greatly indetermined. Indeterminacy is again expressed by way of decentralization - here, too, a "central" element is missing. All elements have equal significance in the structure. The importance of the obtained result is contained in the following basic conclusion. Structural entropy is dependent not only on the number of structural connections, but on its configuration as well, i.e. on the way of combining of these connections. This means that structures with equal number of elements and connections but different configurations have different structural entropy depending on the degree of decentralization.

The calculations for the open chain entropy (see Fig. 1 C) are as follows:

$$H(I) = \frac{1}{2 \times 4} = \frac{1}{8} \qquad\qquad H(I) = \frac{2}{2 \times 4} = \frac{1}{4}$$

for the end elements   for the rest

$$ENTRO = -2 \times \frac{1}{8} \log_2 \frac{1}{8} - 3\frac{1}{4} \log_2 \frac{1}{4} = 2,25 \tag{14}$$

The tearing of the chain decreases structural entropy and approximates it to the minimal.

The conclusions made can be examined by tracing the modification of the simple structures (see Fig.1) and the respective changes in the value of structural entropy with equal number of elements N=5. It becomes clear that the absolute value of the structural entropy depends on the number of connections, their configuration and, naturally, on the number of elements. The latter is best evident in equations (9) and (11) where N is included in clear form. For us, however, this dependence is insignificant.

It is advisable, therefore, to introduce a norming expression of entropy that allows comparing entropies of structures with different number of elements. This norming equation is the following:

$$ENORM = \frac{EMAX - ENTRO}{EMAX - EMIN} \tag{15}$$

The normed entropy thus will be a number between zero and one:

$$\text{ENORM} = 0 \qquad \text{when} \quad \text{ENTRO} = \text{EMAX}$$
$$\text{ENORM} = 1 \qquad \text{when} \quad \text{ENTRO} = \text{EMIN} \tag{16}$$

Making use of equations (3) and (4) we shall introduce a norming expression for the real number of connections in order to plot the interdependence between entropy and the number of connections.

$$\text{NLREAL} = \frac{\text{LMAX} - \text{LREAL}}{\text{LMAX} - \text{LMIN}} \tag{17}$$

The normed number of connections will also be a number between zero and one:

$$\text{when LREAL} \longrightarrow \text{LMIN} : \text{NLREAL} \longrightarrow 1$$
$$\text{when LREAL} \longrightarrow \text{LMAX} : \text{NLREAL} \longrightarrow 0$$

By means of a specially designed programme FORTRAN IV, tables of values were generated for LREAL, NLREAL, ENTRO and ENORM.

The above reasoning can have some practical results that have to be found out. In the process of the system structuring one has, therefore, to search for such variants of the structure where entropy has minimal value. This, however, would bring about only the formation of "star" type structures which in reality is impossible because of the necessity of direct connecting of the elements according to the content of the real systems. Then, obviously the question is of finding of an optimum as a reasonable compromise of the extremely strong requirement for minimal structures. When searching for this optimum we shall make use of the opposing tendencies of centralization and decentralization in the structuring process. To this end we have to find a quantitative characteristic measuring the degree of centralization in a certain structure. In our opinion the best characteristic of this type can be the diffusion of the graph interpreting a certain structure.

Diffusion is quantitatively determined by use of the "distance" characteristic between two nodes in the graph, the distance being equal to the length of the minimal chain (the minimal number of arcs in the graph) connecting two nodes. Each graph can have the distances between its separate nodes simply defined and so it can have the diffusion as a sum of the distances:

$$\text{RAS} = \sum_i \sum_j \delta_{ij} \qquad \text{where } \delta_{ij} \text{ is the distance between} \tag{18}$$
$$\text{the i-th and j-th node}$$

Thus the diffusion characterizes the graph as a whole and changes its value at the addition or elimination of a connection in the structure: some of the distances will become longer or shorter.

A full graph where each element is connected to the rest directly has diffusion of minimal value:

$$RASMIN = N (N-1) \tag{19}$$

And vice versa, with a "star" type graph, diffusion is greatest:

$$RASMAX = 2(N-1)^2 \tag{20}$$

This is due to the fact that all distances between all the nodes of the graph without the main one, become equal to two. Thus structures with a high degree of centralization have big values of diffusion respecting to the existence of longer chains in the graph that present the indirect connections. It becomes clear that this characteristic is a precise quantitative evaluation of the changes that take place in the structure as a result of the centralization tendencies.

In order to make diffusion independent of the number of elements we shall here, too, introduce a norming expression:

$$RASNOR = \frac{RASMAX-RAS}{RASMAX-RASMIN} \tag{21}$$

when $RASNOR \rightarrow 1$ when $RAS \rightarrow RASMIN$
and $RASNOR \rightarrow 0$ when $RAS \rightarrow RASMAX$

If we use the analytic expression for diffusion as a function of the number of elements and number of connections in the graph:

$$RAS = 2\left[(N-1)^2+(N-1)+LREAL\right] \tag{22}$$

and we replace respectively (19), (20) and (22) in the equation in the normed diffusion (21), and we replace (3) and (4) in (17), we get that:

$$RASNOR + NLREAL = 1 \tag{23}$$

A similar simple dependence between the normed structural entropy and the connections cannot be found (because of the participation of a logarithmic function in the expression of the entropy) and that is the reason why an analogic way cannot help to define the optimum number of connections, where the normal values of diffusion and entropy are equal.

Experimental data also shows that normed diffusion appears to be a linear function of the normed number of connections in the structure. On the other hand the overlapping of the RASNOR and ENORM graphics shows that there is a cross point respecting to the searched optimum. All this made it necessary to design an imitation model where through simulation of structural change and continual increase of the number of connections we look for an equation of the normed values of entropy and diffusion and from there the <u>optimum number of connections</u> for structures with different number of elements is defined.The model together with the programme for computing of structural entropy and program for computing of diffusion and for adjustment of the model and change of structure. The structural imitation performed with N=10,20 and 30 elements gives the following results:

N	10	20	30
RASNOR	0,333	0,315	0,298
ENORM	0,343	0,312	0,296
NLREAL	0,666	0,684	0,701
LREAL optimum	21	73	150

      The check for similarity of results with rising N gives grounds to claim that the obtained regularity is of a stable character, which in turn means that any type of structure has an optimum number of strictly defined connections among its elements. The importance of this result is conditioned by the strength of the general validity of the obtained regularity, as well as by its importance for the practice of structural analysis.

      The idea for the use of entropy to the ends of structural analysis can be broadened by discovering additional quantitative characteristics for the intensity of connections (see /3/).

REFERENCES

1. Gleditsch N.P.,Høvik T., Simulating Structural Parameters of Graphs, Quality and Quantity,V,224-227, 1971.
2. Bavelas A., Barret D., An Experimental Approach to Organization Psychology, Homewood, III.:The Dorsey Press, Inc., 1961.
3. Stanchev I., Modelling the Structure of Economic System, Print.,Systems Analysis, Modelling and Simulation 2 ('85) 4, 323-335.

Designing and Systems

Chairperson: W.Gasparski (Poland)

ORGANIZATIONAL HEALTH IN THE SYSTEMS AGE:
A RENAISSANCE SYSTEMS PERSPECTIVE

William J. Reckmeyer
Cybernetic Systems Program
San Jose State University
San Jose, CA 95192-0113
United States of America

Abstract

This paper briefly explores the relevance of a renaissance systems approach - an integrated pragmatic philosophy with a full range of unified epistemological, ontological, and methodological features - for helping modern organizations improve their ability to handle the increasing complexity of life in the Systems Age in a more responsible and effective fashion.

Introduction

Much ado has been made of late regarding the need for better quality in what we do, most notably in terms of a renewed search for excellence that now extends beyond the corporate world into nearly every aspect of modern life. The barriers to excellence can be legion, however, and even the best people are hard-pressed to figure out exactly what to do given the volatility of societal affairs and the extensive advice that has been recently generated by academic specialists and management evangelists alike. What works for one organization often doesn't work for others, though, for everyone's situations and abilities are different. It takes a subtle blend of grand visionaries and dedicated missionaries to build the healthy organizations that are essential to excellence - especially if it is to be done with an appropriate combination of character and competence - so people need to develop means for conducting their affairs that are better suited to handling the complexities of modern life.

I haven't discovered any magic answers, but have found that we urgently need more integrative approaches that are much longer on both theory and practice - pragmatic philosophies that enhance our individual and collective abilities to handle complexity in a more responsible and effective fashion. I have been developing such an approach during the last fifteen years for addressing a

149

R. Trappl (ed.), Cybernetics and Systems '86, 149-156.

variety of complex concerns and have been using it to help people improve their integrity/performance through a better synthesis of thought and action. This renaissance systems approach draws on and extends the basic theoretical insights and practical skills of systems science (a general art/science of relationships) and cybernetics (a general art/science of regulation) as well as key contributions from related fields (systems management, systems engineering, systems dynamics, operations research, information theory, systems analysis, etc) and knowledge from the traditional disciplines and professions. It isn't a panacea, of course, but it has proven particularly helpful in my work with a variety of organizational clients and I would like to briefly clarify its essential points in the hope that others might also find it of some use in their own work.

The Systems Age

Scholars and pundits have been noting for some time now that the world is in the dawn of a new era which is markedly different from the life experienced by earlier generations - a Systems Age where systems of factors synergistically produce an increasingly complex world so dominated by change and death-bets that we find it tough to keep our heads above water, much less to anticipate and deal with what might be coming around the next bend. Changes of this sort are not unparalleled in human history, of course, as anyone familiar with the Enlightenment and Industrial Revolution would be quick to point out. Nor is the transformation as pervasive as many contemporary prophets seem to think, for most of the world remains mired in the Agricultural Age and only its more advanced areas have actually begun moving out of the Machine Age. Still, it is clearly a time of profound change - a crisis in the truest sense - and thus full of opportunities as well as dangers. The challenge facing us all, therefore, is how best to maximize the former while minimizing the latter.

This is no easy matter, especially since Systems Age issues are a good deal more complex than the ones we are used to dealing with. The issues confronting us today rarely fall into the kinds of neat little disciplinary or functional boxes that most of us have been taught in school. They are not problems - reasonably well-defined concerns with linear causal mechanisms that tend to behave in generally predictable ways - so much as they are messes - relatively ill-defined systems of problems with complex mutual causal mechanisms that tend to behave in counter-intuitive ways and often get worse the more we intervene. Nor can we afford to continue viewing all issues as problems to be solved once and for all, so much as we must begin seeing many of them as messes to be managed over long periods of time. The dilemma is that we know a good deal more about solving problems than we do about managing messes and thus tend to treat every issue with approaches that

have worked in the past, even though they may be less appropriate
for the situation at hand - much as the drunk does when looking
for his keys under the light.

Developing the requisite character and competence to succeed
on an individual basis under such conditions is difficult, to say
the least, but doing so on a collective basis poses even greater
challenges. Although there are notable exceptions, most organizations tend to cope with change in an ad-hoc fashion - fighting
fires as needed rather than developing better ways for preventing
them in the first place. Moreover, they generally devote a great
deal of attention and resources to improving specific products as
well as the processes that produce them, but relatively little to
developing processes for ensuring their own long-term viability.
There are no recipes for excellence, even under ideal conditions,
but we do know that the healthier people are the greater is their
generic ability to handle changing conditions. The same is true
for organizations, although we know far less about organizational
health than we do about personal health and even less about what
can be done to enhance it. Thus, the overwhelming need right now
is for more reflective practitioners - visionaries who can dream
and missionaries who can make dreams come true in a collective
setting - armed with approaches that enable them to really build
the healthy organizations that modern conditions warrant.

The principal barriers to organizational health, it seems to
me, derive from the piece-meal fashion in which most of us handle
complex issues and our general inability to work together as well
as we would like. My research and experience, reinforced by that
of others, demonstrate that real innovation essentially requires
a creative tension between divergent and convergent thinking and
acting. We have to open up in order to expand our horizons, but
cannot open up too much or we may find it difficult to get much
done. The Law of Requisite Variety reminds us that only variety
handles variety, so we must either dampen the complexity of the
issue at hand or amplify our own. We tend to do the former more
than the latter, but messes are much tougher to dampen than problems and we need approaches that amplify our capabilities rather
than the other way around. The Law of Requisite Parsimony, however, reminds us that too much variety often hinders more than it
helps. The most suitable resolutions are invariably the simplest
ones that work, so we must develop approaches that help us focus
as well as amplify our efforts. The Law of Requisite Saliency
reminds us that some aspects of an issue are more important than
others, so we need approaches that can help us separate the wheat
from the chaff. Finally, the Law of Requisite Freedom reminds us
that everything cannot be done at once. The concern is to minimize constraints as much as possible, so we need approaches that
maximize flexibility throughout the process and help us operate
in an increasingly refined fashion as we zero in on our goals.

A Renaissance Systems Approach

In their most fundamental sense, approaches are the ways in which people deal with reality. For most of us, they are highly idiosyncratic and largely implicit; we cope as best we can and rarely give much thought to how we do it. In a scientific sense, though, approaches are much more shared and explicit – paradigms for helping people address the world in more structured fashions. As such, it is important to recognize that there are three major features in all approaches: epistemological ones regarding our values and beliefs, ontological ones regarding our concepts and theories, and methodological ones regarding our operations. The epistemological parts concern the nature of observers and help us clarify our role in generating knowledge. The ontological parts concern the nature of observed phenomena and help us describe and explain what we see in the context of what we know of reality as a whole. The methodological parts concern the nature of observational procedures and help us develop blueprints for action. The extent to which these features are consciously manifested in any particular approach can vary considerably, of course, but all are crucial and should be explicitly integrated as much as possible.

Reflecting humanity's inability to make sense of everything all at once, people have developed approaches that deal with the world in terms of parts and wholes. Conventional paradigms have usually treated wholes as equal to the nature of their parts and assumed the existence of an objective reality which can be fully understood by human observers once we figure out the fundamental laws of nature. Epistemologically reductionistic, ontologically mechanistic, and methodologically analytic, these approaches have proven extremely valuable for addressing harder kinds of issues (harder in the sense that they can be satisfactorily treated with a high degree of precision, not harder in the sense of being more difficult to address). Emerging systems paradigms usually treat wholes as greater than their parts and propose a subjective world that can never be fully known by human observers because the fundamental laws of nature are always relational. Epistemologically expansionistic, ontologically holistic, and methodologically synthetic, these approaches have been developed to deal with the softer kinds of issues that have often proven less tractable to conventional approaches.

Considerable progress has been made during the last forty years in developing sundry threads of these systems paradigms, in terms of general contributions as well as specific theories and/or tools, but the systems community has yet to generate the sort of coherent paradigm that I think is both necessary and possible at this time. There are numerous reasons for this, most of which stem from the broad nature of the field and its relative youth, but there seem to be three major trends worth emphasizing: (1) a tendency to develop paradigms for addressing hard or soft issues, but not both; (2) a tendency to develop certain parts of these approaches (epistemological, ontological, or methodological), but not all three; and (3) a tendency to emphasize theory or applications, but not both. The approach described here – what I have been calling renaissance cybernetics or a renaissance systems approach to highlight its comprehensive and integrative nature – reflects my personal belief that people have to deal with a full range of hard-medium-soft concerns and that we benefit most from those paradigms with a comparable range of features. It consists of an explicitly unified epistemology, ontology, and methodology appropriate to the entire spectrum of human affairs and has been consciously developed to ameliorate the historical trends noted above and help people become more reflective practitioners.

Epistemologically, it recognizes the intrinsic subjectivity of all observers and argues that our knowledge is constructed not recieved, the result of an inquisitive rather than an acquisitive process. Rejecting traditional science's Dogma of the Immaculate Perception, cyberneticians as well as a growing number of people in the biological and cognitive sciences are beginning to realize what philosophers and social scientists have known for some time – that knowledge consists of distinctions drawn by observers, not given by God. Knowledge clearly involves a range of hard-medium-soft distinctions, but in the deepest sense our universe is made up of stories not atoms. Perception is reality. All enquiry, therefore, is an inherently purposeful activity biased by underlying attitudes, values, and beliefs – so we always have to be deliberately self-referential about anything we do. In short, it helps us be more comfortable with uncertainty because the process of observation inherently limits what can be known about observed reality – the very point of the General Uncertainty Principle.

Ontologically, the approach recognizes the intrinsic interdependence of all observed phenomena and stresses the relational patterns that connect rather than differences that separate. It posits that all aspects of reality (physical, biological, social, technological, noological) can be better understood when treated as systems – wholes with a range of emergent characteristics that derive from the way they are internally/externally organized and change through time. There is clearly a range of hard-medium-soft phenomena, but it holds that all systems have similar traits and manifest similar behaviors – paying particular attention to the variety of linear, mutual, and circular causal relationships constituting phenomena and the common regulatory processes that enable some of them to pursue a variety of purposeful activities. In short, it helps us be more comfortable with incompleteness and inconsistency because an observed world of infinite relationships can never be fully understood through a process of finite enquiry plagued by rampant uncertainty – the very point of the General Incompleteness Principle.

153

Methodologically, the approach recognizes the intrinsic need for observational blueprints if sophisticated enquiry is to occur and clarifies the broad guidelines and operational procedures for appropriate action that enable people to move from fairly general matters to more specific ones. There is clearly a range of hard-medium-soft tools and techniques for doing this, but it demands a blending of theory and data through an appropriate combination of conceptualization and empirical research that is consistent with the epistemological and ontological portions of the paradigm. It provides systematic steps for research, planning, and action that help people utilize their theoretical and practical knowledge and experience for intervening in a variety of situations. Moreover, it pays special attention to group methods for implementing this in a more interactive fashion since we rarely work in isolation. In short, it helps us be more comfortable with complementarity because the inherent uncertainty and incompleteness of knowledge preclude excessive reliance on singular ways of doing things – the very point of the General Complementarity Principle.

Organizational Health

The critical difficulty facing modern organizations is how best to manage their various changing relationships in ways that enhance their short-term/long-term viability without compromising the viability of their members or the environments in which they exist. This is not too difficult when conditions remain fairly stable; people have time to develop a pretty good sense of what's happening and what it takes to succeed. When conditions begin changing so fast that people have no real sense of what is going on, though, they are far less able to figure out what needs to be done. As a result, we tend to place a premium on maintaining the status quo and reactively deal with new conditions in an ad-hoc, piece-meal fashion that over-emphasizes operational concerns at the expense of strategic ones. More importantly, we tend to lose sight of the human dimensions of what we are doing and zero in on how profitable we can make things – a behavior that is ultimately unhealthy for everyone involved.

Such behavior makes it rather difficult for organizations to develop the foresight and flexibility necessary for excellence in turbulent times and severely limits the extent to which they can adjust to change, much less turn it to their advantage. Success in the Systems Age requires organizations to place a much greater focus on integrative approaches for anticipating and proactively addressing situations that balance concerns for the here-and-now with the there-and-then. This means that organizations have to manage two kinds of change: those that tend to maintain existing conditions and those that tend to transform them. The temptation is to develop specific approaches to specific issues and leave it at that, but the paramount concern should be to develop healthy

154

organizations with generic abilities to handle specific issues as needed. More often than not, this means that organizations have to be sophisticated learners as well as doers, explicitly able to develop insights and skills appropriate to changing conditions through a combination of bootstrapping and reliance on approaches that have proven successful over the years.

So, what is to be done? The fundamental premise, of course, is that planning is an essential part of management and that good planning is a prerequisite for proactive behavior. Over-planning is not the answer, however, any more than crisis management is. All this necessitates a subtle blend of design and evolution, for planning is best seen as a domain for disciplined improvisation. Too much design inhibits the natural evolution of organizational life and limits flexibility, while too little design makes life a crap-shoot and limits organizational ability to pursue collective goals in a coherent fashion. Moreover, the sorts of issues being addressed require gardeners more than they do mechanics; problems can be fixed, but messes need more nurturing and we have to pay more attention to developing systemic modes of intervention. We have to work with the natural order rather than always seeking to impose our will on matters for our own convenience (which is not only irresponsible but often ineffective). No matter how much we amplify our own capabilities, we can never manifest the requisite variety to control everything. So we should treat organizational issues as well as life in general with a combination of chutzpah and humility, regardless of how much power we might have to do as we please at any particular moment.

Building healthy organizations, then, requires an ability to handle the full complexity of organizational life - balancing the here-and-now with the there-and-then across the complete range of typical organizational functions. Managing complexity ultimately involves wrestling with specific issues - from strategic concerns that affect the entire organization to operational ones that only affect a few people - and traditional approaches that have worked well for solving simple problems rarely work as well for managing complex messes. A renaissance systems approach enables people to manage the entire spectrum of hard-medium-soft issues through its focus on context, content, and process - helping people generate appropriate processes for addressing the content of the issues in an appropriate context. The key to renaissance systems practice, therefore, lies in working with the critical stakeholders of any issue in a highly interactive manner - a disciplined conversation if you will - to construct a domain for thought and action which enables us to dream in a more responsible and effective fashion. There are no elixers for ensuring organizational health, needless to say, and details vary according to one's basic situation and resources - but the fundamental goal should always be the same: working on specific concerns to improve here-and-now excellence and generic concerns to improve there-and-then excellence.

Conclusion

Committing cybernetics in public is not always as easy as some people seem to think or hope, especially the sort of systems work advocated here. Unfortunately, there are no guarantees that what works for me will work the same way for others – principally because the power of any approach ultimately lies in the extent to which it affects and reflects the very essence of the person using it. Nevertheless, there are several characteristics that I believe are worth summarizing here. First, it is an explicitly unified approach whose systemic epistemological, ontological, and methodological features help people develop more appropriate means for perceiving, understanding, and tackling concerns in an organized manner. Second, it explicitly includes a hard-medium-soft range of insights and skills that help us treat a comparable spectrum of concerns. Third, it explicitly includes a full set of group methods that help people do all this in a collectively interactive fashion. Fourth, its comprehensive and integrative nature both encourages and enhances our ability to move among the meta-macro-micro aspects of a situation without getting too lost in the clouds or too stuck in the mud. Finally, it is explicitly applied in a systemic fashion – an ecological two-step of sorts – to ensure interventions that draw on and improve people's ability to manage their own affairs, thereby developing autonomy rather than the kind of dependence that normally occurs when people rely on others to provide the answers for them.

It's a long way from rhetoric to reality, though, for people need more than platitudes and pep-talks to develop the individual and collective excellence we all desire. Judging by the numerous born-again companies that have relied on the formulas for success offered by management specialists, most of which tackle symptoms rather than causes, it seems clear that band-aid management isn't the answer. Simply put, organizations need to invest a good deal of time, effort, and money in themselves – for the best return on investment in the long run comes from those investments that most affect the very being, knowing, and doing of the organization as a whole. The key is to help them learn how to speak with a clear voice, better integrating their thoughts and actions to develop a pervasive coherence throughout the organization that ameliorates the sorts of oscillitary behavior that are generally pathological for complex systems. Organizations will always need people who know the details specific to their operation, to be sure, but the really vital need right now is for more reflective practitioners possessing the generic insights and skills required to sail in uncharted waters and not for more technicians with the latest recipes for excellence. In short, we need more people armed with pragmatic philosophies like a renaissance systems approach that enable them to handle the complexity of life in the Systems Age with an appropriate combination of character and competence.

DESIGN AND PLANNING

Dr. Vilmos Nemeny
Karl Marx University of Economic Science
Kuruc u. 4.
H-1021 Budapest
Hungary

ABSTRACT. The paper does investigate the similarities and differences between design and planning. It considers both to be a necessary part of the preparation of rational human action. Design should mean the mental-formal preparation of the creation of a new system, whereas by planning should be designated the mental-formal modelling of the future behavior of an existing system. From this starting point the paper tries to give a short overview of the methods appropriate to and the contents of design and planning respectively.

This paper is, despite its title, not an exercise in semantics. Rather, I have the wish to ease communication across departemental, ideological and territorial borders by contributing to the clarification of the much used and mis-used notions mentioned in the title, by trying to define the aims and contents of the human activities expressed by them.

Much of what follows could be developed in an elegant mathematical form, but my aim being, as mentioned, not as much elegance as better communication /not always being furthered by the use of formal language/ I renounce the use of this language.

In essence, design/planning is a necessary part of the preparation of rational human action. Any rational human action, be it the action of a single person, a group or an organisation, can be divided into four main parts: setting of objectives and criteria /what may be called "policy"/, making a /mental or formal or mixed/ blueprint of the ways and means leading to the realization of the objectives according to the criteria set /that being the object of this paper/, realizing this blueprint /"implementation"/, and then looking back more or less contentedly at our achievement.

It seems obvious that any human action not generated by artificial stimulants or purely emotional motives not only

157

R. Trappl (ed.), Cybernetics and Systems '86, 157–163.

has to, but truly does follow this avowedly very crudely outlined path. Anybody having observed acutely the behavior of
his dog, will have to concede that even higher animals are
behaving in this manner.

Another question is, of course, on what level of con-
ciousness, deliberateness, creative thinking etc. this rationality is realized. We have here a very wide paletta of
possible behaviours, from purely traditional /which nevertheless sometimes has to be creative/ to purely scientifi-
cal. It seems also to be obvious that the complexity of the
preparation of action has to reflect the complexity of the
action itself, extending from the very simple /say, planning
my way to my working place and the means of getting there/
to the very complex /e.g. the planning of the future behaviour of the world financial markets/. But this, alas, does
not concern us here.

For the blueprint mentioned above it was usual to use
the word "planning" /as I did just now/. But planning is
frought with many ideological and political overtones, it is
used in many different senses. In the US planning seems to
be lately rather a dirty word, in England it has very strong
territorial-regional connotations, in other countries again
it is practically a fetish or at least treated as such.

Design on the other hand is from this aspect a neutral
term. Coming, as it does, from the technical sphere, where
it was first used for making the blueprints of, mostly, new
industrial products, later also of "products" of engineering
and architecture, it seems to be very dear to would-be tech-
nocrats, who look at socio-economic systems with the same
eyes as at artificial systems. Lately one can therefore hear
and read about the design of the behaviour of economic systems, say enterprises, national economies etc.

This has two advantages: first, it divests the making
of the blueprints mentioned of all ideological and other
overtones and helps thus open, secondly, the way to treat
socio-economic systems with the same methodology as artificial systems, i.e. to introduce into the planning of systems consisting at least partly of human elements, mathematical and other formal methods, and even computers. This
is, in my opinion, a very important development, especially
considering the very strong countercurrents against such a
development of the so-called human sciences.

The superseding of planning by design would also satisfy the principle of Ockham's razor.

Nevertheless it is very difficult to imagine the re-
christening of, for instance, the National Planning Office
into National Office for the Design of the National Economy.
Not to mention also, that e.g. in the Hungarian language the
same word is used for design and planning /"tervezes"/, with
an appropriate attribute /industrial design sounds e.g.

"planning of industrial forms"/. In the Slavic languages
they have a different word for thechnical planning /"projek-
tovani" for instance in Czech/ and other planning /"planova-
ni"/.

Before losing ourselves in semantic niceties, let us
take a look at the content of making the blueprints mentioned.

Already the first superficial look makes it obvious
that in designing the future we are confronted with two really quite different tasks. Either there is no system existing where we want to have one wants for instance to build a
hospital, an industrial complex or a defensive weapons system - because nobody ever does build offensive weapons systems. Or we are confronted with an existing and working systems, whose future behaviour we want to manage or control
/these two words are used here as synonyms/. These are obviously two basically different situations, although they have
also much in common.

My proposition is now to call the first task "design"
and the second "planning". One could say therefore that
"design" consists in planning the creation of a new system
and "planning" in designing the future behaviour of an
existing system.

Let us now have a look first at the common features of
both tasks and then at the differences between them, from
the aspect of their content as well as of their methodology.

The fact of being wedged in between "policy" and "implementation" is not the only common feature of design and
planning, as defined above. Their praxeology too is identical.

Design/planning involves, like all management actions,
a series or more often a system of decisions. There is, alas,
neither place nor necessity to elaborate here on the library
filling science of decision making. Let us be content with
the following facts:

After the decision to create a new system has been made,
and the necessary specifications of this system are elaborated and the financial and other means /inputs/ being available
have been specified, there begins the design process. By the
way, I am inclined to include into the notion of design not
only the making of a detailed blueprint of the new system,
but also the planning of the process leading to its creation.
These two activities are bound to each other by so many
bonds, feed-backs, iterative processes etc. that it would
lead nowhere to tear them asunder.

In the course of this process all the problems pertaining to decision making are arising - the interplay of man
and machine, the combination of formal and heuristic problem
solving methods, the organisation of teams and other work

159

groups, making choices in hierarchical and non-hierarchical structures etc. To stress a point already made: designing a new system requires knowledge and application of the whole science of praxeology.

But planning the future behaviour of an existing system is from this point of view not at all different from designing a new system. If you are working out the new five-year plan of a national economy, after having received from the political authorities the necessary policy guidelines, or if you are determining the curricula of the next academic year, after knowing /from the ministry of culture or the Board of the University - depending on the university's degree of autonomy/, again you are confronted with all problems treated by the science of praxeology.

Different are the contents of these activities and therefore the methods to be employed for the solution of its tasks. Let us look first at design.

The design of a new system consists of the following tasks:
a/ detailed blueprint of the new system /dependent on its required output, as well as on the means available for its creation/,
b/ listing the different inputs necessary, with qualitative specifications, and possible sources,
c/ computing the necessary quantitives per input,
d/ making a time-table /schedule/ ordering the necessary activities in time and showing which quantities of what inputs have to be available at different points in time,
e/ mobilizing the inputs according to the schedule, which involves the organization of the co-operation of input sources, input transporters, input users and designer,
f/ building feed-back loops into the schedule from implementation to designer and in case of necessity from designer to policy-maker.

It seems obvious, at least to people at home in organisation theory, project management theory and related subjects, that all the methods known in the disciplines mentioned are applicable to design. The methods chosen will depend partly on the complexity of the task of the designer, partly on the cost-benefit relation between the cost incurred through application of more sophisticated methods and the benefit accruing from better design work /although the evaluation of this benefit is mostly very subjective/, and partly on the ability and will to use more sophisticated methods where they would be appropriate.

In relation to a/ we find a very fruitful field for simulation methods. In case of b/ and c/ all the methods of technical and again cost-benefit calculations lend themselves readily, especially the method of value analysis. For d/ we could mention all the methods for planning time-tables

160

from the writing of scenarios to the most sophisticated network planning methods and, in case of especially complex
systems, also PPBS. In case of e/ the knowledge of the designer must include bartering skills, ability to make advantageous contracts, organisational skills - here again praxeology comes into its rights. At last, f/ is a typically cy-
bernatical problem.

The planning of social and socio-economic systems is
quite another kind of problem. These systems differ essentially from physical or artificial /technical/ systems, in
that they are not Ashby machines, but - using the expression
of Oskar Lange - systems with ergodic behaviour. The root of
this kind of behaviour lies in their learning ability /which
is naturally an effect of them containing human elements,
acting mostly in groups - humans being par excellence learning systems/. The learning ability makes the social systems
into goal seeking, goal adjusting, adaptive and, here most
important, self-regulating systems, i.e. systems able to
compensate disturbances autonomously, without outside interference. Therefore these systems are able to define their

own equilibrium state, and in case of being disturbed either
to restore this equilibrium or to seek a new one /this capability is called multi-stability/. Especially their ability
to define a new equilibrium for themselves makes a prediction of their future behaviour extremely precarious.

If social systems are endowed with such advantageous
characteristics, there arises the question, why have they to
be planned at all? The answer lies in what we called earlier
"policy". A social system functions always for the attainment of some objectives and there is no guarantee whatsoever
that its autonomous equilibrium seeking activity will realize the goal having been definde by those who are authorized
or have the power to set goals, i.e. determine policy for
the systems in question /policy is determined practically
always by a group inside or outside the system or divided
between in- and outside/. We cannot go here into the details
of how the different possible goal setting mechanisms work,
although this is one of the most exciting questions pertaining to the control of social systems.
In any case one should never forget that for a system
whose goal is not defined in an absolutely democratic manner
solely by its members /what in reality does practically
never happen/, the plan destined to lay down the future behaviour of the system in the interest of attaining the objective set for it by the policy makers, constitutes really
a kind of disturbance /noise/ and the system will try to
treat it as such.

A well organized plan should consist of three parts:
1/ Description of the end-state of the system, i.e.

that state it has to attain at the end of the plan period in order to realize the objective/s/ set. To this end there has to exist a list of the necessary and sufficient characteristics /parameters/ describing only state of the system. The values taken by these parameters give us the actual state. The description of the end state is therefore equivalent to determining those parameter values whose set bring the system nearest to its goal fulfillment. In the case of relatively simple systems this set of values will be a vector, but if we have to plan some more complex system it is more efficient to construct a model of the system, incorporating the above mentioned parameters and their interaction. Especially because we shall need such models anyway for the further steps of planning.

2/ Determination of the trajectory leading from the present to the end state. For this we have to make a distinction between variables independent of the system and variables whose values can be chosen by it. For the independent variables we make prognoses /using the well known methods from trend extrapolation to simulation models/, select the most probable of these and assign on this basis appropriate values to those variables whose value the system is able to determine. In this way we can derive from our /simple or very sophosticated/ model thus arrived at a series of actions necessary to put and hold our system on the trajectory chosen. It is advisable to define the trajectory not as a narrow path but rather in the form of a broader band, so that in the course of implementation minor disturbances should not be sensed to be deviations from the trajectory. This makes management much more flexible. Even not very complex social systems give rise to very difficult modelling tasks. In my opinion the only kind of model appropriate is computer simulation, for example of the kind known as industrial dynamics. Into these simulation models it is of course possible to incorporate as building blocks any other kind of model representing sub-systems or cross-aspects of the whole system.

3/ Social systems do not willingly accept interference. Looking at the history of economic planning one would be rather often inclined to look at this fact as a rather happy circumstance. Social systems have an astounding resilience which is often a good medicine against all too often maladroit interferences from the part of dogmatically inclined policy makers /the fate of the monetary school or the reform of the Hungarian economy since 1968 are good examples/.

The plan has therefore to contain the ways and means by which the managers will induce the system to travel on the trajectory chosen to the objective set for it. Here we are confronted again with praxeology, as well as the questions of conflict management, material and moral stimulation - mostly the domain of social psychology.

Parts 2/ and 3/ together are called the strategy of the plan. It is advisable to have reserve strategies too.

Lack of time obliged me to cram too much into too small a space, for which I seek your forgiveness.

GENERAL THEORY OF DESIGN AND ITS APPLICATION TO DESIGN /PLANNING/ IN MEDICINE

Jan Doroszewski
Medical Centre of
Postgraduate Education
Marymoncka str.99
01-813 Warsaw, Poland

Wojciech Gasparski
Polish Academy of Sciences
Nowy Swiat str.72
00-330 Warsaw
Poland

ABSTRACT. The study presents an outlined base of the general theory of design, paying special attention to these elements of this theory which are directly related to medicine. One discusses the process of planning a therapeutic and diagnostic procedure by a doctor. The authors stress, among others, a great importance of competence in solving problems of a design type by doctors, and computer-aided doctor's planning.

1. DESIGN AND MEDICINE

The term "design" rarely appears in the context of medicine and when it arrives it is primarily in connection with design of technical devices used in medicine. This kind of design is however a part of technical design and not the design one may call medical. Both kinds of design are instead individual cases of "design in general" similarly to eg. technical or medical sciences which are kinds of "science in general".

In praxiology considerations it is a matter-of-course to call a designer everybody who designs. Separation of the process of design /planning/ is not possible in practical medicine, that is in a therapeutic, preventive procedure or medical care /the situation may look differently in the organization of health service/. There are no doctors whose function would consist in, exclusively or mainly, design. Distinguishing design in medicine as the object of analysis is prescribed by the necessity to define clearly the field of research, not by other reasons. We still use the term "a designer" as a general term in connection with medicine, meaning the doctor whose activity /more precisely: one of the aspects or this activity/ is considered for research purposes from a definite point of view. I.e., we are interested in work of a doctor qua designer though the

165

R. Trappl (ed.), Cybernetics and Systems '86, 165–172.

same person may be investigated as a diagnostician, therapeutist, etc.

2. CONCEPTUAL FOUNDATIONS OF THE GENERAL THEORY OF DESIGN

Make a starting-point the statement that design is the activity aiming at formulating a design, and a design is the description of the state of affairs which is regarded as desired for the realization in reality, we have to count with two ontologically different areas: area of reality for which and in consideration of which design is practised /patient, a group of people, elements of an environment etc./; area of language in which information on reality is contained for the use of design and in which design is practised. Here we face double understanding of design: i.e. the process of design, and a design. Each of the above mentioned areas as well as each of the above mentioned understandings of design and links occurring between these areas and between these understandings completed with the analysis of the third context of design related to a designer himself /a doctor or other person designing for health service/ determine the region of exploration done by the general theory of design.

In real world there are facts, more or less known dependencies occur between them. Facts or their aggregates constitute the object of interest to people behaving actively and making a part of the real world. Facts when interesting to a man become the object of assessment made by him. On the grounds of assessment it follows the relativisation of facts according to the order resulting from criteria of evaluation governing the assessment.

We can call a fragment of reality, i.e. a fact or the aggregate of facts distinguished by any man in respect of his interests, a practical situation and the man: the subject of this situation. One can notice two possible results of practical situation assessment: situation is assessed positively, i.e. it is satisfactory to its subject; situation is assessed negatively, i.e. it is not satisfactory to the subject.

There is no doubt that in the second case the subject desires a change of situation to a satisfactory one and undertakes actions aiming at attaining these desires. However, if one gives a closer look to the first case it shows that also in this case the subject willing to maintain the duration of the situation which satisfies him, cannot behave passively because external course of events infringes the duration of a current situation. In connection with it the subject of the satisfactory situation in order to maintain its duration should undertake actions directed to a change of external course of events. Considering the subject of the practical situation as an ideal type we say that in every case of the practical situation the subject pursuits for a change of events constituting this situation or events external to it, or both kinds of events together.

In relatively simple cases, i.e. in the so called standard practical situations, where the subject possesses knowledge and means, he takes actions leading to providing changes required by him. In remaining cases the realization of the change calls for support: material when one wants to acquire means, informational when one wants to acquire knowledge, the so called non-standard practical situations. Informational support of actions is of three kinds: educational, i.e. resting on providing knowledge necessary to actions; cognitive, i.e. consisting in developing research tending to develop new knowledge; conceptual, i.e. design relying on elaborating the cognitive-based concept of the change and actions necessary to its realization.

Summing-up, in the area of reality we have the practical situation distinguished in respect of the subject with its context. The context of the distinguished situation is the practical situation of other object and at least we have a pair of practical situations: core situation /distinguished situation/, complementary situation /situation constituting the context of the first one/.

Distinguishing two kinds of situations occuring in a pair is very important in design associated with medicine which must consider not only the patient, i.e. his situation /core/ but also many elements of patient's environment /complement/. In schedule of patient medical treatment one should include from one side what changes should be introduced depending on the patient environment.

Two of the states in which the pair of practical situations appears in the area of reality are distinguished: initial state, i.e. a state before a change of the core and/or complementary situation; resultant state, i.e. state of the provided change. In case when the realization of the change requires design, the pair of practical situations is the object of design.

Design occurs in the informational area that demands the transposition of the pair of practical situations from the area of reality to its mapping in the adequate language. In this case the design problem consists in a verbal copy of the pair of practical situations in the language of medicine.

In the process of thinking in problem solving by doctors the main role is played by operations on assessments, i.e. their formation, transformation, association, etc.; these operations often are not fully verbalized. Wording a design problem and its solution with the aid of sentences of a definite language or at least the possibility of such wording constitutes a necessary component of rational design. If it concerns planning in medical procedure so the

167

verbal expression of this plan is important for the fact
that it is the language that enables understanding between
the doctor and other persons. It is worth mentioning that
it is necessary to use a definite language /not always na-
tural/ for application of computer technology in support
of medical problem solving.

The subject carrying out planning in the process of
patient's treatment is the doctor because he directly works
out a plan and then puts into practice and is responsible
for the whole of his activity. In this way the term "the
subject of design" is understood in this paper. One should
not forget that the basic subject in relation patient-doc-
tor is the patient /being the subject of the practical si-
tuation/, the activity of the doctor is satisfying the will
of the patient and aiming at his good.

Correctness of a design result depends on the appropriateness of mapping of the pair of practical situations
in a design problem: suitably of the core situation to the
core and the complementary situation to the complement of
a design problem. The condition for correctness of mapping
is the adequacy of a design problem, so such a formulation
of the problem which includes this and only this what constitutes the substance of the pair of practical situations.
Such mapping is called essential. Procedure of identification essential factors of the pair of practical situations
is diagnostic procedure.

The procedure of formulation a design problem is composed of subprocedures of identification, interpretation
and testing.

Identification of practical situations: a/ measuring
values of characteristic variables for preliminary exploration of the pair of practical situations; b/ hypothetical
formulating the substance of the pair of practical situations; c/ measuring the variable value to test a hypothesis;
d/ possible correcting a hypothesis; e/ testing a corrected
hypothesis; f/ providing description of the pair of practical situations.

Interpretation: a/ accepting the description of the
pair of practical situations as the initial formulation of
the design problem; b/ comparing the initial formulation of
the design problem with formulations of recognized design
problems to assess solvability of the formulated problem;
c/ correcting the initial formulation of the design problem; d/ solvability analysis; e/ recording design problem.

Correcting and testing in both subprocedures are done
so many times as many is necessary to arrive at the formulation of the description of the pair of practical situations respective of the design problem. In the second case
till when one does not make such a formulation which subjective probability of solving is higher than limit probability and moreover subjective probability of finding for-

mulation with higher probability is very low at the time provided and possessed means. Time factor is specially important in medical design in which identification and interpretation procedure should not delay medical assistance to the patient.

Solution of the design problem, in this case the plan of therapy is the result of the process of the problem solving. Activity connected with it is of two kinds: creative - generating candidating solutions, control - testing candidates and selecting of the solution fulfilling adopted criteria in the highest degree.

3. PROCESS OF MEDICAL DESIGN

Among various kinds of planning /design/ or "conceptual preparation of activity" in medicine one distinguishes specially planning of direct actions of doctors or medical staffs in relation to people which require medical care /patients/. Activity of this kind takes place in definite broader situations which must be taken into account in the process of planning, so it always occurs the above mentioned pair of practical situations. For obvious reasons in planning medical procedure, to which kind of planning in medicine we shall limit below remarks, a basis meaning has the problem connected with the patient, the problem of context is subjected to it or consists as its complement.

In planning direct medical activity special importance is rooted in the assessment of the health value of different states of affairs. One should not forget that therapeutic activity is - disregarding special situations - a process in the course of which the two parties involved in it, i.e. the patient and the doctor, exert conscious and optional influence. Planning a therapeutic or preventive activity is the common undertaking for the patient and the doctor.

In the medical design problem the initial situation /initium/ is the present /at a given time/ state of the patient which is not satisfactory from the health point of view. This state is known to the doctor with a lower or higher accuracy and this or other degree of probability. Thus, in mind of the doctor there is a set of assessments of the present state of the patient /S/ which are expressed in the linguistic sphere by a set of sentences. The doctor arrives at these assessments relying on observations /results of examinations/ of the patient and his general knowledge. On a similar basis the doctor forms an assessments /sentences/ of desired /more desired than present/ state of the patient /S^+/. The third set of assessments which occur in doctor's mind in the problem situation are assessments of possible actions /A/ or manners of procedure /behaviour/ which may evolve a desired change in the patient's state or transition of the patient from the present undesi-

red state into a desired one. Solution of a medical design
problem consists in such a mutual matching of assessments
sets S, S^+, A so that assessment A occurring in finally
selected three of these assessments would achieve possibly
the best basis for taking decision on therapeutic doctor's
activity. Doctor's plan is formed of accepted by the doctor
/as the basis for further decisions/ set of assessments -
alternative in majority - of his /doctor's/ future activity
and of the desired state of the patient possible to attain
with the aid of these actions.

The final phase of medical problem solving takes place
when assessments S, S^+ and A /and also others/ are stated
precisely, i.e. when the doctor knows everything about the
patient what he should know /from the point of view of the
dependence on assessments S^+ and A/, when he has clearly
defined assessments S^+ of activity aims /attainable in the
light S and A/, and explicitly separated elements of set A
relating to the accessible and effective in a given situation kind of activity. Before making the decision, the doctor as a rule must be acquainted /additionally to what he
knows/ with the present state of the patient, he must get
to know something about the desired state of the patient
and about possible actions, i.e. he must modify assessments
S, S^+ and A. In medical practice a major role is played by
the study of patient's state /modification of assessments
S/ and to this process one usually refers the term diagnostic procedure /examination/. In many cases a better study
of desired states of the patient /eg. by learning his desi-
res/ and more precise determination of accessible actions
may be also important. One may shortly say that medical
procedure is composed of solving diagnostic /cognitive/ and
therapeutic /realization/ problems.

Medical activity is a very complex goal-directed procedure in which the condition of effectiveness consists in
constant awareness of action ends and means which may reach
these ends, in the mind of the doctor. This awareness is
the essence of the doctor's plan. In case when individual
steps depend not only on those already done but also on
steps which will follow - and it is a characteristic feature of every intentional activity - anticipating those latter is equally important as recording the first one.

If in any phase of procedure the doctor knows sufficiently the present state of the patient and his desired
state, i.e. if he knows what is the desired change in the
patient's state /if assessments belonging to sets S and S^+
are sufficiently precise/ he looks for such actions which
may cause such a change. In such a case the doctor works
out a therapeutic plan. If a required change in the patient's state is known enough to the doctor /if assessments
S or S^+ are not made sufficiently precise/ the doctor sets
a diagnostic plan. When some elements of a required change

are known to the doctor, others are not sufficiently settled /when some assessments S and S^+ are precise enough/
the plan elaborated by the doctor is mixed, diagnostic and
therapeutic.

Elaborating and accepting the plan of the procedure
by the doctor is based on separating and selecting a set
of assessments of actions; this set describes actions which
occur in definite time interrelations and show alternative
character. For example: after accomplishing act a, act b
will be done, then act c, etc. but depending on the result
of act a, act b_1 or b_2 will be performed and then if b_1 so
c_1 but if b_2 so c_2 or c_3, etc. Foreseen results of these
acts, i.e. potentially changing patient's states and the
state of doctor's knowledge /received information/ also
form the plan. Acceptance of this plan lies in the decision
of committing the first from planned acts and - in proper
sequence - remaining acts determined explicitly and alternatively included in the plan.

In many cases the doctor thinking over how he intends
to treat his patient /including diagnosis and therapy in
it/ - has some alternative plans to choose. It is usually
the case, but often one of the plans is so obvious to be
carried out /sometimes deceptively/ that this problem is
not the object of conscious deliberation. The problem of
choosing one of plans A_1, A_2, etc. is similar to the problem of selecting separate acts, but it is much more complex
and the process of its solving takes place in a greater,
as it were, shadow of uncertainty. Effect evaluation of
actions included in the plan, considered separately and
together, is the obvious basis for selection the plan in
medicine. First of all it is important to evaluate effects
from the point of view of the patient's health state /and
other elements of his state/ and the person who makes this
assessment is the patient as well as the doctor. Effects
with positive value /desired effects/ and with negative
value /undesired side effects/ are also important; in other
words some kind of the resultant value of the activity is
considered.

One should stress that values which are the object of
this assessment show various character, among others - and
on the first place, a moral one. The effects of doctor's
activity are not limited exclusively to the patient's state so - coming back to the previously applied expressions
- to the core situation, but refer also to the second ele-'
ment of the pair of the practical situation. To important
criteria of the plan selection it belongs also the probability /degree of certitude/ of evoking various effects of activity, positive as well as negative, and time characteristics of these effects, first of all the time of their appearing after the moment of action and the time of their duration.

4. CONCLUDING REMARKS

At the present stage of medical knowledge and technology, solving medical problems and performing treatment becomes more and more difficult and complex, and takes also new moral dimensions. Limits of this what the doctor may know about the patient and diversity of possible ways of patient's treatment find its expression, among others, in the increasing importance of planning in medicine.

Along with the development of medical specialization and improvement of health service organization, the medical care becomes a collective undertaking to more and more extent: the patient /ill man, man threatened with illness or crippled/ is treated not only - as before - by the individual doctor, but by the whole team of doctors and other workers of health service.

It is known how great are difficulties connected now with assigning a proper kind of education and the scope of activity of a so called general practitioner. In connection with this, one should stress that efficiency in planning doctor's procedure is the basic matter for the doctors of this kind. This competence should be possessed certainly by every doctor-specialist, "specialistic" plan refers, however, in most cases only to the fragment of treating a patient and concerns often relatively narrow and homogeneous group of problems. Mastery of a specialist shows mainly in solving detailed design problems, while from a general practitioner one expects rather settling broad, long-term plans deciding on the entity of patient's treatment along with episodes and aspects of the specialistic care and only in some limited-range - individual solving of definite detailed problems. Just for these reasons it is worth postulating that programmes of doctor's education, perhaps especially general practitioners, provide acquiring knowledge and skills from the field of general rules of the art of planning in medicine by them. The main form of this kind of complementary education should introduce theoretical, homogeneous, invariant structures in various specific situations.

REFERENCES

1. Gasparski W., Doroszewski J., 1984, Design in medicine, in: W. Gasparski, Understanding Design, Intersystems Publ., Seaside CA.
2. Kotarbiński T., 1966, Gnosiology, Pergamon Press, Oxford.

THE DEVELOPMENT OF DESIGN METHODOLOGY
IN ARCHITECTURE, URBAN PLANNTNG AND INDUSTRIAL DESIGN

Nigel Cross
Design Discipline
Faculty of Technology
The Open University
Milton Keynes
U.K.

ABSTRACT. This paper reviews the development of design methodology in
the period since the first conference on design methods, in 1962.
Four inter-related areas of research are identified: the management of
design process, the structure of design problems, the nature of design
activity, and the philosophy of design method. It is concluded that
methodology has valid roles to play in design research, education and
practice.

INTRODUCTION

I have recently (Cross, 1984) attempted to provide an overview of the
development of design methodology in the two decades since the first
Conference on Design Methods (Jones and Thornley, 1963). Drawing on
the principal papers included in my overview, my intention here is to
suggest some of the conclusions that might be drawn in each of the
main areas that have been studied by design methodologists.

THE MANAGEMENT OF DESIGN PROCESS

Jones' (1963) 'Method of Systematic Design' was one of the first
attempts to provide a completely new way of proceeding with design.
It did not, however, attempt to replace every aspect of conventional
designing; it was based on the recognition that intuitive and
irrational aspects of thought have just as important roles to play in
design as logical and systematic procedures. The clear intention to
supplement, rather than to supplant, traditional design methods was
often ignored by the early critics of systematic design procedures,
who tended to assume that the 'systematic' must be the enemy of the
'intuitive'.
    Another early, radical review of the design process – this time
for urban design – was provided by Alexander (1964). Using a process
of hierarchical decomposition, he sought to conceptualise new
components, to design totally new, more appropriate artefacts,

173

R. Trappl (ed.), Cybernetics and Systems '86, 173–180.
© *1986 by D. Reidel Publishing Company.*

structures and systems; he argued that a radically new structure for a city, for example, cannot emerge from simply rearranging the accepted conventional components.

A third influential, early contribution to design methodology was a series of articles on 'Systematic Method for Designers' by Archer (1965). He distinguished designing from artistic creation, musical composition, scientific discovery and mathematical calculation, and also made it clear that systematic designing does not imply automatic designing.

There were several similarities between Archer's view of design and that of Luckman (1967) in his paper 'An Approach to the Management of Design', which was concerned with architectural design. Luckman perceived from his observations of architects that at each level of design detail, the components of a solution are always highly interdependent, and the designer's difficulty therefore lies in finding a compatible set. There is no guarantee that optimum sub-solutions will combine into an overall optimum solution.

In reviewing these four early contributions to the development of systematic design procedures, several common aspects become quite clear. For instance, there is considerable overlap in the reasons given for the emergence, and the necessity, of systematic approaches to designing. The late nineteen-fifties and early nineteen-sixties had seen increasing technological change and concomitant increasing complexity in the designer's task. Alexander referred to 'changes in technology and living habits happening faster all the time', and Luckman referred to a 'rapidly changing technological world'. There had also been the emergence of the systems approach to design, which was implicit in the procedures of all four authors. There was also a common concern with increasing both the efficiency and the reliability of the design process in the face of the increasing complexity of design tasks. This common concern resulted in a considerable commonality of approach. In particular, for all four authors there was an emphasis firstly on extensive problem exploration and analysis to identify all the factors that have to be taken into account, and secondly on systematically establishing the interconnections between all these factors so that all the sub-problems are identified. They all also adopted the common approach of first breaking-down the overall problem into its sub-problems and then attempting to synthesise a complete solution by combining partial solutions.

The fact that in four different fields - engineering design, urban design, industrial design and architectural design - such similar approaches were being recommended gave some support to the notion that there is an underlying common design process.

THE STRUCTURE OF DESIGN PROBLEMS

A second principal area of study for design methodologists has been to understand the special nature of design problems, and to describe their particular structure. The authors already referred to made many assumptions about the nature and structure of design problems - that they consist of many interacting factors, that they can be decomposed

174

hierarchically into sub-problems, and so on. In particular, Luckman's 'decision graphs' clearly expressed certain aspects of problem structure, such as the way decision areas, or sub-problems, are often interlinked in a cyclical manner and thus require comprehensive resolution rather than piecemeal, step-by-step approaches.

Very similar problem structures were encountered by Levin (1966) in his study of 'Decision Making in Urban Design'. For example, the relationships between the population to be accommodated, the population density and the required area imply a 'tree-like' decision path - i.e. separate 'branches' (or 'roots') leading to a common 'trunk'. However, Levin found it difficult to identify any clear hierarchy of decisions; the designer 'exercises discretion' in choosing where to start on the decision path. It was also clear that there occur in practice many feedback loops, or cycles of decisions from which it is difficult to escape.

It was the apparent arbitrariness of design that Alexander found so unsatisfactory, and which he sought to remove from design in his paper on 'The Atoms of Environmental Structure'. (Alexander and Poyner, 1966.) He objected that not only is most design arbitrary, in that the programme or brief does not define the ultimate geometry, but also that the programme is itself arbitrary, in that there is no way of testing it objectively.

However, the view that values inevitably conflict in many areas - including environmental design and urban planning - was adopted by Rittel and Webber (1973) in their discussion of "Wicked Problems'. They argued that any search for scientific bases for solving problems of social policy is bound to fail, because of the very nature of these problems. Science has been developed to deal with 'tame' problems, whereas planning problems are 'wicked' problems. Rittel and Webber's analysis led them to a criticism of the early 'systems approach' methods of planning, which relied on exhaustive information collection followed by data analysis and then solution synthesis or the 'creative leap'. Such methods they regarded as 'first generation' ones, which needed to be replaced with a 'second generation'.

A strong alternative view was presented by Simon (1973). He argued that there is no clear boundary between 'well structured' and 'ill structured' problems, which, in Rittel and Webber's terms, might be interpreted as their being no real distinction between 'tame' and 'wicked' problems. Simon showed that some apparently well structured problems are not always so, and gave examples of theorem proving and chess playing, which Rittel and Webber classified as 'tame' problems.

Clearly there are some significant differences of view between the above authors on the implications of problem structure for how design problems are, could, and should be tackled. The one point of agreement is that design problems are inherently ill defined, but all offered different views about how to cope with ill defined problems. According to Levin, the designer copes by adding an 'extra ingredient', such as an ordering principle. Alexander and Poyner attempted to eliminate such arbitrariness by devising an objective, externalised body of design knowledge. For Rittel and Webber it is morally objectionable to turn wicked problems into tame ones, and they suggested the need for a participatory, 'argumentative' design process. Simon insisted that we already have adequate logical procedures for coping even with apparently ill structured problems.

We are therefore left with a clash of views between those who want to develop an objective 'design science' and those who want to reconstitute the design process in recognition of the ill defined, wicked, or ill structured nature of design problems.

THE NATURE OF DESIGN ACTIVITY

A third main area of study and research in design methodology has been the investigation of what it is that designers actually do when they are designing. In general, the intention has been to try to develop an objective understanding of how designers design, which might then in turn lead to the development of improved design procedures.

Darke's (1979) starting point was a dissatisfaction with the early systematic design procedures which presumed an objective analysis-synthesis approach to designing. She used evidence from her interviews with architects to support an alternative approach of 'conjecture-analysis' (derived from Hillier et al., 1972; see below) and to suggest that, in addition, designers rely firstly on the formulation of a 'primary generator'. Very early in the design process, the designer imposes (or identifies) a particular generating concept or limited set of objectives.

Akin's (1979) empirical study of the design process – using protocol analysis – involved setting up quasi-laboratory conditions for recording the behaviour and the spoken thoughts of a designer performing a design task. Akin likened the designer's general solution-search strategy to 'hill-climbing', i.e. the designer starts more or less at any point in the solution space and then tries to move from there towards a local improvement.

A controlled experimental approach to studying designers' problem solving behaviour was taken by Lawson (1979). He compared the performance of 5th-year architectural students and 5th-year science students on a variety of problem-solving tasks involving the layout of coloured blocks. Lawson discovered that, in general, the scientists were selecting blocks in procedures which were aimed at uncovering the problem structure (i.e. the hidden rule), whereas the architects' procedures were aimed at generating a sequence of high-scoring solution attempts until one proved acceptable. Lawson called these two different problem solving strategies 'problem focussed' (scientists) and 'solution focussed' (architects). The implication is that designers' methods are quite different from scientists' methods.

A consistent view of how architects design emerges from these studies of their behaviour. For example, it seems clear that architects have a 'solution-focussed' approach to design and that they begin to generate solution concepts very early in the design process. This is presumably typical of ill defined problem solving approaches; because the problem is ill defined there is an inevitable emphasis on the early generation of a solution so that an understanding of the problem-and-solution can be developed. An ill defined problem is never going to be completely understood without relating it to a potential solution.

The other general conclusion which is stressed by these authors is that most systematic procedures are ill matched to the conventional design process. Systematic procedures tend to assume or require an extensive phase of problem analysis, which seems an unrealistic approach to ill defined problems. Darke, Akin and Lawson all criticised the systematic analysis-synthesis procedure, in the light of their observations of how designers design. However, it would be tautologous simply to argue that conventional designing is unlike systematic designing; the systematic procedures were developed specifically to be a change from conventional design practices, which were seen to be inadequate for the complexity of the tasks facing modern designers.

THE PHILOSOPHY OF DESIGN METHOD

There is a school of thought within design methodology which believes that little knowledge of any real value will be gained simply from observing what designers do when they are designing. If one acknowledges that conventional design procedures are inadequate in some way, then what is needed is innovation of improved procedures rather than observation of faulty ones. New ideas for improved procedures are unlikely to arise merely from observation, it is argued. Instead, one needs as a starting point a tenable theory of design - a philosophy of design method.

In developing such a philosophy, Hillier, Musgrove and O'Sullivan (1972) referred to, and used as an analogy, developments in the philosophy of science. Like science (according to Popper), design relies on conjectures, they suggested. Conjectures must necessarily come early in the design process, to enable the designer to structure an understanding of the problem and because a vast range of design decisions cannot be taken before a solution in principle is known. Conjectures become more sharply defined as relevant data is collected and used to test the conjecture. Conjecture and problem specification therefore proceed side-by-side rather than in sequence. The model of a rational design process developed by Hillier, Musgrove and O'Sullivan is based substantially on Popper's 'conjectures and refutations' model of science. However, according to March (1976), design is in conflict with Popper's views on science, which oppose inductive logic, seek falsifiable hypotheses and reject subjective probability statements. March said that Popper's criteria 'must be stood on their heads in order to maintain an approach which is rational' in design.

March introduced Peirce's concept of 'abduction' as a third mode of reasoning besides deduction and induction. March prefers to call abduction 'productive' reasoning, and specifies three tasks for rational designing: '(1) the creation of a novel composition, which is accomplished by productive reasoning; (2) the prediction of performance characteristics, which is accomplished by deduction; and (3) the accumulation of habitual notions and established values, an

177

evolving typology, which is accomplished by induction'.

Analogies with, and distinctions between, design and science have also been made by Broadbent (1979). He began with Kuhn's concept of 'paradigms' in science, which he compared to the concept of 'style' in design. Broadbent then went on to consider what might constitute theory in design. He suggested that there cannot be any true theories of design as such, and so design will continue to be susceptible to 'pseudo-theories'. He concluded by distinguishing between the designer and the scientist, and between designing and theory-building. He insisted that the differences should not be regarded as a weakness of design, but perhaps quite the opposite: design activity is more difficult than scientific activity.

The nature of design knowledge has been considered by Daley (1982). She suggested that perhaps the propositional knowledge which is regarded as the principle content of intellectual activity represents only a small area of overlap of a set of knowledge systems. This led her to some important conclusions about design, and about the limits to verbal discourse about design. In particular, she suggested that 'The way designers work may be inexplicable, not for some romantic or mystical reason, but simply because these processes lie outside the bounds of verbal discourse: they are literally indescribable in linguistic terms.'

Where does such a conclusion leave design methodology? It seems to place some potentially severe - but as yet undefined - boundaries to any discourse about the way designers work, and it therefore suggests that many of the concerns of design methodology may be untenable. Perhaps a more positive way of viewing the outcomes of this set of philosophical papers is that they represent a freeing of design methodology from any naive adherences to science and to the ideology of science. Hillier, Musgrove and O'Sullivan provided an updating on the epistemology of science and emphasized the necessity of cognitive 'prestructues'; March differentiated design from science and established the logic of abduction or productive thinking alongside induction and deduction; Broadbent identified territories for design which make it more difficult and rewarding than science; and finally Daley claimed types of non-propositional knowledge in design which are not amenable to verbal description. What we are left with, then, is a greater confidence in design as a way of knowing and thinking, a new set of axioms for design methodology, and a recognition that much of the discourse must be transferred to new and more fundamental levels of epistemology.

CONCLUSION

One of the surprising things in the relatively brief history of design methodology has been the way attitudes and opinions have changed quite dramatically. In some cases, protagonists have become antagonists, and internal debate has become internecine conflict. It is time to return the discussion and study of design methodology to an appropriate level of discourse.

Here, I have offered a sub-division of the field into four major

178

interest areas which might be pursued. This four-part structure also suggests that the design methodology 'movement' has progressed through four stages: prescription of an ideal process, description of the intrinsic nature of design problems, observation of the reality of design activity, and reflection on the fundamental concepts of design. Progressing through these stages might well have been an inevitable process of maturation. In any event, design methodology now seems in a much stronger condition to return to the prescription of realistic ideals.

There is a newly confident view (expressed for example by Archer, 1979) that design methods must not try to ape the methods of science (nor of the humanities) but must be based on the ways of thinking and acting that are natural in design. It is from this viewpoint that design methodology can be seen to have a valid role to play in the development of design research, design education and design practice.

REFERENCES

Akin, O., 'An Exploration of the Design Process', Design Methods and Theories, Vol. 13, No. 3/4, pp. 115-119.

Alexander, C., (1964), Notes on the Synthesis of Form, Harvard University Press, Cambridge, Mass., USA.

Alexander, C. and Poyner, B., (1966), The Atoms of Environmental Structure, Ministry of Public Building and Works, London, U.K.

Archer, L. B., (1965), Systematic Method for Designers, The Design Council, London, U.K.

Archer, L. B., (1979), 'Whatever Became of Design Methodology?', Design Studies, Vol. 1, No. 1, pp. 17-18.

Broadbent, G., (1979), "Design and Theory Building', Design Methods and Theories, Vol. 13, No. 3/4, pp. 103-107.

Cross, N., (1984), Developments in Design Methodology, Wiley, Chichester, U.K.

Daley, J., (1982), 'Design Creativity and the Understanding of Objects', Design Studies, Vol. 3, No. 3, pp. 133-137.

Darke, J., (1979), 'The Primary Generator and the Design Process', Design Studies, Vol. 1, No. 1, pp. 36-44.

Hillier, B., Musgrove, J. and O'Sullivan, P., (1972), 'Knowledge and Design' in Mitchell, W. J. (ed), Environmental Design: Research and Practice, University of California, Los Angeles, U.S.A.

Jones, J. C., (1963), 'A Method of Systematic Design' in Jones, J. C. and Thornley, D. (eds), Conference on Design Methods, Pergamon Press, Oxford, U.K.

Lawson, B., (1979), 'Cognitive Strategies in Architectural Design', Ergonomics, Vol. 22, No. 1, pp. 59-68.

Levin, P. H., (1966), Decision-making in Urban Design, Building Research Station, Garston, U.K.

Luckman, J., (1967), 'An Approach to the Management of Design', Operational Research Quarterly, Vol. 18, No. 4, pp. 345-358.

March, L. J., (1976), 'The Logic of Design and the Question of Value', in March, L. J. (ed), The Architecture of Form, Cambridge University Press, Cambridge, U.K.

Rittel, H. and Webber, M., (1973), 'Dilemmas in a General Theory of Planning', Policy Sciences, Vol. 4, pp. 155-169.

Simon, H.A., (1973), 'The Structure of Ill-structured Problems', Artificial Intelligence, Vol. 4, pp. 181-200.

Thomas, J. C. and Carroll, J. M., (1979), 'The Psychological Study of Design', Design Studies, Vol. 1, No. 1, pp. 5-11.

METHODICAL DESIGN IN ENGINEERING - BASIS AND APPLICABILITY

W. Ernst Eder
Royal Military College of Canada
Kingston, Ontario,
Canada K7L 2W3

Vladimir Hubka
ETH   HG   F-48
CH-8092 Zürich
Switzerland

ABSTRACT. The activity of engineering design is broadly described in the context of modelling and thinking. A general model of artifacts is introduced, and the design process is shown as an example of a process within the artifact model. The nature and contexts of the designer's tasks is presented, and the needs for computer aids discussed.

1.   DESIGNING

One of the most challenging activities for human beings is to imagine and create a new (not yet manufactured) product to fulfill a recognised purpose. The product may be an artifact or a procedure, it may be for sale or for own use, but it always has some social and technical significance. This activity is called _designing_. It has traditionally been carried out by persons using intuition and know-how, assisted by science. Progress has usually been accomplished by a combination of evolution (small changes to existing items) and invention. The most visible aspect of such design work has been "the designer sitting at a drawing board", particularly the work of drawing.
      This view raises some interesting questions:
- Are "well established" practices also scientifically sound ? Can they be supported by scientific investigations and theories ?
- Can "scientifically based and established" practices be useful in design work ? To what extent can any of the sub-tasks be completed by computer ? How should information be presented to the designer ?
- When is designing regarded as having been "successful" ?

2.   PERCEIVING AND DESIGNING

Interactions of human beings with their environment involve physical and mental (thinking) processes, and require the human to form impressions and models of reality. Three basic processes are active as shown in Fig. 1 (compare [1]): (a) _perceiving_ reality to form a mental model, by abstracting, isolating, simplifying, investigating, interpreting,

181

R. Trappl (ed.), Cybernetics and Systems '86, 181–188.
© _1986 by D. Reidel Publishing Company._

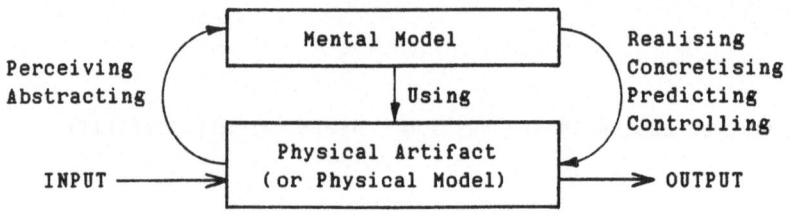

Fig. 1   Formation and Use of Models

categorising, etc., (b) <u>using</u> a relatively well-formulated mental
model on existing reality, by predicting, acting, observing and controlling, etc., (c) <u>designing</u>, moving from a relatively poorly-formulated
mental model to a future reality, by defining perceived needs, imagining
and concretising, realising (including manufacture), etc.

    <u>Thinking</u> requires the human being to have a set of abilities that
can be learned or practiced [2], and generally involves manipulating
(building and transforming) models in the mind [3]. Models may be
classified [4] according to: (a) the nature of their context and content
(on a spectrum from abstract/conceptual to concrete/material), (b) the
purpose or function for which the model will be used (descriptive,
predictive, explorative, planning and designing, prescriptive), (c) the
medium, or combination of media, in which it is formulated (verbal,
mathematical/symbolic, imagal/graphical), and (d) the mode of usage
(iconic, similitic, metaphoric). <u>Designing</u> involves using mental and
external models [3] in a dialogue which may range between a propositional mode (formal logical and relational operations) to an appositional
mode (informal and intuitive operations which frequently involve a
creative element).

    Knowledge, as a constituent of thinking, can be classified :
a)   <u>with respect to its origin</u>:
 - scientific, verifyable by repeatable experiment, predictable, usually mathematically modellable
 - technological, verifyable by experience, predictable within the
   limitations of large variances and many interacting factors, usually
   with a significant component of human judgement
 - mythological, not verifyable, but also not readily refutable
b)   <u>with respect to the way it is structured</u> [5]:
 - integratively   - hierarchically   - selectively
c)   <u>with respect to the nature of its content</u>:
           *** knowledge FOR design ***
 -§ general nature of artifacts, their properties and constituents
 - phenomena, their behaviours and influencing factors
 - human beings, their physical and mental capabilities and needs
 -§ processes of designing, stages of progress and intermediate products
 - types of problem (related to the number of possible or acceptable
   results or solutions) : algorithmic, diagnostic, open-ended need-
   directed, open-ended free-form (artistic)
           *** knowledge ABOUT designing ***
The items marked § need to be further clarified in sections 3 and 4.

3. GENERAL THEORY OF THE NATURE OF ARTIFACTS

Science has concentrated on individual phenomena, and attempted to provide a descriptive and predictive theory, usually based on experiments and formulated in mathematical terms (but sometimes the theory or speculation precedes the experiment). Theory is thus the result of simplifications. Philosophy has usually attempted to formulate pictures of the whole world, with generalisations about meanings and purposes.

Between these extremes, systems theory has attempted to extend science towards the interaction of phenomena, and to predict large-scale and non-linear behaviours of complex artifacts. Cybernetics has attempted to bring the behaviour of human beings into the scientific framework, with the aim of providing largely mathematical models.

A general theory about artifacts should cover their components and relationships, the life stages of an individual artifact, the development of families of artifacts over longer time periods, the general properties of such artifacts, and their internal structures.

By performing its duty the artifact changes a part of its environment, and will also change a part of itself. In a broad sense, such an artifact can be called a system. We exclude pure arts objects by this assumption. A system can only be "useful" if it fulfills some human purpose. Ropohl has attempted to explain the role of technology in society [6]. Similarly, Hubka tries to explain the context and nature of artifacts [7]. Elements of these theories are combined here.

A system can be considered from three conceptual viewpoints [8]. The functional concept shows its main constituents as **inputs, outputs,** and **characteristics,** including any feedback functions. The structural concept shows that separable **elements** are bound by **relationships** inside the system. The properties of the whole system result from the sum of the elements, but the total effect includes the synergistic effects of the relationships. The hierarchical concept shows that any system is a constituent of a **super-system,** and can be divided into **sub-systems.** A single piece-part can be regarded as a system within that hierarchy, it has inputs and outputs (typically force and motion), internal characteristics (typically non-uniform stress and inertia), elements (of form or geometry, and of crystals and atoms), relationships between these elements, it is a part of a larger system, and can be divided into smaller parts (but these are generally no longer of interest to the mechanical engineer).

Fig. 2 [8] shows that a system receives inputs from the environment, and delivers outputs, both of which contain those that are desired and those that are unintentional or even harmful. An external feedback indicates that this system is not static. Within the boundaries of the system, the inputs are divided into two streams that may not always be obvious to the observer.

One stream feeds into the operators : the **human beings** who run the system, the **technical system** proper that helps the human being to perform the tasks, and the active **environment.** Goals are set for the system, and information is generated, stored, retrieved and used. The operators deliver the necessary effects at "output 1" to enable, guide and control the second stream; this is their function. They also de-

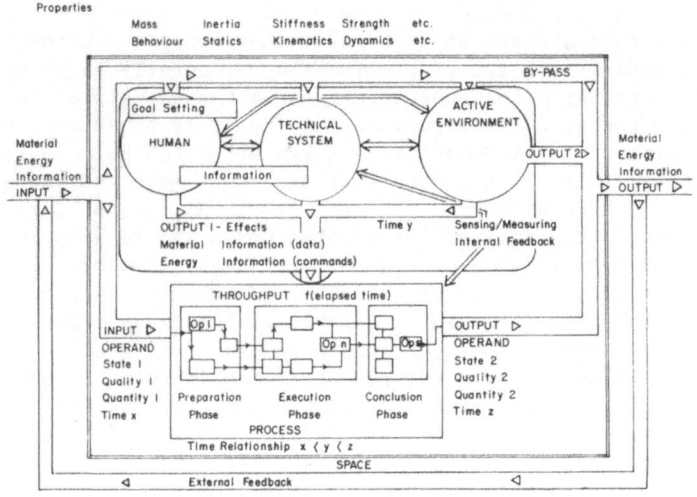

Fig. 2   Socio-Technical Transformation System

liver secondary products at "output 2".

The second stream consists of the <u>operand</u>, that part of the input that the system should actively transform from a less desirable to a more desirable state.   This process is under the direct control of the operators, who receive feedback from the operands.   This usage is analogous to the concepts of mathematical function, operator, and operand.

Each system passes through a number of processes and life stages, Fig. 3 [9].   These include the mental stages of preparing, designing, and planning, which result in the information for manufacturing a large number of nominally identical systems (or if the results are not deemed favourable no system is ever manufactured).   The physical stages of manufacture, distribution, operation to transform operands, and eventual liquidation follow.   Over a longer period of time, a family of nominally similar systems usually evolves that have different sizes and capabilities, or show developments in sophistication, ease of maintenance, user-friendliness, etc.

The properties of any system consist of (a) demands which the system is intended to fulfill (function, quality, price, appearance, operation, etc.), (b) externally observable properties, the capabilities of the system (functional, operational, ergonomic, aesthetic, economic, law conformance, etc.), (c) internal properties that can be observed over long time periods (durability, strength, corrosion resistance, etc.), (d) properties established directly in the design process (structure, form, dimensions, tolerances, materials, etc.).

Many different products are covered by these models of a system, they show different observable characteristics.   Fig. 4 implies that products tend to progress in maturity by being more amenable to routine prediction of design properties.   Their complexity tends to increase, but within relatively narrower limits.   Their novelty tends to decrease.

184

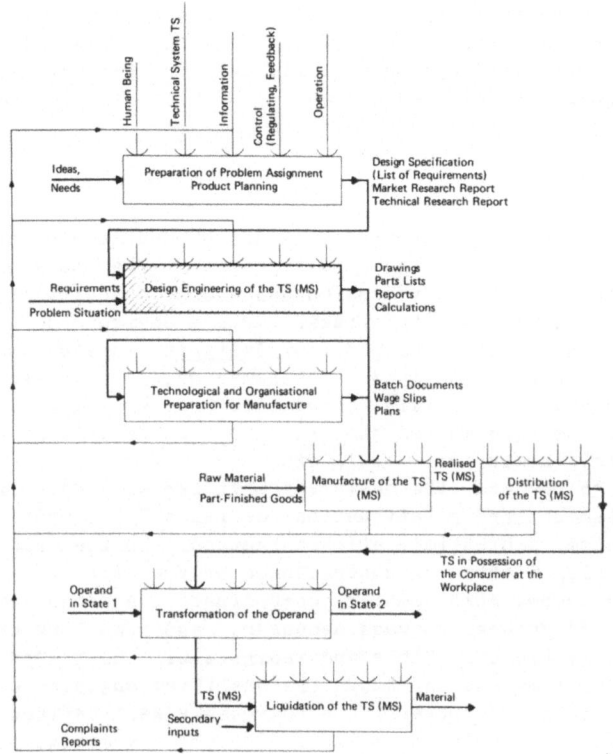

Fig. 3   Origination and Life Stages of Technical Systems

The risks of failure and damage (e.g. to human life) tend to increase
directly with novelty and complexity, and inversely with maturity.
Maturity manifests itself in (a) codes of practice, laws and standards,
(b) empirical knowledge and know-how, and small evolutionary changes,
and (c) quality and quantity of the scientific foundation to knowledge

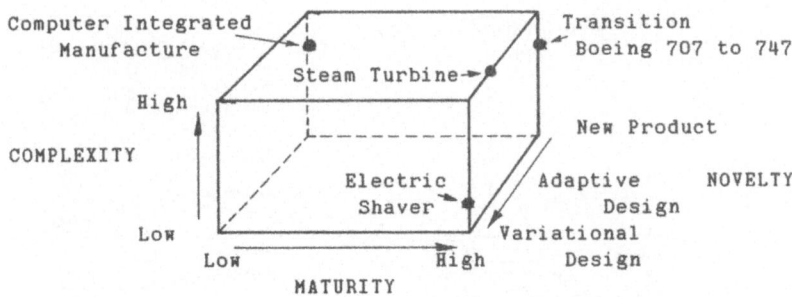

Fig. 4   Characteristics of Systems Development

185

about products and principles. Novelty manifests itself in unconventional ideas, features and conceptual combinations that "are not obvious from the state of the art" (patent definition) and that are incorporated as innovations into a usable product.

4.   THE NATURE OF DESIGNING

A problem that requires as its solution a new product and/or procedure is the subject and **operand** of the design process. The **operators** are designers, and the technical systems (drawing boards, calculators, computers, etc.) that they use within their working environment (managerial, mental and physical). The model of <u>designing</u> is thus analogous to the model of a technical system. The human being (a design engineer) needs to set the goals, to obtain information from existing reference sources, and provide information that is novel, integrative, creative, judgemental, moral, human and social, etc.

In the design process, the designing engineer must establish all the necessary elements and relationships, define all the properties of the proposed system, and satisfy all the factors. In the traditional intuitive view, Fig. 5 shows an unstructured progression.

As products become more complex, co-ordination and management of the design team and process becomes necessary, and some form of structure and control is needed. Tools and insights will be needed to aid intuition, and for some routine tasks the qualified engineer can be replaced by automatons (computers). A reasonably well-defined structure and procedure that is likely to be imposed by company management can be recognised in the design process, see Fig. 6, the right side of the tree-trunk. The left side shows a more detailed structure for the

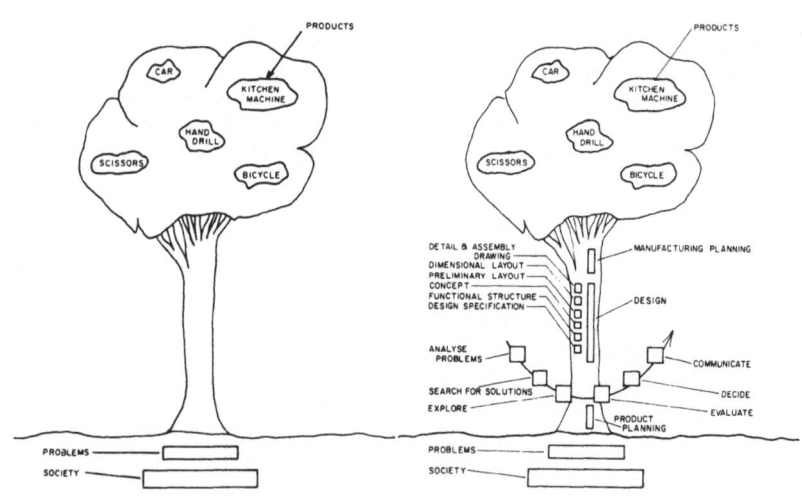

| Fig. 4 | **Model of Intuitive Design** | Fig. 5 | **Model of Design Steps and Stages** |

design process. Such a sequence is a useful guideline, and allows the designer and management to control work, and to view progress more rationally. It indicates that at least in the first three stages there are processes that require large mental effort, and which show little tangible results in the form of writing or drawing. Nevertheless, these stages are essential for a well-prepared solution. The encircling arrow shows a division of a problem-solving process (with some psychological advantage) into smaller sectors. This cycle must be performed many times to achieve progress. Each step should ideally be brought to completion before the next is started.

In practice, in a "natural" progression, the human designer tends to jump from abstraction to detail and back (Fig. 1), using and manipulating different models. At any one stage, he should create a number of different principles and/or arrangements which could solve the problem, and select from these the most promising. Work at a more concrete level inevitably reveals that further work is needed at the more abstract levels. A number of design methods and procedures have been proposed to aid the designer in his work, especially to assist completing a design stage. By providing (self and external) control they can enhance the designer's operation. These methods cannot be proved to yield success, but this cannot justify any claim that they are worthless.

Even with the best available methods, procedures and equipment, the designer's tasks are very complex and difficult requiring creativity, judgement and critical abilities, and using and combining many sources of information (most of which will be incomplete and of limited applicability). He must also be versatile in using available knowledge, he must therefore be aware of a wide range of existing knowledge, and by consultation to find it [10]. He needs to satisfy a wide range of requirements, many of which will not be quantifyable because they have a subjective basis. Many will tend to conflict, and need to be resolved by judgement and compromise, especially because the interactions (and synergy) between items of knowledge are not readily predictable. Three-dimensional visualisation and thinking is essential, especially for the mechanical engineer. These abilities must be acquired and practiced for the designer to be able to use computer and other aids effectively.

5.   COMPUTER AIDS

Many analytical aids exist, e.g. finite element programs. Linking these to other partial systems still presents major difficulties. It should be possible to develop expert systems to assist the designer in the conceptual stages (some work has been started [11]), to be able to store and retrieve large funds of information about existing sub-systems and components, and known properties and characteristics of scientific nature, covering materials and their behaviour, etc. The major problem in this context is entering the data in a way that is useful and accessible to the designers, without creating unwieldy data structures and programs. Can and should OEM-catalogues be computerised ?

Much work has also been done on graphical representations by computer aids. These are at present not very user-friendly, except in the

very detailed phases of component drawing. The difficulties include
providing the designer with means for easy entry and manipulation of
models, changing these and making consequent changes automatic (but
easily reversible), giving easy combinatorics for alternative solution
arrangements (morphology), making distinct differences in appearance of
the displays between tentative ideas and firmly decided features, and
assisting legibility and recognisability of model forms.

6.   CONCLUSIONS

Progress in computer applications, even within the design process has
been rapid.   Further developments need guidance from the theory of
technical systems, and from practical applications in industry, such
that this progress can be maintained in a controlled and beneficial
fashion.

7.   REFERENCES

[1]   Yoshikawa, H., 'Extended General Design Theory', in IFIP W.G.5.2:
   Design Theory for CAD, Amsterdam: North Holland, 1985 (in press)
[2]   Kurajian, M.A., & Kurajian G.M., 'Expanding Design Creativity',
   in WDK 12 : Proceedings of ICED 85 (Vol.2), Zürich: Heurista, 1985,
   p. 1075-1083
[3]   Archer, B., 'The Implications for the Study of Design Methods
   of Recent Developments in Neighbouring Disciplines', in WDK 12 :
   Proceedings of ICED 85 (Vol.2), Zürich: Heurista, 1985, p. 833-840
[4]   Eder, W.E., 'Engineering Design :   Context and Procedures for
   Creativity', in Proceedings Fourth Canadian Conference on Engineering Education, Fredericton, N.B.: Univ. N.B., 1984, p. 283-295
[5]   Müller, J., 'Denkpsychologie und Ingenieurmethodik - Wege zur
   Empirisch Fundierten Methodikforschung', in WDK 12 : Proceedings of
   ICED 85 (Vol.2), Zürich: Heurista, 1985, p. 841-854
[6]   Ropohl, G., Eine Systemtheorie der Technik, München: Carl
   Hanser Verlag, 1979
[7]   Hubka, V., Theorie Technischer Systeme (2 ed), Berlin: Springer-
   Verlag, 1984
[8]   Eder, W.E., 'Structures as Models in the Design and Development
   of a System', in IFIP W.G.5.2: Design Theory for CAD, Amsterdam:
   North Holland, 1985 (in press)
[9]   Hubka, V., Principles of Engineering Design, London: Butterworth
   Scientific, 1982 (Translated and edited by W.E. Eder)
[10]   Hales, C., 'Designer as Chameleon', Design Studies, 6, No. 2, 1985,
   p. 111-114
[11]   MacCallum, K.J., Duffy, A. & Green, S, 'An Intelligent Concept
   Design Assistant', in IFIP W.G.5.2: Design Theory for CAD, Amsterdam: North Holland, 1985 (in press)

THE CYBERNETIC MODEL OF THE ORGANISATION: AN ASSESSMENT

Michael C. Jackson
Department of Management Systems and Sciences
University of Hull
Hull
HU6 7RX
United Kingdom

ABSTRACT. Cybernetics offers an extremely sophisticated account of the
nature of organisations. In spite of its strengths, the cybernetic
model is not widely known or used in organisation and management
theory. One reason might be that perceived weaknesses in the model are
seen to outweigh the strengths. In this paper criticisms of the model
are examined against two distinct versions of the cybernetic account of
organisations - here distinguished as 'management cybernetics' and
'organisational cybernetics'. It is argued that while the criticisms
hold against management cybernetics, they cannot be sustained against
organisational cybernetics. Those who dismiss the cybernetic model
because of problems with management cybernetics should take a fresh
look at organisational cybernetics. It is an approach rich in insight
and with much potential for future development.

INTRODUCTION

The cybernetic model offers excellent prospects for the analysis and
design of organisations. It is of sufficient generality to apply to a
wide range of organisations. The model is capable of dealing with
complex systems the parts of which are in varying degrees of interdependence. It demands that attention be paid to the sources of command
and control in the system and recognises that information is the true
cement holding organisations together. The organisation is represented
as being in close interrelationship with its environment. The
cybernetic model is well able to yield specific recommendations for
improving the performance of organisations.
     In spite of all this, the cybernetic model is not widely known or
used in organisation and management theory. The work of Buckley (1),
Weick (2) and Beer (3,4,5), for example, remains of marginal concern to
many researching and teaching in this area. Perhaps the reason for the
neglect is that the weaknesses of the approach outweigh whatever
strengths it may have. If this is the case then the model can quite
reasonably be ignored. In this paper the criticisms that have been
made of the cybernetic model are examined to see whether they should

189

R. Trappl (ed.), Cybernetics and Systems '86, 189–196.
© 1986 by D. Reidel Publishing Company.

condemn it to neglect. The criticisms are first set out. Two versions of the cybernetic model are then identified and briefly described. These are labelled 'management cybernetics' and 'organisational cybernetics' respectively. The criticisms are then assessed against these two versions. It is argued that while many of the criticisms are relevant and damaging to management cybernetics, they are usually inappropriate when addressed to organisational cybernetics. It follows that those who ignore or write off the cybernetic model because of weaknesses in management cybernetics should think again and give a fair hearing to organisational cybernetics.

CRITICISMS OF THE CYBERNETIC MODEL

Criticisms of the cybernetic model may be grouped under three headings – methodological, capacity to provide understanding and usefulness in practice. Eight different criticisms are considered.

First, two perceived methodological weaknesses.

1. The cybernetic model is often accused of adherence to misplaced mechanical and biological analogy. Checkland (6) criticises Beer's The Heart of Enterprise because he sees it as based on the idea that organisations are like machines. Rivett (7) in clear reference to Beer's Brain of the Firm, asks why the human brain and nervous system should necessarily tell us anything about how organisations should be structured. Ulrich (8) provides a detailed critique of the use of the mechanistic and organic systems models in cybernetics.

2. At the centre of many expressions of the cybernetic model is the concept of 'variety' – the number of possible states a system is capable of exhibiting. Rivett (7) argues that this concept is a poor measure, subjective in nature and not adequate for scientific work. Ulrich (8) argues, by contrast (!) that the concept is deficient because it is employed in cybernetics as an absolute, observer-independent measure of complexity. Checkland (6) finds Ashby's 'law of requisite variety' to be "unexceptional."

Next, four criticisms can be listed which relate to the ability of cybernetics to provide a good understanding of organisations.

3. The cybernetic model is held to give an impoverished picture of organisations. Thus, Thomas (9) argues that the ability of the model to aid understanding of social systems is severely limited. Checkland (6) points out that regarding an organisation as a machine reveals some of its characteristics, but it could equally legitimately and usefully be seen as a social grouping, an appreciative system or a power struggle.

4. The point is frequently made that the cybernetic model emphasises stability at the expense of change. Ulrich (8), for example, argues that the model cannot deal with change of goal-state in a stable environment.

190

5. A question has been raised by Morgan (10) about the way the cybernetic model represents the relationship between organisations and
their environments. Morgan argues that 'cybernetics as technique' is
designed to aid organisations achieve pre-determined goals without
regard to the field of relationships in which they find themselves.
This, 'cybernetics as epistemology' reveals, may be ultimately self-
defeating; bringing ruin on the organisation as well as the environment.

6. Perhaps the most frequent criticism of the model is that it under-
plays the purposeful role of individuals in organisations. Morris (11)
(while not agreeing with this criticism) captures the flavour of the
argument nicely with his phrase - "the big toe also thinks!". For
Adams (12) the viable system model of Beer implies that man, the basic
unit in organisational systems, is free only in the same way that the
knee is free to jerk; as a reflex action. In Ulrich's view (8)
cybernetic models leave out perhaps the most important feature of
socio-cultural systems - human purposefulness and self-reflectiveness.
    Finally, two criticisms can be mentioned relating to the
application of the model.

7. Following on very much from 6, the point is made that underplaying
the role of the individuals can carry autocratic implications when
cybernetic models are used in practice. This is an old criticism.
Lilienfeld (13) comments on a 1948 review of Wiener's Cybernetics in
which a Dominican friar, Père Dubarle, expresses his fear that
cybernetic techniques might help some humans to increase their power
over others. Thomas (9) and Adams (12) have, more recently, argued the
same point. Adams, indeed, paints Beer's work in Chile as representing
a fully elaborated and computerised model of a tyranny. Checkland (6)
charges the Beer model with offering the prospect of a "negative
utopia" - a monolithically defined system in which the operational
units possess only that freedom compatible with systemic cohesion.
Rivett (7) is concerned about the "frightening" (for personal liberty)
use of computers in Beer's proposals. Ulrich (8) argues that Beer's
cybernetic tools are likely to be used to serve undemocratic purposes.
He points out that, although in 'organic' versions of the cybernetic
model control is spread throughout the architecture of the system, the
source of motivation - the determination of the goal state - still
remains outside. Both Ludz (14) and Holloway (15) comment on the way
cybernetics can be employed to increase control in bureacratic
societies.

8. It is also argued - and perhaps this is a blessing given 7, that
cybernetic recommendations are very difficult to apply in practice.
Rivett (7) argues that people tend to resist the implementation of
Beer type macro-systems. In Thomas' view (9) cybernetic approaches do
not pay enough attention to the need to alter attitudes in successful
change management.

THE CYBERNETIC MODEL 1: MANAGEMENT CYBERNETICS

Almost as soon as Wiener's definition of cybernetics - the science of
control and communication in the animal and the machine (16) - was
coined, it appeared to be too limiting. Interest in the new science
soon spread beyond engineers and physiologists to psychologists, sociologists, anthropologists and political scientists. In 1959, Beer
published Cybernetics and Management (17) and the list of those
interested began to include managers and management scientists.
      The early pioneers of cybernetics frequently employed analogies in
their work to illustrate particular insights. Not surprisingly,
perhaps, a tendency grew up in the secondary literature to treat
organisations as if they were actually like machines or organisms.
This comes through, for example, in the discussions of management
cybernetics in George (18) and Pask (19) and in the chapters on
cybernetics in P.P. Schoderbek et al. (20). A recent book by Strank
(21) demonstrates that this tendency is not yet dead. It is this kind
of cybernetics, as applied to organisations, which will be referred to
here as 'management cybernetics'.
      The starting point for the management cybernetic model of the
organisation is the input-transformation-output schema. This is used
to describe the basic operational activities of the enterprise . The
goal or purpose of the enterprise is, in management cybernetics,
invariably determined outside the system. Then, if the operations are
to succeed in bringing about the goal, they must, because of inevitable
disturbance, be regulated in some way. This regulation is effected by
management. Management cybernetics attempts to equip managers with a
number of 'tools' which should enable them to so regulate operations.
Chief among these are the black box technique and managing by inducing
self-regulation into organisations. Systems which are so complex that
they cannot be easily examined in order to discover what processes are
so complex that they cannot be easily examined in order to discover what
processes are responsible for system behaviour, are called in
cybernetics 'black boxes'. Organisations and their environments are to
some extent black boxes. The 'black box technique' of input
manipulation and output classification can be used by managers to gain
some knowledge of system behaviour. If managers understand the
nature of self-regulation they may be able to induce it in the
organisations they manage. The work of Cannon (22) and Wiener (16)
has established that an effective way to ensure self-regulation is by
means of the negative feedback mechanism. Strank (21) notes that this
needs to be supplemented by 'strategic control' - based upon feed-
forward information and 'external control'.

THE CYBERNETIC MODEL 2: ORGANISATIONAL CYBERNETICS

There is another strand of cybernetic work concerned with organisations
that breaks completely with the mechanistic and organismic thinking
that characterises management cybernetics. This is found in fully
developed form in Buckley (1) and Weick (2); in Beer's later work (4)
(5) (23) (24); and in the writings of two adherents of Beer's thinking,

192

Clemson (25) and Espejo (26) (27). This strand is here labelled 'organisational cybernetics'. The account which follows is based upon the work of Beer.

Beer's version of 'organisational cybernetics' seems to have emerged from 'management cybernetics' as a result of two intellectual breakthroughs. First, in The Heart of Enterprise (4), Beer succeeds in building his 'viable system model' (VSM) in relation to the organisation from cybernetic first principles. This enables cybernetic laws to be fully understood without reference to the mechanical and biological manifestations in which they were first recognised. Second, more attention is given in organisational cybernetics to human purposefulness and the role of the observer. Clemson (25) makes a distinction between a first order cybernetics appropriate to organised complexity because it studies matter, energy and information, and a second order cybernetics capable of tackling relativistic organised complexity because it studies, as well, the observing system. Organisational cybernetics is second order cybernetics.

Beer's VSM encapsulates the most important features of organisational cybernetics. For Beer, a system is viable if it is capable of responding to environmental changes even if those changes could not have been foreseen at the time the system was designed. In order to become or remain viable, a system has to achieve 'requisite variety' with the complex environment with which it is faced. The exact level at which the balance of varieties should be achieved is determined by the purpose that the system is pursuing. Thus variety is a strictly subjective measure - a measure of relevant states given some defined purpose. It should also be noted that the purpose or goal of the system is not something defined externally to it, but is a compromise at which the system arrives given constraints imposed by different internal functions and the environment (5). Now according to Beer, all viable systems need to possess five functions - Systems 1-5. The System 1 of an organisation consists of the various parts of it directly concerned with implementation. Each part of System 1 should be autonomous in its own right so that it can absorb some of the massive environmental variety that would otherwise flood higher management levels. This means the parts themselves must be viable systems - Beer's model is 'recursive'; the structure of the whole is replicated in each of the parts. System 2 - co-ordination - is necessary to ensure that the various elements making up System 1 act in harmony. System 3 is the control function, ultimately responsible for the internal stability of the organisation. System 4, or the intelligence function, captures for the organisation all relevant information about its total environment. System 5 is responsible for policy. One of its most difficult tasks is balancing the sometimes antagonistic internal and external demands placed on the organisation, as represented by the requirements of System 3 and System 4 respectively. S5 must also represent the essential qualities of the whole system to any wider system of which it is part. Much attention is also given in the model to the information channels linking the different Systems and the organisation and its environment. The model can be used to design new organisational systems or as a diagnostic tool to check the viability and effectiveness of existing systems.

ASSESSING THE CRITICISMS OF THE CYBERNETIC MODEL

To what extent do the criticisms previously outlined carry weight against these two versions of the model?

1. The charge that cybernetics is too ready to identify organisations with mechanical and biological systems holds against management cybernetics. In organisational cybernetics, however, it is clear that what is being studied are the properties inherent in systems themselves, with machines and brains being used simply as examples of complex systems. The principles that emerge from this study can legitimately be applied to organisations as systems. The point is forcibly made by Beer in The Heart of Enterprise (4) when the VSM is derived from cybernetic first principles rather than being based upon insights derived from neuro-physiology.

2. The concept of variety is little used in management cybernetics. When it is, it falls foul of Ulrich's criticism. In organisational cybernetics variety is a strictly subjective measure and Ulrich's criticism is inappropriate. Rivett's argument that observer-dependent measures are not adequate for scientific work carries little weight when such measures are the only proper ones available. The law of requisite variety may seem "unexceptional" in itself, but its working out in terms of effective organisational form is far from trivial. Its operation in practice is exceptionally thought provoking.

3. Management cybernetics does offer a pretty impoverished picture of the organisation. Strank (21) finds many parallels between management cybernetics and the classical model of organisation. This classical, or rational model, has been heavily criticised by such as Gouldner (28) and Abrahamsson (29). The same criticism is difficult to sustain against organisational cybernetics. Beer's VSM stands comparison with the most advanced theories produced in the organisational sciences. For example, there are similarities with Thompson's (30) three levels of responsibility and control in organisations, with the concern in socio-technical thinking about autonomous work groups (31) (32), and with Galbraith's (33) sophisticated statement of contingency theory. Organisational cybernetics does perhaps neglect politics and power. Even here, however, progress is being made. In Buckley (1) and in Beer (5,23) the starting point for a cybernetic theory of power can be discerned.

4. The charge that cybernetics emphasises stability at the expense of change is probably justified against management cybernetics. Interest is centred on deviation-counteracting systems. Change can only come about as a disturbance from the environment or as an alteration in the externally determined goal state. Maruyama (34) calls this the

194

'first cybernetics' and argues that there is no reason why equal
attention cannot be given to a 'second cybernetics' which emphasises
deviation-amplifying effects. Maruyama is correct, and organisational
cybernetics is capable of dealing with structure elaboration and
change as successfully as with system maintenance. See, for example,
Cadwallader (35). Also, Beer's idea that an organisation converges on
a compromise purpose, suggests that change can be internally, as well
as externally, generated.

5. Management cybernetics is 'cybernetics as technique' designed to aid
organisations achieve predetermined goals. It could help an organisation damage the field of relationships on which its existence
depended. In organisational cybernetics the emphasis is as much upon
'viability', upon surviving in a set of relationships, as upon goal-
seeking.

6. In management cybernetics (Strank's book is an honourable
exception) little attention is usually paid to individuals in the
organisation. In organisational cybernetics the tendency has been to
pay increased attention to the perceptions and roles of individuals.
Beer recognises that: "The laws of viability lie at the heart of any
enterprise. So too do human beings" (4). His model suggests that it
is to the advantage of organisations to grant maximum autonomy to
individuals. In general it is doubtful whether organisational
cybernetics implies any greater unanimity among members of an
organisation about purposes than is normally found. In formal
organisations, almost by definition, individuals sacrifice certain
freedoms for what are seen as the benefits that stem from co-operation.
This is not to say that Beer's model would not benefit from taking into
account some socio-technical insights about what makes satisfying work
for individuals and how autonomous work groups should be organised.

7. Management cybernetics sees the organisation's goal as determined
externally and presents the organisation as an hierarchical control
system – as "... a series of hierarchically arranged supervisory
feedback loops", according to Strank (21). It clearly has autocratic
implications and is likely to serve those who already possess power.
Beer sees the organisation's purpose emerging as a compromise from
among the various internal and external influences on the organisation.
Further, despite the terminology of Systems 1-5, the VSM should not be
seen as hierarchical – all five functions are dependent upon each other.
Some of the criticisms levelled at the autocratic nature of
cybernetics are therefore misplaced when directed at organisational
cybernetics. What organisational cybernetics achieves when it is
applied to organisations is an increase in efficiency and effectiveness. This will occur whatever the nature of the organisation.
There is nothing to prevent the application of organisational
cybernetics to democratic organisations in which individuals
participate fully in the process of goal-setting and in which the goal
changes frequently, as required by the democratic process - and by
Ulrich's criterion of intrinsic motivation. Similarly misplaced is

195

the criticism that Beer's model implies autocratic control over individuals. The model requires only that degree of control over individual freedom necessary in order to maintain cohesiveness in a viable system. If less control were exercised the result would not be greater freedom for the parts, but anarchy. This would inevitably bring in its wake more severe and unpredictable constraints on individual liberty. If then, the individuals within a system are agreed about the goal to be pursued, the model would seem to offer them a means of pursuing this goal with only those constraints on individual autonomy necessary for the achievement of that goal. Of course, the problem still arises of the model being misused by a powerful group. Ulrich (8) argues that Beer's model does in fact lend itself to this kind of usage. He insists that design tools should be so constructed that they are impossible to subvert for authoritarian usage. Beer replies (36) that the risk of such subversion does exist but that safeguards can be built into the system to minimise the danger. Clemson (37) dismisses Rivett's arguments about the frightening use of computers in Beer's proposals.

8. The recommendations of management cybernetics are very likely to be difficult to implement since little is offered except a more efficient control system. Organisational cybernetics can, by contrast, offer the prospect of increasing personal freedom, as well as efficiency, in pursuit of more widely agreed goals. Implementation is always likely to be a problem, however, when specialised knowledge is imported from outside an organisation. Organisational cybernetics has not perhaps addressed this issue as fully as it might. However, recent books by Clemson (25) and Beer (5) do make useful suggestions about implementation.

CONCLUSION

It seems that while management cybernetics is subject to most of the criticisms that have been levelled at the cybernetic model of organisation, organisational cybernetics largely escapes. Cybernetics should not be dismissed because of the failings of the management cybernetic variant. Organisational cybernetics provides a model for the analysis and design of organisations that is at least as useful as any other currently available in the literature of organisation and management theory. Critics of the cybernetic approach to organisations should take a fresh look – at organisational cybernetics, and see what can be learned from it. It repays close study, providing a model capable of integrating much modern theory. It is open to being developed to even higher degrees of sophistication.

References can be obtained from the author.

FUNCTIONAL APPROACH EVOLUTION IN ORGANIZATIONAL DESIGNING

Zbigniew Martyniak
Institute for Organization and Management
Cracow Academy of Economics
31-510 Cracow
ul. Rakowicka 27
Poland

ABSTRACT. The paper presents the ways of penetration of functional approach into organizational designing - sociological, engineering and linguistic. Shaping of functional approach in social sciences from B. Malinowski to C. Lévi-Strauss is discussed as well. Especially the role of D.L. Miles and G. Nadler in formation of functional approach within a framework of engineering approach is exposed. Also the main ideas of functionalism in linguistics are presented starting from the Prague Linguistic Group to Osgood's semantic analysers. Besides, the criticism of classical functionalism represented by E. Nagel is introduced. That criticism allows to illustrate some contemporary concepts of organizational designing - P. Hussenot's verification of quasi-objectives - a case study of French National Employment Agency, author's formulation of Value Organization, H. Wellenreuther's concept of Value Analysis, J. Trzcieniecki's prognostic designing method - 1979 version and F. Liptak's method called RAPPOS.
        In conclusion the typology of the main strategies of organizational designing is elaborated. This typology includes following approaches: descriptive-improving, pattern-functional and functional-diagnostic.

1. INTRODUCTION

Three ways of penetration of functional approach into organizational designing can be distinguished. First, it was accomplished by psychologists and sociologists whose role was constantly increasing in organizational research in the twenties of our century. Then, after the Second World War, the penetration was facilitated by the development and introduction of functional approach to engineering designing. Value Analysis and Value Engineering may serve as adequate examples of the above mentioned trends. Finally, in the

197

R. Trappl (ed.), Cybernetics and Systems '86, 197–204.
© 1986 by D. Reidel Publishing Company.

last decades, one can observe the introduction of linguistic methods to management theory with their structural approach. In all of the above trends functionalism reflected negation of the approach in which the entity was treated as a simple sum of isolated parts. In contrary, they all reflected system approach to problems solving.

2. BEHAVIOURAL SCHOOL

Psychologists W. James, J. Devey and others, established functional approach based on the concept of transferring interest from the anatomy of psychical processes to the problem of their role in the life of an individual [11]. On the other hand, the forerunner of functional analysis in sociology, social anthropologist B. Malinowski wrote that field researchers collected rather dispersed data instead of analysing natural, essential and constantly repeated relations. Malinowski maintained that functional approach to culture reflects the principle that in every kind of civilization, every custom, every material object, concept or belief performs certain vital function and each of them has a special task and constitutes an indispensable part of the entity [5, p. 132-133]. If Malinowski identified function with the task to accomplish then A.R. Radcliffe-Brown maintains opinion that the role in the entity of every regularly repeated activity can be treated as its function and can be also treated as a contribution to structural continuity [10, p. 179-180]. The concepts of functionalism proposed by Malinowski and Radcliffe-Brown passed through significant evolution in sociology thanks to such scientists as T. Parsons and R.K. Merton. They both, as sociologists of organization, played an important role in the origin of new management technique - Management by Objectives /MBO/.

3. ENGINEERING SCHOOL

Similarly, in engineering designing D.L. Miles in his Value Analysis and Value Engineering put the stress on the functional structure and not on the material one [7]. In classical approach to rationalization the key question was: How does a system work? In functional approach to technical designing the major problem became: What is the objective of a system? Stressing functions and tasks of a product and not a product as such marked a radical change in methodological approach to improvement of industrial structures and processes. If in classical approach heuristic foundation of improvement was based on the observation of an improved product then in the approach connected with Value Analysis or Value Engineering it is necessary to 'wipe out' from memory the existing object.

Functional approach to engineering designing originated by Miles was fully expressed in G. Nadler's concept of
ideal system. That concept was created as an opposition to
the tradition of Taylor exposing the registration of the
actual state of a subject and critical evaluation of that
state [8].

The principal idea of Nadler's IDEALS concept consists
in contradiction of conventional 'improvement' and seeking
patterns distant from existing solutions. In the systemic
strategy of Nadler the starting point of creative organizational thinking is not connected with analysis of existing
systems, but with the objectives of those systems. Instead
of looking for particular improvements of elements /'shares'/
of the system one is seeking for a general concept of total
improvement of given system. In this end designing starts
from the theoretically ideal concept and gradually comes
to the concept considering limitations. In certain sense
the induction is replaced by deduction. From the point of
view of systems theory the entity is always more than a sum
of its components. Properties of any entity can not be reduced to properties of its parts and every system has its
specific characteristics. Considering any entity as a system, in opposite to analytical approach, is very conducive
to heuristic inspiration.

4. LINGUISTIC SCHOOL

In the thirties of 20th century the Prague Linguistic Group
represented by N. Troubetzkoy and R. Jakobson arraigned
'atomistic' ideas of traditional linguistics and introduced
the concept of functionalized phonological system. They objected to considering words as the independent units and
postulated to take into consideration the relations between
words. The ideas of the Prague School were further developed by many scientists and the achievements of phonology
were implemented to social sciences by C. Lévi-Strauss. He
noticed particularly that phonology was of such great importance in behavioural science as nuclear physics was in
exact sciences [2, p. 31].

According to the opinion of B. Lussato, the development of computer science and automation disengaged managers
from work scheduling, from layout planning and from the
form rationalization as well. But that could not solve difficult problems facing all trends in management practice
an theory based on the integration of men and systems [4,
p. 122].

An attempt to solve those problems was made within
linguistic school with the contribution of such disciplines
as: semantics, semiology, psycholinguistics, theory of

automata. The semantic analysers are the tool of linguistic
approach applied to designing of information processes.
Their application allows to eliminate excessive precision
of computing, redundant information, empty indicators and
absurd numbers. The first semantic analysers were: 'Goal'
elaborated by A. Mc Donough in 1963 and 'Modsin' elaborated
by F. Peccoud in 1967. Nowadays there exist a substantial
number of semantic analysers and Ch. Osgood proposed an
analyser 'measuring' the meaning of words. But unfortunately the above results are not well-known among organizers
though they could play an important role in marketing, advertising and promoting.

5. CRITICISM OF TRADITIONAL FUNCTIONAL APPROACH

Functional approach represented in organizational designing
by linguistic approach includes virtually all the contemporary achievements. In order to display the evolution of
functional approach in organizational designing it is necessary to look back and evaluate the tools created within
behavioural and engineering schools. Frequently the implementation of Management by Objectives, IDEALS concept and
mechanical attempts of application of Value Analysis to organizational problems ended fruitlessly in practice. The
criticism of orthodox functional approach that emerged in
methodology of science in the sixties explains easily the
above presented phenomena. This trend is represented by
E. Nagel - the most consequent and also the most authorita-
tive cristic of functionalism in social and natural sciences. He noticed that the activities of living system can
be analysed without assumption that objectives are motivating factors [9, p. 354]. Criticising teleological concepts
of T. Parsons, E. Nagel expressed opinion that the analysis
of functions performed by different elements of social system leads to justifiable results only when supported by the
precise description of conditions and states of given system [9, p. 454-455]. In opposite to teleological explanations E. Nagel stresses the elucidation arising from analysing of the elementary factors setting up the system. As
a result he proposes an approach based firstly on thorough
description of the system examined and secondly focused
upon the analysis of its functions.
    Practical obstacles and theoretical criticism caused
a radical change in methodology of organizational designing.
The new methodological concepts try to link teleological
/functional/ approach with a diagnostic /genetic/ one. This
way, the triad of Hegel: thesis - antithesis - synthesis
finds place in methodology of organizational designing.

6. HUSSENOT'S VERIFICATION OF QUASI-OBJECTIVES /A CASE STUDY OF FRENCH NATIONAL EMPLOYMENT AGENCY/

The new modified Management by Objectives technique first stresses the actual outcome of research and the actual values of parameters characterizing an institution. Subsequently, functions are identified and explained and then following steps of the procedure of Management by Objectives are accomplished.

P. Hussenot describes a case of French National Employment Agency founded in 1967 in order to co-ordinate the labour force transfers throughout the country [1]. It had been planned that in the 6th National Plan the Agency would have participated in 30% of transactions on the French labour market. But despite the considerable development of the Agency between 1970 and 1979 when the number of employees increased from 4500 to 9000 and the number of branches increased from 200 to 619, the main objective was not achieved even in half. In 1979 the share of the Agency was about 11% /690 thousand transactions when the total number was 6254 thousand/. The results of research conducted in 1979 and in 1980 displayed that the inefficiency of classical Management by Objectives technique was caused by the change of the main objective. The real objective of the Agency was social control of the unemployed who had to register. Growing stream of unemployed people was registered and verified by the growing staff of the Agency. A great number of clients were not interested in looking for employment opportunities but they only sought for unemployment benefits. The staff was occupied with registration and arranging benefits for the unemployed. Only 10% of working hours were spent on contacts with employers. The outcome obtained in research made possible to introduce several changes creating proper circumstances for accomplishing the main objective.

In this case the following changes were adapted:
- Exemption of registration of the unemployed seeking to obtain benefits,
- Transfer of files of the unemployed to Regional Employment Agencies,
- 30% of working hours had to be spent on the preparations of new offers,
- Opening an advertisement campaign: 'National Employment Agency - the biggest labour exchange in service of employers'.

Thanks to the changes made in management structure of the Agency and its environment only in 1980 the growth of number of transactions was approximately 5%.

As a conclusion of above and similar cases P. Hussenot presented a modification of traditional MBO based on the verification of quasi-objectives. He defined a quasi-objective as: '... a result which is achieved by an organization in relations with environment and which presents certain determinism if the result can be associated with the state variables expressing the conditions indespensible that result was achieved and would be achieved' [1].

In order to verify quasi-objectives the following steps should be made:
- Verification of actual results,
- Identification of the state variables of actually existing organization,
- Determination of functions realized by variables,
- Verification of the model.

According to the opinion of Hussenot the identified state variables are not the measures leading to planned objectives. The state variables are conditions allowing to achieve any given result in constant circumstances. Prior assigning of the objectives of an organization describes only one of the circumstances. Such results can be achieved even in absence of any earlier determined objectives but settlement of the new objective not always leads to the change of results [1].

Hussenot's proposition can not be treated as a simple modification of functional approach to organizational designing. In fact, it means deviation from classical functionalism. Instead of saying that Y is a consequence of X, Hussenot points out that X is a cause or condition for Y. Such return to the genetic approach with preserving typically functional tools, especially to quantitative problems, confirms Nagel's statement saying that every teleological system /teleologically oriented/ can be divided into parts conditioning certain property of the system. Those parts are related to each other and to the environment. The relations can be formulated within a framework of general regularities [9, p. 360].

The above statement enables us to draw a conclusion that the characteristics of systems teleologically oriented can be described without referring to objectives as to motivating factors.

7. MODIFICATION OF CLASSICAL FUNCTIONALISM OF MILES' VALUE
    ANALYSIS

In Value Analysis proposed by D. Miles causal analysis was omitted in favour of functional analysis. In modern research functional analysis is usually associated with causal /genetic/ analysis and the last one is treated with priority.

7.1. Author's Approach to Value Organization

This concept, presented for the first time in 1977 was later

published in French in 1980 [6]. The procedure typical for Value Organization includes following stages:
- Selection of the subject of analysis,
- Identification of system,
- Gathering information,
- Analysis of functions and searching for new designs,
- Detailed designing,
- Implementation of design.

The first stage is based on the organizational diagnostics referred to the whole 'organism' of an institution to which Value Organization is applied. Appropriate analysis in the framework of discussed approach is preceded by identification in which the needs and the requirements of the environment are determined. Identification includes also description of faults of the system. Moreover, the analysis of functions is preceded by information gathering. It seems necessary to add that gathering of internal information concerns functioning of an existing system.

Presented concept clearly shows that identification of the external functions /system identification/ and of the elementary functions /gathering information/ is strictly connected with methodological analysis of conditions and processes accomplished within the system and its environment.

7.2. Wellenreuther's Concept of Value Analysis

Similar tendency of modification of classical Value Analysis is displayed in the work of H. Wellenreuther [14]. It is not a simple compilation of Anglo-Saxon monographs but contains new proposition of procedure of Value Analysis referred to products and processes. Taking into consideration the criticism of traditional functionalism Wellenreuther describes the procedure in following stages: Preliminary measures; Description of subject; Evaluation of subject; Descriptions of designs; Evaluations of designs; Presentation and implementation of design.

The procedure does not ignore the actual state of the subject but strongly express it in analysis. Additionally, he recommends to intensify genetic analysis previously opposed to functional analysis. He simply writes that designer, as one of the members of Value Analysis team, should, among other things, consider the history of manufacturing of a product and its constructional changes in the past and should also determine the reasons of changes [14, p. 41]. Wellenreuther emphasizes also that description of the actual state takes a lot of time and efforts and some participants of Value Analysis teams do not pay enough attention to that stage trying as soon as possible to search for new solutions. He also warns that such early searching often means losing the right way [14].

8. CONTEMPORARY MODIFICATIONS OF NADLER'S CONCEPT

8.1. Prognostic Method of J. Trzcieniecki

The modification of dominant functional /teleological/ approach, that takes into consideration omitted by G. Nadler analysis of the actual state, was proposed by J. Trzcieniecki /version of 1979/ [13]. It comprises following stages: Determination of objectives; Determination of tasks; Analysis of the actual state; Pattern organization designing; Determination of limitations and preparation of variants; Selection of the most favourable design; Implementation of design.

Treating the analysis of the actual state of a system as an indispensable element of improvement of existing organizations and underlining the role of that analysis indicate that prognostic method of J. Trzcieniecki includes also the diagnostic element. It means that the discussed method has much in common with causal /genetic/ approach.

8.2. The RAPPOS Method

The method proposed by Slovak researcher F. Lipták called RAPPOS /after an acronyme of Slovak name: Improving Analysis and Designing of Organizational Systems/ shares some common principles with the IDEALS concept of G. Nadler but differs from it essentially [3]. The main difference lies in fact that Nadler prefers prognostic element and RAPPOS underlines the importance of diagnostic one. The RAPPOS method proposes following stages of organizing:
- Separation of organization and defining complex problems to be solved,
- Systemic disaggregation of problems,
- Solution of disaggregated problems,
- Systemic aggregation of partial problems - modelling,
- Synthetizing evaluation of systemic aggregation of partial problems - optimization,
- Design of improving changes - application,
- Implementation of improving changes,
- Evaluation of effects of improving changes,
- Correcting changes,
- Control of functioning of the modified system.

System separation as such performs certain diagnostic purpose. But the proper diagnostics finds its place in a separate stage and is based mostly on quantification of system characteristics /parameters/. Summing up this method we can say that in the first two stages diagnostics plays a predominant role.

References can be obtained from the author.

SYSTEM - ORIENTED DESIGNING PROCEDURES

Jan Petr
Prague Technical University
Faculty of Civil Engineering
Thakurova 7
166 29 Praha 6
Czechoslovakia

ABSTRACT. There are two basic conceptions of a design process:"top-down" and "down-top".The first one is more popular and usually more efficient.But in some special cases
the "down-top" process is more advantageous.Specially in
case of existence of a standard build elements set.This
paper aims at indicating a way of formalization of this
problem and at forming main ideas of proper algorithm.The
matrix of compatibility between structure elements is presented and so is the matrix containing relations between
standard functions of designed object and basic structure
elements.The concept of a "genetic code" is introduced for
technical objects.It is used for controlling the "down-top"
composition of a structure.

1. SYSTEM FEATURES OF DESIGNED OBJECTS

The large projects of recent decades, which we have
been witness to in the technological and social field,have
drawn attention to those features of real objects to which
the general system theory began to refer to as systemic.We
have in mind the features which represent the "organism"
of the object,i.e. the quality which distinguishes the objects composed of interacting constituents from the mere
summary of these constituents.This quality was already mentioned in Aristoteles´statement that "the whole is more
than just a mere aggregate of its parts".The representative of these features is the interaction of parts of the object among themselves, the cooperation (frequently antagonistic) of a separate part with the remainder of the object,
the interaction of the object with its enviroment,the goal-
seeking behaviour of the object, its adaptability, etc.
The existence of the system features in the entities
of the real world is objective, i.e. even in objects which
are subject to the activity of designers. It can,therefore,

R. Trappl (ed.), Cybernetics and Systems '86, 205–211.
© *1986 by D. Reidel Publishing Company.*

be said that, apart from the other features of the object, the designer also designs the system features, the "organism" of the object. Up to a certain time and, with some objects, to this day, these features were and are being designed as if indirectly, implicitly. This is possible if the object being designed is more or less homogeneous as regards the types of parts of which it is composed, and if the number of these parts is not too large.

However, in objects whose significant characteristics are complexity and heterogenity, the system features become more important and decisive for the resultant quality of the object.It is, therefore, necessary to devote appropriate attention to them already at the design stage, to consider their design explicitly, using objective engineering methods and techniques. This task in fact represents the mission of the constructive system theory and the system engineering related to it, and emphasizes the necessity for the system method of designing contemporary and future objects. Designing which explicitly deals also with designing the system features of the object is referred to as system designing. Its objective is to achieve optimum system characteristics of objects.

We have so far been emphasizing the importance of the system features, as well as mastering them, in connection with extensive projects. However, it also has been found that mastering (in the sense of analysis and synthesis) the system features of objects is also very important with regard to the automation of designing, especially for the automation at a higher level, i.e. the automation of creative operations in the designing process. The system approach to a future object in the form of a system model is in many cases a convenient point of departure for algorithmization and, consequently, also for the automation of the design phases which at present still seem to be the exclusive domain of man. This applies namely to the operations related to the generation of the object structure. One of the approaches to the algorithmization of generating the object structure, based on the principles of system modelling,is discussed below.

2.   THE USE OF SYSTEM PROCEDURES IN DESIGNING "DOWN-TOP"

2.1. Principle of formalization

The "down-top" procedure assumes the existence of the fundamental constructional parts of the structure, a kind of catalogue of the basic elements or, in more general terms, of a dictionary. They are used to generate gradually the higher structures which are required to fulfil the functions the object has to provide.

The algorithms, which generate the structure in this manner, are manageable and satisfy the specific requirements of computer procedures.The present state of technology also provides sufficient useful practical applications for this (automated) method of designing.

The formalization of the "down-top" procedure is based on the structural record of the object in the form of the traditional concept of the system model: the system elements, which are the function carriers, are interconnected. These connections are labelled by the parameters characterizing the represented relation. The fundamental algorithm of generating the structure must:

- respect the condition of compatibility of the elements being connected,
- aim at the fulfilment of the conditions imposed on the function of the structure being generated.

The condition of compatibility of the connections being generated may, in the simplest case, be restricted to the condition of keeping to a unique interface in the parameters which can be distinguished in the connections being introduced. If these parameters were understood to be just inputs or outputs of the functions of the elements, the problem of compatibility would be trivial, nevertheless, from the constructive point of view quite effective. However, the category of connection parameters enables the relation between two elements, expressed in terms of a connection, to be specified much more broadly. For example, the parameters and their values can be used to express the condition of their mutual time-space configuration, etc.

The parameters of process character symbolize the values transmitted in a particular process, which activize the function of the element which they enter, are transformed or consumed within this element, and transmitted to other elements. (In these deliberations, one must bear in mind that the connections carry out no functions.) The values of the parameters of this type are additive and distributive in the sense of group compatibility. They express an amount as a rule.

However, a parametric vector may simultaneously contain parameters to which we shall refer as descriptive. The descriptive parameters characterize or describe the relation between two elements.

2.2. The compatibility matrix

The compatibility of the basic elements of a particular set can be described in terms of the compatibility matrix K , which reads

$$K \equiv \begin{array}{c|cccc|c}
 & \varepsilon_1 & \varepsilon_2 & \varepsilon_3 & \cdots & \varepsilon_n \\
\hline
\varepsilon_1 & \mathbf{D}_{1,1} & \mathbf{D}_{1,2} & \mathbf{D}_{1,3} & \cdots & \mathbf{D}_{1,n} \\
\varepsilon_2 & \mathbf{D}_{2,1} & \mathbf{D}_{2,2} & \mathbf{D}_{2,3} & \cdots & \mathbf{D}_{2,n} \\
\varepsilon_3 & \mathbf{D}_{3,1} & \mathbf{D}_{3,2} & \mathbf{D}_{3,3} & \cdots & \mathbf{D}_{3,n} \\
\vdots & \vdots & \vdots & \vdots & \vdots & \vdots \\
\varepsilon_n & \mathbf{D}_{n,1} & \mathbf{D}_{n,2} & \mathbf{D}_{n,3} & \cdots & \mathbf{D}_{n,n}
\end{array}$$

Here ε_i represents the element of the set and $\mathbf{D}_{i,j}$ the matrix of the connections of elements ε_i and ε_j .

The compatibility matrix $\mathbf{K}$ describes the compatibility of the elements from the formal point of view in a quite simple way: it only considers the input and output parameters of the basic elements. However, this is sufficient because any relation, even if quite complicated, between two elements and, consequently, also their degree of compatibility, can be expressed in terms of the parameters. Its simplicity gives good hope of practical utilization. The diagonal elements of matrix $\mathbf{K}$ indicate the possibility of arranging elements of the same type in series. We can thus claim that matrix $\mathbf{K}$ represents the syntax, i.e. the rules of formation for generating structures from the "dictionary" of basic elements.

The connection matrix $\mathbf{D}_{i,j}$ of elements i and j reads

$$\mathbf{D}_{i,j} \equiv \begin{array}{c|cccc|c}
 & p_1^j & p_2^j & p_3^j & \cdots & p_n^j \\
\hline
p_1^i & \sigma_{1,1} & 0 & 0 & \cdots & 0 \\
p_2^i & 0 & \sigma_{1,2} & 0 & \cdots & 0 \\
p_3^i & 0 & 0 & \sigma_{3,3} & \cdots & 0 \\
\vdots & \vdots & \vdots & \vdots & & \vdots \\
p_n^i & 0 & 0 & 0 & \cdots & \sigma_{p,n}
\end{array}$$

In this matrix, the rows refer to the output parametric vector of element i , the columns to the input parametric vector of element j . To avoid confusion, the process parameters are not distinguished from the descriptive.

The coefficients $\sigma_{k,k}$ express the degree of correspondence of the values h_k^i and h_k^j of parameter p_k . If a process parameter is involved, coefficient $\sigma_{k,k}$ is an arithmetic variable denoted $\overline{\sigma}_{k,k}$ for which it holds that

$$\overline{\sigma}_{k,k} \in < 0,1 >$$

If a descriptive parameter is involved, coefficient $\sigma_{k,k}$ is a logic variable denoted $\overline{\overline{\sigma}}_{k,k}$ which takes the logic values 0 or 1.

The determination of coefficients $\sigma_{k,k}$ is one of the procedures of solving an actual problem which depends on the material content of the adopted parameters.

In determining the logic value of coefficient $\bar{\sigma}_{kjk}$ the principle of fuzzy sets has to be used if a descriptive parameter is involved, and the value 0 or 1 is determined depending on whether the threshold value of the membership function of the set of values satisfying or not satisfying the condition of correspondence, respectively, is satisfied.

Distinguishing between arithmetic and logic values of coefficient σ_{kjk} is advantageous in judging the compatibility of groups of elements.

Matrix K describes the compatibility of the separate elements among themselves, but also the compatibility of groups of elements with a single element, in both directions. In this connection, we shall introduce the term degree of compatibility of elements. We shall denote this degree $k(a,b)$, i.e. the degree of compatibility of elements a and b. The symbols a and b may in this case stand for groups as well as elements.

In assessing the combinability of elements, it is ideal if $k(a,b)=1$.

If the compatibility of the elements is known in the sense described by the compatibility matrix K, structures, to which we shall refer as legal, can be generated by means of a suitable algorithm. In this connection, one refers to a structure as legal if it displays sufficient coherence and capability of goal-seeking behaviour, conditioned by the values of the input parameters, and producing certain values of the output parameters. For practical purposes, this means that at least the minimum (threshold) degree of compatibility, which we shall denoted $k_{min}(a,b)$, must be preserved in all connections of such a structure.

An algorithm capable of generating legal structures without further conditions imposed on the generated values, would be simple. Since it would contain some random steps, also the behaviour of the resultant structures would be more or less random. Consequently, also the function of the system, generated in this manner, would be random.

2.3. The genetic code

The randomness in generating the system structure can be eliminated by introduction a controlling mechanism of the structure composition, to which we shall refer as the genetic code in analogy with a similar mechanism in biology. The genetic code governs the generation and growth of the structure.It must contain and respect the rules and data concerned with the kinds, and in the case of technical systems, with the field to which the designed system belongs, as well as data related to the generated system as an individual. The part of the genetic code which, controlling the structure composition, concerns the rules and data on kind, is universal for all objects of a particular field. We shall refer to it as the universal part of the genetic code. For a particular field, it is established once and for all. The part, which controls the structure growth with regard to the individual features of the system, will be referred to as the individual part of the genetic code.

The rules in a particular field are defined by the appropriate natural laws, legislation, standards, customs and construction rules of the appropriate systems, the components of which are the basic elements used. They are described by the theories of the corresponding scientific disciplines, norms and standards of the construction systems. These data and rules are objective, and the designer cannot change them directly. The properties mentioned enable them to be encoded directly in the compatibility matrix, which thus presents the objective (i.e. universal) part of the genetic code related to the features of the generated system as a type. This provides for their formalization.

The data on the generated system as an individual are of a subjective nature and they differentiate this individual from the other individuals of its kind. They represent a tool which enables the system designer to incorporate the required individual features of the object in the system project. They are thus an active part of the genetic code. They can be expressed in the form of standard functions of the designed object and of the values of their parameters. The standard functions define the activity and the dimensions necessary for the fulfilment of the function of the whole successfully. In other words, they represent the components of the overall dynamics of the system.

The composition of the system structure then consists in finding the basic elements (or groups of elements) which satisfy, to an acceptable (optimum) degree, the conditions of the standard functions as well as the conditions of the objective part of the genetic code – the conditions of compatibility. This procedure is analogous to that used in morphological analysis.

To formalize the indicated relation, it is convenient to introduce matrix $\mathbf{F}$ expressing the membership function of the individual basic elements ε_i with respect to the standard functions φ_j . The membership function is assessed according to the capability of the appropriate basic element to satisfy the standard function. This capability is again determined with the aid of the values of the parameters at the inputs and outputs, the process and descriptive parameters being distinguished in the same way as for the compatibility matrix $\mathbf{K}$.

Matrix $\mathbf{F}$ has the form

$$F \equiv \begin{array}{c|cccccc} & \varphi_1 & \varphi_2 & \varphi_3 & \cdots & \varphi_m \\ \hline \varepsilon_1 & \mu_{1,1} & \mu_{1,2} & \mu_{1,3} & \cdots & \mu_{1,m} \\ \varepsilon_2 & \mu_{2,1} & \mu_{2,2} & \mu_{2,3} & \cdots & \mu_{2,m} \\ \varepsilon_3 & \mu_{2,1} & \mu_{3,2} & \mu_{3,3} & \cdots & \mu_{3,m} \\ \vdots & \vdots & \vdots & \vdots & & \vdots \\ \varepsilon_n & \mu_{n,1} & \mu_{n,2} & \mu_{n,3} & \cdots & \mu_{n,m} \end{array}$$

The values μ_{ij} express the membership function of element ε_i with respect to the set of elements satisfying the standard function φ_j.

3. CONCLUSION

The "down-top" procedure enables structures to be generated in hierarchic order, in variant design and under full application of the catalogue principles of designing. However, it only realizes one stage in the designing process, i.e. the stage of generating the design. It does not contain the next important stage, the stage of assessment of the design. But it does create the conditions for the latter by providing variants of legal structures from which the designer can choose the optimum variant, using the appropriate procedures.

The "down-top" procedure represents the exploitation of explicit system methods for algorithmizing the generation of structures with application to designing objects which have a clearly defined base of constructional elements.

References

Klir G.J.(editor): Trends in General System Theory.Wiley, New York, 1972.
Mesarovic M.D.,Macko D.,Takahara Y.: Theory of Hierarchichal Multilevel Systems.Academic Press,New York 1970.
Petr J.: Algorithmization of Generating Object Structures by "DOWN-TOP" Composition. In:Technical Papers of Technical University of Prague,E2,Prague 1984,p.155-171.
Petr J.: System Analysis:Real Objects Analysis (in Czech). Techn.Univers.of Prague, Prague 1985.
Sadovskij V.N.: General System Theory:Its Tasks and Methods of Construction. General Systems,17,1972,p.171
Vlček J.,Petr J.:System Analysis and Design(in Czech). Techn.Univers.of Prague,Prague 1983.

THE STRUCTURE OF THE DESIGN PROCESS

Wojciech Tarnowski
Silesian Technical University
ul. Katowicka 16
44 100 Gliwice
Poland

ABSTRACT. The notion of the design process structure is given, as well as the reasons for analysis and synthesis of the structure. There are proposed three model structures: the macro-structure, the micro-structure and the model of decomposition in designing. They describe three different approaches to the design process. They are of a wide generality and, where appropriate, they permit a full description of the structure of the real design process, and they can be used in superposition.

1. INTRODUCTION

Design is a discrete process. Several distinct activities can be recognized within its structure, each activity having a defined start and end. These activities together constitute the design process. The structure of any process can be defined as an arrangment or a sequence of interlinked activities conceived according to a specific criterion.

Defined another way, the structure of a process can be considered as an entire system of relationships between the sum or totality of the process and its elements, the latter being arranged according to a specific aspect or criterion. The relevant criterion therefore becomes of the utmost significance since it governs the division of the given process.

In the case of the design process, the criterion may be influenced, or take a form of: /i/ the points in time at which the main decisions are taken, during the sequence of the process; /ii/ the different characteristics of the activities comprising the process; /iii/ the difference in attitude of designers involved in the process.

For many reasons, the analysis and the synthesis of the structure of the design process are two of the most important problems in engineering design. Amongst the literature there are many proposals relating to the structure of the design process; see Amkreutz, Archer, Asimow, Hall, Jones, Krick, Norris et alia. [Lit. 4 to 9]. English [Lit.1] made a comparison of these proposals and demonstrated the similarities amongst the many different models. This prompts the question as to which are the appropiate and relevant models for the actual process of design.

A designer/manager, having identified the structure of a design pro-

213

R. Trappl (ed.), Cybernetics and Systems '86, 213–220.
© 1986 by D. Reidel Publishing Company.

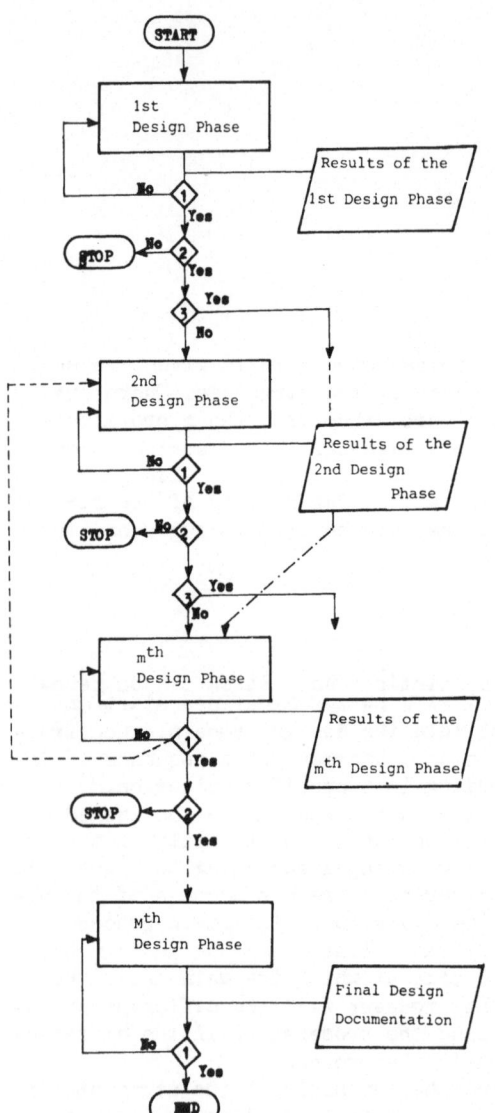

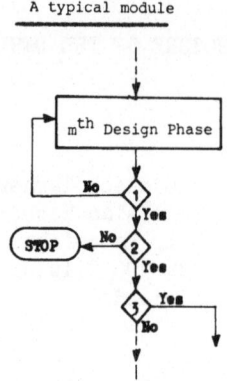

A typical module

m^{th} Design Phase

1-has the mth design phase
been completed properly?

2-do the results of the mth
design phase permit further
progress of the process?

3-is it rational to omit
any of the succeeding
phases? Which?

Fig. 1   General scheme
for the macro-
structure of a
design process

214

cess can logically carry out the following steps:
/i/   the macro-planning, analysis, control and management of the process,
/ii/   the apportionment of tasks among the members of the design team,
       and the co-ordination of their efforts,
/iii/ decision-making at the proper stages and the supplying of the nece-
       ssary data and information,
/iv/   the identification of key decisions and the factors influencing
       them,
/v/   the micro-planning of each individual's task to organise the ef-
       forts of each member of the design team more efficiently, to sug-
       gest a relevant method, for example,
/vi/   the facilitation of a rational description of the design process,
       discovering its characteristics and developing and improving spe-
       cific design methods,
/vii/ the identification of sections susceptible to algorithmisation or
       to computer-aided methods generally,
/viii/the development of the cybernetic approach to design and the reco-
       gnition of the work and the control activities useful to management,
/ix/   the development of the psychological approach and the recognition
       of the sequential phases of design thinking and what may be useful
       for the auto-control of the design process,
/x/   the systematization of research into a design process, and the
       creation of new methods.

2. THE MACRO-STRUCTURE OF THE DESIGN PROCESS /Fig. 1/

A design process is usually completed in a few sequential phases. Each
phase yields information of gradually increasing accuracy about the object that is being designed, and each phase is completed by a decision.
The main aim of the decision is to make screening after each phase, in
order to limit the number of variants to the design. Another reason is
to permit the decision-taker himself to participate in the design process.
This reduces the risk for the designer of his final result not being acceptable at the end of the process.

Since a design process may be broken down in several ways, the question
arises as to which method of division is the most advantageous. Perhaps
the answer to this is that the best division is that which minimises the
cost and maximizes the quality of the final design solution. The costs
may be measured by a certain risk R of recurrence after sequential phases $m = 1, \ldots, M$,

$$\text{thus} \quad R = \sum_{m=1}^{M} pm \cdot C_m ,$$

where pm is the probability and C_m is the cost of the correction of the
m - th phase.

The quality of solution S_y may be measured by the variation of this
solution from the global optimal solution S_o, taken, for instance, as
the difference of their scalar quantities $F/S/$ [Lit. 2, 3] :

$$F = F/S_o/ - F/S_y/.$$

In the general case these two criteria conflict, so the decision is
a matter of compromise, because the greater the number of phases M, the

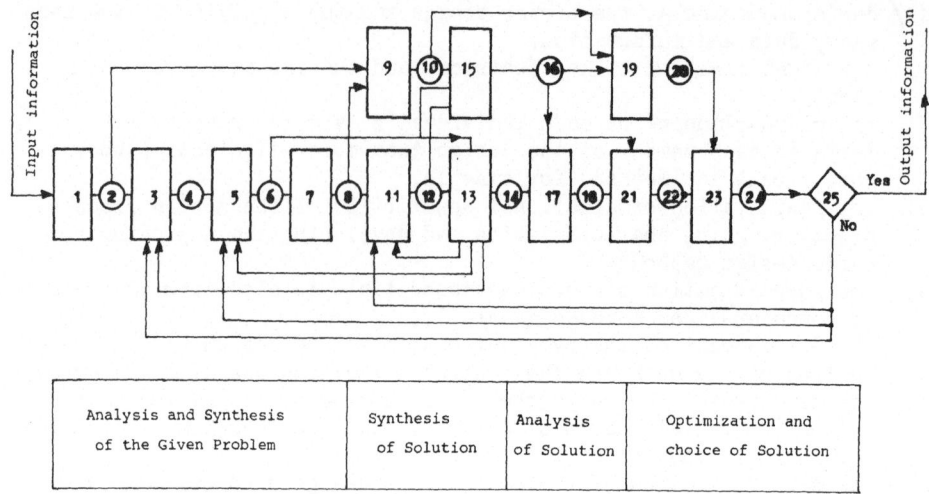

Analysis and Synthesis of the Given Problem	Synthesis of Solution	Analysis of Solution	Optimization and choice of Solution

Fig. 2   Micro-structure of the design process.

1-analysis and identification of the given problem

2-problem formulation and description of the function that must be satisfied by the designed object or project

3-analysis and formulation of the task for design

4-description of the substance of the task

5-defining the requirements

6-design specifications

7-formulating the general value system for the given task

8-formulation of criteria and preferences system

9-formulating the super-criterion of optimality

10-super-criterion of optimality

11-generating alternative solutions

12-set of possible solutions/design variants/

13-rough analysis, appraisal and selection of variants

14-set of correct solutions /variants/

15-identification of the criteria

16-set of criteria

17-analysing and testing of the correct solutions against the criteria

18-assessments of the solutions /in the case of a continous set of variants: their mathematical model/

19-task choice criterion determination

20-choice of optimization criterion

21-appraisal

22-complete assessment set /for all variants, on all criteria/

23-optimization /parametric/

24-set of variants, ranked according to the values of optimization criterion

25-final decision of the given task.

216

less the probability p_m and the less the cost C_m and also the less the probability of obtaining optimal solution S_o.

The structure shown in Fig. 1 is of an idealised character. In a real case, it is a subject of a specific individual planning. Many large companies provide regulations and instructions for its staff covering the procedure for research and development processes and these form good examples of macro-structures for design.

2. THE MICRO-STRUCTURE OF THE DESIGN PROCESS /Fig. 2/

In this case the criterion for division of the process is the difference in nature of the various activities. In contradistinction to the macro-structure covering the whole process, the micro-structure concerns only one task, of whichever scope, large or small, in the transition from decision to decision. No stage of the structure may be omitted. The results and output of each of the sequential stages need not to be recorded. The structure is of a strongly iterative and recurrent character. There are recognized the main activities of a creative process, like analysis, synthesis, assessment, choice, selection and decision. They compose a repetitive module, in which they are arranged many times in a similar sequence. The module repeats like motif and comprise a typical iterative loop.

3. DECOMPOSITION IN DESIGN /Fig. 3/

When a designer, following the sequential steps of a micro-structure, arrives at the panel "Solutions Generation" /11, Fig. 2/ he must attempt to split the given task T into a finite number of sub-tasks T_n :
$$T \; \longrightarrow \; \{ \, T_n \, , \quad n = 1, \ldots , N \, \}$$
in such a way that they envelope and represent the given task T, as shown in Fig. 3. This means that a set of solutions S_n of all T_n is equivalent to solutions S of the task T. This transformation, which is often difficult, is also absolutely crucial to the process of design, and represents a rational change of aim, on the assumption that it is easier to find solutions for all the sub-tasks T_n, than it is to find a solution for the entire task T. For example, to design a central heating system /T/ for a specific building, the following sub-tasks /T_n/ must be designed: a boiler with a heat exchanger unit /T_1/, a pipework distribution system /T_2/, a series of radiators /T_3/ and a control system /T_4/. Each sub-task has its own set of constraints and its own value system. Thus, for each target T_n the designer must develop a seperate design procedure according to the nature of the micro-structure, and starting with panel 1, Fig. 2. Again when panel 11 /Generating Alternative Solutions/ is reached a designer may split the sub-task still further to create less difficult targets of a second stage of hierarchy. This process is admis - sible so long as it is meaningful, logical and advantageous.

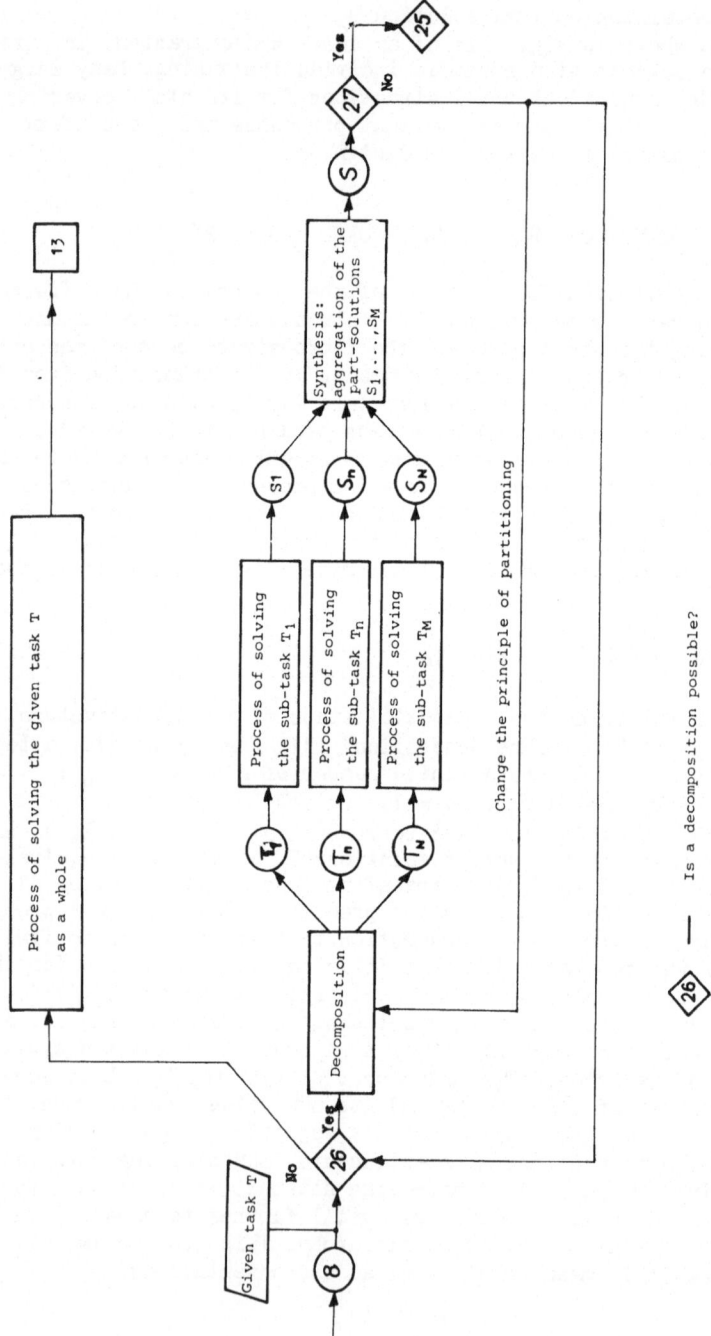

Fig. 3 Decomposition in design. T-given task, T_n - part tasks, S_n - their solutions
/The rest of symbols - see Fig. 2/

218

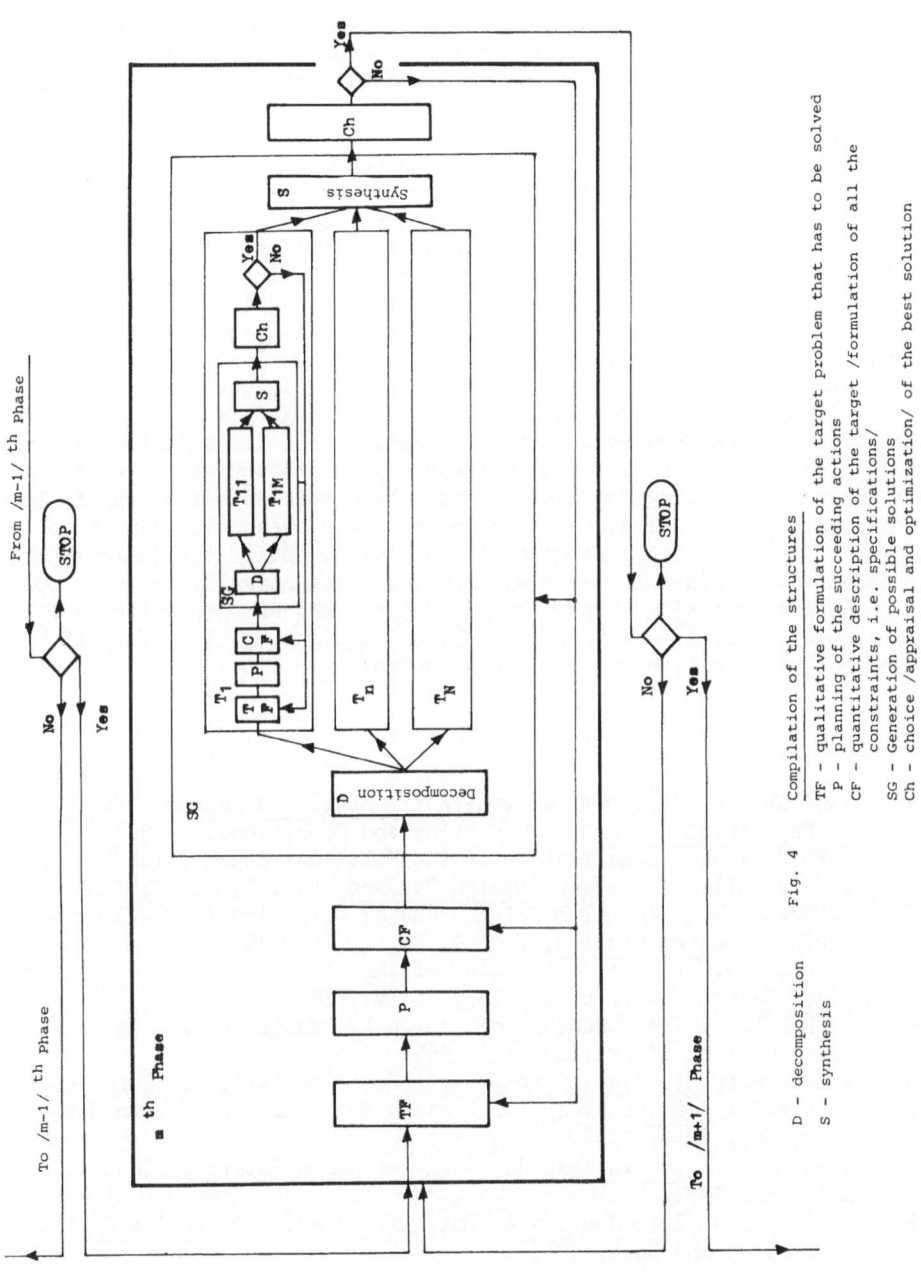

Fig. 4   Compilation of the structures

D – decomposition
S – synthesis

TF – qualitative formulation of the target problem that has to be solved
P – planning of the succeeding actions
CF – quantitative description of the target /formulation of all the
     constraints, i.e. specifications/
SG – Generation of possible solutions
Ch – choice /appraisal and optimization/ of the best solution

219

4. RECAPITULATION

The three models are of an idealised character. Each of them is conceived in accordance with a different but precisely defined aspect and describe three different approaches to the design process. To compare and to contrast them, let examine the Fig. 4, where they are presented in superposition.

An actual design process almost always comprises a complicated sequence of activities. The structure of the process vary from design to design according to the following: /i/ the type of design target /the degree of innovativeness, for example/, /ii/ the character of the design team involved and the qualifications of individual designers, as well as the operating circumstances, /iii/ the magnitude or amount of the output or production, /iv/ the constraints in resources on the design, i.e. time and money.

To conclude, let us insist that it is absolutely essential to structuralize the design process because of its complexity and because of the following features which characterise it: /i/ it comprises various activities, for which different methods may be appropriate, /ii/ logic demands that foregoing activity must be completed before the following activity is started, for example, solution evaluation cannot be started until solution generation is completed, /iii/ the design task is usually visualised in terms of many variables normally too many to be handled in one single task, /iv/ design tasks are generally vast and complex; they cannot be handled by one designer particularly if he is operating intuitively and without control.

REFERENCES

1   ENGLISH J.M. /Editor/: Cost-Effectiveness. The Economic Evaluation of Engineered Systems. John Wiley and Sons, Inc., 1968.
2   TARNOWSKI W.: Formalization of the Multi-Attribute Value System in Probabilistic Terms. Design Studies, Vol. 2, No. 1, Jan. 1981.
3   TARNOWSKI W.: General Model and Choice Criterion in Engineering Design. Design Studies, Vol. 1, No. 1, July 1979.
4   AMKREUTZ J.H.: Cybernetic Model of the Design Process. Computer Aided Design, Vol. 8, ss. 187, July 1976.
5   ARCHER L.B.: The Structure of Design Processes. /Ph.D. Thesis/, Royal College of Art, London, 1968.
6   ASIMOW M.: Introduction to Design. Prentice Hall, New York 1962.
7   HALL A.D.: A Methodology for Systems Engineering. D. Van Nostrand Co., Inc., 1962.
8   JONES J.Ch.: Design Methods. Seeds of Human Futures. John Wiley and Sons, 1973.
9   KRICK E.: An Introduction to Engineering and Engineering Design. John Wiley and Sons, 1969.

PROCEDURAL BUILDING BLOCKS:
THE INTERFACE BETWEEN ARGUMENTATIVE DESIGN DISCOURSE
AND FORMAL EVALUATION PROCEDURES FOR DESIGN

Thorbjoern Mann, Ph.D.
School of Architecture
Florida Agricultural and Mechanical University
Tallahassee, Florida 32307
U.S.A.

ABSTRACT. The concept of 'procedural building block' is proposed to denote small scale procedural steps within the design process, that can be combined in various ways to form different design approaches. Using this concept and suggesting that useful connections can be made between facets of the design process that have mostly been considered separate phases, the paper explores the interface between design argumentation, formalized evaluation procedures, and design decision-making. It is shown how results from one such facet can serve as input for others. This is exemplified with the development of a procedure for design decision-making by systematic argument evaluation. Potential applications of the procedure and its underlying concepts in planning and design practice and the development of planning support information systems are discussed.

1. INTRODUCTION

The following study was triggered by two observations made in the process of trying to develop workable procedures and methods for design decision-making based on systematic argument assessment: The first is that many or most procedural/methodological recommendations for design and planning seem to construct consistent conceptual frames of reference which tend to become exclusive of other concepts and ways of viewing the design process. To the extent they do this (becoming exclusive) they encounter overt or covert resistance from users who seem intent on maintaining some control over how they approach design problems. The other is that there are strong correspondence relationships between the constituent elements in different approaches. It seems plausible to take a closer look at these corresponding elements, to see if they might provide opportunities for being combined into a greater variety of design approaches, or for mutual enrichment from one approach to another.

In the following, two such aspects of the design process are examined for potential interface points: systematic, formal evaluation procedures, and a view that sees the design activity as an argumentative process. (Kunz, Rittel 1970; Rittel 1980). Both have been recommended as vehicles for decision-making in design and planning. While the former has been the subject of much work aiming at making it more systematic, explicit, and transparent not much attention has been given in the design methods literature to similar efforts for the output of design discussions and debate. This is somewhat surprising since decision-making in parliamentary settings is by far the more popular and widespread custom. Thus, a parallel objective of the study is to carry this task a little further.

R. Trappl (ed.), Cybernetics and Systems '86, 221–228.
© 1986 by D. Reidel Publishing Company.

2. PROCEDURAL BUILDING BLOCKS IN THE DESIGN PROCESS

In the literature of what Rittel (1972) calls the "first generation" design methods and systems approach, it was customary to distinguish various types of activities within the design or planning process. These were then taken as the basis for specifying a well-ordered sequence of steps and recommended as the proper design procedure. Examples are: 'stating the problem', 'explaining the problem', 'gathering information', 'generating alternative solutions', 'evaluating the solutions', etc. Each such activity is further broken down into constituent steps which may vary with the particular method or technique discussed.

Rittel argued convincingly that such approaches are not very meaningful, and that the actual design process is a much more fine-grain one, unsystematically alternating between, for example, variety-generating and variety-reducing activities. Nevertheless, the distinctions can be useful for the discussion of problems in design as long as certain points are kept in mind:

- Almost any such activity type can be a legitimate starting point for the design effort;
- The subsequent efforts should not be forced into a procedural straitjacket - especially not with respect to the sequential ordering of the activities;
- Assumptions regarding superior effectiveness of one approach or sequence over another should not be allowed to predetermine the actual process;
- Instead, the role of methodology should be that of making participants in the design or planning process (not all of which are assumed to be experts) aware of procedural options available to them, and of supporting the participants in their selection and use;
- Specifically, efforts should be made to facilitate transitions between various phases and techniques, so as to enhance the work in one phase or approach with results from others.

The concept of 'procedural building block' here should be understood as a constituent activity of designing, or several such activities organized into (partial) procedures for specific purposes within the design process. These building blocks of design or planning procedures use certain forms of information as inputs, and in turn produce information or decisions as outputs. Whereas design procedures usually specify only one sequence of input-output coupling, it is suggested here that many different combinations can be formed, leading to a multitude of possible designs for the overall design or planning process.

In addition to providing a wider range of choice for modifying the design process according to circumstances and user preferences, such combinations can also prove beneficial in terms of improving the power of the individual approaches. In the following, the possibilities of interfacing the argumentative model of design, or specifically its argument assessment extensions as discussed in Mann (1977, 1980) with formal evaluation procedures such as the one suggested by A. Musso and H. Rittel (1969), are discussed as an example.

3. FORMAL EVALUATION (OBJECTIFICATION) PROCEDURES IN DESIGN

To facilitate the discussion of some specific examples of procedural building blocks and their relations, certain assumptions concerning vocabulary and procedures will be made. These should be seen as convenient references to proposals made elsewhere and not as claims to predominant or exclusive validity.

It is assumed that somewhere in the problem-solving effort, an 'evaluation system' (in the sense e.g of Musso and Rittel), has been established, with the following features:

- There is a set of evaluation aspects (ASP) subaspects, sub-sub-aspects etc. according to which participants in the process could evaluate proposed solutions. The aspects can be ordered into a tree-like structure which will be referred to as ASPTREE.
- At least for some aspects or subaspects, participants can specify measures of performance or

criteria (CRIT) which permit (objective) measurement of the extent to which a given solution satisfies a specific aspect.
- A judgment scale has been specified for expressing (subjective) judgments js about the merit or
  goodness of proposed solutions (and the meaning of each of its values agreed upon).
- The evaluators can specify weights aspw of relative importance of aspects and subaspects etc.,
  with the usual condition that for all n aspects on each level of the aspect tree,

$$0 < aspw(i) < 1.0 \quad \text{and} \quad \sum_{i=1,2...}^{n} aspw(i) = 1.0$$

(Ref. the Churchman-Ackoff Approximate Measure of Value, Ackoff 1961).
- For those aspects where a criterion has been established, participants can specify through a graph
  or function, ('criterion function' CF) how their judgment scores will depend on the values of the
  criterion.
- 'Aggregation functions' AF have been agreed upon which specify how partial judgments js(ij) on a
  lower level of the tree will collectively determine the judgment score at the next higher level, and
  ultimately how all partial judgments determine the overall judgment JS(j) for a given solution j.
- Finally, the participants may specify by means of a 'group aggregation function' (GAF) how a set of
  individual overall judgments JS(jk) for solution j and participant k will determine the overall
  group judgment GJS(j) for solution j.

4. THE ARGUMENTATIVE DESIGN DISCOURSE AND SYSTEMATIC ARGUMENT ASSESSMENT

It will also be assumed that the planning process is carried out in such a way as to facilitate the
identification and analysis of various issues, positions, and arguments. Issues are controversial
questions about which participants adopt differing positions. They then seek to support these
positions POS by offering arguments ARG and answers. Distinctions are made between 'factual'
issues (F-issues), 'deontic' issues (D-issues), 'instrumental' issues (I-issues), and 'explanatory'
issues (E-issues). Most important here are the D-issues. Design problems can be expressed as one or
several such issues: "should a state of affairs x be the case?" or should proposal x be implemented?".
Three positions can be adopted: 'YES' (x ought to be), 'NO' (x ought not to be), and 'Inadequate
Question' or IQ (for 'the issue as stated does not address the problem in an adequate way'; 'wrong
question').
    A main advantage of the argumentative model of design is that it seems more in tune with this
popular form of planning decision-making - but it has not yet produced a practical procedure by
means of which decisions can be based on a more systematic analysis and assessment of the arguments
proposed. The aim of any such process can be said to be that producing some judgment relative to the
three positions: what is the degree of support lent to the positions by the arguments brought up in
their favor? Traditionally, parliamentary bodies short-cut this question by means of voting and
making the decision based on the ratio of YES and NO votes. A first outline of such a procedure is
described in Mann (1977, 1980). It will be the basis of the following.

Most design arguments can be transcribed into the following 'standard design argument' pattern:

(a) x should be (done, implemented....) because   formalized: D(x) because
(b) (if x is implemented) x will lead to (is instrumental to) y   F(x INSTR y) and
(c) y ought to be   D(y)

Variations and refinements include patterns with negated claims (formalized by a prefix of N to the
respective part of the statement), and making explicit various unspoken claims and assumptions which
may influence how a decision-maker will assess the argument - for example the conditions c under

223

which the instrumental premiss holds or under which the inference rule R (argument pattern) itself is applicable, or the assumptions regarding whether x or y are already the case.

Evaluation of the arguments begins with assessment of the argument components or premisses. In contrast to calculi of formal logic, where analysis focuses on the implications of the a c t u a l truth-values of factual premisses (and where therefore binary values are adequate, since a state of affairs is either the case or not) the assessment of argument merit should be done in terms of the d e g r e e of certainty or better: degree of p l a u s i b i l i t y a decision-maker is willing to assign to a proposed claim. The suggested scale ranges from +1 ('couldn't be more plausible', or 'virtually certain'; for deontic claims: 'entirely desirable') to -1 ('couldn't be more implausible', 'virtually certain that the claim is not true'; resp. 'entirely undesirable'); the mid-point of zero is interpreted as 'don't know' or 'can't make up my mind'.

These plausibility judgments should not be confused with (in the case of deontic claims) weights of relative importance which will be discussed below. They express, as it were, the balance between the pro's and con's for each claim in the evaluator's mind.

The next task consists of deriving some measure of plausibility for the entire argument as a function of the assigned plausibilities of its premisses. As discussed in Mann (1977) this can be a complex task esp. for combinations of negative plausibility assessments; the surface of the 'argument plausibility function' APF is not necessarily smooth. However, as long as the plausibilities of premisses including that for the applicability of the inference pattern are all on the positive side (between zero and +1) two kinds of functions can be used which have good intuitive interpretation:

APF1: $pl(arg(j)) = MIN \{ pl(premiss\ i)\}$ (1)
for all i premisses including $pl(R)$, or:

APF2: $pl(arg(j)) = PROD \{pl(premiss\ i)\}$ (2)
(the plausibility of argument j is equal to the product of the assigned
plausibility values of all premisses i of argument j).

For the 'Standard Design Argument' SDA, the corresponding argument plausibility functions would be:

APF1(SDA): $pl(arg(j)) = MIN \{pl(F(xINSTRy)), pl(Dy)\}$ (3a)

or, in the expanded version including the conditions and inference rule:

$pl(arg(j)) = MIN\{pl(F(xINSTRy)/c), pl(Fc), pl(Dy), pl(FNx), pl(FNy), pl(R(SDA))\}$ (3b)

and

APF2(SDA): $pl(arg(j)) = pl(F(xINSTRy)) * pl(Dy)$ (4a)

respectively:

$pl(arg(j)) = pl(F(xINSTRy)/c) * pl(Fc) * pl(Dy) * pl(FNx) * pl(FNy) * pl(R(SDA))$ (4b)

Given a set of arguments for and against a design proposal, the next question concerns the development of a measure of position plausibility, which should be expressed as a function of the individual argument plausibilities and of the degree of importance of the deontic premisses in the arguments. Thus, it is first necessary to suggest an 'argument weight function', e.g.:

AWF: $w(arg(j)) = w(y,j) * pl(arg(j))$ (5)

Then, a reasonable first approximation of a 'position plausibility function' POSPLF might be:

$$\text{POSPLF: } pl(pos) = \underset{j=1,2..}{\overset{n}{S\,U\,M}} (w(arg(j))) \tag{6}$$

This expresses the plausibility of the 'YES' position of the issue whether a design proposal should be adopted for implementation. Note that this measure cannot be used for the IQ position since typically, the arguments for this position tend to be suggestions for other issues that should be discussed instead.

A procedure for systematic argument assessment following the above concepts is described in Mann (1977).

5. INTERFACE POINTS BETWEEN THE ARGUMENTATIVE PROCESS AND FORMAL EVALUATION

5.1. Matching argument deontics against evaluation aspects: generating new arguments and aspects

There is a close correspondence between evaluation aspects established for the evaluation of proposed solutions to a design problem, and the deontic premisses of arguments for and against those proposals. Therefore, the tree of evaluation aspects ASPTREE and the list of deontics DLIST compiled from the set of arguments can be used as (partial) mutual checks for 'completeness'. More specifically: if a deontic Dy has been used in an argument about a proposed solution, the question might be raised whether a corresponding aspect (e.g. extent to which a solution achieves y) should not also be included in the aspect tree. Conversely, any evaluation aspect in ASPTREE can be seen as a source for a potential deontic premiss to be used in arguments for or against solution proposals. Whether completeness of the aspect tree or the argument set is really needed depends on the intended basis for making the decision: if the decision is to be based on the results of a formal evaluation, the aspect set should be complete but it is not necessary to generate all potential arguments from the aspects. If the decision is to be based on the result of argument assessment or even mere voting following debate, completeness of the argument set becomes more important.

This correspondence between aspects and argument deontics may seem a matter of course. However, experience with such procedures suggests that in practice, there will be considerable differences between the concerns expressed in arguments and those framed as evaluation aspects. The latter tend to focus more on "stock" issues, such as the criteria listed by Vitruvius under only three respectively five headings: 'durability, convenience, and beauty' (Book I ch. II) or the principles of architecture 'Order, Arrangement, Eurythmy, Symmetry, Propriety, and Economy' (Book I, ch. III) to name only one of the most ancient examples. By contrast, the concerns expressed in arguments tend to be more specific, fine-grain, personalized. But especially if the arguments are generated in a verbal debate, many potentially helpful and worthwhile arguments will not be made for fear of boring the audience. Also, speakers seeking to convince others will select arguments based on deontics they assume to be held by the audience, and avoid those they suspect to be controversial (shared by some and opposed by others). That is, the arguments offered in a debate are systematically incomplete.

5.2. Matching weights of relative importance assigned to evaluation aspects and argument deontics.

The correspondence between argument deontics and evaluation aspects further suggests the possibility of mutual adjustment of the weights of relative importance assigned to each. In general, it will be difficult to arrive at a consistent weighting in DLIST only - the better structure and organization of ASPTREE can be of considerable help. Asssuming that both have been checked and adjusted for completeness, the weights assigned to the aspects in ASPTREE can be used directly for the deontics in the arguments.

Some modification of the argument set may become necessary as a result of this. For example, different arguments may contain deontics which in ASPTREE can be seen to belong to the same 'branch' while this is not at all evident in the argument set. Thus, in the aggregation of pl(pos) as suggested above, the deontics (and arguments) might be "counted twice" unless a provision is adopted to include only arguments based on deontics at the most detailed level of the tree, - and to generate all the corresponding arguments instead of the one referring to the aspect located "higher up" in the tree.

Not all unresolved questions that should be raised in connection with the task of weighting can be discussed here. For example, refer to Grant (1974, 1982); or to Mann (1980) for problems arising from the occurrence of general moral or ethical principles (as opposed to the usually purpose-oriented aspects) in arguments.

5.3. Modifying evaluation scores as a function of argument plausibility.

The aggregation functions of formal evaluation systems treat the judgment scores to be aggregated as if they were all a matter of certainty. In reality, - whether they are terminal 'offhand' (spontaneous) judgments, or taken from a criterion function where the value of the criterion (performance measure) has been calculated by mathematical model - they are all judgments, and as such should be subject to plausibility assessment. More specifically, a judgment score for solution S, based on a criterion c, is the expression of an assessment of the instrumental premiss that 'S will achieve performance level v on criterion c'. This realization suggests that if plausibility assessments of instrumental premisses have been performed somewhere in the process, these pl-values should be used to qualify or modify the judgment 'goodness/badness' scores js of the evaluation system.

This task presents some difficulties arising especially from the question of the proper inter-pretation of negative pl-assessments. However, as long as all pl-values are on the positive side of the proposed scale, one might consider a 'judgment-plausibility adjustment function' JPAF consisting of a simple reduction of the judgment score equivalent to the pl-level of the premiss- for example;

$$\text{JPAF:} \quad js(\text{adjusted}) = js(\text{unadjusted}) * pl(FxINSTRy) \tag{7}$$

6. A DESIGN DECISION-MAKING PROCEDURE BASED ON ARGUMENT ASSESSMENT WITH EVALUATION INTERFACE

The preceding considerations can be applied to practical tasks of design decision-making. This need not lead to excessive complexity of the process, even when refinements such as successive rounds of assessment, feedback, and reassessment (applying principles first suggested in the 'Delphi Method' - Helmer 1966) are added. Figure 1 shows the flow diagram for such a procedure. Its steps are:
- Design proposals are put forward
- Arguments for and against are supplied by concerned or interested parties. To avoid spending much time in meetings, this can be done by circulating folders with argument sheets; arguments are listed in consecutive order. The list should be circulated until all parties have had the opportunity of reacting to all proposed arguments.
- An evaluation aspect tree ASPTREE is developed (in trad. 'top-down' fashion)
- The arguments are analyzed to identify deontics; these are compiled in DLIST
- A match of DLIST and ASPTREE is performed to identify deontics in ASPTREE, these are added to DLIST, aspects from deontics are added to ASPTREE
- DLIST and ASPTREE are edited, with (successive rounds of) feedback to ensure participant consent to revised wording
- Weights of relative importance are assigned to deontics in DLIST and aspects in ASPTR
- A match of weights of corresponding deontics/ aspects in DLIST and ASPTREE is carried out

- Plausibility values are assigned to the instrumental premiss
- If necessary, the premiss is discussed as successor issue before assigning the pl-value
- Applying APF and AWF, each argument's plausibility and argument weight are calculated
- Applying POSPLF, the plausibility (for the 'YES' position) is calculated
- Distribution of plausibility values (for pl(pos) and pl(FxINSTRy) is established, circulated
- Plausibilities are reassessed and re-aggregated
- Results are presented for decision. The group may now, for example, decide by voting according to established procedures, or use the pl(pos) results in lieu of votes (if negative, vote 'NO', if positive, vote 'YES', if zero or close to zero, abstain), or prepare some aggregated group measure of pl(pos).

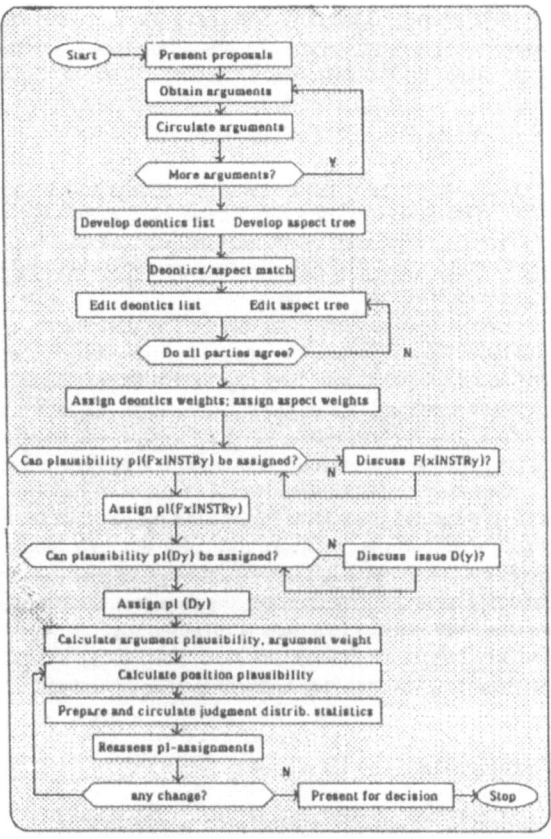

Figure 1
Procedure for design decision-making by systematic argument assessment

7. CONCLUSION

7.1 Possible applications

While the objectives of the study have by and large been met, the effort has not been exhaustive, nor have all questions and controversies been resolved. Quite the contrary: a number of new problems have been encountered which deserve further attention. The relevance of such work can be seen more clearly in the context of possible applications, which will therefore be outlined first.

The straightforward application of the concepts presented above in form of design decision-making procedures is only one possibility. The formalization introduced in the treatment of argument analysis also opens up opportunities in the area of computerized planning support information systems that can interact more actively with users. For example, lists af argument components from actual arguments can be compiled and manipulated by the computer so as to generate new arguments, assess the impact (in terms of plausibility) of new information, suggest possible emerging controversies, etc.

It is interesting to note that the kind of program suggested has many of the features of 'artificial intelligence' systems, yet is significantly different in one crucial aspect. AI systems seek to support human decision-making by eliminating human frailties such as poor memory and especially flawed reasoning: they will aim at logical consistency and valid inferences based on 'true' data. By contrast, the kind of system that seems to emerge from the above ideas not only is tolerant of contradiction and inconclusiveness – it makes it clear that pursuit of consistency and correctness in the data base is futile, even counterproductive (for the purposes of supporting design and planning). The essence of the problems i s contradiction, difference of opinion, controversy.

7.2 Remaining problems; suggestions for further work

One main concern with regard to practical application is that of testing the proposed procedure so as to gain sufficient experience with its use, before applying it in projects of significant scope and consequence. So far, only small-scale test in classroom settings have been carried out. The same applies to the issue of computerized support of the process. No actual programs for the indicated purposes have yet been developed.

Some nagging technical and theoretical questiona demand more satisfactory resolution. The most pressing of these is further development of the position plausibility function; at the current stage, it must be considered a crude first approximation only. This is related to other general issues – such as the proper treatment of 'background knowledge' against which data looking innocuous in isolation may become explosively important, (or vice versa), or the issue of weighting with regard to deontics which are not purpose-oriented but based on general moral or ethical principles (Mann 1980).

On a more practical level, it would seem necessary to conduct a number of experiments for various aspects of procedures such as the one outlined above, aimed at working out such specifics as format for documentation, procedural rules and their required level of formalization, etc. Another area is the development and analysis of a systematic inventory of argument patterns in design and planning discourse. Concurrently, the development of computer programs for the documentation, retrieval, and analysis functions of planning support information systems based on the above ideas should be carried on. Finally, the work of exploring interface points between different facets of the design process that was begun here should be continued.

8. REFERENCES

Ackoff, R. L.:*Scientific Method*, Wiley, New York 1961
Grant, Donald P.:'The Problem of Weighting', *DMG-DRS JOURNAL: DESIGN RESEARCH AND METHODS*, Vol. 8 No. 3, 1974.
- *Design By Objectives*, (Multiple Objective Design Analysis and Evaluation in Architectural, Environmental, and Product Design), The Design Methods Group, San Luis Obispo, California 1982.
Helmer, Olaf:*Social Technology*, Basic Books, New York 1966.
Mann, Thorbjoern:*Argument For Design Decisions*, Dissertation, University of California, Berkeley, 1977.
- 'Some Limitations of the Argumentative Model of Design', in *DESIGN METHODS AND THEORIES*, VOL. 14, No. 1, 1980.
Musso, Arne, and H. Rittel: 'Ueber das Messen der Guete von Gebaeuden' in: *ARBEITSBERICHTE ZUR PLANUNGSMETHODIK* No. 1, Institut fuer Grundlagen der Modernen Architektur (eds.), Karl Kraemer, Stuttgart 1969.
Rittel, Horst W.J.:On The Planning Crisis - Systems Analysis of the First and Second Generation', *BEDRIFTSOEKONOMEN*, No. 8, 1972.
- APIS - A Concept for an Argumentative Planning Information System' Working paper No. 324, Institute of Urban and Regional Development, University of California, Berkeley, Calif. 1980.
Vitruvius Pollio, Marcus: *The Ten Books of Architecture* (transl. M.H. Morgan) Dover, New York 1960.

A FRAMEWORK FOR THE DESIGN OF PROBLEM—SOLVING METHODOLOGIES

P. Keys
Department of Management Systems and Sciences
University of Hull
Hull
HU6 7RX
United Kingdom

ABSTRACT. A framework which can act as a basis for the design of systems—based problem—solving methodologies is presented. The framework is developed from a consideration of difficulties which face problem—solvers in dealing with problem—situations. Two existing methodologies are examined in the context of the proposed framework to illustrate its use in analysis.

1. INTRODUCTION

A number of problem—solving methodologies which involve the use of systems concepts have recently appeared. The approaches of Ackoff (1), Beer (2,3), Churchman (4,5), and Checkland (6) supplement the longer established methodologies embraced by Operational Research (7), systems engineering (8) and systems analysis (9). The scope of this range of methodologies and their application indicates the potential of the systems approach to aid problem—solvers. In order to realise this potential it is necessary to learn from the contributions noted above. It is particularly important to understand how the various strands of systems thinking contribute to the problem—solving process. This knowledge can then be used to aid either the design of novel problem—solving methodologies or the modification of those already in existence.
   In this paper some issues in the design of systems—based problem—solving methodologies are addressed. The intention is to focus attention on a framework within which various problem—solving methodologies can be set. The framework is used to explain the structure of two existing methodologies.

R. Trappl (ed.), Cybernetics and Systems '86, 229–236.
© 1986 by D. Reidel Publishing Company.

The paper consists of four main parts. An initial section contains a formal description of a problem-context. This conceptualisation of the situation where problem-solving is carried out underpins the framework to be developed. Three tasks which problem-solvers must accomplish are then presented in the second section. Third, the framework for methodology design is presented. Finally, the framework is used to provide a basis to discuss the structure of two existing methodologies.

2. PROBLEM-CONTEXTS: A FORMAL DESCRIPTION

Jackson and Keys (10) have suggested that a useful mechanism for discussing the strengths of various problem-solving methodologies is provided by the notion of a problem-context. Use of this has served to identify significant differences in problem types and the methodologies appropriate to them. Here, a formal statement of the nature of a problem-context is given and is used as a basis for the following discussion.

A problem-context consists of three elements which are necessary in order that a problem-solving methodology may be used. The first is a set of people who can both perceive a situation to be problematic and take action to remedy that situation. Such people are referred to as decision- makers. It is not necessary that all decision-makers identify a situation as problematic. It is likely that what is problematic for some will be satisfactory for others. The set of decision-makers will be denoted by {Di} where D_i is the i'th decision-maker.

The second element of a problem-context is a system of interest. This may take on a different appearance to each of the decision-makers. Thus to refer to the system of interest is invalid. Systems of interest should be defined with respect to particular decision-makers.

The system of interest as perceived by D_i at time t will be denoted by $S_i(t)$. That system is problematic for D_i if it differs from a desired system by a significant amount. The system desired by D_i at time t will be denoted by $S_i'(t)$. A decision-maker measures the amount of difference by reference to a measure of utility, U_i. A problematic system will, by definition, have $U_i(S_i'(t)) - U_i(S_i(t)) > \varepsilon$ for ε some small amount. It is possible for a system to be problematic for a decision-maker if a desired system $S_i'(t)$ is unknown. This arises if a decision-maker has an expectation of the utility to be derived from the system and if that is not being met. Then the decision-maker requires an increase in the utility received and requires that a new system is created which provides this.

The third element required in order that a problem-solving methodology can be used is the problem-solver(s) themselves. Problem-solvers are those persons who aid decision-makers to determine the action to be taken. It is the problem-solvers who use a methodology. This methodology takes as input the information regarding the decision-makers and their perceived systems of interest and produces as output recommendations for action. These recommendations will be couched in terms of changes in the perceived systems of interest. The changes based upon the system of interest of D_i and which take place between time t and time t+ δ will be denoted by S_i $(t,t+\delta)$. Only one set of changes may be implemented and these may or may not correspond to those based upon a particular view of the problem. The implemented changes result from considering the set of decision-makers and their individual contributions to the problem-solving process. The implemented changes cause the nature of the system to alter and so allow the decision-makers to revise their perception of the problem-situation. This changed perception may generate a further problem-situation to be overcome. The methodology design process involves specifying the form of a methodology in order that appropriate changes in the system can be identified and the effect of these changes recognised.

It is possible that the decision-makers, individually or collectively, identify the changes to be made for themselves. In such a situation they are acting in the dual role of decision-maker and problem-solver and use a methodology on themselves.

In the next section some difficulties which a problem-solver may face when attempting to design a methodology are considered. These suggest certain aspects of a methodology which must be considered in the design process.

3. PROBLEMS FOR PROBLEM-SOLVERS

Three particular types of difficulty are faced by a problem-solver when attempting to develop a methodology. The means of overcoming each of these difficulties leads to one component of that methodology and their combination leads to an overall design for the methodology.

The first difficulty to be faced is that posed by the presence of several decision-makers who may each have their own perception of the problem. The problem-solver has to decide whether to serve one, several or all of the relevant decision-makers. Such a decision may be governed by the nature of problem or by the way in which the problem-solver is related to the decision-makers. The result of this decision will influence the methodology to be used but the problem-solving methodology cannot directly influence this decision. Consequently this important issue will not be further considered here.

Given that the set of decision-makers is defined the problem-solver must identify how to deal with the fact that rather than one a set of systems of interest, desired systems, utilities and decision-makers are involved. The problem-solver could choose to deal with each decision-maker and their appropriate attributes separately and to combine the results of the analysis after individual recommendations have been achieved. Alternatively, the problem-solver could choose to bring together the individuals first to agree on a statement of the problem and then to form recommended actions. Either of these courses of action are able to bring about satisfactory conclusions provided the individual decision-makers are prepared to take part in a process of debate and exchange of views. If this is not so and a more antagonistic stance is taken by the decision-makers then the difference in views cannot be fully overcome and the result of the problem-solving process will not be as satisfactory.

After the problem-solver has considered this difficulty a second
one appears which is how to determine what action it is appropriate
to recommend. This issue arises if either of the above means of
dealing with multiple decision-makers is adopted. Action needs to be
recommended to the set of decision-makers on the basis of their
individual perceptions of the problem or on their agreed common view
of the problem.

In order that this difficulty is resolved the problem-solver needs
to have a means of evaluating the effects of changes to the system.
If a desired system is known there may be several ways of achieving
it and the most preferable of these should be identified. If an
increase in utility is required then the increases associated with
various changes need to be specified so that a choice can be made on
what action to take. The key to this difficulty is the representation
chosen to model the system of interest. Various modelling tools are
available which range from quantitative models, prevalent in
operational research, to qualitative models, used by Checkland (6) for
example. A suitable model will allow a problem-solver to understand
the nature of the situation and to use this understanding to generate
effective courses of action. The understanding gained by the problem-
solver should also be able to be passed on to the decision-makers in
order that they may benefit from the modelling exercise.

Once recommendations are made and action taken the third
difficulty appears which is that of feedback. It is essential that
some form of feedback is initiated so that the effect of action can be
monitored and if necessary subsequent action taken. Further action will
be necessary if the expected effects of action do not result. The
problem-solver must allow the decision-makers to compare the effects
with their expectations individually. If this is done by a subset of
the decision-makers or by them as a group then some of the richness
which is present by virtue of the range of separate perceptions of the
problem will be lost.

The comparison of effect and expectations may indicate further
action is necessary for two important reasons. First, the model used
to generate the recommended actions may be inaccurate. This could be
due to the model being poorly defined in which case it may be
improved. More likely is the case where the complexity of the real
world makes a good model difficult if not impossible to specify.

Secondly, the problem-solving process may have caused decision-makers
to change their views of the system and its objectives. Events
outside the control of the problem-solver may have a similar effect.
Then the effect of the changes made to the system will be aimed to
achieve a target which has altered and so the changes become
inappropriate and need modification.

Each of these three difficulties has received attention in various
contexts. The problem of the relationship between consultants and
clients is considered, for example, by Churchman and Schainblatt (11)
and by Eden and Sims (12). Model design and the difficulties of
constructing models of complex systems are discussed by Vemuri (13) for
example. The importance of monitoring the results of decisions made
regarding action have been emphasised in operational research and

systems engineering for many years. In the next section a framework for describing a problem-solving methodology is presented in which all of these issues receive attention.

4. FRAMEWORK FOR METHODOLOGY DESIGN

In this section a methodology for problem-solving is described as consisting of three components. Each component corresponds to a means of overcoming one of the difficulties noted above.

The first difficulty to be considered is that posed by the presence of several decision-makers. Two means of overcoming this were outlined above. The first method is to consider each decision-maker's perception of the problem separately then attempt to reach a concensus over the set of recommendations. A second method is to achieve agreement over the nature of the problem first and then to determine appropriate action. To overcome this a process which does not constrain the approach to be adopted more than necessary is required.

A process E is required which engineers agreement between decision-makers over various factors. This process can be generally defined as;

$$E(\{S_i(t)\}, \{S_i'(t)\}, \{U_i\}, \{\Delta S_i(t, t+\delta)\})$$
$$= (S(t), S'(t), U, \Delta S(t, t+\delta)) \qquad (1)$$

The subscript i denotes the attribute of decision-maker D_i and those factors with no subscript denote the attribute which is agreed upon by all decision-makers. It is not necessary for all of the factors to be present in order that the process may function. What is necessary is that no factors may appear as an output of the process unless a suitable set appears as an input. If a set is input which has no corresponding output then no agreement can be reached upon this factor but the information may be used to reach agreement on other factors.

The second difficulty to be considered is that of determining appropriate action. This can be done either for each individual decision-maker or for the agreed view of all decision-makers. The process, D, which overcomes this difficulty can be defined, in two ways to reflect this,

$$D(\{S_i(t)\}, \{S_i'(t)\}, \{U_i\} = (\{\Delta S_i(t, t+\delta)\}) \qquad (2)$$

$$D(S(t), S(t), U) = (\Delta S(t, t+\delta)) \qquad (3)$$

In both cases the form of D is the same but the arguments are changed to indicate whether many or one set of views are being considered. The changes which are implemented are those agreed upon by the decision-makers and which are denoted by $S(t, t+\delta)$.

The third difficulty facing problem-solvers is the need to allow for feedback on the effects of the action taken. The feedback allows adaptation and learning to take place by the decision-makers. The consequence of the feedback process is that decision-makers change their

233

perception of the problem-situation as a result of the effect of the changes on the system as they perceive it. Feedback is therefore a process which acts on individual decision-makers. The process, F, can be defined as,

$$F((S_i(t),S_i^\bullet(t)), \Delta S(t,t+ \delta))=(S_i(t+\delta),S_i^\bullet(t+\delta)) \qquad (4)$$

The task facing the problem-solver is to ensure that the feedback process is effective. This requires that the learning resulting from the process is made use of and that the decision-makers are encouraged to make constructive use of the new knowledge. It is also necessary for problem-solvers to ensure that any modifications to the actions taken are made.

These three components of problem-solving methodologies may be combined in a variety of ways. The only constraint upon their combination is that they yield an overall methodology which is satisfactory. A satisfactory methodology is one which has as inputs the views of the decision-makers at the start of the process and which produces a sequence of actions with which the decision-makers are content. In terms of the logic of the methodology the three processes E,D,F, must be combined to yield a process, M, such that,

$$M(\{S_i(t)\}, \{S_i^\bullet(t)\{,\{U_i\}\})=(\Delta S(t,t+\delta), \Delta S(t+\delta,t+2\delta),...) \qquad (5)$$

The methodology design problem is to choose suitable forms for E,D and F for a given problem. In the next section it is shown how two existing methodologies can be explained according to the structure of this framework.

5. DESIGNING METHODOLOGIES: TWO EXAMPLES

To provide some empirical support for the above framework it is necessary to illustrate the applicability of the proposed approach. Here this will be done by discussing how two existing methodologies fit into the above framework.

The first methodology to be considered is that provided by classical operational research. Various attempts have been made to describe this process and that used here is one of the earliest, that of Churchman et.al (7). Six phases are recognised to exist, formulate the problem, construct a mathematical model to represent the system under study, derive a solution from the model, test the model and the solution derived from it, establish controls over the solution and put the solution to work through implementation.

Each of the three components of a methodology may now be examined in the content of this approach. First, there is no process corresponding to E. Hence it is assumed by a user of this approach that no agreement is required, presumably because either no disagreement is recognised between decision-makers or only one decision-maker is being served. Second, the process $\hat{D}$ is achieved by use of mathematical models of the system of interest. This implies that the system is capable of being adequately represented by means of a quantitative approach. Third, there is no formal role specified for feedback once changes have been implemented. There is room for altering the model of the system if this proves inadequate on being tested. However, the assumption is made that once changes have been made there is little need to learn from their impact and to adapt on the basis of this learning.

Bringing these points together the overall methodology, M, becomes a single process, D. Thus M is defined as,

$$D(S(t), \dot{S}(t), U) = \Delta S(t, t+\delta) \tag{6}$$

The second methodology to be considered in terms of the above framework is Checkland's soft-systems methodology (6). This methodology is constructed to overcome the limitations of the 'hard' systems approaches of which classical operational research is one example. Seven stages comprise the methodology. In stages 1 and 2 the problem-situation is expressed by building a rich picture of the problem-situation. In stage 3 the relevant systems are named by constructing root definitions. Following this in stage 4 conceptual models are made and tested on the basis of the root definitions. These conceptual models are qualitative rather than quantitative in character. The conceptual models are compared with reality in stage 5. Then in stage 6 these comparisons are used to generate a discussion between those involved regarding what feasible and desirable changes are possible. The final phase, stage 7, sees action taken to accomplish these changes. This leads to a new statement of the situation which can be considered by further use of the methodology.

This methodology is more complex than that of classical operational research. Consequently, it involves elements of each of the three processes. First, agreement is reached over what changes are to be made. It is not part of the approach to reach agreement over what the problem is although this may be a valuable by-product. The methodology therefore involves as part of it,

$$E(\{S_i(t)\}, \{S_i'(t)\}, \{U_i\}, \{\Delta S_i(t, t+\delta)\}) = \Delta S(t, t+\delta) \tag{7}$$

The changes $\Delta S_i (t, t+\delta)$ must be the result of taking each individual perception of the problem, the root definitions and conceptual models, and establishing the consequences of these individually. Thus the process D is given by,

$$D(S_i(t), S_i'(t), U_i) = \Delta S_i(t, t+\delta) \tag{8}$$

Finally, it is recognised that once changes are made the character of a situation is changed. Although the mechanisms for feedback are embedded within the methodology they do exist and may be represented as,

$$F(S_i(t), S_i'(t), \Delta S(t, t+\delta)) = (S_i(t+\delta), S_i(t+\delta)) \tag{9}$$

The results of F are then used as inputs to (8) and (7) to provide a further set of changes to be made.

Specifying the nature of the methodologies in this way allows their assumptions to be made explicit and hence their usefulness to be evaluated. Classical operational research is valid when there is no disagreement between decision-makers and when learning and adaptation is not necessary as the system is well-understood. Such situations are referred to as mechanical-unitary problem-contexts by Jackson and Keys (10). In contrast the soft-systems methodology incorporates the means of dealing with many decision-makers and for providing learning about the problem-situation. It is more appropriate for situations when these are needed. Such situations have been referred to as systemic-pluralist problem-contexts.

It should be noted here that in both of the above cases the logical form of methodologies is considered. This ignores the many variations which can be constructed around the core methodologies. The intention here is to illustrate the fundamental structure of the methodologies and not to concentrate upon the detail of either. Hence certain features of the examples used have not been given the prominence which an alternative analysis may have lead to. Further analysis of various methodologies is required if the systems approach is to realise its full potential. The above is one attempt to increase understanding of systems based methodology and to provide a means of designing such methodologies in the future.

6. CONCLUSION

There is much further work required if a suitable operational form of the above framework is to be available. It is only at that time that the validity of the above analysis will be tested. The limited empirical support carried out above suggests that the framework is a useful starting point from which to consider the methodology design issue.

REFERENCES can be obtained from the author.

METHODOLOGICAL PRINCIPLES OF LARGE SCALE COMPLEX ENGINEERING
SYSTEMS DESIGN

Tadeusz Basiewicz
Technical University of Warsaw
Transportation Institute

1. INTRODUCTION

The LSCES designing is a complex process that involves many
spheres of technological, economic, ecological and social
activity. Although there exists an enormous number and variety of studies devoted to diverse particular methodologies
of the LSCES designing, their ideas have not been yet very
well integrated into the main body of an unified general methodology. This paper is an attempt to formulate some general principles of the LSCES designing process. The core of
the approach are the links between physical, economical, pra-
xiological, social and others aspects of designing process
and the efficiency of the entire designing process. The views
presented in the paper are solely those of the writer's and
reflect experience which includes academic research and many years' practice in the field of railway transport systems
design (Basiewicz, 1985).

2. THE CONCEPT OF THE LSCES

When talking about the LSCES designing it seems hardly advisable to introduce definitions of the concepts of large scale
system and complex system. According to Bernussou and Titli
(1982), "we shall call large scale systems which can satisfactory be described by normal, traditional mathematical
tools but which give large scale (often linear) models, bringing into play, for example in the state representation, a
large number of state variables - a hundred or more", whereas complex systems "can be characterized essentially by the
difficulty in representing them with traditional mathematical tools, and of obtaining usable models, or by mathematical complexity of existing models (often obtained from physical and analytical considerations)". With large scale systems a certain spatial distribution is often associated. If
large scale and complexity are common characteristics of a

237

R. Trappl (ed.), Cybernetics and Systems '86, 237–244.
© 1986 by D. Reidel Publishing Company.

single engineering system, then it is called large scale
complex engineering system (LSCES).

Most LSCES design tasks are multi objective decision
problems under uncertainty. To solve them an interaction of
civil engineers, architects, urban designers, economists,
environment engineers, applied mathematicians and other specialists is necessary. In other words, multi disciplinary
interaction is essential to obtain balanced and mutually reinforcing solution to the LSCES design problem.

There is as yet no unified theory of LSCES design. The
attempt to construct a general methodology of LSCES design
still remains in the programmatic stage, despite the long
years of effort by many outstanding specialists (see, for
instance, Jones, 1972 and Koomen, 1985). The untenability of
attempts at unification of the various particular LSCES designing methodologies on a purely formal basis does not, of
course, rule out other approaches to the creation of an unified - perhaps very general - methodology of the LSCES designing. The most promissing seems to be an approach founded
on referrence to modern statistical physics, multi objective
mathematics and systems analysis, and permitting to consider
seemingly quite different LSCES design problems from one
methodologically uniformed point of view.

3.   THE LSCES DESIGNING PROCESS AS A SYSTEM

From the point view of systems analysis and in accordance
with the principle of theory and practice unity (Krayevsky,
1978) each LSCES designing process should be considered as
a system, i.e. as a dialectic triple "designer - design object - design goals" (Basiewicz , 1985). In consequence,
certainty, risk as well as objective and subjective uncertainties manifest as inherent properties of LSCES designing
process, which is multi objective one. When such a process
is to be analysed it is often thought that the first step is
the construction of a mathematical model. In design practice,
however, the construction of a mathematical model is far from
the first step. The LSCES designing is a complex, large scale, multiobjective process with many elements of certainty,
risk and uncertainty, and its full mathematization is unnecessary and simply impossible. This process is executed by
collective interdisciplinary bodies which treat mathematical
models as tools supporting decision making. It is essential
for designers of the LSCES to have mathematical models reflecting various aspects of design problem, but the main body of the design process is carried out by a human being.
Thus, the LSCES designing is a creative process in the course of which a kind of specific dialogue between designer
collective and mathematical models or/and other tools supporting engineering design (computer systems, expert groups,
etc.) takes place.

4.   BASIC CONCEPTS IN THE LSCES DESIGNING

When analysing real LSCES designing processes it seems to be possible to identify a system of nine basic sets of attributes which are common to one and all of them. The sets are as follows (Basiewicz, 1985).

C – set of qualitative and quantitative descriptions expressing customer's needs and desires with regard to designing tasks and giving a sufficiently precise framework for the problem solving;
G – set of constraints;
Q – set of criteria which are measures, rules and standards which should guide designing process;
$\hat{C}$ – set C but defined more accurately by designer;
$\hat{F}$ – set of descriptors characterising functional aspects (technological processes) of the LSCES under design;
F_0 – set of descriptors characterising form, configuration and spatial allocation of material objects under design;
P – set of physically feasible design variants;
$\hat{P}$ – optimal physically feasible variant (basic design);
P_T – technical design, i.e. a detailed form of the basic design.

The sets C, G and Q characterize the design problem and its context and are formulated by the customer which charge the designer with design problems, whereas the others are created in the course of the designing process. The above sets constitute a system of basic concepts in the LSCES designing methodology. The interelations between these concepts as well as the general inference structure of the LSCES design process are presented in Fig.1.

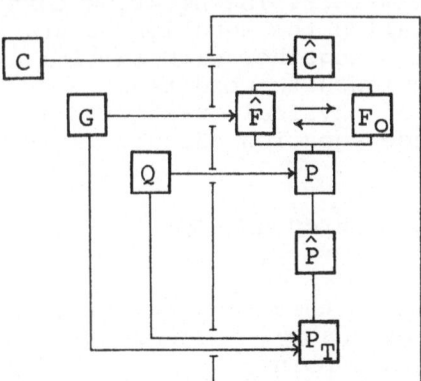

Fig.1. General inference structure of the LSCES design process.

5. PRINCIPLES GOVERNING THE LSCES DESIGNING PROCESS

When analysing the process of the LSCES designing, one can discren some principles with the aid of which it is possible to characterize all its features. The principles are as follows:
(1) physical laws of conservation of energy, momentum, etc.;
(2) law of conservation of biological dynamic equilibrium;
(3) principle of economic rationality;
(4) principle of function and form unity in three-dimensional spaces;
(5) principle of two-level hierarchical decomposition of the designing process;
(6) principle of design feasibility;
(7) principle of optimal design choosing.

The principles (1), (2) and (3) are of universal nature and govern physical, biological and economic aspects of the designing process correspondingly. The principles (4)-(7) reflect some peculiarities of the LSCES designing.

5.1. Conservation laws

It is evident that any LSCES designing process proceeds within certain constraints. This implies a range of physical limits to the choice of the optimal physically feasible · design. To reflect these physical constraints we make use of the laws of conservation. As we know, the physical quantities characterizing every material system are either intensive or extensive. When no external forces act on the system its state is uniquely determined if two intensive independent parameters are given. Any other parameter is a function of two given parameters. The equation that connects any three parameters is called the equation of state for a given system. This equation together with initial and boundary conditions express uniqueness conditions.
The spatial changes of physical quantities are described by differential balance equation (Szucs, 1972):

$$\frac{\partial \rho_i}{\partial t} + \mathrm{div}(\rho_i v + \sum_{k=1}^{n-1} L_{ik}\mathrm{grad}\, y_k) = q_i$$

where: ρ_i — density of the i-th extensive quantity in a given point of space;
v — velocity of this point;
L_{ik} — conductance coefficient corresponding to the intensive parameters i and k;
y_k — intensive parameter;
q_i — source density for the i-th extensive quantity.

This equation (together with initial and boundary conditions) expresses uniqueness conditions. From the equation of differential balance one can deduce mathematical model of any technical system under design. Every technical problem can be recognized to be solved if we know the solution of balance equation under given uniqueness conditions.

5.2. Biological dynamic equilibrium

The LSCES design objective cannot be isolated from the ecological conditions in which it will be materialized. All particular targets of design activity must be subordinated to the biological objective which includes the protection of nature and the prevention of destructions. It corresponds to permanent maintenance of environment in the state of stationary dynamical equilibrium. Such a state is characterized by an extremum principle which states that in the equilibrium state the entropy production has its minimum value compatible with some auxiliary conditions to be specified in each case (Prigogine, 1955). It follows from here that from the view-point of the LSCES design methodology the design activity should not lead to the increase of entropy level in ecological system.

5.3. Economic rationality

The principle of economic rationality (Lange, 1963) asserts that the maximum degree of realization of the goal is achived by proceeding in such a way that either for a given outlay of means the maximum degree of the goal is achived, or that for a given degree of realization of the goal the outlay of the means is minimal. Both variants lead to the same result. In order to apply the principle in the design activity it is sufficient if the goal of designing is a magnitude; it may be need not be a quantity. It is worth noting that the principle of economic rationality is an economic equivalent of the physical principle of least effort. With the equation of the choice of appropriate means for the realization of a particular design when the means are quantitatively measurable and the goal may be realized in varying degrees, one obtain a problem of mathematical programming. A set of particular amounts of the means is called a programme. It is a set of amounts for which the design objective function reaches its maximum.

5.4. Function and form unity

In the LSCES designing the concept of function expresses technological processes $\hat{F}$, whereas form F_0, reflect shapes of material objects (material selection, dimensioning, construction). Two important relations appear, spatio-functio-

241

nal relation and spatio-constructional one. To maintain the spatial harmony the designer must keep in view supperiority of the function over the form.

5.5. Two-level decomposition of the designing process

Superiority of the function over the form in the LSCES design results in the two-level decomposition of the designing process. On the higher of these levels a designer deals with functional aspects of the LSCES under design, while on the lower one he is engaged in the design of the form of material objects entering into the composition of the LSCES. Interactions between these two levels can be expressed by the structural matrix (Fig.2). The construction of a typical structural matrix is schematically illustrated in Fig.2a, where the main-diagonal elements are the sets $\hat{F}$ and F_0 correspondingly. Elements $r(\hat{F},F_0)$ and $r(F_0,\hat{F})$ put the designer up to the existence of linkage (r=1) as well as to the lack of linkage (r=0). If the designing process has some iterative loops, then $r(\hat{F},F_0)=r(F_0,\hat{F})=1$. Figure 2b gives a more detailed description of the structural matrix. It contains as diagonal elements all design variables X_{zi} (objects under design). External influences C, G and Q are linked with diagonal elements standing in the same row of the structural matrix. All non-diagonal elements of the matrix are repre-

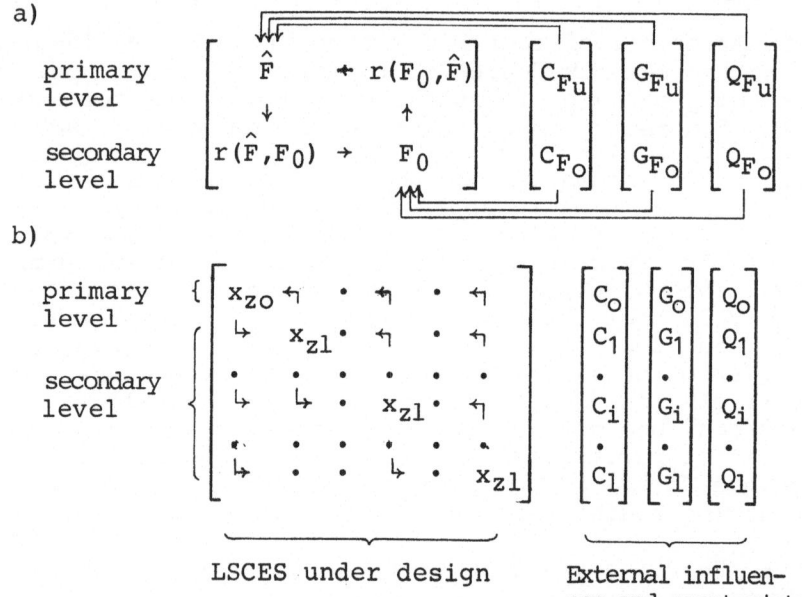

Fig. 2. Structural matrix of the LSCES
a) two-level decomposition; b) more detailed description of second level.

242

sented by the symbol $\llcorner$ (if r=1 and a direct linkage occurs) or by the $\hookleftarrow$ (if r=1 and feedback take place). The lack of these symbols means that r=0.

5.6. Design feasibility

In order to make a design physically feasible, the designer must realize all requirements imposed on the designing process. As a rule the requirements have a form of constraints defined in the following spaces:
- three-dimensional geometric space;
- space of materials and energy;
- space of technologies and exploitation manners;
- ecological space;
- cost space;
- time space, etc.

5.7. Optimal design choosing

If the above principles are respected, then it is possible to find a set of various technically feasible variants of the design. To choose an optimal variant P the designer must make use of the criteria set Q. The problem is multi objective one and to solve it one ought to apply some special mathematical and heuristic techniques (Carlsson, 1983). Unfortunately, because of the great number of the criteria, their different physical sense as well as owing to their incommensurability it is extremely difficult to solve a multi-criteria design problem. As a rule we decide to look for the design which ensures minimization of the total costs of the LSCES constructing and exploitation. In this case the designing problem leads to the mathematical program:

$$\text{minimizes} \quad \{C_0(r) + C_e(r)\}$$

on the set of physically feasible variants of the design, where: $C_0(r)$ is the LSCES constructing cost, $C_e(r) = r^T$ is the LSCES exploatation cost in the period T, r is the LSCES exploitation cost in a time unit. Mathematical form of the functionals $C_0(r)$ and $C_e(r)$ is very complicated. To identify them it is necessary to take advantage of the systems of standards and norms, which are an useful tool supporting designing activity. In accordance with the principle of economic rationality, in the course of the designing process an interaction between principle of design feasibility and that of optimal design choosing take place. This is why standardization is an extremely important and very responsible activity, which supports designers in decision making.

The optimal physically feasible variant of the design is called the basic one. It is used to prepare the technical design P_T which is a detailed form of the basic design.

6.   DESIGN PROCEDURES

The designing process can be considered as modelling of the LSCES and particular elements with the aid of appropriate procedures. Formally, this process can be presented as an ordered pair of sets

$$S(X) = \{H(X), U(X)\}$$

where $H(X) = \{H_1(X), \ldots, H_L(X)\}$ is a set elements of the LSCES under design, $U(X) = \{U_1(X), \ldots, U_M(X)\}$ is a set of designing procedures and X is a design variable. Under the concept of a design procedure we understand here a chain of logically connected mental operations which realize a definite creative process.

The set of all possible design procedures one can divide into two subsets $U_r(X)$ and $U_{nr}(X)$ such that

$$U(X) = U_r(X) \bigcup U_{nr}(X)$$

$$U_r(X) \bigcap U_{nr}(X) = \emptyset .$$

where $U_r(X)$ is a set of routinish procedures and $U_{nr}(X)$ is a set of non-routinish procedures. Next, the procedures belonging to the set $U_{nr}(X)$ can be classified as algorithmic procedures or as heuristic ones. The former can be presented in computer-implemented form, the latter are often realized by designers with the aid of expert systems.

7.   CONCLUDING REMARKS

In the writer's opinion the above considerations would encourage a development of the deductive theory of the LSCES designing. The approach that has been proposed set up certain frames to the general methodology of designing. The ideas making a framework for such methodology reflect writer's experience both in academic research and in the field of large scale compleks railway networks design.

8.   REFERENCES

to be obtained from the author.

ATTRIBUTE-ORIENTED PROJECTS:
CONFIGURATION MANAGEMENT FRAMEWORK AND TWO EXAMPLES

Lech Krzanik
Institute of Control, Systems Engineering and Telecommunications
University of Mining and Metallurgy
Aleja Mickiewicza 30, PL-30-059 Krakow
Poland

ABSTRACT. An attribute-oriented approach to the project configuration management is demonstrated and exemplified with two practical cases.

Keywords: project management, configuration management, requirement engineering, attribute-oriented approach, decision support tools and systems.

1. INTRODUCTION.

Modern project management standards [eg. MIL483, DOD480, ANSI/IEEE729] suggest to encapsulate project's implementation decisions within configuration items, and to follow requirement-oriented rather than technique-oriented project development strategies. Moreover, after assuming two basic requirement types: qualitatively defined functions and quantitative attributes, the standards suggest to apply a mixed function-and-attribute approach, rather than a traditional, function-oriented project planning. In particular, this is advised for high-risk, long-duration projects.

Project functions are (or should be) tightly connected to sets of quantitative attributes. As these connections become clear, project managers are likely to go even further, to an *attribute-oriented* approach. But how such an approach look like in practice? This question, not yet addressed in standards, is often raised when project development strategies are discussed, especially by senior managers who are responsible for attributes. Management responsibilities are the most apparent, but not the only motivation for attribute-oriented projects. Another reason to pursue this approach is an accepted attribute form of detailed project description standards. Also, the approach is motivated by the interface with project users (clients), for whom attribute specifications are usually much more readable than functional ones. The last two points are directly related to project's quality assurance and specification validation.

The present paper gives an outline of an attribute-oriented configuration management methodology and presents two practical examples showing different facets of the subject. On the other hand, the examples make use of two decision support tools, developed lately. Many persons have contributed to the on-going research a small part of which is hereby presented. The author wishes to acknowledge all direct or indirect contributions to this paper.

An immediate stimulus to write this paper was a technical visit to a civil air flight control

R. Trappl (ed.), Cybernetics and Systems '86, 245–252.
© *1986 by D. Reidel Publishing Company.*

center under construction, in central Europe in summer '85, and a stormy discussion within a group of scientists and practitioners that followed the visit. We were presented an informal requirement specification with few functions (such as *radar screen display generation, on-line links to the continental and local neighbouring flight control centers*), and a considerable list of attributes of four kinds: capacities (eg. *200 simultaneous radar tracks*), system response times (eg. *reconfiguartion associated with the loss of track update less than 10 sec.*), availability attributes (eg. *average time between reconfigurations greather than 100 hrs.*), and software size measures (eg. *10000 files under configuration management control*). The project environment, in particular the three reasons mentioned above, namely:

- management responsibilities,
- mostly attribute-like requirement specifications,
- type of interface with clients,

suggested that an attribute-oriented methodology should have been applied. In spite of this, the declared project milestones were system functions, not attributes. The functions implicitly assumed *some* associated attributes at the specified fixed levels, but there was lack of coordination of the manifestations of the same attribute with regard to separate functions (eg. reliability), and some critical attributes were not explicitly stated (eg. usability). Sensibleness of the declared approach was questioned. Having in mind the tight project timing, we discussed the alternative of an attribute-oriented approach and an evolutionary delivery strategy. We extended the attribute list and came to the conclusion that attributes rather than functions are of concern. Finally, issues of attribute-oriented project management were discussed: specification, design, implementation planning, verification and validation: How all this should be coordinated so that required attributes result from appropriate design techniques, and do cover (in specification and in the product) the necessary functions? This paper is intended to clarify some of these issues.

In section 2 we present the general framework in which the attribute-oriented approach can be analysed. In sections 3 and 4 two examples of attribute-oriented project development strategies are presented.

2. THE FRAMEWORK: PROJECT CONFIGURATION MANAGEMENT

The foundation for modern project configuration management is set by the rapidly expanding discipline of requirement engineering [GIL85]. The discipline advises to start with end-user goals and to distinguish between two classes of requirements: qualitative functions that the product or project must be capable of performing and quantitative attributes, such as availability, reliability, usability, defining the product or project resources, performance capabilities and quality metrics. In accordance with the natural project management responsibilities, the higher the analysis level, the more attribute-oriented should be the appearance of the project. The central part of each attribute specification are definitions of a measurement scale, method and tool, and of dependencies between separate attributes. The following is a definition widely used by ski binding manufacturers: *Standard body weight is body height in cm minus 100. Valid from 150 cm on.*

The *configuration management* discipline links the requirements with design decisions and project planning. The discipline uses a notion of *configuration items* that are associations

246

of requirements and design decisions as to which implementation *techniques* should be applied in order to satisfy the requirements. Any operable, improvable or reparable project item designed for separate procurement is a configuration item. Basic configuration management activities are identification, control, audit and status accounting.

Usually the following generic configuration management policies, also called *project control strategies*, are distinguished: monolithic, incremental, prototype-based and evolutionary. The differences are mostly in sequencing of the configuration management activities within the project. The *monolithic* strategy, for instance, requires *all* the configuration items in the project be identified before *any* one of them is implemented. On the contrary, the *evolutionary* strategy allows for independent configuration items' processing – necessary when an item is identified and defined in consequence of the user feedback on already implemented items. The *incremental* strategy is something in between: independent sequencing is possible after a general framework has been monolithically developed, including development plans, stubs for future capabilities, etc.

The term *attribute-oriented* means that all changes to the project state are expressed and evaluated directly in terms of attributes and at this high level. Thus non-attribute specifications may require a translation into attributes before being mapped onto design techniques or development plans. Final attribute profiles of the project, as they appear in the product, should fulfil all the specified requirements. The process leading to the appropriate techniques consists of selection, optimization, tuning and evaluation phases. Usually individual attribute specifications include possible value slack which can be used to select the best trade-off solution in terms of a more general attribute. The process may be performed automatically (first example below) or with an interactive decision support tool (second example).

The evolutionary strategy is unquestionably the oldest, and at the same time the best suited for highly innovative systems. However project managers are often "monolithically biased". Therefore we begin presentation of attribute-oriented projects with a compromised, incremental example. Then we shall present an evolutionary approach. First example regards a continuous case, ie. the one with very small delivery steps. Second example refers to delivery steps of arbitrary size.

3. EXAMPLE I: INCREMENTAL, CONTINUOUS PROJECT

We assume:

- Incremental configuration item delivery.
- Very small delivery steps (during the evolutionary phase), the delivery process can be represented with continuous functions.
- The monolithic phase includes generation of approximate final attribute profiles referenced during the project lifetime. Over the evolutionary phase attributes are automatically controlled so as to conform with all the requirements, in the presence of disturbances representing aspects not conveyed by the profiles. The disturbance may be due to additional dynamic resource constraints, as in this example.
- Project validation is distributed among the two phases. Within the evolutionary phase, on-line validation of design decisions may result in small attribute changes which are included in the disturbance.

The case presented below refers to a large construction project with three very high level attributes (resources): technological equipment, manpower and building machines [GKK85, KK85]. The project is modelled as a two-layer hierarchical system. The lower, resource layer, is a system of objects representing individual attributes-resources, again with a hierarchical object dependence. The upper layer performs on-line parametric coordination and optimization. Whole system structure is shown in Figure 1.

A lower-layer object, presented in Figure 2., is a dynamic difference- differential closed-loop control system with time delays [GOR76], with a local PI-type (proportional-integrating) controller. The cotroller models the behaviour of a local decision maker in the presence of disturbances. A follow-up control law is assumed based on the planned reference profiles. There are two inputs: the reference profile and the disturbance, both are continuous time functions. There are three outputs: undelayed and delayed resource value outputs, and the scaling output. The last two connect the object with lower-level objects. Some of the outputs are available for the system's upper layer.

Sample results are presented in Figure 3. We assume that the upper-level resource is not disturbed. Manpower is disturbed by periodic decreases caused by outflows to agriculture. The Machines resource is disturbed by a typical reliability curve. The optimization criterion applied at the upper layer is a measure of deviation of the actual attributes from the planned profiles: sum of squared deviation integrals over the project horizon, with contrained global project delay. Of course, other criteria are also possible. The disturbances as well as nonzero time delays may cause the output curves to oscillate.

The presented project structure is particularly useful for senior managers. It is flexible, easily restructurable, allows for separate treatment of attributes, and deals with *real* project phenomena such as project delays.

4. EXAMPLE II: EVOLUTIONARY, DISCRETE PROJECT

We assume:

- Evolutionary configuration item delivery.
- Delivery steps of arbitrary size, but for stability reasons small steps are preferred.
- On-line identification, designation and validation of the configuration items based on the end-user feedback.

We will show a tool called *Impact Analysis Table* used in the Design by Objectives set of tools [GIL85], and also employed in an automated project development environment [KG84]. In principle, there is nothing more complex than ordinary cost estimation or budgeting. The originality stems from the fact that we try to estimate the impact of design techniques on *all* specified attributes. The estimates are made in terms of a percentage of the target attribute level. 100% denotes our belief that the technique will allow us to reach the target level. 0% denotes no impact. Estimates less than 0% as well as exceeding 100% are also possible. An example of the tool aplication is given in Figure 4 which shows results as they are acually displayed to the user. Paper [GIL84] gives more detail on the conventions used with the tool. Fagan's Inspection method [FW82] can be used to validate the estimates.

For many reasons, mainly related to the fact that the actual values may depend on unknown implementation particulars, the estimates cannot be particularly accurate. There are several

248

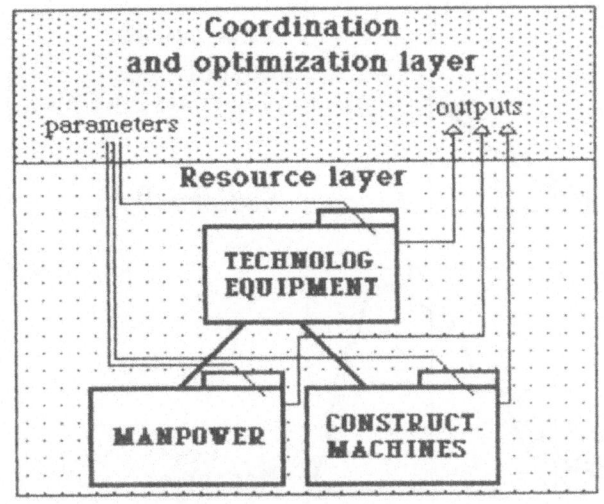

Figure 1. A two-layer project model. Resource objects in the lower layer form a hierarchical multilevel structure.

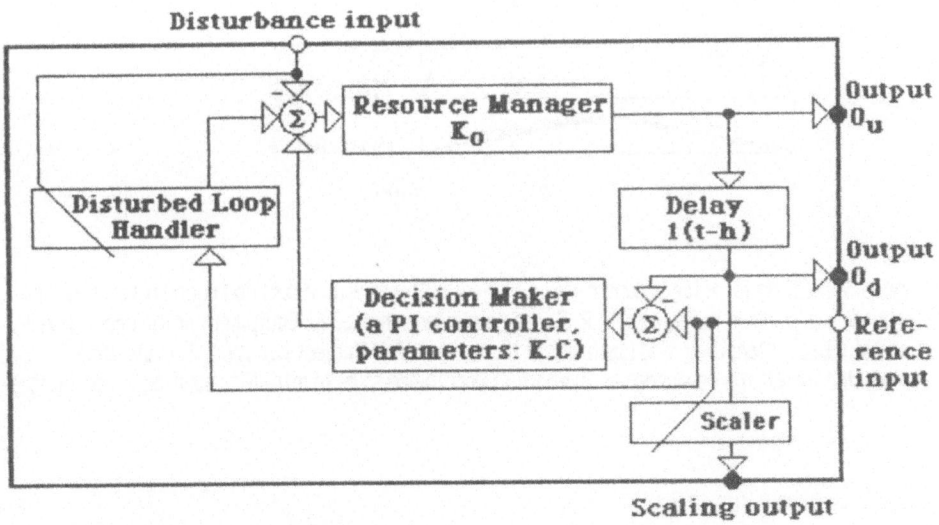

Figure 2. Resource object: a closed-loop control system with time delay. h, K_0, K, C – the object's parameters. O_u – undelayed output, O_d – delayed output.

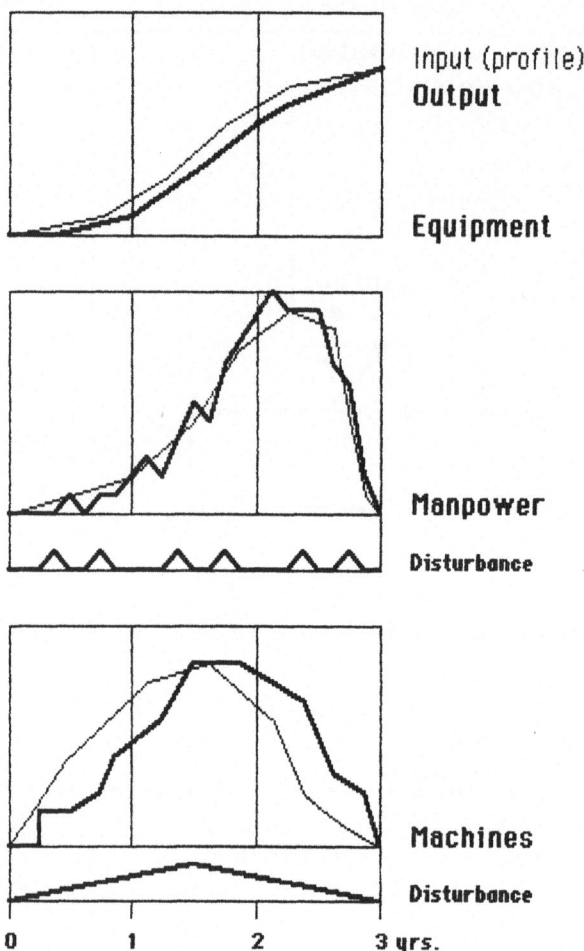

Figure 3. Results for a large construction project obtained with a decision support tool based on the models presented in Figures 1, 2. Three resources considered: Equipment at the upper level (undisturbed), Manpower and Machines at the lower level. Project duration: 3 years. Delay parameter for all the resources h=2 months. Coordinated so as to minimize squared error integral.

ways to overcome this difficulty:

(a) Use uncertainty estimates, eg. 50±10% meaning that the impact is somewhere between 40% and 60%, but 50% is about right.
(b) Use guaranteed estimates – if in doubt, assume the lower limit. There are, however, more advanced, advocated ways:

250

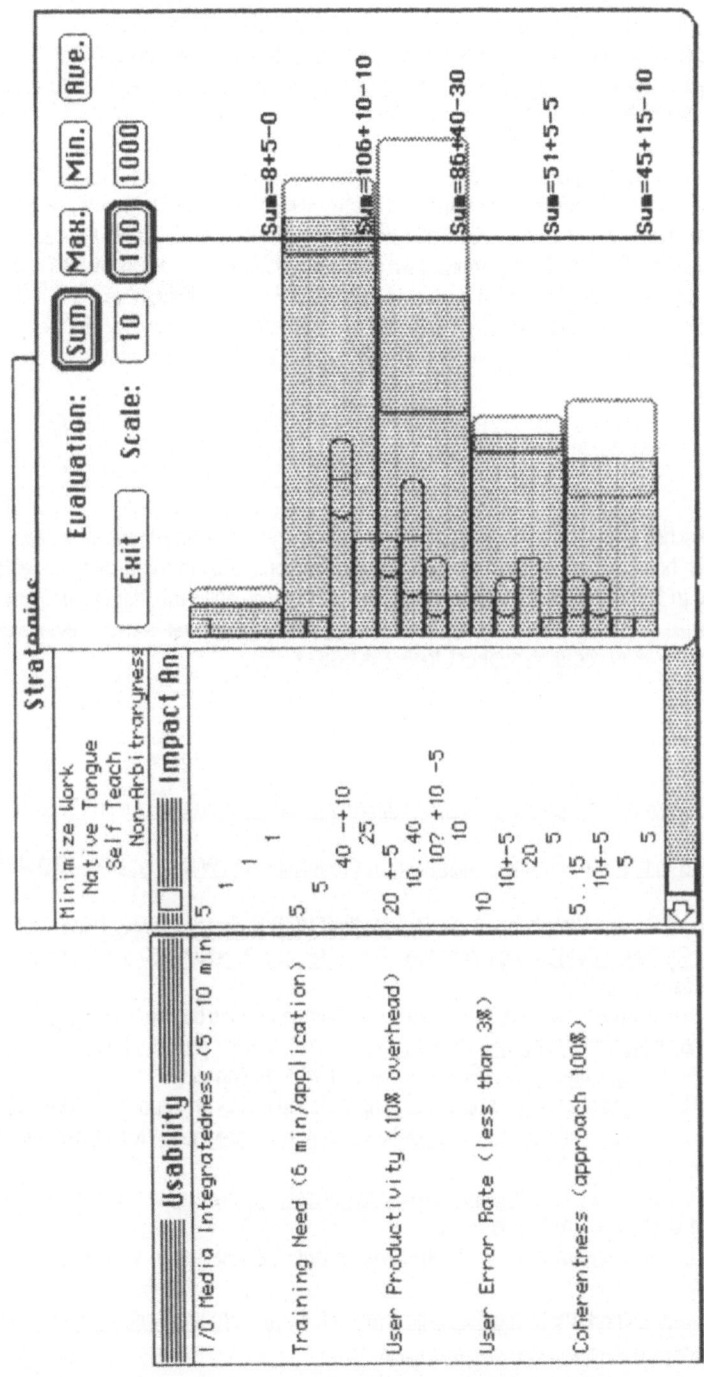

Figure 4. Example of the Impact Analysis Table applied to subobjectives of usability.
Note: Totals shown in chart also include other, not displayed attributes, eg. those defined at lower levels.

(c) Use this tool along with clearly *evolutionary* strategies, with early deliveries to the real environment. Accurate estimates can be based on the user feedback.

(d) Try to *standardize* the attributes as well as the techniques. Use *certified* techniques. Use attribute dictionaries and technique handbooks ([FW82] could serve as a rough example).

To get a *cumulative* impact estimate, several approaches are practised. Simplest are to add the estimates (the corresponding uncertainty estimates also should be added) or to select the maximum value over all relevant techniques. The actual solution depends eg. on how the estimate uncertainty is dealt with. By cumulating impacts we can aggregate complex design data. The tables can be applied at many levels of analysis of both objectives and design techniques.

This tool alows for multiple viewpoint analysis of any design idea in a very simple way. Estimates may be made on paper or with the help of a decision support system providing access to relevant databases.

5. CONCLUSIONS

Two different approaches to attribute-oriented project configuration management have been presented. Both offer handy tools allowing for safe design decisions, also in high-risk projects. The examples speak in favour of the attribute-oriented methodology and evolutionary project development strategies. Another important feature of the presented methods is that they are easily implementable as high-level decision support tools [GKK85, KG84].

6. REFERENCES

ANSI/IEEE729 IEEE Standard Glossary of Software Engineering Terminology, ANSI/IEEE Std. 729-1983.

DOD480 Configuration Control-Engineering Changes, Deviations and Waivers, DOD-STD 480A, 1978.

FW82 Freedman, D.P., and Weinberg, G.M., Handbook of Walkthroughs, Inspections, and Technical Reviews: Evaluating Programs, Projects, and Products, 3rd ed., Little, Brown and Co., Boston, 1982.

GIL84 Gilb, T., "The Impact Analysis Table applied to human factors design", in: Proc. 1st IFIP Conference on Human-Computer Interaction, London, 1984, pp. 97-101.

GIL85 Gilb, T., Design by Objectives, North-Holland, 1985, to appear.

GKK85 Gorecki, H., Kopytowski, J., Krzanik, L., unpublished research reports, 1984-85.

GOR76 Gorecki, H., Analysis and Synthesis of Delayed Control Systems, PWN Publishers, Warszawa, 1976.

KG84 Krzanik, L., and Gilb, T., Automated Design by Objectives, available from UCSD P-System Users Society, La Jolla, CA.

KK85 Krzanik, L., and Kopytowski, J., "High-level resource allocation in large projects", to appear.

MIL483 Configuration Management Practices for Systems, Equipment and Computer Programs, MIL-STD 483a, 1970.

THE FLOW CHART EXPANSION METHOD OF THE DESIGN PROBLEM

Danuta Miller D.S.Engin.
Institute of Philosophy and Sociology
Polish Academy of Sciences
Nowy Swiat 72
00-330 Warsaw
Poland

ABSTRACT. The flow chart expansion method helps the designer to examine the design problem from many aspects. It is an heuristic method useful in the initial stages of the design process. The concept of the chart expansion has certain features in common with systems concepts, although it differs from them in many specific ones. The method allows the designer to look at the problem as broadly as his skills and knowledge permit, without constraining his imagination by rules, regulations and other requirements. The concept emphasizes, in particular, the freest possible, unlimited examination of the problem and the simplicity and ease in obtaining a picture of a given area of reality. The graphic form accepted automatically makes it possible to arrange a picture that is sufficiently clear to create a logical and simulataneously simple and visual construction.

1. THE CONCEPT OF A FLOW CHART EXPANSION

The aim of the flow chart expansion method is to help the designer to examine the design problem from many aspects. This method is useful first and foremost in the initial stages of the design process and also at those crucial points of the process in which the designer searches for unconventional aspects, details, and nuances of the problem solution.

The concept of flow chart expansion – in view of its aim to present the problem as completely as possible – has certain features in common with systems concepts, though it differs from them in many specific features. Flow chart expansion always has a central point which is the basic subject of the design problem. Around this central point the designer gathers selected events, situations, quantities, objects – called elements here – connected in various ways with the subject of a given design problem. These elements

253

R. Trappl (ed.), Cybernetics and Systems '86, 253–259.
© *1986 by D. Reidel Publishing Company.*

form the specific description of the subject.

2.   IDENTIFICATION THE ELEMENTS

For example, fig.1 ahows an expansive flow chart for a basic subject: designing a child's bicycle. As one can see in
the drawing, what is essential in the expansive flow chart
is that its elements are clearly heterogeneous; they differ
ontologically, substantively, formally, in their degree of
importance, minuteness of detail, etc. The common feature
of all of the elements of the expansive flow chart is their
connection with a given design problem, though this connection may be stronger or weaker. So the elements of a flow
chart are a set that is distinguished by the common feature
of "being important" for the solution of a problem, "importance" in this method being treated as gradation.
     There are no special requirements concerning the man-
ner of formulating the substance of individual elements of
the flow chart. They can be expressed in common language,
in the jargon of a given design group or in the jargon usef
to formulate a specific problem.
     The designer, if necessary, adds new elements or eli-
minates those from the flow chart which at the next stage of
the design process turn out to be "unimportant". He can also change the form of certain elements. Elements are identified and included in the flow chart in the course of his
individual thought processes, in accordance with his subjective view of the problem solution. One can assume that
these views differ from each other and that the elements of
the flow chart can be identified according to various criteria. It seems that the most natural way of examining a
problem in creating an expansive flow chart is to follow
the situation and events connected with the life process of
a given object, that is with its design, production, transportation, distribution, use, repair, etc. The elements in
the example given here **were** identified in such a way.

3.   PROPERTY OF A FLOW CHART EXPANSION

The expansive flow chart drawn by the designer can be wide-
ned or narrowed. The designer examines the fragments of the
flow chart in the logical course of the design proceess.
This results in partial flow charts, i.e. local, thematic,
prognostic, etc.
     The expansive flow chart is dynamic, advancing with
the requirements of successive stages of the design process.
     The method allows the designer to look at the problem
as broadly as his skills and knowledge permit, without constraining his imagination by rules. The expansive flow
chart is sort of a freely drawn sketch, made without the
inhibitions imposed by limitations that do not concern the

254

essence of the problem solution. The concept of the expansive flow chart emphasizes in particular the freest possible, unlimited examination of the problem and simplicity and ease in obtaining a picture of a given area of reality. The graphic form accepted automatically makes it possible to arrange a picture that is sufficiently clear to create a logical and simultaneously simple and visual construction.

4.   BOUNDARIES OF FLOW CHART DRAW

The set of elements which the designer includes in the flow chart draw its boundaries; in other words, they delimit the area of reality examined. This is the area which the designer regarded as important at a given stage of the design process. Delimitation of this area is of key importance in creation of the expansive flow chart.

It turns out in practice that - at a given stage of design knowledge - certain kinds of elements are commonly regarded as important for the solution of certain problems. Such elements are routinaly identified and solved by the designer in the design process, so it is obvious that they will be included in the expansive flow chart. Here as examples we can mention such kinds of elements as the functions of a designed object, its features and parameters, the characteristics of the intended users of the object, ways and possibilities of manufacturing it, etc.

With the growth of design knowledge in general the designer identifies more and more details of the problem solution, notices more and more numerous connections of the problem with its context, anticipates more remote effects of design processes; the expansive flow chart widens. Simultaneously, the elements of the flow chart become more distant from the central point, and the links between the elements and this point become hierarchical /fig.2/. The importance of the elements from the standpoint of the design problem become differentiated, becoming less important as the distance of a given element from the central point increases.

Most essential for a correct examination of a problem using the expansive flow chart method is to include in the flow chart all of the elements important to a given problem and to exclude the unimportant ones.

The drawing of the optimum boundaries of the expansive flow chart by the designer is not a routine matter. There are no explicit guidelines containing criteria for distinguishing more and less important elements. In practice drawing the boundaries of the expansive flow chart depends on many factors and conditions, not all of which are directly connected with the design problem. Examples are the social importance of the problem, the size and character of the design team, individual traits of the designer, i.e. his perceptiveness, insight, knowledge, costs and time allocated to the design process, etc.

Generally speaking, the importance of an element is a function of the influence of this element on the solution of a problem. In other words, if a certain important element were not considered, then the problem would be solved less completely /presumably: more poorly/. On the other hand, the inclusion of unimportant elements would unnecessarily widen the expansive flow chart, thereby making the design process more /presumably: needlessly/ complicated.

The expansive flow chart method suggests distinguishing elements according to the criterion of change.

5.   A CHANGE IN THE EXISTING STATE

Design methodology assumes that designing has the aim of conceptually preparing a change in the existing state of things. The purpose of change is improvement, and the designer forceasts and defines the nature of modifications and the boundaries of the area of reality in which the change is to be made. In design practice the change desired is viewed not as an overall, single change but as a series of partial changes. Consequently, individual, successive mini-changes are designed. Such mini-changes are closely coupled with elementary fragments of the area of reality distinguished according to various criteria. The fragments of reality coupled with these mini-changes are presented here in the form of elements.

A suggested change can be presented in the form of a design equation - $Z = \langle z_i = f(e) \rangle$ - where: z - mini-changes, e - elements.

Thereby the previous distinction of elements according to the criterion of importance /important - unimportant elements/ has been replaced by the criterion of change /elements influencing and not influencing change/. The criterion of change has certain important merits for the expansive flow chart. It is more objective than the criterion of importance and is also easier to use in practice and to express.

In deciding whether to include a given element in the expansive flow chart, the designer can express the criterion of change in questions formulated in the language of practice, answaring yes or no to these questions. For example: does a given element make it necessary to meet same condition, does something additional have to be prepared, can the inclusion of a given element have an unexpected effect in the area of reality in question, does this area have to be broadened or narrowad, will it be different in the future, etc?

6. THE AMOUNT OF KNOWLEDGE

The basic function of the expansive flow chart method is to show the designer a simple way of obtaining the fullest and most well-ordered picture possible of a problem solution. Moreover, the expansive flow chart can indicate the amount of knowledge required to solve this problem.

The elements are connected with various fields of knowledge. In other words, in order to evaluate individual elements the designer should have a certain amount of knowledge. For elements that are described in greater detail /see fig.1 and 2/ it becomes apparent that to examine even a single one of them, the designer must have knowledge from various fields.

Generally speaking, knowledge K necessary to solve a design problem is a set of various fields of knowledge K selected in view of the nature of individual elements e, that is: $K = \langle k_j; k_j = \mathcal{Y}/e_j/ \rangle$.

Nowadays only a few design problems can be solved by one designer, among other reasons owing to the different kinds of knowledge required to examine the problem. The designers of the team have various kinds of knowledge and so they can look at a problem from various perspectives. An expansive flow chart may be used to assemble a design team that has sufficient knowledge.

An important advantage of the expansive flow chart is its usefulness in determining the amount of knowledge required for the solution of a design problem.

The child's bicycle already presented here may serve as an illustration of how areas of knowledge are defined on the basis of elements included in the expansive flow chart. It is obvious that designing such a bicycle requires knowledge of mechanics in the broad sense. Without such knowledge, the design of a bicycle cannot be undertaken at all. We could ask to what extent such knowledge is sufficient, however. Let us consider element 2: features of the bicycle /fig.1/. Besides knowledge of mechanics, to examine this element we need the following kinds of knowledge: about the places and conditions of using the bicycle; about the psychological and physical characteristics of the child; about the tastes and preferences of children, their parents, guardians; about safety regulations concerning the use of children's bicycles; about the service network of children's bicycles, etc.

As we can see, these are not typical areas of knowledge taught in colleges; they are hard to define more precisely and even to name. The designer acquires such knowledge not only during his studies but in large measure also during his professional work and through being in a particular social circle.

x x x x

257

The expansive flow chart method appeals first and foremost to the designer's imagination; therefore, it is an heuristic method at the opposite pole – as it were – to formalized mathematical descriptions. It is useful in creating a complete and simultaneously visual picture of the problem solution. It can also be useful in defining the kinds of knowledge required for a comprehensive examination and solution of a given problem.

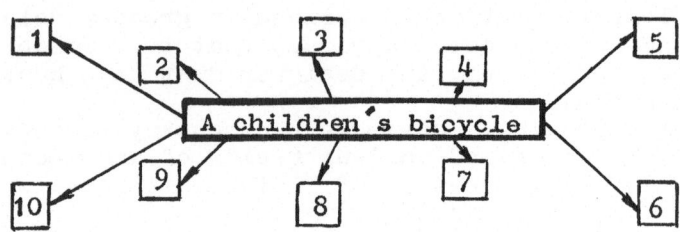

Fig. 1. A children's bicycle

1. Functions of the bicycle: transporting the child, developing the child's dexterity, affording pleasure to the child, parents, satisfying the aspirations of the child, parents, developing tinkering skills, possibility of obtaining benefits, rehabilitation of crippled children

2. Features, characteristics: speed, reliability, safeness, comfort, convenience, aesthetics, repairability ...

3. Persons interested in the finished bicycle: the child – owner of the bicycle, other children, the child's parents, passers-by, merchants, transport workers, repairmen ...

4. Equipment of the bicycle: decorations, lighting, stand, two supplementary wheels, shipping container, set of tools, storage compartment ...

5. Places bicycle will be used: part, street, back yard /riding/, house, cellar cubby-hole /storage/, elevator, stairs, car /transporting/, shop /repairing/ ...

6. Designing the bicycle: the designer, design team, the design process, the designed product, testing prototypes, design conditions, design costs ...

7. Manufacturing the bicycle: manufacturers, manufacturers' equipment, technology, organization of the manufacturing process, materials, parts, norms, waste material, energy, costs, environmental pollution ...

8. Transport, storage: transportation routes, means of transport, conditions of transport, storage conditions, place of storage, time of storage ...

9. Marketing: sales network, prices, advertising, profits, losses ...

10. Disposal: procedures, place, environmental pollution, retrevial, benefits...

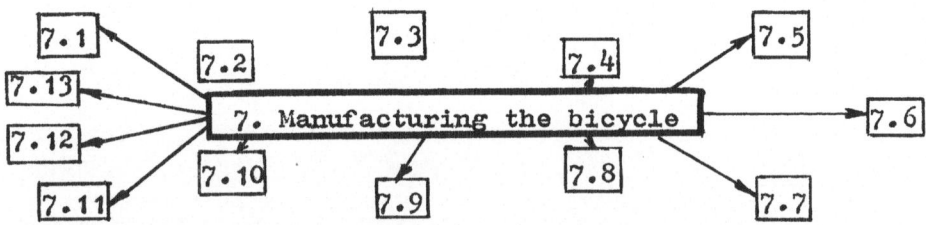

Fig. 2. Details of element 7 /according to fig.1/

7.1. Employees: workers, management, administration, co-operating parties ...

7.2. Organization of production: planning production, production, control, warehouses ...

7.3. Working conditions ...

7.4. Conditions outside work: living conditions, commuting to work ...

7.5. Design documentation ...

7.6. Various information ...

7.7. Energy ...

7.8. Waste materials ...

7.9. Standarized machine elements ...

7.10. Parts, sub-assemblies ...

7.11. Materials ...

7.12. Machinery ...

7.13. Environmental protection ...

QUEUEING SYSTEMS DESIGN, CONTROL AND SIMULATION: THE INTERRELATIONSHIPS

V. Čerić
University Computing Centre
Engelsova bb
41000 Zagreb
Yugoslavia

ABSTRACT. In the past few decades the design of complex queueing
systems has been performed mainly by system modeling methods, like
discrete event simulation and queueing theory. Generally, the discrete
event simulation method enables also the modeling of the system operation control. In this paper we present the results of our investigations on the design of some queueing systems with control by using the
discrete event simulation modeling. The examples of design of a postal
centre for parcel processing and reservoirs in a chemical processing
plant are described. The results of this experience are demonstrating
clearly the influence of alternative system operation control strategies upon the solution of the system design problem.

1. INTRODUCTION

In the past several decades, after the invention of modern computers,
quantitative methods for complex systems modeling, analysis and design
have been developed and used. Such methods have special significance
for contemporary technological systems which generally have both
complex, stochastic and dynamic nature and whose operation has to be
controlled in order to achieve the appropriate and efficient system
functioning.
    In this paper we present an investigation of the design of
queueing systems with control by using the discrete event simulation
modeling. The results of simulation studies of several queueing
systems will be presented, with special emphasis on the relationships
between the alternative system operation control strategies and the
optimum (or at least nearly optimum) design of the system.

2. DESIGN OF QUEUEING SYSTEMS WITH CONTROL

Under the term of a system design we shall understand rational, or
possibly optimum, selection of system parameters which enable the
economical and correct system functioning. More precisely, such kind
of a design belongs to the category of "preliminary system design and

261

R. Trappl (ed.), Cybernetics and Systems '86, 261–265.
© *1986 by D. Reidel Publishing Company.*

optimization" /2/. The system parameters of interest are primarily the system structure, geometry, storage spaces and selection of technological solutions. The evaluation criteria are most often economical ones, like the minimum total system construction and operation costs.

The operation of most complex systems has to be controlled in order to enable the proper functioning of the system and to use system resources as efficiently as possible. While the control theory of the continuous dynamic systems is a well recognized field of investigation with developed modeling and design methods /10/, the control of discrete queueing systems has not been investigated to a larger extent. Some of the investigations have yet revealed that such kind of systems may have quite a complex type of control /1,6,3/.

The main question addressed in this paper is the following: does the alternative system operation control strategies have influence upon the solution of the system design problem, or not?

In searching for the answer to this question it is necessary to have the adequate quantitative methods for modeling of queueing systems with control. Two principal methods for modeling of queueing systems exist, the discrete event simulation method and the queueing theory. Discrete event simulation modeling is especially suitable for modeling of systems with complex structure and operation, and have been used for a long time for design and analysis of the queueing systems /8,9/. The queueing theory, especially with its approximation extensions, has also proved as appropriate for modeling of real complex queueing systems /7/.

Moreover, the discrete event simulation modeling has proved to be suitable also for modeling and design of queueing systems with control. Airport surface traffic control system /1/, manufacturing control system /6/ and postal centre control system /3,4/ have all been successfully modeled by discrete event simulation.

In such a way, a special significance of discrete event simulation within this context is its ability of analysing quantitatively the possible influence of queueing systems operation control strategies upon the solution of the system design problem. In the following, the results of our investigations on two real problems in this field will be described.

3. CASE 1: DESIGN OF POSTAL CENTRE FOR PARCEL PROCESSING

Postal centre for parcel processing is a system which ought to enable the redistribution of consignments from input to output directions. Postal centres are nodes in the postal transportation network, which have to obey the time-table rules of the network. They are complex systems with nonstationary flows of parcels and multiphase parcel service, and with stochastic fluctuations of parcel quantities, parcel arrival and service times. The system operation is taking place during several time intervals, in accordance with the critical arrival/departure times of the transportation network.

Postal processing system analysis /4/ has identified two types of the system operation control, the control of parcel distribution over the output directions and the control of parcel dispatching. The control of parcel distribution over the output directions was shown to be a three-level hierarchical closed-loop type of control, which has to initiate the processing of arrivals, the distribution of parcels over the output directions and the selection of the type of storage conveyers operation. The control of parcel dispatching is a open-loop type of control, which has to ensure the dispatching of parcels prior to the parcel departure time. In general, the system operation control has to enable the appropriate system functioning, to ensure the network time-table fulfilment and to enable a rational usage of the system resources.

The simulation experiments with alternative strategies of parcel distribution control have shown /3,4/ that it has a significant influence on the parcel storage conveyer area necessary for parcel processing system operation. For example, the comparison of two alternative control strategies with different structure of parcel distribution time subperiods has shown that the parcel storage conveyer area can be reduced by approximately 10%.

4. CASE 2: DESIGN OF RESERVOIRS IN PRODUCTION SYSTEMS

Reservoirs for fluids in chemical production systems have to enable stable production. The problem of design of such a reservoire system has been investigated /5/. The system was characterized by the stochastic fluctuations of realization of fluids purchasing and of fluid demand needed for production. The fluid is arriving into the system by various types of tank cars (train, road), and the tank cars of each type can have various capacities.

In the case when the fluid from the tank cars can not be unloaded into the reservoirs, the tank cars have to wait. The waiting costs (penals for waste time) significantly depend upon the type and capacity of tank cars. The system operation control can be performed by using different queueing disciplines for selection of next tank car from the waiting line to be served. The first-come-first-served (FCFS) and the priority discipline (by giving higher priorities for tank cars with higher waste time costs) are most often used.

The design problem for this system can be defined as a problem of finding such total reservoir capacity which gives the minimum total costs of reservoir construction and system operation. Here the reservoir capacity can be upgraded in modules. Sistem operation costs are represented by the waste time costs of tank cars, because other costs (like costs of holding the inventories and costs for lost production due to shortage of raw materials) do not depend upon the reservoir capacity. The comparison of costs is made possible by reducing the reservoir construction cost to one year (by taking into account the reservoir lifetime) and by discounting the tank cars waste time to the present value and summ it up during period of one year. The reservoir contents can be upgraded in fixed reservoir modules.

The results of simulation experiments have shown /5/ that the optimum design solution depends strongly on the selected system operation control strategy. The results are summarized in Table I (costs declared in arbitrary units).

TABLE I   Results of optimum solution of reservoir
               capacity problem

Queueing discipline	No. of reservoirs	Construction cost	Waste time cost	TOTAL COST
	Optimum solution			
FCFS	8	8	14	22
PRIORITIES	3	3	8.7	11.7

5. CONCLUSIONS

The results of studies of two queueing systems design
problems presented in this paper have demonstrated clearly
that the selection of the system operation control strategy
may have significant influence on the optimum solution of
the system design problem. Our recent experience with our
current simulation study of an airport terminal building
demonstrates also the existance of an influence of control
over the dynamics of passenger flow towards the departure
halls on the required area of these halls.
        This interesting and significant interaction of
queueing system design problem with the system control has
been demonstrated with the help of a powerful discrete event
simulation method which enables both the system control
modeling and the solution of the system design problem.
The purpose of this paper is also to increase the interest
in the research on the identification and modeling of the
queueing systems operation control.

REFERENCES

1. S.P. Aranoff and F.D. D'Alessandro, 'Simulation of a
   Surface Traffic Control System for J.F. Kennedy International Airport', Proc. 5th Annual Simulation Symposium,
   Tampa, 1972, pp. 1-5.
2. B.S. Blanchard and W.J. Fabrycky, Systems Engineering
   and Analysis, Prentice-Hall, Englewood Cliffs, 1981.
3. V. Čerić, 'Simulation Modeling of Control in Postal
   Centres', Proc. 2 Symposium Simulationstechnik, Vienna,
   1984, Ed. F. Breitenecker and W. Kleijnert, Springer
   Verlag, Informatik-fachberichte, Vol. 85, pp. 278-283
   (in German).
4. V. Čerić, 'Discrete Event Simulation Model of a
   Consignment Redistribution System', Ph.D. Dissertation,
   Dept. of Management Sciences, University of Belgrade,

Belgrade, 1985 (in Croatian).

5. V. Čerić and M. Mauher, 'Simulation Model for Determination of Optimal Reservoir Capacity in Production Systems', Proc. 12th IFIP Conference on System Modeling and Optimization, Budapest, 1985, pp. 82-83.

6. R.J. Degen and T.J. Schriber, 'On the Use of GPSS to Model Hierarchical Control Systems in a Manufacturing Environment', Proc. Winter Simulation Conference, Gaithersburg, 1976, pp. 115-123.

7. L. Kleinrock, Queueing Systems, Vol. II: Computer Applications, Wiley, New York, 1976.

8. A.M. Law and W.D. Kelton, Simulation Modeling and Analysis, McGraw-Hill, New York, 1982.

9. J. Martin, Design of Real-time Computer Systems, Prentice-Hall, Englewood Cliffs, 1967.

10. H.H. Rosenbrock, Computer-Aided Control System Design, Academic Press, London, 1974.

AN INTERACTIVE MODEL FOR COMPUTER AIDED DESIGN EDUCATION AND RESEARCH ON KNOWLEDGE BASE OF DESIGNERS

Nigân Bayazıt
Istanbul Technical University
School of Architecture
Unit of Architectural Design Methodology
Teknik Üniversite, İstanbul - TURKEY

ABSTRACT. This paper is prepared to formulate an interactive computer-aided design education and research model for the establishment of a micro computer-aided design laboratory in Istanbul Technical University (ITU). The first part of the model is designed for CAD education considering the student, personnel and organization capacities of ITU. In the second part CAD research is modelled in regard to the staff and expert capacities of the University. In this study the term CAD research is taken as the research on the knowledge base of expert system for the purpose of Artificial Intelligence. Two parts of the model, the theory building in CAD research and the application of the theory in education, are planned to work in interaction with each other. The details of the model with proposed specific problem areas are explained as a guide for future studies.

1. INTRODUCTION

Turkey is at the initial stages of high technology but there is a great demand from industry and commerce so that it is advancing rapidly. Foundation of a CAD laboratory at the School of Architecture of ITU has been decided between the initiatives of University of Maryland, Department of Housing and Design (UM) and Istanbul Technical University, School of Architecture (ITU), and a collaborative research proposal has been designed.

1.2. Design Education

In this era learning activity is moving from classical classrooms to computer rooms, even to home. Design education will provide the basis for methodological as well as professional education in the future. Interactive computers provide active learning opposed to passive school learning. Information delivered by school teachers or by books makes the learner passive, absorber of that information, and spectator. Learning must be active if ideas, concepts are to be internalized. Computer can replace the tutors or team members and can query what students know.

R. Trappl (ed.), Cybernetics and Systems '86, 267–273.
© *1986 by D. Reidel Publishing Company.*

Active learning is future oriented, helps people to prepare themselves to probable technological, social, institutional changes as well
as to identify and solve their problems and make decisions having emphasis on the cognitive, critical, participative and cooperative abilities
of the learner.

1.2. Design Research

The broad and generalized definition of design research is to achieve
explanation of the form, composition, objectives, meaning and values in
man-made things and systems. The problems of designing activity, the
behavior and knowledge base of designers, their philosophical, cognitive
capabilities, psychological problems while designing are studied thor-
oughly in design research.

When one considers computer aids in designing, design research is
fundamental to develop new approaches as expert systems, knowledge bases,
studies on design thinking.

Many design theorists dealt with design thinking while they were
developing their design methods and theories.

Since A.M.Turing's "Computing Machinery and Intelligence" (1950),
Newell (1955), Newell, Shaw, Simon (1957), Simon (1969), Feigenbaum
(1963), (1969), Newell (1973), Friedman (1975), Negroponte (1970) ,and
many others directed their efforts to artificial intelligence in their
own areas. Design thinking was one of the main subjects in conferences
on design methods and theories since 1962 conference in Imperial College
(Jones), Thornley, 1962).

Design research in this study is concentrated on the development of
knowledge bases for future computer technology. It is a long and patient
study, before reaching a reliable end, to replace professionals, tutors,
designers. Human experts achieve outstanding performance because they
are knowledgable. The studies on knowledge systems investigate methods
and techniques in man-machine systems, with specialized problem solving
expertise. Expertise consists of knowledge, understanding of domain
problems and skill at solving some of the problems. Expert system is
designed to extract knowledge from humans and putting it in computable
forms that can greatly reduce the cost of knowledge reproduction and
exploitation.

2. CAD EDUCATION AND RESEARCH MODEL

The following model is designed to explain the outlines of the correspondence between design and design research. The main objective of this
correspondence is to start the development of architectural knowledge
bases for future use or to replace design educators and/or design professionals as a long term goal.

The model has three basic parts :
1. Design education,
2. Design research (building knowledge bases of expert system),
3. Evaluation of education, research and their correspondence to each
   other.

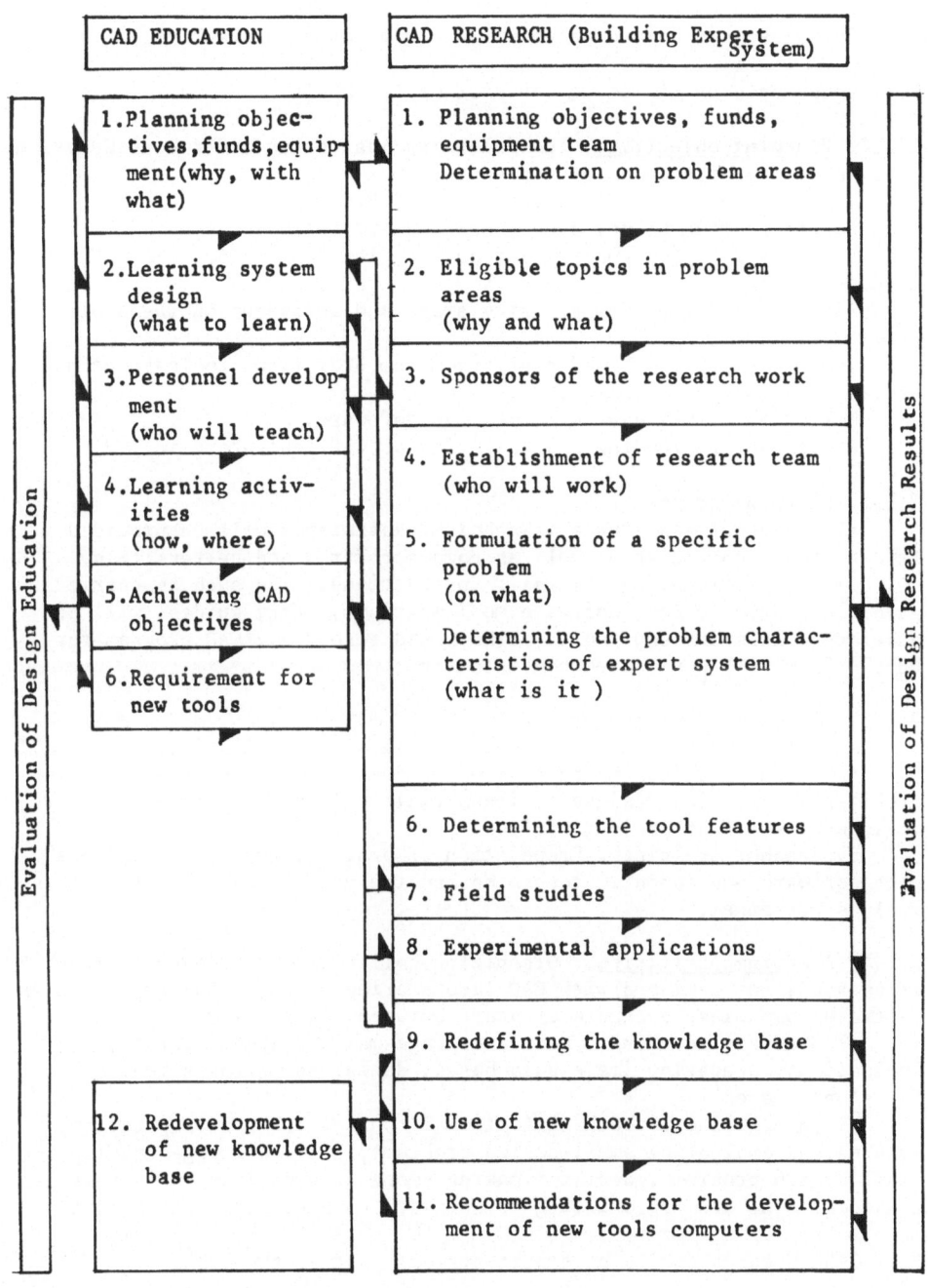

Fig.1 - CAD Education-Research-Evaluation MODEL

The first and second parts will be developed interactively.

2.1. Components of CAD education part of the MODEL

2.1.1. Planning objectives. The following issues are under consideration while planning objectives of CAD education :
Appropriateness of CAD education to ITU.
Identification of key people and funding resources.
Interdisciplinary cooperation on the planning of CAD, ITU, UM, computer firms.
Identification of CAD priority areas and decisions on the basic themes.
Contributions of UM and staff from computer firms to learn computerized learning environment.
Selection of CAD system as well as software.
Provision and funding possibilities of CAD laboratory in ITU.

2.1.2. Learning system.
a) Technical assistance : Technical assistance will be provided from software companies as well as computer firms and universities.
b) Instructional objectives : Instructional aids such as curriculum guide, software guides, software modifications, entry guides, will be developed. Existing CAD tools, methods and resources, CAD program for curricula will be evaluated consistently.

2.1.3. Personnel Development.
a) Decisions on the trainees : The users of the CAD laboratory will be identified, such as undergraduate, graduate, post graduate students, architects, interior designers, industrial designers, graphic designers, government staff of project offices.
b) Teacher training : Preparation of program, and correspondence with software and computer companies and the use of their facilities as well as personnel.

2.1.4. Learning Activities. Organizing collaborative research activities and joint seminars with CAD laboratories of UM, computer companies, software companies, exchange of staff between the ITU and UM.
a) Graduate teaching : Form and image making, space performance evaluations, preparing image data bases, decisions on the selection of forms and images.
b) Undergraduate teaching (optional course) : Image preparation, solving and evaluating small design problems, alternative generation for small design problems, decision making among alternatives with cost consideration, drawing existing buildings, teaching design techniques.

2.2. CAD research (building expert system) part of the MODEL

2.2.1. Planning research objectives, funds, equipment and team. Priorities of workable problem areas will be decided upon. Problems have no tractable solutions, since many important tasks originate in complex social or physical context which generally resists precise description.

The following problem areas of expert systems can be discussed :

a) image analysis, logical, linear, digital, time oriented, signal interpretations, etc.

b) diagnosis of building failures of building spaces, components and elements, building performance studies, etc.

c) design systems researches such as object configurations, preparation of large knowledge bases for market information, product information, building failure information, product cost information.

d) creation of specifications, statements and requirements catalogues for building construction industry.

e) user, student, professional, tutor behavior studies against computer-aided design, non-verbal, synthetic, concrete, analogic, intuitive, holistic, spatial, timeless and diffused characteristics of design behaviours of designers.

2.2.2. <u>Decisions on the eligible topics of the problem areas</u>. Different domains require specific research, design techniques and methods because they contain different design problems. Problem identification methods and approaches can be common to some domains. The functioning of the domain influences the types of the design problems, and hence the methods of investigation to understand the knowledge bases of the experts while solving design problems.

2.2.3. <u>Sponsors of this research work</u>. Computing machine firms and scientific organizations will be supporters of this program.

2.2.4. <u>Establishment of the research team.</u> Ph.D. students, project director and research assistants, educational departments of computing machinery firms, psychologists will be involved in this study.

2.2.5. <u>Formulation of a specific problem.</u> Specific problem on extracting knowledge from experts and encoding it in a program form can be applied to various areas. Here the designers are at the heart of the problem as experts.

The following steps will be considered in the problem formulation. To simplify the design research problem area lay people are selected as the subject of the research. The study on lay people in design will reduce the inputs of previous experience on form perception, conditioning and knowledge of form as designer.

The main knowledge base study will depend on the concept of "form follows form". Transfer of perceived form to formulated new design object and the structuring of knowledge are the main problem areas. The shape, time, speed, scale, number, color, texture, structural patterns are main parameters in this study. There are various difficulties generating from the cultural as well as individual characteristics of the sample people and experiment situation.

2.2.6. <u>Tool features</u>. Proposed tool features are IBM PCXT in ITU in the beginning, and IBM PCXT and PCAT at UM for this project.

2.2.7. Field studies. Observations, definitions, conceptualizations, formulations, structuring, symbolizing, testing steps on lay people. In the next stage application will be made on experts, in a specific field of architecture.

2.2.8. Experimenting with computers. Computer applications will be made in finding a way to symbolize the real world situation applying an appropriate interface or developing a new interface.

2.2.9. Redefining the needs and requirements of knowledge base for new experiments.
     a) Recommendations for the development of new tools, i.e. computers,
     b) Use of new knowledge base in practice,
     c) Redevelopment of knowledge base.

2.3. Interaction between two parts

Interaction between the design education, and research will be established through design practice. Same topics will be applied on students and/or experts and their behavioral responses will be studied. Teachers and trainers will be studied as experts and their learning capabilities and styles will be the indicator for symbolization of expert knowledge base system. Cognitive moddeling will be developed, structures and their effects on designing skills will be searched.

2.4. Evaluation of the whole system

In every step an evaluation procedure will be applied to control the results of education, expert system research and their interaction.

3. CONCLUSION

Development of CAD education and research model brings about a framework for the studies in a CAD Laboratory at the beginning. Design education is the application area of design research which indicates the directions and the results of research on expert system. Design research is a bridge between the design practice world and its application to computers, as they are going to be the basic tools for the design profession in the future. Extracting knowledge from professional experts and putting it in computable forms can greatly reduce the cost of knowledge reproduction redundancy and exploitation. This study will facilitate the transfer of high technology to Turkey and solve the educational as well as research problems of ITU in relation to CAD.
    This study will shed some light to the theoretical brain studies and human thinking problems in the specific area of form perception and design synthesis output. The lack of tool features will be diagnosed and valuable recommendations for computing firms will be developed.

4. REFERENCES

Feigenbaum, E.A., Feldman, J. (Eds) (1963), Computers and Thought, New York : Wiley.

Friedman, Y., (1975), Toward a Scientific Architecture, Cambridge, Mass,; MIT Press.

Hayes-Roth, F., Waterman, D.A., (1983), Building Expert Systems, Reading Mass.; Addison-Wesley.

Jones, C.J., Thornley, D.G., (1962), Conference on Design Methods, New York : Pergamon Press.

Negroponte, N., (1970), The Architecture Machine, Cambridge, Mass.; MIT Press.

Newell, A., (1955), The Chess Machine, An Example of Dealing with a Complex Task by Adaptation, Proceedings of the Western Joint Computer Conference, New York : Institute of Radio Engineers.

Newell, A., Shaw, J.C., Simon, H.A., (1957), Empirical Foundations of the Logic Theory Machine : A Case Study in Heuristics, Proceedings of the 1957 Western Joint Computer Conference, New York : Institute of Radio Engineers.

Simon, A.H., (1969), The Science of the Artificial, Cambridge Mass.; MIT Press.

Turing, A.M., (1950), 'Computing Machinery and Intelligence', Mind, Vol. 59, pp. 443-450.

Humanity, Architecture, and Conceptualisation

Chairperson: G.Pask (UK)

The Way You Look Determines What You See
Or
Self-Organization in Management and Society

Michael U. Ben-Eli   Gilbert J.B. Probst
The Cybertec Consulting Group   and   St. Gall University, Switzerland
New York, N.Y., U.S.A.   and The Wharton School
                                                         Philadelphia, Pa., U.S.A.

The concept of self-organization is reviewed and its implications
are explored in relation to management processes and social
systems. A world view is taken, emphasizing a descriptive
distinction of levels associated with the physical, biological,
social, and mental. Self-organization principles, it is argued,
are operative in all levels of such a stratified scheme, but they
are manifest in different mechanisms and different embodiments.

Management, planning, design, and other "intervention" type of
activities are among the processes through which self-organization is manifest in the social domain. Ultimately they have to
do with maintaining, enriching, and amplifying the potential
variety of the systems concerned. The operationally critical
question involved, it is suggested, is not whether management
activities are "man-made" or "natural," spontaneous" or
"planned," but rather, whether they enhance or supress the
potential variety of a system under consideration.

Introduction

Science, Eddington stated, involves the systematic organization of
humanity's facts of experience. At its best and most creative, science
produces powerful models which for us, human observers, integrate,
interpret, and, in turn, help further interpretation of reality. All
scientific models contribute to the construction of a "world view," but
there is a subtle difference between two type classes of such models.
The most familiar and accepted class of models takes the form of con-
densed quantitative equations, such as Newton's laws of motion, Einstein's $E=mc^2$, and the like. Another class, however, involves the
qualitative interpretation of patterns of phenomena, that is, the
construction of models that take the form of principles of explanation
(Bateson, 1972; von Foerster, 1984). Examples would include the theory
of evolution, notions of relatively, the concept of final cause, and the
like.

The idea of a self-organizing system belongs to this latter class. As
it stands, it does not provide a calculus for predicting single events,
but rather, it provides a conceptual handle with which one can come to

277

R. Trappl (ed.), Cybernetics and Systems '86, 277–284.
© *1986 by D. Reidel Publishing Company.*

grips with complexity that otherwise would elude one's understanding. This is important in so much as it makes a difference if one were to treat a perceived system as being self-organizing or not. The purpose of this paper, accordingly, is to discuss the idea of self-organization, particularly as it relates to management and society.

Self-Organization -- Revisited

What a human observer perceives is largely determined by how he looks at the world and how he looks, in turn, is greatly biased by his sensorial apparatus and also by his experience and socio-cultural background: His values, attitudes, and general view of the world.

In relation to a world view dominated by the second law of thermo-dynamics and pointing, as it does, to the unavoidable increase of homogeneity and indistinguishability, operable not only globally but locally as well, the notion of self-organization can be seen as an attempt, perhaps originally quite unconscious, to compensate for the emphasis on inevitable physical decay and account for the everywhere apparent cases of orderliness and the formation and increase in organi-zation which are typical to all life and social processes; self-organi-zation, because no evident, single isolatable controller can be shown to be responsible for bringing order about.

Intuitively, a self-organizing system is characterized by such terms as complex, dynamic, non-deterministic, and self-referential. It involves active processes and it would typically be interpreted by an observer to have an independent "purpose." It entails some notion of "order," as, for example, when something initially unorganized becomes organized or when an organization develops to become a "better" or more effective organization (Ashby, 1962), both cases being an emergent product of a system's own activity.

However, there is an essentially relativistic connotation immanent in the concept of "organization" and hence also of self-organization. The concept requires a distinction between a system, its environment, and an observer. The latter, in fact, provides the criteria for distinction relative to which a system is identified in the first place. The observer's perspective and purpose determine the frame of reference with respect to which observations are made and conclusions concerning ob-served phenomena are reached.

Discussions on self-organization burgeoned in the late fifties and early sixties, essentially as part of that period's rapid developments in Cybernetics and General System thinking. Early contributions focused on notions involving goal seeking, self-stabilization, homeostasis, adapt-ation, and other concepts typical of the early days of Cybernetics (Yovitz and Cameron, 1960; von Foerster and Zopf, 1962). In recent years, interest in the notion of self-organization has been rekindled (Jantsch, 1980; Prigogine 1984; von Foerster, 1984) with a subsequent shift toward problems in management (Ulrich and Probst, 1981), family therapy (Guntern, 1982), and larger social processes (Luhmann, 1984), with a focus on problems of cognition, intelligence, emergent properties, evolution, creativity, novelty, innovation, and future oriented design. There is, however, a logical continuity that underlies all.

Still perhaps the most elegant and rigorous definition of self-organization is due to von Foerster (1960). Using Shannon's information theoretic concept of redundancy to derive a measure of organization, von Foerster defines a self-organizing system as a system in which the rate of change of its redundancy is always positive. It is precisely this notion of a dynamically continuous positive redundancy which suggests the complexity and richness of behavior found in "living" systems.

Processes of self-organization involving order, complexity, organization, or in some sense, increased effectiveness, always assume an available source of energy. By and large they encompass processes and mechanisms relating to the preservation of autonomy (maintenance) and its creation and recreation (evolution). Typical underlying mechanisms have been characterized by such terms as self-reference, organizational closure autopoiesis, homeostasis, ultrastability, self-reproduction, innovation, learning, and novel emergence. These entail the many rich and complex manifestations ranging from interactions of molecules to the behavior of cells, the dynamics of species, and the many intricate activities and qualities that are special to human societies.

Observable patterns in the evolution of order and complexity are conveniently clustered into levels associated with physical, biological, societal (Boulding, 1978), and, perhaps, "mind" systems. Self-organizing principles are operative in all levels of such a stratified scheme, but they are manifest in different mechanisms and different embodiments. Qualitatively, the products of self-organization across these levels increase in their variety, showing ever greater potency and richness in behavior. From the viewpoint of Cybernetics this expansion in self-realization potentialities can be interpreted as showing a consistent amplification of regulation capabilities (Ben-Eli, 1978), not just in the specialized sense of more efficiently exploiting particular niches, but even more significantly, in the production of ever richer, potentially more comprehensive regulators and the general evolutionary amplification of a property akin to McCulloch's (1965) "redundancy of potential command."

In each of the levels suggested above the dynamics of "becoming" involve essentially processes of production. Production of "self" and the elaboration and expansion of the range of "self," as well as of the means of its self-production capabilities.

As Boulding (1978) suggests, production processes always involve three primary factors: know-how, energy, and materials. It is particularly in the domain of human social systems that the scope of each is significantly expanded and the potential for their availability, development, assembly, combination, and recombination is immensely enhanced, becoming

279

richer and more flexible in its self-realization possibilities.

In the context of human social systems, essentially biological functions of individual humans (sensation, computation, movement) are externalized and amplified many-fold through selective voluntary linkages to vast networks of artifacts and a comprehensive technological infrastructure. This physical aspect of societal variety is further augmented by the more abstract domain of cognitive processes, language, symbolism, and world views, as well as by the rich and varied expressions of culture, including its ethical and esthetical manifestations. All of these involve processes, or mechanisms, through which self-organization is manifest in the social domain.

This domain is increasingly dominated by its own products. But all such products, whether spiritual, cultural, or technological are as much part of nature as other components of the biosphere such as flowers, trees, birds, or butterflies. All are emergent manifestations of evolution. All are "natural." All are native to the complex ecology of Earth.

Self-Organization in Management and Society

In human social systems, the significant amplification in potential variety of self-regulating mechanisms graduates to a qualitatively unprecedented dimension with the advent of choice about purpose and means, as well as the ability consciously to project, pursue, and implement images of entirely new possibilities. Self-organization is operative here in a second order fashion as conscious choices are made subject to self-monitoring, modification, and novel design.

In the core of such processes are human-specific capabilities such as "Management" or "Design" seen not in their specialized professional sense, but as general activities through the wise conduct of which the possibility of human participation in evolution itself is exercised.

Human activities concerned with management, planning, design, and the like, appear at first glance to be contradictory to the notion of self-organization. If human social systems are truly self-organizing, are not managers and planners simply interfering with what would other-wise be a wise benign process?

This seeming contradiction has recently been given a considerable amount of attention focusing on notions of "planned" as distinct from "spontaneous" order. The latter is often portrayed as a positive, desired condition, while the former, at least by implication, is condemned, although the pragmatic need for management-type intervention is never entirely denied (Zeleney, 1985). Confusion exists around this seeming dichotomy. How can it be resolved?

The outline of our own view must have emerged by now. Management, planning, or design type activities, operating as components and not as the "environment" of the social system, are precisely the agents of self-organization in the human-societal "organism." There is no real sense in which they can be separated from the system itself. The entire question concerning the distinction is misconstrued and the contradiction arises because of the way the argument is cast.

The distinction and the confusion which follows, arise, it appears, from at least two important related factors. The first has to do with the relativistic aspects of the concept of self-organization alluded to earlier. Whether management is seen as part of the "spontaneous" activity of a system or as something alien to it, depends very much on where an observer chooses to place his systemic boundaries. A micro view may focus on a management activity isolated from the total social fabric and, in fact, there is important utility in doing so. A bird's eye view, on the other hand, will offer a different perspective. in which the special single case disappears and the overall flow of a history with typical self-organizing characteristics comes to the fore.

The second factor is related, but perhaps even more significant. It has to do with millenia of conceptual conditioning by the predominantly western dogma of creation. The first chapters of Genesis portray the concept of an entirely independent entity bringing order to a "world system" by an arbitrary decree and then interacting and controlling "it" from without. Accept this view concerning the method by which organization and order are brought about and you are but one small step away from transferring it to the domain of social system and from a typical view of management as being applied to a system from "outside" by managers who are "independent" from "it" and who "control" rather than participate in its self-generated, evolving activities.

Understanding the true nature of self-organization, properly identifying management-related activities with its dynamic activities, and bringing a conceptual resolution to the apparent contradiction of the "planned" versus the "spontaneous" are all important for a simple reason: How we manage social affairs and how we judge the results of our actions is deeply conditioned by our view of the nature of the processes involved. The effectiveness of action is much dependent on how effective, as guiding principles, are the models we have of the world and unless we are simply lucky, an erroneous road map is likely to lead us astray. Thus, if we approach a process as if it were an object, a complex system as if it were a trivial assembly of independent parts, or a self-organizing system as if it were a simple clock, we are only likely to be frustrated by unexpected, often undesired, baffling outcomes, resulting from applying an all too primitive notion of management or control.

Managing the Self-Organizing System and Self-Organizing the Managing System

What does it mean, then, to manage a self-organizing system? What are the management-related consequences of the ideas discussed above?

On the face of it, a few important implications emerge, some of which are not entirely unfamiliar, although they are still far from dominating the mainstream of management practice. The newly requisite mode of thinking relates, for example, to a shift from a focus on end results to a process orientation, and from a psychology of viewing the manager as an almost independent focal point of control to an emphasis on distributed intelligence, intimately and inseparably woven into the very fabric of the system itself.

Such shifts are manifest in the growing interest in the idea of "participatory management," in "decentralization," and the push of decision-making responsibility as "wide" and as "low" as possible; in emphasizing the importance of appropriate input to planning processes from all "stake holders"; and in the recognition of the vital need for "entrepreneurial spirit" so that continuous vitality of organizations is ensured. Many such ideas are already apparent in various experimentations with innovative management in government and in the corporate world. When carried to their full conclusion they are bound to bring about a profound change in our management culture and revolutionize the whole concept of what effective management is in the first place, challenging current notions of authority, power, decision making prerogatives, and even the structure of compensation and the distribution of wealth, to their very core.

In a more theoretical vein, Ashby's law of requisite variety combined with McCulloch's concept of redundancy of potential command and von Foerster's definition of self-organization, to which reference has already been made, put into sharper focus not only the pragmatic management strategies referred to above, but the whole general question of managing a self-organizing system. Seen from the viewpoint of these cybernetic theories, the meta function of management is to facilitate, coordinate, integrate, and steer the flow of a system's activities such that its potential variety always remains alive.

Regardless of the scale of systems with which it is involved, the human mind is often tempted to reach for an "ultimate" concept of order or the "genius" one stroke management act. Unless they are entirely trivialized, however, social systems, by definition, cannot be permanently dominated by a single action, no matter how grandly conceived. Their state at any given time is the comprehensive result of a multitude of interacting visions, aspirations, actions, and plans, some well thought out, some incomplete, many mutually antagonistic. The complexity involved defies precise prescription and the resulting condition is rarely exactly "as intended." But this is an inherent synergetic characteristic of systems, the whole behavior of which is unpredictable by the simple sum of their parts. It is precisely here that Adam Smith's "invisible hand" is operating to produce a continuous, self-organizing, balancing act.

Note how self-organization is operating simultaneously on a number of different levels. On one level it is operative in discrete activities, each always accommodating recent pertinent events. On another, it is operative in the ceaseless mutual adjustments of all single activities to produce a meta-systemic whole. On yet another level, however, it operates recursively on "itself," improving on previous norms of self-organization thus ever enhancing the continuous vitality of the self-organizing, process itself.

The meta function of management can thus be made unambiguously clear. True to von Foerster's dictum, it has to do with maintaining, enriching, and amplifying the potential variety of its domain of concern. The critical question is not whether management activities are "man-made" or "natural," "spontaneous" or "planned," but rather, whether they enhance or supress the potential variety of a system under consideration.

Management for Human Development

For any meaningful purpose, variety needs to be channelled. Without qualification, without constraints, the organized landscape of the actually manifest would be impossible. What are the mechanisms, then, for channelling variety? In biology, for example, constraints are applied by the classical process of selection. Among the many tried-out possibilities, that which "works" is allowed to persist. Similar mechanisms operate in society with one important difference. On the level of human social systems, the most powerful device for channelling variety has to do with self-generated purpose. It is precisely in the projection, articulation, elaboration, and refinement of purpose that the most significant function of management in social systems resides.

Here we come immediately against the problem of the relative degree of constraints. Clearly, different activities require a different app-roach. For example, a tight construction schedule with its related budget control requires a great deal of variety constraint, whereas the effective management of pure research or any type of true innovation calls for a much more liberal approach. It appears, interestingly enough, that the tighter the requisite degree of control, the more trivial, with respect to human potential, the pursuit in question is likely to be. There are many special circumstances, nevertheless, which from a management viewpoint, require quick constraint in variety and various crisis situation offer good examples. War would be a case in point although its outbreak can be seen as a social-systemic pathology, the consequence, in part, of inappropriately supressing social variety in the first place. Ultimately, a critically vital management question relates to negotiating the appropriate balance between too much rigidity and too much freedom so that flexibility and the potential for change are ensured.

283

In human social systems -- societies, organizations, corporations, and institutions of various kinds -- channelling and orchestrating variety, "variety engineering" in the sense suggested by Beer (1981), is the very stuff of management. Purpose is the driving force behind shaping the flow of variety. What, then, is the value, the selection criterion, underlying the notion of purpose itself?

The general answer to this question has already been suggested. It has to do with consciously nurturing the self-organizing potentialities of the system involved. In a more specific, pragmatic sense, however, Ackoff's (1981) concept of development offers a powerful working guideline. Beyond questions concerning the bottom line, beyond issues of profits, survival, or annual growth, the primary criteria for judging the effectiveness of management in social systems relate directly to the degree of success it has in enhancing the self-development possibilities for individual participants, as well as the particular social system as a whole.

The ultimate goal, the meta challenge for management in human social systems has to do with how effective it is in creating and recreating environments that increase degrees of freedom and enhance the potential for self-realization of all individuals, while eliminating oppressive advantage-taking of some by others, and minimizing mutually-blocking cross interferences, releasing creative energies enriching to all.

In this concept lies the key to designing management for freedom. But with freedom comes responsibility -- expanding in an ever more encompassing progression from the self to other humans, to all sentient beings, to life itself, and the planet as a whole.

Acknowledgements

Many thanks to Heinz von Foerster, Professor Emeritus, University of Illinois; Prof. Russel Ackoff, Busch Center, The Wharton School; and Michael Parker of The Cybertec Consulting Group, Inc., for their valuable suggestions and help.

References can be obtained upon request by the authors.

CATHEDRALS IN THE MIND:
THE ARCHITECTURE OF METAPHOR IN UNDERSTANDING LEARNING

Kathleen Forsythe
Executive Director, Learning Systems
Knowledge Network
Box 3200
VICTORIA, B.C.
Canada   V8W 3H4

ABSTRACT.

The pervasiveness of metaphor in our conceptual system suggests a
central and basic role in the underlying architecture of thought.
Metaphor represents the ability to understand one thing in terms of
another as we ascribe an understood pattern to an unknown phenomena and
perceive their structural integrity within the environment of our
experience. We can then begin to perceive the environment of learning
as one in which analogical thinking serves as architecture, analytical
thinking serves as engineering and the imagination ensures that the
interactions which create life and meaning are always being realized
anew. The implications for this approach to applied epistemology
provides insight into the design and development of learning systems
that support the creative nature of learning.

1.0   It can be argued that metaphor is at the fundamental core of
our conceptual system as surely as the logic of form which we use in
argument and debate. However, because our conceptual system is not
something we are normally aware of, we have failed to account for its
metaphorical nature in our discussion of truth and meaning. Yet its
pervasiveness suggests a central and basic role in the underlying
architecture of thought. Metaphor can create new meaning, create
similarities and so define a new insight and new perception of reality.
Such a view has no place in the dominant objectivist picture of the
world. Metaphor is the architecture of similarity and relation where
whole pattern is created from the composite unity of both our
subjective and objective points of view as they are experienced. Thus
metaphor is part of the vitality of our interactions in both the inner
and outer environment through a living language of pattern. And so,
the repeated discovery of coherent patterns in both nature and our own
inner system of symbols suggests that our ordinary conceptual system,
in terms of which we both think and act, is fundamentally metaphorical
in nature. Gregory Bateson, just before his death, had the following
insight:
"...metaphor is not just pretty poetry, it is not either good or bad

285

R. Trappl (ed.), Cybernetics and Systems '86, 285-292.
© 1986 by D. Reidel Publishing Company.

logic, but it is in fact the logic upon which the biological world
has been built, the main characteristic and organizing glue of this
world of mental process..."[1]

1.1   Sample sees the metaphorical mind and the metaphorical way of
learning as linked to hemispheric ways of knowing.[2]
Von Bertalanffy's General Systems Thinking has been termed "the
science of similarities", which are called "isomorphisms", by which
he meant structural likenesses that reflect a commonality in the way
the parts of a system relate to each other.[3] Pribam has suggested
that there is no such thing as metaphor because, in a sense, all
metaphor is true, "Everything is isomorphic."[4]

1.2   Analogy and its poetic expression, metaphor, may be the
"meta-forms" necessary to understanding those aspects of our mind
that make connections, often in non-verbal and implicit fashion, that
allow us to understand the world in a whole way.

2.0   THE CATHEDRAL - A PARADOXICAL METAPHOR

"We were led into a large cavern. At first, it was dark and the size
was felt rather than seen. Then it began to change - the elegant
thrust of a vaulted roof, the exquisite detail on this protuberance,
on that wall - it must be some kind of cathedral but what a
cathedral! shimmering and changing with light and colour, the walls
breathing with life, organic forms that shifted like a kaleidoscope,
now structural, now softly organic. I wanted to stop and examine
each change but the guide made me go on. The idea came that if I was
to understand I must see the whole of the cathedral. Then I would be
free to travel through it at my leisure. We went on - the shifting
magical forms compelled us. Then I knew I was alone - inside this
pulsing glowing cathedral. The shifts had meaning! The structure
was elegant, labyrinthine yet organic. The colours altered seeming
at will. As I breathed, it breathed; as it breathed, I breathed.
Could it be my will? I was somehow affecting this structure and it,
affecting me! Then, as suddenly as the dream began, I moved from
here to there. I was outside and inside at once. Just as suddenly,
I knew I had been on a tour of my own mind as it was thinking. I had
been the conscious architect of the cathedral as well as being in it
and of it. I had participated in the process of learning and I felt
it."[6]

2.1   The above experience was not induced by drugs or a meditative
state. It was a very vivid example of insight. These very powerful
flashes of insight, usually follow periods of intense study or
emotional or intellectual activity. From them, it is possible to
learn 'guiding principles' which help one to understand one's
relationship to the world around and the world within. Such
experiences validate both an introspective and extrospective journey
of trying to understand the process of learning, to describe it and
to try and find a metaphor which may prove useful to others who also

seek to understand and <u>feel</u> their own learning.

2.2   The concept of the cathedral has proved to be a seminal metaphor in trying to describe the process of 'ideational architecture'. It is paradoxical that such an enduring stone structure as the cathedral should seem such an apt description of the elegant process of thinking which is such a dynamic dance of activity. However, paradox seems to be a common thread in any discussion of the nature of thinking.

2.3   The concept of 'structure' as a root to understanding is certainly not a new one. However, the growth in the application of 'systems' thinking to social and individual behaviour is providing a context for modelling dynamic structures at both a meta, macro and microcosmic level. As Von Bertalanffy pointed out, we are a 'denizen of two worlds', the physical universe and a universe of our own construction – the world of symbols. Symbol triggering patterns may lie at the root of meaning and may be our guide posts to the universe of understanding.

2.4   Indeed, no sooner had the cathedral metaphor presented itself than it seemed to change, and its greatest strength seemed in its incipient instability. It was as if, when we take in information, what we are doing is mentally asking:

> "Is this the tile for the mosaic down the left corridor of the nave? I've been waiting for years for that piece! Zap! That tile is in its place!"
>   or
> "Is this a whole new left nave? Zap! the cathedral is altered!"
>   or
> "Is this a whole new cathedral? Wow! That one is gone and another one is in place."

and we look around to see universes of cathedrals of which we are both the conscious architects as well as the substance of their structure.

2.5   All of this is done with a rapidity of analysis, synthesis, judgement and decision-making that is so intense and collapsed in time as to be unrecognized.

Thus the process of taking in information, assessing it and discarding or integrating with what is already known is a process of <u>qualitative</u> and <u>quantitative</u> change that can occur with incredible rapidity Conversely, like the cathedrals of old, it can also be a process or rumination over years. As one teacher remarked after hearing the above cathedral analogy, "At last, I understand Piaget's accommodation and assimilation and I have found a metaphor for my own learning."

2.6   Learning is the process of changing one's mind – literally –
and the cathedral metaphor provided a structure to describe the
nature and order of the changes. Thomas Kuhn's theory of scientific
progress via 'paradigm shifts' is particularly apropos of the
cathedral metaphor. In the face of accumulating experience that is
not explained by existing models, the mind searches for a more
workable model. Thus the metaphorical dissolving cathedral is also
an image for paradigm shift. And just as the great cathedrals took
almost one hundred years to built, the enormous capacity of the mind
is exemplified by the speed of change of mind. The process of this
change is not without order but is analogous to the dissipative
nature of open systems as they constantly dissolve to re-form into
new synthesis of complexity as meta-forms.

2.7   The cathedral is only one metaphor. The architectural
modelling process, however, is a way to think about visual,
ideational, emotional and social knowledge structures in order to
examine the thesis that experiencing and examining one knowledge
structure in depth will facilitate the ability to recognize and
develop other knowledge structures i.e. experiencing one's own
thought while one is thinking will improve one's thinking ability.
Concomitant with this thesis is the notion that we could design a
learning system to enable one to consciously experience one's own
process of learning while one is learning. Being able to comprehend
both content and process is fundamental to achieving a new way to
think about learning. We have to be able to self-reference in order
to see our minds changing. We have to find our own personal metaphor
to provide a way to give feedback to our minds on the mind's own
terms.

3.0   Yet how are we to find a way to talk about such a phenomena
without entering into that infinite regress so characteristic of
"thinking about thinking about thinking etc." Hofstadter, in asking
what is the key to understanding creativity, describes a difference
between the human process and the machine process:

> "I would summarize it by saying that it is a general
> sensitivity to patterns, an ability to spot patterns of
> unanticipated types in unanticipated places at unanticipated
> times in unanticipated media."

He goes on to point out that clearly there is something lacking in a
machine.

> "The thing that is lacking can be described in a few words:
> it is the ability to watch oneself as one deals with the
> world, to perceive in one's own activities a pattern and to
> be able to do so at many levels of abstraction."

3.1   To use Hofstadter's analysis further, "In a way "pattern"
means "the underlying logic of a given structure", yet perhaps more

accurately "pattern" means "a structure possessing an underlying logic."[9] It is the ability to "order" one's perception. As Bohm says, a general way of perceiving what is meant by order is to say that order means "to give attention to similar differences and different similarities."[10]

3.2   The issues of content and process are no longer the key issues in the new ways of thinking about learning. What both behaviourists and cognitivists have had in common, is their assumption that analytical thinking based on logical deduction and logical inference is evidence of use of cognition and that the form of our thinking can be separated from its content. The point of interface, and the exclectical point of the new way, is a much older philosophical question: "What is the precise relationship between thought and thinking." Bohm suggests ...."indeed, content and process are not two separately existent things, but rather, they are two aspects or views of one whole movement."[11]

3.3   The key words here are relationship, process and movement because thought is not static, which is precisely why it is too mercurial to discuss using direct referential language. We can only catch the kinetic and relational nature of our thought through a relational language such as a calculus or through analogy and metaphor, the connection making algebra of language.

3.4   If we accept this view, we may then begin to look for an analogy to describe the "patterns" of relationship between ideas or "knowables", their relational architecture and the process of learning. Construction of new knowledge or finding our way through the entailment of idea structures - the web of imagination - can then be based on shared concepts and meaning and can be ordered through our agreement or disagreement.

3.5   The fundamental difference in this new view of learning is to see analogical thinking as the architecture and analytical thinking as the engineering of our mind's view of the world. Thinking and learning then becomes a dynamic "open" geometry (Fuller, 1979)[12] characterized by increasing complexity and transformation as a dissipative structure (Prigogine, 1977)[13] based on a kinetic, relational calculus (Pask, 1976)[14]. The meta design is not built on inference and syllogism but on analogy and relation thus allowing form to develop from an underlying logic - the morphogenesis of an idea. (Sheldrake, 1981).[15] Knowledge is seen not as an absolute to be known but always in relation to agreement and disagreement, to coherence and distinction in terms of individual, cultural and social points of view. The language we use to communicate then takes on a heightened importance (Wittgenstein 1933)[16] whether that be the language of words or the metaphor language of pattern (Alexander, 1979)[17]

4.0   In order to try and understand the implications of the

architecture of metaphor in understanding learning, the author
designed and developed a prototypical learning system, Project
Unicorn, that endeavoured to create an architecture of metaphor
applied through a variety of media. A number of questions were
intriguing.

1. How do we conceive of "newness?"
   Where does "newness" come from?

2. Is there a skill of complex pattern fluency that underlies our
   conceptual ability? If so, does child- thought give us a gateway
   to understand how we develop this skill?

3. Can children grasp the insights of Conversation Theory if it is
   presented through metaphor. What if the metaphor is contained in
   a learning system that utilizes television and print?

4. How do media such as television and print provide a means for
   conversation?

4.1   Because every system with a purpose has a purpose in it, it
was essential that the design and development of this prototype also
practise the principles it was trying to communicate. For this
reason, Project Unicorn modelled the architecture and design of
creative television production exemplified in the Treasure Hunters -
a television special for children that is designed to evoke
conversation in the imagination of viewers. The design of a
conversation book, Hunting the Treasure, intended to evoke
conversations between adults and children, was also based on
metaphorical architecture.

4.2   The metaphor chosen as the kernel of the architecture was one
that is also fundamental to understanding Conversation Theory. When
"argument is war" is the metaphor used in conversation then we build
walls of disagreement. When we choose the metaphor "argument is a
journey of discovery of difference" then we build bridges leading to
new understanding. [19]

4.3   In presenting this metaphor as a children's allegorical
adventure, the author intended to present in a powerful, visual and
dramatic way, an alternative pattern that was based on the
multi-varied logic of Conversation Theory - a logic of process not
only a logic of proposition. The patterns, derived from the above
kernel, were exemplified in the language patterns of drama, colour,
landscape, music, poetry and images of the product.

Just as the author's experience of understanding her own thinking as
a constantly dissolving cathedral had led her to perceive the power
of metaphor in describing the self-referential quality of thought, so
Project Unicorn endeavoured to provide a dynamic universe of coherent
patterns that would connect with deeply formulated patterns in the

minds of those who would use the learning system. It was anticipated that the story would evoke new patterns that could begin to bridge inner and outer reality, thus providing metaphorical tools with which to conceptualize their own thought. This is the power of metaphor in understanding and it lies at the essence of our humanity.[20]

4.5   In this view, learning is understood as the perception of newness. The essential distinction in this approach is to predicate the act of learning as an individual perceptual decision, that the individual makes, based on the feedback from interaction with the environment. The interaction with the environment is the behaviour.[21]   In this there is both the perception of newness of things previously unknown to the learner but known to others in the environment and there is the perception of newness that has not been known. It is arguable that insight and understanding are always new to the individual regardless of whether there seems to be a body of knowledge. The interaction of these public and private "quests for newness" involve the imagination, i.e. the ability to conceive of what has not been known before. Learning, then, is a creative act.

5.0   Metaphor is also the ability to understand one thing in terms of another. This is a function of the imagination – we are able somehow to ascribe an understood pattern to an unknown phenomena and perceive their structural integrity in the environment of our experience. This function of imagination is one measure of the autonomy of the cognitive faculty that allows us to distinguish personhood from which we derive our sense of individual freedom and responsibility.[22]   The architecture of how we structure the reality of our imagination is metaphoric. Metaphors are bridges that order the nature of our collective and individual humanity. Metaphor provides the vitality to the pattern language of thought for it is the mechanism of ordering newness. Language only lives when each person has his or her own version that must constantly be re-created in each person's mind as he or she interacts with others in the environment. It is only through understanding these inner patterns that we can begin to consciously bring the outer pattern of our lives into harmony.

"Imagine that one day millions of people are using pattern languages and making them again. Won't it impress itself then, as extraordinary, that these poems which they exchange, this giant tapesty of images, which they create, is coming alive before their eyes. Will it be possible then, for people to say stonily, that poems are not real, and that patterns are nothing but images; when, in fact, the world of images controls the world of matter.

In early times the city itself was intended as an image of the universe – its form a guarantee of the connection between the heavens and the earth, a picture of a whole and coherent way of life. A living pattern language is even more. It shows each person his connection to the world in terms so powerful that he can re-affirm it daily by using it to create new life in all the places round about him. And in this sense, finally, as we shall see, the living language is a gate."[23]

6.0   FOOTNOTES

1.   Bateson, Gregory - "Form, Substance and Difference" STEPS
2.   Samples, Bob   - The Metaphoric Mind,
        Addison-Wesley Publishing Company, Don Mills, 1981
3.   Davidson, Mark - Uncommon Sense: The Life and Thought of
        Ludwig von Bertalanffy,J.P. Tarcher, Inc.,Los Angeles, 1983
4.   Wilber, Ken - Editor, The Holographic Paradigm and
        other Paradoxes, Shambhala, Boulder, 1982
5.   Bohm, David - Wholeness and the Implicate Order
        Routledge & Kegan Paul, London, 1980
6.   Forsythe, Kathleen - original insight
7.   Kuhn, Thomas   - The Structure of Scientific Revolutions
        University of Chicago Press, Chicago, 1970
8.   Buzan, Tony - Using Both Sides of Your Brain
        Dutton, New York, 1983
9.   Hofstadter, Douglas The Mind's I Barton Books, Toronto 1982
10.   Bohn, David - Op Sit.
11.   Ibid.
12.   Fuller, Buckminster - Synergetics 2
        MacMillan Publishing Co.Inc., New York,1979
13.   Prigogine, Ilya Order Out of Chaos Bantam Books,Toronto 1984
14.   Pask, Gordon - Conversation, Cognition and Learning,
        Elsevier, Amsterdam and New York, 1975
15.   Sheldrake, Rupert A New Science of Life, Granada,Toronto 1983
16.   Wittgenstein, Ludwig- The Blue and Brown Books
        Basil Blackwell, Oxford, 1972
17.   Alexander, Christopher - The Timeless Way of Building,
        Oxford University Press, Berkeley, 1979
18.   Forsythe, Kathleen - "In Search of Unicorns", paper given
        American Society for Cybernetics, Philadelphia, 1984
19.   Lakoff, George,Johnson,Mark - Metaphors We Live By
        University of Chicago Press, Chicago 1980
20.   Forsythe, Kathleen,/Haughey, Margaret - Learning Metaphors,
        The Knowledge ConnectorsPaper given to the International
        Council for Distance Education, Melbourne, 1985
21.   Powers, William T. - Behaviour, the Control of Perception,
        Wildwood House, London, 1983
22.   Ibid.
23.   Alexander, C. - Op Sit.

NEW SOCIO-CYBERNETIC FOUNDATIONS FOR VALUE SYSTEMS

Arnold CORNELIS
University of Amsterdam,
Epistemological Foundations and Research Methods
Oude Hoogstraat 24,
1012 CE Amsterdam
The Netherlands

ABSTRACT. Research on values has been developed in the past without taking to account the social nature of the problems involved or without using the framework of cybernetics. As a result we have Moore's theory of the naturalistic fallacy in ethics and Weber's theory of value-free social sciences. However, the presuppositions behind these epistemological positions cannot be maintained in view of the changes in the conception of the social and cultural role of science and technology. The new foundations for social assessment offer a reconstruction of the problem of values in the socio-cybernetics of scientific thought.

1.THE NEW REPRESENTATION OF SCIENTIFIC IDENTITY PARADIGMATA

In the evolution of species we can distinguish two different strategies for survival. One strategy consists in making the individual invisible, or almost invisible, by a systematic adaptation to the external characteristics of the environment. The animal hides itself, making the differences between the own identity and the structural characteristics of the environment as small as possible. On the other hand, there is a strategy of survival of making the individual conspicuous, that means as prominent and striking as possible. Thus, instead of hiding for fear, there is a demonstration of easiness, like lions yawning when the cameraman comes too near or like showing its presence by shouting loud cries and boasting in the case of the gorilla.

If we apply this idea to the construction of knowledge systems, we have a similar distinction in logical categories. This is not so astonishing as it might seem to be because knowledge can be conceived as being an abstraction of survival strategies of human beings. We can distinguish on one side knowledge as adaptation up to the point that the scientific researcher is totally absent from the epistemological

293

scene, or almost absent. This logical strategy is easily recognized in the self-image of objective knowledge. The scientific identity makes itself invisible and survival takes the
form of empirical truth. We have the epistemological form of
what we have defined as descriptions.

On the other hand, there is a point of development in
the learning process of technology and organization where
the creative act becomes visible in a very conspicuous way.
In the case of building a motorcar or writing a computerpro-
gram it makes no sense to talk about objectivity. We are in
the domain not of descriptions but of representations and
the new standard of truth becomes scientific identity. In order to survive, that means very often to obtain credits or
to sell the products,the scientific identity has to present
itself as being as strong as possible.The scientific identity
becomes a name, like Einstein or Skinner, Marx or Freud, de
Saussure or Chomsky, Durkheim or Weber. The scientific identity develops in a conspicuous way as a set of paradigmata
which must show their postulates and their specific social
characteristics in order to survive. So in this epistemological strategy, objectivity is replaced by publicity, fame
and quotation rates. This is in our view the new representation form of scientific identity paradigmata. The survival
value of truth is affiliated to the situation in industrial
production, like cars or computers. Instead of the convergence of adaptation, we have the divergence of scientific identity specification as a set of alternative paradigmata in
the field. The more alternatives, the more possibilities for
making a choice and hence the best foundation for assessment
analysis.

2. THE LOGICAL PRINCIPLE OF REVERSIBILITY AS AN UNDER-BOUND
   OF VALUE FOUNDATION.

The distinction between objectivityand identity, or between
convergence and divergence in scientific thought, or again
between description and technology does not imply that we have no foundations for values.In the field of objective description there is no need for values because no choices can
be made. In the field of scientific paradigmata we need foundations for values.They have to be logical in nature and hence their foundations escape the argumentations of the naturalistic fallacy theory of Moore. They have to be logical because the values are supposed to be criteria for assessment
analysis. We will distinguish an under-bound and an upper-
bound in the socio-cybernetic foundations for values.

As a zero-level foundation for value-systems, we introduce the logical principle of reversibility. This principle
has been advanced in his theory of human learning by Jean
Piaget. He conceives reversibility to be the criterion for

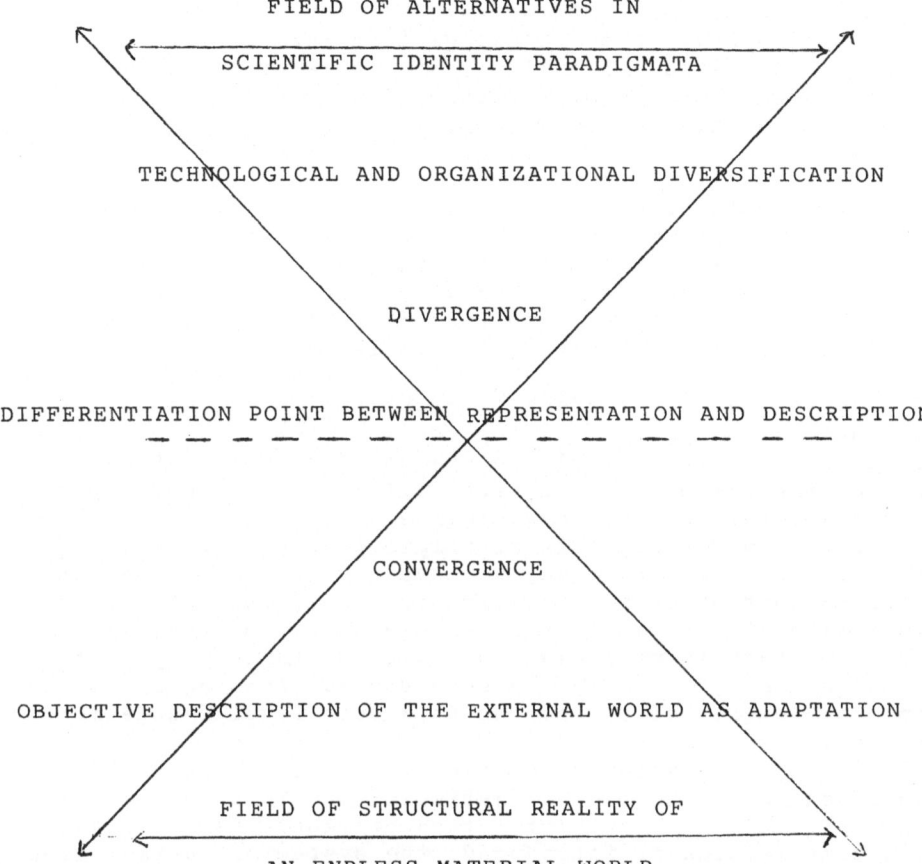

FIELD OF ALTERNATIVES IN

SCIENTIFIC IDENTITY PARADIGMATA

TECHNOLOGICAL AND ORGANIZATIONAL DIVERSIFICATION

DIVERGENCE

DIFFERENTIATION POINT BETWEEN REPRESENTATION AND DESCRIPTION

CONVERGENCE

OBJECTIVE DESCRIPTION OF THE EXTERNAL WORLD AS ADAPTATION

FIELD OF STRUCTURAL REALITY OF

AN ENDLESS MATERIAL WORLD

Fig.1. The basic strategy of living beings for survival consist in either adaptation making themselves invisible in the environment or in making themselves conspicuous. In scientific learning which can be conceived as an abstraction of these survival strategies, this logical distinction becomes specified as objective description of the external world on one hand and diversification of scientific identity alternatives on the other hand.

judging whether a child has reached the level of an equilibrium in relation to the environment in which it learns. This equilibrium is precisely the basic feature of intelligence in the view of Piaget. In our approach we extend this idea of intelligence into the field of the foundations of scientific learning. Therefore the logical principle of reversibility can be elaborated further as a criterion for science and technology assessment. While we can ask that descriptions shall be objective, we have the right to ask that

representations shall be intelligent. Technology and social
organization have to be intelligent in term of their relationship to the social environment. Therefore we introduce
the logical principle of reversibility as a zero-level
foundation of all value-systems.

As an illustration of the logical principle of reversibility let us start from the observations of Piaget in the
development of child intelligence. A child playing with a
puppet hides this object by putting a blanket over it, the
puppet has disappeared. Then the blanket is taken away and
the puppet is there again. The second act shows the principle of reversibility because the original situation is restored. Children like to hide and rediscover objects and
themselves in endless plays, learning thus to reach the intelligence level of representing objects and persons in a
way that is independent from perception. When the puppet is
not perceived, it is still an object of representation as
soon as the criterion of reversibility has been developed
as fundamental for the intelligence.

Let us now apply this principle to a problem like the
pollution of the North-Sea. We have a criterion for a zero-
level foundation of ecology assessment here because the original situation of an unpolluted sea cannot be reached any-
more. So there is no social intelligence in the application
of science and technology in such a case. The logical principle of reversibility applies as a zero-level foundation
for ecological values.

Another illustration of the principle of reversibility
can be shown in the case of jurisdiction. This becomes urgent in view of the automatization of legal texts. As soon
as automatization is introduced, the system of jurisdiction
becomes epistemologically closed. So we have to introduce a
metaprogram which controls the automated program. This metaprogram is in fact a model of the judge who represented
the epistemological openness in the tradition of jurisdiction. The model of the judge is again a beautiful example of
the logical principle of reversibility, showing the zero-level of the value-system of jurisprudence. We can distinguish
structural(or spatial in the sense of a social space) reversibility in the sense that justice claims that the role of
the judge and the role of the person who is judged might be
reversed in principle. Would the judge punish in the same
way if he had done the things at charge and had to punish
himself? This structural reversibility is an elaboration
and a logical formalization of the zero-value of justice in
a social system. If we add temporal reversibility, we can
understand why slowly death sentences have disappeared in
the history of civilization, or at least why the capital
sentences have strongly diminished. Here we have a temporal
reversibility principle because the zero-level asks that no
actions are undertaken that cannot be undone. At the same

time we can understand why crimes like murder are always
wrong, because precisely the temporal reversibility is
transgressed.

3. THE HUMAN CAPACITY DEVELOPMENT PRINCIPLE AS AN UPPER-BOUND FOUNDATION FOR VALUE-SYSTEMS.

In order to develop foundations for value-systems, we
need not only an elaboration of what is forbidden, but also
a principle that indicates in what direction choices have
to be taken in processes of social steering. We introduce
therefore the human capacity development principle as an
upper-bound foundation of values in socio-cybernetics.
The range of choice between what is possible and what
is impossible determines the logical space for social steering. As we do not know what is possible, there is a constant need for human learning in order to discover new aspects of human capacities. For this reason, learning is a
socio-cybernetic indicator of value research. Learning is
the basic drive of human beings as well as the basic value
foundation for steering social processes in a positive way.
As our model shows, the problem of foundations is first
of all a relationship between parts and wholes. To this logical principle, we add the cybernetic principle of learning which consists in presenting anticipations receiving
feedback information for confirmation or rejection. The
first feedback cycle can be recognized as being in accordance with the principle of falsification developed in the
logic of scientific inquiry by Karl Popper. But in our model, the number of anticipation and feedback cycles is extended, which implies that we have postulates about the
world at large incuding the social and ecological environments. The extension of the anticipation-feedback cycles
means also that we can distinguish possible falsifiers that
were not defined in such a way in the naturalistic epistemology of the Popperian type. Therefore in our model, there
is more possibility for learning and the foundations of values are an illustration of this larger learning capacity
that our model shows.
We can explain now why Moore arrived at his naturalistic fallacy argument in matters of value foundation. His argumentation concerns the nature of empirical observation and
is hence the most elementary step of learning. In cybernetic terms, this is even not yet learning, but only a way of
becoming acquainted with signals from the external world,
what is called sense-data in Moore's epistemology. However
this is not yet learning, because the feedback lines are
lacking. We obtain learning of the first order, the second
order and the third logical order when larger epistemological loops can function as a basis for learning.

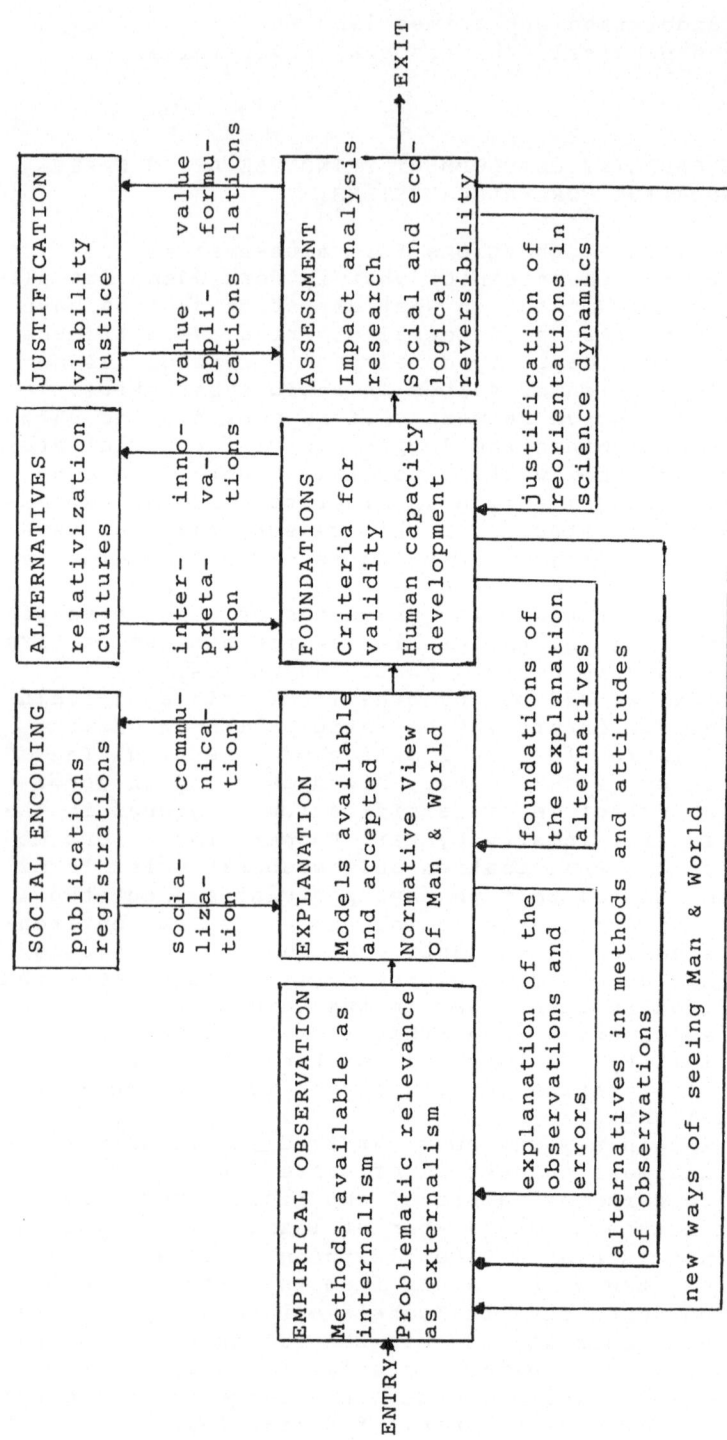

Fig.2. Foundations for values are essentially relating parts to wholes and conversely. The basic pattern of cybernetics where anticipations function as hypotheses or postulates and where feedback confirms or rejects determines the dynamics of value learning.

298

The position of Weber goes further in the sense that the nature of explanation is part of his epistemology theory. However, he does not question the validity of criteria, staying in the position of accepting the social encoding of the world. His epistemological attitude is normative in the sense that he accepts the values and choices made by the social system he is living in. The position of a value-free social science means not a denial of the role of values, but a refusal to propose any changes or reorientations in matters of value.

REFERENCES.

ARBIB, M. and CORNELIS, A.,'The role of Systems Theory.',in: The Social Sciences, Journal of Social and Biological Structures, 1981,4,375-386.
CORNELIS, A.,'Identity in Society as a Process of Natural Learning',in: Robbert TRappl, Luigi RICCIARDI and Gordon PASK, eds., Progress in Cybernetics and Systems Research, Vol. IX(Cybernetics in Cognition and Learning)p.387-394, Hemisphere Publishing Corporation, Washington, London, 1982.
CORNELIS, A.,'Anthropological Transformations in the Dynamics of Scientific Learning', in: Robert TRAPPL,ed., Cybernetics and Systems Research, North-Holland Publishing Company, 1982, 371-8.
CORNELIS, A.,'Epistemological Indicators of Scientific Identity', in: Robert TRAPPL,ed., Cybernetics and Systems Research II, Elsevier Science Publishers(North-Holland), 1984, p.683-690.
CORNELIS, A.,'The Human Capacity Development Model(HCDM)' in: Proceedings of the 6th International Congress of Cybernetics and Systems, Ed. AFCET, Paris, 1984, Vol I, p.259-264.
CORNELIS, Arnold, 'Is it possible to Program an Ethical System?' in: Proceedings of the Second International Congress on Logic, Informatics and Law, Florence, 1985, in press.
CORNELIS, A.,'Three Concepts of Learning', in G. DE ZEEUW e.a.eds, Societal Development, Social Policy and Helping Professions, Amsterdam, in press.
CORNELIS, A.,'The Idea of a Transcultural Plateau'in: G.DE ZEEUW ed., Problems of Disappearing Knowledge, Systeemgroep Nederland, 1985, in press.
MOORE,G.E., Principia Ethica, London, 1903.
POPPER, K.R., The Logic of Scientific Discovery,(1935)1959.
WEBER, M.,'Science as a Vocation(Wissenchaft als Beruf' in: Gesammelte Aufsätzezur Wissenschaftslehre,Tübingen, 1922.)

THE PARADIGM-SHIFT FROM ARCHITECTURED INHUMANITY TO HUMANIZED ARCHI-
TECTURES IN CORPORATE REALITY

Gerrit Broekstra
Rotterdam School of Management
Erasmus University Rotterdam
P.O. Box 1738, 3000 DR ROTTERDAM
The Netherlands

ABSTRACT. This paper is a somewhat philosophical discourse on the para-
digm- and culture-shifts presently occurring in corporations to overcome
the prevailing crises in adaptability and commitment. With the help of
the so-called Consistency-model it is argued that these shifts are basically pointing to a restoration of the balance between a masculine and
feminine business ethics emphasizing the complementarity of the two,
rather than the primacy of the first.

1. THE RATIONALE FOR THE C-MODEL

The working hypothesis underlying the C-model and the associated management logic is that the quality of top management, and hence corporate
performance in terms of competitive advantage, rate of innovation, productivity, organizational 'health', and so on, are closely correlated
with the degree of holistic conceptualization of corporate reality. In
other words, the more top management is inclined to base its informa-
tion-gathering, problem-solving and decision-taking approaches on a
holistic perspective, the better are the odds for corporate excellence.
    A holistic perspective implies that corporate functioning is view-
ed as a whole entity in its own right with emerging properties like
competitive advantage, organizational health and stability, cohesiveness, culture and climate, etc. It also implies a hierarchical view of
the corporation. That is, it is perceived as a part of a larger business structure with its own logic and success factors. And, it is also
seen as consisting of part components between which a good balance,
harmony, fit, match, or consistency is crucial for attaining effectiveness. In a sense, one could contend that the search for excellence is
a quest for a dynamic equilibrium between a variety of key factors both
under and outside control of the corporate inhabitants.
    A holistic perspective also entails a humanistic and phenomenolo-
gical stance. Fundamental to the movement of holism is the idea of
system. And, surely, systems are 'an act of mental recognition' and,
'mappings of our own brains on to the world' (Beer, 1966). Objective
reality appears to be no longer a reality. The central role of subject-

301

R. Trappl (ed.), Cybernetics and Systems '86, 301–308.
© 1986 by D. Reidel Publishing Company.

ivity and consciousness in holism is being recognized even in the alledgedly hard realm of physics (Jones, 1982). Mind and matter are a unity. Dualities are the products of reductionist thinking and counterproductive in understanding the human condition.

There still exists a persistent misunderstanding that a systems approach is some nuts-and-bolts mechanistic way of dealing with problem situations. As systems scientists, we likely have to continue to work doggedly into the next century to make headway to the common-sense stage of understanding systems as the hearts-and-minds holistic way of improving the human predicament. In this paper, I will try to make a modest contribution towards that goal of understanding the true meaning of the systems approach in organization theory and management practice.

In addition, and contrary to another tenacious misunderstanding particularly among social scientists, I will try to convey that systems theory is far removed from the structural-functionalism realms. It is sorely harmful to organizational development to suppose that 'The System exists', and that parts of the system are subjected to an institutional imperative to be functionally integrated into the system. I concur whole-heartedly with Berger's viewpoint that 'the requirement for integration is not at the institutional level but at the individual level, the level of meaning, the way the social order is legitimated' (Wuthnow, e.a., 1984).

And, from what I have observed in the context of discussing humanizing corporate architectures as a prerequisite for improving business performance, a process of delegitimation of many a corporate social order would be highly beneficial. This, indeed, implicates a phenomenological stance for systems thinking as the work of Peter Checkland (1981) also gracefully elucidates. Taken to its consequences, the systems approach to social problem situations thus implies a humanistic rather than a positivistic epistemology. Although considerable headway has been made, we undoubtedly have still some way to go in intermingling systems ideas with such diverse strands as are presently emerging from fields like modern phenomenology, cultural anthropology and so on, to their mutual benefit.

2. THREE LEVELS OF COMPLEXITY

An essential feature of a systems approach is to take a hierarchical view of certain problem situations. Such a hierarchy has nothing to do with the notion of a boss-subordinate pyramid so familiar to classical organization theory. We should, nevertheless, be aware of the fact that, by some cultural lag, this objectified social construct is still deeply engraved in today's managerial mind almost as the most obdurate fact of corporate life.

By a hierarchy we mean a pattern of levels of complexity representing, for example, the levels of supersystems, systems, and subsystems. To simplify the discussion, I distinguish conceptually between three levels of decreasing complexity: Environment, Organization, and People. At the first level, the E-level, our concern is with the environment or business structure (competition, suppliers, customers, new entries, etc.) as perceived and enacted by management, and the wider or contextual environment where socio-economic, political, technological, and so on, developments originate that may have their impact on the corporation.

I would like to capture the characteristics of many a business environment by one familiar term: Turbulence. Markets, customer attitudes, technologies, etc. are perceived to be in such a state of upheaval that they tend to obfuscate the manager's mind. Clearly, change is a relative matter, and largely a phenomenon at the surface level of life. Nevertheless, and perhaps fortunately, the future is no longer a mere linear extrapolation of the past as many corporate, and government, planners and number crunchers have found to their dismay. Uncertainty abounds with a consequent increase of the information- and meaning-processing loads causing quite some anxiety and stress at the top management echelons. An overriding concern with creating and sustaining a competitive advantage has become the almost daily preoccupation of many top managers.

At the second level, the O-level, we locate the organization itself as an entity which may be perceived as possessing a typical identity and social configuration struggling as it were with a whole range of disturbances luring in the background. At this level, our interest turns to the internal constitution of the corporation, its structure, culture and climate, its internal stability and cohesiveness, its responsiveness to disturbances originating at the higher, environmental, and lower, human, levels, its degree of formalization, its moral codes and belief systems, and so on. Again, capturing the problematic state of some corporations, needless to say as an oversimplification, in one term, I would choose: Inertia.

In a masculine culture dominated by the psychological value of separateness (Gilligan, 1982), we find this ideology institutionally reflected in typically segmented organizations where units are fenced off from each other (Kanter, 1984). The necessity of integration or coordination of these separate units occurs almost as an afterthought, and virtually always as one of the major organizational problems. Microcultures develop inside these units as a natural, or biological imperative, result of humans to provide themselves with stable environments. This state of affairs inhibits integrated learning of the organization as a whole, and is often the major obstacle to internal change.

Ironically, humans tend to forget that the organization, its structure and culture, is their own social construction; man is the architect of 'reality'. However, through an intricate and subtle process of social exchange the subjective meanings attached to organizational life by individuals become objectified. The organization attains a 'thing-like quality - the quality of objective facticity' (Wuthnow, e.a., 1984) with objectified, morally sanctioned, codes of behavior. Man's anthropological propensity to externalization, at least in the Euro-American cultures, oddly enough imprisons him in the, more often than not, inhuman architectures of his own making, which, though largely a subconscious process, ultimately originate from his own consciousness. Thus, it may not be far-fetched to suggest that the study

303

of consciousness, turning inwards, may be one important key to humanized change in 'outside reality'. Would it therefore be bad advice to a top manager to think less and meditate more?

Finally, at the third level of complexity, the P-level, we locate the constituent parts of an organization, the people or 'human resources'. Here we may be concerned with such variables and characteristics as their personal goals and aspirations, educational levels, leadership styles, skills, and so on, as well as the quality of the social relationships. The one term I would use to characterize people's feelings about the often poor state of QWL (quality of work life) is: Alienation. In many cases, the everyday organizational situation individuals have to face has reached a state of meaninglessness which they feel powerless to change. They feel alienated from an 'objective reality' which 'manifests itself most unmistakably in its coercive power, in its capacity to direct behavior. impose sanctions, punish deviance and at the extreme, destroy human life' (Wuthnow,e.a.,1984).

Quite frequently, in interviewing people in corporations, I am astonished by their awareness of and insight into the nature of certain problems their company is confronted with. At the same time, they feel utterly powerless to do anything about them as an individual. A general feeling of paralysis has crept under their skins. To them, the organization has become 'The System out there', which oppresses their own individual needs for mental and emotional, let alone spiritual, growth. They have long learned to accept as a fact of organizational life that the company apparently has no need of their ideas and full capacities. The corporation to them is not the life-world that infuses their individual consciousnesses with meaning. It has become de-meaning.

3. A SYSTEMS VIEW OF CORPORATE CRISES

Having broadly untangled by means of a hierarchical perspective of corporate complexity three levels, the E-O-P-levels, caught up in their own emergent problematique, I now pay heed to the interrelatedness of these levels. Clearly, one may discern two interfaces; one between the E- and O-level; the other between the O- en P-level. It is here at these two interfaces that, again with some oversimplification, we may locate the origin of two fundamental crises haunting corporations. At the E-O-interface one may speak of an Adaptability crisis, at the O-P-interface of a Commitment crisis (see also Beer, 1980).

Due to the inertia at the O-level, corporations are continuously experiencing difficulties in adapting to the demands of a turbulent environment. As a consequence, the corporation is unremittingly exposed to the threat of an external stability problem. Relaxation times of the organization to absorb rapid successive shifts in their environments appear too long. The degree of organizational resilience is too low. The dialectical interplay between the E- and O-level becomes unbalanced with a consequent loss of corporate identity and effective demeanor.

Fed by external cultural changes, shifting value and belief systems, increasing concerns for spiritual growth, frequent exposures to new provinces of meaning that undermine the taken-for-granted paramount realities, and so on, alienated people tend to lower their commitment to an organization unable to respond to their individual needs. Thus, an internal stability problem arises as well. People refuse, perhaps mostly unconsciously, to identify with the organization. That world is no longer their world.

At the junction of these two interfaces sits the organization in all its ponderosity with segmented structures, tedious processes, and inflexible cultures. Visionary top managers armed with high-minded missions and elaborated strategic plans run to pieces into the inertial massivity of the organizational architectures. In as much as these crises are seriously threatening to the survival of the corporation, the above admittedly caricature description also reveals the main intervention point, the O-level. And, within this level it is undoubtedly the organizational culture that should become the prime target for attack.

If all present-day crises are essentially different facets of one and the same crises, a Crisis of Perception as Capra (1982) calls it, top managers would do well to make culture their business. And, culture means meaning (Weick,1985), meaning means consciousness and consciousness means holism. Indeed, the successful manager of the future may well turn out to be an experienced meditator founding the effectiveness of his worldly actions on a mind geared to a holistic logic, which in turn is infused with the humanistic values and natural energy from a rediscovered absolute source or unified field (Maharishi, 1968). This, at least, will be one beneficial potential result from the synthesis of Eastern and Western thinking presently unfolding before those eyes that can see.

4. FOUR STRATEGIC CARDINAL GENERIC SYSTEMS

Without attempting to be complete, I will now briefly summarize the key features of the C-model. For a more extensive treatment and further references the reader may consult my previous publications. The model starts to unfold from the above hierarchical perspective as follows. As far as top management is concerned, the matching between the E- and the O-level is subjected to the first fundamental choice, the Business Choice. Likewise, the match between the O- and P-level may be accomplished by a second fundamental choice, the Organizational Choice, which in turn should be consistent with the Business Choice. I am using the term Organization here in a slightly different sense as above as I will clarify shortly.

Each of these two fundamental choices are subsequently divided into two subchoices. These lead to the four corner-stones of the Consistency-model. I refer to them as the strategic Cardinal Generic Systems (CGSs), which are subject to a set of consistently interdependent policies.These are the strategic CGSs:
BUSINESS CHOICE:
      1. Entrepreneurial System (ES)
      2. Technological System (TS)
ORGANIZATIONAL CHOICE:
      3. Administrative System (AS)
      4. Human-Resources System (HRS)

Some examples may help clarifying the content of the CGSs.

ES: the choice of what customers to serve, what products/services to offer, what marketing mixes, what service-image to create,etc.

TS: the business logistics, the productive axis, the service-delivery system, the know-how, and so on; what we sometimes refer to as the 'hardware' of the corporation.

AS: the formal structure, the budgetting-, control-,reward-,etc. systems, the decision-making processes, the degree of differntiation and integration, and so forth; the 'orgware'.

HRS: the skills, educational levels, leadership styles, morale, turnover, the quality of the social relationships,etc.; the 'software'.

The general idea is that these cardinal generic systems are closely interrelated, and ideally should form a pattern or configuration where each choice is consistent or matched with the others; hence Management by Matching. Each of the internal CGSs is thought to be directly related to an external counterpart. So, the quest for a dynamic equilibrium between the internal CGSs is continuously threatened by external events. In making one particular choice with respect to some CGS, management is compelled to look at the whole picture for possible side-effects, further change implications with respect to other CGSs, and so on. Arising inconsistencies among the internal CGSs or between the CGSs and their external counterparts should either be removed, or, and this is of particular importance in times of rapid change, though sometimes psychologically difficult to accept, should be evaluated as signals of an emerging new trend providing an opportunity rather than a threat to the existing way of doing business.

5. SEVEN MAIN CRITICAL CHANGE LEVERS

The model is not yet complete with the four CGSs. At the centre of the model we locate the Dominant Coalition (DC), or 'metaware' of the corporation to emphasize its central role in making strategic decisions, and setting the stage by its vision, guiding beliefs, management philosophy, and so forth. In a way, all four systems may be regarded as strategic in the sense that it is the emerging overall pattern rather than one individual CGS that largely determines the corporation's competitive edge in the market place.

Next, concentrically with the DC we place the Political System (PS) to symbolically indicate that the DC has to work through power and influence distributions to realize its policies. The latter may either productively enhance the corporate functioning, or oppressively inhibit it (Kanter, 1984).

Finally, the C-model is completed with the seventh system which I basically tend to regard as the third fundamental choice at the discretion of the DC, the Cultural System (CS). Although in actual practice the CS may be largely regarded as the softest variable or the Organizational Unconscious (Allen and Kraft, 1982), and thus not as subject to real choice, I contend that neglect of the SOUL ('Soft Organizational

Unconscious Level') of the corporation is a major error in managerial thinking. To emphasize its significance as a 'meaning-generator', I have drawn it as a concentric circle encompassing all other systems as the umbrella under which all the corresponding choices and the ensuing human conduct resort (see Figure 1). So, in view of the above discussion on strategy, I tend to concur with Weick (1985) that Strategy and Culture are as the two sides of the same coin.

Within the larger Cultural System, I conceptually distinguish between a 'left- and right-hand side'. Around the TS and AS I locate a rational, analytical logic driven by a 'masculine business ethics' based on the premises of separation and a morality of justice and individual rights. Around the ES and HRS I posit a holistic, synthetic logic infused by a 'feminine business ethics' based on the primacy of connectedness and a morality of care and responsibility for others (see also Gilligan. 1982).

Needless to say that I consider the two cultural halves as complementary rather than as opposed (Broekstra, 1986). Nevertheless, in practice the two halves are more often than not greatly out of balance. It is the primacy of 'The System' consisting of the TS and AS, the preoccupation of the DC with rationality and analysis, and the oppressive

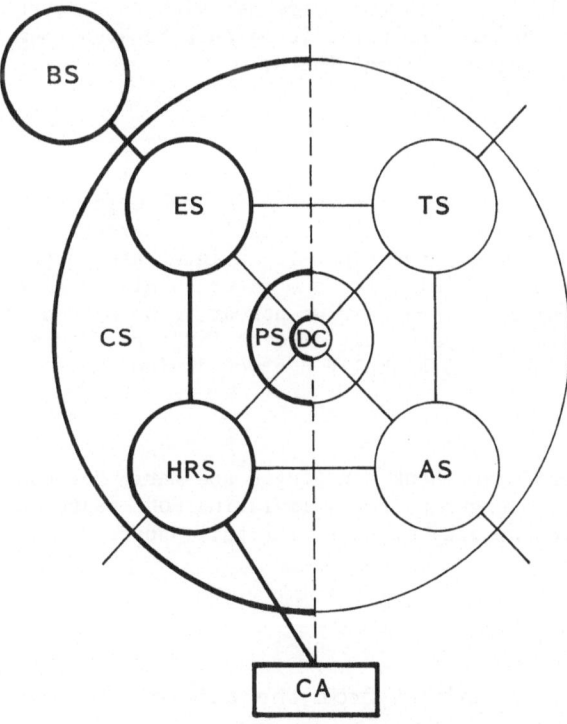

Figure 1. The C-model (see text for explanation of symbols; CA stands for Competitive Advantage; BS for Business Structure)

307

power structure reinforced by a dominant masculine, if not macho, culture and ethics that form the major obstacles to change and innovation. For, as Kanter (1984) argues forcefully, it is not The System, but people and their idea power that are responsible for success in present-day business circumstances.

My plea is for a restoration of the balance between the two halves, which in fact implies a culture or value-shift and a paradigm-shift with respect to the management logic. It means a larger emphasis on the, for the outside observer, left-hand side of the model, which incidentally is essentially the 'right-mind' side from the point of view of the DC sitting inside the model. This is expressed symbolically in Figure 1 by the thick lines. The ES and HRS should regain much larger prominence in managerial thinking to overcome the organizational crises in adaptability and commitment. The organizational architecture should become supportive to these systems infused with a feminine arethics of care for customers (ES) and people (HRS). In actual practice, to facilitate this shift, one might even suggest to pay special attention within human-resource policies to woman-resource policies. But this is only one of the seven CCLs (Critical Change Levers) that management has at her disposal. A holistic management logic requires a consistency-view of all seven 'levers' together with the external systems. But, as argued, to restore the harmonic balance between them some have to attain a larger dominance than others.

6. CONCLUSION

It appears to me that organization theory is developing at an accelerating pace. Particularly the rapidly increasing interest in the SOUL of the corporation, as well as the emphasis on integrated organization development hold a lot of promise for the future. This is an exciting area to work in, especially because we appear to be approaching a point of convergence where many seemingly diverse findings from various disciplines come together into a wholly new world view.

ACKNOWLEDGMENT

I am indebted to Professor Henk van Dongen and Marie Molenaar of the Rotterdam School of Management for stimulating SOUL-searching discussions pertaining to the subject matter of this paper.

REFERENCES

References to be obtained from the author.

Cybernetics in Biology and Medicine

Chairpersons: G.Porenta (Austria)
               L.M.Ricciardi (Italy)

ON SOME FRESH AIR IN NEURAL MODELING

J. Mira and A.E. Delgado
Department of Electronics
Faculty of Physics
University of Santiago de Compostela.
SPAIN

ABSTRACT. Neural modeling is becoming a purely mathematical exercise due mainly to some methodological faults in the steps of modeling. We consider as weak points in the basic strategy of neurocibernetic modeling the wrong selection of description levels, significance tables and formal tools suited to describe the neuronal dynamics.
   The antropomorphycal viewpoint is considered and a new theoretical frame (anastomotic net) is included. This frame is general enough to embody non trivial neural processes like co-opertivity. The software description level leads to neuronal computational frames and algorithms. The hardware level consider that among the composition rules used to describe neuronal events also are included instructions of high level programming languages and pragmatic aspects of natural languages.
   In caming from anatomy to function we propose the speculative assumption that the topological structure we meet in neural nets can be associated to the control structures in the Bohn-Jacopini sense. As we are drawing a net we are printing the embodied function.

1. INTRODUCTION

Neural modeling is becoming a pure mathematical exercise separated from the anatomy and physiology of the real neural nets as well as from the psichophysical and behavioural data relating global phenomena to subserving neuronal mechanisms. This claim is not new; W.S. McCulloch about 1950 said "... The theory of automata is separate from biophysics of brains and the engineering of computing machines, and both factions indulge in those reductionisms that Donald Mackay has cristened "Nothing Buttery".
   More recently V. Braitenberg (Brainterbeg, 1976) has said that work and symposia on "neural networks" were based on "fleeting abstractions from electrophysiological data, quickly provided by neurologists who were eager to see their terminology become food for thought in mathematical circles. By now the mathematiciens have made pure mathematics out of the original models,...".
   These facts are due to methodological faults in the steps of

311

R. Trappl (ed.), Cybernetics and Systems '86, 311–318.
© *1986 by D. Reidel Publishing Company.*

neural modeling, mainly in the selection of appropriate computational frames for the data under consideration and also the mathematical operators needed to cope with the complexity of the neuronal dynamics. This can no longer be considered only as a spatio-temporal adder followed by a threshold element and a delay in a way related to the original McCulloch -Pitts work of 1943, the McCulloch proposal in "Agath-Tyche" (McCulloch, 1959) or the Caianello's Neuronic and Mnemonic equations (E. Caianello, 1965; Caianiello et al., 1967), to name the more extended mathematical frames.

Anatomical data provided by Ramón y Cajal (1911) and Lorente de No (1933, 1938) and later Barlow (1972), Szentagothai (1975) and Eccles (1984) has suggested the belief that neural nets are really complex information processing systems that cannot be described using only integro-differential equations (Mira and Delgado, 1981; Mira et al., 1983, 1984, 1985). The multisynaptic local circuits on part of a neuron, as proposed by Shepherd (1973) is an example of this new point of view of the organizational complexity of the nervous system. The review of Schmitt and Worden in the Fourth study program on Neuroscience (Schmitt and Wordem, 1978) and the points selected in the work on Biophysics of Computation by Christof Koch and Tomaso Poggio: "dendrodendritic synapses, gap junctions, dendritic spikes, nonsynaptic release of neural transmitters ..." (Koch and Poggio, 1985) also indicate the avoidance of reductionism in the computational complexity inherent in neurons and neural nets.

In this paper we comment on some methodological aspects of neural modeling, and introduce a theoretical frame, general enough to embody non-trivial neural models as well as a speculative proposal on the interpretation of anatomical data as control structures in the Bohn-Jacopini sense (Bohn-Jacopini, 1966). This suggests some computational structures inspired by the antomy of neural nets.

2. WEAK POINTS IN NEUROCYBERNETIC MODELING

The basic strategy in neural modeling (Mira et al., 1984.b) starts by selecting a **level of description** (L_i) and a set of **empirical data** (X_i) at this level as well as an initial **table of significance** ($X_i S_i$) that describes in natural language the meaning of the physiological variables under consideration. The next step is the selection of a **computational frame** as well as the **formal tools** (O_{ij}) best suited to describe the neuronal dynamic at this level (integro-differential equations, automata theory, algorithms,...). The operation of O_{ij} on X_i generates the **formal results**, $Y_j = O_{ij} |X_i|$, and a new table of significance (Y_j, S_j) closes the neuro-cybernetic model,

$$\text{Model} = (L_i, X_i, S_i; O_{ij}; Y_j, S_j)$$

which is then used to "explain" the experimental results, to predict new ones and to suggest new experiments (fig. 1).

A great part of "**neural modeling**" is actually concerned with the formal manipulations of symbols that produce Y_j starting from X_i ignoring the level selection, the significance tables and the support arguments in the O_{ij} selection. In this way pseudo-models simply pose formal questions on analysis and synthesis. These questions are irrelevant to the mores genuine properties of neural nets and have all been solved long ago anyway.

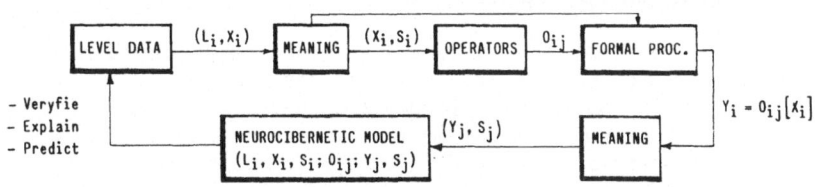

Fig. 1. Modeling schema

The first weak point in neural modeling is the **level and meaning selection** (L_i, X_i, S_i). That is to say the specification of the level most suitable for the nature of the neural processes varies according to the nature of the experimental results as well as the significance assignation, which must be at the same level (Mira, 1984.b). Following mainly the suggestions of David Marr and Tomaso Poggio (Marr-Poggio, 1977; Marr, 1982; Poggio, 1982) we can distinguish at least, five levels of description:

1. Subcellular phenomena
2. Neuronal integration level and Shepherd type local process
3. Particular mechanisms (reflex arch, lateral interaction, Lorente de No, C and M chains ...)
4. Intermediate algorithms
5. Global computations

In general each level is strongly influenced by the others but extreme care is needed when trying to explain high level data by low level structures and/or viceversa. The same is true for the assignment of significance. For example it would obviously be erroneous to associate high level meaning such as perception or purpose to a physical variable such as degree of excitation or post-synaptic potential of a neuron. These errors are associated with the meaning steps association (X_i, S_i) and (Y_j, S_j) of input and output variables.

The next weak point concerns the selection of the operators O_{ij}. At different levels we need different mathematical tools to cope with the dynamics of the level: e.g. **Integro-differential equations** and nonlinear processes (modulation, thresholds, rectification ...) for lower levels, **Automata theory** for intermediate levels and **Computational algorithms** as well as some **pragmatic aspects of natural languages** for the higher level. We can also suppose that the formal tools needed to cope with the more genuine aspects of the nervous system are not yet at our disposal. The **abductive logic** and the calculus of **irreductible triadic intentional relations** of the Stoics and W.S. McCulloch as well as the calculus of Signification and Intention of J. Simoes da Fonseca and J. Mira (1970 and 1975) are failed attempts.

Finally, another weak point in neural models is the confusion

313

between "**fitting the data**" to a curve and obtaining the **neurophysiological law** that produces the data (the "transfer function" in the linear case). The first is to mimic without any relation to the underlying physiological mechanisms, the latter is modeling in physical terms. If we know the input and the decision rules used by the system we can predict the outputs.

Some fresh air is needed in neural modeling with more emphasis on the tables of significance and in the use of neuroanatomical data as well as in the speculative proposal of neural operators. The computational skills of neural tissue must include more than products and sums. Per contra less stress is needed in purely formal developments.

3. THE ANTHROPOMORPHICAL VIEWPOINT ON NEURONAL SOFTWARE

If we consider the brain from an anthropomorphic point of view in which we assume that evolution and genetics have used the same strategies in designing the neural nets that human beings are using in the design of complex information processing systems like computers, we can distinguish between neuronal **hardware**, **software** and **firmware**.

Following this line of reasoning, it is possible to assume that from the software viewpoint we need to deal with computational frames, data structures, algorithms, procedures, formal languages, compilers, assemblers and so on to cope with the understanding of the overall computations in neural nets (levels 4 and 5). This knowledge, as Marr and Poggio (1977) pointed out, is expressed independently of the hardware of the machine in which they are going to run, although for some computations the hardware determines the facilities for solving some kind of problems (LISP machines, array processor, ...).

Some **fresh air** can be obtained in the area of neural modeling that is linked to "artificial intelligence", cognitive process, perceptual mechanisms, speech understanding, language production and learning algorithms to name a few. The feeling of W.S. McCulloch (Sutro, 1985.a) concerning the "special purpose" design of biological computers and the fact that the hardware of a man made machine affects the difficulty of implementing and running an algorithm (Ballard et al., 1983; Marr-Poggio, 1977) can be used to lead an **UP-DOWN analysis** in neural modeling, suggesting possible neuronal architecture, required connectivities and so on.

4. ANASTOMOTIC NETS

Some **fresh air** would be welcome in neuronal hardware. Following the above stated anthropomorphical line of reasoning, we can assume that the brain programs (Young, 1978) are running on neural nets which are, at least, **anastomotic tridimensional distributed processors**. Together with W.S. McCulloch (Sutro, 1985.b; McCulloch, 1963) we speak of neither series nor parallel but **anastomotic** nets, in the sense that neural nets are neither only performing sequential processes nor independent parallel processes on segmented information, but a tridimensional processing with local series and parallel paths **meshed** together in a generally **irreductible manner**.

314

The concept of anastomosis comes from Greek medecine: "The union of artery and vein or the rejoining of branches of a common vascular trunk to form a network by which the circulation of a part is maintained when the usual channel is obstructed" (Webster's Dictionary). Warren replaced blood by neural information and signals but retained the essentially anastomotic quality of the net. "In fact we conceive our nervous system to be so anastomotic that every efferent peripheral neuron can be affected over a multiplicity of paths by every afferent peripheral neuron" (McCulloch, 1963).

In some cases the anastomotic nets can be considered as **columnar** or **layered** computational frames according to the weakness of the anatomical and/or functional connections. If we pay more attention to the density of the dendritic processes we have **"layered computation"**. Per contra, if we focus on axons and local circuits neurons (Rakic, 1975) we obtain **"columnar computation"**. In both cases a computational frame should be powerful enough to cope with neuronal hardware, and can be of the kind we show in figure 2 where the elements, m_{ijk}, of M are the **local computing modules** (LCM) at position (i,j,k) and c_{ijk}^{lmn} specify the connectivity between the (i,j,k) and (l,m,n) local computing modules. This irreducible mesh is adecuate to cope with non-trivial formulations of co-operative processes in Cerebral Dynamics,

$$\text{Net} \triangleq \left[M(m_{i,j,k}), \ C(C_{ijk}^{lmn}); \ \{m_{i,j,k}, \ C_{ijk}^{lmn}\} \ \text{repertories} \right]$$

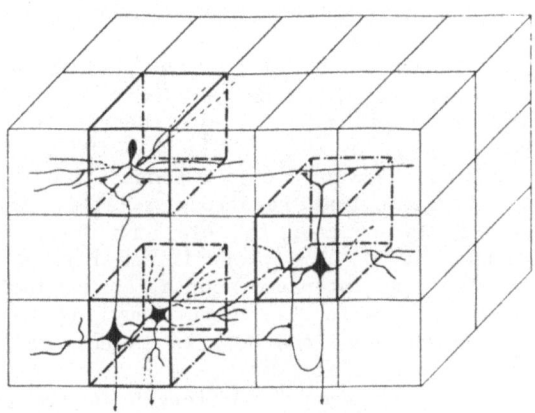

Fig. 2. Anastomotic net

In each node we have an LCM that can be a pool of neurons, a neuron, or a functional unit of integration in the sense of Shepherd which only involves pieces of neurons with specific synaptic organization. Figure 3 shows a table of some of these morpho-functional units (LCM) at neuronal and synaptic levels.

A second point in this theoretical frame is the function associated with the LCM. We wish to consider LCM as complex computing

315

units that perform **microprogrammes** on the afferent, efferent (feedback) and stored (local memory) information. The results of these programmes are spread out to other points of the anastomotic net.

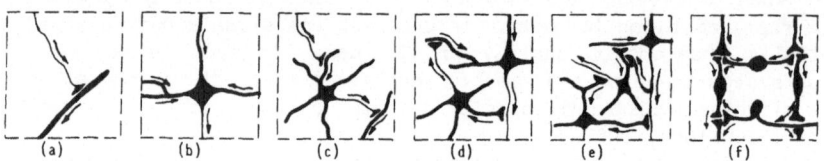

Fig. 3. Possible LCM. Adapted mainly from Shepherd 1975. Local circuits in a spinal motoneuron: (a), (b); with interneuron, (c) and (d); loops, (d), (e); and receptor-bipolar-horizontal-amacrine, in re tina (f)

Finally, we feel it would be convenient to include in these programmes not only analytic and/or logical instructions, but other instructions closer to the pragmatic aspects of natural languages (Mira et al., 1984; Winograd, 1983): descriptions, orders, conditional statements and interrogations. All these instructions must have the nature of **composition rules**. If these composition rules are **analogic**,

$$\{k_1 \, x^n + k_2 \, y^m, \frac{d}{dx}, \frac{d}{dt}, \int_R f(x,t)dx, \int_T f(x,t)dt\}$$

we obtain local analytic processes that give rise to spatio-temporal integro-differential equations.

If these rules are boolean or threshold like, { AND, OR, NOT, MUX, DEMUX, ADD, DELAY } , the frame projects on combinational logic models, sequential machines and automata theory. The McCulloch-Pitts model has been the paradigm of this level: "... to conceive the response of any neuron as factually equivalent to a **proposition** which proposed its adequate stimulus. Physiological relations existing among the nervous activities correspond, of course, to relations among the propositions ..." (McCulloch-Pitts, 1943). The propositions here are considered in logical terms. So, after the interaction of afferents included by M. Blum, a formal neuron of McCulloch-Pitt can compute any logical function of its inputs and previous outputs and can be used as universal modulus in the synthesis of finite state automata.

What makes our proposal different is the possibility that among the composition rules used to describe neuronal events there are also included instructions of high level programming languages and pragmatic aspects of natural languages, such as:

GOTO, IF-THEN-ELSE, WHILE-DO, ANALOG, INVERSION, TRANSPOSITION

If we do not consider the neural function restricted to logical propositions, the McCulloch-Pitts statement is also valid. Thus, we consider the response of anatomo-functional unit (LCM) as factually equivalent to a measure on the result of a local **microprogram** which proposes its adequate stimulus.

5. FROM ANATOMY TO FUNCTION

As a result of the LCM microprogram, the global function emerges. To gain some insight on how it happens we use the V. Braintemberg concepts (1976) concerning the importance of the anatomy: "(a) neuronal wiring may in some cases be very precise; (b) the synaptic junctions may be functionally very diversified; (c) some of the wiring take place while the nerve net is already operating; (d) there are in born constraints to this kind of plasticity".

If we study from this point of view the **topology** of the neural nets (Ramón y Cajal, 1911; Lorente de No, 1933; Eccles, 1984; Rakic, 1975; Schmitt and Worden, 1979; Szentágothai, 1975, ...) we find: linear chains, convergent and/or divergent processes, reflex arches, loops and M and C Lorente de No's multineuron chains. We now speculate saying that the neural nets have the macroprogram "printed" in their anatomy. That is to say, as we are drawing a net we are printing the embodied function. Following this line of reasoning, it is possible to associate the elementary **topological nets** connecting LCM nodes with a complete set of **control structures** (D and Ω_k) as we do in figure 4, including the associations: 1) **Basic action** (assignment statements, proce dure call, input-output statements) to **individual neurons** 2) **Compositions,** "s_1, s_2" of two D structures to **linear chains**. 3) **Conditional statements** "If p then s_1 else s_2" to **convergent/divergent** nets with interneurons. 4) Loops of the form **"while p do s"**, where p is a predicate and s is a D structure, to **loops** and C **and M chains**.

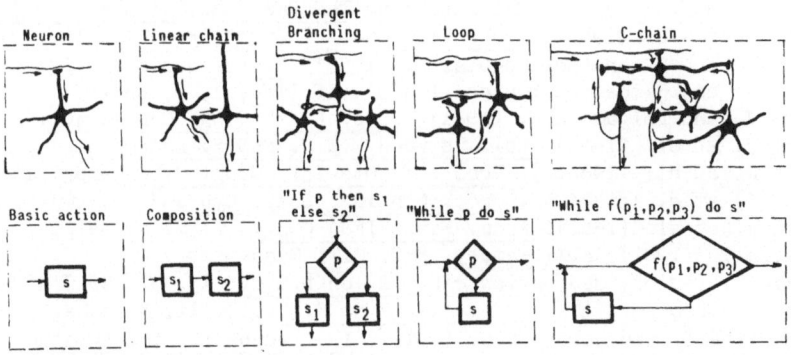

Fig. 4. Topological elementary nets and control structures associated

So we speculate proposing that the anastomotic nets of the cortex perform distributed programmes synthesized from the anatomic wiring of different combinations of the **control structures** previously mentioned.

There are many ways of describing neural nets. The point is to decide on the one which is most appropriate to the present state of knowledge in neurology and systems science. As conclusion we have proposed a possible way based on: a) The by-pass of formal calcula. b) The McCulloch concept of anastomotic net. c) The rigorous pursuit of neuroanatomical data and the following speculative assumptions:

d.1. It is natural and convenient to include **high level instructions** in the description of neural processes, in addition to the more frequently used analytic and logical ones.

d.2. The **anatomy determines the computational structure of the** net (neuronal firmware). The topological structures that we meet in the neural net embraces the control structures found in most algorithmic languages. Thus, if would be useful to explore this analogy. The adventure invites the pioneers.

Finally, this proposal may be discarded as soon as neurophysiological data   points in another direction. Speculation is neither right nor wrong but is more or less useful in leading experimental research and gaining insight on the understanding of present-day data.

REFERENCES

1. Ballard D.A. et al. (1983). Nature, **306**, pp. 21-26.
2. Braitemberg V. (1976). Progress in Brain Research, **45**, pp. 197-204.
3. Caianello E.R. (1965). Cybernetics of neural processes. pp. 1-27
4. Caianello E.R. et al. (1967). Kybernetik, **4**, pp. 10-18.
5. Eccles J.C. (1984). Cerebral Cortex, ed. by Jones & Peters, 2, pp. 1-36
6. Koch C. and Poggio T. (1985). New insights into synaptic function.
7. Lorente de No M.D. (1933). J. für Psychol. un Neurol., 45,6, pp. 381-438
8. Marr D.C. and Poggio T. (1977). Neurosci. Res. Prog. Bull. 15,3,470-488
9. Marr D. (1982). Vision. V.H. Freeman, San Francisco.
10. McCulloch W.S. and Pitts W.H. (1943). Bull. of Math. Bioph. **5**, 115-133
11. McCulloch W.S. (about 1950): Lekton. The Res. Lab. of Elect. MIT Mass.
12. McCulloch W.S. (1959). Mechanisation of Thought Proc. II, 10, 611-634.
13. McCulloch W.S. and Moreno-Díaz R. (1968). Neural Networks, 78-86.
14. Mira J. and Simoes da Fonseca (1975). If life, 1, 7, 32-44.
15. Mira J. and Delgado A.E. (1981). Proc. Fifth Cong. Cyb. Mexico. 2-24
16. Mira J. et al. (1983). Rel. between M.W.P. and S. Learning, II, 687-690
17. Mira J. et al. (1984.a). Proc. of 10th Int. Cong. Cyb. Namur, 17-29.
18. Mira J. et al. (1984.b). Proc. 6th Int. Cong. Cyb and S., París 2, 819-24
19. Mira J. et al. (1985). Proc. First IFSA Cong., I, P. de Mallorca.
20. Poggio T. (1982). A.I. Memory, **683**, MIT, Mass.
21. Rakic P. (1975). Neuroscience R.P.B. on L.C.N., **13**, 3, 299-314. Boston.
22. Ramón y Cajal S. (1911). Histologie du S.N.,..., II, Maloine. París.
23. Schmitt F.O. and Worden F.G. (1979). The neurosci.: fourth study prog.
24. Shepherd G.M. (1975). Neurosci. R.P.B. on L.C.N., **13**, 3, 344-352.
25. Simões da Fonseca J. and Mira J. (1970). Signif. and Intention, 5-11.
26. Szetágothai J. (1975). Brain Research, **95**, 475-496.
27. Sutro L. (1985.a). Personal communication on McCulloch viewpoints.
28. Sutro L. (1985.b). Personal communication on McCulloch concept of Anas tomotic Net. also included in McCulloch's paper: "Anastomotic nets combating noise" in Information storage and neural control (1963).
29. Winograd T. (1983). Lang. as a cognitive process, I. Addison-Wesley.
30. Young J.Z. (1978). Programs of the Brain. Oxford Univ. Press.

ON THE PROBABILITY DENSITIES OF AN ORNSTEIN-UHLENBECK PROCESS WITH A REFLECTING BOUNDARY

L. M. Ricciardi [*] and L. Sacerdote [**]

[*] Department of Mathematics and Applications, Univesity of Naples, Via Mezzocannone 8, 80134 Naples, Italy

[**] Department of Mathematics, University of Turin, Via Principe Amedeo 8, 10123 Turin, Italy

ABSTRACT. We show that the transition p.d.f. of the Ornstein-Uhlenbeck process with a reflection condition at an assigned state S is related by integral-type equations to the free transition p.d.f., to the transition p.d.f. in the presence of an absorption condition at S, to the first-passage-time p.d.f. to S and to the probability current. Such equations, that are seen to be useful also for computational purposes, yield as an immediate consequence all known closed form results for Ornstein-Uhlenbeck process.

1. INTRODUCTION

In recent years one dimensional diffusion processes have been increasingly used as models for various phenomena of physical, biological, psychological and engeenering interest (see for instance Blake and Lindsey /3/; Holden /10/; Maruyama /11/; Ricciardi /15/; Ricciardi and Sacerdote /17/; Ratcliff /14/; Heath /9/; Ricciardi et al. /18/; Ricciardi /16/). In these context for instance first passage time problems have been studied both by theoretical and computational methods (Siegert /21/; Favella et al. /6/; Abrahams /1/; Ricciardi and Sato /20/; Ricciardi et al. /19/; Nobile et al. /12/ and /13/; Balossino et al. /2/; Giorno et al. /8/). It has been shown that the first-passage-time probability density function (p.d.f.) can be obtained as the solution of Volterra-type integral equations whose kernel is either the free transition p.d.f. of the process or the probability current (see Favella et al. /6/; Ricciardi et al./19/; Nobile et al. /12/). Alternatively an integral relation connecting the first passage time p.d.f. with the free transition p.d.f. and with the transition p.d.f. in the presence of an absorbing boundary has also been prooved to hold (Siegert /21/; Favella et al. /6/; Ricciardi et al. /19/).

However, in some instances it is necessary to refer to diffusion processes in the presence of a reflection condition. Typical such examples arise in population dynamics studies in which the total number of individuals at each instant is the result of forces acting in opposite directions, i.e. spontaneous growth and immigration effects on the one

319

R. Trappl (ed.), Cybernetics and Systems '86, 319–326.
© 1986 by D. Reidel Publishing Company.

hand and random harvesting or predation on the other hand. Then the population size is bound to take non negative values which can be accounted for by setting a reflection condition at zero population size (Ricciardi /16/). Similarly, diffusion approximations to queueing systems may naturally lead to a reflection condition (Giorno et al. /7/). Hence, the interest of determining the transition p.d.f. for diffusion processes in the presence of reflection conditions is understood.

Similarly to the case of the first passage time p.d.f.'s, also transition p.d.f.'s in the presence of reflecting conditions are known only in very few and special cases. In this paper we shall refer to the Ornstein-Uhlenbeck process and analyze the problem of determining its transition p.d.f. in the presence of a reflecting boundary. Thus doing, we shall disclose some relations holding among first passage time densities, transition p.d.f.'s, both free and in the presence of reflection or absorption conditions, and probability currents. We shall also show that the few known results obtained by the method of images (Cox and Miller /4/) are immediately recovered by means of our equations.

2. MAIN NOTATIONS AND DEFINITIONS

Let $\{ X(t); t \geqslant 0 \}$ be a one dimensional diffusion process defined in $I \equiv (r_1, r_2)$ and such that $P \{ X(t_0) = x_0 \} = 1$, with $x_0 \in (r_1, r_2)$. Furthermore, for any $\tau < t$ set:

$$F(x,t|y,\tau) = P \{X(t) \leqslant x \, |X(\tau) = y\}$$

$$f(x,t|y,\tau) = \frac{\partial}{\partial x} F(x,t|y,\tau)$$

$$F^{(a)}(x,t|y,\tau) = P \{X(t) < x \, |X(\tau) = y \text{ and } X(\theta')>S, \forall \; \theta< t\}$$

$$f^{(a)}(x,t|y,\tau) = \frac{\partial}{\partial x} F^{(a)}(x,t|y,\tau)$$

$$T \equiv \inf \{t: X(t) > S \, |X(0) = x_0\}$$

$$g(S,t|x_0) = \frac{\partial}{\partial t} P \{T < t\}$$

$$j(x,t|y,\tau) = A_1(x)f(x,t|y,\tau) - \frac{1}{2}\left[\frac{\partial}{\partial x} A_2(x)f(x,t|y,\tau)\right],$$

where $A_1(x)$ and $A_2(x)$ denote the drift and infinitesimal variance of $X(t)$, respectively.

As is well known, the functions f, $f^{(a)}$ and g satisfy the following identity (Siegert /21/):

(2.1) $f(x,t|x_0) = f^{(a)}(x,t|x_0) + \int_0^t d\tau \, g(S,\tau|x_0)f(x,t|S,\tau)$, $x>S$.

Here and throughout this paper the specification of the zero initial

320

time is omitted. It can also be shown that

(2.2) $\lim_{x \downarrow S} f^{(a)}(x,t|x_0) = 0$

(2.3) $\lim_{x_0 \downarrow S} f^{(a)}(x,t|x_0) = 0.$

Finally, let us denote by $F^{(r)}(x,t|y,\tau)$ and by $f^{(r)}(x,t|y,\tau)$ $\equiv \frac{\partial}{\partial x} F^{(r)}(x,t|y,\tau)$ the transition distribution and the transition p.d.f., respectively, of the process $X(t)$ in the presence of a reflection condition at S. As is well known (Cox and Miller /4/), $f^{(r)}(x,t|x_0)$ satisfies the Fokker-Planck equation:

(2.4) $\frac{\partial}{\partial t} f^{(r)}(x,t|x_0) = \frac{\partial}{\partial x}\left\{-A_1(x)f^{(r)}(x,t|x_0)+ \frac{1}{2}\frac{\partial}{\partial x}\left[A_2(x)f^{(r)}(x,t|x_0)\right]\right\}$

with the following initial and boundary conditions:

(2.5) $\lim_{t \downarrow 0} f^{(r)}(x,t|x_0) = \delta(x-x_0)$

and

(2.6) $\lim_{x \downarrow S} -A_1(x)f^{(r)}(x,t|x_0)+ \frac{1}{2}\frac{\partial}{\partial x}\left[A_2(x)f^{(r)}(x,t|x_0)\right] = 0.$

For further details and auxiliary notations we refer to Nobile et al. /12/. Here we limit ourselves to mentioning that by a notation such as $k_\lambda(\cdot|\cdot)$ we mean the Laplace transform with respect to time of a function $k(\cdot,t|\cdot)$.

3. BASIC INTEGRAL RELATIONS

Let $\{X(t); t \geqslant 0 \}$ be a one dimensional Ornstein-Uhlenbeck (O.U.) process (cf., for instance, Ricciardi et al. /19/) defined in the interval $[S,\infty)$, and such that $P\{X(0) = x_0\} = 1$, $x_0 > S$. For brevity, throughout this paper the case in which the diffusion interval is $(-\infty,S]$, and hence $x_0 < S$, will not be considered as it can be treated by similar arguments. Let

$A_1(x) = -\frac{x}{\theta}+ \mu \qquad (\theta > 0, \mu \in \mathbb{R})$

(3.1)

$A_2(x) = \sigma^2 \qquad (\sigma^2 \in \mathbb{R}^+)$

be the drift and the infinitesimal variance of $X(t)$, respectively. It is possible to prove (cf. Ricciardi and Sacerdote, in preparation) that the following theorem holds:

Theorem 1. For all $x > S$ the transition p.d.f.'s $f^{(r)}$ and f are such that

$$(3.2) \quad f^{(r)}(x,t|x_0) = f(x,t|x_0) - \frac{\sigma^2}{2} \int_0^t d\tau\, e^{-(t-\tau)/\theta} f^{(r)}(S,\tau|x_0) \frac{\partial}{\partial x} f(x,t|S,\tau)$$

$$x \geqslant S$$

Corollary. On the boundary S the transition p.d.f. $f^{(r)}(x,t|x_0)$ satisfies the equation

$$(3.3) \quad F(S,t|x_0) = \frac{\sigma^2}{2} \int_0^t d\tau\, e^{-(t-\tau)/\theta} f(S,t|S,\tau) f^{(r)}(S,\tau|x_0).$$

Proof. It immediately follows from (3.2) after integrating both sides between S and $+\infty$ and after making use of the normalization conditions

$$\int_{-\infty}^{\infty} dx\, f(x,t|x_0) = 1$$
$$(3.4)$$
$$\int_S^{\infty} dx\, f^{(r)}(x,t|x_0) = 1.$$

We explicitly remark that due to the above Corollary, use of (3.2) can be made to evaluate the function $f^{(r)}(x,t|x_0)$ for any $x > S$. Note that due to the weakly singular nature of its kernel eq.(3.3) can be numerically solved with the initial condition $f^{(r)}(S,0|x_0) = 0$ by using the computational methods discussed in Favella et al. /6/ for the evaluation of first passage time p.d.f.'s.

We point out that eqs. (3.2) and (3.3) include convolution integrals. Hence we have the following

Remark 1. The Laplace transforms $f_\lambda^{(r)}(x|x_0)$ and $f_\lambda^{(r)}(S|x_0)$ are given by

$$(3.5) \quad f_\lambda^{(r)}(x|x_0) = f_\lambda(x|x_0) - \frac{\sigma^2}{2} f_\lambda^{(r)}(S|x_0) \frac{\partial}{\partial x} f_{\lambda+1/\theta}(x|S)$$

and

$$(3.6) \quad f_\lambda^{(r)}(S|x_0) = \frac{2}{\sigma^2} \frac{F_\lambda(S|x_0)}{f_{\lambda+1/\theta}(S|S)},$$

respectively.

Remark 2. The function $f_\lambda^{(r)}(x|x_0)$ can be written as

$$(3.7) \quad f_\lambda^{(r)}(x|x_0) = f_\lambda(x|x_0) - \frac{f_{\lambda+1/\theta}(x|S)}{\partial x} \frac{F_\lambda(S|x_0)}{f_{\lambda+1/\theta}(S|S)}.$$

4. ALTERNATIVE INTEGRAL EQUATIONS

To avoid unnecessarily heavy notations, without loss of generality in this Section we shall refer to the normalized O.U. process, i.e. we shall take $\mu=0$ and $\sigma^2=\theta=1$. Denoting by $D_\upsilon(\cdot)$ the parabolic cylinder function and by $\Gamma(\cdot)$ the Euler gamma function (Erdelyi et al./5/), it can be shown that for $x_0>S$ and $x>S$ the following results hold:

$$(4.1a) \qquad f_\lambda(S|S) = \frac{2^{\lambda-1}}{\pi} \Gamma(\lambda/2)\Gamma\left(\frac{\lambda+1}{2}\right) D_{-\lambda}(-\sqrt{2}\,S)D_{-\lambda}(\sqrt{2}\,S)$$

$$(4.1b) \qquad F_\lambda(S|x_0) = \frac{2^{\lambda-1/2}}{\lambda\pi} e^{-(S^2-x_0^2)/2}\Gamma\left(\frac{\lambda}{2}+1\right)\Gamma\left(\frac{\lambda+1}{2}\right)D_{-\lambda}(\sqrt{2}x_0)D_{-\lambda-1}(-\sqrt{2}S)$$

$$(4.1c) \qquad f_\lambda(x|y) = \begin{cases} \dfrac{2^{\lambda-1}}{\pi} e^{-(x^2-y^2)/2}\Gamma(\lambda/2)\Gamma\left(\dfrac{\lambda+1}{2}\right)D_{-\lambda}(\sqrt{2}x)D_{-\lambda}(-\sqrt{2}y), & x \geqslant y \\[3mm] \dfrac{2^{\lambda-1}}{\pi} e^{-(x^2-y^2)/2}\Gamma(\lambda/2)\Gamma\left(\dfrac{\lambda+1}{2}\right)D_{-\lambda}(\sqrt{2}y)D_{-\lambda}(-\sqrt{2}x) & x<y \end{cases}$$

$$(4.1d) \qquad \frac{\partial}{\partial x}f_{\lambda+1}(x|S)=- \frac{2^{\lambda+\frac{1}{2}}}{\pi} e^{-(x^2-S^2)/2}\Gamma\left(\frac{\lambda+1}{2}\right)\Gamma\left(\frac{\lambda}{2}+1\right)D_{-\lambda-1}(-\sqrt{2}S)D_{-\lambda}(\sqrt{2}x)$$

$$(4.1e) \qquad \frac{D_{-\lambda-1}(-\sqrt{2}S)}{D_{-\lambda-1}(\sqrt{2}S)} =- \frac{D_{-\lambda}(-\sqrt{2}S)}{D_{-\lambda}(\sqrt{2}S)} + \frac{\pi\, 2^{-\lambda+\frac{1}{2}}}{\Gamma\left(\frac{\lambda}{2}+1\right)\Gamma\left(\frac{\lambda+1}{2}\right)D_{-\lambda}(\sqrt{2}S)D_{-\lambda-1}(\sqrt{2}S)}$$

$$(4.1f) \qquad j_\lambda(S|S) = \frac{2^{\lambda-\frac{1}{2}}}{\pi} \Gamma\left(\frac{\lambda}{2}+1\right)\Gamma\left(\frac{\lambda+1}{2}\right)D_{-\lambda-1}(\sqrt{2}S)D_{-\lambda}(-\sqrt{2}S) - \frac{1}{2}$$

$$(4.1g) \qquad j_\lambda(S|x_0) = - \frac{2^{\lambda-\frac{1}{2}}}{\pi} \Gamma\left(\frac{\lambda+1}{2}\right)\Gamma\left(\frac{\lambda}{2}+1\right)D_{-\lambda-1}(-\sqrt{2}S)D_{-\lambda}(\sqrt{2}x_0)e^{-(S^2-x_0^2)/2}$$

$$(4.1h) \qquad g_\lambda(S|x_0) = e^{-(S^2-x_0^2)/2}\frac{D_{-\lambda}(\sqrt{2}x_0)}{D_{-\lambda}(\sqrt{2}S)}$$

<u>Lemma 1.</u> The Laplace transform $f_\lambda^{(r)}(S|x_0)$ is given by

$$(4.2) \qquad f_\lambda^{(r)}(S|x_0) = \frac{\sqrt{2}}{\pi} e^{-(S^2-x_0^2)/2}\frac{D_{-\lambda}(\sqrt{2}x_0)}{D_{-\lambda-1}(\sqrt{2}S)}.$$

<u>Proof</u>. It immediately follows from (3.6),(4.1a) and (4.1b).

<u>Lemma 2</u>. The Laplace transform $f_\lambda^{(r)}(x|x_0)$ is given by

(4.3) $f_\lambda^{(r)}(x|x_0) = f_\lambda(x|x_0) +$

$$+ \frac{2^{\lambda-1}}{\pi} e^{-(x^2-x_0^2)/2} \Gamma\left(\frac{\lambda+1}{2}\right)\Gamma\left(\frac{\lambda}{2}+1\right) \frac{D_{-\lambda}(\sqrt{2}x_0)D_{-\lambda-1}(-\sqrt{2}S)D_{-\lambda}(\sqrt{2}x)}{D_{-\lambda-1}(\sqrt{2}S)}$$

<u>Proof</u>. It follows from (3.5),(4.1d) and from Lemma 1.

<u>Theorem 2</u>. For all $x,x_0 \in [S,\infty)$ one has

(4.4) $\qquad f^{(r)}(x,t|x_0) = f^{(a)}(x,t|x_0) + \int_0^t d\tau g(S,\tau|x_0)f^{(r)}(x,t|S,\tau).$

<u>Proof</u>. Substituting (4.1e) in (4.3) we obtain

(4.5) $\qquad f_\lambda^{(r)}(x|x_0) = f_\lambda(x|x_0) + A + B$

where we have set

(4.6a) $\qquad A = -\frac{2^\lambda}{\lambda \pi} e^{-(x^2-x_0^2)/2} \Gamma\left(\frac{\lambda+1}{2}\right)\Gamma\left(\frac{\lambda}{2}+1\right) D_{-\lambda}(\sqrt{2}x)D_{-\lambda}(\sqrt{2}x_0)\frac{D_{-\lambda}(-\sqrt{2}S)}{D_{-\lambda}(\sqrt{2}\,S)}$

(4.6b) $\qquad B = \frac{\sqrt{2}}{\lambda} e^{-(x^2-x_0^2)/2} \frac{D_{-\lambda}(\sqrt{2}x_0)D_{-\lambda}(\sqrt{2}x)}{D_{-\lambda}(\sqrt{2}S)D_{-\lambda-1}(\sqrt{2}S)}.$

Recalling (4.1c) and (4.1h) one sees that

(4.7) $\qquad A = -g_\lambda(S|x_0)f_\lambda(x|S).$

We now take the Laplace transform of both sides of (2.1) to obtain

(4.8) $\qquad f_\lambda^{(a)}(x|x_0) = f_\lambda(x|x_0) - g(S|x_0)f_\lambda(x|S).$

Substituting (4.7) in (4.5) and making use of (4.8) we find

(4.9) $\qquad f_\lambda^{(r)}(x|x_0) = f_\lambda^{(a)}(x|x_0) + B.$

Taking the limit of (4.9) and (4.6b) as $x_0 \downarrow S$ and recalling (2.3) one obtains

(4.10) $\qquad f_\lambda^{(r)}(x|S) = \frac{\sqrt{2}}{\lambda} e^{-(x^2-S^2)/2} \frac{D_{-\lambda}(\sqrt{2}\,x)}{D_{-\lambda-1}(\sqrt{2}S)}.$

324

Hence, by virtue of (4.1h) and making use of (4.10) from (4.6b) one gets

$$(4.11) \qquad B = g_\lambda(S|x_0)f_\lambda^{(r)}(x|S).$$

After substituting (4.11) in (4.9) and taking the inverse Laplace transform of both sides one finally obtains eq. (4.4).

Remark 3. Differently from eq.(3.2), eq.(4.4) admits the following straighforward interpretation. The set of the sample paths originating at time t in the neighborhood of the state x in the presence of the reflecting boundary S can be partitioned into two disjoint subsets: One contains the sample paths that end in the neighborhood of x at time t and that have never attained the state S while to the other set belong the sample paths that reach the reflecting boundary S before time t for the first time and that terminate in the neighborhood of x at time t.

Remark 4. Eq. (4.4) has been derived for the O.U. process. However, it is expected to hold for any Markov processes for which the functions $f^{(r)}(x,t|x_0)$, $f^{(a)}(x,t|x_0)$ and $g(S,t|x_0)$ are defined.

It is possible to prove (cf. Ricciardi and Sacerdote, in preparation) that the following theorems hold:

Theorem 3. For all x, $x_0 \in (S,\infty)$ one has

$$(4.12) \qquad f^{(r)}(x,t|x_0) = f(x,t|x_0) - \int_0^t d\tau\, j(S,\tau|x_0)f^{(r)}(x,t|S,\tau).$$

Theorem 4. For all x>S one has

$$(4.13) \qquad f^{(r)}(x,t|S) = 2f(x,t|S) - 2\int_0^t d\tau\, j(S,\tau|S)f^{(r)}(x,t|S,\tau).$$

Theorem 5. For x_0>S one has

$$(4.14) \qquad f^{(r)}(S,t|x_0) = 2f(S,t|x_0) - 2\int_0^t d\tau\, j(S,t|S,\tau)f^{(r)}(S,\tau|x_0).$$

Remark 5. Since j(0,t|0)=0, form (4.13) and (4.14) we obtain the well known closed form solutions (Cox and Miller /4/) $f^{(r)}(x,t|0)=2f(x,t|0)$ and $f^{(r)}(0,t|x_0)=2f(0,t|x_0)$.

Remark 6. Eqs.(4.13) and (4.14) must be solved with the aid of the initial conditions $f^{(r)}(x,0|S)=f^{(r)}(S,0|x_0)=0$. Once the function $f^{(r)}(x,t|S)$ has been determined also the function $f^{(r)}(x,t|x_0)$ can be obtained via (4.12).

Remark 7. The kernel of eq. (4.14) coincides with the kernel appearing in the first passage time integral equation of Ricciardi et al. /19/ for which various solution methods have already made avaible.

By a simple space-time transformation the validity of theorems 2÷5 finally seen to hold for the more general O.U. process of Section 3.

Acknowledgements. This work has been performed under CNR-JSPS Scientific Cooperation Programme, Contract No. 84.00227.01 and under MPI financial support.

REFERENCES

/1/   Abrahams, J. (1983). A survey of recent progress on level crossing
325

problems for random processes'(preprint).

/2/ Balossino, N., Ricciardi, L.M. and Sacerdote, L. (1985).'On the evaluation of first passage time densities for diffusion processes! Cybernetics and Systems (in press).

/3/ Blake, I.F. and Lindsey, W.C. (1973).'Level crossing problems for random processes!I.E.E.E. Trans. on Information Theory IT-19, 295.

/4/ Cox, J.R. and Miller, H.D. (1965). The Theory of Stochastic Processes. Wiley, New York.

/5/ Erdelyi, A., Magnus, W., Oberhettinger, F. and Tricomi, F.G. (1953). Higher Trascendental Functions.Vol. II, McGraw Hill, New York.

/6/ Favella, L., Reineri, M.T., Ricciardi, L.M. and Sacerdote, L. (1982).'First passage time problems and some related computational methods'. Cybernetics and Systems. 13, 95-128.

/7/ Giorno, V., Nobile, A.G. and Ricciardi, L.M. (1985).'On some diffusion approximations to queueing systems.'(preprint).

/8/ Giorno,V., Nobile, A.G., Ricciardi, L.M. and Sacerdote, L.(1985). 'Some remarks on the Rayleigh process'. J.Appl.Prob. (in press).

/9/ Heath, R.A. (1981).'A tandem random walk model for psychological discrimination.' British J. Math. Psychology. 34, 76-92.

/10/ Holden, A.V. (1976). Models of the stochastic activity of neurons. Lecture Notes in Biomathematics. Springer-Verlag, Berlin.

/11/ Maruyama, T. (1977). Stochastic problems in population genetics. Lecture Notes in Biomathematics. Springer-Verlag, Berlin.

/12/ Nobile, A.G., Ricciardi, L.M. and Sacerdote, L. (1985). 'A note on first-passage time and some related problems.'J. Appl. Prob. 22, 346-360.

/13/ Nobile,A.G., Ricciardi, L.M. and Sacerdote, L. (1985).'Exponential trends of the Ornstein-Uhlenbeck first-passage time densities'. J. Appl. Prob. 22, 360-369.

/14/ Ratcliff, R. (1980).'A note on modelling accumulation of information when the rate of accumulation changes with time.' J. Math. Psych. 21, 178-184.

/15/ Ricciardi, L.M.(1977).Diffusion processes and some related topics in biology.Lecture Notes in Biomathematics.Springer-Verlag,Berlin.

/16/ Ricciardi, L.M. (1985).'Stochastic population models.II.Diffusion models.'Lecture Notes at the International School of Mathematical Ecology. (in press).

/17/ Ricciardi,L.M. and Sacerdote,L. (1979).'The Ornstein-Uhlenbeck process as a model for neuronal activity.I.Mean and Variance of the firing time.'Biol. Cybernetics. 35, 1-9.

/18/ Ricciardi, L.M., Sacerdote, L. and Sato, S.(1983).'Diffusion approximatio and first passage time problem for a model neuron.II.Outline of a computation method.' Math. Biosc. 64, 29-44.

/19/ Ricciardi,L.M., Sacerdote, L. and Sato, S. (1984).'On an integral equation for first passage time probability densities'. J.Appl. Prob. 21, 302-314.

/20/ Ricciardi,L.M. and Sato, S. (1983).'A note on the evaluation of the first passage time probability densities'. J. Appl. Prob. 20.

/21/ Siegert, A.J.F. (1951).'On the first passage time probability problem.'Phys. Rev. 81, 617-623.

MORPHOGENESIS AND PROPERTIES OF NEURONAL MODEL NETWORKS

Ingolf E. Dammasch
Universität Göttingen
Zentrum Anatomie
Kreuzbergring 36
D-34oo Göttingen (W.Germany)

ABSTRACT. The behavior of small groups of neurons can be described with certain types of networks, consisting of "logical" (McCulloch-Pitts) neurons. A morphogenesis algorithm compensating initial disturbances by a feed-back process is applied to model networks that are randomly connected in the beginning and equilibrate via selective stabilization and elimination of synapses. The structure and the resulting ability of the networks to generate cyclic activity patterns before and after morphogenesis is analysed mathematically and with computer simulation experiments.

1. THE COMPENSATION THEORY OF SYNAPTOGENESIS

Neurons can react in two ways (on two time levels) to disturbances of their (postsynaptic) membrane potential: The electrophysiological response (millisecond range) consists of action potentials which are produced when the threshold potential is being crossed. In contrast, the morphogenetic response (hour to day range) seems to depend on long-term changes of the average membrane potential or any related parameter (Joó et al 1979, Wolff et al 1979). Neurocytological results lead to the following hypotheses:

Table I. Morphogenetic responses to changes of input

	long-term excitation	long-term inhibition
presynaptic elements	(+)	(−)
exc. postsynaptic elements	(−)	(+)
inh. postsynaptic elements	(+)	(−)

(+) : formation promoted, break down reduced
(−) : formation inhibited, break down accelerated

327

R. Trappl (ed.), Cybernetics and Systems '86, 327–334.
© *1986 by D. Reidel Publishing Company.*

With a behavioral repertoire like this, the neurons interconnected in a network try to change their initial deviations in an inter- active, self-organizing process. During this process, the state of each neuron can be described by three different aspects (Figure 1):

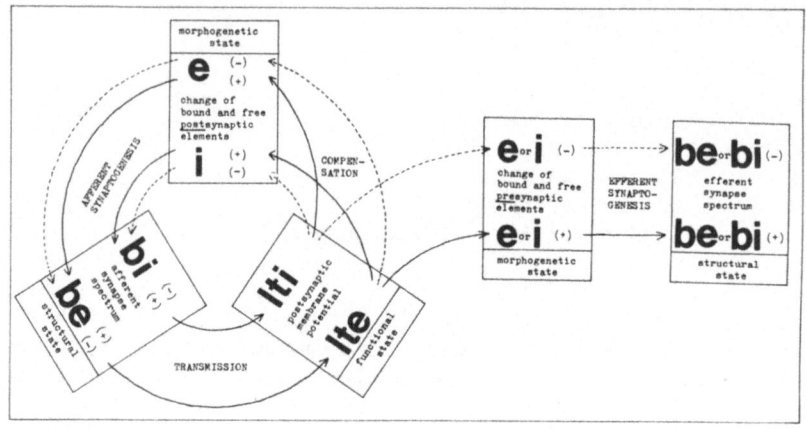

Figure 1. Aspects and interactions in the compensation process
e,i : excitatory, inhibitory synaptic elements
be,bi : bound excitatory, inhibitory synaptic elements
lte,lti : long-term excitation, inhibition
(+),(-) : increase, decrease

The afferent synapse spectrum influences - via transmission - the functional state of the neuron. An average membrane potential cor- responding to "long-term excitation" or "long-term inhibition" leads to a morphogenetic state that tries to compensate that deviation. It is done by changing the neuron's bound and free pre- and postsyn- aptic elements in the right direction. This in turn leads - via de- generation of bound and recombination of free synaptic elements - to a new structural state. The new afferent spectrum transforms the neuron into a new functional state again, etc. (Wolff&Wagner 1983, Wagner&Wolff in prep).

The compensation theory of synaptogenesis has been formalized and applied to neuronal model networks (Dammasch,Wagner&Wolff sub- mitted). Under certain conditions, the networks remain stable and functional.

2. THE EXTENDED McCULLOCH-PITTS MODEL NEURON

The compensation algorithm was tested with networks of logical neu- rons as introduced by McCulloch&Pitts (1943).

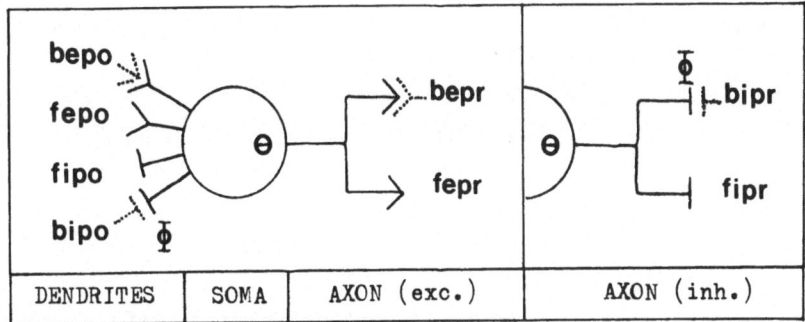

| DENDRITES | SOMA | AXON (exc.) | AXON (inh.) |

Figure 2. Schematic model of the neurons used in the networks

Each neuron in the network consists of the following sets:
bepo : bound excitatory postsynaptic elements
bipo : bound inhibitory postsynaptic elements
bpr : bound presynaptic elements (of excitatory neurons: bepr, of inhibitory neurons: bipr)
The following features are introduced to enable the combination of new synapses:
fepo : free excitatory postsynaptic elements
fipo : free inhibitory postsynaptic elements
fpr : free presynaptic elements (of excitatory neurons: fepr, of inhibitory neurons: fipr)
All neurons in the network have the following values in common:
θ : threshold above which the neuron "fires"
Φ : relative weight of inhibitory synapses
The postsynaptic elements are inputs from other cells, the presynaptic elements are outputs to other cells (see Figure 2).

If the postsynaptic potential (sum of active excitatory inputs minus weighted sum of active inhibitory inputs) reaches the threshold, the cell becomes active itself and influences others.

In the beginning, the synaptic strengths are randomly distributed on a connectivity matrix.

3. PROPERTIES OF THE NETWORKS

For certain values of threshold, inhibitory weight, ratio of excitators to inhibitors, and a certain stochasticity of inputs, the networks are able to produce cyclic oscillations and obtain a medium integrated activity without reaching zero or full activity fixpoints (Dammasch&Wagner 1984). This behavior is considered "functional".

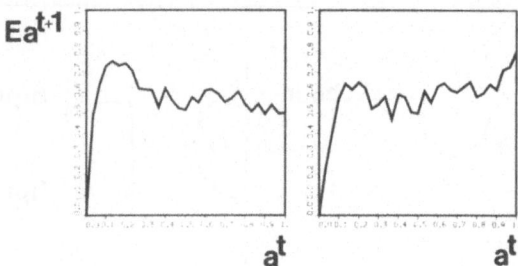

Figure 3. Activity transition function before and after morphogenesis

The activity transition function shows the expected network activity at time t+1, given the activity at time t. The different shape reflects the order that the network has gained concerning the afferent spectrum of the cells (cf. chapter 5).

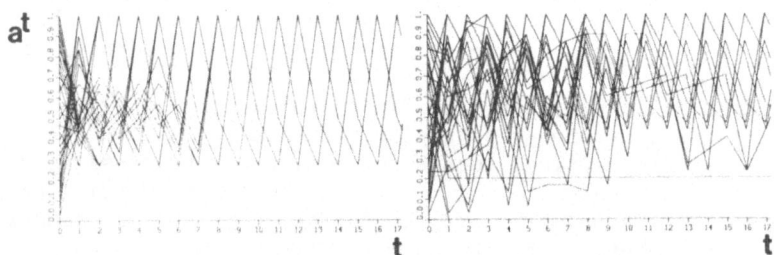

Figure 4. Oscillations before and after morphogenesis

The fraction of active cells is plotted over time. The behavior of the network appears to be more complex after morphogenesis, but it remains functional in the majority of cases.

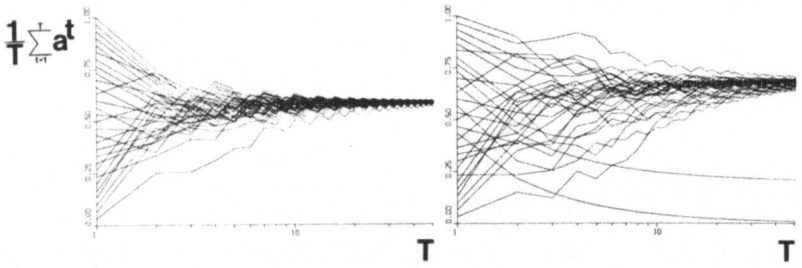

Figure 5. Medium activity before and after morphogenesis

The integrated medium activity is plotted over a logarithmic time scale. Again, it can be observed that the majority of cases lead to a higher but non-degenerate behavior in the end.

4. THE COMPENSATION PROCESS

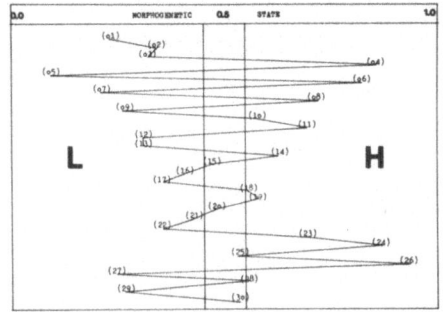

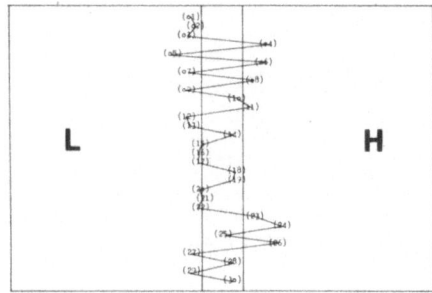

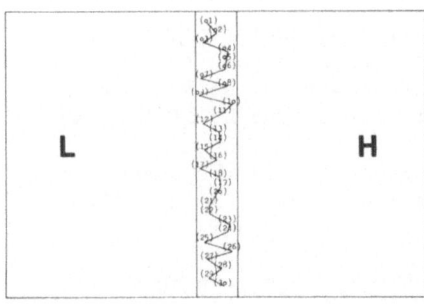

Figure 6. Profiles of morphogenetic states before, during,
and after morphogenesis

Before each morphogenetic step,
the network produces several oscillations to determine the type
of its cells. Neurons that are
outside of an excitation-inhibi-
tion-equilibrium can be either
type H or type L.

H-cells ("high-activity",
corresponding to long-term excitation, cf. Figure 1) try to reduce the excitation and increase
the inhibition they receive. Additionally, they try to increase
their contacts to others.

L-cells ("low-activity",
corresponding to long-term inhibition, cf. Figure 1) react in
the opposite way: increase the
excitation and reduce the inhibition they receive, decrease their
contacts to others.

(H) : bepo,fepo↓ fipo↑ fpr↑

(L) : fepo↑ bipo,fipo↓ bpr,fpr↓

All neurons in the network move
their morphogenetic state into
the desired range by successively
changing their pre- and postsynaptic elements. When this task is
achieved, the network is in equilibrium and morphogenesis comes
to an end.

As a result of this process,
the input spectrum of the cells
converge to a certain order.

Figure 6 shows morphogenetic
states of the various cells k
(1 ≤ k ≤ 3o) of a successful model network in the course of the
compensation process. The morphogenetic state is mapped onto the
unity interval [o,1], the desired
range is defined to be the interval [o.45,o.55].

331

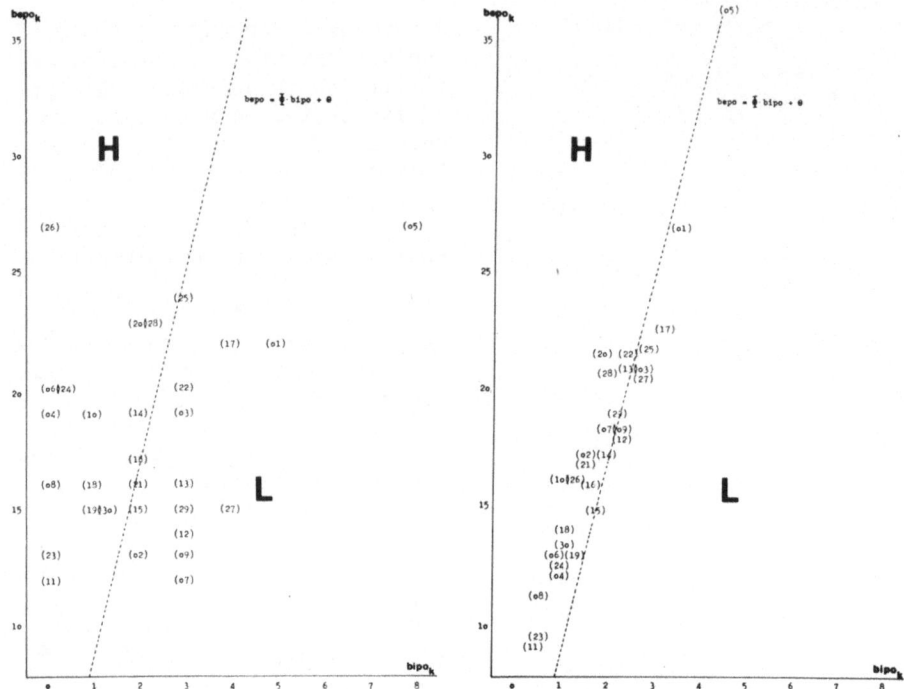

Figure 7. Profiles of structural states before and after morphogenesis (cell numbers $1 \leqslant k \leqslant 3o$ correspond to Figure 6)

Before morphogenesis, possible combinations of excitatory and inhibitory input numbers are scattered over a wide range after the random distribution of connectivities. Neurons tend to be type H, if
they are situated left of the dotted line, and type L, if they are
on the right.
    After morphogenesis, the inputs are ordered in the sense that
they converge to a similar ratio, bepo:bipo ~ const. (Figure 7).

5. ANALYTICAL CONSIDERATIONS ABOUT STRUCTURAL STATE AND ACTIVITY

Given a network activity a^t (=fraction of cells active at time t),
then the probability that exactly ke of ne excitatory inputs and ki
of ni inhibitory inputs are active in a certain cell is

$$p(ke,ki) = \binom{ne}{ke}\left(a^t\right)^{ke}\left(1-a^t\right)^{ne-ke} \cdot \binom{ni}{ki}\left(a^t\right)^{ki}\left(1-a^t\right)^{ni-ki}$$

If we consider a randomly connected network with N cells (of which
NE are excitatory), each cell having an average of n in/outputs,

then the probability that a certain cell has exactly (ne+ni) inputs from other cells is

$$p(ne+ni) = \binom{n \cdot N}{ne+ni}\left(\frac{1}{N}\right)^{ne+ni}\left(1-\frac{1}{N}\right)^{nN-ne-ni}$$

The probability that exactly ni of these (ne+ni) inputs are inhibitory is

$$p(ni) = \binom{ne+ni}{ni}\left(\frac{N-NE}{N}\right)^{ni}\left(\frac{NE}{N}\right)^{ne}$$

Therefore, the expected activity in the next time step is equal to the summed probabilities of all possible cases leading to an active cell:

$$Ea^{t+1}(a^t) = \sum_{\substack{0 \le ne+ni \le n \cdot N \\ 0 \le (ke,ki) \le (ne,ni) \\ ke - \Phi \cdot ki \ge \theta}} p(ne+ni) \cdot p(ni) \cdot p(ke,ki)$$

During the compensation process, the afferent spectrum of each cell k ($1 \le k \le N$) changes from an initial $(bepo^o_k, bipo^o_k)$ to an equilibrated $(bepo^T_k, bipo^T_k)$.

The transitory states can be described by a matrix M^t as follows:

$$(bepo^t_k, bipo^t_k) = M^t \cdot (bepo^o_k, bipo^o_k)$$

M^t starts as the unity matrix $\begin{pmatrix} 1 & 0 \\ 0 & 1 \end{pmatrix}$ and changes gradually. Its values depend on the kinetic parameters of the morphogenesis algorithm.

The activity transition function for a network <u>after</u> morphogenesis is then identical with the formula stated above, except one change: The summation of the possibly active inputs must now include the new possible limits

$$0 \le (ke,ki) \le M^T \cdot (ne,ni)$$

This — analytically determined — graph shows indeed an ascending branch near $a^t=1.o$ that moves closer to the full activity fixpoint $Ea^{t+1}(1.o) = 1.o$, the more M^T converges to a degenerate matrix of rank=1 . When the afferent spectra of all cells are situated on the same straight line (i.e. they all have the same ratio of excitatory to inhibitory inputs, and M^T has rank=1), then the network permanently loses its ability to produce cyclic oscillations and degenerates to a network that is either "on" or "off" after a number of steps.

6. REFERENCES

Dammasch IE, Wagner GP: 'On the properties of randomly connected McCulloch-Pitts networks: Differences between input-constant and input-variant networks'. Cybernetics and Systems 15,91-117. 1984

Dammasch IE, Wagner GP, Wolff JR: 'Self-stabilization of neuronal networks I: The compensation algorithm for synaptogenesis'. submitted

Joб F, Dames W, Wolff JR: 'Effect of prolonged sodium bromide administration on the fine structure of dendrites in the superior cervical ganglion of adult rat'. Progr Brain Res 51,1o9-115. 1979

McCulloch WS, Pitts WH: 'A logical calculus of ideas immanent in nervous activity'. Bull Math Biophysics 5,115-133. 1943

Wagner GP, Wolff JR: 'A kinetic model of synaptogenesis based on morphogenetic consequences of excitation and inhibition'. in prep

Wolff JR, Joб F, Dames W, Fehér O: 'Induction and maintenance of free postsynaptical memebrane thickenings in the adult superior cervical ganglion'. J Neurocyt 8,549-563. 1979

Wolff JR, Wagner GP: 'Selforganization in synaptogenesis: Interaction between the formation of excitatory and inhibitory synapses', in: Basar E, Flohr H, Haken H, Mandell AJ (Eds): Synergetics of the brain. Springer Verlag, Berlin, Heidelberg, New York, 5o-59. 1983

PATTERN FORMATION IN NEURAL SYSTEMS

I. Autorhytmicity, entrainment, quasiperiodicity and chaos in neurochemical systems

P. Érdi , G. Barna : Central Research Institute for
Physics of the Hungarian Academy of Sciences ,
H-1525 Budapest, P.O.B. 49., HUNGARY

ABSTRACT. The skeleton model of transmitter recycling hypothesis
describes rhytmic neurochemical behaviour due to the integrated synaptic
activity. Interaction among neurochemical oscillators are modeled by a
periodically perturbed nonlinear oscillator. Complex arrhytmic dynamics
oocuring as transient phenomena might have connected with neurological
disorders: synaptic level rhytmic generator requires a fine-tuned
neurochemical control system.

1. INTRODUCTION

Rhytmic behaviour is characteristic for biological systems
(Winfree, 1980). The stability of most biological rhytmic phenomena can
be understood by the concept of limit cycle. The independence of the
amplitudes and frequencies from the initial conditions might be
associated to regular temporal patterns.

The mutual interaction among different biological oscillators,
however, might imply different phenomena as entrainment (phase locking),
complex oscillations, as quasiperiodicity even chaos. Entrainment, i.e.
the frequency locking of autonomous oscillator by externally imposed
frequencies has been demonstrated in the Selkov model of glycolitic
oscillation (Richter, 1984). Multiperiodic behaviour due to interactions
of two 'instability generating' mechanisms in biochemical systems have
been illustrated (Decroly & Goldbeter 1982, 1984; Goldbeter & Decroly
1983). Numerical simulation of periodic perturbation of glycolitic
oscillatory model led to entrainment, quasiperiodicity and chaos (Markus
et al 1985).

Whether aperiodicity (ultimately identified by chaos) is
'undesirable' or 'useful' is non-issue. Chaotic behaviour was founded in
a model of the central dopaminergic neuronal system, and it was
associated to schisophrenics (King et al, 1984). Many neural disorders
are characterized by changing the 'normal' temporal patterns to
'abnormal' behaviour. This abnormal dynamics might be interpreted as a
result of disease occuring in a physiological control system operating
within a range of control parameters (Guevara et al, 1983). In contrary
(more precisely parallely) Holden and Muhamed (1984) argued that chaotic
irregularity might have positive role at least at evolutionary time
scale.

The motivation of this work is the very fact that at least three
different neurochemical and neurophysiological oscillatory phenomena

335

R. Trappl (ed.), Cybernetics and Systems '86, 335–342.
© *1986 by D. Reidel Publishing Company.*

appear at different hierarchical levels of cholinergic synaptic transmission (Èrdi & Tòth 1980, Èrdi 1983). A complete theory of hierarchical regulation mechanism of dynamic synaptic activity would require the study of cooperation and competition among the three oscillators. As a first step, the model for transmitter-recycling (TRC) hypothesis adopted to explain the 'integrated' synaptic activity has been supplemented by an independent, harmonic oscillator.

The neurochemical background is shortly analyzed (Sect.2.). Periodic external excitation ('forcing') is known to be an important tool for investigating systems, which have inherent oscillatory character (Sect. 3.). Detailed (but far from 'necessary' and 'sufficient') numerical calculations have been done for a driven TRC model. The possibility of disorders due to change in the parameters of the choline (Ch) transport systems and the sensitivity of the system has been demonstrated (Sect. 4.). Further difficulties and problems are mentioned (Sect. 5.).

2. NEUROCHEMICAL BACKGROUND

As it was mentioned, different oscillators can operate at the cholinergic synapse. The 'rapid' and 'slow' oscillations of free, presumably cytoplasmic acetylcholine (ACh) were presented (Dunant et al, 1977; Israel et al,1977). Another oscillatory phenomenon is the series of miniature - end-plate potential (Fatt & Katz 1952).

We restrict ourselves to study the skeleton model of slow oscillation due to the 'integrated synaptic activity'. In principle instead of setting up lumped, skeleton model, more complex model could be defined to take into account the details of subprocesses (synthesis, storage and release of ACh, cleft processes, transmitter-receptor interaction, diffusion, reuptake). However, experimental informations certainly would not be sufficient to parametrize such kind of models. Similar mental strategy, i.e. the use of lumped, mass-action kinetic based models, was adopted by Leibovicz & Andrietti 1977, Kaufmann 1977, Markov & Venkov 1980, Fritzsche 1985, Kostova & Markov 1985 .

According to the basic assumptions of our four-compartmental model the state of the system is characterized by

-cytoplasmic ACh concentration:X
-ACh concentration at the postsynaptic membrane surface:Z
-Ch concentration near postsynaptic cell:W
-Ch concentration near presynaptic cell:Y.

The subprocesses of the model:

1., transmitter release, cleft processes, transmitter-receptor
   interaction ;
2., ACh hydrolysis (this is the most rapid subprocess);
3., metabolic products (mostly choline) diffuse to the
   vicinity of the presynaptic cell ;
4., (re)uptake of Ch ;
5., autocatalytic synthesis of ACh.

The slow oscillation is perturbed by another, more rapid oscillation connected to the ACh synthesis. ACh synthesis is controlled by the sodium dependent high affinity choline uptake (Barker & Mittag 1975) and by the transport of acetyl group (Jope 1979, Tucek 1983). It could be

336

strong connection between the oxidative metabolism of carbohydrates and the ACh synthesis. The hypoxia and hypoglycemia due to disturbance of the metabolism leads to reduced ACh synthesis and neurological disorders (Gibson & Blass 1976a,b).

According to the idealized neurochemical picture the rhytmic integrated synaptic activity is perturbed by another oscillation due to the presynaptic metabolism, and complex oscillatory phenomena might occur in consequence of the competition and cooperation of the distinct frequencies.

3. PERIODICALLY PERTURBED OSCILLATION:SOME CONCEPTS AND TECHNIQUES

The system of differential equations
$$x(t)=f(x(t)) \quad , \quad x(t) \in \mathbb{R}^n , x(0)=x_0 \quad (1)$$ might
be supplemented with a term $a^*=(0,0,...0,a \cdot \cos(wt+\varphi))$ leading to
$$x(t)=f(x(t))+a^* \cos(wt+ \varphi) \quad (2)$$
It means that one component is perturbed by a amplitude, w frequency and φ phase. In the last years particular attention has been dedicated to the response of nonlinear oscillators perturbed periodically. The celebrated Brusselator model of oscillatory chemical reactions
$$x^2y-Bx+A-x \qquad a \cdot \cos(wt+\varphi)$$
$$Bx-x^2y \qquad 0$$
has been studied (Tomita & Kai 1979, Kai & Tomita 1979, Tomita, 1982). The undriven system shows limit cycle behaviour in a certain region of the parameter space. It was clearly demonstrated that four different types of region may be recognized on the a-w plane, entrainment, quasiperiodic oscillation, periodic doubling cascade and chaos have been found. Albeit elaborated mathematical techniques exist to analyze bifurcations from and to on the regions just mentioned (e.g. Ioos & Joseph 1980) , numerical methods are often offer a technically simpler 'down to earth' treatment of dynamic problems. The analyisis of systems, when the unperturbed system is higher than threedimensional is particularly difficult (but not hopeless; Rössler & Hudson 1985).

To study our neurochemical-oriented problem a program-package have been prepared. The building blocks of the package are:
    i., a numerical integrator (Gottwald & Wanner 1981);
    ii.,phase plane (i.e. twodimensional projection of
        trajectories) plotter ;
    iii., Lorenz plotter (subsequent maxima are detected and
        the x_{n+1} versus x_n function is plotted);
    iv.,Poincare plotter (a stroboscopic phase portrait is
        obtained ; i.e. the phase plane is given by points
        taken at regular intervals of period);
    v., spectral density function plotter.

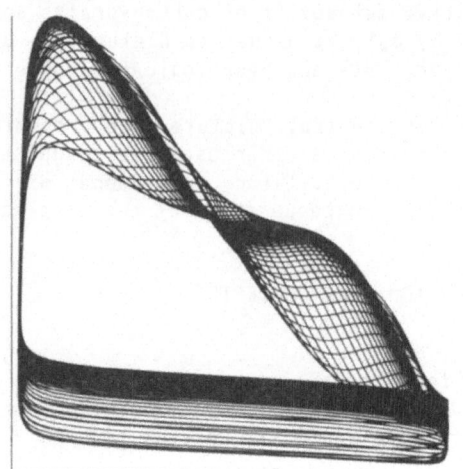
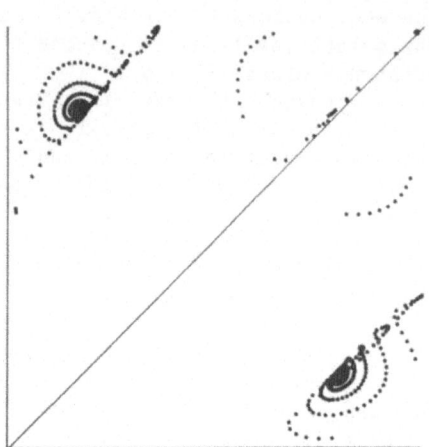

Figure 1. Phase plane and Lorenz plot of the perturbed variable for $w^*/w_0 \cong 2$

4. THE EFFECT OF PERIODIC PERTURBATION ON TRANSMITTER-RECYCLING

The four-compartmental formal chemical model

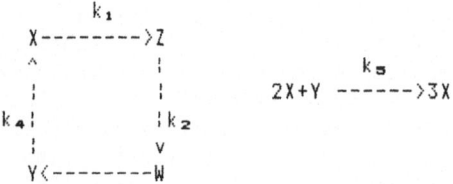

can be associated to the five subprocesses of integrated synaptic activity mentioned in Sect.2. The massconserving model reaction having a single nonlinearity can exhibit sustained oscillation. The 'limit shell' character of the oscillation has been visualized (Tóth 1985). Utilizing the neurochemical assumption according to which the choline uptake (however, not exclusively) controls the process, an independent choline oscillation is assumed. Therefore the model is:

$x(t)=-k_1 x(t)+k_4 y(t)+k_5 x^2(t)y(t)$
$z(t)=k_1 x(t)-k_2 z(t)$
$w(t)=k_2 z(t)-k_3 w(t)$
$y(t)=k_3 w(t)-k_4 y(t)-k_5 x^2(t)y(t)+a \cdot \cos(wt+\varphi)$

To give a rough estimation for the first order rate constants the $k_3 \sim k_4 \ll k_1 \langle k_2$ relations were adopted. (Simulation experiments to be documented here were done with parameter value $k_1=1$, $k_2=10$, $k_3=k_4=0.01$, $k_5=0.1$, the value of the total mass is 110.)

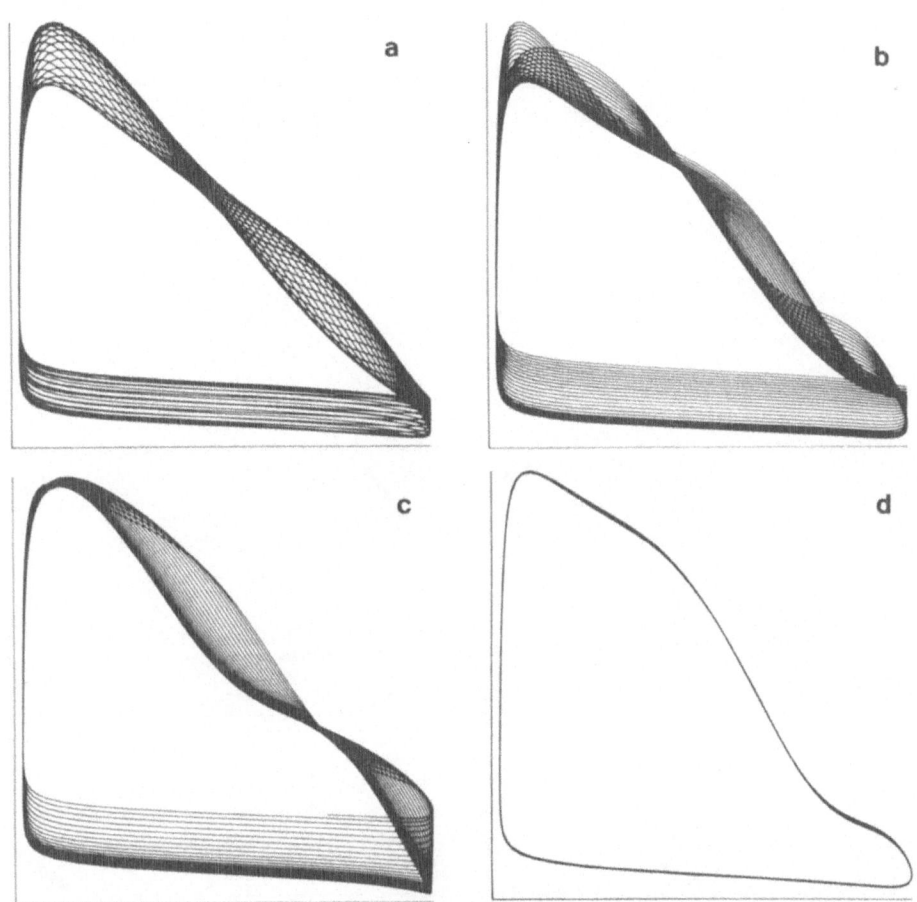

Figure 2. Phase plane diagram in different time regime
a.) approaching to the 'phantom attractor' b.) c.) intermediate
regime d.) near the true attractor.

The evaluation of simulation experiments:
  i., Phase locking
  The main entrainment band ($w^*/w_0 \cong 1$) and its neighborhood was
examined (w_0 is the inherent frequency of the undriven system). In
certain range around w_0 , its width increasing with a , the perturbing
signal ($a/a_0 \cong 0.01$, where a_0 is the amplitude of the inherent oscillation)
the width of the main entrainment band is about 0.02 ($w_0 \cong 0.23$). Other
entrainment bands have also been studied (e.g. Fig.1.)

  ii., Transients: they can be interesting
  In principle it is well known that infinite computational accuracy
as well as infinite computational length would be necessary to obtain
'complicated', asymptotic behaviour. The study of attractors does not

339

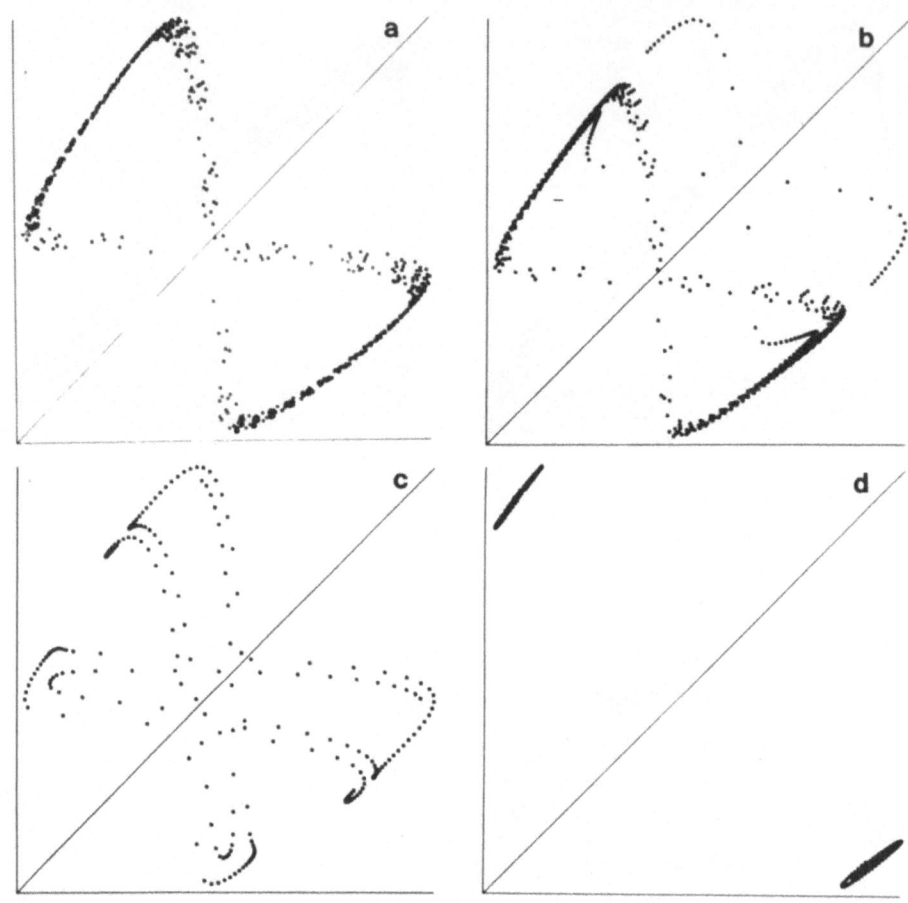

Figure 3. Stroboscopic representation of perturbed variable
a.) quasistable 'butterfly' shape b.) decay of the quasi-stable
shape and start to tend a new shape c.) tending to a new
attractor d.) arriving to a fix point of the Poincare plot.

make superfluous to follow the complicated transient dynamics during
intermediate time regimes (for the role of transient chaos see Kantz &
Grassberger 1985). In the vicinity of $w^*/w_o \cong 2$ for $a \cong 0.5$ numerical
calculations demonstrated the existence of 'phantom attractor' which
seems to show 22T periodicity. It can be interpreted as a quasistable
temporal structure. Though the 'phantom structure' seemed to be
stabilized, a very slight spontaneous modification of the trajectory
implied 'destabilization' leading to 'simple' limit cycles (Fig. 2-3).

5. CONCLUSIONS

From formal point of view it is clearly demonstrated that slight modification of the parameters of perturbation might imply transition to different kind of complex periodic phenomena. It is well-known that periodically perturbed oscillatory system might give rise to 'complex' phenomena, as phase locking, quasiperiodicity and chaos, and the fact have been illustrated as well in neurophysiological experiments and models (see references in Guevara et al, 1983). However, neurochemistry adopts a much more static approach than the Hodgkin-Huxley equation based neurophysiology of single nerve cells. What we wanted to verify is that the regular periodic operation of synaptic level rhytmic generator requires a **fine-tuned neurochemical control system**. Mild impairment of transport processes might impy 'abnormal' dynamic synaptic activity. From formal point of view the model - being a fourdimensional autonomous system (four variables minus one constraint plus perturbation) - could be a candidate to exhibit hyper-toroid and hyperchaotic (Rössler 1983) phenomena. Though the detailed examination of the model would be very important , speculations based on calculations partially presented here seem to be beyond on the experimental realm.

REFERENCES

Barker,L.A. & Mittag,T.W.:Comparative studies of substrates and inhibitors of choline transport and choline acetyltransferase. J.Pharmac.exp.Ther.192(86-94)1975

Decroly,O. & Goldbeter,A:Birhytmicity,chaos, and other patterns of temporal selforganization in a multiply regulated biochemical system. Proc.Natl.Acad.Sci.USA 79(6917-6921)1982

Decroly,O. & Goldbeter,A.:Multiple periodic regime and final state sensitivity in a biochemical system.Phys.Lett. 105A(259-262)1984

Dunant,Y.,Israel,M.,Lesbats,B. Manaranche,R.:Oscillation of acetylcholine during nerve activity in the Torpado electric organ. Brain Res.125(123-140)1977

Érdi,P:Hierarchical thermodynamic approach to the brain. Int.J.Neurosci.20(193-216)1983

Érdi,P & Tóth,J:Oscillatory phenomena at the synapse.Adv. Physiol.Sci.34(113-121)1981

Fatt,P. & Katz,B.:Spontaneous subthreshold activity at motor nerve endings. J.Physiol.(London) 117(109-128)1952

Fritzsche,B.:Das Übertragungsverhalten der neuromuskularen Synapse: Deutung experimenteller Befunde durch ein Modell. Biol. Cybernetics 51(335-346)1985

Gibson,G.E. & Blass,J.:Inhibition of acetylcholine synthesis and of carbohydrate utilization by maple-syrupurine disease metabolites. J.Neurochem. 26(1073-1078)1976a

Gibson,G.E. & Blass,J.:Impaired synthesis of acetylcholine in the brain accompanying mild hypoxia and hypoglycemia. J.Neurochem.27(37-42) 1976b

Goldbeter,A. & Decroly,O.:Temporal self-organization in biochemical systems:periodic behavior vs. chaos. Am. J. Physiol.245(R478-R483)1983

Gottwald,B.A. & Wanner,G.:A reliable Rosenbrock Integrator for stiff differential equations. Computing 26 (355-360)1981

Guevara,M.R.,Glass,L.,Mackey,C. & Shrier,A.:Chaos in neuorobiology. IEEE Trans. Systems, Man, and Cybernetics. SMC-13(790-797)1983

Holden,A.V. & Muhamed,M.A.:Chaotic activity in neural systems. Cybernetic and System Research 2, Trappl,R.(ed) (North-Holland, Amsterdam, 1984)pp.245-250.

Iooss,G, & Joseph,D.D.:Elementary Stability and Bifurcation Theory. Springer, New York-Heidelberg-Berlin (1980)

Israel,M.,Lesbats,B.,Manaranche,R.,Marsal,J. & Mastour-Frachon,P.: Related changes in amounts of ACh and ATP in resting·and active torpedo nerve electroïaque synapse. J.Neurochem.28(1259-1267)1977

Jope,R.S.:High affinity choline transport and acetyl CoA production in brain and their roles in the regulation of acetylcholine synthesis. Brain.Res.Rev.1(313-344)1979

Kai,T. & Tomita,K.:Stroboscopic phase portrait of a forced nonlinear oscillator. Prog.Theor.Phys.61(54-73),1979

Kantz,H. & Grassberger,P.:Repellers, semi-attractors, and long-lived chaotic transients. Physica 17D(75-86)1985

Kaufmann,K.:On the kinetics of acetylcholine at the synapse. Naturwissenschaften 64(371-376)1977

Kostova,T.V. & Markov,S.M.:A model of synaptic transmission. In:Dynamic phenomena in neurochemistry and neurophysics:theoretical aspects(Erdi,P.ed.)Budapest,1985, pp.44-51.

Markus,M.,Müller,S.C. & Hess,B.:Observation of entrainment, quasi-periodicity and chaos in glycolyzing yeast extracts under periodic glucose input. Ber. Bunsenges. Phys. Chem.89(651-654)1985

Leibovic,K.H. & Andrietti,F.:Analysis of a model for transmitter kinetics. Biol.Cybernetics 27(165-173)1977

Richter,P.:Entrainment of chemical oscillators and resonance dissipation. Physica 10D(353-368)1984

Rössler,O.E.:The chaotic hierarchy. Z.Naturforsch. 38a(788-801)1982

Rössler,O.E. & Hudson,J.L.:A piecewise-linear hierarchy (Int.Symp. on Math.Biol. Nov.1985,, Kyoto, Japan; Abstract)

Tomita,K.:Chaotic response of nonlinear oscillators. Phys.Rep. 86(113-167)1982

Tomita,,K. & Kai,T.:Chaotic response of a limit cycle. J.Stat.Phys. 21(65-86)1979

Tóth,J.:A mass action kinetic model of neurochemical transmission. In:Dynamic phenomena in neurochemistry and neurophysics:theoretical aspects (Erdi,P.ed.), Budapest, 1985. pp.522-55.

Tucek,S.:Acetylcoenzyme A and the synthesis of acetylcholine in neurons.Review of recent progress. Gen.Physiol.Biophys. 2(313-324)1983

Venkov,L. & Markov,S.M.:Dynamical model of cholinergic synapse transmission. Cell.Mol.Biol. 26(541-546)1980

Winfree,A.T.:The geometry of biological time (Springer,New York)1980

PATTERN FORMATION IN NEURAL SYSTEMS

II. Noise-induced selective mechanism for the
ontogenetic formation of ocular dominance columns

G. Barna & P. Érdi: Central Research Institute for
Physics of the Hungarian Academy of Sciences ,
H-1525 Budapest, P.O.B. 49., HUNGARY

ABSTRACT
A model for the formation and plastic behaviour of
ocular dominance columns is given in terms of modifiable
synapses. The activity-dependent self-organizing mechanism
presented is in accordance with the concept of noise-induced
transition.

1. INTRODUCTION

The visual cortex is considered as the best paradigm of modular
organization of the neural centers (Szentágothai,1983). We are far from
understanding the ontogeny of columnar structures in the cortex. Ocular
dominance columns or stripes are characteristic examples of ordered
neural structures. It is well known, that the term 'ordered' is here in
connection with the fact that projections between the eye and brain are
arranged retinotopically. This means that neighbouring presynaptic cells
project through their fibres onto neighbouring cells of the postsynaptic
sheet. Retinotopic map of the cortex might be considered point-to-patch
rather than point-to-point representation (e.g. Gilbert 1985).

One of the greatest challenges for neurobiology is the problem
of the mechanism of ontogenetic formation of ordered neural structures.
It is more ore less accepted that the establishment of neural networks
during embryonic and postnatal development does not result from
exclusively genetic mechanisms but interactions with the environment
contributes to the formation of adult connectivity. The environment
could either operate through direct, instructive or indirect, selective
mechanisms (Changeux, 1984).
A selection-based model for the formation and plastic behaviour
of ocular dominance columns was given by v.d.Malsburg.(1979;for some
comments see Érdi,1984). In this model existence of chemical marker
molecules have been assumed to direct the axon growth.'...Newer results
allow to postulate the role of the patterns of spontaneous activity for
the segregation of the ocular dominance bands (Stryker: in Rakic and
Goldman-Rakic 1982), but here a new story starts.' (Érdi 1984).
The general idea that synapses can be modified by activity was
put forward by Hebb (1949) and had many applications. Willshaw &
v.d.Malsburg (1976) gave an activity-dependent mechanism for the
formation of the retinotectal connections. Our model (Érdi & Barna 1984,
Érdi & Barna 1985, Érdi & Szentágothai 1985) differs from the other
models at least one essential point. According to our approach the
formation of ordered neural structure might be interpreted with the

343

R. Trappl (ed.), Cybernetics and Systems '86, 343–350.
© 1986 by D. Reidel Publishing Company.

concept of noise-induced transition. In accordance with the spirit of the theory (Horsthemke & Lefever 1984) fluctuations (noise) do not destroy the structure, on the contrary, they may operate as 'organizing forces'.

In this paper an algorithm is given for the formation of ocular dominance columns. The algorithm is a direct extension of our model for the formation and plastic behaviour of retinotectal connections to a situation , when axons coming from two presynaptic sheets compete for forming synapses with neurons of layer IV of visual cortex establishing partially overlapping bands. The neurobiological background is shortly presented (Sect. 2.). Examples of pattern formation by selective mechanisms are mentioned in Sect.3. An activity dependent mechanism for the formation of ocularity domains is given. Simulation experiments support the view, according to which the superimposition of noise are necessary to produce 'globally ordered' structures (Sect.4). Conclusions and further problems are mentioned (Sect.5.).

2.NEUROBIOLOGICAL BACKGROUND

In normal cats and monkeys the afferents from lateral geniculate nucleus (LGN) laminae corresponding to the two eyes innervete common target structures, e.g. layer IV of visual cortex and form partially overlapping bands. This alternating termination of LGN afferents showing about 300-400 μm wide periodicity is thought to be the anatomic substrate for the ocular domains (Hubel & Wiesel 1972, see also Hubel 1982). Some further readings:LeVay et al 1975, Ferster & LeVay 1978, Schatz et al 1977, Swindale 1982.

The measure of arborization of a single geniculocortical afferent exceeds the 1000 μm. Using computer reconstruction technique Blasdel and Lund (1983) demonstrated that three patches of terminals coincide with one set of ocular dominance band.
After the discovery of columnar architecture the cortex was considered as a structure containing independent modules. Arguments for the existence of connections among columns and of the role of horizontal integration in the cortex seems to be convincing.(See e.g. Szentagothai 1978, Gilbert 1985.)

It is likely that ocularity domains are incompletely formed in monkeys and absent in kittens immediately after birth. While the normal development leads to near-periodic spatial patterns, visual deprivation during the critical period results in severe symmetry-breaking of the width of ocularity domains (Wiesel 1982). The plastic behaviour of ocular dominance columns is still under investigation (see e.g. Tieman 1984, Mower et al. 1984.
Activity patterns heavily influence the formation and plastic behaviour of ocularity domains. It was demonstrated (Stryker 1981, Meyer 1982, see also Stryker 1982, Cotman & Nieto-Sampedro, Schmidt and Edwards 1983, Fraser 1985) that treatment with tetrodotoxin (TTX) of one

eye of kitten from 2 to 6 weeks of age prevent the normal development of ocular dominance columns. Since ocular dominance columns develop at least to some extent before birth in monkeys '...if activity does play a role in columnar segregation, spontaneous activity must be sufficient...'(Stryker 1982).

3. PATTERN FORMATION BY SELECTION

The formation of ocular dominance columns, and more generally, of different ordered neural structures can be considered as prototypes of biological pattern formation. The term pattern is one of the most popular expression of present-day science, and perhaps its scope is overdimensionalized (e.g. Haken 1979). However, biological pattern generating mechanisms occuring at different hierarchical levels might have quite common structure (see Rosen 1981).

The most popular pattern fo ng theories adopt the notion of selection (Eigen 1971, Changeux et al. 1984, Edelman & Finkel 1984.). While the first gives the framework of a selective kinetic theory of the prebiological evolution, the latters deal with the ontogeny of neural patterns. Changeux and his coworkers emphasize that spontaneous activity of neurons is the subject of the selection. According to Edelman & Finkel the stages of selection of neural patterns are the group confinement (i.e the limitation of group size), group selection and group competition.

The term competition and cooperation are useful to give a conceptual framework of neural pattern formation (Amari 1982, Bienenstock, 1983). Our previous and present models for the formation and plasticity of ordered neural structures describe also selective mechanisms. In contrary to the other models we emphasize the positive role of noise to eliminate 'wrong' connections. The concept of environmental noise during growth has successfully been adopted in biological context (May 1972, Nobile & Riccardi 1984). Furthermore, the theory of 'noise-induced transition' (Horsthemke & Lefever 1984) states that noise might play active and constructive role in the organization of orderd structures. Noise superimposed might change the qualitative behaviour of the deterministic system by destabilizing temporary, 'metastable' structures. The often used but not always clearly defined concept of ' self-organization' might get a more precise meaning in the light of the results of the theory of noise-induced transition.

4.FORMATION OF OCULAR DOMINANCE COLUMNS:AN ACTIVITY - DEPENDENT MECHANISM

The formation of mapping between two one-dimensional presynaptic and one postsynaptic arrays of cells is investigated (k_L and k_R are the length of the two presynaptic chains, l is the length of the postsynaptic chain; the subscripts refer to the terms left and right), m^L , m^R and a denote the two presynaptic and one postsynaptic activity vectors. The activity of the presynaptic chains are determined by unstructured stimuli, only one randomly selected element in both

345

presynaptic activity vector has non-zero value.

The activity of the postsynaptic chain increases due to the transfer of 'presynaptic information' and decrase by a first-order decay process. The evolution equation is:

$$a_j := a_j + k_2 \left(\sum_i m_i^L S_{ij}^L + \sum_i m_i^R S_{ij}^R \right) - k_3 a_j \qquad (1)$$

where S_{ij}^L and S_{ij}^R are the elements of the the matrices of synaptic strengths. Synaptic strength can be modified by three different factors (the superindex * means that it refers both to L and R):

$$S_{ij}^* := S_{ij}^* + k_4 m_i^* a_j - k_5 (m_i^* - S_{ij}^* a_j) \qquad (2)$$

This equation might be associated to a Hebb's rule supplemented with a selective decreasing term (Hirai 1980). The second factor is the modification due to the effects of immediate neighbours (the motivation of this step comes from the work of Kohonen 1982). For a general element (being not on the boundary):

$$S_{ij}^* := S_{ij}^* + k_a (S_{i-1,j}^* + S_{i+1,j}^*)/2 \qquad (3)$$

Similarly the effects of the other two elements are taken into consideration, the precise formulation will not be given here. The third factor is the result of normalization procedure. (For our comments on the normalization procedure see Érdi & Barna 1985):

$$S_{ij}^* := S_{ij}^* / \left[\left(\frac{e}{k_1 + k_2} \right)^{1/2} \cdot \left(\sum_n S_{nj}^L + \sum_n S_{nj}^R \right) \right] \qquad (4)$$

Normalization procedure is introduced not only for rows as in (4), but also for columns, specification is again neglected.

Simulation experiments can be carried out with deterministic and stochastic 'learning rule':

$$S_{ij}^* := \max \{ S_{ij}^* + k_6 \xi_{ij}, 0 \}, \quad \xi_{ij} \in N(0,1) \qquad (5)$$

(Even in case of $k_6 = 0$ the model is not completely deterministic, since the presynaptic activities have random character).

Deterministic simulation experiments (i.e. $k_6 = 0$) led mainly locally ordered structures (Fig.1.). The inclusion of external noise can drastically modify the macroscopic structure: globally ordered near-periodic structure appears during the simulation of ontogeny (Fig.2.). The model is also capable of describing plastic properties. Partial postsynaptic lesion and rearrangaments of synaptic connections are illustrated (Fig.3 and Fig.4).

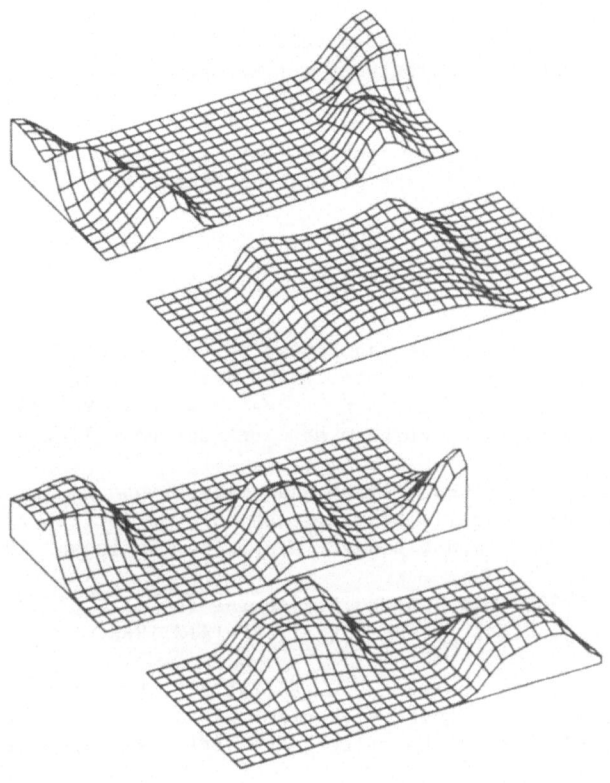

Figure 1. & 2. Locally and globally ordered structures with pure
deterministic and superimposed learning rules, respectively.

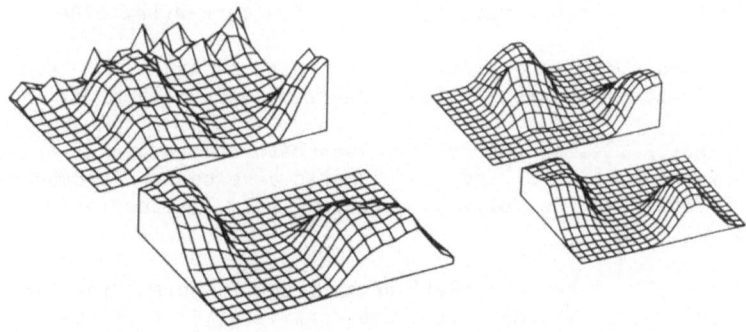

Figure 3. & 4. Structure after partial postnatal lesion;
ocular dominance is preserved after plastic rearrangement.

347

CONCLUSIONS

Motivations and the skeleton of a model for the ontogenetic development of ocular dominance columns have been given. According to the model the connections between cells are not preprogrammed, only an algorithm is given to select favourable connections. Our two main poins are the following:the formation of ocular dominance columns strongly depends on the activity of the system; environmental noise may have positive role in the structure generating mechanism.

REFERENCES

Amari,S.:Competitive and cooperative aspects in dynamics of neural excitation and self-organization.In:Competition and cooperation in neural nets.Lecture Notes in Biomathematics, Vol.45, Amari,S. & Arbib,M.S.,eds.,Berlin-Heidelberg,New York:Springer 1982,pp.1-28.

Bienenstock,E.:Cooperation and competition in central nervous system development: a unifying approach.In:Synergetics of the brain. Basar,E; Flohr,H.;Haken,H & Mandell,A.J., eds. Springer, 1983

Blasdel,G.G. & Lund,J.S.:Termination of afferent axons in macaque striate cortex. J.Neurosci.$\underline{3}$(1389-1413)1983

Changeux,J.-P.,Heidmann,T. & Patte,P.:Learning by selection. In:The biology of learning,Marler,P. & Terrace,H.S.,eds.Dahlem Konferenzen 1984. Berlin- Heidelberg-New York-Tokyo:Springer,pp.115-133.

Cotman,C.W & Nieto-Sampedro,M.:Brain function, synapse renewal, and plasticity. Ann. Rev. Psychol.$\underline{33}$(371-4011982

Edelman,G.M. & Finkel,L.M.:Neuronal group selection in the cerebral cortex.In:Dynamic aspects of the neocortical functon. (Edelman,G.M.,Cowan,W.M.Gall,U.E. eds.) New York-Wiley 1984.

Eigen,M.:Selforganization of matter and the evolution of biological macromolecules. Naturwissenschaften $\underline{58}$(465-523) 1971.

Érdi,P.:System-theoretical approach to the neural organization: feed-forward control of the ontogenetic development.In:Cybernetics and System Research, Vol.2. Trappl,R.ed., Elsevier:North-Holland 1984,pp.,229-235.

Érdi,P. & Barna,G.:Self-organizing mechanism for the formation of ordered neural mappings.Biol. Cybernetics $\underline{51}$(93-101)1984

Érdi,P. & Barna,G.:Self-organization of neural networks: noise-induced transition.Phys.Lett $\underline{107A}$(287-290)1985

Erdi,P. & Szentágothai,J.:Neural connectivities:between determinism and randomness. In:Dynamics of macrosystems. Springer (in press)

Ferster,D. & LeVay,S.:The axonal arborization of lateral geniculate neurons in the striate cortex of the cat. J.Comp.Neurol.182(923-944)1978

Fraser,S.E.:Cell interactions involved in neuronal patterning:an experimental and theoretical approach. In:Molecular basis of neural development. Edelman,G.M.;Gall,W.E.&Cowan,W.M., eds. Neuroscience Res.Found. 1985, pp.481-507.

Gilbert:Horizontal integration in the neocortex. TINS 8 (160-165) 1985

Haken,H.(ed.):Pattern formation by dynamic systems and pattern recognition, Springer,1979.

Hebb,C.O.:The organization of behaviour.New York:Wiley, 1949.

Hirai,Y.:A new hypothesis for synaptic modification: an interactive process between postsynaptic competition and presynaptic regulation.Biol. Cybernetics 36(41-50)1980.

Horsthemke,W. & Lefever,R.:Noise-induced transition. Theory and applications in physics, chemistry and biology, Springer: Berlin-Heidelberg-Tokyo,1984.

Hubel,D.H.:Exploration of the primary visual cortex, 1955-78. Nature 299(515-524)1982

Hubel,D.H. & Wiesel,T.N.:Laminar and columnar distribution of geniculo-cortical fibers in the macaque monkey. J.Comp.Neurol. 146(421-450)1972.

Kohonen,T.:Analysis of a simple self-organizing process. Biol. Cybernetics 44(135-140)1982.

May,R.M.:Stability in random fluctuating versus deterministic environments. Am.Nature 107(621-650)1972.

Meyer,R.L.:Tetrodotoxin blocks the formation of ocular dominance columns in goldfish.Science 218(589-591)1982

Mower,G.D.,Caplan,C.J.,Christen<W.G. & Duffy,F.H.:Dark rearing prolongs physiological but not anatomical plasticity of cat visual cortex. J.Comp.Neurol.235(448-466)1985

Nobile,A.G. & Ricciardi,L.M.:Growth with regulation in

fluctuating environments. Biol.Cybernetics 49(177-188)1984.

Rakic,P. & Goldman-Rakic,P.S.:Developmet of modifiability of the cerebral cortex. Neurosci.Res. Program Bull.20, 1982.

Rosen,R.:Pattern generation in networks. Progr.Theor. Biol.6(161-209)1981

Schmidt,J.T. & Edwards,D.L.:Activity sharpens the map during the regeneration of the retinotectal projection in goldfish. Brain Res.269(29-39)1983.

Shatz,C.J., Lindstrom,S. & Wiesel,T.N.:The distribution of afferents representing the right and left eyes in the cat's visual cortex. Brain Res.131(103-116)1977.

Stryker,M.P.:Late segregation of geniclate afferents to the cat's visual cortex after recovery from binocular impulse blockade. Soc.Neurosci.Abstr.7(842)1981.

Stryker,M.P.:Role of visual afferents activity in the development of ocular dominance columns.In:Rakic,P. & Goldman_Rakic,P.S. 1982(see there)

Swindale,N.V.:A model for the formation of ocular dominance stripes. Proc. R. Soc. Lond. B208(243-264)1980

Szentágothai,J.:The local neuronal apparatus of the cerebral cortex. In: Buser,P.A.; Rougeul-Buser,A., eds.:Cerebral correlates of conscious experience. North Holland,Amsterdam,New York,Oxford 1978. pp.,131-138.

Szentágothai,J.:The modular architectonic principle of neural centers. Rev.Physiol.Biochem.Pharmacol.98(11-61)1983.

Tiemán,S.B.:Effects of monocular deprivation on geniculocortical synapses in the cat.J.Comp.Neurol.222(166-176)1984.

von der Malsburg,Ch.:Development of ocularity domains and growth behaviourof axon terminals. Biol. Cybernetics 45 (49-56)1979.

Wiesel,T.N.:Postnatal development of the visual cortex and the influence of environment.Nature 299(583-591)1982

Willshaw,D.J. & v.d. Malsburg,Ch.:How patterned neural connections can be set up by self organization. Proc. R. Soc. Lond. B194(431-445) 1976

SOME ASPECTS OF MODELING NEURONAL INTERACTIONS IN THE BASAL GANGLIA

G. Porenta
Dept. of Medical Cybernetics
and Artificial Intelligence
University of Vienna
Medical School
Vienna, Austria

P. Riederer
Ludwig Boltzmann Institute
of Clinical Neurobiology
Neurochemistry Group
Lainz Hospital
Vienna, Austria

ABSTRACT. Qualitative models of neuronal interactions in the basal ganglia have helped to improve the treatment of patients suffering from diseases that affect the extrapyramidal motor system. As part of a model simulating the nigro-striatal feedback loop a model of the dopaminergic synapse in the striatum is presented. A compartment model simulates the metabolic pathways of dopamine in the presynaptic neuron and the synaptic cleft. An extended Hodgkin-Huxley model describes the behaviour of membrane voltage and currents of the presynaptic and postsynaptic membrane. Procuring numerical values for model parameters poses some problems. Kinetic constants of receptor kinetics and uptake mechanisms are especially difficult to obtain. Parameters concerning the part of the model which simulates the electrical processes can be found more easily.

1. INTRODUCTION

Diseases affecting the extrapyramidal motor system have attracted much research effort within the last two decades when investigations of post-mortem tissues established a correlation between clinical symptoms and disturbances in transmitter metabolism [3,5]. In the wake of these findings new methods of treatment have emanated.

As to Parkinson's disease the attempt to correct the severe deficit of a specific transmitter substance, dopamine (DA), in the corpus striatum led to the development of the DOPA substitution therapy [2], still the therapy of choice at present. Based on the assumption that in healthy subjects dopaminergic and acetylcholinergic neural systems in the basal ganglia concert to maintain a balanced interaction, current therapeutical strategies are aimed at reestablishing a new state of equilibrium in patients suffering from Parkinson's disease and include actions to increase dopaminergic activity and reduce cholinergic activity.

Recently, however, shortcomings and side effects of this therapeutical concept have been of major concern, and various investigative efforts focus on optimal treatment plans. A more detailed model of the neuronal pathways in the basal ganglia may provide hints

351

R. Trappl (ed.), Cybernetics and Systems '86, 351–358.

for new therapeutical strategies.

The purpose of the present work is to present a mathematical model of the synapse joining dopaminergic and cholinergic neurons in the caudate nucleus and to discuss some problems encountered in the process of procuring parameters.

2. MATHEMATICAL MODEL

The model describing the transmission of information at the dopaminergic synapse can be divided into two main components: (1) a compartment model simulating the metabolic pathways of dopamine at the presynaptic and subsynaptic site, and (2) a model based on the Hodgkin-Huxley equations [6] simulating the behaviour of membrane voltage and ionic currents at the presynaptic and postsynaptic neuron. Both model components interface at two points: At the presynaptic site, the calcium current controls the release of dopamine into the synaptic cleft and at the postsynaptic site, receptor transmitter complexes open ion channels and induce changes in the postsynaptic potential.

2.1 Compartment Model

Figure 1 shows the schematics of a simplified model describing dopamine metabolism. Synthesis in the cytoplasmatic compartment is considered to follow zero order kinetics. From the cytoplasmatic pool dopamine is either taken up into vesicles or metabolized by processes assumed to obey first order kinetics. Dopamine stored in the vesicles can return to the cytoplasma or upon arrival of a presynaptic action potential be released into the synaptic cleft. In this model, release and calcium current are assumed to be proportional with the factor of proportionality chosen in a way that one action potential sets free one quantum of dopamine taken to consist of 300 molecules. In the synaptic cleft, dopamine can bind to free receptor molecules in order to form a receptor transmitter complex. Also, free dopamine can either reenter the presynaptic neuron through an uptake mechanism following Michaelis Menten kinetics or is degraded by a first order process.

The mathematical equations corresponding to this compartment model can be found in the appendix.

2.2 Hodgkin-Huxley model

Figure 2 shows the equivalent circuit diagram of synaptic membrane currents for excitatory and inhibitory synapses. The presynaptic part of this model corresponds to the original model of Hodgkin and Huxley [6] with an additional calcium channel taken from [8] with minor modifications (constant driving force E).

As to the dopaminergic synapse in the striatum, most studies found the postsynaptic potential to be inhibitory. In the present work, chloride ions were assumed to mediate an inhibitory postsynaptic potential. The mathematical equations corresponding to this equivalent circuit diagram are given in the appendix.

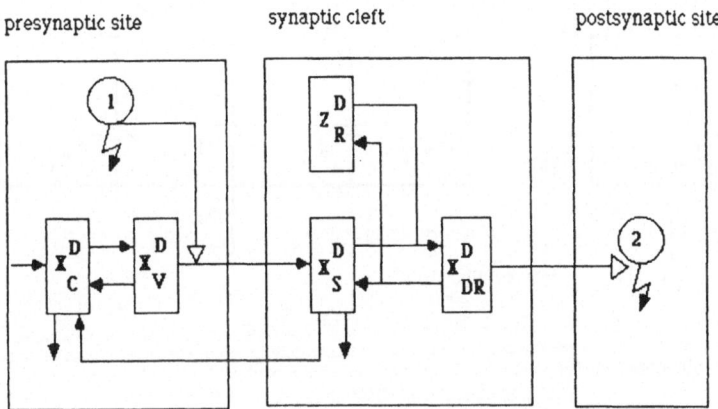

presynaptic site   synaptic cleft   postsynaptic site

Figure 1.   Compartment model of a dopaminergic synapse.
             Presynaptically, the transmitter, dopamine, is synthesized into
             the cytoplasmatic compartment which also gets influx from the
             synaptic cleft through an uptake mechanism and from the
             vesicular compartment. From the cytoplasmatic compartment
             transmitter is either metabolized or transfers into the
             vesicular compartment to be released upon arrival of a
             presynaptic action potential (1). Dopamine in the synaptic cleft
             combines with receptor molecules activating ion channels and
             inducing changes in the postsynaptic membrane potential (2).

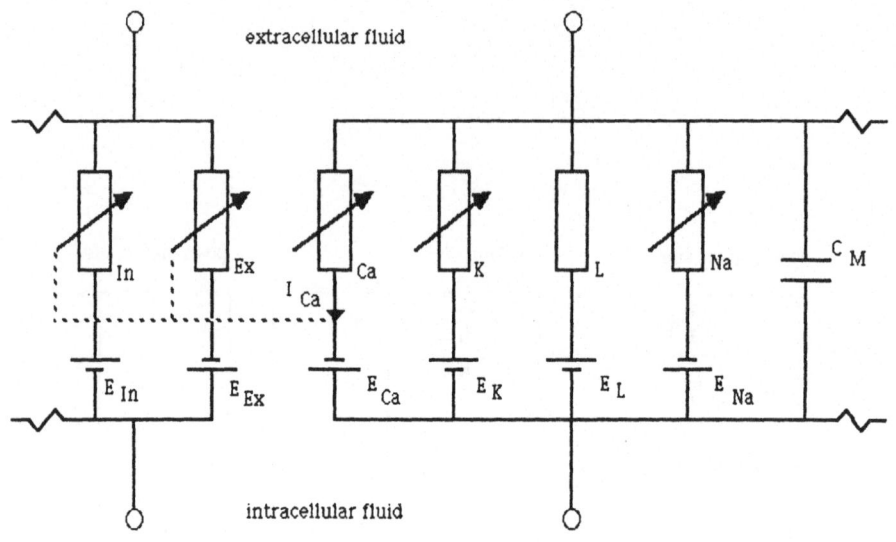

extracellular fluid

intracellular fluid

Postsynaptic potential   Action Potential

Figure 2.   Equivalent circuit diagram of synaptic membrane currents.
Presynaptically, three voltage controlled channels (Na ... sodium, K ... potassium,
and Ca ... calcium) and one passive channel (L ... leakage) determine membrane
conductances. Equations for the sodium, potassium, and leakage currents are
taken from the original paper of Hodgkin and Huxley (1952). Equilibrium
potentials of the individual ions are designated by E with the appropriate
index. Equations for the calcium current was taken from the work of Llinas et al.
(1981) with minor modifications (constant driving force E). As shown by the
broken line, calcium current induces the release of transmitter substance into
the cleft and consequently the opening of postsynaptic channels. Depending on
the equilibrium potential of the corresponding ion, either excitatory or
inhibitory postsynaptic potentials occur. In the present study, sodium and
cloride ions were assumed to mediate excitatory and inhibitory membrane
potentials respectively.

3. PARAMETER VALUES

3.1 Compartment model

Most commonly, values of dopamine concentration are given in units of moles/g tissue wet weight, g/g tissue wet weight, moles/g protein, or g/g protein. As the molecular weight of dopamine is 153 and protein accounts for approximatly 10% of the total tissue, conversion among these units can be accomplished fairly easily.

The structure of the model, however, requires that transmitter concentration should be given in mole/l of presynaptic compartment. Assuming that (1) the ratio between vesicular and cytoplasmatic compartments is 3:2, (2) 0.3% of the total tissue volume can be attributed to presynaptic dopaminergic endings [1], and (3) post-mortem studies measure the vesicular dopamine only, a value of $3.84 \mu g/g$ wet weight [4] can be converted to 0.014 mole/l vesicular compartment.

The rate of dopamine synthesis is considered to be constant and equal to the activity of tyrosine hydroxylase, the enzyme limiting the rate of dopamine synthesis. Assuming that dopamine synthesis occurs in the cytoplasmatic compartment only, a value of 27.8 nmol/g/hr [4] can be converted to 6.44 nmol/ms/l cytoplasmatic compartment. The rate of dopamine elimination from the cytoplasma is obtained by dividing synthesis rate by steady state concentration of dopamine.

The estimation of parameters of receptor kinetics is still somewhat speculative. Usually, in analogy to Michaelis Menten kinetics of enzymes, two parameters B_{max}, a measure of receptor density, and K_d, the substrate concentration necessary for halfmaximal binding, are given as characteristic values. Nevertheless, concern has been raised whether the measurement procedure commonly used in receptor binding studies does indeed yield accurate estimates of kinetic properties [9]. Also, knowledge of the K_d value is not sufficient to allow the computation of the kinetic constants specified in the model so that an additional assumption concerning the velocity of the reaction has to be made.

Parameter values for the uptake mechanism have been published [7], but, again, can only be used as tentative estimates of the corresponding in-vivo values applying to the synaptic level.

3.2 Hodgkin Huxley model

As the general mechanism of neuronal function does not seem to be very typical of the individual species, the assumption that the Hodgkin Huxley model also applies to dopaminergic neurons in the striatum does not limit the model validity significantly. All the parameters occuring in this part of the model can be easily retrieved from the respective literature [6,8].

4. CONCLUSIONS

The presynaptic part of a quantitative model of the dopaminergic synapse in the striatum at a model level of synaptic events can be built from data published in the respective literature. Also, model structures applying to the electric processes occuring at a synapse can be retrieved from earlier studies. However, to complete the model equations, assumptions and speculations about the processes occuring in the synaptic cleft have to be made scince required data are still lacking in the literature.

ACKNOWLEDGEMENTS

The supervision and encouragement provided by Prof. Trappl are gratefully acknowledged. Part of this work was supported by Schering AG, Austria.

REFERENCES

[1] Anden N.E., Fuxe K., Hamberger B., Hoekfelt T.: A Quantitative Study on the Nigro-Neostriatal Dopamine Neuron System in the Rat, Acta physiol. scand. 67:306-312, 1966.
[2] Birkmayer W., Hornykiewicz O.: Der L-3,4-dioxyphenylalanin (=dopa) Effekt bei der Parkinson-Akinese, Wien. Klin. Wschr. 73:787-788, 1961.
[3] Birkmayer W., Hornykiewicz O.: Advances in Parkinsonism, Editiones Roche, Basle, 1976.
[4] Birkmayer W., Riederer P.: Die Parkinson-Krankheit, Springer, Wien-New York, 1980.
[5] Ehringer H., Hornykiewicz O.: Verteilung von Noradrenalin und Dopamin im Gehirn des Menschen und ihr Verhalten bei Erkrankungen des extrapyramidalen Systems, Wien. Klin. Wschr. 38:1236, 1960.
[6] Hodgkin A.L., Huxley A.F.: A Quantitative Description of Membrane Current and its Application to Conduction and Excitation in Nerve, J. Physiol. 117:500-544, 1952.
[7] Holz R.W., Coyle J.T.: The Effects of Various Salts, Temperature, and the Alkaloids Veratridine and Batrachotoxin on the Uptake of 3-[H] Dopamine into Synaptosomes from the Rat Striatum, Mol. Pharmacol. 10:746-758, 1974.
[8] Llinas R., Steinberg I.Z., Walton K.: Presynaptic Calcium Currents in Squid Giant Synapse, Biophys. J. 33:289-321, 1981.
[9] Seeman P., Ulpian C., Wregget K.A., Wells J.W.: Dopamine Receptor Parameters Detected by 3-[H] Spiperone Depend on Tissue Concentration: Analysis and Examples, J. Neurochem. 43(1):221-235, 1984.

The model equations for the dopaminergic synapse and the equations describing the membrane potential and membrane currents are given in this section. The symbol m(X;K,V) denotes Michaelis Menten kinetics.

Equations of the dopaminergic model synapse

$$V_c^D \frac{dX_c^D}{dt} = K_{co}^D + K_{cv}^D X_v^D - K_{vc}^D X_c^D - K_{oc}^D X_c^D$$

$$+ m(X_s^D; K_U^D, V_U^D)$$

$$V_v^D \frac{dX_v^D}{dt} = K_{vc}^D X_c^D - K_{cv}^D X_v^D - K_{sv}^D I_{Ca}^D X_v^D$$

$$\frac{dX_s^D}{dt} = -K_{P1}^D Z_R^D X_s^D + K_{M1}^D X_{DR}^D + K_{sv}^D I_{Ca}^D X_v^D / V_s^D -$$

$$- K_{os}^D X_s^D - m(X_s^D; K_U^D, V_U^D) / V_s^D$$

$$\frac{dX_{DR}^D}{dt} = K_{P1}^D Z_R^D X_s^D - K_{M1}^D X_{DR}^D$$

$$Z_R^D = P_{RO}^D - X_{DR}^D$$

Equations describing membrane currents

$$-C_M \frac{dV}{dt} = I_E + I_{PS} + I_{Ca} + I_K + I_L + I_{Na}$$

$$I_K = g_K (V - E_K) n^4$$

$$I_{Na} = g_{Na} (V - E_{Na}) m^3 h$$

$$I_{Ca} = g_{Ca} (V - E_{Ca}) s^5$$

$$I_L = g_L (V - E_L)$$

$$I_{PS} = g_{PS} (V - E_{PS}) r$$

$$I_E = I_E(t)$$

$$\frac{dx}{dt} = a_x(V) (1 - x) - b_x(V) \qquad x = m, h, n, s$$

$I_E(t)$ .. external stimulus
r .... ratio of open ion channels (0 ... 1)

A NEW ALGORITHMIC APPROACH TO FIRST-PASSAGE-TIME PROBLEMS

A. Buonocore$^{(*)}$, A.G. Nobile$^{(**)}$ and L.M. Ricciardi$^{(*)}$

(*) Dipartimento di Matematica e Applicazioni, University of
     Naples, Naples, Italy
(**) Dipartimento di Informatica e Applicazioni, University of
     Salerno, Salerno, Italy

ABSTRACT. Motivated by some biological applications, a new integral
equation is proposed to determine first-passage-time p.d.f.'s for one
dimensional diffusion processes, which is particularly suitable for computational purposes. The cases of Wiener and Ornstein-Uhlenbeck processes are discussed into some details both with respect to closed form
solutions and to approximate evaluations.

1. INTRODUCTION

In a variety of problems of biological interest one has to evaluate
first-passage-time probability density functions. For instance, in population biology the fixation of a gene can be viewed as the process leading the frequency of that gene to become unity (see, for instance, Crow
and Kimura, 1970); the extinction of a population can be mathematically
described as the first passage through some threshold value for the
process representing the number of individuals (Nobile and Ricciardi,
1984 a) and b)); the firing of a neuron may be depicted as the first
crossing of some threshold value by the process modeling the membrane
potential difference (Ricciardi, 1977), and so on. In all such instances
the random process considered is a one dimensional diffusion process.
In particular, for models of neuronal activity Wiener and Ornstein-
Uhlenbeck (O.U.) processes have been often derived to describe the
fluctuations of the membrane potential (Gerstein and Mandelbrot, 1964;
Capocelli and Ricciardi, 1971; Ricciardi and Sacerdote, 1979). Unfortunately, the determination of the firing distribution is a formidable task.
So far, only numerical procedures could be used to obtain an approximation to firing distributions. Such procedures are highly time consuming,
and thus not suitable to obtain systematic informations on the firing
distribution for various types of threshold functions and for a wide
class of parameter values (see, for instance, Favella and De Griffi, 1981;
Ricciardi et al., 1983).
    In the present paper we address ex novo to first-passage-time
problems for diffusion processes. We prove that a new integral equation
for the first-passage-time p.d.f. can be written down, which is parti-

359

cularly suitable for computational purposes.In particular,this equation
immediately yields the closed form solutions for Wiener and O.U. process
holding for special threshold functions.

2.   THE INTEGRAL EQUATION FOR FIRST-PASSAGE-TIME DENSITIES

Let $\{X(t); \ t \geqslant t_o, t_o \in R\}$ be a one dimensional time homogeneous diffusion
process defined over the intervall $I \equiv (r_1, r_2)$, with r_i (i=1,2) natural
boundaries (Feller,1952) and let $P\{X(t_o) = x_o\} = 1, x_o \in (r_1, r_2)$.Further,let
$A_1(x)$ and $A_2(x)$ denote the drift and infinitesimal variance of X(t),re-
spectively.For all $\tau < t$ and $x, y, \varrho \in (r_1, r_2)$ we define the following functions:

$$F(x,t|y,\tau) = P\{X(t) \leqslant x|X(\tau)=y\} \qquad (2.1a)$$

$$f(x,t|y,\tau) = \frac{\partial}{\partial x} F(x,t|y,\tau) \qquad (2.1b)$$

$$j(x,t|y,\tau) = A_1(x) \ f(x,t|y,\tau) - \frac{1}{2} \frac{\partial}{\partial x}\left[A_2(x) \ f(x,t|y,\tau)\right] \qquad (2.1c)$$

$$A^{(\varrho)}(x,t|y,\tau)=\begin{cases} P\{X(t)<x|X(\tau)=y \ \underline{and} \ X(\vartheta)<\varrho, \ \forall \vartheta<t\}, \ x,y<\varrho \\ P\{X(t)>x|X(\tau)=y \ \underline{and} \ X(\vartheta)>\varrho, \ \forall \vartheta<t\}, \ x,y>\varrho \end{cases} \qquad (2.1d)$$

$$a^{(\varrho)}(x,t|y,\tau) = \frac{\partial}{\partial x} A^{(\varrho)}(x,t|y,\tau) \qquad (2.1e)$$

$$T = \begin{cases} \underset{t \geqslant t_o}{\inf}\left\{t \ : \ X(t) > \varrho \ |X(t_o)=x_o\right\} & , x_o < \varrho \\ \underset{t \geqslant t_o}{\inf}\left\{t \ : \ X(t) < \varrho \ |X(t_o)=x_o\right\} & , x_o > \varrho \end{cases} \qquad (2.1f)$$

$$g(\varrho,t|x_o,t_o) = \frac{\partial}{\partial t} P\{T \leqslant t\} \qquad (2.1g)$$

Relations (2.1b) and (2.1e) define the free transition p.d.f. and the
transition p.d.f. in the presence of an absorbing barrier at ϱ ,respec-
tively; (2.1f) and (2.1g) define the first-passage-time and its p.d.f.,
respectively[1]; (2.1c),finally, is the definition of the probability
current.There are several relations relating these functions to one
another.In particular,one has :

$$f(x,t|x_o,t_o) = \int_{t_o}^{t} d\tau \ g[S(\tau),\tau|x_o,t_o] \ f[x,t|S(\tau),\tau], \qquad (2.2a)$$

$$\text{if } [x_o < S(t_o) \ \underline{and} \ x \geqslant S(t)] \text{ or } [x_o > S(t_o) \ \underline{and} \ x \leqslant S(t)]$$

---

[1] Note that T can be a dishonest r.v.In such case g is the first-passage-time p.d.f. conditional upon the passage through ϱ .

$$\int_{r_1}^{S(t)} dx \; \alpha^{[S(t)]}(x,t|x_0,t_0) = 1 - \int_{t_0}^{t} d\tau \; g[S(\tau),\tau|x_0,t_0], \text{if } x<S(t_0) \tag{2.2b}$$

$$\int_{S(t)}^{r_2} dx \; \alpha^{[S(t)]}(x,t|x_0,t_0) = 1 - \int_{t_0}^{t} d\tau \; g[S(\tau),\tau|x_0,t_0], \text{if } x_0>S(t_0) \tag{2.2c}$$

$$\frac{\partial f(x,t|y,\tau)}{\partial t} + \frac{\partial j(x,t|y,\tau)}{\partial x} = 0 \tag{2.2d}$$

where $\varrho = S(t)$ denotes a continuous function of time. We recall that (2.2a) is due to Fortet (1943),(2.2b) and (2.2c) are identities of straightforward probabilistic interpretation and (2.2d) is the continuity equation expressing the conservation of the probability mass (Stratonovich,1963).

Lemma 1. Let $S(t)$ denote a function of class $C[t_0,\infty)$ and let

$$\varphi(x,t|y,\tau) \equiv \frac{d}{dt} \; F(x,t|y,\tau) \tag{2.3}$$

for all $y \in I$ and $\tau < t$. One then has:

$$g[S(t),t|x_0,t_0] = \begin{cases} -2\varphi[S(t),t|x_0,t_0]+2\int_{t_0}^{t} d\tau \; g[S(\tau),\tau|x_0,t_0]\varphi[S(t),t|S(\tau),\tau], \\ \quad\quad\quad\quad\quad\quad\quad\quad\quad\quad\quad , x_0<S(t_0) \\[4pt] 2\varphi[S(t),t|x_0,t_0] -2\int_{t_0}^{t} d\tau \; g[S(\tau),\tau|x_0,t_0]\varphi[S(t),t|S(\tau),\tau], \\ \quad\quad\quad\quad\quad\quad\quad\quad\quad\quad\quad , x_0>S(t_0) \end{cases} \tag{2.4}$$

Proof. Assume first that $x_0 \leqslant S(t_0)$. By integration of both sides of (2.2a) with respect to x between $S(t)$ and r_2 and by use of Fubini's theorem one obtains:

$$1 - F[S(t),t|x_0,t_0] = \int_{t_0}^{t} d\tau \; g[S(\tau),\tau|x_0,t_0]\{1 - F[S(t),t|S(\tau),\tau]\}, x_0 < S(t_0). \tag{2.5}$$

Taking the derivative of (2.5) with respect to t and making use of the relation (Fortet,1943):

$$\lim_{\tau \uparrow t} F[S(t),t|S(\tau),\tau] = \frac{1}{2} \tag{2.6}$$

the first of (2.4) follows. Let now $x_0 > S(t_0)$. By integration of (2.2a) with respect to x between r_1 and $S(t)$ we now obtain:

$$F[S(t),t|x_0,t_0] = \int_{t_0}^{t} d\tau \; g[S(\tau),\tau|x_0,t_0] F[S(t),t|S(\tau),\tau] \quad x_0 > S(t_0). \tag{2.7}$$

The second of (2.4) then immediately follows by differentiation of both sides of (2.7) with respect to t and by making use of (2.6).

Theorem 1. Let $S(t)$ and $K(t)$ be continuous functions in $[t_o, \infty)$. Setting for all $y \in I$ and $\tau \leqslant t$

$$\psi[S(t),t|y,\tau] = \varphi[S(t),t|y,\tau] + K(t) \ f[S(t),t|y,\tau] \ , x_o \neq S(t_o) \tag{2.8}$$

where φ is defined by (2.3), one has:

$$g[S(t),t|x_o,t_o] \begin{cases} -2\psi[S(t),t|x_o,t_o] +2\int_{t_o}^{t} d\tau \ g[S(\tau),\tau|x_o,t_o]\psi[S(t),t|S(\tau),\tau], \\ \qquad\qquad , x_o < S(t_o) \\ \\ 2\psi[S(t),t|x_o,t_o] -2\int_{t_o}^{t} d\tau \ g[S(\tau),\tau|x_o,t_o]\psi[S(t),t|S(\tau),\tau], \\ \qquad\qquad , x_o > S(t_o) \end{cases} \tag{2.9}$$

Proof. For brevity, we omit the proof. This will appear elsewhere (Buonocore et al, in preparation).

3. CLOSED FORM RESULTS

a. The Wiener Process

Let $\{W(t); t \geqslant t_o, t_o \in R\}$ be a Wiener process with drift such that $P\{W(t_o) = x_o\} = 1$, $E[W(t)] = x_o + \mu(t-t_o)$ and $Cov\{W(t),W(s)\} = \sigma^2 \min(t,s)$ with $x_o \neq S(t_o)$, $\mu, \sigma \in R$. Then, for all $y \in R$ and $\tau < t$ one has:

$$f(x,t|y,\tau) = \frac{1}{\sigma\sqrt{2\pi(t-\tau)}} \ \exp\left\{ - \frac{[x-y-\mu(t-\tau)]^2}{2\sigma^2(t-\tau)} \right\} \tag{3.1}$$

and

$$F(x,t|y,\tau) = \frac{1}{2} \left\{ 1 + Erf\left[\frac{x-y-\mu(t-\tau)}{\sigma\sqrt{2(t-\tau)}} \right] \right\} \tag{3.2}$$

where $Erf(z)$ denotes the error function:

$$Erf(z) = \frac{2}{\sqrt{\pi}} \int_0^z dy \ \exp(-y^2) \tag{3.3}$$

Lemma 2. Let $S(t)$ be differentiable in $[t_o, \infty)$. Then for the Wiener process $W(t)$ and for all $y \in R$ and $\tau < t$ one has:

$$\psi[S(t),t|y,\tau] = h(t,\tau,y) \ f[S(t),t|y,\tau] \ , x_o \neq S(t_o) \tag{3.4}$$

where the function $h(t,\tau,y)$ is defined as follows:

362

$$h(t,\tau,y) = S'(t) - \frac{\mu}{2} - \frac{S(t)-y}{2(t-\tau)} + K(t). \tag{3.5}$$

Proof. We first calculate the function φ given by (2.3). To this end we set $x = S(t)$ in (3.2) and then differentiate both sides with respect to t to obtain:

$$\varphi[S(t),t|y,\tau] = \left[S'(t) - \frac{\mu}{2} - \frac{S(t)-y}{2(t-\tau)} \right] f[S(t),t|y,\tau]. \tag{3.6}$$

Equation (3.4) then follows from (2.8) and from (3.6).

Theorem 2. Let $S(t)$ be a $C^2[t_0,\infty)$-class function and let $W(t)$ be the Wiener process. Then,

(i) $\quad \lim_{\tau \uparrow t} \psi[S(t),t|S(\tau),\tau] = 0$ iff $K(t) = \frac{1}{2}\left[\mu - S'(t)\right]$

(ii) $\quad \psi[S(t);t|S(\tau),\tau] = 0 \quad \forall\, t,\tau : t_0 < \tau < t$ and $\lim_{\tau \uparrow t} \psi[S(t),t|S(\tau),\tau] = 0$

$\qquad$ iff $S(t) = at+b, (a,b \in R), K(t) = \frac{\mu-a}{2}$

Proof. In order for $\lim_{\tau \uparrow t} h[t,\tau,S(\tau)] \quad f[S(t),t|S(\tau),\tau]$ to exist, one easily sees that, due to the divergence of $f[S(t),t|S(\tau),\tau]$ as τ approaches t, it must be

$$\lim_{\tau \uparrow t} h[t,\tau,S(\tau)] \equiv \lim_{\tau \uparrow t} \left[S'(t) - \frac{\mu}{2} - \frac{S(t)-S(\tau)}{2(t-\tau)} + K(t) \right] = 0$$

which implies :

$$K(t) = \frac{1}{2}\left[\mu - S'(t)\right] \tag{3.7}$$

Using (3.7) and the assumption that $S(t)$ is a $C^2(t_0,\infty)$-class function, by use of l'Hospital rule one can then prove that

$$\lim_{\tau \uparrow t} h[t,\tau,S(\tau)] \quad f[S(t),t|S(\tau),\tau] = 0, \tag{3.8}$$

which concludes the proof of the necessity of (i). Vice versa, if (3.7) holds it is immediately seen that the limit in (i) is zero, which proves the sufficiency of the condition. To prove (ii) we note that by assumption it also follows

$$\lim_{\tau \uparrow t} \psi[S(t),t|S(\tau),\tau] = 0 \tag{3.9}$$

From (3.9) and from (3.4) and (3.5) it then follows $K(t) = [\mu - S'(t)]/2$

so that one has

$$\psi\left[S(t),t|S(\tau),\tau\right]_{=}\frac{1}{2}\left[S'(t)-\frac{S(t)-S(\tau)}{t-\tau}\right]f\left[S(t),t|S(\tau),\tau\right]$$

$$(3.10)$$

However,the left hand side of (3.10) vanishes by assumption for all $t_o\leqslant\tau<t$ and for $\tau\uparrow t$.Hence,it must be $S'(t)=[S(t)-S(\tau)]/(t-\tau)$,which implies that $S(t)$ is a linear function of t,i.e. $S(t)=at+b$.In turn,this implies $K(t)=(\mu-a)/2$,which proves the necessity of (ii).The sufficiency is immediately proved since from (3.4) and (3.5) it follows that $\psi[S(t),t|S(\tau),\tau]=0$ for all $t_o\leq\tau<t$ and for $\tau\uparrow t$ if one takes $S(t)=at+b$, $K(t)=(\mu-a)/2$.

Corollary 1   For the Wiener process $W(t)$ the first-passage-time p.d.f. through the linear boundary $S(t)=at+b$ is given by

$$g(at+b,t|x_o,t_o)\quad\frac{|at_0+b-x_0|}{t-t_0}\quad f(at+b,t|x_o,t_o)\ ,\ x\neq at_o+b$$

$$(3.11)$$

Proof. It follows from (2.9) and from (ii) of Theorem 2.

Corollary 2. Let $S(t)$ be a function of class $C^2[t_o,\infty)$ and let $W(t)$ be the Wiener process.If $K(t)=[\mu-S'(t)]/2$ then equation (2.9) possesses a unique continuous solution.

Proof.   It follows from the theory of integral equations and from the remark that with such choice of $K(t)$ both functions $\psi[S(t),t|S(\tau),\tau]$ and $\psi[S(t),t|x_o,t_o]$ are continuous.

b. The Ornstein-Uhlenbeck Process

Let $\{X(t);t\geqslant t_0,t_0\in R\}$ be the O.U. process characterized by the drift and infinitesimal variance $A_1(x)=ax+\beta$ and $A_2=\sigma^2,a,\beta$ and $\sigma\neq0$ being arbitrary real constants[2],and let $P\{X(t_0)=x_0\}=1$.Then,for all $y\in R$ and $\tau<t$ one has:

$$f(x,t|y,\tau)_{=}\left\{\frac{a\,e^{-2a(t-\tau)}}{\sigma^2\pi\left[1-e^{-2a(t-\tau)}\right]}\right\}^{\frac{1}{2}}\exp\left\{-\frac{a\left[(x+\beta/a)e^{-a(t-\tau)}-(y+\beta/a)\right]^2}{\sigma^2\left[1-e^{-2a(t-\tau)}\right]}\right\}$$

and

$$(3.12)$$

$$F(x,t|y,\tau)_{=}\frac{1}{2}\left\{1+\text{Erf}\left[\left[(x+\beta/a)e^{-a(t-\tau)}-(y+\beta/a)\right]\left\{\frac{a\,\sigma^{-2}}{1-e^{-2a(t-\tau)}}\right\}^{\frac{1}{2}}\right]\right\}$$

$$(3,13)$$

Lemma 3. Let $S(t)$ be differentiable in $[t_o,\infty)$.Then for the O.U. process $X(t)$ and for all $y\in R$ and $\tau<t$ one has:

$$\psi[S(t),t|y,\tau]=H(t,\tau,y)\ f[S(t),t|y,\tau]\ ,x_o\neq S(t_0)\quad(3.14)$$

---

[2]Here we are purposedly making a slight abuse of terminology as we do not require, as in the O.U. process, that a is negative.

where the function $H(t,\tau,y)$ is defined as follows:

$$H(t,\tau,y)=S'(t)-\alpha\left[S(t)+\frac{\beta}{\alpha}\right]-\frac{e^{-\alpha(t-\tau)}}{1-e^{-2\alpha(t-\tau)}}\alpha\left\{\left[S(t)+\frac{\beta}{\alpha}\right]e^{-\alpha(t-\tau)}-y-\frac{\beta}{\alpha}\right\}+K(t)$$

(3.15)

Proof. We calculate the function φ defined in (2.3) by setting $x=S(t)$ in (3.13) and then taking the derivative with respect to t:

$$\varphi\left[S(t),t|y,\tau\right]=\left\{S'(t)-\alpha\left[S(t)+\frac{\beta}{\alpha}\right]-\frac{e^{-\alpha(t-\tau)}}{1-e^{-2\alpha(t-\tau)}}\alpha\left\{\left[S(t)+\frac{\beta}{\alpha}\right]e^{-\alpha(t-\tau)}-y-\frac{\beta}{\alpha}\right\}\right. \times$$

$$\times\ f\left[S(t),t|y,\tau\right]$$

(3.16)

Equation (3.14) then follows from (2.8) and from (3.16).

Theorem 3. Let $S(t)$ be a function of class $C^2[t_0,\infty)$ and let $X(t)$ be the O.U. process. Then,

(i) $\lim\limits_{\tau\uparrow t}\psi[S(t),t|S(\tau),\tau]=0$ iff $K(t)=\frac{1}{2}\left[\alpha S(t)+\beta -S'(t)\right]$

(ii) $\psi[S(t),t|S(\tau),\tau]=0$ $\forall t,\tau:t_0\leqslant\tau<t$ and $\lim\limits_{\tau\uparrow t}\psi[S(t),t|S(\tau),\tau]=0$

iff $S(t)=-\frac{\beta}{\alpha}+A\ e^{\alpha t}+B\ e^{-\alpha t}$ $(A,B\in R),K(t)=B\alpha\ e^{-\alpha t}$

Proof. For brevity we omit the proof and refer to Buonocore et al in preparation.

Corollary 3. For the O.U. process $X(t)$ the first-passage-time p.d.f. through the hyperbolic boundary $S(t)=A\ \exp(\alpha t)+B\ \exp(-\alpha t)-\beta/\alpha$ is given by

$$g\left[A\ e^{\alpha t}+B\ e^{-\alpha t}-\frac{\beta}{\alpha},t|x_0,t_0\right]=\frac{2\alpha\ |B\ e^{-\alpha t_0}+A\ e^{\alpha t_0}x_0-\beta/\alpha|}{e^{\alpha(t-t_0)}-e^{-\alpha(t-t_0)}} \times$$

$$\times\ f\left[S(t),t|x_0,t_0\right]$$

(3.17)

Proof. It follows from (2.9) and from (ii) of Theorem 3.

Corollary 4. Let $S(t)$ be a function of class $C^2[t_0,\infty)$ and let $X(t)$ be the O.U. process. If $K(t)=[\alpha S(t)+\beta -S'(t)]/2$ then equation (2.9) possesses a unique continuous solution.

Proof. As in Corollary 2.

4. NUMERICAL SOLUTION OF THE INTEGRAL EQUATION

In this Section we limit ourselves to considering the case $x_0<S(t_0)$ so that the first of integral equations (2.9) holds. The case $x_0>S(t_0)$ can be treated in a similar way.

Let $h>0$ be a fixed constant and let $t=t_0+kh$ $(k=1,2,\dots)$ so that equation (2.9) reads:

$$g[S(t_0+kh), t_0+kh|x_0, t_0] = -2 \ \psi[S(t_0+kh), t_0+kh|x_0, t_0] +$$

$$+2 \int_{t_0}^{t_0+kh} d\tau \ g[S(\tau), \tau|x_0, t_0] \psi[S(t_0+kh), t_0+kh)|S(\tau), \tau]$$
$$(k=1, 2, \ldots). \qquad (4.1)$$

If the process X(t) is such that

$$\lim_{\tau \uparrow t} \ \psi[S(t), t|S(\tau), \tau] = 0 \qquad (4.2)$$

(which can take place for Wiener and O.U. process as shown by Theorems 2 and 3),then by evaluating the integral on the right hand side of equation (4.1) by means of a composite trapezoidal rule one obtains the approximate first-passage-time p.d.f. $\tilde{g}$:

$$\tilde{g}[S(t_0+h), t_0+h|x_0, t_0] = -2 \ \psi[S(t_0+h), t_0+h|x_0, t_0]$$

$$\tilde{g}[S(t_0+kh), t_0+kh|x_0, t_0] = -2 \ \psi[S(t_0+kh, t_0+kh|x_0, t_0] +$$

$$+2h \sum_{j=1}^{k-1} \tilde{g}[S(t_0+jh, t_0+jh|x_0, t_0] \ \psi[S(t_0+kh), t_0+kh|S(t_0+jh), t_0+jh]$$
$$(k=1, 2, \ldots) \qquad (4.3)$$

Note that the evaluation of g by means of relations (4.3) is particularly simple as compared to the other numerical procedures discussed in the literature (Favella and De Griffi,1981;Ricciardi et al,1983).Indeed, differently from such procedures,our method does not require use of large computing facilities but it is suitable even for implementation on personal computers.The underlying reason is that the kernel of equation (2.9) is a now continuous function due to assumption (4.2),whereas the kernel appearing in other numerical procedures exibits a singularity as τ approaches t.

As for the convergence of $\tilde{g}$ to g ,we limit ourselves to stating without proof the following result (Buonocore et al ,in preparation):
Theorem 4   Let (4.2) hold.Then the differences

$$\triangle_{kh} = \left| g[S(t_0+kh), t_0+kh|x_0, t_0] - \tilde{g}[S(t_0+kh), t_0+kh|x_0, t_0] \right|$$

go to zero as h$\downarrow$0 with kh fixed.

In conclusion ,we stress that,by virtue of the outlined computational procedure,novel and more efficient attempts to first-passage-time evaluations in biologically motivated problems become feasible.

REFERENCES can be obtained from the authors

SELFDUAL AND OTHER STRUCTURES OF OPTIMAL CYCLES IN NEURAL NETWORK BEHAVIOUR

E.Labos
Semmelweis Medical School.1st Department of Anatomy.
1450 Budapest.Tuzolto u.58.Hungary.

1.PRELIMINARIES.

Formal neuronal networks(FNNs) are nontypical $B^n \to B^n$ functions,where B^n is the n-dimensional Boolean cube.An FNN is realized by an N square matrix and a T threshold vector of real entries so that for any $b \in B^n$ $f(b)=u(bN-T)$ holds,where $u(r)=1$ iff $r>0$ and it is 0 otherwise.

It is hard to design an FNN function whose functional digraph consists of a single cycle of $L=2^n$ length.On this point,even a general existence theorem is lacking.A cycle is regarded LONG if it is displayed by n neurons and its length exceeds the half of the possible maximum,i.e.2^{n-1}.A necessary condition and solutions for n=1,...,6 have been published(Labos,1980,1984).

THEOREM 1: A vectorial Boolean function which is FNN and its state-transition graph consists only of cycles(i.e. it is transient-free,TF) should have selfdual threshold gates components pairwisely in Hamming-distance of 2^{n-1},forming regular Hamming-polyhedron.

REMARK:Selfduality is crucial property which does not necessarily hold for nonFNN TF functions.It determines the "internal structure" of cycles.

2.EXTREMAL CYCLES AS THE NUMBER OF NEURONS GROWS.

2.1.Networks with 1 neuron:the case n=1.

The 4 networks of 1 neuron are FNNs ,and 2 of them are invertible,selfdual,regular Hamming polyhedra.These are n-tuples of functions each with 2^{n-1} true vectors.Two functions have no such properties.

2.2.The case n=2.SELFDUAL NETWORKS(SD).

Among the 256 Boolean nets 196 belong to the class of FNNs of which 16 are selfdual:8 are invertible and 8 have transient states.Among the 60 non-FNN nets 16 are permutations on B^2.44 items "have no face".Out of the 19 possible functional digraphs(Harary and Palmer,1973) 1 cannot be found among FNNs:it is the permutation with (3,1)

R. Trappl (ed.), Cybernetics and Systems '86, 367–374.
© *1986 by D. Reidel Publishing Company.*

cycle decomposition.The cause of this lies in the
selfdual(SD) property of TF-FNNs, since $\bar{f}(b)=f(\bar{b})$.
Thus either DISJOINT TWIN-cycles of W and its negated $\bar{W}$,of
equal lengths or GLUED $W\bar{W}$ cycles of even lengths occur in
the state transition graph.

2.3.The case n=3.RC and C-PERMUTATIONS.

Since 104 of the 256 3-inputs truth functions are
threshold gates(Muroga,1971),it follows that among the
16777216 Boolean nets only 1124864(=104^3)are FNNs.Among
the latters 2744 are SD FNN of which 240 are
TF(Labos,1980).Out of the 240 FNN-Permutations only 48 have
L=8,i.e. maximum length cycle,while,144 nonFNN selfdual and
39936 nonFNN and non selfdual TF Boolean nets exist.The
selfdual permutations form a subgroup in the symmetric
group of order 8.On the contrary,the 240 invertible FNNs do
not form a subgroup,however they generate the group of 384
selfdual permutations.Thus,at n=3 the majority of
cases(15606024) lack the properties in question.
THEOREM 2 :The set of SD permutations on B^n represents a
subgroup of symmetric group of order 2^n.The order of this
subgroup is k!*2^k where k=2^{n-1} .
Certain partitions of 8 do not occur among the 240
relevant FNNs or 384 SD permutations.Thus e.g.no (7,1) or
(4,2,1,1) cycle decompositions are possible with FNNs of 3
inputs.These appear among the 39936 remaining cases.Thus
"random net statistics" considered on Boolean
nets(Gelfand,1982) cannot be applied directly to the FNN
subclass.The 48 optimal FNNs may be derived from 6
"essential" cases by relabeling the variables which is a
simultaneous permutation of rows and columns in the matrix
of network.Lengths cycles are invariant against these
RC-permutations,while those of columns(C-permutations)
strongly influence the cycle decomposition of states but do
not destroy selfduality.At n=3 the THEOREM 1 is still a
sufficient condition for reversibility,but this does not
hold from n=4 on as it is shown by counterexamples.

2.4.CONNECTED and SPLIT numbers.MARGINAL states.4 units.

22 primitive networks are required to get the 10752 nets
with L=16 cycle length.The further required ways of long
cycle(L=9...16) synthesis are listed:
(a) - INDEPENDENT SUBCLOCKS with "local" cycle lengths
which are primes to each other and whose total number of
variables equals to 4 yield solutions.E.g.-2 FNNs,each with
2 neurons and with L=3 or L=4 lengths provides L=12.This
net splits into two disjoint parts.Lengths 10,12,14 are
available in this way,supposed that the primitive or
connected lengths were obtained for n=1,2,3.
(b) - Primes (11,13) or prime powers (9,16) or a third

category of numbers(here 15) require CONNECTED networks and a new method of synthesis.

DEFINITION:The natural number L is called connected if $Q(L)<Q(z_1)+Q(z_2)+...+Q(z_k)$,where $Q(x)$ is the upper integer of $\log_2(x)$ and z_i-s are the relative prime factors of L in such a decomposition.E.g.L=45=9*5 is connected since $Q(45)=6<Q(9)+Q(5)=4+3=7$.

REMARK:the DIAGNOSIS of CONNECTEDNESS of a number L,needs $B(r)-1$ investigations,where r is the number of prime divisors of L and $B(r)$ is the r-th BELL-number.The smallest connected number is 15.The primes and prime powers are also taken as connected numbers since such cycle lengths cannot be designed by non-connected FNN with a minimum number of variables(neurons).The non-connected numbers will be called split ones.E.g.even numbers between $2^{n-1}+1$ and 2^n-1 are split ones.

The synthesis of connected lengths is called selective state transition or SHUNT METHOD based on special modifications of a start (N,T) pair generating lengths usually higher than the length to be constructed.Transitions of certain states may be selectively modified.This states are called marginal ones.

DEFINITION:Let (N,T) be an FNN and $f=(c,t)$ one of its component threshold gates.The $b\in B^n$ points are called marginal with respect to f,which are true or false vectors and their effects are equal to $U(f)=\min(S*c)$ or equal to $D(f)=\max(K*c)$ respectively.S and K are the sets of true or false vectors of f and * denotes inner product.$U(f)-D(f)=g$ is the gap of f at the realization $f=(c,t)$

We give an FNN for n=4 which provides all cycle lengths if suitable modifications are applied.The state cycle is as follows:0.10.9.14.13.7.4.12.15.5.6.1.2.8.11.3.

2.5.The case n=5.CODES of matrix columns,modifications.

Columns of certain square matrices are given by an array of decimal numbers.E.g.(11,20,19,8,10) is a 5x5 matrix code.How to decode?Write n-2 as diagonal entries.It is here three.Write the binary form of COLUMN CODE.E.g the 1st column corresponds to 01011.Write -1s instead of non-diagonal 0s and leave +1s unchanged.Compute the 1st threshold:it is the amount of 1s in the column minus 1.Thus the first function is specified by (3,1,-1,1,1) and (2).Decoding all function codes,the partial negation has to be specified.The NEGATION CODE 1 means 00001,a command to negate the 5th function.This is available by changing signs of entries of the column and writing -(t+1)instead of the original threshold t.The negated 5th function is given by :(1,-1,1,-1,-3) and (-2).The next matrix transformation is a C-permutation given by an array of column subscripts.E.g. (13542) means (235) permutation with two fixed columns.

Now,we deal with the M=(11,20,19,8,10) * neg(1) *

369

(13542) specification.The result is an optimum length
generating FNN with the following state
sequence:(0.4.12.5.8.7.10.3.2.6.14.15.11.18.22.30.31.27.19.
26.23.24.21.28.29.25.17.16.20.13.9.1).These 32 numbers
encode the 32 state-vectors if converted to binary
form.Thus 01010 -> 00011 is a state transition in this
optimal cycle.Investigating the 120 column permutations and
32 negations,3840 cases emerge of which in this special
case 346 have L=32 cycle length.

Finally we give modifications M by which specific shunts
inside its cycle can be evoked.To do this,it is necessary
to look for the marginal states of each component.Each
component have 5-5 upper and lower marginal states.E.g.
state 10 is upper marginal of the 5th function.If state 10
was jumped into state 2 instead of 3,then the cycle length
would be L=31.This is achieved by increasing the (5,5)
entry and decreasing the (5,4) entry,together with
increasing the thresold.The value of all changes is
uniformly 0.5.This modification is coded as follows :
a=5(5,4) which commands to increase the 5th entry and
decrease the 4th entry in the 5th column and also to
increase the 5th threshold.

Now we list the modification codes for various connected
lengths:a=5(5,4),b=4(3,1),c=1(5,2),d=3(1,3),e=1(4,5) which
have to be applied to the negated-permuted M matrix as
follows:31=Ma,29=Mab,27=Mc,25=Mbc,23=Mabcd,19=Meb,17=Mabde.
Thus to reach L=23,it is sufficient to modify 2-2 entries
in the following columns:5th(a),4th(b),1st(c) and
3rd(d).The realized shunts
are:10(3..)2,19(26..)24,14(15..)11,28(29..)13 resp.Other
lengths are accesible by the subclock method using a
disjoint collection of smaller networks.

2.6.The case n=6.STRUCTURAL STABILITY and its limits.

The code of start matrix is (31,15,7,3,1,0).That is the
value of all its diagonal entries is 4 while in the upper
triangle there stand -1s,in the lower one +1s.This matrix
(defined for any n) will be referred as matrix A .The
0-negated of the (123456) identical column permutation
results in a behavior including one L=12 cycle and 52 fixed
points.Scanning through the 64 negated of this permutation
the length spectrum of cycles enclosing the state 0
contains 1,2,3,5,6,7,9,10,14,18,24.Neither of these are
long enough.However,among the negations of other
permutations - e.g. (2,6,5,1,3,4) - L=64 appears 10 times
besides 34,38,40,52 which are also long cycles.

Now,we list certain C-permutations and negations of the A
matrix which provide L=64
cycles:(241635)*25,(351264)*4,(215364)*17,(125364)*17,(1356
24)*9,(315624)*3,(365241)*19,(451623)*6,(634251)*3,(315264)
*25,(152364)*13,(321564)*15,(132564)*15,(213564)*23,(564213

>*4,<635241>*58,<352614>*44,<251346>*7.The complete
negations of any of such nets also yield L=64:e.g
<251346>*56.The efficacy of finding these nets by computer
aided searching was 3-4%.

   In the synthesis of the "strange" cycle lengths the
following procedure proved to be effective:A matrix -->
neg(32) --> <265134> column-permutation --> M.Now 7
column-modifications are
listed:a=1(3,4),b=2(4,3),c=2(1,2),d=3(4,5),e=(1,1),f=5(5,4)
,h=6(2,3).Applying suitable patterns to M ,we get connected
cycle lengths
:63=Mb,61=Ma,57=Mc,55=Mbf,53=Maf,51=Mch,49=Mcf,47=Mafh or
47=Maef,45=Mceh,43=Md,41=Maefh,37=Mdh.However,for L=59 a
new matrix was required:A --> neg(5) --> <564321>
--> N.Modification for shunt is:x=5(3,4).The result is
59=Nx.

   Experience shows that the modifiability of a network is
limited.The cause of this is not yet known.However,FNNs are
structurally stable in the following sense.
THEOREM 3:An FNN is designed always with <N,T> so that
between the effects of upper and lower marginal states a
positive g>0 gap lies.All the matrix entries as well as the
thresholds may be modified by an ε >0 quantity so that the
behavior remains unchanged.
REMARK:The term "effect" of state $b \in B^n$ is its inner product
with c column.If a g gap is given,then ε <g/(2n+2) must
hold.Thus this kind of stability decreases if the amount of
neurons increases.The question is open how the ratio of the
g gap and the range of effects could be MAXIMALIZED.The
range is the difference or maximal and minimal effects when
b runs over B^n.The problem is related to the maximalization
of structural stability.The practical consequences are
evident:the reliability,the tolerance against noise,the
VULNERABILITY of formal neurons or technical threshold
gates strongly depend on this issue.Related topics is found
in Muroga(1971).

2.7.Networks with 7 formal neurons.

   As n grows ,the THEOREM 1 becomes less and less
efficient.Nevertheless,a program (AUTODESIGN) after some
thousands of trials resulted in two solutions for
L=128.These are as
follows:1.B-matrix:<62,30,14,6,3,1,124>,neg(1),<7365124>.2.
C-matrix:<31,64,96,48,56,60,32>,neg(1),<5627431>.Ultimately
   the A-matrix-<63,31,15,7,3,1,0>,neg(79),<5762314> is of
interest producing L=126.The shunt method was applied to
reach connected cycle lengths.Fifteen column
transformations were
necessary:a=7(5,6),b=7(1,2),c=6(3,4),d=5(5,4),e=4(6,7),f=4(
2,1),g=5(5,6),m=2(2,3),n=1(2,3),t=3(4,5),o=4(1,2),z=7(7,4),
u=5(6,7),x=6(5,2),w=1(1,2).The list of their applications

371

to the B,C and A networks is as
follows:127=Cu,125=Ba,123=Ax,121=Cuw,119=Bb,117=Bac,115=Bad
,113=Be,111=Bbc,109=Bbd,107=Bf,103=Bde,101=B9,99=Bcf,97=df,
95=B9b,89=B9e,85=Bmoz,83=B9f,81=Becz,79=Bmnz,73=Bme,71=B9nz
,67=Bf9t.

2.8.The case of 8 and 9 threshold gates

For n=8 5 solutions are presented:1.Start
matrix:<127,63,31,15,7,3,1,0>,i.e.the A -matrix.the column
permutation:<42856317> with 6 and 101 negations.2.The same
start matrix with <68374125> C-permutation and 21 partial
negation code. 3.Start
matrix:<63,191,31,15,7,3,1,0>,C-permutation:<14856237>,part
ial negation:6 or 90.
At n=9 optimal solutions were obtained with 0.18%
efficacy.Take the
matrix <255,127,63,31,15,7,3,1,256>.Negation code:40 or
99.Apply the next C-permutation:<579243168>.

2.9.TRACTABILITY OF LARGE OPTIMAL NETWORK DESIGN.

If an FNN of n neurons displays a cycle of lenght L,- the
case <n,L> - NETWORK SEQUENCES whose cycles increase
rapidly are obtained.The enlargment of a net by state
recognizer neurons permits a jump from a state x to y if x
is not an endpoint.By a second enlargement any length may
be duplicated providing <n+2,2L>.A more rapid evolution is
obtained by a recognizer to reach from <n,L> the case
<n+1,L+1> and by these two subclocks to reach
<2n+1,L*(L+1)>.Iterations provide net sequences.These
procedures result neither in optimal nets nor in long
cycles.However,the a set of solutions up to n=9 give long L
solutions up to n=71,using subclocks of strange
lengths.This results in non-dense wiring of nets with
locally strong or even complete connections.The hardest
open problem is to find an iterative design which still
keeps the network-sequence long or even maximal.The group
structures in sets of FNNs represents also a hard
subject.Enumeration of special FNNs is hindered by the fact
that even the threshold gates are not yet
counted(Muroga,1971).It seems also interesting to clarify
the tractability status of threshold logic including a
search of NP-complet problems(Garey and Johnson,1979:see
L09 in their catalogue).

2.10.TAXONS OF BOOLEAN AND THRESHOLD GATES AND NETS.

2.10.1.Finite 0,1-strings can be classified according to
their cycle length,recursive order and amount of 1s
inside.These problems can be effectively handled with
Moebius-inversion and by a Theorem of De Bruijn.

2.10.2.Concerning $B^n \rightarrow B^1$ functions the threshold gate
property and self-duality as well as Chow-parameters seem
to be important.The concept of ANTIDUAL functions is also
important.A truth function is antidual if its dual pair is
equal to its negated.With dual comparabilities an
exhaustive classification is available with 12 taxons.If at
fixed n the sets of threshold
gates(T),selfdual(D),antidual(A)and the two sets(V and W)of
dual-comparable functions,or finally the set of functions
with 2^{n-1} true vectors(H),is represented by logical
variables then the nonvoid and empty classes can be
characterized by a "taxon-function" as follows:

$$F(T,H,V,W,D,A)=\overline{T}.\overline{V}.\overline{W}.\overline{D} + \overline{H}.\overline{D}.(V o W).(T.A+\overline{A})+H.V.W.D.\overline{A}$$

where ".":=and,"+"=or,"o"=exclusive or,X is the negated of
X.The disjunctive normal form of this expression consists
of 12 terms determining 12 classes.At n=4 the sizes of
these classes are:104,888,888,1,1,152,70,12544,5416,5416,18
4,39872.The last class is the largest in which none of the
listed properties is satisfied(having no face).
2.10.3.The census of functional digraphsaccording to the
amounts of endpoints or initial states(i),true
transients(t),nonfixed recurrent states(c) and fixed
points(f) as parameters is relatively easy.The labeled case
of this problem leads to a special counting of forests(of
transients).If x=i+t+c+f is the number of arguments,m=c+f
is the attractor's size,s=i+t,then altogether $(1/6)*(x^3$
$+5*x)$ classes exist.Let denote by h(i,t,c,f) the size of
such a class.Then

$$h(i,t,c,f)= \sum_{k=1}^{i} F(s,k,i).m^k .\binom{x}{m}\binom{m}{f} P(c)$$

where F(s,k,i) is the number of forests with s points,k
rooted trees and i endpoints in the forest.P(c) is the
subfactorial of c.
2.10.4.The behaviour of nets is influenced by the
excitatory and inhibitory innervations(i.e. by the + or -
matrix entries) and by the pacemaker units.A neuron is
pacemaker if its threshold is negative.Thus each wiring
gives a digraph with 2-labeled points and 2-labeled edges:a
wiring is defined here as a 2P2q labelled digraph.At n=4 218
digraphs exists.The numbers of 2P , 2q or 2P2q labelled
digraphs are about 3000,20000 or 360000.

3.DISCUSSION.PROBLEMS.

   Questions of indirect biological relevance merit
attention. (1) In what sense are the real neural nets
optimal? (a) Performing a task with the fewest units:in
special case generate the longest "activity control" with a
given amount of neurons. (b) Realize a physiological

given amount of neurons. (b) Realize a physiological
function with the sparsest wiring and fewest parts. (c)
Solve (a) and (b) with the maximal robustness or
structutral stability.(2) Whether some kind of duality
principle plays a role in brain function or not?
Anyhow,selfduality was required to get transient free
behaviours in FNNs.(3) Whether an idealized
autonomous(closed) neural activity is transient free or it
consists mainly of extremely long transients or even it is
essentially aperiodic?(4) At last out of the immense
collection of FNNs which(analogous)wirings and behaviours
occur in fact?Analysing FNN properties,the generic networks
"have no face" ,while the extremal ones are very rare.

REFERENCES

Andrews,G.E. (1976) The Theory of Partitions.
  Adison-Wesley,Reading,Mass.
Biggs,N.L. and White A.T. (1979) Permutation Groups and
  Combinatorial Structures. Cambridge Univ.Press,Cambridge.
Cameron,P.J. (1983) Automorphism Groups of Graphs. In
  Selected Topics in Graph Theory 2 (eds.Beineke,L.W. and
Wilson,R.J.) 90-127.Academic Press New York.
Garey,M.R. and Johnson,D.S. (1979) Computers and
  Intractability. Freeman & Co,San Francisco.
Gelfand,A.E. (1982) A behavioral summary for completely
  random nets. Bull.Math.Biol.44(3):309-320.
Goulden,I.P. and Jackson,D.M. (1983) Combinatorial
  Enumeration.Wiley-Interscience, New York.
Harary,F. and Palmer,E.M. (1973) Graphical Enumeration.
  Academic Press,New York.
King,R.B. (1980) Chemical Applications of Group Theory and
  Topology.Theoret.Chim.Acta(berl.) 56:269-296.
Labos,E. (1980) Optimal Design of Neuronal Networks. In
  Neural Communication and Control (eds.Szekely,G. & al.)
  Adv.Physiol.Sci.30:127-153.Pergamon Press, Oxford.
Labos,E. (1984) Periodic and non-periodic motions in
  different classes of formal neuronal networks and chaotic
  spike generators.In Cybernetics and System Research 2
(Ed.R.Trappl)
  237-243.Elsevier,Amsterdam.
Moon,J.W. (1970) Counting Labelled Trees.Canadian
  Mathematical Monographs No.1,Alberta.
McCulloch,W.S. and Pitts,W. (1943) A Logical Calculus of
  the Ideas Immanent in Nervous Activity.Bull.Math.
  Biophys.5:115-133.
Muroga,S.(1971) Threshold Logics and Its Application.
  Wiley-Interscience.New York.
Nijenhuis,A. and Wilf H.S. (1975) Combinatorial Algorithms.
  Academic Press,New York.

SIMULATION OF A NEURAL NETWORK FOR ADAPTIVE COLOUR PERCEPTION

N.IOANNIDES, N.PARITSIS, and C.P.MELETIS
Institute of Childs Health,
Agia Sophia Children Hospital
Athens - Greece
and
Greek Systems Group

ABSTRACT. The basic network's unit (neuron) have been designed using a number of logical elements. This neuron has been simulated and tested previously. In the network model three neurons for colour coding are used at each point of the visual field. Three levels of coding are considered. The final level "recognizes" a colour as a point in a three dimensional space of the outputs of the three colour coding neurons. Two of them mainly encode hue and the third one encodes luminosity. Colour contrast is simulated using in addition a set of three neurons, the so-called "adaptors", one for each type of colour coding neurons. Each adaptor receives excitatory inputs from the same type of colour coding neuron and then inhibits them. In the present simulation of the network's model, 57 neurons are used for 6 points of the visual field. The results of the simulation have shown that the network "perceives" colours and exhibits adaptive properties of colour contrast and constancy.

1. INTRODUCTION

Neural networks for colour perception can be devided in two main categories. The first basically includes the manystage theories for colour vision (DONDERS 1881, ADAMS 1923, HURVITCH and JAMESON 1957, WALRAVEN 1962, HASSENSTEIN 1968, RUDDOCK 1971,KOENDERING 1972, DEVALOIS 1972). The other category is about network models and it is refereed to adaptive phenomena of contrast, constancy or after effects (GROSBERG 1970, 1976).

A neural network model which covers both these aspects is the so-called "polytropic" model described in PARITSIS and STEWART (1983). To our knowledge it is the only one concerned with adaptive colour vision. This is the main reason that the polytropic model have been chosen for the present computer simulation with the purpose of studing and testing its behaviour. Furthermore, the specification of some of the model's parameters would enable the model (i.e. the artificial network) to exhibit a behaviour closer to the natural one which realizes the hyman colour perception.

R. Trappl (ed.), Cybernetics and Systems '86, 375–381.

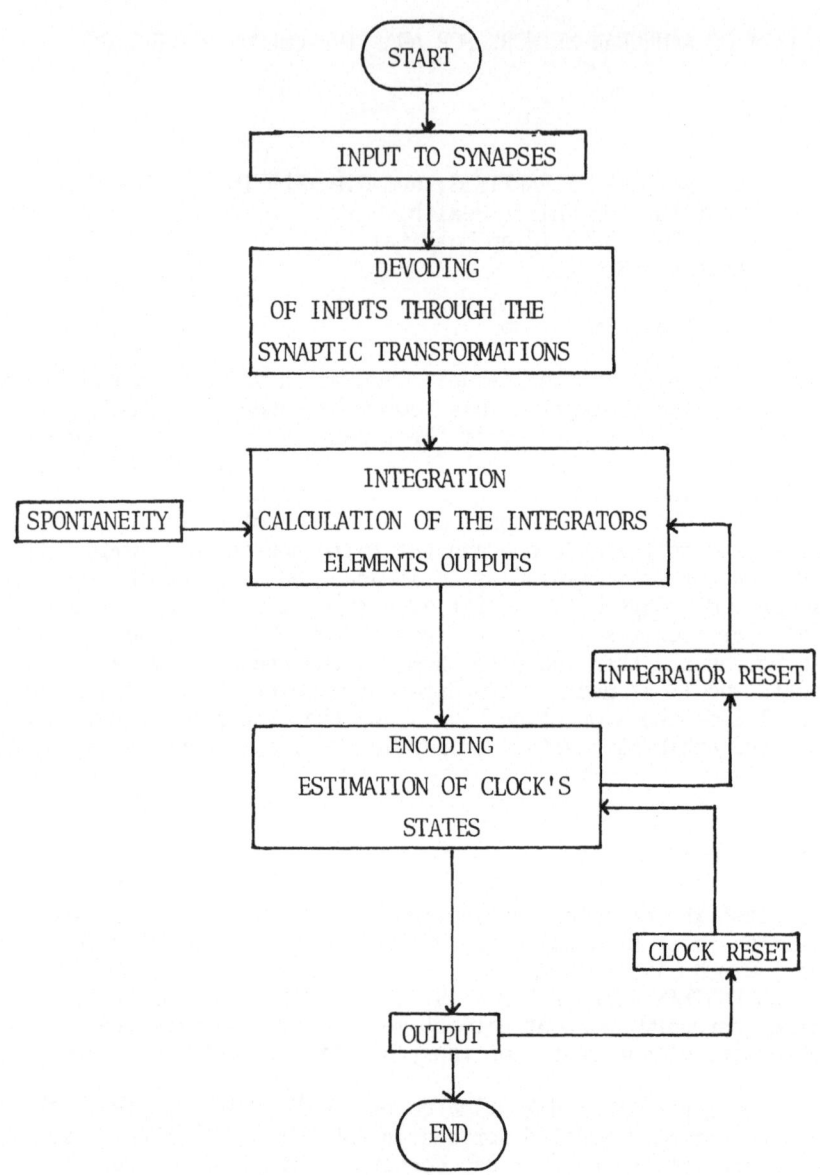

FIG. 1. A FLOW-CHART OF NEURON'S MODEL SIMULATION.

2. THE SIMULATION METHOD

The simulation uses as a basic unit the neuron model (PARITSIS and MELETIS 1984).

2.1. The simulated neuron's model

The neuron used in the network model is conceived as a kind of a logical network and is designed using a number of logical elements (Mc CULLOCH and PITTS 1943) or threshold elements (DERTOUZOS 1965). This conceptualisation has been choosen since we are viewing neurons as finite automata with communicative properties. The neuron's model includes the following main parts : decoding; input transformation; integration; output transformation; and encoding (PARITSIS and STEWART 1983). FIG. 1. is a flow-chart of the simulation of the neuron's model (PARITSIS and MELETIS 1984) and (IOANNIDES 1982). The Fortran computer programming language and a WANG computer at the National Technical University of Athens have been used for the simulation purposes. The simulation of the neuron's model realizes the following main functions :
a. Estimate the Interpike Interval Time (IIT) between two successive spikes ;
b. Transforms IIT into the intensity of neural excitation/inhibition ;
c. Transforms the result of (b) through a polynomial function ;
d. Integrates the values of (c) ;
e. Transfoms the result of integration through another polynomial function ;   and
f. Encodes, using a clock, the result of (e) into the IIT code.
 The output of neuron-automaton is a spike (pulse) which resets the clock and causes inhibition in the integration part of the neuron's model (FIG. 1).

2.2. The neural network

The present neural network is based on the proposed one in PARITSIS and STEWART (1983). To avoid a large neural network, the minimum requirement of three neurons has been applied for colour coding at all levels of the simulated network. The hypothesis that three variables are enough for the perception of any colour has been put forward by YOUNG (1803), has been elaborated by HELMHOLTZ (1911) and is presently well accepted (e.g. WRIGHT 1972).
 To simulate colour contrast and constancy six points of a hypothetical receptive field have been considered.
 The network realizes a stage theory which, from a trichromacy approach at the first stage of YOUNG-HELMHOLTZ, is transformed to an opponent process of HERING type at the second stage. The present network model encodes blue (B) versus orange (O) by a neuron; and red (R) versus green (G) by another neuron. Luminosity and white (W) are encoded by a third neuron, (FIG. 2).
 For a specification of the parameters of the network's model the average of spectrum absorption curves of cones (MARKS et al 1964) are considered as the outputs of the level's 1 receptors. Similarly the

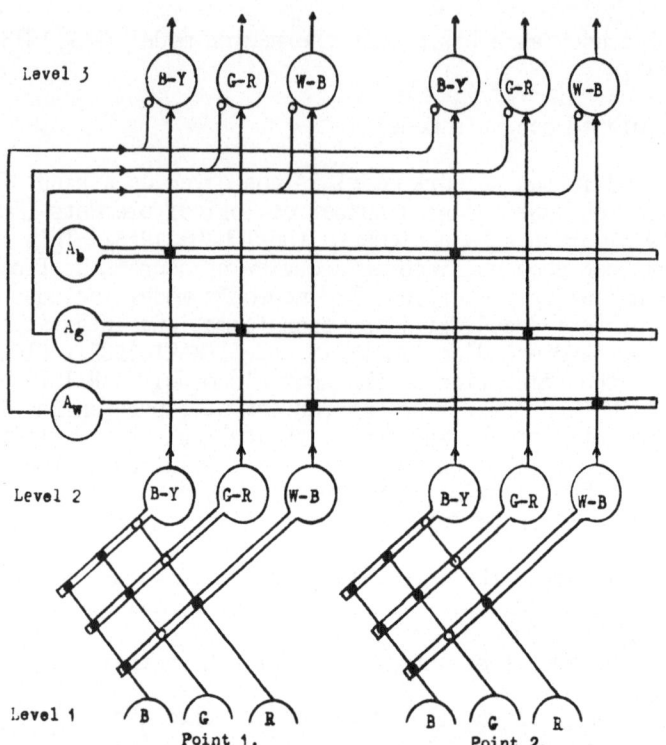

Level 3

Level 2

Level 1

Point 1.   Point 2.

Figure 2. The neural network model for an adaptive classification of colour perception, (o) excitation, (●) inhibition.

average responses of L.G.N. cells (DE VALOIS 1966) are considered as the output of level's 2 neurons. Regarding synaptic transformations as second order polynomial functions their coefficients are specified.

The output (V) of each neuron (Ni, i = 1,2,3) at level 2 can be considered as a single dimension (D) in a 3-D space, where the perceived colour can be represented as a point (V_{N1}, V_{N2}, V_{N3}).

The outputs from level 2 are inputs to level 3 and also to another set of three neurons called adaptors. The functions to each adaptor are:

a. to receive inputs from only one type (out of the existing three) of colour coding neurons from all of the six points to the receptive field,

b. to average these inputs, and

c. to inhibit at level 3 the same type of colour coding neuron.

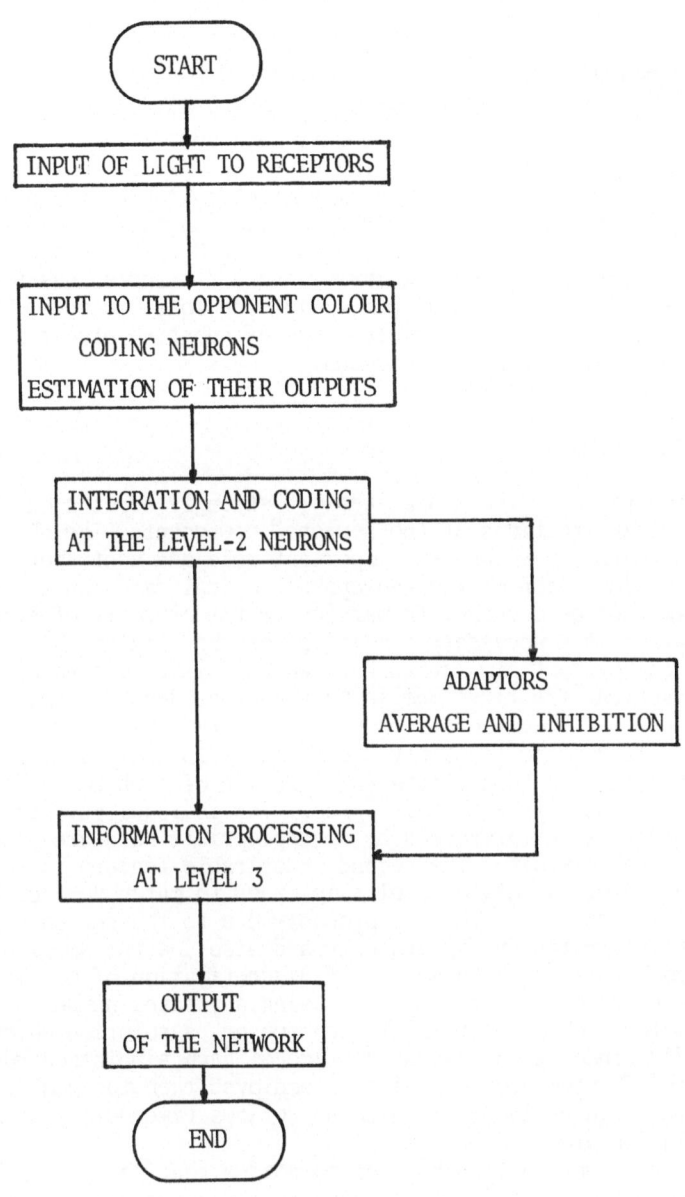

FIG. 3. A FLOW-CHART OF NEURAL NETWORK SIMULATION.

FIG. 3 is a flow-chart of neural network simulation.

3. RESULTS

The computer simulation showed, at each successive level of the network
an increased deviation from the expected results of the model. This
deviation appeared to be random and not following any particular rule,
which indicated that the observed deviation is due to the small number
of logical elements that have been used. Despite this deviation, colour
classification has been achieved, and a "triangle" has been formed in
the 2-D space of the two "hue coding" neurons' outputs. The network
also demonstrated the expected type of adaptive properties for colour
contrast and constancy phenomena.

4. DISCUSSION

The behaviour of the neural network strongly depends on the properties
and the interactions of the neurons' components. The characteristics of
the network's neurons play important role and contribute to the success
of the simulation of the neurophysiological data concerned with colour
information processing. In particular the property of synaptic transformation is a necessary condition for the simulation.
    The present simulation has two undesirable features regarding its
utilisation. The first one is that a great deal of computer time (about
20 mins) was required for each run in a WANG mini computer during 1982.
This disadvantage is mainly due to the relatively long period of time
which is needed to simulate the function of each network's neuron. However if a network with these properties is required then the above disadvantage can be overcomed by an appropriate hardware simulation using
integrated circuits. The second undesirable feature is that we do not
get extremely accurate results in order to match perfectly the neurophysiological data. This is probably due to the neuron's part (FIG. 1)
which integrates the spontaneity and also due the small number   of
logical elements which a sort of discretization of continuous variables.
The consistency can be improved using a greater number of logical elements for the realization of each neuron, a solution which has been
avoided since it increases the time of each simulation run. If the approach of integrated circuits is employed then the number of logical
elements can be increased with no serious time delay in the overall
simulation process.
    It is interesting however to notice that real neurons exhibit also
the important feature of spontaneity and not a deterministic behaviour
so that only after averaging the neurophysiological data then a more
clear picture is emerged (see the example DE VALOIS 1966).
    Despite some technical limitations, due to the previously described
undesirable features, the present computer simulation showed :
a. That the neural network classifies, recognizes and perceives colours
   in a way which conforms with the neurophysiological and physiological
   data as far as colour vision and colour contrast and constancy are

concerned ; and,

b. the existence of such a working network model is appropriate prior to the construction of a hardware (IC) network prototype which can realizes colour perception, for various applications.

5. REFERENCES

Adams E. (1923). 'A theory of colour vision', Psychol. Rev. 30, 56.

Dertouzos M. (1965). 'Threshold logic : a synthesis approach'. Research Monograph No. 32. The MIT press.

De Valois R., Abramov I., and Jacobs G. (1966). 'Analysis of response patterns of LGN cells', J. Opt. Soc. Amer., 56, 7, 966.

Donders F. (1881). Arch. F. Opht. XXVII, 1, 155 quoted by Parsons J. in 'An introduction to the study of colour vision', Cambridge (1924).

Grosberg S. (1970). 'Neural pattern disvrimination' J. Theor. Biol., 27, 291.

Grosberg S. (1976). 'Adaptive pattern perception and universal coding' Biol. Cybernetics, 23, 187.

Hassenstein B. (1968). 'Modellzechrung zur Datenverbeitung bein Farbenseitung des Menschen', Kybernetic, 4, 209.

Helmholtz H. (1911) 'Physiological optics' 3, english translation of the third edition, Opt. Soc. Amer. Rochester, New York (1924).

Hurvich L. and Jameson D. (1955) 'Some quantative aspects of an opponent colour theory. I. Chromatic responses and spectral saturation'. J. Opt. Soc. Amer. 45, 7, 546.

Ioannides N. (1982). 'Computer simulation of an adaptive neural network based on a communicative neuron model'. Graduate Dissertation, Dept. of Electrical Engineering, National Technical Univ. of Athens, Greece.

Koendering J., Van de Grind W., and Bouman M. (1972). 'Opponent colour coding :a mechanistic model and a new metric for colour space'. Kybernetik, 10, 78.

Marks W., Dobelle W., and Macnichol E. (1964) 'Visual Pigments of single primate comes'. Science, 143, 1181.

McCulloch W. and Pitts W. (1943). 'A logical calculus of the ideas immanent in nervous activity' Bulletion of Math. and Biophys. 5, 115.

Paritsis N. and Meletis C. (1984). 'A communicative neuron model and its computer simulation' in Cybernetics Systems : Recognition, Learning and Self-organisation, (Caianiello E. and Musso G. eds.), John Wiley and Sons Inc., New York.

Paritsis N. and Stewart D. (1983). 'A Cybernetic approach to colour perception' Gordon and Breach, New York.

Ruddock K. (1971) 'Parafoveal colour vision responses of four dichromats'. Vision Res., 11, 143.

Young T. (1801) 'On the theory of light and colours' Bakerian Lecture in the Royal Institution, cories at the Libary of the Royal College of Arts, London.

Walraven P. (1962) 'On the mechanisms of colour vision', Thesis, Utrecht.

Wright W. (1972) 'Colour Mixture' in Handbook of sensory physiology 7, 4th ed., eds. Jameson D. and Harvich L., Spinger - Verlag, New York.

ON THE STATISTICAL PREDICTION OF NIPTS DUE TO INDUSTRIAL STATIONARY
NOISE EXPOSURE*

Lin Li and Wanrong Zhou
Beijing Institute of Otorhinolaryngology
Beijing,China

Zhongjie Xie
Department of Probability & Statistics
Beijing University,Beijing,China

ABSTRACT. This paper investigated 1 to 10 years prediction problem of
the individual hearing loss induced by industrial noise. The prediction
formular given in the paper is based on data of TTS(Temporary Threshold
Shift) and PTS(Permanent Threshold Shift). Since 1980, we have made 260
times, 1 - 5 years, individual hearing loss predictions for Beijing textile workers and check individually with the practical testing data each
year. The results showed that more than 80% of the prediction errors are
less than 10 dB.

1.   INTRODUCTION

The main purpose of this paper is to investigate the individual prediction method of Noise Induced Permanent Threshold Shift (NIPTS) based on
the data of TTS & PTS.
   As we know, the individual prediction of NIPTS is a very important
problem in health care (see /1/, /2/, /3/, /4/ and /5/), but up to now
there are no satisfactory method for practical use. A number of researchers conjectured that the TTS (after working in a heavy noise environment) will refer to a future NIPTS, say 20 years later. But after 20
years observation, Soviet researcher Arvid Luts /1/ reported that the
examination of the TTS does not refer to a Permanent threshold shift.
Daniel L. Johnson investigated the population percentage prediction problem in /2/ but no individual prediction involved.
   This paper gives a 1 - 10 years statistical individual prediction
formula of the NIPTS for each person who works in the noise enviroment
with 100 dB (A).

- -

   * This research work partially supported by the Fund of the Ministry
of Education, PRC and The Public Health Bureau of Beijing Municipal.

R. Trappl (ed.), Cybernetics and Systems '86, 383–386.
© *1986 by D. Reidel Publishing Company.*

2. STATISTICAL PREDICTION FORMULA

As an important index, we are interested in the average value of NIPTS at the frequencies of 3, 4 and 6 kHz and it will be denoted by APTS in the sequel.

According to the statistical theory and some mathematical derivation, the prediction formula of APTS can be simply represented as follows:

Suppose that we have several observations this year on APTS and ATTS of a worker, listed as

$$P_1(0),\ P_2(0), \cdots\cdots,\ P_m(0)$$

$$T_1(0),\ T_2(0), \cdots\cdots,\ T_m(0), \qquad (5 \leq m \leq 12)$$

and let

$$\overline{P}_0 = \frac{1}{m} \sum_i P_i(0),\ \overline{T}_0 = \frac{1}{m} \sum_i T_i(0),$$

also suppose that τ is an integer positive number, then the APTS of the worker in τ years later can be predicted by

$$\hat{P}(\tau) = A \exp^{(B/(T+\tau))},\ \tau = 1,2,\cdots\cdots,10,$$

where

$$B = \log(\overline{P}_0/G)/(1/T - 1/(T+10))$$

$$A = 0.9\overline{p}_0\ \exp(-B/T),$$

$$G = 0.798\ \overline{T}_0(T+10)^{0.098} - 21 \cdot \exp(\ -0.091(T+10)\ )$$

and T is the standing (year) value of the worker.

3. PRACTICAL CHECK ON THE INDIVIDUAL PREDICTION OF APTS

All of the workers we tracked in the last 5 years satisfied the following conditions:

1. They work for 8 hours (in workday)in the noise environment with 100 dB (A).

2. They never used any protective articles

3. They never suffered with any diseases which may cause hearing loss

4. They never used any medicine which can lead to the hearing loss such as streptomycin, etc.,.

During 1980 - 1985 we have made 260 times, 1 - 5 years,individual APTS prediction for Beijing Textile workers and check individually with the practical testing data each year.

Let $e_{\tau,1}^{(i)}$ be the error of τ years prediction for the ith person, i.e.

$$e_{\tau,1}^{(i)} = \hat{P}_i(\tau) - P_i(\tau), \quad i = 1,2,\cdots\cdots,52; \quad \tau = 1,2,\cdots\cdots,5,$$

Where $\hat{P}_i(\tau)$ and $P_i(\tau)$ are predicting and real testing values of APTS respectively.

Let

$$\bar{e}_1 = \frac{1}{N} \sum_{\tau=1}^{m} \sum_{i=1}^{n} e_{\tau,1}^{(i)}, \qquad n + m = N, m = 5, n = 52$$

$$\overline{|e_1|} = \frac{1}{N} \sum_{\tau=1}^{m} \sum_{i=1}^{n} \left| e_{\tau,1}^{(i)} \right|$$

$$\sigma_1 = \text{S.D. of} \left\{ e_{\tau,1}^{(i)} \right\}$$

our research work showed that the average predicting error is

$$\overline{|e_1|} = 5.997 \quad (dB)$$

there are 84% of $\left\{ |e_{\tau,1}^{(i)}| \right\}$ less than 10 dB, 52% less than 5 dB, only 6%

more than 15 dB and $\sigma_1 = 7.07$, $\bar{e}_1 = 2.8$ (dB).

Another 24 times, 6 - 10 years predicting error (started from 1976 and checked during the years 1981 - 1985) is

$$\overline{|e_2|} = 8.11 \quad (dB), \quad \sigma_2 = 5$$

and about 67% of the error $\left\{ |e_{\tau,2}^{(i)}| \right\}$ less than 10 dB, 38% less than 5dB.

4.   ACKNOWLEDGEMENTS

Many thanks to the managers and workers of Beijing Wollen Mill and Beijing Flannelette Blanket Factory for their cooperation and help on our research work. Many thanks to Mr. Xie Hui, he helped us a lot for the numerical calculation of this paper .

5.   REFERENCES

/1/. Arvid Luts, 'The results of the aural-overload test for the determination of the individual sensibility to intensive noise: 20 years later', XII World Congress of Otorhinolaryngology, June, Budapest, Hungary 1981.
/2/. Johnson, D.L., ' Prediction of NIPTS due to continuous noise exposure', AMRL-TR-73-91 (AD 767205), U.S.A.
/3/. Robinson, D.W., 'Relationships betwee hearing loss and noise exposure', National Physical Laboratory, Report Ac 32, England, 1968.
/4/. Baughn, W.L., 'Relation between daily noise and hearing loss as

based on the evaluation of 6835 industrial noise exposure cases' ,
<u>AMRL-TR-73-53 (AD 767204)</u>, <u>Wright-Patterson AFB</u>, Ohio, June 1973.
/5/. Nixon J'C. & Glorig, A, 'Predicting hearing loss from noise-induced
TTS ', <u>Arch Otolaryngol</u>. <u>81</u>, March 1965.

* *   Dr. Li Xin and Zhao Xiaoyan joined our research work.

POSITIVE PROTOSYSTOLIC PEAK OF CORONARY ARTERIAL BLOOD FLOW. A NEW IN-
DEX OF EPICARDIAL COMPLIANCE?

Verlato G., Cevese A. and Poltronieri R.
Institute of Human Physiology
Strada Le Grazie
37134 Verona
Italy

ABSTRACT. In open-chest anesthetized dogs left circumflex Coronary Blood
Flow (CBF), recorded with an electromagnetic flowmeter, displays a posi
tive peak simultaneous with the upstroke of Aortic Blood Pressure (ABP),
which is hardly detectable in normal conditions, but becomes quite rele
vant during pharmacologically-induced hypotension. We suggested that
this phenomenon represents filling of the epicardial compliance (EPI.
C.). To test this hypothesis we examined the instantaneous relationship
between ABP and flow during the positive peak. As in a compliant system,
instantaneous flow appeared linearly related to the I derivative of ABP
(r > 0.95). The ratio of the positive peak area to pulse pressure is pro
posed as a new index of EPI.C.. A Significant nonlinear inverse correla
tion was found between estimated EPI.C. and transmural pressure (diasto
lic ABP + 1/2 pulse pressure), in accordance with current literature.

INTRODUCTION

In many vascular beds the relationship between pulsatile pressure and
flow has been satisfactorily understood by modeling the arterial tree
through three basic elements: a resistance, a compliance and an inertan
ce (Westerhof et al., 1979).
     The coronary circulation is particularly complex since during sy-
stole cardiac contraction squeezes intramyocardial vessels, while it
does not affect large epicardial arteries. Therefore, to adequately model the coronary circulation it is necessary to take into account both
an epicardial compliance (EPI.C.), in which transmural pressure is roughly proportional to aortic pressure, and an intramyocardial compliance,
whose transmural pressure is the difference between intravascular and
extravascular intramyocardial pressure.
     As a consequence, EPI.C. should undergo volume changes completely
out of phase with respect to intramyocardial vessels and it should be
charged during systole, when aortic pressure rises. Recently, Chilian
and Marcus (1985) provided experimental support to this hypothesis; they
found that blood flow in systole is greater in superficial coronary arteries than in intramural branches, particularly in the first half of
387

ventricular ejection.

At the onset of ventricular ejection a positive peak is often observed in left circumflex flow traces, recorded both with electromagnetic (Adams et al., 1979) and with Doppler flowmeters (Chilian and Marcus, 1984), especially when aortic diastolic pressure is low. Since vessel compliance increases when distending pressure decreases (Spaan, 1985; Klocke et al., 1985), we supposed that the coronary "proto-systolic" peak could represent the charging of EPI.C.. To test this hypothesis we utilized data from previous experiments in which a sudden, profound and reversible hypotension was induced by i.v. injection of Bitis Gabonica Venom.

MATERIALS AND METHODS

Experiments were performed on 2 mongrel dogs weighing 13 and 21 Kg, anesthetized with nembutal (30 mg/Kg i.v.) and artificially ventilated.

The chest was opened through a midline sternotomy and electromagnetic flow probes were positioned at the root of the aorta and on the left circumflex artery to record cardiac output (CO) and coronary blood flow (CBF) respectively. Coronary flow baseline was periodically checked by mechanical occlusion of the vessels. In vitro calibration of coronary flow probes was performed by timed collection of saline flowing through an isolated artery.

Arterial Blood Pressure (ABP) and Left Ventricular Pressure (LVP) were measured with fluid-filled catheters, connected to Statham P23Gb strain gauge pressure transducers.

After completion of the surgical procedure the animals received Bitis Gabonica Venom (0.125 mg/Kg i.v.). As shown in Fig. 1, this substance causes a huge vasodilation, which affects first the coronary circulation and somewhat later the other systemic districts. Thus at 15" a large increase in CBF is observed, while a fall in ABP and a rise in CO is fully apparent at 25". Later on, systemic vasodilation fades gradually and arterial pressure recovers.

Bitis Gabonica Venom causes a number of additional detrimental effects, such as impairment of cardiac contraction and relaxation, hemorrhages and plasma losses. However, these effects appear at least 10' after injection, much later than the peripheral vasodilation (Adams et al., 1979). Thus, we assumed that within the first 10' after injection of the venom its outstanding hemodynamic consequences were the fall and subsequent recovery of peripheral resistance. Therefore we limited our study to this time interval.

Pressure and flow signals were transferred online into a computerized acquisition system (Cevese, 1984), after A/D conversion (250 Hz per trace). Data were stored on floppy disks for subsequent offline automatic elaboration. The beginning of each cardiac cycle was recognized by shifting back from the maximum first derivative of LVP to the point where the derivative started to rise.

For each cardiac cycle the following parameters were automatically elaborated: Heart Rate (HR), Average ABP (AVG ABP), Diastolic ABP (DIAST ABP), Pulse Pressure (PULSE ABP) and the maximum positive I derivative of ABP (dP/dt max +).

Another parameter, EPI.C. was calculated by visually selecting the
limits of each positive peak on the computer monitor (Fig. 2). The beginning was easily recognized, since it coincides with the rise of the
ABP curve and it was marked by a change in CBF derivative from negative
to positive. Also the end was usually marked by a change in the I derivative of CBF from negative to less negative or from negative to positi
ve; however, this point was not clearly evident in a few cardiac cycles,
which were excluded from statistical analysis, especially when ABP AVG
was in the normal range. The computer integrated the curve within the
selected intervals and subtracted the half-sum of the initial and the
final values, thus giving the area of the peak (hatched areas in Figg.
1 and 2), which represents a volume, as integral of a flow curve.

Assuming that this volume represents storage of blood in the EPI.
C. during early systole (ΔV), the area of the peak was divided by PUL-
SE ABP (ΔP) for each cardiac cycle and the obtained quotient was consi
dered a measure of EPI.C. ($C = \Delta V / \Delta P$).

To calculate instantaneous flow into EPI.C. we considered as reference baseline the segment joining the initial and final points of the
peak.

RESULTS

Values of HR, AVG ABP and "Protosystolic peak" duration before and after Venom injection are reported in Table I.

TABLE I

		Before Venom	1' After Venom
Dog A	HR	135.0 bpm	124.0 bpm
	AVG ABP	135.8 mmHg	44.6 mmHg
	PEAK DURATION	37.0 msec	93.0 msec
Dog B	HR	146.0 bpm	148.0 bpm
	AVG ABP	113.1 mmHg	61.0 mmHg
	PEAK DURATION	38.0 msec	75.5 msec

Hemodynamic conditions before and after Venom injection.

Typical pressure and flow patterns before Venom injection (CON-
TROL) and 15", 25", 2' after injection are shown in Fig. 1. "Protosystolic peaks" on CBF traces (hatched areas) were hardly detectable when
ABP was normal (CONTROL and 15"), but became quite apparent during hypo
tension (25" and 2').

Fig. 2 shows three typical cardiac cycles recorded 3' after injection in dog B. Since in a compliant system the flow-driving force corresponds to the I derivative of transmural pressure rather than to tran
smural pressure itself, we calculated the linear correlation between
the I derivative of ABP and the instantaneous flow into EPI.C.. The re-

389

sults were highly significant (r = 0.96, 0.97 and 0.96 in the I, II and III cycles respectively; P < 0.01).

The existence of this relationship was also verified during the fall of ABP in late systole; CBF was measured considering as reference zero the last value of CBF before ABP started to decrease. Correlation coefficients of 0.37 (Not Significant), 0.57 (P <0.01), 0.52 (P < 0.01) were found in the I, II and III cycle respectively.

As shown in Figg. 3 and 4, the estimated values of EPI.C. in normo tensive situation varied between 0.2 and $1.9 * 10^{-12} \, m^4 \, s^2 \, Kg^{-1}$ in dog A and between 1.7 and $4.4 * 10^{-12} \, m^4 \, s^2 \, Kg^{-1}$ in dog B respectively.

An inverse relationship was observed between estimated EPI.C. and transmural pressure (DIAST ABP + 1/2 PULSE ABP). The best fit of the experimental data was an hyperbola (Figg. 3 and 4). Correlation coefficients were statistically significant (P < 0.01) both in dog A (r = 0.888) and in dog B (r = 0.548).

DISCUSSION

The hypothesis that the "Protosystolic peak" on coronary blood flow records represents the filling of EPI.C. is addressed to by the following observations:

1) The Instantaneous Flow into EPI.C. is directly proportional to the I derivative of aortic pressure (r > 0.96), as in compliant systems. On the contrary, in rigid tubes as well as in blood vessels flow is usually determined by the pressure gradient between inflow and outflow ports. For instance, Bellamy (1978) reports that during diastole coronary flow is proportional to the difference between aortic pressure and zero-flow pressure, while Cevese and Versini (1985) observe, during mechanically uneffective beats, a linear relationship between coronary flow and the aortic-left ventricular pressure gradient.

2) EPI.C., estimated as the ratio of peak area to PULSE ABP, was inversely related to DIAST ABP + 1/2 PULSE ABP in a nonlinear fashion, in accordance with the current literature (Spaan, 1985; Klocke et al., 1985).

3) The estimated values of EPI.C. in our studies are in agreement with results obtained by Burattini et al. (1985), but they are one order of magnitude smaller than those reported by others (Douglas and Greenfield, 1970; Spaan et al., 1981). However we studied, like the first group, the EPI.C. of the left circumflex territory, while the other Authors considered the EPI.C. of the whole left ventricle.

4) The "Protosystolic peak" is a short-lasting phenomenon (Table 1) which outlasts the ABP upstroke by a few msec. Likewise, the time constant of EPI.C. should be equally small.

5) The "Protosystolic peak" is present in CBF traces recorded both with electromagnetic (Adams et al., 1979) and with Doppler flowmeters (Chilian and Marcus, 1984). Thus it is not an artifact due to the recording device.

If EPI.C. is charged during ABP upstroke, one should expect, con-

390

versely, its emptying with the ABP fall. Indeed, a CBF negative wave is often observed when ABP decreases (Figg. 1 and 2). However its boundaries are not well defined and the correlation between the I derivative of ABP and instantaneous CBF is weak. Probably other phenomena, obscuring the emptying of EPI.C., take place at this moment.

In conclusion, the results of this study support the hypothesis that the coronary positive peak in early ejection represents the charging of epicardial compliance. However, the phenomenon is hardly detectable in normal conditions but it becomes quite relevant during hypotension.

ACKNOWLEDGEMENTS

The authors are warmly grateful to Miss Giuliana Cerutti, for her precious technical help in all steps of this work. They thank Dr. Nico Westerhof, Dr. Rob Kramps and Dr. Peter Duÿst for fruitful discussions.

REFERENCES

1. Adams Z'S, Alella A, Di Lavore P, Gattullo D, Losano G, Vacca G (1979) 'Il circolo coronarico nella fibrillo-vibrazione atriale'. G. Ital. Cardiol., 9: 678-686.
2. Adams Z'S, Gattullo D, Losano G, Marsh NA, Vacca G, Whaler BC (1979) 'Haemodynamic effect of the venom of Bitis Gabonica in the dog'. Boll. Soc. It. Biol. Sper., 55: 1693-1699.
3. Bellamy RF (1978) 'Diastolic coronary artery pressure-flow relations in the dog'. Circ. Res., 43: 92-101.
4. Burattini R, Sipkema P, van Huis G, Westerhof N (1985) 'Identification of canine coronary resistance and intramyocardial compliance on basis of the waterfall model'. Ann. Biomed. Eng., 13: 385-404.
5. Cevese A (1984) 'Automatic elaboration of hemodynamic phasic curves including coronary blood flow'. Boll. Soc. It. Biol. Sper., 60: S3, 139-140.
6. Cevese A, Versini W (1985) 'Pressure-flow relations in coronary arteries during inefficient beats'. Proc. 37th Meeting SIF, Pisa.
7. Chilian WM, Marcus ML (1984) 'Coronary venous outflow persists after cessation of coronary arterial inflow'. Am. J. Physiol., 247: H984-H990.
8. Chilian WM, Marcus ML (1985) 'Effects of coronary and extravascular pressure on intramyocardial and epicardial blood velocity'. Am. J. Physiol., 248: H170-H178.
9. Douglas JE, Greenfield JC (1970) 'Epicardial coronary artery compliance in the dog'. Circ. Res., 27: 921-929.
10. Klocke FJ, Mates RE, Canty JM, Jr., Ellis AK (1985) 'Coronary pressure-flow relationships. Controversial issues and probable implications'. Circ. Res., 56: 310-323.
11. Spaan JAE (1985) 'Coronary pressure-flow relation and zero flow pressure explained on the basis of intramyocardial compliance'. Circ. Res., 56: 293-309.
12. Spaan JAE, Breuls NPW, Laird JD (1981) 'Diastolic-systolic coronary

flow differences are caused by intramyocardial pump action in the anesthetized dog'. Circ. Res., **49**: 584-593.
13. Westerhof N, Murgo JP, Sipkema P, Giolma JP, Elzinga G (1979) 'Arte
rial impedance'. In Quantitative Cardiovascular Studies, edited by NHC
Hwang, DR Gross, DJ Patel. Baltimore, University Park Press.

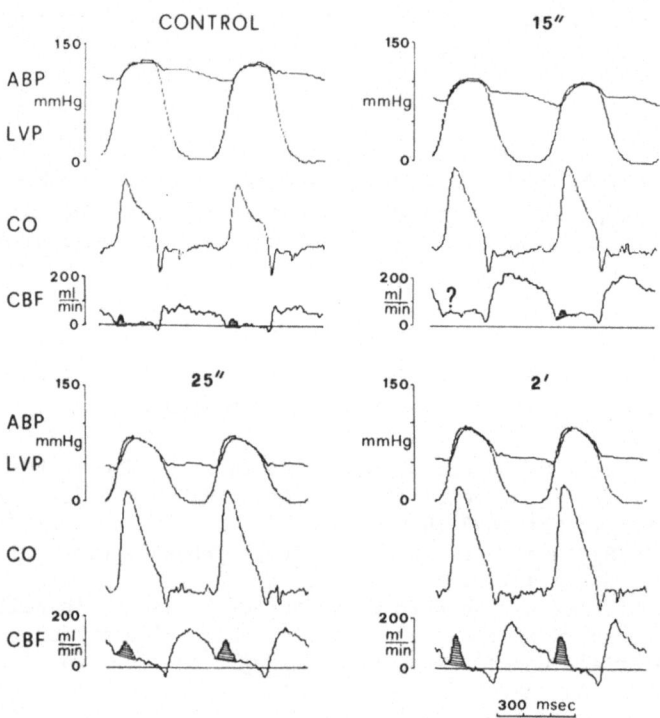

Figure 1. Arterial Blood Pressure (ABP), Left Ventricular Pressure (LVP),
Cardiac Output (CO) and Coronary Blood Flow (CBF). Amplification of pro
tosystolic peak in CBF curves (hatched areas) during hypotension induced
by venom injection. ? = "Protosystolic peak" not detectable.

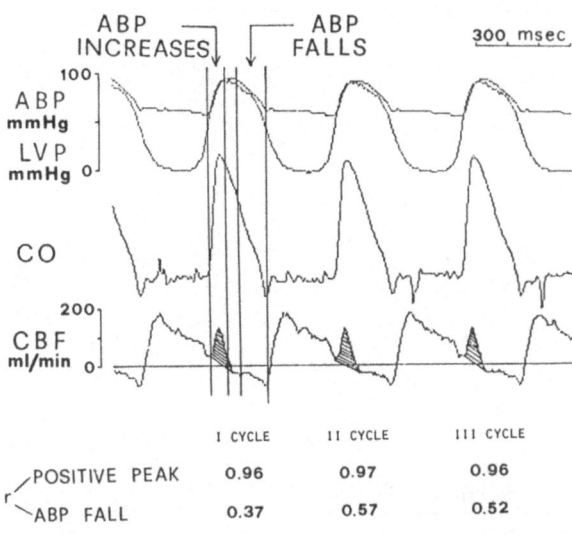

	I CYCLE	II CYCLE	III CYCLE
POSITIVE PEAK	0.96	0.97	0.96
ABP FALL	0.37	0.57	0.52

Figure 2. Arterial Blood Pressure (ABP), Left Ventricular Pressure (LVP), Cardiac Output (CO) and Coronary Bood Flow (CBF) recorded 3' after venom injection. Hatched area in CBF = Protosystolic peak, which is simultaneous with the upstroke of ABP. While ABP falls down, a negative wave is observed on CBF, which however has no clear boundaries. r = linear cor relation coefficient between the I derivative of ABP and instantaneous CBF.

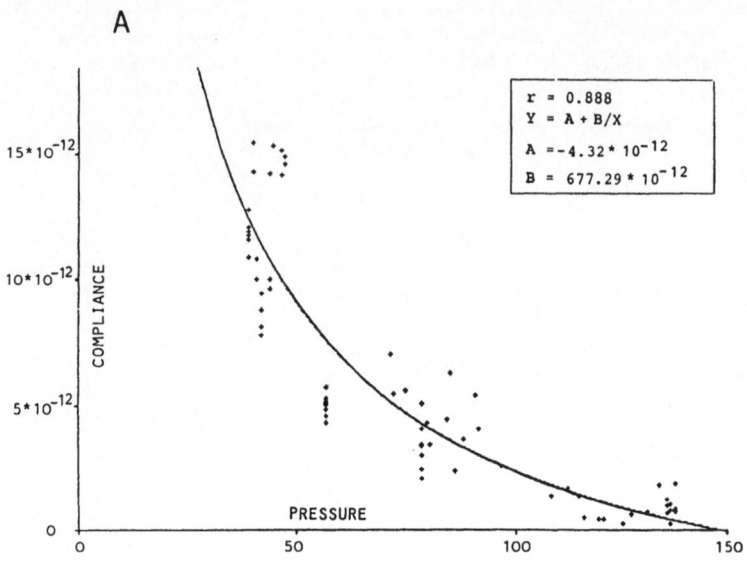

Figure 3. Relationship between epicardial compliance and transmural pres̲sure in dog A.

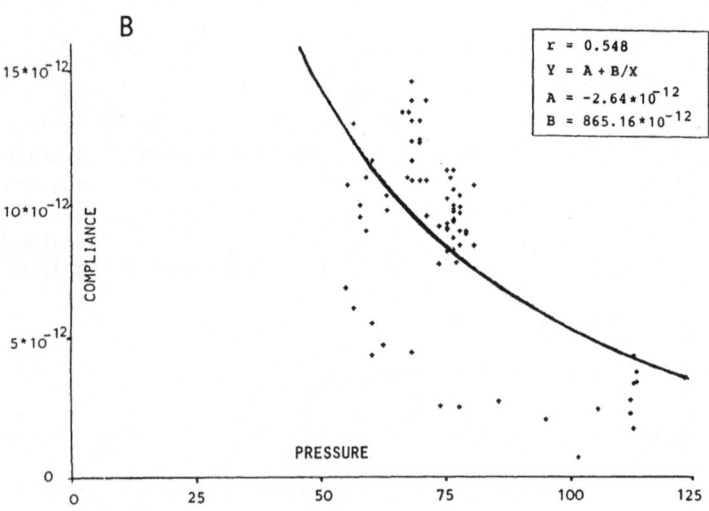

Figure 4. Relationship between epicardial compliance and transmural pres̲sure in dog B.

PLASTICITY OF THE CELL MEMBRANE RECEPTORS (A MODEL)

A. S. Koch and Rózsa Nienhaus*
Second Department of Pathology
Semmelweis University of Medicine
 H-1091 Budapest
Hungary
*Computer Centre, University of Münster
A.-Einstein-Strasse 60
D-4400 Münster
Federal Republic of Germany

ABSTRACT. A model is proposed to visualize the concept of
dynamic receptor generation on the surface of the animal
cell. It consists of a hexagonal network of automata, each
having four possible states. The state of a central automaton at t time depends on its own and its six nearest
neighbours'state at t-1 time. The transitions are simultaneous for the total network of 1801 automata. Receptors
may consist of one or more automata simply connected in
the plane. The enumeration of patterns containing five or
more units is a non-trivial problem. The units being "coloured", the enumeration of the possible allocations for
all possible patterns with any kind of symmetry also is
non-trivial. It is suggested that similar principles may
be involved in the dynamic production of receptors for
"unknown" ligands.

Cells as open systems are in a continuous interaction
with their environment. This means - in other words - a
continuous screening of the environment for relevant in-
formation.For the cell, information means molecular
patterns representing food, stimulus, inhibition or danger.
The potential number of such informative molecules is very
large and still tends to increase with the increasing
production of new non-natural molecules by the chemical
industry.
How can a cell cope with such a challenge? The genetic apparatus available to a cell is clearly insufficient,
however versatile it may be, like in the case of antigen
receptors. It is hard to imagine that a cell should have
pre-designed during its evolution a genetically encoded

395

receptor for any new organic molecule synthesized yesterday. Thus the concept of stable, preformed receptors cannot be generalized. This would also contradict the apparently universal biological law of simultaneous conservativism and plasticity. It should be remembered that only the
primary structure of a polypeptide is fully deterministic.
The formation of secondary and higher level structures is
considerably affected by the environment, thus it is a
probabilistic process. Local environmental changes may
cause dramatic local changes in the availability of
radicals at the protein surface. The necessity of instantaneous cellular response presupposes the existence of some
dynamic regions on the cell membrane, which are able to
form, from pre-existing units, "ad hoc", a wide variety
of receptors for binding "unexpected ligands. The
principle of our approach to the problem had originally
been formulated by Bichat, in his "Traité des membranes"
published in Paris in 1816, as follows: "Nature applies
the same principles everywhere, only the results achieved
are different; she is greedy in her tools, but generous
in the effects produced with them".

A model for a possible theoretical solution of these
problems has been proposed recently by our group (1, 2, 3,
4). Let us regard the two-dimensional surface of a cell
as a lattice of closely packed units, which are free to
rotate and to be translated laterally. This obviously
simplified interpretation is based on the fact that the
cell membrane consists of an orderly system of protein and
lipid molecules, each of which possesses different free
radicals (units) of limited mobility, and the entire
system has the fluidity of a thin motor oil.Qantum chemical maps of the molecules show that their surfaces exhibit
characteristic patterns of relatively positive or negative
electric charges and inducible or neutral sites represented by appropriate atoms or atomic groups. The dynamics of
molecules, especially of larger ones in solution, e.g. of
proteins in the cell membrane, greatly affect the actual
"accesibility" of the different surface groups.

With these basic notions in mind, the following
model was constructed: Have a regular triangular plane
network of closely packed circles of identical radiuses
(units). Assign to each unit one of the four possible
states, i.e. neutrality, positive charge, negative charge,
inducibility (s_0, s_1, s_2, s_3) and $S:(s_0,..., s_1)$.

Consider a centered hexagon of the lattice, and close it
to torus by projecting identical hexagons to each side of
tHe primary hexagon, as shown in Fig. 1.

Set the pattern in motion by applying to it a set of
deterministic transition rules, $F:S^7 \longrightarrow S$ representing the
relation of the 4^7 (16384) neighbourhood configurations

to all four possible states of the central automaton. The
state of the central automaton of the unit hexagon at t+1
time depends on its own and its six nearest - and only its
six nearest - neighbours'
rules are applied simultaneously to all units of the set
under study. The rotationally symmetrical neighbourhood
configurations are considered equivalent.

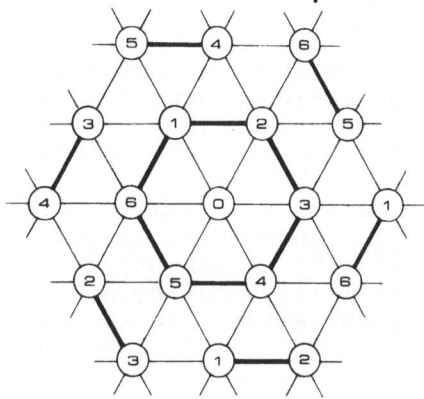

Figure 1. Closing a unit hexagonal lattice to a torus

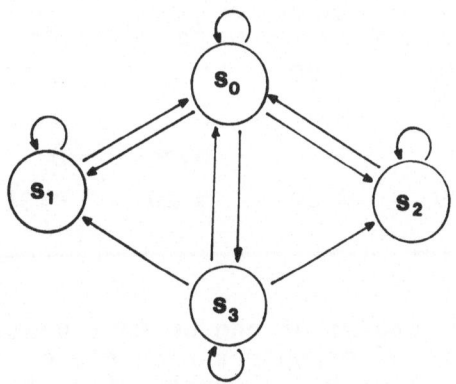

Figure 2. Graph of transition rules
neutral = s_0, positive = s_1, negative = s_2, inducible = s_3

The transition rules have been constructed intuitive-
ly-empirically, so as to provide for a constant mean
relative frequency of the individual states within the
finite 1801 unit lattice studied. Constancy was checked
empirically through a maximum of three thousand iterations.
The problem was not trivial, for the coordinates of units
in a given state were allowed to vary freely. This condi-

tion was necessary to simulate both the genetically determined constant average molecular composition of the membrane and the dynamics of accessibility of the individual
chemical groups as described above. A graphical presentation of the local transition rules is shown in Fig. 2.
Note that the graph is not complete, for the transitions

$$s_{12}; \; s_{21}; \; s_{13}; s_{23}$$

are missing. There is a relative conservativism in the
system, for all states remain unchanged at a relatively
high probability. This statement is illustrated by presenting the local transition rules as a probability matrix
(Table I). Based on the probability function providing for
the constancy of mean relative frequency of states in the
total network, a function generating system was developed
(5), which made possible the construction of "domains"
controlled by different local transition functions (i.e.
of different local "dynamics") within the network.

TABLE I. Transition probability matrix

	s'_0	s'_1	s'_2	s'_3
s_0	0.34	0.02	0.02	0.62
s_1	0.62	0.38	0	0
s_2	0.61	0	0.39	0
s_3	0.29	0.20	0.20	0.31

Receptors may consist of one or more units. The two-
dimensional geometry of receptors with one or two units
is trivial. With an increasing number of units the problem of enumeration of the possible simply connected, non-
holey patterns - called "animals" by Harary and Palmer
(6) - becomes more sophisticated. With unit numbers higher than 10, there is only the laborious iterative method
available, because explicit formulas for computation have
not yet been found. We first limited our studies to the
case isomorphic to the problem of constructing solid(non-
holey) animals from hexagons in the plane. The three-,
four- and five-unit "animals" were enumerated and graphically presented. Fig. 3 shows the basic modules, i.e. the
structures not transformable into each other by rotation
or reflection. It is, however, clear that the latter may
be of great importance in biology, where chirality plays

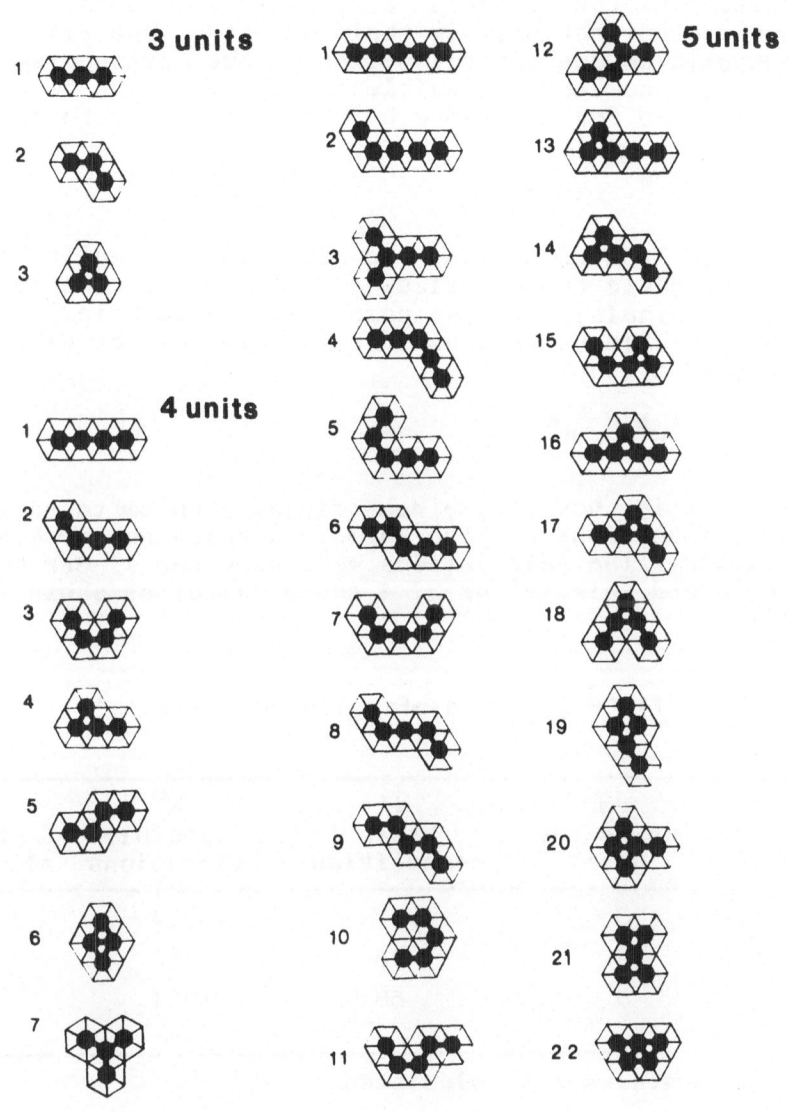

Figure 3. Three-, four- and five-unit "animals"

399

a central role.

The model operates with four possible states of each unit. Thus the "animals" serving as receptors differ from one another not only in their geometry, but also in their composition and the allocation of the distinguished units.

The number of possible compositions can be easily calculated for all cases by the combination formula

$$c_n^{k,i} = \binom{n+k-1}{k}$$

It is more tedious and often non-trivial to enumerate all possible four-labeled, non isomorphic receptors (coloured animals). For the completely asymmetrical patterns the possible variations of allocation can be easily calculated by the formula

$$V_n^{k,i} = n^k$$

It is, however, a non-trivial problem to enumerate the allocations for the animals displaying any kind of symmetry. The calculations were done for linear hexagonal "coloured animals" of 3, 4 and 5 units, as shown in Table II.

TABLE II. Data of coloured "animals"

N^o units per "animal"	N^o basic compositions	N^o possible allocations	N^o basic allocations
3	20	64	40
4	35	256	132
5	56	1024	n.c.

n.c. = not calculated

It is thus clear that each geometrical structure may represent a variety of allocations and that each allocation may appear in a variety of geometrical structures. Reminding that each unit of the network is both center and nearest neighbour, it is clear that none of them can be definitely assigned to a single receptor, but may participate in the formation of any receptor of which it may be a simply connected component.

400

We are aware that the model presented is a drastic
simplification of the molecular biological reality. Nonetheless it seems to be reasonably useful for drawing
attention to the considerable local variability in a network of constant average composition. This points to the
possibility that while the average molecular composition
of the membrane of a cell is fully determined genetically
at any time, the intrinsic dynamics of the molecules -
especially of proteins - allow for a broad range of plasticity. This seems to be a remarkable selection advantage,
since it enables the cell to "get acquainted" with hitherto unknown molecules of potential information value. Local
dynamics also permit direct, instantaneous "recognition"
processes by avoiding the involvement of the relatively
slow and circumstantial genetic regulation.

REFERENCES

1. Koch, A.S., Fehér, G., Lukovits, I.: 'A simple model of
   dynamic receptor pattern generation'. Biol. Cybern. 32,
   125-138 (1979).
2. Koch, A.S.: Theoretische Grundlagen und Computersimula-
   tion von dynamischen Zellrezeptormodellen. Schriften-
   reihe des Rechenzentrums der Universitaet Münster, 44.
   Münster (1979).
3. Koch, A.S., Nienhaus, R., Lautsch, M., Lukovits, I.:
   'An advanced version of the dynamic receptor pattern
   generation model: the flux model.' Biol. Cybern. 39,
   lo5-lo9 (1981).
4. Koch, A.S., Nienhaus, R., Lautsch, M.:'Metastable equilibrium with random local fluctuations: simulations of
   dynamic receptor pattern generation in a fluid mosaic
   membrane.' Biol. Cybern. 44, 121-128 (1982).
5. Nienhaus, R., Koch, A.S., Legendi, T.: Synthese und
   parallele Durchführung von lokalen Überführungsfunk-
   tionen für die 2 1/2 D Zellularautomatenmodelle der
   dynamischen Rezeptoren. Parallel Computing 83, ed.:
   M. Feilmeier, J. Joubert and U. Schendel. Elsevier Sci.
   Publ. (North Holland), 1984, pp. 463-467.
6. Harary, F., Palmer, E.N.: Graphical Enumeration. Acad.
   Press New York - London. 1973. pp. 235-236.

PREDATOR- PREY AND 'EVOLON'- BEHAVIOUR MODELLED BY RANDOM-WALK PROCESSES

F.Breitenecker
Technical University Vienna
Wiedner Hauptstrasse 8-10
A-1040 Vienna

M.Peschel, W.Mende
Academy of Sciences of GDR
Rudower Chaussee 5
DDR-1199 Berlin

ABSTRACT. In this contribution mathematical models for a global evolution and growth process ('evolon') and for the corresponding predator-
prey processes are discussed. First by means of a general structure
building principle a model for the evolon represented by the
hyperlogistic growth law is transformed into a Lotka-Volterra system,
where due to well known results on these systems qualitative analysis
can be done. It turns out that within this three- dimensional Lotka-
Volterra system a twodimensional predator- prey relation is responsible
for all phenomena. Generalizing the special parameters of this predator-
prey system results in a generalized deterministic evolon- model. In the
following the question of the randomness of the process is dicussed. In
order to treat also the 'random basis' of the process - the process is
partially a random one, the deterministic continuous models are only
approximations - a discrete model based on a random walk process for
predator and prey is developed and investigated. Several rules in this
random walk process are discussed. This discrete model based on random
walk shows in the time domain the same qualitative behaviour as the
deterministic model for the predator- prey process, the deterministic
model has to be seen as approximation of the behaviour of the random
model. Furthermore the randow walk model gives much more insight into
the process because in each step interesting clusters representing the
building of stable and unstable structures of the process can be
observed.

1. EVOLON- AND VOLTERRA- MODELS

In our world we meet dynamic processes, interactions and competitions on
all levels. Growth and structure- building are the impressing phenomena
of evolution in biology, ecology, energy consumption, etc.

R. Trappl (ed.), Cybernetics and Systems '86, 403–410.

One approach for the simulation of these phenomena is based on the decomposition of the system to be investigated into subsystems, which are linked by certain relations. As the number of unknown parameters increases with the number of subsystems this approach soon results in too complex high-dimensional models.

Another approach is based on the assumption, that the system to be investigated develops as a whole. Consequently the interrelation between the subsystems has to fulfill a certain uniform evolution law for the entire system. This approach drastically reduces the dimension of the model to be formulated, but an appropriate overall evolution law and evolution model is much more difficult to find.

In their works Peschel and Mende (/2/,/3/) start with the second outlined approach. Observing the growth process · of a 'general' variable in a complex process (for instance the total biomass) one usually meets a s-formed state transition curve, which is called 'evolon' (fig.1).

This curve starts with an extensive phase well represented by an autocalytic growth law and approaches a saturation limit B well represented by an autacatalytic saturation law which both are combined to the generalized hyperlogistic growth law

$$dx/dt = k.x^P.(B-x^r)^q \qquad\qquad ..(1)$$

From experience it is known, that within the extensive phase many small but unstable structures are built up while within the intensive phase (saturation phase) the number of different structures decreases to few but stable and large structures.

Causal reasons for this growth law are found in chains of rate-coupled exponentially growing systems, which can be seen as realization of the first outlined approach for the processes under consideration. Neglecting feedback from previous levels and autocatalytic influences within a level these chains have the form

$$dx_i^N/dt = k_i.x_i^N.x_{i+1}^N \ , \quad i=1,..,N \qquad\qquad ..(2)$$

where i and N are the indices of hierarchical level and chain length. Basic rate-coupled chains are the finite exponential tower and the so-called hypercycle which has been extensively studied by Eigen and and Schuster (/1/).

Mende and Peschel (/2/) found out that under weak assumptions an infinite exponential tower (2) converges to the fore-mentioned autocatalytic growth law if N tends to infinity. The corresponding autocatalytic saturation law can be also approximated by an infinite exponential tower so that consequently the hyperlogistic growth law (1) can be approximated by coupled infinite chains.

It is to be noted that the logarithmic differential operator F = dln/dt generates these chains where the coefficients k_i of each level are related to the initial values of the levels.

404

Considering now the growth law (1) and the representation as infinite chain (which is not unique) the question arises whether the process could be represented also by a finite structure consisting of coupled finite chains and hypercycles.
Following Mende, Peschel, Grauer, Breitenecker (/2/,/3/,/4/,/5/) such finite structures exist and can be constructed if in generating a chain (2) the operator F (logarithmic derivative) is used more flexibly.

These more flexible structure-building principle consists of the following steps:

- The operator F is applied to any intermediate state (level) x_i:

$$Fx_i = A_i$$

- The arithmetic expression A_i now is not interpreted as new state (level) as in case of building up an infinte chain; but it is decomposed into states (levels) already known, states unknown up to the current stage of the structure-building principle and nonlinear expressions of both types.
- The known states are identified and linked by feedback to their previous appearance, the unknown states and nonlinear expressions are introduced as new states.
- The operator F is applied on the new states.
- This process stops if all arithmetic expressions in the last stage contain only known states (levels).

Consequently the representation (2) becomes more complex but finite.
It is to be noted that the outlined structure building principle may be applied on each function defined by a system of differential equations. As results this function $x(t)$ can be represented by a Lotka-Volterra system of the form

$$Fx_i = \sum_{j=0}^{N} G_{ij} \cdot x_j \, , \quad x(t)=x_0(t), \ i=1,..,N \qquad ..(3)$$

Applying this principle on the hyperlogistic growth law (1) results in the following Lotka-Volterra system (3) with $b=B-1$, $\bar{p}=p-1$, $\bar{q}=q-1$:

$$Fx_0 = k \cdot b^q \cdot x_1$$

$$Fx_1 = \bar{p} \cdot k \cdot b^q \cdot x_1 - r \cdot q \cdot k \cdot b^{\bar{q}} \cdot x_2$$

$$Fx_2 \ (\bar{p}+r) \cdot k \cdot b^{\bar{q}} \cdot x_1 - r \cdot \bar{q} \cdot k \cdot b^{\bar{q}} \cdot x_2 \qquad ..(4)$$

It is now of great interest and importance that the global evolon- model (1) for an evolution and growth process can be interpreted as a result of two competing 'driving forces', which obey a special two-dimensional Lotka- Volterra system (4), which is a predator-prey system with special coefficients (fig.2). Due to these special coefficients it is a property of this predator-prey system that both driving forces (predator and prey) are extincted if time tends to infinity. This fact generates an evolon with a 'fixed' saturation limit B.

2. PROPERTIES OF THE MODELS

Now soon the question arises, what happens if a more general predator-prey system of the form

$$dx_1/dt = a.x_1 + b.x_2 \ , \quad dx_2/dt = c.x_1 + d.x_2 \qquad ..(5)$$

is used for modeling the driving forces of the evolon.
It follows immediately that now besides the extinction of both variables both may oscillate (as common known from predator-prey systems), both may approach an equilibrium point not equal zero and both may 'explode'.

The first case results in a sequence of evolons where the beginning of a new evolon can be interpreted as mutuation too. The second case leads to an 'exploding' behaviour after one evolon, the last case gives only 'exploding' behaviour.
These additional behaviours, especially the sequence of evolons enrich the features of the model used for describing a global growth and evolution variable. The predator-prey model (5) were investigated in (/6/) for modeling social systems; it turned out, that 'weakly coupled' systems of form (5) with the corresponding evolon function are suitable models.

But now immediately the main question arises, and that is the question of random behaviour. The outlined models describe namely a very complex process which consists of 'random' parts too but using deterministic equations. Using these deterministic models the random influences and the random 'basis' of the processes under investigation are neglected.

One way is now to study the sensibility of the deterministic equations under random influences and random disturbances.
It can be shown (/6/) that the deterministic evolon model shows significant behaviour under random influences. Disturbing the evolon with an additive noise source and by adding stochastic variables to the velocity parameter k and to the saturation limit B results in case of Gaussian white noise in closed analytical formulas for the stationary distributions.
Theoretical investigations and investigations by simulation show that within the extensive phase of the evolon (before reaching the point of maximal growth rate) the stochastic disturbances have almost no influence, in contrary, they seem to stabilize the process. But in the following intensive phase small disturbances result in instabilities so that the saturation limit B may not be reached. This phenomen gives hints to possible mutuations.

But the more interesting questions, what happens with the basic random behaviour in the process, cannot be answered by the outlined investigations.
In order to take into account this basic random behaviour another model approach has to be used. There a successfull approach can be made by discrete modeling.

3. RANDOM-WALK PROCESSES AS MODELS

Discrete modeling is an alternative approach for modeling the evolon. Using this approach the competition of the two driving forces (predator and pray) which 'generate' the evolon has to be described by a discrete model using for instance the two partially independent variables time and space. The relations between predator and prey then can be interpreted as two-dimensional game.

A simple but efficient discrete model for such a process can be based on a predator-prey game on a toroidal surface.
Doing so, first a rectangular is discretized giving points where predator and prey may stay on.
Now it is assumed that the region has no border, but it is finite. That means, an individual which leaves the region at the right border appeares immediately at the left one (and vice versa); the same should hold for upper and lower border. Consequently the region can be interpreted as toroidal surface which is generated by first 'rolling' the rectangular up to a torus and by 'closing' the torus to a ring (fig.3).

At each discretisation point of the toroidal surface now a predator or a prey may stay or not. Within a time instant each individual is moving to an adjacent point under special circumstances; the direction of the moving is choosen in a random way (there are six possibilities). It is clear that preys may move only to a free point, whereas predators preferably move to points where a prey stays.
Depending on initial values of predator and prey, on the initial distribution of predator and prey at the toroidal surface, on breeding times for both and on average age for both now interesting ecological clusters appear if the individuals are moving. Accounting the numbers of predators and preys at each time instant then shows the behaviour of the process in the time domain.

The rules of this ecological games are the following one, where 'intelligent' behaviour can be used optionally:

* If a prey moves, it chooses in a random way an adjacent unoccupied position. There the following actions take place:
  - The age of the prey is updated by one.
  - If the new age equals the breeding time a new prey is 'generated' at the old position.
  - The prey dies either after reaching the maximal age or after breeding by creating two new preys, the one at the old position, the other at the new one.
  - If all adjacent points are occupied the prey does not move nor breed, the prey may only die.
  - Choosing in a random way an unoccupied adjacent position can be influenced by intelligent behaviour of the prey:
    - If in a certain direction there stay predators the prey preferably chooses the opposite direction.
    - If in a certain direction there stay many preys, the prey chooses prefereably this direction (swarm).

* If a predator moves, it chooses in a random way an adjacent position where a prey stays to be eaten. There the following actions take place:

  - The age of the predator is updated by one.
  - If the age of the predator equals the breeding time, a new predator is 'created' at the old position.
  - The predator dies either by reaching his individual maximal age or after breeding by 'creating' two new predators, the one at the old position, the other at the new.
  - The individual maximal age is the maximal average age minus the times a predator did not find a prey within one step of moving (starvation)
  - Choosing in a random way an adjacent position occupied by a prey can be influenced by 'intelligent' behaviour:
    - If in a certain direction there stay (many) preys the predator chooses preferably this direction.
    - If in a certain direction there stay (many) predators, the predator chooses preferably the opposite direction

The evolon itself now can be computed easily from the current number of predators $x_{1,k}$ and the number of predators in the previous stage $x_{1,k-1}$ using the formula

$$\overset{\circ}{x}_k = \exp(h \cdot \overset{\circ}{x}_{1,k} \cdot (t_k - t_{k-1})) \cdot \overset{\circ}{x}_{k-1}$$

where the '$\circ$' denotes the calculation by random walk and h denotes a normalization factor.

This random walk model with the above outlined rules can be interpreted as two- dimensional semi- Markov process.

While the deterministic model requires for simulation computers with appropriate simulation and integration software, the random walk model can be implemented easily on a personal computer (8 bit too); we implemented it on a COMMODORE 64 where for documentation a 'supergrafic' software was used.

The results with the random walk model were surprising. Depending on initial number of predator and prey, on initial distribution and on breeding age and maximal age of both individuals one can can distinguish between three different types of behaviour (fig.4):

  - Extinction of predator and prey if time tends to infinity after reaching a maximal value (resulting in one step of an evolon)
  - Prey and predator reach an unstable equilibrium not equal zero (small disturbances change the behaviour) giving one evolon with following unstable behaviour
  - Oscillating but not periodical behaviour of predator and prey giving a sequence of evolons.

Comparing with the results of the deterministic model now the case of 'exploding' behaviour is missing. This fact is caused by the 'unbounded bounded' toroidal surface where the process acts at. From the point of view of ecology this results is a real one, because each predator- prey action has natural bounds.

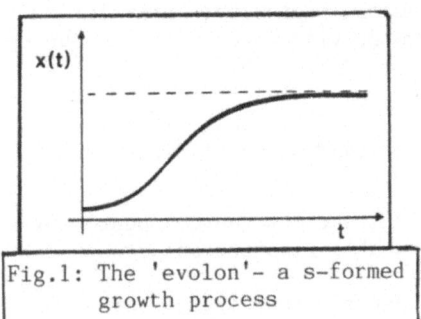

Fig.1: The 'evolon'- a s-formed growth process

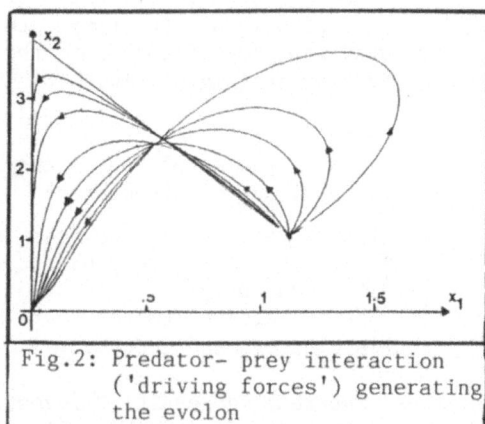

Fig.2: Predator- prey interaction ('driving forces') generating the evolon

Fig.3:

Toroidal surface of the random-walk model for the driving forces

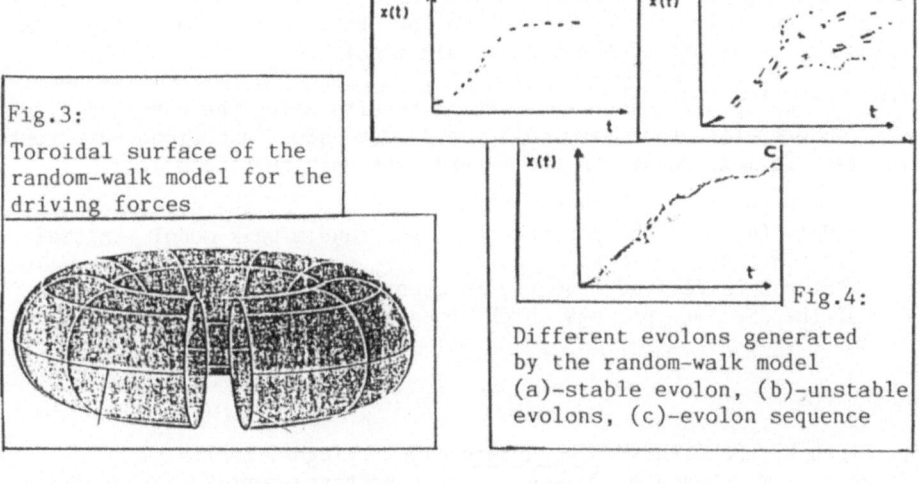

Fig.4:

Different evolons generated by the random-walk model (a)-stable evolon, (b)-unstable evolons, (c)-evolon sequence

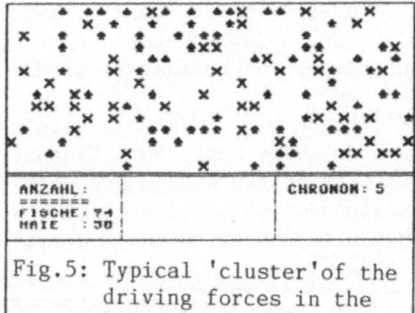

Fig.5: Typical 'cluster'of the driving forces in the extensive phase

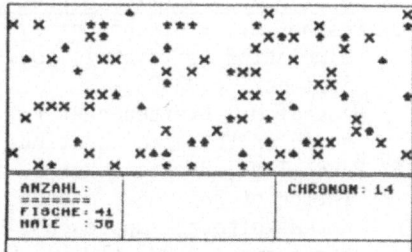

Fig.6: Typical 'cluster'of the driving forces in the intensive phase

The results of the random walk model for the 'evolon'- process offer more information than the behaviour in the time domain. At each time instant where both individuals are moving interesting clusters and groups of predators and preys (to remember: predator- prey action is interpreted as competition of the two driving forces for the evolon) appear and vanish (fig.5, fig.6).

The perhaps most interesting result is the fact, that extensive phase and intensive phase of the generated evolon are accompanied by the following behaviour of structures:

- In the extensive phase on the toroidal surface there appear many short-living small complex but unstable clusters and groups of predators and preys.
- In the intensive phase there appear few long-living large but stable clusters and groups.

Another interesting result of investigation of the random walk model is the fact, that the different qualitative behaviours of the deterministic model have to be seen as idealized nonlinear approximation of the real 'evolon'- process. This fact is at most evident in case of the typical oscillating periodical behaviour of the deterministic model, which has to be seen only as approximation of the oscillating only quasi-periodical behaviour of the random walk model.

Although we could show interesting results using the outlined random walk models for the 'evolon'- behaviour some questions are to be discussed in more detail in the future. The main questions are:

- Exist relations between the parameters of the deterministic model (4) and the parameters of the random walk model (initial distribution, breeding time, etc.) ?
- What can be derived from the interesting structures and clusters of the discrete process which appears at each time instant ?

REFERENCES

/1/ Eigen M., Schuster P. The Hypercycle .Springer, Berlin, 1979.
/2/ Peschel M., Mende W. Do we live in a Volterra-World? - An ecological approach to applied system analysis .Akademie-Verlag, Berlin, 1983.
/3/ Peschel M., Breitenecker F., Mende W. 'On a new concept for the simulation of dynamic systems. Informatik-Fachbericht 71 (1983), Springer, p.93-98.
/4/ Peschel M., Breitenecker F., Grauer M., Mende W. 'System analysis based on Volterra equations'.Proc. SWIISS 1983, Sept.1983, Vienna.
/5/ Peschel M., Breitenecker F. 'Interactive structure design and simulation of nonlinear systems under multiobjective aspects with the Lotka-Volterra- approach'. Lecture Notes in Economics and Mathematical systems 229 (1984), Springer, p.63-76.
/6/ Peschel M., Breitenecker F. 'Socio - economic consequences of the Volterra- approach for nonlinear systems'. Cybernetics and System Research 2 (1984), North Holland, p.423-428.

REPRESENTATION OF COMPLEX ONTOGENETIC TRAJECTORIES

István Molnár[1], Gábor Vida[1] and Elemér Lábos[2]
1. Department of Genetics, L. Eötvös University,
Budapest, Muzeum krt.4/a,H-1o88
2.1st.Department of Anatomy,Semmelweis Medical
School, Budapest,Tüzoltó u.58.H-145o

ABSTRACT.Representations of generation of size and shape
in ontogeny and phylogeny are presented.

1. INTRODUCTION

The concept of ontogenetic trajectory is a generalization
of the developmental path,and it has been proposed as an
organizing principle for the description of evolutionary
transformation of biological forms/1/."This is a step
towards creating a unified view of developmental biology
and evolutionary ecology in the study of morphological
evolution."/1/.The aim of this paper is the investigation
of the geometrical behavior of coupled ontogenic growth
trajectories.
    In the analysis of the relationship of development
and evolution a traditional approach is the investigation
of the relation of size and form, or their generative
processes, the growth and morphogenesis/1,1o/.D'Arcy
Thompson's book,the On Growth and Form, is long argument
supporting the generative role of growth in the unfolding
of the form.
    The recent picture of growth /1,3,4,9/ and morphoge-
nesis /1,2,4,6,7/ shows that the generative role of the
anisotropic growth in the genesis of shape can be more
systematically explored in both ontogenetic and
evolutionary perspective. After presenting the geometrical
representation of ontogenetic trajactories and a shape
generator, the noise induced shape diversity and the
metastability of shape are discussed.

2. METHODS OF REPRESENTATION OF COMPLEX TRAJECTORIES

If the number of variables and/or parameters of a system

411

R. Trappl (ed.), Cybernetics and Systems '86, 411–417.

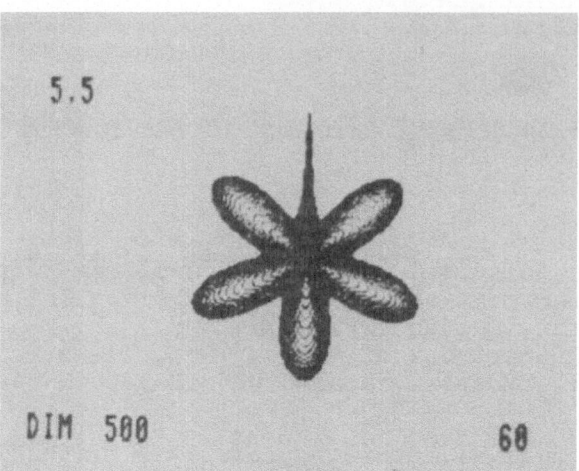

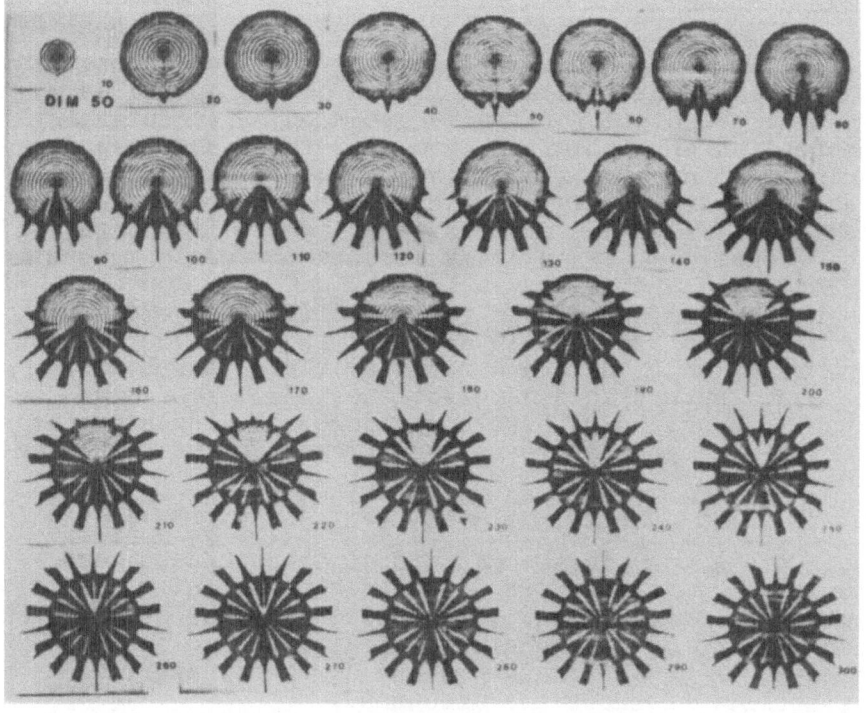

Figure 1. A. An 500 dimensional phase space portrait of an ontogenetic motion.B.A 50 dimensional ontogenetic trajectory from 10 to 300 iteration .

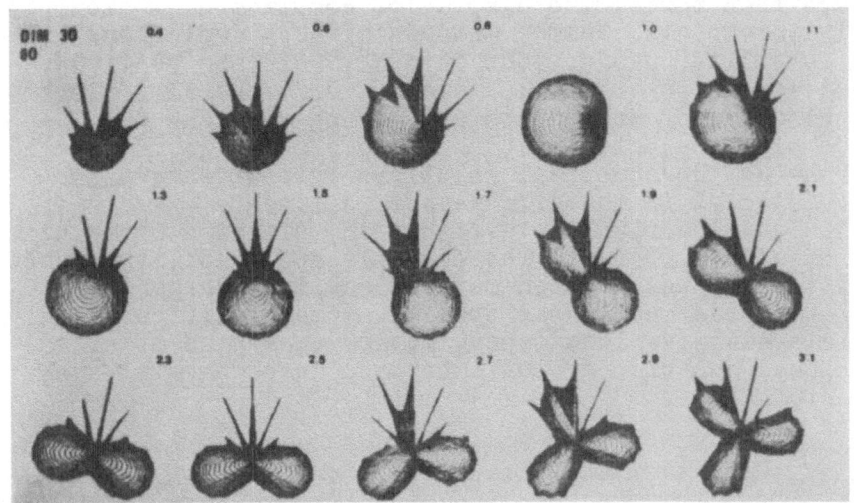

Figure 2. Representations of 30 dimensional ontogenetic
trajectories, after 60 iterations ,with changing parameters.

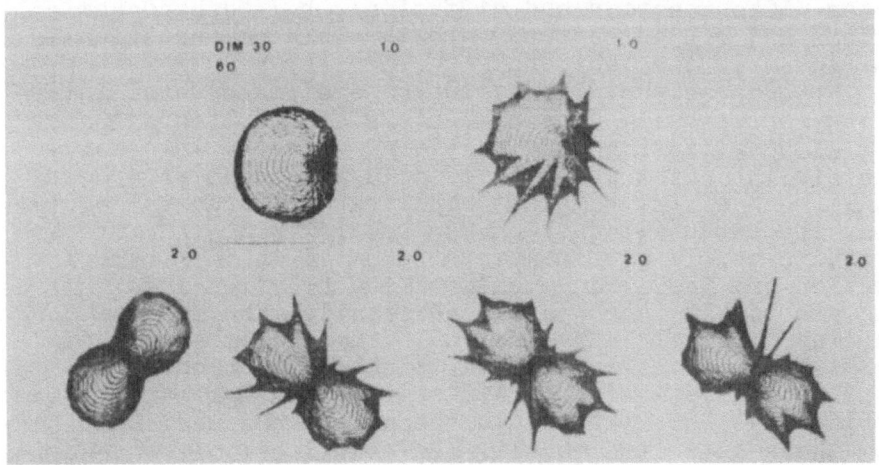

Figure 3. Noise-induced shape diversity.The first
shapes are noise-free.

are more than three, the display of complicated motions is usually incomplete. Common methods of such depictions are phase portraits, projections into R^2, Poincaré sections, reduced system portraits , iterative or temporal trajectories, diagrams of components and moving polygons /5/.

Complex trajectories can be represented geometrically by arranging the numerical solutions into different geometric objects. If the arrangement is linear, circular, spherical, cylindrical, etc., then the diagrams of solutions are quite different. The possible applicability of the geometrical representation methods may include general high /$n \geq 4$/ order nonlinear systems, more specifically multivariate adaptive landscapes, motion equations of multi-dimensional genetic, evolutionary and developmental systems, etc.

3. GENERATION OF SHAPE

A survey of the relevant literature /1,2,4,7/ shows that the principal mechanisms of biological shape generation can be ordered into a few classes: a./ Chemical field processes /like reaction and diffusion/, b./ Mechanochemical systems and c./ Anisotropic growth. This presentation is restricted to the last one.

We suppose that in developing systems several interacting logistically growing centers or moduli are operating with activating and inhibiting effects. In order to generate the joint dynamics of a large amount of growing moduli, one of the simplest nonlinear differential equation, the Verhulst equation was used: $\dot{x} = x - x^2$. The hypercyclic coupling of numerous /from 10 to 500/ Verhulst equations and the arrangements of the solution into various diagrams result in shapes. Specifically, the mode of coupling was "chain-like". A set of sequentially arranged Verhulst equations were taken. Each was coupled to its first, second, third ... left and right neighbours. The coupling was "excitatory" to the neighbours and inhibitory from these activated moduli. The moduli are of self-activating nature. The equation of motion of the shape generator is as follows:

$$^i x_{n+1} = {^i x_n} + h\left[\left(^i a - 1 - {^i u_n}\right)x_n - \left(^i a - {^i u_n}\right)x_n^2\right], \text{ where}$$

$$^i u_n = \sum_{j=1}^{r}\left(^i z_j \; ^{i-j}x_n + {^{i+j}x_n}\right)$$

and $^{B}x_{A}$ is the variable in time A and at the site B.

Other letters denote parameters.

In figure 1 an ontogenetic trajectory, in Figure 2 state vectors of different ontogenetic trajectories are demonstrated.

The following possibilities made this system surprisingly versatile: a./ Giving suitable assignments to the initial values the "handicap-effect" appeared: smaller initial values remained small. b./ The interaction parameter vectors /the first, second, third ... paradiaginal entries of the coupling matrix/ was assigned in homogenous monotonous changing or periodic way. This resulted in various contours. c./ Each modul also has parameter: to this set a pattern also represented a control possibility. d./ The number of growing centers, i.e. the dimension of the whole system influenced the smoothness of shapes.

It is an interesting consequence of the inhibitory coupling the fact that the individual component motions in time will not remain monotonous. The question arises whether an externally or network controlled - otherwise /in isolation/ monotonous solution - still represents a growing process or not.

4. NOISE-INDUCED SHAPE DIVERSITY

By rearranging the nature of the attractors external and internal noise effects are capable of producing qualitative changes in deterministic systems. As a symmetry breaker, the noise might induce self-organizing evolutionary diversity transformations /11/. If $h^2 = V_A / V_p$ and $R = h^2 S$, V_A and V_p are the additive genetic and phenotypic variance respectively, moreover R is the response to selection and S is the selection differential, then the noise-induced transitions evidently enter into selective effects. Thus, the transmission of noisy developmental transitions are of evolutionary importance. The evolutionary effects of noise is manifesting in the diversity of the phenotype, on which the selection acts/ see Fig. 3. /

The interaction of developmental and evolutionary noise is an unexplored question both methodologically and theoretically. In the bifurcation theoretic approach of evolution /8/ the stochastic fluctuations are not taken into consideration despite of the fact, that fluctuations might select different combinations of bifurcation sets.

The noise can be regarded as input or cause for developing systems. It is plausible to separate the cause and the effect of the noise, where the final outcome of the noise-induced developmental changes might be called ontogenetic drift.

5. METASTABILITY OF THE SHAPE

One of the most surprising aspects of the investigated
nonlinear growing system is the presence of slow instabilities occuring in properly parametrized class of shape.
Two categories of the slow instability can be observed in
the numerical solutions obtained. In one category there
is an inflexion point in certain trajectories, in the
others certain trajectories change monotonously.

6. DISCUSSION

The applied geometrical representations of complicated ontogenetic motions may contribute to the understanding of
the dynamics and evolution of development. By the visua-
lization of complex trajectories it is easy to detect the
nature of monomorphism and the polymorphism in complex ontogenetic trajectories. Thus, the gap between the genetic
polymorphism and the phenotypic variability can be bridged
over with the intercalation of diverse ontogenetic trajectories.
    The applied techniques may shed light on the deve-
lopmental constraints arising from the network character
of the coupled ontogenetic trajectories, on the cellular
coevolution, on the fractional phenotypic shape dynamics,
on the relation of temporal and spatial behavior in nonlinear dynamic systems, on the multivariate, generalizable
heterochronic behavior of the ontogenetic trajectories
and on their interrelationships. Consequently the comparative discussion and further classification of evolutionary motions is still necessary and possible.
    We reinforce the old, computer-free D'Arcy Thompso-
nian lesson that the variable anisotropic growth may generate rich shape diversity. It is open question what is
the connection between the hereditary basis of form and
the mechanochemical basis of morphogenesis. In the absence of genetic components of the models of morphogenesis
there is no evolutionary model class for the description
of the evolutionary shape transformations. The genetical
constraints play important role in the morphogenesis /4/,
which we tried to take into account by considering elementary activating and inhibiting interactions between the
coupling of different trajectories being the activation
and inhibition the most ancient effects of genetic systems. The most apparent disadvantage of our model class is
the application of lateral inhibition producing prickly
shape world. Hovever, tha nature is not always prickly,

nor a family of hopeless monsters, which can be transformed by increasing the number of the interactions of growing units in further studies.

REFERENCES

1. Alberch,P., Gould, S.J., Oster, G.F. and Wake, D.B.: Size and shape in ontogeny and phylogeny.Paleobiology 5:296-332 /1979/.
2. Bookstein, F.L.: The Measurment of Biological Shape and Shape Change, Springer, Berlin, /1978/.
3. Bryant, P.J. and Simpson, P.: Intrinsic and extrinsic control of growth in developing organs. Q.Rev.Biol. 59:387-415 /1984/.
4. Cook, A.G.: Genetical aspects of metrical growth and form in animals. Q.Rev.Biol. 41:131-19o /1966/.
5. Lábos, E. and Turcsányi, B.: On the reversible and irreversible representations of motions in R^n to R^2. Psysica 16D, 124-132 /1985/.
6. Meinhardt, H.: Models of Biological Pattern Formation. Academic Press, London /1982/.
7. Murray, J.D. and Oster, G.F.: Generation of biological pattern and form. IMA J.Math.Appl.Med.Biol. 1:57-75 /1984/.
8. Oster, G. and Alberch, P.: Evolution and bifurcation of developmental programs. Evolution 36: 444-459 /1982/.
9. Savageau, M.A.: Growth equations: a general equation and a survey of special cases. Math.Biosci. 48:267-278 /1982/.
1o.Thompson, D.W.: On Growth and Form. Cambridge Univ. Press. Cambridge /1942/.
11.Waddington, C.H.: The strategy of the genes. Allen and Unwin, London /1957/.

COUPLINGS BETWEEN MOLECULAR AND CELLULAR LEVELS :
SIMULATION OF DRUG ACTION

P. Auger * C. Julien **
* 8 rue Jean Menans 75019 Paris, France
** Laboratoire de Cytofluorométrie CNRS ARC
7 rue Guy Moquet B.P.3, 94800 Villlejuif, France

ABSTRACT. We present a model of coupled molecular and cellular kinetics.
From molecular level fundamental equations, we compute equations ruling
the cellular kinetics, i.e. the physiological progression between phases
G_0, G_1, S, G_2, M.
Our model is connected to Kendall-Takahashi models. We present simulations of the time evolution of a population of cells synchronized in S
phase. We study the effects of multi-phase acting drugs, for example
drugs controlled by cells in G_1 phase killing cells in M phase, that
correspond to non-linear terms added to the cellular kinetics equations.
These particular drugs control and regulate the growth of the cellular
population evolving towards a constant size.

INTRODUCTION

In molecular and cellular biology, two large classes of dynamical models
are generally considered : chemical kinetics and cellular kinetics
models. In chemical kinetics models, the considered variables are the
concentrations C_b of different chemical species b which are related each
other by chemical reactions. These models reproduce the time evolution
of these concentrations, $C_b(t)$. As the set of chemical reactions inside
cells is very complex, simplified models have been proposed, such as
the Weinberg-Zeigler's one (1,2).
In cellular kinetics models, the considered variables are the numbers of
cells $n^i(t)$ at time t, which are in a particular phase of the cell cycle
(G_0, G_1, S, G_2, M) and belong to a given cellular population. i is an
index for the phase. (i = 1, G_0, i = 2, G_1, and so on). These models
represent the time evolution of the demography of a population of cells.
Many models have been already suggested, such as the Kendall-Takahashi
models (3,4) or the Smith and Martin model (5).
Recently, it has been possible to measure by new technical means such
as cytofluorometry, the concentrations of different chemical species
inside cells in a given physiological phase. In this context, we propose
a new class of dynamical models coupling molecular and cellular kinetics
models. The purpose of this work is to present a dynamical model in

419

R. Trappl (ed.), Cybernetics and Systems '86, 419–426.

which considered variables are the concentration $n_b^i(t)$ of molecules b
inside cells ine the phase i, at time t. We have already developped a
similar model involving simultaneously demographic and chemical aspects
(6). In section 1, we describe fundamental equations at molecular level.
In section 2, we derive the dynamical equations at cellular level for
the previous ones. In section 3, we study coupling effects between
molecular and cellular levels, and we present simulations of drug actions
on the growth of a cellular population. We study multi-phase drugs which
allow to regulate the cellular growth.

1. A MODEL FOR COUPLED CELLULAR AND CHEMICAL KINETICS :

Consider a given population of cells that can be in different phases
such as G_0, G_1, S, G_2, or M. Let i be the index for the phase compartment $i \in \{1,K\}$. K is the last compartment. The cells contain many different chemical species b, and b is the index for the chemical species,
$b \in \{1,B\}$ where B is the total number of chemical species. Let $n_b^i(t)$ be
the number of molecules b inside all the cells in the phase i at time t.
Consider the following dynamical system (1), see Fig. 1.

$$i \neq 1, \quad \dot{n}_b^i(t) = \frac{dn_b^i(t)}{dt} = \tag{1}$$

$$= \underbrace{\sum_{b'} k_{bb'}^i n_{b'}^i(t) + e_b^i(t)}_{=(I)} - \underbrace{(\mu^i + \lambda^i) n_b^i(t) + \lambda^{i-1} n_b^{i-1}(t)}_{=(II)}$$

For i = 1, one must replace λ^{i-1} by λ^i.

System (1) is a sum of two terms. The term (I) concerns chemical kinetics
inside cells in phase i. $k_{bb'}^i$ is the rate of transformation of molecules
b' into molecules b inside cells in phase i. e_b^i is the rate of exchange
of molecules b with the extra-cellular medium, for cells in phase i. We
used a very simplified linear model for the chemical kinetics in the same
way as Weinberg and Ziegler (1.2). The term (II) concerns phase changes.
λ^i is the rate of aging for cells in compartment i. μ^i is the rate of
death for cells in compartment i. For more details, we refer to previous
papers (6.7).

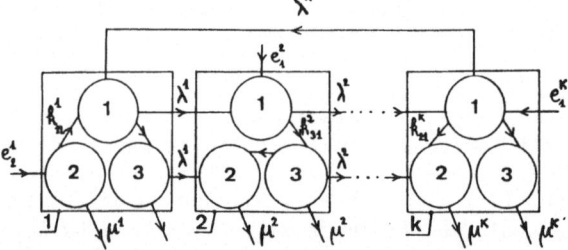

<u>Figure 1.</u> : **graph of coupled molecular and cellular kinetics models**
Each square corresponds to a phase compartment. The circles
correspond to molecular species. Arrows correspond to transitions. $k_{bb'}$ is the chemical rate of reactions b'-->b in cells
in compartment i. δ_b^i is the rate of exchange of molecules b
with outside world for cells in compartment i. All possible
arrows are not represented, it is only an example.

2. CELLULAR KINETICS EQUATIONS

Let $n_b^i(t)$ be the number of cells in phase i at time t. Let m^i and m^b be respectively the average mass of a single cell in phase i and the molecular mass of chemical species b. We have the next relation between variables $n^i(t)$ and $n_b^i(t)$:

$$n^i(t) = \sum_b \frac{m_b}{\bar{m}^i} \, n_b^i(t) \tag{2}$$

By time derivation of equations (2) and by using (1), one gets :

$$\dot{n}^i(t) = \sum_b \frac{m_b}{\bar{m}^i} \, \dot{n}_b^i(t) = \sum_b \frac{m_b}{\bar{m}^i} \, (I) + \sum_b \frac{m_b}{\bar{m}^i} \quad (II) \tag{3}$$

(I) and (II) correspond to the terms defined in system (1), assuming the average mass of cells in phase i as constant. Then it is easily understandable that the first term $\sum_b m_b/m^i$ (I) vanishes. For details, we refer to (6,7). Under these conditions, system (3) is written more simply as :

$$\begin{cases} \dot{n}^i(t) = \lambda^{i-1} n^{i-1}(t) - (\mu^i + \lambda^i) n^i(t), \ i \neq 1 \\ \dot{n}^1(t) = 2\lambda^k n^k(t) - (\mu^1 + \lambda^1) n^1(t), \ i = 1 \end{cases} \tag{4}$$

To get equations (4), we assume that $\bar{m}^{i-1} = \bar{m}^i$ and $\bar{m}^k = 2\bar{m}^1$. System (4) is identical to Kendall-Takahashi models (3,4).

3. COUPLED CHEMICAL AND CELLULAR KINETICS :

Let us consider the introduction of a drug in the system acting specifically on cells in the phase i. Then, many chemical reactions are going to take place and the number of molecules b in phase i cells is going to vary. The global effect of this drug is to modify the rates of aging λ^i and death μ^i of cells in compartment i. Let $\delta\lambda^i$ and μ^i be respectively the variations of the rates λ^i and μ^i, which are assumed to be proportional to the concentration of the drug b, C_b.

$$\delta\lambda^i = \alpha_b^i \, C_b$$
$$\delta\mu^i = \beta_b^i \, C_b \tag{5}$$

α_b^i and β_b^i are constant parameters. Under these conditions, the drug b slows the cellular cycle and kills cells in phase i. Figure 2 gives a simulation of the action of a drug acting on cells in S phase. These cells, initially partially synchronized in S phase, (60% of the population at time t = 0). At t = 0, we have 1 000 cells with 600 in S phase. The values of the parameters are the followings :

421

$$\begin{cases} \lambda^1 = 0.035 & \lambda^2 = 0.3 & \lambda^3 = 0.26 & \lambda^4 = 0.075 & \lambda^5 = 0.4 \\ \mu^i \text{ is } 1\% \text{ of } \lambda^i, \text{ i.e. } \mu^1 = 0.00035 & & (6) \\ \delta\lambda^2 = -0.25 & \delta\mu^2 = 0 \end{cases}$$

We have five phases, G_1, early S, late S, G_2 and M. λ^2 correspond thus to the transition from early S to late S. Figure 2-a gives the time evolution of the percentages of cells in G_1, S, and G_2 + M. Figure 2-b gives the time evolution of the whole population which grows exponentially. The population grows slower than when $\delta\lambda^2 = 0$. But the growth is not stopped, it is only slowed.

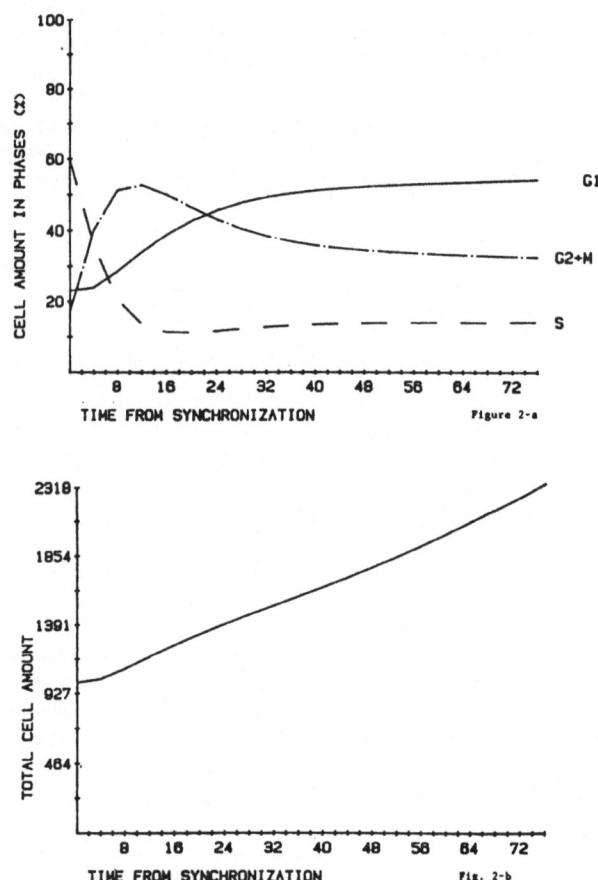

Figure 2-a

Fig. 2-b

<u>Figure 2</u> : **Evolution of cellular demography after a blocking step**

Figures 2-a and 2-b show respectively the time evolutions of the percentages of cells in G_1, S, G_2+M phases and of the whole population initially synchronized in S phase (60%) with a drug blocking partially the cells in S phase.

422

To regulate the population, it appears that one must consider multi-phase drugs. For this, let us assume that the concentration of the drug b acting on cells in phase i is piloted by cells in another phase j. For example, let b' be a drug acting on cells in phase j which transform b' into b at rate $m^j_{bb'}$,

$m^j_{bb'}$ is the rate of transformation of b' into b for a single cell in phase j. Under these conditions, the n^j cells produce $m^j_{bb'} n^j$ molecules b per second.

Now, assuming that the drug b is spontaneously transformed into another molecule b" at rate $k_{b"b}$, we can write the following equation for the total number of molecules b, n_b :

$$\dot{n}_b(t) = m^j_{bb'} n^j(t) - k_{b"b} n_b(t) \qquad (7)$$

Considering that $n^j(t)$ varies very slowly compared to $n_b(t)$ then we are in a steady state and $\dot{n}_b(t) = 0$

Then, at equilibrium, n_b can be expressed as :

$$n_b = \frac{m^j_{bb'} n^j}{k_{b"b}}, \text{ when } \dot{n}_b(t) = 0 \qquad (8)$$

To obtain the concentration of the drug b, C_b, one must divide the total number n_b by the cellular volume V, assuming that the drug b is extended in a uniform way in the medium.

Under these assumptions, the term (5) must be rewritten as :

$$\delta\mu^i = \beta^i_b C_b(t) = \frac{\beta^i_b}{V} \times \frac{m^j_{bb'}}{k_{b"b}} n^j(t) \qquad (9)$$

These terms seem to us very interesting because they correspond to non linear terms added to Kendall-Takahashi models. For example, let us consider a drug b' acting on cells in phase G_1 producing a drug b. b is then spontaneously transformed into b". b" acts on M phase cells as killing factor. Then, the Kendall-Takahashi model is not modified except for its fifth equation :

$$\dot{n}^5(t) = - (\lambda^5 + \mu^5) n^5(t) + \lambda^4 n^4(t) - \alpha^{51} n^1(t) n^5(t)$$
$$\alpha^{51} = \frac{\beta^5_b}{V} \times \frac{m^1_{bb'}}{k_{b"b}} \qquad (10)$$

One must note that the correspondance between chemical parameters $m^j_{bb'}$ and $k_{b"b}$ and cellular parameters λ^i, μ^i is now known as factor α^{51} in this example. Thus, a change at the chemical level induces a change at the cellular level and the coupling effect is known.

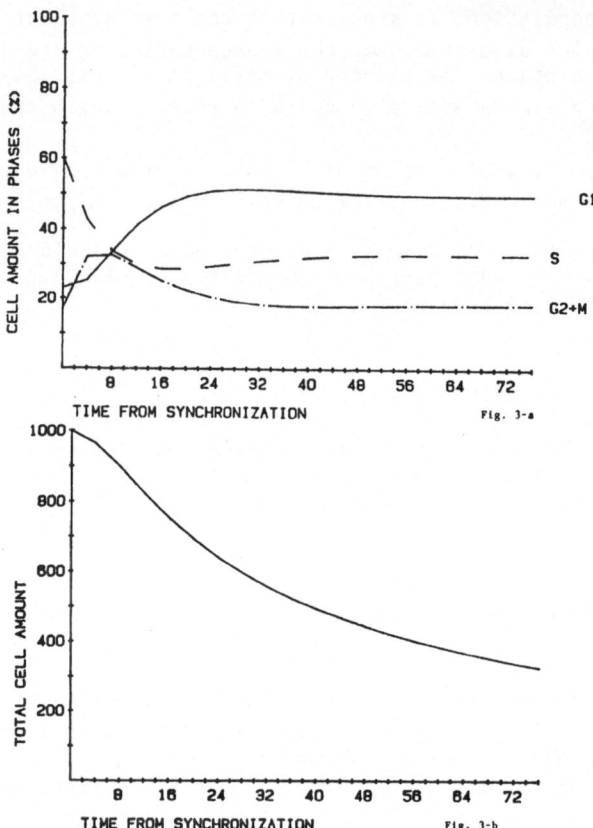

CELL AMOUNT IN PHASES (%)

TIME FROM SYNCHRONIZATION   Fig. 3-a

TOTAL CELL AMOUNT

TIME FROM SYNCHRONIZATION   Fig. 3-b

Figure 3 : Simulation of cellular demography after action of a multi-phase drug.

    Figures 3-a and 3-b show respectively the time evolution of the percentages of cells in G_1, S, G_2+M phases and of the whole population initially synchronized in S phase (60%) with a drug piloted by cells in G_1 phase killing cells in M phase.

  On another hand, these multi-phases drugs are very interesting because they correspond to non-linear terms added to the Kendall-Takahashi models wich allows to regulate the cellular growth of the population. Figure 3-a gives the time evolution of the percentages of the cells in G_1, S, G_2+M phases for α^{51} = 0.005. Figure 3-b gives the time evolution of the whole population whose growth is stopped and which evolves towards an equilibrium. This equilibrium corresponds to $\dot{n}^i(t)=0$ and can be calculated by solving the following system :

$$\begin{cases} -(\mu^1 + \lambda^1)\hat{n} + 2\lambda^5\hat{n}^5 = 0 \\ -(\mu^i + \lambda^i)\hat{n} + \lambda^{i-1} = 0, \ i = 2, 3, 4, \\ -(\mu^5 + \lambda^5)\hat{n}^5 + \lambda^4\hat{n}^4 - \alpha^{51}\hat{n}^5\hat{n}^1 = 0 \end{cases} \quad (11)$$

  $\hat{n}^i$ are the equilibrium populations and may be not equal to zero (see Fig. 3-b).

CONCLUSION

The purpose of this work is to propose a model of coupled molecular and cellular kinetics by establishing the connections between molecular parameters, such as rates of chemical reactions, and cellular parameters such as rates of aging and death in each phase. The study of the links between models at different levels of organization has been developped by many autors in hierarchy theory in general and has been applied to very different fields. This model is a supplementary contribution among other studies of multi-level models (8, 11).

The use of non-linear terms added to cellular kinetics models presents the advantage of imagining feed-back effects, control and regulation of the cellular growth. The existence of such multi-phase drugs may be related to actual biological systems. A simple example of such a model would be represented by the steady state in fibroblast growth in a monolayer culture.

Our model is very incomplete and many other effects such as inter-actions between cells of different populations or different probabili-ties of aging and of death for cells of the same population must be added to the model to make it more realistic. This could fit with the description of proliferative and quiescent tumor cells.

REFERENCES

1. Weinberg R. Ziegler B.P. Theor J. Biol. 29, 1970

2. Segel L.A. Mathematical Models in molecular and cellular biology Cambridge University Press, Cambridge, 1980

3. Kendall D.G. Biometrika, 35, 1948

4. Takahashi M. J. Theor. Biol.13, 1966, and 18, 1968

5. Smith J.A. Martin L. Proc. Natl. Acad. Sci. USA, 70, 1973

6. Auger P. Proceedings of the 28th meeting of the SGSR, Intersystems Publications, New York, 1984

7. Auger P. accepted for publication by the Int. J. of Systems research 1985

8. Allen T.F.H. Starr T.B. Hierarchy : perspectives for Ecological complexity, University of Chicago, 1982

9. Whyte L.L. Wilson A.G. Wilson D. : Hierarchical structures, Elsevier New York, 1969

10. Weiss P. Hierarchically Organized systems, Hafner, New York, 1971

11. Auger P.Int. J. Gen. Sys. 6 n°2, 1980, and 8, n°2 1982, Math Biosci.

65, 1983, J. Theor. Biol. 112, 1985.

PSEUDORANDOM INTERVAL MAPS FOR SIMULATION OF NORMAL AND EXOTIC NEURONAL ACTIVITIES

E.Nógrádi and E.Lábos
Semmelweis Medical School
1st Dept. of Anatomy
Tüzoltó-u. 58.
145o Budapest, Hungary

1. INTRODUCTION

The systems studied in this presentation are iterations of piecewise linear maps /PLM/ of interval 0,1 occasionally with a narrow neighbourhood of this region. In its standard version for neurobiological modelling it was first introduced by Lábos /1981; 1984/ and was extensively tested /Nógrádi and Lábos 1981; Lábos 1981/. The motivation to work with such models is multiple: they run quite rapidly in computer simulation, display rather realistic behaviours and still quite amenable for deeper analysis despite of their explicitly complicated phenomena. These properties correspond well to May's /1976/ criteria. The standard version was called by Lábos /1984/ UPG /=universal pattern generator/. It was given by a single parameter $a \in (0,1)$ and by two lines:

$$Y_{n+1} = mY_n \text{ if } Y_n \leq a \text{ and } Y_{n+1} = /uY_n7u \text{ if } Y_n > a$$

where $m=1+(1-a)^2$ and $\mu=1/(1-a)$. Fixing a=0,1, we have m=1.81. The two lines are denoted by L_1 and L_2.

In its extended version /Lábos 1985/ m is independent of the a threshold /fixed at o,1/ and the motion is bounded if 10 m 0. If m 1 then this "neuron" is an oscillating pacemaker. For further purpose its behaviour was also defined below 0 by a third line: $Y_{n+1} = wY_n+e$, where the slope $w \in [0,1]$ and e=0 or small positive number. This makes possible the coupling of such units into networks.

A survey of some interesting properties follows: /1/ The iteration has two kinds of periodic solutions obtained by solving the following equations to initial value x: $x=xL_1^k L_2^2$ A periodic solution is called simple if between the start and return values only one spike occurs. The solution is called complex if in a period the spikes generate a parti-

427

R. Trappl (ed.), Cybernetics and Systems '86, 427–434.
© *1986 by D. Reidel Publishing Company.*

tions of iterations into a "pattern" of interspike intervals. /2/ The majority of solutions is aperiodic.Starting
by non-rational initial value, the rational formula of periodic solutions contradicts periodicity. /3/ At reasonable values
of m,periods of any p natural number can be obtained except
some smaller values. For a given p, usually more than one
solution exists. The smallest interspike interval is 3 if
$m=1+(1-a)^2$. /4/ In simulations the periodic solutions show an
easily computable finite life-time. Trajectories started at
different values diverge rapidly. /5/ Patterns of preassig-
ned transients and prescribed spike-partition of cycle can
be designed. /6/ This units simulate surprisingly well real
neural network properties if connected into small nets. The
units have dead /or refractory/ time, may excite or inhibit
each other according to the plan of a matrix. Their excur-
sions may remain bounded even after strong inhibition or excitation. The manner of coupling may be different: e.g. the
influences are added to the autonomous values after /+ or - /
amplifications or parameter-controls are introduced to influence time-constants etc. The former piecewise linear units
may be generalized in order to simulate a broader spectrum
of normal and pathological excitable cell behaviour /Nógrá-
di and Labos, 1981/.

The system UPG can be regarded chaotic essentially in the
sense of Li and Yorke /1975/ since it is typically aperiodic
but has /extremely unstable/ periodic solutions, its trajectories sensitively diverge. However, it is - contrary to many
similar systems /Collet and Eckman, 1981/ and to that of Li
and Yorke the maps applied here are typically not continuous.
Many of their interesting features takes their origin from
this character.

2. THE GOALS OF THESE SIMULATIONS

No doubt, the coupled PDE&3ODEs of Hodgkin and Huxley /1952/
still represent a starting point - at least in principle -
for the majority of nerve equations aiming to reproduce the
behaviour of excitable tissues /see e.g.Holden, 198o/. However, as soon as nerve cell shape is more complicated than
a cylinder or sphere with few branching cylinders or cones
or moreover when large networks of such systems have to be
taken into account in model building, then the HH-equations
become too slow to achieve sufficient amount of experience
even if the computers are rather quick. In order to reach a
reasonable tractability of the problems faced with in brain
function simulations, quick tools are necessary which still
imitate the "essential" properties of living neurons and this
is done with short, simple algorithms. We believe that the
piecewise linear interval maps are capable of satisfying this
condition and precisely their piecewise linearity permits
even an exhaustive theoretical analysis over computer experiments.

3. GENERAL DESCRIPTION OF THE MODEL

The entries of a short $(2 < r < 10)$ finite sequence $a_r \in [0,1]$ numbers are called separatrices or thresholds. Here $a_1 < a_2 < \ldots < a_r < 1$.

For each $(a_j, a_{j+1}]$ semiclosed subinterval a linear first /or higher/ order iteration is defined as follows:

$$Y_{n+1} = m_j Y_n + b_j \quad \text{if} \quad Y \ (a_j, \ a_{j+1}]$$

An additional line is defined also below 0 $(a_1 = 0)$.
The set of lines are denoted by $L_1, L_2 \ldots L_r$

It is obvious that after many iretaions any value of the generated number-sequence can be expressed symbolically by a sequence of linear operators /the Ls/ applied to the x initial value:

$$y = x L_{j_1}^{k_1} \ L_{j_2}^{k_2} \ L_{j_3}^{k_3} \ldots L_{j_s}^{k_s}$$

where the k_{j_i} -s are non-negative integeres.

4. SUBTHRESHOLD PROCESSES

The real subthreshold processes may be reconstructed with 1 or 2 Ls resulting in 1 or 2 time-constants process. This passive cable model is sometimes as simple as those of Blair, Hill, Rashewsky or Monnier. Very often to reconstruct merely the subthreshold parts of single cell records, these are unsufficient. The case occurs when we meet oscillatory happenings or are close to the rapid /nonlinear/ part of discharge. In this period the "degree of nonlinearity" increases.

The method is suitable to simulate almost all kinds of synaptic potentials or low amplitude partial discharges.

This part of the system plays a role in the control of discharge frequency.

5. SPIKE GENERATION

Spikes like in UPG are generated by an L with high value of b and usually negative m. This line has a "hidden" focal equilibrium point. This focal equilibrium usually "participates" in spike generation only indirectly.

6. THE CONTROL OF FREQUENCY AND REGULARITY OF SPIKE DISCHARGES

The L operators mentioned in SECTION 4 are suitable to determine the very characteristic property of the model- neuron. If they have unstable /resting/ equilibria then the unit will be autoactive and we see spontaneous firing or in the contrary that part may be settled at stable singularity which results in silent but activable cell.

The trick mentioned before is not sufficient to design spike sequences in an arbitrary way. For this purpose a further line is necessary and its (a_i, a_{i+1}) operating region is near to the peak value of spike. This line may determine at least three features: /a/ Regularity of firing from the exact periodicity to the chaotic interspike interval distributions; /b/ Mean value of interspike intervals; /c/ Maximum and minimum value of interspike intervals.

The methods mentioned until this point are suitable to reproduce BEATING pacemaker activity and at certain parameters groups of firing, i.e. burst-like discharge sequences. However, a true well-controllable burst activity cannot be achieved. Additional operators are necessary.

7. BURST ACTIVITY

For bursting activity various tricks are applicable. Two of them were applied by Nógrádi and Lábos /1981/ and Lábos /1981/. The principles are different. A method deals with two-virtual equilibrium design, the other introduces a decomposition of spike generating L operator into at least two Ls. The following properties become well or exactly controllable: /1/ The number of spikes in one burst; /2/ The interburst interval; /3/ The shape of repolarization which follows the last spike in the burst. However, many "morphological" properties of spike-burst records are difficult to keep in hand. Such are for example: the lower and upper enveloping contour of the spike amplitudes or the frequency variation in the burst.

8. PLATEAU POTENTIALS. PAROXYSMAL DEPOLARIZATION SHIFTS.

These well-known abnormal discharges are also reproducible with usually 4,5 or 6 lines. The number of parameters in such a system thus does not exceed that of the HH system. Consequently it is not more complicated than the corresponding traditional simulations. Both the duration of plateaus, the time between them, the decay phase of plateaus are reproducible.

The category which we call complex plateau is usually accompanied with introductory and end oscillations. These are in the reality very multiform. Some of them can be obtained by simple tools. However, there are cases the design of which need higher order iterations.

The alternation of spikes and plateaus - as a real phenomenon in abnormal or "pharmacological" milieu" - was also successfully reconstructed.

9. COUPLING PIECEWISE LINEAR MAPS/PLM/ INTO SMALL NETWORKS

From two to four we coupled either UPG or more complicated units.

The number of possible nets is very high even at few
units. To become better oriented in this immense diversity
we classified the nets according to their digraph skeleton-
wiring, by the number and allocation of pacemakers in the
net, allocation of the excitatory and inhibitory wiring,
allocation of abnormal and normal units.

The basic well-known phenomena like feed-forward and
feed-back control, divergence or convergence, temporal
and spatial summation, lateral inhibition etc. are easily
and quickly reproducible. The additional advantage of our
model is that beside wiring-requirements the effect of
parameter allocation can also be investigated.

The results are demonstrated by numerous examples. To
get a clear picture in this huge zoopark of nets a more extensive analysis is necessary.

However, we mention some·findings: /1/ Regular bursts may
appear in nets of units which are non-burster in isolation;
/2/ Regularity emerges in networks of otherwise chaotic
modules; /3/ The prediction of activity solely on the basis
of wiring is not usually possible. Even if the pacemaker
allocation is known, some surprising phenomena may occur.
What is necessary to know for a more conscious design, it
is the equilibrium structure of the modules including
stability pattern.

REFERENCES

Collet,P. and J.P.Eckmann /1980/ Iterated Maps on the Inter-
    val as Dynamical Systems.Progr.Phys.1.Birkhauser,Boston,
Farmer,J.D. /1981 Order Within Chaos.Doctoral Thesis.
    University of California, Santa Cruz,
Garey,M.R. and Johnson,D.S. /1979/ Computers and Intractabili-
    ty. Freeman and Co., San Francisco,
Gelfand, A.E. /1982/ A behavioral summary for completely
    random nets. Bull.Math.Biol.44/3/:3o9-32o
Goulden, I.P. and Jackson,D.M. /1983/ Combinatorial
    Enumeration. Wiley-Interscience, New York
Harary,F. and Palmer, E.M. /1973/ Graphical Enumeration
    Academic Press, New York.
Hodgkin,A.L. and Huxley,A.F. /1952/ A quantitative descrip-
    tion of the membrane current and its application to con-
    duction and excitation in nerve.J.Physiol.117:55-544,
Holden,A.V./1984/ Why is the nervous system not as chaotic
    as it should be? Abstract of a Workshop held in Budapest.
Holden,A.V./1982/ The Mathematics of Excitation. In Bio-
    mathematics 1980 /eds. Ricciardi,L.M. and A.C.Scott/,
    North-Holland, Amsterdam,
King, R.B. /1980/ Chemical Applications of Group Theory and
    Topology.Theoret.Chim.Acta/berl./ 56:269-296,
Lábos,E. /1981/ A Model of Dynamic Behaviour of Neurons and
    Networks.Lecture Abstract of Annual Meeting of Hung.
    Physiol.Soc.Budapest.I.S4.p.117./in Hungarian/

Lábos,E. /1984/ Periodic and non-periodic motions in
    different classes of formal neuronal networks and chaotic
    spike generators. In Cyberenetics and System Research 2
    /Ed.R.Trappl/ 237-243.Elsevier,Amsterdam,
Li,T.Y. and Yorke,J.A./1975/ Period Three Implies Chaos.
    Am.Math.Monthly 82:985-992,
May,R.M. /1976/ Simple Mathematical Models with complicated
    Dynamics. Nature 261:459-467,
Misiurewicz,M. /1983/ Maps of an Interval. In Comportement
    Chaotique des System Deterministes./eds. Iooss,G. et al./
    pp.567-59o.North-Holland, Amsterdam.
Nogradi,E. and Labos E. /1981/ Simulations of Spontaneous
    Neuronal Activity by Pseudo-Random Functions.Abstracts
    of Ann.Meeting of Hung.Physiol.Soc. Budapest.I.P 74 p.
    151. /in Hungarian/,
Pounder,J.R. and Rogers,T.D./198o/ The Geometry of Chaos:
    Dynamics of a Nonlinear Second-Order Difference Equation.
    Bull.Math.Biol. 42:551-597.

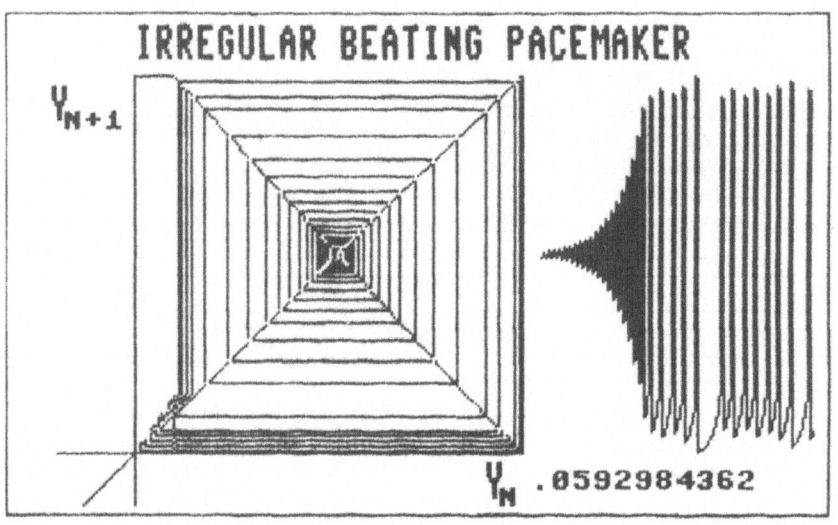

Fig.1.
Separatrices: 0,1; 1,0; 1,0; 1,0; 1,0;
Lines: L1: 1,5; 0,0; L2: -1,11111111; 1.11111111; L3: 0,0;
0,0; L4: 0,0; 0,0; L5: 0,0; 0,0; L6: 0,0; 0,0; Initial value:
0,52

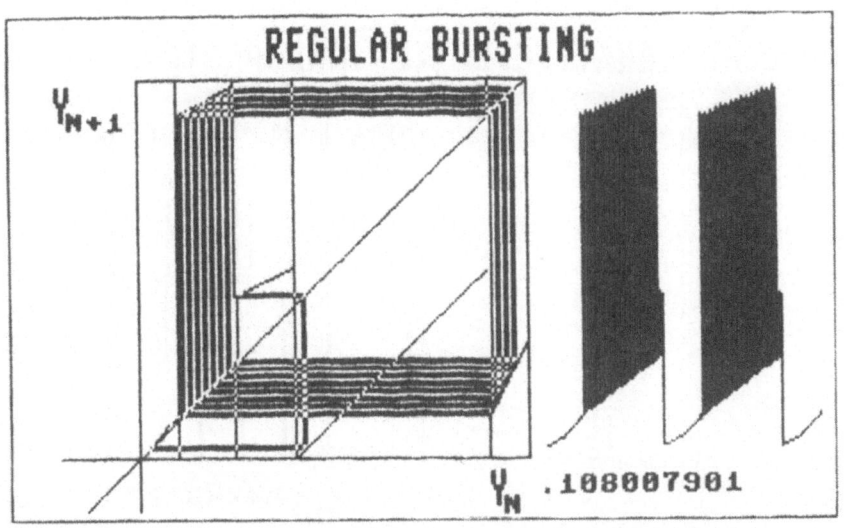

Fig.**2.**
Separatrices: 0,1; 0,25; 0,4; 0,9; 1,0;
Lines: L1: 1,1; 0,0; L2: 0,5; 0,85; L3: 0,5; 0,3; L4: 1,0;
- 0,4;L5: 2,0; -1,69; L6: 0,0; 0,0. Initial value: 0,03.

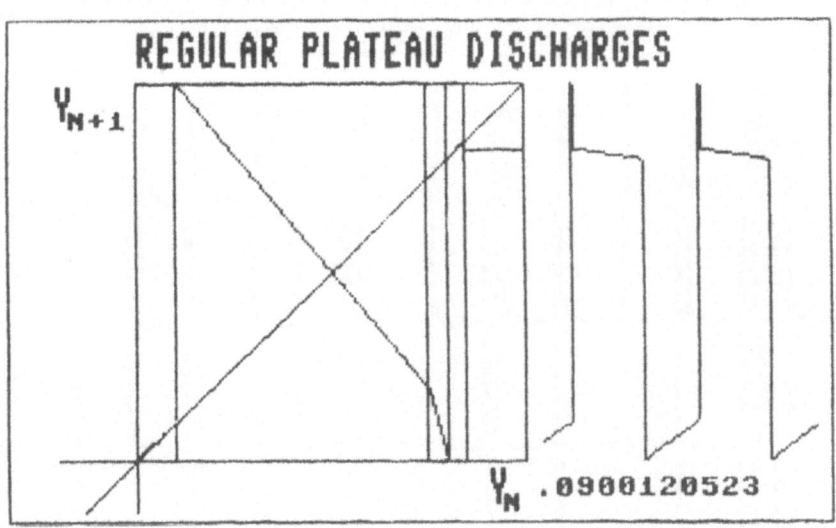

Fig.3.
Separatrices: 0,1; 0,75; 0,8; 0,85; 1,0;
Lines: L1: 1,0; 5E-03; L2: -1,23; 1,12; L3: -4,0; 3,2; L4:
1,0; -1E-03; L5: 1E-03; 0,825; L6: 0,0; 0,0;
Initial value: 0,05

433

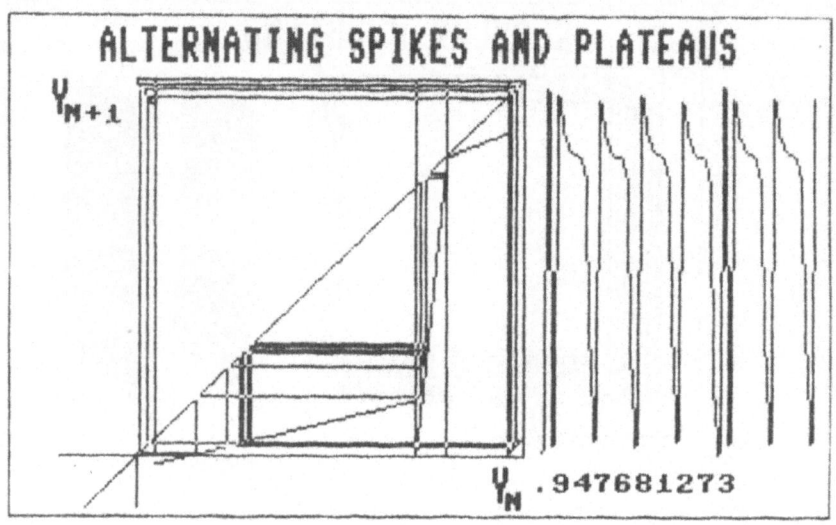

Fig.4.
Separatrices: 0,05; 0,72; 0,8; 0,96; 1,0.
Lines: L1: -1,2; 0,985; L2: 0,25; -0,0375; L3: 9,8125;
-7,055; L4: 0,375; 0,495; L5: 0,8; -0,755; L6: 0,0; 0,0;
Initial value: 0,01

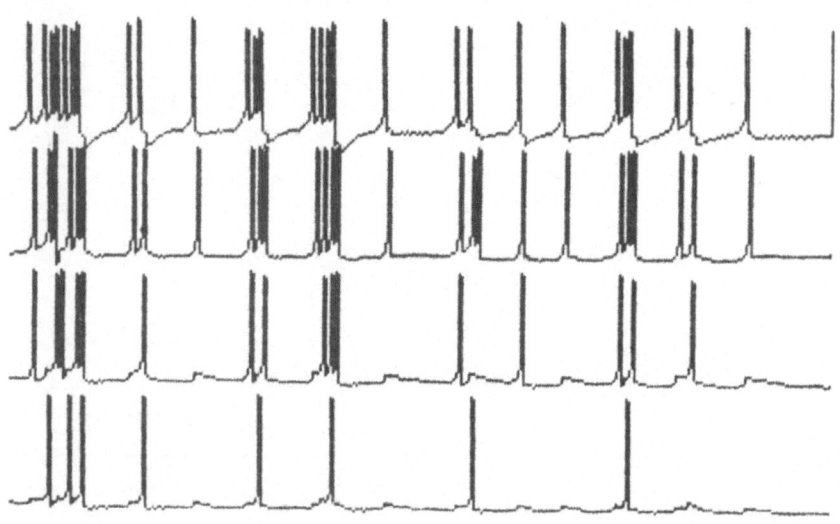

Fig.5.
Network consisting of four units. The 1st unit is a pacemaker
and excites the 2nd, 3rd and 4th unit, which, in turn, inhibit the 1st one.

434

THE GOORE GAME AND DAISYWORLD - SUBSTRATES FOR SELF-ORGANIZATION

Alex M. Andrew
Viable Systems, Splatt Mill
Chillaton, Lifton
Devon PL16 0JB
England

ABSTRACT. Much thinking under the heading of Cybernetics has been
concerned with self-organization, a rather ill-defined but nevertheless
important idea. A self-organizing system modifies itself during
interaction with an environment so as to come to display behaviour which
is, in some sense, advantageous or "expedient". It is clearly desirable
to study self-organization in simple situations, both because they are
easier to think about and because they may indicate how properties
conducive to complex self-organization were evolved in natural systems.
A number of alternative environments, or substrates for simple self-
organization, are compared here, namely neural nets, populations of
simple automata, and an environment with continuous variables termed
"Daisyworld" by Lovelock.

1. VIABLE SYSTEMS

Cybernetics is concerned with systems having the property of viability,
and in particular with living systems at all levels. The Oxford
Dictionary gives alternative definitions of "viable" as "capable of
living" and "able to maintain a separate existence". Neither of these
quite captures the meaning that is appropriate to Cybernetics and
Systems Theory; what is needed in this context is a hybrid of the two.
Since attention is not restricted to living systems, only the second of
the alternative definitions is strictly applicable, but if it is adopted
the term "viable systems" is intrinsically redundant. This follows from
the observation that, however a "system" is defined, one essential
property is that it survives for a sufficient time to be observed and
recognised as an entity with some kind of internal cohesion. Hence the
term "system" implies the possibility of separate existence, even when
not qualified as "viable".

In the Cybernetics context, however, the term "viable system" is
understood to indicate one that achieves longevity by some complex
dynamic interaction with its environment, in a manner characteristic of
living systems. This is in contrast to the relatively static means by
which it is achieved by, say, the solar system, which (at least in the

435

R. Trappl (ed.), Cybernetics and Systems '86, 435–442.
© *1986 by D. Reidel Publishing Company.*

time-scale in which it can readily be observed) retains its structure through sheer inertia, or by a crystal structure. The distinction cannot be a sharp one, but it seems to be useful nevertheless.

The idea of a "viable system", or a particular viewpoint for considering it, has frequently been indicated by the term "self-organizing system". This suggests that the interactions with the environment alter the structure of the system itself in some fundamental way. Precise definition of terms is extremely difficult, and whether or not a given system is seen as self-organizing depends on how it is described. As Glushkov [1] has pointed out, description of a system as self-organizing implies its decomposition into a "learning automaton" and an "operative automaton". There is no firm rule for making the decomposition, so the whole idea is essentially subjective. On the other hand, the same subjectivity applies to many terms in everyday use such as "learning", and the idea of a self-organizing system, though imprecise, is useful. These questions are treated at length in a work currently in preparation [2].

1.1. Substrates for Self-Organization

Forms of behaviour which merit recognition as self-organization have been studied in simple contexts. It is not usually appropriate to judge the performance of an experimental system by its survival, and the criterion of self-organization has to be something else. Tsetlin [3] simply says that his systems are of interest if they come to show behaviour that is "expedient". Where inputs to the system are described as rewards or punishments, "expedient" behaviour is that which evokes the former and avoids the latter.

Much of the discussion has been in the context of nets of neuron-like elements. This is not surprising since the self-organizing capability of the brain presents a formidable challenge to science. The substrate is then a network of neurons unable to perform some task (e.g. one of pattern recognition), and the self-organization is seen to be effective if it alters the network so that the task becomes possible. It is also interesting to consider simpler environments, and in particular to compare two approaches which assume very simple substrates. One of these is the study of networks of simple automata, associated with Tsetlin [3] and his group and the other is the "Daisyworld" discussed by Lovelock [4] in connection with his Gaia hypothesis [5]. The two approaches involve very different paradigms of thought, that of Tsetlin being based on classical automata with discrete states, while Lovelock's system uses continuous variables and is best described by differential equations.

Tsetlin describes a number of types of simple automata and considers the behaviour of large populations of them. His interest is in living systems and particularly the nervous system, in which there are often numerous units acting in parallel. The simplest type of automaton is the "automaton with linear tactic", described also by Glushkov [6]. In its simplest form this is termed an automaton type $L_{2n,2}$, and has 2n states, where n is an integer greater than zero, and output signals which are two-valued.

The automaton is such that a state-transition diagram may be drawn as a line of nodes representing states. Every transition is between adjacent nodes, except when the current state is one of the extreme ones, in which case the transition may be back to the same state. When the automaton gives an output, the binary digit transmitted depends on whether its current state is in the left or right half of the linear arrangement. It can accept two types of input producing a change of state; one of these is termed a reward and the other a punishment. A reward causes a state transition represented on the diagram by a move away from the middle of the line, unless the state representation is already at one end, in which case it does not change. A punishment causes a move in the opposite direction and may cause the state representation to cross over the mid-point, so that the next output signal is different from the last.

It is interesting to note that George [7, 8] has described "belief networks" of model neurons whose behaviour can be shown to be exactly that of the $L_{2n,2}$ automata. They are quite complex networks, and their introduction does not aid Tsetlin's aim of finding a conceptually-simple substrate for self-organization. However, it is interesting that there is this link with neural-net theory.

A very simple situation in which a population of $L_{2n,2}$ automata interacts with an environment is described by Tsetlin as the "Goore game", and it is further treated in an Appendix due to B.G. Pittel. The present author's experiments with computer simulation of this game have proved disappointing, as will be seen later. First the alternative approach represented by "Daisyworld" will be reviewed.

2. GAIA AND DAISYWORLD

In recent years Lovelock [5] has advanced his "new look at life on Earth", conveniently referred to as the "Gaia hypothesis", the name Gaia being one given to the Greek Earth Goddess. He rejects the common assumption that environmental conditions on the earth (temperature, oxygen concentration, ocean salinity, etc.) just happen to be compatible with life, and suggests instead that they are best seen as being regulated at levels conducive to the existence of living systems. The regulation is imposed by the totality of living organisms in the biosphere, acting like one giant animal, or Earth Goddess. It is not difficult to show that the environment is much influenced by biological activity - without it, for example, there would be almost no atmosphere at all. Lovelock suggests various channels through which biological activity might control environmental variables.

To show how such control might be established, Watson and Lovelock [4] have discussed a simple model of a planet on which two species of plants ("daisies") can grow. One of these is dark in colour ("black" for convenience) and the other light (referred to as "white"). The spread of black daisies causes the planet to become warmer, and white daisies reflect radiation and cause it to become cooler. The bare ground of the planet has an albedo intermediate between those of the two species.

It is assumed that the growth rate of daisies is a function of the temperature of the planet, such that a certain temperature is optimal. The function is the same for both species, and Lovelock has verified (private communication) that its exact form is not critical. It is assumed that the two species are sufficiently segregated in their growing areas that the local temperature for black daisies is higher than that for white ones; the model incorporates simple and plausible assumptions about the thermal conductivity of the planet.

Computer simulation shows that this simple model is effective in keeping the mean temperature of the planet close to the optimum for daisy-growth, over a wide range of levels of incident radiation on the planet. The system thus produces behaviour that is "expedient" in that it favours the survival of the biota of the planet. There is evidence that the earth's surface temperature has remained remarkably constant over a period when the sun's power has increased by at least 30 per cent [5].

The problems of control are of course more complex for a planet with atmosphere, and a simple mechanism such as that of Daisyworld can be described either as a control system or as a rather fortunate form for the solution of the differential equations. Nevertheless, something of the sort could well be the forerunner of more complex control networks.

3. THE GOORE GAME

Tsetlin [3] describes a simple game in which each of a group of individuals is invited to produce a binary signal - say by raising either one or two fingers. The individuals have no communication with each other. The proportion who signal in a particular way - say by raising one finger - is computed and used to determine a value p according to a single-peaked function such as that represented in Fig. 1. Each of the individuals is then either rewarded or punished, the choice between the two being made independently for each individual, such that p is the probability of reward and q = 1-p is the probability of punishment.

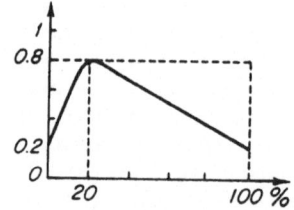

Figure 1

It is claimed that, if the individuals are automata of type $L_{2n,2}$ as described above, the behaviour of the population comes to be "expedient" in that it maximises the probability of rewards being

438

obtained. For the function shown in Fig. 1 this would happen when the proportion of individuals raising one finger is 20%.

The Goore game is not treated analytically for n > 1 (i.e. for automata having more than two states). Where the number of automata is N, the total number of states of the population of automata is $(2n)^N$, and Pittel indicates that the game can be represented as a Markov process having this number of states. In fact, a much smaller number of states is sufficient if the automata are not distinguished from one another, since all that is necessary is to know how many are in state 1, how many in state 2, and so on. The number of states of the population to be distinguished is then the ordered partition of 2n elements of N [9], and it can be shown that this is equal to the number of combinations of (N + 2n - 1) objects taken N at a time, or to:

$$(N + 2n - 1)! / [N! (2n - 1)!]$$

For N = 100 and n = 5 the number of states of the population, according to this formula, is approximately 3×10^{12}, whereas it is 10^{100} when the automata are distinguished from one another. However, even with this vast reduction in the number of states of the associated Markov process the Goore game does not seem to be amenable to rigorous analysis.

It is not difficult to analyse the behaviour of an $L_{2n,2}$ automaton in an environment in which the occurrence of the two types of input (reward and punishment) have respective probabilities p and q, and their occurrence is unrelated to the state of the automaton. If the two states nearest the middle of the linear transition diagram are considered to be merged into a single state (state 1, say), and other symmetrically-placed states are similarly combined to give n states in all, the resulting n-state automaton corresponds exactly to a simple random walk with reflecting barriers [10]. It follows that, in statistical equilibrium, the probability of the automaton being in state k is proportional to:

$$(p/q)^k$$

and this is easily normalised so that the sum of the probabilities is unity.

This result does not depend on the condition that the probabilities of the two types of input (reward and punishment) should be independent of the state of the automaton. Where such independence holds it is possible to deduce, from symmetry, that the corresponding states on the two sides of the transition diagram are equally probable, so the probability of each is half of the normalised value above, or:

$$(1 - (p/q))(p/q)^{k-1} / [2(1 - (p/q)^n)]$$

The condition of independence of input and output to the automaton holds when the population of automata is equally divided between those responding with one form of binary signal and those responding with the other. It can therefore be seen that this is a stable situation according to the above analysis, with the automaton states distributed in accordance with the last expression. It is not clear from the analysis here that this is the only stable state, but informal arguments suggest that it is and that the system will converge on it from any starting-point. It appears that the Goore game has asymptotic stability, but does not converge on the state of maximum "expediency".

3.1. Experimental Study of the Goore Game

The Goore game is easily simulated on a digital computer. For a complete simulation, the state of a large number of automata may be stored in an integer array. The language PASCAL allows the declaration of subrange types of variable, and for the particular system used the space required to store a value is only one byte (eight bits) if the value is of a subrange integer within the range 0 .. 255. This made it possible to represent 40000 automata in a program running on a 64K machine under CP/M. The running time was very long - for N = 40000 and n = 10 the time taken to simulate 100 steps of the game was about 70 minutes.

In this "exact" simulation the automata are distinguished from one another, and a more efficient one is possible in which the population is represented by an array of 2n integers, these being the numbers of automata currently occupying each of the 2n states. It is possible to represent a very large population of automata by storing 2n real numbers corresponding to the proportions of the automata occupying the states. The proportion of automata responding in a particular way is obtained by summing the proportions in the n lowest-numbered states (or, alternatively, the n highest-numbered). This proportion is converted to the probabilities p and q by reference to a function as represented in Fig. 1, and these are used to modify the entries in the matrix in an obvious way.

In some runs the function of Fig. 1 was approximated by two straight-line segments. In others a continuous function was used to derive the probability p as a function of the "score" or proportion s of automata responding in one of the two possible ways. The function was computed as follows and has its maximum at s = 0.8.

$$p = 0.6 + 0.8*x*(1-x)$$

where the asterisks indicate multiplication, and:

$$x = s^a \text{ where } a = \log 2/\log 5$$

Simulation runs were made with values of n from 1 to 10 and with both the piecewise-linear and continuous probability functions. The results for large populations of automata are easily summarised; there was always convergence on a state in which the two types of binary response were equiprobable. The distribution of the automata among the states was then in accordance with the above analysis based on random-walk theory.

The result was unaffected by the use of automata of type $D_{2n,2}$, which respond to punishment in exactly the same way as the $L_{2n,2}$ ones, but respond to a reward by moving immediately to an extreme state. It was also unaffected when the reward-or-punishment decision (at each step, with probability $\underline{p}$) was made collectively for all the automata, instead of independently for each one.

Tsetlin describes two further types of automata which have not yet been tested in this way. One of these, the "automaton with comparing tactic" due to Ponomarev, differs significantly from the others, as it could be said to introduce experimental variations in its response. These may enable the population of automata to move towards the optimum.

3.1.1. <u>Results</u> <u>for</u> <u>Small</u> <u>Populations</u>. It has been found that very small populations (10 members or less) of simple automata gave convergence on "expedient" behaviour. Tests were made with linear automata of type $L_{12,2}$ and $L_{20,2}$ (i.e. n=6 and n=10), and with corresponding D-automata, and with automata with comparing tactic having the same numbers of states. This is a recent finding which will be reported more fully in a paper to the workshop on self-organizing systems arranged by Dr. Gerhardt Dalenoort in conjunction with EMCSR 1986. The appearance of the effect only with small populations is contrary to the views of Tsetlin and his colleagues, and makes it implausible as a basis for self-organization as usually visualised.

4. CONCLUSIONS

Unless some crucial point has been missed, it appears that the Goore game, as played by sizeable populations of the simplest automata, does not produce behaviour more expedient than would be produced randomly. It is difficult to see how it could, since there is nothing to direct the population of automata towards behaviour eliciting the optimum response.

It must be emphasised that this conclusion applies only to the Goore game and not to the other situations discussed in Tsetlin's book. For example, in the Appendix in which he treats the Goore game, Pittel goes on to discuss a problem of assigning accommodation in a town so as to minimise the time spent by people in travelling between home and place of employment. Here the moves of the iterative procedure are steered in a favourable direction by letting their probability be determined as a function of the associated travelling times. Such steering allows an effective algorithm but also renders the situation less plausible as a model of spontaneous self-organization.

It is probably significant that Tsetlin and the distinguished group of workers around him were keen to find forms of automata more effective in their adaptive behaviour than the $L_{2n,2}$ type. That due to Ponomarev has been mentioned. Although they claim that a population of the simple automata is successful in the Goore game they have also looked for improvement in some respect, presumably in rate of convergence.

The failure to produce expedient behaviour in the Goore game situation suggests that, of the two simple substrates for self-organization postulated earlier, Lovelock's Daisyworld may be the more useful. Other simple substrates may be possible, so too much should not

441

be read into this finding. It is, however, consistent with previous discussions [11, 12] in which it has been argued that continuous-variable information processing is more primitive than concept-based processing, and that concept-based processing has evolved from the continuous kind.

REFERENCES

1. V.M. Glushkov, Introduction to Cybernetics, New York: Academic Press, 1966, p. 140 (Russian original 1964)

2. A.M. Andrew, Self Organizing Systems, Chichester: Wiley, in preparation.

3. M.L. Tsetlin, Automaton Theory and Modeling of Biological Systems, New York: Academic Press, 1973 (Russian original 1969)

4. A.J. Watson and J.E. Lovelock, 'Biological homeostasis of the global environment: the parable of Daisyworld', Tellus 35B, pp. 284-289, 1983

5. J.E. Lovelock, Gaia, a New Look at Life on Earth, Oxford: O.U.P., 1979

6. V.M. Glushkov, Introduction to Cybernetics, pp. 166-8

7. F.H. George, The Brain as a Computer, Oxford: Pergamon, 2nd ed. 1973, p. 128

8. F.H. George, Precision, Language and Logic, Oxford: Pergamon, 1976, p. 183

9. J.G. Kemeny, J.L. Snell and G.L. Thompson, Introduction to Finite Mathematics, London: Prentice-Hall, 1960, p. 105

10. D.R. Cox and H.D. Miller, The Theory of Stochastic Processes, London: Chapman and Hall, 1965, pp. 41-43

11. A.M. Andrew, 'The concept of a concept', in Applied Systems and Cybernetics, ed. G.E. Lasker, New York: Pergamon, 1981, vol. 2, pp. 607-612

12. A.M. Andrew, 'Logic and continuity - a systems dichotomy', in Cybernetics and Systems Research, ed. R. Trappl, North-Holland, 1982, pp. 19-22

NONPARAMETRIC METHODS FOR MEASUREMENT OF HEIGHT GROWTH

Danuta Rutkowska
Department of Electrical Engineering
Technical University of Częstochowa
Zawadzkiego 17
42-200 Częstochowa
Poland

ABSTRACT. Nonparametric methods, developed in mathematical statistics for the estimation of regression function, are applied for measuring height-growth. The general form of these procedures is presented and the various algorithms are treated as particular examples of this form.

1. INTRODUCTION

A wide variety of different methods has been proposed to analyse longitudinal growth data, such as height (see e.g. [4], [5], [6]). In former papers an a priori fixed functional model was assumed and a parametric approach was developed. Unfortunately, in many cases such models are chosen in an arbitrary manner and parametrization leads to erroneous conclusions. Recently, some nonparametric methods have been studied by statisticians to estimate a regression function [1]-[9]. An application of these methods does not assume a unique form of the growth process of all individuals. The aim of this paper is to adopt recent nonparametric methods for the measurement of height growth. Moreover, we shall generalize the available procedures and present a general algorithm.

2. FORMULATION OF THE PROBLEM

The following regression model is assumed:

$$h_j(t_i) = H_j(t_i) + e_j(t_i), \quad \begin{aligned} i &= 1, \ldots, n \\ j &= 1, \ldots, m \end{aligned} \qquad (1)$$

where:

$h_j(t_i)$ - height measured at age t_i of subject j

443

R. Trappl (ed.), Cybernetics and Systems '86, 443–446.
© *1986 by D. Reidel Publishing Company.*

$e_j(t_i)$ - random variation of height measurements

$H_j(t_i)$ - true height at age t_i

This model describes the measurement of human height growth when height $H_j(t_i)$ of individual j ($j=1,2,\ldots,m$) is measured at ages $t_1^j, t_2^j, \ldots, t_n$ (see [4]).

Based on the data $(t_1, h_j(t_1))$, $(t_2, h_j(t_2))$,..., $(t_n, h_j(t_n))$, $j=1,2,\ldots,m$, we wish to estimate the individual j-th growth curve $H_j(t)$.

3. NONPARAMETRIC METHODS

The estimate of $H_j(t)$ we present in the following general form:

$$\hat{H}_j(t) = \sum_{i=1}^{n} h_j(t_i)\, w_{ni}(t), \qquad (2)$$

where $w_{ni}(t)$ is a sequence of weights.
Let a positive integer n be given and let t_i be known without errors, satisfying the following order condition

$$t_1 < t_2 < \ldots < t_n.$$

Priestley and Chao [8] proposed the estimator (2) with

$$w_{ni}(t) = (t_i - t_{i-1})\, a_n^{-1}\, k\big[(t-t_i)/a_n\big], \qquad (3)$$

where $k(z)$ is a kernel function satisfying: (i) $k(z) \geqslant 0$ for all z, (ii) $k(z) = 0$ for $z \notin [-L,L]$ for some positive constant L, (iii) $\int_L k(z)\, dz = 1$, and where a_n is a sequence of positive constants converging to 0 as $n \to \infty$.

Georgiev [4] presented algorithm (2) with

$$w_{ni}(t) = (t_i - t_{i-1})\, r_n^{-1}\, k\big[(t-t_i)/r_n\big], \qquad (4)$$

where $r_n = r_n(t,k_n)$ - the Euclidean distance beetween t and k-th nearest observation of t among all t_i; k_n - a sequence of positive integers, which is determined by the experimenter.

Clark [2] proposed the estimator (2) with

444

$$w_{ni}(t) = \begin{cases} \int_{t_0}^{t_1} c_n(t,z)\, dz + \int_{t_1}^{t_2} c_n(t,z)\, \frac{t_2-z}{t_2-t_1}\, dz & \text{for } i=1 \\[4mm] \int_{t_{i-1}}^{t_i} c_n(t,z)\, \frac{z-t_{i-1}}{t_i-t_{i-1}}\, dz + \int_{t_i}^{t_{i+1}} c_n(t,z)\, \frac{t_{i+1}-z}{t_{i+1}-t_i}\, dz & \\[2mm] \qquad\qquad\qquad \text{for } i=2,3,\ldots,n-1 & \\[4mm] \int_{t_{n-1}}^{t_n} c_n(t,z)\, \frac{z-t_{n-1}}{t_n-t_{n-1}}\, dz & \text{for } i=n, \end{cases} \qquad (5)$$

where $c_n(t,z) = a_n^{-1}\, k\big[(t-z)/a_n\big]$.

Cheng and Lin [1] considered algorithm (2) with

$$w_{ni}(t) = \int_{t_{i-1}}^{t_i} a_n^{-1}\, k\big[(t-z)/a_n\big]\, dz \qquad (6)$$

and they showed that (3), (5) and (6) are asymptotically equivalent in various senses. Moreover, consistent results are established and rates of uniform convergence obtained.

Georgiev [7] studied the following algorithm

$$w_{ni}(t) = \int_{t_{i-1}}^{t_i} r_n^{-1}\, k\big[(t-z)/r_n\big]\, dz. \qquad (7)$$

It is obtained from (6), in a similar way as (4) from (3).

Rutkowski [9] proposed another nonparametric algorithm derived from expansion of the regression function $E\big[h_j|t\big] = H_j(t)$ in the orthogonal series. It has form (2) with

$$w_{ni}(t) = \int_{t_{i-1}}^{t_i} \left[\sum_{k=0}^{N(n)} g_k(t)\, g_k(u) \right] du, \qquad (8)$$

where $g_k(\cdot)$, $k = 0,1,2,\ldots$, is the orthogonal system of functions defined on $[0,1]$, such that $|g_k(t)| \leqslant c$ for all $t \in [0,1]$, where c is a positive constant; $N(n)$ is a sequence of integers such that $N^2(n)/n \xrightarrow{n} 0$, $N(n) \xrightarrow{n} \infty$. The last conditions guarantee convergence in the mean square error.

4. CONCLUSIONS

It should be noted that the presented algorithms are easily computed. Procedures (6) and (7) become very simple for uniform kernels of type

$$k(t) = \begin{cases} 1 \text{ for } |t| \leqslant 1 \\ 0 \text{ otherwise.} \end{cases}$$

The algorithm (8) can be expressed in simpler forms using Dirichlet's or Fejer's kernels of Fourier orthogonal expansions. The bandwith sequence a_n in procedures (3), (5) and (6) does not depend on the data contrary to procedures (4) and (7). It would be interesting to study procedures (8) with sequence $N(n)$ depending on the data $(t_1, h_j(t_1))$, $(t_2, h_j(t_2)), \ldots, (t_n, h_j(t_n))$, $j=1,2,\ldots,m$. Finally, we note that nonparametric algorithms can also be applied for estimation of velocity and acceleration of longitudinal growth curves.

REFERENCES

[1] Cheng, K.F. and Lin, P.E. (1981). 'Nonparametric estimation of regression function', Zeit. Wahrscheinlichkeitsth., 57, 223-233.
[2] Clark, R.M. (1977). 'Nonparametric estimation of a smooth regression function', J.R. Statist. Soc., B, 39, 107-113.
[3] Gasser, T. and Muller, H.G. (1979). 'Kernel estimation of regression functions, Smoothing Techniques for Curve Estimation', 23-68, Lecture Notes in Math. 757, Springer-Verlag.
[4] Gasser, T., Kohler, W. Muller, H.G., Kneip, A., Largo,R., Molinari, L., and Prader, A. (1984). 'Velocity and acceleration of height growth using kernel estimation', Annals of Human Biology, 11, 397-411.
[5] Gasser, T., Muller, H.G., Kohler, W., Molinari, L., and Prader, A. (1984). 'Nonparametric regression analysis of growth curves', Annals of Statistics, 12, 210-229.
[6] Georgiev, A.A. (1984). 'Nonparametric mathematical model for individual human growth curve', Cybern. Syst. Research 2, R. Trappl (ed.), Elsevier Science Publishers B.V. (North Holland), 277-279.
[7] Georgiev, A.A. (1984). 'A nonparametric algorithm for identification of linear dynamic SISO systems of unknown order', Syst. Contr. Letters 4. 273-280,
[8] Priestley, M.B. and Chao, M.T. (1972). 'Nonparametric function fitting', J.R. Statist. Soc., B, 43, 385-392.
[9] Rutkowski, L. (1982). 'On system identification by nonparametric function fitting', IEEE Trans. Autom. Control, AC-27, 225-227.

Cybernetics of Socio-Economic Systems

Chairpersons: K.Balkus (U.S.A.)
               O.Ladanyi (Austria)

OPTIMAL STABILIZING AND DESTABILIZING "STABILIZATION" POLICIES

Reinhard Neck
Institut für Volkswirtschaftstheorie und -politik
University of Economics, Vienna
Augasse 2 - 6
A-1090 Vienna, Austria

ABSTRACT. We consider a dynamic Phillips curve model of the trade-off
between unemployment and inflation subject to exogenous regular
fluctuations of aggregate demand, which can be influenced by demand
management policies. Optimal "stabilization" policies both for an
"altruistic" and an "egoistic" government are derived by optimal
control methods. We show that the optimal policy for an infinite time
horizon eliminates the business cycle and thus stabilizes the economic
system. If the government is myopic, on the other hand, the optimal
policy may generate a political business cycle and thereby destabilize
the entire system.

1. INTRODUCTION

One of the main controversies in the theory and practice of economic
policy centers around the question whether political actions of
economic policy makers contribute to the stabilization of the economic
system. On the level of macroeconomic policy-making, by "stabilization"
one usually refers to the reduction or elimination of fluctuations
arising out of the business cycle and manifesting themselves in such
key variables as the rates of inflation, of unemployment, and of real
income growth. The view of economic policy stabilizing economic
fluctuations is held in particular by Keynesian economists; they
maintain that responsive governments actually pursue stabilization
goals, acting like a "benevolent dictator" in the best interest of the
society. This position has been criticized both in by Monetarist
economists, who doubt governments' ability of pursuing successful
stabilization policies, and by public choice theorists, who don't
believe in governments' willingness to act according to the public
interest. Instead, public choice sees politicians as selfish and short-
sighted, being primarily concerned about their re-election into office
when they are responsible for government measures. Therefore, according
to this view, stabilization of economic fluctuations is not of primary
importance for the government; instead it might even destabilize the
economy by introducing "political" business cycles.

R. Trappl (ed.), Cybernetics and Systems '86, 449–456.

Clearly this debate, which is far from being settled today, involves many diverse aspects, such as differing (sometimes hidden) value judgements and differing views about the structure and the working of both the economic and the political system. However, whereas the arguments of Monetarists have been analysed within the context of fairly sophisticated theoretical models in depth, this is much less true of the public choice viewpoint. Because the latter is essentially concerned with the questions of the relative stability of the political and the economic system and the interactions between them, concepts and notions of systems theory and related techniques of cybernetics and control theory might be useful for an analysis of these issues. In the present paper we use optimal control theory to investigate the problem of "economic" versus "political" business cycles. We start from a very simple economic model of the trade-off between unemployment and inflation, which is subject to exogenous regular fluctuations of aggregate demand. The particular model used has a Keynesian structure, thus the government is able to affect macroeconomic variables in a systematic way. We examine both the optimal policies of an "altruistic" government aiming at stabilizing the economic system, and of an "egoistic" government being interested in its record with the electorate at the next election. It will be shown that the "economic" fluctuations are eliminated in both cases; the "egoistic" government, however, introduces new, purely "political" fluctuations into the system. Thus we are generalizing Nordhaus' (1975) analysis of the political business cycle, which does not consider economic cycles; "stabilization" policies can have both stabilizing and destabilizing effects in our model.

2. THE MODEL

We consider the same basic model of the trade-off between unemployment and inflation as does Nordhaus, retaining also his linear specification for the sake of analytical convenience, namely an expectations-augmented Phillips curve, where expectations are formed according to an adaptive adjustment to actual inflation, formulated in continuous time. This model is extended in two ways: First, instead of regarding the rate of unemployment as a policy instrument, we introduce an instrument variable $b(t)$ which directly affects aggregate excess demand in the markets for goods and labor, denoted by $h(t)$, which in turn influences the rate of inflation according to

$$p(t) = \alpha h(t) + \lambda p^e(t), \quad \alpha > 0, \ 0 < \lambda \leq 1 \text{ const.}, \tag{1}$$

and the rate of unemployment according to

$$u(t) = \varepsilon_0 - \varepsilon_1 h(t) \quad \text{for } u(t) > 0, \ \varepsilon_0, \ \varepsilon_1 > 0 \text{ const.}, \tag{2}$$

where $p(t)$ denotes the actual, $p^e(t)$ the expected rate of inflation, and $u(t)$ the rate of unemployment. The variable $b(t)$, which is regarded as the control variable in the government's decision problem, may be interpreted as a fiscal policy instrument, such as the budget deficit or its growth rate (cf. Breuss 1980), or as a monetary policy instrument, e.g. the (growth rate of) real money supply (cf. Ramser 1977), or a combination of both. The expected rate of inflation is given by

$$\dot{p}^e(t) = \gamma[p(t) - p^e(t)], \quad \gamma > 0 \tag{3}$$

with initial condition for (present) period $0 : p^e(0) = p_0^e > 0$, given.

The second way in which we depart from Nordhaus' model is the explicit introduction of economic business cycles, that is, of regular fluctuations of the economic variables. In particular, we assume that there are oscillations of aggregate excess demand around the general equilibrium in the goods and labor markets, which is given by $h(t) = 0$. This "economic" component of $h(t)$ is assumed to be given by $A.\cos(\theta t - \varepsilon) + G,$ where A is the amplitude and $2\pi/\theta$ the period of the oscillation, $A, \theta, \varepsilon, G$ const. We do not provide an economic explanation of these kinds of business cycles but assume them to be inherent in the unregulated economic system. Dynamic models of the goods market provide some justification of such periodic movements, such as multiplier-accelerator models, although it is well known that they can be derived from linear ordinary differential equations models only under specific assumptions on the parameters. Non-linear differential equations, on the other hand, can give rise to limit cycles without such restrictions on the parameters (see e.g. Laven 1982); our model might be interpreted as an approximation to the time path of such a business cycle model. Combining both the "economic" and the "political" component of aggregate excess demand, we have

$$h(t) = \delta b(t) + A \cos(\theta t - \varepsilon) + G, \tag{4}$$

where $\delta > 0$ const. is the impact multiplier of the policy instrument $b(t)$ on $h(t)$. Long-run changes shall be excluded from our analysis, which is concerned only with short-run business cycles. In order to make sense of the linear formulation of the system, we have to restrict the values of $u(t)$ to the positive. For the optimization problem, we also impose a non-negativity condition upon $p(t)$.

Our model of the economic system is a dynamic model with one control variable; by substitution, it can be reduced to a first-order differential equation, which for $p^e(t)$ as state variable gives

$$\dot{p}^e(t) = -\gamma(1-\lambda) p^e(t) + \alpha\gamma\delta b(t) + \alpha\gamma A \cos(\theta t - \varepsilon) + \alpha\gamma G, \quad p^e(0) = p_0^e, \tag{5}$$

and the politically relevant (target) variables are

$$u(t) = -\varepsilon_1\delta b(t) - \varepsilon_1 A \cos(\theta t - \varepsilon) + \varepsilon_0 - \varepsilon_1 G, \tag{6}$$
$$p(t) = \lambda p^e(t) + \alpha\delta b(t) + \alpha A \cos(\theta t - \varepsilon), \tag{7}$$

which shows the cyclical components of both the rates of unemployment and of inflation. As in Nordhaus (1975), we assume that the political

451

preferences of the society under consideration can be expressed by an objective function including both u(t) and p(t), which may be interpreted as some kind of "social welfare function" or simply as the objective function of the majority of the electorate. Specifically, assuming the same functional specification as Nordhaus, the government's objective is to minimize

$$g(u(t), p(t)) = u^2(t) + \beta p(t), \quad \beta > 0 \text{ const.}, \tag{8}$$

for $p(t) \geqq 0$ at each relevant point of time t. (5) constitutes the dynamic constraint the government's policy has to observe. In the following we will consider two different optimization problems, both for the same instantaneous objective function (8) and the same system (5), but with different dynamic preferences of the government.

3. OPTIMAL STABILIZING "STABILIZATION" POLICY

First we consider a government behaving like a "benevolent dictator" in the Keynesian view of stabilization policy. The government has an infinite time horizon, but uses a positive rate r of discounting the future, which seems plausible also for the electorate and hence also for the most impartial government. Hence its problem is to maximize, over all admissible trajectories b(t),

$$\int_0^\infty \exp(-rt)[-g(u(t), p(t))]dt \tag{9}$$

subject to the constraint (5). This is a scalar infinite horizon optimal control problem, which can be solved by Pontryagin's maximum principle (see, e.g., Sethi and Thompson 1981). The current-value Hamiltonian is given by

$$
\begin{aligned}
H\,(p^e(t), b(t), \psi(t),t) =\ &- \beta\lambda p^e(t) - \varepsilon_1^2\delta^2 b^2(t) + \\
&+ [2\varepsilon_0\varepsilon_1 - 2\varepsilon_1^2\delta G - \alpha\beta\delta - 2\varepsilon_1^2\delta A \cos(\theta t-\varepsilon)]b(t) - \\
&- \varepsilon_1^2 A^2 \cos^2(\theta t-\varepsilon) + [2\varepsilon_0\varepsilon_1 - 2\varepsilon_1^2 G - \alpha\beta]A \cos(\theta t-\varepsilon) - \\
&- (\varepsilon_0 - \varepsilon_1 G)^2 - \alpha\beta G - \gamma(1-\lambda)\psi(t)p^e(t) + \alpha\gamma\psi(t)b(t) + \\
&+ \alpha\gamma A \cos(\theta t-\varepsilon)\psi(t) + \alpha\gamma G\psi(t),
\end{aligned}
\tag{10}
$$

where $\psi(t)$ is the current-value adjoint (costate) variable determined by

$$\psi\,(t) = r\psi(t) - \frac{\partial H}{\partial p}e(p^e(t),\ b(t),\psi(t),t) = [r +$$
$$+ (1-\lambda)]\psi(t) + \beta\lambda. \tag{11}$$

Further necessary conditions are the state equation (5) and the requirement that the Hamiltonian be maximized over all admissible b(t) as each instant of time t. Assuming an interior maximum (which will be checked later on), the latter condition gives for the optimal control:

$$b(t) = \left(\frac{1}{2\varepsilon_1^2\delta^2}\right)[\alpha\gamma\delta\psi(t) - 2\varepsilon_1^2\delta A \cos(\theta t - \varepsilon) +$$

$$+ 2\varepsilon_0\varepsilon_1\delta - 2\varepsilon_1^2\delta G - \alpha\beta\delta]. \tag{12}$$

Because of the exogenous oscillations our problem is not an autonomous one, so we cannot define the usual optimal long-run stationary equilibrium; however, as we shall see, in the optimal state trajectory the fluctuations disappear. We determine a candidate for the optimal state trajectory from the necessary conditions and show afterwards that it fulfills sufficient conditions for infinite horizon problems and hence is the optimum indeed.

First we determine the general solution of the linear costate equation (11), giving

$$\psi(t) = \exp\{[r+\gamma(1-\lambda)](t-t_0)\}.\{\psi(t_0) + \frac{\beta\lambda}{[r+\gamma(1-\lambda)]}\} - \frac{\beta\lambda}{[r+\gamma(1-\lambda)]} \tag{13}$$

for $t \geq t_0$, t_0 an arbitrary point of time. Since we have an infinite time horizon, the sufficient transversality condition

$$\lim_{t\to\infty} \exp(-rt)\ \psi(t) = 0 \tag{14}$$

can be used instead of a terminal condition, implying

$$\exp\{-[r+\gamma(1-\lambda)]t_0\}.\{\psi(t_0) + \frac{\beta\lambda}{[r+\gamma(1-\lambda)]}\} \cdot \lim_{t\to\infty} \exp\ [\gamma(1-\lambda)t] -$$
$$- \frac{\beta\lambda}{[r+\gamma(1-\lambda)]} \cdot \lim_{t\to\infty} \exp(-rt) = 0. \tag{15}$$

The first term of (15) is divergent for $t\to\infty$ unless $\psi(t_0) = -\beta\lambda/[r+\gamma(1-\lambda)]$; since t_0 is arbitrary, we must have:

$$\psi(t) = - \frac{\beta\lambda}{[r+\gamma(1-\lambda)]} \quad \text{for all } t \geq 0. \tag{16}$$

By substituting for the constant costate variable into (12) we get:

$$b(t) = (\frac{1}{\delta}) \cdot \{(\frac{\varepsilon_0}{\varepsilon_1}) - (\frac{\alpha\beta}{2\varepsilon_1^2}) \frac{(r+\gamma)}{[r+\gamma(1-\lambda)]} - A \cos(\theta t-\varepsilon) - G\}. \tag{17}$$

This shows that the optimal control trajectory follows a cyclical movement, designed in amplitude and phase exactly such as to iron out the fluctuations in $h(t)$. Solving the state equation (5) with (17) substituted for $b(t)$ gives:

$$p^e(t) = \exp[-\gamma(1-\lambda)t] \cdot \{p_0^e - (\frac{\alpha}{1-\lambda}) \cdot [(\frac{\varepsilon_0}{\varepsilon_1}) - (\frac{\alpha\beta}{2\varepsilon_1^2}) -$$
$$- \frac{(r+\gamma)}{[r+\gamma(1-\lambda)]}]\} + (\frac{\alpha}{1-\lambda}) \cdot \{(\frac{\varepsilon_0}{\varepsilon_1}) - (\frac{\alpha\beta}{2\varepsilon_1^2}) \cdot \frac{(r+\gamma)}{[r+\gamma(1-\lambda)]}\}. \tag{18}$$

The usual sufficient concavity condition for the Hamiltonian is obviously fulfilled for our model. Applying the sufficient condition for infinite horizon optimal control problems due to Michel (1982), which demands that the optimal value of the standard Hamiltonian converges to zero for $t\to\infty$, shows that we have in fact found the optimal solution for our problem. (18) reveals that the "economic" fluctuations in $p^e(t)$ vanish, too, due to the countercyclical policies of the "benevolent" dictator.

The optimal trajectories for the aggregate excess demand, the rate of unemployment, and the rate of inflation are given by:

$$h(t) = \bar{h} = (\frac{\varepsilon_0}{\varepsilon_1}) - (\frac{\alpha\beta}{2\varepsilon_1^2}) \frac{(r+\gamma)}{[r+\gamma(1-\lambda)]}, \tag{19}$$

$$u(t) = \bar{u} = (\frac{\alpha\beta}{2\varepsilon_1}) \frac{(r+\gamma)}{[r+\gamma(1-\lambda)]}, \tag{20}$$

$$p(t) = \{p_0^e - (\frac{\alpha}{1-\lambda}) \cdot [(\frac{\varepsilon_0}{\varepsilon_1}) - (\frac{\alpha\beta}{2\varepsilon_1^2}) \frac{(r+\gamma)}{[r+\gamma(1-\lambda)]}]\} \cdot$$
$$\cdot \lambda \exp[-\gamma(1-\lambda)t] + (\frac{\alpha}{1-\lambda}) \cdot \{(\frac{\varepsilon_0}{\varepsilon_1}) - (\frac{\alpha\beta}{2\varepsilon_1^2}) \frac{(r+\gamma)}{[r+\gamma(1-\lambda)]}\}. \tag{21}$$

This shows that the optimal values of the aggregate excess demand and the rate of unemployment are constant. The optimal trajectory of the rate of inflation converges towards a stationary state for $t\to\infty$:

$$\lim_{t\to\infty} p(t) = \lim_{t\to\infty} p^e(t) = (\frac{\alpha}{1-\lambda}) \bar{h}. \tag{22}$$

$p(t)$ converges more slowly towards its stationary state than $p^e(t)$, showing the lagged adaptation of inflationary expectations to actual inflation. The stationary aggregate excess demand will in general be non-zero, leading to continuous inflation or deflation. The behavior of $p(t)$ and $p^e(t)$ depends upon the relation of initial inflationary expectations to the stationary value of the rate of inflation; in any case, the movements of $p^e(t)$ and $p(t)$ will be monotonical. Checking whether $u(t)$ and $p(t)$ are really non-negative, as has been assumed in formulating the government's problem, we note that $u(t) = \bar{u}>0$ can be seen immediately from (20). Furthermore, $\bar{h}\geqq0$ is a sufficient condition for $p(t)\geqq0$ for all t; hence our analysis is applicable only for the case of long run inflation or constant price level, which is clearly what we (and Nordhaus) had in mind when formulating our objective function.

4. OPTIMAL DESTABILIZING "STABILIZATION" POLICY

As an alternative, we consider also an optimization problem for a government which is not a "benevolent dictator", but is instead inter-ested in improving its chances at the next election, assumed to take place at a fixed known point of time T, $0 < T < \infty$. With Nordhaus, we assume that voters are myopic in that their memory of the government's performance, expressed in the instantaneous and past values of the objective function, is declining. In addition, they don't look into the future when electing the new government. The idea of a declining memory is expressed by a "backward discounting" factor $\rho\geqq0$ applied to the instantaneous objective function for the election period [0,T]. The best thing a government can do under these circumstances is to look only at the time period until the next elections take place; that is, it has a finite time horizon T for its dynamic optimization problem.

Generalizations of this framework to a multi-election period analysis have shown the persistence of Nordhaus' central result, the existence of a political business cycle (Kirchgässner 1983); we extend his analysis to a model where "economic" business cycles are already present. The problem of the "selfish" government is now to maximize, over all admissible trajectories $b(t)$,

$$\int_0^T \exp(\rho t)\, [-g(u(t), p(t))]\, dt \tag{23}$$

subject to the constraint (5). The current-value Hamiltonian now is

$$H(p^e(t), b(t), \phi(t), t) = -g[u(t), p(t)] + \phi(t)\, \dot{p}^e(t), \tag{24}$$

where $\phi(t)$ is the current value costate variable given by

$$\dot{\phi}(t) = [\gamma(1-\lambda) + \rho]\phi(t) + \beta\lambda \tag{25}$$

with terminal condition $\phi(T) = 0$, because the government does not look beyond T. Maximizing the Hamiltonian over all feasible $b(t)$ at each t and assuming again an interior maximum we get for the optimal control variable:

$$b(t) = (\frac{\alpha\gamma}{2\epsilon_1^2\delta})\phi(t) + (\frac{1}{\delta})\cdot[(\frac{\epsilon_0}{\epsilon_1}) - G - (\frac{\alpha\beta}{2\epsilon_1^2}) - A\cos(\theta t - \epsilon)]. \tag{26}$$

Because of the linear-quadratic nature of our problem and of the finite time horizon transversality condition, there are no additional problems for verifying the sufficiency of the derived candidate for the optimum solution.

Solving the costate equation and substituting into (26) gives:

$$b(t) = \frac{\alpha\beta\gamma\lambda}{2\epsilon_1^2\delta[\gamma(1-\lambda)-\rho]} \cdot \exp\{-[\gamma(1-\lambda)-\rho](T-t)\} +$$
$$+ (\frac{1}{\delta})\cdot\{(\frac{\epsilon_0}{\epsilon_1}) - (\frac{\alpha\beta}{2\epsilon_1^2})\cdot\frac{(\gamma-\rho)}{[\gamma(1-\lambda)-\rho]} - A\cos(\theta t - \epsilon) - G\}. \tag{27}$$

Thus here, too, we have a cyclical movement of the policy instrument. However, provided $\gamma(1-\lambda)-\rho>0$, the first term in the right-hand side of (27) now is positive, generating increasing aggregate excess demand. The optimal movements of $u(t)$ and $p(t)$ for the period $[0,T]$ are given by:

$$u(t) = -\frac{\alpha\beta\gamma\lambda}{2\epsilon_1[\gamma(1-\lambda)-\rho]}\cdot\exp\{-[\gamma(1-\lambda)-\rho](T-t)\} +$$
$$+ (\frac{\alpha\beta}{2\epsilon_1})\frac{(\gamma-\rho)}{[\gamma(1-\lambda)-\rho]}, \tag{28}$$

$$p(t) = \lambda\{p_0^e - (\frac{\alpha}{1-\lambda})[(\frac{\epsilon_0}{\epsilon_1}) - (\frac{\alpha\beta}{2\epsilon_1^2})\frac{(\gamma-\rho)}{[\gamma(1-\lambda)-\rho]}] -$$
$$- \frac{\alpha^2\beta\gamma^2\lambda\exp\{-[\gamma(1-\lambda)-\rho]T\}}{2\epsilon_1^2[\gamma(1-\lambda)-\rho][2\gamma(1-\lambda)-\rho]}\}\exp[-\gamma(1-\lambda)t] + \exp\{-(\gamma-\gamma\lambda-\rho)(T-t)\}.$$
$$\cdot \frac{\alpha^2\beta\gamma\lambda[\gamma(2-\lambda)-\rho]}{2\epsilon_1^2[\gamma(1-\lambda)-\rho][2\gamma(1-\lambda)-\rho]} + (\frac{\alpha}{1-\lambda})\{(\frac{\epsilon_0}{\epsilon_1})-(\frac{\alpha\beta}{2\epsilon_1^2})\frac{(\gamma-\rho)}{[\gamma(1-\lambda)-\rho]}\}. \tag{29}$$

As in the infinite horizon case the "economic" cycles are eliminated here; on the other hand, the behavior of the policy instrument intro-

duces a new element of variability, which leads to a monotonically
decreasing behavior of the rate of unemployment over the election
period from $u(0)$ to its minimum $u(T) = \alpha\beta/2\varepsilon_1$. Since $u(T)>0$, we must
have $u(t)>0$ for all $t\varepsilon[0,T]$ as required. The behavior of $p(t)$ and $p^e(t)$
is less easily characterized, and there exist more possibilities than
in Nordhaus' model; a monotonic movement of these variables cannot
generally be established. However, the general pattern of the political
business cycle discovered by Nordhaus does occur here, too: The
"selfish" government will raise unemployment by cutting down $b(t)$
immediately after the election in order to reduce inflationary expectations. During the election period it will increase its policy instrument gradually in order to reduce the unemployment rate down to its
minimum, which is hit exactly at the election date. Afterwards the same
pattern starts again. One could derive the structure of these cycles in
the same way as Kirchgässner (1983) does for the Nordhaus model for our
model, too, since we have shown that the behavior of the unemployment
rate during the election period is the same in both models. Thus,
whereas an "altruistic" government will actually "stabilize" the
economic system, the "egoistic" (short-sighted) government will perform
both a "stabilizing" and a "destabilizing" task.

5. CONCLUDING REMARK

In this paper only a first attempt has been made to study the possibilities for stabilizing and destabilizing macroeconomic policies. More
sophisticated models should be used to introduce modifications of our
results. But we think to have shown that a system-theoretic and optimal
control analysis of the impact of stabilization policies on the economy
can provide valuable insights into such relevant questions as the
possibility and desirability of macroeconomic intervention.

REFERENCES

F.Breuss (1980), 'The Political Business Cycle: An Extension of Nord-
haus's Model'. Empirica 1980/2, 223-259.
G.Kirchgässner (1983), 'The Political Business Cycle if the Government
is not Myopic'. Mathematical Social Sciences 4, 243-260.
G.Laven (1982), 'Persistierende Zyklen in der dynamischen Wirtschafts-
theorie: Ein Beispiel zum Satz von Poincaré und Bendixson'. Jahrbuch
für Sozialwissenschaft 33, 320-332.
P.Michel (1982), 'On the Transversality Condition in Infinite Horizon
Optimal Problems'. Econometrica 50, 975-985.
W.D.Nordhaus (1975), 'The Political Business Cycle'. Review of
Economic Studies 42, 169-190.
H.J.Ramser (1977), 'Anmerkungen zur Theorie politischer Konjunktur-
zyklen'. Diskussionsbeiträge des Fachbereichs Wirtschaftswissenschaf-
ten der Universität Konstanz, Nr. 105.
S.P.Sethi, G.L.Thompson (1981), Optimal Control Theory. Applications
to Management Science. Boston et al.

MACROSYSTEM OF THE SOCIETAL SELF-ORGANIZATION

Kozmas Balkus
Florida State University
Tallahassee, FL   32306
U.S.A.

ABSTRACT. The macrosystem of the societal self-organization was developed under the hypothesis that the societal organization surfaces as a result of the interface between two forces of nature; on the one side is the human creativity that strives to secure human needs and to enrich individual's existence; on the other side is the entropy that tends to degrade all things that are created and to inflict disorder where order exists. By means of holistic concepts representing the various aspects of the societal organization first the study depicts the society's organizational design for encountering entropy. The second part of the model introduces the operational processes through which the organizational design is sustained and altered. The concluding discussion of equilibration, progress, and development relates the study to societal development.

1.   INTRODUCTION

Human societies are organized in a large number of ways ranging from communities of primitive tribes to developed nations. Diverse artifacts, organization styles, forms, and values constitute a complexity that masks the order and purposes of the organization as a whole. Without comprehending the "big picture", however, societal problem solutions can turn out to be erratic and ineffective.

In this study, a society is taken to consist of a complex structure of autonomies each possessing the authority for exercising self-organizatio and management. As an aggregate, such autonomous activities constitute the over-all societal self-organization process. Order and purposes of this process can be detected by placing it into a systems framework.

Self-organization, as an area of investigation, received attention from cybernetics and systems research in the early 1960s. Two inter-disciplinary conferences on this subject were sponsored by the Information Systems Branch, U.S. Office of Naval Research in 1960 and 1962. In the latter, W.Ross Ashby presented his classical paper "Principles of the Self-Organizing Systems" in which he envisioned the constraint, that acts upon a continuous chain of events, to be the vehicle of

R. Trappl (ed.), Cybernetics and Systems '86, 457–464.

self-organization.[1] In subsequent applications the self-organization
was interpreted as "self-regulation" or "self-direction."[2] Recent
book on General Systems thinking replaces the self-organization paradigm
with selected topics on development.[3]

Contrary to this trend, Erich Jantsch was trying to revive the
self-organization as an area of systems investigation. In his book
Design for Evolution, Jantsch links self-organization with the phenomenon
of a human system.[4] In later studies he associated the self-organization
dynamics with "dissipative structures" consisting of closed circles
of transformatory or catalytic processes (hypercycles) in which one
or more of the participants act as cross-catalysts and provide a "driving
force".[5] By this the circle theory also identifies the role for autonomy's
leadership. In their hypercycles, autonomies constitute the societal
space-time structures. Two or more interacting structures co-evolve
through a "learning process" (ultracycle) which increases the complexity
of systems components and enhences their stability. As explained
by Jantsch, social self-organizing systems are: open in their relations
with the environment; internally far from equilibrium; organized in
hypercycles; autopoietic in their function; arranged in dissipative
space-time structures; evolving through an indefinite sequence of
structures; and co-evolving with other systems in ultracycles.[6] According
to Jantsch, the function of autopoiesis occupies a special place.
It is geared to self-renewal. An autopoietic system refers to itself
and it is therefore called self-referential. In contrast, an allopoietic
system, such as a machine, refers to a function given from outside.[7]

The self-organization processes, however, are shaped by the larger
framework within which they operate. The framework is the main concern
of the study.

2.   STUDY DESIGN

In his book General Systems Thinking, Bowler identifies five central
macrosystems modelling problems[8]:

1.   "real" aspects of civilizations as opposed to intellectual
     inventions

2.   differences between primitive societies and advanced
     civilizations

3.   civilization boundaries

+.   regularity, necessity and sequence of development steps

5.   development patterns of societal systems

Bowler dealt with these problems by drawing upon the works[9] of Melko,
Quigley, Redfield, and Coulburn. His macrosystem utilizes a few General
Systems concepts; but primarily it deals with processes related to
individual's experiences as well as to sociological notions regarding the
behavior of human aggregates.

As the term macro implies, the macrosystem is to interrelate
components of the highest aggregation level. Thus far in General
Systems research no standards have been set as to how the highest
aggregates are to be identified and how one can be sure that a given
macrosystem addresses the highest level of aggregation. Although
Bower did not bring up this matter, the number one of his modelling
problems revives one of the perennial issues of philosophy, namely,
the ways of seeing. With our eyes we perceive shapes, colors, and
other particulars of observed phenomena. In contrast to the particularistic seeing, we also can visualize things and events in terms of
"universals" through the Eye of the Mind - alternatively known as
thought, intellect, insight, and "gut feeling".[10] Human mind also
enables the individual to think in "holistic" terms. Each holistic
concept or a metaphore represents one aspect of a complex system.
A set of holistic concepts may be selected for representing a complex
system as a macrosystem from a desired point of view. Social sciences
terminology is pervaded with universals and holistic representations.
Terms such as development, politics, political processes, economy,
ideology and religion represent aspects of a macrosystem beyond the
particular realm. Discoursing about topics involving complex systems
requires operating with universals, metaphores and holistic concepts.

Sciences concepts and paradigms can become universals and holistic
representations if they are adopted by other fields, such as social
sciences. Entropy was first detected in thermodynamics and defined
by measurable quantities. In its broad interpretation, however, entropy
became a universal force leveling off the world we know. By this,
the entropy became a universal and a holistic concept representing
one aspect of the world system.

We attain knowledge about the societal make-up by internalizing
its holistic universalistic images, and this knowledge can be changed
by internalizing new insights. Particularistic activities can change
the images of conceptual structures. In macro modelling one must
deal with both the particularistic operations, their impacts upon
holistic structures, as well as impacts of holistic structures upon
each other. Consequently the macro modelling of social systems must
be divided into holistic and particularistic levels.

3. HOLISTIC CONCEPT STRUCTURE IN THE SOCIETAL SELF-ORGANIZATION

Individuals find it fascinating to discuss holistic explanations,
but prefer to forget them after the discussion is over. Holistic
awareness as yet has to penetrate school textbooks and proceedings
of learned societies. Because of the lack of this awareness, societies
are paying a price. For instance, United States cities are afflicted
by decay and blight. If the urban society had lived with the awareness
of inevitable deterioration, American cities would have established
permanent institutions for obsolescense management. This, however,
has not taken place. As a consequence, sporadic urban renewal and
redevelopment has been a major public cost which produced only limited
achievements.

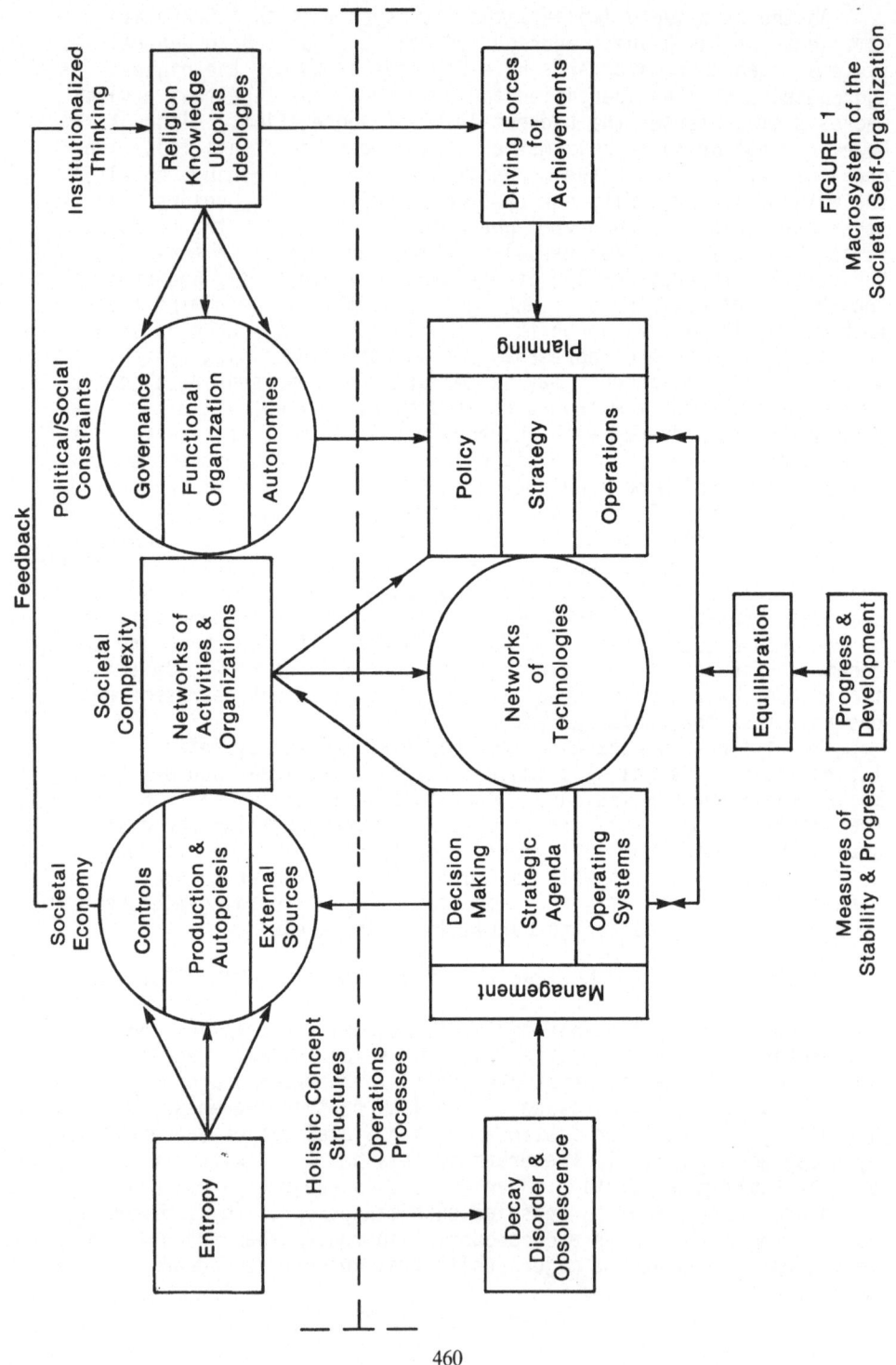

FIGURE 1
Macrosystem of the
Societal Self-Organization

460

The upper part of Figure #1 represents the holistic aspect of
the societal macrosystem. Four major holistic structures: religion,
knowledge, utopias, and ideologies are the results of human creativity.
Religions date back to infathomable prehistory. Several millenia
ago priests began paving way for scientific investigations by engaging
in astronomy, mathematics, and other branches of knowledge.[15] Utopias
for new social order surfaced by synthesizing religious norms and
scientific evidence. Ideologies followed utopias; they consist of
strategies for action and for attaining an envisioned social order
and anemity.[16] The four components constitute the "collective thinking"
formation process. The collective thinking contains norms and other
behavioral constraints. The forms of human creativity are impacted
by these constraints.

The upper middle block, in Figure #1, represents the "network
of activities and organizations". This holistic concept, however,
remains structureless until the networks are identified. Two circles,
one at each end of the networks block, are shown for this purpose.
The right hand side circle includes governance, functional organization,
and autonomies. The constraints of this circle give structure to
the "network of activities and organizations" by reflecting the principles
of prevailing ideologies. The scope of the study permits identifying
only the major constraint characteristics for each of the three holistic
aspect of the societal organization.

Governance function is closely linked with the political power
distribution and its exercise in the societal self-organization.
Governance styles range between two extremes: centralized and decentralized.
Most governance issues are associated with the political power concentration.
Autonomies, shown at the bottom part of the circle, possess boundaries
and limited privilages for self-governance as well as creation of
their own environments. The structure of autonomies and the extent
of their privilages are related to government centralization. Functional
organization addresses human needs, such as housing, food, health
care, education, recreation and welfare. Urban systems include government,
basic services, transportation, security, infrastructure, and production.
At one extreme of the institutionalized thinking all functions are
considered to be the responsibility of the government. At the other
extreme societies believe that individuals and settlements should
be responsible for their needs. Functional organization occupies
the central position in the societal self-organization. It opens
up the opportunities for population's creativity, sets standards for
well-being and amenity, and controls activities and organizations.

The left side circle shows the structure of societal economy;
it represents the organizational structure of productive capabilities.
The three holistic aspects of this structure include controls, production
and autopoiesis, and external resources. From organizational point
of view, the circle represents the over-all societal fitness for confronting
entropy. Obsolescense, decay, and disorder become evident if any
one or all of the three societal organization aspects are insufficient.
The central position of the circle is occupied by production and autopoiesis
representing processes and enterprises engaged in repairing, renewing,

and improving the existing production capability. Like in biological
organisms, maintenance and replacements of productive capabilities
constitute a vital function of the national economy. Autopoiesis
stands in a direct confrontation with the entropy. Controls aspect
of the societal production is shown at the top of the circle. The
range of control styles spans between state control of all production
activities to a minimal state control in "free enterprise" economies.
External resources are shown at the bottom part of the circle.

A feedback loop links the "economy" circle with the processes
counstituting the formation of the institutionalized thinking. If
problems develop in the societal economy, the information is channeled
to the institutionalized thinking formation process for assessing
the prevailing beliefs and principles and for adjusting appropriate
constraints. Institutional inflexibility in effectuating adjustments
and insensitivity to feedback information could weaken production
capabilities and open up the societal economy to disorganization,
obsolescense, and decay.

4. MACROSYSTEM OF THE SOCIETAL SELF-ORGANIZATION

In the final model the holistic structures are linked with corresponding
operations. On the right hand side the "institutionalized thinking"
above is liked with the "driving forces for achievements" below.
In some cultures the institutionalized thinking stresses the importance
of achievments more than in others. The striving for individual and
collective achievements is the vehicle that gives pace for operational
activities.[17]   On the opposite side, the block denoted "decay, disorder,
and obsolescense" is linked with the entropy above. These are the
operational manifestations of entropy. The two opposing tendencies
are mitigated through planning and management.

The circle located in the middle of the lower part is labeled
"networks of technologies". Each civilization possesses its peculiar
mix and networks of technologies. Technology networks underlie the
"networks of societal activities and organizations". Technologies
are also the medium by which planning an management are seeking to
achieve their objectives.

Adjacent to the technologies circle, on the right hand side there
is the block containing three levels of planning. A similar block
on the other side shows three levels of management activities. The
planning function is under the pressure to seek achievements through
ingeneous issue solutions. Planning constriants come from the top.
Governance practices, functional organization, and the structure of
autonomies constitute the existing framework of constraints for operations,
strategic, as well as policy planning. Operations planning addresses
issues related to production of goods and services. The horizons
of operational planning are broadened by strategic planning. New
outlooks, designs, products, activity patterns and organizations are
the objectives of strategic planning. Policy planning addresses autonomies.
Programs are designed to give the operational expression to policies.

The management side is part of the societal economy in three
major ways: by developing and managing operating systems, by formulating

and pursuing strategic agenda, and by making decisions. Management also is attending to the autopoietic side of productive processes. It exercises controls to the extent permitted by the institutionalized thinking and utilizes external resources for the benefit of the societal economy. Networks of existing technologies are utilized by planning and management for enhencing the societal economy and for advancing the self-organization process.

Of the two lowest level blocks, in Figure #1, one represents "equilibration" and the other "progress and development". Equilibration is a standing issue of planning and management. Stability of societal economy depends upon a successful equilibration of major areas of the societal organization. Progress and development accrues as a result of individual and collective achievements. By making progress in arts, science, and philosophy individual contributors enhence the environment for development. Collective achievement have been made in space technology, communications, and automation. What kind of impacts these innovations will make on future life styles and community forms, it remains a speculation.

5. CONCLUSIONS

The macrosystems model of the societal self-organization, which was developed by this study, shows how human societies are endeavoring to survive and to enhence the quality of their existence by utilizing their creativity potential. The success of these endeavors is spotty. On the same continent some nations are better off than others, and within a wealthy nation there are pockets of poverty and blight.

Putting it into holistic terms, societies pursue achievements through self-organization. In this sense the self-organization represents a growing network of interdependent and interrelated activities and organizations. However, the network can consist of uneven density and of irregular weave. There can be weak and strong areas in the network. Utopian designs and ideological systems have been proposed for improving the societal fabric and for closing weak spots of the self-organization network.

Organizational forms of the societal economy are imposed by controls. The production processes are autopoietic, depending upon high quality operations, including knowledge and skill of production, maintenance, replacements, and improvements. The societal economy is under the pressure of entropy; it needs frequent and thorough tuning as well as updating; new economy forms and processes surface as a result of evolving autopoietic capabilities.

Equilibration is one of the most difficult management's tasks. Recent imbalances of budgets, trade, currency values, and loans threaten the stability of societal economies. These imbalances are also impediments to progress and development. The effects of the entropy persist and assume new forms.

REFERENCES

1. Ashby, Ross W. "Principles of the Self-Organizing Systems" in Modern Systems Research for the Behavioral Scientists,ed. Walter Buckley. Chicago: Aldine Publishing Co., p. 109.

2. Breed, Warren. The Self-Guiding Society, New York: The Free Press, 1971.

3. Bowler, Downing T. General Systems Thinking Its Scope and Applicability, New York: North Holand, 1981.

4. Jantch, Erich. Design for Evolution, New York: George Braziller, 1975 Chapter 4.

5. Jantch, Erich. "Autopoiesis: A Central Aspect of Dissipative Self-Organization", Chapter 5 in Autopoiesis A Theory of Living Organization, ed. Milan Zeleny, New York: North Holland, 1981, pp. 81, 85; Zeleni, Milan ed. Autopoiesis, Dissipative Structures, and Spontaneous Social Orders, Boulder Colorado: Westview Press, Inc., 1980; Jantsch, Erich ed. The Evolutionary Vision, Boulder, Colorado: Westview Press, Inc. 1981.

6. Jantsch, (Ref. #5) pp. 85-6.

7. Jantsch, (Ref. #5) p. 83.

8. Bowler, 1981, p. 177.

9. Bowler, 1981, p. 176.

10. Rorty, Richard. Philosophy and the Miror of Nature, Princeton: Princeton University Press 1979 p. 41.

11. Schrodinger, Erwin. What is Life? & Mind and Matter, Cambridge: At the University Press, 1969 p. 72.

12. Ibid., p. 75.

13. Toffler, Alvin. Future Shock, New York: Bantam Books, 1970.

14. Bowler, 1981, p. 4.

15. Childe, Gordon V. Mand Makes Himself, New York: The New American Library 1951, Chapters VIII.

16. Ibid., p. 106.

17. McNeill, John T. The History and Character of Calvinism, New York: Oxford University Press, 1967.

PEACE AS A CYBERNETIC CONTROL PROBLEM

F. Breitenecker, P .Kopacek
Technical University Vienna
Karlsplatz 13
A-1040 Vienna

M. Peschel
Academy of Sciences of GDR
Rudower Chaussee 5
DDR-1199 Berlin

ABSTRACT. Today peace research is mostly concentrated on non-mathe-matical and non-technical describing methods. In the paper first steps in the direction of a mathematical approach based on methods of cybernetics, system theory and control engineering will be given. Various ideas for model concepts are shortly discussed and reviewed and also 'conventional' as well as 'advanced' control concepts are introduced for these purposes. An outline of applications conclude the investigations.

1. INTRODUCTION

Througout history nations have sought to improve the national security by increasing their military forces. Cybernetics and especially control theory and closely related fields of research indicate that there may be alternative or supplemental methods employed for improving the solution of various conflict situations.
Today a mathematical approach based on methods of cybernetics, system theory and control engineering will be used more intensively for describing and solving such problems and conflicts. Few publications are known with more or less theoretical background while a lot of publications base on verbal descriptions of the phenomena without giving mathematical realisations of the problem.
First ideas and approaches for such mathematical realisations are included e.g. in /1/, /2/, /7/. But they are mainly dealing with pure mathematical concepts without practical applications.
Therefore we will go to try introducing cybernetical and system theoretical concepts in this field where control theory has the role of a direct connection to practice. For this approach firstly models for the static and dynamic behaviour of a nation and for interactions between nations are absolutely necessary.

R. Trappl (ed.), Cybernetics and Systems '86, 465–471.

These models are to be seen as basis for the application of well known or absolutely new methods for investigation of the phenomena.
In the paper firstly the problem of model building will be discussed and various approaches are sketched. For this reason three model philosophies namely 'macroeconomical models', 'power models' and 'ideological models' are investigated. Based on this models various control concepts seem to be useful for this purpose are shortly reviewed. As application a model for socio-political conflicts is discussed.

2. MODEL CONCEPTS

One of the main questions is how to build up an appropriate model, and the first question is how to define, how to name and how to interpret 'measures' and 'quantities' which are able to describe the behaviour of a nation and the interrelations between nations.
The question which immediately follows is which quantities are the states (the quantities which have their own dynamics and which can be influenced only on behalf of control quantities), which are the control quantities (quantities which are able to influence states and which can be changed by an 'operator') and which are the output quantities (states which can be 'observed' and consequently be measured for getting information for building up a certain control quantity).

Both questions depend mainly on a 'philosophical' approach to model building, which is based on how we think about the dominant quantities within a nation.
In our opinion there exist three possible options for considering appropriate models for static and dynamic behaviour of nations and of the interrelations between them, namely:

- The macroeconomical approach:
  Bases of these types of models are economic relations between various input-, output- and state variables within a nation and/or between nations. These type of variables are well known from literature.
  Certain economic control variables have to be seen as controls which guarantee the peace within a nation and/or the peace within nations. The later-mentioned controller or 'operator' (see 'control concepts') influences in choosing appropriate control algorithms these controls resulting in peace or not.
  This concept naturally leads to the consideration of such important subprocesses as population dynamics, production factors, resources and environments.

  The 'power'- approach:
  Basis of these types of models is the decomposition of the overall power within a nation and/or between nations into special kind of powers: political power, mental power, economic power, nature's power, individual groups' power, etc.

Input-, output- state- and control variables correspond to these powers. Some of them may be 'mixed' variables (input and control variable, state and control variable) depending on the phenomena to be described.

The controller or 'operator' influences one of powers mentioned before. But also only parts of the powers may be used for controlling the system. As example the political power can be decomposed into political military power, political parlamentary power, etc.

The 'ideological approach':
Bases of this 'philosophical' approach are interactions between almost undefinable variables like measures for ideology, society, structure, acceptance, pressure, tension, etc.
This basis seems to be a very suitable one for our purposes, but problems soon arise because of too uncertain definitions and because of an amount of model parameters.

In practice the model used will be a mixed approach, but based mainly on one of the three mentioned possibilities. The 'ideological' approach seems very suitable, but is difficult to use. Therefore the macroeconomical approach and the 'power'- approach will give results in a shorter time. In this context it is to be noted, that also behind these two approaches the 'ideology' appears as background, so that the third approach, the 'ideological' approach, seems to be a general common nominator.

Another question in model building is the modeling technique. There exist two well known general techniques:

- Model building using bottom-up technique
- Model building using top-down technique

The technique used depends naturally on the kind of the problem. On the one hand the macroeconomical approach offers well kown economic laws and relations between small subcomponents, so that in this case top-down techniques naturally are used. But there exists due to the complexity of the investigated problems great difficulties with an amount of model parameters.

On the other hand the remaining approaches tend to bottom-up techniques, because one tries first to use small 'overall' models. But doing so informations resulting from the complexity of the problem are lost.

Consequently in our opinion a certain mixed technique is useful for the problems under investigation, where for the mathematical modeling bottom-up techniques are mainly used:

- Decomposition of the system into subsystems which can be overlooked (decomposition in top-down technique)
- Mathematical description of the subsystems in bottom-up technique
- Combining the submodels resulting in complex interactions

467

Now the question remains, which subsystems are 'enough' decomposed for our purposes. This is a very difficult question, but there a 'dialectic' way seems to be successful (/4/, /5/).
This dialectic approach which has proven suitable for socio- economic processes (/5/) proposes to decompose the system into subsystems which are dominated by two competing variables (states) in the sense of dialectic. These two variables should build up a stable behaviour within the submodel; instabilities then may arise by coupling the various 'dialectic' subdynamics.

3. CONTROL CONCEPTS

The goal of each control concept in this field is to secure the peace within a nation or between nations. This goal can be interpreted as a stability problem in the sense of control theory.
A controller therefore in our opinion is an 'operator' who (which) sets appropriate 'actions'. This 'operator' or controller works with a set of prescribed control algorithms where the actions to be choosen depend on different informations (inputs in the sense of control theory). From the viewpoint of control theory and system theory, 'classical' as well as 'advanced' control concepts are available.

Classical control algorithms are well known a long time and therefore rules for application of a distinct algorithm and also for the determination of optimal controller parameters are available. The efficiency of these classical concepts is strongly limited to linear or linearized decoupled models. As before pointed out the models for the dynamics of nations and the interactions between nations are highly nonlinear and also strongly coupled.
The classical control concepts are therefore only applicable for very simplified models which are only valid for a distinct 'working point' and for the nearest surrounding. The controller can be arranged with and without feedback. In most cases a negative feedback will be absolutely necessary for stabilization of the system (in order to guarantee the peace). Consequently the classical control concepts may be only successful for a first level of investigations.
In addition to conventional control algorithms 'advanced' or'modern' algorithms will be available since few years. They base on state space approaches or similar models and are suitable for realization on digital computers. State space models consist of state variables and therefore the actual values of these must be available online for a control. The different model approaches mentioned before require different choices of state variables. These state variables are in most cases not available or not determinable and.they have to be estimated by special algorithms named 'observers' in control theory.
Another problem arises in the determination of the structure of the control algorithm and also in the calculation of optimal 'controller parameters'. The controller means in this special case a device which gives informations about appropriate actions for securing the peace within a nation and between nations.

A higher level of investigations in control theory is the so called adaptive control. Starting with a simple model with appropriate control algorithms the 'operator' gets for each conflict situation suggestions for actions. If the 'operator' carries out these actions he has to report the results to the model. The 'operator' has also the possibility to neglect these proposals and to act in own response. These own decisions together with expected results have to be given also to the model. In this way the model will be able to learn personal conflict solution and after a distinct time span it will be able to reproduce the reality. For the 'operator' the model works like an expert system with many degrees of freedom for him. In some sense the model then will have a kind of intelligent behaviour.

4. APPLICATIONS

As application now a socio-political model describing the peace within a nation using economic well being and depreviation as measures for the peace is discussed. The peace is guaranted if a certain amount of economic well being does not decrease under a limit and a certain amount of depreviation does not increase beyond a certain limit.
This socio-political model can be seen mainly as an example for the fore-mentioned 'power'- approach. But it should be noted, that the way how to define 'powers' is based on the structure and ideology of the society under consideration (and on the structure and ideology of the modeller's society) and on the resources a government has to act in some way. Consequently this model has to be seen as modelled by the 'power'- approach with influences from the economical approach and from the ideological approach.

The scenario is the following one: a government acts with a certain exercising control, the second key actors are dissidents opposing the government (from inside or outside).
Due to the fore-mentioned idea in decomposing the system into subsystems consisting of controlled competing (dialectic) behavior and due to the idea of negative and positive feedback loops (the latter one lead to instability of the system) one may decompose the process into more and less important negative feedback loops (of two main variables) and into (important) positive feedback loops.

The variables based mainly on the 'power'- approach are dissidence, threat, depreviation, civil liberty and economic well being; the variables with economic background are total resources, resources for economic activities and resources for defense activities.
The controller ('operator') is able to influence the dynamics using different algorithms - but in certain constellations instability may appear due to not suitable algorithms.
This model was studied extensively in /6/ for the dynamics of political revolutions and fundamental socio-political changes; the model is based on ideas sketched in /3/, where a lot of interesting facts and assumptions on the investigated problem can be found.

One of the important negative feedback loops describes the interaction of dissidence and depreviation: dissidence can be suppressed by more control; but an increase of control results in depreviation resulting in pressure for reform, consequently the 'controller' has now the possibility to limit the control with an appropriate algorithm (fig.1).

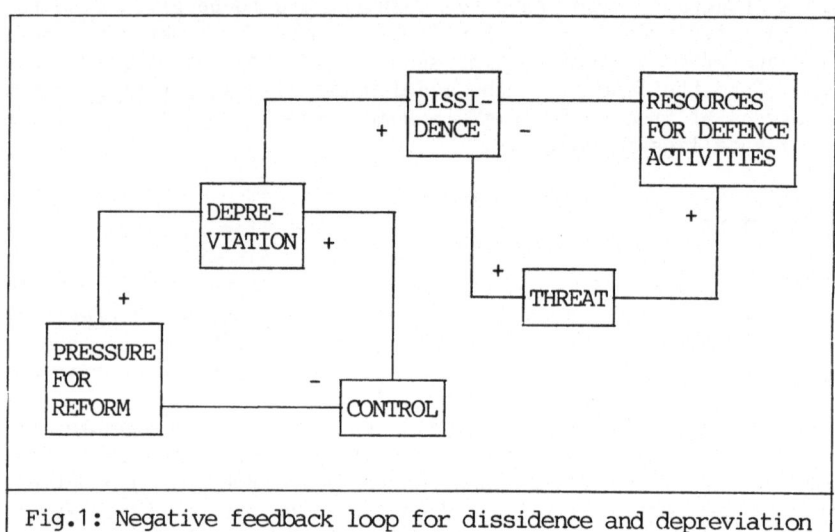

Fig.1: Negative feedback loop for dissidence and depreviation

Based on the stable (peaceful) dynamics one tries to build up the interactions leading to instability. These positive feedback loops are for instance control - resources for defence activities - threat, control - depreviation - dissidence - threat, etc.
Combining the subsystems of positive feedback may result in a dangerous unstable loop (used in /6/ for modeling the development of stressful pre-revolutionary conditions). Figure 2 shows these positive feedback loops resulting in instability.

It should be noted, that these feedbacks may change on other levels of the investigations. Also there exist feedback loops in the control itself.

5. SIMULATION

The simulation of the sketched models and of the outlined application may be done by computer simulation. It seems in our opinion suitable to use interactive program packages (simulation languages, simulation packages) in order to simulate the behaviour of the controller ('operator'). An appropriate simulation language for this purpose is DYNAMO; implementations of the outlined model in DYNAMO (on 16 bit PC) and in ACSL (on mainframe) are now in preparation.

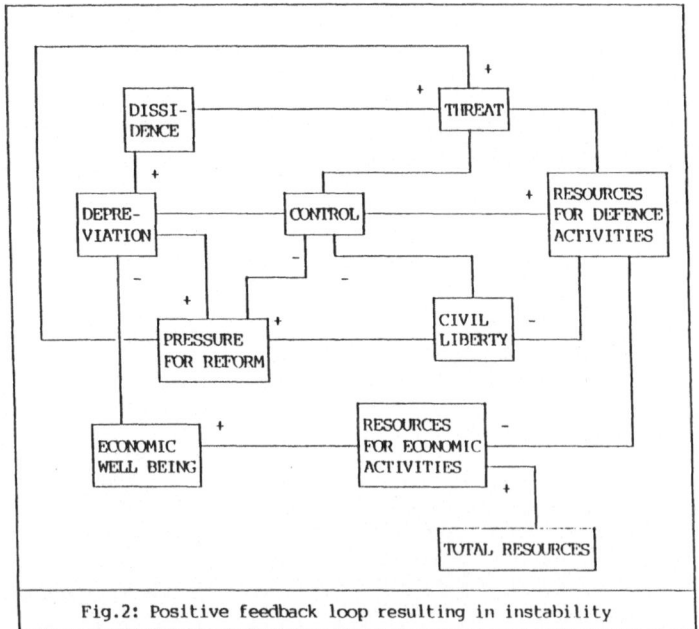

Fig.2: Positive feedback loop resulting in instability

Finally an idea should be sketched briefly. The controller should have in some sense the possibility for learning and intelligent behaviour. Imlementing this features in simulation would be / is nothing more than AIP (Advanced Information Processing) – and consequently our approach to peace as a cybernetic control problem can be implemented at a computer as an AIP- problem.

REFERENCES

/1/ Chestnut H.(Ed.).'Modeling large scale systems as national and regional levels'. Report to NSF, of Workshop at Brookings Institution, Washington, DC, Feb.1975.
/2/ Chestnut H. 'Methodologies useful for improving international stability'. IEEE Transactions on Systems, Man and Cybernetics, Vol.SMC -12, No.5, p.714-721.
/3/ Forrester J. Industrial Dynamics. MIT Press.
/4/ Peschel M., Breitenecker F., Grauer M., Mende W. 'System analysis based on Volterra equations'. Proc.of SWIIS-Workshop, Vienna 1983, p.277-283.
/5/ Peschel M., Breitenecker F. 'Socio-economic consequences of the Volterra-Approach for nonlinear systems'. Cybernetics and System Research 2 , North Holland (1984), p.656-660.
/6/ Saeed K. 'Political revolutions and fundamental socio - political change: a system dynamics analysis'. Proc. of the Applied Modelling and Simulation Conference, Paris, July 1982, p.21-31.
/7/ Wierzbicki A. 'Negotiation and Mediation in conflicts. The role of mathematical approaches and methods'. Proc. of the SWIIS-Workshop, Vienna 1983, p.163-177.

PROBLEMS IN THE DESIGN OF LARGE DATA-BASES

Owen J Hanson
Director of the Centre for Business Systems Analysis,
The City University,
Northampton Square, London EC1V OHB
United Kingdom

ABSTRACT. This paper examines the factors limiting the data-base designer's choice of storage medium, data-base organization and mode of access. It is shown that size alone limits the alternatives; in addition, the effect of a requirement for direct, sequential or mixed accessing capability, the pattern of accesses - both in terms of distribution through time, and distribution through the physical data-base - and whether one or more keys are used to identify records for retrieval, and the impact of security and backup considerations, are all analyzed.

1. INTRODUCTION

The term 'data-base' means different things to different computer users. In this paper it is used in the sense of being the operating data of a given user, and the meaning is not restricted to data that is organized according to the requirements of IBM's IMS, a Codasyl data-base package, a relational data-base or their equivalent. All the examples are cases that require large but homogeneous sets of data, and in which direct or indexed-sequential file organizations are superior to proprietary data-base packages because they are simpler, and so take up less storage capacity and on average provide more rapid access.

2. THE EFFECT OF SIZE ON DESIGN

If a data-base is small, the effects of poor design will not be so marked as they would have been if it had been large. However, there are good reasons for holding small data-bases on magnetic disk. First, it is usual to hold only one file on a magnetic tape. This is because all but the first file would have to be accessed by spacing along the tape until the desired file was found, which involves considerable waste of time. An average time might be 25-30 seconds, while the wait could be as long as three minutes for data at the far end of the tape. Second, if many files are held on a single tape, they are all available to the operator as soon as the tape has been issued. Disk, on the other hand, allows immediate access to only one file, providing a defence against unauthorized reference to files other than that intended.

R. Trappl (ed.), Cybernetics and Systems '86, 473–480.
© 1986 by D. Reidel Publishing Company.

There is a further factor favouring disk for small data-bases. Knight (1976) pointed out in an internal report to his employers that, unless it was possible to pre-load a tape, the time required to load it in his installation was 74 seconds. It turned out that only 28% of job steps in the installation used tape, but that these job steps accounted for 64% of all processing time (including allocation time). As a graphic demonstration of what this meant to the installation, he pointed out that the time lost in tape mounting was equivalent to turning off both computers for two hours out of every 24. In addition, he observed that pre-mounting of tapes only saved time when the operators did not have to delay any other operation in order to carry out the pre-mount. His main recommendations were:

- Move small data sets to disk, adding disk capacity as required.

- Introduce self-loading tape drives.

- Have spare tape drives, to allow for pre-mounting and backup.

- Position tape drives to minimise operator walking distances.

Implementation of these points led to much improved performance.

At the other extreme, data-bases can be so large that it is impractical to store them on magnetic tape. Table 1 shows the tape passing times required for sequential data-bases of varying sizes; this takes no account of the time required for processing, and is made up of the time required to read the data, and the time lost due to traversing IBGs (inter-block gaps). The limits on minimum and maximum data, and on minimum and maximum number of records have been chosen to cover the range from large commercial data-bases to national insurance files in countries such as Germany, France and the United Kingdom. For a full discussion of the considerations involved in optimizing tape operations, see **Blocking and Buffering**, Chapter 4 of (Hanson, 1982).

As the time required to update the whole file increases, the system designer's options are reduced. If the hit-rate is very high, as would apply for a payroll, for example, there is no way to avoid long run times. In fact, a high hit-rate data-base is almost always best held on magnetic tape - see (Hanson, 1980). However, whenever the hit-rate is relatively low, the designer will consider transferring the data-base to direct-access storage.

If the hit pattern is bunched - as happens when meter readers provide data on the gas or electricity consumption of users whose customer numbers are arranged in a sequence that shows physically close users as close in the user number sequence, it may be possible to **section** the data, so that the active part of the data is updated, while the rest is not. This is a very effective technique, so long as there is no need for direct access to the data. A good example of a data-base that would perform very well in sectioned form, but for the need for direct access, is an insurance data-base. Policy renewal dates, retirement dates, benefit payment dates are all predictable, and could be handled by arranging the data in date order. Only the records to be processed on any given day would need to be accessed, which would cut the run time on any given day to about one 250th of the total data-base. Unfortunately, direct accesses to the data as a result of accidents, deaths and the like will span the full extent of the data-base, and this has lead to most of these data-bases being held as indexed-sequential files. More details of sectioning, with a full discussion of the pros and cons, are given in **Sequential File Organization**, Chapter 5 of (Hanson, 1982).

TOTAL DATA	NUMBER OF RECORDS									
	150K	300K	500K	1M	2M	4M	8M	16M	32M	64M
25MB	4.05	7.50	12.50	25.20	50.20	1.40	3.20	6.40		
50MB	4.25	**8.10**	13.10	25.40	50.40	1.41	3.21	6.41	13.21	
125MB	5.25	9.10	14.10	26.40	51.40	1.42	3.22	6.42	13.22	26.42
250MB	**7.05**	10.50	15.50	**28.20**	53.20	1.43	3.23	6.43	13.23	26.43
500MB	10.25	14.10	**19.10**	31.40	56.40	1.47	3.27	6.47	13.27	26.47
1GB	**17.05**	20.50	25.50	**38.20**	1.03	1.53	3.33	6.53	13.33	26.53
2GB	30.25	34.10	39.10	51.40	1.17	2.07	3.47	7.07	13.47	27.07
4GB	57.05	1.01	1.06	1.18	1.43	2.33	4.13	7.33	14.13	27.33
8GB	1.50	1.54	1.59	2.12	2.37	3.27	5.07	8.27	15.07	28.27
16GB	3.37	3.41	3.46	3.58	4.23	5.13	6.53	10.13	16.53	30.13
32GB	7.12	7.16	7.21	7.34	7.59	8.49	10.29	13.49	20.29	33.49
64GB	14.17	14.21	14.26	14.38	15.03	15.53	17.33	20.53	27.33	40.53
128GB	28.30	28.34	28.39	28.52	29.17	30.07	31.47	35.07	41.47	55.07
256GB	56.57	57.01	57.06	57.18	57.43	58.33	60.13	63.33	70.13	83.33
512GB	113.50	113.54	113.59	114.12	114.37	115.27	117.07	120.27	127.07	140.27
1024GB	227.37	227.41	227.46	227.58	228.23	229.13	230.53	234.13	240.53	254.13

TABLE 1

The figures tabulated above show the time required to read the total quantity of data given in the left hand column, when it is held in the number of records shown at the top of each column. Values in **bold** type show minutes and seconds, while those in normal type represent hours and minutes. Processing is not included in these times, so they are minima, not averages.

For swift direct reference to data, it has to be online. This can present a problem when the volume of data is large. However, the IBM 3850 Mass Storage Facility, the CDC 38500, the Braegen 7110 Automated Tape Library and the Masstore M860 provide from 16GB to 1400GB of storage that is accessible in 5 to 30 seconds, so that these devices provide an ideal medium to hold data-bases that have a low volume direct access requirement. Insurance data fits this definition, but booking systems do not. The more successful an insurance application is, the less it is referenced – the less claims the better. A booking system is more successful, the more references there are. Thus, large booking systems will generally require IBM 3380 disks or their equivalent.

3. TYPE OF ACCESS REQUIRED

3.1 Sequential, Direct or Mixed

The choice has been discussed for a number of specific cases above; in general, the obvious choice for **sequential** access only is tape. As the hit-rate reduces, at some point skip-sequential processing becomes more efficient. On tape, all records have to be read, whether they are required or not, so as soon as skip-sequential processing is justified the storage medium changes to disk. The file organization to be used **has** to be sequential while the storage medium is tape, but can be either sequential or indexed-sequential on disk. Note that the separate key format for record storage has to be available if a **sequential** disk file is to be skip-sequentially processed.

Direct processing has to be on a direct access device, and the only question is whether the throughput is low enough to allow the use of the relatively cheap, slow mass storage devices. If it is, the cost can be very low. If not, disk or – for page data sets or reference tables – semi-conductor 'disks' such as the STC 4305 or Intel Fast 3805 must be · used. These latter devices can be accessed about seven times faster than a fixed head disk and fifty times faster than a 3380. For pro cessing that is direct **only,** a directly organized file will be at least 10% faster than an indexed-sequential file, and roughly twice as fast if the Cylinder Index is too large to be held in main storage. More complex data-base software is very much slower than this, so it should only be used if there is a need for multiple indexing, linked records, multiple key reference or some other facility offered by the software.

Mixed processing generally implies direct access devices and an indexed-sequential file organization. If the **sequential** element of the processing requirements is low, there may be an argument for using a direct file with an ancillary file of actual addresses in sequential key order. If the **direct** element in the processing requirements is low, it may be possible to meet it by a binary or statistical binary ('interpolation') search. These choices are discussed in detail in (Hanson, 1982).

3.2 Single or Multiple Keys

Much of data processing involves retrieving records for a given customer, stock item or member of staff. In each of these cases a single key is all that is required to reference the record. However, in retrieving documents from a data-base holding the contents of a library, the situation is quite different. There are no longer any 'keys' that uniquely define the document or documents that are wanted by the user. Generally, a combination of words or phrases is used as **descriptors** that can be combined to select data items that meet the user's needs. As an example, a Company in Austria may wish to assign an engineer to work in Japan for some months. The personnel file might be examined to list all the employees who meet the following criteria:

476

Speaks Japanese **AND** Graduate Engineer **AND** Single.

The personnel department would make the final choice, from the list produced by this enquiry. If the resulting list were too large, further descriptors could be added to reduce it. If it were too small, the 'single' restriction might be removed, adding to the assignment costs.

Multiple key applications present new and interesting problems. For smaller data-bases, magnetic tape becomes important once more – an example is the International Food Information Service – (Larbey, 1972). Small data-bases that demand multiple key handling are usually stored on magnetic tape and processed sequentially. A data-base arranged as shown in Figure 1 has considerable advantages by comparison with the other main file organization used in these applications, which is inverted.

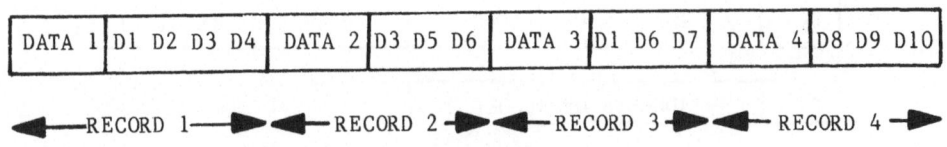

Figure 1

Each record (such as a text) is represented by the descriptors D1, D2 etc. Records 1 and 2 have a common descriptor D3, records 2 and 3 have D6, while records 1 and 3 share D1. Record 4 has no shared descriptors with the other three records, although it may have with later records.

This type of file has to be scanned completely before a single query can be answered. Each record is examined in turn, and its descriptors are compared with those of the search request (which might be like that for a graduate engineer with other attributes shown above). Because only one record is examined at a time, it is possible to test the descriptors against very complex Boolean conditions, expressed in terms of the desired descriptors expected by the user to obtain a match. The work areas required in main storage are relatively small, as only one record is being examined. However, as the data-base increases in size, the time taken to search through the data increases in proportion. At between 20000 and 60000 records, the search time becomes so much slower than that for the alternative inverted technique, that most users prefer to change to inverted files. However, the sequential file still finds a very important place in integrated systems, as shown in Figure 3.

At some point that depends on a number of factors such as complexity of requests in terms of Boolean conditions, speed of access of the medium in use and size of data-base, each individual reference takes too long. This is shown by an inacceptably high average wait time before service. If, instead of looking at the application in terms of records, attention is focussed on the descriptors, a more efficient and rapid method of reference can be arranged. This is to arrange the records in **inverted** form, as shown in Figure 2 below.

477

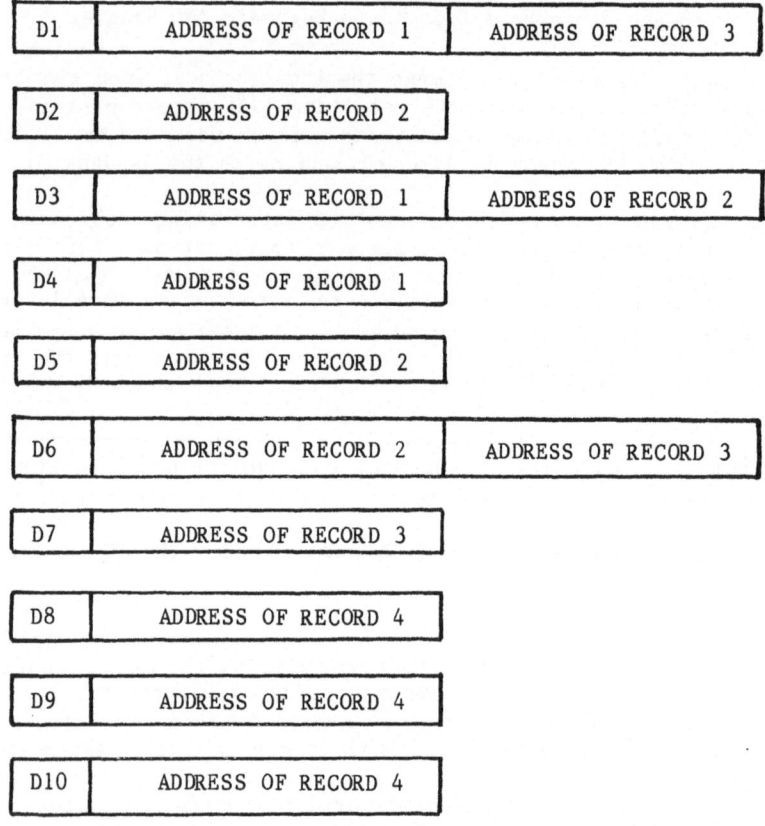

D1	ADDRESS OF RECORD 1	ADDRESS OF RECORD 3
D2	ADDRESS OF RECORD 2	
D3	ADDRESS OF RECORD 1	ADDRESS OF RECORD 2
D4	ADDRESS OF RECORD 1	
D5	ADDRESS OF RECORD 2	
D6	ADDRESS OF RECORD 2	ADDRESS OF RECORD 3
D7	ADDRESS OF RECORD 3	
D8	ADDRESS OF RECORD 4	
D9	ADDRESS OF RECORD 4	
D10	ADDRESS OF RECORD 4	

Figure 2

The main index is of descriptors, and each has a reference for every record to which the descriptor applies. Data is that used in Figure 1.

When an inverted organization is employed, a number of limitations follow. First, the data base may not be able to support such complicated search conditions as can a sequential data-base, because the size of work area required to process a request is now much larger; instead of dealing with one record at a time, the system now deals with them all at once. This speeds request handling, but greatly increases work area size. Second, addition of records to the file is no longer a matter of adding to the end of the data-base. Each descriptor record throughout the data-base that applies to this new record has to be updated, so the process is relatively slow. Third, the space requirements for such a data-base are considerably greater than those for a sequential file. Spiegel and Miller, (1978) investigated IBM's STAIRS/AQUARIUS system (Storage and Information Retrieval System/A Query and Retrieval Interactive Utility System). The system uses four main data sets: a dictionary, a text data set, a text index data set and an inverted file of all descriptors used in the data-base. These files are indexed by the use

478

of BDAM (basic direct access method) and in a typical data-base of just
over 2 gigabytes, which they found was the average size of those they
examined, the number of characters in the data sets comprising the database was as follows:

TEXT	864000000
TEXT INDEX	83000000
INVERTED	781000000
DICTIONARY	442000000

It is clear that the basic text file has been increased by around 150%
in order to provide the retrieval capabilities offered by the package.
This is typical, and should be borne in mind before abandoning single
key reference, which usually involves an overhead of only 5-20%.

The system described by Spiegel and Miller could handle up to one
thousand queries per hour, but many of them were relatively
straightforward. Larbey (1972) described a tape-based system in which
the text file contained a maximum of 1400 items, each of maximum size
4300 characters - six megabytes at most. This system provided SDI
(selective dissemination of information) on current data only to eighty
scientists using a set of thirty eight separate query profiles. Each
profile averaged twenty six distinct search terms, and production of the
complete SDI output took 12 minutes - or just under 200 queries an hour.

Because sequential and inverted organizations each have strengths and
drawbacks for information retrieval work, many systems combine the two.
The latest accessions to the data-base provide an SDI service to users
who request it. This part of the system is held in a sequential file;
at intervals that are determined by the size of the file or, if the
accession rate is low, by the time the main data-base is permitted to be
out of date, the sequential file contents are used to update the main
inverted data-base. Any user who wishes to consult the total data-base
would ask for a **retrospective search** and an SDI. The arrangement is
shown in Figure 3 below:

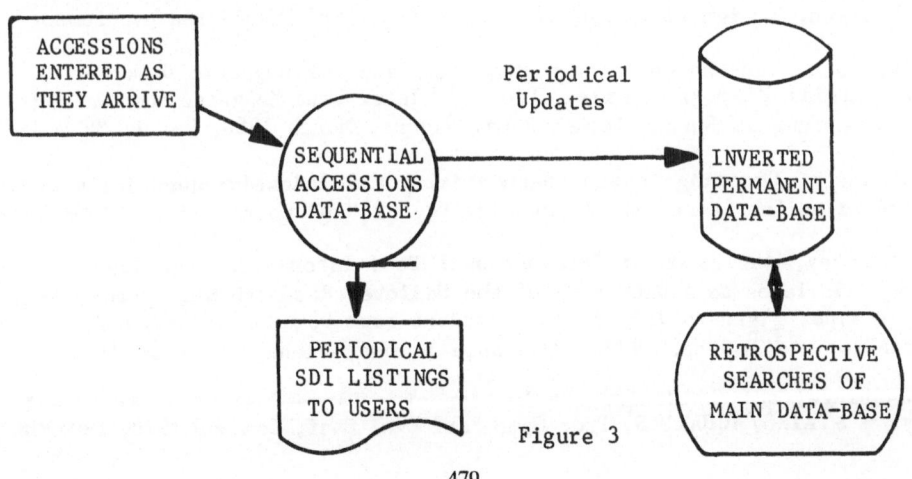

Figure 3

479

4. THE PATTERN OF UPDATES TO THE DATABASE

It is very important to analyze the access pattern to a data-base. If
it is absolutely even - say records are arranged in day order and there
is one or n records for each day, and if only the records for a particular day are updated on a given run, the file should be sectioned. It
is in effect a number of separate files that can be separated. The much
more typical random distribution of updates through the data-base may
eliminate sectioning as an option, and so prevent the use of tape. If
updates are grouped, sectioning may still be possible, depending on how
predictable the grouping is. Often the access or update pattern is
grouped plus random; in this case the decision depends on the designer.

5. SECURITY AND BACK-UP

Unlike tapes and removable disks, the larger fixed disks and mass
storage devices cannot be used for storage at a distance. However, some
users remove the modules from data cells to provide this facility. For
this reason, most users still retain magnetic tapes for back-up
purposes. This can be exploited by the designer, as any data-base which
can be processed efficiently on tape will release direct access devices.

6. CONCLUSION

This paper has examined the inter-relationship between many factors in
the design of data-bases. It is not possible to cover so wide a field
exhaustively in a single paper, but it is hoped that the data-base
designer will be able to use the rules mapped out as a guide, leaving
only the details of design to be determined.

7. REFERENCES

A.J.Knight, **The Use of Magnetic Tape Drives at The Royal Bank of
Scotland**, 1976, Internal Report.

O.J.Hanson, **Design of Computer Data Files**, 1982, published by Pitman.

O.J.Hanson, **The Choice Between Magnetic Tape and Magnetic Disk for
Sequential File Processing**, Proc. 6th Internatnl Kongress fuer Datenverarbeitung im Europaeischen Raum, Vienna, March 1980, Vol I, 89 - 122.

O.J.Hanson, **Choosing Between Sequentially and Indexed-Sequentially Organ
ised Files for Sequential Processing** Proc 6th NZ Comp Conf Auckland 1978

D.W.Larbey, **Inclusion of International Food Information Service's
Magnetic Tapes as a Data-Base of the Unilever Research SDI System**, text
of a paper given to IFIS at the Institut fuer Dokumentationswesen,
Frankfurt, 7th Sept, 1972. Available in microfiche only from IFIS.

M.G.Spiegel and C.M.Miller, **Evaluation of a Large Scale Data Retrieval
Sys - STAIRS/AQUARIUS**, Proc Comp Perf Eval Conf, London, 1978, 189-208.

THE DEVELOPMENT OF AN EXPERIMENTAL DISTRIBUTED DATABASE SOME PRACTICAL EXPERIENCE

M FLOWER*   J LONG   N REVELL   M SHAVE**
CENTRE FOR BUSINESS SYSTEMS ANALYSIS
CITY UNIVERSITY
LONDON

* Bristol University, Dept of Computer Science
** Liverpool University, Dept of Computer Science

ABSTRACT In a previous paper presented at EMCSR 84 the development of methodologies for the design of small database systems were reviewed [1]. This paper describes some practical experience gained in using a heterogeneous distributed database system where the nodes represented a variety of Database Management Systems (DBMSs) and system types. This latter ranged from microcomputers to mainframes with a preponderance of minicomputers. Database technology as such has only evolved for single centralised systems, and although networking techniques have also been available for some years, the merger of the two , ie distributed databases has not yet been widely implemented. One exception to this has been provided by Computer Manufacturers with their own proprietary systems, for example IBMs SNA. These represent a special case and may be classified as "homogeneous" systems. This paper concentrates on the general ie "heterogeneous" approach to distributed systems. The emphasis of this project has been to develop a common protocol for the handling of database queries which may be translated into the local query language of each site.

INTRODUCTION

The database concept has evolved over the past ten years in response to the growing volume and complexity of the data processed in many organisations, and the need to rationalise this by establishing an integrated view of its logical structure. Yet, whatever the need for corporate control over strategic decisions, the centralisation traditionally associated with databases conflicts with the current interest in the devolution of routine responsibilities to local groups.

This interest has itself been encouraged by technological developments which have made local computing systems economically justifiable, such as powerful microprocessors and networking facilities. In addition, when much of the data has strongly localised relevance, there can be considerable savings in transmission costs if the processing of the data can also be localised, and a wider view of the database invoked only when necessary.

In discussions about distributed databases the example quoted most often is the case of a large group or corporation with a number of

481

R. Trappl (ed.), Cybernetics and Systems '86, 481–488.

largely autonomous departments or companies, and where the volume of data involved, even at local level, is considerable. However, one consequence of the dramatic reduction brought about by microprocessors in the scale and cost of computing is the growth of "personal" computer systems, and in particular "personal" databases. These may hold, for example, a personal bibliography, experimental results or current client orders. The volume of data may be of modest size but a database approach gives the owner much more flexibility in its use. Furthermore a number of such small systems could jointly form a significant distributed database, so that one research worker could gain access to (say) details of literature in specialised areas other than his own, or a sales manager can investigate all outstanding orders obtained by his sales team.

OBJECTIVES

A distributed database can be defined as a system "where logically related data is physically distributed between a number of separate information processors linked by telecommunications. The data must be defined by and controlled under the constraints of one common schema" [2].

Given the widely varying characteristics of hierarchical, network and relational database systems the choice of a common schema is not easy, and there are significant differences even within these broad categories. The simplest implementation of a distributed database would of course be a homogeneous system in which the same database management system (DBMS) was used locally at each constituent site.

In practice it is more likely that a distributed system will be required to capitalise on existing investment, and integrate a number of existing databases rather than making a completely fresh start. In these circumstances it is probable that two or more distinct DBMS will be in use, so that a heterogeneous approach is necessary in designing the distributed system.

The project to be described in this paper has adopted a position between these extremes, namely a distributed database in which each local database is based on the relational model, but the sites may nevertheless use different DBMS - INGRES, MRDS, etc. This model, which has been the subject of research at the University of Bristol, could thus be described as a semi-homogeneous distributed database.

The Bristol team were, however, part of a wider research group, the Proteus project, which has involved seven teams at sites throughout the UK. Within this wider group a non-homogeneous approach was necessary, and this led to the use of a specially designed low-level schema, the ACS or Abstract Conceptual Schema [3], as the common base for the Proteus project.

Previous research on distributed databases has concentrated on systems in which control has been exercised through a single central node. One of the objectives of the research at Bristol was to set up a distributed database which could operate as a sub-network within the overall Proteus system. Thus the sub-network would appear as one site to any node elsewhere in the Proteus group, and conversely the Proteus network would look like another local site to the node controlling the

Bristol sub-network. This was achieved without too much difficulty, since the ACS and its associated network query language (NQL) were both designed on relational lines, and in so doing a heterogeneous distributed database became feasible. Some other aspects of the original plans proved more difficult to implement.

THE PROJECT ARCHITECTURE

The first priority in getting the project underway was to establish at Bristol a stand alone relational database network The network was to be heterogeneous only in the sense that it would contain a number of relational systems exhibiting different characteristics. There was no plan initially to include network or other types of database systems, though an interface to systems of this type was subsequently established through collaboration with other sites in the Proteus project, as described later in this paper.

Preliminary investigations were carried out into the structure of the query languages of the Honeywell MRDS (MULTICS Relational Data Store) and the results revealed no major problems in employing MRDS as one element in a heterogeneous relational database network.(At the implementation stage,however,this initial investigation proved too optimistic.) Similar preliminary work was done on the INGRES database management system, which runs under UNIX on the PDP 11/44, and its query language QUEL. The necessary communication between the Honeywell mainframe and the University of Bristol Computer Science Department's PDP 11/44 looked feasible.

Having established that MRDS and INGRES were suitable database management systems for inclusion in the network, attention was turned toward setting up a central distribution mechanism that would enable these database management systems to be incorporated as nodes in a heterogeneous relational database network controlled by the central hub.

The fundamental features of this central hub are set out by Bocca in a project working paper [4]. The basic elements of this design are:

-an internal query language (IQL) which functions as a common interface query language between the query languages in the network, in this case between MRDS and QUEL.

-a network processor which receives IQL queries and decomposes them into subqueries with the support of the central distribution mechanism's own database management system. This hub DBMS has as its query language the internal query language,IQL, and is designed to hold data about the location,relations, and attributes of data in the network. In other words, a "database of databases".Decomposed queries are distributed to the proper site, as determined by information in the database of databases, for local processing. The network processor has the task of recomposing replies received from local sites and distributing the composite reply to the proper site. Recomposing of queries may call upon the central hub's own

483

database management system to perform another function.It may be used to perform 'joins' between data files returned from the nodes.

-a stand alone database management system, custom built to perform the functions described above, also holds, maintains and supports a Global Schema which reflects the structure of the database network as a whole.

IMPLEMENTING THE ARCHITECTURE

Several pieces of software were written during the first year of the project as steps toward implementing the original version of the central distribution architecture. Some,but not all, of these could still be incorporated in revised plans which were subsequently adopted, as described below.

First a translator was written in PASCAL to convert queries written in the Proteus project's Network Query Language (NQL) into equivalent queries written in the Bristol project's Internal Query Language(IQL). The source language syntax for NQL is described in [5] and that of the target IQL in [6]. A translator was then written in PROLOG to translate the IQL syntax to a low level version of IQL that resembles a 'C' language program. Two other items of software, which were abandoned under the revised plans,were a DBMS written in 'C' and intended to control the data used by the central hub, and an IQL to QUEL translator which was superceded by other software.

Finally, a substantial part of a translator was written during the first year to translate low level IQL queries into an equivalent form in the query language of MRDS. As work progressed,it became apparent that it was not feasible to have a MRDS node in the Bristol network. This conclusion was drawn despite preliminary work which had indicated the opposite. The major problem in producing a good translator centred around the way the MRDS query language handles temporary relations. MRDS is designed to be primarily an interactive language. Consequently, the query format that produces database retrievals displayed on a screen won't produce a temporary relation to hold that retrieval.A distinct query format must be used to create temporary relations under MRDS. The difficulty here is that the temporary relation which is created is given a unique index number by the system, whereas the IQL translator expects to refer to the temporary relation by name.The index number cannot easily be determined by the IQL translator.It would not be an impossible task to overcome this difficulty if this was the only drawback to using MRDS. However,in the environment in which it was running,where there were a large number of student programs with high priority,MRDS proved to be too time consuming. Translating a relatively simple query from IQL to MRDS and retrieving the data from a MRDS test database containing less than 50 tuples could take as little as 5 minutes when the Honeywell mainframe was not busy but as much as 30 minutes when reasonably busy. This time factor was not acceptable when coupled with the difficulty over temporary relations.

RETROSPECTIVE COMMENTS ON THE ARCHITECTURE OF THE NETWORK

The internal query language,IQL, used in the Bristol project proved to be both powerful and flexible.However, the architecture of the central hub as outlined above was undoubtedly overly ambitious. The design was intended to cater for different databases at different sites, and to provide a mechanism for 'joins' when necessary- a task which has caused considerable problems. The system would almost certainly have proved too sophisticated to implement in the time available,but at a crucial point shortly after the outline design was produced the team was disrupted by major changes in staffing.

When work was resumed on the hub architecture, a number of serious deficiencies in the early documentation became apparent, such as the precise algorithm for decomposing queries and a method for query recomposition from partial results. These weaknesses are perhaps understandable in the early stages of design and could doubtless have been overcome more easily with more continuity of staff. However, enough work had been done to make clear the ambitious nature of the design, and it was decided instead to take an alternative approach, as described below, in which work elsewhere in the Proteus group could be used to avoid "reinventing the wheel".

RETHINKING PRIORITIES

The reassessment of the project took place against the background that one of our original goals had been to cooperate with related distributed database projects. With this in mind it was decided that immediate benefit could be obtained by enabling Bristol to operate as a simple node in the wider Proteus network pending the implementation of a fully distributed local network.

As described above,a translator had already been written to convert Proteus NQL queries to Bristol's IQL, and the IQL queries to a lower level form. These translators were first modified to overcome syntax difficulties which had arisen.A further translator was written in PL/1 to convert the low level IQL form of a query into QUEL,since INGRES had replaced MRDS as the main database management system for the project. It was, however,possible to use the front end of the aborted IQL to MRDS translator, thereby reducing the new work significantly.Bristol began participating in the Proteus network testing in September 1984.

The use of PL/1 and the previous MULTICS work was seen as a quick and relatively unproblematic way of getting a Proteus node up and running.Later a more efficient link was written in 'C' language running under UNIX to translate queries directly from IQL to QUEL.

Software was acquired from several Proteus sites in setting up the Bristol Proteus node. The ability to translate NQL queries to QUEL and execute them is only a part of the total job which a node must perform successfully. A Proteus node must be able to identify the type of message being sent to it and process it according to that type. If the incoming message is mail, it is sent to the recipient's mailbox. If the message is a reply to a query, it is also sent to the recipient's mailbox. If the message is a query it is sent through the query translators,executed under INGRES and the response is then sent back to the University of East Anglia hub with the appropriate header attached. Software from other Proteus sites was used to do two tasks- to identify incoming messages and to repackage responses being returned to UEA.In addition a translator from QUEL to NQL was modified to run in the Bristol environment. Following this work it became possible for incoming files from the Proteus hub at UEA to be translated, processed by Ingres and the response repackaged for return to UEA in less than five minutes.

THE CENTRAL HUB RECONSIDERED

Having established a node for the Proteus project, attention was turned again to the original problem of setting up a central distribution node at Bristol.

It was decided that the best course of action was to set up a central hub on a more modest operational scale than the original design called for. The design settled on was from the functional point of view on a similar level of sophistication to the University of East Anglia central hub. By this is meant that the assumption is made that all sites in the network have the same database schema, but of course with different instances of data. The network exhibits two kinds of transparency. The types of database management systems used in the network need not be known by the user, and the physical source of the data need not be known.

The architecture of the revised and simplified central hub used the Proteus project's Network Transfer Language to identify incoming messages. These message files are received in the central hub directory by UNIX and identified by type of message (mail,query,response etc.), destination site,destination system, source site,source system, sequence number, original sequence number,version number, date time, and person originating the message.By opting for the Proteus project's Network Transfer Language as the mechanism for distributing messages, the project can easily integrate incoming Proteus messages and outgoing Bristol message traffic into the Proteus network. This aspect is an improvement on the mechanism originally proposed for the hub.

A new item of software was written in PASCAL to analyze Network Transfer Language headers,replacing an earlier and larger routine produced by another Proteus site. The results of the analysis produced by this new routine are manipulated by UNIX shell script and the appropriate action is taken depending on the type of message being analyzed.

If the incoming message is determined to be a query ,the central hub passes the query portion of the message to the query decomposer. Since the current state of the network is such that each node has the same database schema, though not the same data, the entire query is passed on to the destination system with a revised header attached. The hub is designed so that a more sophisticated query decomposer can be added as research progresses.

Since the same query is sent to each site when the original query called for global distribution, the query recomposer algorithm is one that simply concatenates the results of the replies received from the

486

network. Once all the replies have been received, the composite reply is given a new header and the result is sent back to the original site initiating the query.

The type of queries currently being processed by the Proteus heterogeneous network and the Bristol relational network are artificial in one fundamental sense. Both networks assume that all nodes in the network use the same database schema. In the real world, this is an unlikely case. Furthermore, it is not at present possible to perform 'joins' across different database schemas. That is to say, if node A has a relation called staff with an attribute called 'id_no' and node B has a relation called ADDRESS with an attribute called 'id_no' the following query cannot be processed:

'JOIN   STAFF*ADDRESS where id_no=id_no   into RESULT'.

The redesigned hub running under UNIX at Bristol can however be adapted to handle more sophisticated queries. The hub is written in such a way that the problem of query decomposition and recomposition can be isolated from the other functions performed by the central hub.

It is undoubtedly true that the central hub must have its own database management system in order to perform 'joins' efficiently across databases.A hub DBMS would also be required to hold metadatabase information such as the schemas of the databases in the network. What is not clear now is that it is necessary to build a tailor made database management system to perform this task as originally proposed [4]. Instead it was suggested that INGRES could serve as a meta-database management system as well as a hub DBMS to perform network 'joins'.This proposal is described more fully in the project paper by Long [7].   Since the Bristol hub runs under UNIX, the INGRES database management system should be entirely suitable to perform the functions of a metadatabase, keeping track of what relations and attributes are in the network, and where they are. It can also perform 'join' functions between relations in the network.

This proposal has been taken up as part of a M.Sc. thesis by Sweet [8]. Sweet has successfully implemented a distributed database system using the hub architecture described above with INGRES as the database management system for the controlling hub. The system uses VAX machines on two distinct sites,both running under UNIX.In fact,the database at each site is managed by INGRES but,as described above,other database systems could easily be incorporated. A further development has been the use in this distributed system of two quite distinct schema. This has enabled the project to carry out 'joins' across databases which are based on distinct schemas, a task not previously demonstrated in the project.

CONCLUSION

The project has successfully completed most of its objectives. The relatively simple hub architecture offers advantages.It is relatively small in its current form and can run on a small UNIX machine. This could lend itself to research in heterogeneous distributed networks with multiple central control points, which in turn may have important applications where a distributed system must stay operational in cases where a hub is out of action.

The Bristol network differs from Proteus in emphasizing locally distributed DBMS.There are a number of situations in which such systems could arise and local communication problems are likely to be less expensive and more trouble free than PSS or JANET links.

The architecture of the hub makes it possible to tackle problems of heterogeneous distributed networks more systematically. There are clear criteria for attaching additional nodes to the network; the translator between IQL and local sites can reside either at the local site (as in the current Bristol and Proteus implementations) or at the hub site. Furthermore,research on query decomposition and recomposition can proceed in relative isolation from other problems of distributed networks.In short ,the project network to date offers a good platform from which to launch more sophisticated distributed heterogeneous networks and an environment which provides good overall system control.

At a wider level the use of such a system as a basis for a more generalised architecture of Decision Support Systems (DSS) needs to be practically developed. Just as distributed database systems incorporate networking and database technology, the DSS environment will involve the integration of these plus other components such as Expert Systems

REFERENCES

[1] Revell, Systematic Methodologies for the Design of Small Database Systems, proc EMCSR 84
[2] British Computer Society Distributed Database Working Group
[3] Stocker & Cantie,A Target Logical Schema: The ACS, 9th International Conference on Very Large Data Bases,Florence,October,1983
[4] Bocca , CDS Summary,Bristol Project Internal Working Paper,May,1983
[5] Proteus Project Internal Working Paper E2
[6] Bocca , Control of Distributed System,Bristol Project Internal Working Paper,December,1982
[7] Long,A Network Transfer Language Mechanism,Bristol Project Internal Working Paper,December,1984
[8] Sweet,MSc Thesis,Bristol University,1985

ADDRESSING SOCIAL CONFLICTS THROUGH NATURALIZED PROGRAMMING

Irad Dean Cole
System Development Corporation—A Burroughs Company
McLean, Virginia

ABSTRACT. Conflicts erupt in democracies when advocates of competing, monistic philosophies seek political control. Computer programmers can address such conflicts to resolve them by writing and publishing naturalized programs that present argumentations based on Perelman's theory of new rhetoric. Naturalized programs may surpass conventional argumentations by bringing programming literacy to bear upon the conflict. Citizens can use programming literacy to discover and evaluate new linkages between policy choices and desired results. The following discussion defends this claim by explaining related topics and applying them to a real problem.

1. NATURALIZED PROGRAMMING

Naturalized programming promotes programming literacy through readable programs (Cole 1982). The idea is to publish programs that ordinary people can read, so that elements of programming languages become part of the natural language. Over time, a natural programming language should evolve that addresses the needs of a population at a given time, place, and circumstance.

To make the concept work, programmers must know how to write programs that people will read. Three papers on this subject illustrate the use of traditional rhetoric (Cole 1982, 1983, 1984). Let it suffice here to repeat that traditional rhetoric is the art of persuasion. To be persuasive, the programmer must know the interests and reading abilities of his audience, what he wants the audience to do, and how to achieve his ends through the rules of traditional rhetoric.

2. PERELMAN'S NEW RHETORIC

Perelman calls the new rhetoric a theory of argumentation (Perelman and Olbrechts-Tyteca 1971; Perelman 1979). An argumentation is a discourse, oral or written, based on practical reasoning. Its purpose is to persuade an audience to accept the author's thesis. Using practical

R. Trappl (ed.), Cybernetics and Systems '86, 489–496.

reasoning to influence human action contradicts popular precepts of
western philosophy. Since Plato, practical reasoning has been suspect because it is based on opinion, and gullible audiences are vulnerable to flattery and deception. Plato initiated western philosophy's
quest for rational truth, and Descartes led it into the cul-de-sac of
formal reasoning.

Today rationality and formal reasoning are synonymous.

Perelman equates rationality with mechanical reasoning. Rationality is based on calculation -- logical or mathematical. Once premises
underlying the calculation are accepted, reasoning can be performed
mechanically, and the results appear compelling. There is no apparent
need for argumentation. But, the underlying premises are subject to
judgement; people must be persuaded to accept them. At that point,
argumentation and practical reasoning enter the scene.

Perelman counters Plato's objection to rhetoric by basing the
quality of an argumentation partially upon the quality of its intended
audience. An appropriate argumentation seeks the adherence of a competent body or, as Perelman calls it, a universal audience.

An argumentation must start from a point of agreement with the
audience and proceed toward the author's thesis. The author may wish
to strengthen the audience's adherence to the point or gain adherence
to a new point. The author pursues his goal by applying processes of
association and dissociation to objects of the real and the preferable.
Association unifies elements, and dissociation separates them. Objects
of the real include facts, truths, and presumptions held by the universal audience, and objects of the preferable include values, hierarchies,
and lines of reasoning relating to choices held by particular audiences
(Perelman and Olbrechts-Tyteca 1971, 66).

3. THE NEW RHETORIC AND SOCIAL CONFLICT

Perelman relates the new rhetoric to conflicts arising from philosophical monism by using the findings of sociological pluralism (Perelman
1979, 62-71). He claims that monistic ideologies lead to sociological
conflicts in democratic societies when opposing groups compete for
political control. Each monistic group believes it possesses the ultimate truth and that opposing groups are deceived. Individuals faced
with the dilemma of embracing one group and rejecting the other may
reject both and form a new group. In the process, balance may be
restored, unless the state takes the side of one group. To retain
order with freedom, the state must play the role of arbitrator.

The new rhetoric can play a role in this problem through the pluralist philosopher, one who doesn't try to impose an eternal truth but
presents a view acceptable to a universal audience. This approach can
engulf a society in a dialog that resolves controversy with a well-
balanced solution.

4. PROGRAMMING LITERACY

A social aspect of programming literacy for the citizen programmer
is using naturalized programming to play the role of the pluralist
philosopher. A naturalized program can enhance communication by
providing readers with an algorithm that presents the conflict as a
programming problem. The problem must be defined to deal with the
objects of the real and the preferable used within the argumentation.
Its objective is to illustrate relationships between the real and the
preferable in a way that enhances chances of a well balanced solution
to the conflict. The following paragraphs describe how this might
be done.

Programming literacy is the ability to read and write computer
programs. A program contains three literary parts: comments, coding,
and user interface. Coding must be written in a programming language:
however comments and user interfaces may be written in a natural language. Coding is written to solve a computing problem, comments are
customarily written to help programmers read the coding, and user
interfaces are written to help users execute the coding to solve a
computing problem.

A program may be read interactively through a terminal or from a
hardcopy. In the latter case, a naturalized program contains two
parts: a copy of the source code and an interface dialog between a
surrogate user and the executed program. Of course, the source code
also contains the comments and the embedded user interface. The interface dialog appears first to present the argumentation in its natural
language form and to illustrate how the program is used. The source
code appears next and is designed for easy reference between dialog
and coding.

After reading the dialog, the reader's computing problem depends
upon his reaction to the author's objectives. If the reader accepts
the author's problem, then the reader accepts the programming challenge
from a positive viewpoint. But, if the reader rejects the author's
problem, then he is confronted with justifying his rejection and is
tacitly challenged by his rejection but from a negative viewpoint. In
either case dialog is enhanced, and chances of resolution are increased.

5. THE REAL CONFLICT

The United States is confronted with conflicting views on economic
justice. A study of the ecumenical movement shows that some people
correlate economic justice with equalizing income through government
action, while others correlate economic justice with compensation for
economic activity (Cole 1970). For convenience, the first form of
economic justice is called normative justice, and the second is called
market justice.

Those who favor normative justice are generally critics of capitalism. They believe some form of government intervention is needed
ranging from socialism to welfare. Those who favor market justice
advocate capitalism as the economic cure-all. Members of both groups

take moralistic stands. Each group believes it is right and the enemy
is wrong. Each group seeks followers to gain political control. Each
group paints the darkest possible portrait of the other. That favoring
capitalism calls its enemies socialists or communists, and that favoring control calls its enemies libertarians or anarchists.

As a result, the United States' economic system is vulnerable to
two dangers. On the one hand, the economy may vascillate between the
opposing positions of a warring electorate. Or, on the other hand, it
may plunge into the extremism of a victorious group.

Attaining balance requires a rhetorical position that softens the
monistic positions with a dose of practical tolerance.

6. DEMOCRAN_86

DEMOCRAN_86, a naturalized Ada program, presents a pluralistic argumentation addressing the conflict between monistic views of economic justice in the United States. The argumentation associates the conflict
with harmful monistic policies, proposes traditional principles for
qualifying the policies, and encourages the reader to help qualify
policies and pursue programs leading to more desirable results. The
source program contains an algorithm for demonstrating the computing
problem and structuring future solutions. Figure 1 presents the package specification, and Figure 2 presents the main program.

6.1 The Conflict

The TYPES package depicts the conflict over economic justice in terms
of four political/economic types: Extreme Liberal Democrats, Moderate
Liberal Democrats, Moderate Liberal Anarchists, and Extreme Liberal
Anarchists. Popular views of economic justice reduce to six policies
that are significant to the conflict. Members of the extreme types
have favored policies from which they never deviate. Members of each
moderate type may select the policy of their extreme partners or select
more moderate policies depending upon circumstances.

The potential results of policies are divided into two sets:
democratic (D_RESULT package) and anarchistic (A_RESULT package). Each
set contains results ranging from least harmful to most harmful. The
least harmful liberal democrat result improves normative justice but
decreases market justice. The most harmful result destroys the political freedom of the anarchists. The least harmful liberal anarchistic
result improves market justice and normative justive. The most harmful
result leads to terrorism.

Each potential result is associated with a probability based on
current conditions.

6.2 The Computing Problem

From each monistic viewpoint, the computing problem is that of attaining a favored form of economic justice. But, from a pluralistic viewpoint, the problem is that of protecting both freedom and democracy

492

```
Package FRONT is -- a library of front end material.
   Procedure Title_Page;
End FRONT;------------------------------------------------
With D_RESULT, A_RESULT; Use D_RESULT, A_RESULT;
Package PRESENCE is -- a library of devices
   POLICY_NR:  integer; -- for making the subject
   PROBABLE:  integer;   -- present to the reader.
   Procedure The_Policy_Game;
      Procedure Computer_Probable_Result (POLICY_NR:  in integer);
End PRESENCE;----------------------------------------------
Package TYPES is -- a library of arguments establishing
                 -- political types.
   Procedure Extreme_Liberal_Democrats;
   Procedure Moderate_Liberal_Democrats;
   Procedure Moderate_Liberal_Anarchists;
   Procedure Extreme_Liberal_Anarchists;
End TYPES;------------------------------------------------
Package LOCI is -- a library of arguments based on commonplaces.
   Procedure Least_Government_Ideal;
   Procedure Majority_Rule_Ideal;
End LOCI;-------------------------------------------------
Package MODEL is -- a library of solution methods.
   Procedure Democratic_Short_Term_Solutions;
   Procedure Anarchistic_Long_Term_Solutions;
   Procedure Involving_The_Reader;
End MODEL;------------------------------------------------
Package BACK is -- a library of back end material.
   Procedure Bibliography;
End BACK;-------------------------------------------------
Package A_RESULT is -- a library of likely results for
                    -- anarchistic policies.
   Procedure A_Policy_Results(POLICY_NR, PROBABLE:  in integer):
      Procedure A_Result_1;
      Procedure A_Result_2;
      Procedure A_Result_3;
      Procedure A_Result_4;
      Procedure A_Result_5;
End A_RESULT;---------------------------------------------
Package D_RESULT is -- a library of likely results for
                    -- democratic policies.
   Procedure D_Policy_Results(POLICY_NR, PROBABLE:  in integer);
      Procedure D_Result_1;
      Procedure D_Result_2;
      Procedure D_Result_3;
      Procedure D_Result_4;
      Procedure D_Result_5;
End D_RESULT;---------------------------------------------
```

Figure 1. Package specifications. The argumentation is organized in rhetorical sections contained in Ada packages.

```
With FRONT, PRESENCE, LOCI, TYPES, MODEL, BACK;
Procedure DEMOCRAN is
Begin
  FRONT.Title_Page;
  PRESENCE.The_Policy_Game;
  TYPES.Extreme_Liberal_Democrats;
  TYPES.Moderate_Liberal_Democrats;
  TYPES.Moderate_Liberal_Anarchists;
  TYPES.Extreme_Liberal_Anarchists;
  LOCI.Least_Government_Ideal;
  LOCI.Majority_Rule_Ideal;
  MODEL.Democratic_Short_Term_Solutions;
  MODEL.Anarchistic_Long_Term_Solutions;
  MODEL.Involving_The_Reader;
  BACK.Bibliography;
End DEMOCRAN;
```

Figure 2. Main program. The argumentation is produced by calling
procedures using the Ada dot notation.

while pursuing total economic justice. Pluralists need a process for
maximizing the probabilities of the least harmful results. Assuming
that the argumentation properly presents the objects of the real and
the objects of the preferable associated with the conflict, one method
is to associate policy results with objects of the preferable that have
more universal appeal. To do that, the argumentation invokes two principles (LOCI package): the least government principle -- the traditional American viewpoint that the least government is the best government,
and the majority rule principle -- the traditional American acceptance,
at least since the Civil War, of majority rule.

The traditional principles provide criteria for qualifying the
harmful results of policies (MODEL package). Liberal policies should
implement the least government principle by devising programs that are
adaptable to voluntary initiatives, thus giving anarchists the opportunity to act. Anarchistic policies should implement the majority
rule principle by deploying programs convincing to the voting majority,
thus offering liberals some proof of their workability.

The computing problem now has the following IPO form: input =
policy, process = principle application, and output = qualified result.
The form has two cases: 1) the liberal democratic case, where input
= liberal democratic policy, process = least government principle
application, and output = adaptable program; and 2) the liberal anarchistic case, where input = liberal anarchistic policy, process =
majority rule principle application, and output = acceptable program.

6.3 The Reader's Algorithm

The reader's algorithm is contained within the context of a policy game
presented by the procedure The_Policy_Game (PRESENCE package). The
reader receives a set of six policies and is asked for his choice.

When the reader selects a policy, The_Policy_Game sends it to Compute_
Probable_Result. This procedure computes a random variable and calls
A_Policy_Results for anarchistic selections and D_Policy_Results for
Democratic selections. These procedures select a policy result based
on the value of the random variable. The result is presented to the
reader and the reader may continue the game or turn to the argumentation.

The algorithms for selecting policy results are placed in the
packages A_RESULT and D_RESULT for the readers' convenience. Readers
may revise them for their solutions. See Figure 3.

The MODEL package challenges readers to pursue the American dream
of an ideal society by searching for probable solutions to the problem
of economic justice. They are encouraged to modify A_RESULT and
D_RESULT and to discuss their solutions with friends and neighbors.
Initially solutions may be based entirely upon rhetoric, but experience
may lead to pluralistic models.

The hardcopy program contains coding forms to help the reader
formulate solutions.


```
With Text_IO; Use Text_IO;
Package body A_RESULT is
Procedure A_Policy_Results(POLICY_NR, PROBABLE:  in integer) is
Begin
  ...
  If POLICY_NR = 5 then
    If PROBABLE < 00 then A_Result_1; return; end if;
    ...
    If PROBABLE < 00 then A_Result_5; return; end if;
  end if;
end A_Policy_Results;
  ...
  Procedure A_Result_5 is
  Begin
    Put_line("First line of reader's solution                    ");
    ...
    Put_line("Last line of reader's solution                     ");
  end A_Result_5;
end A_RESULT;
```

Figure 3. A_RESULTS skeleton. The reader may change result probabilities and produce a solution in procedure A_Result_5.

7. CONCLUSION

The foregoing discussion and example show that naturalized programs
can present argumentations that apply programming literacy to social
conflicts. The question of their usefulness is a matter that time
may tell. The results depend partly upon the skills of the programmers
and partly upon human nature as a whole. The process might be linked

to Wittgenstein's language games and Bloor's social theory of knowledge (Bloor 1983), but that is a subject for other papers. Meanwhile time waits for the prime mover -- the programmer. Additional material on the conflict between western philosophy and rhetoric may be found in the work of Ijsseling (1979). A paper describing relationships between argumentation structures and Ada structures was submitted for publication in a volume of selected conference papers (Cole 1985).

8. REFERENCES

Bloor, D. 1983. Wittgenstein: A Social Theory of Knowledge. New York: Columbia University Press.

Cole, I. D. 1970. "An Inquiry Into the Problems of Classifying a Christian Economic System." Master's Thesis, University of Nebraska at Omaha.

Cole, I. D. 1982. 'Naturalized Programming: A Method of Naturalizing Programming Languages.' Cybernetics and Systems Research. Edited by Robert Trappl. Amsterdam: North Holland Publishing Company.

Cole, I. D. 1983. 'The Roles of Rhetoric and Metaphor in Naturalized Programming.' Sixth International Conference on Computers and Humanities. Edited by Sarah K. Burton and Douglas D. Short. Rockville, Maryland: Computer Science Press.

Cole, I. D. 1984. 'Naturalized System Development.' Cybernetics and Systems Research 2. Edited by Robert Trappl. Amsterdam: North Holland Publishing Company.

Cole, I. D. 1985. 'Ada, Rhetoric, and the Humanities.' Paper presented at the Seventh International Conference on Computers and the Humanities, 26-28 June, at Brigham Young University, Provo, Utah.

Ijsseling, S. 1979. Rhetoric and Philosophy in Conflict: An Historical Survey. Translated by Paul Dunphy. The Hague: Martinus Nijhoff.

Perelman, Ch. and L. Olbrechts-Tyteca 1969. The New Rhetoric: A Treatise on Argumentation. Translated by John Wilkinson and Purcell Weaver. Notre Dame: University of Notre Dame Press.

Perelman, Ch. 1979. The New Rhetoric and the Humanities: Essays on Rhetoric and its Application. Dordrecht: D. Reidel Publishing Company.

INSTITUTIONAL REVIEW BOARDS AS COMPLEX SYSTEMS

Patricia M. Trussell, Retired Professor
University of Central Arkansas
8 Fernwood Drive
Conway, Arkansas 72032
United State of America

ABSTRACT. Institutional Review Boards (IRBs) are required by Public
Law 93-348 of the Congress of the United States to assure that research
involving human subjects is conducted in ways that demonstrate ethical
principles of respect for persons, beneficience, and justice. Though
an IRB may involve as few as five persons, evidence is presented to
support the view that IRBs are complex systems. The aim of this paper
is to describe IRBs in terms of their history, purposes and functioning,
to indicate their relations to macro and micro systems of society,
and to conceptualize IRBs as complex systems.

INTRODUCTION

In 1974 the United States Congress passed the National Research
Act (Public Law 93-348) which was designed

> To amend the Public Health Service Act to establish
> a program of National Research Service Awards to
> assure the continued excellence of biomedical and
> behavioral research and to provide for the protec-
> tion to human subjects involved in biomedical and
> behavioral research and for other purposes. (U.S.
> Statutes at Large, 1974, Vol. 88, Part 1, p. 342)

Title II of this Act concerns the Protection of Human Subjects of
Biomedical and Behavioral Research and established a Commission with
responsibilities to consider

> (i) The boundaries between biomedical and behavioral
> research involving human subjects and the accepted
> and routine practice of medicine.
> (ii) The role of assessment of risk-benefit criteria
> in the determination of the appropriateness of re-
> search involving human subjects.
> (iii) Appropriate guidelines for the selection of
> human subjects for participation in biomedical
> and behavioral research.
> (iv) The nature and definition of informed consent

497

R. Trappl (ed.), Cybernetics and Systems '86, 497–504.
© *1986 by D. Reidel Publishing Company.*

in various research settings.
(v) Mechanisms for evaluating and monitoring the
performance of Institutional Review Boards established in accordance with Section 474 of the Public
Health Service Act and appropriate enforcement
mechanisms for carrying out their decisions. (Ibid p. 349)
Discussion in this paper focuses on Institutional Review Boards as
entities, their purposes, their composition, their characteristics
corresponding to those of complex systems and their relations to macro
and micro systems all of which contribute to the view of IRBs as
complex systems.

Institutional Review Boards were legislatively initiated in 1966
for Public Health Service grants. However, it was the National
Research Act of 1974 that extended their use by making them a necessity
to all research projects/programs involving human subjects and funded
wholly or in part through the Department of Health and Human Services
(HHS). In 1981 regulations were revised and directed specifically
to HHS funded research involving human subjects. Current regulations
were most recently revised in 1983.

What is an Institutional Review Board?

By law, an Institutional Review Board is a generic term for
a multidiscipline board, Committee or group named by an institution
conducting research that involves human beings as research subjects.
Universities, medical schools, medical centers, hospitals or any
agency interested in conducting biomedical or behavioral research
involving human subjects and applying for HHS funds to do so are
required to have an Institutional Review Board. For example, the
American Nurses Association has an IRB because the organization
receives HHS funding for some of its research projects and some of its
research projects involve human subjects. I have been a member of the
IRB Committee of the American Nurses Association since 1981. It is
from that experience and concomitant ones that I write this paper.

Specific purposes of an IRB

Specific purposes of an IRB are to assure that
1. risks to human subjects are minimized by
    a. sound research design.
        A research project in which all the human subjects in the
        project are subjected to the same experimental treatment may
        not be sound. For this may depend upon the nature of the
        evidence. (Achinstein, 1983, pp 1-10)
    b. unnecessary exposure to risk.
        What is necessary risk as differentiated from unnecessary risk?
        For example, under what conditions is exposure to repeated
        X-Ray a necessary or unnecessary risk?
    c. use of procedures already being performed for diagnostic and
        treatment purposes on the subjects.
        Asking human beings to undergo many additional procedures is

considered to involve unnecessary risk.
2. risks to subjects are reasonable in relation to anticipated benefits to them and to the importance of the knowledge to be gained. For example, an experimental surgical procedure should potentially benefit the human subject as well as provide scientific information.
3. selection of subjects is equitable. That is to say, for example, that human beings in institutions for the mentally retarded are not selected just because they are easily accessible and compliant.
4. informed consent is to be sought. If obtained, an informed consent is to be documented from each prospective subject or the subject's legally authorized representative. This is to preclude human subjects of research being unaware of their participation in a research project. In the cases of children, mentally retarded individuals or unconscious persons, a legally authorized represent- ative decides for the person in giving or not giving informed consent.
5. the research plan, when appropriate, provides for monitoring the data being collected during the process to ensure the safety of the human subjects. Further, in the event of adverse effects, such effects will be picked up promptly and will not impinge on the safety of the subjects.
6. privacy of human beings who are subjects of research and confiden- tiality of data are part of the research plan. One way this is done is use of a numbering system rather than names. When a medical record number is used, an extra precaution is to employ a second numbering system.

Members of an IRB

An IRB must have at least five (5) and may have more members of varying backgrounds to include both men and women capable of promoting complete and adequate review of the research activities of the institu- tion. Diversity in education and experience as well as cultural and racial backgrounds is desirable to reflect sensitivities to community issues and to safeguard the rights and welfare of human subjects. One member of an IRB needs to have a primary concern in a nonscientific area (lawyer, ethicist, clergyman), another member needs to be unaffil- iated with the institution both by unemployment and kinship. No member is to have a conflicting interest in terms of a particular project. An IRB may invite persons with particular expertise in special complex problems. However, such persons may not vote.

The six persons on the IRB of the American Nurses Association include three women and three men from three different states representing nursing, research, community health, the law and the community.

Responsibilities of IRB Members

IRB members need to be knowledgeable and willing to prepare for meetings by reading and digesting written materials ahead of meetings

and by coming to meetings prepared to be analytical and fair.
Different projects at different stages of development and implementation
are presented at every meeting. Thus, though an IRB may consist of as
few as five persons, it involves knowledge, experience, cultural values
and a willingness to contribute to scientific advances in biomedical
and behavioral research that involves human subjects in ways that
demonstrate respect for human beings, beneficience, and justice.

Credibility of an IRB

Levine (1981, p. 226) states credibility is the most important
factor contributing to an IRBs successful functioning. An IRB's
credibility needs to exist both within the organization and the
community served by the organization. Levine points out that an IRB
can create a facade of credibility but not have substance.

Factors contributing to an IRB's credibility (Levine, 1981,
pp 226-238) include: 1) acting as agent of an organization, not
as a 'deputy sheriff' of government regulations, 2) avoiding double
standards with inconsistent procedural regulations, 3) questioning
defective regulations in ways to promote change, 4) focusing on
essentials rather than trivia, and 5) having competent membership.

Who Monitors IRBs

The work of each IRB is monitored through the Office for Protection
from Research Risks (OPRR) from the HHS regulations dated March 1983.
OPRR requires rosters of current IRB members. Each organization
maintains documentation of research proposals, minutes of IRB meetings,
records of continuing review activities, copies of correspondence
between the IRB and investigators, and statements that new findings
have been made available to research subjects.

An IRB as Part of a Complex Hierarchical System

An IRB comprised at the minimum of five English speaking persons
might seem like a small uncomplicated system. However, this is not
the case. This small group functions with features of a complex
system. It has entity (i.e. the whole being more and different from
the sum of the parts) and hierarchy (i.e. it interrelates with larger
and smaller systems); is adaptive (i.e. has the capability to altar
itself) and mutually interactive (i.e. is effected by and effects
both larger and smaller systems). Further, interrelationships are
mediated by symbolic information and increasing flexibility, complexity
and negentropy. A model of an IRB is depicted as

Hierarchy
- Individual investigator (entity) (microsystem)
- IRB of an institution
  (entity)
- HHS, fed govt agency
  (entity)
- Society (entity)
  (macroorganism)

500

Broken line indicates communication between and among entities.

A microsystem (entity) is an investigator who develops a proposal designed to benefit human society. The proposal involves human beings as research subjects. The investigator requests funding from the Department of Health and Human Services (HHS) of the United States through the National Institutes of Health (NIH) and the Office of Protection from Research Risks (OPRR). A hierarchy in itself! The proposal is required by law to be reviewed by an IRB to assure fulfillment of the purposes previously stated.

A hierarchy of entities concerned with biomedical and behavioral research involving human beings as research subjects and funded by HHS is depicted in the diagram.

Other interrelationships exists between and among society, HHS, a particular IRB and a specific investigator. These include the sharing of verbal and written information via regulations, written reports and minutes, through person to person communications via committee meetings, site visits, and telephone conversations.

Members of given entities within hierarchies also interact with each other formally and informally. The exchange of information within committee meetings is supplemented with information acquired in other settings and contributes openness and flexibility resulting in modifying and updating regulations and procedures.

Relations with Other Agencies

Relations exist with other kinds of agencies. These include independent, non profit, educational entities such as The Hastings Center and Public Responsibility in Medicine and Research (PRMR) as well as institutes associated with universities, such as the Kennedy Institute at Georgetown University, Institute for Medical Humanities at the University of Texas at Galveston and Center for Ethics at Baylor College of Medicine. Such organizations raise peoples' awareness of ethical issues in biomedical and behavioral research in which human beings are research subjects.

There has also been a trend in medical schools and undergraduate colleges to employ as faculty a philosopher by discipline with expertise in medical ethics to contribute to the education of medical and pre-professional students in the various health care disciplines. Interneships and residency programs also include discussions of ethical issues.

Relations may exist with private funding agencies, either a foundation or a business. The relations of an IRB to a funding agency require careful delineation. It has happened that those who control the funds may also wish to influence the design of the research project in ways that can raise dilemmas for the IRB as well as for participating physicians. For example, who controls the random selection of subjects? And what does a physician do in a situation where he truly believes that patient is in a control group?

In different ways the influence of non governmental agencies on IRBs is extensive. One organization is the Hastings Center, officially the Institute of Society, Ethics and Life Sciences, which has existed since 1969 and is probably the best known. It came into being

"as a response to advances in medicine, the natural
sciences, and the social and behavioral sciences.
Organ transplants, human experimentation, prenatal
diagnosis of genetic disease, life extending technologies, recombinant DNA, health policy and control of human behavior are among the focal topics of
the Center's interdisciplinary research groups."
(Inside Cover, Hasings Center Report, June 1985)
The Hastings Center publishes a bimonthly journal, Hastings Center
Report, IRB, A Review of Human Subjects Research, and books on a
variety of relevant topics. It conducts workshops in biomedical
and applied and professional ethics.

When this writer was first named to the IRB Committee of the
American Nurses Association in 1981 she attended a week long conference
on IRBs conducted by the Hastings Center. This meeting had more than
100 participants representing many disciplines and community members.

In July 1985 The Hastings Center in conjunction with the Department of External Studies of Oxford University in England conducted at
Queen's College the first International Conference titled "Medicine,
Ethics and Society". Over 100 persons including this writer attended;
approximately one third were from the U.S.A., one third from the
United Kingdom and the others from other parts of the world. Again,
program content was informative and instructive.

Presidents' Commissions

Of indirect and yet highly significant to present IRB activities
is the work of the two Commissions established by Title II of the 1974
National Research Act. President Carter named the members of the
National Commission for the Profection of Human Subjects of Biomedical
and Behavioral Research which was charged with preparing recommendations
to the then Department of Health, Education and Welfare. President
Reagan in 1980 named the members of the President's Commission for the
Study of Ethical Problems in Medicine and Biomedical and Behavioral
Research which went out of existence in March 1983, and no further
Commission has been named.

The deliberations and Reports of these two Commissions provided
recommendations from which in part the Office for Protection from
Research Risks of the Department of Health and Human Services (HHS)
considered in revising regulations in 1981 and again in 1983.
Coordination with the Food and Drug Administration (FDA) was also
accomplished in the revision process.

Titles of some of the Reports of the two Commissions indicate
relevance to the work of an IRB. They include Report and Recommendations, Institutional Review Boards, Implementing Human Research
Regulations, Defining Death, and Compensating for Research Injuries.

An early and very significant Report of the National Commission
for the Protection of Human Subjects of Biomedical and Behavioral
Research was the Belmont Report, subtitled Ethical Principles and
Guidelines for Research Involving Human Subjects. The Belmont Report
identified boundaries between practice and research as they are

502

sometimes blurred because of loose definitions of "experimental" and "research" and because sometimes they do overlap as when a particular research project involves the administration of a new drug as therapy.

The Belmont Report identified three ethical principles underlying research involving human subjects accepted in our cultural tradition as 1) respect for persons, manifested by autonomy and informed consent, 2) beneficience, manifested by benefits/harms considerations, and 3) justice that is fair in its distribution. These three ethical principles underlie the regulations of the Office for Protection from Research Risks (Porter, Unpublished paper, 1985).

A Specific Project

An example follows of a completed project that came under review by the IRB of the American Nurses Association. Originally sponsored by the American Nurses' Foundation and later partially funded federally, the project concerned the identification in school age children of risk factors associated with later chronic diseases. Titled Independence, Missouri/Health Education Project (IM/HEP), the first three years were funded by a local foundation and focused on the development and implementation of a model for screening school age children in four school districts and, in addition, offering the program to parents and the community. Wellness concepts and health life styles were incorporated into a previously developed Know Your Body (KYB) program. Some 4000 students and 2500 adults participated.

The next phase, partially federally funded, added specific smoking and alcohol risk reduction activities to junior and senior high school students in the target population. The immediate impact of the second three year program was reflected in a) a reduction of smoking in that age group from 14.2 percent to 10.9 percent, b) a 30% reduction in alcohol consumption between high school seniors in the program since its inception and those just entering the program, and c) a positive effect on weight control. (Building Community Support for Health Promotion Programs: A Model, 1985, pp 52-53.)

A sample of participating adults with identified risk factors were surveyed six months later. Depending on the specific risk factors percentages ranged from 58 to 95 percent of those who had taken specific steps to counteract the risk factor (Ibid, p 53).

The report, titled Building Community Support for Health Promotion Programs: A Model provides a model that can be replicated as a guide for others. In addition, data are available for a longitudinal study of identified risk factors in school age children who will be adults in the late 1980s and 1990s.

Such projects are not as dramatic or headline grabbing as those involving new drugs to combat cancer or AIDS. In the long haul, however, decisions young people make regarding their health habits may have lasting influence on later illnesses.

Summary

Analyzed from a systems view an IRB is a complex system that is part of a hierarchy in which members interact not only within the group but in a larger society in which people are becoming increasingly aware of a variety of ethical issues in biomedical and behavioral research involving human subjects.

REFERENCES

Achinstein, Peter, Ed. The Concept of Evidence. Oxford, England: Oxford University Press, 1983.

American Nurses Association, Minutes, IRB Committee, 1981-1985.

Building Community Support for Health Promotion Programs: A Model Kansas City, Missouri: American Nurses Foundation, 1985.

Buckley, Walter, Modern Systems Research for the Behavioral Scientist, Chicago: Aldine Publishing Company, 1968.

Hastings Center Report, June 1985.

Levine, Robert J., Ethics and Regulation of Clinical Research, Baltimore, Maryland: Urban and Schwarzenberg, 1981.

Porter, Joan, 'Protection of Human Subjects - Requirements of the United States Department of Health and Human Services for Foreign Research Involving Human Subjects,' Unpublished Paper, 1985.

Protection of Human Subjects, OPRR Reports, NIH, PHS, HHS, March 1983.

United States Statutes at Large, 1974, **88**, Part 1.

A Directable Ashby System

J. Lynn England
W. Keith Warner
Department of Sociology
Brigham Young University
Provo, Utah, USA

ABSTRACT. A directable Ashby system is a system that may operate at several different hierarchical levels. Each level has a collection of laws or rules that are not reducible to other levels. In human systems, the distinct levels require views of humans that are dramatically different from each other. At some levels traditional scientific concepts and methods are applicable. A person may be said to have been caused to act in a certain way. At other levels, human choice and creativity must be accounted for by using neo-scientific concepts such as rule construction and rule governed activity. People may shift from one hierarchical level to another in so far as the essential variables, such as agency, have certain values. The scientific accounts at the two levels will be fundamentally different. A directable Ashby system is a system in which the values of the essential variables change as a result of the manipulation of control variables such as repression and lifeworld constructs.

Introduction.

One of the major problems for social science has been the wide range of human activities that seem to require highly disparate descriptions and explanations. For example, Rollo May (1981) offers an account of a patient he calls Philip who, when he entered therapy, was unable to cope effectively in his relation to a female friend named Nicole. He could not break the realtionship off, was unwilling to marry her, and was extremely unhappy in the relationship. May took him through several sessions and found ways to bring to awareness the sources of the inability to cope with the pressures arising from the relationship. The problems arose from a combination of his past experiences with his mother and sister and his beliefs about the rightness and wrongness of some of Nicole's behavior. May also assisted Philip in finding ways to act

505

R. Trappl (ed.), Cybernetics and Systems '86, 505–512.
© 1986 by D. Reidel Publishing Company.

with greater freedom or agency by creating new, more personally acceptable patterns of action. The therapeutic process used by May is one of several alternative procedures; each of which appears to result in success in certain cases and failures in others. Typically, the successes are attributed to a change in the client from a condition in which his action sequences do not appear to be alterable by him to one in which he is able to conceptualize a set of alternative courses of action, evaluate them as to their anticipated consequences, and endeavor to enact one of the sequences with a desired set of consequences.

If accounts of successful therapy, such as May's, are accepted, then serious problems are posed for the social scientist interested in explaining the full richness of human behavior as it ranges from the pre-therapy automaton to the post-therapy actor. Models of the menatlly ill person view the individual as having lost control of his behavior so that questions of the causation of the disability arise. In the model of the post-therapy person, he is described as having achieved new levels of control and freedom. He becomes a more or less rational decision maker. In the first case, a natural science of human mental illness seems to be called for. In the second case, the description calls for an explanation that substitutes reasons, heuristics, and choices for causes. The distinction is captured by the difference between being acted upon and acting. We (England and Warner, 1984) have attempted to provide a solution to the dilemma through the concepts of hierarchy theory and essential variables. The hierarchy theory we have developed is based on work by Simon (1981) and Polanyi (1969) and consists of four basic assumptions.

1. The laws and rules that govern events at one hierarchical level are not reducible to those of other levels above or below it.

2. Systems are nearly-decomposible due to the loose coupling of subsystems.

3. The principle of boundary conditions operates in such a way that the laws applicable to a hierarchical level may not be violated at any other level, but no level is so completely constrained by its own laws and rules that some of its actual structures and dynamics cannot be influenced by those of neighboring hierarchical levels.

4. Dual control supplements boundary conditions so that events at a given hierarchical level are the products of laws and rules at that level plus the control that may arise from the operation of the laws and rules of the next higher level.

A hierarchy forms an <u>Ashby System</u> when a set of

essential variables is present. An essential variable has some values which, once they are attained, produce dramatic changes in many of the other variables characterizing the entity, the relationships among many of the variables are modified, and the entity, itself, becomes different in significant ways from what it was before the value was attained. In other words, essential variables have values which result in a shift in hierarchical level for the entity. When May's client succeeds in shifting from the person who is compulsively tied to his female friend and becomes someone who can either restructure the relationship to satisfy himself or leave it, he has shifted hierarchical levels. The rules and laws that controlled him initially are replaced by those that govern an agent who is free to make choices. Such a shift requires a change from concepts such as natural law and causation to concepts such as rules of rightness and rules of constraint: to principles which indicate to a person how to accomplish a task well and honorably.

The view that a person may shift from one hierarchical level to another is not new. Jaynes (1976) argues that over the course of recent human evolution mankind has moved through autogenic, bicameral, and modern hierarchical levels; each level requires distinct laws and rules to understand the activities of the persons operating at those levels. He argues that the movement from one level to the next results from changes in language, symbol, and culture: the essential variables. Stamps (1980) argues for a similar view of the role of language in changing mankind from one hierarchical level to another.

In the discussion to this point, agency, language, symbol, and culture operate as essential variables. The persons affected by these changes in hierarchical level did not consciously seek to attain the next hierarchical level. The changes in the essential variables occured as part of a natural progression, usually produced through an evolutionary process. In the case of the therapist, such as May, a fundamental question that must be dealt with in the science is the issue of how a therapist or other practitioner is able consciously and systematically to move a person or group from one hierarchical level to another by intentionally changing the values of the essential variables. The same issue arises when a person wills and accomplishes a change in essential variables to reach a desired hierarchical level. The change is effected by an agent's choice and plan, not by a process present in nature. They do not simply change a person's state on the agency continuum, but they formulate an intention to change it and then go about accomplishing the task with a plan or program. A concept from catastrophy theory and Ashby's (1952) work appears to be promising: control variables. A

507

control variable is a variable that will move an essential variable from a value that induces a given system-structure in a particular hierarchical level to a different system-structure at another hierarchical level. The basic effort of a therapist such as May is to identify the set of control variables that are susceptable to manipulation by the well trained therapist to move a person to a more desirable level. Some tyrannical societies have sought to discover control variables that will reduce a person from a hierarchical level where agency is high to one in which agency is reduced and behavior becomes subject to causal law. One of the sources of contention among therapists and other practitioners seems to be over the collection of variables that will serve as control variables.

In summary, we have now defined a directable Ashby System. It is a system with essential variables and control variables that influence its hierarchical level. In the final two sections of this paper we will attempt to apply these concepts to show how they resolve the two problems raised by the May example: the dramatic change in the nature of the determinants of the actions of some patients and the effort to find ways to achieve such change. We will use the notion of agency as the essential variable and lifeworld and repression as the control variables.

Agency as an Essential Variable.

Agency is a concept that has had a long philosophical history, but has not been popular is mainstream social science: a state of affairs that may be due to the theological and metaphysical connotations of the term. The old reluctance to adopt the term for scientific purposes has been declining as the positivist tradition has come under attack. More and more social scientists have recognized that the old assumption of an ontologyless science carries an ontology within itself (Feyerabend, 1975). The concept of agency has been used by several important social scientists (Fromm,1962; Giddens, 1976, 1981; Harre, 1984; and Ricoeur, 1984).

Giddens defines agency as a state in which
>   (a) ... a person "could have acted otherwise" and
>   (b) ... the world as constituted by a stream of events-in-progress independent of the agent does not hold out a predetermined fate. (Giddens, 1976:75)

In addition choices are efficacious. Efficacy means that the alternative selected is assumed to "bring something about (Ricoeur, 1984:136)." The enactment of the alternative results in a state of affairs in the environment that occurs, in part, because of the enactment. Giddens (1984) points out that "Whatever happened would not have happened if the individual had not intervened (p. 9)."

Agency does not mean that the alternative cannot be predicted in advance in most cases, but that there is always the potential for the unpredictable and novel solution. The definition and the assertion that people possess agency to one degree or another constitute a theory of man. The theory contends that man is "a mind-making, self-mastering, and self-designing animal...in...a search for meaning (Giddens, 1981:p. 155)." In addition, Marcuse (1941) contended that

Man alone has the power of self-realization, the power to be a self determining subject in all processes of becoming, for he alone has an understanding of potentialities and a knowledge of notions (p. 9).

Agency is the capacity to make reality over in line with states of affairs that are both desired and possible, where possibility is established by the laws of the hierarchical levels of the entities involved as part of the environment. Agency is a variable where certain conditions limit the degree to which self-mastery and actualization are attained and other conditions enhance them.

The consequences of the functioning of agency as an essential variable are illustrated through the types of scientific theories that are applicable to a persons who are at different levels on the agency variable. The activities of a person who is low on the agency variable can be expected to conform to the rules and laws proposed by B. F. Skinner(1971) and George Homans (1974). The methods appropriate to study such a person would be highly similar to those used in experimental and survey techniques. Statistical analyses such as causal modeling should fit well. The activities of a person whose agency variable is high would not ordinarily conform to such rules and laws. Traditional methods and statistical techniques would not usually work because of the potential for creative and open-textured activities. The work of scholars such as Gadamer, Giddens, Habermas and Ricoeur become increasingly relevant. Issues of language and understanding, knowledge and choice become the focus of the theorizing instead of reenforcement and conditioning. The methodologies proposed by hermeneutics, linguistics, and symbolic interaction replace the traditional approaches.

Limits to the values agency can take are a combination of biological, psychological, and sociological conditions. Studies of genetics and evolution (Wilson, 1978), brain functioining (Springer and Deutsch, 1981), and memory (Simon, 1981) establish some of the biological limits. Habermas (1971) and Marcuse (1966) build on Freud by using his notion of repression as one of the psychological limits. They also argue that domination of one social class by another is a sociological limit to agency. Marcuse (1966) points to false needs (such as needs

509

to relax, consume, and mass conformity) created by the
dominant interests of the society as being beyond the
control and awareness of most individuals. Giddens' (1979)
theory of structuration is another example of limits to the
agency variable. He holds that "structure is both enabling
and constraining (p. 70)." However, as structure changes,
so does the capacity to act as an agent. At one extreme, a
person may not be able to conceive of options, nor believe
that he can alter the course of events due to the structure
of beliefs and meanings he holds. At the other, a person
may be trained to construct or create options and believe
in his or her ability to effect a selected course of
events, again due to the structure of his meanings

A Directable Ashby System for Agency.

The discussion above establishes a view of agency
suggesting that it acts as a critical variable and that it
varies as a consequence of several biological,
psychological, and sociological variables. Efforts to
increase agency may be successful in those contexts in
which some of the variables that influence agency can be
altered. The problem is to determine the control variables
and the nature of their relationships to agency. The
literature reviewed above indicates that there are two
variables which are especially important: repression as
developed by those influenced by Freud and lifeworld as it
has been elaborated by Giddens and Habermas.

Lifeworld is a notion that is usually traced to
Husserl. He (1970) argued that it is that part of our
knowledge that is taken for granted: it is self-evident and
unquestioned. It is the ground against which judgments are
made and actions engaged in. Schutz (1962) describes it as
the background "within which inquiry starts and within
which alone it can be carried out (p. 57)." Schutz does
contend that while it is unquestioned, it is always
questionable. Habermas (1981) contends that it is the
cultural tradition or situation definitions.

Lifeworld is related to agency in a straight forward
way. Lifeworld acts without the conscious awareness of the
actors (Giddens, 1984). As such, it restricts the
alternatives for action that can be formulated in
consciousness. For example, in a traditional family in the
western United States, a woman may not be able to formulate
alternatives to a position as wife and mother in which she
is totally subservient to her spouse. No other life comes
to mind because that is the way things are meant to be. She
may not be able to articulate the beliefs that lead her to
her particular life. It will be similarly accepted by her
neighbors and community.

Habermas' (1981) argues that lifeworld is more subject
to change and conscious manipulation than do many of the
other developers of the concept. He contends that it may be

made open to critique and rational discussion with a discussion among equals as the most fruitful place for the opening of lifeworld to occur. As the discussion and analysis of the content of a lifeworld proceeds, it will be recognized that many unquestioned beliefs are in fact questionable. There are formulable alternatives that have not been formulated before. Husserl (1970) describes the impact of an encounter with a new and dramatically different culture and its way of bringing to consciousness the beliefs involved in lifeworld. Berger, Berger, and Kellner (1973) also argue that as people come into contact with persons of other lifeworlds, they begin to doubt and question their lifeworlds. In summary, the lifeworld acts as a control variable that left unexamined restricts the agency of the actor. In so far as the lifeworld is articulated, challenged by other lifeworlds, and subjected to critique and discussion, it will open an actor's agency. It is not unreasonable that a therapist might be involved in this process and in training a client to construct alternatives outside of his original lifeworld.

Repression is a concept that was first developed by Freud. It has since been adopted by such thinkers as Marcuse (1966) and Habermas (1968). It functions in many ways as the psychological counterpart to the sociological phenomenon of lifeworld. It is a component of the actor's world that is not in his consciousness. Just as discussions with others and exposure to other cultures may bring lifeworld to consciousness and prepare the actor to change it, explorations into the unconscious of an actor provide opportunities to bring to awareness those items that are repressed. Habermas thinks that introspection and social discourse will suffice to overcome repression. However, many psychoanalysts contest this and suggest that repressed information can only be brought to consciousness through expert assistance. The basic issue concerns the degree to which there are resistances in the psyche to admitting the repressed information to consciousness. In so far as repressed desires and recollections can be brought to consciousness, the theory argues that the actor then achieves increased agency.

In the case of both control variables, they serve to change a person from low agency to a higher level with the concomitant change in hierarchical level of the actor. The therapist is involved in a process which places the actor in a mode that requires a very different type of model and methodology than was originally present. The shift that results is a consequence of changing the control variables so that the essential variable passes through its boundary conditions to produce a distinct type of actor. A directable Ashby system is in operation.

Bibliography

Ashby, R. Design for a Brain (New York: Wiley; 1952)
Berger, P., Berger, B., and Kellner, H. The Homeless Mind (New York: Vintage Books; 1973)
England, L and Warner, K. `An Ashby Hierarchy for Human Action' Cybernetics and Systems Research; 2(1984):665-670
Feyerabend, P. Against Method (London: Verso; 1975)
Fromm, E. Beyond the Chains of Illusion (New York: Simon and Schuster; 1962)
Giddens, A. New Rules of Sociological Method (New York: Basic Books; 1976)
---- Central Problems in Social Theory (Berkeley: University of California Press; 1979)
---- A Contemporary Critique of Historical Materialism (Berkeley: University of California Press; 1981)
--- The Constitution of Society (Berkeley: University of California Press; 1984)
Habermas, J. Knowledge and Human Interests (Boston: Beacon; 1968)
---- Theory and Practice (Boston: Beacon; 1973)
---- Reason and the Rationalization of Science (Boston: Beacon Press; 1981)
Harre, R. Personal Being (Cambridge, Mass.; Harvard University Press; 1984)
Homans, G. Human Behavior (New York: Harcourt, Brace and Janovich; 1974)
Husserl, E. The Crisis of European Sciences and Transcendental Phenomenology (Evanston, IL; Northwestern University Press; 1970)
Jaynes, J. The Origin of Consciousness in the Breakdown of the Bicameral Mind (Boston: Houghton-Mifflin; 1976)
Marcuse, H. Reason and Revolution (Boston: Beacon; 1941)
--- Eros and Civilization (Boston: Beacon; 1966)
May, R. Freedom and Destiny (New York: Dell; 1981)
Polanyi, M. Knowing and Being (Chicago: University of Chicago Press; 1969)
Ricoeur, P. Time and Narrative (Chicago: University of Chicago Press; 1984)
Schutz, A. The Problem of Social Reality (The Hague: Martinus Nijhoff; 1962)
Simon, H. The Sciences of the Artificial (Cambridge, Mass.: MIT Press; 1981)
Skinner, B. Beyond Freedom and Dignity (New York: Alfred Knopf; 1971)
Springer, S. and Deutsch, G. Left Brain, Right Brain (New York: Freeman; 1981)
Stamps, J. Holonomy (Seaside, CA: Intersystems Press; 1980)
Wilson, E. On Human Nature (New York: Bantom; 1978)

USING MATHEMATICS FOR INTRODUCING SYSTEMS THINKING TO CHILDREN

Andrea Graebe
San Jose State University
Cybernetic Systems Program
San Jose, Ca 95192

ABSTRACT: How well can children of different ages comprehend and utilize systems concepts? This paper describes the author's one and a half years of experiences in trying to teach systems concepts to children on a one-to-one-basis during math tutoring lessons. Preliminary observations indicate that the mathematical language might offer some unexplored possibilities for formally and effectively introducing systems concepts to elementary and highschool children.

1. INTRODUCTION

Who has not seen the fascinated expression on a toddler's face as it pulls on its wooden duck's string and discovers that the wooden duck will move? This child has just discovered a relationship: its own actions affect those in its environment. The persistence and joy with which a toddler repeats such a discovery suggest above all that young children have a natural drive to explore not just objects but the various ways in which they interact.

How can this initial drive be fostered in a child's education to lead to a cybernetic understanding of our world? A "cybernetic under-standing" could be defined in L. J. Perelman's words as: "cultivating a child's inherent capacity to... think in systems, reinforcing the habit of persistent and critical questioning, by permitting children to see manifestations of their own decisions and actions in the broadest space and time horizons possible" (Perelman, 1972: 36).

Cybernetic concepts tend to be of such abstract nature that they need to be introduced carefully to children. Children move through a learning hierarchy in their intellectual development, and--even though they might be natural systems thinkers--cannot understand abstract concepts before a certain age (Miller, 1981: 253-260) (Piaget, 1971).

One possible approach for teaching systems concepts to children of different ages is therefore described by Ruth-Ellen and J. P. Miller as:

"Rather than, for instance, demonstrating the interconnected-ness of elements through flow diagrams, the early childhood

513

R. Trappl (ed.), Cybernetics and Systems '86, 513–520.

educator is more likely to point out the importance of sun-
light, water, and worms in the soil where the children garden--
perhaps letting them experiment by doing without one or more of
these....".
Such concrete, day-to-day experiences would "...offer the
prepubescent child the opportunity to use non-abstract, pre-
logical thinking processes to move through the learning hierarchy with a systems perspective... Then later, when more
abstract concepts (e.g. cybernetics, nonlinearity) are introduced, they will be associated with and supported by meaningful
experiences, and hence, more easily apprehended." (Miller,
1981: 254).

2.0 USING MATHEMATICS TO EXPLAIN SYSTEMS CONCEPTS

St. Augustine said: "The good Christian should be aware of mathematicians and all those who make empty prophecies. The danger already
exists that the mathematicians have made a convenant with the devil to
darken the spirit and confine man in the bonds of hell" (Kline, 1953:
3). And the Roman jurists ruled: "concerning evil-doers, mathematicians, and the like" that "to learn the art of geometry and to take
part in public exercises, an art as damable as mathematics, are forbidden" (Kline, 1953: 3). And the philosopher Schopenhauer described
arithmetics as being the lowest activity of the spirit, as is shown by
the fact that it can be performed by a machine (Kline, 1953: 4).

With the rise of the systems age, mathematics can take on yet
another meaning: it can be viewed as man's most sophisticated language
for describing relationships among objects rather than the objects
themselves. Taught to children as such rather than as a technical tool
for specific tasks I have found that mathematics creates fascination
and an awareness of systems concepts rather than the usual boredom,
confusion, and fear.

I have experimented on two levels with teaching mathematics to
children as their first formal language for learning about relation-
ships--stimulating students to start asking "systems questions" in the
process.

On one level, I use mathematics as a medium through which
students can experiment with different ways of relating to a complex
subject and improve their mind's inherent ability to grasp complex,
interrelated phenomena. The emphasis is not only on understanding
multiplication, for example, but on becoming aware of and experimenting
with this process of understanding. My overall goal on this level is
to help students develop the cognitive abilities necessary for understanding the multi-level dynamics of social, natural, and global
systems by first learning to control the complexity in mathematical
systems.

On a second level, I use the rules according to which numbers
behave as analogies for introducing systems concepts. The nature of
concepts such as evolution, complexity, simplicity, hierarchy, organization, assumptions, system, wholeness, emergent properties, bound-

aries, multiple perspectives, decision-making and many more can be
simulated and explained in a metaphoric (rather than cause-and effect)
way by using mathematical models.

The great benefit of using mathematics for introducing students
to systems thinking lies in the fact that numbers in and of themselves
have less internal complexity than the components of any other system
(even an electron has more inherent complexity than a number). The
entire complexity of mathematics arises from the multitude of interactions, not from the components themselves. The lack of complexity
within the components helps direct a student's entire focus towards the
interactions between the parts.

2.1 First Level: Improving a Child's Ability to See Patterns and Relationships in Mathematics

When tutoring children on a one to one basis I frequently did not
have the time to prepare for the lessons. As a result, the child and I
often learned the material together during the lesson. This was an
ideal opportunity for comparing learning strategies and pinpointing
what allowed me to understand the material faster than the child did. I
found that most students not only had difficulties with extracting
useful information from their mathematics books, but had poor
strategies in general for comprehending material that required an
ability to think in patterns and networks of simultaneous, dynamic
events. Once I understood this, it occurred to me that if I could
improve a child's strategies for understanding its mathematics book, I
could probably also enhance its receptivity to systems concepts.

In order to enhance a child's ability to first of all see the
patterns and connections within mathematics, I experimented with
viewing the child and myself as two cybernetic systems, each possessing
detector (for detecting relevant information), selector (for selecting
goals or motives), and effector (muscular) functions as well as a feedback loop informing the 'detector' about the success of the 'effected'
action in terms of achieving the 'selected' goal.(Alfred Kuhn, 1975:
47-48), (see figure 1).

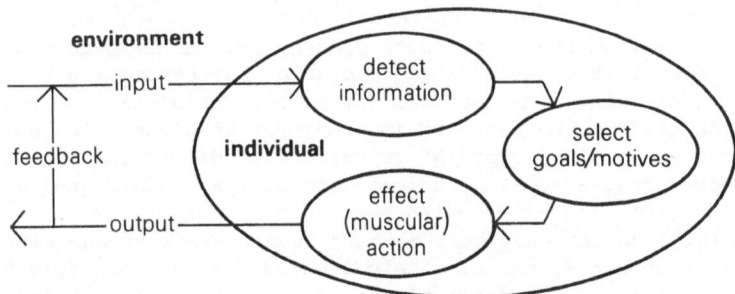

Figure 1. Alfred Kuhn's model of a cybernetic system.

My overall goal was to improve the student's detect, select, and
effect strategies for picking up patterns and relationships.

515

Using mathematics as the medium, I take the child through four stages in trying to improve its ability to first of all see the patterns and relationships in mathematical systems.

First, we try to 'select' the child's goal. Why is it learning mathematics? Commonly, the first problems arise at this level. Most children are not quite sure why they are really studying these "meaningless" techniques. This means the child has no sense of the relevant context within which it can place the isolated pieces of information presented to it. A "brain writing session" (brainwriting is a technique by which the brainstorming process of a group or individual is recorded) usually creates a first awareness of the fact that the subject is not just an isolated body of knowledge but something that is highly interconnected with other events in the child's life. One child for example discovered through a brain writing session that failing in mathematics meant that it would lose its network of friends. This student then easily understood why it had developed such a fear of the subject.

The important aspect of this first stage is that the child has experienced the interconnectedness of the different aspects in its life and created a personal meaning around the subject of mathematics. Within this context it can now 'select' a personally meaningful goal for learning mathematics. Only now will a child really be motivated to receive ('detect') the information in the book. Interestingly enough, all these children, given the freedom to develop their own motives, abandon the traditional goal of learning mathematics in the hope of someday applying it towards "balancing checkbooks and building bridges".

At this point, I also share my goal with them (I am a separate cybernetic system with separate goals). I tell them that I teach mathematics because I believe that it will train their minds to think in systems and that this will help them be more effective problem solvers. So far, the prospect of being a better problem solver has seemed interesting enough to my students (I have tried this with about twenty children from age 8 to 17) that, with occasional minor changes, they have decided to 'select' this as one of their motives for learning mathematics.

Once the overall goal has been 'selected', I then use a series of questionnaires from the German book Denken, Lernen, Vergessen (Vester, 1978) to initiate the second stage: to help them become aware of their style for 'detecting' information. These tests help evaluate how information needs to be packaged in order for this specific child to receive it. A child might prefer visual over auditory information, graphs over words, a somewhat threatening over an understanding teacher, a formal learning environment, etc..

Again, I do not only help a child become aware of and alter its own 'detect' channels, but also help a child discover my style for teaching information (my 'effect' channels) so that each child can develop an awareness of my habit of giving overviews of chapters (for example) whereas the child's 'detect' channels might be geared towards being introduced to one detail at a time. I practice with the child to recognize and mention such situations in order to enhance children's control over their own learning experience. Having the ability to initiate, maintain and control their learning process independently of the external learning environment is one of the goals of this phase.

After going through these tests, we then start using the mathematics book to further improve the child's ability to 'detect' patterns and relationships. Rather than explaining the contents of a chapter, I try to guide the child to 'detect' the relevant information itself as well as the overall pattern that connects the single bits of it into a whole. I make the child aware of the fact that chapter headings, highlighted sentences, examples, etc., all carry pieces of information that the child can utilize in its overall attempt to extract the key message of a specific chapter. We analyze the style of the book and identify where the child has strong and weak points in understanding the given style. While doing so, children usually discover very much to their own surprise that within a chapter, the same information is repeated over and over again from many different angles. This discovery usually surprises them and gives them feedback about their growing ability to consciously notice the many pieces of information within the chapter. At this point I introduce a new distinction: I encourage them to distinguish between information and noise within the chapter (whereby I point out that what might be noise for this child--given her 'detect' channels--might be information for another) and to connect the single information bits into a meaningful whole. So far, I have been amazed at how little time it takes most children to learn how to learn mathematics from their own textbook--without my help as a tutor--by this method. This has reinforced my view that children have a latent ability to think in systems (given my assertion that understanding mathematics requires an ability to think in systems) and do not have to learn this as something completely foreign to them.

To further practice "seeing the whole" behind all the details, and also to practice the 'effect' function, we then move into the third stage: in the child's own copy book we create "an abbreviated model" of the contents of a chapter. The child summarizes in its own style --sentences, graphs, flowcharts, comic strips or whatever--the key information of the chapter and highlights this summary with color.

In the fourth stage, we go back to the book and the child is free to pick as many exercises from the newly learned chapter as it needs for reassuring itself whether it really understood the new material. (most of the children enjoy picking the hardest examples!). This feedback brings closure to the learning process. The most common comment I receive from children at this point is that they don't understand why math used to be such a problem for them. This change in ability to "read" mathematics I believe is intitiated by teaching the child how to learn rather than teaching mathematics directly.

As a "meta-closure" process, I then allow children to add a reflective statement expressing their own feelings about the newly learned material. I found that coming in touch with these underlying feelings is so valuable to children that just for this alone they would sit through an hour of math lessons.

2.2 Second Level: Drawing Analogies between Mathematical and Systems
    Concepts

    Once children are comfortable with the densely packaged
information style of the mathematical language, I then start calling
children's attention to the patterns in which numbers interact and
introduce systems vocabulary or concepts that describe this type of
behavior. We then explore whether and how this systems concept is
relevant within their own immediate life.
    In geometry, for example, 11-year-old children learn to take a
cube apart so that it becomes a two-dimensional pattern of connected
squares (see figure 2). In the process they discover, much to their own
surprise, that, depending on how they take the cube apart, very
different two-dimensional patterns emerge. This serves as a direct
example for the general notion of the systems field that more than one
perspective is possible of any piece of reality (this is a profound
insight for children). Vocabulary such as alternatives, model building,
appropriateness, constraints, resources, can be introduced at this
point. I commonly apply the discovery of multi-perspectivity to some
recent conflict situation within the child's life, and we try to
explore alternative interpretations of the situation (just like finding
alternative two-dimensional patterns hiding in the cube). This whole
concept is then carried further by encouraging a child to experiment
with the relativity of other problem situations and with more
consciously searching for several alternatives.

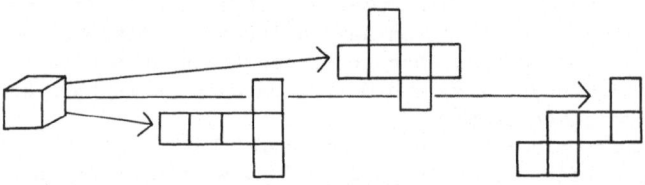

Figure 2. Different ways of disassembling a cube into two-dimensional
patterns.

    For more advanced students, the process of taking derivatives
serves as an example of how complexity and simplicity are intimitely
related and form an equilibrium (which is then also expanded to point
out that most variables act together to form a larger homeostatic
situation). The more complicated the meaning of a graph becomes (i.e.
it is the derivative of the derivative of the derivative), the simpler
the graph itself will be (figure 3).

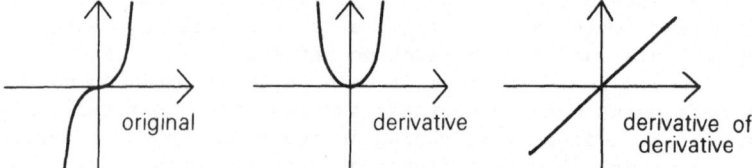

Figure 3. Decrease of the graph's geometric complexity is coupled to
an increase in the complexity of the graph's meaning.

518

Or children learning sine and cosine functions can play the "Heinz von Foerster game" of picking some number of "reasonable" size, then taking the sine of it, taking the cosine of the result, taking the sine of the new result and so on, back and forth. After a few iterations, an equilibrium is found; further iterations keep producing the same two numbers (von Foerster, Heinz. Videotape: <u>Understanding Understanding</u> and personal discussion. 1985. Heinz von Foerster uses this metaphor to introduce the concept of "eigen-values".) (see figure 4). I use this as an analogy for introducing the concept of "emerging properties", "eigen values", and "stability".

sin 16 = 0.275   cos 0.275 = 0.999   sin 0.999 = 0.0174

cos 0.0174 = 1   sin 1 = 0.0174   cos 0.0174 = 1

Figure 4. Taking the sin and cos of some initial number in an iterative fashion will always lead to the two numbers 1 and .0174.

Almost any mathematical phenomena can be used to illustrate a systems concept because mathematical systems are dynamic, highly interconnected, holistic, and so abstract that they practically beg to be filled with meaning--even if it is on a symbolic, metaphoric rather than literal level.

After I have pointed out a few analogies in this way, children usually start viewing mathematics as an abstract world of patterns within which they are free to use all their creative abilities to discover connections and assign real life meanings to them, and, in my experience, come to truly enjoy the subject.

With younger children (below age 10), I do not use mathematics for introducing formal systems vocabulary but just try to detect their style for seeing the patterns and relationships and try to guide them towards an awareness of relationships. Most young children, for example, have a hard time learning the times tables for the number eight. After they have struggled for a while, I tell them that "a trick is hiding in the number sequence of the eight". While the front digits go from 0 to 8, the back digits go 8 6 4 2 0//8 6 4 2 0. The only spot where the front digits "become stuck for a second" (they repeat themselves at one point) is at the point where the sequence of the back digits starts over. This is very easy for most children to understand and remember, and suddenly the eight-sequence is among the easier ones to learn (the nine sequence is even simpler). After several times of pointing out these underlying patterns in which numbers tend to behave and the child each time experiences that seeing these patterns makes the memorization process easier, it searches for these patterns without much further input.

3. CLOSING

Systems concepts can be taught to children through a variety of experiences, including math--the original language of systems. Once children's strategies for understanding mathematics have been improved so that the subject no longer evokes fear and confusion, systems concepts can be introduced during math lessons by using the behavior of numbers as a metaphor. This process should be supplemented through real life examples demonstrating the relevance of these systems concepts. In teaching systems thinking, it should be kept in mind that not all students relate well to teaching through metaphors and that some students feel uncomfortable with the abstract and holistic thinking necessary for understanding many systems concepts. Given these precautions, I have found that most children are interested in, can understand, and spontanously enjoy utilizing systems concepts.

4. ACKNOWLEDGEMENTS

I wish to express thanks to Dr. Balkus for encouraging me to write this paper, to Heinz von Foerster and my thesis advisor Ruth-Ellen Miller for their continued and patient support throughout the production of the paper, to my colleague Elin Smith for several good ideas concerning both the paper and my work with children, to my friends Bob Kelsey and Adrian Bourne who did not let me give up on this paper, and especially to all the children who gave me their continued and valuable feedback when I asked them to evaluate my "new math tutoring lessons".

4. REFERENCES

Argyris, Chris. Reasoning, Learning, and Action. San Fransisco: Jossey-Bass Inc. 1982.

Kuhn, Alfred. Unified Social Science. Homewood: The Dorsey Press. 1975.

Miller, Ruth and Jack. 'Systems Concepts for Early Grades.' General Systems Yearbook, Vol XXVI, 1981, p. 253-260.

Perelman, L.J. 'Developing an Ecological Curriculum for 'Sesame Street'.' Unpublished ms., Harvard Graduate School of Education. 1972.

Vester, Frederic. Denken, Lernen, Vergessen. (Thinking, Learning, Forgetting). Munich: DTV. 1983.

THE ART OF NEGOTIATIONS: A SYSTEMS PERSPECTIVE

Amit K. Maitra
Technology Consultant
1204 Linden Hill
Lindenwold, NJ 08021
U.S.A.

ABSTRACT. This paper discusses the art of negotiations using a quantitative framework to highlight tradeoffs in a given situation. It does not include empirical data to explain how the quantifiable information can be integrated into a nego- tiating process. Its basic intent is to elucidate the appli- cation principles of a systems concept in the form of a Multi- national Control System (MCS). To that end, it argues that the MCS puts in perspective the remedies and dispute settle- ment procedures relevant to international joint ventures, coproduction, and licensing negotiations and transactions.

1. INTRODUCTION

The operations of a Multinational Corporation (MNC) are gov- erned by economics. Its financial objectives are to maximize profit on a global basis. It invests in foreign countries, provides them with technology, incomes, foreign trade earnings new employment, and management education. The size and nature of the MNC, once this global objective is seen, gives rise for concern in host countries in the areas such as transfer pricing, and profit maximization which could affect the count- ry's foreign exchange rate as a result of currency transfers. Therefore, the host country has a right to know, in advance, what the likely cash flows will be for things such as capital expenditure, patents, licenses, know how, and management fees. In so far as possible, all such details should be negotiated beforehand and finally specified in an agreement to avoid future recriminations.

The intent of this paper is to present an approach for business negotiations between large MNCs and foreign colla- borators for international joint venture, coproduction, and licensing arrangements. The approach can best be characterized as a systems framework wherein all functional tools of busi- ness administration (e.g., financing, production, location,

521

R. Trappl (ed.), Cybernetics and Systems '86, 521–526.

marketing, etc.) are integrated. As these tools are used in the context of a multinational control system, a basis for negotiation of all the common and conflicting interests of the various parties involved [foreign investors(MNC), host country government, local partners, international agencies, **etc.**] develops. Here, the underlying assumption is that the individual issues involved in international joint venture, coproduction, and licensing arrangements - whether concerned with equity matters, or host country's other economic and welfare aspirations - are so complex, their "natural" linkages are so little understood, and the capacity of the negotiators to create and manipulate "synthetic" linkages for corporate and/or national advantages is so perplexing that only a systems approach, in the form of a multinational control system, has the potential for establishing a basis for negotiation.

2. MULTINATIONAL CONTROL SYSTEM

The operations of an MNC present formidable problems to corporate executives responsible for negotiating international agreements. Each nation exhibits unique characteristics; distance and differences in practices also create communication problems. Any negotiation, therefore, has to be planned and conducted in the context of uncertainty about most of the major internal (corporate) and external (host country) forces which could either favorably or unfavorably influence the negotiation process in a given situation. Market growth, competitive moves by other MNCs, government regulations, and costs are just a few of the uncertain factors about which assumptions must be made. A company should consider these uncertain factors as gray areas where appropriate adjustments in its overall policies, practices, and conditioning factors for international business arrangements can often produce satisfactory results in terms of consumating a particular deal.

Companies use budgeting as a basic technique for making adjustments in domestic marketing. It is conceivable that the same technique can be extended to international marketing environments, generating perhaps a new framework that can be termed as a multinational control system. In what follows, some purely conceptual arguments as to how a multinational control system can be perceived are presented. The discussion is continued further to determine if the system can be used for mutually profitable adjustments in negotiation processes between an MNC and any other host country government. The control system is being characterized as multinational, because in the process of negotiations, an MNC must constantly seek avenues to systematically and comprehensively integrate the various controls that it exercises over several territories or nations.

3. ACCOUNTING FOR MANAGEMENT CONTROL

Budget, in its normal domestic usages, spells out the objectives and also the expenditures that will be incurred to achieve any particular set of production goals. It expresses planned sales and profit objectives and production programs in unit and money terms. Control, on the other hand, consists of measuring actual sales and expenditures. This budget - control mechanism is a good candidate for export because (1) it works, (2) there are people who understand it, and (3) these people can in most instances transfer their "knowhow" to a foreign environment. The question is how the underlying principles of this knowhow can be applied to international negotiations.

If there is no variance or a favorable variance between actual and budget, as normally observed in a company's domestic operations, no action would be required in a company's international operations. If, on the other hand, variance is unfavorable, this is a red flag that attracts the attention of corporate managers; they immediately investigate and attempt to determine the cause of the unfavorable variance and what might be done to improve the domestic operation.

The international arrangements for the same company or, for that matter, any other company can be handled somewhat the same way, with, of course, objective considerations given to the different scope of operation. First, the executives must perceive and identify the possible unfavorable variances at the time of negotiations with foreign collaborators. For control purposes, they then will have to use budget not merely to show appropriate quantitative clarification of a particular company's narrow profit or loss objectives, but also to justify how such profit or loss objectives impact the host country's own economic goals and welfare aspirations. In this process, it must be emphasized that perfect arrangements, either from a company's or a host country's standpoint are impossible; but if the company and the host country representatives maintain continuing interest in the dynamic process of negotiation, particularly to isolate sensitive areas where changing circumstances can be taken into account, a good agreement can be negotiated.

A good agreement is one which leaves no unreasonable future constraints. The definition of what is unreasonable can be argued at length. To that end, a rudimentary analysis of the types of common and conflicting interests in international joint venture, coproduction, and licensing arrangements is presented in the following section. Its more important purpose, however, is to put in perspective how an accounting methodology, in the form of a multinational control system, renders explicit the implicit preferences of all parties (e.g.,MNC, host country government and business collaborator, etc.) in a negotiating situation.

4. INTERNATIONAL NEGOTIATION: MISSION IMPOSSIBLE

Certain restrictive practices, often put in as clauses in
agreements, impinge on the economic, political, and security
considerations of a particular joint venture, coproduction,
and licensing agreement. These deal with various issues, including (a) limitation on export, and (b) restricting field
of activity of licensee. The primary reason for insisting on
these two issues is to evoke here the analysis of major an-
tagonisms that are at play in international negotiations, involving an MNC and a foreign collaborator.

The first tension arises from the manner in which different parties view technology in the context of development.
Most host countries argue that development is dependent unless the production of a basket of goods, capital accumulation, and technical progress are all integrated into the
national economy. Concern over capital accumulation and relative independence gives rise to host country's desire for
production of sufficient quantity of goods that will meet
not only the domestic demand but also future export possibilities. Thus, the host country government argues for prohi-
bition of:

> "clauses and/or practices
> prohibiting or limiting in any
> way the export of products
> manufactured on the basis of the
> technology in question including
> restrictions on exports to certain
> markets, permission to export only
> to certain markets; and requirements
> of prior approval of the licensor
> for exports;"

> "clauses and/or practices requiring
> higher technology payments on goods
> produced for exports vis-a-vis goods
> for the domestic market;"

Here lies the built in propensity of international
negotiations to give rise to serious conflicts. Most MNCs
view technology as a marketable commodity. Technology, they
argue, costs money to produce; therefore, it is a commodity
to be marketed. The owners of the technology at times venture
to operate temporarily at a loss in the hopes of creating a
market and eventually earning a fair return. In many circumstances, a licensor has exclusive licensee in more than one
territory and may wish to protect one licensee's market from
competition by goods imported by another licensee. The point
is made that the sale of technology to a country or its use
therein must be carefully planned so that the MNCs which

develop, own, or transmit technology can sooner or later
generate an acceptable return for their technological capital.
Other than these business considerations, there are also
donor country's national security interests which at times
require that the MNCs put export restrictions.

A second conflict takes us straight to the dynamics of
development economics. Much of the technological property
available from MNCs can be used to produce diverse products
or be used in diverse fields of activity. What the host countries want today is a degree of autonomy required to define
their technology policy with respect to their own needs. Thus
they voice their opinions against "field use of restrictions"
in an agreement, referring to:

> "clauses and/or practices
> restricting the recipients
> volume, scope, and range of
> production or field of activity;"

Any restriction on volume, scope, and range of production or field of activity has a clear limiting effect on the
licensee's potential competitive posture in world markets.
More importantly, it gives a sense of infringement by the
licensor on the host country's desire for self guidance.
These are negative consequences of legitimate concern to representatives of the host country viewpoint.

However, restriction of this nature is usually there to
preserve the competitive positions of the licensor and his
other licensees. Where the licensor holds a product patent,
the argument that it thereby has legitimate power to control
competition in the licensed product has some force. By recognizing a reasonable correlation between the scope of the
transferror's propertyrights and the restriction on production or field of use in such a case, a beneficial effect on
technology transfer can be achieved. For instance, host
countries can use any concession respecting production in
seeking concessions on other negotiable conditions of the
agreement. To justify such conditions, the host country representatives must constantly advert to their development
priorities, their resource capacities, the possible effects
of different technologies on a whole range of social,economic,
and political indicators.

5. CONCLUSIONS

The quick review of the above environmental forces suggest
that in multinational operations, marketing control presents
numerous challenges. The rate of environmental change in an
MNC is a dimension of each of the national market in which
the company operates, and the multiplicity of environments,
each changing at different rate and each exhibiting unique

characteristics adds to the complexity of this dimension. In addition, the multipilicity of multinational environments challenges the multinational control system with much greater environmental heterogeneity and therefore greater complexity in its control. It is this complexity that makes simple linear arrangement almost invalid. So the paper has attempted to raise the possibility of a valid quantitative method of measuring trade-offs in a given negotiation situation. The materials presented here do not contain any empirical data to further ascertain what and how the quantifiable information can be integrated into a negotiating strategy. Because of corporate confidentiality, such information is not readily available. The paper has, therefore, dealt with the principles of applications of a systemic concept of a multinational control system concerning remedies and dispute settlement procedures relevant to international joint venture, coproduction, and licensing negotiations and transactions.

INFORMATION VALUE ANALYSIS

W.L. Gage
Professor, Polytechnic of Central London.
Director, Harold Whitehead & Partners Ltd.

Systems analysts use information technology to provide on-line
integrated systems.   There is a requirement for system cost/benefit
analysis.   Information Value Analysis is recommended for this stage of
a project.

1.   MANAGEMENT SYSTEMS ANALYSIS

The search for a better regulator (Beer, 1984) may be defined as the
process of analysing requirements and designing the procedures by which
work will be carried out by computer.   (British Standard 3138)

It comprises a series of tasks:-
  . select application
  . survey for feasibility
  . analyse existing system
  . define requirements
  . design
  . cost/benefit analysis
  . implement
  . evaluate
  . maintain
which may require several iterations as features of the terms of
reference constrain the design.

As an exercise in management the analysis and design should be
structured (Davis, 1982) and constitutes a project, with the attendant
organisational, motivational and control problems.

The case for teamwork in systems analysis and design rests on:
  . the need for information
  . the need for co-ordination
  . the creativity benefit from hitch-hiking

R. Trappl (ed.), Cybernetics and Systems '86, 527–532.
© *1986 by D. Reidel Publishing Company.*

. the need to find consensus regarding the sociological
paradigm.   (Burrell & Morgan, 1985)
. the negotiation and reconciliation of perspectives
(Antill & Wood-Harper, 1985)
. a measure of departmental commitment to implementation

When requirements are defined the participatory design process
involves Information Mapping (Best, 1984) to consider options for
providing outputs which fulfil the requirements.

2. <u>COST BENEFIT ANALYSIS</u>

The systems analysis project team is expected to prepare cost benefit
analysis on two occasions. During feasibility assessment it must
justify the study and later it must justify implementation. The
second and more rigorous cost benefit analysis creates the budget for:
. asset investment (storage requirements keep growing)
. system operating costs
. change costs, including any training or parallel run
expenditure and any payroll additions
. maintenance/insurance/security

The exercise will call for variety control when the initial sizing
calculations are complete.

. Do we need to retain all customers on file for our mailing
list, or is it possible to eliminate some ?
. Will a stock classification exercise (Pareto; ABC) enable
us to omit class C items from the systems ?
. Must every work order be entered, or could we leave Friday
afternoon for rectification jobs and other internally
generated load ?

Cost may be reduced by the application of variety reduction to
the database, which like inventory can be searched for inactive data.
A further reduction may be attainable by limiting the reports, or the
flexibility of interrogation for ad hoc reports. But the latter
curtailment may alienate users. The development of information
technology as a merging of computing and data transmission is believed
to have been driven by a demand for this kind of management information system (Gage, 1980), and helped by government subsidies which may
or may not be used wisely.

A new survey (U.K.D.T.I., 1985) challenges this belief. "It is
an absolute myth to say that senior managers need access to the
company database. Yet it makes companies spend more on computers and
software systems than anything else."

Certainly the myth has sustained system builders intending to
provide intangible benefits which could arise if executives can
retrieve information for spreadsheet manipulation about any fields

within the organisations's database. ESSO (UK) is concerned about justification and control and in a conference paper (Ibbotson, 1985) called for "a systematic approach to benefit analysis".

3. VALUE ANALYSIS

Its originator (Miles, 1961) defined Value Analysis as an organised procedure for the efficient identification of unnecessary cost.

Miles discloses in the definition his conviction that wherever cost is generated in an organisation, unnecessary cost is likely to occur, and his procedure will disclose it.

In practice its application to products was considered most useful. Teams challenged the design and specification of multi-component hardware, including cabinets and packaging, and usually found savings exceeding 10% of factory cost.

Hardware applications lasted about 10 years in UK, from 1964 to 1974. Burnout (Lawler & Mohrman, 1985) was rapid in the seventies, as Management by Objectives replaced value analysis as flavour-of-the-month.

The technique was distinguished (Gage, 1969) from other approaches to cost reduction by the following:-
. a multi-function team, not necessarily peers, and not necessarily insiders
. a predetermined work plan
. analysing, listing and ranking of function
. marginal costing which supported allocation to function
. commitment to a theory of group creativity, now called innovation culture.

Function cost analysis survived burn-out in several parallel management productivity teams, such as Unilever's Large Scale Value Analysis and Allegheny's Product Innovation groups. More widespread were the administrative function studies described as Value Administration by Mead, Carney Ltd., Value Management by Whiteheads, and Overhead Value Analysis by McKinsey.

Miles had formulated a useful package for deploying process consultancy in support of cost reduction teams. Assignments may differ according to the cost reduction targets and the culture in the host organisation. At RACAL the Chief Design Engineer channelled the speculation; at Cadbury the team addressed itself to yield controls on ingredients and packaging; at United Biscuits there was no marketing delegate in the team.

But pre-occupation with function and its cost survived diversification.

(Process consultancy, of course, survived and diversified.
Facilitators work as animateurs of project teams, and in Boeing a
structured participation program called Consensus is attributed to
Klamm.)

4. INFORMATION VALUE ANALYSIS

The shopping list approach to systems analysis tends to cause
unnecessary cost. Frankel & Gras (1983) list 85 features to be envi-
saged in the shopping list for choosing materials management software.
Who could resist the opportunity to store three price levels and
individual vendor lead times ? For many inventory applications real-
time access for material users, for production scheduling, for cost
accountants and field service engineers must be attractive. But this
means sophisticated software for networking, with plenty of memory for
each workstation and a spooled printer. The table offers some bench-
marks in the function cost analysis for a material control system to
provide operational and management reports in a contract service
organisation (central heating, maybe, or building or electrical
repairs) with
. 2000 line items held in custody
. 100 in/out transactions per day
. maintenance included.

FUNCTION	3-YEAR LIFE CYCLE COST IN £		
	Hardware	Software	People
KNOW STATUS	4,000	500	45,000
(16-bit business computer, MS-DOS operating system, daily update on floppy discs; one operator; dBASE II)			
KNOW STATUS (on line) KNOW VALUE KNOW TURNOVER	16,000	1,000	75,000
(16-bit, MS-DOS, ports for additional VDU in warehouse and purchasing; printer; three operators part-time, Kewill MICROSS)			
-as above plus KNOW SUPPLIER GENERATE REQUISITION GENERATE INVOICE	50,000	12,000	120,000
(mini-computer with VDU and printer in material control, purchasing, sales and warehouse; four operators part-time, CINCOM MRP)			

530

Cost is generated for the above table by:-

(1)   Knowledge required.

(2)   Speed of retrieval required (the on-line requirement demands a local area network).

(3)   Quantity of data on file (the reason for variety control).

(4)   Accuracy required.

(5)   Modelling requirements, including historical data for trending.

(6)   User stipulations for extras (often subjectively perceived as important).

(7)   IT strategy and standards of the host organisation.

(8)   Training costs imposed by lack of user friendliness.

The value analysis protocol requires that secondary functions, such as GENERATE REQUISITION, and other desirable features, such as ranking by turnover to automate the stock classification, should be identified and the associated incremental cost considered. A similar discipline derived from cybernetic principles is recommended by Carter (1984).

Rigour in cost/benefit analysis implies associating a cost to each increment of benefit. The discipline of value analysis imposes a duty on the systems analysis team to speculate, without inhibition at that stage, on other ways of achieving the output, then costing the other methods.

A sequenced activity list for systems analysis and design may be taken to imply that cost/benefit analysis is a discrete phase which discloses information for the decision to implement or abort.

Information value analysis entails a duty to be aware of costs during the design process, but in a way which does not inhibit creativity.

5.　REFERENCES

Antill, L. & Wood-Harper, A.T. : Information Systems Definition
　　　(Blackwell 1985)

Beer, S. : Keynote address to EMCSR-84

Best, D.P. : A Cybernetic Approach to the Application of Information
　　　Technology in EMCSR-84 Proceedings (Elsevier 1984)

Burrell & Morgan : Sociological Paradigms (Gower 1985)

Carter, M.P. : The Cost of Management Information in Management
　　　Decision Vol.22 No.5 (MCBU Press 1984)

Davis, W.S. : Systems Analysis & Design (Addison-Wesley 1983)

EOSYS Consultancy for UK Department of Trade and Industry
　　　(HMSO 1985)

Frankel, P. & Gras, A.: Software Sifter (MacMillan 1983)

Gage, W.L. : Value Analysis (McGraw-Hill 1967)

Gage, W.L. : Why Managers Prefer Interrogation Facilities in MIS
　　　(Hemisphere EMCSR-78 proceedings)

Ibbotson, A. :The Information Centre (Xephon Conference 1985)

Lawler, E.E. & Mohrman, S.A. : Quality Circles after the Fad
　　　(HBR Jan-Feb 1985)

Macintosh, N.B. : Social Software of Accounting and Information Systems
　　　(Wiley 1985)

Miles, L.D. : Techniques of Value Analysis and Engineering
　　　(McGraw-Hill 1961)

Perry, W.E. : The Micro-mainframe Link (Wiley 1985)

MODEL FOR INTERDISCIPLINARY COOPERATION IN THE CONSTRUCTION OF
INDUSTRIAL PLANTS BY A GROUP OF PRODUCERS

Otmar G. Ladanyi
University of Technology Vienna
Theresianumgasse 27
1040 Wien
Austria

Hans Ladanyi
University of Illinois at
Urbana-Champaign;
University of Vienna
Austria

ABSTRACT. Consortia producing industrial plants are faced by ever increasing demands and risks in implementing key-turn contracts. *a) The paper analyzes the specific problems in designing and constructing operations of this sort, discusses possible coping strategies, and proposes a computerized system intended to improve the communication and cooperation among consortia members.

1. INTRODUCTION

Engineering industries face more and more difficulties in marketing single appliances, they must offer complete systems which can solve particular problems. (1) Companies, who are active in international business - especially in developing regions - are often required to combine their systems to turn-key-industrial plants. According to the UNIDO 51 % of Germany's (Fed. Rep.) exports of engineering products (value), are combined systems. (2)
      Besides the mostly difficult financing of the project and the clarification of the general conditions for investing in the country of destination, exporters have to solve primarily two problems which are: research for new system concepts or the adaptation of these to the climatic, legal and socio-economic conditions of the specific region, to infrastructure, supply of raw materials (type, amount and quality), the particular construction site and establishing of effective communication/coordination structures among the organizations involved (departments, partners, suppliers).
      This paper approaches primarily the design of such structures. (3) Establishing of effective policies to employ heuristics for planning (4) and profitable decision making will be discussed.

2. CONSORTIA - HISTORICAL AND CONTEMPORARY ASPECTS

A company that wants to bid for a project, but cannot do so alone due to lack of capacity, funds, experience, equipment, licenses or necessary

533

R. Trappl (ed.), Cybernetics and Systems '86, 533–540.

materials and parts, has basically two options:

It can buy the missing share, implement it and resell it as a part
of the whole plant. In this case the company must dispose of sufficient
capacity and know how to cover risk to develop and sell the general
concept.

It can form a consortium and become part of a group of independent
companies, which share - according to the contract among them - profit
and losses. The biggest of the partners usually coordinates among them
and represents the consortium towards outsiders.

Consortia are mainly formed in the field of surface and underground construction, mining and crude oil businesses. Generally huge capacities are
necessary due to the overwhelming extent of the work and the big risk
involved. (5) But the projects per se are planned and therefore easier to
organize. Consortia in the engineering industries on the other hand, face
the problem, that the (most important) partners must plan together and
have often to adapt existing concepts to changed conditions within a very
short time.

3.   SPECIFIC PROBLEMS

3.1   Sale and Presentation

Factory-projects are usually done in different stages: Conception,
planning and construction. (6) The decisions taken during the concep-
tion-phase determine success and failure of the project far more, than
those taken later. Additional requests of the client can easily be
considered, necessary modifications easily been made. Changes in design
tend to become more expensive and more difficult later on. Therefore the
activities of the salesperson are crucial for the project. Under normal
circumstances product knowledge makes the seller's work more interesting,
builds confidence, meets objections and satisfies the needs of the
prospect. (7) Selling industrial plants means, that the salesperson is
the "first designer", whose experience and knowledge are extremely
important. Therefore the people responsible for the first contact with a
client should be salespersons and product specialists at the same time.
They need intuition and a contact to an expert-group for questions beyond
their knowledge. However there are some more important points such as:
reluctance to decide, the tendency to burden the supplier with as much
responsibility as possible, contribution to the politics of a country or
its reputation by the purchaser; pressure to succed, gaining personal
contact and even friendship with important partners by the salesperson.

3.2 Adaption of Design

Every plant has to be adapted to its designated environment. Special requirements are occasionally mentioned in the tender, but they arise often
long after the contract has been signed. Disturbances interfere with the
goal of the contractors, that is to produce good technology in time using
the available resources efficiently. Many organisations use interdisci-

plinary principles to meet emergencies. For this purpose they assemble diversified task forces to carry out crash programs (under the supervision of a senior executive). Unfortunately, when the crises have been passed, the advantages of intimate coordination of specialized skills are lost sight of, and the customary cellular structure of responsibilities is resumed. (8) Interdisciplinary team or task force procedures face more difficult problems when team members are employees of different companies. The flow of information among the partners can be endangered by interfering organizational structures, the complexity of the relation between decisions and their impact in the future, and the role of all participants, who can be partners for one project but competitors for another.

Due to the lack of algorithmic rules for most of these activities and since the time available to test new technologies before the application decreases steadily, many problems have to be solved by heuristic methods - moving by trial and error, evaluating past experiences, assisted by data-bases and expert systems. All this requires an appropriate communication system.

3.3 Variety

Consortia of the type described above are basically faced by a problem of increased variety. According to Ashby's law (9) of requisite variety and the conforming theory of Galbraith *b) (10), in order to survive, they can increase their information and decision processing capacities, lower the variety in the environment or learn to cope with a gambling type of business by raising funds elsewere or government guarantees.

Feasible strategies to reduce the environmental variety are i.e. not to offer the ready designed plant alone, but the solution of problems by an experienced, reputationable consortium, since first contacts among the future partners or with the potencial clients pin down in fact a good part of the whole plant.

But in this purchaser's market clients tend to shift variety to the producer whenever possible. To avoid the risks of a random-strategy, at least the possibilities for a better communication and cooperation have to be established.

4. AN ORGANIZATION CHART DERIVED FROM THE EXCHANGE OF ACTION AND INFORMATION BETWEEN CUSTOMERS AND SUPPLIERS

In Figure 1 and 2 five main activities drain the flow of action and information from a contractor to a customer. Purchase, as an alternative to production, normally is arranged by the planning and design offices. The organizational structure provides four departments, sales, planning/production, processes/projects, set up and testing.

The flow of information among the departments (action units) and five feedback-loops - cost/price control, timing, profitability/feasibility, market-inquiry and technological assessment - characterizes the processes of the organizational system.

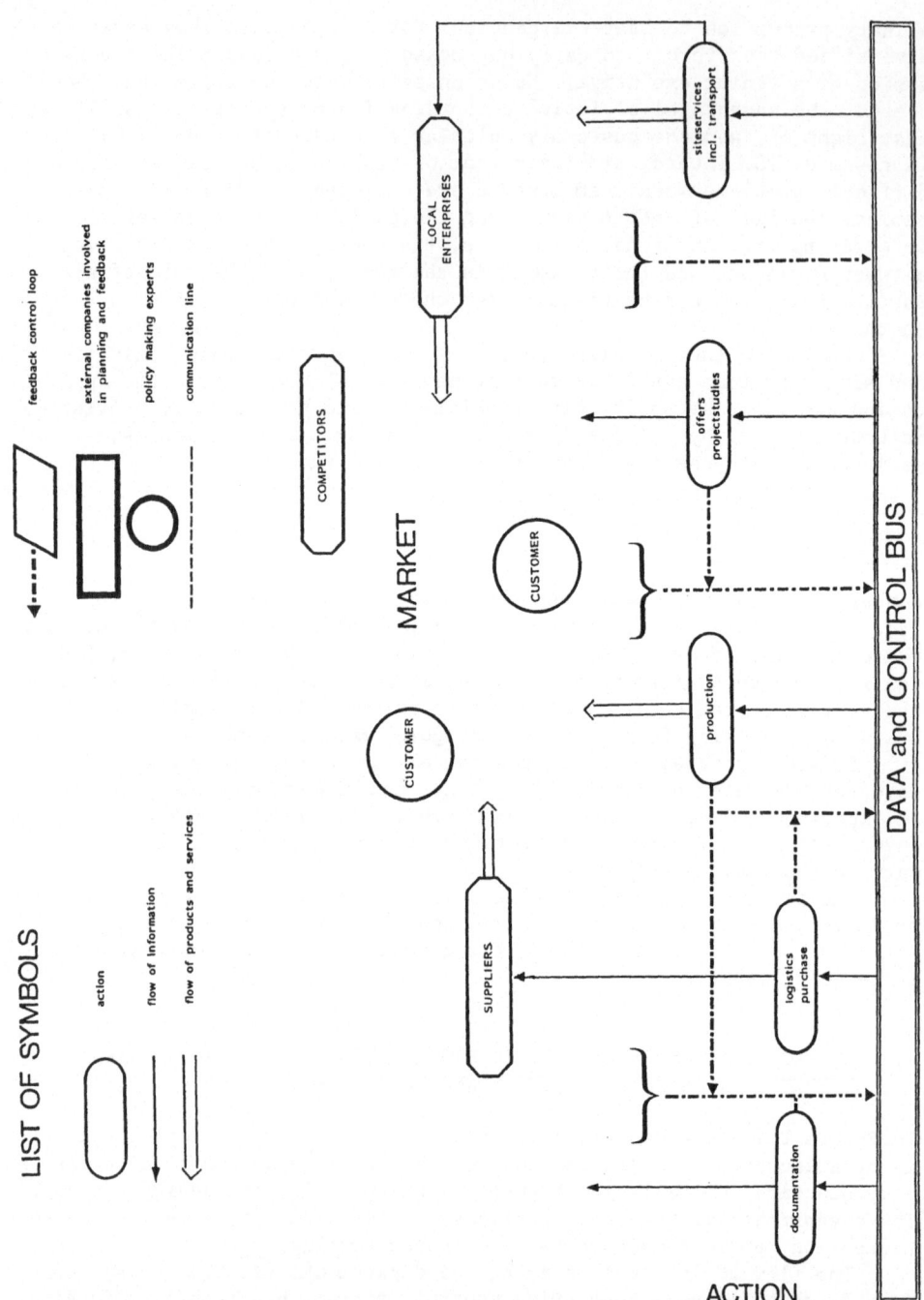

Figure 1. Main activities related to the construction of turnkey industrial plants. Flow of information, products and services between a consortium of independent companies, suppliers and customers.

536

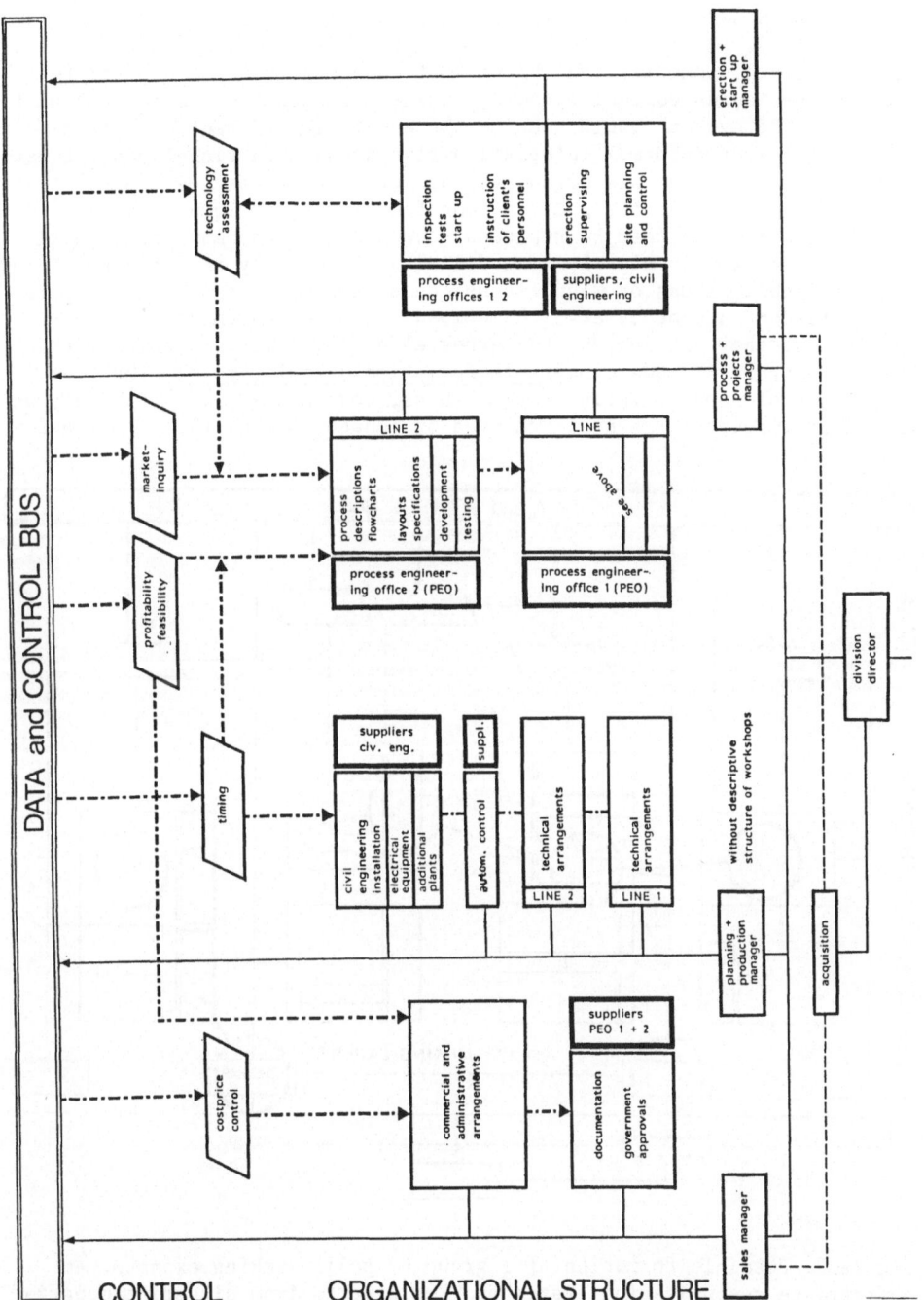

Figure 2. Organizational and control structure. The organizational structure of the maincontractor provides four departments affiliated with engineering offices and suppliers. Five feedback control loops characterize the intensified cooperation.

5. A COORDINATION AND COMMUNICATION SYSTEM ALLOWING HEURISTIC FLOWS OF DECISIONS

An appropriate communication system must enable a <u>group of experts</u> to stay in continuous contact without interfering with their other responsibilities. The system should combine the advantages of meetings and a valuable flow of informal information with those of official contact between each partner and his organisation. For that purpose each participating company should designate a competent member or members of its staff and authorize them to represent and bind the company for a particular project within clearly stated limits. Especially in the case of new financial obligations or when extensions or alternations of the cooperation agreement are necessary, the companies' top management must be involved so they can approve the experts' decision or veto and suggest changes. Figure 3 shows a <u>possible formation of this system.</u> The four components of good decisions – timeliness, correctness, acceptability and maximized results – are best achieved by <u>consensus.</u> *c) (11) The idea,

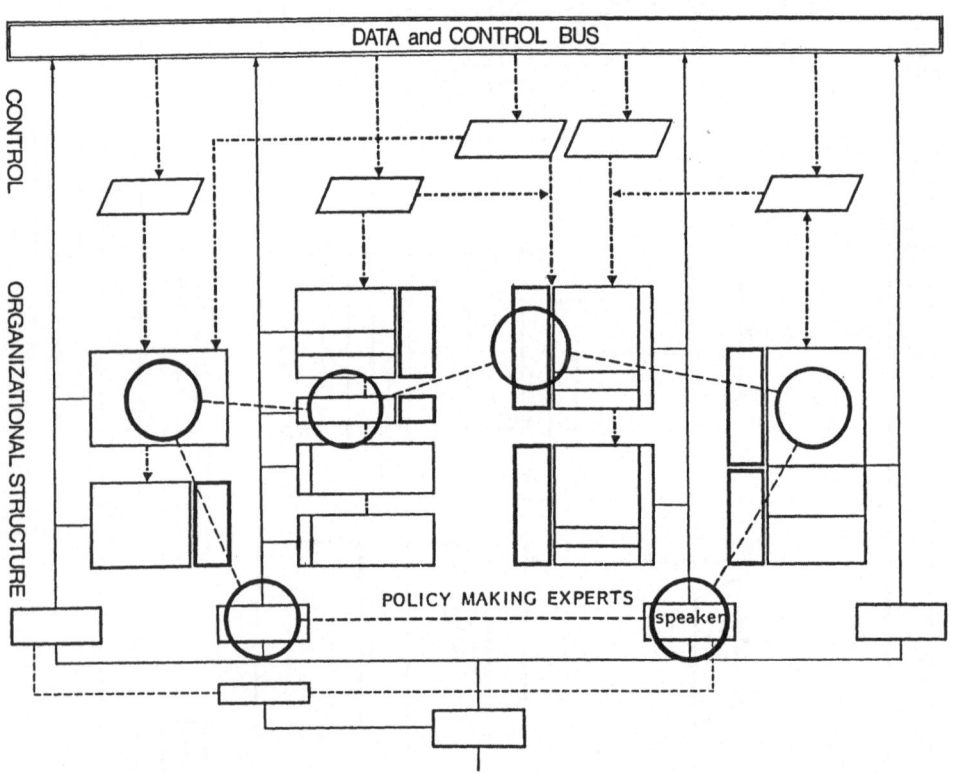

Figure 3. Possible formation of a group of policy making experts. An appropriate communication system enables experts from different departments or the affiliated companies to consider problems in time.

that an appointed project-manager has contact with every member of his team and can lead them like a conductor of an orchestra, (12) does not

seem to be the best solution for Matrix- and Global Project Organisations.
(13) This would block the formal flow of communications between the
partners and would require organizations to accept the authority of
outsiders for certain projects. This is not likely to occur. It rather
stands against the regulations and intentions of the commercial (corporate) law.

The partners should avoid voting, assign the same status to every
member regardless to his status in the home-organization. The groups
should treat their business as confidential in order to allow all members
to express their opinions freely and openly (11). They also must have the
possibility to get instructions from their management if needed. The
group appoints a speaker or coordinator. Costly personal meetings of all
members should be reserved for general outlines and decisions concerning
the cooperation within the group itself. The consortium can set up rules,
maintain and access databases and seek the advice of outside consultants.

6.   A COMPUTERIZED COMMUNICATION SYSTEM

Contacts which are essential also between the personal meetings can be
arranged by means of a communication system especially designated for
this purpose, such as
   acoustic connections, where the group members have priority, which
can be switched to conference mode and equipped with devices for keeping
user's hands free for other activities also.
   A system for transmitting and storage of data with terminals enabling every user, to load, read and edit. The access should be controlled
by codes and/or keys, to avoid misuse and enable the group to conclude
binding agreements.
   Whenever a problem arises, a member can contact one or more others
and try to find a solution. Decisions are concluded via terminals and
computer. Other group-members will be informed via this network and can
check, if these decisions are of importance for them or not. When all
members have indicated satisfaction with a solution, the agreement is
binding, provided the limits are not exceeded and/or no vetos arise.
There are little difficulties in installing computerized communication
systems as described above; comparable equipment is widely used in
various organizations. If interactions between the executives are frequent, a similar communication system can be installed for them (with
possible connections with the experts' system).

7.   CONCLUSION

Technical plants producing consortia are often forced to accept additional risk due to increased variety/uncertainly of the environment.
   The partner companies of these consortia must be involved in the
planning, the information and feedback-flow for mutual benefit.
   The adaptation of existing concepts to particular construction sites
and the fast technological development require a heuristic problem
solving.

The proposed computerized communication/coordination system enables group-decision-making, heuristic problem solving and the settling of agreements on-line, without unnecessary interferences with the experts' other responsibilities.

Consortia which install and use such systems gain the possibility to avoid risks of random strategies.

ACKNOWLEDGEMENTS

We would like to thank Charlotte M. Teuber und F. de P. Hanika † for many long discussions and encouragement. We are grateful to Marya Leatherwood, whose advice in ways of improving the paper was of great value. We acknowledge the help of Robert W. McCloy, with the manuscript.

REMARKS

*a) "Key-turn" refers to industrial plants, where the contractor organizes and is responsible for all activities from the scratch to the testing.
*b) Galbraith uses the term uncertainty, which is a result of increased variety and a lack of improved control structures
*c) Although the decision per se might take longer the whole period including the implementation should be shorter due to increased acceptability.

REFERENCES

1   Hinterhuber, H.H.; Strategische Unternehmensführung.
    Berlin, New York: de Gruyter, 1977
2   Bauer, J.; Lecture: 'Investment Promotion Services'. Graz, 10.10.85
3   Ladanyi, O.; Unternehmensplanung in der Investitionsgüterindustrie.
    Berlin: Duncker & Humblot, 1974
4   Wojda, F.; Planungsheuristik für eine partizipative Arbeitsge-
    staltung. Köln: Z.Arb.wiss., 1982/4
5   Wöhe; Allgemeine Betriebswirtschaftslehre. München: Vahl 1984
6   VDI 2222; Düsseldorf
7   Anderson, B.R.; Professionel Selling. Englewood Cliffs, New Jersey,
    1977
8   Bass, L.W.; 'Interdisciplinary Team Procedures integrate Modern
    Theory of Management'. Washington, D.C.: Little Inc., 1969
9   Ashby, W. Ross; An Introduction to Cybernetics. New York: 1958
10 Galbraith, J.R.; Organizational Design. Reading Mass. 1977
11 Murphy, J.; 'Profitable Decision Making'; in Warrick D.; Ed.,
    Contemporary Organization Development. Glenview (IL), London, 1985
12 Kharbanda O. & Stallworthy E.; How to learn from Project Disasters.
    Aldershot, 1983
13 Harrison, F.; Advanced Project Management. Aldershot, 1981
14 Lakain; How to get control of your time and your Life. New York,
    1973

EXPERIENCE IN APPLICATION OF THE DIALECTICAL SYSTEMS THEORY THROUGH "USOMID" FOR MASTERING OF BUREAUCRATIC RELATIONS IN AN ENTERPRISE

Matjaž Mulej, University of Maribor, School of Business
Economics, Professor of Dialectical Systems Theory
Vlado Sauperl, M.A., manager, Mariborska plinarna Maribor
Yugoslavia

ABSTRACT. The authors report on their new methodological model for
mastering of the danger that the paperwork people, office clarks and
other hourly workers become a bureaucracy with poor effectivness. The
approach starts from the process of work and the objectives and
information requirements resulting from the process.

1. SELECTION OF THE PROBLEM AND VIEWPOINT

Not only in Yugoslavia, the paper work people, office clarks and
other horly workers are considered a latent danger to be a bureaucracy,
which diminishes effectivenees and efficiency. In Yugoslavia, the fight
against bureaucracy is a constituional goal, but the solution lags
behind Constitution.

The research, which we have been doing in several teams and
enterprises has demonstrated that a lot can be done to solve this
problem if one starts from the statement that:
"ORGANISATION" MEANS INSIGHT INTO AND MASTERING OF THE ENTIRE PROCESS OF
WORK AS A WHOLE, NOT MERELY SUBORDINATION AND REPORTING WHICH CREATES
THE RIGHT OF IRRESPONSIBILITY AND ROUTINISM WITH ALL SUBORDINATES.

To get away from irresponsibility, we have developed in Maribor on
the basis of Mulej's DST (= Dialectical Systems Theory) (Mulej 1979), a
methodology for creative cooperation of many (even nearly everybody),
called USOMID in Slovene abbreviation which has been reported about in
several (also international) papers by M. Mulej (Mulej et al.1983, 1984,
1985).

V. Sauperl, in his master thesis (Sauperl 1985) under mentorship of
M. Mulej tried to find out how can USOMID be applied to solve the
problem of mutual relations of common offices and other (producing)
parts (subsystems) of the enterprises so to avoid the threat of
bureaucratisation or to abolish it.

Here, we briefly report on the findings.

2. A BRIEF SUMMARY ABOUT DST AND USOMID

The interconnection of DST and USOMID, in a scheme, is as follows:

541

R. Trappl (ed.), Cybernetics and Systems '86, 541–548.
© 1986 by D. Reidel Publishing Company.

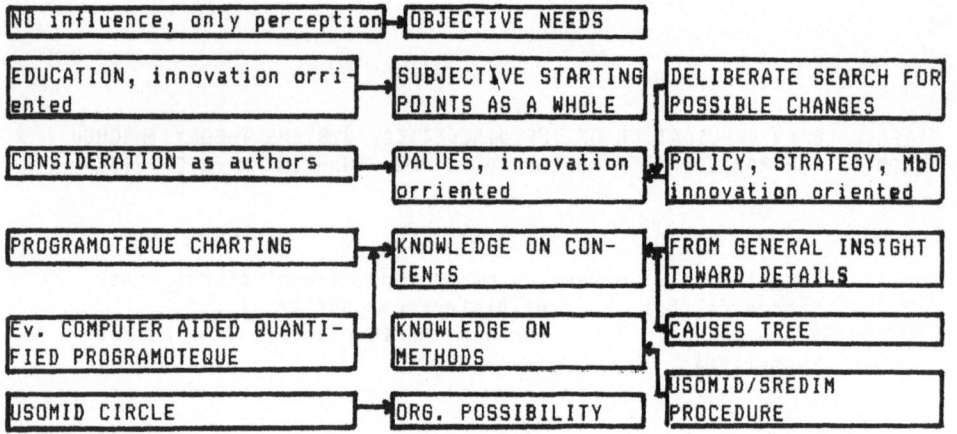

Fig.1: Influences over the starting points by components of USOMID

3. METHODOLOGY TO MASTER POSSIBLE BUREAUCRATIC RELATIONS IN ENTERPRISE

3.1. THE STEPS OF THE PROCESS IN THE ENTERPRISE

We applied USOMID to find a way to objectively define the tasks of the common offices, and to monitor their performance. For this end, a standardisation of the elements of the process and of its costs (measured phisically and financially), aswell as mutual relation of the measures applied, all dependent on actual circumstances in subsystems of the common offices and the process of management,can be very useful.

Therefore, we did not start from the definition of subordination, but rather from the general model of the process (see Fig. 2).

1. PLANNING OF OBJECTIVES - by creative vision for grouded objectives,
2. DESIGNING OF THE REALISATION OF OBJECTIVES - by creative ingeeniring and coordination, to elaborate designs and define tasks for all subsystems,
3. IMPLEMENTATION WORK BY DESIGNS AND TASKS - by smart, dedicated work,
4. MONITORING OF THE RESULTS - by inspection (from the technical and business viewpoints).

Fig. 2: The four basic steps of a wholistic process in an enterprise

We see from Fig.2 that the most influentiàl jobs are the least influenced ones, which needs to be changed.

3.2. THE PROGRAMOTEQUE CHARTING AND PLANNING OF WORK - A WAY TOWARD THE INFLUENCE OVER THE MOST INFLUENTIAL ONES

The title says the way to detect the interdependence of all jobs, the process depedendent need for each one of them and the subsystems place of them. It also allows for formulation of time standards and cost-benefit relations. Since all these elements are parts of legal documents to support mutual interdependence and cooperation called "income relations" by the Yugoslav constitution of 1974, so far mostly lawyers used to take care of them. So, the process used to start from the bylaws etc. instead in the process from Fig. 3:

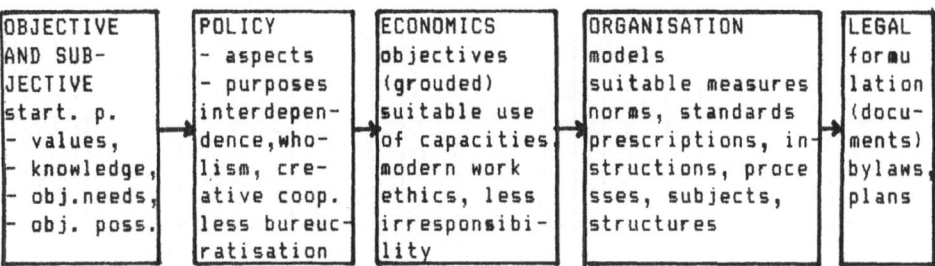

Fig. 3: The (dialectical) succession of making of basis for "income r."

The yearly plan is made as in the Fig. 4 (based on Fig. 2 and 3), which is, at the same time, the interlinking program of the programoteque (= its general part). So, it provides for rough insight into the whole and so the basis for the partial programs, i.e. the other parts of the programoteque. They are all needed for a rather detailed insight into the process of programming and monitoring of the work of the common offices.

Such a way of work activates the possibilities and capabilities for creative cooperation. The result of such work expresses wholism, openess, interdisciplinarity and probability, demanded by (D)ST, since the entire process involves everybody who is concerned by the plan. Their agreement is achieved in a process of three steps, which are   and (in DST) correspond to:

1. the offered program   1. the estimated needs and poss.
2. the demanded program   2. the pref. needs and corr. poss.,
3. the agreed program   3. the objectives.

If the process does not go in such a way as in Fig 3., people feel and are disregarded instead of being considered, and so may real circumstances be, too. The consequence is an unacceptable and refused system of objectives (= plan), which leads to poor results. Here you are also the connection between Fig. 1-4.

In the given case, the programoteque charting has demonstrated that the basis for mastering of possible bureaucracy (= an alienated power with the right to decide without consideration of reality) lies in the following procedure (see Fig. 5):

1. THE INSIGHT into the ENTIRE process and the ROLE of the so called COMMON OFFICES in it, based on the PROGRAMOTEQUE charting with USOMID
2. THE DEFINITION of the business objectives for a longer term and for a single year (BUSINESS POLICY and ECONOMICS)
3. THE PLANNING of tasks for the COMMON OFFICES.

FIG. 4: THE STEPS OF THE ELABORATION OF THE YEARLY BUSINESS PLAN

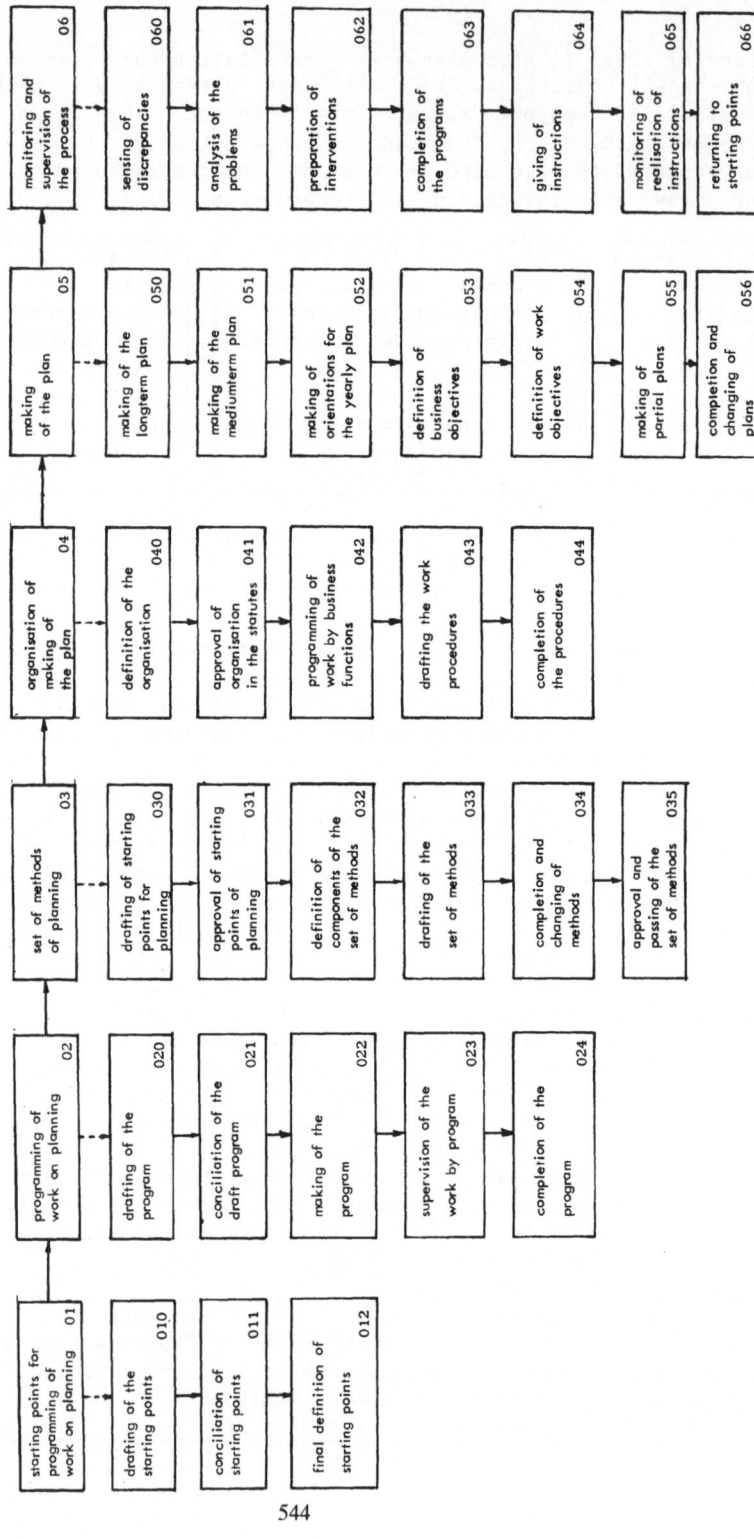

544

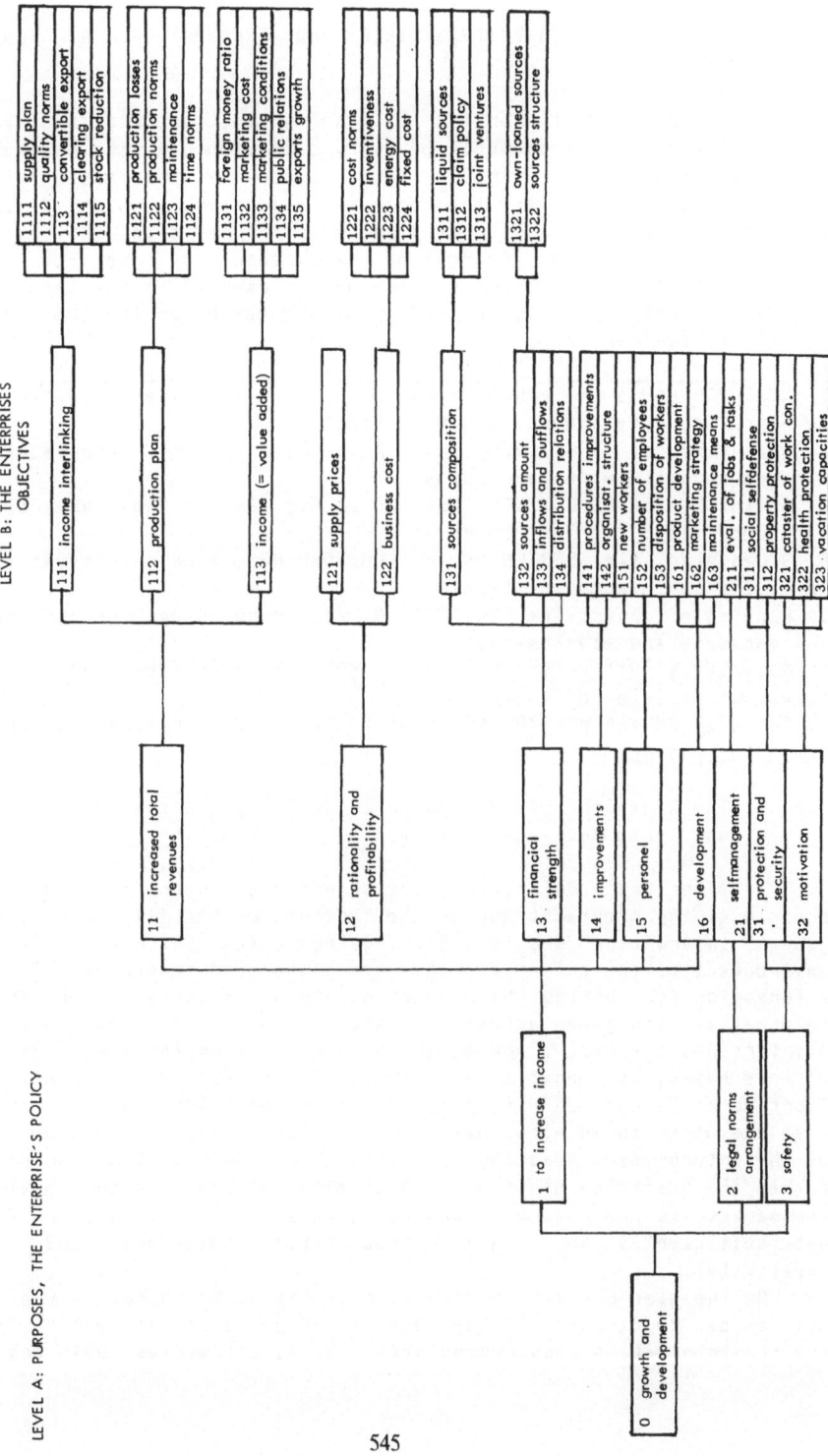

Fig. 6: SYSTEM OF BUSINESS OBJECTIVES AND TASKS TO MAKE THE YEARLY
BUSINESS PLAN
(AN EXAMPLE OF THE BUSINESS OBJECTIVES TREE FOR THE YEAR X)

LEVEL A: PURPOSES, THE ENTERPRISE'S POLICY

LEVEL B: THE ENTERPRISES
OBJECTIVES

LEVEL C: (DERIVED) WORK OBJECTIVES

545

3.3. THE BUSINESS OBJECTIVES TREE AND INFORMATION R EQUIREMENT DEFINITION

The programoteque charting of the entire process and all its essential steps shows the role of every subsystem in the process. It also shows that, every year,the main source of information for the running of the process are the business objectives, which define the contents of the yearly business plan, with the basis in the estimation and evaluation of the information requirement of everybody in the process. The business objectives are well presented in the form of the business objectives tree, as in Fig. 6. The making of the bus. obj. tree runs as in the Fig. 7:

```
1. RESEARCH BASES FOR PURPOSES AND OBJECTIVES (by experts  offices, esp.
Research and Development, and Marketing)
2. Definition of OBJECTIVES, level A in Fig.  6  (by  management  team,
workers council, workers reunion)
3. Definition of OBJECTIVES, level B in Fig. 6, for the yearly plan  (by
management team, workers council)
4. Organising, i.e. DESIGNING and PROGRAMMING - work objectives, level C
in Fig. 6 (by management team)
5. Running of objectives REALISATION, according to designs and  programs
(by managers and middlemanagers)
6. Objectives realisation by DAILY WORK  (by everybody acc.  to  the
technical division of labour)
7. SUPERVISION and MONITORING of work (by quality  office,  bookkeeping,
invention and innovation circles etc.).
```

Fig. 7: The hierarchy of succession in defining and realising the bus.
        obj. tree and acquiring of needed information

After their definition, the objectives enter the interlinking program of the programoteque as the contents of the (1) indirect and (2) general information (see Fig. 8). Together with information from the environment of the enterprise they are elaborated to become (3) direct information for running the production and other current work. Now, the information flow comes across the material and energy flow, so the Fig. 8 interlinks the Fig. 2 and 6, and elaborates them for a specific case. On this basis, no longer only the phase 3 from Fig. 2 (the routine shop floor work) is covered with planning and information and insight, but also the other three with their even greater influence over the destiny of the enterprise.. Also the production of information, which later serves the mastering of production of material products and services for the market, is now plannable and manageable (of course, not in details, but sufficiently to fight bureaucratic relations and support creativity).

On the same basis, the structure of the work program of the common offices can be defined with an objectified basis in the entire process and its information requirement (see Fig. 4, activities 054 and 055).

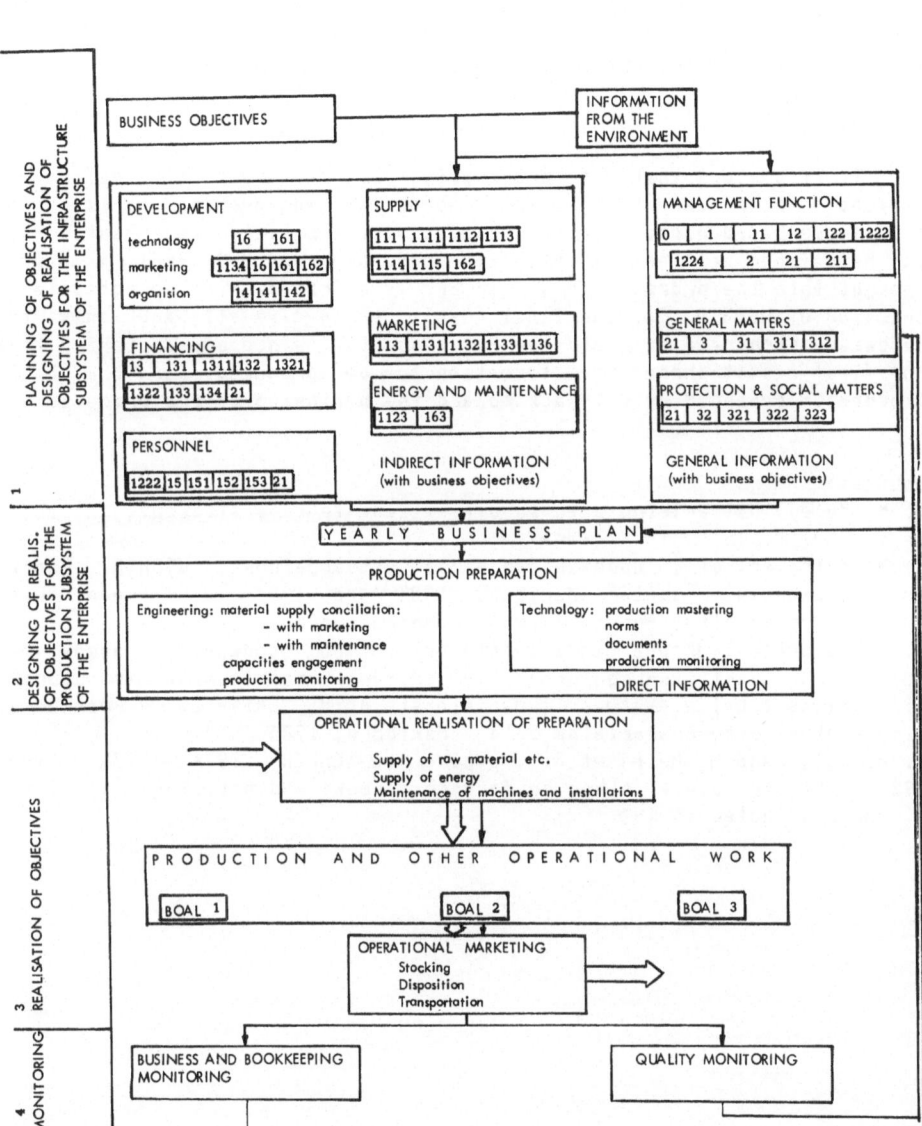

Fig. 8: THE INTERLINKING PROGRAM OF INFORMATION,
NEEDED FOR THE BUSINESS PROCESS

information flow
material flow

PLANNING OF OBJECTIVES AND DESIGNING OF REALISATION OF OBJECTIVES FOR THE INFRASTRUCTURE SUBSYSTEM OF THE ENTERPRISE

BUSINESS OBJECTIVES

INFORMATION FROM THE ENVIRONMENT

DEVELOPMENT

technology	16	161
marketing	1134	16	161	162
organision	14	141	142

FINANCING

| 13 | 131 | 1311 | 132 | 1321 |
| 1322 | 133 | 134 | 21 |

PERSONNEL

| 1222 | 15 | 151 | 152 | 153 | 21 |

SUPPLY

| 111 | 1111 | 1112 | 1113 |
| 1114 | 1115 | 162 |

MARKETING

| 113 | 1131 | 1132 | 1133 | 1136 |

ENERGY AND MAINTENANCE

| 1123 | 163 |

INDIRECT INFORMATION
(with business objectives)

MANAGEMENT FUNCTION

| 0 | 1 | 11 | 12 | 122 | 1222 |
| 1224 | 2 | 21 | 211 |

GENERAL MATTERS

| 21 | 3 | 31 | 311 | 312 |

PROTECTION & SOCIAL MATTERS

| 21 | 32 | 321 | 322 | 323 |

GENERAL INFORMATION
(with business objectives)

DESIGNING OF REALIS. OF OBJECTIVES FOR THE PRODUCTION SUBSYSTEM OF THE ENTERPRISE

YEARLY BUSINESS PLAN

PRODUCTION PREPARATION

Engineering: material supply conciliation:
 – with marketing
 – with maintenance
capacities engagement
production monitoring

Technology: production mastering
 norms
 documents
 production monitoring

DIRECT INFORMATION

REALISATION OF OBJECTIVES

OPERATIONAL REALISATION OF PREPARATION

Supply of raw material etc.
Supply of energy
Maintenance of machines and installations

PRODUCTION AND OTHER OPERATIONAL WORK

BOAL 1   BOAL 2   BOAL 3

OPERATIONAL MARKETING
 Stocking
 Disposition
 Transportation

MONITORING

BUSINESS AND BOOKKEEPING MONITORING

QUALITY MONITORING

The tasks are found out and the amount of work rougly defined with the procedure from Fig. 5, their duration (in frame-work time norms) is found out with programoteque charting, which shows also the number and expertise of the doers needed. So the cost of the common offices can be foreseen and agreed upon, monitored together with the results, paid for etc. - with clear relations and no bureaucracy. The measurement of the work performed and the results achieved is possible too, at least in a framework estimation, but a quite and ever more grounded one.

4. CONCLUSIONS

It is obvious that in programming of the work of the common offices, which can not be on industrial engineering norms, the experience based norms of time and cost etc. are very important. They can be defined well enough only if they are derived from a shared insight into the process. This can be elaborated with programoteque charting by USOMID. So, the final result can involve all and only the necessary steps and so avoid the Parkinson law, since one proceeds from the final result (here the information to be produced for the basic process or demanded by it) back toward the beginning of the process.

Sources:
1. M. Mulej, Ustvarjalno delo in dialektična teorija sistemov, Razvojni center Celje, 1979 (in Slovene)
2. M. Mulej et. al., Usposabljanje za ustvarjalnost, USOMID, kratki prikaz, Ekonomski center Maribor, 1983 and 1984 in Slovene, with Radnički univerzitet Subotica 1985 in SerboCroate
3. V. Sauperl, Svobodna menjava dela kot pot do dohodkovnih odnosov med TOZD in združbami skupnega pomena v delovni organizaciji (z uporabo dialektične teorije sistemov), Magistersko delo, Univerza v Mariboru, Visoka ekomnomsko komercialna šola v Mariboru, 1985
4. M. Mulej and M. Mulej et al., papers to EMCSR 1976, 1978, 1980, 1982, 1984 and several other conferences, books and articles
5. sources quoted in 1-4.

THE GRADUATE MANAGEMENT ADMISSIONS TEST - PREDICTOR OR PRETENDER?

Owen Hanson
Director, the Centre for Business Systems Analysis,
The City University Business School,
Northampton Square,
London, EC1V OHB,
United Kingdom

ABSTRACT. The GMAT has been used by many Schools of Business Studies
since it was developed at Princeton University (originally as the
ATGSB). This is the case in the City University Business School,
London. A careful test of the performance of the then ATGSB was
apparently carried out around 1970; since then the results achieved by
candidates for the MBA programme offered by the Business School have
been used as a discriminator, and candidates who do not reach predetermined scores in the test are generally rejected.

When an MSc programme in Business Systems Analysis and Design was set up
in 1973, the same test was applied to all candidates in order to build
up a base of experience, rather than to select students. After four
years, it was found that the results of the GMAT showed negative
correlation with those achieved by students in the MSc examinations in
two of these years; as a result, it was dropped as a pre-condition for
the course. That result cast some doubt on the GMAT as a selection
tool, and this paper describes the results of an investigation into the
effectiveness of the GMAT in predicting the likely success of candidates
on the MBA programme in their final examinations.

1. INTRODUCTION

For the last fifteen years, the City University Business School has used
the Graduate Management Admission Test developed by Princeton University
in the USA as one of the factors that are taken into account in deciding
whether a candidate should be accepted for one of its specialist MBA
courses (and, earlier, the MSc in Administrative Sciences run by the
School). Generally, candidates are required to have a GMAT Total score
of at least 50% below - in other words, to be in the top half of
candidates who have taken the test - if they are to be considered for a
place on the MBA programme. Naturally, other criteria need to be
satisfied in addition, if a candidate is to be accepted.

An MSc in Business Systems Analysis and Design, with an associated
Postgraduate Diploma, has been run in the School since 1973. All

549

R. Trappl (ed.), Cybernetics and Systems '86, 549–555.

candidates for this course were required to take the GMAT (or its
forerunner, the ATGSB) in the first four years that it was offered; the
correlation of GMAT scores with results in the final examinations was
discussed in (Hanson, 1975, 1977, 1979). As a result of this study, the
GMAT was dropped as a factor in the selection of students, except when
they could not be interviewed. Even in this case, only the GMAT Verbal
score was considered, as the requirement was for a test of ability in
the English language. If possible, candidates from non English-speaking
countries are expected to have taken the TOEFL (Test of English as a
foreign language) instead.

With the results of the earlier studies in mind, it was decided to
examine the relationship between results in the final MBA examinations
and a number of possible selection factors, including age, prior
experience, class of degree and the three values provided by the GMAT
test – Verbal, Quantitative and Total. All the records of students who
have studied on the nine years of the MBA and its precursor, the MSc in
Administrative Sciences, were analysed by Miss Carine Lim (Lim, 1985).
Of these, 257 had taken the GMAT, and it was possible to establish a
number of relationships on a sound statistical basis.

At this point it is important to make clear that this paper does not
seek to investigate the value or relevance of the GMAT test in general,
and particularly not to challenge the findings of Harrell (1970). The
intention was to find out whether the GMAT test could be used as a
predictor of success in the MBA examinations set by the City University
Business School, London.

2. RESULTS

One widely held belief in the Business School was that, although there
might not be a linear relationship between GMAT scores and performance,
low GMAT scores were a pointer to an unsuitable candidate. Table 1
shows the **lowest** and **highest** GMAT Total scorers in each of the nine
years investigated, with other low or high scorers when their results
seemed to be of interest. There seems to be a trend, albeit very faint, that
high scorers in GMAT score higher than **low** scorers. However, more high
scorers than low scorers dropped out of the course, or failed. On the
basis of the data presented in this Table, it does not appear
justifiable to assume that low GMAT scores are an indication of a
candidate's likely success in the MBA examinations.

In order to test any possible trends, regression analyses and analyses
of variance were carried out on the data. For brevity, only a part of
this data is presented here; the remainder is available in (Lim, 1985).

Academic Year	GMAT Verbal	GMAT Quant.	GMAT Total	Examination
1976/77	1	10	2	45
	84	89	90	fail
	89	97	96	53
1977/78	30	63	43	59
	89	93	94	58
	89	99	98	fail
1978/79	1	10	2	fail
	16	20	17	50
	91	92	95	62
1979/80	21	40	26	68
	80	99	96	fail
	95	99	99	46
1980/81	37	63	49	56
	89	67	85	fail
	92	94	96	62
1981/82	3	40	8	59
	21	4	10	58
	77	98	95	62
1982/83	4	45	10	48
	9	23	12	53
	23	10	13	57
	81	91	90	58
	89	92	94	65
1983/84	26	23	20	55
	20	50	28	59
	69	99	95	58
	96	92	97	65
	99	93	98	59

TABLE 1

The figures presented here give the verbal, quantitative and total
scores achieved in the GMAT (Graduate management admissions test) by a
number of students on the MBA programme run by the City University
Business School, London. In each year the student with the lowest and
highest GMAT total score has been shown, and in each year some other
students have also been selected. The examination results achieved by
these students at the end of the MBA course have also been given.
Scores tabulated give the percentage of students in the total population
tested in the year in question who achieved results below those of the
student quoted.

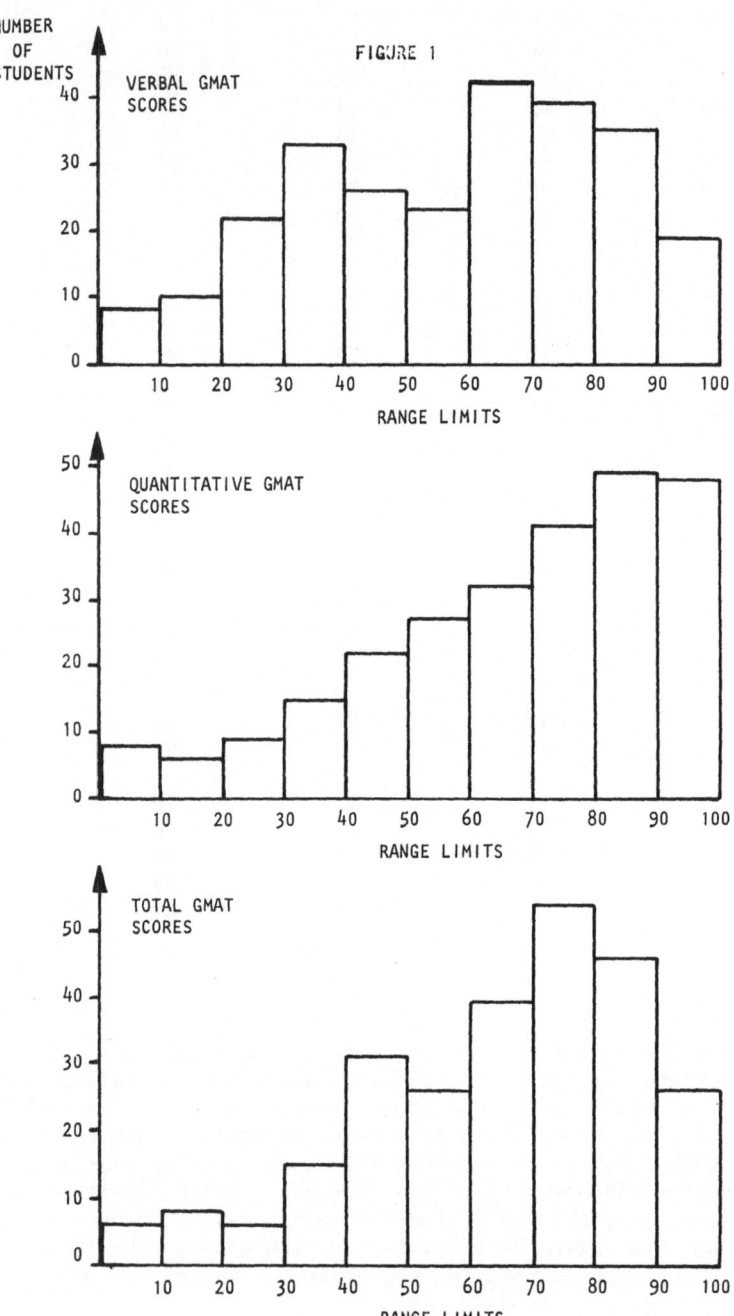

552

Before applying further statistical tests, it was necessary to ensure that the student body being examined contained at least some candidates in every range of ability, as determined by the GMAT. Although Figure 1 shows that students are above average in GMAT score, sufficient low scorers were present to analyse the full range of abilities in the GMAT in terms of later success in the final MBA examinations.

A regression analysis of the 238 sets of GMAT scores for students who sat and passed the final MBA examinations provided the correlation coefficients that are set out in Table 2. **Positive** coefficients imply that higher GMAT scores are linked to higher MBA results, while **negative** coefficients imply that higher GMAT scores are linked to lower MBA results.

Year	Students in group	GMAT Verbal	GMAT Quantitative	GMAT Total	Age	Experience
1975/76	3	− 0.895	0.977	− 0.291	0.034	− 0.206
1976/77	8	0.498	0.524	0.504	0.193	0.184
1977/78	17	0.002	0.145	0.006	− 0.180	− 0.010
1978/79	9	0.517	0.335	0.501	− 0.280	0.140
1979/80	6	− 0.432	− 0.719	− 0.524	0.104	0.270
1980/81	11	− 0.245	0.403	0.102	− 0.003	0.225
1981/82	38	0.002	− 0.080	− 0.005	0.012	0.007
1982/83	56	0.321	0.176	0.361	0.008	0.007
1983/84	90	0.215	0.000	0.153	− 0.072	0.006

TABLE 2

Some of the figures given here are significant; however, it should be noted that **none** of the factors is consistently positively correlated with success in the final MBA examinations. On the whole, however, it seems that greater age, and higher GMAT scores, are linked to MBA examination success.

Reference to the original paper by Lim shows that, with the exception of the GMAT Quantitative score in 1975/6 − when the number of students in the group was only 3 − the trend line was in every other case not far from the horizontal. The implication is that, however highly correlated the factor considered is with·results in the final MBA examinations, it does not alter those results very much. This is emphasized by the figures given in Table 3, showing the predicted final examination results on the basis of a **Nil** GMAT score in each test value.

Year	Students in group	GMAT Verbal	GMAT Quantitative	GMAT Total	Age	Experience
1975/76	3	71.4	9.0	76.2	52.9	55.6
1976/77	8	46.0	43.8	45.2	64.4	54.0
1977/78	17	59.6	55.8	58.0	70.6	60.9
1978/79	9	47.8	53.4	46.9	54.5	57.4
1979/80	6	67.0	79.3	70.5	54.5	55.3
1980/81	11	60.3	50.4	54.9	58.7	55.1
1981/82	38	56.0	57.8	57.3	55.9	56.0
1982/83	56	50.9	52.5	49.1	52.5	55.1
1983/84	90	52.1	56.0	52.4	58.9	56.3

TABLE 3

Figures tabulated show the predicted final examination marks in the MBA, based on a nil score in the factor concerned.

The final view expressed about GMAT scores was that a low Verbal score might lead to failure. Of the 257 students who had taken the GMAT, 18 had scores of 20% or less below in the Verval test. Their results are tabulated below.

GMAT Verbal	GMAT Quantitative	GMAT Total	MBA Exam
1	10	2	45
14	54	27	fail
9	23	12	53
3	40	8	59
20	72	39	59
1	10	2	fail
12	15	10	47
20	81	46	38
16	20	17	50
20	50	28	59
11	91	46	59
4	45	10	48
9	91	35	56
16	23	17	55
8	79	26	52
9	87	35	52
15	64	32	51
18	89	50	53

CONCLUSION

The GMAT scores achieved by students on the MBA course at the City
University Business School do appear to be correlated with their results
in the final MBA examination. However, this correlation varies from
year to year, and even when it appears consistent the effect of a low
score on results in the examination is so small that it does not provide
satisfactory evidence on which to base a decision of such importance.
It is noteworthy, however, that these results are more consistent than
those reported by (Hanson, 1979) for a computer orientated course, which
suggests that the GMAT is indeed well-designed to test skills that are
specific to business education.

REFERENCES

HARRELL,T.W, Predicting Job Success of MBA Graduates, Research and
Development Brief No. 1, Princeton ATGSB Programme

HANSON, O.J, A Systems Approach to the Training of Systems Analysts, in
Progress in Cybernetics and Systems Research, Vol 2, 1975, 203-212, publ
by Hemisphere Publishing Corporation.

HANSON, O.J, A Systems Methodology for the Design, Assessment and
Development of Training Courses, presented at the 3rd European Meeting
on Systems and Cybernetics, Vienna, April 1976.

HANSON,O.J, The Problem of Providing and Assessing Feedback in an
Educational System, presented at the 4th European Meeting on Systems and
Cybernetic Research, Linz, March 1978.

LIM, C.C, Analysis of the Significance of GMAT Scores for MBA Student
Entry, 1975/84, Using a Number of Different Statistical Packages, MSc
Thesis 1985, obtainable from the Librarian, The City University,
Northampton Square, London, EC1V OHB.

COMPUTER-AIDED SIMULATION OF CONTROL PROCESSES IN ENTERPRISES

S. von KÄNEL and G. SCHÄFER
Dresden University of Technology
Mommsenstraße 13
8027 Dresden
GDR

ABSTRACT. The aim of this paper is to demonstrate a principal methodology for the computer-aided simulation of control processes in enterprises. Both the characteristics of process and its control and some results of process simulation are considered. The paper is a contribution to the CAM-problems.

1. INTRODUCTION

It is fact the carrying out of economic processes and their control on the base of a balanced plan is a complicted task in practice. Why?
Now, above all for that reason, because of production processes many are influenced by disturbances of various kinds.
In the case that control of production processes is only on the principle of feedback-control the control organs (here: manager of production) are in a difficult situation: They can only influence the processes after the effect of disturbances in an intervall t, therefore at the earliest to the beginning of intervall t $\neq$ 1.
The following question is of especially importance, both for considering control theory and for the practice of management in enterprises:
Is it possible to design and to carry out a control process which - in addition to feedback-control - is based on a principle of control with prediction of effect of disturbances?
The answer to this question leads to the principle "control with experimental-aided process simulation.
Fig. 1 will illustrated this principle.
The subject of this paper is to demonstrate the basic idea of this principle in its context to the use to control of production processes in enterprises.

557

R. Trappl (ed.), Cybernetics and Systems '86, 557–564.
© 1986 by D. Reidel Publishing Company.

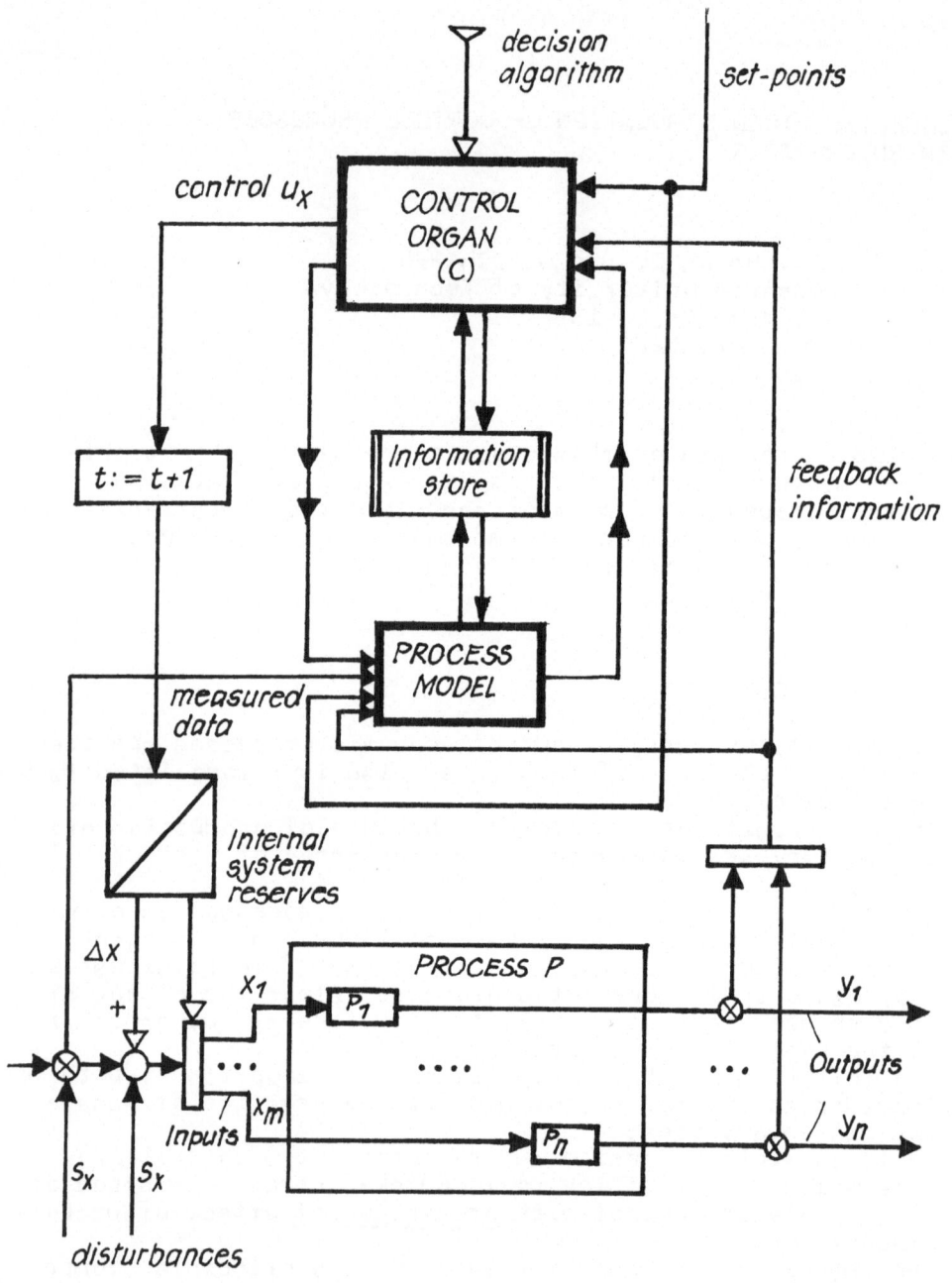

Fig. 1: Control with experimental-aided process
simulation

2. CHARACTERISTICS OF PROCESS AND ITS CONTROL

The process, which we have examined in detail, has following characteristics:
It is a manufacturing process of parts in a machine-building enterprise with "n" technological homogeneous production cells. The sequence of technological operations is not a branch-network.
Inputs of process are labour-time of workers, raw material and semi-finished products and other ressources.
Outputs are the quantities of parts in various kinds.
The relations existing between inputs and outputs are reflected in model by linear transfer coefficients (s. Figure 2).

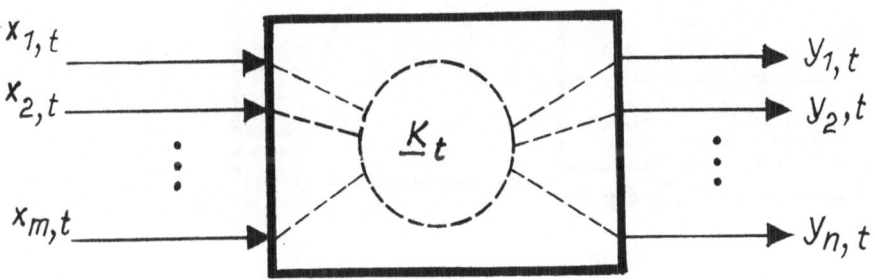

Fig. 2 : Process model with linear transfer
coefficients (with influence of disturbances)

Therefore is valid:

$$\underline{y}_t^{(r)} = \underline{K}^{(r)} \cdot \underline{x}_t^{(r)} \cdot \tag{1}$$

It means:

$\underline{y}_t^{(r)} = (y_{i,t}^{(r)})_n$ vector of outputs (quantities of parts)

$\underline{x}_t^{(r)} = (x_{j,t}^{(r)})_m$ vector of inputs (quantities of resources)

$\underline{K}^{(r)} = (k_{ij})_{n,m}$ matrix of transfer coefficients (reciprocal of specific expense quantities)

$r = 1(1)n$ number of production cells
$t = 1(1)N$ time intervall .

559

In the case that the total process is balanced altogether we can write in model:

$$y_{i,t}^{(r)} = w_{i,t}^{(r)} = k_{i1,t}^{(r)} \cdot xw_{1,t}^{(r)} = \ldots = k_{im,t}^{(r)} \cdot xw_{m,t}^{(r)}. \quad (2)$$

It means:

$w_{i,t}^{(r)}$ set-point for output $y_{i,t}^{(r)}$,

$xw_{j,t}^{(r)}$ set-point for input $x_{j,t}^{(r)}$.

In practice of carrying out of production process disturbances effect the process in various kinds, especially in direction to inputs (s. <u>Fig. 3</u>).

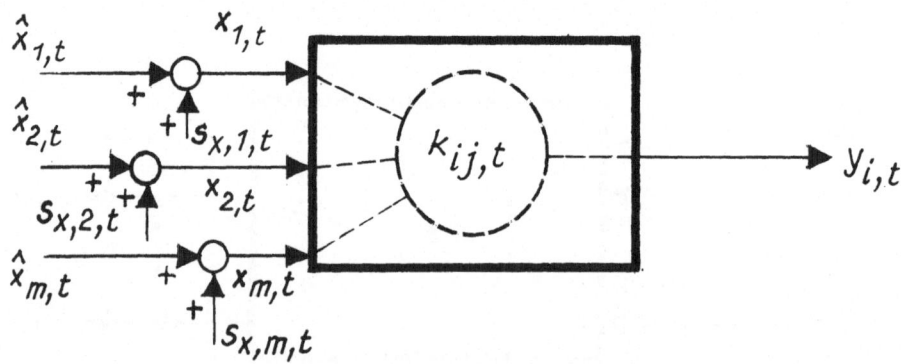

Fig. 3: Process model with marking of disturbances
in direction to inputs

It this case it is valid:

$$y_{i,t}^{(r)} = \min_{j} \begin{cases} k_{i1,t}^{(r)} \, (xw_{1,t}^{(r)} + s_{x,1,t}^{(r)}) \\ \ldots \ldots \ldots \ldots \\ k_{im,t}^{(r)} \, (xw_{m,t}^{(r)} + sx_{m,t}^{(r)}) \, . \end{cases} \quad (3)$$

where

$s_{x,j,t}^{(r)}$ disturbance to input $x_{j,t}^{(r)}$.

It is the basic task of control organs to ensure a continuous carrying out of the production process, especially in case that disturbances will injure the process cource.

560

In our concrete situation it was necessary to realize three kinds of control processes:

- pre-adaptive control for the purpose of checking all inputs;

- feedback-control for the purpose of controlling the total process;

- internal adaptive control for the purpose of optimizing the process course according to priorities.

This different control processes are connected together.

3. COMPUTER PROGRAMMES FOR THE SIMULATION OF CONTROL PROCESSES

In order to solve the task which we have described it was necessary to design and to implement two programm systems:

With our programm system PRIOPS it is possible to calculate an optimum vector of process outputs which is characterized by minimum deviation of actual quantities of the set-points. For the optimization we use the simplex-algorithm. The programm system PRIOPS realizes a sequential simulation. The files which we need for the simulation are structured by turns of intervalls t.

Our second programm system is called SIMPROS. This programm system has a modular basic structure with main programm and 20 subroutines. SIMPROS enables the simulation of control process in a man-machine-dialogue. It is possible to use both programm systems in practice as components of CAM-projects or in economic research or in teaching.

4. SOME RESULTS OF PROCESS SIMULATION

With the aid of SIMPROS it was possible to prove the concrete effects of control in a production system:

Tab. 1 : Results in a modelled process without control (example)

quantity	value
output (total)	11.2 million marks
fulfilment of plan	90.0 per cent

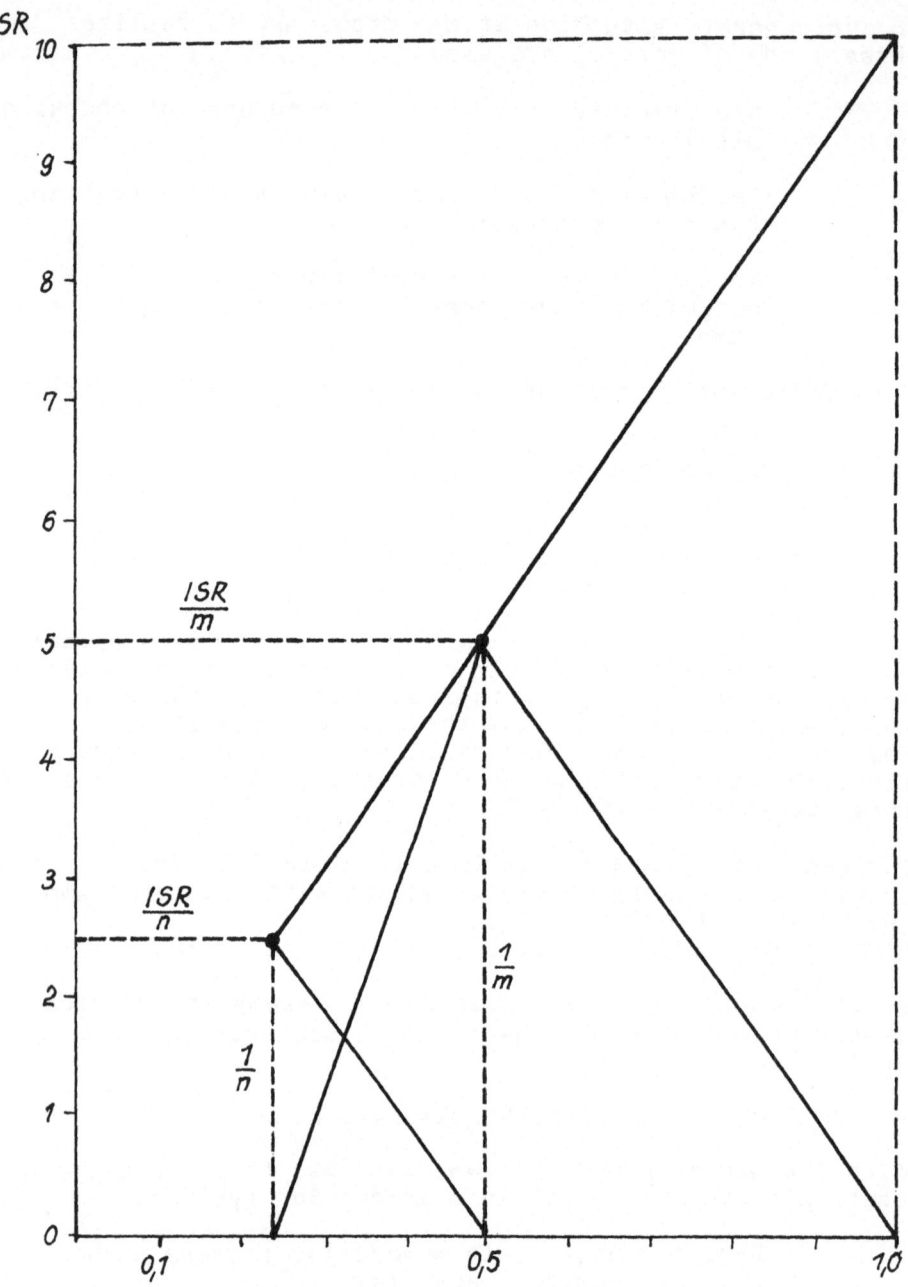

Fig. 4 : Determination of ISR-portions of control levels
in dependence on centralization degree
(n = 4, m = 2, ISR = 10 units)

It this case was the quantity of funds which were not used
very high, concrete 81 thousand marks.

Tab. 2 : Results in a modelled process (with
control)

quantity	value
output (total)	12,9 million marks
fulfilment of plan	97.8 per cent

It was possible to reduce the quantity of funds which
were not used to 7 thousand marks.

This results were attained without extra labour-time of
workers and material, only by means of an optimum disposition of the concrete available resources!

Furthermore, we have examined the determination of internal system reserves in dependence on the centralization
degree of this reserves.
Fig. 4 will illustrate this dependence in case of n = 4
sub-processes, m = 2 control levels and ISR = 10 units
(ISR = internal system reserves).

The influence of the reaction-time in control process is
of likewise importance:
Shorter the reaction-time in the first and in the second
control level greater the centralization degree of system
reserves in order to attain a high stability in carrying
out production processes.
Our experiments confirm that computer-aided simulation of
control processes delivers results which are of important
interest both from the aspect of theory and practice.

REFERENCES

/1/   FRANK,M./LORENZ,P.: Simulation diskreter Prozesse.
       Leipzig, VEB Fachbuchverlag, 1979.

/2/   FRIEDRICH,D. : Systemtheorie und ökonomische Modelle.
       Freiburg im Breisgau, R. Haufe-Verlag, 1984.

/3/   von KÄNEL, S./ LAUENROTH, H.-G.: Kybernetik für Öko-
       nomen. Leitfaden. Dresden 1984.

/4/   von KÄNEL, S., u.a.: Kybernetik in der Organisations-
und Leitungspraxis der Kombinate und Betriebe.
Dresden 1985.

/5/   SCHÄFER, G.: Modellierung und Simulation von Prozes-
sen der Lenkung und Kontrolle der Produktionsdurch-
führung unter Nutzung kybernetischer Erkenntnisse
und Methoden. Dissertation, TU Dresden, 1982.

/6/   von KÄNEL, S. : On the problem of the Controllability
of Economic Systems.
Economic Computation and Economic Cybernetics Studies
and Research. Bucharest - Romania. 1(1984), p. 75-
82.

COMPUTER AIDED SYSTEMS ANALYSIS AND MODELLING OF INNOVATION STRATEGIES IN THE FIELD OF FLEXIBLE AUTOMATION

H.-G. Lauenroth
Academy of Sciences of the GDR
Institute of Theory, History and Organization
of Science
GDR.1100 Berlin, Prenzlauer Promenade 149/52

ABSTRACT. The aim of the systems analysis of industrial innovation processes is to study the characteristics, laws and dynamics of these processes and develop innovation strategies. This requires the identification of the innovation fields of demand, solution and realization. The main tasks of the computer aided decision system REMISA are the ascertainment of the potential worthy of innovation, the formation of variants of strategies and their evaluation in order to select the most effective variants with the help of an algorithmic system. This concept was realized in the field of the innovation process of flexible automation by scenarios and interactive computer programmes.

1. SYSTEMS ANALYSIS OF INNOVATION PROCESSES

Scientific and technological innovation processes are processes of the creation, development, use, and diffusion of new products with improved parameters as well as new and more efficient technologies.

Product innovations and process innovations are the result of the connection

- of an already existing or latently existing demand,
- with usable scientific and technological problem solutions,
- under given or possible conditions of realization.

Innovation processes show essential characteristics of large-scale systems. Therefore it is expedient to use the thinking way, the methodology, and the methods of applied systems analysis for the study, the projecting, and the realization of innovation processes.

On the basis of the tasks in terms of the content the approach to the study and the project preparation of innovation

565

R. Trappl (ed.), Cybernetics and Systems '86, 565–569.
© 1986 by D. Reidel Publishing Company.

processes aimed at elaborating efficient innovation strategies can be summarized in a heuristic algorithm /1/.

Essential elements of the innovation field flexible automation include the fields of demand, solution and realization. The field of demand in the area of industrial enterprises consists of

- production processes to be automatized (pre-manufacturing, assembling, measuring and control, transport, storage),
- information processes to be automatized (computer aided planning/CAP, computer aided design/CAD, computer aided manufacturing/CAM,)

and the field of solution

- automatic production technology, devices, and equipments (NC machines, industrial robots, integrated flexible production systems),
- automatic information technology, devices, and equipments (microprocessors, small computers, process control computers, data processing systems, telecommunication systems).

Quantity, quality, and availability of hardware, software, material resources, their costs and prices, the level of qualification of specialists, and sociological factors are relevant parts of the field of realization to be regarded in the formation and evaluation of automation strategies.

In this context, two main directions in strategy formation of flexible automation can be identified:

I. The extension of existing elements of flexible automation, especially by opening up new fields of utilization, e.g. in assembling processes, or the accelerated introduction of industrial robots of the second generation;

II. The design of complex large-scale projects of hierarchical production, control, management and information systems with integrated CAP/CAD/CAM systems and manless production units /2/.

2. COMPUTER AIDED DECISION SYSTEM 'REMISA'

The systems analysis of scientific and technological innovation processes is covering the solution of three main tasks:

- analysis of innovation situations to ascertain the potential Pt worthy of innovation,
- synthesis of innovation processes to form and vary innovation strategies St,
- evaluation E of innovation strategies to select the most effective strategy variants.

Potential algorithms, strategy variation algorithms and evaluation algorithms are necessary for the computer aided realization of these tasks. This applies to the three classes of strategies in the innovation field of flexible automation: research strategies R, production strategies P and utilization strategies U.

From this results the structure of the system S of algorithms π

$$S_{\pi} = \left[\left\{ \pi_R, \quad \pi_P, \quad \pi_U \right\} , \quad \left\{ R_{ij} \right\} \right] \qquad (1)$$

with

$$\pi_1 \in S_{\pi} = \left[\left\{ \pi_i^{Pt}, \quad \pi_i^{St}, \quad \pi_i^{E} \right\} , \quad \left\{ R_{mn} \right\} \right] \qquad (2).$$

This system S_{π} (Fig. 1) is the object of modelling

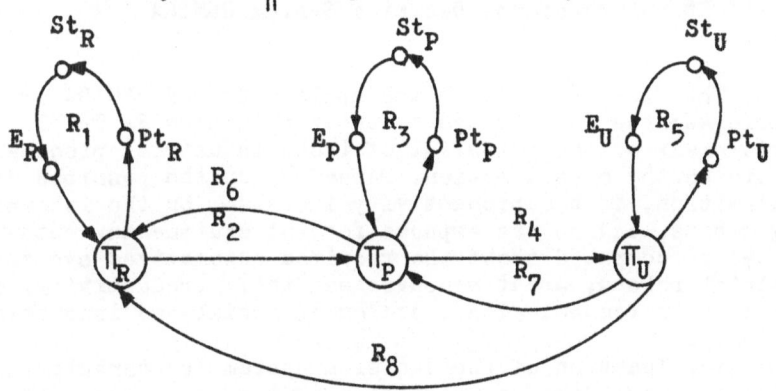

Fig. 1: Graph of the Algorithmic Model System

in the computer aided decision system for the variation, evaluation and selection of innovation strategies REMISA /Rechnergestütztes Entscheidungs-Modell für die Innovations-Strategien-Auswahl/ (Fig. 2).

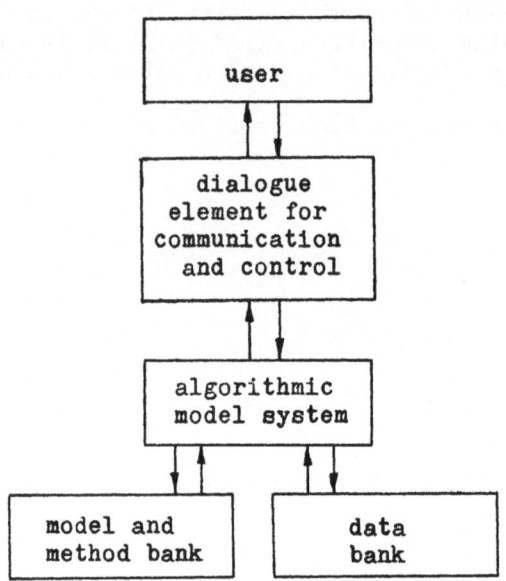

Fig. 2: Structure of the Decision System REMISA

The first results of the application of REMISA are the scenario and the interactive computer programme FA TREND for the ascertainment of the potential of those industrial processes that are worthy of automation. Depending on the possible degree of automation, on the productivity increase, on the intensity of using robots, and on the expense for the equipments, output data can be computed about the required automatized systems and industrial robots, about manpower and their productivity, about costs and the technological, economic, social and innovational efficiency.

The function of the decision system is characterized by flexibility regarding the variation of targets, restrictions, parameters, and methods of simulation and evaluation. Therefor the model and method bank contains

- analysis methods
- synthesis methods
- simulation models
- evaluation models.

The data bank contains prognostic, actual and historical data.

A conception was elaborated for a computer aided innovation game for automation strategies regarding the existing conflicts between the elements research, production and utilization, their strategy variants and their complex evaluation.

/1/ Lauenroth, H.-G., Weber, M.: Inhalt, Prinzipien und Methoden der Systemanalyse von Innovationsprozessen. In: messen.steuern.regeln, Berlin, 10/11, 1983.

/2/ Haustein, H.-D., Maier, H.: Flexible Automatisierung - Aufbruch einer Schlüsseltechnologie der Zukunft. Akademie-Verlag, Berlin, 1984.

PRESENT STATUS AND EXPECTED DEVELOPMENTS IN COMPUTER INTEGRATED MANUFACTURE IN THE SOCIALIST COUNTRIES

F S DRECHSLER,
University of Dublin
Trinity College
Dublin 2
Ireland

A M HUSKA
Building Economics and
Organisation Institute
Bratislave (CSSR)

ABSTRACT   This paper outlines some of the developments which are taking place in Computer Integrated Manufacturing in Eastern Europe. The topic of Flexible Manufacturing is intentionally not covered however the developments leading up to it are.

Introduction

This paper deals with one very small part of a study carried out under the EEC-ESPRIT program. The task in the EEC project was to develop design rules for Computer Integrated Manufacture; specifically to examine the relevance of CIM to the medium size firm.[1]

In the way of a summary one might say that most medium size manufactures have a computer; this computer is used for performing most of the Accounting Functions but very little else. Many (even large) manufacturers talk about MRP (materials requirements planning) but few understand its implications.[2] Perhaps the key issue that came out of the search for some answers why this is so were that computer application programs were just too complex and took too long to learn to make them readily available to an average user. A comprehensive system may consist of more than eleven modules (Accounting, Order Processing, Faculty Control, MRP, Shop Floor Management etc.) and each module apart from its cost (about £1,000) takes days even to become familar with and six months to a year to know well.

It was not difficult to learn about west european practices and compare user differences with standard Nixdorf, IBM, ICL, DEC or similar software. But what about the Socialist countries? It became clear that very little was known in the event about developments of CIM in the Socialist countires. This paper is the result of this part of the study.

R. Trappl (ed.), Cybernetics and Systems '86, 571–578.
© *1986 by D. Reidel Publishing Company.*

1 Historical background

Central and East European countries began their industrial development in quite a different way. Countries like Czechoslovakia (CSSR) and East Germany already had an industrial tradition for over 100 years before World War II. Others, like Bulgaria or Rumania, were under-developed.

Since World War II, developments in the socialist camp began, in the light of their historical past, with a considerable time lag; and apart from the disadvantage that other countries pay in the international market, a penalty or rent for innovation to the developing countries, this development had its advantages.

When socialist countries built new manufacturing facilities after World War II they avoided conventional methods used by capitalist countries, where industrial development had begun a century ago.

As far as the Capitalist countries are concerned, the development of their manufacturing activity is taking place in the post industrialisation era in the age of electronics. As far as the socialist countries are concerned, this development is taking place in the electronic age of a scientific cum technical revolution, which is a planned process of change which is taking place in the context of both the capitalist as well as the socialist conditions.

Planning of all the developments of the socialist society as a whole, affects not only where an activity is located, but also the type of activity that takes place and the time, when it takes place, as well as the alocation of the work force so that developments in the "electronic age" appear as a development of the hierarchicaly organised management structures, now aided by computer technology. These systems of management are referred to as "automated systems of management" (AMS), and are in effect what in the west would be a combination of Management Information Systems (MIS) and Decision Support Systems DSS). The structure is illustrated in the following diagram (Jakabcin 1978).[3]

Automated system of management (ASM) for:

1 Whole National Economy
2 Branches
3 Association of firms
4 Independent Concerns
5 Technological Processes

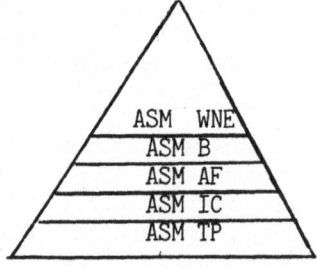

The area that we are specifically concerned with here is ASM TP i.e., automated systems of management of the technological processes and inspite of the fact that in socialistic countries standard conditions for the setting up and the design of automated systems exist there can be great variety in computer based management systems (CBMS) and indeed in ASM TP.

2 ASM TP AS A FRAMEWORK OF COMPUTER INTEGRATED MANUFACTURE

ASM TP represents a system of production and transmission of management information in manufacturing. It is different in different branches of manufacturing. In the machining industry for example it basically has the following structure (Jakabcin 1978)[3] :

Environment
↓
Capacity Planning and Accounting
↓
Term Planning and Decision Making
↓
Process Control and evidence of Manufacturing
↓
Management of Technological Processes
↓
Actual Management Process (manufacturing)

The basis of an automated system of manufacture of components in the machining sector are NC machines, NC measurement, NC handling as well as Robotics devices, and these are shown as block 4 in the above diagram.

2.1. Direct Management of Production in Industrial Concerns

Direct management of production as indicated in part 4 of the diagram (process control and output measurement) are different in a centralised ASMTP and a decentralised system. (G Tomek and J Cermak 1984).[4] The structure of a centralised or decentralised system is defined basically by the fact whether the ASM has been developed TOP DOWN or BOTTOM UP. For example in the building industry, the construction process is only partly mechanised (and complex mechanisation exists only in engineering structures) and basically the actual building construction is not automated, with the exception of the manufacture used in building, such as the mixed concrete of mixed mortar, concrete slabs etc., where manufacturing has been automated in many instances.

573

It was for this reason that computerisation and automation in the building industry started BOTTOM UP - first there were ASM F systems (computarised undertakings and ASM of economic units) and it was only later on that one began to develop ASM TP.

In manufacturing industry, on the other hand, ASM started BOTTOM UP that is starting with stage 4. First one began to link NC machines and local measuring and control lines, then isolated Robots and later complex Robotic work stations. Following this one automated stage 3 then 2 and 1; and all this in the context of ASM TP. Later on development of higher ASM (of enterprises and economic units) started to take place i.e., ASM IC and ASM AF. An example of a combination of a decentralised and central computer system in one manufacturing economic unit is shown in the following diagram (G Tomek - J Cermak 1984) :

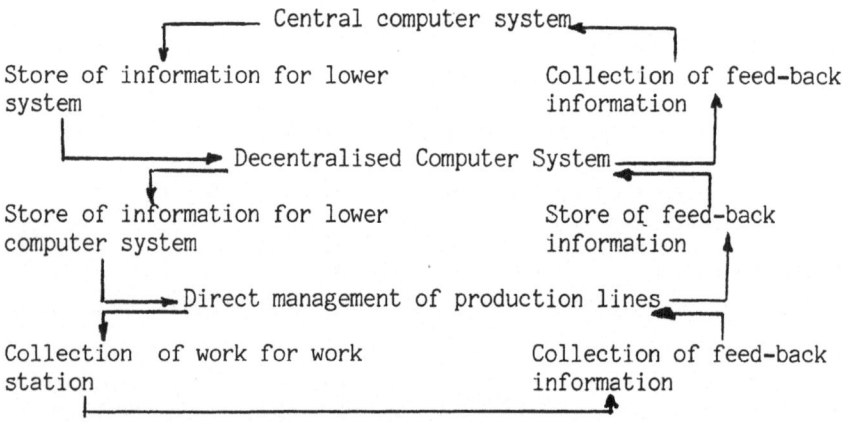

Computarisation allows one to limit workforce, and also the management of production and its concentration on a central or local system.

One insures in this way that the entre of management directly affects all participants, who are engaged in the manufacturing process, and this in the framework of management of the total system such as: transport and materials handling within the concern, the activity of manufacturing and maintenance stores, technical control, materials stores, tool stores, jiggs and fixture design and manufacture etc. A horizontal linkage is thus formed in the sub-system ASM TP. This is discussed in some detail by G Tomek and J Cermak 1984.[4]

Direct management of production from the central level, or local management requires the acceptance of the following pricnples of management:

574

- it concerns the whole of ASM TP (namely all four levels)

- management is concentrated in the management centre and is the only place where the efficient operation of the manufacturing process can be assessed

- in order to insure the success of the planned production runs, the central office manages the work of all the components that participate in the manufacturing activity.

All this is insured by means of one time coordinated allocation of work carried out as follows (G Tomek, J Cermak, 1984)[4] :

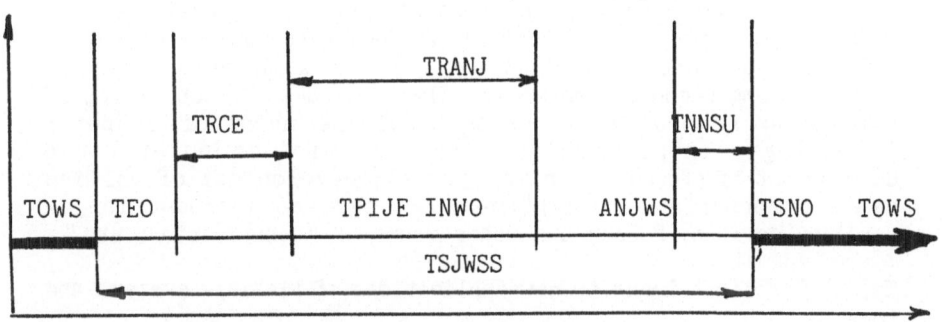

TOWS	Time of operation at work station
TEO	Time of end of operation
TSNO	Time of start of new operation
TSJWSS	Time in which the store of job at work station has to suffice
TRCE	Time required for control and evidence
TRANJ	Time requireed for alocation of next job
TPIJE	Time when planner is informed about job end
ANJWS	Alocation of next job at work station
TNNSU	Time needed for new set up
INWO	Issue of new work orders

So called direct management of production by means of computers of the ·integrated systems is the progressive methiod of direct management and it substitutes both the classical dispatching management and classical operation planning.

In the German Democratic Republic (DDR), according to B Schutze (1984),[5] they verified experimentally the use of specific modifications of CAD (Computer Aided Design) where a whole range of technical aids are in use.

There is every indication that the socialist countries are looking for more and more complex solutions. At the same time it has been shown, that it is not enough to solve computer support for individual management tasks, but that it is necessary to integrate this support, even at the identification stageof a system, and that not only at the pre-production stage, but also at the post-production stage (outcome - records - statistics) stage. Of course this includes a qualitative change in technology of individual production systems (by gradual introduction of NC machines, handling devices, Robots and total systems with artificial intelligence) which requires new approaches to the solution of problems in the context of strategies of the eighties. O Bogomolov (1983)[6] in his essay on the economic strategy on the eighty years in the socialistic countries states, that "for the eighties countries of the Council of Mutual Economic Cooperation (COMECON) selected common aids in line with priorities in knowledge and technical advances. This includes the automation of manufacturing processes, using available means of computer technology, in particular micro and mini computers; the development of programs for management; development of unified basic components for electro-technology; an introduction of handling devices, Robots and other means of mechanisation; etc.".

The whole effort leads to new applications of flexible systems and this by:

- the creation of various modifications of CAD (Computer Aided Design)

- the creation of integrated work stations (made up of NC machines, handling devices and Robots)

- creation of special units with so called artificial intelligence.

In the report "USSR: the use of micro-processors" it is suggested, that in the years 1982 and 1990 one is to build around 100 automated factories and by 1990 there should be 100 thousand handling and Robotic devices in integrated work centres.

2.2. Trends in the applications of special computer systems

In so far as the use of special computers is concerned, the originator and principle developer are the USSR, however there also are some joint ventures (for example USSR and CSSR).

During the years 1976-1983, the centre of gravity were in the USSR AMS TP based on computers SM-2M with a main store capacity of 256 MB and an operating speed up to 0.5 mil operations per second.

"In world wide news are the new parallel micro-processors type PS 3000 with a main store of 8 MB and speeds of 3 or 10 million operations per second; these have up to four processors for multi-process operations with a fast series accumulator for parallel connection of individual processors. The channel input/output capacity is MB(s)", (Halek, 1984).[7] Developments in production (for example in the cooperative IMPULS in the USS) are directed towards single purpose macro-computers, which solve one kind of problem (e.g., transport problem) and they will insure the further developments in ASM TP. A further development in the USSR is the introduction of the Micro-processor PS 2000. According to J Halka (1984)[7] its first prototype was introduced into a long test run in the geophysics offices of the science-manufacture cooperative Neftegeofyzika. The PS 2000 micro-processor has an operating speed of up to 1 thousand million operations per second and is basically the central micro-processor with 64 parallel processor connected to it.

Into this design is introduced the theory of systems with variable structure, which was developed in the Institute for management problems AV SSSR (St Stibor 1983). For the optimal use of the new computers, the firm IMPULS supplies user application programs (user software) in the form ASPO, which has 2 million instructions taking up 60 million bytes.

Petr Sapatyj (1984) suggests, that the cybernetics institute V.M.Gluskova in Kijev in cooperation with the Technical institute of cybernetics of Slovak Academy of Sciences, Bratislave, is developing a new computer based on an "active network of information" architecture, which is capable of solving tasks that are not in the traditional form of an algorithm, with divisions between data and their computation, but in the form of active self organised network models of data, which in a natural way represent the real world - for example real factories and production lines. The principle component of this computer - according to P Sapatyj - is a universal area, which allows one to introduce and include complex structural methods from different areas, where it is necessary to find a solution. The method for the solution from the point of view of logic and dynamics reminds one of similar solutions for physical and biological roblems. P Sapatyj writes in Pravda on the 16 May 1984, that the computer is based on an organic link of results obtained by the Russian experts in Kyjev, working in the area of the so called interpretative computers with higher intellect and the results of Czechoslovak experts in Bratislava graftech and networks using so called derivative computers and the technology of large integrated enterprises.

1 Drechsler F S, Design Rules for Computer Integrated Manufacture ESPRIT Project 23, EEC.

2 Drechsler F S and Zamzeer M J, Major Problems of Computerised Production Planning and Control; The Institute of Production Control, December 1985.

3 Jakabcin M, Priemyselne Roboty a Nacrt Ich Zapojenia Do Automatizovanych Systemov Riadenia, ASR, Bulletin Inorga, Ustav Pro Automatizaci Rizeni Prumyslu, Vol 12, No 2, Praha 1078 1978.

4 Tomek G and Cermak, Systemove O Primem Rizeni Vyroby, Magazine Podnikova Organizace, Vol 38, No 1, Federalni Ministerstvo Vseobechneho Strojirenstvi, Nakladatelstvi Sntl Praha, 1984.

5 Bchutze B.

6 Bogomolov O, Sev - Chozjajstvennaja Strategija Dlja Osemdesiatyje Gody, Magazine Komunist, No 7, Kpss, Moskva, 1983.

7 Halek A, Vypocetni Technika Pro ASR (MIS) Technologickych Procesu Vedecko Vyrobniho Zdruzeni impuls, Severodoneck, .SSSR, Magazine Automatizace, Vol 27, No 3, Federalni Ministerstvo Hutnickeho a Tezkeho Strojirenstvi, Praha 1984, (Monthly).

Fuzzy Sets - Meeting of the EURO Working Group

Chairperson: C.Carlsson (Finland)

SEMI-LATTICE ISOMORPHISM OF THE EXTENSIONS OF POSSIBILITY MEASURE AND THE SOLUTIONS OF FUZZY RELATION EQUATION

Zhenyuan Wang
Department of Mathematics
Hebei University
Baoding
Hebei
China

ABSTRACT. The extensions of possibility measure may be obtained by solving a certain fuzzy relation equation, and the semi-lattice formed by all extensions of possibility measure is isomorphic to the semi-lattice formed by all solutions of this fuzzy relation equation.

The possibility measure is a nonadditive measure, it may be used in system research as expert's subjective evaluation to a family of events. The extension theory of the possibility measure provides a theoretical basis and a practical method for profiting fully from rough and incomplete information.

Let X be a nonempty set, $P(X)$ be the power set of X, $\mathcal{E}$ be an arbitrarily given nonempty subset of $P(X)$. Throughout this paper, the following conventions are made:

$$\bigcup_{t\in\phi}\{A_t|A_t\subset X\}=\phi\ ,\ \sup_{t\in\phi}\{a_t|a_t\in[0,1]\}=0,\ \inf_{t\in\phi}\{a_t|a_t\in[0,1]\}=1.$$

Definition. A mapping $\pi: P(X)\to[0,1]$ is called possibility measure on $P(X)$, if

$$\pi(\bigcup_{t\in T}A_t)=\sup_{t\in T}\pi(A_t),\ \forall\ \{\ A_t|t\in T\ \}\subset P(X),$$

where T is arbitrary index set.

Here, we do not require $\pi(X)=1$, and this definition is more general than Zadeh's one [6].

The following extension theorem of possibility measure has been proved by author [5].

Theorem 1. A mapping $\mu: \mathcal{E}\to[0,1]$ can be extended to a possibility measure on $P(X)$, if and only if μ is P-consistent on $\mathcal{E}$, i.e.,

$\forall\{A_t|t\in T\}\subset\mathcal{E},\ \forall A\in\mathcal{E},$

$$A\subset\bigcup_{t\in T}A_t\implies\mu(A)\leq\sup_{t\in T}\mu(A_t),$$

where T is arbitrary index set.

Moreover, if we denote all of the possibility measure extensions

R. Trappl (ed.), Cybernetics and Systems '86, 581–583.
© 1986 by D. Reidel Publishing Company.

of μ from $\mathcal{C}$ onto $\mathcal{P}(X)$ by ξ , and define a partial order "$\leq$" on ξ:
$\forall\ \pi_1 \in \xi,\ \forall\ \pi_2 \in \xi,$

$$\pi_1 \leq \pi_2 \iff \pi_1(A) \leq \pi_2(A),\ \forall\ A \in \mathcal{P}(X),$$

then, we also may prove the following theorem.

Theorem 2. If μ is P-consistent on $\mathcal{C}$, then $(\xi,\ \leq)$ is an upper semi-lattice, and the extension π^* given by the expression

$$\pi^*:\ \mathcal{P}(X) \longrightarrow [0,1]$$
$$B \longmapsto \sup_{x \in B}\ \inf_{x \in A \in \xi}\ \mu(A)$$

is the greatest element of $(\xi,\ \leq)$.

As we all know, a possibility measure π on $\mathcal{P}(X)$ is determined uniquely by its possibility distribution $p(x) = \pi(\{x\})$ with

$$\pi(A) = \sup_{x \in A}\ p(x),\ \forall\ A \in \mathcal{P}(X).$$

Thus, the extension problem of possibility measure also may be stated as follows: arbitrarily given a mapping $\mu:\mathcal{C} \longrightarrow [0,1]$, we ask whether there exist some possibility distributions $p(x)$ satisfying the condition

$$\mu(A) = \sup_{x \in A}\ p(x),\ \forall\ A \in \mathcal{C},\tag{*}$$

It is quite interesting that all such possibility distributions can be obtained by solving a certain fuzzy relation equation.

Let S be a singleton. Then, the possibility distribution $(p(x))_{x \in X}$ may be considered as a fuzzy relation on $S \times X$, and $(\mu(A))_{A \in \mathcal{C}}$ as a fuzzy relation on $S \times \mathcal{C}$. Furthermore, let $(R(x,A))_{x \in X, A \in \mathcal{C}}$ be the characteristic function family of $\mathcal{C}:\forall x \in X,\ \forall\ A \in \mathcal{C},$

$$R(x,A) = \begin{cases} 0,\ \text{if}\ x \notin A \\ 1,\ \text{if}\ x \in A, \end{cases}$$

then, it is an ordinary relation (of course, also a fuzzy relation) on $X \times \mathcal{C}$. Thus, the condition (*) may be expressed by a fuzzy relation equation:

$$(R(x,A))_{x \in X, A \in \mathcal{C}} \circ (p(x))_{x \in X} = (\mu(A))_{A \in \mathcal{C}}.\tag{**}$$

Every solution $p(x)$ of this equation is a possibility distribution, it determines uniquely a possibility measure π which is an extension of μ from $\mathcal{C}$ onto $\mathcal{P}(X)$. All of the solutions (if they exist) of fuzzy relation equation (**) forms an upper semi-lattice when we define a partial order "$\prec$" on $X^I:\forall p_1 \in X^I,\ \forall\ p_2 \in X^I,$

$$p_1 \prec p_2 \iff p_1(x) \leq p_2(x),\ \forall\ x \in X,$$

where I is the unit closed interval $[0,1]$. By a theorem given by Sanchez [2], the greatest element p^* of the solution set of (**) is

$[(R(x,A))\otimes(\mu(A))^{-1}]^{-1}$. And, in this context, we have

$$p^*(x) = [(R(x,A))\otimes(\mu(A))^{-1}]^{-1}(x)$$
$$= \inf_{A \in \mathcal{E}} [R(x,A) \propto \mu(A)]$$
$$= \inf_{x \in A \in \mathcal{E}} \mu(A), \quad \forall x \in X.$$

The possibility measure determined by p* is just the greatest extension π^* of μ from $\mathcal{E}$ onto $\mathcal{P}(X)$.

If we denote the solution set of the fuzzy relation equation (**) by $\mathcal{R}$, then it is easy to prove the following theorem.

Theorem 3. $(\mathcal{E}, \leqslant)$ is isomorphic to $(\mathcal{R}, \prec)$.

REFERENCES

[1] E. Czogala, J. Drewniak and W. Pedrycz, 'Fuzzy relation equations on a finite set', Fuzzy Sets and Systems 7(1982)89-101.
[2] E. Sanchez, 'Resolution of composite fuzzy relation equation', Information and Control 30(1976)38-48.
[3] Z. Y. Wang and Z. P. Zhang, 'On the extension of possibility measure', BUSEFAL 18(1984)26-32.
[4] Z. Y. Wang, 'Extension of possibility measures defined on an arbitrary nonempty class of sets', Proceeding of the First I.F.S.A. Congress, Palma de Mallorca, 1985.
[5] Z. Y. Wang, 'Semi-lattice structure of all extensions of possibility measure and consonant belief function', BUSEFAL 24(1985)18-22.
[6] L. A. Zadeh, 'Fuzzy sets as a basis for a theory of possibility', Fuzzy sets and Systems 1(1978)3-28.

MAXIMAL NUMBER OF LOWER SOLUTIONS IN FUZZY RELATION EQUATION

Józef Drewniak
Department of Mathematics
Silesian University
40-007 Katowice
Poland

ABSTRACT. This paper discusses an estimation of the maximal number of incomparable solutions in a fuzzy relation equation, and presents an algorithm for calculation of this number.

1. INTRODUCTION

Let $m, n \in \mathbb{N}$ and L denote a bounded chain. We consider properties of fuzzy relation equation

$$x \circ A = b,$$

where $x \in L^m$, $A \in L^{mn}$, $b \in L^n$, i.e.

$$\max_i \min(x_i, a_{ij}) = b_j \quad \text{for} \quad j=1,\dots,n.$$

If the family $X(A,b)$ of all the solutions $x \in L^m$ is nonempty, then it has the form (cf. [1] or [3])

$$X(A,b) = \bigcup_{i=1}^{K} [1_i, u], \qquad (1)$$

where u is the greatest solution and $1_1, \dots, 1_K$ are lower solutions. These lower solutions are incomparable as minimal elements of $X(A,b)$ under the partial order induced in L. The number $K = K(A,b)$ of lower solutions depends on the characteristic matrix $C \in B_2^{mn}$,

$$c_{ij} = \begin{cases} 1, & \text{if } \min(u_i, a_{ij}) = b_j, \\ 0, & \text{if } \min(u_i, a_{ij}) < b_j, \end{cases}$$

where $B_2 = \{0,1\}$.

R. Trappl (ed.), Cybernetics and Systems '86, 585–590.
© 1986 by D. Reidel Publishing Company.

The problem of determination and estimation of K(A,b) was formulated in [1] and considered in [2]. We present here some new informations about it.

2. CALCULATION

The determination of K(A,b) is connected with the following (cf. [3])

2.1. <u>Algorithm A(C)</u>. Let c^i denote the i-th row vector of C for i =1, ..., m.

Step 0. Put s:= 1, u:= 0 $\in$ L^n, I:= $\{1,...,m\}$, J:= $\{1,...,n\}$.

Step 1. Choose an indeks $k_s \in I$ such that $c_{k_s,s} = 1$.

Step 2. Put u:= max(u,c^{k_s}), P:= $\{j \in J|\ u_j = 0\}$.

Step 3. If P $\neq \emptyset$, then put s:= max P and go to Step 1.

The above algorithm produces different sequences k_1, ..., k_s according to the different selections in the Step 1. The number of different results of the algorithm will be denoted by M(C). After [3] we know that

$$K(A,b) \leqslant M(C),$$

and this upper bound is attained for suitable A and b.

2.2. <u>Example</u>. For an explanation of the presented algorithm let us consider a characteristic matrix

$$C = \begin{bmatrix} 1 & 1 & 0 & 1 \\ 1 & 0 & 1 & 0 \\ 1 & 1 & 1 & 0 \end{bmatrix}.$$

There are five different ways in A(C) and we obtain the following sequences: a) 1, 2; b) 1, 3; c) 2, 1; d) 2, 3, 1; e) 3, 1. Thus M(C)=5.

The Algorithm A(C) does not work if the matrix C contains a zero column (case M(C) = 0). If any column has exactly one unit, then we obtain exactly one sequence (cf. [4]). Otherwise the different sequences are possible but they have no repetitions and s is bounded by m-1. So the number of different sequences in the algorithm is bounded by the number of all the permutations of I and we have (cf. [3])

$$M(C) \leqslant m! \quad \text{for} \quad C \in B_2^{mn}. \tag{2}$$

The permutations of a finite set can be ordered lexicographically (as the sequences in the above example). So we can describe the procedure of counting of all the sequences in the Algorithm A(C). We write it as the following

2.3. <u>PASCAL function</u>.

```
FUNCTION maxnols(m,n:integer; c:x1):integer;
{TYPE x1 = ARRAY[1..m,1..n] OF Boolean}
```

586

```
TYPE x2 = ARRAY[1..m,1..m] OF Boolean;
     x3 = ARRAY[1..m] OF 1..m;
VAR i, r, row, step: 1..m;
    p, q: 1..n;
    repetition: integer;
    u, colset: x2;
    colnr, rownr: x3;
BEGIN
repetition:=0;
FOR row:=1 TO m DO
  IF c[row,1] THEN
    BEGIN
    step:=1;
    FOR p:=1 TO n DO u[step,p]:=c[row,p];
    q:=1;
    WHILE q<=n DO
      BEGIN
      IF NOT u[step,q] THEN
        BEGIN
        colnr[step]:=q;
        FOR r:=1 TO m DO colset[r,step]:=c[r,q];
        i:=1;
        WHILE i<=m DO
          BEGIN
          IF colset[i,step] THEN
            BEGIN
            rownr[step]:=i;
            step:=step+1;
            FOR p:=1 TO n DO u[step,p]:=u[step-1,p] OR c[i,p];
            GO TO 2
            END;
          1:i:=i+1
          END;
        GO TO 3
        END;
      2:q:=q+1
      END;
    repetition:=repetition+1;
    3:step:=step-1;
    IF step< 1 THEN GO TO 4;
    i:=rownr[step];
    IF i>=m THEN GO TO 3;
    q:=colnr[step];
    GO TO 1;
    4:END;
maxnols:=repetition
END.
```

If a characteristic matrix $C \in B_2^{mn}$ is transformed into the Boolean matrix c, then the above procedure calculates $M(C) = \text{maxnols}(m,n,c)$.

3. OPTIMIZATION

Let us define

$$k(m,n) = \sup\{M(C) \mid C \in B_2^{mn}\}. \tag{3}$$

Obviously

$$k(1,n) = 1, \quad k(m,1) = m \quad \text{for} \quad m, n \in \mathbb{N}. \tag{4}$$

Now (2) implies

3.1. Theorem. For any $m, n \in \mathbb{N}$ we have

$$k(m,n) \leqslant m! \tag{5}$$

After (4) the bound (5) is obtained for $m = 1$. We shall show that for every $m \in \mathbb{N}$ there exists $n = n(m)$ such that $k(m,n) = m!$ So the maximal number of lower solutions is exactly $m!$ for fixed m.

At first we list some properties of function (3):

3.2. Theorem. Function k is strictly increasing with respect to the first and increasing with respect to the second variable.

3.3. Theorem. For any $m \in \mathbb{N}$ there exists $n^* = n^*(m)$ such that the function k is strictly increasing with respect to the second variable for $n \leqslant n^*$ and

$$k(m,n) = k(m,n^*) \quad \text{for} \quad n \geqslant n^*. \tag{6}$$

After Theorem 3.3 we can distinguish an important family of characteristic matrices:

3.4. Definition. A matrix C is optimal in B_2^{mn} if $n \leqslant n^*(m)$ and $M(C) = k(m,n)$.

3.5. Definition. The number of the unit entries in $c \in B_2^m$ is called the weight of this vector.

As an elementary consequence of the Algorithm $A(C)$ we get the following properties of optimal matrix:

3.6. Lemma. No optimal matrix has two equal columns.

3.7. Lemma. Columns of the optimal matrix are ordered increasingly with respect to their weights.

3.8. Lemma. No optimal matrix has a column of weight 1.

3.9. Lemma. Any optimal matrix has the column of the maximal weight (m).

3.10. Lemma. Any optimal matrix in B_2^{mn} has at most $\binom{m}{k}$ columns of the weight $k \leqslant m$.

3.11. Theorem. Any optimal matrix with m rows has at most $2^m - (m + 1)$ columns and can be divided into m-1 submatrices of constant weights:

$$C = [c_0, c_1, \ldots, c_{m-2}] , \tag{7}$$

where c_i has at most $\binom{m}{i}$ columns of the weight m-i.

3.12. Corollary. For any $m \in \mathbb{N}$ we have

$$n^*(m) \leqslant 2^m - (m + 1). \tag{8}$$

Now we consider C^* – the greatest admissible matrix for fixed m in (7). Submatrice c_i^* will be called an i-th section of C^* for i = 0, ..., m-2. Section i has exactly $\binom{m}{i}$ different columns of the weight m - i.

In the Algorithm A(C) the Boolean sum of some rows of C is calculated in order to obtain the row vector without zero entries. Now we describe the consequences of A(C^*).

3.13. Lemma. The Boolean sum of arbitrary s rows in C^* has no zero entries in the sections from 0 to s-1 and has exactly one zero entry in the section s.

3.14. Lemma. Any repetition of the Algorithm A(C^*) produces a sequence of m-1 numbers.

3.15. Lemma. There are exactly m-i+1 possible values of k_s in the i-th execution of the Step 1 in A(C^*).

3.16. Lemma. $M(C^*) = m!$ for $m \in \mathbb{N}$.

3.17. Lemma. For any submatrice C' of C^* we have $M(C') < M(C^*)$.

3.18. Theorem. For any $m \in \mathbb{N}$ the maximal optimal matrix has the form of C^* and we have

$$n^*(m) = 2^m - (m + 1), \tag{9}$$

$$k(m,n^*(m)) = m! \tag{10}$$

A determination of k(m,n) for $n < n^*$ is more complicated. However by consideration of submatrices C' without one section of C^*, we get

3.19. Theorem. If $m \in \mathbb{N}$ and $n \geqslant n^*(m) - \binom{m}{i}$, then

$$k(m,n) \geqslant \frac{m-i-1}{m-1} m! \quad \text{for } i = 0, 1, \ldots, m-2. \tag{11}$$

589

4. CONCLUSION

Our considerations show that the fuzzy relation equations can have a great number of incomparable solutions. So in the application of fuzzy relation equations an additional criterion is necessary in order to determine one of the incomparable branches of the solution family (1). The above results give an information about how many cases can appear in such a criterion.

The above considered problem is not a marginal one because of the great number of different optimal matrices. E.g. number

$$\sum_{i=1}^{m-2} \binom{m}{i}!$$

for matrices from Theorem 3.18.

5. REFERENCES

[1] E. Czogała, J. Drewniak, W. Pedrycz, 'Fuzzy relation equations on a finite set', *Fuzzy Sets Syst.* 7 (1982), 89-101.

[2] A. Di Nola, W. Pedrycz, S. Sessa, P.Z. Wang, 'How many lower solutions does a fuzzy relation equation have?', *BUSEFAL* 18 (1984),67-74.

[3] J. Drewniak,'System of equations in a linear lattice', *BUSEFAL* 15 (1983), 88-96.

[4] A. Lettieri, F. Liguori, 'Characterization of some fuzzy relation equations provided with one solution', *Fuzzy Sets Syst.* 13 (1984), 83-94.

A DOMINANCE OF ALTERNATIVES FOR DECISION MAKING
IN PROBABILISTIC FUZZY ENVIRONMENT

E. Czogała
Silesian Technical University
ul. Pstrowskiego 16
44-100 Gliwice
Poland

ABSTRACT. Three main types of dominance of alternatives
i.e. stochastic dominance, statistical dominance, and
stochastic-statistical dominance are presented in this
paper. The purpose of it is the choice of optimal alternatives in uncertain and imprecise environment. For the decision set (as well as for the sets representing goals and
constraints) the concept of probabilistic set in a sense
of Hirota is applied.

1. INTRODUCTION

The concept of fuzzy set defined by a membership function

$$A: \mathcal{X} \longrightarrow [0,1] \tag{1.1}$$

to the decision problems was applied by Bellman and Zadeh
[1] firstly and continued by many authors e.g. Zimmermann
[8], Yager [7], Kacprzyk [5] and others. $\mathcal{X}$ represents a
set of possible alternatives and A may denote decision
criteria, objective functions, restrictions or goals. In
fuzzy approach $A(x)$ may indicate the degree to which x
satisfies the criteria A. In decision making problems an
aggregation operator of decision criteria plays a significant role when one desires to satisfy more then one criteria. In particular, if $A_1, A_2, \ldots, A_n$ are decision criteria that one wish to satisfy then the overall becomes

$$O_n: \left\{ (A_1, A_2, \ldots, A_n) | A_j : \mathcal{X} \longrightarrow [0,1] \quad j = 1, 2, \ldots, n \right\}$$
$$\longrightarrow \left\{ D | D : \mathcal{X} \longrightarrow [0,1] \right\} \tag{1.2}$$

R. Trappl (ed.), Cybernetics and Systems '86, 591–598.

where O_n denotes the n-ary operation on the membership functions of fuzzy sets. The optimal solution is then $x_{opt} \in \mathcal{X}$ which satisfies e.g.

$$D(x_{opt}) = \max_{x \in \mathcal{X}} D(x) \qquad (1.3)$$

$$x_{opt} = \frac{\int\limits_{\mathcal{X}} x \, D(x) \, dx}{\int\limits_{\mathcal{X}} D(x) \, dx} \qquad (1.4)$$

where in (1.4) x_{opt} is respected to be the centre of gravity of the fuzzy set D. An important feature of this approach is worth noticing namely the symmetry between the goals and the constraints which allows to treat both of them in the same way.

In some situations, however, especially in the uncertain decision making environment the membership grade may be of probabilistic random nature or of possibilistic nature. The possibilistic type of uncertainty leads to fuzzy sets of type II and it will be not considered here. For the membership function being a random variable for each $x \in \mathcal{X}$ the concept of probabilistic set introduced by Hirota [4] seems to be convenient. A probabilistic set A of $\mathcal{X}$ is essentially defined by the defining function

$$A: \mathcal{X} \times \Omega \longrightarrow [0,1] \qquad (1.5)$$

Similarly as in fuzzy approach we can find situations, that goals and constraints constitute classes which can be described by means of probabilistic sets. In these situations a probabilistic fuzzy goal (constraint) is a probabilistic set in the set of alternatives $\mathcal{X}$, characterized by its defining function. The probabilistic fuzzy decision is the probabilistic set satisfying simultaneoulsly the goals and constraints. Denoting the respective n-ary operation on the probabilistic sets $A_1, A_2, \ldots, A_n$ by O_n, we may write for each $x \in \mathcal{X}$ as follows

$$O_n: \left\{ (A_1, A_2, \ldots, A_n) \mid A_j: \mathcal{X} \times \Omega \longrightarrow [0,1] \quad j = 1,2,\ldots,n \right\}$$

$$\longrightarrow \left\{ D \mid D: \mathcal{X} \times \Omega \longrightarrow [0,1] \right\} \qquad (1.6)$$

Taking into account the distribution function description
of probabilistic sets [2] we have the following equality
for each $x \in \mathcal{X}$

$$F_{O_n(A_1,A_2,\ldots,A_n)(x)}(z) = F_{D(x)}(z) \tag{1.7}$$

The problem of evaluating the optimal alternatives may be
solved in many ways, using various criteria. In this paper
the criteria based on some types of dominance are proposed.
These criteria should help for choosing the optimal alternatives in the respective decision situations.

2. STOCHASTIC DOMINANCE

Let $Z = [0,1]$ be an attribute set and $z \in [a,b]$ be a specific level of the attribute Z, where $a < b$ and the endpoints
may be 0 and 1. Let $\mathcal{X}$ denote a set of all feasible alternatives and $u(z)$ be a utility function on Z. In risky decision problems, suppose that the possible impacts of two
alternatives x_i, $x_j \in \mathcal{X}$ can be described by the probability distributions $F_{D(x_i)}$ and $F_{D(x_j)}$ on Z, respectively

($D(x)$ denotes the defining function of probabilistic set D
i.e. the decision set). Then the following axiom is appro-
ved under the expected utility criterion

$$x_i \succcurlyeq x_j \quad \text{means} \quad E[u, D](x_i) \geqslant E[u, D](x_j) \tag{2.1}$$

where the symbol $\succcurlyeq$ means "preferred or indifferent to",
and $E[u, D](x)$ denotes mathematical expectation with respect to the utility function u and probability distribution of $D(x)$ on $[0,1]$ i.e.

$$E[u, D](x) = \int_0^1 u(z) \, dF_{D(x)}(z) \tag{2.2}$$

Under the above axiom the probability distributions themselves are viewed as risky alternatives. As the available
partial knowledge about the utility function the following
classes of utility functions are defined

$$\mathcal{U}_1 = \left\{ u(z) \,\middle|\, u \in C^1, \quad \frac{du}{dz} > 0 \right\}$$

$$\mathcal{U}_2 = \left\{ u(z) \,\middle|\, u \in C^2, \quad u \in \mathcal{U}_1, \quad \frac{d^2u}{dz^2} \leqslant 0 \right\} \tag{2.3}$$

$$\mathcal{U}_3 = \left\{ u(z) \,\middle|\, u \in C^3, \quad u \in \mathcal{U}_2, \quad \frac{d^3u}{dz^3} \geqslant 0 \right\}$$

where C^i represents the set of bounded i-th differentiable functions. These classes are of importance for attitude of decisionmaker's preference toward risk. Obviously $\mathcal{U}_1$ is the class of utility functions for which the decisionmaker prefers an increase of the attribute level. $\mathcal{U}_2$ is the class for the decisionmaker to be risk-averse, and $\mathcal{U}_3$ is the class for the decisionmaker to be decreasingly risk-averse. With these classes the stochastic dominance is defined as follows.

For r = 1,2 or 3, the distribution $F_{D(x_i)}$ dominates the

distribution $F_{D(x_i)}$ in the sense of r-th degree stocha-

stic dominance, written as

$$F_{D(x_i)} \geqslant_r F_{D(x_j)} \quad \text{if} \quad E\left[u, D\right](x_i) \geqslant E\left[u, D\right](x_j)$$

for $u \in \mathcal{U}_r$ and r = 1,2,3 $\tag{2.4}$

The symbol $\geqslant_1$ refers to first-degree stochastic dominance, $\geqslant_2$ to second-degree stochastic dominance, and $\geqslant_3$ to third-degree stochastic dominance.

The necessary and sufficient conditions for stochastic dominance are the following ones [6].

Provided that $F_{D(x_i)}$ and $F_{D(x_j)}$ are distribution functions of a single variable

1. $F_{D(x_i)} \geqslant_1 F_{D(x_j)}$ iff $F_{D(x_j)}(z) \geqslant F_{D(x_i)}(z)$

$$\forall z \in [0,1]$$

2. $F_{D(x_i)} \geq_2 F_{D(x_j)}$ iff $\int\limits_0^z F_{D(x_j)}(t)dt \geq \int\limits_0^z F_{D(x_i)}(t)dt$

$$\forall z \in [0,1]$$

3. $F_{D(x_i)} \geq_3 F_{D(x_j)}$ iff $^m F_{D(x_i)} \geq {}^m F_{D(x_j)}$ and

$$\int\limits_0^z \int\limits_0^y F_{D(x_j)}(t)dtdy \geq \int\limits_0^z \int\limits_0^y F_{D(x_i)}(t)dtdy$$

$$\forall z \in [0,1] \qquad (2.5)$$

where $m_{(\cdot)}$ denotes the mean value with respect to distribution function $(\cdot)$ i.e.

$$m_F = \int\limits_0^1 z\ dF(z) \qquad (2.6)$$

3. STATISTICAL DOMINANCE

Statistical dominance of alternatives will be formulated by the following components:

1. A decisionmaker who is faced with a choice of two alternatives, x_i, $x_j \in \mathcal{X}$, and whose criterion is the expected utility

2. A set of m mutually exclusive and exhaustive states of nature $\{N_1, N_2, \ldots, N_n\}$, whose probabilities p_k, $k \in M = \{1, 2, \ldots, m\}$, are known exactly

3. An n×m matrix of utility values in which u_{ik} is the known utility value evaluated by the decisionmaker, if he applies alternative x_i and state N_k is the true state, $i \in I = \{1, 2, \ldots, n\}$, (n denotes the total number of alternatives taken into account), $k \in M$.

According to the statistical character of the consequences states, u_{ik} may be interpreted as the following two cases:

i when only a single consequence z_{ik} can possibly prevail then

$$u_{ik} = u(z_{ik}) \quad \text{for} \quad i \in I \quad \text{and} \quad k \in M \tag{3.1}$$

ii when it is possible for two or more different consequences to occur then

$$u_{ik} = \int u(z^1_{ik}, z^2_{ik}, \ldots) \, dF_{D(x)}(z^1_{ik}, z^2_{ik}, \ldots) \tag{3.2}$$

$$(z^1_{ik}, z^2_{ik}, \ldots) \in Z \quad \text{for} \quad i \in I \quad \text{and} \quad k \in M$$

where $F_{D(x)}(z^1_{ik}, z^2_{ik}, \ldots)$ are the conditional probability distributions of the consequences, given the state N_k, for alternative $i \in I$.
Under the above formulation, the expected utilities for alternatives x_i and x_j are written as

$$E[u, D](x_i) = \sum_{k=1}^{m} P_k u_{ik}$$

$$\tag{3.3}$$

$$E[u, D](x_j) = \sum_{k=1}^{m} P_k u_{ik}$$

respectively.
Provided that complete knowledge about probabilities of the states of nature is available, if

$$E[u, D](x_i) \geqslant E[u, D](x_j) \tag{3.4}$$

we say that alternative x_i dominates alternative x_j in the sense of statistical dominance.

4. STOCHASTIC-STATISTICAL DOMINANCE

Stochastic-statistical dominance of alternatives is formulated under the following circumstances

1. The decisionmaker is faced with a selection of two alternatives, x_i and $x_j \in \mathcal{X}$, and prefers an alternative maximizing the expected utility.

2. The decisionmaker's utility function may be not identified completely but it is known which class of utility functions is preference attitude belongs to.

3. There exists a set of m mutually exclusive and exhaustive states of nature i.e. $\{N_1, N_2, \ldots, N_m\}$. One and only one of them is the true state but the decisionmaker is uncertain which N_k, $k \in M = \{1, 2, \ldots, m\}$, is the true state. Probability p_k of the state is known exactly.

4. The decisionmaker is not certain which consequence is the true one even if we knew the true state of nature. The conditional probability distributions of consequences given for each state of nature are completely assessed for each alternative.

Let $F_{D(x_i)}^k$ and $F_{D(x_j)}^k$ denote the conditional distributions respectively with respect to attribute Z. Then distributions with respect to attribute Z are given by

$$F_{D(x_i)}(z) = \sum_{k=1}^{m} p_k \, F_{D(x_i)}^k(z)$$

$$(4.1)$$

$$F_{D(x_j)}(z) = \sum_{k=1}^{m} p_k \, F_{D(x_j)}^k(z)$$

Provided that complete knowledge about probabilities of the states of nature is available, if

$$E[u, D](x_i) \geqslant E[u, D](x_j)$$

for all $u \in \mathcal{U}_r$ and $r = 1, 2, 3$ $\qquad (4.2)$

we say that distribution $F_{D(x_i)}$ alternative x_i dominates distribution $F_{D(x_j)}$ alternative x_j in the sense of r-th degree stochastic-statistical dominance.

5. CONCLUDING REMARKS

The presented types of dominance of alternatives are based on the expected utility criterion. In particular case a respective mean value may be considered.

The moment analysis of probabilistic sets shows that the main information is concentrated on lower moments such as a mean a mathematical expectation called a "membership function" of probabilistic set and a variance called a "vagueness function". In order to characterize a probabilistic set it is sufficient practically to consider both a membership function and a vagueness function.

Taking into account both these functions it is easy to see that the expected utility criterion may be extended. It way be important when the maximum of $E[u, D](x)$ is not unique. It means that there exists a set

$$M = \left\{ x \in \mathscr{X} \mid E[u, D](x) = \max \right\} \tag{5.1}$$

In that case an additional information from the variance may be used

$$x_{opt} = \left\{ x \in M \mid V(u, D)(x) = \min \right\} \tag{5.2}$$

where $V[u, D](x)$ denotes the variance defined as

$$V[u, D](x) = \int_0^1 u^2(z) dF_{D(x)}(z) - (E[u, D](x))^2 \tag{5.3}$$

The above given formulas are extensions of the criteria presented in [2]. Some further extensions may be made on the base of e.g. [6]. Formulas derived in this paper should be helpful for the choice of optimal alternatives in probabilistic fuzzy environment.

REFERENCES can be obtained from the author.

THE INFORMATION ENERGY GAIN AS A CRITERION OF COMPARISON BETWEEN FUZZY INFORMATIONS SYSTEMS

L. PARDO
Department of Statistics
Facultad de Matemáticas
Universidad C. de Madrid
Spain

M.L. MENENDEZ
Department of Mathematics
E.T.S. de Arquitectura
U.P. de Madrid
Spain

J.A. PARDO
E.U. de Estadística
U.C. de Madrid
Spain

ABSTRACT

In this paper we stablish a comparison criterion between Fuzzy Information Systems based on the concept "Information Energy Gain" give by Pardo(1984).This criterion is called "Information Energy Gain's Criterion".

1.-INTRODUCTION

Let A be a random experience whose results $s_1,\ldots,s_n$ have probabilities $p(s_1),p(s_2),\ldots,p(s_n)$ respectively $(p(s_i)\geqslant 0, i=1,\ldots,n \quad \sum_{i=1}^{n}p(s_i)=1)$, $X=\{x_1,\ldots,x_p\}$ is an observation space, $p(x_j/s_h),j=1,\ldots,p$, is a conditional probability distribution and $S=\{s^1,\ldots,s^r\}$ is a set of fuzzy events on A named "Fuzzy Results Space" . We suppose that S is a fuzzy partition of fuzzy events on A.Now we consider the fuzzy messages $X^1,\ldots X^t$ which are fuzzy events on X and we suppose that $\{X^1,\ldots,X^t\}$ is a fuzzy partition on X.Finally,let us define the fuzzy information as the observation of a fuzzy message from $\{X^1,\ldots,X^t\}$.We will call $E=\{X^1,\ldots,X^t\}$ the "Fuzzy Information System".The set of Fuzzy Information Systems is denoted by E^*.

Pardo(1984),in analogy with Onnicescu's Information Energy,gives a measure of the information quantity of a Fuzzy Information System E, concerning the Fuzzy Results Space S in the following terms:

Definition 1

The Information Energy Gain about the Fuzzy Results Space S obtained by the Fuzzy Information System E is defined by

R. Trappl (ed.), Cybernetics and Systems '86, 599–606.

$$GW(S,E)=W(S/E)-W(S)$$

where

$$W(S/E)=\sum_{j=1}^{t}P(x^j)W(S/x^j) = \sum_{j=1}^{t} (P(x^j) \sum_{i=1}^{r} (P(s^i/x^j))^2), \quad W(S)= \sum_{i=1}^{r}(P(s^i))^2$$

and

$$*P(s^i)= \sum_{j=1}^{n} f_S^i(s_j)p(s_j) \quad \text{(Prior probability distribution on S)}$$

$$*P(s^i/x^j)=(P(x^j))^{-1} \sum_{k=1}^{n} \sum_{m=1}^{p} f_S^i(s_k)f_X^j(x_m)p(x_m/s_k)p(s_k) \quad \text{(posterior probability distribution on S)}$$

Pardo(1985) studies the properties of the W(S/E),W(S) and propose the "Information Energy Gain" as a measure of the amount of information about the partition S obtained by the partition E. In this paper we sta_blish a comparison criterion between fuzzy information systems based on definition 1. This criterion is called "Information Energy Gain's Criterion".

Let $E,F \in E^*$ be fuzzy information systems on $X= \{x_1,...,x_p\}$ and $Y=\{y_1,..,y_q\}$ respectively.

Definition 2

The fuzzy information system E is prefered or indifferent to fuzzy information system F, written $E \succsim F$, if and only if $GW(S,E) \geq GW(S,F)$ for the prior distribution $(P(s^1),...,P(s^k))$. $E \sim F$ if and only if $E \succsim F$ and $F \succsim E$.

For a prior distribution on S, it is easy to prove that $\succsim$ is a complete preording on E^*.

2.-PROPERTIES OF THE INFORMATION ENERGY GAIN'S CRITERION

In this section, the properties of the criterion previously defined are studied.

A fuzzy information system from which exact information can be obtained with a probability irrespective of the state is called Null fuzzy information system(M.A.Gil, M.T. Lopez and P. Gil 1984).

Theorem 1

If $N \in N^*$ is a Null fuzzy information system, then $E \succsim N \; \forall \; E \in E^*$. For all prior distribution on S.

Proof.

By properties of the conditional Information Energy(Pardo 1985),
$GW(S,E) \geq 0$. Moreover, to be $P(S^i/N^j)=P(S^i) \; \forall \; N^i \in N$

$$GW(S,N)= \sum_{j=1}^{t} P(N^j) \; \sum_{i=1}^{r} (\frac{P(S^i.N^j)}{P(N^j)})^2 \; - \sum_{i=1}^{r}(P(S^i))^2 \; =0$$

Where $P(S^i.N^j)=P(S^i/N^j)P(N^j)$. Therefore $E \npreceq N$.

Let E,F be fuzzy information systems, we consider the fuzzy information system

$$ExF= \{ X^i.Y^j \; / \; X^i \in E, \quad Y^j \in F, \; 1 \leq i \leq t \; , \; 1 \leq j \leq u \}$$

The membership function of the fuzzy set $X^i.X^j$ is $f_X^i(x_r).f_Y^j(y_s), 1 \leq r \leq p$
$1 \leq s \leq q$. It is easy to see that ExF is a partition of fuzzy events on
XxY.

We say that the fuzzy information systems E and F are independent
if and only if
$$P(X^i.Y^j/S^k)= P(X^i/S^k) \; P(Y^j/S^k) \; \forall \; X^i \in E \; , \; \forall \; Y^j \in F \; \forall \; S^k \in S.$$

where
$$P(X^i.Y^j/S^k)=(P(S^k))^{-1} \sum_{l=1}^{p} \sum_{s=1}^{q} \sum_{r=1}^{n} f_X^i(x_1)f_Y^j(y_s)f_S^k(s_r)p(x_1,y_s/s_r)p(s_r)$$

Theorem 2

Let E,F be fuzzy information systems, then $E.F \npreceq E$. Furthermore, if
$P(X^i/Y^j.S^k)$ does not depend on $S^k \; \forall \; X^i \in E, \; \forall \; Y^j \in F$, it follows that
$$E.F \sim E$$

Proof.

Let Z be a random variable taking the value $Z_j=P(S^k/X^i.Y^j)$ with
probabilities $P(Y^j/X^i)$ respectively and consider the convex function
$f(x)=x^2$, then
$$E(Z)= \sum_{j=1}^{u} P(S^k/X^i. Y^j)P(Y^j/X^i)= \sum_{j=1}^{u} \frac{P(S^k.X^i.Y^j)}{P(X^i)} = P(S^k/X^i)$$
$$f(E(Z))=(P(S^k/X^i))^2 \text{ and } E(f(Z))= \sum_{j=1}^{u} (P(S^k/X^i.Y^j))^2 \; P(Y^j/X^i)$$

We may now apply Jensen's inequality to obtain
$$\sum_{j=1}^{u} (P(S^k/X^i.Y^j))^2 \; P(Y^j/X^i) \; \geq \; P(S^k/X^i))^2 \quad (1)$$
Multiplying the inequality by $P(X^i)$ and summing over k and i we have

$$\sum_{i=1}^{t} \sum_{j=1}^{u} P(X^i.Y^j) \; \sum_{k=1}^{r} (P(S^k/X^i.Y^j))^2 \geq \sum_{i=1}^{t} P(X^i) \; \sum_{k=1}^{r} \; (P(S^k/X^i))^2 \text{ i.e.}$$
$W(S/ExF) \geq W(S/E)$. Hence

$$GW(S,ExF) \geqslant GW(S,E)$$

In the expresion (1) we obtain the equality if,and only if,

$$P(S^k/X^i.Y^j)=P(S^k/X^i)$$

Then,

$$P(X^i/Y^j.S^k)= \frac{P(X^i.Y^j.S^k)}{P(Y^j.S^k)} = \frac{P(S^k/X^i.Y^j)P(X^i/Y^j)P(Y^j)}{P(S^k/Y^j)P(Y^j)} = P(X^i/Y^j)$$

does not depend on S^k, $\forall\ Y^j \varepsilon\ F$, $\forall\ X\varepsilon\ E$.

If $P(X^i/Y^j.S^k)$ does not depend on S^k $\forall X^i$ E, $\forall\ Y^j$ F , it follows that

$$P(S^k/X^i.Y^j) = P(S^k/X^i)$$

whence

$$W(S/ExF)= \sum_{i=1}^{t} \sum_{j=1}^{u} P(X^i.Y^j) \sum_{k=1}^{r} (P(S^k/X^i))^2 = \sum_{k=1}^{r} \sum_{i=1}^{t} (P(S^k/X^i))^2 \sum_{j=1}^{u} P(X^i.Y^j))$$

$$= \sum_{i=1}^{t} P(X^i) \sum_{k=1}^{r} (P(S^k/X^i))^2 = W(S/E) \quad i.e.$$

$$GW(S,ExF)=GW(S,E).$$

Let $E\varepsilon\ E^*$ be a fuzzy information system.The fuzzy information system $E^{(n)}=Ex\overset{(n}{...}xE$, $n\varepsilon N$ is called a fuzzy random sample of size n from the fuzzy information system E (M.A. Gil 1984).It is easy to prove that if $E^{(n)}$ is a fuzzy sample of size n from the fuzzy information sys_ tem E, then

$$GW(S,E^{(n+1)}) \geqslant GW(S,E^{(n)}) \quad \forall\ n\varepsilon\ N$$

This results suggest that the greater the size of a fuzzy random sample, the greater the information it provides, and consequently a fuzzy sample is more preferred as its size is greater.

Theorem 3

Let $E,F,G\varepsilon E^*$ .If $E\geqslant G$ for any prior distribution on S,with E and F independent and,G and F independent,then

$$ExF \gtrsim GxF$$

Proof.

We suppose that $G=\{Z^1,..,Z^h\}$ is a fuzzy information system on $Z=\{z_1,...,z_v\}$ .By hypothesis $E \gtrsim G$ for any prior distribution on S.

Taking $P_o(s_h)= \sum_{i=1}^{q} f_Y^r(y_i) \frac{p(y_i/s_h)\ p(s_h)}{P(Y^j)}$ ($\sum_{h=1}^{n} P_o(s_h)=1$)

602

we have

$$P_o(s^h) = \sum_{t=1}^{n} \sum_{i=1}^{g} f_Y^r(y_i) \frac{p(y_i/s_t)p(s_t)}{P(Y^j)} \quad f_s^h(s_t) = P(s^h/Y^j)$$

and

$$P_o(s^h.x^i) = P(s^h.x^i/Y^j) \quad , \quad P_o(x^i) = P(x^i/Y^j)$$

For the prior distribution on S, $(P_o(s^1),..,P_o(s^r))$, we have,

$$GW(S,E) = \sum_{i=1}^{t} P_o(x^i) \sum_{k=1}^{r} \left(\frac{P_o(s^k.x^i)}{P_o(x^i)} \right)^2 - \sum_{k=1}^{r} P_o(s^k)^2 =$$

$$= \sum_{i=1}^{t} P(x^i/Y^j) \sum_{k=1}^{r} (P(s^k/x^i.Y^j))^2 - \sum_{k=1}^{r} (P(s^k/Y^j))^2$$

and by (1), we have

$$\sum_{i=1}^{t} \sum_{k=1}^{r} P(x^i/Y^j)(P(s^k/x^i.Y^j))^2 \geqslant \sum_{m=1}^{h} \sum_{k=1}^{r} P(z^m/Y^j)P(s^k/z^m.Y^j)$$

Multiplying by $P(Y^j)$ and summing over j we have $ExF \geqslant GxF$ for all prior distribution on S.

It is easy to prove that if E,F,G and $H \in E^*$, $E \geqslant F$ and $G \geqslant H$ for any prior distribution on S; E,F and G,H are independent, then

$$GW(S,ExG) \geqslant GW(S,FxH)$$

Let $E = \{ x^1,..,x^t \}$ and $E_o = \{ x_o^1,..,x_o^r \}$ be fuzzy information systems on X. The fuzzy information system E_o is said to be a refinement of E if for each $x^i \in E$ there exist a subset $J(i)$ of $\{ 1,...,r \}$ such that

$$f_X^i(x) = \sum_{t \in J(i)} f_{X_o}^t(x) \quad , \quad J(1) \cap J(h) = \emptyset \text{ for } 1 \neq h \text{ and } \bigcup_{1=1}^{t} J(1) = \{ 1,...,r \} (\text{Ken}$$

Kuriyama 1983).

Theorem 4

Let $E,E_o \in E^*$. If E_o is a refinament of E, then $E_o \geqslant E$

Proof.

Since E_o is a refinement of E, for each x^k there is a subset $J(K)$ of $\{ 1,..,r \}$ such that

$$f_X^k(x) = \sum_{j \in J(k)} f_{X_o}^j(x) \quad , \quad \bigcup_{k=1}^{t} J(k) = \{ 1,..,r \} \text{ and } J(r) \cap J(v) = \emptyset, r \neq v.$$

Let Z be a random variable taking on the values $Z(x_o^j) = P(s^i.x_o^j)/P(x_o^j)$ and probabilities $(P(x_o^j)/\sum_{j \in J(k)} P(x_o^j))$ respectively. Considerer the convex function $f(x) = x^2$, then

603

$$E(Z)=\sum_{j\epsilon J(k)}\frac{P(s^i.x_0^j)\,P(x_0^j)}{P(x_0^j)\sum_{j\epsilon J(k)}P(x_0^j)} = \sum_{j\epsilon J(k)}\frac{P(s^i.x_0^j)}{\sum_{j\epsilon J(k)}P(x_0^j)}$$

$$f(E(Z))=(\sum_{j\epsilon J(k)}P(s^i.x_0^j))^2\sum_{j\epsilon J(k)}(P(x_0^j))^{-2}$$

$$E(f(Z))=(\sum_{j\epsilon J(k)}(\frac{P(s^i.x_0^j)}{P(x_0^j)})^2\frac{P(x_0^j)}{\sum_{j\epsilon J(k)}P(x_0^j)}$$

We may now apply Jensen's inequality to obtain

$$(\sum_{j\epsilon J(k)}\frac{P(s^i.x_0^j)}{\sum_{j\epsilon J(k)}P(x_0^j)})^2 \leqslant \sum_{j\epsilon J(k)}(\frac{P(s^i.x_0^j)}{P(x_0^j)})^2\frac{P(x_0^j)}{\sum_{j\epsilon J(k)}P(x_0^j)}$$

Multiplying the inequality by $\sum_{j\epsilon J(k)}P(x_0^j)=P(x^k)$ and simplifyiend, we ha

ve

$$P(s^i.x^k)\frac{P(s^i.x^k)}{P(x^k)} \leqslant \sum_{j\epsilon J(k)}\frac{P(s^i.x_0^j)}{P(x_0^j)}P(s^i.x_0^j)$$

summing over i and k, we have

$$\sum_{i=1}^{r}\sum_{k=1}^{t}P(s^i.x^k)\frac{P(s^i.x^k)}{P(x^k)}\leqslant\sum_{i=1}^{r}\sum_{k=1}^{t}\sum_{j\epsilon J(k)}\frac{P(s^i.x_0^j)}{P(x_0^j)}P(s^i.x_0^j)$$

Hence

$$W(S/E_0) \geqslant W(S/E)$$

i.e.

$$E_0 \succeq E$$

Let $E=\{x^1,..,x^t\}\epsilon E^*$ and let $E^{(n)}$ $(n\epsilon N)$ be a fuzzy sample from E. Let T^0 be a mapping from $E^{(n)}$ so that $T^0(E^{(n)})\epsilon E^*$, with

$$P(s^k.T_a^0) = \sum_{(x^{i_1}..x^{i_n})\epsilon\Lambda(T_0^0)}P(s^k.(x^{i_1}....x^{i_n}))$$

where $\Lambda(T_a^0) = \{(x^{i_1}....x^{i_n})/T^0(x^{i_1}...x^{i_n})=T_a^0, 1\leqslant i_j\leqslant t, j=1,..,n\}$
and a=1,..,b.

Then we have the following result.

Theorem 5

$$E_i^{(n)} \succeq_i T^0(E^{(n)}). \text{Furthermore, } E_i^{(n)} \sim_i T^0(E^{(n)}), \text{if and only if,}$$

$$P(S^k/(X^{i_1}...X^{i_n})) = P(S^k/T_a^0) \ \forall \ (X^{i_1}...X^{i_n}) \ \varepsilon \ \Lambda(T_a^0), \ \forall \ T_a^0 \varepsilon \ T^0(E^{(n)})$$

Proof.

Let $Z_{ka}(X^{i_1},..,X^{i_n})$ be a random variable taking on the values $P(S^k/(X^{i_1}...X^{i_n}))$ with probabilities $(P(X^{i_1}...X^{i_n})/P(T_a^0))$, respectively and consider the convex function $f(x)=x^2$, then

$$E(Z_{ka}(X^{i_1},..,X^{i_n})) = \sum_{(X^{i_1}..X^{i_n}) \varepsilon \Lambda(T_a^0)} P(S^k/(X^{i_1}....X^{i_n})) \frac{P(X^{i_1}...X^{i_n})}{P(T_a^0)} =$$

$$= \sum P(S^k.(X^{i_1}....X^{i_n})) (P(T_a^0))^{-1} = P(S^k/T_a^0)$$

$$f(E(Z_{ka}(X^{i_1},..,X^{i_n}))) = (P(S^k/T_a^0))^2$$

$$E(f(Z_{ka}(X^{i_1},..,X^{i_n}))) = E(P(S^k/(X^{i_1}....X^{i_n}))^2) =$$

$$= \sum_{(X^{i_1}..X^{i_n}) \varepsilon \Lambda(T_a^0)} P(S^k/(X^{i_1}....X^{i_n}))^2 \frac{P(X^{i_1}....X^{i_n})}{P(T_a^0)}$$

we may now apply Jensen's inequality to obtain

$$P(S^k/(X^{i_1}...X^{i_n}))^2 P(X^{i_1}...X^{i_n}) \ \geqslant \ P(T_a^0) \ P(S^k/T_a^0)^2$$

with equality if and only if

$$P(S^k/(X^{i_1}....X^{i_n}))=P(S^k/T_a^0) \ \forall \ (X^{i_1}...X^{i_n}) \ \varepsilon \ \Lambda(T_a^0), \ \forall \ T_a^0 \varepsilon \ T^0(E^{(n)}) \quad (1)$$

summing over a and k , we have

$$\sum_{k=1}^{t} \sum_{(X^{i_1}..X^{i_n}) \varepsilon E} (P(S^k/(X^{i_1}...X^{i_n}))^2 \ P(X^{i_1}...X^{i_n}) \ \geqslant \ \sum_{a=1}^{b} \ P(T_a^0) P(S^K/T_a^0))^2$$

Hence

$$W(S/E^{(n)}) \ \geqslant \ W(S/T^0(E^{(n)}))$$

i.e.

$$E^{(n)} \succeq T^0(E^{(n)})$$

605

By (1) it is immediate to prove that

$$E^{(n)} \sim T^0(E^{(n)})$$

REFERENCES

Gil, M.A. ; Lopez,M.T. and P.Gil .- "Comparison Between Fuzzy Informa-
    Systems". Kybernetes,Vol.13,1984,pp.245-251.

Gil, M.A. ; Lopez,M.T. and P. Gil.- "Quantity of Information; Compari-
    son Between Information Systems: 1. Non-Fuzzy States" . Fuzzy
    Sets and Systems 15,1985,pp.65-78.

Gil, M.A. ; Lopez,M.T. and P.Gil .- "Quantity of Information;Comparison
    Between Information Systems: 2. Fuzzy States. Fuzzy Sets and Sys-
    tems 15, 1985,pp.

Kuriyama,K.- "Entropy of a finite Partition of Fuzzy Sets". Journal of
    Mathematical Analysis and Aplications 94, 1983, pp. 38-43.

Onicescu,O.- "Energie Informationnelle". C.R. Acad. Sci. Paris. Ser.A
    1966,pp. 841-842.

Pardo,L. .-"Information Energy of a fuzzy Event and a Partition of fu-
    zzy Events". IEEE Transactions on Systems Man and Cybernetics.
    Volume 15. Number 01,1985,pp. 139-144.

Zadeh,L.A. .- "Fuzzy Sets" . Information and Control 8,1965,pp.338-353.

Zadeh,L.A. .-"Probability measures of fuzzy events".Journal of Mathema-
    tical Analysis and Aplications. 23, 1969,pp. 421-427.

AN INTERACTIVE METHOD FOR MULTIOBJECTIVE NONLINEAR PROGRAMMING PROBLEMS
WITH FUZZY PARAMETERS

Masatoshi Sakaka*   and   Hitoshi Yano**
* Department of Systems Engineering, Faculty of Engineering
   Kobe University, Kobe 657, Japan
** Department of Information Science, College of Economics
   Kagawa University, Kagawa 760, Japan

ABSTRACT. An interactive method for solving multiobjective nonlinear
programming problems with fuzzy parameters characterized by fuzzy
numbers is presented and examined.   The concept of α-Pareto optimality
is introduced in which the ordinary Pareto optimality is extended based
on the α-level sets of the fuzzy numbers. In our interactive method, if
the decision maker (DM) specifies the degree α of the α-level sets and
the reference objective values, the minimax problem is solved and the DM
is supplied with the corresponding α-Pareto optimal solution together
with the trade-off rates among the objective functions and the degree α.
Then by considering the current values of the objective functions and as
well as the trade-off rates, the DM responds by updating his reference
objective values and/or the degree α .   In this way the satisficing
solution for the DM can be derived from among an α-Pareto optimal
solution set.   A numerical example illustrates various aspects of the
results developed in this paper.

1. INTRODUCTION

In the multiobjective nonlinear programming problem, there is no optimal
solution due to the inherent conflict between these objectives.
Consequently, the aim is to find the satisficing solution of the
decision maker (DM) which is also Pareto optimal. However, when
formulating the multiobjective nonlinear programming problem which'
closely describes and represents the real decision situation, various
factors of the real system should be reflected in the description of the
objective functions and the constraints. Naturally these objective
functions and the constraints involve many parameters whose possible
values may be assigned by the experts.   In the conventional approach,
such parameters are fixed at some values in an experimental and/or
subjective manner through the experts' understanding of the nature of
the parameters.
     In most practical situations, however, it is natural to consider
that the possible values of these parameters are often only ambiguously
known to the experts.   In this case, it may be more appropriate to

607

R. Trappl (ed.), Cybernetics and Systems '86, 607–614.

interpret the experts' understanding of the parameters as fuzzy numerical data which can be represented by means of fuzzy subsets of the real line known as fuzzy numbers [1] . The resulting multiobjective nonlinear programming problem involving fuzzy parameters [2] would be viewed as the more realistic version of the conventional one.

In this paper, in order to deal with the multiobjective nonlinear programming problems with fuzzy parameters characterized by fuzzy numbers, the concept of α-Pareto optimality is introduced by extending the ordinary Pareto optimality on the basis of the α-level sets of the fuzzy numbers. Then an interactive decision making method to derive the satisficing solution of the decision maker (DM) efficiently from among an α-Pareto optimal solution set is presented as a generalization of the results obtained in Sakawa et al.[4] .

2. α-PARETO OPTIMALITY

In general, the multiobjective nonlinear programming (MONLP) problem is represented as the following vector-minimization problem:
MONLP

$$\left.\begin{array}{l} \min f(x) \triangleq (f_1(x), f_2(x), \ldots, f_k(x))^T \\[2mm] \text{subject to} \quad x \in X = \left\{ x \in E^n \mid g_j(x) \leq 0, \ j=1,\ldots,m \right\} \end{array}\right\} \quad (1)$$

where x is an n-dimensional vector of decision variables, $f_1(x), \ldots,$ $f_k(x)$ are k distinct objective functions of the decision vector x, $g_1(x)$ $,\ldots, g_m(x)$ are inequality constraints, and X is the feasible set of constrained decisions.

In practice, however, it would certainly be appropriate to consider that the possible values of the parameters in the description of the objective functions and the constraints usually involve the ambiguity of the experts' understanding of the real system. For this reason, in this paper, we consider the following fuzzy multiobjective nonlinear programming (FMONLP) problem involving fuzzy parameters:
FMONLP

$$\left.\begin{array}{l} \min f(x,\tilde{a}) \triangleq (f_1(x,\tilde{a}_1), f_2(x,\tilde{a}_2), \ldots, f_k(x,\tilde{a}_k))^T \\[2mm] \text{subject to} \quad x \in X(\tilde{b}) \triangleq \left\{ x \in E^n \mid g_j(x,\tilde{b}_j) \leq 0, \right. \\[2mm] \hspace{4cm} j = 1, \ldots m \left. \right\} \end{array}\right\} \quad (2)$$

where $\tilde{a}_i = (\tilde{a}_{i1}, \ldots, \tilde{a}_{ip_i})$ and $\tilde{b}_j = (\tilde{b}_{j1}, \ldots, \tilde{b}_{jq_j})$ represent respectively a vector of fuzzy parameters involved in the objective function $f_i(x,\tilde{a}_i)$ and the constraint function $g_j(x,\tilde{b}_j)$.

These fuzzy parameters are assumed to be characterized as the fuzzy numbers introduced by Dubois and Prade [1] .

We now assume that $\tilde{a}_{ir}$, $r=1,\ldots,p_i$, and $\tilde{b}_{js}$, $s=1,\ldots,q_j$ in the FMONLP are fuzzy numbers whose membership functions are $\mu_{\tilde{a}_{ir}}(a_{ir})$ and $\mu_{\tilde{b}_{js}}(b_{js})$ respectively. For simplicity in the notation, define the following vectors:

$$\mu_{\tilde{a}_i}(a_i) = (\mu_{\tilde{a}_{i1}}(a_{i1}),\ldots,\mu_{\tilde{a}_{ip_i}}(a_{ip_i})),$$

$$\mu_{\tilde{b}_j}(b_j) = (\mu_{\tilde{b}_{j1}}(b_{j1}),\ldots,\mu_{\tilde{b}_{jq_j}}(b_{jq_j})),$$

$$\mu_{\tilde{a}}(a) = (\mu_{\tilde{a}_1}(a_1),\ldots,\mu_{\tilde{a}_k}(a_k)),$$

$$\mu_{\tilde{b}}(b) = (\mu_{\tilde{b}_1}(b_1),\ldots,\mu_{\tilde{b}_m}(b_m)),$$

$$a_i = (a_{i1},\ldots,a_{ip_i}), \quad b_j = (b_{j1},\ldots,b_{jq_j}), \quad a = (a_1,\ldots,a_k),$$

$$b = (b_1,\ldots,b_m), \quad \tilde{a} = (\tilde{a}_1,\ldots,\tilde{a}_k), \quad \tilde{b} = (\tilde{b}_1,\ldots,\tilde{b}_m).$$

Then we can introduce the following α-level set or α-cut [1] of the fuzzy numbers $\tilde{a}$ and $\tilde{b}$.

Definition 1. (α-level set)
The α-level set of the fuzzy numbers $\tilde{a}_{ir}$ ($i=1,\ldots,k$, $r=1,\ldots,p_i$) and $\tilde{b}_{js}$ ($j=1,\ldots,m$, $s=1,\ldots,q_j$) is defined as the ordinary set $L_\alpha(\tilde{a},\tilde{b})$ for which the degree of their membership functions exceeds the level α:

$$L_\alpha(\tilde{a},\tilde{b}) = \{(a,b) \mid \mu_{\tilde{a}_{ir}}(a_{ir}) \geq \alpha, i=1,\ldots,k, r=1,\ldots,p_i,$$

$$\mu_{\tilde{b}_{js}}(b_{js}) \geq \alpha, j=1,\ldots,m, s=1,\ldots,q_j\} \quad (3)$$

It is clear that the level sets have the following property:

$$\alpha_1 \leq \alpha_2 \text{ if and only if } L_{\alpha_1}(\tilde{a},\tilde{b}) \supset L_{\alpha_2}(\tilde{a},\tilde{b})$$

For a certain degree α, the FMONLP (2) can be understood as the following nonfuzzy α-multiobjective nonlinear programming (α-MONLP) problem.
α-MONLP

$$\left. \begin{array}{l} \min \ f(x,a) \triangleq (f_1(x,a_1),f_2(x,a_2),\ldots,f_k(x,a_k))^T \\[2mm] \text{subject to} \\[2mm] x \in X(b) \triangleq \{x \in E^n \mid g_j(x,b_j) \leq 0, j=1,\ldots,m\} \\[2mm] (a,b) \in L_\alpha(\tilde{a},\tilde{b}) \end{array} \right\} \quad (4)$$

It should be emphasized here that in the α-MONLP the parameters (a,b) are treated as decision variables rather than constants.
On the basis of the α-level sets of the fuzzy numbers, we introduce

609

the concept of α-Pareto optimal solutions to the α-MONLP.

Definition 2. (α-Pareto optimal solution)
$x^* \in X(b)$ is said to be an α-Pareto optimal solution to the α-MONLP (4), if and only if there does not exist another $x \in X(b)$, $(a,b) \in L_\alpha(\tilde{a}, \tilde{b})$ such that $f_i(x, a_i) \leq f_i(x^*, a^*)$, $i=1,\ldots,k$, with strict inequality holding for at least one i, where the corresponding values of parameters (a^*, b^*) are called α-level optimal parameters.

In order to generate a candidate for the satisficing solution which is also α-Pareto optimal, the DM is asked to specify the degree α of the α-level set and the reference levels of achievement of the objective functions, called reference levels. For the DM's degree α and reference levels $\bar{f}_i$, $i=1,\ldots,k$, the corresponding α-Pareto optimal solution, which is in a sense close to his requirement (or better, if the reference levels are attainable) is obtained by solving the following minimax problem.

$$\min_{\substack{x \in X(b) \\ (a,b) \in L_\alpha(\tilde{a}, \tilde{b})}} \quad \max_{1 \leq i \leq k} \ (f_i(x, a_i) - \bar{f}_i) \tag{5}$$

or equivalently

$$\min \quad v \tag{6}$$

subject to

$$f_i(x, a_i) - \bar{f}_i \leq v, \quad i=1,\ldots,k, \tag{7}$$

$$\mu_{\tilde{a}}(a) \geq \alpha, \quad \mu_{\tilde{b}}(b) \geq \alpha , \tag{8}$$

$$x \in X(b) . \tag{9}$$

The relationships between the optimal solutions of the minimax problem and the α-Pareto optimal concept of the α-MONLP can be characterized by the following theorems.

Theorem 1.
If (x^*, v^*, a^*, b^*) is a unique optimal solution to the minimax problem for some $\bar{f} = (\bar{f}_1, \ldots, \bar{f}_k)$, then x^* is an α-Pareto optimal solution to the α-MONLP.

Theorem 2.
If x^* is an α-Pareto optimal solution and (a^*, b^*) is an α-level optimal parameter to the α-MONLP, then there exists $\bar{f} = (\bar{f}_1, \ldots, \bar{f}_k)$ such that (x^*, v^*, a^*, b^*) is an optimal solution to the minimax problem.

If (x^*, v^*, a^*, b^*), an optimal solution to the minimax problem, is not unique, then we can test the α-Pareto optimality for x^* by solving the following problem:

$$\max \quad \sum_{i=1}^{k} \epsilon_i$$

subject to

$$f_i(x,a_i) + \epsilon_i = f_i(x^*,a_i^*), \qquad i=1,2,\ldots,k.$$

$$x \in X(b), \quad (a,b) \in L_\alpha(\tilde{a},\tilde{b}).$$

$$\left.\begin{array}{c}\\\\\\\\\\\end{array}\right\} \quad (10)$$

Let $(\bar{x},\bar{a},\bar{b})$ be an optimal solution to (10). If all $\bar{\epsilon}_i = 0$, then x^* is an α-Pareto optimal solution. If at least one $\bar{\epsilon}_i > 0$, it can easily be shown that $\bar{x}$ is an α-Pareto optimal solution.

It is significant to note here that from the property of the α-level set, the following relation holds for any two optimal solutions (x^1,v^1,a^1,b^1) and (x^2,v^2,a^2,b^2) to the minimax problems corresponding to α_1 and α_2 with the same reference levels:

$$\alpha_1 \leq \alpha_2 \quad \text{if and only if} \quad f_i(x^1,a_i^1) \leq f_i(x^2,a_i^2) \quad i=1,2,\ldots,k .$$

3. TRADE-OFF RATES

Now given the α-Pareto optimal solution for the degree α and the reference levels specified by the DM by solving the corresponding minimax problem, the DM must either be satisfied with the current α-Pareto optimal solution, or update the reference levels and/or the degree α. In order to help the DM express his degree of preference, trade-off information between a standing objective function and each of the other objective functions as well as between the degree α and the objective functions is very useful. Fortunately, such a trade-off information is easily obtainable since it is closely related to the strict positive Lagrange multipliers of the minimax problem.

In the following for notational convenience we denote the decision variable in the minimax problem (6)-(9) by $y = (x,v,a,b)$ and let us assume that the minimax problem has a unique local optimal solution y^* satisfying the following three assumptions.

Assumption 1.
y^* is a regular point of the constraints of the minimax problem.
Assumption 2,
The second-order sufficiency conditions are satisfied at y^* .
Assumption 3.
There are no degenerate constraints at y^* .

Then the following theorem is derived by using the implicit function theorem [3] .

Theorem 3.
Let $y^* = (x^*,v^*,a^*,b^*)$ be a unique local solution of the minimax problem (6)-(9) satisfying the assumptions 1,2 and 3. Let $\lambda^* = (\lambda^{f*},\lambda^{a*},\lambda^{b*},$

λ^{g*}) denote the Lagrange multipliers corresponding to the constraints
(7)-(9). Also assume that all the constraints (7) of the minimax
problem are active. Then it holds that

$$
\frac{\partial f_i(x,a_i)}{\partial a}\Bigg|_{a=a*} = \sum_{i=1}^{k} \lambda_i^{a*} + \sum_{j=1}^{m} \lambda_j^{b*} , \quad i=1,\ldots,k. \tag{11}
$$

Regarding a trade-off rate between $f_1(x)$ and $f_i(x)$ for each $i=2$,
...,k, it can be proved that the following theorem holds [5] .

Theorem 4.
Let all the assumptions in Theorem 3 are satisfied. Also assume that
the constraints (7) are active. Then it holds that

$$
\frac{\partial f_i(x,a_i)}{\partial f_1(x,a_1)}\Bigg|_{a=a*} = -\frac{\lambda_1^{f*}}{\lambda_i^{f*}} , \quad i=2,\ldots,k. \tag{12}
$$

It should be noted here that in order to obtain the trade-off rate
information from (11) and (12), all the constraints (7) of the minimax
problem must be active. Therefore, if there are inactive constraints,
it is necessary to replace $\bar{f}_i$ for inactive constraints by $f_i(x*, a_i*)$
and solve the corresponding minimax problem for obtaining the Lagrange
multipliers.

4. INTERACTIVE ALGORITHM

Following the above discussions, we can now construct the interactive
algorithm in order to derive the satisficing solution for the DM from
among the α-Pareto optimal solution set. The steps marked with an
asterisk involve interaction with the DM.
Step 1. Calculate the individual minimum and maximum of each
objective function under given constraints for $\alpha = 0$ and $\alpha = 1$.
Step 2*. Ask the DM to select the initial value of α ($0 < \alpha < 1$)
and the initial reference levels $\bar{f}_i$, $i=1,\ldots,k$.

Step 3. For the degree α and the reference levels specified by
the DM, solve the minimax problem and perform the α-Pareto optimality
test.
Step 4*. The DM is supplied with the corresponding α-Pareto
optimal solution and the trade-off rates between the objective functions
and the degree α . If the DM is satisfied with the current objective
function values of the α-Pareto optimal solution, stop. Otherwise, the
DM must update the reference levels and/or the degree α by considering
the current values of the objective functions and α together with the
trade-off rates between the objective functions and the degree α and
return to step 3 . Here it should be stressed for the DM that (1) any
improvement of one objective function can be achieved only at the
expence of at least one of the other objective functions for some fixed
degree α, and (2) the greater value of the degree α gives worse values

of the objective functions for some fixed reference levels.

5. NUMERICAL EXAMPLE

To clarify the concept of α-Pareto optimality as well as the proposed method, consider the following three objective nonlinear programming problem.

$$
\left.
\begin{aligned}
\min \quad & f_1(x,\tilde{a}_1) = \tilde{a}_1(x_1-9)^2 + (x_2-6)^2 \\
\min \quad & f_2(x,\tilde{a}_2) = 3x_1 + x_2 - \tilde{a}_2 \\
\min \quad & f_3(x,\tilde{a}_3) = 3x_1 + 5x_2 - \tilde{a}_3 \\
& \text{subject to} \\
& x \in X = \{ x \in E^2 |\ g_1(x) = -x_1 \leq 0,\ g_2(x) = -x_2 \leq 0 \},
\end{aligned}
\right\} \quad (13)
$$

where $\tilde{a}_1$, $\tilde{a}_2$, and $\tilde{a}_3$ are fuzzy numbers whose membership functions are given below :

$$
\left.
\begin{aligned}
\mu_{\tilde{a}_1}(a_1) &= \max (\ 1 - |a_1 - 1.2|\ ,\ 0\ )\ , \\
\mu_{\tilde{a}_2}(a_2) &= \max (\ 1 - 2\ |a_2 - 5.4|\ ,\ 0\ )\ , \\
\mu_{\tilde{a}_3}(a_3) &= \max (\ 1 - 0.5\ |a_3 - 17.1|\ ,\ 0\ )\ .
\end{aligned}
\right\} \quad (14)
$$

Now, for illustrative purposes, we shall assume that the hypothetical DM selects the initial value of the degree α to be 0.8, and the initial reference levels ($\bar{f}_1$, $\bar{f}_2$, $\bar{f}_3$) to be (20, 7.5, 7.5) . Then the corresponding α-Pareto optimal solution can be obtained by solving the following minimax problem.

$$
\min \qquad v \qquad\qquad\qquad (15)
$$

subject to

$$
\left.
\begin{aligned}
a_1(x_1 - 9)^2 + (x_2 - 6)^2 - 20 &\leq v \\
3x_1 + x_2 - a_2 - 7.5 &\leq v \\
3x_1 + 5x_2 - a_3 - 7.5 &\leq v
\end{aligned}
\right\} \quad (16)
$$

$$
\left.
\begin{aligned}
\max\ (\ 1 - |a_1 - 1.2|\ ,\ 0\ ) &\geq 0.8 \\
\max\ (\ 1 - 2\ |a_2 - 5.4|\ ,\ 0\ ) &\geq 0.8 \\
\max\ (\ 1 - 0.5\ |a_3 - 17.1|\ ,\ 0\ ) &\geq 0.8
\end{aligned}
\right\} \quad (17)
$$

$$
-x_1 \leq 0, \quad -x_2 \leq 0 \qquad\qquad (18)
$$

Solving this problem, we obtain a unique optimal solution
$(x_1^*, x_2^*, v^*) = (5,3,5)$, $(a_1^*, a_2^*, a_3^*) = (1,5.5,17.5)$ and objective
values $(f_1^*, f_2^*, f_3^*) = (25,12.5,12.5)$. This unique optimal solution
clearly satisfies the assumptions 1,2 and 3. Considering the second-
order sufficiency conditions, the corresponding Lagrange multipliers
become $(\lambda_1^{f*}, \lambda_2^{f*}, \lambda_3^{f*}) = (3/11,1/2,5/22)$ and $(\lambda_1^{a*}, \lambda_2^{a*}, \lambda_3^{a*}) = (48/11,1/4,$
5/11) by solving $\nabla L = 0$. Since all the constraints (16) and (17) of
the minimax problem (15)–(18) are active, using the results of Theorem
3, the values of the trade–off rates between f_i, i = 1,2,3 and α can
be obtained as follows :

$$\frac{\partial f_i}{\partial \alpha}\bigg|_{\alpha=\alpha^*} = \lambda_1^{a*} + \lambda_2^{a*} + \lambda_3^{a*} = \frac{223}{44}, \quad i=1,2,3.$$

Concerning the trade–off rates among the objective functions, from
the results of Theorem 4, we have

$$\frac{\partial f_1}{\partial f_2}\bigg|_{\alpha=\alpha^*} = -\frac{\lambda_2^{f*}}{\lambda_1^{f*}} = -\frac{11}{6},$$

$$\frac{\partial f_1}{\partial f_3}\bigg|_{\alpha=\alpha^*} = -\frac{\lambda_3^{f*}}{\lambda_1^{f*}} = -\frac{5}{6}.$$

Observe that the DM can obtain his satisficing solution from among
an α–Pareto optimal solution set by updating his reference levels and/or
the degree α on the basis of the current values of the objective
functions and α together with the trade–off rates among the values of
the objective functions and the degree α.

References

[1] D.Dubois and H.Prade, *Fuzzy Sets and Systems : Theory and Applications*, Academic Press, (1980).
[2] S.A.Orlovski, 'Multiobjective programming problems with fuzzy parameters', *Control and Cybernetics*, 13, 3, 175–184 (1984).
[3] A.V.Fiacco, *Introduction to Sensitivity and Stability Analysis in Nonlinear Programming*, Academic Press, (1983).
[4] M.Sakawa, T.Yumine and H.Yano, 'An Interactive Fuzzy Satisficing Method for Multiobjective Nonlinear Programming Problems', *Collaborative Paper* CP-84-18, International Institute for Applied Systems Analysis, Laxenburg, Austria (1984).
[5] H.Yano and M.Sakawa, 'Trade–off rates in the weighted Tchebycheff norm method', *Trans. S.I.C.E.*, 21, 3, 248–255 (1985) (in Japanese).

Systems Engineering for Design Automation

Chairpersons: K.Kellermayr (Austria)
F.Pichler (Austria)

MATHEMATICAL SYSTEMS THEORY AND DESIGN AUTOMATION

Franz R. Pichler
Institute of Systems Science
Department of Systems Theory and Information Engineering
Johannes Kepler University Linz
A-4040 Linz/Austria

ABSTRACT. This paper discusses some aspects for the application of
systems theory in CAD workstations for computer design. The main
concern is to consider multi-strata systems specifications as a useful
framework to model the design process.In addition systems theory is
considered to provide fundamental means for the construction of optimal
specifications at the different levels.Furthermore it provides the
right source for the selection of proper mappings to relate the
different levels to each other.As an example the introduced concepts
are demonstrated by a 4-strata systems specification 4-STRAT-SPEC-S
which uses finite state machines.As a research-goal,the paper discusses
some of the motivations for the use of finite state machine theory
to enhance current existing design stations to improve "Design For
Testability" features.

1. INTRODUCTION

The task of design automation is to automate the system design process.
In this paper we discuss some problems of design automation where the
systems to be designed are components of computers, e.g. certain types
of processors,interfaces or bus-systems.But also more primitive
components such as for example controllers,ALU's,multipliers or adders
are considered by us as design goals.Today,the tools for supporting the
design process are computerized at a high degree.The design of computers
without using a computer is not efficient **any more**.By the steady
progress of semiconductor-and high-integrated circuit technology and
since in the development of computer design workstations the computer
designer are envolved on their own part very strongly,the art of
design automation has in the field of computer design a high standard.
    Naturally,the computer industry is very much interested on their
own to find an optimal design environment for computer engineering
(e.g. Gonauser (1983)).Today there exist a number of CAD workstations
for computer design and the industry is strongly engaged to automate
the process for VLSI circuit design by the development of "silicon
compilers".

R. Trappl (ed.), Cybernetics and Systems '86, 617–624.
© *1986 by D. Reidel Publishing Company.*

Besides of artwork and practical experience,design automation requires
an exact systems theory-instrumented approach.There are of course many
different ways to apply results of systems theory in design automation.
Examples are provided by the formal specification of the design process
where the results of hierarchical multi-level systems theory can be
used,or also by the application of systems theory to specify the
different operations of the design process. The design engineer can
use the methods and results of systems theory to improve his artwork
and he gets tools which enable him to deal with complex problems,
such as for example the computation of realizations with optimal
internal structure ore the model-based construction of simulators,
directly.

Any implementation of tools for enhancing a design workstation
by theoretical results should be completely transparent to the designer.
It is not realistic to require that the designer has an insight into
the different applicable theories on which the tools are based.
The designer,however,should be able to ask the proper questions at the
right step and has to be an expert by the interpretation of the results
which are computed by tools.

In this paper we want to discuss some concepts of systems theory
which seem to be basic for the construction of design automation tools.
In the last chapter we outline a possible application of these concepts
in the problem area "Design For Testability",a research topic which
deserves strong interest today.

2.   MULTI-LEVEL SYSTEMS SPECIFICATIONS

It is quite common to describe technical products in the different
possible levels of usage and abstraction.Similarly it is very useful
to model the design process "top down" by the world of multi-strata
systems,which have been introduced earlier by the fundamental work
of Mesarovic (Mesarovic (1970), Kellermayr (1976)).There each level
(=stratum) models the whole system as seen from a certain abstract point
of view.Figure 1 shows the general structure of a multi-strata system
specification by a block-diagram.

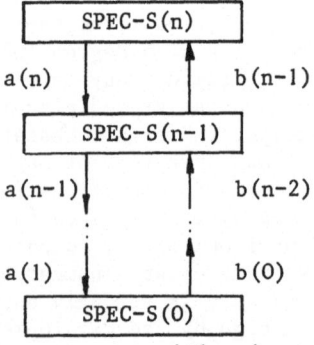

Figure 1:Multi-strata system specification m-STRAT-SPEC-S

For every k'th level system specification SPEC-S(k),k=1,2,...,n-1, there exist two operations a(k) and b(k),called _refinement_ (refining operation) and _coarsing_ (coarsing operation),respectively,which relate SPEC-S(k) to the specifications situated at the levels above and below, respectively.For the top-level only a(n) is defined;for the bottom-level,on the other hand,only b(0) exists.

The kind of operation which is performed by a(k) and b(k), respectively,depends on the type of the associated system specification SPEC-S(k) (for a discussion of different types of general systems specifications compare with Pichler (1984,1986)).As a general requirement it can be stated,that the composition a(k)oSPEC-S(k)ob(k-1) where k=1,2,...,n,is assumed to simulate SPEC-S(k) in a certain well-defined sense.Then,as a consequence,the top-level specification SPEC-S(n),which represents in many cases the user-system,is simulated via the intermideate specifications by the bottom-level specification SPEC-S(0).This level represents usually the implementation-system.

The _design problem_ which can be related to our multi-strata modelling philosophy can be defined as follows:

For a given top-level system specification SPEC-S(n),called the start-specification,determine a sequence of pairs of operations (a(n),b(n-1)),(a(n-1),b(n-2)),...,(a(1),b(0)) consisting of refinement and coarsing operations,such that the related intermediate systems specifications SPEC-S(n-1),SPEC-S(n-2),...,SPEC-S(1) meets certain level-specific realization requirements and the computed bottom-specification SPEC-S(0),the finish-specification,realizes the design goal.

There are many examples of engineering design problems of this kind.Furthermore,there also exist many examples for engineering design tools,which can be applied for the solution of such problems.In the case that these tools are realized my methods of systems theory,we call them instruments and we use the phrase "systems theory instrumented-design" (STI-design).As examples of STI-design tools which are in practical use we mention the work of Rammig (1984),Toussant (1984) and ZTISOF3 (1985).

The following advantages of STI-design tools can be stated:
(1) a STI-design process is formally specified in every design step; therefor all data which are necessary for computerized processing are available.
(2) for every level of a multi-strata specification there exists a rich source forchoosing the right type of systems specifications and related refinement-and coarsing operations.
(3) the formal verification of the design process can be proven automatically.

Our discussion of a systems approach for design automation has been so far very general.In our further discussion we want to be more specific. We do this by a "text book example" of small size taken from the area of hardware design.

3. MULTI-STRATA MODELLING BY SYSTEMS THEORY INSTRUMENTS

3.1 General structure of the example

In order to demonstrate the STI-design approach by a simple example
which shows the characteristic features of the method we choose
4-strata systems specification 4-STRATA-SPEC-S of a system S as
represented in Figure 2.

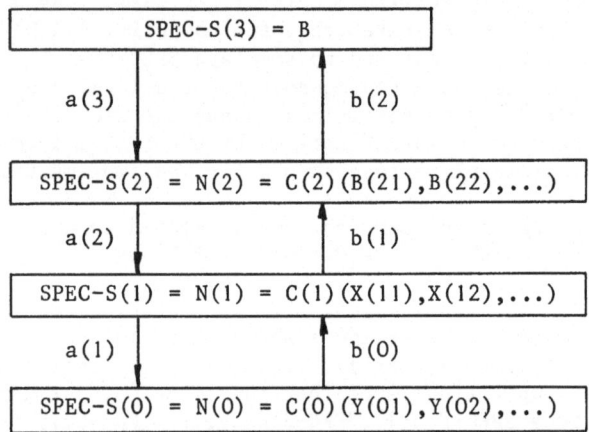

Figure 2 : 4-strata systems specification 4-STRAT-SPEC-S:
Implementation of a black box B by a network N(0)
consisting of a coupling of elementary building blocks Y(Oi).

In 4-STRAT-SPEC-S of Figure 2 it is assumed that the top-level systems
specification SPEC-S(3) is a black box B. The systems specification
SPEC-S(2) on the next level below is by assumption a network N(2)
consisting of black boxes B(21),B(22),... coupled together by the
coupling operation C(2). The systems specification SPEC-S(1) on level 1
is required to be a refinement of the network N(2) in that sense, that
now the components X(11),X(12),..., are assumed to be of generative
or algorithmic type. But also black boxes in form of (partial) functions
are allowed as components on this level. Finally, for the bottom-level
we assume a specification SPEC-S(0) which is a network N(0) consisting
of building blocks Y(01),Y(02),...,for which an implementation in
hard-or software in a certain realization technology is known.

The example shown in Figure 2 reflects in a simplified form an
important structure of practically existing cases. The black box B can
be associated with a given user I/O specification. The refinement N(2)
which is reached by the first design step constitutes the architecture
of the design-goal. On this level the black box B is structured into a
network consisting of smaller black boxes B(21),B(22),..., the modules
of N(2). By the next design step these modules are refined further and

realized by computational effective systems specifications of generator-algorithm-or function-type.The kind of specification which is chosen for this level reflects strongly the <u>realization</u> of the design-goal.The bottom level,finally,shows how the systems S can be implemented by a set of building blocks.This level shows in the finish the final <u>implementation</u> of the systems S which is reached by 4-STRAT-SPEC-S.

So far our example has been of general systems type.For a good demonstration of the potential power of the STI-design approach it would be necessary to specify the different systems specifications which are used in 4-STRAT-SPEC-S so that they appear as (mathematical) objects of special systems theories.For the user I/O specification on level 3, for example,black boxes given by relations or functions would constitute a class of such objects.In the next level,where the architecture of the system S ist determined,again black boxes as components therefore also relations (e.g. specialized to I/O time systems in the sense of Mesarovic) and functions are important mathematical objects for the specification of the network-components.For the coupling-operation relations,directed graphs or petri-nets would be candidates to be used.The realization-level is in our point of view dominated by computational effectiv constructs of systems theory such as finite state machines,difference equation systems,discrete event systems ,different-ial equation systems or formal grammars (all are examples of general systems of generator-type) or they are specified by algorithms written in some pseudo-programming language (e.g. ALGOLIC or PSEUDOPASCAL). This is a level where also the decision wether some component should be realized in hardware or in sofware is done. Finally the bottom-level on which the implementation of the system S in form of a "blue print" is specified,uses special types of systems specifications needed for the different building-blocks of this level.In computer hardware design this is very often the level where the systems specifications are given in the form of gate-functions,flip-flops,latches, PLA's,RAM's or other elementary building blocks of hardware implementations.

Unfortunately space does not allow us to work out an example for 4-STRAT-SPEC in detail.However,to give the reader an idea we will sketch the procedure to design an adding device (of simple nature and of text-book size).

3.2 Design of a mod 4-adder

The I/O specification SPEC-S(3) of a mod 4-adder ADD(mod 4) can be given by the table ADD(mod 4) of the function ADD(mod 4):$X(1) \times X(2) \rightarrow Y$, where $y:=(x(1)+x(2)) \bmod 4$ and $X(1):=X(2):=Y:=\{0,1,2,3\}$. In the next level ADD(mod 4),which is of course a black box,will be refined in a serial composition of two functions B(21) and B(22).B(21) computes the concatenation $x(1)x(2)$,B(22) is a serial-mod 4-adder, which computes from the string $x(1)x(2)$ the desired value $x(1)+x(2) \bmod 4$.With the serial composition $B(21) \rightarrow B(22)$ we have reached the systems-specificat ion STRAT-SPEC-S(2) of level 2. On level 1 we realize both functions, B(21) and B(22) of level 2 by corresponding finite state machines FSM(11) and FSM(12). FSM(11) is basically a mod 4-shiftregister of

length 2,FSM(12) is a usual mod-4 counter.Therefore the serial
composition FSM(11) → FSM(12) is the specification N(1)=STRAT-SPEC-
S(1) on the realization level of 4-STRAT-SPEC-S.In the final step,
to reach STRAT-SPEC-S(0) of the implementation level,we realize
the finite state machines FSM(11) and FSM(12) by sequential switching
circuits SSC(01) and SSC(02) by solving the "state assignment
problem" to get an optimal solutation for efficient implementation.

We learn from our example that even in a simple case of a design
process,the construction of a multi-strata systems specification is a
rather complex task if we depend on paper & pencil implementation
techniques.In the real case,when the design should be performed by the
means of a CAD workstation,all the STI-methods have necessarely to be
implemented for immediate use in software.It seems to be difficult to
find a detailed description of such implementations in the open
literature.However,results reported for existing workstations (e.g. for
the VLSI design tool VENUS of Siemens AG,Munich,West Germany) show
the high standard of the state of the art.Because of the educational
needs in computer design methodology at the universities it would be
desirable to put strong efforts in STI-design methodology research.
The work done previously by Zeigler (1976,1984) in the modelling and
simulation field can serve as a guideline for it.However,also other
results of research,e.g. the work established by Klir (1985) and his
coworkers with the general systems problem solver GSPS may be a milestone in that direction.The STIPS framework (STIPS stands for
"systems theory instrumented problem solving" which is under
investigation by the author (Pichler (1984,1984a,1986)),will be used
to develop STI-enhanced tools for "Design For Testability".In the next
concluding chapter we explain some of the ideas which guide currently
our research in that special design automation task.

4. DESIGN AUTOMATION FOR TESTABILITY

In "Design For Testability" (DFT) the designer is required to take
a fault model caused by the production process into account.In addition
to the existing reqirements put on the design-goal,it has to be
testable in a "nice" sense.Many important results have already been
derived in DFT-research.For a survey paper we refer the reader to
Williams (1982) and to the text-book of Fujiwara (1985).The results
which have been derived so far apply to different levels of systems
specification.The priority,however,is given to the register transfer-
and gate-level.Our purpose here is to discuss some results and research
ideas for the solution of DFT problems which are related to finite state
machine specifications.In the past,this level of systems specification
has found considerable interest,both,from the theoretical point of view
(e.g. Kohavi(1967),Zech(1977),McCluskey(1981)) and from the practical
side (e.g. Eichelberger-Williams(1978)).
    For finite state machines we want to discuss the following DFT-
problems:

We assume that FSM(11) starts always from initial state (0,0).Further-
more,that it receives an input-word w:=(x(1)00,x(2)00) of length 3.
Under these conditions it can be shown quite easy that the resulting
output-word of FSM(11) is 0x(1)x(2) which is basically the concatenation
of x(1) with x(2).

Figure 5 is showing a circuit diagram for the finite state machine
FSM(11) using a mod 4-adder and two mod 4-storages.It is a shift
register in mod 4-arithmetic.The reader should not get confused by the
fact that we need a mod 4-adder for realizing FSM(11),which on the
other hand is in our design process a part for realizing a mod 4-adder.
From a logical point of view this fact would require a mod 4-adder for
realizing a mod 4-adder,which would be a kind of design contradiction.
In reality,since FSM(11) starts from initial state (0,0) and receives the
special input-word (x(1)00,x(2)00),the mod 4-adder of Figure 5 has only
to compute trivial values.

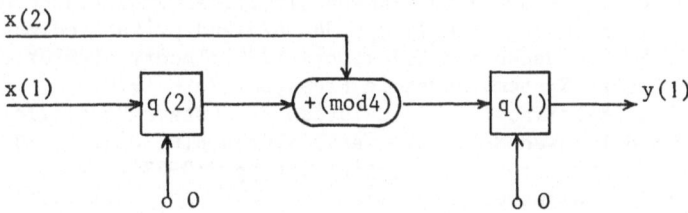

Figure 5 : shift-register diagram of the finite state machine FSM(11).

In the next "hozontal" step of our design we want to realize the
serial mod 4-adder B(22) of the architectural level by a finite state
machine FSM(12).With some little experience in finite state machine
realizations we conclude,that FSM(12) can be defined as follows:

FSM(12):=(X,Y,Q,δ(2),λ(2))   where

X:=Y:=Q:={0,1,2,3}   and

δ(2) and λ(2) are given by the following table

δ(2)	0	1	2	3	λ(2)
0	0	1	2	3	0
1	1	2	3	0	1
2	2	3	0	1	2
3	3	0	1	2	3

We observe that the state-transition function δ(2) of FSM(12) is
algebraically given by δ(2)(q,a):=(q+a)mod 4.Again this fact will not
contradict our design,since δ(2) is realized by recursion.

623

5. REFERENCES

Eichelberger E.B. and T.W.Williams(1978):A logic design structure for LSI testability.J.Design Automation and Fault Tolerant Comp. 2(2),pp.165-178.

Fujiwara H.(1985):Logic Testing and Design for Testability The MIT Press,Cambridge,Mass.1985.

Gonauser M.,R.Kober and W.Wenderoth(1983):A Methodology for Design of Digital Systems and Requirements for a Computer Aided Design Environment.IFIP Working-Conference on"Methodology for computer systems design",Lille,France,Sept. 15-17,1983.

Kellermayr K.H.(1976):Hierarchische Mehrebenensysteme:Konzept von Mesarovic,Report SYS-PED-9,Systemtheorie,University Linz,1976.

Klir G.J.(1985):The Architecture of Problem Solving.Plenum Publishing Corp.233 Spring Street,New York,N,Y,10013,1985.

Kohavi Z.and P.Lavallee(1967):Design of Sequential Machines with Fault-detection Capabilities.IEEE Trans.Electron.Comp.EC-16,pp.473-484.

McCluskey E.J. and S.Bozorgui-Nesbat(1981):Design for autonomous test. IEEE Trans.Comp. C-30(11),pp.866-875 and private communication.

Mesarovic M.D.,D.Macko and Y.Takahara(1970):Theory of Hierarchical Multilevel Systems.Academic Press,New York 1970.

Pichler F.(1984):Symbolic Manipulation of Systems Models.In:Simulation and Model-Based Methodologies.T.I.Ören,B.P.Zeigler and M.S.Elzas (eds.),Springer-Verlag Berlin 1984,pp.217-234.

Pichler F.(1984a):General Systems Algorithms for Mathematical Systems Theory.In:Cybernetics and Systems Research 2.R.Trappl (ed.) Proc.EMCSR 84,Vienna,Austria.North-Holland,amsterdam 1984,pp.161-164.

Pichler F.(1986):Model Components for Symbolic Processing by Knowledge Based Systems:The STIPS framework.In:Modelling and Simulation Methodology in the Artificial Intelligence Era.M.S.Elzas,T.I.Ören and B.P.Zeigler (eds.),North-Holland,Amsterdam 1986 (in press).

Rammig F. et al.(1984):A Unified Multilevel Simulation Technique.Proc. IEEE ICCAD 84,Santa Clara,CA,Nov.12-15,1984.

Toissaint I.(1984):Algorithmen zur Vergröberung und Verfeinerung von netzartigen Diagrammen.GMD-Studien Nr.90.GMD St.Augustin,BRD,1984.

Williams T.W. and K.P.Parker(1982):Design for testability-A survey. IEEE Trans Comp. C-31(1),pp.2-15.

Zech K.A.(1977):Zum Entwurf prüfgünstiger Automaten nach Kohavi und Lavallee.Elektron.Inf.und Kybernetik,EIK 13,4/5,pp.231-242.

Zeigler B.P.(1976):Theory of Modelling and Simulation. Wiley,New York 1976.

Zeigler B.P.(1984):Multifacetted Modelling and Discrete Event Simulation. Academic Press,London 1984.

ZTISOF 3 (1985):Modellierung und Simulation informationstechnischer Systeme.Siemens AG,ZTI,Softwaretechnik,München 1985.

SYSTEM PARADIGMS AND DESIGN PRACTICE

Maurice S. Elzas, Chairman,
Computer Science Department
Wageningen Agricultural University
Hollandseweg 1
6706 KN Wageningen
The Netherlands

ABSTRACT.   In this paper the relations between style of design, design, scope, verifiability and a systems-engineering design framework are explored.
A central assumption in the whole analysis is the widely accepted top-down, stepwise-refinement approach.
This approach is enhanced in the sense that the generation of test protocols has been directly linked to the design steps associated with this technique.
Evidence is presented for assessing limited adequateness of the incremental approach to design excercises if truly novel ideas have to be implemented.

1.   INTRODUCTION

Among the group of people that play a decisive role in the creation of new (technological) objects, one can recognize two main categories: the craftsmen and the designers.

The craftsman is basically a talented optimist, who − through intuition acquired by learning in practice − has an adequate (holistic) feeling for the selection of the raw material in which he fashions the desired object directly − himself − in the correct final form.

The designer, on the other hand, is a pessimist, a worrier − who has to rationalise about his goals, his means, his customers, etc. − in other words: to plan everything in detail, (long) before he can trust his ideas to paper or any other communication vehicle, in order to have the actual object made by others.

Can an objective choice be made between these creative attitudes, depending on the goal of the exercise?
Most probably not in a decisive way. But we can ascertain that, at a certain degree of complexity of the resulting object, the craftsman is bound to fail in one or more aspects of the result of his activity, unless of course he is a genius (of which we seem to have too few).
Thus the idea of (system-oriented) design can rest on three reasons for support:

R. Trappl (ed.), Cybernetics and Systems '86, 625–632.

- it allows one to create complex objects composed of a myriad of (known) components, in response to some, formalised, requirement
- it can be learned - to a large extent - in a curricular fashion
- as such a type of design activity depends heavily on the generation of documents of some kind, it allows design to be teamwork and thus to be more objective (in the sense of less limited in scope or biased by personal taste) and based on a multidisciplinary systems approach (C. West Churchman 1968, W. Wymore 1976).

The above seems to entail that we can approach all design in a completely rational way. Even for engineering tasks this is not always the case: "engineers first turn to science for answers and help, then to mathematics for models and intuition and finally to the seat of their pants" (Richard Hamming).

In general it appears that the larger the divergence of the new "product" with known practice, the more the "seat of the pants" (or skirts) is needed. The negation of this effect can have far reaching consequences in the realisation of innovative designs, as has been evident during the last decade in the area of development of computing tools (e.g. IBM-360/67 project, DEC-Jupiter project).

2. SYSTEM AXIOMS AND DESIGN PARADIGMS

It is generally assumed that - in practice - the "designer" has a decisive advantage over the "craftsman" in the sense that he is supposed to be able to verify the adherence of this system to specifications at every step of the design process, by testing his intermediate results. However, this assumption is by and large based on specific axioms about systems that - quite often - cannot either be rigorously proven to be right or negated out of hand. (See for example: Whitehead 1926.)

Four important ones are:

a. *any system to be designed can be sufficiently described by a finite set of symbols and symbol-relations*
b. *any design of such a system can be realised if it consists of a finite set of finite subassemblies of determinate components which can be manipulated as a series of entities related to each other by explicit rules (known a priori)*
c. *all systems which fullfil condition a. can be described by symbols which are intelligible by man. With this finite set enough information can be transferred to provide a satisfactory level of knowledge about the system being designed*
d. *system designs which fullfil requirements a. and c. are sufficiently independent of their exogeneous context to be analyzeable as invariant (or at least adaptive by determinate rules) with reference to considerable changes in their environment. (Or: only determinate objects are suitable for design activity.)*

Thus the scope for application of system-concepts to objects to be designed is clearly limited.

Axiom a. in practice requires proof a priori of the possibility to
describe goal and requirements of the system to be designed.
Axiom b. requires a priori knowledge of all possible components and
possible inter-component relations, in order to be able to
evaluate finiteness and manipulation rules.
Axiom c. being an intelligible documentation requirement, is central to
the feasability of multidisciplinary design.
Axiom d. limits the time-horizon of applicability of the design, in the
sense that changes in the exogeneous context can at best be
foreseen within a restricted time-frame.

For many simple cases, where new objects are to be designed with
known components for a well defined environment, it is clear that these
axioms do not form an impediment to the system design concept.
However, whenever the system to be designed should represent a clear
departure from current practice, lack of testable evidence for support
of these axioms often result in a lack of a priori insight in the
feasibility, adequateness and verifiability of the design. Consequently
the size and precise nature of the job that is to be tackled can only be
very roughly estimated and milestones for success are hard to define
beforehand.
Seen in this light, the structured systems design approach can be
said to be incremental by nature, while the craftsman-approach can be
thought of as holistic.
Thus there seems to be a relation between the scope of a design activity
and the applicability of specific design styles (see Fig. 1).

DESIGN STYLE \ DESIGN SCOPE	CONVENTIONAL SYSTEMS	INNOVATIVE SYSTEMS	MAJOR BREAKTHROUGH
HOLISTIC DESIGN	X	X	X
CREATIVE DESIGN	X	X	□
INCREMENTAL	X	□	—

X : SUITABLE
□ : APPLICABLE IN SOME CASES
— : INADEQUATE

Figure 1. Design styles versus design scope

The design style called "incremental style" above and in Fig. 1., is in fact the same as what is commonly known as the structured design approach consisting of consecutive top-down and bottom-up steps applied in direct relation to the knowledge available at every stage of the process and needed for the decomposition/aggregation phases which are essential to the systems approach.
The style is called incremental here because every step is essential for the final result and there are no "quantum jumps" in the process, which is clearly deducive.

Creative design (much like the style in which e.g. architects operate) on the other hand knows discontinuous transitions between the (traditional) phases based on extraevidental knowledge or creative intuition. In this way "unexpected" new avenues can be opened to produce novel approaches to previously resolved design problems.

Holistic design (the craftsman approach) displays the intuitive creation jump even more strongly, without often following any evident structured path. The approach is clearly inducive because it values a priori (intuitive) knowledge more than (conventional) design experience or detailed requirements and specifications. This style is typical of the great artists, scientists and inventors and requires - as yet unexplored - techniques to use elements of extraevidential consideration and is not concerned a priori whith any requirements or customer base.

Yet this is, clearly, what major breakthroughs are made of.

3. A FRAMEWORK FOR INCREMENTAL DESIGN

Formal evidence has been presented elsewhere (Elzas 1984, Aggarwal 1979, Hegner 1979) for the fact that models of systems fullfilling conditions very similar to the axioms presented in the previous paragraph, can be modelled in a systematic way (either top-down or bottom-up).

As incremental design is totally dependent on models (at least one that reflects the requirements and another that represents the system being designed), we can state - without furhter proof for lack of space - that systems complying with aforementioned axioms, can be rationally designed if a proper design procedure is followed throughout.

A framework for the necessary procedure is outlined in Fig. 2. The framework is based on the following assumption:
- There exists a "requirements base" which is an (informal) set of requirements which is capable for accounting for all expectations that (e.g. a "customer base", a "market" etc.) exist - however informal - for the system to be designed.

This requirement base has to be extracted out of the persons in whose minds it resides, in a systematic way in order to be amenable to translation into specifications (requirement analysis).

At the end of this stage we will have obtained an informal requirement specification. Informal because the representation of this specification need not yet fullfil the conditions of axioms a. and c. of paragraph 2.

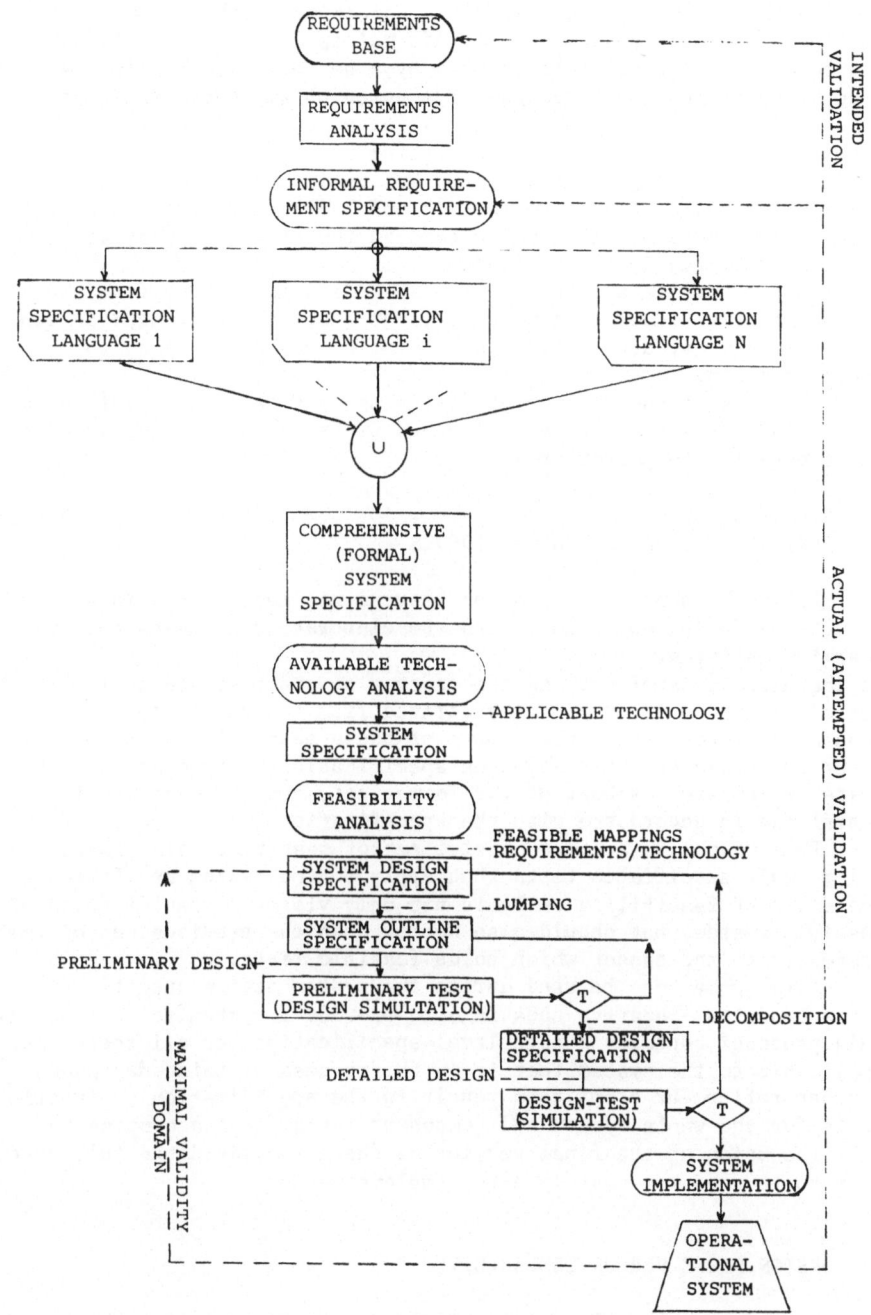

Figure 2. System-design and validation framework.

Assuming the existence of system specification languages (which will certainly fullfil the axiomatic conditions although possibly not all facets in one language), the informal specification is formalised (as to all its formalisable facets) by a set of documents in one or several specification languages. The union of all these documents results in a formal system specification at the highest level of comprehensiveness, formalisms permitting.

Following the path laid out by Wymore in his tricotyledon system engineering methodology (Wymore 1982 and 1984), the next stage is to filter this system specification through the sieves of available technology an feasibility criteria.
The outcome then is a system design specification which, from the viewpoint of top-down design, will first lead to the (rough) design of a system outline, after which only detailed design can lead to implementation.
To keep track of the quality of design as many tests as possible have to be carried out during actual design (a priori) and immediately after implementation (a posteriori).

4. DERIVABILITY OF TESTING PROTOCOLS

Figure 3. shows the relation between the major steps in a structured design environment and the elaboration of tests for the emerging entities.
At the highest level (during the process of requirements analysis) the set of potential tests directly derived from the requirements can, and should be, formulated. Only a part of those tests will still make sense after the stage of formal systems specification is reached. But those tests, which are a subset of the former set, can be described in a formal way in accordance with the specification.

Thus we obtain a comprehensive set of test protocols, containing all formaly specifiable tests that apply to the system specified.
The stage of feasibility analysis not only yields a specification of a feasible system, but should also narrow down the previous set of test protocols to the subset which holds feasible tests.

This subset can be used during the system design specification phase (and its iterative updating) to provide a system test protocol. This protocol contains a high level specification for all tests that are applicable to the system that is in the process of being designed. Further refinement steps then result in the specification of functional tests for the whole system and component tests for its components.

The union of the final version of these two yield the full system test to be used immediately after implementation.

5. DESIGN SCOPE VERSUS TESTABILITY

In order to be able to globally evaluate the relation between the scope of the design and the possibility to test its results, a simplified version of the design style vs design scope matrix (shown in

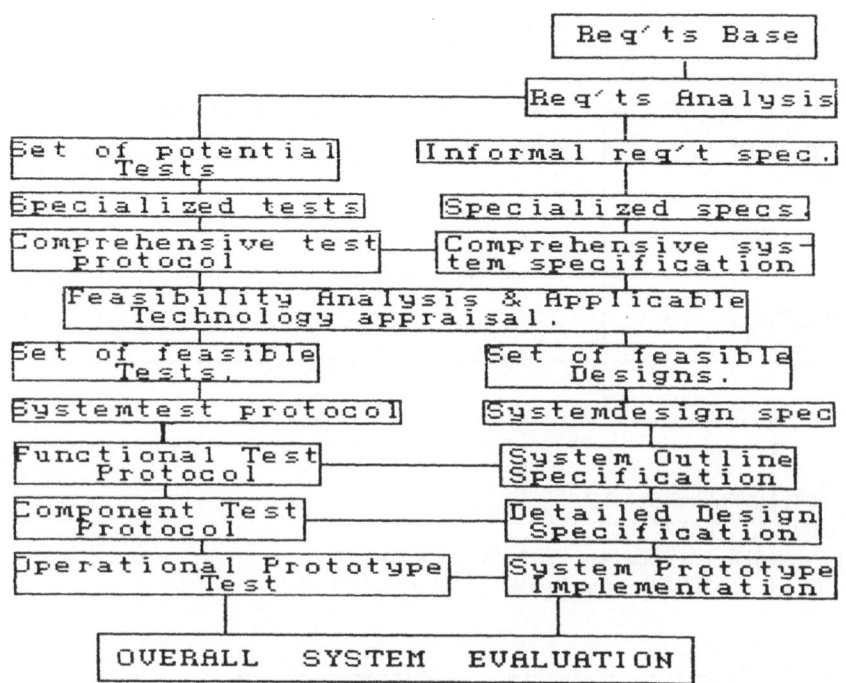

Figure 3. Test derivation and structured disign.

Fig. 1.) has been used. This simplification entails the use of the maindiagonal of that matrix to provide a one to one correspondence between style and scope.
If we also make use of the knowledge that systems can be tested during the design phase (a priori) and - immediately - after implementation (a posteriori), we can combine the two in an attempt to ellicit the relation mentioned in the title of this paragraph.

In this way the relation diagram illustrated in Fig. 4 can be constructed.
As in the incremental design approach (which is the best solution for the design of "conventional" systems), all tests are derived during the step by step system specification/system design procedure, all aspects of the system can (and should) be tested both a priori and a posteriori. Due to the assumption that conventional design makes use of previously tested components, even reliability of the system can be roughly assessed in a very brief time after implementation.

TEST ABILITY \ DESIGN SCOPE	A PRIORI		A POSTERIORI		
	of CONCEPT	of FEASIBILITY	of CONCEPT	of IMPLEMENTATION	
				ADEQUATENESS	RELIABILITY
CONVENTIONAL	X	X	X	X	~
INNOVATIVE	~	□	X	~	□
MAJOR BREAKTHROUGH	□	—	~	□	—

X : COMPLETELY TESTABLE
~ : ROUGHLY VERIFIABLE
□ : AMENABLE TO PARTIAL TEST IN SOME CASES
— : NOT TESTABLE/NO NORMS FOR TESTING AVAILABLE

Figure 4. Design scope versus design verification.

In the case of creative design, which is to be used in the innovative case, the feasibility can only be partially assessed beforehand. Therefore only a rough outline of a system test can be generated, which can possibly supply an adequate functional test. Component tests can obviously be thorough for conventional assemblies. The final system test can certainly offer an estimate for the adequateness of the design but will generally yield no - short term - data on reliability.

A major breakthrough, which has necessarily been "designed" in the holistic way, clearly only allows very limited pre-implementation verification.

In general post-implementation, immediate, testing has to be limited to rough testing of concepts and an estimation of adequateness. With other words: a long shake-down period is required to show the world the real value of the invention, as we already knew from experience.

6. REFERENCES
   to be obtained from the author.

TOOLBOX OR COOKBOOK?   THE FUTURE DEVELOPMENT OF STRUCTURED
SYSTEMS METHODOLOGIES

by John Crinnion

Centre for Business Systems Analysis,
The City University, London

This paper examines the approach to systems analysis taken by the current plethora of what are referred to as systems methodologies, what their contribution is to solving the problems of systems development, and where the trend of which they are an illustration seems to be directing us. It proposes an approach for DP departments and training organisations, aimed at providing a systems development method appropriate for all their various types of project.

INTRODUCTION

During the last five or so years, there has been a gradual movement away from the more traditional systems analysis and design techniques, as perhaps represented by those propagated by the NCC Basic Systems course during the 1970's [1], and towards the use of new groupings of tools which provide a variety of benefits for both user and DP management. Most of the tools themselves are not new, in fact one of the main claims of the effectiveness of the new approach is that it is based on tried, tested and proven techniques. The novelty stems from the way the tools are employed, to cross-check and to provide input for each other within an organised and integrated structure of project stages, the whole constituting a complete and continuous process of system development. This combination of tools and integrating framework is referred to as a 'systems methodology', and there are now in the market place many of these methodologies, most having many common tools but all having their own unique framework. In fact it is the uniqueness of the framework, along with the occasional extra tool, and some variations in the symbols and interpretations of the common tools which make the different methodologies marketable by the originating companies. There have been a number of studies recently which have examined the features of selected different methodologies,[2,3], though because the methodologies themselves are still in a development stage there is a need for constant review.

It must be stressed that any methodology only represents part of the overall range of required systems analysis skills and expertise. Very few for example deal with interviewing techniques or communications skills. Fitzgerald, Stokes and Wood,[4] have analysed the different stages in the systems development life cycle

633

R. Trappl (ed.), Cybernetics and Systems '86, 633–640.
© 1986 by D. Reidel Publishing Company.

addressed by seven of the leading methodologies and point out for example that few concern themselves with the feasibility stage of a development project, several address themselves only to the analysis stage, leaving the detailed design process to the discretion of the individual DP department, while others include a rigorous design stage. The point is important because some organisations are equating methodology training with systems analysis training and are substituting a two week methodology course for a full basic systems analysis course. Many training organisations are attempting to incorporate a detailed new methodology into an existing course, and as a result often failing to give a balanced view of the whole subject.

DEVELOPMENT OF METHODOLOGIES SO FAR

So a systems methodology consists of a collection of tools and a framework. The tools are many and varied, the commonest being the data flow diagram, as popularised by Constantine and DeMarco,[5], though different methodologies take different approaches for instance, to physical and logical DFDs, to how materials flow is to be diagrammed, to how different levels of diagram are to be linked, and even to the shape of the symbols to be used. Almost equally common is the use of hierarchical decomposition diagrams to illustrate the structures of both functions and data. For the more detailed analysis of data, common tools include Codd's normalisation and relational model, (to various levels of complexity), as well as several forms of the more intuitive entity attribute relationship modelling technique, (though there are conflicting views put forward in some as to what constitutes an entity). The use of walkthroughs, data dictionaries and structured English are stressed to varying degrees. Several of the fuller methodologies that contain a design component make use of adaptations of Jackson's entity life history tool,[6] to produce a design based on the structure of the data and taking into account its time dependency. Others base their design approach more on the structure of processes. The previously mentioned studies,[2,3], together with a recent small study done by the City University,[7] give a fuller account of the different tools used in each methodology.

It is however the framework which is the most interesting aspect of each of the methodologies. The frameworks, with their emphasis on different project stages, their breakdown of stages into tasks, their checklists of activities and their interrelating, overlapping and cross-referencing of tools, give us a clear picture of what the methodology originators consider to be the most important aspects of systems development.
Many methodologies for example stress user involvement, especially in the early stages,. Experience has shown that some users, when faced with a complex technical specification, will opt out of their continuing responsibility for the developing system, transfering it to the systems team. To counteract this, several of the methodologies physically force the user to participate by means

634

of formal walkthroughs, user design teams for various parts of the design stage, the insistence on a user as project manager, etc. The framework of such a methodology reflects this concern in that it ties together very simple stages in a very formal way, making use of simplified user-friendly versions of the main structured techniques, and insisting on continuous iteration and quality assurance.

Some of the most popular methodologies, for example those originated by LBMS,[8] but now available in three slightly different forms,[9,10], include a thorough, detailed and formalised design phase. This imposes a very formal approach to the analysis phase, where products from each task-stage are considered to be essential prerequisites for following tasks. Clearly this tackles the problems of inadequate analysis and poor specification, though it does make the assumption that the problem being faced lends itself to this type of analysis.

Several methodologies are based on the view that the structure of the designed system should mirror the structure of the data involved in the system. This approach, it is claimed, reduces later maintenance problems, and allows the full potential of the data to be realised. The frameworks for these methodologies vary in their degrees of formality and complexity, but one of the most important, Jackson Structured Design Methodology, has its roots firmly in the detailed design and programming stages of the project. This aspect of the methodology is arguably visible in the framework, which begins with a requirements specification, and moves through comprehensive design and implementation stages, working inexorably towards the in-house production of a computer solution.

On the other hand, a number of the methodologies, including for example BIS Modus [11], and a particularly good in-house methodology originally built for the Exxon Corporation and now marketed under the name Extim [12], clearly are more concerned with the business view of the system . This is emphasised by the attitude to business functions and requirements inherent in the framework, and the inclusion of an optional DP strategy stage, with appropriate tools, (for example, an adaptation of IBM's Business Systems Planning tool).

This variety is only to be expected; different companies because of their nature and experience have different views of what constitute the main problems of systems analysis and design, and choose a particular approach to overcome them.

TOOLBOX AND COOKBOOK

A simple analysis of the framework aspect of the various methodologies shows a continuum based on the degree of rigidity and complexity inherent. At one extreme there is the 'toolbox' approach, where the framework is minimal, and the individual tools are used as and when they are felt to be worthwhile. This approach is obviously only suitable where the systems required vary in size and type, and where experienced analysts are employed. There is clearly a danger in using this approach in larger and more complex systems, where detailed plans and estimates are required.

At the other end of the continuum is the 'cookbook' approach, where great emphasis is placed on the framework, with its ordered stages, its checklists, its interdependency of tools and its rigidity of approach. Please note that the use of the term rigidity does not necessarily imply criticism; some level of imposition has always been recognised as necessary for large and complex projects where many of the tasks are performed by junior staff.

All of the current methodologies can be mapped onto this, most of the ones mentioned more towards the cookbook end of the scale.

THE PROBLEMS

Most of these methodologies have now established and proved themselves on a variety of system types. However, this success is only relative. Each methodology has its own strengths and weaknesses, and although the better ones can produce a working system for almost all types of problem, the solution is not always as efficient as it might be . Also, the development of the system is often longer and more costly than it perhaps need be; the use of a cookbook methodology on a relatively simple information system can result in unnecessary stages being performed and too rigorous application of some techniques. This has been recognised by some of the suppliers, who have tried to provide a 'fast path' method of applying their methodology.

In spite of the possible inefficiency, DP management are often prepared to accept such an overhead in return for the level of control that is possible, and the level of guarantee of a worthwhile finished product. The manager is prepared to sacrifice the possibility of an efficient and elegant solution in three months with some risk of a poor solution taking nine months, for the probability of a satisfactory solution in seven months.

The ideal situation for a DP organisation would be to have several different cookbook methodologies from which it could select the most appropriate for any particular large project, and to have a standard toolbox from which analysts could select their best approach to smaller systems. However, most methodologies are so extensive and require such a large training overhead that for any organisation to support more than one is out of the question. Moreover, there are problems in allowing a cookbook and a toolbox to work alongside each other in the same department. One of the critical aspects in the success of a cookbook approach is that the rules and standards must be adhered to, and evidence from the previously mentioned City University survey [7] suggests the necessity of some method of enforcement within the DP department.The existence of one or more systems analysis teams who are not subject to the same discipline can make this difficult to apply.

The problem with which this paper is mainly concerned is that of a DP department or organisation who are considering changing from their existing approach to some form of structured systems analysis

636

and design approach. What should they do? Should they go for a toolbox or cookbook? It obviously depends on the type of projects normally undertaken. However nearly all Dp departments will have some medium or large size projects requiring tight control. If a cookbook approach is to be adopted, which is the best option for the type of work being handled? Would it be better to build an in-house methodology, perhaps adapted from one of the existing methodologies?

In practice, as pointed out by Nolan in his work on applications portfolios [14], most DP organisations of any size have to be able to provide a variety of large and small systems, some at the operational level, others concerned with management information and decision support. Some of these systems are of the type which suit a data-driven approach as used in SSADM or JSD, whereas others might better suit the more function oriented approach of, say, Yourdon. Many of the small systems which are created, perhaps using fourth generation languages, relational DBMS packages or other special software,(a growing proportion of the DP workload), are little suited to any form of rigid cookbook methodology [15]. Do we then need an entirely separate approach for these?

A different problem exists for the major DP training organisations. They are expected to provide systems analysis training for a range of public and private organisations some of whom are not yet concerned with structured analysis, while others are making use of all varieties of different methodologies. Should the DP training companies restrict themselves to general systems analysis training, leaving the methodology training to the methodology suppliers? Should they perhaps specialise in one methodology, hoping to find enough clients who use it , or to help persuade some of their existing clients to change? Ideally for these companies, one methodology should establish a dominance to the extent of almost being accepted as an industry standard; this would solve the problem of what and which to teach. It is interesting to see the vested interests of this powerful lobby being aligned with those of the equally commercial interests of the methodology suppliers, in an attempt to hasten the arrival of an industry standard. The methodology which seems to benefit the most from this hastening is probably that of LBMS and its variants, the important factor being the contract with the Civil Service, who employ probably the largest number of systems analysts in the country. This possible trend is not welcomed by all disinterested observers, many of whom feel that SSADM, when applied to small and medium sized systems is unnecessarily rigorous and cumbersome.

The position is made additionally complicated by the important advances in the marketing and use of application development tool packages, such as Excelerator from ITC and Auto-mate from LBMS, which not only provide graphical facilities for creating and adjusting the tool diagrams for specific methodologies, but also automatically incorporate a high level of validation and cross-checking. This again tends to support the formality rather than the flexibility of the framework, making it difficult to take a toolbox approach.

THE FUTURE

We are quite obviously in the middle of a major change in the way in which the process of systems analysis and design is conducted. On one side, the benefits of the new structured approach are beginning to make themselves obvious. However, the approach brings not only benefits. The previous generation of computer systems in this country were developed for the most part using a subset or variant of the very full NCC set of techniques and documentation, which served as a very flexible industry standard. The replacement of this by a multitude of different sets of methodology standards has in one sense caused the industry to take a step backwards.

There is clearly a need for further development, not only to provide the level of flexibility necessary to handle diverse system types, but also to restore the advantages of some level of recognised standard approach throughout the industry.

My feeling is that the major tools, although some of them are still developing, are more or less right, and the new development must occur by building flexibility into the framework aspect of the structured approach. The methodology suppliers have developed and patented particular frameworks, but it seems that no one framework will suffice for a DP organisation. In fact different frameworks suit different types of system, and it would serve an individual firm better if it could choose for itself the framework and tools to apply to each particular project.

This would require the development of a new skill within DP departments; an experienced and specially trained analyst would be required to examine each project at the feasibility stage and decide which tools would be used and how they would be integrated. The person taking on this new and senior role of 'framework builder' within a DP department would have a standard toolbox from which to select for each stage or aspect of a project, and would be able to describe and document the decided framework structure using one or more of the tools; (it is common practice, for example, to use the data flow diagram to illustrate the steps involved and the tools used in the different stages of the systems development process).

The one critical gap in the potential framework builder's armoury is knowledge of a comprehensive range of framework crosschecking techniques etc., and, more importantly, the structure. In what circumstances for example does it cease to be worthwhile to use an entity life history diagram? When is it wise to use both an entity-relationship modelling technique and a full normalisation? and under what conditions would each be the better choice of approach? Much of the research now being done is directed at comparing full methodologies, and although some approaches to tailoring a methodology for a specific project are being explored [16], it seems to me that there is still major scope for research into individual framework components and their interactions. Some of this has obviously already been done by the methodology developers, and part of the task may well be a synthesis of this by disinterested parties.

The advantages to a DP organisation of having such a role in their structure are many. Firstly, the overheads mentioned earlier, incurred in the name of risk management would be minimised. Secondly, the whole systems department would gain an extra level of flexibility; the more skilled analysts within the organisation would have new opportunities for creative use of their talents, while the more junior staff would still be able to function effectively within a cookbook situation. It would be possible for new analysts to be trained in a limited range of tools, and they could then be given projects which incorporated those limitations. This contrasts with the current situation, where junior analysts are taught the full range of tools, some, of necessity, at a superficial level, in order to be able to see the methodology in perspective. This can be a particular problem with some of the more sophisticatd tools like for example the entity life history from LBMS and JSD, where some of the concepts involved really require time to digest, and some inexperienced staff are confused and put off. In the proposed new approach, the learning of advanced tools could be spread throughout the early part of the analyst's career, to be followed later perhaps by a standard advanced course in framework building, run by one of the DP training organisations.
Finally, the extra flexibility of such an approach should allow a natural growth in systems development science, as new concepts, tools and techniques are added, while less effective ones fall by the wayside.

While research in this area is going ahead, (and such a programme is being conducted here at the City University), what can the many DP departments faced with these problems do? Shackleton [17] gives some good criteria for selecting a methodology, though his examples refer more to the situation for companies in the United States, and recent articles by Aitken [18] might give guidance by example to large DP organisations Perhaps the best advice might be to select what is considered to be the most appropriate of the existing structured methodologies for their particular circumstances, build up a level of expertise within the organisation, and then gradually and carefully begin to experiment with small adjustments, attempting to tailor the framework for individual projects. Care must be stressed because of the real danger of uncontrolled tampering with a proven and trusted set of standards. However, at the moment there seems little alternative; we are all at the same development stage of the systems' development process.

References

1.   NCC Data Processing Documentation Standards Manual   NCC. (1977)
2.   TW Olle, HG Sol and C.J. Tully (eds)
     Information Systems Design Methodologies

A Feature Analysis (CRISZ)
North Holland (1983)
3.   R.N. Maddison, et. al
Information Systems Methodologies
Informatics Series
Wiley Haydon Ltd.,
4.   G. Fitzgerald, N. Stokes, JRG Wood
Feature Analysis of Contemporary Information Systems
Methodologies
Computer Journal Vol 28. No 3 1985.
5.   T. DeMarco
Structured Systems Analysis and System Specification
Prentice Hall
6.   M. Jackson
Systems Development
Prentice Hall (1983)
7.   M. Lee
An Investigation into the use of Structured Systems
Methodologies in U.K. Organisations
M.Sc Thesis, City University (1985)
8.   Introduction to the LSDM Methodology
LBMS (1984)
9.   SSADM Reference Manual
(internal Civil Service document)
10.   Model Systems Training Package volumes 3 & 4
Model Systems Training Ltd (1984)
11.   G. Collins and G. Blay
Structured Systems Development Techniques
Pitman (1982)
12.   SSA Reference Manual
(internal Exxon Corp. document)
13.   R. Nolan
Managing the Data Resource Function
West (1984)
14.   E. Yourdon
Design if On-line Systems
Prentice Hall (1972)
15.   J. Martin
Application Development without Programmers
Prentice Hall (1982)
16. D.M. Episkopou and A.T. Wood-Harper
A Multi-View Methodology, Applications and
Implications
17.   J. Shackleton
Systems Development Methodology Packages
from 'A Practical Guide to Systems Development
Management'
Aurbach (1982)
18.   I. Aitken
'Tools to Clean up a Tarnished Image' and
'Shopping for Productivity Gains'
Computing, the Magazine (June 1985)

TOOL SUPPORT FOR MODEL DESCRIPTION WITH SDL AND SIMULATION

Dieter Hogrefe
SIEMENS AG, ZTI SOF3
Otto-Hahn-Ring 6
8000 Munich 83
Germany

ABSTRACT: This paper gives some ideas for the development of a tool where the simulation program is described in the language SDL. In a brief introduction the reason for using SDL as a model description language is explained. Then a short description of the language SDL is followed by the tool concept. Here it is shown how top-down modelling using SDL can be supported from inception up to the simulation program. We suggest using existing tools and have thus made some restrictions on the standard SDL. These are restrictions though, which do not effect the basic descriptive power of SDL. The ideas for the tool concept came from several years of experience with simulation of SDL-specified systems.

1. INTRODUCTION

Today the behaviour of many real systems is specified or described in the language SDL (1). The language is especially suitable for systems with a lot of concurrency, such as telecommunication systems, multiprocessor systems, and so on. Since mankind is not used to thinking in concurrent terms, it is hard to fully understand the behaviour of parallel processes just by their formal description. Computer simulation is a frequently used technique of evaluating a concurrent system in an early development phase. There is always the problem of writing a simulation program which is consistent with the specification of the system. Usually not all parts of the system specification are relevant for the simulation. Thus the non-relevant elements have to be abstracted in some way. If the abstractions are valid and we take the relevant parts of the system as they are and put them together with the abstracted parts, we should get a valid simulator for the real system.

An SDL description of a system can be viewed as a discrete event system specification, DEVS (5), which is a well-established formalism for simulation models (2). This means that SDL can also serve as a model description language. Therefore many parts of the real system description can be used in the model description without much change.

Tools that support a description in SDL or support the simulation of DEVS are being developed (6). But there is not yet an overall concept for a tool that derives a simulation model out of an SDL description, such that the

641

R. Trappl (ed.), Cybernetics and Systems '86, 641–648.

result can be further treated by existing tools. In the following chapters the reader will find a first approach to this problem.

2. SPECIFICATION AND DESCRIPTION LANGUAGE (SDL)

SDL (1) is a language developed by the CCITT for the specification and description of telecommunication systems. It can of course also be used for the description of any behaviour capable of being described using a discrete model, for instance the behaviour of a simulation model. SDL describes the behaviour of a system in a stimulus/response fashion assuming that both are discrete.

To any sequence of inputs received by one or more channels the system will respond with a sequence of outputs through one or more channels.

The language also provides structural concepts, so that the behaviour of the system can be described by stepwise refinement. The system itself is represented by a block. The behaviour of this block can be described by the behaviour of a set of interconnected blocks as shown in figure 1.

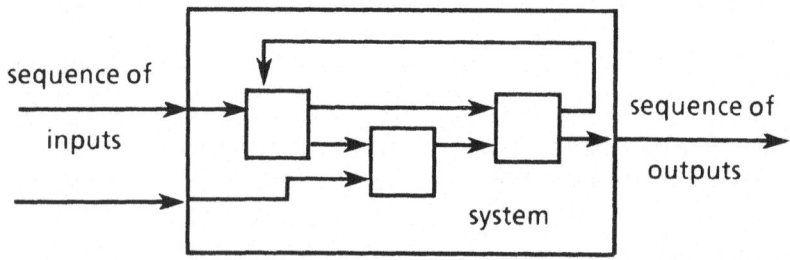

Figure 1. A blockstructured system with inputs and outputs

The interconnected blocks can themselves be described by a set of interconnected blocks.This structuring implies a hierarchy of blocks, that can be viewed as a tree, figure 2. The leaves of the tree are called *leaf blocks* and all the other nodes are called *inner blocks*.

The leaf blocks of this tree structure contain *processes*. In general, one block can contain zero or more processes. The reason for having more than one process in a block is, that, if two processes want to share data, they have to be in the same block.For simplicity we will concentrate on blocks that contain only one process, thus processes and blocks have basically the same meaning here.

SDL processes may retain and manipulate *data values*. The data values are bound to *variables*, which are local to a process. Data values may be sent between processes, and to and from the environment by means of signals. Local variables for a process are defined in the process definition. The data treated is typed. A number of predefined data types are defined in SDL and these are listed in (1). The user may also define new data types.

The interconnections between blocks are called *channels*. Each channel can carry different *signals*. The incoming signals to a block are recieved by *input ports*, the outgoing by *output ports* of the block. There is one input

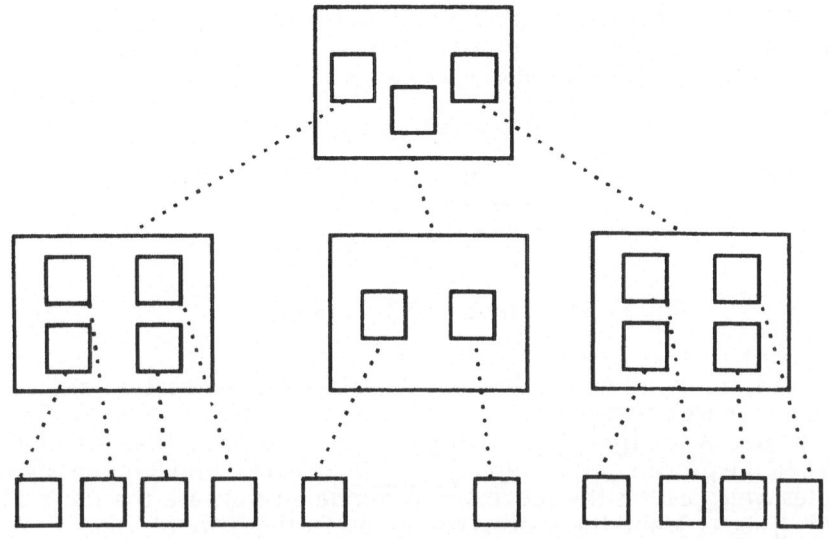

Figure 2. Refinement tree of a system

port to each incoming channel and one output port for each outgoing channel. The input port delivers a signal to the pertinent inner block, or if it was a leaf block, to the process. The output of the process is delivered to the correct output port. The signals are distinguished by names. Signals may also be used to carry data from one process to another. Usually, channels like blocks can be subject to refinement. A refined channel then consists of various blocks and channels. Examples can be found in the literature (1). In the following, we will not allow channel refinement.

We still have to make another restriction on the common SDL. During the refinement process of a block, a channel can be split up into various subchannels leading to subblocks so that the incoming signals are distributed among the subblocks. This shall not be allowed.

A process that is contained in a leaf block is described by a state transition diagram. It can be represented graphically with SDL/GR as well as a textually with SDL/PR. We will only concentrate on the graphical representation. There are 5 basic symbols that are used to describe the stimuli/response behaviour of a process, shown in figure 3.

state symbol

input symbol

output symbol

task symbol

decision symbol

Figure 3. The 5 basic symbols

643

In addition to these symbols we shall use two more symbols, figure 4, that are not standard SDL graphic symbols but are used in CCITT recommendations (0) to describe time behaviour.

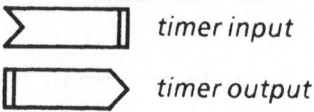

    timer input

    timer output

Figure 4. Non-standard SDL symbols

These symbols are not declared in the CCITT standardisation, therefore their meanings are declared here. Timers have names, for example T1. Once a timer is started with [start T1⟩ two things can happen. Either the time T1 elapses and the process gets an input ⟩ T1 ‖ , or something happens before T1 elapses which causes the process to continue. In this case the timer T1 is stopped [stop T1⟩ and the process continues. Further symbols can be found in the literature (1).

A process is either in a state or active performing a transition. It can only leave a state through an input that is received by one of the channels. During a state transition the process can produce an output intended to stimulate another process. The output signal is carried via a channel to the other process, and there it serves as an input.

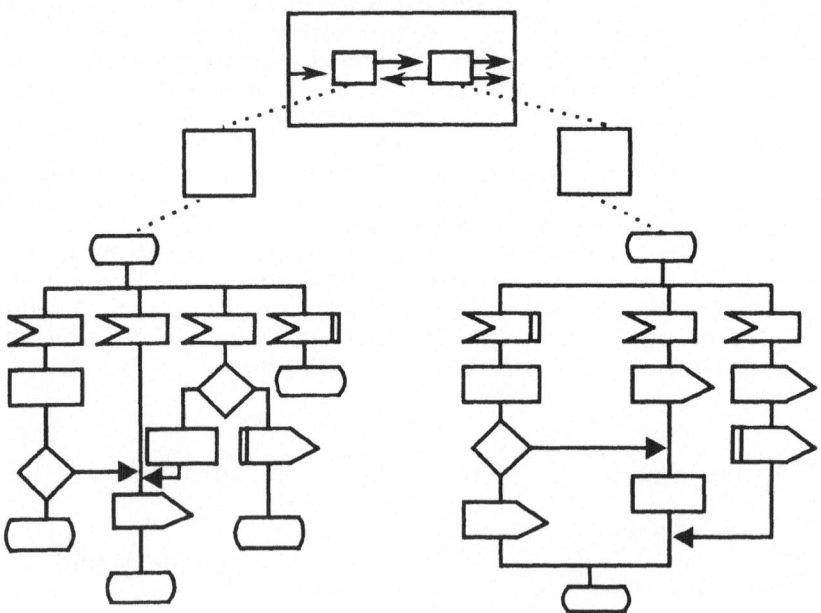

Figure 5. Two refined leaf blocks

To conclude, here are the three restrictions we made in order to develop the tool concept explained in the next chapter

- only one process per block
- no channel refinement
- no subchannels leading to different subblocks

This is very simple and incomplete introduction to SDL but it can serve as a basis for the following. It is impossible for the reader to now be familiar with the whole semantics of SDL so that for further detail the reader is referred to the appropriate literature (1). The extent of the SDL as described here is about the same that is used in most SDL recommendations, e.g. (0).

3. THE TOOL CONCEPT

What should a support tool look like which encompasses both the description of a simulation model in SDL and the simulation of the model on a computer?

We will develop our simulation model in a top-down manner. On the top level of description our simulation model is represented by a single block that has input ports and output ports. The input- and output ports are connected by channels with the environment. The model environment, also called the experimental frame (3), figure 6, is absolutely semantically equal to the model itself. Thus, we will concentrate on the description of the model. The experimental frame can be described in the same way.

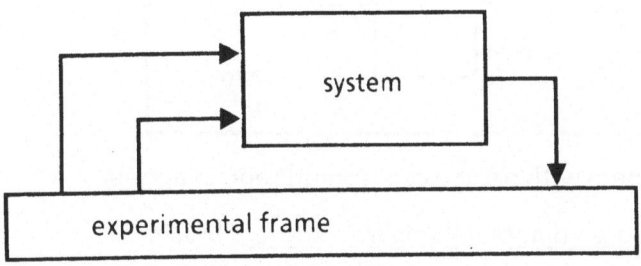

Figure 6. System model with experimental frame

The single block on the top level can be viewed as a discrete event system, DEVS (2,3) with a readout function. In fact, the idea of the DEVS is very similar to that of an SDL-block (5). The mathematical foundations for structuring a DEVS by a tree structure are developed in (4) where the system theoretic idea of system coupling (7) is used. Also an exact simulation relationship between a structured DEVS and a computer program can be found in (4). The DEVS is a model description in algebraic terms, whereas the SDL description is a description in a flow diagram form. This makes it quite easy to derive a sequential program from it. We will see how part of this derivation can be performed automatically with an appropriate tool.

Refinement of blocks

Let us now suppose that we have a block with input ports and output ports, which we want to refine. We go inside the block; i.e., the block fills the whole terminal screen. The ports are also visible together with the channel name of the channel that a port is connected to. Each port gets a name and the block gets another name. The block now has two names, a type name, that may be equal to the type names of other blocks, and an instance name, which identifies the block uniquely. The two names are seperated by a point. We can now use this block in a hierarchical higher construct at different places and connect it with different channels. Next, we draw the refinement blocks with their input- and output ports. Each refinement block gets an instance name. Later the refinement blocks will get a type name as well, either in their refinement phase or, if the type already exists, the type name is added to the instance name. The type names of the leaf blocks are process names. After having drawn the refinement blocks we interconnect them by channels or perhaps connect them with the input- or output ports of the block.

Since we are dealing with SDL we now have to define a signal list for each channel. Since the data carried by the different signals of the signal list of a channel have well defined data structures we give one data type name to each channel which is a synonym for the respective structures.

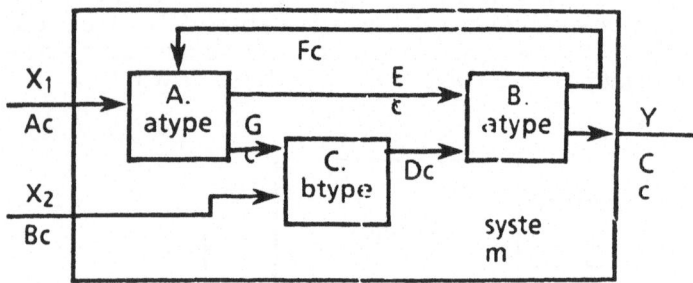

Figure 7. System with named components and channels

Derivation of a transition diagram frame from the leaf blocks

In this section we will see how the tool can use the information we have given so far to derive a transition diagram frame from the leaf blocks of the refinement tree. We remember that the leaf blocks contain one and only one process. So far we know that the signals can arrive at a block but we have not said anything about the states and the state transition. Thus the tool assumes that we only have one state and it draws the following diagram fragment.

The name of the process which is described is "btype" and the process frame is shown in figure 8. "x_i" and "x_k" are the names of the input ports of the block containing the currently described process "btype". "atype" is the name of the process connected to "btype" by a channel. "aname", "bname" and "cname" are the names of the signals, which can be carried by the channel connected to "x_i". And so on ... .

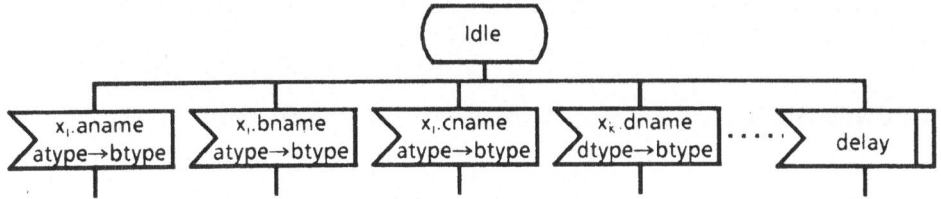

Figure 8. Process diagram frame

The timer input symbol will be followed by the action, which is performed when an elapsed time causes a state transition. The elapsed time mechanism is a construct of the DEVS-Formalism. To fully understand its meaning, the reader is referred to the literature (2,3). This diagram fragment is the maximum that can be derived from the information given so far.

Filling up the diagram

Now we must consider the number of states of the process. These should not exceed four or five including the standard state "Idle". We should be able to give a different name to the standard state if we wish. Let us suppose we have another state "α" in addition to the state "Idle". Next we have to define the local variables with their data type used by the process. We do so by selecting the state "idle" with a joy stick. This opens another window where we do our definitions. After having defined the variables once, they are automatically defined at every other state symbol.

Now we remove every input symbol for which the input is not allowed or ineffective in the state "Idle". The rest of the input symbols now begin the action that is to be taken by the process after having received the respective input. If there was a timer running when the process recieves the external input, the first action to be taken by the process is a "stop timer" output. We fill up the diagram with output, task, and decision symbols until we reach another state. This can be "Idle" again or "α". In the second case the tool creates the same diagram frame as before only with the state "α" at the beginning. Now we proceed the same way as before. When the process recieves a timer input, a certain time has elapsed which defines an autonomous state transition. Autonomous means that the state transition is not caused by an input from an external.

Towards a simulation program

There is a rather straight forward way of translating the process diagram into a program procedure similar to the ones used (6), if the information in the diagram is complete. If the information is not complete, for example if there are some textual explanations in the SDL-symbols, the tool will ask about their meanings. If no further information is input the text will be interpreted as a comment. Otherwise, it is interpreted as a macro call and the macro must be defined.

The complete mechanism for translation cannot be given here but it is quite obvious. The basic principles can be found in (5).

4. CONCLUSION

We could not give a complete tool description here, but the basic ideas were presented. To sum up, here is the chronology of the design process for a simulation model. First we define the static block structure of the model. We do this by stepwise refinement. After having reached the lowest level, we further describe the function of a block with a graphic state transition diagram. The frame of this diagram is produced by the tool. The diagram is then translated into programming code as far as possible. This translated code must be completed by hand if a high level of abstraction was used in the graphic description.

Some aspects, such as alteration of an already defined model, are not treated here. We have only concentrated on top-down design so far, but for practical reasons there have to be some bottom-up mechanisms as well, especially for the of changing of a model. We will leave this for further study.

5. LITERATURE

(0)   CCITT: *Specification of Signalling System No. 7, Recommendations Q.701-Q.741*, I.T.U., Geneva, 1981.

(1)   CCITT: *Specification and Description Language SDL, Recommendations Z.100-Z.104*, I.T.U., Geneva, 1983.

(2)   Zeigler, B. P.: *Theory of Modelling and Simulation*, Wiley, New York, 1976.

(3)   Zeigler, B. P.: *Multifacetted Modelling and Discrete Event Simulation*, Academic Press, London, 1984.

(4)   Hogrefe, D.: *Über Hierarchisch Konstruierte Modelle und deren Simulation: Systemtheoretische Aspekte*, Dissertation, Hannover, 1985.

(5)   Hogrefe, D., Zorn, S.: 'Simulation of SDL Specified Models' (in Shoemaker: *Computer Networks and Simulation III*), North Holland, Amsterdam, 1986 (to appear).

(6)   Siemens: *BORIS-Manual*, Siemens, München, 1985.

(7)   Wymore, A. W.: *A Mathematical Theory of Sytems Design*, Techn. Rpt., College of Engineering, Univ. of Arizona, Tucson, 1980.

A SYSTEMS ENGINEERING ORIENTED FRAMEWORK
FOR COMPUTER BASED DESIGN AUTOMATION SYSTEMS

Karl H. Kellermayr
Institute of Systems Science
Johannes Kepler University Linz
A-4040 Linz/Austria

Abstract: For future design automation systems it will not be enough, to use sophisticated tools. We will be increasingly forced by complexity, to use scientific principles, scientifically and operationally well founded methodologies, to get directly from concepts to total systems. "Hard evidence" for the improvement and development of the design process can be considered as the operativ words. In this paper suggestions are made on how models and theories of the design process can be reached, using concepts from systems science and systems engineering. The six categories of the structural scheme for a scientifically founded general system theory, introduced by J.L.Elohim, and M.D.Mesarovic´s concept of functional multilayer decision hierarchy will be used as a modeling frame. For a detailed modeling of the higher layer submodels within this hierarchical model, G.J. Klir´s approach to general systems problem solving is suggested.

1. Introduction

As the advanced countries prepare for the information age or for the information society (Klir 1985a), and the developing countries still struggle to provide the basic goods, necessities and services to their people (while at the same time planning to leapfrog into the information age) the investment in the computer based information industry is literally exploding all over the world. The resulting large expenditures involved in planning, designing, procuring, operating, and maintaining modern computer based information systems (networks) are justifications enough for making the engineering and management of such systems in general, and of computer based design automation systems in special, a subject of critical importance all over the world.

The origins of computer based design automation systems can be dated back to 1940 and George Stibitz´s Model I Relay Computer (Mayo 1983). This was one of the worlds first electrical digital computer, and it was in service at Bell Labs from 1940 to 1949. It was used for arithmetical operations on complex numbers to aid the design of circuits and filters and for other purposes. 1962 was another most important milestone for design automation (Sutherland 1962). At this time, at MIT a conceptual framework for computer aided design and computer aided manufacturing systems was established. This work was highly and substantially supported by important companies like General Motors, Lockheed, Mc Donald Douglas, Ford and others, in expectation of

R. Trappl (ed.), Cybernetics and Systems '86, 649–656.

a revolution in engineering methodologies and tools. But, this did not happen as swiftly nor as completely as had been envisioned. However, since that time computer based design tools evolved very fast and allowed in many fields to take a quantum leap in improving the efficiency of engineering activities. But there is also an intuitive feeling, that the early anticipated goals have not been reached, and that simply adding further tools to the design automation process, will not suffice.

For future computer based systems it seems important, that they are to be considered under a very broad view, in order to reflect more than just the few most important aspects of them. Focus should be given not only on engineering and management, but also on system aspects such as: human and social factors, performance, flexibility, expandability, capabilities, reliability, availability, serviceability. Considering this focus, it becomes obvious, that an interdisciplinary and scientifically as well as operational well founded approach to both, the future evolotion of the design process and the future development of computer based tools is needed, in order to be able to manage scope and complexity of this development. A systems engineering approach is considered to be best suited, to provide a scientific and operational basis for such undertakings. But what exactly is meant by "systems engineering" approach? If one were to randomly select ten persons who consider themselves systems engineers, chances are good that one would get ten different descriptions (or even more) of sytems engineering, much as in the story of different blind men describing an elephant. Of course each of them would be right from his own point of view.

This paper tries to high-light some aspects of systems engineering and of computer based systems in general. Suggestions are made for a systems engineering based framework for computer based design automation systems, in order to provide an overall structure within which the various aspects of such systems can be developed and handled in a rational, scientifically well founded way. G.J.Klir´s General Systems Problem Solver (Klir 1985b) is suggested to provide deeper insight and to develope such aspects , models or theories.

2. Computer based systems for design automation

Computer based services in support of design automation are evolving very fast. On the one hand, this is due to the fact, that innovation in the field of computers is moving very fast and the cost reduction in processing power over the last few years was enormous, so that computers are attainable for a broad range of applications. On the other hand, problems to be solved are getting more and more complex, and require sophisticated, powerful theories, concepts, techniques and efficient operational tools. This is not only true for the engineering branches. There are also many complex systems in other areas that need to be designed: communication, transportation, health, education, law enforcement, social services, ecological, defense and others. For engineering branches like aircraft mechanical electrical and computer engineering, very advanced design concepts have been developed. But, health delivery and other above mentioned systems are no less complicated than a modern airoplan or a computer.

Many theories, concepts and techniques can only be applied to real-world design situations via a computer because of the large number and complexity of information processing operations (search, calculation,...) involved. Even when a manual approach is feasible, investment in the development of a computer based tools may make more efficient use of the designers time, if the same or a similar situation occurs repeatedly. Side benefits of using a computer based tool include fewer chances of an error, and consistency in results obtained by different designers for the same complex situation (design homogenuity, know-how stability).

As computers still become more powerful and inexpensive, their use can only be expected to increase with time. This is another fact, that leads to an evolution of methods and tools in general. However, one must be careful about putting too much faith in the use of computer based tools. It is also very important, to concentrate on the overall design process as framework, within which such tools have to be used. Design and design automation are not a matter of tools alone, it is a careful coordination and cooperation of processes, people, and tools. Unless used carefully by experienced people, computer tools can easily lead one astray. Design is largely a heuristic process, aimed at satisfying predicted client needs through the use of predicted scientific and technological changes in the most effective manner. Computers are good for making millions of searches and calculations, but cannnot judge the accuracy and quality of modeling assumptions and input data. Computers therefore cannot properly interpret the relevance of the output results which can only be done by experienced humans. Franz Pichler (Pichler 1984) does not like for that and related reasons, in the context of the computer based problem solving process, to put too much focus on (computer based) tools . He prefers to use "instrument" instead of "tool".

3. Systems engineering

General speaking, engineering is defined as the application of scientific principles to practical ends as the design, construction and operation of efficient and economic structures, equipment, and systems (Morris 1976). Over the years as the body of scientific and technological knowledge was broadened and multipled, new (engineering) disciplines were born. The rapid growth and complexity of industry has created unusual opportunities, but also new big problems. On one hand, our society is such, that people aspire to do more complex things, and there are complex sets of solutions from which one can choose to make them possible. On the other hand, the advent of automation and the emphasis on increased productivity coupled with higher levels of systems sophistication, and the awareness of constraints in resources, social and environmental factors are providing impetus to the demand for new engineering approaches and a new type of engineer. No engineering discipline alone has the total design potential for transforming modern scientific discoveries to practical use under the realized constraints. Each (engineering) discipline is focusing on its very special aspects, the gaps between the different disciplines tend to become broader and deeper. Systems engineering can be considered as bridging the gaps.

A basic difference between systems engineering and other engineering disciplines is one of approach. A systems engineer should be trained to approach problems from the "top down". He should accept problems in all its complexity and should be able to translate a problem into quantitative terms, including objectives, restrictions, and means of comparing various alternatives which he may propose. Like every engineer, the systems engineer should be concerned with achieving a "best" of desired solutions. But due to the broader scope of his view he shall be aware, that a best solution might not exist, if he is considering (as it becomes more and more important) multivalued performance (optimization) criterias. So, in many situations, a "good solution" might be best.

Systems engineering may be most effectively conceived as a process, that starts with the detection of a problem and continues through problem definition, planning and designing of a system, manufacturing or other implementing action, its use, and finally ends at its obsolescence. There are many ways of defining systems engineering, because of the many facets one can focus on. It is (Hall 1965): "as if the subject were enclosed in a multisided box, each side having a window which permits an outside viewer to see something new and worthwile." Hall named eight sides of the "box" (subjects), which might be considered as eight ways to answer the question: What is systems engineering: (1) evolution, (2) procedure, (3) objectives, (4) classification of work, (5) organization structure, (6) tools and techniques, (7) people who do it, (8)relation to other fields

There are different aspects which may be enforced in an systems engineering approach. They allow a classification of systems engineering approaches into four categories:

-management oriented systems engineering approaches (Sage 1977, 1981)
-engineering oriented systems engineering approaches (Hall 1965,1969),
 (Chesnut 1966)
- systems engineering approaches oriented towards mathematics
-systems science oriented systems engineering approaches (Wymore 1976)

However in any systems engineering approach the basic objectives are about the same, and all are to a great amount oriented toward management and engineering aspects, all are based on systems thinking (systems philosophy,systems science) and all use to an great extend mathematical concepts. Another important aspect in common is, that all of them are model oriented. As any other discipline, system oriented disciplines have a body of knowledge regarding its domain and its methodologies for the acquisition of new knowledge as well as for the utilization of the knowledge for dealing with relevant problems. System oriented disciplines are first of all, always considered in the context of specific problems. This attitude toward problem solving is considerably different from that of mathematics (Klir 1985a).

4. A Systems engineering oriented design framework for design automation

Design automation has evolved from a supportive position to a leading-edge technology in its own right. There is a broad acknowledgement, that certain functions of design can and should be automated. Computer based systems have dramatically effected the way, products or complex systems are designed these days. User invest in such powerful systems in order to improve the design process. Improvements may lay in the area of increased productivity, improved quality, reduced cost and shorter development times. Changing markets are demanding those improvements. Experience has shown, however, that these benefits are realized only when the systems are included in proper environments, have been properly selected and installed, and if they are properly used, maintained and further developed. As in any "white colour" professional area, measurable improvements are very difficult to document. Except for improvements in document preparation (by means of text processing within office automation systems), engineering drafting (based on CAD tools) and very special design tasks (CAE-FEM), there is little hard evidence of *genuine* productivity improvement resulting from design automation systems. The operative words are "hard evidence" for improvements. One problem in demonstrating the hypothetical improvements (companies selling such systems are very good in producing such hypotheses) is the translation of qualitative benefits into concrete, quantitative terms. A second problem is the lack of funds to develop and perform measurement methodologies that would be adequately, rigorous and comprehensive. In order to develop such measurement methodologies which include the qualitative aspects of design systems, it is necessary to use models, in order to allow a rational attitude towards the reality of the design process.Three ways of rational attitudes may be taken in an rational approach (Elohim 1982) :an **empirical,** a **heuristic** and a **scientific** (which seems to relieve one another in a permanent dialectic sequence). While so far improvements in design automation was to a great amount technology oriented and empirical and heuristic in nature, for the future evolution a rational, scientific attitude towards the design automation process is considered very important for at least three reasons:(1) classification of design tasks, (2) study the construction and the relation between design tasks, (3) study the evolution of the design and design automation process.

In systems engineering, great attention has been given to the classification of design tasks and towards the relation between different design tasks. The design process is in many fields like architecture, mechanical and electrical engineering relatively old and well established. However, since only a few years we realize an effort to treat the design process as a scientific discipline. There is a strong need for this due to the evolution of computer based tools (Lauber 1982). We need a formal, theoretical, model based fundament, if we try to teach a computer how to perform or aid the design process. Considering the evolotion of the design and design automation process is most important if one is thinking on the high amount of investment which is spent in equipment and in research projects. To the best of the authors knowledge, only very little is known about this evolution process.

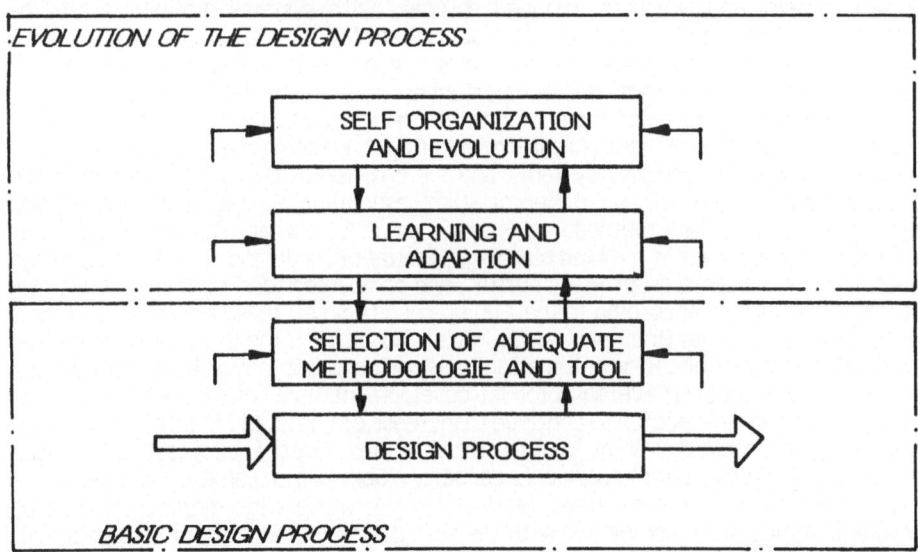

Figure 1: Fundamental multilayer decision hierarchy for the future development of the design process

J.L.Elohim consideres six categories (submodels) of the structural scheme for a scientifically founded general sytem theory (Elohim 1982). These six categories may be agregated to four, and in our case used as a modeling frame for the overall design automation process. The categories are sumodels, which have to be modeled. This is a difficult task, because there are qualitative as well as quantitative factors to be taken into account. Each submodel reflects specific functional aspects, and so they may be arranged to a hierarchical multilevel system. This hierarchy emerges naturally, in reference to the three essential aspects of the decision problem related to the uncertainities in the further development of design automation: (1) the selection and further development of adequate methodologies and tools to be used in a design process, (2) the reduction and elimination of uncertainities in a learning and adaption process, and (3) the search for a preferable or acceptable course of action under the conditions of the technological, economical and social conditions. This functional hierarchy, as shown in figure 1 (as an application of Mesarovic´s functional multilayer decision hierarchy (Mesarovic 1970)), contains four layers: the design process and three decision layers. While the lower two layers may be subsumed to a **"basic design process"** model, the higher two may form a model for the **"evolution of the design process"**.

For the basic design process many different models exist and have beer published (Lauber 1982).They may be classified into the following categories: (1)management oriented models, (2) flow of activity oriented models and (3) design level oriented models. To the best of the knowledge of the author, only very little "hard evidence" is known for the "evolution of the design process". To develop such hard evidence, appropriate methodologies (metamethodologies), capable for modeling the relevant characteristics of the design process, have to be determined. George J.Klir´s General System Problem Solver (Klir 1985b), which is utilized in a computer expert system, and which is designed to deal with systems problems, may be considered as an approproate concept. Much has been written about this methodology, and we do not have enough space at this point to describe it. Rather than this we want to proceed in describing some of the important aspects which needs to be modeled.

Modeling the issues of the evolution of the design (design automation) process, leads to the question of what is really controlling it. Heading the list of forces is the growing demand for complex systems, and the position of design automation at the leading edge of competitive differentiation, especially among large enterprises. Strong design tools and methodologies are a powerful competitive advantage. This position has been a bit of a mixed blessing. Because of its competitive impact, design automation has been a proprietary pursuit, and companies tend to develop their own standards and tools, according to their unique needs. So all these standards and tools differ from each other (this was so far quite a powerful force in the evolution). The competitive impact of design automation tools and concepts may be best described, by two industry-trends: (1) average product development time has increased over the years, and it can be expected to continue to increase dramatically in this decade. (2) At the same time, estimates show, that the lifespan of products is decreasing. One good example is the growth of memory chip capacity (256k, 1M). Japan and North America are competing to introduce these products in the world wide market as soon as possible. The country (company?) with the best design methodologies and tools will most likely succeed and will capture this multi -billion US $ market.

It is an established fact, that it is better to know about systems characteristics before putting it into practice or expand it. This is because a designer has more freedom, and it is less costly to adjust various alternatives in the early planning stage rather than in the operational stage. Only computer based tools can provide this information in early design phases. Typical relationships for degree of freedom to

654

adjusting various design alternatives (parameters) and the cost of doing so (cost for changes), are shown in figure 2, togther with a typical relationship of the relative effort (i.e. designers manpower) and the design automation strength for different phases in the design cycle (for a polycell VLSI circuit). The design phases included are: planning and conception P&C, architecture design AD, functional design FD, logic design LD, timing T, layout L, and test development TD. This figure shows quite clearely, that so far design tools are focusing on the later design phases, while it would be very much needed to have them in the very early phases available too.

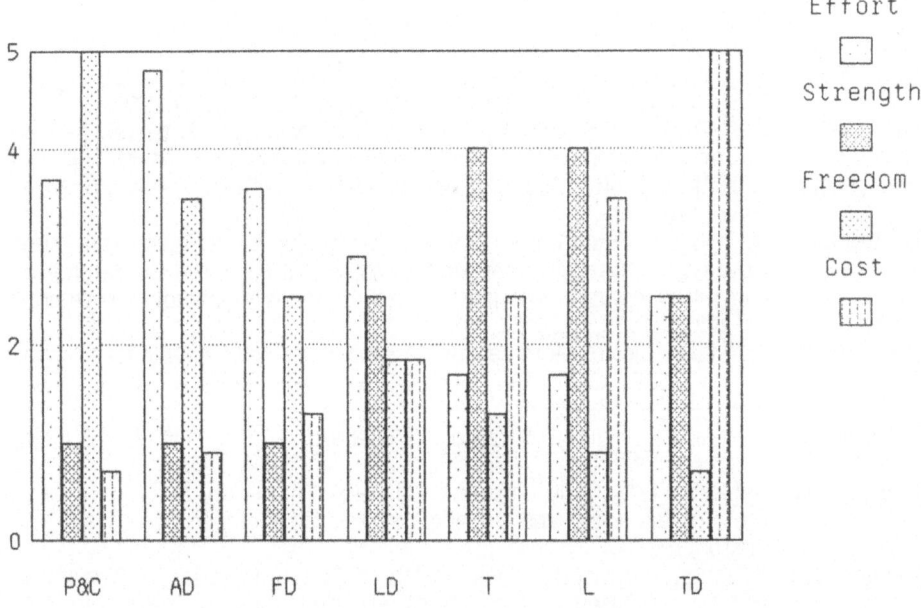

Figur 2: Relative effort and design automation strength in the phases of polycell VLSI subsystem design, and cost and freedom to adjust alternatives at different design phases

5. Conclusions

Design automation has evolved from a supportive position to a leading edge technology in its own right. While so far improvements in design automation has been to a great extend technology driven, and empirical as well as heuristic in nature, for the future evolution a rational, scientific attitude towards the further development of design automation systems is considered very important. Therefore, a systems approach for modeling the complex design automation process is suggested in this paper, and some of the important issues of its evolution are discussed.

6. References

(Chesnut 1966) H.Chesnut, ´Systems Engineering Tools´, John Wiley & Sons, New York, 1966

(Elohim 1982) J.L.Elohim, ´Theory and Practice of Systems Methodology´,in: R.Trappl, G. Klir, F.Pichler (edts.):Progress in Cybernetics and Systems Research, Vol VIII, Hemisphere Pub.,1982, pp.109–118

(Hall 1965) A.D.Hall, ´Systems Engineering from an Engineering Viewpoint´, IEEE Trans.Syst.Sci.Cybern., Vol.SSC-1, pp.4–8, Nov.1965

(Hall 1969) A.D.Hall, ´Three-Dimensional Morphology of Systems Engineering´, IEEE Trans.Syst.Sci.Cybern., Vol.SSC-5, pp.156–160, Apr.1969

(Klir 1985a) G.J.Klir, ´The Emergence of Two-dimensional Science in the Information Society´, Systems Research Vol.2, No.1, pp.33–41, 1985

(Klir 1985b) G.J.Klir, ´Architecture of Systems Problem Solving´, Plenum Press, New York, 1985

(Lauber 1980) R.Lauber, ´Design Methods for Computer Controlled Real-Time Automation Systems´, Preprints of the 6 th IFAC / IFIP Conference on Digital Computer Applications to Process Control, Düsseldorf, 14–17.Oct.1980, pp.25–34

(Mayo 1983) J.S.Mayo, ´Design Automation: Lessons of the Past, Challenges for the future´,IEEE Computer Graphic and Applications, Vol.3, No.6, Sept.1983, pp.13–18

(Mesarovic 1970) M.D.Mesarovic, D.Macko, Y.Takahara, ´Theory of Hierarchical, Multilevel, Systems´, Academic Press, New York, London, 1970

(Morris 1976) W.Morris, edt., ´The American Heritage, Dictionary of the English Language´, Houghton Mifflin Company, Boston, 1976

(Pichler 1984) F.Pichler, ´Symbolic Manipulation of System Models´,in: Simulation and Model-Based Methodologies–An Integrative View,T.I.Ören, B.P. Zeigler,M.S. Elzas (eds), Springer Verlag Berlin, 1984, pp.217–234

(Sage 1977) A.P.Sage (edt.), ´Systems Engineering:Methodology & Applications´ IEEE Press, 1977

(Sage 1981) A.P.Sage, ´Systems Engineering: Fundamental Limits and Future Prospects´, Proceedings of the IEEE, Vol.69, No.2, Feb.1981, pp.158–166

(Sutherland 1962) I.E.Sutherland, ´Sketchpad: A Man-Machine Graphical Communication System´, Ph. D. Thesis, Massachusets Institute of Technology, 1962

(Wymore 1976) A.W. Wymore, ´Systems Engineering for Interdisciplinary Teams´, John Wiley & Sons, New York, 1976

COMPUTER AIDED SYSTEM DESIGN

Stephan Zorn
SIEMENS A.G.
Otto-Hahn-Ring 6
D 8000 München 83
Federal Republic of Germany

ABSTRACT.   This paper presents a sytematic way to a computer
aided system design process. In this context a sytem means a
computer system. The main focus is put on the design of the
hardware of a computer system, but not on the abstraction
levels that are usually handled by conventional CAD - systems.
It is our goal, to develop an integrated computer aided system
design environment, that supports the design of digital
computer systems in all phases of the system design process.
By this way the process is made more systematic and more
efficient.

This work has been supported by the Federal Department of
Research and Technology of the Federal Republic of Germany.
The author alone is responsable for the contents.

1.   INTRODUCTION

The permanently growing need for more computer power leeds to
computer systems that must fulfill the requirements much
better than formar computer generations. This fact enlarges
the requirements for new CAD-systems. The growing complexity
requires suited design methodologies and design tools. But
these tools must provide their support much earlier in the
design process than CAD-systems are doing it today. An
integrated tool support for requirement specification, design
of the architecture and design of the modules isn't offered up
to now. Our system design environment will be such an
integrated design tool, beginning at the derivation of the
requirements, leading over several abstraction levels down to
the interface to conventional CAD-systems.

R. Trappl (ed.), Cybernetics and Systems '86, 657–660.
© *1986 by D. Reidel Publishing Company.*

2. PRESENT SITUATION

First we started an analysis of the present situation in the area of computer design. Our result was the structure of the design process over several levels, that we called abstraction levels:
- first ideas and descriptions of the planned system
- requirement specification
- design of the architecture
- design of the modules
- usage of conventional CAD-systems (register transfer level).
Within each abstraction level there is a constant sequence of steps for all levels:
- requirements for this level
- design and specification
- validation and verification of the design
- deduction of new requirements from the results for the remaining design levels.

3. SYSTEM DESIGN ENVIRONMENT

From this analysis of the present situation we deduced the basis for the design process that we want to support: the combination of the abstraction levels and the design steps builds a matrix that is the basis of our system design environment. Each design step may be placed in one square of this design matrix. For all the levels of the design process there are things that are common for every level as for example
- the user interface
- description and design languages
- tools for the valuation by simulation or analytical methods
- a data base for descriptions, specifications, models and results.
Zeigler /1/ showed some ideas that together with the experimental frame concept of Rozenblit /2,3/ have some basic concepts that are very similar to our design matrix.
The main requirements for the system design environment are:
- support of all the design steps as there are specification of the requirements, design, validation, verification
- a formal design methodology
- a uniform user interface for all design levels
- a formal description of the design object
- an integrated documentation and information sytem for the developper and the project manager.
Finally there must be defined interfaces to the software design process and to conventional CAD-tools.

4. INTEGRATED TOOLS

4.1 User interface

The user interface must be adapted to the usual way the designer works. It must provide a uniform interface to the design system and to the integrated design tools themselves. All the power and the possibilities of a graphic workstation are offered to the user. Help functions and an information system can guide new users of the system design environment.

4.2 Description and design languages

The description and design languages are the interface between the designer and the design object. The design system should provide one language for all design levels; this language must be problem oriented, that means adapted to the world of computer design. The language constructs should have a graphical representation too. The use of graphics is adapted to the conventional design method. From the language you can deduce models of the design objects; these models should be usable in more design levels, we call this multi level modelling.

4.3 Valuation

The valuation tools will be mostly simulation systems, but we try to get some experience in analytical methods too. Simulation will serve for the validation and verification of a design. It may help to show the function of a planned system and to gather performance data already at the design level. It should be possible to integrate the results of a higher abstraction level into a simulation model on a lower level. For those models that can be analyzed by analytical methods we try to get this integration too. An other possibility is the combination of simulation and analytical methods, because each of them has its special scope.

4.4 Data base

Finally the design data base will provide a support for all the information that is produced in the system in all steps at all levels of the system design process. Actual information about all documents must be available for every designer, who works with this system design environment. Because the system design environment will not consist out of one workstation alone, there must be a distributed data base. Depending on the number of data they may be put on a main frame computer too. So the data consistency is one important goal of the data base.

5. ACTUAL SITUATION

Actually the first version of our computer aided system design environment is running. With this system we try to get more experience for its further development. In the first version there is at least one tool for each design step integrated. In a next version there may be a choice of tools for each design step. The next version of the system design environment will have a better integration of the tools, an optimization of their interfaces and a unification of the user interfaces.

6. REFERENCES

/1/ Zeigler, B.P., Multifacetted Modelling and Discrete Event Simulation, Academic Press, London 1984

/2/ Rozenblit, J.W., Experimental Frames for Distributed Simulation Architectures, Proc. of the 1985 Distributed Simulation Conference, San Diego, California, January 1985

/3/ Rozenblit, J.W., Structures for a Model-Based System Design Environment, Technical Report, Siemens AG, West Germany, 1984

SOME EXPERIENCES WITH AI METHODS IN CAD

M. Gams, M. Spegel
"Jozef Stefan" Institute,
Jamova 39, P.O.B. 100
61000 Ljubljana
Yugoslavia

ABSTRACT. We present three attempts to implement AI methods in CAD,
CAT and CAPP. The first approach is an implementation of a modified
A* algorithm in the process of routing of printed circuit boards
(PCB's). The second approach consists of a rule-based program for
a simulation of PCB's, whereas the last one is an expert system for
process planning (CAPP).

1. INTRODUCTION

Artificial intelligence is getting wide attention in several areas
including different kinds of computer-aided fields like CAD, CAT, CIM,
CAL, CAP, CASA and CAPP [1-8]. So far, most of the results in the
literature have been rather encouraging. In this paper, we present
results of our efforts [9,10,11] to solve three difficult and interesting problems by use of AI methods.

2. PRINTED CIRCUIT BOARDS

CAD systems for design of printed circuit boards usually consist of
several parts such as specialized programs for I/O, logical testing
and simulation of logical plans, programs for placement, routing and
interactive editing. Our experience shows that two of these tasks are
especially suitable for artificial intelligence methods; these are
logical testing (simulation) and routing.

2.1. Logical Testing and Simulation

In the production process, testing and simulation of logical design is
of central importance [1,3,10,12]. It is much easier to correct mistakes in logical plan before actual placement and routing is done. We
think that one of AI methods [13,14] is especially suitable for this
purpose, namely a rule-based expert system built in PROLOG. The idea
here is to express elements' reactions (chips or gates) in a form of

R. Trappl (ed.), Cybernetics and Systems '86, 661–668.
© 1986 by D. Reidel Publishing Company.

simple production rules as can be seen in the example in Figure 1.

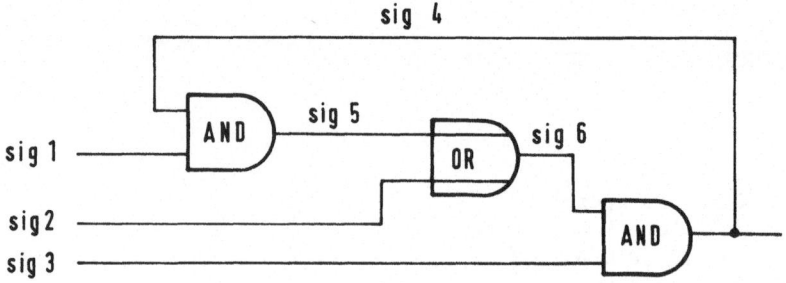

Figure 1. Example of a logic circuit

```
/*description of a circuit*/
signal (s1, [and/1/2]).
signal (s2, [or/1/2]).
signal (s3, [and/2/2]).
/*signal values - input data*/
signal - value (s1, [1:0, 0:2, x:5], init).
signal - value (s2, [0:2, 1:3, 0:5], init).
signal - value (s3, [0:1], init).

Results:
signal - value (s4, [0:2]).
signal - value (s5, [0:1]).
signal - value (s6, [0:2, 1:3, 0:5]).
```

The program uses a catalogue of all elements. For example, for the
AND gate we have:
chip (and, [and Op (1,2,3)/2]).

We can also define our own PAL, for example:
chip (and, [and Op(1,2,ml)/2, neg Op(ml,3)/1]).

The methods to interpret rules and explain changes in the circuit are
similar to those applied in [13,14] which proved to be especially
useful for explanations. In our system, the signals (Figure 1) and
their evaluation are actually not bound to any time discretization as
could be wrongly understood in our simple example. However several
complications can arise because time delays and cycles are allowed.The
true interpreter works like this:
```
1  repeat
2     stop := true;
3     check all components in the system
4        if anyone triggers then stop := false
5  until stop
```

In line 4, the system tries to compute the output values of the component by checking whether at any time there are sufficient input data and if this result hasn't yet been computed. This method promises to be more efficient then present widely used methods based on discretizating time and computing in small time increments.

Namely, the proposed method computes complete series of results at some component if all input signals are already computed. However, the trouble is that all input signals are usually not yet completely computed when certain component is taken under consideration. It can happen that during computation at some component at some cycle the system wrongly computes some output state since the system cannot know which input signals are completely computed and which only partially. Three things can happen:

1. The system cycles endlessly and in practise stops when cycle limit is overriden with a warning and explanation.
2. The system stops in some stable state with some signals with unknown values. Then the system tries to suppose some unknown value and repeats the computation but only once more. That is usually enough to find out what happens although some internal states of elements (like RS cell) may have been left unitialised.
3. The system stops with some stable state where all signals have some values.

In case 2, the user is asked to fill insufficient data and return the system. The values that are not instantiated retain their value "x".

2.2. Routing

The routing problem is to find optimal connections between some points on the board and at the same time satisfying some technological demands such as the width of connections etc. As it can be seen in Figure 2, even quite "normal" boards have rather complicated rats nets and hence quite complex real life NP problems.

Our routing program consists of two main parts: first part deals with logical connections and only tries to rearrange connections for the second part that actually routs them.

The logical connections part again consists of two parts: one tries to rearrange connections to detect patterns (and to make a minimal spanning tree with remaining connections), whereas the other part tries to combine patterns. This second part is a simplified global router and is supposed to stay on logical (qualitative) level.

Actual routing is done with a modified A* search algorithm (or general ordered search algorithm or Dijkstra's two-point shortest path algorithm) [17,18] as AI algorithm on one side and the modified Lee's algorithm as routing algorithm in CAD of printed circuit boards [15,16] on the other side. But we added several modifications to this algorithm: a) We usually do not connect only two points but rather two subsignals. That is why instead of a start node we have a set with many start nodes with different initial estimates and the goal is not one point but again a set of goal points as seen in Figure 3. We solve the problem of guiding search by putting the target area in some rectangle and then guide search from start area to target rectangle. If there are no

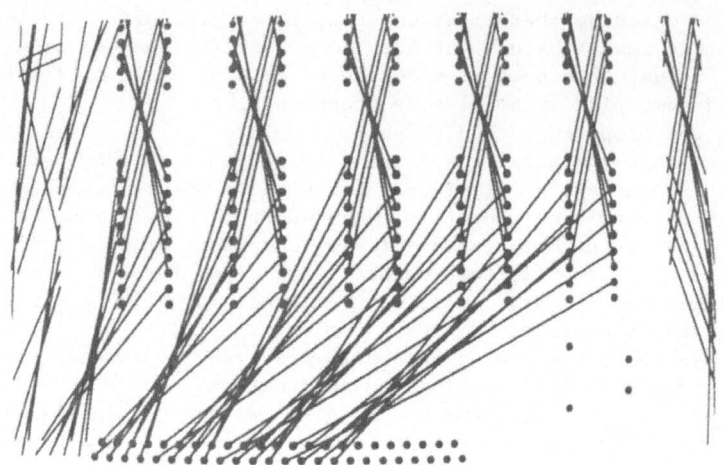

Figure 2. Rats nest for a placed circuit before routing

unexpected obstacles between target rectangle and current expanding
node, the search will not bactrack until reaching target rectangle.
Inside target area the search is completely blinded (basic Lee's algorithm). Nevertheless the results again guarantee optimality when
estimates are correctly combined. Maybe it is interesting that steps
parallel (inside x-y projection segments) to target rectangle must also
be blinded in the opposite direction in order to guarantee optimality
as can be seen in Figure 3 and Table 1.

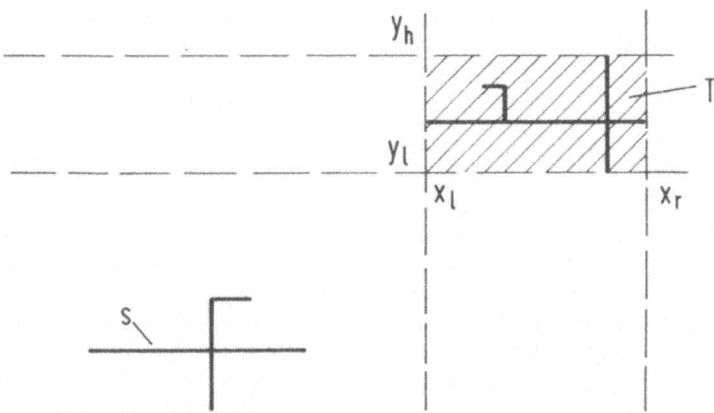

Figure 3. Connecting subsignals

TABLE I. Costs for ordered search using target rectangles

position	direction of move	cost
yl <= y <=yh	y to Ty	py
yl <= y <=yh	y from Ty	py
elsewhere	y to Ty	0
elsewhere	y from Ty	2*py
xl <=x <= xr	x to Tx	px
xl <=x <= xr	x from Tx	px
elsewhere	x to Tx	0
elsewhere	x from Tx	2*px

px and py are prices for one step in x or y direction

b) Several other (original) modifications are introduced, such as:

- putting several extra restrictions on the form of connection, on search area and deviations compared to the ideal optimal connection;
- changing path cost so that fittness of the developing line according to the nearest obstacles such as other lines is taken into account - this is especially important in the routing problem since the most important factor here is the interaction between connections;
- algorithm is not bound to equidistant cells and is often much faster in other e.g. vector or rectangle representations. The same philosophy holds for other shapes of cells [16];
- several mechanisms allow the user to define his own routing strategy, like "first route long and good fitting connections in the left central part of the board ...".

The ratio between search area developed by original Lee's algorithm and our is about $r * r : r = r : 1$, where r is the distance between start and target point. In real-life examples the measured ratio between Lee and our pure algorithm without other features was about the order of magnitude. The reason for this is that actual boards are more or less dense meaning there are many obstacles between target and start. It is interesting to notice that G usually produces less dense boards than theoretically computed by minimal spanning tree. There are two reasons for this:

a) designers usually draw some redundant connections in theirs logical plan;

b) our system actually finds better solutions than minimal spanning tree. It is understandable if we think about a "simple" problem of connecting only one signal net.

When observing theoretically computed density, it is gradually dropping when more and more connections are done. But in case of one extremely dense board, theoretically computed density grew and finally resulted in a number greater than one. The only answer in that situation was a multi-layer board.

Note that our system doesn't guarantee global optimality although it is locally optimal and globally suboptimal. If the heuristics about the danger of unconnected connections never fails the results are optimal. In reality system makes small deviations from optimal

665

heuristics but it should at least stay close to the optimal solution.

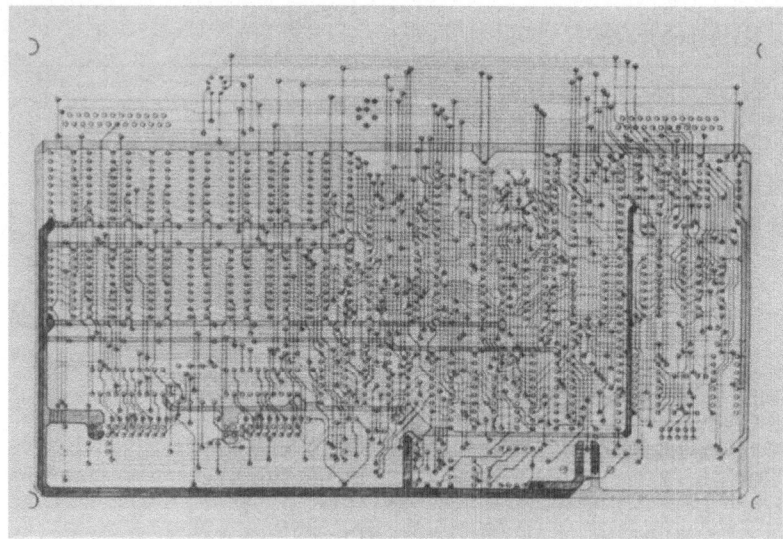

Figure 4. First automatically routed board.

3. PROCESS PLANNING

In process planning, the task is to compute the right (in a sence
optimal) sequence of operations for a given task. For example in
Figure 5 we can see a workpiece that has to be produced from a blank.
It consists of two cylinders with different diameters.
    In cooperation with Faculty of Mechanical Engineering, University
of Ljubljana, we experimentally developed a CAPP system, described in
[11]. It is a classical expert system with a typical rule:

```
operation drilling
if
   gdb:  fc is_a cylinder_in           and
   gdb:  dc included interval (3,40)    and
   gdb:  lc / max(gdb:dc) =<  10        and
   gdb:  nc subset interval (11,12)
then
   fc := is_a blank                     and
   dc := 0 m                            and
   nc := undefined
end.
```

telling what are preconditions to applaying drilling and what are
changes.

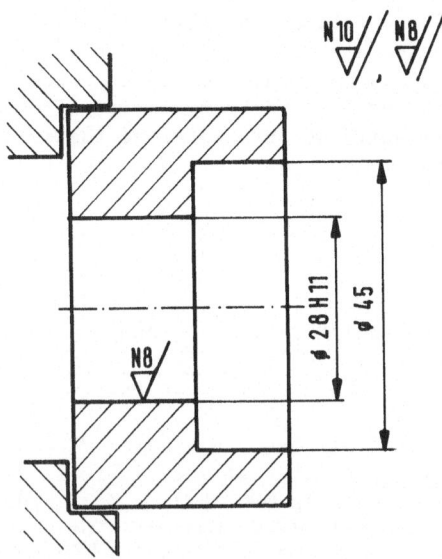

Figure 5. The master part

The system OPEX actually has 3 levels of rules:
- rules for applaying basic operations
- rules for combining basic operations within individual feature
- rules for combining operation sequences.
    This system is a classical expert system with a three level hierarchy.

4. DISCUSSION

Implementation remarks: routing program is written in PASCAL having about 5500 lines and is only a part of some 10000 lines program. The other systems were written in PROLOG having less then 1000 lines each. Router was developed in two man-year, the other systems in less then 6 man-months.
    Our experiences are the following:
a) about computer languages
    - it is much easier to implement quite a good prototype in PROLOG than in any other procedural language for a lot of problems;
    - it is much easier to change the program if it is written in PROLOG;
    - the program in PROLOG is several times smaller than equivalent program in any other procedural language;
    - the program in PROLOG is several times slower and more memory greedy than equivalent program in any other procedural language;
b) about methods
    - in many fields it is quite easy to procedure quite solid systems based on AI methods in a short time that is in most characteristics superior to classic ones;

- many classical algorithms and methods are very difficult to change or adapt and therefore inadequate for implementations especially in great systems. There is also a great difference between "classical" AI methods and expert systems. The flexibility of expert systems design is not only suitable for tailoring the system according to user's needs but is also very suitable for modernisations or integrations into some bigger system.

5. REFERENCES

1. A. Fusaoka, H. Seki, K. Takahashi:"Description and Reasoning of VLSI Circuit in Temporal Logic", 79-91, New Generation Computing, An International Journal on Fifth Generation Computers, Springer-Verlag NGC Vol. 2, No. 1, 1984
2. T. Uehara, N. Kawato:"Logic Circuit Synthesis Using PROLOG", 187-195, New Generation Computing, An International Journal on Fifth Generation Computers, Springer-Verlag NGC, Vol. 1, No. 2, 1983
3. K. Matsumo, T. Wake, T. Sakaguchi: "Fault Diagnosis of a Power System", Expert Systems, Vol. 2, No. 3, 1985
4. H. Mori, K. Mitsumoto, T. Fujita, S. Goto: "Knowledge-based VLSI routing system - WIREX", Proc. of ICOT 1984
5. H.J. Rothermel, D.A. Mlynski: "Routing Method for VLSI Design using Irregular Cells", No. 20 Design Aut. Conf. 1983, USA, pp. 257-263
6. Y. Descotte, J.C. Latombe: GARI: "A Problem Solver that Plans How to Machine Mechanical Parts", Proc. IJCAI, 1981
7. K. Matsushima, N. Okada, T. Sata: "The Integration of CAD and CAM by Application of Artificial-Intelligence Techn." Annals of the CIPR, Vol. 31, 1982
8. I. Darbyshire, B.J. Davis: "EXCAP - An Expert Systems Approach to Recursive Process Planning", 16th CIRP, Tokyo, 1984
9. M. Gams: "Routing" Informatica, no. 2/3, Ljubljana, 1983
10. M. Spegel et al: "A System for Printed Circuit Board Design", Automatika 1-2, pp. 89-99, 1984
11. A. Sluga et al: "An Attempt to Implement Expert Systems Techniques in CAPP", II. Int. Conf. on CAM, Ljubljana, 1985
12. M.A. Breuer (ed.): Design Automation of Digital Systems, Pr.-Hall, 72
13. M. Gams, I. Bratko: "A Circuit Analysis Program that Explains its Reasoning", Cybernetics and Systems Research 2, Elsevier Science Publishers B.V, (North-Holland), 1984
14. R.M. Stallman, G.J. Sussman: "Forward Reasoning and Dependency-Directed Backtracking in a System for Computer-Aided Circuit Analysis", Artificial Intelligence 2, 1977, pp. 135-197
15. J. Soukup: "Fast Maze Router", IV. No. 15 Design Automation Conference, 1978, USA, pp. 100-102
16. F. Tada, K. Yoshimura, T. Kagata, T. Shirakawa: "A Fast Maze Router with Iterative Use of Variable Search Space Restriction", No. 17 Design Automation Conference, USA, 1980
17. N.J. Nilsson: "Principles of Artificial Intelligence", 1980
18. J. Pearl:"Heuristics: Intelligent Search Strategies for Computer Problem Solving", Addison-Wesley, 1984

LOBSTER-M: A MIXED MODE SIMULATOR FOR CAD

A. Jávor
Central Research Institute for Physics
of the Hungarian Academy of Sciences
P.O. Box 49
H-1525 Budapest, HUNGARY

ABSTRACT. The LOBSTER-M mixed mode simulation system for CAD in micro-electronics is described. Some special features such as *Quasideterministic State Representation* for handling significant hazards, switch level simulation of MOS circuit segments with bidirectional propagation of signals, tristate logic and dynamic storage as well as hierarchical model building and interactive graphic display of the simulated waveforms are discussed.

1. INTRODUCTION

Because of the high and rapidly increasing complexity of digital logic circuits [1] it is certain that designers commit errors that must be corrected before any circuit is mass produced. In the days of classical discrete-component-system building, "breadboard models" and pilot production were used to check the design and correct the possible errors. For designing LSI and VLSI circuits the utilization of simulation programs is unavoidable. The reasons are obvious.

- The expenses of model building are comparable with those of the whole of mass production.

- It is practically impossible to execute the measurements for locating and determining the design errors.

- The correction of even a single error on a chip requires the production of a completely new chip.

This means that

a) A simulation system for the modelling of digital logic circuits is essential for computer aided design.

b) The simulation system has to supply a modelling tool that is not only as realistic as a physical model but supplies the information gained by a whole series of models available from pilot production. In this sense it has to provide a model that is "better" than a classical physical model.

c) The concept of the design methods has to be seriously considered. The reason for this is that whereas in the early days of electronics (i.e. in the days of transistors - and even tubes) the circuit

669

R. Trappl (ed.), Cybernetics and Systems '86, 669–676.
© *1986 by D. Reidel Publishing Company.*

and the system design were tightly coupled and the designer had to deal with both aspects. The advent of integrated circuits has meant that designers and their models were divided into two, more or less distinct subgroups (i) system designers ("outside the case") (ii) circuit designers ("inside the case").

The design (and custom design) of LSI and VLSI circuits means that the whole system has to be built from the circuit components "inside the case" so the two formerly separated areas had to be coupled again and this was the reason that the need for mixed mode simulation combining both logic and quasicircuit level models arose [2][3][4][5][6][7][8][9].

These were the guiding principles in the development of the LOBSTER (Logic Operational Behaviour Simulator for Time and Effort Reduction) system [8][10][11][12][13][14][15]. The original version of the system was conceived in the early 70's and since then there have been several completely new versions incorporating the latest results from theoretical research as well as experience gained from its widespread use. The original version was developed for simulating logic circuits built from discrete logic elements, i.e. SSI integrated circuits, later versions and applications were for simulating LSI circuits as a CAD tool in the custom design of microelectronic systems. The present version is the LOBSTER-M (where M stands for "mixed mode"); this was completed in 1985.

2. MAIN FEATURES OF THE SYSTEM

(a) The system consists of two separate phases. In the first - model building phase; the model network is constructed from the building block elements available in the system library, in accordance with the topology of the network. The system element library is extendable and contains building blocks (gates, flip-flops, etc.) with fixed and with user definable time parameters. That means that, for example, a NAND gate is available with two inputs where the time delays, and the rise and fall times have to be defined by the user for every individual model element.

On the other hand, it is convenient if fixed parameter elements are also available. If an SN7400 model is used then the above mentioned gate will have the time parameters defined in the TEXAS INSTRUMENTS catalog. In the same way if you have your own set of elements for "library custom" or "gate array" design you may have an XNAND in your library with the specific time parameters given by yourself.

The model building has another facility: *hierarchical model building*. The possibility of building (eventually testing) subnetworks then to insert them as arbitrarily located blocks in arbitrarily many instances in a larger model and also the hierarchical extension of this (i.e. these models may be inserted in still hierarchically higher ranking models is possible. The principle is illustrated in Figure 1 showing the hierarchical insertion of the different blocks. The block types are denoted by capital letters, the subscript numbers indicate their individual instances. Such blocks may be stored in a block library and

670

used similarly to the building elements by referring to them by their names.

The model building phase – beyond constructing the model and storing it on a disc – undertakes the structural investigation of the model. Here it is worth mentioning that beyond the information supplied concerning the load conditions of the outputs of the gates, *analysis for the detection of all feedback loops and connected loop systems* is undertaken. This may call the attention of the designer to possible design errors that can be corrected prior to the dynamic simulation run.

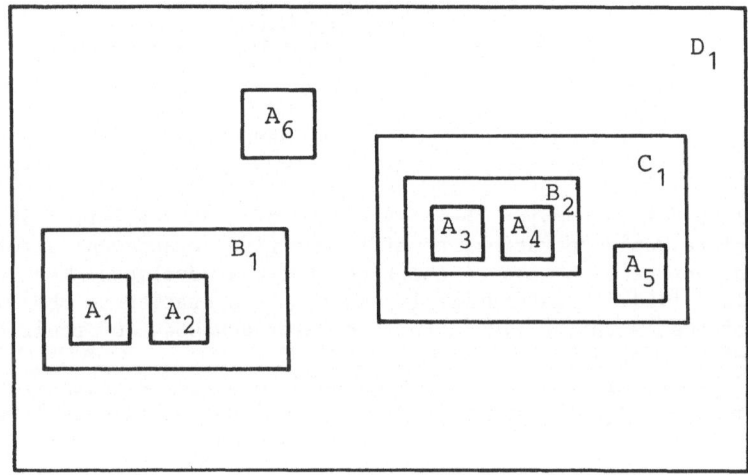

Figure 1. Hierarchically built model structure.

The second phase deals with the actual dynamic simulation using the model built in the first phase with appropriate input sequences and conditions of investigation determined by the user.

This architecture, i.e. the separation of model building and experimenting, enables convenient investigation of the same model under different conditions and also the distinct possibility of model modification.

(b) For realistic description of events in the time domain, *asynchronous time representation* is used. This means that time delays as well as transfer times between logic states or dynamic storage times are handled. The representation provides for taking into consideration the "worst case" deviations resulting from operating under marginal conditions, the range of the distribution of time parameters in mass production, and the cumulative effect of these factors. Thus the longest possible undetermined periods will appear in the model. The worst case principle is illustrated in Figure 2. Here t_{dmin} and t_{dmax} denote the minimum and maximum delay values of an element. In this way the minimum number of time parameters – for a simple combinational gate

671

taking into account different rise and fall times - is four.

UNDETERMINED (TRANSIENT) STATE

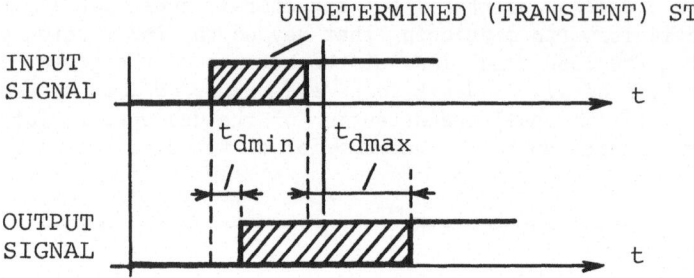

Figure 2. Timing conditions for worst case design.

In order to combine the possibility of high resolution in time and to achieve rapid operation, an efficient time advancement algorithm serving as the executive of the simulator was developed. The Delft Algorithm [16][17] automatically adapts its operation to the distribution of events during simulation and takes advantage of their usually burst-like occurence.

(c) Special attention has been paid to state representation in the system. Handling of undetermined situations was an essential requirement. Although transient states during the rise and fall times of the signals could be described adequately, due to the inherent inconsistence of three-valued logic {1,u,0} significant hazards could not be described appropriately as was shown by Breuer [18]. The problem is shown on the simplest example of an RS flip-flop built from NAND gates and driven by the "forbidden" input signal combination (see Figure 3).

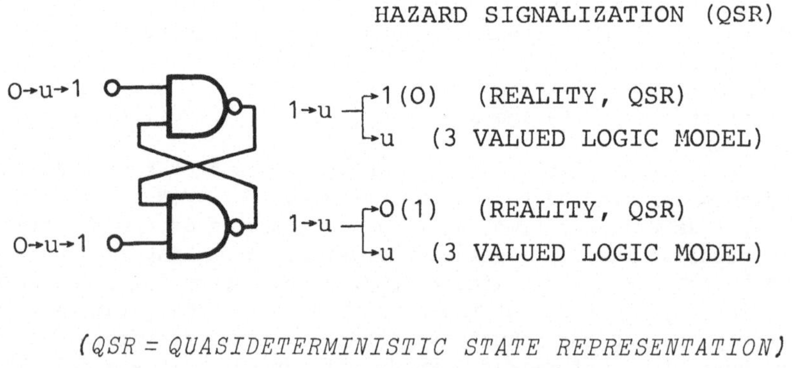

HAZARD SIGNALIZATION (QSR)

0→u→1 $1→u$ ┌→1(0) (REALITY, QSR)
               └→u   (3 VALUED LOGIC MODEL)

0→u→1 $1→u$ ┌→0(1) (REALITY, QSR)
               └→u   (3 VALUED LOGIC MODEL)

(QSR = QUASIDETERMINISTIC STATE REPRESENTATION)

Figure 3. Operation of an RS flip-flop driven by the forbidden input combination.

672

In three-valued simulation the circuit would be stuck at the value u whereas in reality it would go into one of the possible (0,1) or (1,0) states. The *Quasideterministic State Representation* [19] solves this problem. During runtime a special procedure treats the model network segments consisting of feedback loop systems that are liable to cause significant hazards. If such a situation occurs, the state of the network segment is forced into one possible value (thus imitating the real physical situation) and it simultaneously signalizes that this is not the only possible next state, i.e. a *significant hazard* is present. In this way this second feature gives more than a physical model would and this warning enables the erroneous operation to be detected in advance that otherwise could only have been detected during mass production. The method is utilized for explicitly or implicitly (in the form of, for example, flip-flops as building elements) given feedback loops.

As follows from the above mentioned features, simulation of both combinational and sequential circuits including those that contain feedback loops is enabled.

(d) In LSI system simulation, besides the increasing complexity of the digital logic networks to be modelled another important requirement has been raised by the widespread use of MOS technology. The circuits built up from a network of MOS transistors have enabled the designers to construct networks using less elements by using them as switches, and a network of switched capacitors may realize the logic. The simplest example is the use of a transfer gate (see Figure 4/a) where the opening voltage on the gate electrode connects the source and drain electrodes; however, without knowing the impedance relations at the two ends we cannot determine in which direction the propagation of the signal takes place. This means that the element itself has to provide for bidirectional transfer possibilities in contrast to the classical logic gates where the transfer of signals was always clear, i.e. from input to output.

Another practical example is shown in Figure 4/b. Here the bridge circuit realizes the function $F = AD + BC + BED + AEC$ and as either $B = E = D = 1$ or $A = E = C = 1$ results in $F = 0$ the transistor controlled by signal E obviously plays the role of a bidirectional gate. A third example – frequently used – is the case of dynamic storage (see Figure 4/c) where after the input level is stored in the capacitor on the output the gate is closed and the "floating" electrode stores the value until it is refreshed or after a given time it "forgets" the information. Such high impedance "floating" nodes or tristate logic are used in other cases as well, e.g. buses.

The task is to build models that are almost as effective (with regard to runtime and storage space) as classical simulators and simultaneously to provide a "quasi circuit level" modelling possibility to take care of the above requirements.

The LOBSTER-M mixed mode simulator solves this model-building so that classical circuit segments may be mixed in the model with switch level segments that can describe such circuits in those parts where realistic modelling is necessary. The most general facility in the system is that arbitrary networks of MOS transistors can be inserted in the model, such as a special element or block using the name MOSNET and

673

describing the topology of the subnetwork. During operation the effects of bidirectional signal propagation, floating "high impedance states", finite storage time, propagation delays at the gate as well as due to the capacitors at the nodes of the network, worst case effects of un-determined (transient) states on the gates are solved [12].

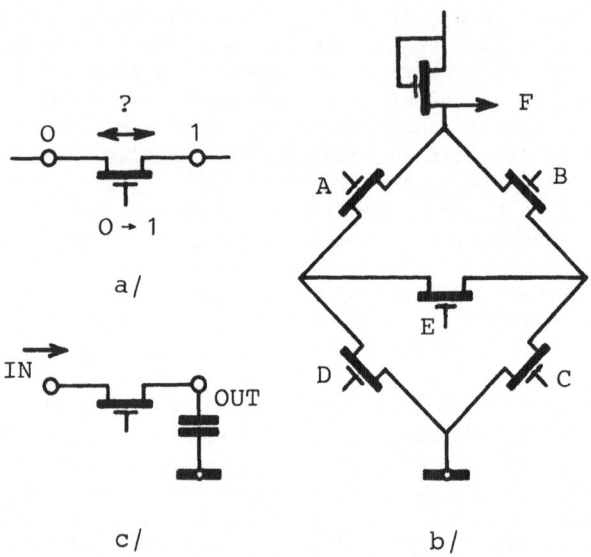

Figure 4. Examples of the use of MOS transistors in digital logic.

(e) A very important aspect when using the simulator is the man-machine communication. The input language of the system is a structural description of the model that can easily be coded from the block scheme of the model to be simulated.

Concerning the output, it has to be emphasized that although a number of options are available to provide the results in the conven-ient form of printouts the most appropriate form of obtaining them is not this.

For real investigations and testing of a system a tool that is equivalent to a multitrace measuring oscilloscope with all its options is a necessity. Therefore a postprocessor is included in the system that provides this by using a graphic display (see Figure 5) enabling: flexible display of 16 signals simultaneously on 16 "traces", variation of the nodes, time resolution, time domain displayed, accurate measure-ments of time values and intervals using a light pen, etc.

3. CONCLUSIONS

The simulator described above has already been used with success in Hungary and abroad. It is written in FORTRAN and is therefore easily portable. It has been installed on several IBM, DEC compatible and also on ICL machines.

Figure 5. The multitrace measuring scope equivalent output display facility.

4. ACKNOWLEDGEMENTS

The author is indebted to all those who have contributed to the development of the system and in particular to M. Benkö, A. Vigh and B.K. Szabó.

5. REFERENCES

[1] Moore, G., 'VLSI: Some Fundamental Challenges', *IEEE Spectrum*, April (1979) 30-37.
[2] Jávor, A., Benkö, M., Tarnay, K., 'Multimode Simulation Concepts, in Jávor, A. (ed.), *Simulation in Research and Development*, (North-

Holland, Amsterdam, 1985) 135-138.

[3] Ruehli, A.E., 'New Aspects of Large-Scale Circuit Analysis and Simulation', Proc. 1981 European Conf. on Circuit Theory and Design, The Hague 25-28 August 1981. 151-155.

[4] Lightner, M.R., Hachtel, G.D., 'MOS Switch Level Simulation Macromodelling and Testing', ISCAS'82 Rome, 63-67.

[5] Chawla, B.R., Gummel, H.K., Kozak, P., 'MOTIS - An MOS Timing Simulator', *IEEE Trans. on Circuits and Systems*, 22(12) (1975) 901-910.

[6] DeMan, H., 'Computer-Aided Design for Integrated Circuits: Trying to Bridge the Gap', *IEEE J. Solid-State Circuits*, 14(3) (1979) 613-621.

[7] Sakuma, H., Fujinami, Y., Kurobe, T., 'NELSIM: A Hierarchical VLSI Design Verification System', in Anceau-Aas (ed.), *Computer Hardware Simulation Languages*, (Elsevier North-Holland, 1983) 109-118.

[8] Jåvor, A., Keresztes, P., Benkő, M., 'A Solution for MOS-LSI Gate Level Simulation', Simulation of Systems IMACS Congress 1979 Sorrento, September 24-28 1979. (North-Holland, Amsterdam) 365-374.

[9] Lightner, M.R., Hachtel, G.D., Byrd, R.H., 'A Theory and Algorithmic Frame for Switch Level Simulation', in Jåvor, A. (ed.), *Simulation in Research and Development* (North-Holland, Amsterdam, 1985) 151-159.

[10] Jåvor A., Benkő T.né, *Simulation of Discrete Systems* (Müszaki Könyvkiadő, Budapest, 1979) (in Hungarian)

[11] Jåvor, A., Benkő, M. Mrs., 'A User-Oriented System for the Simulation of Digital Logic', CAD Seminar, Budapest, 3-5. November 1976, 178-191.

[12] Jåvor, A., Szabó, B.K., 'Switch Level Extension of a Logic Simulator', in Jåvor, A. (ed.), *Simulation in Research and Development* (North-Holland, Amsterdam, 1985) 139-149.

[13] Benkő, M.Mrs., Jåvor, A., Keresztes, P., 'LSI System Simulation: an Interdisciplinary Approach', Zbornik Radova JUREMA 1977 (April 19-22) G1

[14] Jåvor, A., Révész, Á., Tóbiás, P., 'Simulation System with a Single Core and Several Outer Layers', in Jåvor, A. (ed.), *Discrete Simulation and Related Fields* (North-Holland, Amsterdam, 1982) 65-85.

[15] Jåvor, A., Révész, Á., Tóbiás, P., 'A Closed-Loop Feedback Controlled Simulation System', in Jåvor, A. (ed.), *Discrete Simulation and Related Fields* (North-Holland, Amsterdam, 1982) 87-95.

[16] Jåvor, A., 'An Adaptive Time Advancement Algorithm for Discrete Simulation', *Information Processing Letters* 6(3) (1977) 83-86.

[17] Jåvor, A., 'Ereignis-Behandlung mit dem Delft Algoritmus', Simulationstechnik 2. Symposium Simulationstechnik Wien, September 1984. (Springer Verlag) 349-353.

[18] Breuer, M.A., 'A Note on Three Valued Logic Simulation', *IEEE Transactions on Computers* 21(4) (April 1972) 399-402.

[19] Jåvor, A., 'An Approach to the Modelling of Uncertainties in the Simulation of Quasideterministic Discrete Event Systems', *Problems of Control and Information Theory* 4(3) (1975) 219-229.

COMPUTER IN THE ARCHITECT'S WORKSHOP - NEW INTERNATIONAL
STYLE IN ARCHITECTURE

J. Kłos
Centre of Building Systems Research and Develop-
ment
Wierzbowa 11
00-094 Warszawa
Poland

ABSTRACT. We may observe a phenomenon that can be called
the universality of development of the CAAD concepts in
the world. This is a result of the difficulty in identyfi-
cation of architectural design specifity and of the supremacy of some countries in the development of CAD. In the
universality of CAAD one should seek the lack of full acceptance of a computer by architects in their workshop.
This universality - called here the international style -
cannot be accepted. We may expect the evolution of design
form as a result of CAD development universality.

1. INTRODUCTION

A comunity of architects is not commonly interested in
available computer-aided systems. Moreover, architects
often negate the new technique to be introduced usefully
to their workshop. The researchers in computer-aided architectural design /CAAD/ increasingly search for reasons
why great potential of computer-aided architectural design is not fully used. They wonder whether after more
than twenty years of development CAAD will finally serve
its turn. And those hopes have been connected with various directions of computer usage development. The seventies were marked with optimism and faith in technical
possibilities of computer science. The dynamic development of equipment and software in computer graphics has
played a significant part. From the architect's point of
view, the computer graphics systems available nowadays
influence creative activities in architecture both in
positive and negative ways. The possibility of obtaining
complex images on a colour display, the possibility of
their immediate modification and geometrical transformations, may be understood as the straight goal /Selby 1984/
Then the apparently correct and certainly striking

677

R. Trappl (ed.), Cybernetics and Systems '86, 677–683.
© *1986 by D. Reidel Publishing Company.*

applications of the systems which have been implemented
seemingly properly are a factor influencing the intensifi-
cation of negative phenomenon in contemporary practice in
architecture - the phenomenon of "documentation production"
/Cross 1977/. The effectivness of computer graphics depends much more as it would have seemed on the range and
way of computer use.

At the end of seventies, we noticed a distinct conceptual crisis in the field of CAAD. Much more attention
than before has been paid since then to the revision of
hitherto concepts and their methodological background
/Bijl 1890, Purcell 1978/. Only the concepts established
in a cognitive way should initiate the search for proper
formal methods, methods of programming, and technical solutions proper in specific architectural applications.
This very direction is represented by the concepts of expert systems where one assumes the necessity of knowledge structures in architecture to be systematized. Yet the
cognitive grounding of CAAD development is more difficult
for two reasons:
- science in architecture is not systematized, which
  makes it more difficult, among others, to formulate methodological research problems,
- there appears a strong pressure "from the outside"
  on the growth of rationality in architectural design.
In this second case, in relation to computer applications,
two facts deserve some stressing.
Firstly the whole range of design problems in building
including structural problems, environmental problems,
economic problems is developed today with the aid of formal apparatus, mathematical methods. As soon as the computer is introduced into design practice those building
problems appear in a privileged situation, and in consequence it may lead to the dehumanization in architecture.
People making decisions, who has a whole range of measurable criteria at their disposal, prefer them to non-
measurable social criteria, often intuitive criteria of
an architect. In such a case the reluctance of architects
understanding their profession in a social /humanistic/
way towards computer techniques is understandable.
Secondly, computer industry for obvious reasons prefers
"for today" type of solutions which enable manufacturers
to enter user market. Yet, we may still hope that concerning the microcomputer industry, due to full supply on
the market and low cost of equipment, the market entering
will proceed with the presentation of rich and attractive
offer of system programming /for instance the system graphic software, or data base/. Such a situation may considerably ease developments in CAAD.

2. DESIGN SPECIFITY IN ARCHITECTURE

For a CAAD systems developer the computer-aided process
is his design subject, the knowledge of which should be
supplied by general design methodology and its detailed
sections. As much as methodology is recognized by practi-
cians of various practical disciplines /ways of designing/
as useless, yet it is different in the field of CAD - numerous unsolved and yet important methodological problems
are perceived. What is more, many problems are undertaken
just on the initiative of the CAD researchers, as in the
case of design representation theory /Eastman 1981/ or
information communication in a graphic form /Aish 1979/.
  Still, the problems connected with identification
of architectural design specificity deserve particular
attention. It is difficult nowdays to find satisfactory
definition of architecture, it is difficult to identify
the sphere of architecture, and it is even more difficult
to state features that distinguish architecture among
others ways of designing. Let us formulate two features,
bearing in mind that considering the lack of deep research, they should be treated hypothetically. The first
may be denoted as follows: individual character of graphic
design languages. The second - variety of participation
forms of numerous specialists and non-professionals in
the design process.
  This is one way of understanding this specificity.
The second, and no less important, is distinction between
the conditions of carrying out the profession in different countries - let it call the "place specificity".
Architects do not solve everyday problems in housing in
every country - they are only engaged in prestige problems, and houses are designed by technicians and engineers. The role of individual participants in design process is also different, including an architect. There are
countries where an architect is more a social planner
than a building engineer. The operational definition of
architectural design, proposed by A. Kotarbiński, well
characterizes the problem of place specificity: architecture is the sphere of practical activity in a given place and time, entrusted to architects and accepted by them.

3. UNIVERSALITY OF DEVELOPMENT OF CAAD

The necessity and simultaneously the difficulty in considering specificity depends on that the CAD develops in
direction of methodological specialization in interdisciplinary cross-sections, it means that specializations emerge, connected with seperate design activities and methods
irrespective of way of designing. It leads to the searching

in the CAD for the features more common than differences
between ways of designing. Still, optimization understood by an architect is different from that of a doctor
or an economist - they apply different design languages
and different methods of design representation. In the
aspect of place specificity, its dynamical development
is carried out only in a small number of countries.
Because of lack in methodological knowledge on design
specificity in architecture /in both meanings of speci-
ficity/ and in view of above difficulties, we may observe a phenomenon that can be called the universality of
development of the CAAD concepts in the world. Yet similar universality characterizes concepts of system design
methods, such as in the case of a classical mathod of
Alexander /developed, as a matter of fact, on the example of an Indian village/ or Friedman's method. It may
be stated generally that any way of aiding design by
means of modern methodological knowledge and knowledge
on facts in architecture has the features of universality.

4. STYLE IN ARCHITECTURE

How can be understood then the technical revolution in
architecture, signalled by the research workers in the
context of the above universality of design methods development? This revolution is accompanied by the evolution of design form, and also the transformations in the
scope of architecture or the role of individual participants in the design process. Any methodological transformations in architecture, because of their universal and
international character, seem analogous to the development of artifact concepts of the first half of the twentieth century, that is to the phenomenon known under the
name of the "international style". The background of the
phenomenon thirty years ago was significant development
of knowledge on facts in architecture. It was then, when
an architect came across the social problems, town sociology, and the new techniques appeared in building. The
notion of style, up till now connected with the artifact
understanding of architecture, now gains a new quality
in the methodological considerations - the methodological style /Simon 1981/. The artifact style is understood
as that derived from description of a completed architectural object /product of architectural design/, and methodological style is understood as that derived from
design process of this object.
    In methodological works, particular attention is
paid to the meaning of individual design methods, psychical predispositions of a designer; generally - on the
meaning of methodological conditions of design

effectivness, and the quality of design solutions. Nowdays, it is the team that designs more and more often, and the cooperation methods, style of team work, ways of communication of information influence the final form of artifact concepts - the methodological style decides upon the artifact style.

5. NEW INTERNATIONAL STYLE IN ARCHITECTURE

The international style of the beginning of the twentieth century has not been accepted bacause of the reasons understood nowadays - the cultural, social and regional differences were omitted in the theory of architecture. The development of the international methodological style in architecture seems similarly wrong. The place specificity is also the result of many years tradition of carry - ing out the profession, and the methods of teaching architecture. That is why in the universality of CAAD one should seek the lack of full acceptance of a computer by architects in their workshop.
       Summing up, we may state that the architectural computer-aided design universality results particalarly from:
- big supremacy of some countries in the development of CAD
- insufficient development of science in architecture in the field of knowledge on facts and methods,
- strong influence of computer industry on the form of CAD concept,
- new methodological specialization in CAD, leading to the identification of various design problems, inconsistent with tradition.
The reasons of the international methodological style are numerous. In the case of the thirty years ago, the international style developed in this way:
- The theoretical achievement in the theory of architecture and architectural sciences have been preserved /such as town sociology/,
- simultaneously, big emotional load has been introduced into architecture, in the course of searching for connections with cultural tradition understood very freely.
On the other hand, in the case of the present methodological style, we may expect the evolution of design form meeting half-way the reasons of universality of CAD development. We may expect in particular:
- the increase of importance of the methodological specialization in architecture. Just at present we may observe the appearance of companies specialized in elaboration of architectural design in technical stage /documantation/ based on the conceptual design prepared earlier, independently, and by other teams,
- the drive to team elaboration of design concepts

in interdisciplinary teams.

In order to create conditions favourable for such evolution
one should dynamically develop the science in architecture and design methodology. It is indispensable to systema-
tize the architectural design languages and the ways of
decomposing the design problem - these actions will allow
for the communication of information between the participants of design process to be more efficient. Yet simultaneously, one should aim at taking into consideration
the specificity of place, and the decrease of universality
of CAD concept. It seems that in this case the following
simultaneous actions may play a significant part:
- architect are supplied with a rich offer of effective
  methods of system and computer design, and
- architects are equipped with methodological knowledge,
  it means the methodological concience is increased.
  It will enable the proper and conscious choice of these
  methods in the conditions of a given design task, in
  given conditions of carrying out profession, and according to individual predispositions of a designer.

6. CONCLUSION

The above considerations are the result of confronting
theory with practice. In 1983-85 the author carried out
research works in the field of architectural design methodology and simultaneously took part in the works of
a team designing and impementing the URBOS system - computer-aided urban design. It found its expression in the
development of concept of computer-aided architectural
design, and this development is well characterized by
a change in attitude the computerization problem, which
has occured during these three years. In 1983, in elaborating the concept of URBOS system, the universally understood the advetages that can be obtained through the
automation of such and such time-consuming and difficult
activities of the design process, were stressed quite
strongly. After three years work, many different problems
were stressed - the usefulness of automation in the context of specific features such as:
- complexity of analyses /measurements/ of design solutions in architecture and urban planning,
  accessibility , especially accessibility to information
  in design process,
- way and scope of communication of information between
  the participants of the design process /specialists
  and non-professionals/,
and not in the context of universally understood "usual"
design activities.
      The paper tries to show that one of the most

important research problems within the methodology of architectural design is to identify special features of architectural design that means its specific character. This problem has been tackled insufficiently as fa is the importance of the design practice in architecture and specifically in context of computer-aided architectural design.

References

Selby, P.L. 1984   - 'The impact of CAD on architectu-
                          ral practice-challenges, benefis
                          and prospects', CAD 84 Proceedings,
                          Brighton, April 1984

Cross, N. 1977   - The Automated Architect: Human and
                          Machine Roles in Design, London,
                          1977

Bijl, A. 1980   -'The revolution is here to stay',
                          CAD No 3, 1980

Purcell, P. 1978   -'Computing and architecture: a fresh
                          conspectus, CAD, No 4, 1978

Eastman, C. 1981   -'Recent development of representa-
                          tion theory in the science of de-
                          sign', 18th Design Automation Con-
                          ference Proceedings, Neshville,1981

Aish, R. 1979   -'3D input for CAAD systems', CAD,No2
                          1979

Simon, H.A. 1981   -'Style in design',/in:/ Gasparski,W.,
                          Miller,D. Projektowanie i systemy,
                          vol. III, Ossolineum, Wrocław,1981
                          /in Polish/

Kłos,J.,Pawelec,A.   -'1985 - URBOS - a system for compu-
                          ter-aided building site planning',
                          INFOPRO-85 Conference proceedings
                          /in Polish/.

A SEQUENTIAL ALGORITHM FOR THE SYNTHESIS OF TREE AUTOMATA

I. Sierocki, W. Jacak
Institute of Technical Cybernetics
Technical University of Wrocław
50-370 Wrocław
Poland

ABSTRACT. The paper deals with the synthesis problem for tree automata. A sequential synthesis algorithm is presented based on the hypothesis formulation-verification-modification scheme.

1. INTRODUCTION

One of the important problems in Systems Engineering is the synthesis of a cybernetic system from samples of its behaviour i.e. the problem of de-termining a cybernetic system with behaviour containing a given set of input-output pairs (computations). For a dynamical system (sequential ma-chine), a grammar (an automaton), a program, this problem is referred to as the identification, the grammar inference, the automatic programming, respectively [2],[3],[5].
This paper is concerned with the inference problem for tree automata. The choice of this class of cybernetic systems is motivated by the fact that an ordinary (one-dimensional) automaton is the special case of a tree automaton and, moreover, by the fact that the theory of tree auto-mata has found many interesting applications in areas such as computer science, VLSI systems, and syntactic pattern recognition [7],[6],[3]. For instance in syntactic pattern recognition a pattern can be represen-ted by a tree which describes a relationships between basic elements of the pattern. In this case, a synthesis problem (called also a learning problem) is interpreted as follows: on the basis of learning examples and if possible, counter-examples one should construct a pattern recognizer a tree automaton .
Known tree automata-synthesis algoritms are based on k-tail method [8],[10], [9]. However, the algorithm presented here is sequential i.e. the algo-rithm generates a sequence of automata $M_1,..,M_k,..,M_n$ such that the first k input-output pairs of the sample set are contained in the behaviour of M_k, while M_k and k+1 -th input-output pair is the initial data for the procedure generating M_{k+1}. Our algorithm is organized on the basis of the hypothesis formulation - verification - modification scheme. During the first phase hypothesis are formulated cocerning the value of any transi-tion-state relation. Roughly speaking, this is done by assigning to every

685

R. Trappl (ed.), Cybernetics and Systems '86, 685–691.

tree t a set of states which is a preimage of the output function with
respect to the output letter corresponding to a tree t. When a state assigned to the tree can be deduced from the assumed hypotheses then a verification procedure is performed which relies on a comparison of the
predicted-and-observed output letters. When a contradiction appears then
a modification procedure is applied by introducing a new state and by re-
formulating some transition-state relations. Finally, we would like to
emphasize that the approach of this paper is particularly influenced by
the papers [1],[2],[4] which are concerned with the inference problem for
one-dimensional automata.

2. BASIC NOTIONS

Begin by introducing a definition of a ranked alphabet which is a pair
(U,r), where U is a finite set of function symbols and $r:U \to N$ is a finite function called the ranking function. Let $U_n = r^{-1}(n)$. The set $T(U)$
of U-terms is defined as follows:

(i) $U_0 \subset T(U)$

(ii) $u \in U_n$ and $t_1,..,t_n \in T(U)$ then $u(t_1,..,t_n) \in T(U)$,

Additionally, we introduce some terminology which is due to S. Gorn [11].
The Gorn's formalism allows to interpret any U-terms as a certain labelled tree. Let A be a free monoid generated by N^+ and $\cdot$ be a concatenation
operation and e the identity of A. Let $D \subset A$ be a tree domain. A U-term
(U-tree), (for short tree t)is a function $t:D \to U$. The domain of a tree
t is denoted by $D(t)$. Let $a \in D(t)$ then $t/a = \{(b,x) | (a \cdot b, x) \in t\}$ is a
subtree of t at a. The set of frontier nodes of a tree t is denoted Ft
and defined as $Ft = \{a \in D(t) \mid a \cdot i \notin D(t)\}$ for every $i \in N^+$. So, from
now on we say U-tree instead U-term. Let $U = \{u_1,..,u_p\}$.

A nondeterministic, finite tree-automaton M over (U,r) is a system
$M = (X, f_{u_1},..,f_{u_p}, Y, g)$ where:

(i) X is a finite set of states

(ii) for each $n \neq 0$ and $u \in U_n$, $f_u \subset X^{r(u)} \times X$, and for $u \in U_0$, $f_u \subset X$,

(iii) $Y = \{y_1,..,y_l\}$ is a output alphabet and $g \subset X \times Y$ is called an

output relation.

For a given nondeterministic tree-automaton M, one can define so-called
run relation $f_M^* \subset T(U) \times X$ as follows:

(i) for $t \in U_0$, $(t,x) \in f_M^* \Leftrightarrow x \in f_t$

(ii) for $u(t_1,..,t_n) \in T(U)$; $(u(t_1,..,t_n),x) \in f_M^* \Leftrightarrow$ there exist $x_1,..,x_n$

from X such that $(t_i,x_i) \in f_M^*$ for $i=1,..,n$, and $((x_1,...,x_n),x) \in f_u$.

A composition of relations g and f^* gives the relation $g_M^* \subset T(U) \times Y$ which
will be called a response relation. Additionally, for every $t \in T(U)$ we
define an output-labelled tree $\bar{t}$ as a function $\bar{t}:D(t) \to Y$. The set of an
output-labelled trees will be denoted by $T(Y)$. Now, we are able to define an input-output relation $g_M^* \subset T(U) \times T(Y)$ for an automaton M as fo-
llows: $(t,\bar{t}) \in g_M^* \Leftrightarrow D(t) = D(\bar{t})$ and $\bar{t}(a) = g_M^*(t/a)$ for every $a \in D(t)$.

3. SYNTHESIS OF A TREE AUTOMATON

Given a ranked alphabet (U,r) and an output-alphabet Y. A sample set E is defined as a finite, partial function $E:T(U) \to T(Y)$ satisfying the following conditions:

(i) $E(t) = \bar{t} \iff D(t) = D(\bar{t})$

(ii)   if $t,t' \in D(E)$ and there exists $a \in A$ such that $t/a = t'/a$ then $E(t)/b = E(t')/b$ for every $b \in D(t/a)$.

Let us assume that $E = \{(t_i, \bar{t}_i) \mid i=1,..,n\}$. The synthesis problem for tree automata is formulated as follows: given a sample set E, determine a finite tree-automaton M over (U,r) such that $E \subset g_M^{**}$.

Synthesis algorithm.

A step k of the algorithm is determined by an analysis of the tree t_k from the sample set E. All subtrees of the tree t_k (this set is denoted by $\mathcal{T}_k$) are analysed in an inner loop which is indexed by the number of applications of the modification procedure (Time i). This procedure is called out when a contradiction appears and then it creates a new state. By T_k we will denoted a set of trees accepted after a step k.

Step 0.

  Initial data: E, (U,r), $Y = \{y_1,..,y_1\}$

  Result: initial automaton $M_0 = (X_0, f_{u_1}^o,..,f_{u_p}^o, Y, g_0)$ where

$$X_0 = \{x_1,..,x_1\}, \quad g_0(x_i) = y_i \text{ for } i=1,..,1 \text{ and } f_u^o = \emptyset \text{ for each}$$

  $u \in U. T_0 = \emptyset$ is the set of accepted trees.

Step k.

  Initial data: automaton $M_{k-1} = (X_{k-1}, f_{u_1}^{k-1},..,f_{u_p}^{k-1}, Y, g_{k-1})$ inferred

    at step k-1, and the set of accepted trees T_{k-1}.

  Result: automaton $M_k = (X_k, f_{u_1}^k,..,f_{u_p}^k, Y, g_k)$ obtained as a result of

    analysis of trees from $\mathcal{T}_k$ and the set T_k.

Inner loop of analysis of trees from $\mathcal{T}_k$.

Time 0

  Initial data: initial automaton $M_{k-1}^o = (X^o, \psi_{u_1}^o,..,\psi_{u_p}^o, Y, g^o) = M_{k-1}$

  and the set of accepted trees $T^o = T_{k-1}$.

Time i

  Pick a tree $\tau \in \mathcal{T}_k$ such that the following conditions hold:

  A/ $\tau \in Ft_k$ or

  B/ If $\tau = u(\tau_1,..,\tau_n)$ then $\psi^{*i}(\tau_j) \neq \emptyset$ for $j = 1,..,n$.

  Remark: These conditions determine the succesion of analyzed trees
        with respect to their height.

Time ia

  If the condition A holds then define a function ψ_τ^i according to the procedure I and go to time ib.

687

If the condition B holds then for $\bar{x} \in \prod_{j=1}^{n} \psi^{*i}(\tau_j)$ there may occur three situations:

1. $\psi_u^i(\bar{x})$ is undefined, then define $\psi_u^i(\bar{x})$ with the help of the procedure I and take next $\bar{x}$,

2. $\psi_u^i(\bar{x})$ is defined and the contradiction condition

$\psi_u^i(\bar{x}) \cap (g^i)^{-1}(g^*(\tau)) = \emptyset$ does not hold, then leave $\psi_u^i(\bar{x})$

without change and take next $\bar{x}$

3. $\psi_u^i(\bar{x})$ is defined and the contradiction condition holds, then

create a new state, increase i by 1, modify the functions

ψ_u^{i+1}, ψ^{*i+1}, g^{i+1} according to the procedure II (an automaton

M_{k-1}^{i+1}) and take next $\bar{x}$ from the modified $\prod_j \psi^{*i+1}(\tau_j)$.

If all $\bar{x}$ have been analyzed then set $\psi^{*i} = \bigcup \{\psi_u^i(\bar{x}) | \bar{x} \in \prod_j \psi^{*i}(\tau_j)\}$
and go to time ib.

Time ib

Set $T^i = T^i \cup \{\tau\}$ and check if $\mathfrak{T}_k \subset T^i$. If no, then repeat time
i for a next subtree of a tree t_k without change of the index
i, else set the following as a result of the step k:

$M_k = M_{k-1}^i$ and $T_k = T^i$ and go to step k+1.

Procedure I: Hypothesis Formulation

Result: values of $\psi_{u_1}^i$,.., $\psi_{u_p}^i$

I1. If $\tau \in Ft_k \subset U_0$ then define ψ_τ^i as:

$$\psi_\tau^i = \psi^{*i}(\tau) = \begin{cases} f_{k-1}^*(\tau) \text{ if } f_{k-1}^*(\tau) = f_\tau^{k-1} \neq \emptyset \\ (g^i)^{-1}(g^*(\tau)) \text{ otherwise} \end{cases}$$

I2. If $\tau = u(\tau_1,..,\tau_n)$ and $\psi_u^i(\bar{x})$ is undefined for $\bar{x} \in \prod_j \psi^{*i}(\tau_j)$

set $\psi_u^i(\bar{x}) = (g^i)^{-1}(g^*(\tau))$.

Procedure II: Modification

Result: automaton $M_{k-1}^{i+1} = (X^{i+1}, \psi_{u_1}^{i+1},.., \psi_{u_p}^{i+1}, Y, g^{i+1})$ and the set
of accepted trees T^{i+1} .

II1. Create a new state x_{new}^{i+1} and set $X^{i+1} = X^i \cup \{x_{new}^{i+1}\}$.

II2. Chose any subtree τ_m of a tree τ (if it is possible chose such
τ_m that $\psi^{*i}(\tau_m) \subset X^i - X_0$) and define a function $g^{i+1}: X^{i+1} \to Y$
as follows $g^{i+1}/X^i = g^i$ and $g^{i+1}(x_{new}^{i+1}) = g^*(\tau_m)$...

II3. For every t from T^i, define the value of $\varphi^{*i+1}(t)$ as follows:

$$
\varphi^{*i+1}(t) = \begin{cases}
\{x_{new}^{i+1}\} & \text{for } t = \tau_m \\
\varphi^{*i}(t) & \text{for } t \neq \tau_m \text{ and } t \in Ft_k \text{ or if} \\
& t = u(t_1 \ldots t_n) \text{ then } \varphi^{*i+1}(t_j) = \varphi^{*i}(t_j) \\
& \text{for each } j . \\
(g^{i+1})^{-1}(g^*(t)) & \text{otherwise}
\end{cases}
$$

Using the function $\varphi^{*i+1}(t)$, define new value of the function φ_u as follows:

If $t = u(t_1, \ldots, t_n)$ then for each $\bar{x} \in \prod_j \varphi^{*i+1}(t_j)$ set

$$
\varphi_u^{i+1}(\bar{x}) = \begin{cases}
\varphi_u^i(\bar{x}) & \text{for } \bar{x} \in D(\varphi_u^i) \text{ and } t \neq \tau_m \\
(g^{i+1})^{-1}(g^*(t)) & \text{for } \bar{x} \notin D(\varphi_u^i) \text{ and } t \neq \tau_m \\
\{x_{new}^{i+1}\} & \text{for } t = \tau_m
\end{cases}
$$

If $t \in Ft_k \subset U_0$ then $\varphi_t^{i+1} = \varphi^{*i+1}(t)$

As the set T^{i+1} put the set T^i.

Remark: This procedure does not change the set of accepted trees T^i. Now we will show that our algorithm is correct. At first, one should show that $E \subset g^{**}$. This follows directly from the fact an automaton M_k inferred at the k step $k = 1, \ldots, n$ accepts trees $t_1, \ldots, t_k \in T_k$ from $D(E)$. Next, one should prove that the algorithm possesses the stop property. To do so, it suffices to show that the modification procedure does not lead to the appearance of new contradictions.

Stop property

For every $t = u(t_1, \ldots, t_n) \in T^i$ and for every $\bar{x} \in \prod_j \varphi^{*i+1}(t_j)$ the condition of contradiction: $\varphi_u^{i+1}(x) \cap (g^{i+1})^{-1}(g^*(t)) = \emptyset$ does not hold.

Proof: First, let us notice that for every $t \in T^i$ and for each $\bar{x} \in \prod_j \varphi^{*i}(t_j)$ the following condition holds: $\varphi_u^i(\bar{x}) \cap (g^i)^{-1}(g^*(t)) \neq \emptyset$. In turn, it is easy to observe that for $\bar{x} \in \prod_j \varphi^{*i}(t_j) \cap \prod_j \varphi^{*i+1}(t_j)$, $\varphi_u^{i+1}(\bar{x})$ is equal to $\varphi_u^i(\bar{x})$ or to $\{x_{new}^{i+1}\} \subset (g^{i+1})^{-1}(g^*(t))$ (if $t = \tau_m$). It is also true that $(g^i)^{-1}(g^*(t)) \subset (g^{i+1})^{-1}(g^*(t))$. From these statements it follows that for $\bar{x} \in \prod_j \varphi^{*i}(t_j) \cap \prod_j \varphi^{*i+1}(t_j)$ the thesis of the theorem is valid. Clearly, for another $\bar{x}$ the thesis is also satisfied.
Q.E.D.

As an illustration of this algorithm, consider the following example: Let $U = \{u, v, w, \alpha, \beta\}$ where $r(u) = r(v) = r(w) = 0$, $r(\alpha) = 1$, $r(\beta) = 2$, and let the sample be of the following form: $E = \{(t_1, \bar{t}_1), (t_2, \bar{t}_2)\}$

where $t_1 = \alpha(\beta(\beta(u,v),\beta(w,u)))$, $t_2 = \alpha(\alpha(\beta(\alpha(u), \beta(v,u))))$
$t_1^1 = 0(1(0(0,1),0(0,0)))$ $t_2^1 = 1(0(1(1(0), 0(1,0))))$

Step 0: Result: initial automaton $M_o = (X_o, f_u^o, f_v^o, f_w^o, f_\alpha^o, f_\beta^o, Y, g_o)$ where
$Y = \{0,1\}$, $X_o = \{x_o, x_1\}$, $g_o(x_o) = 0, g_o(x_1) = 1$, $f_u = f_v = f_w = f_\alpha = f_\beta = \emptyset$

Step 1: During this step the tree t_1 is analyzed. The set $\mathcal{T}_1$ is defined
as $\mathcal{T}_1 = u, \mathcal{T}_2 = v, \mathcal{T}_3 = w, \mathcal{T}_4 = \beta(\mathcal{T}_1, \mathcal{T}_2), \mathcal{T}_5 = \beta(\mathcal{T}_3, \mathcal{T}_1), \mathcal{T}_6 = \beta(\mathcal{T}_4, \mathcal{T}_5), \mathcal{T}_7 = \alpha(\mathcal{T}_6)$.

Time 0: initial automaton $M_o^o = (X_o^o, \mathcal{Y}_{uo}^o, \mathcal{Y}_{vo}^o, \mathcal{Y}_{wo}^o, \mathcal{Y}_{\alpha o}^o, \mathcal{Y}_{\beta o}^o, Y, g_o^o) = M_o$.

During the determining of the relation $\mathcal{Y}_{zo}^o$ by the analysis of
the tree $\mathcal{T}_6$ there appears a contradiction. Before the modification procedure the inferred automaton M_o^o is of the following
form: $\mathcal{Y}_{uo}^o = \{x_o\}, \mathcal{Y}_{vo}^o = \{x_1\}, \mathcal{Y}_{wo}^o = \{x_o\}, \mathcal{Y}_{\beta o}^o = \{((x_o, x_1), x_o), ((x_o, x_o),$
$x_o)\}, \mathcal{Y}_{\alpha o}^o = \emptyset$. As a result of the modification procedure one
obtains the automaton M_o^1 where $X_o^1 = \{x_o, x_1, x_2\}$, $g_o^1(x_2) = 0, \mathcal{Y}_{uo}^1 = \{x_o\}$
$\mathcal{Y}_{vo}^1 = \{x_1\}, \mathcal{Y}_{wo}^1 = \{x_o\}, \mathcal{Y}_{\alpha o}^1 = \emptyset, \mathcal{Y}_{\beta o}^1 = \{((x_o, x_1), x_o), ((x_o, x_o), x_2)\}$.

Time 1: During the analysis of successive trees from $\mathcal{T}_1$ there do not
appear any contradictions. As a result of the step 1 one obtains
the automaton $M_1 = (X_1, f_u^1, f_v^1, f_w^1, f_\alpha^1, f_\beta^1, Y, g_1)$ where $X_1 = X_o^1, g_1 = g_o^1$,
$f_u^1 = \{x_o\}, f_v^1 = \{x_1\}, f_w^1 = \{x_o\}, f_\alpha^1 = \{(x_1, x_o), (x_1, x_2)\}, f_\beta^1 = \{((x_o, x_1), x_o),$
$((x_o, x_o), x_2), ((x_o, x_2), x_1)\}$.

Step 2: The tree t_2 is analyzed. Initial data: automaton M_1.

Time 0: initial automaton $M_1^o = M_1$.

During the analysis of the tree $\mathcal{T}_{10} = \beta(\alpha(u), \beta(u,v)) \in \mathcal{T}_2$ which
is used to determine the relation $\mathcal{Y}_{\beta 1}^o$ a contradiction appears.
In order to eliminate this contradiction the value of the tree
$\mathcal{T}_m = \mathcal{T}_8 = \alpha(u)$ is modified by introducing a new state $\dot{x}_3$. The modification procedure produces the following automaton M_1^1 where
$X_1 = \{x_o, x_1, x_2, x_3\}$, and $g_1^1(x_3) = 1$.

Time 1: The analysis of succesive trees do not cause the contradiction
and as the result of the step 2 one obtains the automaton
$M_2 = M_1^1 = (X_2^2, f_u^2, f_v^2, f_w^2, f_\alpha^2, f_\beta^2, Y, g_2)$ where : $X_2 = X_1^1, g_2 = g_1^1$,
$f_u^2 = f_u^1, f_v^2 = f_v^1, f_w^2 = f_w^1, f_\alpha^2 = f_\alpha^1 \cup \{(x_o, x_3), (x_2, x_1), (x_2, x_3), (x_3, x_o), (x_3, x_2)\}$
$f_\beta^2 = f_\beta^1 \cup \{((x_1, x_o), x_o), ((x_1, x_o), x_1), ((x_3, x_o), x_3), ((x_3, x_2), x_1),$
$((x_3, x_2), x_3)\}$.

End - Stop.

It is easy to observe that a transition relation f_u for $u \in U$ depends on the choice of a tree τ_m which is applied in the modification procedure. One should also emphasize that a form of an inferred automaton depends on the succession of analyzed trees from the sample set E.

REFERENCES

1. Luneau P., Richetin M., Cayla C., Robotica, "Sequential learning of automata from input-output behaviour", 7, 1984, pp. 151-159.
2. Booth T.L., Sequential Machines and Automata Theory, Wiley, New York 1968.
3. Fu K.S., Syntactic Pattern Recognition and Applications, Prentice Hall, Englewood Cliffs, New York 1982.
4. Veelenturf L.P.Y., IEEE Trans. on Computers, "Inference of sequential machines from sample computations", 27, 1978, pp. 167-170.
5. Biermann A.W., IEEE Trans. on Syst. Man and Cybern,,'The inference of regular LISP programs from examples', 8, 1978, pp. 585-600.
6. Culik K., Salomaa A., Wood D., RAIRO Theoretical Informatics, "Systolic tree acceptors", 18, 1984, pp. 53-68.
7. Gecseg F., Steinby M., Tree Automata, Akademiai Kiado, Budapest, 1984
8. Gonzalez R.G., Edwards J.J., Thomason M.G., Intern. J. of Comp. and Inform. Science, "An algorithm for the inference of tree grammars", 5, 1976, pp. 145-164
9. Fu K.S., J. of Chinese Institute of Engineers, "Inference of hihg dimensional grammars", 1, 1977, pp. 64-73.
10. Jacak W., Sierocki I., Reports of Institute of Techn. Cybern. Technical University of Wrocław, "On determining the k-th Nerode equivalence for tree automata inference", 77, 1985.
11. Brainerd W.S., Information and Control, "Tree generating regular systems", 14, 1969, pp. 217-231.

MULTIRATE ADAPTIVE CONTROL FOR LATERAL DYNAMICS OF AIRCRAFTS

by I. Eiguren, P. Esgueva, and M. de la Sen.
Departamento de Física
Facultad de Ciencias
Universidad del País Vasco, Spain

ABSTRACT. In this paper, we apply multirate adaptive control to the lateral dynamics of an aircraft by making use of the projection algorithm of Goodwin, Ramadge, and Caines. The algorithm is modified for the use of two inputs (namely, aileron deflection and rudder deflection) being sampled at different rates. An appropriate selection of the sampling periods can attenuate the effects of additive output disturbances.

Numerical results have been obtained by computer simulation of the "F-8" airplane dynamics.

1. INTRODUCTION

We turn our attention to the multirate adaptive control of linear, time invariant, deterministic systems. The basic formulation of this work involves the idea of considering two or more system parameter vectors being estimated at diffetent sampling intervals. For this reason, the projection algorithm (Goodwin G.C., P.J. Ramadge, P.E. Caines, 1980) is modified for parameter estimation and obtention of control inputs. Its convergence and stability properties are proved.

A practical application for multiple sample rate control systems arises from the study of aricraft dynamics. In this paper simulation results of our multirate control design are obtained for the lateral dynamics of the "F-8" airplane. The variable to be controlled is the airplane yaw rate by using two control channels. One control channel, U_f (aileron deflection), is updated at a fast rate, T^{-1} samples per second; and the other U_s (rudder deflection), is calculated at a slower rate, $(LT)^{-1}$ samples per second, with L being an appropriate positive integer which must be chosen in accordance with the technical constraints of the on-board computer. The results of the simulation show that a better steady-state performances for the accumulated regulation error are achieved with the combined multirate design in the presence of additive output disturbances if the

693

R. Trappl (ed.), Cybernetics and Systems '86, 693–700.
© *1986 by D. Reidel Publishing Company.*

sampling periods are appropriately selected.

The paper is organized as follows:
The structure of a multirate adaptive controller for the case of two sample rates is shown in section 2. Aeronautic terms related to the airplane dynamics, are recalled in section 3. Computer simulation is presented in section 4, under two headings:
- "F-8" equations and characteristics of simulation (4.1)
- Simulation results and performance of the design (4.2)
(the behaviour of the scheme against errors in the output measurements is also illustrated in this section).
Conclusions are given in section 5.

2. MULTIRATE ADAPTIVE CONTROL

Consider a continuous time-invariant plant described by the equation
$$\dot{\underline{X}} = F\underline{X} + G_f U_f + G_s U_s \tag{2-1}$$
Where $\underline{X}$ stands for the n-state vector, U_f stands for the scalar fast test control input, U_s stands for the scalr slowest control input. With a little effort the above equation could be transformed to obtain the discretized input-output equation in the d-step predictor form:
$$Y(t+d) = \alpha(q^{-1})Y(t) + \beta_f(q^{-1})\,U_f(t) + \beta_s(q^{-1})\,U_s(t) \tag{2.2}$$
Where q^{-1} is the backward shift operator correspondent to the shortest period (i.e., $q^{-1} U_s(t+1) = U_s(t)$).

Let us define the parameter and measure vectors as follows:
$$\theta^T = (\alpha_0 \cdots \alpha_n \beta_0^f \cdots \beta_m^f, \beta_0^s \cdots \beta_{m2}^s)$$
$$\phi^T(t) = (Y(t)\ldots Y(t-n)U_f(t)\ldots U_f(t-m_1)\,U_s(t)\ldots U_s(t-m_2)) \tag{2.3}$$
Eqn. (2-2) can be written in a more compact way by using (2-3) as follows:
$$Y(t+d) = \theta^T \phi(t) \tag{2.4}$$
Note that one of the two sampling periods is L times greater than the other one which is the base sampling period. This circumstance is not introduced in the notation of equations (2-2) through (2-4) in order to not complicate it. Due to presence of two inputs we could use two parameter estimators in order to implement an adaptive control scheme for the system eqn. (2.1).

The updating schemes of the adaptive controller are :

$$\hat{\theta}_1(t) = \hat{\theta}_1(t-1) + \frac{a_1(t)\,\phi(t-d)\,\phi^T(t-d)\,\tilde{\theta}_1(t-1)}{c_1(t) + \phi^T(t-d)\,\phi(t-d)} \tag{2.5}$$

$$\hat{\theta}_2(t) = \hat{\theta}_2(t'-L) + \frac{a_2(t')\,\phi(t'-d)\,\phi^T(t'-d)\,\tilde{\theta}_2(t'-L)}{c_2(t') + \phi^T(t'-d)\,\phi(t'-d)}$$

With $t' = Lt$ and t represents a generic sampling instant for the base period.
The control law is obtained from the equations:

694

$$Y^x(t+d) = \hat{\theta}_1^T(t)\,\phi(t); \text{ with } U_s(t)=U_s(t-1) \text{ for } t \neq t' \tag{2-6a}$$

$$\begin{cases} Y^x(t+d) = \hat{\theta}_1^T(t)\,\phi(t) \\ \\ Y^x(t+d) = \hat{\theta}_2^T(t)\,\phi(t) \end{cases} ; \text{ for } t=t' \tag{2.6b}$$

Where Y^x is the bounded reference sequence. At shortest sampling points the fast input ($U_f(t)$) is obtained from eqn (2-6a) taking $U_s(t)=U_s(t-1)$, where $U_s(t)$ is the slow control input. The fast and slow inputs at largest sampling points ($U_f(t')$, $U_s(t')$) follow from eqns (2.6b), These last equations (2-6b) could not have a well-posed solution from a mathematical point of view. If this happends, we get $U_s(t')$ from eqn (2-6a) taking $U_f(t')=U_f(t'-1)$.

Thus, under the following hypothesis and "a priori" knowledge
A-1 $0 < a_1(t) < 2;\ i=1,2$
A-2 $c_1(t) > 0;\ i=1,2$
A-3 The system to be adapted is a minimum phase one (this is to say in a more appropriate way, it has a stable inverse).
A-4 The reference sequence $Y^x(t)$ is bounded.
A-5 In the non-deterministic case, it is assumed that lower and upper bounds for the frequency of an additive output sinusoidal disturbance are know.

We can get the following convergence properties (the proofs are not presented by space limitation reasons)

i) $\|\tilde{\theta}_1(t)\|^2 - \|\tilde{\theta}_1(t-1)\|^2 \leq 0$

ii) $\lim\limits_{t\to\infty} \dfrac{e^2(t)}{c_1(t) + \phi^T(t-d)\,\phi(t-d)} = 0$

iii) $\lim\limits_{t\to\infty} \|\hat{\theta}_1(t) - \hat{\theta}_1(t-1)\| = 0$

iv) $\|\tilde{\theta}_2(t')\|^2 - \|\tilde{\theta}_2(t'-L)\|^2 \leq 0$

v) $\lim\limits_{t\to\infty} \dfrac{[\phi^T(t'-d)\,\tilde{\theta}_2(t'-L)]^2}{c_2(t') + \phi^T(t'-d)\,\phi(t'-d)} = 0$

vi) $\lim\limits_{t\to\infty} \|\hat{\theta}_2(t') - \hat{\theta}_2(t'-L)\| = 0$

vii) $\lim\limits_{t\to\infty} \dfrac{\varepsilon(t)}{[c_1(t) + \phi^T(t-d)\,\phi(t-d)]^{1/2}} = 0$

viii) $\|\phi(t-d)\| \leq C_1' + C_2' \max\limits_{0 \leq \tau \leq t} |\varepsilon(\tau)|$

ix) $\lim\limits_{t\to\infty} \varepsilon(t) = 0$

695

x) $\|\phi(t-d)\|$ is bounded

xi) $\lim\limits_{t \to \infty} e(t) = 0$

xii) $\lim\limits_{t \to \infty} \sum\limits_{i=0}^{t-1} e^2(i)$ is bounded

Note that results of Goodwin, Ramadge, and Caines (Adaptive filtering, prediction and control, 1984), are generalized (properties (i) through (xii)) for the multirate adaptive control case mutatis-mutandis. Thus, the scheme has all the classical suitable properties

3. AERONAUTIC TERMINOLOGY

Here we describe briefly planes balancer systems, which allows the plane to maneouver around the three spatial axis:

(1) OX is the plane longitudinal axis, towards the fuselage.
(2) OY is the plane transversal axis
(3) OZ with OX and OY defines a direct thriedron, its vertex is the gravity centre.
The terminology involved is:
- A rotation around OX axis is called "Roll"
- A rotation around OY axis is called "Pitch"
- A rotation around OZ axis is called "Yaw"
    The maneuvers regarded to the lateral dynamics of planes are carried through the ailerons and the direction rudder. The ailerons control the airplane maneouver around its longitudinal axis. The direction rudder controls the airplane movements around its vertical axis.
Litle variations of course requires the combinate action of direction rudder and ailerons, however, greater changes of course only needs the direction rudder action. In this case the plane maintains its transversal plane of flight.

4. COMPUTER SIMULATION

4.1 "F-8" plane equations and characteristics of simulations

For the computers simulation in this paper, we use the lateral dynamics of an "F-8" aircraft described by the following equations under the flight conditions, h=20000 feet, =0.078 rad (equilibrium angle of attack, V_o= 620 ft/sec (total equilibrium velocity).

$$\frac{d}{dt} \begin{bmatrix} p \\ r \\ B \\ \phi \end{bmatrix} = \begin{bmatrix} -2.6 & 0.25 & -38 & 0 \\ -0.075 & -0.27 & 4.4 & 0 \\ -0.078 & -0.99 & -0.23 & 0.05 \\ 1 & 0.078 & 0 & 0 \end{bmatrix} \begin{bmatrix} p \\ r \\ B \\ \phi \end{bmatrix} + \begin{bmatrix} 17 & 7 \\ 0.82 & -3.2 \\ 0 & 0.046 \\ 0 & 0 \end{bmatrix} \begin{bmatrix} U_p \\ U_s \end{bmatrix}$$

$$(4.1-1)$$

with
   P: roll rate
   r: yaw rate
   β: sideslip angle
   ϕ: pitch attitude
   U_f: aileron deflection
   U_s: rudder deflection

Our claim is to control the yaw rate by means of a multirate adaptive control. Discretizing the plant equations with a base period of 0.65 seconds, one gets:

$$Y(t+1)= Y(t)-0.667\ Y(t-1)+ 0.775\ Y(t-2)-0.084\ Y(t-3)+ 0.399\ U_f(t)$$
$$-0.0337\ U_f(t-1)+0.129\ U_f(t-2)-0.184\ U_f(t-3)-1.336\ U_s(t)+$$

$$1.992\ U_s(t-1)-1.124\ U_s(t-2)+0.113\ U_s(t-3) \qquad (4.1-2)$$

Where $Y(t)$ is $r(t)$, the yaw rate. The time delay for this specific plant is 1 $(d=1)$, and the stable inverse condition imposed by assumption A-3 is verified for a base period ranging between 0.51 and 1.01 seconds. For the simulation the initial values of the system parameters are changed in a 5% from the real ones. The range of the rudder input is maintained bounded by using a saturation of a unytary step.

A periodic signal is added to the output for testing the capacity of filtering sensor measurement errors of the multirate design $(\Lambda(t))$. This is one of the main reasons for the use of two controllers with two sampling periods. The other reason is that the rudder and aileron rates are different in practice.

$$Y(t+1) = \theta^T \phi(t)\ \text{real output}$$

$$Y'(t+1)= Y(t+1) + \Lambda(t+1);\ \text{output measured by the algorithm} \qquad (4.1-3)$$

with $\Lambda(t)= 0.008\ \text{sen}\ \dfrac{\Pi t}{4} + 0.001\ \text{sen}\ \dfrac{\Pi t}{16}$

$t=$number of sampling $(0,1,2,3,4,\ldots)$

Note that the faster controller has as main objective to accelerate the transient behaviour while the slowest one must filter the noise effects. This must be tajen into account when choosing the relative values of these sampling periods related to the forecasts on the possible additve output noise. The slowest controller must have small gains at the beginning of the adaptation process in order not to lead to excessive input-output peaks. The values of algorithm parameters are $a_1=1.5$, $a_2=0.5$, $c_1=5$

$$c_2(t) = \begin{cases} c_2(t-1).\ 0.95\ ,\ \text{if}\ c_1 < c_2(t-1) \\ a_2(t-1)\qquad\ ,\ \text{if}\ c_1 \geqslant c_2(t-1) \end{cases} \quad \text{with}\ c_2(0)=500$$

4.2 Simulation results

Figures 4.2-1, 4.2-2, 4.2-3, and 4,2-4 illustrate the performances

697

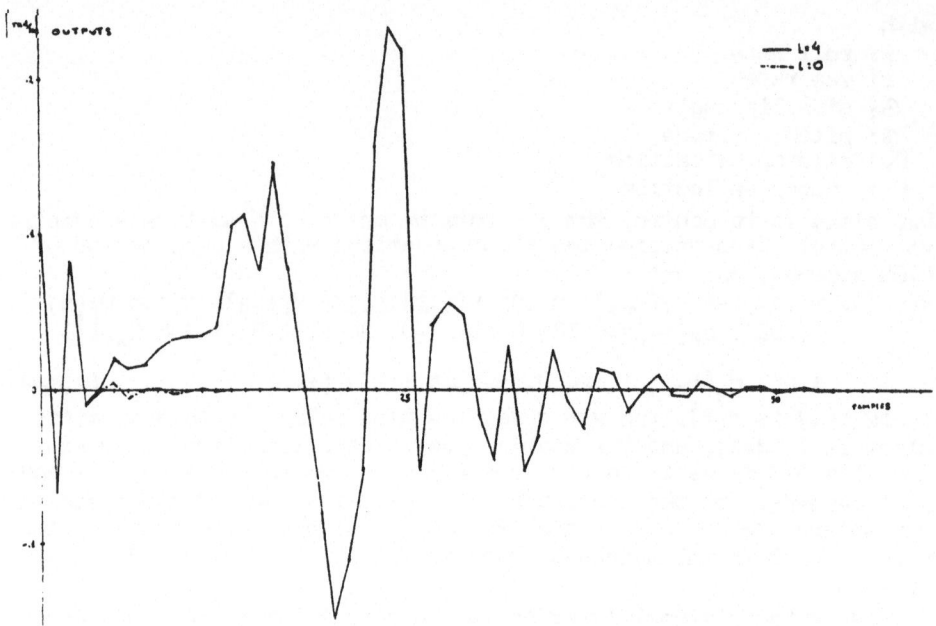

Fig.4.2-1   Real outputs using algorithms (2-5) and control law
            (2-6a, b), without considering errors in output measures.

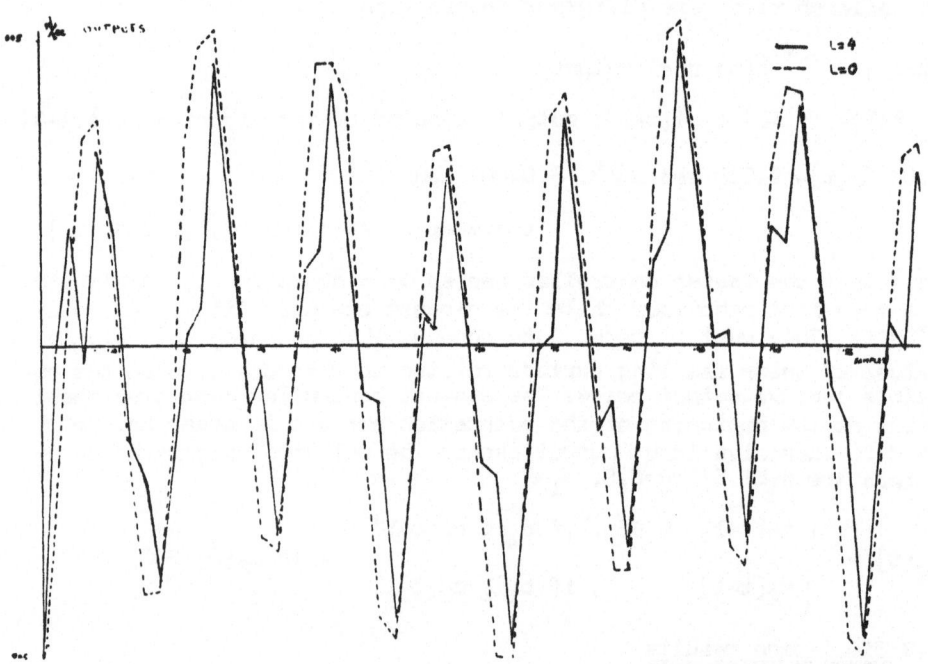

Fig. 4.2-3 Steady-state behaviour, case of additive output noise,

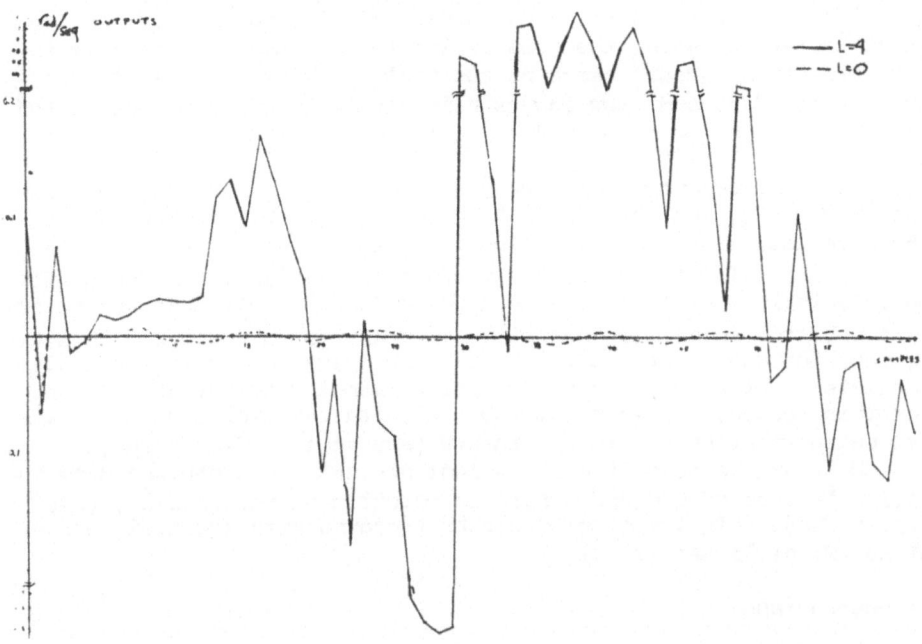

Fig. 4.2-2 Adaptation transient behaviour using algorithms (2-5) and control law (2-6a,b), considering an additive output noise (4.1-3)

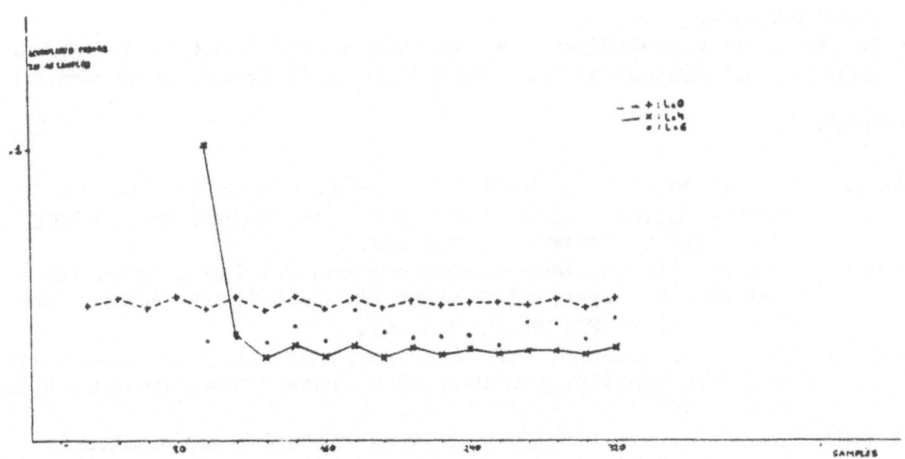

Fig. 4.2-4 Case of additive output noise.

of the multirate adaptive control with L=0 and L=4 used for regulation $(Y^*(t))=0)$. The case L=0 involves only the control of the fast
input (ailerons) using the base period (0.65 seconds), the slow input (direction rudder) reamains constant. Case L=4 implies the control of the fast and slow inputs using respectively the base period
(T=0.65 sec for the fast input) and another period of T and T_S values has been motivated by the knowledge of lower and upper bounds
for the additive output disturbances frequency (4.1-3). In both cases (L=0, L=4), the initial disturbance is Y(0)=0.1 rad/sec and the
characteristics of the simulation heve been shown in section 4.1.

As shown in figure 4.2-1 a perfect regulation is achieved after
an acceptable transient behaviour. When there is not measurement errors a better regulation objective is achieved for case L=0 than case L=4. The choice of ratio L equal four leads to update the system
parameter vector $\hat{\Theta}_2$ when the additive output disturbance is zero.
For this reason, the multirate control with L=4 yields better filtered measurement errors than when L=0 (see Figs. 4.2-3, 4.2-4).

However the adaptation transient presents an important deterioration in case of L=4 and errors in output measures (4.1-3), (see
Fig. 4.2-2). This transient could be improved with aperiodic sam -
pling (M. de la Sen 1984).

5. CONCLUSIONS

The experimental study reported in this paper provides the following
significant conclusions:
- Regulation and tracking objectives have been achieved for multirate adaptive control.
- Errors in sensor measures can be filtered in part by appropriately selecting the L ratio (for instance, L=4) between the two sampling periods.
- We economize calculation time, because second input U_s is controlled each LT seconds instead each T as U_f (T is the base period).

REFERENCES

Douglas P. Glasson (1981). Research in multirate estination and con-
        trol - Optimal sample rate selection. Report No. TR-1356 of
        the analytic sciences corporation.
Jarrel R. Elliot (1977). NASA s advanced control law program for the
        F-8 digital fly-by-wire aircraft. IEEE Trans. Autom. Con-
        trol, Vol. AC-22, No.5, 753-757.
Goodwin G.C., P.J. Ramadge, P.E. Caines (1980). Discrete time multi-
        variable adaptive control. IEEE Trans Autom. Control, Vol.
        AC-25, 449.
Goodwin G,C., K.S. Sin (1984). "Adaptive filtering and control".
        Prentice Hall.
M. de la Sen (1984). A new modelling for aperiodic sampling systems.
        Int. J. Systems, Vol.15, No. 3, 315-328.

SYMBOLIC ALGORITHM FOR OBSERVING THE STATES OF A CLASS OF NONLINEAR
SYSTEMS

Mladen Luksic
Division of Mathematics, Computer Science, and Systems Design
The University of Texas at San Antonio
San Antonio, Texas 78285
USA

ABSTRACT. The problem of estimating the states of a class of nonlinear
systems is considered. Necessary and sufficient conditions for existence
of such method, along with a constructive, computer implementable algorithm are presented.

1. Introduction

Nonlinear systems appear in model design of many complex engineering
problems (robotics, aircraft control, spacecraft maneuvering, attitude
control of rotating satellites, etc.). An extensive work of many researchers shows that nonlinear systems differ significantly from their linear counterparts. In particular, it seems that many of their properties
depend on a certain geometric structure, which in return, represents a
serious difficulty when practical implementations are needed.

One of the problems that has received a lot of attention lately is
the construction of a state observer for nonlinear systems. The parameters describing the functioning of the system may not be accessible for
direct measurement. Therefore, it is important to estimate the actual
states of the system based on some available outputs. Such methods for
linear systems are well-known ([2]), and can be implemented using algorithms with predictable numerical behavior.

The purpose of this paper is to introduce a new algorithm for observing the states of a class of nonlinear control systems with outputs.
The systems considered are those that are locally state space equivalent
to time invariant linear controllable and observable systems under the
conditions of Hunt, Luksic and Su ([5]). (Also [7], [8], [9]). These
conditions classify the adequate group of nonlinear systems and, when
placed in the linear setting, they implement themselves naturally into
the algorithm for asymptotic estimator for linear systems.

As mentioned earlier, the dependence on the geometric structure represents a problem in the numerical work. Fortunately, with the development of computer software capable of symbolic computations, this problem
can be avoided, and numerical instability of the method kept at the level not higher then the one known for linear systems.

701

R. Trappl (ed.), Cybernetics and Systems '86, 701–708.
© *1986 by D. Reidel Publishing Company.*

2. Preliminaries

Consider the nonlinear control system with outputs

$$\dot{x}(t) = f(x(t)) + \sum_{i=1}^{m} g_i(x(t))u_i(t)$$

$$y(t) = h(x(t)) = (h_1(x(t)),\ldots, h_p(x(t))) \qquad (2.1)$$

$$x_0 = x(0)$$

where f, $g_1,\ldots, g_m$ are real analytic vector fields defined on a connected analytic n-dimensional manifold M. Also, h: M $\rightarrow$ N is an analytic output map, where N is a p-dimensional analytic manifold.

Definition 2.1   The system (2.1) is (locally) state space equivalent to a linear time invariant system

$$\dot{w}(t) = Aw(t) + Bv(t)$$

$$z(t) = Cw(t) \qquad (2.2)$$

$$w_0 = w(0)$$

if there exists a local, nonsingular, smooth coordinate transformation $w = T(x)$ taking (2.1) to (2.2). Here, A, B, and C are n $\times$ n, n $\times$ m and p $\times$ n constant matrices, respectively.

The inputs (controls) u_i, i = 1,..., m of (2.1) are not affected by the state space coordinate change. Hence we can take $(u_1, u_2,\ldots, u_m)^{tr}$ to be the input vector v in (2.2). Here, tr indicates the transpose.

Definition 2.2   The linear system (2.2) is controllable and observable if its controllability and observability matrices

$$W = [B\ AB\ \ldots\ A^{n-1}B] \quad \text{and} \quad V = [C^{tr}\ (CA)^{tr}\ \ldots\ (CA^{n-1})^{tr}]^{tr}$$

have rank n. Here, A, B and C are as in (2.2).

Definition 2.3   The (full-dimensional) asymptotic estimator (observer) for the system (2.2) is the linear, time invariant system

$$\dot{\hat{w}} = (A - LC)\hat{w} + Lz + Bu, \quad \hat{w}_0 = \hat{w}(0) \qquad (2.3)$$

where A, B, C, u and z are as in (2.2), L is a constant n $\times$ p matrix and $\hat{w}_0$ is an arbitrary initial condition ([10]).

The error $e = w - \hat{w}$ which measures the difference between the actual and the estimated states shows an exponential behavior. This may cause problems if noises are present in the system (11). To simplify the discussion, we will assume that systems considered in the rest of the text are noise free.

<u>Definition 2.4</u> For C^∞ vector fields f and g on a manifold M, the Lie bracket, $[f, g]$, is given by

$$[f, g] = \frac{\partial f}{\partial x} g - \frac{\partial g}{\partial x} f$$

where $\frac{\partial f}{\partial x}$ and $\frac{\partial g}{\partial x}$ are Jacobian matrices. The successive Lie brackets are given by

$$(ad^0 f, g) = g, \quad (ad^k f, g) = [f, (ad^{k-1} f, g)], \quad k = 1, 2, \ldots .$$

<u>Definition 2.5</u> For a C^∞ real valued function h and a C^∞ vector field f on a manifold M, the Lie derivative of function h with respect to vector field f, $L_f h$, is given by

$$L_f h = < dh, f >$$

where dh is the gradient of h and $<\cdot,\cdot>$ denotes the dual product of one-forms and vector fields. The higher order Lie derivatives of h with respect to f are given by

$$L_f^0 h = h, \quad L_f^k h = L_f L_f^{k-1} h, \quad k = 1, 2, \ldots .$$

Also, given another C^∞ vector field g, the mixed derivatives, $L_g L_f^k h$, for $k = 0, 1, 2, \ldots$, are given by

$$< dL_f^k h, g > .$$

<u>Theorem 2.1</u> (4 , 11) Let f, g_i, $i = 1, \ldots, m$, and h be as in (2.1). Suppose that there exist nonnegative integers $\kappa_1, \kappa_2, \ldots, \kappa_m$ and $\beta_1, \beta_2, \ldots, \beta_p$ such that

(i) $\kappa_1 + \ldots + \kappa_m = n$ and the vector fields g_1, (adf, g_1),

$\ldots, (ad^{\kappa_1 - 1} f, g_1), \ldots, g_m, (adf, g_m), \ldots, (ad^{\kappa_m - 1} f, g_m)$

are linearly independent at each point x near x_0.

(ii) $\beta_1 + \ldots + \beta_p = n$ and the one-forms dh_1, $dL_f h_1, \ldots,$

$dL_f^{\beta_1 - 1} h_1, \ldots, dh_p, dL_f h_p, \ldots, dL_f^{\beta_p - 1} h_p$ are linearly

independent at each point x near x_0.

Then, the system (2.1) is state space equivalent to a controllable and observable linear time invariant system if and only if there exist constants c_{ijk} with

$$L_{g_i} L_f^k h_j = c_{ijk},$$

where $k = 0, 1, \ldots, \kappa_i + \beta_j - 1$, for $i = 1, \ldots, m$ and $j = 1, \ldots, p$.

The conditions (i) and (ii) may seem restrictive at first, but they are usually present in the systems model design. In fact, in engineering literature they are often quoted as generic. ([3], [6])

3. Observing Algorithm

For the sake of simplicity we will describe only the single-variable case. The result for the multi-variable case can be found in ([11]).

In the single-variable case $m = p = 1$. Then, (2.1) becomes

$$\dot{x}(t) = f(x(t)) + g(x(t))u(t)$$

$$y(t) = h(x(t)) \tag{3.1}$$

$$x_0 = x(0)$$

where f and g are real analytic vector fields defined on a connected analytic n-dimensional manifold M and h: $M \rightarrow \mathbb{R}$ is an analytic output map.

<u>Corollary 3.1</u> (4 , 11) Let f, g and h be as in (3.1). Suppose that

(i') the vector fields g, (adf, g),..., $(ad^{n-1}f, g)$ are linearly independent at each x near x_0.

(ii') the one-forms dh, $dL_f h$,..., $dL_f^{n-1}h$ are linearly independent at each point x near x_0.

Then the system (3.1) is state space equivalent to a controllable and observable linear time invariant system if and only if there exist constants c_k with

$$L_g L_f^k h = c_k$$

where $k = 0, 1,..., 2n-1$.

The coordinate transformation, $w = T(x)$, which realizes the equivalence is given by $w_i(x) = L_f^{i-1}h(x)$, $i = 1,..., n$. It converts (3.1) to (2.2) with

$$A = \begin{bmatrix} 0 & 1 & 0 & \cdots & 0 \\ 0 & 0 & 1 & \cdots & 0 \\ \vdots & \vdots & \vdots & & \vdots \\ -a_n & -a_{n-1} & -a_{n-2} & \cdots & -a_1 \end{bmatrix}, \quad B = \begin{bmatrix} b_n \\ b_{n-1} \\ \vdots \\ b_1 \end{bmatrix} \quad \text{and } C = (1\ 0\ \ldots\ 0)$$

where $b_1,..., b_n$ are some constants and $a_1,..., a_n$ are the coefficients of the characteristic polynomial $\det(\lambda I-A) = \lambda^n + a_1\lambda^{n-1} + ... + a_n$ of A. A surprising fact is that the coefficients $a_1,..., a_n$ are the solutions of the linear system of equations

$$c_0 a_1 + c_1 a_2 + \cdots c_{n-1} a_n = c_n$$
$$c_1 a_1 + c_2 a_2 + \cdots c_n a_n = c_{n+1}$$
$$\vdots \qquad \vdots \qquad \vdots \qquad \vdots \qquad (3.2)$$
$$c_{n-1} a_1 + c_n a_2 + \cdots c_{2n-2} a_n = c_{2n-1}$$

The single-variable system

$$\dot{w} = Aw + Bu$$

$$z = Cw \qquad (3.3)$$

$$w_0 = w(0)$$

generated in Corollary 3.1 can be transformed into its canonical observable form

$$\dot{\bar{w}} = \bar{A}\,\bar{w} + \bar{B}u$$

$$\bar{z} = \bar{C}\,\bar{w} \qquad (3.4)$$

$$\bar{w} = \bar{w}(0)$$

where

$$\bar{A} = \begin{bmatrix} 0 & 0 & \cdots & 0 & -a_n \\ 1 & 0 & \cdots & 0 & -a_{n-1} \\ \vdots & \vdots & & \vdots & \vdots \\ 0 & 0 & \cdots & 1 & -a_1 \end{bmatrix}, \quad \bar{B} = \begin{bmatrix} \bar{b}_n \\ \bar{b}_{n-1} \\ \vdots \\ \bar{b}_1 \end{bmatrix}, \quad \bar{C} = (0 \ \ 0 \ \cdots \ 0 \ \ 1),$$

and $\bar{b}_1, \bar{b}_2, \ldots, \bar{b}_n$ are some constants ([2]). This transformation is established by the following relations: $\bar{A} = PAP^{-1}$, $\bar{B} = PB$ and $\bar{C} = CP^{-1}$. Here, $P = \bar{V}^{-1}V$, where V and $\bar{V}$ are observability matrices for (3.3) and (3.4), respectively.

A simple calculation shows that $V = I$, the identity matrix, and

$$\bar{V} = \begin{bmatrix} 0 & 0 & \cdots & 0 & s_1 \\ 0 & 0 & \cdots & s_1 & s_2 \\ \vdots & \vdots & & \vdots & \vdots \\ s_1 & s_2 & \cdots & s_{n-1} & s_n \end{bmatrix}$$

where

705

$$s_1 = 1, \quad s_i = (-a_i) + \sum_{k=1}^{i-1} (-a_{i-k})s_k, \quad i = 2,\ldots, n. \qquad (3.5)$$

Now, the problem of finding P^{-1} reduces to calculating $\overline{V}$, which, using (3.5), is numerically more stable than calculating the inverse of a matrix.

Notice that if L is as in (2.3), and $\overline{L} = PL$, then $A - LC$ and $\overline{A} - \overline{L}C$ have the same eigenvalues. Since L can be chosen arbitrarily, we can assign arbitrary eigenvalues to the matrix $\overline{A} - \overline{L}C$. Let its characteristic polynomial be $\lambda^n + \sigma_1\lambda^{n-1} + \ldots + \sigma_n$. If we take $\overline{L} = (\sigma_n - a_n,\ldots, \sigma_1 - a_1)^{tr}$ then

$$\overline{A} - \overline{L}\,\overline{C} = \begin{bmatrix} 0 & 0 & \ldots & 0 & -\sigma_n \\ 1 & 0 & \ldots & 0 & -\sigma_{n-1} \\ \vdots & \vdots & & \vdots & \vdots \\ 0 & 0 & & 1 & \sigma_1 \end{bmatrix},$$

hence, $A - LC$ has arbitrarily chosen eigenvalues.

Finally, we can present the algorithm.

Algorithm 3.1

Step 1: Determine whether or not the conditions $L_g L_f^k h = c_k$, $k = 0,1,$ $\ldots$, 2n-1 are satisfied for the system (3.1). If not, the linearization as described in Corollary 3.1 cannot be completed and consequently, the state observer cannot be built.

Step 2: Determine $a_1,\ldots, a_n$ by solving the system of linear equations (3.2) where c_0, $c_1,\ldots, c_{2n-1}$ are generated in Step 1.

Step 3: Form $P^{-1} = \overline{V}$ by using (3.5).

Step 4: Choose n complex numbers $\lambda_1,\ldots, \lambda_n$ with negative real parts to be the eigenvalues of $\overline{A} - \overline{L}\,\overline{C}$ and calculate the coefficients $\sigma_1, \sigma_2,\ldots, \sigma_n$ of the polynomial $P(\lambda) = (\lambda - \lambda_1) \ldots (\lambda - \lambda_n)$.

Step 5: Determine $L = P^{-1}(\sigma_n - a_n,\ldots, \sigma_1 - a_1)^{tr}$.

Step 6: Solve the system

$$\dot{\hat{w}} = (A - LC)\,\hat{w} + Lz + Bu, \quad \hat{w}_0 = \hat{w}(0)$$

where A, B, C, z, u are as in (3.3) and $\hat{w}_0$ is an arbitrary initial condition.

Step 7:   Determine $x(t) = T^{-1}(w(t))$. Here, $x(t)$ is the estimated state
          of the nonlinear system

The coordinate transformation T is not, in general, linear. Thus,
it may not be always possible to find an explicit relation $x = T^{-1}(w)$.
If this is the case, we have to apply one of the standard numerical methods for function inversions. In practice, an observer is often used in
combination with control generator. Since the controls are not affected
by state space coordinate change, it usually suffices to observe the
system from the w-coordinate system. Then, the inverse T^{-1} is not needed.
    We have applied the algorithm for the single-variable and multi-va-
riable case in simulations of real-life examples. The symbolic algebraic computations were performed in MACSYMA on VAX 11/780 ([11]).

4. Conclusion and Future Research

The method for observing the states just presented depends on the fact
that the state equivalence is a local property. This means that a non-
singular, smooth coordinate change $w = T(x)$ exists only near x_0. To be
more precise, there are neighborhoods U of x_0 and W of w_0 such that $w_0 =$
$T(x_0)$ and $W = T(U)$. A possible problem is that an arbitrarily chosen i-
nitial state for the observer, $\hat{w}_0$, may not belong to the closure of W.
Then there exists a neighborhood $\hat{W}$ of $\hat{w}_0$, disjoint from W and the inverse $T^{-1}(\hat{w}(t))$ may not be defined. However, in practice, an observer is
used for estimating inaccessible states, so a proper design always provides a good approximation of at least one initial state, say w_0. Then,
the problem described above can be overcome by choosing $\hat{w}_0$ close to w_0.

    In engineering applications this can be interpreted as having a pro-
cess with several tasks (states). Often, these tasks differ in nature
(for example, moving arm and then rotating wrist, in control of a robot
arm). At each state a different model is employed and the problem can be
considered as the sequence of subproblems for which there is a good chance that mathematically generated neighborhoods will be sufficiently large. Notice that the initial state x_0, and consequently, every other state, were taken at time $t = 0$. However, there is no restriction on any
other later time, i.e., initial state can happen at any $\tau > 0$.
    If we look back at the algorithm, and if a simulation consists of a
single stage, all steps (except possibly Step 7), can be prepared prior
to execution. However, if the operation consists of several stages,
there will be several initial states, which means that the simulation
has to be synchronized with the operation of the system. Since our algorithm favors symbolic calculations, this synchronization calls for the
ability of doing symbolic manipulations in real time. Notoriously slow
execution of such computer operations is still a big problem. Improvements in this direction represent an open field for research in computer
and symbolic software engineering.

707

Similar problem occurs if the locality on which linearization is possible is not large enough for a single operation state. Then the analyticity of the objects involved and paracompactness of manifolds allow us to consider a sequence of localities, and the problem becomes similar to the one with several stages. However, an ideal solution would be to find necessary and sufficient conditions to generate an algorithm for global linearization. Although some progress has been made in this direction ([1]), many issues of global analysis of nonlinear systems are stil open problems.

5. References

[1]   Ayels, D., 'Global Observability of Morse-Smale Vector Fields' preprint, 1976.

[2]   Chen, C.T., Linear System Theory and Design, HRW Series in Electrical and Computer Engineering, 2nd Ed., CBS College Publishing, 1984.

[3]   Hunt, L.R., Su, R. and Meyer, G., 'Design for Multi-Input Nonlinear Systems', Differential Geometric Control Theory, Birkhauser, Boston, R.W. Brockett, R.S. Millman and H.J. Sussman eds., 27(1983), 268-298.

[4]   Hunt, L.R., Luksic, M. and Su, R., 'Recognizing Linear Systems' Proceedings of 23rd Conference on Decision and Control, Las Vegas, Nevada, December 1984.

[5]   Hunt, L.R., Luksic, M. and Su, R., 'Exact Linearizations of Input-Output Systems', International Journal of Control, to appear.

[6]   Hunt, L.R., Su, R. and Luksic, M., 'Nonlinear Input-Output Systems', International Journal of Control, to appear.

[7]   Isidori, A., 'The Matching of a Prescribed Linear Input-Output Behavior in a Nonlinear System', preprint, 1983.

[8]   Krener, A.J. and Respondek, W., 'Linearization by Output Injection and Nonlinear Observers', System and Control Letters, 3(1983), pp. 419-431.

[9]   Krener, A.J. and Respondek, W., 'Nonlinear Observers with Linearizable Error Dynamics', preprint, 1984

[10]   Luenberger, D.G., 'Oserving the States of s Linear System', IEEE Transactions on Military Electronics, Vol. Mil-8, pp. 74-80, 1964.

[11]   Luksic, M., 'Nonlinear Observers', Ph.D. Dissertation, Texas Tech University Press, December 1984

COORDINATION OF CONCURRENT PROCESSES: AUTOMATIC PROGRAM SYNTHESIS

Z. Banaszak
Institute of Technical Cybernetics
Wrocław Technical University
ul. Janiszewskiego 11/17, 50-372 Wrocław
Poland

ABSTRACT. This paper deals with the Petri net approach to the automatic synthesis of a control procedure ensuring deadlock-free coordination of concurrently flowing processes. The control programs are represented by net models derived with the help of an algorithm transforming the given process specification into the related net model of processing. The main result of the paper concerns the necessary conditions which should be satisfied in the course of net models synthesis. Presented approach to automatic design of net models reflecting required behaviour of concurrently flowing processes can be applied to designing errorless logical controllers as well as computer aided planning systems.

1. INTRODUCTION

Problems arising in the field of the control system design for concurrently acting processes cause growing needs for automatic tools supporting their programming. The process of control procedures designing usually includes some of performance constraints ensuring the required flow of parallel processes. To achieve their objectives, the system designers use computer assisted analysis and design methods based on the high level languages. While developed packages allow to automatize the evaluation of derived control programs, for example by means of computer simulation, yet however there is a lack of techniques allowing to design such programs automatically.

In most cases it is required that designed control procedure, besides of its optimal design and operation, should also respect some performance constraints reflecting required /feasible/ execution of controlled processes. Such constraints may include requirements for asynchronous, deadlock-free, concurrent, etc. controlled process flow. The above observation leads to the following concept of two stage program synthesis. At the first stage a program satisfying some general performance constraints is developed. Obtained program, containing feasible flows of controlled processes, serves as a basis for further performance optimization at the second stage. The latter means the subsequent restriction of feasible flows to those which satisfy additional decision

709

R. Trappl (ed.), Cybernetics and Systems '86, 709–716.
© *1986 by D. Reidel Publishing Company.*

/optimizing/ rules.

Our considerations are focused on the task of automatic synthesis of the control procedure ensuring deadlock-free coordination of concurrently flowing processes, i.e. at the first stage of the above mentioned methodology of the program design. To explain the approach, let us consider a finite set of concurrently acting and asynchronously executed processes in a system consisting of a finite number of components which may function concurrently. Each process realizes the pipeline flow of standard operations. Some of the operations may be shared among different processes as well as performed in different system components. It means that process specifications, i.e. the order of carrying on operations, can be described by chains of sets of operations. Each set contains the description of the same operation performed in different system components.

The central problem of this paper is stated as follows: Design an algorithm deriving a control procedure which ensures the asynchronous and deadlock-free performance of concurrently flowing processes. The process specifications serve as input data for the algorithm.
Our approach to this problem is based on the Petri net concept. While doing this, the control programs are represented by net models derived with the help of an algorithm transforming the given process specification into the related net model of processing.

As a solution of the above task we propose a method for the description and construction of a class of a priori regular Petri nets reflecting required behaviour of concurrently flowing processes.
First, in section 2, we give basic definitions and present the formalism employed. Then, in section 3, we present necessary conditions essential for the algorithm design. We state our theorems without proofs which will appear elsewhere. Section 4, contains a brief explanation of the algorithm operation. Short review of possible aplications of our results is contained in section 5.

2. NOTATION

Throughout this paper a class of simple, self-loop free and safe general Petri nets /or place/transition nets/ will be considered.
Definition 1
We define a self-loop free and safe place/transition net /PT-net for short/ by a quadruple $PN = (P,T,E,M_o)$, where
P and T are finite sets of places and transitions, respectively, such that $P \cup T \neq \emptyset$ and $P \cap T = \emptyset$,
$E \subset (P \times T) \cup (T \times P)$ is a flow relation such that $dom(E) \cup cod(E) = P \cup T$, $M_o : P \longrightarrow \{0.1\}$ is an initial marking.

Since our considerations are restricted to the self-loop free PT-nets hence the net topology will be completely specified by the incidence matrix C [5]. In what follows PN will be described either by the tuple $PN = (C,M_o)$ or by the quadruple $PN = (P,T,E,M_o)$. Also, we write down $C[i]$ for the i-th row ($C[i,j]$ for the j-th column in the i-th row) of the matrix C.

Because of the space limitation definitions of the next state function δ, of the reachability set of markings $R(C,M_o)$, and of the firing sequence $\mathfrak{S}$ are omitted. They can be found in [1,5].

Definition 2

A matrix $[d_{ij}]_{g \times n}$, $d_{ij} \in \{0,1,-1\}$, is said to be a process performance matrix /PPM for short/ if the following conditions hold:

/i/ for each two rows $D[k]$, $D[l]$ of the matrix D there exists a sequence of rows $(D[i_j] \mid j \in \overline{1,r})$ such that

   i. $(\exists j \in \overline{1,n})(D[k,j]=1 \ \& \ D[i_1,j]=-1 \lor D[k,j]=-1 \ \& \ D[i_1,j]=1)$,

   ii. $(\exists j \in \overline{1,n})(D[l,j]=1 \ \& \ D[i_r,j]=-1 \lor D[l,j]=-1 \ \& \ D[i_r,j]=1)$,

   iii. $(\forall q \in \overline{1,r-1})(\exists j \in \overline{1,n})(D[i_q,j]=1 \ \& \ D[i_{q+1},j]=-1 \lor$
                                $\lor D[i_q,j]=-1 \ \& \ D[i_{q+1},j]=1)$,

/ii/ there is a family of sets $\mathbb{D} = \{\mathbb{D}_i \mid i \in \overline{1,v}\}$, $\mathbb{D} \subset P(\{D[i] \mid i \in \overline{1,g}\})$,

   where $\mathbb{D}_i = \{D[i_k] \mid k \in \overline{1,v_i}\}$, such that

   i. $\bigcup_{i \in \overline{1,v}} \mathbb{D}_i = \{D[i] \mid i \in \overline{1,g}\}$

   ii. $(\forall \mathbb{D}_i \subset \mathbb{D})(\forall j \in \overline{1,n})(\sum_{k=1}^{v_i} D[i_k,j]= 0)$,

   iii. $(\forall \mathbb{D}_i \subset \mathbb{D})(\forall l \in \overline{1,v_i})(\sum_{k=1}^{l} D[i_k] + X \in \{0,1\}^n)$,

       where dim X = dim $D[i]$ for $i \in \overline{1,g}$ and

$$X[j] = \begin{cases} 1 & \text{if } D[i,j]=-1 \text{ and } (\forall k \in \overline{1,i-1})(D[k,j]= 0). \\ 0 & \text{otherwise} \end{cases}$$

Definition 3

A PT-net is said to be repetitive for M if there is a sequence $\mathfrak{S}$ of minimal length which contains every transition of T and such that
$$M = \delta(M, \mathfrak{S}).$$

Corollary 1

If D of size $g \times n$ is a PPM, then there exists a PN $= (C,M_0)$ being a repetitive for M_0 PT-net, where $[c_{ij}]_{m \times n}$ and M_0 are defined as follows

$(\forall i \in \overline{1,n})(\exists! l \in \overline{1,g})(\forall k \in \overline{1,1-1})(C[i]= D[l] \ \& \ i \leq 1 \ \& \ D[k] \neq D[l])$,

   dim M_0 = dim $D[1]$ and

$$M_0(j) = \begin{cases} 1 & \text{if } D[i,j]=-1 \text{ and} (\forall k \in \overline{1,i-1})(D[k,j]= 0) \\ 0 & \text{otherwise} \end{cases}$$

   Consider a set $B \subset B_1 \times B_2 \times \ldots \times B_i \times \ldots \times B_r$, where $B_i = \{B_i^j \mid j \in \overline{1,w_j}\}$ such that $(\forall i,k \in \overline{1,r})(B_i \cap B_k = \emptyset)$ holds.

Assumption 1

Let $PN = (P,T,E,M_0)$, where $T = B_1 \cup B_2 \cup \ldots \cup B_r$, be a PT-net such that $(\forall \mathfrak{S} \in B)(\delta(M_0,\mathfrak{S})= M_0$ and $\bigcup_{\mathfrak{S} \in B} \{crd \ \mathfrak{S} \mid i \in \overline{1,|\mathfrak{S}|}\}= T$, here $|\mathfrak{S}|$ stands for the length of $\mathfrak{S}$.

Definition 4

A PN $= (C,M_0)$, where C is of size $m \times n$ is said to be extended pipeline for M_0 and B PT-net if there exists a set $A \subset P(\bigcup_{\mathfrak{S} \in B} \{\mathfrak{S}_i \mid i \in \overline{1,|\mathfrak{S}|}\})$, such that the net's reachability set is as follows

$R(C,M_0)=\{M \mid M = \delta(\ldots \delta(\delta(M_0,\mathfrak{S}_a),\mathfrak{S}_b)\ldots,\mathfrak{S}_s) \ \& \ \{\mathfrak{S}_a,\mathfrak{S}_b,\ldots,\mathfrak{S}_s\} \in A \ \&$

$$\& \ |\delta_a| > |\delta_b| > \cdots > |\delta_s| \ \& \ M \epsilon \{0,1\}^n \ \} \ .$$

Assumption 2.

Let $F = \{ PN^i = (P^i, T^i, \Xi^i, M_o^i) \mid i \epsilon \overline{1,z} \}$ be a set of extended pipeline PT-nets such that

$$(\forall PN^i, PN^j \epsilon F)(i \neq j \longrightarrow T^i \cap T^j = \emptyset) ,$$

$$(\forall PN^i \epsilon F)(\exists PN^j \epsilon E)(i \neq j \ \& \ P^i \cap P^j \neq \emptyset).$$

Further we will use the following notation for the set F

$$F = \{ PN^i = (C^i, M_o^i) \mid i \epsilon \overline{1,z} \ \& \ [c_{kl}^i]_{m_i \ x \ n} \} .$$

Definition 5

A $PN = (C, M_o)$, where C is of size g x n, is said to be extended open queueing for M_o and F PT-net if the following conditions hold

/i/ $\qquad g = \sum\limits_{i \epsilon \overline{1,z}} m_i$,

/ii/ $\quad$ there exists a set $A \subset P(\bigcup\limits_{k \epsilon \overline{1,z}} A^k)$, where $A^k = \bigcup\limits_{\delta \epsilon B^k} \{ ^k \delta_i \mid i \epsilon \overline{1,|\delta|} \}$,

$\quad$ such that the net's reachability set is as follows

$$R(C,M_o) = \{ M \mid M = \ \delta(\ldots \delta(\delta(M_o, \delta_{k_1,i_1,l_1}) \ \delta_{k_2,i_2,l_2}) \ldots , \delta_{k_s,i_s,l_s}) \ \&$$

$$\& \ \{ \delta_{k_1,i_1,l_1}, \ldots, \delta_{k_s,i_s,l_s} \} \epsilon A \ \& \ (\forall i,j \epsilon \overline{1,s})((k_i = k_j) \ \&$$

$$\& \ (i < j) \longrightarrow l_i > l_j) \ \& \ M \epsilon \{0,1\}^n \ \},$$

$\quad$ where

δ_{k_j,i_j,l_j} - is the i_j-th firing sequence of the l_j-th length in the k_j-th extended pipeline TPT-net.

Note that the construction of the last two definitions restricts our considerations to a class of Petri nets including sources and sinks.

3. RESULTS

Our main task is to derive the necessary conditions for the design of a deadlock-free extended queueing PT-net /DFQ-net for short/ ensuring the occurence of intended firing sequences. At first, consider the necessary conditions which should be satisfied by PPM if related PN must be DFQ-net.

Assumption 3

Let D of size g x n be a PPM such that each submatrix D^k consisting of rows $D[i_{k-1}+1], D[i_{k-1}+2], \ldots, D[i_k]$ be also a PPM. $D[i_{k-1}+1]$ ($D[i_k]$) stands for the first (last) row of the submatrix D^k. Clearly, for D^1 its rows are as follows $D[1], D[2], \ldots, D[i_1]$.

Theorem 1

If PPM D satisfies the following conditions then there exists a DFQ-net.

/i/ for each D^k there exists a set $\mathbb{D}^k = \{ D_1^k \mid 1\epsilon\overline{1,z_k} \}$, where D_1^k is a PPM and for each D_1^k there exists a set

$\mathbb{D}_1^k = \{ D[i_{k-1}+1_i] \mid 1_i \epsilon U_1^k \ \& \ U_1^k \epsilon \overline{1,q} \ \& \ q = i_k - i_{k-1} \}$, such that for each $k \epsilon \overline{1,v}$ the following conditions hold

i-i $\quad D[i_{k-1}+1] \epsilon \{0,1\}^n$, $\qquad D[i_k] \epsilon \{0,-1\}^n$,

i-ii $\quad \bigcup\limits_{1\epsilon\overline{1,z_k}} U_1^k = \{1,2,\ldots,q\}$,

i-iii $\quad (\forall 1,1' \epsilon \overline{1,z_k})(|U_1^k| = |U_{1'}^k| = y)$, $\ y \geq 3$,

i-iv $\quad (\forall 1,1' \epsilon \overline{1,z_k})(\forall n \epsilon \overline{0,Y})(D[i_{k-1}+1_j] = D[i_{k-1}+1'_j] \& \ j = 3n+1)$,
$\qquad\qquad\qquad\qquad\qquad\qquad\qquad\qquad\qquad Y = (y-1)/3$,

i-v $\quad (\forall 1\epsilon\overline{1,z_k})(\forall j,j' \epsilon \overline{1,y})(D[i_{k-1}+1_j] \neq D[i_{k-1}+1_{j'}])$,

/ii/ $(\forall k,k' \epsilon \overline{1,v})((\bigcup\limits_{1 \epsilon \overline{1,z_k}} \mathbb{D}_1^k) \cap (\bigcup\limits_{1 \epsilon \overline{1,z_k}} \mathbb{D}_1^{k'}) = \emptyset)$,

/iii/ for $X \epsilon \{0,1\}^n$ defined as in Definition 2 the following conditions hold

iii-i $\quad$ there exists a set $S \subseteq P(\bigcup\limits_{1 \epsilon \overline{1,z_k}} \mathbb{D}_1^k)$ such that

$$(\forall s \epsilon S^k)(\exists u \epsilon \overline{1,q})(\forall j \epsilon \overline{1,n})((D[i_{k-1}+u,j] = 1 \longrightarrow$$

$$\longrightarrow \sum\limits_{w_1 \epsilon A^k} \sum\limits_{i=1}^{w_1} D[i_{k-1}+1_i,j] + X(j) = 0) \ \&$$

$$\& \ (D[i_{k-1}+u,j] = -1 \ \sum\limits_{w_1 \epsilon A^k} \sum\limits_{i=1}^{w_1} D[i_{k-1}+1_i,j] + X(j) = 1) \&$$

$$\& \ (D[i_{k-1}+u,j] = 0 \longrightarrow \sum\limits_{w_1 \epsilon A^k} \sum\limits_{i=1}^{w_1} D[i_{k-1}+1_i,j] + X(j) \epsilon \{0,1\}^n)),$$

where $A^k = \{w_1 \mid D[i_{k-1}+1_{w_1}] \epsilon s\}$,

$$\sum\limits_{i=1}^{w_1} D[i_{k-1}+1_i] = D[i_{k-1}+1_1] + \ldots + D[i_{k-1}+1_i] + \ldots +$$

$+D[i_{k-1}+1_{w_1}]$ for $1_{w_1} \epsilon U_1^k$ and $1_i \epsilon U_1^k$

iii-ii $\quad$ there exists a set $S \subseteq P(\bigcup\limits_{k \epsilon \overline{1,v}} S^k)$, where

$S^k = \bigcup\limits_{1 \epsilon \overline{1,z_k}} \mathbb{D}_1^k$ such that

$$(\forall s \epsilon S)(\exists i \epsilon \overline{1,g})\,(\forall j \epsilon \overline{1,n})\,((D[i,j]=1 \longrightarrow$$

$$\sum_{A^k \epsilon A}\sum_{w_1 \epsilon A^k}\sum_{i=1}^{w_1} D\left[i_{k-1}+1_i,j\right] + X(j) = 0)\ \&$$

$$\&\ (D[i,j]=-1 \longrightarrow \sum_{A^k \epsilon A}\sum_{w_1 \epsilon A^k}\sum_{i=1}^{w_1} D\left[i_{k-1}+1_i,j\right] + X(j) = 1)\ \&$$

$$\&\ (D[i,j]=0 \longrightarrow \sum_{A^k \epsilon A}\sum_{w_1 \epsilon A^k}\sum_{i=1}^{w_1} D\left[i_{k-1}+1_i,j\right] + X(j)\epsilon\{0,1\}^n\,)),$$

where $A = \{A^k | A^k = \{w_1 | D[i_{k-1}+1_{w_1}] \epsilon s^k\}\ \&\ s^k \subset s\}.$

Now, let us focus our attention on necessary conditions under which D becomes PPM satisfying the conditions of Theorem 1.

The problem may be stated as follows: Let B be a set of chains spanned on a set of operations performed on a set of machines. Each chain is a sequence of sets of alternatively executed operation, i.e. $b \epsilon B$,

$b = (b_i | i\epsilon\overline{1,r})$, $b_i = \{b_i^j | j\epsilon\overline{1,r_i}\}$, where b_i^j - is a j-th operation performed on the i-th machine. Find an algorithm transforming the process specification, i.e. its set of chains, into the PT-net model of control flow of feasible performances of the process. According to Corollary 1 and Theorem 1 the task of DFQ-net design is equivalent to the task of design of the proper matrix D.

Necessary conditions for the design of such a matrix are presented in the theorem given below.

Theorem 2

If a matrix D of size g x n satisfies the following conditions then it is a PPM and the conditions of Theorem 1 hold.

/i/ $(\forall i,i' \epsilon \overline{1,g})\,(D[i] \neq D[i'])$,

/ii/ matrix D contains a set of submatrices $\{D^k | k\epsilon\overline{1,v}\}$, where each D^k consists of rows $D[i_{k-1}+1],\ldots,D[i_{k-1}+1],\ldots,D[i_k]$, and where i_k - is an index of the $D[i_k]$ row of D being the last row of the submatrix D^k.

/iii/ for each D^k there exists a set $\{a_i | i\epsilon\overline{1,z}\} \subset \overline{1,i_k-i_{k-1}}$ and a set $G_k = \{j_i | i\epsilon\overline{1,z-1}\ \&\ j_i\epsilon\overline{1,n}\}$, such that $(\forall i\epsilon\overline{1,z-1})(a_{i+1}-a_i-1 = r_i\ \&\ \bar{r}_i$ is even) and $D[i_{k-1}+a_1] \epsilon \{0,1\}^n$, $D[i_{k-1}+a_z] \epsilon \{0,-1\}^n$ and for each $i\epsilon\overline{1,z-1}$, $D[i_{k-1}+a_i,j]= 1$ and $D[i_{k-1}+a_{i+1},j_i] = -1$,

/iv/ for each D^k and for each $i\epsilon\overline{1,z-1}$ there exists a set $H_k^i = \{j_i^1 | l\epsilon\overline{1,r_i+2}\ \&\ j_i^1\epsilon\overline{1,n}\}$ such that

714

$$D[i_{k-1}+a_i, j_i^1]=1 \ , \quad D[i_{k-1}+a_{i+1}, j_i^2]=-1 \ \text{ and for } \ n \le r_i/2$$

$$D[i_{k-1}+a_i+2n-1, j_i^1]=-1, \quad D[i_{k-1}+a_i+2n-1, j_i^2]=1$$

$$D[i_{k-1}+a_i+2n-1, j_i^{2(n+1)}]=-1 \ , \quad D[i_{k-1}+a_i, j_i^{2(n+1)}]=1$$

$$D[i_{k-1}+a_i+2n, j_i^{2(n+1)-1}]=-1 \ , \quad D[i_{k-1}+a_i+2n-1, j_i^{2(n+1)-1}]=1 \ ,$$

/v/ $\quad (\forall k, k' \in \overline{1,v})(\mathbb{H}_k \cap \mathbb{H}_{k'} = \emptyset \ \& \ G_k \cap G_{k'} = \emptyset)$

$\quad (\forall k \in \overline{1,v})(\exists k' \in \overline{1,v})((\mathbf{H}_k \setminus \mathbb{H}_k) \cap (\mathbf{H}_{k'} \setminus \mathbb{H}_{k'}) \ne \emptyset)$

$\quad (\forall k \in \overline{1,v})(\mathbf{H}_k \cap B_k = \emptyset)$

where
$$\mathbb{H}_k^i = H_k^i \setminus \{ j_i^{2(n+1)-1} \mid n \in \overline{1, r_i}/2 \ \& \ j_i^{2(n+1)-1} \in \overline{1,n} \}$$

$$\mathbb{H}_k = \bigcup_{i \in \overline{1,z}} \mathbb{H}_k^i \ , \quad \mathbf{H}_k = \bigcup_{i \in \overline{1,z-1}} H_k^i \ , \quad \mathbb{H}_k \subset \mathbf{H}_k \ .$$

4. IMPLEMENTATION

Obtained results are of fundamental significance for the design of an algorithm transforming sets of chains /see section 3/ into the DFQ-nets. The following example presents the main idea about the operation of the above mentioned algorithm.

Let $B = \{ b, b' \}$, where $b := (\{ b_1^1, b_3^1 \}, \{ b_2^1 \})$ and $b' := (\{ b_1^2, b_3^2 \}, \{ b_2^2, b_4^2 \})$, be a set of considered input data, i.e. a symbolic description of the process specification. An illustration of the considered case is shown in Fig.1.

According to condition /iv/ of Theorem 2 one can consider the following sequences $t_1 b_1^1 t_2 b_3^1 t_3 t_4 b_2^1 t_5 t_6$, $t_7 b_1^2 t_8 b_3^2 t_9 t_{10} b_2^2 t_{11} b_4^2 t_{12} t_{13}$ modelling elements of the set B. Due to Theorem 2, elements of concatenation of the above mentioned sequences specify the rows of PPM D which in turn determine the considered PT-net. The graphical representation of the control procedure is presented in Fig. 2.

5. CONCLUSIONS

The emphasis in this paper has been put on the formal investigation of properties of a net incidence matrix useful for the design of deadlock-free PT-nets. Presented approach to the automatic design of net models reflecting required behaviour of concurrently flowing processes can be applied for the design of errorless and reliable logical controllers[2] as well as for the process performance evaluation by means of computer simulation. A practical implementation of the introduced concept has been done in the design of a computer aided planning system [3].

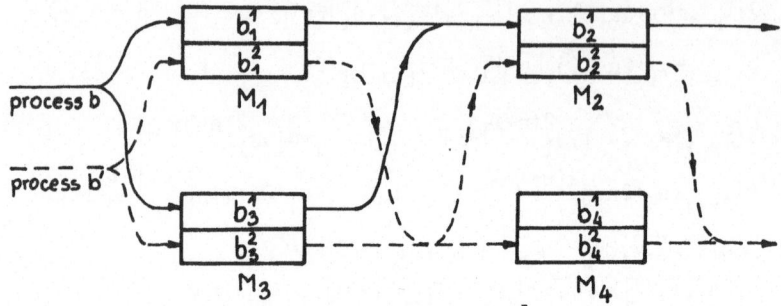

Fig.1 The structure of a production system. $/b_i^j$-is the j-th operation performed on the i-th machine, M_i-is the i-th machine of production system/

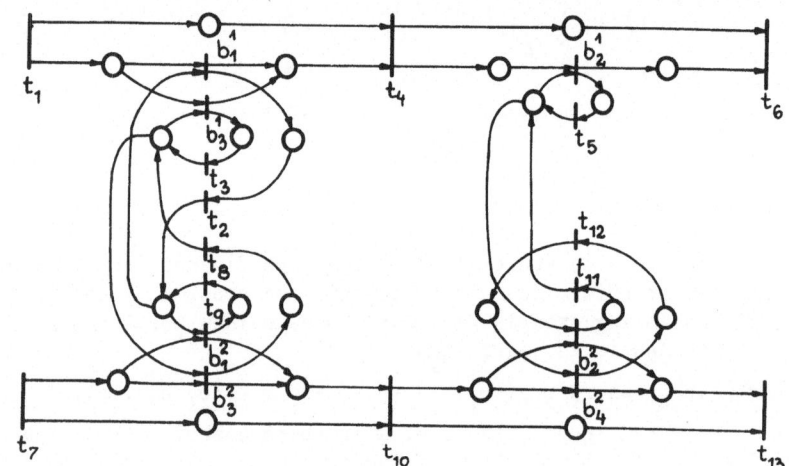

Fig.2 Net model of the control procedure

6. REFERENCES

[1] Banaszak Z., 'An application of Petri nets to automatic design of control flow models', Proc of CYBERNETICS'85 Conference, Warsaw, May 27-29, 1985, pp. 15-24.

[2] Banaszak Z., Mazur M., 'Self-programmable controller of concurrent processes', Proc of First International School MICROCOMPUTER'85, Bierutowice, Sept., 24-27, 1985, pp. 5-12.

[3] Banaszak Z., Mazur M., 'Computer aided planning system of concurrent processes', /in Polish/, Proc. of First National Conference on Robotics , Wrocław, Sept., 18-20, 1985, 117-124.

[4] Banaszak Z., 'Algorithms for the automatic modelling of asynchronously acting concurrent processes', /in Polish/, Proc. of First National Conference on Robotics , Wrocław, Sept., 18-20, 1985, pp. 105-116.

[5] Peterson J.I., Petri net theory and the modelling of systems, Prentice-Hall, Englewood Cliffs, New York, 1981.

SOME OPTIMIZATION METHODS FOR EXPERIMENTAL INVESTIGATION DIALOGUE SYSTEMS

Aram Arakelian
Computing Center of Academy of Sciences
of Armenian SSR
Ul. P. Sewaka, 1
375044 G. Yerevan-44
USSR

ABSTRACT. A formulation and investigation of optimization principles and their realization for some experimental investigation dialogue systems optimization problems are discussed. These problems are connected with optimal choice of experimental investigation dialogue system variation, modelling and optimization of systems under incertainty conditions, optimization of diagnostic provision, aggregation in optimization problems, method of statistic solutions in control problems.

1. INTRODUCTION

In the program report [1] devoted to the development prospects of scientific investigation automation systems (SIAS) it was pointed that successful realization of main directions is connected with creation of "complex optimization program for blocks, units and the whole optimization systems." But, it is known [2-7] that generally solution of optimal synthesis problem for experimental investigation dialogue systems (EIDS) is practically insoluble question since it is connected with necessity of consideration the various groups of particular criteria.

This report is the development of the papers [8-19] . It is devoted to formulation and investigation of optimization principles and their realization for some EIDS optimization problems connected with
    a) optimal choice of the EIDS variation [2-6,8] ;
    b) organization of statistics gathering systems about SIAS [1,9,10] ;
    c) creation of translators from algorithmic languages of high level [1,11] ;
    d) creation of EIDS software [1,12,13] ;
    e) development of software methods for parallel

R. Trappl (ed.), Cybernetics and Systems '86, 717–724.

solution of problems in multiprocessor computing systems [11-13];

f) elaboration of high level languages for description of specialized systems [1];

g) elaboration of EIDS diagnostics methods, control objects (CO), and methods and aids to optimization of their diagnostic provision [1,13-15];

2. FORMALIZED ALGORITHMIC MODEL OF EIDS

Formalized algorithmic model (FAM) of EIDS is the set of algorithms, programs and rules allowing the description of action sequence for realization of CO measurement, control and recovery.

EIDS must provide the possibility of the following generalized functions:

a) realization of toleranced quantitative control and conducting on its basis an CO classification by principle "works - does not work" or by virtue of belonging to one of possible states [11];

b) diagnostics of hardware and software faults [1,14, 15];

c) failure prediction in equipment, hardware and software systems (HSS) on the basis of failure data gathering [1,10];

d) CO state recovery by means of reduction of control parameter spread relative to their nominal values.

The experience of EIDS realization, installation and exploitation calls for necessity of properties connected with systemological features [1,8-15], namely;

a) trainingness, modification and development by means of designing and realization of new algorithms for functioning and measurement and control, problem-oriented languages (POL) of programming, translators from these languages, and hardware realizing the program models created [1,11-13,16,17];

b) effectiveness and function optimization by means of choice of optimal dialogue procedures [1,16];

c) "survival rate" that is the ability to adopt for hardware and software over a wide range [1,13];

d) principle of moduleness that is relative independence of components contained in hardware and software [1,9,11-13];

e) selfcontrol that is the function control of EIDS [12,13] and its fault diagnostics by means of hardware and software.

EIDS providing the possibility of requirements mentioned is a complex man-machine system (MMS) allowing the dialogue with user, development and training by means of new hardware and software creation, and choice of optimal dialogue procedures.

718

According to [1] these EIDS are from the class of programm-cybernetics systems capable of selftraining and adaptation for variable environment by means of new hardware and software there, variation of environment can be considered by both user's knowledge level and CO technical specifications.

According to [5,6] let us divide EIDS on 2 independence parts, subsystem of stimulating action generation and subsystem of transformation and reaction analysis.

Denote by $x_1, x_2, \ldots, x_n$ a set of OC parameters, by X_i a set of their values. Let us denote by $B_0, B_1, \ldots, B_n$ a set signals on inputs and outputs of EIDS transformators' at the different transformation stages during OC control. Here, B_0 is the set of signals providing the direct data transformation from CO and other B_j, $1 \le j \le m$ signals refer to the transformators at next control stages. Let us denote by f_{ij} representations of signal set B_i into signal set B_j. Let us take $B_{m+1} = \bigcup X_i$ define on set B_i, $i = 1, 2, \ldots, m+1$ relation families R_i. Denote the HSS of EIDS by Q. Then by system we will denote the relation family $\{R_i\}_{i=1,2,\ldots,m+1}$ matching the values of variables from B_i with the values of variables from B_j for obtaining the purpose set C. Hence, EIDS is

$$S = \langle X, \{B_i\}, \{R_i\}, \{f_{ij}\}, Q, C \rangle \qquad (1)$$

For extension and more precise definition of EIDS (1) let us consider auxiliary parameters defining by γ_i the quantitative characteristics of transformator system elements. As the quantitative characteristics, we can consider such quantities as trustworthiness and transformation time of signals from B_i set to B_j set. EIDS as the complex man-machine system representing a set of interconnecting and interacting elements operating for achievment of certain purposes, stipulates introduction of a parameter which specifies the time required for attaining these purposes. Let us denote the control time, by $T = \bigcup t_{ij}$ a set consisting of time characteristics defining the time t_{ij} of the signal transformation from B_i set into B_j set. Let M be a set of CO's including also perspective ones which must be served using EIDS. Let us denote by $\{\theta_i\}_{i=1,2,\ldots,m}$ a set of requirements for EIDS which provides the control possibility for objects of M set. Then EIDS can be represented in the form

$$S = \langle X, \{B_i\}, \{R_i\}, \{t_{ij}\}, Q, f, \{\gamma_u\}, T, C, \{\theta_i\} \rangle \qquad (2)$$

3. OPTIMIZATION OF DIAGNOSTIC PROVISION OF EIDS

A number of papers [14,15] was devoted to construction of function control tests (FCT) for discrete devices (DD).

In these papers an assumption was made concerning an agreement with FCT designers about the test choice. However, as a matter of fact the FCT designers may act independently that is for each designer indefinite factors represent tests which are at other's disposal.

Here we consider the problem of construction of a complete FCT set of microprocessor (MP) LSI in the presence of incertain factors exerting influence on their construction process. Advisability of such approach is explained by increasing complexity and scale of MP LSI integration.

Let us assume that in an MP n function complete units (FCU) and $I = \{1, 2, \ldots, n\}$ sets of FCT designers are chosen. Here i-th designer designs FCT of the i-th FCU. Denote by X_i a FCT set which is at i-th designer's disposal, $i \in I$. The process of FCT construction is as follows: i-th designer chooses a test $x_i \in X_i$, $i \in I$, and so we have a situation $x = (x_1, x_2, \ldots, x_n)$, $x \in X = \prod_{i \in I} X_i$. Here, the designers choose the tests independently.

Let's denote [18] by $N_i(x_1, \ldots, x_n)$ a set of faults of i-th MP LSI FCU detected by $x_1, \ldots, x_n$ tests. Let N_i be a set of i-th MP LSI FCU faults, .

Thus, if we consider FCT designers as players, FCT set X_i which is at i-th designer's disposal as i-th player's strategies, $X = \prod_{i \in I} X_i$ set as a situation set, and a preference relation ρ_i defined as follows:

$$(x, y) \in \rho_i \text{ if and only if } x_i \neq y_i, x_j = y_j, j \neq i, j \in I, N_i(y) \subseteq N_i(x)$$

then we get a general coalitionless game

$$\Gamma = \langle \{X_i\}_{i \in I}, \{\rho_i\}_{i \in I}, I \rangle \tag{3}$$

where ρ_i is the relation of partial ordering.

We will say that a FCT set $X' \subset X$ is complete [18] if

$$N_i = \bigcup_{x \in X'} N_i(x) \text{ for any } i \in I \tag{4}$$

Since the preference relation ρ_i is a relation of partial ordering, then there is a skew-symmetric function of relative usefullness $u_i(x, y)$ for it, that is a function $u_i(x, y)$ such that

$$(x, y) \in \rho_i \text{ if and only if } u_i(x, y) > 0$$

Define the relation $\rho \subset X \times X$ as follows.

$$(x, y) \in \rho \text{ if and only if there is } i \in I$$
such that $(x, y) \in \rho_i$

A subset $V_\rho(X)$ is called the Naumann-Morgenstern solution (NM-solution) if

1) $(x, y) \notin \rho$ for any $x, y \in V_\rho(X)$;

2) for any $x \notin V_\rho(X)$ there is $y \in V_\rho(X)$ such that

$(y,x) \in \rho$.

Let the set of tests X_i which is at i-th designer's disposal satisfies the relation

$$N_i = \bigcup_{x_i \in X_i} N_i(x) \text{ for any } i \in I \tag{5}$$

It follows that $\bigcup_{x \in V_\rho(X)} N_i(x) = N_i$, $i \in I$.

For the microcomputer from [14] an FCT example is given for which the ρ-relation is not even. That implies consideration of probability distribution on the FCT set.

Let us denote by $\tilde{X}_i$ a probability distribution on Σ-algebra of strategy set X_i, $i \in I$. Set

$$u_i(\tilde{x}, \tilde{y}) = \sum_{x,y \in X} u_i(x,y) \tilde{x}(x) \cdot \tilde{y}(y)$$

Let us denote by $\tilde{\rho}_i$ relation defined as follows:

$(\tilde{x}, \tilde{y}) \in \tilde{\rho}_i$ if and only if $u_i(\tilde{x}, \tilde{y}) \geq 0$.

Then the game

$$\tilde{\Gamma} = \langle \{\tilde{X}_i\}_{i \in I}, \{\tilde{\rho}_i\}_{i \in I}, I \rangle \tag{6}$$

is a mixed expansion of the coalitionless game (3).

Here the mixed strategies can be interpreted as follows. Instead of choice of an concrete test $x_i \in X_i$ the player i choses a probability measure $\tilde{x}_i$ defined on Σ-algebra $\mathcal{X}_i$ of X_i subsets and x_i test is chosen by means of a random device constructed such that for an arbitrary $X_i' \in \mathcal{X}_i$ the probability of (chosed test) $x_i \in X_i'$ is

$\tilde{x}_i(X_i')$, $i \in I$.

Theorem. If I is a finite set, X_i are compact subsets of linear convex topological spaces, ρ_i relations are acyclic and continuous, ρ_i are convex then ρ relation has an NM - solution.

Corollary. For any FCT set such that $\tilde{\rho}_i$ are acyclic, $i \in I$, there is an NM -solution $V_{\tilde{\rho}}(\tilde{X})$.

5. AGGREGATION IN OPTIMIZATION PROBLEMS OF FCT FOR DISCRETE DEVICES (DD).

Let's assume that X_0 is a set of FCT for a controlled device and provides the probability of checking of some fault set.

Assume that on X_0 a preference relation ρ_0 is given and $N(x)$ is a fault set of the controlled device, detected by a x test. If we denote by N_0 a set of all faults then [18]

$$N_0 = \bigcup_{x \in V_\rho(x)} N(x) \qquad (7)$$

We will define X_0 as a set of 0-level aggregated FCT. It is often impossible to solve (7) by single designer, since the sets of faults and tests are defined by the collective of designers each of them designs a FCT of a certain functional complete unit of the controlled device.

One of the methods of this problem solution is construction of FCT designing problem hierarchy for DD.

Define the 1-level aggregated FCT set.

$$X_1 \supseteq \{x(1) = \varphi_1(x(0)) \mid x(0) \in X_0 \}$$

Denote by Ψ_1 a mapping from X_1 into X_0 that is

$$X_0 \supseteq \{x(0) = \Psi_1(x(1)) \mid x(1) \in X_1 \}.$$

Here we assume that X_1 is a FCT set allowing the possibility of checking of fault set $N_1 \subset N_0$. Denote by ρ_1 the preference relation specified on X_1. By continuation of FCT aggregation process we get the following expressions:

$$X_2 \supseteq \{x(2) = \varphi_2(x(1)) \mid x(1) \in X_1 \},$$

$$X_1 \supseteq \{x(1) = \Psi_2(x(2)) \mid x(2) \in X_2 \},$$

ρ_2 is the preference relation on X_2, $N_2 \subseteq N_1, \dots,$

$$X_{k+1} \supseteq \{x(k+1) = \varphi_{k+1}(x(k)) \mid x(k) \in X_k \},$$

$$X_k \supseteq \{x(k) = \Psi_{k+1}(x(k+1)) \mid x(k+1) \in X_{k+1} \},$$

ρ_{k+1} is the preference relation on X_{k+1}, $N_{k+1} \subseteq N_k, \dots,$

$$X_m \supseteq \{x(m) = \varphi_m(x(m-1)) \mid x(m-1) \in X_{m-1} \},$$

$$X_{m-1} \supseteq \{x(m-1) = \Psi_m(x(m)) \mid x(m) \in X_m \},$$

ρ_m is the preference relation on X_m, $N_m \subseteq N_{m-1}$.

For the choice of aggregation steps m let us assume that the set N_m is low-power and the preference relation ρ_m is not complex. It is clear that with rational aggregation we can ensure the realization of $N_{k+1} \subseteq N_k$ inclusions and the possibility of the problem solution on m-th step that is determination of NM-solution $V_{\rho_m}(X_m)$.

5.1. I equality of FCT designing process.

Suppose that all aggregation steps are finished namely, $X_k, \rho_k, k = 0, 1, \dots, m$ are defined. Then the FCT designing

722

problem can be solved as follows:
Define the NM – solution $V_{\rho_m}(X_m)$ and a set

$$\left\{ x(m-1) \in X_{m-1} \left| \begin{array}{l} \varphi_m\,(x(m-1)) = x(m), \\ \psi_m\,(x(m)) = x(m-1), \quad x(m) \in V_{\rho_m}(X_m) \end{array} \right. \right\}$$

This set is $\bar{X}_{m-1} = \psi_m\,(V_{\rho_m}(X_m))$

Then define the NM – solution $(\bar{X}_{m-1},\,\rho_{m-1})$ that is a
set

$$V_{\rho_{m-1}}(\bar{X}_{m-1}), \quad \bar{X}_{m-2} = \psi_{m-1}\,(V_{\rho_{m-1}}(\bar{X}_{m-1})).$$

By continuation of construction process for NM – solutions at each aggregation step we get the NM – solution
$V_{\rho_0}(X_0)$.
So, the aggregation process offered can be represented as the following recurrent equation :

$$V_{\kappa} = V_{\rho_{\kappa}}\,(\psi_{\kappa+1}\,(V_{\kappa+1})),\,\kappa = m-1, m-2, \ldots, 1,\, 0 \qquad (8)$$
$$V_m = V_{\rho_m}\,(X_m)$$

Solution of FCT optimal set construction process we
will understand construction of V_0 set. In the report a
solution method for equation (12) based on the results of
[19] is given.

REFERENCES

1. Petrov B.N., Kuklin G.N. Development Program In Field
   Scientific Investigation Automatization.'Problemy Cybernetiky Avtomatyzacia Experimentalnich Issledovany', M.,
   1979.
2. Wittich W.A., Kuklin G.N. Informational Approach to
   Rational Designing of Test Automatization Systems. 'Problemy Cybernetiky·Avtomatyzacia Experimentalnich Issledovany', M.; 1979.
3. Yegipko W.M. Organization and Designing of Automatization Systems for Scientific-Technical Experiments
   'Naukova Dumka', Kiev, 1978.
4. Wittich W.A., Kuklin G.N., Tomnikov G.N., Tsibatov W.A.
   Topological Optimization of Information Gathering Systems. Problemy upravlenia·i·theoria informatzii
5. Ponomarev N.N., Frumkin I.S., Gusinskij W.N. et al.
   Automatic Test Equipment. M., 1975.
6. Dolgov W.A., Kasatkin A.S., Sretenskij W.N; Radioelec-
   tronic Automatic Control Systems. M., 1978.
7. Kaljavin W.P., Chusin R.S. Optimization of Element Base
   of Automatic Diagnostic Facilities. 'Izvestija LETI',

v.278, 1980;

8. Arakelian A.H. Modelling and Optimization of Dialogue Control Systems Under Incertainty Conditions. 12th IFIP Conference on System Modelling and Optimization. Budapest, 1985.

9. Arakelian A.H., Kocharian R.A. ASSDT As a Result of HMC Electric. Parameter Measurements. 'Electronnaya Technica, ser.3. Microelectronica, N2(100), 1978.

10. Arakelian A.H., Agaian C.C. On an Algorithm of Spectral Analysis, Cybernetics and Systems Res.2, R.Trappl. North-Holland; 1984.

11. Haikazian E.M., Arakelian A.H. Problem Oriented Language DISTM Proc. of III All-Union Conf. 'Dialog - 83', Protvino, 1983.

12. Haikazian E.M.; Arakelian A.H. ARM of REE Engineer-Designer. Math. Problemy Cybernetiky i Vychislitelnoy Techniky, Yerevan, N. XIII; 1984.

13. Arakelian A.H., Papian S.S. System Software of Continuous Supervision Complex for Cardiacs. Proc. of I Repub. Conference On Med. Technics and Cybernetics, Yerevan, 1984.

14. Arakelian A.H., Sajadian G.A., Ohanjanian S.R. Automatic Synthesis Algorithms for LSI Functional Control Microprograms. Automatica Vichislitelnaya Technika. NI,1983

15. Amirbekian W.C., Arakelian A.H. et all. Standard Progr; Package for Automatic Test Synthesis for Microcomputer. Elektronnaya Technika. ser.3, Microelectronica, N4(94), 1981.

16. Arakelian A.H. Automatic Control System Optimization of MP BIS Parameters Under Incertainty Conditions. Proc. of III All-Union Meeting 'Reliability and Effectiveness of 'ACYP' MP AMS. M., 1984.

17. Arakelian A.H., Krkeian A.M. et al. Construction of Specialized Processor for LSI Memory FCT Generation.'Electronnaya Technika'. ser 3. Microelectronica N1(107), 1984.

18. Arakelian A.H. SDT Diagnostics Optimization On Microprocessor Basis Proc. of II All-Union Meet. On Standard Module SDT Synthesis Methods. M., 1985.

19. Arakelian A.H. Existence of Solutions for Expandable Ratio. Math. Problemy Cybernetiky i Vychislitelnoy Techniky N XV, 1985.

Methodological Improvements and New Applications of Expert Systems

Chairpersons: W.Horn (Austria)
              C.A.Kulikowski (U.S.A.)

HAS THE TIME COME FOR A MEDICAL EXPERT SYSTEM TO GO DOWN IN THE BULLRING: THE TROPICAID EXPERIMENT.

B. Auvert, P. Aegerter, V. Gilbos *, E. Benillouche,
P. Boutin, G. Desve, M-F. Landre and D. Bos
   INSERM U88. 91, Bd de l'Hôpital. 75013 PARIS. FRANCE
* MEDECINS SANS FRONTIERES. 68, Bd St Marcel.
   75005 PARIS. FRANCE

ABSTRACT. Competent medical personnel is a condition of a good health service but it is still lacking in developing countries. Along with a humanitarian organization, we defined the specifications of a helping and teaching system for paramedical personnel in tropical dispensaries. With the results of a field trial, we present the system we are now working on: a hand-held computer including an expert system which deals with knowledge bases on drugs, treatments and diseases. It provides an aid in diagnosis and therapy. Moreover, it is easy to use and can be adapted to its working environment. Finally, we discuss the condition of suitability and acceptability of such systems and the place they could take in health system network.

1. INTRODUCTION

In many developing countries, much of the population still lives in rural areas where health care services are rather limited. Dispensaries, where they exist, often have few beds, material sufficient for only the most minor surgery and less than a hundred medications. Staff generally have had no more than six months to two years of training which is not helped by distance from more competent practitioners and the lack of continuing education. While, as emphasized at the Alma-Ata Conference (1) in 1978, the existence of competent medical personnel is an indispensable condition to the amelioration of the level of health of a country, qualified doctors are reluctant to remain where there are no resources. There are difficulties in training para-medical personnel (bush medics, "bare-foot" doctors) and, once trained, people tend to seek more remunerative positions.

   Our main objective is to offer to rural health workers a tool to augment their diagnostic and therapeutic skills and to provide reinforcement. This tool would provide immediate help without needing major changes in their working conditions. Portable computers for para-medical personnel have already been proposed with this aim in view (2). So, with the humanitarian organization "Médecins Sans Frontières" (MSF), we defined the specifications of such a system.

727

R. Trappl (ed.), Cybernetics and Systems '86, 727–734.
© *1986 by D. Reidel Publishing Company.*

2. HARDWARE

The material used is an HHC (Blaise) intended for biomedical applications (3). The device is made autonomous by running on NiCad batteries which are rechargeable (via a solar panel). The prototype measures 29x20x5 cm and is light-weight (1.5 kg). The waterproof and shock-resistant keyboard has 51 alphanumeric and 5 function keys. The liquid crystal display can show 8 lines of 40 large-size characters. There is also a standard RS232c serial interface. On the inside, two circuit boards include: an 8- bit Z80- compatible CMOS microprocessor (NSC800), CMOS RAM memories totaling 128 K bytes and MMOS EPROM memories (up to 500 K bytes), containing programs and data, which are activated by VMOS only when they are to be read by the processor. Information may be updated by simple replacement of the EPROM modules. The device it will run continuously for 20 hours whithout recharge. Data in the RAM are saved up to seven weeks on stand-by current.

3. OPERATING SYSTEM

The operating system is the Softech P-System because of its portability and (due to the dynamic code segment swapping) the fact that extremely large programs can be implemented. It is used with Pascal-UCSD, a high-level language for structured programming, dynamic data structures and recursive procedures. The program was developed on a Victor S1 then transferred to the prototype's storage by an EPROM programmer.

4. APPLICATION SOFTWARE

A system of aid to medical practice intended for use by para-medical personnel should cover the four following areas: knowledge and use of medications, treatment of a given disease, diagnostic decision and collection of epidemiological data. Moreover, it should be easy enough to be used by people with no informatic training. We present now the solutions provided by the first system called Tropicaid 1.

4.1. Information on drugs

We created a data base of 64 drugs used by MSF in health centers and appearing among those classed to be "essential" by the World Health Organization (WHO) (4). For each drug, information include the following: brand name, international name, indications, contra-indications, side-effects and how to control them, interactions and how to manage them, signs of overdose and the way to treat it, recommendations for use, posology including dose, duration and route of administration and depending on indication, patient's characteristics and drug form, pharmacological properties and forms.
This information, except numeric values, is coded into thesauri. So a drug record contains only references to these thesauri. After

packing, the size of a drug record is less than 100 bytes.

Successive selection grids allow the user to choose at first the drug and then the various characteristics. The average access time to a drug record is about ten seconds starting from the main menu.

4.2. Information on treatments

A therapeutic data base concerning the 200 main diseases includes, for each disease, the following information: a) clinical description and therapy management, b) therapeutics: it lists the drug(s) in order of preference and with the posology as above. It also includes rules for selection of a treatment according to the clinical appearance, the patient type, and the epidemiological situation; c) general remarks.

All this information is codified using thesauri, except for the clinical description and the remarks both of which appear as text.

The interrogation uses successive selection grids. For each treatment, the selection of a drug allows access, not only to the posology according to the treatment, but also to the whole set of information about the drug. This module thus encompasses the previous one. To study a treatment takes about 30 to 45 seconds.

4.3. Decision-aid

The "diagnostic decision-aid" module of the first system uses symptom-oriented flowcharts derived from the diagnostic pathways of B.J. ESSEX (5) by which one can obtain possible diagnoses through successive questions and answers.

The pathways are represented as a set of nodes. Each node contains the code number of the question to ask and, for each possible answer, the code number of the next node or the code of a diagnosis. Answers may be "yes", "no", "don't know" or a choice from a list. For certain questions, the "Help" key allows the display of an explanatory text. The complete network includes 464 nodes with 412 different questions and 72 explanatory messages and 210 diagnosis.

Once arriving at a diagnosis, the user may either continue the interrogation, or access its specific therapy as described in the previous module. It takes generally about 30 seconds to obtain a diagnosis if it is not too complicated.

4.4. Data collection

This module allows the storage in non volatile memory, for each patient and up to 2000 patients, of the following characteristics: age, sex, month of consultation, geographical origin, symptoms, diagnosis and medical action. It is possible to define for each of these items the number of possibilities and their labels. The recording of a patient's data takes about 20 seconds. A program may give numbers according to selected criteria. A sort among 2000 patients is about 15 seconds long.

5. SOFTWARE ORGANIZATION

Programs and files are stored in ROM. The whole program, which represents 48 K bytes of code for the first version, is divided into segments. During operation, only index files and needed segments are present in active memory.

All the data files are packed. We used direct access files with variable length records. The whole set of data and index files occupies 164 K bytes in this first system. The use of a data transfer function such as "blockread" allows a quick access to the data. By using indexed files, response time is independent of the quantity of data.

6. FIELD TRIAL

A first trial of this prototype (6) took place in Chad in Spring 1984 during which around 50 doctors (MSF and Chadian) and para-medical workers who tried it found the device easy to use, fast and very useful. One Chadian para-medic managed to use it successfully during a consultation after only 30 minutes of prior initiation. The systematic use of selection-menus (7) with only three function keys (RESTART, NEXT and HELP) appears responsible for this ease of learning. The dominant impression of the users is the feeling of conversing with a system which "knows" a lot of information. This trial also demonstrated the physical resistance of the device despite numerous trips into the field (around 1000 km of rough road, heat and dust). In addition, recharging the batteries via a solar panel proved entirely satisfactory (7).

7. DISCUSSION ABOUT TROPICAID 1

7.1. Data bases

The data bases concerning medications and treatments in our system appeared to be satisfactory, from the point of view of both information and interrogation. Needed modifications were minor.

7.2. Decision-aid flowcharts

7.2.1. The path of a graph which is evolved according to the given clinical situation is of a rigid structure and can't take into account seasonal or geographic variability in the frequency of a disease. Nor can it be adapted to avoid vain answers, such as those beyond the user's level of training or material means. In the same way, the separation from the treatment modulemay lead to one or more diagnoses whose treatments are beyond the possibilities of the user.

7.2.2. This method does not reproduce the medical diagnosis process in which hypotheses are formulated based on a few signs, using further examination to reject or reinforce a hypothesis before deciding on the "best" treatment, that is one that will be simple and effective relative to one or more diagnoses that may be more or less "certain".

7.2.3. This method offers no explanation for the diagnoses it derives. Each decision point appears to be independent from the others. The lack of any physio-pathological underlying model impedes any justification. Thus, it deprives the user of a potential learning situation.

7.2.4. Lastly, this explicit representation is not compact; it would require an enormous amount of memory to consider all the possible sequences of situations. On the other hand, the simplification of the domain studied yields a diagnosis after only a few questions and this rapidity is an important factor in user acceptability.

8. TROPICAID 2

8.1. Improvements since Tropicaid 1

The field trial involved several modifications, mainly in order to make the system more powerful in diagnosis decision and more adaptable to local conditions of use.

8.1.1. The pharmacological data base is extended to 160 essential drugs. This sample might cover any possible situation in different dispensaries where drugs not available can be "masked" in the program.

8.1.2. The therapeutic data base concerns about 500 diseases likely to be usually encountered in all developing countries. The informatiom for each of those is stored into records including: as before, 1) a clinical description; 2) the rules by which to determine the treatment (drug(s) and/or other treatment) as a function of the following conditions: type of patient, clinical form of the disease, epidemiological context and causal agent; and newly, 3) a priority index for the treatment; 4) a reference to a more generalized treatment; 5) the symptoms for which the treatment is effective.

8.1.3. The diagnostic data base concerns the same diseases as the therapeutic data base, whch are now represented by a "frame" (8) made up of two fields.
    A selection field includes a set of rules of evocation concerning 350 basic symptoms likely to be recognized by health workers having received a basic medical training; these signs are sufficient to activate a diagnosis and may also, separately or in association, lend a weight of evocation to the diagnosis under consideration.
    A diagnosis field contains rules of two types: obligatory and optional. Non-verification of an obligatory rule leads to the elimination of that diagnosis. These rules, separately or in association, participate in the attribution of a degree of certainty for each diagnosis ("certain", "highly probable", "probable"). The premises of these diagnosis rules rest either on some 2000 clinical or para-clinical signs or on other diagnoses. Certain of these symptoms,

such as intense pain, are classed "to be treated" and such a patient should at least receive symptomatic relief.

8.1.4. For each sign considered in the preceding bases, there is a corresponding question. Explanatory messages are provided for difficult questions. Each question belongs to a category so as to avoid questions beyond the capacity of the user's knowledge or material circumstances. A set of conditional rules links all the signs into a network which assures the consistency of the interrogation.

8.1.5. In order to adapt TROPICAID-2 to the environment in which it is to be used, the different knowledge bases take into account several parameters: 1) the level of knowledge of the user; 2) the diagnostic tools available; 3) the therapeutic means available; 4) the epidemiological situation of the diseases. These parameters may be interactively defined by the user and remain in a non-volatile RAM thus making one system useable in widely diverse situations.

8.2. Operation

8.2.1. TROPICAID-2 may still be used as a series of data bases which may be consulted using successive menus of selection. TROPICAID-2 uses the rules of the therapeutic data base to select the best treatment and those of the pharmacological data base to determine the best posology. The rules of the diagnostic data base allow to check a diagnosis before treatment or entry in the data collection module.

8.2.2. Especially, in developing countries, rather than make an accurate diagnosis leading to a specific treatment, the problem remains of choosing the optimal therapy in the face of more or less probable diagnostic hypotheses and limited means of healing. We propose a solution to this problem in three steps.

The first step is the registration of the main symptoms of the the patient using selection grids concerning the 350 basic signs.

The second step begins by the selection of suspected diseases using the rules of evocation. The diagnoses thus selected are ordered relative to an index relative to the frequency of the disease, its priority rating, the concordance with clinical presentation, the weight of suspicion and the degree of certitude. Then, the choice of the most pertinent question calls into play the diagnosis rules of the top classed diseases. Anamnestic signs are asked before clinical examination signs and both of them before lab signs. The answers update the findings base and permit the elimination of some diagnoses and the imputation to others of a degree of certitude. It permits also possibly, as the system iterates to the beginning of step 2, the addition of some new diagnoses. This cycle continues until the verification of a stop criterion which may depend on the signs not explained by a disease and the "priority" diseases still unverified.

The last step consists of choosing a therapy based on the diagnoses retained which are now classed according to their frequency, degree of certitude, degree of priority and therapeutic possibilities.

Diseases which are "certain" receive their specific treatment. For those which are "highly probable", the specific treatment is recommended unless it falls within several "highly probable" for which there is a common generalized treatment which is then selected. For those diagnoses which are only "probable", only the generalized treatments are proposed. In any case, no more than two treatments are suggested, and the second only if the first doesn't "cover" all the signs classed "to be treated" complained of by the patient.

9. CONCLUSION

During the development of this advanced version, we were invited by Ivory Coast Ministry of Health to present our work. This lead us to consider and prepare two trials: as a teaching and reinforcement tool for doctors and nurses in the school of medicine and as a decision-aid system for nurses in dispensaries. It will also be used by Public Health teams for data collection among dispensaries.

Indeed, from a general standpoint, a computer aid for para-medics could serve three major functions. Certainly, it serves as an aid to decision during consultation, but this requires a speed and an ease of use which must be reconciled with the quality of the response given. The time constraint is partly removed for the second function which is training and continuing education, intended not only for the local para-medic, but also possibly for foreign professionals whose field experience is limited. This teaching aim appears to be the most realistic use for the moment. Lastly, epidemiological surveillance would benefit from direct recording and immediate verification of data just as from the means of analysys and transmission of such data. There it would also be possible to monitor the activities of local dispensaries and in addition coordinate the distribution of resources.

Such a system could certainly be operational on a desk-top computer although all this capacity in a dedicated, ready-to-use HHC is even more interesting, especially as an aid to decision-making. In addition, HHCs have shown themselves to be particulary well-adapted to the conditions of use in developing countries by their ruggedness, internal mass storage, energy autonomy and relatively low cost.

The use of systems like TROPICAID faces some constraints. At the present time it would appear difficult to create a decision aid system to encompass all medicine, at least as it is practiced in the West. Aside from INTERNIST (9), medical expert systems are confined to highly specialized fields and are of limited size: glaucoma, antibiotic therapy (10). Although INTERNIST covers 600 diseases, it requires a mainframe computer and takes one hour to interrogate. However to consider all the pathology likely to be encountered at an outpost dispensary in a developing country is not unrealistic since it represents only a rather small sub-group of all known medicine, especially considering the inability to perform the more demanding sorts of diagnosis and the unavailability of a large number of treatments thus preventing an "explosion" of information due to greater refinement of the possibilities. Nevertheless, the current data bases already represent the work of six men during a year. Another problem is to associate developing countries' doctors into the elaboration and the updating of these bases. Of course, a decision aid system is of little use if the user hasn't training sufficient to register the signs and symptoms and to understand the systems replies, as well as needing a certain amount of willingness to learn and appreciation of what the system can offer. These, being human qualities, technology can do little to change directly. Lastly, such systems remain relatively costly, more than 10% of an annual dispensary budget, but maintenance is minimal, and they could contribute to a better all-around functioning of a dispensary.

We are convinced of the future of portable systems in this domain. Their performance continues to improve while their size is decreasing. While their cost is tending to fall, it will surely remain more expensive than paper but will permit a wide distribution of systems such as the one we describe. The widespread use of large numbers of such devices will give rise to a certain "standardization" of practical education and thus of the conduct of medicine throughout a country or beyond. One can only hope that such an improvement to the organization of health care will lead to positive consequences in the public health as well as the general development of a developing country.

REFERENCES

1- Alma-Ata Primary Health Care. Health for All Series (Number 1). World Health Organisation, 1978.
2- GOLDBERGER H. and SCHWENN P., 'Man-Machine Symbiosis in the Assistance and Training of Rural Health Workers: A Proposal'. Meeting the Challenge: Informatics and Medical Education (JC Pages, A.H. Levy, F.Gremy and J. Anderson, eds), IFIP-IMIA, 1983, pp 295-306, Elsevier Science Publishers B.V (North Holland).
3- TAVERNIER H., AUVERT B. and LE BEUX P., 'BLAISE: A portable CMOS Bio-Terminal Programmable in Pascal'. The Best of Computer Fairs, Vol VII, pp 250-253, 1982.
4- Selection of essential drugs. Technical Report Number 641. World Health Organisation, 1980.
5- ESSEX B.J.,Diagnostics Pathways in Clinical Medicine. Churchill
6- AUVERT B., GILBOS V., AEGERTER Ph., LE THI HUONG DU, BOUTIN Ph., MONIER J-L. and EMMANUELLI X. 'A hand-held system usable by rural health workers for medical decision making'. MIE 85, Proceedings, Helsinki, Aug. 22-29, 1985, pp 349-353, Springer Verlag Ed.
7- LE BEUX P. "Frame selection system and language". PhD Thesis, University of San Francisco Medical Center, 1974.
8- MINSKY M. 'A framework for representing knowledge'. The Psychology of computer vision. Winston eds. Mc Graw-Hill 1975 pp 211-277.
9- MILLER R.A, POPLE H.E., MYERS J.D. 'INTERNIST-1, an experimental computer-based diagnostic consultant for general internal medicine'. New-Engl. J. Med, 307, pp 468- 476, (1982).
10-SZOLOVITS·P. Artificial Intelligence in Medicine. Westview; 1982.

MULTILEVEL INFERENCE CONTROL IN EXPERT SYSTEM CODEX

F. Gyárfáš, M. Popper
Research Institute of Medical Bionics
83308 Bratislava, Jedľová 6
Czechoslovakia

ABSTRACT. Applications of expert systems in real-life
setting require many enhancements which are not in focus
of attention while they are developed and used in research
laboratories. Among many aspects which are in this respect
worth for consideration is the computational complexity
when extended and complex knowledge bases are used, say
thousands of represented entities and tenthousands
(implicit or explicit) rules. In such cases simple interpretation of production rule systems may not be sufficient.
In our contribution we aim to characterize a hierarchical
and dynamic inference mechanism control together with
the corresponding structuralisation of knowledge represen-
totion in frame-like data structures employed in CODEX
expert system.

1. INTRODUCTION

Thousands of expert systems (ES) have been reported
already. Most of them, however, work with rather small
knowledge bases (KB) of not more than some hundreds of
rules. The architecture of those systems is well known.
Their inferemce mechanism (IM) mostly embody rather simple
control strategies. The quality of their performance is
determined by adequate rule construction and efficiency
of the approximate reasoning.
  Nowadays there are not many ES working with large
KBs comprising thousands of rules. In such systems besides
increasing necessity for a knowledge base management
system methods for efficient control for search space
reduction, early prunning, hierarchical problem solving,
etc. are becoming inevitable integral parts of the inference. So that the inference control mechanism, whose
strategies can be seen as some sort of metaknowledge, is
to be considered as an important and equivalent part

R. Trappl (ed.), Cybernetics and Systems '86, 735–741.

of the established basic inference techniques as are
forward and backward chaining, conflict resolution, etc.
   In our contribution we focus on description of some
control techniques yielding more sophisticated possibilities for IM. We will mention those ones which are implemented as integral parts of the multilevel inference
control mechanism in our expert system CODEX. In it
frame-like knowledge representation is employed as well as
a mixture of two methods for approximative reasoning:
a numerical one for weighting associations and a nonnumer-
ical qualitative endorsement-like method (1) for concept
evaluation. The latter is based on monotonically ordered
rules in accordance to their rigorousity in matching
available facts, i.e. in determining the modality of
truth-values assigned to their consequences. However, we
omit description of those CODEX features as well as its
architecture, instead the reader is refered to (2-5).

2. CONCEPT SELECTION

The ES performance can be characterized by its capability
to search for correct response to a not predefined situation. In searching for such a response the ES employs
knowledge from the domain in which the situation occures.
This knowledge embodied in the KB can be considered as a
problem domain model. A KB comprises concepts - as basic
building blocks of a model - which are mutually interrelated. The response to a particular situation means that
a specific subset of concepts from KB must be selected
and the most adequate correspondence between the real
situation - represented by known facts - and related
models must be found.
   In our case the inference control mechanism has to
perform two tasks: to select concepts for evaluation
in searching for given problem solution and to determine
a proper sequence of their evaluation. These tasks could
be complex due to dynamically changing content of the
reasonable set of concepts for evaluation and changes
in the evaluation priorities. To handle this it is necessary to organize the IM control processes dynamically and
hierarchically.
   The CODEX control mechanism is backed by a hierarchical data structure (we call it agenda) which serves proper
concept scheduling for evaluation - see Fig.1.
   The stack of hierarchical dependencies (SHD) enables
the IM to evaluate concepts according to their generalization hierarchy in the KB. If a concept is to be evaluated
and it is a specialization in sequences of more general
concepts (multiple hierarchies are considered), the IM
responses by inserting the lower hierarchical elements

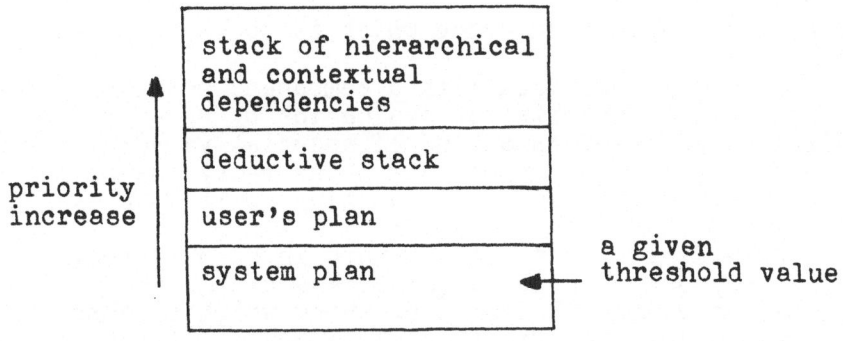

Fig.1.

into the SHD while attempting evaluate the higher one.This causes the most general concept is evaluated first. Refutation (the false-value assignment) of a more general concept yields refutation all of its specializations in any level of depth. This may result in a dramatical reduction of the needed number of concepts with explicit evaluation.

The stack of contextual dependencies has a similar function. Evaluation of a concept, especially such one which gets its value assigned by observation, is frequently reasonable in a context, i.e. in a sequence of concept evaluations. Then, if a given concept should be evaluated only after another one, it is placed to the stack while attempting evaluate those one whose evaluation should precede. This is, however, not based on generalisation dependencies but rather on practical, organizational, or technological ones. Therefore this stack does not yield an implicit truth-value propagation as in previous case. If there are implication dependencies they must be represented in the corresponding frame structure.

The deductive stack (DS) is an efficient tool for handling cases in which evaluation of a concept is based on evaluation of other ones. In such cases a concept evaluation must be frequently interrupted and suspended. The information specifying the interruption, i.e. the exact situation in which the interruption occured, must be stored in order to resume latter the suspended evaluation and conclude it. The DS is the structure in which these information are stored. A concept evaluation is resumed only if all latter interrupted concepts have been evaluated.

The user is allowed in the initial phase of the session with CODEX as well as in the course of its inference to specify its own concepts for evaluation. The user's plan serves for recording those concepts in a queue. Besides by the user specifically selected sequence of concepts it is possible to activate the inference also by a

737

predefined default sequence which is to be prepared in the KB.

The IM is provided with a component enabling selection of reasonable concepts for evaluation by association. The selection is based on a kind of associative relations among concepts in KB. The IM employs those relations as a byproduct of concept evaluation in setting up its own system plan.

Relations of associations are in KB weighted. The weight expresses the strenght of association according to the belief of the KB designer. Those weights cannot be considered as any qualification of concepts truth or falsity. They simply represent a kind of ranking the concepts associated to a given one for evaluation. As various concept can be associated several times the related association weights should be summed up. This gives rise the priority queue of associated concepts in the system plan. Priorities are given by the resulting weighting values. In order to ensure proper selectivity of concept evaluation due to this plan a threshold value may be employed. Only those concepts are actually evaluated whose association weighting value exceeds the threshold value. This value can be either set up as a default or it can be specified by the user either at the beginning of the session or even dynamically in the course of the inference.

3. CONCEPT EVALUATION

Concepts as the main building blocks of knowledge representation are in CODEX represented in a frame-like form. They correspond either to the entities of the problem domain or to (auxiliary) control objects of the given model. Their evaluation means matching the concepts with the given facts related to a particular situation and evaluation of the strenght of this match. For this purpose there are defined certain criteria expressed by production rules or procedures which support evaluation of the match. Each frame contains usually several criteria (dozens). This is due to:
  (a) different possible ways of finding the correspondence among concepts as well as different possibilities of their extensional specification
  (b) approximative nature of matching
  (c) inner structure of the concepts - their various features should be evaluated as well

A concept evaluation is generally a complex and 'expensive' operation. Making this operation more efficient and faster yields faster inference and thus makes markedly more efficient the whole ES performance. A hierarchical concept evaluation, as it is performed in CODEX, is a powerful mean for attaining inference efficiency. The related principles are described in the following.

The concept representation includes an evaluation part which consist of an ordered set of criteria whose evaluation priorities correspond to the following order (from the highest to the lowest): inheritance, undecidability, refutation, definitive confirmation, modal confirmations (endorsments), and for concept attributes evaluation - see Fig.2. Actually neither of those criteria is obligatory in the concept representation, however, at least one kind from the three last listed criteria must be specified. In different concepts combinations of various types of criteria are allowed.

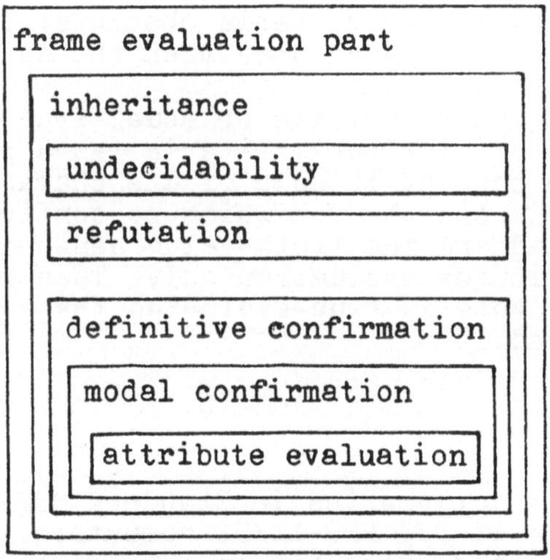

```
┌─────────────────────────────────────────┐
│ frame evaluation part                   │
│  ┌───────────────────────────────────┐  │
│  │ inheritance                       │  │
│  │  ┌─────────────────────────────┐  │  │
│  │  │ undecidability              │  │  │
│  │  └─────────────────────────────┘  │  │
│  │  ┌─────────────────────────────┐  │  │
│  │  │ refutation                  │  │  │
│  │  └─────────────────────────────┘  │  │
│  │  ┌─────────────────────────────┐  │  │
│  │  │ definitive confirmation     │  │  │
│  │  │  ┌───────────────────────┐  │  │  │
│  │  │  │ modal confirmation    │  │  │  │
│  │  │  │  ┌─────────────────┐  │  │  │  │
│  │  │  │  │ attribute       │  │  │  │  │
│  │  │  │  │ evaluation      │  │  │  │  │
│  │  │  │  └─────────────────┘  │  │  │  │
│  │  │  └───────────────────────┘  │  │  │
│  │  └─────────────────────────────┘  │  │
│  └───────────────────────────────────┘  │
└─────────────────────────────────────────┘
```

Fig.2.

The inheritance criterion, which is simple in its construction, ensures the false-value and undecidability inheritance from more to less general concepts. If such inheritance occures no other criteria evaluation takes place.

The undecidability criterion tests whether facts needed for concept evaluation are available at all. If not, further evaluation is sensless so that the concept is marked as undecidable.

The refutation criterion frequently allows to find out in a simple way the mismatch of a given concept to a given situation (facts) and its positive evaluation causes false-value assignment to the concept. Naturally, such a criterion should be considered only if the observation and computational complexity of its evaluation is lesser as in the case of conceptconfirmation. This can be frequently the case. If the refutation criterion is true-evaluated

739

then evaluation of the remaining criteria is omitted.

For many concepts it is possible to design a criterion for their definite (categorial) confirmation. If this criterion is true-evaluated the concept gets true-value assigned, the modal confirmation criteria evaluation is omitted and only attribute criteria are evaluated if are specified.

The modal confirmation criteria (endorsements) correspond to different possible matches between a concept and facts. They enable to evaluate the strenght of the match. If there is a match then the concept gets a modal true-value assigned, e.g. possibly-true, likely-true, nearly-true, etc. Successful evaluation of a more rigorous criterion makes evaluation of weaker criteria obsolete. If all modal criteria have been false-evaluated then the concept gets false value assigned.

If a concept has a definite or modal true-value assigned the evaluation of attribute criteria takes place. Attributes specify the concept in some of its characteristics. There are cases of concepts for which no confirmation criteria are specified and the truth-value assignment is based on the attributes evaluation only. Then in CODEX if at least one attribute is true-evaluated the concept gets true-value assigned.

4. CONCLUSION

The CODEX has been implemented in Standard MUMPS and it runs on TESLA SM-4 or DEC PDP-11/50 computers. It was developed for diagnostic consultation in real clinical practice. Till now several medical knowledge bases were developed or are under developement in domains of lung diseases, localised peripheral nerve lesions and entrapments, cerebellum syndrommes, classification of epileptic seizures, evaluation of acid-base equilibrium distortions, and endogenuous psychiatric diseases. The average number of concepts in KBs exceeds the number of five hundreds and the number of criteria is in order of several thousands.

The structure of multilevel inference control embodied in the system CODEX enables real-time consultation which does not overflow the patience of physicians.

References

(1) Cohen,P.R.,Grinberg,M.R.:'A theory of heuristic reasoning about uncertainty', The AI Magazine,17-23, Summer 1983

(2) Gyárfáš,F.,Popper,M.:'CODEX: Prototypes driven backward and forward chaining Computerised Diagnostic Expert System',Cybernetics and System Research,(ed. R.Trappl),North-Holland,821-824,1984
(3) Popper,M.,Gyárfáš,F.:'CODEX: A Computer-based Diagnostic Expert System',Artificial Intelligence and Information-Control Systems of Robots,(ed.I.Plander),North-Holland,297-300,1984
(4) Popper,M.,Gyárfáš,F.:'Two flows of approximativeness in diagnostic expert systems',Medical Informatics Europe 85,(eds.F.H.Roger,P.Gronroos,R.Tervo-Pellika, R.O'Hoore),Helsinky,Springer-Verlag,163-167,1985
(5) Popper,M.,Stanek,J.:'Approximativeness of expert system inference: Is a uniform mechanism sufficient?',Medical Decision Making: Diagnostic Strategies and Expert Systems,(eds.J.H.van Bemmel et al.),North-Holland, 373-376,1985

ANALYZING, REPRESENTING AND INTERPRETING
EXPERT STRATEGIC KNOWLEDGE

L. Johnson and E.T. Keravnou
Centre for Information Technology
Brunel, The University of West London,
Uxbridge,
Middlesex UB8 3PH, UK.

ABSTRACT. We discuss how the strategic knowledge of an expert
can be conceptually analysed, and how this analysis can be
represented and interpreted in the context of an expert system.

1. TASK ANALYSIS TREES

Task analysis is a decomposion of tasks into subtasks. We extend this
notion to cover the intellectual complexity encountered in knowledge-
intensive tasks.

This extended task analysis tree is a static representation of the
means for discharging some global knowledge based task such as diagnosing.
A task is either primitive or non-primitive. A primitive task manipulates
facts. A non-primitive task (sometimes referred to as a control task) can
be refined into a set of subtasks that collectively define the means for
discharging the higher task. Only non-primitive tasks have specified
termination conditions. As subtasks can themselves be non-primitive, a
task tree is defined whose leaf nodes represent primitive tasks.

A particular strategy under a task has specified **enabling** and **disabling** conditions. Conditions are evaluated using the problem specific
data. A strategy may be selected if its enabling condition is satisfied
and its disabling condition is not satisfied. Hence disabling conditions
override the enabling conditions. These conditions constitute the logical
bases for the strategies. Default information can also be included whereby
the specified default strategy is always selected in the absence of any
contrary evidence. The ordering of strategies under some task can be of
significance. Furthermore, the set of strategies for some task can be
partitioned into groups of alternatives.

In dynamic terms, therefore, an instantiation of a non-primitive task
is accomplished by going through its specified strategies, selecting the
one to apply next, executing the selected strategy and repeating this
cycle until the task's termination condition is satisfied.

R. Trappl (ed.), Cybernetics and Systems '86, 743–750.

```
( <TASK>
 (PARAMETERS  <parameter₁> ... <parameterₙ>)
    (TRACE  <token> ... <token>)
    (SITUATION  <token> ... <token>)
    (ENTERED-FROM
         ( <supertask-id 1>
            (message
              (concrete
                 (why-text      <token> ... <token>)
                 (enablingc     <token> ... <token>)
                 (disablingc    <token> ... <token>) )
              (abstract ....   )))
         ( <supertask-id 2>)
               .
               .                    ))
    (STRATEGIES
         ((( <strategy-id> <description>) ...)
          (( <strategy-id> <description>) ...) ....))
    (ACHIEVED-THROUGH
         ($or ( <action-on-completion>
             (enabled-if  <termination condition>))
           ( <subtask call 1>
             (enabled-if   <condition>)
             (disabled-if  <condition>))
           ( <subtask call 2>
               .
               .                    ))))
key: a  <token> is either a word or a function call
```

Figure 1   Task frame format.

2.   REPRESENTATION STRUCTURE FOR REASONING TASKS

The conceptual structure of a reasoning task is mapped into frames.
Referring to figure 1, SITUATION contains, more concisely than TRACE, the
information on what the task performs. This information is stored in an
explanation tree (see section 3) when the task is performed. The ENTERED-
FROM slot gives all the supertasks that employ the given task as one of
their strategies; each supertask is associated with concrete and abstract
messages. An abstract message expresses the conditions defining the
selection of the task in the context of pursuing any instance of the
particular supertask. For example, in a diagnostic domain, the abstract
message for some DISCRIMINATE-REFS strategy ENTERED-FROM some supertask
EXPLORE would say "we discriminate between the possible refinements to a
hypothesis, if none of these refinements has yet been suggested". This
message involves general terms like 'hypothesis' and 'possible refinement', rather than an actual hypothesis and an actual possible refinement.
Concrete messages, on the other hand, indicate why the task was selected
in a particular instantiation of the supertask. Hence concrete messages,
like TRACE and SITUATION, consist of text nested with function calls which

744

embed the particular values qualifying the specific task instantiation. This information is also stored in the explanation tree. The STRATEGIES slot applies only for a non-primitive task. It gives the set of strategies for the task (each strategy being accompanied by a short description) partitioned into groups of alternatives. The ACHIEVED-THROUGH slot also refers to non-primitive tasks. It specifies the calls to the various subtasks and the action to be undertaken when the particular task instantiation has been accomplished (this is usually to re-enter the supertask tnat invoked the given task in the first place). The calls to subtasks are associated with enabling and disabling conditions. In the case of primitive tasks the list of subtask calls is replaced by an unconditional call to the task itself.

3. TASK INTERPRETER

The task interpreter is called with the name of a task and a parameter list. Its function is to create an instantiation of the task pertaining to the particular parameters, to link such task instantiations into a strategic explanation tree, to display the particular trace message and to execute the task. Initially the task interpreter is invoked for the particular global task.

Task executions range from single unconditional calls to procedures manipulating facts and/or requesting actions, to requests for executing a sequence of subtasks in a specified order, or to requests for cycling through a sequence of subtasks, selecting for execution, the first subtask whose enabling condition is satisfied and its disabling condition (if any) is not satisfied. A request for a subtask execution is a recursive call to the task interpreter. The interpreter maintains a stack whose top points to the task instantiation that is currently executing. Thus a pointer to the subtask instantiation to execute next, is pushed onto the stack prior to execution and the stack is popped when the subtask instantiation has been achieved. When a non-primitive task is reentered through one of its subtask instantiations, on the latter's completion, the interpreter recognizes the particular request as a recursive call to an already existing task instantiation. This is because the particular task can not be called from within the subtask, an instantiation of which is pointed at by the top of the stack. The stack is thus popped to point to the non-primitive task instantiation concerned. (More care should be taken when two tasks, have each other as a subtask.) The function of the interpreter, especially the generation of strategic explanation trees, is analyzed in more detail below.

Constructing a case specific picture: During a problem solving activity a picture, that presents a (partial) solution to the particular problem, is gradually being built. The resolution of the picture is enhanced as the activity progresses. It is being constructed by primitive task instantiations, and directs the selection of the next task to execute.

Creating task instantiations: A task instantiation is created by retrieving the particular task frame and substituting for every instance of each

745

parameter specified in the PARAMETERS slot the corresponding value that has been passed to the interpreter. Each function call in the TRACE, SITUATION, and ACHIEVED-THROUGH slots, and the relevant concrete message in the ENTERED-FROM slot, is then replaced with the value returned by it (see section 2).

Generating strategic explanation trees: A strategic explanation tree, for a particular problem solution, is dynamically generated from the task tree which is the analysis of the relevant problem solving task. The generation of the explanation tree is guided by the available problem specific data (see above). An instantiation of a non-primitive task is accomplished by generating instantiations of selected subtasks until the task's termination condition is reached. An instantiation of a primitive task is accomplished by performing the appropriate manipulations on the facts. Explanation trees, therefore, consist of all the task instantiations that needed to be accomplished in order to reach some 'solution' concerning the particular problems, i.e. in order to complete the particular picture. The root node of an explanation tree corresponds to the particular instantiation of the global task and the leaf nodes correspond to instantiations of primitive tasks. The 'entered-from' property specifies the supertask instantiation that set up the particular task instantiation. The 'how' property, for instantiations of non-primitive tasks, gives the list of subtask instantiations that were needed to accomplish the particular task instantiation. 'Situation' properties were explained in section 2. The 'why' property specifies the concrete message corresponding to the particular task instantiation (see section 2).

The 'alternatives' property needs some clarification. The alternatives to some task instantiation depend on its application context, i.e. on the particular supertask instantiation entering it.

On the one hand the alternatives to a task, under some supertask, are made explicit in the STRATEGIES slot of the particular supertask frame. Two subtasks under the same task are alternatives if they constitute alternative means for achieving the same (sub)ends, and two subtasks are non-alternatives (but co-operators) if the one could yield a situation enabling the subsequent selection of the other. Although this is a necessary condition, it is not sufficient since two alternatives, as indicated below, may also be related in this fashion. Thus, an additional condition is that two non-alternatives must not operate towards the achievement of the same immediate (sub)ends. For example, each of a set of information acquisition heuristics operates towards the abduction of some refinement to the focus hypothesis, but each with a different means. Thus they constitute alternatives to each other. However, choosing a particular heuristic might give rise to a picture whereby that heuristic is no longer the best choice for achieving the particular ends and thus an alternative heuristic is selected halfway through the processing. Thus one heuristic can lead to the selection of one of its alternatives (which in reality represents a different form of co-operation). This, in fact, is often the case. Thus in this case the alternatives to a task instantiation are those tasks that could be alternatively applied to the same factual entity or entities.

On the other hand alternatives are implicitly defined and need to be explicated for particular instantiations of the task. The alternatives are implicit when the particular task performs some sort of a selection operation on a finite set of case specific entities, such as information acquisition actions associated with relevant hypotheses' predictions or the suggested refinements to the current focus. Thus the alternatives to such a task instantiation are the remaining choices to the one encoded in the task instantiation. These 'alternatives' do not constitute alternative choices for the task to undertake next, but alternative choices for the particular generic entity involved.

Explicit alternative choices are determined by the interpreter during the execution of the particular supertask instantiation, together with the reason for turning each one down as: "the enabling condition was not satisfied", "the disabling condition was satisfied", "the selected task is always preferred to the particular alternative if both tasks are applicable (ordering constraint)". Implicit alternative choices (if any) are explicated by the interpreter when the task instantiation has been achieved. The information on alternatives to task instantiations is used to answer "WHY-NOT" questions. The incorporation of a strategic explanations facility is discussed in [6].

Displaying trace messages: The trace message corresponding to a particular task instantiation is displayed prior to its execution. Primitive task instantiations can display additional messages from within their associated execution code. Trace messages are indented to reflect the nesting of task instantiations for the particular problem case.

Executing task instantiations through the ACHIEVED-THROUGH slot: A primitive task instantiation is executed by invoking, with the parameter values concerned, the associated code that performs the relevant factual manipulations. For non-primitive task instantiations there are two cases:
(i) The execution amounts to executing a sequence of subtasks in order.
(ii) The execution amounts to selecting and executing one subtask; this involves cycling through the subtasks, for the particular task, selecting the first whose enabling condition is satisfied and its disabling condition (if any) is not satisfied. When the particular subtask is achieved, the selection process may be repeated until the task's termination condition is met. This "repeat-selection" aspect of a non-primitive task execution, captures the fact that a human problem solver employs strategies in a collaborative fashion to achieve a task, and that he/she switches from one strategy to an alternative strategy when the currently selected strategy seizes to be in his/her mind the best choice for achieving the particular (sub)ends. In the NEOMYCIN system, a non-primitive task is associated with a set of meta-rules (if-then statements whose consequents refer to subtasks) and a control regime that indicates how the meta-rules are to be applied to achieve instantiations of the particular task 3 . It seems to us, however, that these control regimes have no theoretical foundations. In our task representation structure, the real driving force behind the selection of a task are the enabling and disabling conditions (with the relaxation conditions as a future addition). It is the combination of the particular selection conditions for the respective subtasks under a particular task that defines the

particular invocation regime. The general "repeat- selection" regime is
then sufficient to yield the required behaviour as captured in these conditions. We have checked that each one of the NEOMYCIN control regimes can
in fact be captured via some combination of enabling and disabling
conditions, which leads us to hypothesise that control regimes as NEO-
MYCIN's are ad hoc constraints, concealing the true application conditions
for the strategies concerned. Since the antecedents of the NEOMYCIN meta-
rules are not refined into enabling, disabling and relaxation components,
the incorporation of a selection procedure that reasons from the logical
bases (captured in the above condition types) of the subtasks under some
task, is not possible.

4. EXTENDING THE TASK STRUCTURE

Strategy Relaxation Conditions and Defaults: The immediate extension to
the task representation structure would be to incorporate strategy relaxation conditions and defaults. The analysis and subsequent use of relaxation conditions in some system must reflect the way in which the
particular experts tend to relax their tactical choices. For example,
relaxation conditions may need to be refined into those for relaxing the
enabling conditions and those for relaxing the disabling conditions. If a
first cycle through the strategies specified under a task fails to select
a strategy through the satisfaction of its enabling condition and the
disatisfaction of its disabling condition (if any), a second cycle may
attempt to select a strategy by relaxing its disabling condition, which if
also unsuccessful, a third cycle may attempt to select a strategy by
relaxing its enabling condition. If all this fails then the specified
default (if any) is to be selected, whose enabling condition in a sense is
relaxed if no other strategy can be selected. This discussion concerning
the role of relaxation conditions is purely speculative. The important
thing is that it is natural, in problem solving, to attempt to relax
(within an allowable or feasible range) the current constraints (as
captured in the enabling and disabling conditions) guarding the selection
of strategies when no choice is possible. The inclusion of relaxation
conditions in our task representation structure and their appropriate
manipulation is therefore necessary.

Reasoning with Unknown Strategy Selection Conditions: Up till now we have
assumed that the truth status of the strategy selection conditions can be
established as either "true" or "false". However, when dealing with
problem domains, such as the diagnostic domains, that are guarded by
incomplete information, it is more natural to assume that the truth status
of such conditions may simply be "undetermined". In such cases the problem
solver must make the best possible choice given the available information.
This may be to abandon the relevant task as currently unachievable, and
attempt to achieve the particular supertask via a different means. Our
explication of the strategy selection criteria into enabling, disabling
and relaxation factors, rather than compiling them into arbitrary boolean
expressions, gives **flexibility** to the problem solver by allowing it to
reach reasonable decisions even in the light of unknown information. The

748

problem solver can, therefore, succeed in cases where systems employing compiled applicability criteria would have failed. This is because each selection condition type serves a different purpose and should be treated accordingly. For example if the enabling condition for a strategy is true and its disabling condition is undetermined, the strategy could still be selected if the condition relaxing the disabling condition is true. Similarly if the enabling condition is undetermined and the condition relaxing it is true then the strategy could still be selected etc. If such conditions were compiled, their overall truth value would resolve to "undetermined" if one condition were "undetermined", thus preventing the selection of a strategy (which in actual fact should have been selected at the particular choice point). If the combinations of truth values for the conditions, that would allow the selection of a particular strategy under some task, are specific to the particular ⟨task, strategy⟩ pair, then these combinations of truth values should be made explicit.

Task Termination Conditions: A further extension to the task analysis is concerned with task termination conditions. Since the same strategy can be invoked under more than one tasks the termination conditions for the strategy could be specified by the particular tasks invoking it. Further, a default termination condition can be specified which is assumed if no other termination condition is specified. Termination conditions can either be included as extra values under the various facets of the ENTERED-FROM slot of the strategy frame or they can be passed as extra parameters to the task interpreter. In the latter case termination conditions can even be dynamically formulated.

Concept Dependent Applications of Strategic Principles: In the current task analysis structure we assume that the means for achieving any instantiation of a particular task are independent of the factual entities (domain concepts) corresponding to such instantiations. For example the means for refining a hypothesis are independent of the particular hypothesis. We can envision a situation however, whereby the means for refining some hypothesis are specific to that hypothesis. The diagnostic principles, e.g. "if the hypothesis can not be directly tested for confirmation then you need to refine it" in the above example, are independent of the instances of the relevant domain concepts. It is the application of a principle (e.g. how to refine a concept) that may vary from concept to concept (c.f. the CENTAUR 1 and MDX 2 systems whereby application instances of a diagnostic principle are distributed amongst the domain concepts concerned (i.e. each concept is associated with the particular means for refining it) -- in these systems the actual generic principles are not made explicit and thus can not be communicated). Below we outline the changes, needed in our task analysis structure and its subsequent representation and implementation, in order to cover for principles whose application may be concept specific.

Since a concept dependent application of a principle would most probably be an exception rather than the rule (i.e. a principle's application would generally be uniform in relation to instances of the domain concepts), the overheads to be incurred in storing and executing the information concerning the concept specific applications of a principle should not be significant. Such domain concepts are to be linked to their specific analyses of the application of the particular principle and similarly the generic definition of the principle is to be linked to these concepts. At the representation level such pointers are to be specified as additional slots for the domain, concept and task, frames. At the implementation level, the task interpreter when instantiating tasks, must recognize a particular task instantiation as one that diverges from the task's normal execution procedure and should therefore transfer control to the specific execution procedure.

Thus by treating tasks as data we facilitate extensions in their organizational structure. A change to the task structure can be introduced simply by incorporating the relevant changes to the task interpreter.

REFERENCES:

1   Aikins, J.S., 'Prototypical knowledge for expert systems', Artificial Intelligence, **20**, 1983, 163-210.

2   Chandrasekaran, B. & Mittal, S., 'Conceptual representation of medical knowledge for diagnosis by computer: MDX and related systems', Advances in Computers, **22**, 1983, 217-293.

3   Clancey, W.J., 'Acquiring, representing and evaluating a competence model of diagnostic strategy', in Chi, Glaser and Farr (eds.) The Nature of Expertise, 1985.

4   Johnson, L., 'The need for competence models in the design of expert consultant systems', Int. J. Systems Research and Information Science, **1**, 1985, 23-36.

5   Keravnou, E.T., Building expert systems that model competence: a case study in fault diagnosis, Ph.D Thesis, Centre for Information Technology, Brunel University, UK.

6   Keravnou, E.T. & Johnson, L., 'Design of expert systems from the perspective of conversation theory methodology', in Trappl, R. (ed.) Cybernetics and Systems Research, **2**, 1984, 651-654.

REPRESENTING LEGAL TEXTS BY LOGIC PROGRAMS

K. Yalumov and G. Gargov
Institute of Mathematics
P.O. Box 373, 1090 Sofia
Bulgaria

ABSTRACT   Current results of the work on the ESIM project for developing a knowledge-based expert system on a set of business regulations are
presented. Knowledge is extracted from natural language documents by an
informal analysis. It is then encoded manually in the PROLOG-like logic
programming language NESY. NESY is an instrumental, domain-independent
expert system which is being developed in parallel with the domain knowledge base. The project is sponsored by the Bulgarian Industrial Association.
     Some characteristic features of the process of legal text formali-
zation are discussed as well as possible solutions of several essential
problems in this area. Proposals are put forward for the improvement of
the logic power of PROLOG-like programming languages.

1.   INTRODUCTION

Below are reported some current results obtained in the course of
developing ESIM - a knowledge-based expert system on a set of business
regulations concerning small-scale enterprises. Legal knowledge is extracted from the relevant natural language documents by an informal
analysis. The next step is a manual encoding in a PROLOG-like logic
programming language called NESY - an instrumental, domain-independent
expert system which is developed simultaneously with the knowledge base
for the project /1/.
     We discuss several characteristic features of the process of legal
texts formalization as well as solutions of some essential features in
the area. Proposals on improving the expressive and deductive power of
PROLOG-like programming languages are given.

2.   FEATURES OF THE LEGAL TEXT FORMALIZATION PROCESS

There is a number of peculiarities and difficulties when formalizing a
normative text. Some of them arise due to the inherent incompleteness
and ambiguity of the language exploited there, others are results of

751

R. Trappl (ed.), Cybernetics and Systems '86, 751–758.

shortcommings in the present technology of drafting normative documents, but the main problem is of course that these documents are designed for use by humans and not by computers. Although usually very carefully worded, legal texts in fact presuppose familiarity with a substantial volume of extra-linguistic knowledge which is accepted as self-evident by an intelligent user but which has to be explicitly included in the knowledge base in the form of "additions". For instance, the system should explicitly know that a statute-book is a normative document, and moreover - that all normative documents are documents. The same is also true for the set of domain-specific equivalence statements by which synonymy is defined.

Our experience with the ESIM project confirms the greater logical complexity of consultative expert systems based on formalized text compared with the predominant number of "diagnostic" expert systems. Most known expert systems are driven by knowledge bases containing rule sets defining appropriate actions for specific "symptoms". The development of an automatic consultant on a knowledge of normative texts requires solutions of more difficult logic and linguistic problems. In the latter case for instance queries have more variations in respect to form, complexity, content and expected interpretation.

In order to keep an as close as possible correspondence between the formalized knowledge and the original text we have decided to follow "the letter of documents". Formal predicates' names are chosen so as to match the natural language text with the intention at the same time to keep them context independent. When one recognizes some interdependencies appropriate rules are included as specific additions. In this way we avoid a crucial dependence on some basic "canonical" relations and relax the restrictions on the query form.

However the necessity to explicate in a best possible way the domain-specific relations is not rejected - it remains an important work connected with the better understanding of the problem domain and the knowledge base structure. This is a substantial part of the original text analysis. The latter includes a text restructuring and development of a dictionary of the basic domain consepts. This work was done by the legal experts in collaboration with the knowledge engineers.

3. AN EXAMPLE

Some typical aspects of the formalization process will be illustrated here by means of an example. We intentionally present a hypothetical text in order to relieve the reader from the irrelevant and somewhat misleading details of the real text. All essential from formalizational point of view features however are preserved:

"Bulgarian Industrial Association may use as a financial source for its funds part of the profit formed as a difference between the provisional and the regular prices of the new production reduced by the corresponding abatements. The amount of the above is determined by a contract between BIA and the investor of the small enterprise. The funds established by this routine are special purpose funds."

The meaning of the above text is represented by several implicatio-

nal rules. Three of them directly correspond to the original text and
the rest are contained in the knowledge subbase "Additions". The first
three rules run as follows:

```
is_a_fund_of(X1,bia), is_a_source_for(X2,X1),
is_a_small_enterprise(X3), is_a_profit_of(X4,X3),
is_a_new_production_of(X5,X3), is_a_provisional_price_of(X6,X5),
is_a_regular_price_of(X7,X5), is_the_difference_between(X8,X6,X7),
is_formed_as(X4,X8), is_an_abatement(X9),
is_the_reduction_of_with(X10,X4,X9), is_a_part_of(X11,X10)
==> may(use_as(bia,X11,X2)).

is_a_fund_of(X1,bia), is_a_source_for(X2,X1),
is_a_small_enterprise(X3), is_a_profit_of(X4,X3),
is_a_new_production_of(X5,X3), is_a_provisional_price_of(X6,X5),
is_a_regular_price_of(X7,X5), is_the_difference_between(X8,X6,X7),
is_formed_as(X4,X8), is_an_abatement(X9),
is_the_reduction_of_with(X10,X4,X9), is_a_part_of(X10,X11),
use_as(bia,X11,X2), is_the_amount_of(X12,X11),
is_an_investor_of(X13,X3), is_a_contract_between(X14,bia,X13)
==> is_determined_by(X12,X14).

is_a_fund_of(X1,bia),
is_established_by_routine_from(X1,norm(doc(abc123), article(2),
paragraph(1), ))
==> is_a_special_purpose_fund(X1).
```

All X-es here represent variables, the comma sign - conjunction, and
the arrow sign - implication. The "norm" functor is used when referring
to portions of original text, in this case the part "... by this routine...". Some of the additions (used not only here) are:

```
is_a_fund_of(X,Y) ==> is_a_fund(X).
is_a_special_purpose_fund(X) ==> is_a_fund(X).
X(Y1) ==> may(X(Y1)).
X(Y1,Y2) ==> may(X(Y1,Y2)).
X(Y1,Y2,Y3) ==> may(X(Y1,Y2,Y3)).
```

The example is more complicated then the typical case - our observations
based on about 200 rules presently encoded indicate 6 to 7 predicates
per rule on the average. The logic rules are less compact then natural
language representation for many reasons, the most obvious of which is
that users of the latter representation are more intelligent and informed. One can expect the domain knowledge in this project (i.e. without
pure linguistic data and interpreting procedures) to contain ultimately
about 1500 rules and facts. Additions are almost trice the rules directly representing original text. However additions are usually much
simpler.

The ESIM knowledge base consists of three subbases, or main knowledge sources (KS): the domain knowledge base NORM, the linguistic knowledge base LING to handle quasi-natural language interaction (its deve-

lopment is intentionally delayed) and the base PROG containing clause
sets which define various interpreting and utility procedures. The knowledge base structure has a depth more than 1. Any KS has a meta-level
part and an object-level part. A meta-component can for instance contain
a text fragment from documents (as an argument of the 'text' predicate)
and some descriptors too, while the associated object knowledge is the
formal representation of the text. The meta-knowledge facilitates retrieval of potentially relevant object knowledge and serves the implementation of a detailed explanation concerning the way a query answer is
generated.

4. QUERY TYPES

When logically representing a normative text one is at the same time
obliged to consider how this representation will be interpreted and what
kinds of questions one could ask on the basis of this knowledge. These
two issues are in fact closely interdependent.
    In the ESIM problem domain there are not so much data for specific
documents, organizations, quantities, etc. Hence queries about concrete
values such as WHICH, HOW_MUCH, ACC_TO_WHICH are rare - the fact is consistent with the well known difference between a knowledge base and a
conventional data base. The larger part of normative knowledge is related to general object classes and has the form of universally quantified
implications. In our case the majority of queries is of the types HOW TO,
IS_IT_PERMITTED, WHAT_IS, etc. These are equivalent of logic implications
with or without additional restrictions. It is not expected usually to
get specific variable bindings as an answer, but a query confirmation/
rejection together with some additional details. In many cases a positive answer has the form of a conditional statement. An answer with a small
number of conditions would be acceptable but more complicated answers
have to be simplified. In this case the user is asked to supply additional restrictions and possibly some reduction of the interconnected items
in the conditions is performed. The basic query types are interpreted by
specialized procedures which rely on a more realistic notion of inference. Upon failure to relate a query to some basic type a general procedure (see below) is directly invoked and it is possible the user to be
prompted to reformulate his question. Some queries require pure knowledge
retrieval which is fortunately facilitated by the knowledge base organization which preserves the connection between the meta- and the object
knowledge. In such cases there are searched those rules which mention
relations and constants (or their synonymes) from the query.

5. THE NESY SYSTEM

The formalized text in ESIM is a declarative logic program interpreted
by the PROLOG-like system NESY. An earlier version of the system, designed as an expert system shell, is described in /7/. At present NESY is
more closely oriented to PROLOG (cf. e.g. /2/) but possesses features of
a more advanced logic programming language.

At an intuitive level a data set is viewed as a conjunction of its elments with no need this connective to be made explicit. Lists are a natural representation in this case hence NESY represents conjunction by a list link, externally - by a comma. Besides lists are known to be an extrimely flexible data structure. In PROLOG they are playing (unjustifiably) a secondary role: lists are implemented as a special case of terms and one expects to use them "if needed only". Depending on the implementation, the clause head and body may not be the head and tail of a list and the data base may not be a list of clauses neither a conjunctive term. The basic data structure (the term) is also not a list.

NESY preserves the data logic structure representing them at the same time as lists. Thus the list representation flexibility for both data and programs is combined with the PROLOG procedures for list processing. These procedures which are multi-purpose and so even more elaborated than their LISP analogs, are exploited more fully than in PROLOG. Each NESY term is a list but a convenient external functor and operator notation is supported. The data base and any its part are regular data structures and can appear as normal variable bindings. So one can easily combine structural and logic means for dynamic data analysis, interpretation and modification. Some of the positive effects of this implementation are the better system comprehension, convenient knowledge structuring and easier definition of various utilities and interpreters. Examples of these are a LISP interpreter and the interpreter CallOn answering complex logic queries upon an explicit indication of accessible data. Varying both goals and data allows a dynamic focus of attention. CallOn presents the most advanced representational and deductive facility of NESY which is crucial for the successful encoding and interpretation of normative texts.

5.1. The CallOn procedure

The predicate call_on(Goals,Data,Result) calls Goals as a goal assuming to be known only Data. Goals and Data range over arbitrary combinations of atomic formulas by means of connectives AND, OR, NOT, XOR, EQV and ==> , i.e over universally quantified propositional combinations of basic assertions. The PROLOG built-in predicate call(X) invokes X as a goal assuming as accessible the whole data base. The NESY call(X) is a particular case of call_on where Data is instantiated to the data base.

CallOn is the procedure allowing to dynamically control the knowledge accessibility - by an interactive or automatic analysis based on deduction or pattern matching. So one can isolate particular fragments of the base and persue subsequent goals by taking into account these fragments only. It is also possible to restrict the Goals structure. Besides the better goaldirectedness, a modular knowledge base organization is facilitated too. One can use the same relational names for predicates with different meaning and used in different KSs. The implementation of an explanation capability with explicitly controlled level of details is based on CallOn as well.

CallOn is in fact an extension of pure PROLOG towards a three-valued logic: the Result returned is yes, no or fail. Negation is treated more realistically and broader classes of query types are correctly answered.

The procedure is defined as a clause set expressing various logic transformations for goal-subgoal reduction and for alternative uses of data
acc. to their logical structure. For instance such well known logical
equivalencies are applied as the de Morgan lows which are valid in the
three-valued logics (cf. /4/).

It is appropriate to distinguish the domain-independent (or pure
logic) equivalencies applied by CallOn from the domain-specific ones.
The former are built into the procedure definition while the latter are
used via the Data argument. Domain-specific equivalencies are in general
counterparts of synonymes in the problem domain. For instance, in the
ESIM world establishes(X,Y) and organizes(X,Y) are equivalent. Expert
opinion was taken into account to decide which pairs of relations to be
declared equivalent. Note that the above equivalence is not purely linguistic one as is e.g. the case with establishes(X,Y) and
is_established_by(Y,X).

The boundaries of CallOn applicability as an automatic theorem prover are not yet fully understood. All we can say at present is that the
procedure is by no means complete. If the Result returned is yes then
Goals are correctly inferred from Data. The Result no means that the
search for Goals has been unsuccessful but the Goals negation has been
successfully inferred. If neither is the case then we have fail.

5.1.1. Answering implicational queries. An extr mely important case of
query is when an universally quantified implication is called as a goal.
In PROLOG a query of the form   ?- (c(X,Y) :- a(X), b(Y))
usually fails and the definition   (X1 :- X2) :- clause(X1,X2)
will in general not remedy the situation because goals of the rule body
in a query can be arbitrarily ordered, query variables should not be instantiated (as it is in PROLOG), etc. CallOn at first searches an implicational rule through the data, such that from its consequent(s) one can
infer the goal's consequent(s) and its antecedent(s) can be inferred
from the goal's antecedent(s). Goal consequent variables should not be
instantiated, i.e. on unification they should not share neither directly
nor indirectly (via data variables) and they should not be bound to any
data constants and structures. Implicational queries can require longer
inference chains (based on more than one data rules) than here described.

5.2. The NOT procedure

Independently from CallOn NESY achieves a more realistic negation compared with PROLOG where a failed call to prove the argument of a NOT goal
is treated as a proof of the goal itself. The very nature of legal knowledge requires a more subtle approach to negation. Hence NESY supports
1) negation as failure and 2) a "real", or as we call it, logic negation
for such relations for which it is explicitly stated. For a goal with
main functor NOT first the domain-dependent reductions are tried (see
the figure below). This is an attempt to prove the negation directly as
it is treated like a normal, user-defined relation. When/if this option
is exhausted a number of domain-independent reductions are tried. After
that there is an attempt to reject the NOT goal. Ultimately (in case the
above attempt fails) the rules NOT(X) :- LOGNOT(X), !, FAIL and

NOT(_)   decide whether NOT succeeds or fails:

```
/*                    The NOT procedure                    */

/*        User-defined (domain-specific) clauses:          */
                LOGNOT(a).           /* relations for which  */
                LOGNOT(b(_)).        /* negation by failure is */
                LOGNOT(c(_,_)).      /* inacceptible          */
          ............
                NOT(d) :- e, f.
                NOT(r(X,Y)) :- NOT(s(X)), h(Y).
/*        Domain independent (logic) clauses:              */
                NOT( X;Y ) :- NOT(X), NOT(Y).
                NOT( X:-Y ) :- CALL(Y), NOT(X).
/*        Attempt to reject the goal:                      */
                NOT(X) :- CALL(X), !, FAIL.
/*        Distinguishing a failed logic negation           */
          from a negation by failure:                      */
                NOT(X) :- LOGNOT(X), !, FAIL.
                NOT(_).
```

5.3. Pragmatics

Our design philosophy and some implementational decisions reflect intuitions and observations based on the current experience on formalizing
legal knowledge in the project. For instance, the CallOn definition
takes into account the expected frequences of different logic connectives. It is interesting that there is no perfect symmetry between these
frequences for data and goals respectively. One can judge our findings
from the following (to some extent hypothetical) diagram.

Main logic functor	Used in Goals	Used in Data
AND	OFTEN	OFTEN
==>	OFTEN	OFTEN
OR	OFTEN	seldom
XOR	seldom	OFTEN
NOT	seldom	seldom
EQV	seldom	OFTEN

6. CONCLUSION

The experience gained from the work on the ESIM project for developing
an expert system on business regulations was briefly discussed. Our results confirm the intricacies of the formalization problem but are as a
whole encouraging. To the best of our knowledge some essential issues
such as answering questions about rules are not adequately treated in
PROLOG as well as in the general AI deductive production systems /6/.

The expert systems based on knowledge of legal texts are undoubtedly an extremely attractive area of AI. There are not so much relevant projects around the world and most of them are at initial stages of development (cf. /3/). Legal expert systems are scientifically interesting and practically important. A major implication of their development is the possible improvement of present day technology for legal document drafting. About such a positive side-effect of the normative text formalization writes R. Kowalski /5/ in connection with his work on formalizing "The British Nationality Act 1981". Finally, some important advances in the general expert system theory can be expected from the work on such a relatively complex logical and linguistic problem area compared with the now popular "diagnostic" expert systems.

7. ACKNOWLEDGEMENTS

Authors would like to thank their colleagues B. Kavaldjiev (Bulgarian Association for Tourism and Recreation), D. Natchev (Software Products and Systems Corp.) as well as G. Krustev and K. Georgiev (BIA) for the fruitful discussions and collaboration through the common work on the ESIM project.

8. REFERENCES

/1/ K. Yalumov,'Preliminary Design of ESIM - an Expert System on Business Regulations', 1984 (in Bulgarian)

/2/ W. Clocksin and C. Mellish, Programming in Prolog, Springer-Verlag, 1981

/3/ J. Fain, F. Hayes-Roth, H. Sowizral and D. Waterman, 'Programming in ROSIE: An Introduction by Means of Examples', A RAND Note, 1982

/4/ G. Gargov, 'Logics for Knowledge Representation', International Conference on AI (AIMSA'84), Varna, Bulgaria, 1984

/5/ R. Kowalski, 'Logics for Knowledge Representation', FST&TCS, Bangalore, Dec. '84 (LNCS, Springer-Verlag, 1984)

/6/ N. Nilsson, Principles of Artificial Intelligence, Tioga Publ. Company, Palo Alto, 1980

/7/ K. Yalumov, 'KET: A Knowledge Engineering Tool', International Conference on AI (AIMSA'84), Varna, Bulgaria, 1984 (to appear in Computers in Industry, North-Holland)

MIXING PROLOG AND LISP

Bernhard Pfahringer
Christian Holzbaur
Austrian Research Institute for Artificial Intelligence,
and Department of Medical Cybernetics
and Artificial Intelligence, University of Vienna

ABSTRACT. Mixing PROLOG and LISP appears as a possible synthesis emerging out of the debate betweens adherents of these two languages. Examples are LOGLISP [7], YAQ [2], POPLOG [8], VIE-KET [6], TAO [9] and others. This article first shows briefly some of the advantages of such a mixture. This is augmented with a short example. A second part describes the interface between PROLOG and LISP, as it is implemented in VIE-KET.

1. IDEA

PROLOG's philosophy (namely unification as strategy for procedure invocation (no 'read tape' info in the head of a procedure), and backtracking to cope with indeterminism) is well tailored for certain kinds of problems (part 3. mentions some of them). If PROLOG programs can call programs written in other languages and vice versa, one can choose the 'best' language for every subtask.

2. WHAT DOES LISP WIN IN THIS CONTRACT?

As we developed VIE-KET, a hybrid knowledge engineering tool implemented in LISP combining both frames and PROLOG, we finally decided to use PROLOG as an interpreter for production rules. Working with VIE-KET we realized that PROLOG is a useful add-on for any LISP system, not only good for interpreting rules, but also quite useful for parsing tasks and generate-and-test problems. PROLOG allows to specify problems of one of these kinds in a straightforward and very natural way. One could say that 'the specification is (almost) the implementation'.

R. Trappl (ed.), Cybernetics and Systems '86, 759–765.

3. DOES PROLOG WIN, TOO?

First of all PROLOG gets access to a lot of useful utilities like a window system, graphics, etc. All that could be implemented in PROLOG, no doubt, but why should already existing tools not be used. Especially if implementing in PROLOG seems to be difficult. Mescheder [5] states problems of writing well understood and purely procedural algorithms in PROLOG.

Second: In some cases it is possible to increase time and/or space efficiency of a PROLOG program by using features of an other language. We for instance had the following problem: A program to generate a time-table created lots of relations of the following form:

(table ?day ?hour ?class ?subject)

(A short remark on the syntax we use for representing Horn clauses: It is similar to that used in PiL [10] with the exception of starting names of logical variables with a question mark. So

    son(Son, Father) :- father(Father, Son),
                        male(Son).

in Clocksin/Mellish syntax [3] is written as:

    ((son ?son ?father) (father ?father ?son)
                        (male ?son))

). And now back to our problem. That time-table generating program also frequently checked if a certain entry was already there. Todays PROLOG implementations allow either no indexing of clauses at all or use only the first argument. So at every check the system has to search sequentially. In the worst case this is a clause that is not known yet. This fact can only be discovered after searching through all of the list of clauses. That time behavior made it impossible to simply assert (and retract) the clauses. So why not use a LISP hashtable with the three keys ?day, ?hour, and ?class ? But how to integrate backtracking and the hashtable? Here is a simple solution:

    ((new-subject ?day ?hour ?class ?subject)
     (lisp-ignore put-subject ?day ?hour ?class ?subject))

    ((new-subject ?day ?hour ?class ?subject)
     (lisp-ignore remove-subject ?day ?hour ?class ?subject)
     (fail))

'Put-subject' and 'remove-subject' are LISP functions for accessing the data structure. 'Lisp-ignore' is a built-in predicate that is part of the interface between PROLOG and LISP (see 4.). So the predicate 'new-subject' first fills our hashtable and on backtracking clears it again and our problem is solved. Picture 1 tries to sketch the way this predicate works.

```
                    on call:
                    First clause adds hashtable
                    entry and succeeds.

                              │
    head -                    │
            clause1,          │
                              │        ↑
              ...             │        │
              ...             │        │
            new-subject(Day,Hour,Class,Subject),
              ...             │        │
              ...          │  │        │
            clauseN.       ↓           │
                                       │
                                       │
                                       │
                    on backtracking:
                    Second clause of new-subject
                    removes hashtable entry  and
                    invokes further backtracking ('fail').
```

Picture 1. How 'new-subject' works.
(this time Clocksin/Mellish syntax)

4. THE INTERFACE: PROLOG TO LISP

Three built-in predicates provide access to LISP functions out of
PROLOG: 'is', 'lisp' and 'lisp-ignore'.

4.1 'Is'

'Is' is the general way to invoke a LISP function and unify the result returned by this LISP function call with a given template:

```
(is template (lisp-function-call))
```

Variables used in the function call must be instantiated to a non variable term. Here is an example for the use of 'is':

```
(is ?subject (get-subject ?day ?hour ?class))
```

?subject will be unified with the result, that 'get-subject' (assumed to be a LISP function for accessing the hashtable of the above example) returns.

4.2 'Lisp'

```
(lisp lisp-function arg1 .. argN)
```

just evaluates (lisp-function arg1 .. argN). If this returns NIL, it is interpreted as 'failure', nonNIL values mean 'success'. This predicate is useful for tests that one wants to formulate in LISP:

```
(lisp leap-year ?year)
```

If ?year is bound to e.g. 1984, the LISP function leap-year returns T and for PROLOG this means 'success'. If ?year is not a leap-year, then the LISP function returns NIL, which will be 'failure' for the PROLOG interpreter.

4.3 'Lisp-ignore'

```
(lisp-ignore lisp-function arg1 .. argN)
```

This function is analoguos to 'lisp', but always yields 'success'. It has no effect on PROLOG's control mechanism. So it is called merely for side-effect, e.g. output:

```
(lisp-ignore print ?subject)
```

5. THE INTERFACE: LISP TO PROLOG

This part is divided into two cases:

a) Just starting any PROLOG program out of LISP. This is done via the function 'Prove'.

(prove goal1 .. goalN)

If called with more than one PROLOG goal, 'Prove' establishes an implicit 'and'. In any case it computes all solutions. (This is only half the truth: computing all the solutions is a default. Any user can define his own 'successfn', that will be invoked by 'prove' upon success. The functions appearing in part b) are implemented via that feature).

b) Starting PROLOG programs which return a value to the calling LISP function. For this purpose three different functions can be used: 'One', 'Any', and 'All'. This part of the interface is similar to the one known from LOGLISP.

(one template goal1 .. goalN)

(any n template goal1 .. goalN)

(all template goal1 .. goalN)

All three functions instantiate 'template', when a solution for goal1 .. goalN is found. 'One' returns the template according to the first solution, 'Any' a list of the first 'n' templates and 'All' a list of all the templates.

The following example will help to clarify the use of these functions. Our database shall consist of just three assertions:

    (hobby john tennis)
    (hobby mary tennis)
    (hobby jack tennis)

If we want to find two persons to play tennis with each other, we could call:

    (one (?player1 plays against ?player2)
        (hobby ?player1 tennis)
        (hobby ?player2 tennis)
        (not (= ?player1 ?player2)))

This call returns the 'template' with the variables instantiated according to the solution found for 'goal1 .. goalN' :

    (john plays against mary)

To get two pairs of players, you have to use 'any':

    (any 2 (?player1 plays against ?player2)
        (hobby ?player1 tennis)
        (hobby ?player2 tennis)
        (not (= ?player1 ?player2)))

763

Giving you the result:

```
((john plays against mary)
 (john plays against jack))
```

6. DISCUSSION

Mixing PROLOG and LISP appears as a possible synthesis emerging from the sometimes almost 'religious' debate between PROLOG and LISP adherents. On the other hand that mixing (at least the way we have done it) bears one major weakness: Data passed from PROLOG to LISP (via 'is', 'lisp' or 'lisp-ignore') must not(!) contain any uninstantiated logical variable. Otherwise results are unpredictable. So LISP functions cannot modify partially instantiated PROLOG terms and pass them back afterwards. To achieve such a tight coupling, one would need a functional language working with PROLOG's kind of data. An interesting model for this integration can be found in [2].

7. ACKNOWLEGDEMENTS

We would like to thank W.Horn for fruitful discussions on the topic and R.Trappl, without whom this work would not have been possible at all. This work has been supported by the Austrian Federal Ministry for Science and Research.

8. REFERENCES

[1] Bellia M., Dameri E., Degano P., Levi G., Martelli M.: A formal model for lazy implementations of a Prolog-compatible functional language, in Campbell J.A.(ed.), Implementations of Prolog, John Wiley and Sons, New York, 1984.
[2] Carlsson M.: (Re)Implementing PROLOG in LISP or YAQ - Yet another QLOG, UPMAIL 81/1, Box 2059, S-75002, Uppsala, Schweden, 1981.
[3] Clocksin W.F., Mellish C.S.: Programming in Prolog, Springer, Berlin, 1981.
[4] Kahn K.M., Carlsson M.: How to implement Prolog on a LISP Machine, in Campbell J.A.(ed.), Implementations of Prolog, John Wiley and Sons, New York, 1984.
[5] Mescheder B.: Prolog - Implementierungssprache der kuenstlichen Intelligenz, in Savory S.(ed.), Kuenstliche Intelligenz und Expertensysteme, Oldenbourg, Muenchen, 1985.
[6] Pfahringer B., Holzbaur C.: VIE-KET: Frames + Prolog, in Trost H., Retti J.(eds.), Oesterreichische Artificial Intelligence - Tagung, Springer, Berlin, 1985.
[7] Robinson J.A., Sibert E.E.: LOGLISP: An Alternative to PROLOG, in Hayes J.E., et al.(eds.), Machine Intelligence 10, John Wiley and

Sons, New York, 1982.
[8] Sloman A., Hardy S., Gibson J.: POPLOG: A Multilanguage Program Development Environment, Information Technology: Research and Development, 2, 109-122, 1983.
[9] Takeuchi I., Okuno H., Ohsato N.: TAO --- A harmonic mean of Lisp, Prolog and Smalltalk, SIGPLAN Notices, 18(7)65-74, 1983.
[10] Wallace R.S.: An Easy Implementation of PiL (PROLOG in LISP), SIGART, 85,29-32, 1983.

IMPLEMENTING INFERENCE STRATEGIES IN PROLOG BASED EXPERT SYSTEMS

Luca Console and Gianfranco Rossi
Dipartimento di Informatica-Universita' di Torino
Via Valperga Caluso, 37
10125 Turin
Italy

ABSTRACT. One of the most controversial question about the suitability
of Prolog for implementing expert systems is its built-in, non-
modifiable control strategy. In this paper a technique for implementing
different inference strategies in Prolog is described, based on the use
of suitable preprocessing facilities. Various inference mechanisms are
implemented as Prolog programs which are generated automatically through
preprocessing. It is argued that this approach has several advantages
over other more traditional uses of Prolog in the implementation of
expert systems. Implementations of forward and backward inference
mechanisms, both with and without uncertainties are presented. Also an
explanation mechanism and a technique for user level program debugging
are suggested.

1. INTRODUCTION

Prolog is now considered by many people as an interesting and promising
tool for implementing expert systems (see for instance [1] and [2]). It
is very natural comparing Prolog to a production rule system. Rules and
facts are naturally expressed as clauses and assertions in Prolog. The
inference engine is the Prolog interpreter itself. Therefore, the inference process is goal driven, and the search strategy is depth-first,
left-to-right, with backtracking. Matching takes place in the form of
usual unification of symbolic terms.

Various real expert systems have been implemented directly in Prolog, so far (e.g. [3] and [4], among others). In spite of this, the
suitability of Prolog for implementing expert systems is still a source
of great debate. One of the most controversial aspect resides in its
built-in control strategies, since Prolog does not allow the user to
substantially alter them. As experiences in production-rule based systems have pointed out, a purely backward mechanism can be both inefficient and too limitative, in many practical cases. The user is not
always able to suggest a goal to be proved and an exaustive exploration
of all the goals is indeed very inefficient. Moreover, non-classical
inference techniques, such as inexact reasoning, are often required in

R. Trappl (ed.), Cybernetics and Systems '86, 767–774.

practical applications.

Implementing different control strategies directly in ordinary Prolog can result largely unsatisfactory, mainly because clauses for guiding the control strategies may be mixed with clauses which represent domain knowledge, so that readability of the resulting system is strongly reduced. Alternative solutions can be achieved either by adding an extra level of interpretation on the top of Prolog [5] [6] or by extending it with suitable features [7] [8]. However, both cases present some drawbacks, as we point out at the end of this section. A more detailed analysis of these three possible uses of Prolog for implementing Expert Systems can be found in [9].

In this paper we show that various control strategies (including inexact reasoning) and other useful features of expert systems can be implemented in Prolog, but the required Prolog programs can be generated automatically by preprocessing an higher level rule based specification. This allows the user to do not take care of the details of the actual Prolog code. Readibility of programs is strongly enhanced. User is only concerned with the logic component of the system at hand, while control details are embedded in the preprocessor.

This technique has several advantages over other possible uses of Prolog for implementing Expert Systems [9].
With respect to extending Prolog:
 - easier and more inexpensive implementation;
 - higher portability of programs;
 - no overhead in the execution of ordinary Prolog programs;
 - more comprehensibility of control strategies.
With respect to using directly ordinary Prolog:
 - more comprehensibility of both the knowledge base and control strategies;
 - modularity, that is the possibility of modifying control strategies without affecting the knowledge base.
With respect to using Prolog for implementing new interpreters:
 - better overall performance; using preprocessing no extra level of interpretation is added, but Prolog programs are executed directly.
 - better suited to compiled Prolog.

2. FORWARD INFERENCE

Forward inference on a system of production rules can be easily simulated by a Prolog program which uses the built=in predicates 'assert' and 'retract' for storing and deleting facts in the program data base.

As an example, let us consider the trivial system composed of the following three Prolog-like rules:

        a1 if b1 or b2.
        a2 if a3 and b4.
        a3 if b3 and a1.
        goal(a2).

                    Figure 1.

768

At least one fact of the form goal(A) must appear in the rule system, where A is a left-hand side predicate of any rule in the system. It specifies that A must be considered as a final goal of the system.

The Prolog program which simulates a forward inference process on this system is shown in Figure 2. Edinburgh Prolog syntax is used in our examples. A knowledge of Prolog is assumed throughout (for reference see [11]).

```
start :- a2,!,write(a2).
start :- rule1.
start :- rule2.
start :- rule3.

rule1 :- not(a1), (b1;b2), insert(a1), start.
rule2 :- not(a2), a3,b4, insert(a2), start.
rule3 :- not(a3), b3,a1, insert(a3), start.
```

Figure 2.

Initial facts must be supplied in the form of usual Prolog assertions. For instance, b1, b3, b4 is a possible set of facts for the program above. Execution is activated when 'start' is specified as the current goal for the Prolog interpreter. The first clause for 'start' contains the goal of the system. If it is satisfied, then execution stops with success. Otherwise the next alternative for 'start' is selected, activating the first rule. If the rule condition part is satisfied and the fact in its conclusion part is not present yet, then this fact is inserted in the program database, and 'start' is called again. Otherwise execution backtracks and another rule is selected. If no 'start' alternative can be satisfied, execution stops with failure.

Predicate 'insert' is used in place of the built-in predicate assert which is not "backtrackable".It is defined as follows :

```
insert(C):- assert(C).
insert(C):- retract(C),fail.
```

Each time the clause C is stored in the database, an alternative in the search tree which is able to remove C is left open. This alternative will be selected in case of backtracking over 'insert'.

In a similar way we have implemented a forward scheme with a phase of heuristic conflict resolution wich allows to select the 'best' rule to be executed at each step [12].

It is easy to see that program of Figure 2 can be easily derived from rules of Figure 1. This transformation can be carried out automatically by means of a suitable preprocessing tool. Such a tool has been implemented as a runnable Prolog program with a quite small effort. The complete Prolog program is reported in [12]. Its input are production rules with the following simple format:

A if b1 and b2 and ... and bn.

or   A if b1 or b2 or ... or bn.

with n>0, where A, b1, ..., bn are first order predicates, like in Prolog. The implementation of this tool has been clearly simplified by the simple format of input rules, and by the use of Prolog flexible operator syntax. Rules are stored in the program database as Prolog assertions. Unification is used as the only mechanism for retriving rules and analysing them. Non matching rules are detected, too, and errors are reported.

3. INFERENCE WITH UNCERTAINTIES

Real applications often require inexact reasoning capabilities. Thus, in a rule based expert system, it must be possible specifying certainties of rules and facts, and computing certainties of conclusions given certainties of conditions. We tackled this problem in the same way as the previous one. Rules are defined so that they allow uncertainties to be expressed in a suitable manner. Then a preprocessing program (written in Prolog) for transforming them into a Prolog program is built. Both forward and backward inference with uncertainties are addressed.

The mechanism for inexact reasoning we adopted is in the style of Mycin. However, if a different mechanism is required, it is easy modifying Prolog procedures which deal with uncertainty evaluation. We assume rules have the following simple format:

A with C if B.

where C is a certainty value and 'with' is as an infix operator with lower precedence than 'if'.

3.1. Backward inference with uncertainties

In the classic (categorical) case early evaluation is used. For instance, evaluation of a disjunction of conditions can be suspended as soon as one of the predicates is found to be true. Inexact reasoning, on the contrary, requires all predicates and clauses to be evaluated, so that the best one - as far as its certainty value is concerned - can be selected.

For each rule, the preprocessor generates a Prolog clause which performs the following actions: calling each predicate which appears in the condition part of the rule; evaluating the certainty value of conditions by calling the 'min' or 'max' functions, in the case of conjunction or disjunction of conditions, respectively; controlling if the same conclusion has been already reached (procedure 'is_present'); computing the certainty value of the rule; inserting the conclusion in the program database as a new fact, along with its certainty factor C.

As an example, let us consider the simple rule system of Figure 3. It is a lightly modified version of the system in Figure 1. Rules have been augmented with a certainty factor. Two rules with the same conclusion a1 (but a different premise part) are now present in the system. An assertion 'threshold(C)' specifies that only solutions with a certainty value greater than C are accepted. No predicate 'goal' is present. The actual goal must be specified dynamically by the user, as a parameter of the predicate 'start'. The certainty value of the goal is also returned as a further argument of 'start'.

```
a1 with 0.5 if b1 or b2.
a2 with 1    if a3 and b4.
a3 with 0.8 if b3 and a1.
a1 with 0.9 if b5.
threshold(0.6).
```

Figure 3.

The Prolog program which simulates backward inference over the sample system above is partially described in Figure 4. It has been generated by means of a preprocessor, as in the previous case. General
purpose functions, such as min, max, insert, remove (the opposite of
insert) and clauses for other rules are defined in an obvious way.
Notice that, the operator 'rwith' is used in place of 'with', to avoid
erroneus reactivations of rules, within procedure 'is_present'.

```
best(0).
start(G,C) :- go(G,C),!.
start(G,C) :- best(C), write('certainty below the threshold').

go(G,Cbest) :- G rwith Cg,
               retract(best(Cmax)), max([Cmax,Cg],Cbest),
               assert(best(Cbest)), Cbest > 0.6.

a1 rwith C :- a1 with C.
a1 rwith C :- (b1 with Cc1; Cc1 is 0), (b2 with Cc2; Cc2 is 0),
              max([Cc1,Cc2],Cmax), not(Cmax = 0),
              is_present_1(Cold),
              Cnew is Cmax * 0.5, max([Cnew,Cold],C),
              insert(a1 with C).

is_present_1(C) :- ((a1 with C,!, remove(a1 with C)) ; C is 0).
....
```

Figure 4.

Some comments on the program above. If a fact is already present
with a certainty value Cold and if Cold is greater than the new certainty value Cnew, nothing is changed in the program data base (see
is_present_1(C)). If a solution is found, but its certainty factor is
below the given threshold, then other solutions are searched, by backtracking. If backtracking is no more feasible, 'go' fails. The second
alternative for 'start' is then selected; 'best(C)' will return the best
certainty value (below the threshold) computed during the various
attempts for satisfying the goal.

3.2. Forward inference with uncertainties

Ideas from both the previous two inference mechanisms are combined in
this last case. Rules have the same format as rules in Figure 3. However, a goal must be specified in this case, as we did in Figure 1. The
Prolog program which is generated by preprocessing is an extension of
the program we presented in Figure 2. Most of the new predicates in the

771

former were already used in the case of backward inference with uncertainties (see Figure 4). An example for the rule system of Figure 3 is shown below.

```
start :- a2 with C, not(usable(_)), C > 0.6,!, write(a2 with C).
start :- rule_1.
start :- rule_2.
start :- rule_3.
start :- rule_4.
start :- a2 with C,!, write(a2 with C),
         write('certainty below the threshold').

rule_1 :- usable(rule_1),
          (b1 with Cc1 ; Cc1 is 0), (b2 with Cc2 ; Cc2 is 0),
          max([Cc1,Cc2],Cmax), not(Cmax = 0),
          remove(usable(rule_1)), is_present_1(Cold),
          Cnew is Cmax * 0.5, max([Cnew,Cold],C),
          insert(a1 with C),
          retry(C,Cold,[rule_3]), start.

/* is_present_1(C) - see Figure 4 */
....
```

Figure 5.

The main difference with the previous cases is the introduction of the notion of "usable" rules. Initially all rules are usable. So that, the data base of our sample system will contain an assertion 'usable(rule_i).' for each rule_i. After a rule has been activated, the fact that it is usable is removed. Before calling another rule the predicate 'retry' is called: the certainty value C of the conclusion is compared with the previous value (Cold) for the same conclusion. If the actual certainty value of the conclusion is higher than the previous one, then all the rules which refer to this conclusion are set to be usable again. It is assumed that the preprocessor is able to determine for each conclusion a list of all the rules where the conclusion is used. These rules can be subsequently activated and better certainty values may be obtained. As a consequence, other rules may be set to be usable, and so on. This process is repeatedly applied until the goal can be proved with a certainty value above the given threshold, and no rule is usable. Thus, the solution with the best possible certainty value is computed. On the contrary, if no rule is usable and a goal is proved but with a certainty value below the threshold, then the last alternative for the start procedure is selected.

4. EXPLANATIONS WITH FORWARD INFERENCE

The forward inference mechanisms we have presented prove themselves to be naturally well suited to supporting explanation facilities. Let us verify this statement by looking into the behaviour of Prolog programs which implement forward inference (see Figures 2 and 5). When the goal

772

of the system is finally proved to be true, also the related clause
'start' succeeds. This causes the calling clause to be successfully completed. This in turn completes the evaluation of another call to the
'start' procedure; and so on, until the beginning of the chain of nested
calls to 'start' is reached.

   This suggests a straightforward implementation of an 'how' explanation mechanism. A new predicate 'explain(rule_i)' is added at the end of
each clause rule_i:
         rule_i :- not(...), ..., start, explain(rule_i).
A simple implementation of 'explain' could be
         explain(R) :- write(R),nl.
which produces the sequence of all activated rules, in reverse order
(i.e. from goal to basic facts). Obviously, more powerful definitions of
explain are possible, too. The same technique applies also to forward
inference with uncertainty. On the contrary, the case of backward
inference seems more difficult to be dealt with.

5. PROGRAM DEBUGGING

A critical problem is debugging of programs which have been translated
by preprocessing. Prolog debugging facilities can be used. But they
force users to be aware of the precise Prolog code which is generated by
the preprocessor. It is very hard for the user to understand the activation flow of rules if he/she is provided only with informations about
activation of Prolog predicates. A better solution can be easily
obtained in the following way. Prolog debugging facilities are not used
at all. Prolog clauses generated by the preprocessor are augmented with
calls to suitable new procedures. These procedures allow informations
about rule activation and termination to be reported to the user. For
instance, the first rule of Figure 1
         a1 if b1 or b2.
is transformed in the following Prolog clause:
         rule_1 :- not(a1), trace_in(rule_1),
                   (b1;b2), insert(a1),
                   trace_out(rule_1), start.
and predicate 'trace_in' can be defined as follows:
      trace_in(R) :- ((dbg, write('entering'), write(R),nl); true).
      trace_in(R) :- ((dbg, write('exiting_back from '),
                       write(R),nl,!, fail); fail).
   Predicate 'trace_out' is defined in a very similar way. The fact
'dbg' is used for dynamically switching on/off the tracing facility. It
is asserted in the data base if the user requests tracing. Generation of
tracing predicates is considered as an option of the preprocessor. So
that, it can be suppressed if not required. Also a step by step tracing
mechanism has been implemented with the same technique [12].

6. CONCLUSIONS

We have shown that using ordinary Prolog [11] in conjunction with a suitable preprocessing tool can be a good technique for the implementation of rule based expert systems.

This technique is advocated also by other authors. In [10], preprocessing is used for building various extensions to Prolog, such as modules, macros, functional notation, etc.. In [1], it is proposed as a means to allow some irrelevant details to be hidden from the user. What is new in our work is applying preprocessing for building different inference strategies in Prolog, in the framework of expert systems development.

The production systems described in this paper have been used also as part of a frame+rules expert system shell implemented in Prolog [13].

7. REFERENCES

[1] Clark, K.L. and McCabe, F.G.: 'PROLOG: A Language for Implementing Expert Systems', Machine Intelligence, 10 (Hayes & Michie eds.), 1982.
[2] Parsaye, K.: 'Database Management, Knowledge Base Management and Expert System Development in Prolog'; Proc. Logic Programming Workshop '83, Algarve, Portugal, 28 Jun-1 July, 1983.
[3] Walker, A. and Porto, A.: 'KB01: A Knowledge Based Garden Store Assistant', in Proc. Logic Programming Workshop '83, Algarve, Portugal, 28 Jun-1 July, 1983.
[4] Poe, M.D.: 'Control of Heuristic Search in a PROLOG-based Microcode Synthesis Expert System'; Proc.of the Int. Conf. on 5th. Generation Computer Systems 1984, Tokyo, Japan, Nov. 6-9, 1984.
[5] Pereira L.M.: 'Logic Control with Logic', in Proc. of the First International Logic Programming Conference, ADDP, Marseille, Sept. 1982.
[6] Sterling, L.: 'Expert System = Knowledge + Meta-Interpreter'; Tech. Rept. CS84-17, Weizmann Institute, Israel, 1984.
[7] Clark, K. and McCabe, F.: 'The Control Facilities of IC-PROLOG', in Expert Systems in the Micro Electronic Age, (D. Mitchie, ed.), Edinburgh University Press, 1981.
[8] Porto, A.: 'Epilog: a language for extended programming in logic', in Proc. of the First International Logic Programming Conference, ADDP, Marseille, Sept. 1982.
[9] Rossi, G.: 'Uses of Prolog in the Implementation of Expert Systems'; Technical Rept., Univ. of Turin, March 1985.
[10] Eggert, P.R. and Val Schorre, D.: 'Logic enhancement: a method for extending logic programming languages'; in Proc. of the ACM Conf. on Lisp and Functional Programming Languages, August, 1982.
[11] Clocksin, W.F. and Mellish, C.S.: Programming in Prolog, Springer Verlag, Berlin, 1981.
[12] Console, L. and Rossi, G.: 'Implementing inference strategies in Prolog by preprocessing', (in italian), Technical Rept., Univ. of Turin, April 1985.
[13] Console, L. and Rossi, G.: 'Frame based expert systems in Prolog' Technical Rept., Univ. of Turin, November 1985.

DOXASTIC LOGIC AND DOXASTIC-EPISTEMIC META-REASONING IN EXPERT SYSTEMS

K. Mohyeldin Said
Dept. of Computer Science,
University of California, Santa Cruz, USA.
Dept. of Psychology, University of Oxford, England.

G. Provan,
Mathematical Institute, University of Oxford, England.

ABSTRACT. In this paper we argue that doxastic logic (DL) and other doxastic-epistemic principles can enhance the reasoning process of expert systems (ESs). The basic idea is to include a doxastic logic module in the inferential engine of the ES. We start by discussing two different approaches to uncertainty, which we call the numeric approach and the structural-semantic approach, and their respective implementation in expert systems. The importance of augmenting uncertain belief with the "logical" principles of doxastic logic is made explicit. We cover some meta-level doxastic and epistemic principles that have potential usage in ES. We then incorporate these and other doxastic principles (in a DL module) in two types of expert systems (each based on one of the above mentioned approaches to uncertainty). Various augmented inferential capabilities thus made possible are discussed.

1. DOXASTIC LOGIC AND EXPERT SYSTEMS

1.1. Introduction

Knowledge and beliefs play a major role in human information processing. Experts, for example, derive their conclusions from, among other things, a set of beliefs and knowledge. Awareness of the importance of the concept of knowledge (e.g. epistemic logic) and of beliefs (e.g. doxastic logic) in artificial intelligence is increasing (Cohen and Levesque, 1985; Fagin, Halpern and Vardi, 1984; Halpern and Moses, 1985; Mohyeldin Said, 1985a, 1985b; Moore, 1980).

Doxastic logic formalizes principles and logical relationships between propositions of beliefs. In this system, false beliefs are allowed because humans, in general, are not completely rational in their beliefs, and this irrationality is in itself an important part of the reasoning process. That is, they do not have infallible, objective justifications for their beliefs. In fact, this emphasizes the fundamental difference between the logic of beliefs and that of knowledge in which false knowledge is not allowed.

R. Trappl (ed.), Cybernetics and Systems '86, 775–782.
© *1986 by D. Reidel Publishing Company.*

1.2. Two Approaches to Uncertain Belief

There are two basic approaches to uncertainty in AI: the <u>numeric</u> approach and the <u>structural-semantic</u> approach. The former uses numerical weights to represent the degree of uncertainty (and hence the degree or strength of belief). Examples, among others, are: degrees of beliefs (Shafer, 1976); belief functions (Gordon and Shortliffe, 1985); certainty factor-based (e.g. MYCIN: Buchanan and Shortliffe, 1984); Bayesian-based (e.g. PROSPECTOR: Duda et al 1978); fuzzy logic (Zadeh, 1965; Zadeh et al., 1975; Gaines, 1976).

Most current expert systems dealing with uncertainty use similar methods of weight-generation, propogating these weights throughout the system using combination algorithms, most of which are probability-based. A difficulty of these numerical approaches is that they are normative and do not necessarily represent human's performance under uncertainty: "It does not seem that probability theory is in general used by decision makers" (Halpern and Rabin, 1983, p.310). That is, human uncertain reasoning is non-normative and heuristic-based (Edwards, 1968; Tversky and Kahneman, 1973, 1974; Kahneman, Slovic and Tversky, 1982).

A recently proposed method, which we call the structural-semantic approach, uses propositions represented by strings, as opposed to numerical weights, to represent uncertainty. The adequacy of the evidence and the strength of belief is represented in the form of the <u>reasons</u> for believing and disbelieving (called "endorsements" by Cohen and Grinberg, 1983; Cohen, 1985). The main advantage of this approach is that the many factors which lead to a belief are not "compacted" into a single number. The main disadvantage is the difficulty of finding (a) "semantic rules" (corresponding to numeric ones) to combine reasons for believing and disbelieving, and (b) endorsement propagation rules across inferences. Obviously, the value of having both numerical degrees of belief as well as reasons for (dis)believing is debatable. We suggest that this is the case. Furthermore, we believe that <u>logical</u> principles holding between "full" or "certain" belief (see section 2.3) should be present as well (see section 2.4). We do that by incorporating a doxastic logic module in the inference engine of expert systems (see section 3). In the following section we consider some principles of doxastic logic.

1.3. Doxastic Logic: Principles of Certain Belief

As mentioned above the notion of belief is a weaker one than that of knowledge. While in the logic of the latter we have $K_a p \text{ -- } p$, in the logic of the former we have the weaker principle:

(1) $B_a p \rightarrow P_a^B p$

where "$P_a^B p$" stands for "it is possible for all that $\underline{a}$ believes that p".

Other rules are:

(2) $B_a p \wedge B_a (p \rightarrow q) \rightarrow B_a q$; (3) $\vdash \bowtie \Rightarrow \vdash B_a \bowtie$; (4) $B_a p \rightarrow B_a B_a p$

If (1), (2) and (3) are added to propositional logic, the $>M_D$ system results. Further, adding (4) gives the $>S4_D$ system (following the terminology of Mohyeldin Said, 1985b).

After this brief presentation of doxastic principles let us consider how it could be augmented.

1.4. Augmenting Doxastic Logic with Uncertain Beliefs and Other Belief Constructs

In the previous section we did not allow for "degrees" of belief. That is a either believes (fully) that p or does not. The rules (1), (5) and (6) hold regardless of how the belief came to be, i.e. independent of the reasons to believe and disbelieve. In other words, these doxastic rules are "logical" ones. The reasons for believing or disbelieving that p can be attached to the doxastic principles and can propogate through the inferences smoothly (as they are logical rules and not domain-specific uncertain rules - see section 3.4.2). Hence, they augment the transparency capabilities of expert systems by explaining the reasons for believing or disbelieving the conclusions.

However, it would be advantageous to also have degrees of belief. In that case the reasons of belief take an important role. It is those very reasons of believing and disbelieving which determine the degree of belief. One of the earliest works taking such reasons into account is Lenat's (1976) AM program, where "interestingness criteria" were attached to concepts (in a mathematical hypothesis space). Similarly, Doyle (1979) developed a "truth maintenance system," in which reasons for believing and disbelieving hypotheses revise sets of beliefs and construct explanations, thereby establishing one belief over competing ones. The hypotheses, however, are checked whether they have support without the more important analysis of the type of support or reasons for the support. As mentioned above, Cohen and Grinberg (1983) and Cohen (1985) point to the importance of reasons of belief and disbelief ("endorsements") in uncertain contexts. That avenue of research has produced the expert system SOLOMON.

In addition to the reasons for believing and disbelieving there is the importance of (a) the believer him/herself, and (b) the context of applicability of the belief. Different believers weight evidence differently. Furthermore, besides having different reasons, they have different (quantitative and well as qualitative) criteria for deciding, say, when a given set of endorsements is adequate for believing the conclusion of a given inference. In other words, people have different justification criteria: what is "objectively justified" for some is "subjectively justified" for others. For example the justification criteria of Khomeini's believing that God exists are, presumably, drastically different than those of a Christian Professor of Theology at Oxford University. Also, personality traits are of relevance. A naive character believes more easily than a suspicious one.

The context where the belief is applied also plays a role. For example, propositions could constitute adequate evidence in a given context but not in another. Similarly, the justification criteria of a judge believing that a is guilty will be different if the sentence is three months than if it is life-imprisonment.

2. DOXASTIC, EPISTEMIC AND META-LEVEL REASONING IN EXPERT SYSTEMS

2.1. Introduction

Of its many potential uses in expert systems (ESs), the most powerful contribution of DL is its ability to formulate meta-level knowledge. Meta-level knowledge is basically knowledge which dictates how other knowledge (e.g. rules, knowledge-base contents) is to be processed. In a sense it reasons about the reasoning process itself.

Meta-level knowledge can be both user-supplied or system-derived, with the latter being the more powerful. System-derived meta-level reasoning capabilities can be enhanced by using meta-principles of DL and other meta doxastic-epistemic principles (e.g. those presented in section 3.2). Because these capabilities are an important feature of ESs (the more powerful this meta-level reasoning the more powerful is the ES in terms of efficiency and reasoning capabilities), the incorporation of a DL module thus represents an advance in ES design and function.

In section 2.2 we introduce a few meta-level doxastic-epistemic principles. In the next section (2.3) we briefly mention the meta-level knowledge capabilities of a typical numeric expert system (ES using the numeric approach to uncertainty), MYCIN, and discuss a few areas in which a DL module can enhance or augment such capabilities, not only within MYCIN but within any such numeric ES. In the following section (2.4) we illustrate the use of the DL module in a structural-semantic expert system (ES using the structural-semantic approach to uncertainty), such as SOLOMON.

2.2. Some Meta-Level Doxastic-Epistemic Principles

$K_a p \;\rightarrow\; K_a K_a p$, which says that if a knows that p then a knows that he knows that p. It seems that in many cases this meta-knowledge capability is present (especially in rational minds, e.g., scientists and logicians). But in other cases it is not. For example, experts know much expertise knowledge but the task of the knowledge engineer is to make that expert's implicit knowledge explicit. In other words, the expert has certain types of intuitive knowledge of which he is not aware. Also, rule (a) does not apply for procedural knowledge.

Examples of other rules include $B_a p \rightarrow K_a B_a p$, $B_a p \rightarrow B_a B_a p$, $K_a p \rightarrow B_a K_a p$, $K_a B_a p \rightarrow B_a B_a p$ (see Mohyeldin Said, 1985b).

2.3. Doxastic Logic in Numeric Expert Systems

2.3.1. Meta-Level Knowledge in MYCIN. TEIRESIAS (Davis, 1978) incorporates some meta-level knowledge rules about MYCIN. The three major types are knowledge about: (a) rule content, (b) syntax, and (c) strategies.

The rule-content meta-level knowledge is basically a set of domain-specific rule models (rule models being abstract generalizations of groups of rules) used for inferring more general information about the rule base. The representation-specific syntax meta-level knowledge generalizes information about each piece of knowledge to provide enhanced knowledge base capabilities, including both data base updating and correction, and knowledge acquisition. Meta-level knowledge strategies are a set of domain-specific meta rules used to organize processing of other program knowledge.

2.3.2. Incorporating a Doxastic Logic Module in MYCIN. DL can, among other inferential powers, both enhance and augment existing program meta-level knowledge, primarily in the areas of rule-content and strategies. Let us discuss these capabilities by dividing them into: first, those affecting the system before processing begins; and second, those affecting the system during processing.

2.3.2.1. Pre-processing capabilities. In the area of rule-content, the DL module has many functions. Such functions involve system rule-base self-examination and clarification prior to actual processing. This involves the system checking

778

all of its rules to ensure that none provide contradictory conclusions. DL meta-rules, because they are based on a logical system, form a consistent set. Since these rules are more consistent than the heuristic (or experience-derived) rules which constitute the MYCIN rule base, DL can be used to check the MYCIN rule base to eliminate inconsistency, as described above. In addition to this consistency-check, the DL module can not only formalize these rules but also augment them. This is done by hypothetically converting high certainty factors (CFs) into "full" beliefs and comparing the inferences and conclusions derived by the DL module with those derived by the MYCIN system. Any discrepancies can then be analysed further. Moreover, because DL holds for any given belief, these meta-rules are not domain-specific.

Beliefs (in the DL module) must be consistent, but CFs may have similar meaning but have different values, and hence different consequences. CFs of 0.6 and 0.7 have similar meaning but different values, a difference which can have significant consequences. Let us use the MYCIN rule in which an inference with CF $\leqslant$ 0.2 is rejected and $\geqslant$ 0.8 is accepted. In a chain of reasoning we may obtain CF combinations upon which conclusions are based, such as:

hypothesis 1: 0.6 x 0.3 = 0.18 ($\leqslant$ 0.20) reject--below threshold
hypothesis 2: 0.7 x 0.3 = 0.21 (> 0.20) retain--above threshold.

Hence, hypothesis 1 is rejected and hypothesis 2 is retained, and the CF difference is seen to be important.

Thus, for example, if in the reasoning process a rule (when converted to a belief within the DL module) leads to a belief in p, and a subsequent rule, after several CF combinations have taken place, leads to a belief in -p, then a contradiction flag is raised in the DL module. This contradiction might not have occurred in MYCIN because of the clouding effect of the CFs, but it does in the DL module, because of its consistency and the greater strength of the DL principles, namely that it forbids simultaneous belief in both p and ¬p.

The DL module can also enhance knowledge acquisition. Belief consistency checks can be made to indicate the presence of data errors. This may crop up when the DL module detects errors once the data is encoded into beliefs. In the area of meta-level knowledge strategies, DL with the basic epistemic operators added immediately introduces a host of meta-rules. These rules are used while processing is being done, and ensure the wisest and broadest possible use of every piece of information. A sampling of these rules was given in section 2.2.

2.3.3.2. Processing capabilities. Hypothetically doxastic rules can increase processing speed. Inference chains for "full" beliefs can also be cut down.

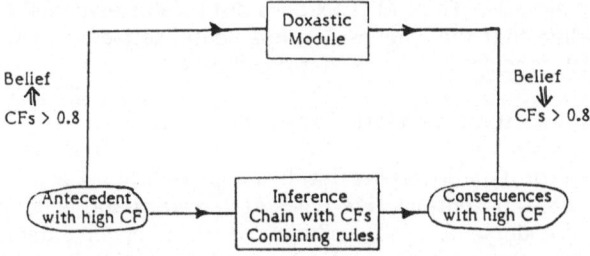

Figure 7.1: A clause with high CF can go through a long chain of combining CFs before reaching the conclusion. Translating the clause into belief statements in DL and then processing it before retranslating the conclusion into a CF could, hypothetically, cut down the long chain of CF combining mechanisms.

779

Furthermore, search for any solution (e.g. a diagnosis) can be speeded up in at least one of the following ways: 1. reducing the search space; 2. reordering the branches of the tree; 3. generating additional information given the knowledge of the belief set.

Consider the following examples, which explain how the DL module can affect processing in each of the three above-mentioned ways. Firstly, translate the MYCIN thresholds in the DL module as follows:

Prob (p) < 0.2 $B_a \neg p$
Prob (p) > 0.8 $B_a p$

Suppose that test T1 implies the presence of bacteria b1 and b2 with probabilities 0.85 and 0.10 respectively. This implication is converted into the following belief within the DL module: $B_a p_1 \wedge B_a \neg p_2$, where p1 and p2 stand, respectively, for "bacteria b1 is present" and "bacteria b2 is present."

Suppose further that a subsequent test T2 implies the presence of bacteria b1 and b3 with probabilities 0.15 and 0.70 respectively. The corresponding belief here is $B_a \neg p_1$. In this case, evidence for b3 cannot be converted into a belief since its probability lies between both the upper and lower threshold, so only a belief in $\neg p_1$ is generated.

Now the DL module registers inconsistency, since, as described in section 2.2, it knows (assuming that a is the system) that it believes that p1 is present (from test T1), yet it simultaneously knows that it believes that p1 is absent (from test T2). Consequently, the DL module initiates further analysis of tests T1 and T2 (such as accuracy, reliability, etc.). If a resolution can be made, e.g. that test T2's results are discarded, errors introduced by the propagation of T2's results throughout the system are avoided, and substantial processing time may be saved, as test T2 could have led the system down a blind alley. The avoidance of the blind alley is a search space reduction, in the sense that any implications from test T2 are discarded.

Secondly, if the contradiction is not resolved, the branches of the processing of test results (i.e search tree) could be reordered to try to resolve that contradiction, hopefully avoiding error and any unnecessary processing.

Thirdly, the generation of additional knowledge (and the inherent power of such a capability) is displayed in the following example. Suppose that both $B_a p$ and $B_a q$ exist in the DL module, and the presence of both these two symptoms (p,q) result in a diagnosis. Without the belief encoding, the system could be processing probabilities for a while before (a) the threshold for diagnosis were reached or (b) the correct probabilities were combined is such a way as to indicate establishment of the diagnosis. Thus, MYCIN does not (in this example) have the capabilities to realize that the diagnosis is, in a sense, self-evident to the system, whereas the DL module does have that capability.

2.4. Doxastic Logic in Structural-Semantic Expert Systems

2.4.1. Introduction. A prototype incorporating this approach to uncertainty is SOLOMON (Cohen 1985). It contains five types of knowledge:(a) endorsements (b) adequacy criteria of endorsements (c) ranking criteria of endorsements (d) rules for generating resolution tasks, and (e) rules for propogating endorsements over inferences. SOLOMON uses this knowledge to reason about uncertainty instead of numeric weights. Semantic methods for combining endorsements replace the numerical combination mechanisms.

2.4.2. Incorporating a Doxastic Logic Module in SOLOMON. A doxastic logic module can be added to an expert system irrespective of the inference generation methodology (e.g. through numerical mechanisms in MYCIN-type systems and endorsement mechanisms in SOLOMON-type systems). In other words, the doxastic-logical rules of a DL module augment the type of influence mechanism the given expert system uses.

For example, in SOLOMON there are domain specific uncertain inference rules. Endorsements are attached to these rules. Doxastic rules could be added in the system and endorsements could be attached as well to these. Endorsements propogate according to certain "semantical rules" through the uncertain domain-specific rules. Endorsements propogate "smoothly" across the doxastic rules as they are "logical" principles (see figure 2).

3. CONCLUSION

This paper has discussed the benefit of incorporating Doxastic-Epistemic principles within ESs. The use of DL to augment uncertain beliefs was introduced, along with other belief-related constructs. Together, these more closely simulate general characteristics of belief systems. Such a formulation could enhance many aspects of ES processing, for both the numeric and structural-semantic ES.

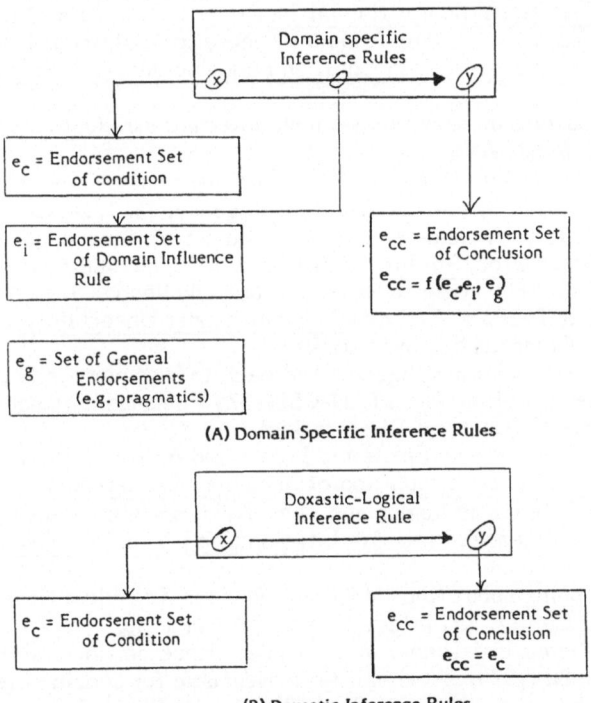

(A) Domain Specific Inference Rules

(B) Doxastic Inference Rules

Figure 7.2: Two types of inferences dealing with beliefs: (A) Domain-specific infererence rules, and (B) doxastic infererence rules. In the former, endorsements of the conclusion result from a complex function of condition, inference rule, and general endorsements. In the latter, endorsements propogate "smoothly" from condition to conclusion as the rule is "logical".

781

6. REFERENCES

Buchanan, B. & Shortliffe, E. (Eds.) (1984) Rule Based Expert Systems: The Mycin Experiments of the Stanford Heuristic Programming Project. Addison-Wesley.

Cohen, Paul R., & Grinberg, M. (1983) 'A Theory of Heuristic Reasoning About Uncertainty.' The AI Magazine, Summer 1983, 17-24.

Cohen, Paul R. (1985) Heuristic Reasoning About Uncertainty: An Artificial Intelligence Approach. Pitman Publishing Ltd.

Cohen, Philip R. & Levesque, H. (1985) 'Speech Acts and Rationality.' Unpublished revised paper appearing in Proc. 23rd Annual Meeting of the Association for Computational Linguistics, Chicago, July 1985.

Davis, R (1978) 'Knowledge Acquisition in Rule-Based Systems: Knowledge about Representations as a Basis for System Construction and Maintenance.' In D.A. Waterman & F. Hayes-Roth (Eds.) Pattern-Directed Inference Systems, Academic Press: New York, pp. 99-134.

Doyle, J. (1979) 'A Truth Maintenance System.' Artificial Intelligence, 12, 231-272.

Duda, R., Gasching, J., Hart, P., Konolige, K., Reboh, R., Barrett, P. & Slocum, J. (1978). Development of the PROSPECTOR Consultation System for Mineral Exploration. Final Report, SRI Projects 5821 and 5415, SRI Int., Cal., USA.

Edwards, W. (1968) 'Conservatism in Human Information Processing' In B. Kleinmuntz (Ed.) Formal Representation of Human Judgement, New York: Wiley.

Fagin, R., Halpern, J. & Vardi, M., (1984) 'A Model-Theoretic Analysis of Knowledge: Preliminary Report.' Proc. 25th Conf. on Fundamentals of Computer Science, 268-278.

Gaines, B. (1976). 'Foundations of Fuzzy Reasoning.' International Journal of Man-Machine Studies, 8, 623-668.

Gordon, J., & Shortliffe, E. (1985). 'A Method for Managing Evidential Reasoning in a Hierarchical Hypothesis Space.' Artifical Intelligence, 26, 323-358.

Halpern, J. & Moses, T. (1985) 'A Guide to the Modal Logics of Knowledge and Belief: Preliminary Draft' Proc. 9th Int. Joint Conf. on AI, pp. 480-490.

Halpern, J. & Rabin, M. (1983) 'A Logic to Reason About Likelihood.' J. of ACM.

Kahneman, D., Slovic, P. & Tversky, A. (Eds.) Judgment under Uncertainty: Heuristic and Biases. Cambridge University Press.

Lenat, D. (1976) AM: An Artificial Intelligence Approach to Discovery in Mathematics as Heuristic Search. Rep. No. STAN-CS76-570 Computer Science Dept., Stanford University (Doctoral Dissertation).

Mohyeldin Said, K. (1985a) 'Axiomatic Epistemic Logics and Artificial Intelligence'. Proc. Artificial Intelligence and Simulation of Behaviour Conference, 1985.

Mohyeldin Said, K. (1985b) 'Doxastic Logics and Their Relation to Epistemic Logics in Artificial Intelligence'. Proc. 5th Int. Conf. on Computer Science, Chile, 1985.

Moore, R.C. (1980) Reasoning about Knowledge and Action. Technical Note 191, Artificial Intelligence Center, SRI International, October 1980.

Shafer, G. (1976). A Mathematical Theory of Evidence. Princeton University Press.

Tversky, A. & Kahneman, D. (1973) 'Availability: A Heuristic for Judging Frequency and Probability' in Kahneman, D., Slovic, P. & Tversky, A. (Eds.) Judgement under Uncertainty: Heuristics and Biases, 163-178, Cambridge University Press.

Tversky, A. & Kahneman, D. (1974) 'Judgement and Uncertaintly: Heuristic and Biases.' Science, 185, 1124-1131.

Zadeh, L. (1965) 'Fuzzy Sets.' Information and Control, 8, 338-353.

Zadeh, L., Fu, K., Tanaka, K., & Schimura, M. (Eds.) (1975). Fuzzy Sets and Their Applications to Cognitive and Decision Processes, Academic Press Inc.

GENERALIZATION AND PARTICULARIZATION OF PRODUCTION RULES IN EXPERT SYSTEMS

Witold Pedrycz
Department of Automatic Control and Computer Sci.
Silesian Technical University,44-100 Gliwice,Poland
and Research and Development Center of Electronic
Medical Instrumentation,Zabrze

ABSTRACT. A problem of validation a knowledge base for production-rule expert systems is studied.Considered are several
shortcomings which could appear in any data acquisition pro-
cess.Furthermore appropriate methods for their detection and
resolution(generalization and particularization)are derived.
Some numerical examples are also presented.

1. INTRODUCTION.PRELIMINARY REMARKS

A rapid development of expert systems forming an applied
branch of Artificial Intelligence imposed several important
methodological issues.They have to be solved in order to pro-
wide the knowledge engineer/user with a spectrum of methods
general enough to attack the problems of:
i/knowledge acquisition,
ii/choice of the appropriate form of the inference engine,
iii/processing of uncertainty manifesting in the expert's
   knowledge and the inference mechanism.
Among well-known and widely accepted schemas with which the
expert systems are realized it is worthy to recall production
rules [9], [13],semantic nets [16],and frames [2], [3].Each of
them has obvious advantages and disadvantages.Nevertheless,
the choice is application-driven and relies mainly on experience of the knowledge engineer and the expert.

In this paper we will discuss rule-based expert systems.
In its basic background it is assumed that the knowledge ac-
quised can be included in a form of the set of " if then"
statements,
                if condition$_i$ then action$_i$
where the index i stands for the number of the rule,i=1,2,
,...,N.In more compact and formal fashion they can be put
down as

$$\underline{A}_i \Rightarrow B_i \tag{1}$$

783

R. Trappl (ed.), Cybernetics and Systems '86, 783–790.
© 1986 by D. Reidel Publishing Company.

with A_i and B_i standing for the condition$_i$ and action$_i$,respectively.And,as usually $\underline{A}_i$ consists of conjunction($\&$) of some parts(subconditions) $A_{i1},A_{i2},\ldots,A_{in}$,
$$\underline{A}_i = A_{i1} \& A_{i2} \& \ldots \& A_{in} \tag{2}$$
As underlined in many research studies on rule-based expert systems,cf.[4],a process of knowledge acquisition is very time-consuming and error-prone.Remembering the knowledge base may contain hundreds of production rules,it is unrealistic to expect they would be free of errors.In [14]dealing with validation of the knowledge base four types of errors have been specified,i.e.:

a.conflict(two rules succed under the same condition but make contradictory conclusions),
b.redundancy(two rules make the same conclusion in the same situations;it cause problems for scoring mechanisms e.g.realized by aggregation certainty factors of the rules,see [13]),
c.subsumption(two rules are similar except that one contains additional restrictions),
d.missing rules(there is no rule which can be fired by the given condition).

Here we will pay attention to two important cases:
i.two rules have different conditions but lead to almost the same actions,
ii.two rules have almost the same conditions but the actions emitted are totally different.

Both of them indicate inconsistencies in the set of production rules.The second one corresponds to the conflict situation mentioned above.A main source of these two deficiencies appears in the process of knowledge acquisition.Bearing in mind the condition part consists of several or many subconditions,the appearence of the two cases can be explained as follows.If for the two rules the same action is caused by different condition parts,then some of subconditions can be simplified,or in extreme situation are irrelevant with respect to the action specified.Then some subconditions can be modified;this means the rules are generalized and replaced by a new one.The procedure leading to it will be called generalization.In the situation (ii)we deal with the case in which the expert has missed some subconditions,perhaps due to its obvious evidence,which are different for both the rules.Thus some subconditions should be added,viz.the rules are to be particularized(specified).The way leading to this goal is called particularization.

One can notice that in (i)we force the user of the expert system to feed more data that it is really required or more rules have to be checked in the system.Thus we deal with redundancy which stands in out of accordance with requirements of any effective man-machine interface.The second situation is awkward as well:for the given condition two contradictory actions are suggested,and,of course,this is unaccep-

table.
Below we present several illustrative examples.The
first one is an excerpt from a control protocol forming a basis of the fuzzy controller[8],

R_1: If(error is small & change of error is large)then
control is medium ,

R_2: If(error is small & change of error is small)then
control is medium

Here the condition part consists of two subconditions expressing the state of the process under control.The state is
formulated by fuzzy labels given in space of error and change of error,viz. small,medium,large,and small,large,respe-
ctively.At a first glance one can detect the rules R_1,R_2 are
to be generalized,and the subcondition expressing the change
of error can be skipped.So we get:

R_{1g}:If error is small then control is medium,
R_{2g}:If error is small then control is medium,
so finally by one rule,

R_g:If error is small then control is medium.
In situation the space of change of error consists of three
labels:small,medium,large then R_1 and R_2 are read as follows

R_g:If(error is small & change of error is medium)then
control is medium.

In the second example consider two production rules being a
bit simplified advices for a car driver,
R1:If the weather is fine then drive slowly,
R_2:If the weather is fine then drive fast,
where as before all the underlined ntions are fuzzy in their
nature(e.g.fine weather consists of several subconditions
that describe temperature,rains,...,also in a fuzzy way).But
for these rules the same condition leads to quite different
actions(slowly,fast).This can be resolved by adding next subcondition,

R_1 R_{1s} If(the weather is fine &...) then drive slowly,
R_2 R_{2s} If(the weather is fine &...) then drive fast
Of course,the extra subcondition should be added by the expert,but indication of such a situation is given automatical-
ly.For instance take,

R_{1s}: If (the weather is fine & it is almost weekend) then drive slowly

R_{2s}: If (the weather is fine & it is middle of the week)then
drive fast

or

R_{1s}: If (the weather is fine & you are a weak driver) then
drive slowly

R_{2s}: If (the weather is fine & you are a good driver) then
drive fast

Now we will propose some mechanisms that allow to recognize
the rules which require particularization or generalization.
Due to a natural way fuzzy notions appeared in the abovesta-
ted examples,we will consider the conditions and actions are

formulated in terms of possibility distributions(fuzzy sets),
namely A_i and B_i are treated as fuzzy relations and fuzzy
sets.For details explaining the role of fuzzy sets in expert
systems,inference engines for rule-based ones the reader is
referred to [1],[5], [10], [12],[17].

As the main point of our algorithms makes use of matching conditions and actions of the rules,we concentrate our
attention on basic notions of degree of equality of fuzzy relations.

2. DEGREE OF EQUALITY OF FUZZY RELATIONS

Consider two fuzzy relations A_1 and A_2 forming the conditions
of the rules and expressed in cartesian product denoted by
A.An expression to which extent A_1 and A_2 are equal each other comes from a logical background.By definition[7],the degree of equality $[\![.]\!]$ is given by,

$$[\![A_1 \equiv A_2]\!] = (A_1 \rightarrow A_2) \& (A_2 \rightarrow A_1) \qquad (3)$$

where implication $\rightarrow$ and conjunction $\&$ are modelled by Gö-
delian implication α and lattice intersection $\wedge$ =min,respe-
ctively, $a \alpha b = 1$, if $a \leqslant b$, and b if $a > b$, $a, b \in [0, 1]$ .Then (3) translates into

$$[\![A_1 \equiv A_2]\!] = \{ \inf [A_1 (a) \alpha A_2 (a))] \} \wedge \{ \inf [A_2 (a) \alpha A_1 (a)] \} \qquad (4)$$

Note that if supports of A_1 and A_2 are disjoint,supp$(A_1) \cap$
$\cap$ supp$(A_2) = \emptyset$,supp $A_1 = \{ a | A(a) > 0 \}$,then $[\![A_1 \equiv A_2]\!]$ is equal to
zero.This may form a certain disadvantage of the above de-
finition.An other definition of equality can be constructed
as follows(assume A is a finite space).Introduce a pointwise
equality index of A_1 and A_2 equal to

$$\Gamma(a) = [A_1 (a) \rightarrow A_2 (a)] \wedge [A_2 (a) \rightarrow A_1 (a)] = [A_1 (a) \alpha A_2 (a)] \wedge [A_2 (a) \alpha A_1 (a)] \qquad (5)$$

Then the degree of equality of A_1 and A_2 is formulated by a
specifity measure cf. [15],

$$1 - \int_0^1 \frac{dc}{\text{card}\{ a | \Gamma(a) \geqslant c \}} \qquad (6)$$

DETECTING THE RULES FOR GENERALIZATION OR PARTICULARIZATION

Making use of the grade of equality introduced above put
down notation,

$$\alpha_{ij} = [\![A_i \equiv A_j]\!] \qquad \beta_{ij} = [\![B_i \equiv B_j]\!] \qquad (7)$$

Then the degree to which the rules i and j are to be generalized is articulated by,

$$\gamma_{ij} = \beta_{ij} \rightarrow \alpha_{ij} = \beta_{ij} \alpha \alpha_{ij} \qquad (8)$$

The lower γ_{ij} is,the more required generalization is.For binary values of the grades of equality,a behaviour of γ_{ij} is

displayed below,

	α_{ij}	β_{ij}	γ_{ij}		Remarks
$\underline{A}_i \neq \underline{A}_j, B_i = B_j$	0	1	0		generalization
$\underline{A}_i = \underline{A}_j, B_i = B_j$	1	1	1	np	generalization
$\underline{A}_i = \underline{A}_j, B_i \neq B_j$	1	0	1	no	generalization
$\underline{A}_i \neq \underline{A}_j, B_i \neq B_j$	0	0	1	no	generalization

The values of all pairwise evaluations γ_{ij} are arranged in the form of $(N \times N)$ symmetrical matrix,

$$[\gamma_{ij}] = \begin{bmatrix} 1 & \gamma_{12} & \gamma_{13} & \cdots & \gamma_{1N} \\ & 1 & \gamma_{23} & \cdots & \gamma_{2N} \\ & & 1 & & \\ & & & 1 & \\ & & & & 1 \end{bmatrix}$$

The following index expresses the degree to which the two rules i and j require specialization,

$$\delta_{ij} = \alpha_{ij} \rightarrow \beta_{ij} \tag{8}$$

As before, for all the pairs of the rules, the values of δ_{ij} are put into a matrix form.

The performance indices as above characterize all the rules with respect to their requirement to be generalized or specialized. The matrices $[\gamma_{ij}]$ and $[\delta_{ij}]$ will be treated as similarity matrices; then any hierarchical clustering method[6] generates a dendrogram. It allows the knowledge engineer to visualize the subset of the production rules that need modifications and indicate clearly their hierarchical interrelationships.

3. AN ALGORITHM FOR RULES GENERALIZATION

Having a look at the table in the previous section, in order to increase the value of γ_{ij} without modification of β_{ij}, one has to decrease the value of α_{ij}. It means for fixed values of the membership function B_i and B_j, A'_i and A'_j being generalized versions of $\underline{A}_i$ and $\underline{A}_j$ differ slightly. One of plausible way is to perform projections of $\underline{A}_i, \underline{A}_j$ on one or several axis of the cartesian product A. The following proposition specifies it in a compact manner.

For any two fuzzy relations $\underline{A}_i$ and $\underline{A}_j$ defined in A, the following inequality holds,

$$[\![\underline{A}_i = \underline{A}_j]\!] \leq [\![\text{Proj } \underline{A}_i \equiv \text{Proj } \underline{A}_j]\!] \tag{9}$$

where $\text{Proj}(.)$ denotes symbolically projections on the respective coordinate of A.

Proof of (9) forms a straightforward consequence of the following inequality:

787

$a \leftrightarrow b \leq a' \leftrightarrow b'$ for $a' > a, b' > b$, and $a \leftrightarrow b = (a \rightarrow b) \wedge (b \rightarrow a), a, b \in [0,1]$.

If $\text{Proj } \underline{A}_i$ will be sought as the projection of $\underline{A}_i$ on exactly one axis, then the values of $[\text{Proj}_{A_1-i_A} \underline{A}_i \equiv \text{Proj}_{A_1-j_A} \underline{A}_j]$ for $l=1, 2,\ldots,n$ indicate which coordinate of $\underline{A}_1-i_A$ $\underline{A}_1-j$ has to be changed. The higher the value of the $[\text{Proj}_{A_1} \underline{A}_i \equiv \text{Proj}_{A_1} \underline{A}_j]$ the more preferable the l-th axis is as a potential candidate to modify.

Returning to the example, establish the following membership functions in the space of error and change of error,
-for error,

	e_1	e_2	e_3
small	0.7	1.0	0.6

-for the change of error,

	de_1	de_2	de_3	de_4	de_5
large	0.3	0.4	0.5	0.7	1.0
small	1.0	0.8	0.5	0.4	0.2

Then the fuzzy relation $\underline{A}_1$ viewed as the cartesian product of the linguistic labels (fuzzy sets) small and large and $\underline{A}_2$ (small × small) yield,

	$\underline{A}_1$					$\underline{A}_2$				
	de_1	de_2	de_3	de_4	de_5					
e_1	0.3	0.4	0.5	0.7	0.7	0.7	0.7	0.5	0.4	0.2
e_2	0.3	0.4	0.5	0.7	1.0	1.0	0.8	0.5	0.4	0.2
e_3	0.3	0.4	0.5	0.6	0.6	0.6	0.6	0.5	0.4	0.2
e_4	0.3	0.3	0.3	0.3	0.3	0.3	0.3	0.3	0.3	0.2

In sequel we calculate $[\underline{A}_1 \equiv \underline{A}_2] = 0.2$. Now perform projections on the axis of error and change of error,

$$\underline{A}'_1 = \text{Proj}_{\text{error}} \underline{A}_1 = \max_{de} \underline{A}_1(e, de) = [0.3 \ 0.4 \ 0.5 \ 0.7 \ 1.0]$$

$$\underline{A}'_2 = \text{Proj}_{\text{error}} \underline{A}_2 = [0.7 \ 0.8 \ 0.5 \ 0.4 \ 0.2]$$

and

$$\underline{A}''_1 = \text{Proj}_{\text{change of error}} \underline{A}_1 = \max_{e} \underline{A}_1(e, de) = [0.7 \ 1.0 \ 0.6 \ 0.3]$$

$$\underline{A}''_2 = \text{Proj}_{\text{change of error}} \underline{A}_2 = [0.7 \ 1.0 \ 0.6 \ 0.3]$$

Now, $[\underline{A}'_1 \equiv \underline{A}'_2] = 0.2$, $[\underline{A}''_1 \equiv \underline{A}''_2] = 1.0$. In virtue of the above statement following the proposition, the subcondition expressed in the space of the change of error may be skipped.

4. CONCLUDING REMARKS

We have indicated some open questions relevant to the acquisition of expert knowledge and its representation in terms of production rules (rule-based expert systems). A special attention has been paid to the generalization and particularization of the rules enabling to attain a consistent form of

the knowledge base.Some indices proposed here may be useful
for detecting inconsistencies resolved by the generalization
and particularization of the respective production rules.
Nevertheless,the problems formulated are not completely solved,some algorithms have been only outlined and require
further development.

REFERENCES

1. K.P.Adlassnig,G.Kolarz,W.Scheithauer,Present state of the
   expert system CADIAG-2.Meth.Inform.Med.24,1985,13-20.
2. D.G.Bobrow,GUS,a frame driven dialog system,Artificial
   Intelligence,8,1977,155-173.
3. D.G.Bobrow,T.Winograd,An overview of KRL,a knowledge representation language,Cognitive Science,1,1977,3-46.
4. B.G.Buchanan,R.O.Duda,Principles of rule-based expert system,Fairchild Tech.Rep.no.626,1982.
5. A.Di Nola,W,Pedrycz,S.Sessa,Fuzzy relation equations and
   algorithms of inference mechanism in expert systems.In:
   Approximate Reasoning in Expert Systems M.M.Gupta,A.Kandel
   eds. North Holland,Amsterdam,1985.
6. R.O.Duda,P.E.Hart,Pattern Classification and Scene Analysis
   J.Wiley,New York,1973.
7. S.Gottwald,Characterization of solvability of fuzzy equations,EIK,to appear.
8. E.H.Mamdani,Advances in the linguistic synthesis of fuzzy
   controllers,Int.J.Man-Machine Stud.,10,1978,313-322.
9. W.van Melle,MYCIN:a knowledge-based consultation program
   for infectious disease diagnosis.Int.J.Man-Machine Stud.
   10,1978,313-322.
10. C.V.Negoita,Expert Systems and Fuzzy Systems.Benjamin Cum-
    mings Publ.Comp.Menlo Park Calif,1985.
11. W.Pedrycz,Applications of fuzzy relational equations for
    methods of reasoning in presence of fuzzy data,Fuzzy Sets
    and Systems,16,1985,163-175.
12. H.Prade,A computational approach to approximate and pla-
    usible reasoning with applications to expert systems.
    IEEE Trans.Pattern Analysis and Machine Intelligence,7,
    1985,260-283.
13. E.H.Shortliffe,Computer-Based Medical Consulatation:MY -
    CIN.Elsevier,New York,1976.
14. M.Suwa,A.C.Scott,E.H.Shortliffe,An approach to verifying
    completeness and consistency in a rule-based expert sys-
    tem.Rep.HPP-81-5,June 1981,Stanford.
15. R.R.Yager,Measuring tranquility and anxiety in decision-
    making:an application of fuzzy sets.Int.J.Gen.Systems.
    8,1982,139-146.
16. S.M.Weiss,C.A.Kulikowski,S.Amarel,A model-based method
    for computer-aided medical decision-making,Artificial

Intelligence,11,1978,145-172.
17.L.A.Zadeh,The role of fuzzy logic in the management of uncertainty in expert systems,Fuzzy Sets and Systems,11, 1983,199-227.

Knowledge Based Natural Language Processing

Chairpersons: R.Brachman (U.S.A.)
               H.Trost (Austria)

CONCEPT - CLASS - PROTOTYPE: *unum an trinum* ?

Cristiano Castelfranchi
Oliviero Stock
I.P.- Consiglio Nazionale delle Ricerche
Via dei Monti Tiburtini 509, 00157 Roma, Italy
Tel. 0039-6-451204

ABSTRACT: In this paper we discuss if concepts, classes and prototypes are different entities and should be treated as such in a knowledge representation system. In particular we postulate the presence of a class in the memory if and only if this results in having generic assertions about it, and discuss how classes can be diiferently related to concepts and prototypes.

1 Introduction

After the criticism by W.Woods (19/ɔ) and extensive work by R. Brachman (1979), a number of relevant distinctions have been introduced in semantic networks, and some requisites that semantic networks must satisfy have become apparent. Nonetheless it seems to us that an overall and solid organization of the different levels and types of formal objects necessary for KR has not emerged, in particular in relation to natural language. Not always is it clear the necessity and appropriateness for the introduction of one component of KR. For example, KLONE has had the merit of clearing the distinction between extension anc intensional definition of concepts, between set-based relations and structural relations ɔi intensional hierarchies. It has drawn a distinction, in this way, between terminological and assertional parts; but while it has expressed an apparatus for representing the first one, it did not so for the second one, except for simply calling in predicate calculus, in one or another form, i.e. without significant *desiderata* or functional specification (see for instance KRYPTON, Brachman et al. 1983).

Actually, one of the central problems of semantic networks has been the organization (not only hierarchical) of assertions, in particular deriving from language understanding. KLONE, in this perspective, has not solved the problems with semantic networks, or their hierarchical organization, but instead has put the emphasis on one perspective (in this sense rather than a complete KR language, KLONE is a language for representing concepts). KLONE and KRYPTON have shown that "intensional hierarchies" are distinct from extensional organizational axes, but therefore "concepts" or "terms" cannot play entirely the role of "classes" (see next paragraph). In our discussion we consider the knowledge representation necessary for such natural language processing tasks as: representing the meaning of a sentence, interact with an encyclopaedia of world knowledge for

793

R. Trappl (ed.), Cybernetics and Systems '86, 793–798.
© *1986 by D. Reidel Publishing Company.*

comprehension and disambiguation, organization and maintainance of knowledge extracted through text reading and so on.

2 Classes

Classes are particular mental entities in an assertional network, to be intended as generic individuals (e.g. *a protestant priest* or *protestant priests*). They are introduced a) to support generic assertions (e.g. ..... *are allowed to get married);* b1) to generalize and sinthetize in one place assertions that would concern various entities in the memory, other classes (subclasses, such as *Calvinist priests*), sets (see next paragraph) and individuals (e.g. *Vater Schmidt* and *Domine Van der Broek)*; b2) to collect knowledge that would be true of more entities, not already defined c) to organize a network in search spaces, grouping together exemplars.

We postulate the presence of a class in the memory if and only if this results in having generic assertions about it.

A class, in this connection, is something that we can look at as the extension of a concept (a term or a structured predicate), a kind of "open" set of possible entities. Sets (e.g. *protestant priests now in London)* share with classes functions b1) (not b2) and c). A characteristic of human languages is that they tend to assimilate sets and classes (hence the origin of one of the many ambiguities of the ISA link, Brachman, 1983). They share many properties and many linguistic expressions are actually ambiguous (e.g. "is a", or "the priests who ... "). Some, nonetheless, realize a discrimination: in "<u>one of the</u> protestant priests", "the protestant priests" can refer only to a set and not to a class.

3 Concepts (or terms)

We call "nodes" entities introduced to "give support" to assertions or allow accumulatior of assertions. Concepts are not nodes in a knowledge network. Assertions are propositions not made *on* concepts , but *using* concepts. Concepts are the constituents of properties or relations that are attributed to nodes through assertions. In linguistics the problem of terms or concept analysis was widely dealt with through lexical decomposition or semantic analysis (Lakoff, 1970, Dowty, 1979, Miller and Johnson-Laird, 1976, Parisi and Antinucci, 1976). In the lexical decomposition tradition there was an intensional viewpoint, but the organization lay only in the fact that predicates were "composed" of common "ingredients" (predicates, features, primitives, components and so on) and therefore conceptual representations could partially or entirely overlie (e.g. "to die" and "to kill", "to whiten" and "white"). On the other hand, the merit of KLONE, compared to lexical decomposition, has been that it has introduced a well defined theory of how to represent and organize concepts (or terms or structured predicates). There are a) hierarchies of concepts (considering one concept leads to considering other "more" generic ones; b) there is more structure in the concept description. It would make sense that the two traditions meet, in any way.

4 The relation class / concept

Classes are defined by means of one or more concepts. "Defined" means that there are properties that individuals or sets must have to be recognized as certainly belonging to that class, and that differentiate that class from other classes. If a class is defined by means of more than one concept, there is the problem of how these concepts get combined together. If we want to account for the fact that classes can be created through sentences, using a however complex semantic structure (e.g. "the protestant priests that may have decided to get married, because were convinced, thanks to Saint Paul, of the superiority of celibate"), we may accept then that concepts get combined with the same modality with which they are combined in semantic networks that represent sentences. If some concepts (referred through propositions) define a class, we must make a distinction between these propositions and those used to make assertions *on* the class (e.g. "may have decided to get married"). About the importance of propositional nodes for KR, see also Castelfranchi et al. (1984).

Not for every concept there is a class. We do not think it is sensible to have a class for all the things that are <u>not</u> something, or of the things that are <u>above</u> something, or are <u>more</u> <property> <u>than</u> others, though we have concepts for <u>not</u>, <u>above</u>, <u>more</u>. What do we know, in fact, about what is "above" something?

The hierarchical organization of concepts (the fact that one concept subsumes other concepts) is reflected in the hierarchical organization of classes (fig. 1). Similar ideas are also

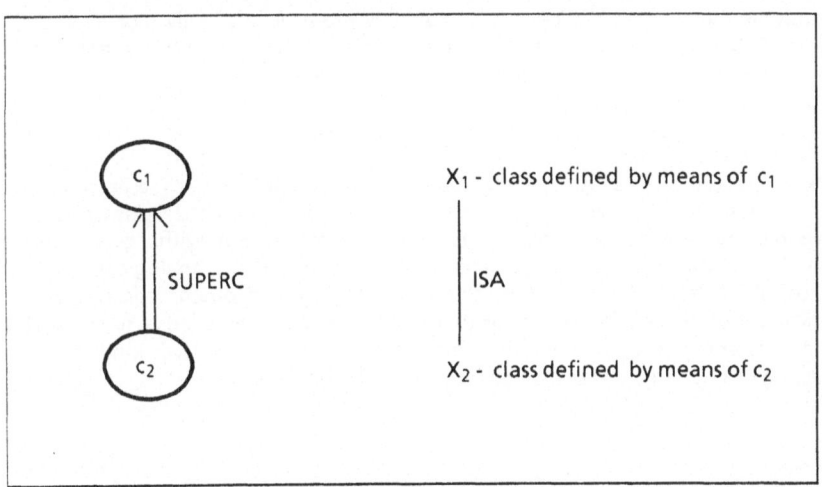

Fig. 1

in Patel-Schneider (1984) and Brachman and Levesque (1984).

The class defined by a concept is a subclass of a class defined by one of its superconcepts. Therefore we have two types of superclass: an analytic superclass (based on superconcepts) and a nonanalytic one (where the relation with the subclass is not definitory). An example: *liquors* are (for conceptual reasons) *drinks*, but they also are a subclass of *luxury items; to eat something with one's fingers* is a subclass (for conceptual reasons) of *to eat* , but also a subclass of *an action that my mother did not want me to do*. The fact that a concept that does not define a class does not imply that its subconcepts will not define a class.

5 Prototypes

Prototypes have been very popular in AI. All the frame based approaches have considered prototypes the key to KR. An insightful discussion on prototypes is in Winograd (1978). Criticism to the prototype centered approach has been levelled by various authors, included Brachman (1985). Nonetheless we all accept that prototypes are something we widely use in our mental processes.

A prototype is a node that is linked to a class, but has some typical properties, and plays a particular role. One aspect of prototypes is that they consent to set defaults for unknown properties of an entity. In fact this is the aspect that has been mostly used in frame based approaches. The other strictly operational characteristic is that the idea of prototype yields a different modality for deciding if an entity belongs to a class: an entity can be accepted as belonging to a class by "analogy" with the prototype, and therefore if a certain "quantity" of relevant properties are shared with the prototype. Belonging to a class not on a definitional base (having all the properties that define a class), but on a prototypical base, is obviously neither certain nor necessary, but only more or less likely. For example, let us consider the concept (or term) *Italian male* (a male person born in Italy), and the class of Italian males, defined by that concept (the class of male persons born in Italy), about which we have some knowledge (e.g. *they are subject to the draft; they can be married to at most one woman at a time*) and that we have the node of a prototypical Italian male (induced by experience, prejudice or other processes). Knowledge attached to that node may be that he is dark-haired, quite fat, a latin lover, and adores spaghetti and wine. If a person x is known to be "born in Italy", he will be put safely and necessarily in the class of Italians; if he is known to be dark-haired, a woman molester etc., he may be put, with a certain likelihood in the class of Italians, but maintaining associated to him the analogical origin of this hierarchical relation. Without this, things would soon go out of control, while with specifications of this kind, a processor that would use the knowledge base could allow for certain inferences and inhibit other inferences. This implies two kind of processes interacting in a non trivial way on a common knowledge base.

6 Prototypes and classes

A prototype is such for a certain class. Some classes may not have a prototype (e.g. ideas, catholic Melanesians), at least for a lack of experience with instances. Other classes may not have a conceptual definition (or complete conceptual definition). "Natural kinds" belong to this group. Classes not created "by definition" may be built on an exclusively prototypical base, even on a single example. For instance: "this jacket (this kind of jacket) is on sale only in Paris". This means that a class may be created by generalization of attributes of instances (or subclasses): a very important aspect of the human mind's modelling of the world.

A superclass either has a prototype, which is the abstract synthesis of the prototype of its subclasses, or, if this mechanism is not viable, it has as a prototype the prototype of the subclass that is most "relevant" (e. g. most used, or most widely used for teaching). For example, the class of dogs has a prototype, which is neither the prototype of the German shepard, nor that of the bassett-hound or of the boxer, but something more abstract. The class of doors, instead, (whose subclasses include: hinged doors, sliding doors, rotating doors etc.) has as a prototype the prototype of hinged doors.

7 Conclusions

We believe that there are various resources that humans use for representing the world and for making use of that knowledge. Prototype calculus, assertion generalization and analytical concept structuring are different but coexisting mechanisms. In general, we are able to let interact one mechanism with the other ones, but also to maintain its specificity.

If one comes to modelling mental knowledge representation and use, he should be clear in what functions he is considering. If he unifies concepts and/or classes (see for instance Schubert, 1976, Hendrix, 1979) and/or prototypes, this choice should be discussed explicitly, in reference to the facts that are supposed to be accounted for. The problem is not only one of formal elegance and austerity, nor of computational complexity. We think it is important for KR to touch some delicate but essential questions without forgetting human mind and linguistic behaviour. Isn't it that too often in Artificial Intelligence models are underdetermined: critical facts that motivate options are too limited, or not explicitly accounted?

Acknowledgements

We wish to thank F. Cecconi, D. Parisi and G. Romano for discussing with us the ideas presented here.

REFERENCES

Brachman, R. (1979) On The Epistemological Status of Semantic Networks. In N. Findler (ed.) *Associative Networks*. New York: Academic Press.

Brachman, R. (1983) What IS-A Is and Isn't: An Analysis of Taxonomic Links in Semantic Networks. *IEEE Computer* 16 (10), 30-36.

Brachman, R. (1985) "I Lied About The Trees". *AI Magazine*, 6, 3., 80-93

Brachman, R. , Fikes , R. & Levesque, H. (1983) KRYPTON: A Functional Approach to Knowledge Representation. *IEEE Computer* 16 (10), 67-73.

797

Brachman, R. & Levesque, H. (1984) The Tractability of Subsumption in Frame-Based Description Languages. *Proc. of AAAI-84.* Austin, Texas, 34-37.

Castelfranchi, C. Parisi, D. & Stock, O. (1984) Knowledge Representation and Natural Language: Extending the Expressive Power of Proposition Nodes. In B. Bara & G. Guida (eds.) *Computational Models of Natural Language Processing.* Amsterdam: North Holland.

Dowty, D. (1979) *Word Meaning in Generative Semantics and Montague Grammar.* Dordrecht: Reidel.

Hendrix, G. (1979) Encoding Knowledge in Partitioned Networks. In N. Findler (ed.) *Associative Networks.* New York: Academic Press.

Lakoff, G. (1970) *Irregularity in Syntax.* New York: Holt Rinehart and Winston.

Miller, G. & Johnson-Laird, P. (1976) *Language and Perception.* Cambridge: Belknap Press.

Parisi, D. & Antinucci, F. (1976) *Essentials of Grammar.* New York: Academic Press.

Patel-Schneider, P. (1984) Small Can Be Beautiful in Knowledge Representation. Fairchild Technical Report n° 660. Palo Alto.

Schubert, L.K. (1976) Extending the Expressive Power of Semantic Networks. *Artificial Intelligence,* 7, 163-198.

Winograd, T. (1978) On Primitives, Prototypes, and other Semantic Anomalies. *Proc.* TINLAP-2, Urbana, Ill. 25-32.

Woods, W. (1975) What's in a Link? Foundations for Semantic Networks. In D. Bobrow and A. Collins (eds.) *Representation and Understanding.* New York: Academic Press.

THE ROLE OF METAKNOWLEDGE IN TEXT COMPREHENSION

G. Airenti^, M. Colombetti^^, M.C. Gallo^
^ Unita' di ricerca di intelligenza artificiale,
  Universita' di Milano
^^ Progetto di intelligenza artificiale,
   Politecnico di Milano

ABSTRACT. In this paper we present an artificial intelligence model of the cognitive processes involved in text comprehension. In particular we focus on the structure of the knowledge required. Our hypothesis is that a relevant feature in the process of text comprehension is the use of specific metaknowledge which correlates the text structure to the intentionality of the author. We introduce three metaknowledge assumptions and show how they can guide the understanding process when the recognition of an unexpected element causes a discrepancy.

1. INTRODUCTION

In this paper we present an artificial intelligence model of the cognitive processes involved in text comprehension. In particular we focus on the structure of the knowledge required.

We consider text comprehension as the process of subjective reconstruction of the content of the text. A model of such a process should account for the subject's ability to:

- reconstruct the content of the text on the basis of his knowledge of the world and of the text structure

- acknowledge possible discrepancies between his reconstruction and the text

- overcome such discrepancies through a modification of his reconstruction.

Our model deals with these abilities from a competence point of view. This means that we investigate the knowledge structures and the thought processes which enable any cognitive system to understand a text, independently of the type of text and of the individual characteristics of the understander. Such a standpoint has a number of

799

R. Trappl (ed.), Cybernetics and Systems '86, 799–806.

consequences.

First, our model is intended to fit any kind of text, both written and audiovisual like TV programs and movies. In fact, the differences among texts affect the performance but not the structure of the reconstruction process. For instance, if a TV viewer acknowledges a discrepancy, he can neither pause the transmission nor go back and watch again a previous scene, while both actions are possible for a book reader. Here we have a difference in the access to input information which will presumably influence the performance of the understander; on the contrary, the underlying thought processes are identical.

Second, our model is independent of the individual characteristics which heavily affect the performance of an understander, like for instance the richness of general knowledge, the availability of specific knowledge about the text being processed, and the effectiveness of memory mechanisms.

In this paper we suggest an organization of knowledge and briefly analyze the structure of the process of text comprehension. Our hypothesis is that a relevant feature of such a process is the use of specific metaknowledge which correlates the text structure to the intentionality of the author. In our work we make use of representational tools, like frames and scripts, borrowed from AI research in story understanding Schank and Abelson, 1977; Charniak, 1978). Moreover, our model is compatible with the principles of text understanding by Wilensky (1983).

2. THEORETICAL FRAMEWORK

The text comprehension processes of an ideal understander can be characterized on the basis of general principles, which delimit the competence of the understander but do not provide a computational description of his processes. Wilensky (1983) proposes the following five principles: consistent construal, concretion, least energy, exhaustion, and poignancy. For example, the exhaustion principle states that all the elements of the text must be given an interpretation. Wilensky also proposes a set of knowledge management procedures which build up an artificial system able to understand simple stories written in English in accordance with the general principles. For instance, exhaustion is guaranteed by the fact that each element of the story is filled into a slot of a frame by a procedure.

It is important to note that the understanding process involves making hypotheses which may prove discrepant with the subsequent input. In this case, the principles do not indicate how the system could cope with the problem.

We suggest that discrepant situations are dealt with on the basis of metaknowledge on texts. Such metaknowledge relates the structure and content of the text with the intentionality of the author, and is used by the understander to reason on the discrepancy and as a guide in the attempt to recover.

As we shall see in the following, metaknowledge is compatible with the general principles of text comprehension. To anticipate an example, consider the following metaknowledge assumption:

(1)   "All elements of a text have been intentionally inserted by the author in order to reach a specific goal"

Such an assumption, which relates the elements of a text with the intentionality of its author, is in accordance with the principle of exhaustion, which requires that an interpretation account for all elements of the text.

However, general principles and metaknowledge assumptions should not be confused. Principles are theoretical abstractions which constrain the text understanding processes. Instead, metaknowledge assumptions are knowledge structures possessed by real understanders, which guide them in text comprehension.

Metaknowledge assumptions are used together with knowledge about the structure, content and author's goals of different types of texts. For example, let us consider a scene in a thriller where a character lies to the detective investigating on a murder. According to assumption (1), the lie has been inserted intentionally by the author in order to achieve a specific goal. The interpretation depends on what the understander considers to be the author's goal. A naive one will interpret the lie as a positive clue that the character is the murderer. On the contrary, an expert thriller reader will interpret the same element as a move by the author to achieve suspence through the intentional introduction of ambiguity.

In the next section we delineate the elements of a knowledge representation as a basis for our model of text comprehension.

3. KNOWLEDGE AND THOUGHT PROCESSES

All cognitive processes involve the manipulation of knowledge structures by thought processes. A large amount of the knowledge used in the text comprehension is just ordinary world knowledge. In other terms, the knowledge used to understand the word "apple" is essentially the same which is used to interact with a concrete apple in the real world. In a sense, this is not true for words like "dragon" or "angel", which can be found in tales, and can be understood even if there are no such things as dragons and angels in the real world. To cope with this problem, we separate the knowledge which is necessary to conceptualize (build a mental model of) something, and the knowledge about what actually exists in the external world.

We think of conceptual knowledge as a network of entities which represent objects, properties, events which are conceptually possible, independently of their reality: APPLE, DRAGON, ANGEL are examples of such entities.

A second component of knowledge is constituted by real world frames, arranging conceptual entities in scenarios which are likely to be encountered in the real world. A classical example is the frame RESTAURANT, which represents the objects and events constituting such real scenarios as restaurants.

As a further component of knowledge we have possible world frames, accounting for the conceptual entities which are part of possible worlds, i.e. worlds which do not actually exist but can be imagined. Such frames establish the laws holding in the possible world; for example, an angel cannot possibly die, while a dragon can.

Possible world frames are part of knowledge structures that we call text schemes. A text scheme describes a type of text by connecting:

- the narration scheme, representing the intentions of the author (for instance, in a thriller, concealing the identity of the murderer until the end)

- the possible worlds frames describing the possible worlds which can be dealt with (for instance, a science fiction world, the real world, the world of Peanuts)

- the story scheme, which represents the possible intentions of the characters (for instance, the intention of the detective to find the murderer and the murderer's intention not to be found).

An important category of thought processes deal with the interpretation of input information. Among such processes are the comprehension of real people's plans and the understanding of texts. While we think that the competence underlying the comprehension of any type of text is basically the same, there are sharp differences between understanding texts and understanding the behaviour of real people. In other words, we assume that there are a set of specific thought procedures which account for the comprehension of texts in a specific way.

Following Airenti, Bara and Colombetti (1984), we assume that such procedures interpret the input information by building mental models on the basis of general knowledge. Occasionally, the interpretation of the input may be impossible, because it would lead to the construction of an inconsistent model. For example, a character of a story who has been interpreted to have died in Chapter 2, is back in the story in Chapter 3. In such cases, if the discrepancy between the previous interpretation and the new information input is acknowledged by the understander, a possible way to cope with the situation is to reinterpret the previous input to make the discrepancy vanish. In our opinion, such a reinterpretation requires: (i) an explicit representation of the discrepancy; (ii) the use of metaknowledge to reason on the discrepancy in order to overcome it.

In the following section we shall discuss the metaknowledge involved in the analysis of discrepancies which arise in text comprehension.

4. METAKNOWLEDGE

Metaknowledge is a pervasive notion in AI, and has been proved useful both to model cognitive activities (Wilensky, 1983) and to implement artificial systems (see for instance Davis and Buchanan, 1977). Here we are interested in a particular kind of metaknowledge, which is part of a cognitive model of text comprehension.

We can represent such metaknowledge as a set of assumptions on the relations between the structure and content of the text and the intentions of its authors. Our hypothesis is that in the process of comprehension the understander may refer to the intentions of the author both directly and indirectly. In the first case the understander directly investigates the author's intentions. For instance, he may wonder what is the importance of a love affair the author has inserted in the thriller. In the second case the understander analyzes the content of the story itself: this means both to recognize the kind of possible world pertaining to the story, and to reconstruct the plot relying on the supposed coherence in the characters' intentions. Note that referring to a possible world and to coherence in the characters' intentions is meaningful only on the underlying assumption that the author intentionally created them. In fact, when a discrepancy arises, the understander attributes it to an error in his reconstruction, i.e. to his misunderstanding of the author's intentions.

On the basis of what we have just discussed we propose the three following metatheoretical assumptions:

(1) "All elements of a text have been intentionally inserted by the author in order to reach a specific goal"

(2) "All elements of a text have been intentionally inserted by the author in order to describe a coherent possible world"

(3) "All the actions performed by the characters are coherent with standing intentions attributed to them by the author"

The function of metaknowledge assumptions is to guide the process of reconstruction, to make the understander acknowledge possible discrepancies between his reconstruction and the author's intentions, and to overcome such discrepancies.

As we have previously considered our metaknowledge assumptions should agree with the principles of comprehension: in the theoretical framework we have discussed our assumption (1) as related with the principle of exhaustion. Now we can briefly analyze how assumptions (2) and (3) are connected with the principle of consistent construal, which states that the input is interpreted as instantiating knowledge structures in a coherent way. In fact, although texts may describe worlds different from the real one, such worlds are assumed by the understander to be coherent; for instance, in a sword-and-sorcery movie an understander interprets all events as consistent either with real world laws or with the laws of magic. Assumption (3) is

803

particularly relevant for narratives and extends the coherence requirement to characters' plans.

In conclusion, we think that the author's intentionality accounts for basic differences between texts and the real world. Texts are created for being understood: this justifies the centrality of coherence, which is a precondition of understanding.

5. METAKNOWLEDGE AND NOISE

In the process of comprehension different kinds of discrepancies may arise. A discrepancy stems always from the impossibility to make an element of the text fit into the previous reconstruction.

The possible cases are:

(i) an element does not fit the currently recognized narrative scheme; for instance, in a thriller a strong, early clue that a character is the murderer contradicts the assumed author's intention of concealing the true identity of the murderer

(ii) an element does not fit the currently recognized possible world; for instance, the appearance of a flying saucer in an everyday life story

(iii) an element does not fit the currently recognized story scheme; for instance, James Bond betraying Great Britain.

Not necessarily does the understander acknowledge the presence of a discrepancy at the moment it arises. The process of understanding may go on until there is sufficient evidence against the current reconstruction. Eventually, when the understander becomes aware of the discrepancy, we say that subjective noise has been formed. In this case, the understander is likely to analyze the discrepancy in order to overcome it. We suggest that this analysis is carried out relying on the metaknowledge assumptions.

The relation holding between the three components of the text scheme and the metaknowledge assumptions allows us to apply a single assumption to each of the cases (i)-(iii) in order to guide a recovery strategy exploiting the available knowledge.

In case (i) the metaknowledge assumption (1) leads the understander to look for a specific narrative goal which would account for the insertion of the discrepant element in the text. In our example the understander can interpret the strong, early clue as an intentionally misleading insertion by the author.

In case (ii) the metaknowledge assumption (2) suggests to the understander to investigate different possible worlds to identify a suitable one. In the corresponding example the understander will probably assume a science fiction world.

In case (iii) the metaknowledge assumption (3) leads the understander to analyse the characters' intentions in order to justify their actions. In our example a James Bond connoisseur will interpret the apparent betrayal as a stratagem to deceive the baddies.

In a realistic situation the recovery strategies activated by the different metaknowledge assumptions may compete in the search for a new interpretation of the input. For istance, in the case where the discrepancy was originated by a too early clue in a thriller, an analysis of the discrepancy could include reasoning on the story scheme and thus bring to a different interpretation: it is the murderer who forged a track to mislead the detective.   Note that the actual performance of an understander in the treatment of discrepancies depends on individual characteristics like the amount and specificity of knowledge. In the example of case (iii), a nonconnoisseur of James Bond would not even notice a discrepancy and would interpret the betrayal as typical in spy stories.

6. DISCUSSION

The main point of this paper is the introduction of metaknowledge assumptions which guide text comprehension in critical situations like the arising of discrepancies. We consider metaknowledge as fundamental in distinguishing between text comprehension and the understanding of everyday life. In fact, assumptions (1)-(3) explicitly refer to different kinds of intentionality which are distinctive of texts.

We believe that understanding involves knowledge on the determination laws which govern either texts or the real world. Texts are determined by the intentionality of their authors, while in general people do not assume that the real world is ruled by a unique intentionality. Therefore metaknowledge about the real world will be centered on such notions as causality and individual actors' intentionality (see for example Airenti and Colombetti, 1985). Given the role of metaknowledge, it follows that discrepancies in the understanding of real world events will be treated differently. For instance, we are not allowed to shift to a world with different physical laws in order to justify a fact which is difficult to explain. Such constraints also hold in texts describing real world situations. In fact in a normal thriller if a gun does not fire we expect that it is either unloaded or broken and not that the planned victim has magical powers. On the contrary, the last interpretation is possible in a science fiction story.

REFERENCES

Airenti G., Bara B.G., Colombetti M., 1984. 'An intrasystemic approach to belief'. In: Elithorn A., Banerji R., eds., Artificial and Human Intelligence, North-Holland, Amsterdam

Airenti G., Colombetti M., 1985. 'Representing events and actions', Proceedings COGNITIVA 85, Paris

Charniak E., 1978. 'On the use of framed knowledge in language comprehension', Artificial Intelligence, II, 3

Davis R., Buchanan B.G., 1977. 'Meta-level knowledge: overview and applications', Proceedings Fifth International Joint Conference on Artificial Intelligence, MIT, Mass.

Schank R.C., Abelson R.P., 1977. Scripts, plans, goals, and understanding, Erlbaum, Hillsdale, N.J.

Wilensky R., 1983. Planning and understanding, Addison-Wesley, Reading, Mass.

Wilensky R., 1983. 'Memory and inference', Proceedings Eighth International Joint Conference on Artificial Intelligence, Karlsruhe, D.F.R.

ACKNOWLEDGMENTS

This research has been supported by the Istituto Agostino Gemelli, Milano

AUTHORS' ADDRESS:

Istituto di Psicologia della Facolta' di Medicina, Universita' degli Studi di Milano, Via Francesco Sforza, 23 - I.20122 Milano

MICRO-WORLD RECOGNITION BY "RESTLESS DEBUGGING"

Yves Kodratoff
Laboratoire de Recherche en Informatique
Université de Paris-Sud, Bâtiment 490
F - 91405 ORSAY Cedex

ABSTRACT.   We present a new operational model for Computational Linguistics,
based on Logic Programming Debugging, called here **Restless Debugging**.
We also try to clarify a number of implications this model has for Knowledge
Representation.

1.   INTRODUCTION

This paper presents a proposal for the implementation of an error recovery
mechanism that checks the coherence of each character's knowledge.
This mechanism is qualified as "restless" because we would like to underline the
frequency of error detection rather that its depth. Our approch does not favor
long and difficult debugging sessions as the key to learning the Natural
language. It favors rather a kind of very active debugger that works on small
sets of clauses and performs simple inferences.
Hence, the problem resides in providing the debugger with small sets of clauses
from a given text. In this paper we also describe, in a less detailed way than the
debugger itself, the environment that will provide these sets of clauses.

2.   OVERALL PRESENTATION OF THE MODULES.

The whole system is made up of 4 interacting modules.

2.1.   A micro-world recognizer module that recognizes and uses the "micro-
world" about which the text is speaking.

Here, micro-world means any kind of closed environment. For instance, one can
speak of the micro-world of two cubes on a table and describe their relationships. Not only do the words used to describe this micro-world not have exactly
the same meaning as in others, but the sentences themselves have an organization which is that of the micro-world being described.
Micro-worlds recognition is not as huge a task as micro-worlds definition itself.
We shall suppose here that this work is done in the dictionary (see below),
without attempting to hide that we are planning to implement but small sub-
parts of the actual big universe we are living in.

807

R. Trappl (ed.), Cybernetics and Systems '86, 807–814.

This module must also transform each sentence into its "normal" form, meaning that peculiarities (for instance, slang uses of words) linked to a particular micro-world are erased in the internal representation of the sentence.

This module covers the idea of script, and provides an internal representation of the sentence, chosen here to be first order clauses.

It may seem that Natural Language treatment reduces to the obtainment of such an internal representation. Being concerned with an understanding that enables learning from the knowledge base provided by a text, we show that obtainment of internal representation is only a first (but necessary) step.

This module also performs circonscription [McCarthy 1980, AAAI Workshop 1984], in that sense that it gives the theorems that common sense considered valid in the micro-world concerned.

2.2. A syntactico-semantical dictionary with more information than usually dictionaries have.

Our dictionary is supposed to contain all the available information about words, their particular meanings in different micro-worlds, their semantical relationships, as for instance described in [Fahlman 1979].

It also contains the logical representation of each word. For instance, one receives a gift, a confession, or a guest. Associated predicates must reflect the fact that one receives a guest somewhere, a confession from someone on a specific topic etc ...

We shall also suppose here that the problem of variable arities is solved. In reality, a predicate, like say "to hunt" can be of arity one in "He went hunting", of arity two in "He is hunting his phantasms", of arity three in "He hunts small birds for his pleasure", and by further specifications, we can ad libitum increase its arity.

2.3. A semantic analyser under the form of a parallel theorem prover.

This is the most original part of our contribution.

We are well aware that there have already been many contributions presenting First Order Logic (FOL) as good means to understanding Natural Langage [Colmerauer 1979, Dahl & Saint-Dizier 1985, Hayes 1979, Kowalski 1979, Saint-Dizier 1985], but they described logical ways of representing knowledge rather than inferring new knowledge or acquiring new concepts.

The problem of beliefs representation is solved by regarding each chararcter's knowledge as an independant knowledge "box".

2.4. An information exchange management module (IEMM).

A great deal of attention has already been given to the problems treated by IEMM. It contains all the modal treatment of information, all the second order and strategy problems. On this topic, see for instance [AAAI Workshop 1984].

An originality of our approach is that we point out a new difficult problem (that must be solved by IEMM), the one of deciding what information each character of a story should be aware of. In the simplest joke, understood by the dumbest person, there are usually different characters, and the so-called fun comes from the fact that some characters misunderstand something, i.e., that the information available to them is not the same as that available to others. How can an information management module decide which information must go to whom ?

At any rate, we feel that this problem is not specific to our representation, therefore leaving this part in limbo does not make us feel un-scientific. We shall simply give a sketch of its functioning.

The elementary building block of text understanding will be theorem proving or, as could be better said, "logical debugging" very similar to the one that is needed when an attempt is made to debug PROLOG programs [Shapiro 1982, Pereira 1985].

One of the differences here is that Shapiro's oracles are either a professor in the learning phase, or already stored knowledge in the understanding phase. A complete example is given in next section, where it is shown how a clause can be detected as faulty because invalid in the micro-world concerned.

Finally, the motto of this paper is that **"understanding is removing bugs"**. Otherwise, one should not speak of understanding but rather of acknowledging, which relies on "learning by heart". All the rest is a description of the way information can be brought to the bug remover which is the central mechanism of comprehension.

3.   MICRO-WORLD RECOGNIZER

As a summary let us say that the "micro-world problem" can be described, as shown below, by 3 sub-problems.

```
                 1            2
Recognizer -----> micro-world ------> set of rules putting text in normal
                                                             form
                          ----- 3
                          -----> set of specific inference rules
```

3.1. First sub-problem

Several micro-worlds may be simultaneously possible, and one of them can lead to contradictions (bugs). One way of removing bugs is to reject the current micro-world and choose another one, which does not present a bug. It follows that the first choice is a simple device but that successive choices may come after a sequence of attempts for finding the micro-world concerned. Actually, this is a very unusal and un-human situation since most people just do not understand you if you attempt to skip from one micro-world to another (contradictory) one (unless this is the game one is playing : showing off how much clever one is at changing micro-worlds ... this means that there is a special IEMM routine that is able to handle quick changes of micro-world).

If you are reading a criticism of the USSR in a European Communist newspaper, you well know that the meaning of each word is completely different from that in a right wing newspaper. Shifting between the two micro-worlds may cause total misunderstanding.

Usually the game of changing micro-worlds does not go further than explaining to someone else what is "hidden behind the words". Actually, nothing is really hidden, one is just using two sets of different rules that put the texts into two different normal forms.

Usually very apparent banners with very clear keywords on them have to be shown each time there is a change of micro-world. If not, there is no wonder that a complicated process has to take place.

The building of such a set of rules is itself a hard task. At LRI, such a set has been written for the micro-world of 'children solving problems at school'. It contains around 100 rules that put sentences into their normal form, called a "caricature" of the sentence in the concerned work [Karoubi & Nicaud 85].

3.2. Second subproblem

Choosing a micro-world also means choosing a set of rules that can be applied to the text to put it into non-ambiguous "normal" (normal, relative to this micro-world) form.

At this stage, one gets rid of specialists mumbo-jumbo (trivial matters like local slang are also difficult to work out) in order to put the text into a simpler form.

The now famous example "Withdrawal from territories occupied by Isreali forces" takes the normal form "Withdrawal from all territories occupied by Isreali forces" in an anti-Israeli micro-world, and takes the normal form "Withdrawal from some territories occupied by Isreali forces" in a pro-Israeli micro-world.

We claim that this sentence by itself is never ambiguous : one may have ambiguous positions relative to Israel and, therefore may have a varying opinion on the sense of this sentence, but we claim that **the problem does not reside in the sentence, but in its reader mind, who attempts to mix two different micro-worlds.**

This is our understanding of the reason why this sentence had little effect in practice. Since the two worlds are actually simultaneously present, the problem should rather be treated by IEMM than by a module that gives a meaning to sentences : the meanings are clear, their use is complicated. In the mouth of an historian, this sentence would have been really un-ambiguous.

3.3. Third subproblem

Choosing a micro-world will also mean that some specific inference rules will have to be used in the theorem proving module.

Let us suppose that in a micro-world of bankers, a lot of imagination implies "bad" or at best "need for forgiveness".

This knowledge will be represented by a clause like :

$$IF\ imaginative(x)\ \&\ banker(y)\ THEN\ despise(y,x).$$

Since, as we shall see, each character will have his (her) own personal theorem prover, one will simply add, if ,say, John is a banker and Mary has got lot of imagination, the fact : "despise(John, Mary)" into John's data when the above law is found.

3.4 Learning problems.

- building a good hierarchy (or rather, good concurrent hierarchies) of microworlds, i.e. such that a sub-micro-world is actually an instance of its father. This problem is linked to the one of the representation of knowledge relative to the whole micro-world we live in. The present approach is only one of the possible tools that may help in solving this problem.

- representing tangled hierarchies. We suggest use of parallel sub-hierarchies such as the following.

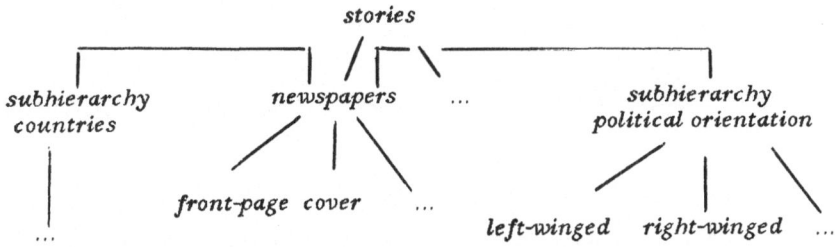

- learning of laws valid in a particular micro-world. Problem of the generalization of behaviours.

3.5. A complete example.

Let us now give an example that will illustrate how the debugger can help in finding the correct micro-world in which reasoning should take place.

Consider the story of a character called here "AI researcher" who attends a congress at a place where he must wear a tie and jacket at dinner, which is considered as quite formal by most "AI researchers".

Suppose that this character reads an advertisement on the congress place, insisting on how relaxed it is, and how informally people dress there.

In "AI researcher" micro-world, there are theorems that indicate that "relaxed area" implies "informal dressing" and "informal dressing implies no jacket & tie at dinner". This information will be given as theorems like

$$C_1 \text{ informal-dressing}(x,y) :- \text{relaxed-area}(y)$$
$$C_2 :- \text{informal-dressing}(x,y), \text{wears}(\text{tie\&jacket}, \text{dinner}, x, y)$$

where x is a character and y is the place where this charater is present.

Notations :

" A :- B, C " means " IF B & C THEN A "

" A " means "A is TRUE"

" :- A" means "A is FALSE"

The fact that he had to wear a tie and a jacket at dinner last night can be written as

$$C_3 \text{ wears}(\text{tie\&jacket}, \text{dinner}, \text{AI-researcher}, \text{Skytop-lodge})$$

On the other hand, while reading the above advertisement, "AI researcher" must add to his knowledge basis the fact that

$$C_4 \text{ relaxed-area}(\text{Skytop-lodge})$$

C_4 and C_1 resolve to give

$$C_5 \text{ informal-dressing}(x,\text{Skytop-lodge})$$

C_5 and C_2 now resolve to give

$$C_6 :-\text{wears}(\text{tie\&jacket}, \text{dinner}, x, \text{Skytop-lodge})$$

C_6 and C_3 resolve to give the empty clause with the substitution {x <-- AI-researcher}.

The contradiction therefore appears as the possibility of obtaining the empty clause from a given set of data and from knowledge deduced from a general data basis representing the micro-world in which text understanding takes place.

The resolution tree is as follows.

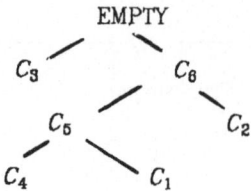

C_3 is part of "AI researcher's" personal experience and cannot be contradicted.
C_6 is a simple deduction from C_5 and C_2.
C_5 is a simple deduction from C_4 and C_1.
C_2 is part of "AI researcher's" knowledge. More information about C_2 should be looked for.
C_4 has been read in the text to be understood. A possible solution is "error in the text".
C_1 is also part of "AI researcher's" knowledge. More information about C_1 is needed : One could also find an explanation by finding reasons why C_1 can be wrong.
Let us consider the explanation linked to a discussion of C_2.
It appears that more information about informal dressing is required. Supposing the existence of a "dictionary" as described in [Kodratoff 1985], one can imagine that there is a mechanism, called here IEMM, that is able to retrieve information from this dictionary.
There should be somewhere a description of micro-worlds where C_1 is right but where C_2 is wrong. For instance, in these micro-worlds C_2 becomes
$$C_2' :\text{- informal-dressing}(x,y), \text{wears}(\text{evening-dress}, \text{dinner}, x, y)$$
that is, informal dressing implies that one does not wear an evening dress. Besides, in this micro-world, wearing a tie and jacket is considered as quite informal, that is
$$C_2'' \; \text{informal-dressing}(x,y) :\text{- wears}(\text{tie\&jacket}, u, x, y)$$
This new knowledge must not be considered at the same time as the first one. This why we use "knowledge boxes" that described in [Kodratoff 1985]. Let us simply say here that now, no contradiction is derived from
$$C_1 \; \text{informal-dressing}(x,y) :\text{- relaxed-area}(y)$$
$$C_2'' \; \text{informal-dressing}(x,y) :\text{- wears}(\text{tie\&jacket}, u, x, y)$$
$$C_3 \; \text{wears}(\text{tie\&jacket}, \text{dinner}, \text{AI-researcher}, \text{Skytop-lodge})$$
$$C_4 \; \text{relaxed-area}(\text{Skytop-lodge})$$
Our interpretation is that one possible reason for the "AI researcher's" contradiction was that he was not in the correct micro-world when reading the advertisement.
There might be other interpretations : that the text he is reading is nonsense, or that C_1 is wrong (i.e. that one can be quite relaxed while wearing a tie and a jacket at dinner). We skip here a more thorough study of the hypothesis that C_1 may be wrong, that advertisement is often intentionally deceptive, etc ... but one should be aware that equally correct explanations could come from these sources.
A last problem is the choice among possible explanations. We do not treat this problem here : we want to illustrate how debugging can bring explanations and comprehension, we do not want to present procedures that choose the best

explanation. Our personal feeling is that Humans have a strong tendency to stick to the first non stupid explanation, but this is completely outside the scope of this paper.

4 - THEOREM PROVER.

This essential module treats knowledge present in "boxes", each of which contains the knowledge of each character. Before explaining the way it works, let us say what is put in these boxes.

Definition : A "box" of knowledge is a set of clauses that describes the instantaneous knowledge of one character.

It will deal with the belief, the temporality and the global understanding problems.

Consider a story of two characters, John and Mary.

There will be at least a "Mary" box containing her knowledge, a "John" box containing his knowledge, and a "Master" box containing the knowledge one can draw from the combined one. If John has beliefs about Mary, they are simple knowledge and need no special treatment. We mean that the fictious "Mary" who lives in John's head is simply a set of clauses in John's box, and that these clauses describe Mary from John's point of view.

This trivialization of beliefs holds for one level of embedding only. As soon as several levels exist in a sentence, there is a need for creating a complicated net of fictious characters, "Mary as seen by John" and so on ...

The clauses describing the state of each knowledge box are put in the corresponding box. What is put in what is decided by IEMM.

The theorem prover treats all these clauses in the same way as a classical theorem prover and "restlessly" tries to deduce the empty clause from them.

As long as it fails, nothing happens.

When it succeeds in deriving the empty clause, the contradictory clauses are brought before a "judge" (this function is done by IEMM), that uses its own rules to solve the contradiction. Some clauses are deleted, some others are starred as explained below. Finally, no contradiction must be left in a box.

Since this process is restlessly taking place, each new clause is instanteanously checked against all the old ones. This avoids a complicated debugging treatment of a whole set of clauses.

In other words, the consistency of each new clause with the information present is restlessly checked.

4. CONCLUSION

Most researchers in Natural Language Understanding have concentrated on syntaxico-semantical analysis, or on problems here attributed to IEMM.

Our approach does not follow this path. It rather aims at

1 - pointing to a new, efficient and simple operational model, called here **Restless Debugging**,

2 - showing some of the implications this model in Knowledge Representation. Specifically, we specify several requirements

   2.1 - taxonomies of generality should be given, together with several semantical indications (see sections 2. and 4.), particularly

      2.1.1 - detection of mutually exclusive actions,

      2.1.2 - range of information transmission among characters

2.2 - micro-worlds of meaning validity should be explicitly given

2.3 - theorems describing the semantics of the words in each micro-world should either be given or easily retrievable.

Our operational model is certainly not the only one possible. But we have taken extreme care in giving its links with its associated Knowledge Representation model.

An implementation is not an easy task since it requires, as a preliminary step, an implementation of knowledge that is both lengthy and disputable (implementation tricks can hide fundamental mistakes in the model). This is why this paper is only an "idea" paper. It is a first step to be followed by a triple effort, refining the model, refining its implications on Knowledge Representation, and implementation that will be done concurrently.

The primary aim of this paper is the illustration of some consequences drawn from our hypothesis that logical debugging is both an elementary building block and a corner stone of Natural Language Understanding.

ACKNOWLEDGEMENTS.

Remarks from a referee have been of much help.

This research has been partially sponsored by GRECO and PRC "Intelligence Artificielle", by ESPRIT AIP contract INSTIL 1063 and by the European Research Office of US Army contract 'Tools for Learning'.

REFERENCES

[AAAI Workshop 1984] *Non-Monotonic Reasoning Workshop*, New Paltz 1984.

[Allen & Hayes 1985] Allen J. F., Hayes P. J., "A Common Sense Theory of Time", Proc. IJCAI-85, pp. 528-531.

[Colmerauer 1979] Colmerauer A., "An Interesting Subset of Natural Language", *Logic Programming*, Clark and Tarnlund eds, Academic Press 1979.

[Dahl & Saint-Dizier 1985] *Natural language understanding and Logic Programming*, Dahl V., Saint-Dizier P. eds., North Holland 1985.

[Fahlman 1979] Fahlman S. E., *NETL : A System for Representing and Using Real-World Knowledge*, The MIT Press 1979.

[Hayes 1979] Hayes P., "The Logic of Frames", reproduced in *Readings in Artificial Intelligence*, B. L. Webber, N. J. Nilsson eds., Tioga 1981

[Karoubi & Nicaud 85] Karoubi M., Nicaud L., "Modéliser le raisonnement sans le figer" ("A Non-clotting reasoning model") Actes congrès *COGNITIVA 85*, Paris 1985, pp. 617-623.

[Kodratoff 1985] Kodratoff Y., "Restless Debugging" = the Key to Understanding & Learning from Texts. A Description of the Necessary Environment", Internal Paper, LRI 1985.

[Kowalski 1979] *Logic for Problem Solving*, North Holland 1979.

[McCarthy 1980] McCarthy J., "Circumscription - A Form of Non-Monotonic Reasoning", Artificial Intelligence 1980, 13, 27-39.

[Pereira 1985] Pereira L. M., "Rational Degugging of Logic Programs", Draft, Lisbon University, July 1985.

[Saint-Dizier 1985] Saint-Dizier P., "An approach to Natural Language Semantics in Logic Programming", Rapport de Recherche INRIA no 389, 1985.

[Shank 1982] Shank R. C., *Dynamic memory*, Cambridge University Press 1982

[Shapiro 1982] Shapiro E. Y., *Algorithmic Program Debugging*, MIT Press, Cambridge MA 1982.

SEMANTIC INTERPRETATION IN
NATURAL LANGUAGE INTERFACE APPLICATIONS

Helmut Horacek
Research Unit for
Information Science and
Artificial Intelligence
University of Hamburg

Abstract
In this paper we will present how the practical relevance of
the semantics in Natural Language utterances can be made
available for database interaction without a complete understanding of the general meaning of such utterances. We will
demonstrate our ideas on the treatment of adjuncts, especially of time adjuncts, on the treatment of the verbal complex and of words representing compound actions like "verify" and "complete". Representation techniques and interpretation heuristics are sketched out that take advantage of
the restricted domain and produce useful relations between
critical parts of an utterance and entities of a database.
This work has been done within the frame of the Hamburg subpart of the ESPRIT project LOKI whose aim is the production
of a Natural Language Interface (German and English) to a
database, concentrating on pragmatics and performance.

Introduction
Research in Natural Language Understanding is confronted
with fairly complex devices of a semantic nature. A lot of
sophisticated approaches have been made in various sub-
fields, from which the consideration of tense, interpretation of quantifier scope and semantic representation on its
own are of relevance for our approach. Unfortunately, most
of the proposed theories and methods are currently of limited relevance for the field of database interaction and are
therefore poorly applied in implemented systems (not to mention incomplete themselves). When a NLU-system is intended
to be used as an interface to a database, the restricted
domain and the reduced model of reality adopted by a database do not require a full understanding of all semantic
phenomena, especially not of the complicated ones. The
effort is concentrated more on efficiency and robustness.
However, the task is to extract just that information from
an utterance that can be used for the database interaction.

815

R. Trappl (ed.), Cybernetics and Systems '86, 815–822.

It is our belief that, even when meta-knowledge about the database, devices like user guidance and external operations with data are provided, only simple approaches seem to be manageable and sufficient to a reasonable degree. We will confirm this assumption by an examination of adjuncts, of the verbal complex and of compound actions like "verify" and "complete". These considerations were made within the frame of the Hamburg subpart of the ESPRIT project LOKI, whose aim is the production of a Natural Language interface (German and English) to a database, mainly concentrating on pragmatics and performance. The area of the pilot application is project management, the task is strongly oriented on the features of the PRADOS system. This is a project management system applying a standard menu technique to deal with the relational database UNIFY and some external calculations, especially arithmetic operations.

Treatment of adjuncts
Finding links for adjuncts is a hard problem and ambiguous solutions and alternative representations occur frequently. This problem is somewhat reduced in database applications because of its restricted capabilities and its fixed model. Actually, this means that in many cases a correct meaning and an appropriate representation can be assigned to some kind of ambiguous utterance within the context of a certain database. To illustrate these conjectures let us look at the sentences

    1.a)   Who wrote the minutes on April the 5th ?
      b)   What is on the agenda from April the 5th ?

where the link to the temporal reference in a knowledge representation formalism heavily depends on the representation chosen for the writing process, the minutes and the agenda. It is far from clear if the time reference actually should be linked to the writing process or some kind of meeting when the minutes were written. The same considerations apply to the second sentence. In a database we are confronted with representations in form of relations like those in Figure 1.

Meeting			
key	date	agenda#	min. writer
...	....	....	....
m#1	0405	a#1	miller john
m#2	0412	a#2	smith jack
...	....	....	....

Agenda	
key	line of text
...	....
a#1	plan of ....
a#1	costs for ..
...	....

Figure 1

816

In both cases the determination of the "meeting"-relation is the relevant source and the indications are high that the time entity there is the appropriate referent for the time adjuncts in the above sentences. If we assume that the entities "min. writer" and "agenda" occur in the "meeting"-relation only (except for the "agenda"-relation itself, which just contains text) the appropriate resolution of the time reference is clearly induced. We will state a general rule for the finding of links based on that line:

If
    an adjunct of some specific type (time in the above case) is syntactically linked to a constituent corresponding to an entity that does not have such a link in the database (it is either not a key in a relation or there is no entity of the specific type in the relation from which it is the key)

then
    look for a component of the same type in the relation(s) where the constituent the adjunct is linked to is such an entity.

It should be noted that this rule is a help only when it leads to a single solution, which can be trusted to be rather plausible. When several entities satisfy this condition, again a disambiguation has to be made according to the context or a clarification dialogue has to be started. Either way, one is no better off then, but all options are still present. On the other hand, if no possible referent entity has been found, it is inconceivable that the above rule is applied recursively. It should be clear that this could lead to rather obscure interpretations. Again, the rule did not help, but it also did no harm. Nevertheless, one has the intuitive feeling that its merits are of no relevance in very many occurrences. In our approach we disregard the problem of interpolation which is urgent when dealing with motion processes, but is also not relevant for our domain. This problem setting has been discussed exhaustively in the panel on Natural Language access to databases /2/.

Country		
name	number of inhabitants	gross national product
. . . .	. . . .	. . . .
Austria	7.000.000	?
Germany	60.000.000	?
. . . .	. . . .	. . . .

Figure 2

We will show how the above rules can be applied to other kinds of adjuncts or to genitive objects. When confronted with a relation containing information about countries like in Figure 2, the expression "the gross national product of the Austrians" can be treated on the same lines. Austrians are supposed to be defined by the lexicon as the inhabitants of Austria (which is the key). Applying the above rule their gross national product can be caught conveniently as an entity in the "country"-relation although it is linked to the inhabitants and not to the country itself in the above noun phrase. It is our belief that this heuristic rule can be applied successfully to many data base requests, but there is a strict limit of complexity. For instance, in the sentence "From whom will we get computing time ?" it is even hard for a human to find out explicitly what inferences are to be drawn by a computer system in order to enable a representation well-suited for the database.

When we refer back to the expression "the gross national product of the Austrians" we are additionally facing the re-ference problem of plural forms. This issue has been treated already by Warren /4/ with respect to the question-answering system Chat and by Saint-Dizier /3/, among others. Chat treats these plural forms as introducing sets and applies a few heuristics enabling the correct interpretation of expressions like "the children of the employees", "the average of the salaries of the part-time employees" and "Do the European countries border the Atlantic ?". This view is commonly accepted to be valid which we agree in general. Nevertheless, in our example, we have to adopt another kind of interpretation for the noun phrase "the Austrians". It has to be treated as a unit in this instance. When we assume that the database does not contain any information about specific Austrians it is a pragmatic approach to specify Austrian(s) as an aggregate. Therefore only the interpreta-tion as a unit makes sense. Similarly, notions like "The United States of America" are usually treated as idioms. As a consequence, this leads to an other interpretation of the question "Do The United States of America border the Atlan-tic" than the same question with the European countries. We are fully aware that this kind of treatment is not a solu-tion for aggregates which have also been considered in /2/. But, if aggregates occur in the database only in this form, the approach should be sufficient.

The verbal complex
Within the verbal complex we will examine time and modality. In the area of databases the representational possibilities of time are admittedly poor. The usual occurrence of time in a database is a concrete timepoint or a concrete duration represented as an entity. As for the verbal complex, tense

can hardly be considered at all, while considerations of
modality bear some more interesting consequences. The common
distinction between point of speech, point of reference and
point of event treated by Kamp /1/ and many others is beyond
the scope of the representation facilities of most of the
databases. Usually, the only reasonable usage of the tense
feature can be made via the relation to the current
timepoint "now". A fundamental distinction has to be made
there between most of the verbs that can express tense and
somehow "timeless" verbs. Consider the following examples:

    2.a)   Who is the manager of project A ?
      b)   Who was the manager of project A ?
    3.a)   What does A stand for ?
      b)   What did A stand for ?

While the relation to the current timepoint is crucial to
find an appropriate answer in example 2, time is not considered at all in example 3. As a consequence, in case project A ended a year ago, 2.a) suggests a presupposition
failure to be recovered by the cooperative answer: "Project
A ended last year, the manager was B.". Moreover, 2.b) suggests over-answering by: "B, and he still is", in case the
project is going on and B. is still the manager. 3.b) is a
rather unusual question either suggesting that A ended a
long time ago or that its meaning has been changed earlier.
3.a), however, does not ensure that A is still going on and
the question has to be answered by the long name for A
regardless of its actual time of existence. These considerations point to a lot of complexity. However, we restrict our
task to the exploitation of the tense feature for the formulation of an appropriate database query.

The consideration of tense in the parsing process can be
enabled by providing a condition "compare-op(timepoint,now)"
that will augment the lexicon entry of a verb and has to be
transferred to the query after the instantiations have taken
place. "Now" will be instantiated to the current date.
"Timepoint" must be inferred as an entity in the database
later on and "compare-op" will be instantiated to "before"
or "after" by the parsing process according to the tense.
The most difficult task is the inference process for finding
an appropriate timepoint. This problem is actually the same
as that one of finding the correct link for an adjunct,
which has been treated in the previous section. Additionally, when facing the appearance of time as points or intervals we are confronted with the problem of multiple word
entities, in a somewhat special form. We have chosen a
method that is relevant for such multiple word entities for
which one word bears most of the meaning and any others
introduce some variations. Typically plan and real data and

from- and to- timepoints belong to these types of entities. We introduce an expression "transf(meta_entity,variant)" for the lexicon entry of the word bearing most of the meaning. "Meta-entity" corresponds to that word and "variant" is a variable for feasible variations. This variable is instantiated by other parts of the sentence and then the functor "transf" which is supposed to be defined for all feasible combinations of meta-entities and variants can be applied to them yielding a unique solution, the required entity name. This task is so complicated because of the necessity of introducing the compare operation by the verb. This cannot be done by any other constituent as none of them is a safe anchor (see also the process of finding a correct link for an adjunct). This way, a feature on sentence level has been made available in the right place. For reasons of efficiency it is better to trigger a general rule for the consideration of the compare expression which has to be blocked for certain exceptions only like for the verb "to stand for".

The usage of modality has even more consequences on the database interaction than the tense aspect. For our purposes we disregard the appearance of modality in speech acts like utterances containing "Can you do ...", "Can I see ..." where the subject is either the user or the system. We just restrict our considerations to the significance for the database access. Especially management databases contain data about the planned and the real state of activities. The request for the plan data can be inferred frequently from the appearance of "must" or "should" in the uttered query. Moreover, the (domain-dependent) model of the database certainly supports the process to select correct referents for the "plan"-feature strongly, as this can hardly be done on the basis of syntax. The usage of the indicative, however, does not exclude a query about planned data. In this case the use of tense will give the right clue, as no information about real things is possible after the current timepoint.

If the database is an advanced one, it often has consistency rules, external operations ranging from a simple average computation to the application of complex algorithms. Additionally, the interface itself may provide some kind of meta-knowledge. These external devices can be triggered by a request containing "can" or "could" other than in the "Can I" or "Can you" utterances mentioned above. To illustrate these considerations compare the examples:

4.a) Did activity A end before April 5th ?
  b) Will activity A end before April 5th ?
  c) Must (should) activity A end before April 5th ?
  d) Can activity A end before April 5th ?
  e) Could avtivity A end before April 5th ?

4.a) is a simple request about real data (assuming April 5th
is in the past), while 4.b) states the possibilities to ask
for plan data (assuming April 5th in the future, otherwise a
different tense would have been selected). Moreover, this
gives a clue for the determination of the correct year in
the above utterances (past, current or next). The further
assumption is made that a reference to another year would
have been expressed explicitly, unless there is a clear
established context. The same is valid for 4.c). 4.d) tends
more to be a request to start a verification process about
the project plan that includes activity A rather than a simple request for plan data. The interpretation of the last
utterance differs from 4.a) insofar that it suggests an
additional explanation for the fact that has been asked. A
summary of the effects of interaction between tense and
modality can be seen in the table of Figure 3. The necessity
can be expressed by "must" and "should", the possibility by
"can", "could" and "may", according to the relation to the
current time point.

modality	past	future
indicative	real data	plan data
necessity	plan data	plan data
possibility	real data, requests additional explanation	plan data, triggers additional verification

Figure 3

The principal method for the consideration of modality in
the technical sense is similar to the choice between a from-
and a to- timepoint (also by "transf"). We did not yet consider explanation and verification processes appropriate for
the utterances containing "can" or "could", we have restricted our task to the determination of appropriate entities.

Semantically complex notions
There are a lot of words (particularly actions) that would
require a fairly complex subgraph as a representation in a
semantic network if they have to be represented there with
sufficient generality and accuracy. In a database application this complexity will be greatly reduced by the restricted domain and the specific context. There are two principal
ways of approaching the goal of simplification: A complex
notion can be distinguished according to the circumstances
(for instance an action according to the feasible classes of
the objects it can be applied to) or its meaning can be reduced to the features relevant for the database interaction.
A very general process like "verification" can be realized
as a few distinct actions according to the facilities the
database or some of its external enhancements provide for.

821

The distinction can be made according to the class of objects and a closer specification of these objects can be used as context setting. In the PRADOS system the request "Verify the expenditures" triggers a fairly complex calculation procedure that checks the equality of the expenditure of a project and the sum :of the expenditures of all its subprojects for all projects that have any subprojects. A specific set of projects can be selected by "Verify the expenditures of the projects from 1984". Apart from this kind of verification , PRADOS provides for checking of consistency of the personnel hierarchy, of the hierarchy of the activities and some more. It can be seen easily that the appropriate kind of process can be selected according to the type of unit to be checked. This approach is mainly apt for the classes of actions the system provides for, like update, query, check and the manner of output. The reduction of a complex notion to the database relevant features seems useful for some kind of words which occur in indirect requests:

5.a)   We are waiting for report A.
       (How long do we have to wait for report A ?)
  b)   When will activity B. be completed ?

In 5.a) the proper meaning of the wait process is not relevant for the database interaction. Strictly speaking, it indicates an indirect request, which is very hard to solve in a sufficiently general way. We treat this speech act by providing a lexicon entry that only represents the endpoint of a process. This is the only aspect of the wait process the database can deal with, which somehow justifies this brute approach for the application. In 5.b) the process of completion itself will be ignored for the same reason, and the interpretation is reduced to a reference of its enddate.

References
/1/ Kamp H., A Theory of Truth and Semantic Representation. In: J.A.G. Groenendijk, T.M.V. Janssen, M.B.J. Stokhof (eds.), Formal Methods in Study of Language – Part 1, Amsterdam, 1981, pp.277-321.
/2/ Moore R.C. (1982), Natural-Language Access to Databases-Theoretical/ Technical Issues, panel on the same topic, Moore (chairm.) et alii, in 20th Annual Meeting of the ACL, University of Toronto, June 1982.
/3/ Saint-Dizier P. (1985), Handling Quantifier scoping ambiguities in a Semantic representation of Natural Language Sentences, in Dahl V., Saint-Dizier P. (eds.), Natural Language Understanding and Logic Programming, North-Holland.
/4/ Warren D. (1982), Issues in Natural Language Access to Databases from a Logic Programming Perspective, in 20th Annual Meeting of the ACL, Univ. of Toronto, June 1982.

THE OVERANSWERING MECHANISM IN THE FIDO SYSTEM

Nicoletta Bersia, Barbara Di Eugenio,
Leonardo Lesmo, Pietro Torasso
Dipartimento di Informatica - Universita' di Torino
Via Valperga Caluso 37 - 10125 Torino - Italy

ABSTRACT. The present paper describes the approach to the problem of overanswering in the FIDO (a Flexible Interface for Database Operations) system. The overanswering process makes use of the various representations of the input query that are generated during the whole process, from parsing to data retrieval, to take into account everything that can be useful to produce a meaningful answer, from the NL structure of the input query to its logical representation.(*)

1. INTRODUCTION

The need of extending direct responses to NL questions, whatever kind of system they are addressed to, has been largely acknowledged (see [1], [2], [3], [4], [5], [6], [7], [8]): it is one of the many consequences of the fact that man - machine interaction should follow the conventions of cooperative conversation, stated in Grice's Cooperative Principle, and in the various reformulations of his Maxims of Quality and Quantity ([9], [4], [5]).

The process of extending direct responses, which can be called overanswering (this definition is for example contained in [5]), has many purposes, among the others:
- correction of user misconceptions, which are often the source of negative answers to question (Consider for example Q1: "How many students took the exam of CS122?": if CS122 does not exist, an answer such as "Zero" can be misleading, as it does not point out the actual reason why there are "Zero" students which took this exam);
- suggestions ("Are there any seats in the stalls?" "No, but there are some left in the balcony");
- formulation of the answer in such a way that it corresponds to the point of view the user expressed in his/her question.
There are many approaches to this problem : some people devised particular formalisms to represent the input query (this is especially true

---

(*) Questions about this paper should be addressed to Pietro Torasso, Dipartimento di Informatica, Via V. Caluso 37, 10125 Torino, Italy.
This work has been partly supported by the Italian Ministero della Pubblica Istruzione.

R. Trappl (ed.), Cybernetics and Systems '86, 823–830.

when the purpose is correction of misconceptions [6], [7]), others claim
that this is not sufficient and that "language-driven inference" systems
(that is, systems where the inference process takes advantage of
language related knowledge) are better (for example, Kaplan's system,
COOP, represents the query in the so-called Meta Query Language, that
is, a graph structure whose nodes and edges are derived from the lexical
and syntactic structure of the input query [1],[2]). It is of course
very useful to take into account NL expressions used in the input query,
as they convey much information on the user's attitude; on the other
hand, it is not possible to rely just on them; for example, in an interface towards a DB system, real data are found by evaluating a query
expressed in some QL, and it is likely that there is no exact match
between what the system looked for and what the user asked for.

In order to produce sound answers, it seems necessary to take into
account various levels of description of the input query, its form, its
meaning and the way it is translated . However, this does not mean that
you need to use all levels each time an extended answer is produced: for
example, we found that syntactic clues were less important in producing
corrective answers than in other kinds of overanswering, as it will be
described in the following paragraphs.

The overanswering module has been inserted in the FIDO system,
which is rapidly reviewed before describing the process of answer extension.

2. THE FIDO SYSTEM

FIDO is a Natural Language prototype system (developed at the Dipartimento di Informatica, Universita' di Torino) which allows the user to
address a relational DB in Italian. The input question is parsed (a
kind of syntactic tree is produced), translated into a conceptual query
and then into a logical one, which will be executed. The conceptual
level concerns the abstract DB objects; it represents the domain as it
is viewed by the user, taking into account its characteristics and the
NL terms by means of which the user can describe it. However, the
higher degree of abstraction should not affect the process of query
evaluation: therefore, the translation from the conceptual to the logical level is not a mere redenomination, but a complex process of optimization.

The translation at the conceptual level makes use of a two-level
semantic net: the external level concerns the surface semantic constraints imposed on the input sentence (selectional restrictions); the
internal level specifies the connections between "content_words" and the
conceptual objects defined in the DB schema. Without giving further
details, it can just be noted that both the semantic checks and the
translation are done while the syntactic analysis is still in process
(see [10] [11], [12], [13]).

The conceptual query is then translated into a logical one, that
is, a final query that makes use only of the stored relations and their
attributes. Conceptual relations are defined by means of relational
operations on the DB relations; as an example we include @lives, which

refers to the addresses of the various people and includes the conceptual attributes $person (the person's name) and $city (his/her address). At the logical level it is defined as the union of the names and addresses of professors (whose data are stored in the relation "faculty"), secretaries (in "secretary"), male and female students (in "studentmale" and "studentfemale", respectively):

```
@lives
    ($person $city)
        (union (personname city)
            ((project faculty (name address))
             (project secretary (name address))
             (project studentmale (name address))
             (project studentfemale (name address)))))
```

This kind of definition is then used in a preprocessing phase, whose results are the conceptual relations' definitions (called Visible Pragmatics, VP) which will be actually used by the translator. The Visible Pragmatic is generated by taking into account empty relations, constant attributes etc, and by trying to foresee possible joins; instead of giving further details, as an example we can consider @lives and the following hypotheses:

- all professors live in Turin: the evaluation process does not need to retrieve their addresses every time, since we can modify the definition of @lives in the following way

```
        @lives
        ($person $city)
        (union (personname city)
            ((cartes (name address)
                     (project faculty (name))
                     (Turin))
             (project secretary (name address))
             (project studentmale (name address))
             (project studentfemale (name address)))))
```

(NB: cartes is short for cartesian product)

- @lives, which stores all people's addresses, is joined with another relation whose logical equivalent concerns a subset of the entity 'person', such as professors, students etc.: in this case it is useless to retrieve all the data concerning all people, as they will be thrown away by the subsequent join: in this case, we can use a simplified definition for @lives; for example, if @lives were joined with a relation concerning professors (such as @teach), its definition would be:

```
    @lives
    ($person $city)
        ((cartes (name address)
                 (project faculty (name))
                 (Turin)))
```

By using the Visible Pragmatics, conceptual operations are substituted by their logical equivalents; other simplification rules allow to

further simplify the query : some conceptual operations are removed (that is, they are not included in the logical query); others are moved (for example, select operations are often moved to deeper levels, in order to reduce the cardinality of the considered relations). (For further details see [12]). This kind of optimization can lead to logical queries completely different from the conceptual ones, as we can see in the following example.
Q2:"Which are the wifes of the male professors who teach CS122?"

Conceptual query:
```
(project
    (join
        (join
            (select @teach
                    (($course eq CS122)))
            (select @sex (($sex eq m)))
          ($professor eq $person))
        @married
        ($professor eq $person))
    ($spouse))
```

Logical query :
```
(project
    (select faculty
            ((spouse ne $)
            (sex eq m)
            (course eq CS122)))
    (spouse))
```

As data about sex, spouse and course taught are all stored in the logical relation faculty, the logical query is a simple selection on it. In the end, we can state that a query has three different representations at three different levels: the parsing tree (which, for our purposes, we can consider equivalent to the NL formulation), the conceptual query and the logical one.

3. OVERANSWERING IN FIDO

FIDO is able to process WH-questions and, in this context, to:
- correct user's misconceptions regarding the data actually stored (that is, not on semantic grounds): it explains the reason why certain data have not been found (for example, in a case like that of Q1, it would answer something like "There is no CS122 course among the courses that are taken by students");
- give summary responses (for the moment only quantifiers, like "All", "Most of them" etc.);
- answer in a sensible way to questions concerning properties, like sex, age etc. (of course a list of ages is useless without the identification of the person each age refers to);
- structure the answer in a way it corresponds to the user's

expectations on the cardinality of the result.

It is useful to define a question towards a DB as the selection of a subset from a particular set of objects ([1][2]): if the question concerns a property, this notion of sets can be applied to the elements it refers, as in Q3 "Which is the age of the male students who live in Turin?" Here we have the first set (students), the second (male students), the third (male students who live in Turin): however it must be noticed that it depends on the translation whether the second set to be actually evaluated is "male students" or "students who live in Turin": we will see that it is important to take this order into account. Correcting misconceptions is equivalent to finding the smallest set which is empty for each independent failure: we define 'independent' those failures that concern data sets which are empty before the relations among them are considered (for example in a case like Q4:"Which old students attend the courses taught by professors who live in Paris?", in the hypothesis that there are nor old students neither professors living in Paris, FIDO points out these two facts separately). On the other hand, giving a quantitative information corresponds to reckoning the ratio of the cardinality of the final subset to the cardinality of the subset from which it has immediately been obtained (immediately refers to the subset whose evaluation is immediately precedent to that of the final subset).

In both cases, the evaluation process (at the logical level) knows nothing about all this, and only finds an empty relation or a final ratio. This information must be taken back to higher levels of query description to be given a meaning.

3.1. Corrective overanswering

As regards correcting misconceptions, it is not possible to only use the logical level to produce the answer, as the logical query is completely unbound from the way the user views the DB domain: it is only a way, presumably the most efficient, to retrieve data, but it knows neither their meaning nor the relationships existing among them. On the other hand, it would be perhaps useless to go back to the NL question: the surface expressions are too many and not formalized enough to convey this notion of sets and subsets; moreover, our purpose is not to use the NL expressions to give an answer but to understand the meaning of the failure detected at the logical level. We found what we needed to give corrective answers at the conceptual level: the conceptual query mirrors that part of the domain semantics contained in the input question and it is the result of the interpretation and translation of the superficial NL expressions by means of the semantic net. The problem is how to go back from the logical level to the conceptual one, that is, to the conceptual context of each failure. This was achieved by observing that in relational algebra those operations which can fail while their operands are not void are join, select, intersection, subtraction; the first two impose conditions on their operands, and if these conditions are not satisfied the operation's result is void. If we simplify strongly our strategy, we can say that the correspondence between the two levels is mainly maintained by these conditions, as they are very little affected by the optimization process which translates a conceptual query into the logical one: if the operation they are linked to is not removed, they are simply redenominated; on the other hand, if they were not present at the conceptual level, they came up in the substitution of a relation with its VP (for example @chair is translated with

```
(project
        (select faculty ((chairflag eq yes))
    (name))
```

In the translation from conceptual to logical query, the conditions are linked in a kind of graph which mirrors their nesting in the logical query. At the same time, this structure provides backward links to the portion of the conceptual query each condition comes from. During the evaluation, this graph will be traversed together with the logical query, so the correspondence between the two levels is maintained. Whenever a failure is found, its conceptual context, that is, the portion of conceptual query it corresponds to is used to generate an answer (it is 'translated' in NL by a particular module). As an example, we can refer to Q2: if there were no CS122 course, we could go back from the logical condition "course eq CS122" to the conceptual one "$course eq CS122" and therefore to the conceptual operation it is linked to, to produce the answer: "There is no CS122 course among courses that are taught by professors".

3.1. Non-corrective overanswering

Its purpose is to structure the answer in a way that corresponds to the user's point of view, as he/she expressed it in the input question. In this case, it is not sufficient to maintain a correspondence between the logical and conceptual levels: the NL formulation of the question must be taken into account as well, as it conveys the user's real intentions. The problem is to find those features of the input question that make an answer more or less suitable, and to combine this information with the way the system interpreted the question and found the result. Before going into further details, it should be pointed out that a NL interface allows to give descriptive or quantitative answers to questions: not always is the user really interested in a list where every element that satisfies his/her restrictions is identified, sometimes a description of this set is sufficient (for example "Which students attend the Greek course?" -> "Those coming from classical studies" or "All"). In a real dialogue, choosing the best answer can make use of the context, the cardinality of the result, perhaps a direct question to the user about his/her intentions; in FIDO we examined isolated questions, so we relied on the way the question was phrased.

The lexical and syntactic level have remarkable impact on the structure of the answer: in the superficial form of the input question there are a lot of clues to understand what the user really wanted, clues that are lost at deeper levels. Some of them can concern the user's expectations on the cardinality of the result: if he asks Q5: "Which professor teaches NL Processing?" it is clear that he thinks one professor teaches that course; if this is not true, expressions such as

828

"There are more than one ..." can be used in the answer to draw the user's attention to this fact. This kind of structuring of the answer would be more useful for more complex questions, like Q6: "Which students attend the course taught by Professor Smith?". If prof. Smith teaches more than one course, an answer that lists the students' names does not show this fact, while it would be more cooperative to point it out. For the meantime, FIDO is able to answer in the way described to Q5.

As far as quantifiers are concerned, syntactic clues are very useful too: not all superficial forms allow a particular answer. For example, we can consider the two questions: "Which professors are male?" and "Who are the male professors?". They have identical translations at the conceptual and logical levels, and therefore identical results: however, in the first case an answer such as "Most of them" is correct too, while in the second it is meaningless.

Our approach was to try to classify the possible input questions according to their interrogative term, the syntactic form it has, the principal verb: roughly speaking, it seems that, at least in Italian, quantifiers are less suitable for questions introduced by an interrogative pronoun and with the verb to be, such as "Who are ...", "Which are ..." etc.

A few words now on the importance of the conceptual and logical levels: it seems strange to take them into account, as a purpose of a (NL or not) interface to a DB system should be to hide the technical details from the user; however, the real way data are retrieved must be taken into account by the overanswering module, otherwise its answers might mislead the user. Using a quantifier X means that there are X elements, chosen imposing some restrictions on them, which satisfy the user's question. As said before, if we regard the question as the selection of a particular subset, this X is the ratio of the cardinality of the final subset to that of the subset from which the previous one has been immediately drawn. For example, Q7: "Which male sex students who live in Milan attend CS122?". An answer like "most of them" is interpreted by the user as the ratio of the male sex students who live in Milan and attend CS122 to the male sex students who live in Milan.

Unfortunately, not always do the conceptual and logical queries reflect the set structuring of the input: what we do in this circumstances is to disregard the quantifier found by the evaluation and to reckon the ratio of the result cardinality to the cardinality of the principal entity (that is, the class of objects the question asks for) and, if it is 100%, to answer "all" (of course if the class of the question allows this answer): this means that the constraints imposed by the user did not actually restrict that set; other quantifiers are not allowed, as they would be misinterpreted.

To maintain the evaluation module independent from all these considerations, this heuristic knowledge is expressed by means of condition-action rules; the condition part concerns lexical and syntactic features of the input sentence, while the action part contains several functions: one of them checks if the conceptual and logical queries are such that a quantifier will be correctly interpreted by the user, another if the user expects a single or multiple result: the last of them, on the basis of all information retrieved, generates the real

NL answer.

4. CONCLUSIONS

In this paper, we have described the way overanswering has been introduced in FIDO: this has been achieved by taking into account the various
levels of description the input query goes into in this system. Future
work should concern the use of semantic constraints in extending
responses (both in correction and in giving quantifiers) and the restructuring of the answer in more complex cases (for example Q6 above).

5. REFERENCES

[1] S.J. Kaplan 'Appropriate responses to inappropriate questions' In
Elements of discourse understanding , Josh, Webber, Sags (eds) 127
- 143, 1982.
[2] S.J. Kaplan 'On the difference between natural language and high
level query language' Proc. ACM National Conference 1978, 27 - 38,
1979.
[3] B.L. Webber, E. Mays 'Varieties of User Misconceptions : Detection
and Correction' Proc. IJCAI 1983, 650 - 652, 1983.
[4] A. Joshi, B.L. Webber, R.M. Weischedel 'Preventing false inferences' Proc. Coling 1984, 134 - 138, 1984.
[5] W. Wahlster, H. Marburger, A. Jameson, S. Busemann 'Over-answering
Yes-No questions: Extended responses in a natural language interface to a vision system' Proc. IJCAI 1983, 643 - 646, 1983.
[6] J.M. Janas 'How not to say 'nil': Improving answers to failing
questions in data base systems' Proc. IJCAI 1979, 429 - 434, 1979.
[7] J. Hirschberg 'Toward a redefinition of Yes-No Questions' Proc.
Coling 1984, 48 - 51, 1984.
[8] J.K. Kalita, M.J. Colbourn, G.I. McCalla 'A response to the Need
for Summary Responses' Proc. Coling 1984, 432 - 436, 1984.
[9] H.P. Grice 'Logic and Information' In Syntax and Semantics , Cole,
Morgan (eds), 1975.
[10] L.Lesmo, P. Torasso 'A flexible natural language parser based on a
two level representation of syntax' Proc. of the First and Inau-
gural Meeting of the Association for Computational Linguistics,
Pisa, 1-2/9/1983, 114 - 121, 1983.
[11] L.Lesmo, P.Torasso 'Interpreting syntactically ill-formed sentences' Proc. Coling 1984, 534 - 539, 1984.
[12] L.Lesmo, L.Siklossy, P. Torasso 'Semantic and Pragmatic Processing
in FIDO: a Flexible Interface for Database Operations' Information
Systems , Vol. 10, no. 2, 219 - 238, 1985.
[13] L.Lesmo, P. Torasso 'Weighted interaction of syntax and semantics
in natural language analysis' Proc. IJCAI 1985, vol. 2, 772 - 778,
1985.

ACHIEVING TEXT COHERENCE IN A GENERATOR FOR GERMAN TEXTS

H. Horacek
Research Unit for
Information Science and
Artificial Intelligence
Univ. Hamburg, FRG

E. Buchberger
Department of
Medical Cybernetics and
Artificial Intelligence
Univ. Vienna, Austria

ABSTRACT. In this paper we present methods for dealing with some classes of text coherence, especially the use of paraphrases and the treatment of contextual links between complex structures in order to produce cohesive text in a natural way. We show how the presented methods fit nicely into the overall construction of our generator that transforms semantic network structures into German sentences. Creation of short verbalizations for a medium-complex semantic network portion (intended for paraphrasing) is described with respect to the problem of avoiding ambiguity. The roles of time and reason in the semantic network are examined for appropriate verbalizations. Finally, organization and selection of paraphrases and global links are discussed in relation to pronominalization.

1. INTRODUCTION

Unsatisfactory treatment of textual coherence is one of the most significant weaknesses of today's NLU-systems. One method to realize coherent text is the use of cohesion /5/. In this paper we present how VIE-GEN, the generator of the system VIE-LANG /2/, is able to deal with some aspects of this linguistic phenomenon /6/. VIE-GEN produces German text out of a semantic network representation. Details on the construction of the generator are to be found in /3/. One of the aspects treated in this paper is paraphrasing, regarded as a summary of a whole paragraph or sentence already uttered by just one word or by a group of words, when referred to later on. Furthermore, treatment of links among semantic network portions is presented with special regard to the links expressing reason and time, as these are most often of importance for the coherence of a text /1/. Other aspects of creating coherent text by VIE-GEN like anaphora, gapping and portioning of text have been treated elsewhere /7, 8/.

831

R. Trappl (ed.), Cybernetics and Systems '86, 831–836.

2. THE PROBLEM

The net portion in Figure 1 expresses Frank's astonishment about the message by John that Peter gave a book to Mary. A straightforward approach leads to:

(1) Weil Hans Franz sagt, daß Peter Maria ein Buch gibt,
    ist Franz erstaunt, daß Peter Maria ein Buch gibt.

The first step towards facilitating easier understanding leads to:

(2) Hans sagt Franz, daß Peter Maria ein Buch gibt.
    Deshalb ist Franz erstaunt, daß Peter Maria ein Buch gibt.

This solution is not much better, however. Although the length of the sentences has been reduced considerably, two unsolved problems remain: The repetition, which suggests a reduced version of the 'Objtrans', and the link realized by 'deshalb' ('weil'). A hearer can easily infer the message to be essential for Frank's astonishment, so the causal relation is obvious and need not be stated explicitly.

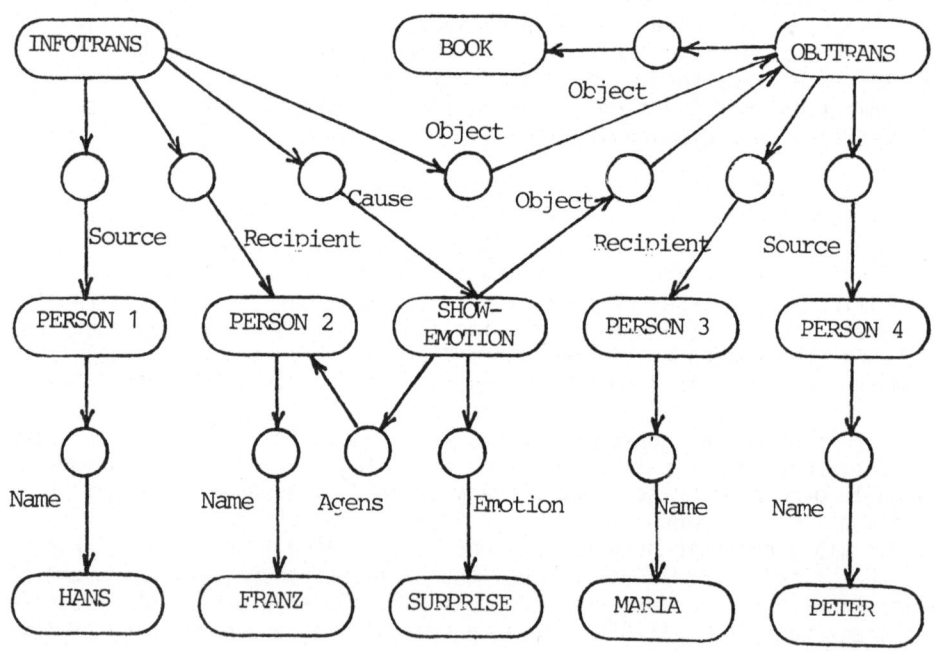

Figure 1

3. CREATION OF PARAPHRASES

A generator usually is supposed to choose the most precise wording for a fact to be uttered. How to select exactly that wording has been the theme of many a former paper on generation. While this idea seems obvious at first sight, it is so only for facts that are not repeatedly uttered. In order to improve the bad style due to repetitions we suggest to use paraphrases for repeatedly occuring facts.

The generator of the system VIE-LANG interprets entries of the syntactico-semantic lexicon /10/, choosing an appropriate verbalization for net structures marked by the dialogue component. Discrimination nets (DNs) provide selection of a possibly suitable utterance. Other than the classical DN /4/ which yields just one result, our DNs return reduced expressions additionally, if the main result consists of more than one word or is a compound noun. The transformational component of the generator selects an alternative when the main result has already been used. A less expensive implementation would be to create the structure for a paraphrase only when explicitly triggered by demand. On the other hand, control becomes very easy this way and the additional effort is partially compensated by a reduction of search. Moreover, the decision to use a paraphrase is not only caused by multiple reference of this concept in the semantic network. Portioning of text from the deep structure on may require an anaphor, which can be realized by this paraphrase.

There are different ways to create a paraphrase all of which are supported by the fact that a semantic network is the basic data structure:

1. Choosing some property already mentioned by the user or obviously known to him due to his general world knowledge. In general, this applies to roles of objects or persons ('the pope', 'the big building with the flags').
2. Utilizing some class the concept belongs to, by the corresponding generic (if the instantiation was verbalized by its name, 'Vienna' -> 'the town'), or by the superconcept's name, if it is not too general ('the city hall' -> 'the building').
3. Verbalizing just the root concept of the involved subtree, ignoring the roles which require additional words: ('general assembly' -> 'assembly', 'x gave y to z' -> 'the transfer').
4. Verbalizing just the name of the role and selectional restriction instead of the object attached to the role. Note, that the user is intended to interpret the name of the role as a designation for its filler ('recipient', 'buyer').

In general, case (1) is preferable to all the others, but most of the time the features necessary for a realization are not available. Cases (3) and (4) are very probably correct concerning comprehension. They are usually accompanied by a demonstrative pronoun. The suitability of a verbalization (realized by a simple value) is a further decision criterion additionally available in the discrimination nets. The selection of case (2) is sometimes critical, but it is necessary if no other realization is possible. Some effort has then to be put into additional tests, in order to ensure unambiguity.

In our example the 'Objtrans' fills a role in 'Infotrans', suggesting a paraphrase by the linking role 'message' rather than by the root concept 'transfer' due to reasons of suitability, leading to:

(3) Hans sagt Franz, daß Peter Maria ein Buch gibt.
    Deshalb ist Franz über diese Nachricht erstaunt.

4. TREATMENT OF CONTEXTUAL LINKS

A causal relation need not be uttered explicitly if the user is familiar with it. This will be the case if either it is part of the corresponding generic concept expressing the common world knowledge, or it is part of the episodic events well known to the user. Both of these cases can be checked by making use of VIE-LANG's dialogue partner model /9/. When the check is positive, the causal link is ignored and a junction of two structures is created. A similar approach is adopted when realizing temporal relations. In case of contemporal events, the temporal relation is expressed explicitly only when focussed.

Applied to our example, the final version is:

(4) Hans sagt Franz, daß Peter Maria ein Buch gibt.
    Franz ist über diese Nachricht erstaunt.

5. ORGANIZATION AND SELECTION

Global links generally form a structure like:

        (Junctor Phrase1 Phrase2 .. Phrase)

This applies for the following junctors:

        SOR...... Select from alternatives for paraphrasing
        AND...... Simple co-ordination (also includes relations of
                  time and reason, when expressed implicitly)
        TIMEQ.... Contemporal events to be focussed
        TIMSEQ... A temporal sequence

An explicit relation of reason is realized by an interior dependency as a constituent in a case frame:

        (Subject Verb ... Cause ...)

When the deep structure is cracked into a sequence of sentences /8/, a decision is made to generate either a subordinate or a main clause. In case of a subordinate clause, the relations of 'AND', 'TIMEQ', TIMESEQ' and 'Reason' are realized by 'und', 'wenn', 'nachdem' and 'weil', whereas in the case of a main clause '.', 'währenddessen', 'danach' and 'deshalb' are used.

Structures with 'SOR' as junctor are processed as follows: When appearing the first time, phrase1 is selected, afterwards the next phrase, and so on, in a cyclic way. Phrase1 is excluded from this cycle if it contains a verb. Note that the transformational part /8/ will effect a pronominalization when the syntactic environment is well-suited.

6. CONCLUSION

Text coherence constitutes an important goal for natural language generators that has not been fulfilled satisfactorily up to now. One of the methods towards reaching this goal is cohesion. We have demonstrated some aspects of cohesion that have been integrated into a German language generator, VIE-GEN, namely the use of short paraphrases for reoccuring facts and the handling of obvious causal and temporal relations. Whereas a general solution to the problem of creating coherent text is still far away, significant enhancements in style and readability have been achieved by the methods demonstrated, as is shown by an example.

ACKNOWLEDGEMENTS

Part of this work has been sponsored by the Austrian 'Fonds zur Förderung der wissenschaftlichen Forschung', grant no.5468. We would like to thank our friends and colleagues Alfred Kobsa, Ingeborg Steinacker and Harald Trost for their support and advice and Prof. Robert Trappl for his supervision.

REFERENCES

(1) Black J.B., Bern H.: Causal Coherence and Memory for Events in Narratives, Cognitive Science Technical Report No. 3; 1980.
(2) Buchberger E., Leinfellner E., Steinacker I., Trappl R., Trost H.: VIE-LANG - A German Language Understanding System, in Trappl R. (ed.), Cybernetics and Systems Research, North-Holland, Amsterdam; 1982.
(3) Buchberger E., Horacek H.: VIE-GEN - A Generator for German Texts, in: Bolc, L., McDonald, D. (eds.): Natural Language Generation Systems, Springer, Berlin; 1986.
(4) Goldman N.M.: Computer Generation of Natural Language from a Deep Conceptual Base, Stanford AI Lab Memo AIM-247; 1974.

(5) Granville R.: Controlling Lexical Substitution in Computer Text, in: Proceedings of the 10th International Conference on Computational Linguistics, Stanford Univ., California; 1984.

(6) Halliday M.A.K., Hasan R.: Cohesion in English, Longman Group Ltd.; 1976.

(7) Horacek H.: Zur Generierung zusammenhängender Texte, in: Proceedings GWAI-83, Dassel/Soling, Springer; 1983.

(8) Horacek H., Buchberger E.: On Generation of Anaphora and Gapping in German, in R. Trappl (ed.), Cybernetics and Systems Research, Vol. II, North-Holland, Amsterdam; 1984.

(9) Kobsa A.: VIE-DPM: a User Model in a Natural-Language Dialogue System, in: J. Laubsch (ed.): Proceedings GWAI-84, Springer, Berlin; 1984.

(10) Steinacker I., Buchberger E.: Relating Syntax and Semantics: The Syntactico-Semantic Lexicon of the System VIE-LANG, in: Proceedings of the First Conference of the European Chapter of the ACL, Pisa, Italy; 1983.

INTERACTIVE SEMI-AUTOMATIC CREATION OF A MORPHOLOGICAL LEXICON

Harald Trost, Georg Dorffner
Department of Medical Cybernetics and Artificial Intelligence
University of Vienna
Freyung 6
A-1010 Wien, Austria

ABSTRACT. Natural Language Understanding (NLU) systems are lexicon based, i.e.only words contained in their dictionary can be processed adequately. Dictionary entries must contain the necessary morphological and syntactic information, which is coded in a system-specific way. To input new entries to such a lexicon an expert familiar with the system is needed. This is no problem with experimental systems with small vocabulary, but the situation is totally different for realistic applications. In this paper we present a system which enables the extension of such a lexicon in a semi-automated way. All technical expertise is supplied by our system, the only knowledge the user must have is a good command of the German language. Classification is performed by a small rule based system with lexical knowledge and language-specific heuristics. The key idea is the identification of three sorts of knowledge which are processed distinctly and the optimal use of knowledge already contained in the existing lexicon.

1. INTRODUCTION

In this paper we describe a system for the semi-automatic build-up of a morphological lexicon. This system forms part of the German language dialogue system VIE-LANG (Buchberger et al. 1982). VIE-LANG serves as a target and as a meta system: on the one hand its lexicon is to be augmented, on the other hand it is used itself to facilitate the augmentation; the parser serves to analyze the input to the acquisition system, the generator is used to provide examples to the user.

In contrast to English morphological analysis of German words is no trivial task, due to two .causes: First there is a rich inflectional system, consisting of about 60 different endings (most endings having various different interpretations), prefixes ('ge-' for PPP, 'zu' for infinitive forms), 'umlautung', and irregular forms; second lemmatization does not suffice but has to be complemented by interpretation, because the functional structure of a sentence is not bound to constituent order but to the case system.

To build up a lexicon, one needs a classification scheme of German

837

R. Trappl (ed.), Cybernetics and Systems '86, 837–844.

words on the basis of their graphemic realization. There are several works on this subject, e.g. Bergmann (1982), Knopik (1984), Schott (1978), Schulze and Heinze (1982), Willee (1979). For VIE-LANG we developed our own classification scheme (Trost and Dorffner 1986), based on Kunze and Ruediger (1968).

All these schemes have in common that it takes an expert to classify new words correctly. Our system contains linguistic expertise in form of different types of rules, which allows for semi-automatic acquisition of lexical knowledge in an interaction with a native speaker who need not have specific linguistic knowledge.

2. THE MORPHOLOGICAL CLASSIFICATION SCHEME

Our classification scheme is based primarily on the sets of suffixes, which can be combined to certain stems. Every different set constitutes a morphological class, and every lexicon entry falls in exactly one of these classes. Altogether there are about 70 different ones.

For each class there is a list stored containing the set of suffixes belonging to the class, and another one containing the syntactical interpretation of these suffixes. Superimposed on this scheme is information about 'umlaut' and prefix 'ge'. They can occur only in a few positions, depending on word category. Every possible combination is represented by a certain numerical value stored with each lexicon entry.

Lexical information is divided between morphological and syntactical information, the latter being a feature of the lexeme itself (and not expressed by inflection), e.g. the gender of a noun. The morphological information consists of the following features:

KL : The class of suffixes the word falls into
UM : Information about 'umlaut'
PF : Information about formation of PPP (only verbs)
FM : Information about other forms (suppletion)

UM and FM serve for filtering out those interpretations delivered by the analysis algorithm which cannot co-occur with an 'umlaut' or prefix 'ge'. As an example, consider the possible interpretations of 't' as a suffix of the stem 'lauf' ('to run'). They are:

a) 3rd person sg present tense
b) 2nd person pl present tense

Whereas a) is always accompanied by 'umlaut' to render a correct interpretation ('läuft'), this is not the case for b) ('lauft').

The syntactic information (which is independent of inflection) is stored in the feature SY. It consists of the following data:
- word category (verb, noun, pronoun, etc.)
- gender of nouns
- subcategory (auxiliary verb, modal verb, proper name, etc.)
- case of prepositions
- auxiliary for present and past perfect ('haben' or 'sein')
- separable verbadjuncts

This information is coded into a number, the first digit representing the word category, the other ones depending on it (e.g. gender only for nouns).

As an example let's look at the entries for the verb 'geben' (to give). There are three forms to be considered, 'geb' is the stem for present tense and PPP, 'gib' for 2nd and 3rd person sg present tense indicative, and 'gab' the stem for past tense. The corresponding dictionary entries have the following form:

```
GEB: Key: LXM#889      GIB: Key: LXM#718      GAB: Key: LXM#754
     KL:  22                KL:  26                KL:  23
     UM:  0                 UM:  0                 UM:  3
     PF:  1                 PF:  0                 PF:  0
     FM:. 8
     SY:  500
     FORR: (LXM#718 LXM#754)
```

The two lists corresponding to morphological class 22 are given below:

```
END22 : (E EN END EST ET T)
INT22 : (E (111 121 123)
         EN (3 6 114 124)
         END (4)
         EST (122)
         ET (125)
         T (115 52))
```

The suffix list gives the possible endings of the words in class 22, the interpretation list gives the code of all forms expressed by any one of these endings.

3. THE PRODUCTION RULES

The acquisition system is a rule based one. Its knowledge base comprises three types of knowledge:
- For each inflectional paradigm there is at least one associated rule package. They describe the basic types of conjugation and declination in German (there is one for adjectivic inflection, six for substantivic one and two for verbs).
- Morphonological Rules. The basic inflectional endings are split up into a much larger set by various morphonological rules which alter the endings and stems to make pronunciation easier.
- Heuristic rules. While the former two types are derived from the German grammar proper, these rules are more like plausible guesses. They help the system to make choices like which category a word belongs to according to knowledge about forms (i.e. all verbs end with -en), actual frequency of classes, etc. According to their nature they may be wrong in certain cases (e.g. some nouns end with -en, too), and have to be verified some way.

These rules are organized in distinct packages. Only rules in active packages are considered. Rules may activate and deactivate rule packages.

4. SYSTEM OUTLINE

According to their different nature, the three types of knowledge mentioned are processed differently. Knowledge about inflectional types serves to partition the words in disjunct classes. Once the inflectional type has been determined, there are relatively clear guidelines as to the inflection of the word. The inflectional type actually is a subclassification of the word type.

A crucial point is determining the word type. The system first tries to make use of its existing vocabulary. It checks whether a new word is composed of words contained in the lexicon or of an existing word stem together with a derivational ending. In German noun-noun-compounds (which are written without spaces or hyphens in between) the morphological class is determined by the last noun. On a similar line reasoning about derivational endings is performed, as those may determine word type as well as inflection. If the word type cannot be determined this way, morphological clues are taken into consideration. There exists a number of them, but ambiguities may arise. In the latter case, a third strategy is applied: the system asks the user to type in a short utterance containing the new word. The utterance is analysed by the parser of VIE-LANG rendering information about the word type by means of the phrase type it appears in. The system relies on the presupposition that the user usually enters an utterance containing the word in a proper linguistic context. This way, a noun will be contained in at least a noun phrase or even a clause, a preposition in a prepositional phrase, etc. We do not argue that the user will always utter the minimal projection, rather that he will not violate phrase borders with his utterance. Knowledge about phrase types as well as the basic vocabulary permits unambiguous determination of the word type in most cases.

The closed word classes (pronouns, articles, auxiliary and modal verbs, etc.) are already contained in the basic lexicon because their number is relatively small, they are often used and their morphology is most irregular. Given that fact, the problem of morphological class determination is reduced to verbs, nouns and adjectives, as the rest of the remaining words have no inflection at all. The most complex morphology is associated with verbs (50 out of a total of approximately 70 inflection classes).

Once the word type has been determined, the rule package associated with it is activated. Let's suppose the new word is a verb. Then, the verb-package is triggered. Here we find in turn packages for strong and weak inflection. Actually the large number of subclasses is implied by morphonological reasons, whereby the small number of general paradigms is multiplied. Morphonological rules have exact matching conditions, therefore classification in this part is automated to a large extent. The only problem is deciding for weak or strong inflection first. As exact rules do not exist, heuristics are applied which are based mainly on word frequency.

An important feature is the dynamic interaction register: the hypotheses evoked by the heuristic rules require to be confirmed by the user. The system knows which word forms will form sufficient evidence for a certain hypothesis. It will generate these forms and ask the user

840

for confirmation. The forms however depend on the hypotheses. Thus, the user is only asked a minimum of questions. The forms to be asked for are kept in a dynamic interaction register which is updated with every hypothesis and every answer from the user.

The overall process can now be seen as follows: The user enters a new word. After having checked whether the word or at least part of it is not already present in the dictionary, the system creates a hypothesis about the word type, based on heuristic rules. Upon success, further rules determine a subclass the word belongs to. Morphonological rules modify the class to create a plausible and acceptable hypothesis. Based on the dynamic interaction register, the user is asked for confirmation. Finally the detailed information is synthesized to fit the lexicon format.

5. AN EXAMPLE SESSION

In this chapter we will show how a new entry is actually created. The user starts the interaction by entering a new word, e.g. 'abgeben' (to deliver). The first thing the system has to decide about is the word category. The best heuristic is to find out if the word is composed of already known parts. Therefore it will try to split off words first from the beginning then from the end. This will result in recognizing 'ab' as a separable verbadjunct. Of course the 'ab' could be part of a totally different stem like 'Abend' (evening) or 'aber' (but). The system must look for facts supporting the verb hypothesis. Verbs are usually typed in in infinitive form and this implies the ending '-en' (in a few cases also '-n'). Again this '-en' could also be part of a stem like 'Magen' (stomach) or 'wegen' (because), but the combination of both verb adjunct 'ab' and ending '-en' on a word belonging to a different category is highly unplausible. Therefore 'abgeben' is split into ab/geb/en.

As a next step the lexicon is looked up for 'geben'. If it is found the rest is easy. All the information from 'geben' is simply duplicated, since compound words behave morphologically like their last part. The only additional information to be stored is about the separable 'ab'. This way the new entry may be created without any other help by the user.

To continue with our example we will assume that 'geben' is not contained in the lexicon. That means the system has to figure out a hypothesis concerning the conjugation type of 'abgeben' (either weak or strong). Since weak verbs make up the vast majority of German verbs, this hypothesis is tried first (see fig.1). Weak conjugation is regular, all forms are built from one stem. To confirm weak conjugation it suffices to show the user the 1st person sg past tense. Before doing so all morphonological rules connected to weak conjugation are tried. None applies, so user interaction can start.

	FORM	CLASS	FM	UM	PF	SY
present tense	abgeb	44	0	0	1	502

Figure 1

1st person sg of past tense in weak conjugation is 'gebte ab'. To make sure the user knows which form is intended, some context has to be provided. This leads to the phrase 'gestern gebte ich ab' (I delivered yesterday) specifying tense and person. Now the user will find out that 'gebte' is incorrect and reject the phrase. This makes the system discard the hypothesis weak and try strong instead.

Strong conjugation is more complicated than weak. There may be a maximum of four different stems for present tense, present tense 2nd and 3rd person sg, past tense and PPP. Accordingly all these possibilities have either to be resolved automatically or asked explicitly from the user. First the system continues to determine the past tense forms. There are three different types of vowel changes in the case of 'e'-stems (e-a-e, e-o-o, e-a-o). They are sorted by frequency, because no other criterion is available. Again all morphonological rules applicable to strong verbs are tried. In our case none applies, so the user is asked again for verification with 'gestern gab ich ab' (see fig.2).

	FORM	CLASS	FM	UM	PF	SY
present tense pres.t.2nd p.sg	abgeb	30				
past tense past participle	abgab	23				

Figure 2

This time the user confirms, so the system can continue. There are two possibilities for the PPP, and again the more frequent one is tried (see fig.3).

	FORM	CLASS	FM	UM	PF	SY
present tense pres.t.2nd p.sg	abgeb	22				
past tense	abgab	23				

Figure 3

After that there is still another irregularity concerning second and third person sg present tense. In most of the cases the stem vowel 'e' becomes 'i'. After verification of this fact the morphological class is finally determined. The system creates three lexical entries 'abgeb', 'abgib' and 'abgab' for present and PPP, 2nd and 3rd person sg present tense and past tense respectively.

Now all of the features have to be filled in. PF of 'abgeb' is set to 1, since the verbadjunct 'ab' implies the use of the prefix 'ge-' for the PPP. UM is set to 8 for 'abgab', indicating 'umlautung' for the subjunctive mode in the past tense. FM of the primary entry 'abgeb' is set to 8 as a result of the combination of classes. Then SY is set to 502 (5 = verb, 0 = present perfect with 'haben', 2 = separable verbadjunct of length 2).

	FORM	CLASS	FM	UM	PF	SY
present tense	abgeb	22	8	0	1	502
pres.t.2nd p.sg	abgib	26	-	0	0	-
past tense	abgab	23	-	8	0	-

Figure 4

As a last step all indicative forms of present and past tense and the PPP are printed and the user is asked for confirmation. This step could actually be skipped but it is another safety measure against faulty entries.

In our specific example there is a final step to be done by the system: Since 'geben' was not found in the lexicon, it has to be included, too, for two reasons. First the analysis algorithm otherwise could not handle all those cases where the particle is actually split off in the text, second there may be many more compound verbs with 'geben', and their incorporation into the lexicon can then be handled fully automatic.

Creation of the new entries is simple anyway. All forms are duplicated, 'abgeb', 'abgib' and 'abgab' are changed to 'geb', 'gib', 'gab' respectively and SY is set to 500 instead of 502.

6. CONCLUSION

While a perfect system for automatic acquisition of all sorts of knowledge for an NLU system is still far from being realized, systems for partial acquisition of knowledge are possible. This is especially true for lexical data. Nevertheless, the task is not trivial, in particular when dealing with languages rich in inflectional forms, like German.

We have presented a system which automates acquisition of lexical data for a natural language understanding system. Knowledge acquisition takes place in graceful interaction with a human who is not supposed to have specific linguistic knowledge. The system relies on the existing natural language system VIE-LANG containing among other sources of knowledge a lexicon with a basic vocabulary such that acquisition does not start from scratch but can be seen as an iterative process. The acquisition system is based on a small rule based system in which three different sorts of knowledge, inflectional, morphonological and heuristic rules are distinguished and processed differently. As for derivational endings as well as compound words the system heavily relies on existing lexicon entries to form its hypotheses.

The described system forms part of an integrated system for acquisition of different sorts of knowledge for natural language understanding (Trost and Buchberger 1985). The final goal will be a system which augments its knowledge automatically in every interaction with the user in a practical and comfortable way.

Acknowledgments
Part of this work was sponsored by the Austrian 'Fonds zur Foerderung der wissenschaftlichen Forschung', grant no.5468.

REFERENCES

Ballard B.W.: The Syntax and Semantics of User-Defined Modifiers in a Transportable Natural Language Processor, in Proceedings of the 10th International Conference on Computational Linguistics, Stanford Univ., California; 1984.

Bergmann H.: Lemmatisierung in HAM-ANS, HAM Memo ANS-10, Universitaet Hamburg; 1982.

Buchberger E., Steinacker I., Trappl R., Trost H., Leinfellner E.: VIE-LANG - A German Language Understanding System, in Trappl R.(ed.), Cybernetics and Systems Research, North-Holland, Amsterdam; 1982.

Haas N., Hendrix G.G.: Learning by Being Told: Acquiring Knowledge for Information Management, in Michalski R.S., et al.(eds.), Machine Learning: An Artificial Intelligence Approach, Tioga, Palo Alto, Calif.; 1982.

Knopik T.: MORPHY - Die morphologische Komponente zu einem Generierungssystem fuer das Deutsche, Diplomarbeit, Inst.f.Informatik, Univ.Stuttgart; 1984.

Kunze J., Ruediger B.: Algorithmische Synthese der Flexionsformen des Deutschen, Zeitschrift fuer Phonetik, Sprachwissenschaft und Kommunikationsforschung 21,245-303; 1968.

Schott G.: Automatische Deflexion deutscher Woerter unter Verwendung eines Minimalwoerterbuchs, Sprache und Datenverarbeitung 1, 62-77; 1978.

Schulze W., Heinze G.: Die Morphosyntaktische Komponente in der Wortdatenbank des Deutschen, Sprache und Datenverarbeitung 1-2,34-42; 1982.

Trost H., Buchberger E.: Knowledge Acquisition in the System VIE-LANG, in Trost H., Retti J., Oesterreichische Artificial-Intelligence-Tagung 1985, Springer, Berlin; 1985.

Trost H., Dorffner G.: A System for Morphological Analysis and Synthesis of German Texts, in Hainline D.(ed.): New Developments in Computer Assisted Language Learning, Crooms Helm Ltd., London; in print.

Willee G.: LEMMA - Ein Programmsystem zur automatischen Lemmatisierung deutscher Wortformen, Sprache und Datenverarbeitung 1-2,45-60; 1979.

ERROR MESSAGES IN SPOKEN NATURAL LANGUAGE

Dr. Christopher C.R.Turk
University of Wales
Institute of Science and Technology
Aberconway Building,
Colum Drive,
Cardiff CF1 3EU
U.K.

ABSTRACT. UWIST is studying Robot/Human communication, combining expertise in Robotics, NL Processing, and work-study techniques in Applied Psychology. The project will investigate the combined robot/user system, by creating dialogue between user and automaton to disclose the interaction of the constraints in the automaton, the NL generator, and the user's beliefs and attitudes. The work design is based on an evolutionary paradigm of robotic development.

The system will update a 'corrective action database' using a simple learning algorithm. Error conditions will be input from the robot end effector, and when the correction required is not recognized, be output to the NL generation system, the user input read, and added to the list of errors with known corrective actions.

Updating a database in NL presents a different problem then designing a NL query front-end, because it requires the NL input to be parsed, compiled into an IL (Intermediate Language), and the database to be modified. A purpose designed IL is used to store and index corrective actions in a form mid-way between the CD (Conceptual Dependency) form of the NL generator, and the instruction set of the automaton itself.

1. THE WORK

The University of Wales Institute of Technology (Cardiff, U.K.) is planning to study Robot/Human communication, combining expertise in Robotics, NL Processing, and work-study techniques in Applied Psychology. The project uses available state-of-the-art knowledge in robotics, language processing, and work-study techniques, to investigate the combined robot/user system as a whole. The work creates intensive interaction between user and automaton to investigate the interaction of the constraints in the automaton, the NL generator, and the user's psychology. It is based on an evolutionary paradigm of robotic development. This paper describes the plan of work; because of funding constraints at present in the UK, work has not yet commenced.

845

R. Trappl (ed.), Cybernetics and Systems '86, 845–852.
© *1986 by D. Reidel Publishing Company.*

1.1 Practical Pruning

A representative current project, the Edinburgh Speech Transcription Project accepts that the most viable way forward in Intelligent Systems lies in intimate computer interaction between user and machine:-

> It is a widely shared opinion that continuous speech recognition and machine translation are tasks which are fundamentally beyond the reach of current computational technology, if we stipulate automatic performance at human levels on unrestricted materials. This is because such performance is crucially dependent on understanding of the materials involved, and such understanding is in turn based on far greater and more detailed knowledge of the world than we can currently represent in computer systems.[Thompson 84]

Thompson points out that there are two ways of pruning this infeasible knowledge requirement:

o Abandoning the demand that the domain be unrestricted

o Abandoning the demand that the system perform automatically at a human level

The Edinburgh project adopts the second technique, aiming to recognize unrestricted speech by a human assisted incremental process.
The present project adopts both pruning techniques. The domain is restricted to error, status or inquiry messages from a robot system operating in an automated assembly environment. The ideal of Fully Automatic Intelligent Performance (FAIP) will be restricted to a system which is designed to request information and directional support in an interaction with a human user. This design is based on the assumption that, if realistic systems are to be at a marketable stage within the present decade, the automaton can be expected only to assist the human effort, not replace it. To achieve this aim, it is necessary to construct convenient, rapid, well-researched and robust interaction systems.
The present project envisages that robotic tools will, for some decades, fail to provide sufficient vision, error recovery, and 'common sense' problem solving methods to operate unassisted. Rather than abandon the aim of creating automata, able to operate usefully in hostile, unpredicted, or error rich environments, it is consistent with current thinking in the AI community to expect an automaton to interact frequently with its user. The machine may be expected to inquire from its user for assistance when unrecognized conditions are met, or some unexplained error is encountered. Such an automaton will be of practical use if it is able to report the detail of errors and failures without hostile verbosity. This requires a sensitivity in the NL generator mechanism to the discourse structure of the interaction between automaton and user. Few results are available which enable

'verbosity' to be described, and a central aim of the UWIST project is to provide such results.

1.2 Spoken Error/Status Messages

Of the various methods available for interaction between automaton and user, all those depending on human vision have serious disadvantages:

o They require the user to be <u>watching</u> constantly
o There may be a significant time delay between an urgent message being generated, and the next time the user 'checks' a display system
o Visual messages can compress information greatly especially with graphic icons, but cannot so easily use anaphora to reduce verbosity.

For reasons probably similar to these, human communication systems constantly employ speech, especially for urgent messages. It therefore seems plausible to investigate robotic speech messages, especially in the field of error messages. Such messages are more immediately available to the human user, who may not be watching, but cannot stop listening. They are more convenient, since humans find speech interaction more natural. They are also quicker, since understanding of spoken language is typically faster than reading, and human replies in spoken language are faster than typed responses. The natural interaction system uses speech in both directions; a VDU display for message output, with typed input, can seem cumbersome, and distract the smooth flow of interaction.

For these reasons, we can expect future generations of automata to interact with their users using speech. The Hamburg HAM-ANS project [Nebel 82] surveyed users, and found that: 'An NLS (Natural Language System) was judged a useful support for flexible (indicated by 62.2% of the interviewees) and time sensitive <u>working processes</u> (71.4%). It is expected that the information gets into the information seeker's hands sooner with the help of NLS.' [Morik 83] This research, and almost all NL systems so far have been for data base query ('the most often chosen background system for a NLS was a data base system (66.2%).'), and no system using an assembly automaton is known.

There has been considerable work on voice recognition, both for data base query, and automaton control. The present project uses commercially available voice recognition boards, and concentrates on the generation of messages, and the refinement of the overall interaction. Its purpose is to explore the way current technologies will interact when used together in practical assembly tasks, and the way the spoken error message technique facilitates incremental interactions between user and system.

847

1.3 Automatic Assembly

The chosen domain for the initial system is a familiar problem in automatic assembly, the insertion of a component into an aperture. In the first stage, the corpus of possible error message codes generated by the end effector system will be initially constrained to 20-30. These will be output to the NL system. The NL generator will have lexical resources of some 2-300 tokens, a verb form generator, a quantifier algorithm, and a simple anaphora mechanism. The speech synthesizer is current commercial technology, and the psychological tests controlled response tests.

2. THREE PROJECT PHASES

2.1 The First Phase Establishes a Minimal Interaction

In this first phase of the project, the simple error messages fall into three categories: unexpected errors encountered, current status of process, termination notification. As examples of the system, some of the unexpected errors in this simple automated assembly device may be 'hole not found,' 'peg binding in hole.' Status messages may be '25th peg inserted,' 'work continuing,' and the termination messages may be 'work complete,' 'job terminated with four errors reported,' or 'unable to continue because of errors.' Initial work shows that the complexity of these messages depends on two things: the error detection sensors incorporated in the automaton, e.g. whether it can report 'hole too far to left,' or 'peg bent, causing binding,' and the extent to which the messages can be actioned, e.g. whether reporting that the hole is left or right of the desired position is useful, in terms of successful corrective action which can be taken by the user, and how far the robot can automate the corrective action for these conditions.

The research explores what error message can be generated, and what inquiries form the most useful interactions between user and automaton. The work in the first stage includes the design of a simplified NL generator for the limited domain. The work in the first phase also studies the human user's reactions to the type, phrasing, and frequency of the messages.

2.2 The Second and Third Phases

The second phase of the project will consist in controlled diversification of the complexity of each component. The contributing components will be elaborated, using more complex assembly paradigms, visual component selection systems, and multiple component assembly tasks. As the error messages are diversified, the NL generator will acquire a procedure to refer back to the automaton for clarification and generalization of the output message. This section of the system will be based on a discourse model of the interaction, and will include some user modelling, and comparisons of user model and discourse history. The speech synthesizer will incorporate intonation control, based on user context and knowledge of the domain world. The third phase of the project is intended to construct an experimental robot mechanism, perhaps including automaton controlled movememt in a naturally constrained work-space, with voice interactive control, and a learning mechanism.

3. MACHINE LEARNING

3.1 Corrective Action Database

The architecture of the interactive message structure is derived from a modified version of the message passing techniques of the HEARSAY 'blackboard.' The driving conception of the project being the application of existing technologies, to establish a pattern of interaction for the whole automaton/control-architecture/user system.

The problem of updating a database in NL is a 'fundamentally different problem from enquiry,' [Sylvester 84] because it requires the NL input to be parsed, compiled into an IL (Intermediate Language), and the database to be modified. An important element is the choice of internal representation for the corrective action database. A purpose designed IL, similar to many current database NL query systems, will be used, to store and index corrective actions in a form mid-way between the CD (Conceptual Dependency) form of the NL generator, and the instruction set of the automaton itself.

3.2 Learning

A major element in the software design of the third phase is the incorporation of a learning system. This section of the paper outlines a software design, not yet implemented. The robotic device which encounters an error condition, and needs to ask for human direction, will record the condition which produced the error, together with the solution in a corrective action database. Pattern matching routines will search this database when another error condition is encountered, and attempt the proposed solution offered last time. If the solution still produces an error condition, the database can be updated with discriminatory information, providing a distinction between the two error conditions, and the new human-input corrective action recorded as the solution to the new error condition.

Early thinking about learning [McCarthy 58] resulted in descriptions of the actions needed, such as [Hayes-Roth 81]:

1. Request - get advice
2. Interpret - Assimilate into internal representation
3. Operationalize - convert into usable form
4. Integrate - add to knowledge base

The error correction learning system follows this general structure. At a simple level, this learning pattern is theoretically equivalent to

849

the Schankian [Schank 84] 'expectation failure' driven learning automaton. The expectation is that the system already recognizes the error condition. If the first clause in the automatic error correction function fails, the expectation has failed, and the system enters an inquire and learn sequence.

Such a simple learning design is possible because of the limited domain, and because the user-assisted context provides constraints on the types of unexpected events encountered. Error conditions are input from the robot, and when the correction required is not recognized, they are output to the NL generation system, and the user input read, and added to the list of error conditions which have recognized solutions. A major part of the research is observing how the numbers of conditions needing to be recognized escalate for various classes of automatic assembly robots, and at what points on this curve of growing complexity the human user becomes exasperated by the error messages. A further constraint to be quantified by the research is the machine time used by realistic levels of error condition complexity.

3.3 Natural Language Generator

[McKeown 83] succinctly summarizes the processing needed in a NL generator interface: 'A system that communicates with its users must be able to decide what information to communicate, when to say what, and which words and syntactic structures among many possibilities best express its intent.'

Work on NL generation by McKeown and Danlos [Danlos 84a] form the basis of the simple generator, purpose designed for a limited domain (automatic assembly), and a limited function (error/status messages). Nevertheless, the problems to be addressed are significant: 'A generation system must carry out two operations: lexical choices and selection of a discourse structure. The latter choice is made by means of a discourse grammar which indicates the list of linearizations into sentences available to formulate a given semantic relation. These two operations are dependent on one another.' [Danlos 84b].

Recent work on quantifiers in NL generation is adapted to the basic generator [Saint-Dizier 84]. If later psychological tests show that the simplicity of the NL strings generated are the principal barrier to acceptance by human users, the level of complexity in anaphora, quantifier, and verb form generation will be enhanced, since no changes beyond the boundaries of the NL generator are required in the first phase.

A significant component in the interaction is the discovery of what the user's belief system about the automaton contains, and how it changes, i.e. what the typical user believes the automaton knows at a given stage in the interaction, how this changes, and what changes it. One aspect of this is whether the style of the error/status messages, and the extent to which they use anaphora, and knowledge about the previous discourse (discourse structure) in their spoken messages affects the user's perception of the automaton.

REFERENCES

[Danlos 84a]   Danlos, Laurence, Génération automatique de texts
en langues naturelles Thèse d'Etat, Université de Paris 7.

[Danlos 84b]   Danlos, Laurence, 'An Algorithm for Automatic
Generation,' Proceedings of the Sixth European Conference on
Artificial Intelligence, ed. T.O'Shea (Elsevier, 1984), pp.
213-215.

[Hayes-Roth 81]   Hayes-Roth, F., Klahr, P., and Mostow, D., 'Advice
Taking and Knowledge Refinement: An Iterative View of Skill
Acquisition,' Cognitive Skills and their Acquisition ed.
J.R.Anderson (Lawrence Erlbaum, 1981), pp.231-253.

[Jameson 82]   Jameson, A., and Wahleter, W., 'User Modelling in
Anaphora Generation: Elipsis and Indefinite Descriptions,'
Proceedings of the Sixth European Conference in Artificial
Intelligence (Orsay, 1982), pp. 222-227.

[McCarthy 58] McCarthy, J., 'Programs with Common Sense,' in
Semantic Information Processing, ed. M. Minsky (MIT Press,
1968).

[McKeown 83]   McKeown, Kathleen R., 'Focus Constraints in Language
Generation,' Proceedings of the Eighth International Joint
Conference on Artificial Intelligence (William Kaufmann,
1983), pp. 582-587.

[Morik 83] Morik, Katharine, 'Demand and Requirements for Natural
Language Systems,' Proceedings of the Eighth International
Joint Conference on Artificial Intelligence (William Kaufmann,
1983), pp. 647-649.

[Nebel 82] Nebel, B., and Marburger, H., 'Das Naturlichesprachliche
System HAM-ANS: Intelligenter Zugriff auf heterogene Wissens-
und Datenbasen,' in Nehmen, J. (ed.), GI-12 Jahrestagung
(Springer, Heidelberg, 1982), pp.192-402.

[Saint-Dizier 84]   Saint-Dizier, Patrick, 'Quantifier Heirarchy in a
Semantic Representation of Natural Language Sentences,'
Proceedings of the Sixth European Conference on Artificial
Intelligence, ed. T.O'Shea (Elsevier, 1984), pp. 233.

[Schank 84] Private communication

[Salveter 84] Salveter, Sharon, 'A Model of Action that Supports
     Natural Language Database Update,' <u>Proceedings of the Sixth</u>
     <u>European Conference on Artificial Intelligence</u>, ed. T.O'Shea
     (Elsevier, 1984), pp.185-194.

[Thompson 84] Thompson, H., 'Speech Transcription: An Incremental,
     Interactive Approach,' <u>Proceedings of the Sixth European</u>
     <u>Conference on Artificial Intelligence</u>, ed. T. O'Shea, Pisa
     1984 (Elsevier, 1984), pp. 697-&04

Artificial Intelligence / Symbolic Computation

Chairperson: B.Buchberger (Austria)

A FORMAL FRAMEWORK FOR MODELLING AGENTS

Nigel Seel
Standard Telecommunication Laboratories
London Road, HARLOW
Essex, CM17 9NA
England

ABSTRACT. The notion of agent underlies many disciplines including biology, cybernetics, psychology and AI. It has proved notoriously difficult to capture the concept using traditional mathematical techniques found, for example, in systems engineering and control theory. The approach explored here uses ideas from discrete mathematics in an approach reminiscent of both Varela [4] and Ashby [2].

1. INTRODUCTION

The notion of agent is a pervasive one in science. Intuitively we describe human beings as agents, and extend the concept to deal with the higher animals, social systems and the artificial systems resulting from AI research etc. But formal theories of animal, human and social behaviour (and of our cognitive tools) continue to prove intractable. As a result, fields of study which in some sense are "agent-based", such as ethology, sociology, psychology have been termed "soft" sciences as compared to fully formalised disciplines such as physics.

A "naive" approach to defining agents might be to say that "an agent is any system which has a goal, and tries to achieve it". Many difficulties and further questions arise from this kind of definition. We therefore attempt to develop a mathematical model in which such a definition can be unambiguously stated and the consequences explored.

2. PRELIMINARY DEFINITIONS

In what follows, $\mathcal{N} = \{0, 1, 2, \ldots\}$, the set of natural numbers with s the successor function, Z is the set of integers, $bool$ is the set $\{true, false\}$. If X is a set, then $P(X)$ is the powerset of X.

Suppose we have a product $U = (u_1, \ldots, u_r, \ldots, u_n)$. Then p_r will denote the r-th projection function, so that $p_r(U) = u_r$, alternatively we write the r-th component in functional notation, so that $u_r = U(r)$, $r \in [1 \ldots n]$. $U - U(r)$ will denote $(u_1, \ldots, u_{r-1}, \perp_r, u_{r+1}, \ldots, u_n)$ where $\perp_r$ is an undefined element of the same type as u_r.

Let SORTS be a set whose elements are called *sorts*. Let $\{A_s\}$, $s \in$ SORTS be a family of countable sets indexed by SORTS , where we say that A_s is the carrier of sort s. Intuitively SORTS is a collection of names of properties, $\{A_s\}$ is a collection of sets of corresponding property values.

855

R. Trappl (ed.), Cybernetics and Systems '86, 855–861.
© 1986 by D. Reidel Publishing Company.

We define the state of an object to be a product of properties, of type

$$\text{OBJSTATE} = A_{s_1} \times \cdots \times A_{s_n}$$

where $s_1 \ldots s_n$ is an enumeration of SORTS .

(For convenience all objects have the same properties, with the proviso that certain carrier sets may contain a $\perp$ element). Likewise we define an environment state type, ENVSTATE, where an environment state is a product of $m \in \mathcal{N}$ object states, so that

$$\text{ENVSTATE} = \text{OBJSTATE}^m$$

We write e_i as the i-th environment state.

We will need to define invariant "laws" true of environment states or environment state transitions, hence we need environment state properties and relations. Let $k1 \subset$ ENVSTATE $\rightarrow$ *bool* be a collection of properties of environment states: we let $\psi :$ ENVSTATE $\rightarrow$ *bool* range over $k1$. Let $k2 \subset$ [ENVSTATE $\times$ ENVSTATE] $\rightarrow$ *bool* be a collection of relations between environment states: we let $\rho :$ [ENVSTATE $\times$ ENVSTATE] $\rightarrow$ *bool* range over $k2$. Let $\kappa = k1 \cup k2$, and $K =$ [ENVSTATE $\rightarrow$ *bool*] $\cup$ [(ENVSTATE $\times$ ENVSTATE) $\rightarrow$ *bool*].

Finally we introduce a function type ENVSTATE $\rightarrow$ ENVSTATE, the set of environment continuations which take environment states to environment states, with object continuations of type ENVSTATE $\rightarrow$ OBJSTATE as coordinate function types. Intuitively, if $f \in$ ENVSTATE $\rightarrow$ OBJSTATE, then f applied to a particular environment state will construct the next state of an object. We can write f itself in terms of coordinate functions, which we shall call continuation property functions (cpf's), for the various properties of X. So $f = (\phi_1, \ldots, \phi_n)$ where $\phi_i :$ ENVSTATE $\rightarrow A_{s_i}$ for $i \in [1 \ldots n]$, $s \in$ SORTS (see figure 1).

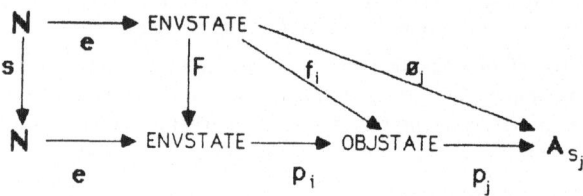

Figure 1:   Environment and Object States, and their Continuations.

We now define objects as a pair consisting of an initial object state with an object continuation, thus: OBJECT = OBJSTATE $\times$ [ENVSTATE $\rightarrow$ OBJSTATE]; we define an environment as a triple consisting of an initial environment state, an environment continuation, and a collection of properties and relations κ which are to hold either invariantly in all environment states, or between successive environment states. So:

$$\text{ENVIRONMENT} = \text{ENVSTATE} \times [\text{ENVSTATE} \rightarrow \text{ENVSTATE}] \times \mathcal{P}(K)$$

856

We will normally write

1. $E = (e_0, F, \kappa)$ as an environment, with $F = (f_1, \ldots, f_m)$ as the environment continuation.

2. We write $X = (x_0, f) = (e_0(r), F(r))$ as a typical object, the r-th object in the environment, $1 \leq r \leq m$.

3. $x_{i+1} = f e_i$ and $e_{i+1} = F\ e_i = (f_1\ e_i, \ldots, f_m\ e_i)$,
    where $\forall i \in \mathcal{N} \,.\, [\forall \psi \in k1 \,.\, \psi(e_i) = true \land \forall \rho \in k2 \,.\, \rho(e_i, e_{i+1}) = true]$. $\square$

Compare the above with systems of autonomous differential equations. We take the (many-sorted) discrete rather than analytic approach simply through abstaining from the assumption that the sets A_s are actually the real numbers with suitably well-behaved functions to model behaviour. Given the strong evidence for computational and representational phenomena in cognition, it seems unwise to develop the theory on the basis of differentiable systems (e.g. this would be appear to be the main problem in the otherwise excellent approach of Ross Ashby in [2]). In particular we need sets with more complex structure than the reals or its subsets to capture cognitive processes (e.g. [5]).

3. INFINITE SEQUENCES

DEF: We define the type SEQ of infinite sequences from some set U by the type equation $SEQ = U \times SEQ$. We use the concrete syntax $[u_1; \ldots; u_n; \ldots]$ to express such sequences, $u_i \in U$, with operations $hd : SEQ \to U$, $tl : SEQ \to SEQ$, $\_.\_ : U \times SEQ \to SEQ$ with defining equation $\forall l : SEQ \,.\, (hd\ l)\,.\,(tl\ l) = l$. Considering a sequence l as a map $\mathcal{N}^+ \to U$, $l(i)$ denotes the i-th member of l. $\square$

Let $\gamma : U \to bool$ be a property defined over members of $l : SEQ$. Then there are three possible cases:

1. if $\exists k \in \mathcal{N} \,.\, \forall\ i > k \,.\, \gamma(l(i)) = true$, then we say that γ eventually holds completely in l which we write as $\#T(\gamma, l)$. If $k = 0$ we say γ holds completely in l.

2. if $\exists k \in \mathcal{N} \,.\, \forall i > k \,.\, \gamma(l(i)) = false$, then we say that γ eventually fails completely in l which we write as $\#F(\gamma, l)$.

3. The third possibility is that $\forall i \in \mathcal{N} \,.\, \exists j, k \in \mathcal{N} \,.\, j, k > i \ \land\ j \neq k \ \land\ \gamma(l(j)) = true$ $\land\ \gamma(l(k)) = false$. In this case we say that γ is changeable in l, which we write as $\#C(\gamma, l)$.

LEMMA 1: $\forall \gamma . \forall l . \#T(\gamma, l), \#C(\gamma, l), \#F(\gamma, l)$ are pairwise mutually exclusive, and there are no other cases.

PROOF: (i) mutually exclusive - immediate, (2) no other case:- (see [3]). $\square$

Suppose we have $\#C(\gamma, l)$. If $[a, b] = \{x \mid a \leq x \leq b, x, a, b \in \mathcal{N}\}$ is an interval in $\mathcal{N}$ with $b \geq a$, then let length $[a, b] = b - a$. Let $I = \{[a, b] \mid a, b \in \mathcal{N}^+\}$ be the collection of intervals in $\mathcal{N}^+$.

Let $I_t = \{\iota \in I \mid \forall n \in \iota \,.\, \gamma(l(n)) = true\}$ and $I_f = \{\iota \in I \mid \forall n \in \iota \,.\, \gamma(l(n)) = false\}$, then if $\exists k \in \mathcal{N}^+ \,.\, sup\{length(\iota) \mid \iota \in I_t\} \leq k$ we say that γ is true-bounded; if $\exists k \in \mathcal{N}^+ \,.\, sup\{length(\iota) \mid \iota \in I_f\} \leq k$ we say that γ is false-bounded. If γ is true-bounded and false-bounded in l we say it is bounded.

4. INFINITE TREES

DEF: Let $P1(X) = \{S \mid S \subseteq X$ and S countable$\}$. We define the type $TREE$ of infinite trees with nodes of type U and unordered successors by the type equation $TREE = U \times P1(TREE)$.

Let T be a set of trees, $u \in U$ a node and let $t = (u, T)$ be a tree. Then we define operations

$root : TREE \to U, \quad root(u, T) = u;$

$succ : TREE \to P(U), \quad succ(u, T) = \{root(t) \mid t \in T\};$

$desc : TREE \to P1(TREE), \quad desc(u, T) = T.$

A path in $(u, T) : TREE$ is an infinite sequence of elements of U formed by appending to u a path in a member of $desc(u, T)$. We define

$$\Pi : TREE \to P(SEQ), \quad \Pi(u, T) = \{u \cdot l \mid l \in \cup \{\Pi(t) \mid t \in T\}\}$$

as a function which given a tree returns the set of all paths within it. $\quad \square$

Given $E = \big(e_0 - e_0(r), F - F(r), \kappa\big)$ as a "punctured" environment with an undefined r-th object, we consider the set of trees of environment states resulting from the combination of all possible initial states with all possible computable continuations of the r-th object. We call a typical tree belonging to this set an *etree*, and construct it by pruning a larger object called a *pre-etree*. Let $\eta1 = \eta1(E, r, x_0)$ be a typical *pre-etree* associated with E and initial state x_0 defined as follows.

(1) $root(\eta1) = \big(e_0(1), \ldots, e_0(r-1), \chi, e_0(r+1), \ldots, e_0(m)\big)$ where $\chi \in$ OBJSTATE.

(2) if $\eta1_\xi = (\xi, T_\xi)$ is a subtree of $\eta1$ rooted at ξ : ENVSTATE,

$$succ(\eta1_\xi) = \big\{\xi' \mid \xi' \in \Delta \ \wedge \ [\forall \psi \in k1 \cdot \psi(\xi') = true \ \wedge \ \forall \rho \in k2 \cdot \rho(\xi, \xi') = true]\big\},$$

where $\Delta = \{(f_1\xi, \ldots, f_{r-1}\xi, \chi, f_{r+1}\xi, \ldots, f_m\xi) \mid \chi \in$ OBJSTATE$\}$,

(3) for all subtrees (ξ, T_ξ) of $\eta1, T_\xi \neq \{\}$. $\quad \square$

Not all environments have an associated *pre-etree* set because of condition (3). The set of all paths in $\eta1$ is $\Pi(\eta1)$.

DEF: ς is a unary node in $\eta1$ if $\mid succ(\eta1_\varsigma) \mid = 1$. $\quad \square$

DEF: Given $\eta1$ for some e_0, if $p \in \Pi(\eta1)$ we say f implements p when

(1) $f = F(r)$, and (2) $p = [e_0; Fe_0; F^2e_0; \ldots]$. $\quad \square$

Now, $\Pi(\eta1)$ may contain paths which cannot be implemented by a function (e.g. $[\ldots; u; u; v; \ldots], u, v \in$ ENVSTATE, $u \neq v$). Since we require F to be well-defined, we remove such paths from $\eta1$ giving us $\eta2$.

It can be shown [3] that if the number of unary nodes in $\eta2$ is finite, then $\Pi(\eta2)$ is uncountable. Since we require f to be computable, and there are only a countable number of paths corresponding to choices of f as a computable function, we remove those paths in $\Pi(\eta2)$ which correspond to non-computable choices for f. The resulting "pruned" tree we will write as $\eta = \eta(E, r, x_0)$ with associated paths $\Pi(\eta)$. Note that a path in η represents a particular future chosen out of all possible futures.

We write the set of *etrees* associated with an environment E and r as $\{\eta\}$. The corresponding collection of paths $\{p \mid p \in \Pi(\theta) \mid \theta \in \{\eta\}\}$ we write as $\Pi(\{\eta\})$.

5. PRE-AGENTS AND AGENTS

D E F : (PRE-AGENT) Let $E = (e_0, F, \kappa)$ be an environment with r-th object $X = (x_0, f)$ and *etree* $\eta = \eta(E, r, x_0)$. Then given $P \mid Q$ as a partition of $\Pi(\eta)$ we say X is a pre-agent with respect to E, P if f implements a path in P. $\square$

This definition is analogous to that of "stability" for continuous systems [1]. We start by considering the possible futures of the world correlated with X's initial condition and possible actions (paths). These futures are considered to be grouped into good futures P and bad futures Q. All we ask is that X have a finite description (motivating f computable) and that it should choose one of the good futures for it to pass the test for pre-agenthood in this environment according to the criterion P.

Note that being a pre-agent is not a property of X taken in isolation: it is a relation which X stands in with respect to its environment and some criterion. Take a given X and put it into a different environment, or apply a different performance criterion, and the resulting system may fail to qualify as a pre-agent system.

We would like to characterise agents in terms of "goals" however, and this notion is missing from the definition of pre-agent. This provides a motivation for the following definition.

D E F : (AGENT - tentative). Let $E = (e_0, F, \kappa)$ be an environment with r-th object $X = (x_0, f)$ and *etree* $\eta = \eta(E, r, x_0)$. Let
(1) $\gamma :$ ENVSTATE $\to$ *bool* be a property defined over environment states,
(2) $P_\gamma \mid Q_\gamma$ be a partition of $\Pi(\eta)$, $P_\gamma = \{p \in \Pi(\eta) \mid \#T(\gamma, p) \vee \#C(\gamma, p)\}$,
then X is an agent with respect to E, γ if f implements a path in P_γ. $\square$

This definition is motivated as follows: γ selects out possible futures P_γ for X in the environment in which it is eventually always true, or in which it "keeps becoming true". There are also futures (in Q_γ) for which eventually γ will never subsequently be true. Provided X has been configured to select a future in P_γ rather than Q_γ (through a correct x_0 and f) then it will count as an agent. For this reason we sometimes call agents "goal-seeking objects". It is important to note that being an agent is a property that pre-existing systems (either naturally occurring systems, or systems that were specified and engineered for some human purpose) may exhibit.

LEMMA 2 : There exist pre-agent systems which are not agent systems.

PROOF : By considering the tree of decimal expansions of elements of the real interval $[0, 1]$ partitioned into rational and irrationals. An argument by contradiction shows that no γ exists which allows an agent system to realise this partition. See [3] for details. $\square$

We now use these ideas to examine the notion of autopoietic system.

6. AUTOPOIETIC SYSTEMS

Autopoietic objects are self-producing systems which require continued access to free energy in their environment to power their self-producing mechanisms [4]. The most obvious examples of such systems are biological systems, whose varied complexity is witness to the varied sources of free energy, and the difficulties of regularly accessing it. Another example might be the case of robot systems which maintain certain state variables within bounds in their transactions with the environment. We now construct a simple model of ("energetically buffered") autopoiesis which directly addresses the problem of capturing the "perturbation" of such an autopoietic object by its environment, which is considered generally problematic in [4].

To make X an autopoietic object we give it as q-th component an energy buffer W which can store up to μ resource units. We allow this buffer to be augmented by a function up just when condition Σ holds, otherwise the buffer is to be decremented by a function $down$. We demand that the object operates so as to keep its buffer within bounds, non-negative but less than or equal to μ. We call up, $down$, Σ, μ, q the parameters of the autopoietic system.

DEF: (AUTOPOIETIC SYSTEM): We consider the environment $E = (e_0, F, \kappa)$ with $X = (x_0, f)$ as r-th component and $\eta = \eta(E, r, x_0)$, with:

(1) $W \simeq Z$ as the q-th component of OBJSTATE called the status property. We write w for a variable ranging over W, possibly indexed so that if x_i is the i-th state of X, $w_i = x_i(q)$.

(2) ϕ_w as the cpf computing the status property of X of the form

$$\phi_w e_i = \text{if } \Sigma(e_i) \text{ then } up(w_i) \text{ else } down(w_i),$$

where $w_i = x_i(q), \Sigma : \text{ENVSTATE} \to bool$ is a property of environment states, $up, down : W \to W$ are functions such that $up(w) > w, down(w) < w$. $\kappa = \{\lambda(e, e') \cdot e'(r)(q) = \phi_w(e)\}$.

(3) Given some $\mu \in \mathcal{N}$, $\iota = \iota_\mu : \text{ENVSTATE} \to bool$ is a property of environment states defined as $\iota(e_i) = 0 \leq w_i \leq \mu$.

Then if $P_\iota = \{p \in \Pi(\eta) \mid \iota \text{ holds completely in } p\}$, we call X an autopoietic system when for some $p \in P_\iota$, f implements p. $\quad \square$

THEOREM 1: If X is an autopoietic system with parameter Σ with respect to an environment E and criterion P_ι, then $\forall p \in P_\iota$, $\#C(\Sigma, p)$ and Σ is bounded.

PROOF. We have from the definition of autopoiesis:

1. $\exists \mu \cdot \forall p \in P_\iota \cdot \forall i \in \mathcal{N} \cdot \iota(p(i)) = true$.
2. $\iota(e_i) = 0 \leq w_i \leq \mu$.
3. $w_{i+1} = \phi_w e_i = \text{if } \Sigma(e_i) \text{ then } up(w_i) \text{ else } down(w_i)$.
4. $up(w) > w, down(w) < w$.

From (1) we see that (2) holds completely $\forall p \in P_\iota$, hence from (3) and (4) we see that the functions up and down must have their application interleaved and that for a given μ the number of compositions of both up and down must be bounded. However, the only way of controlling the sequencing of application of up, down is via the truth or falsity of Σ in the elements of $p \in P_\iota$, hence Σ must be changeable and bounded.

Note that for $p \in Q_\iota = \Pi(\eta) - P_\iota$ we have the following possibilities for Σ: (1) $\#C(\Sigma, p)$, Σ bounded, but ι not holding completely in p, (2) $\#C(\Sigma, p)$ but Σ not bounded, (3) $\#T(\Sigma, p)$, (4) $\#F(\Sigma, p)$. $\quad \square$

So when can an autopoietic system be classified as an agent ?

THEOREM 2: Suppose $X = (x_0, f)$ is an autopoietic system in $E = (e_0, F, \kappa)$ with etree $\eta = \eta(E, r, x_0)$ and parameter Σ. Then if $\exists p \in \Pi(\eta) \cdot \#F(\Sigma, p)$ then X can also be considered an agent with objective Σ.

PROOF. We show that the partition of $\Pi(\eta)$ required in the definition of agent can be constructed in this case with $\gamma = \Sigma$. $Q_\Sigma = \Pi(\eta) - P_\Sigma$ is non-empty because the p for which $\#F(\Sigma, p)$ [given] is in Q_Σ. P_Σ is non-empty because $\#C(\Sigma, p)$ for the path p implemented by f (theorem 1) hence X is an agent with objective Σ [by definition of agent]. $\quad \square$

This theorem states that if we have an autopoietic system for which there is at least one possible behaviour for which Σ is eventually completely false, then since the system rejects that behaviour, we may consider the system to be a (goal-seeking) agent for objective Σ.

Some consequences of this are (1) an autopoietic system which is related to its environment so that it cannot help but maintain regulation cannot be considered an agent [given condition not true]; (2) some agents are not realisable by autopoietic systems as defined (e.g. because they would require unbounded buffering). It appears that the interesting concept to study is that of agent rather than autopoietic system if we are interested in cognitive systems: our results may then transfer across to those agents which are also autopoietic.

7. CONCLUSION

In an extensive discussion in /4/, Varela contrasts the point of view in which autopoietic systems are goal-less, merely implementing homeostatic self-regulation, with a behavioural point of view in which the system is clearly "goal-oriented" in its environment, "doing things for a reason". The discussion above is intended to shed some light on such different levels of description of autopoietic systems, and more generally to begin the examination of the notion of agent. We plan continued work in this area. I am grateful to Roy Simpson of the Intelligent Systems Laboratory at STL for many valuable discussions.

8. REFERENCES

[1] *Introduction to Mathematical Control Theory*, S. Barnett, Clarendon Press, (1975)

[2] *Design for a Brain*, W. R. Ashby, Chapman & Hall, (1952)

[3] 'Agent Theories and Architectures', N. R. Seel, ISL/STL (1985)

[4] *Principles of Biological Autonomy*, F. J. Varela, Elsevier North Holland (1979)

[5] 'An analysis of a simple learning system', N. R. Seel, in *Proceedings of ECAI-84*, Elsevier Science (1984)

MENTAL MODELS AND INFERENCES IN EVERYDAY REASONING

B.G. Bara, A.G. Carassa, G.C. Geminiani
Unita' di ricerca di intelligenza artificiale
Istituto di Psicologia della Facolta' Medica
Universita' di Milano, via F. Sforza 23 - 20122 Milano ITALY

ABSTRACT. This paper presents a psychological theory of everyday reasoning, based on the concept of mental models. Mental models are considered as a unitary representational structure which may be manipulated by different cognitive functions. We used a story understanding task for the analysis of different types of inferences: Connected (linking two models), Stabilized (expliciting the essential relations within a model), Developed (expanding a model along a temporal line). Experimental results confirm in general the predictions generated by the theory. Predictions not verified are explained by the analysis of points in the stories, liable to subjective interpretations, alternative to the straightforward ones given by the majority of subjects.

1. INTRODUCTION

Inferences have been studied in all types of reasoning problems. The most complete results, however, have been obtained in formal reasoning, i.e. in an area where only the abstract processes are concerned, often regardless of the mundane meaning of the premises.

The risk of the formal approach is its limited generality, because the corresponding theories apply only to a particular kind of problems, where it is possible to assume the irrelevance of the general knowledge for the correct execution of the inference algorithms.

Our aim in this paper is to develop a model of how people cope with everyday inferences, in order to define a set of general processes possibly underlying the different types of reasoning problems. The theory proposed is based on the concept of mental model, considered as a unitary representational structure which may be used by different processes.

From a psychological point of view, a descriptively and explanatory adequate theory of deductive reasoning based on mental models has been proposed by Johnson-Laird (1983). His basic hypothesis is that reasoners do not apply logic rules of inference to draw valid

863

R. Trappl (ed.), Cybernetics and Systems '86, 863–870.
© 1986 by D. Reidel Publishing Company.

conclusions, but mentally manipulate models of the state of affairs from which inferences are drawn.

A mental model is finite, computable and contains tokens and relations that represent entities in a specific situation. A mental model is an analogic representation of the state of affairs, analyzed under certain relevant aspects. Its structure conveys the necessary informations about the way in which the model may be manipulated.

2. EVERYDAY INFERENCES

If inferences have to be drawn on propositions, the propositional representation of a sentence is the starting point for the construction of a mental model. According to this point of view, the basic ability requested to make inferences is the ability to create an integrated model of the premises.

We single out two main reasoning steps peculiar to the processes underlying everyday inferences:

i) Interpretation.
For each sentence a mental model is constructed, basing it on the meaning of the sentence and on implicit inferences drawn from general knowledge. The model represent a fact (state or event) described by the sentence. Since the model embodies some arbitrary assumptions, it may be considered a single representative sample from the set of models satysfying the assertion.

ii) Integration.
Each initial model, representing a fact, is treated as a token in the construction of a global higher level model. The global model represents the story described by the sentences in terms of facts linked, in our hypothesis, by temporal and causal relations.
In order to give an account of our schema of causal relations, we have to introduce a few basic concepts.
We define:
- fact as the representation of a property holding for an individual, or of relation holding among a number of individuals;
- state as a collection of facts which keeps itself unchanged in a fixed time interval;
- event the occurring of a change in the state of the world; this change occurs in a interval of time one cannot furtherly split.
We consider the cause-effect relation as a basic relation between the two events, event (cause) and event (effect).
When the cause-effect relation is used in the area of everyday reasoning, it can never be considered as necessary. In fact, no mundane inference is ever certain, but always probable.
From the point of view of the cognitive processes, establishing a cause-effect relation is a creative activity, based not on necessity, but on a subjective judgment. In particular, we claim that the event (effect) follows the event (cause) with a high degree of expectation when some enabling conditions subsist. Both the establishing of the

relation cause-effect and the introduction of different enabling conditions depend upon the general knowledge of the system.

Interpretation and integration are the basic steps also in syllogistic reasoning (Johnson-Laird and Bara, 1984). We suggest indeed that the distinctive features of formal inferences do not rely on specific procedures distinctly differentiable from those that guide everyday inferences, but on the particular constraints that the task of formal reasoning imposes. When people have to draw syllogistic inferences, the task obliges them to concentrate only on the relations explicitly mentioned, regardless of the meaning of the premises.

Another peculiar feature of formal problems is that as the reasoners know that only one correct conclusion exists, they do not limit themselves to draw valid inferences, but they try to gain the unique correct conclusion.

As far as this particular point is concerned, the theory proposed by Johnson-Laird and Bara (1984) assumes a test procedure to evaluate the conclusion on the basis of a semantic principle according to which an inference is sound, if there are no counterexamples to it. Consequently, reasoners search for alternative models that could falsify putative conclusion. In conclusion, formal reasoning appears to be a subset − a special case − of everyday reasoning.

3. A MODEL OF EVERYDAY INFERENCES

In order to make the theory outlined below easier to follow, we present here a sketch of the experiment that is described in Bara, Carassa, Geminiani (1985). As experimental material we constructed triplets of sentences (A, B, C) describing a short story. Three patterns of couples of sentences (AB, AC, BC) were composed from these triplets and presented to the subjects. For the purpose of an analysis in terms of mental models, we chose the two sentences configuration, as it seems the simplest possible one.

Following Figure 1, after describing the general structure of the schema, we shall explain in detail each part of it.

3.1. The global schema

The upper part of the model (see Fig.1) corresponds to the comprehension processes all subjects exhibit when dealing with the experimental material. We assume that the processes implicit in the functions READ and BUILD are equivalent to the ability to construct an internal model (M1 or M2) from a written sentence (respectively, P1 or P2).

The central part of the schema corresponds to a series of tests confronting the models generated by the two premises. The models are submitted to two subtests, one is based on the presence of tokens in common between the models M1 and M2, and the second one on causal relations. The tests described are not claimed to cover any possible discontinuity between the models, but they are sufficient to explain our data.

The first outcome of the schema corresponds to the connected response, i.e. the building of a third model (M3) which causally links the initial ones in a new structure (see 3.4)

In the lower part of the schema is analyzed the giving of the integrated response (see 3.5.). After integrating M1 and M2 in a unique model M12, a plausibility test is used to examine the plausibility of M12. Again, this test relies on a subjective judgement of the subjects. The two possible outcomes of the test correspond to the two different types of integrated responses found:
- if M12 is valued as plausible enough, then it is developed along a line of probable future (M123);
- if M12 is valued as not plausible, then it is strenghtened by expliciting some internal relations (M12*).

3.2. Comprehending the story

READ: it transforms the written sentences into mental representations, tokens and relations.

BUILD: it connects the tokens and relations in a finite model. It is assumed that a different model is built for each of the sentences presented.

Both models, once built, are stored in working memory for further processing (see Fig.1).

3.3. Testing the initial models

The test for discontinuity is decomposed in two subtests. The global purpose of the subtests is to discover if there is a significant discontinuity between the two initial models M1 and M2. After describing each test in detail, we shall discuss their validity.

The first sub-test is based on the tokens present in the two models. If at least one token is present in both models, the models will go to the INTEGRATE function, otherwise they will go to the CONNECT function (see 3.4.).

INTEGRATE: It takes M1 as the basic model and it iserts on M1 the tokens and the relations described by M2. Its output is model M12, presenting all the features of M1 enriched by the novelties introduced by M2. We outline that this function produces an integrated model only at lower level.

The integrated model is submitted to the second subtest. This subtest is applied on the higher level model only when M1 and M2 represent two events: it detects a causal discontinuity. In particular, it examines if a postulated cause-effect relation between the two events is already structured within knowledge representation.

3.4. Connecting the models

Whichever the type of discontinuity detected by the two subtests previously described, the models are submitted to the CONNECT function.

CONNECT: If you have a token discontinuity, this function correlates M1 and M2 by introducing new tokens and relations; the result is a complex model M12 which contains both M1 and M2.

If you have a causal discontinuity, this function introduces an event M3 in the higher level model so as to generate two relations M1---M3 and M3---M2. The reasoner breaks the postulated relation between M1 and M2 in a two steps one, in order to increase the global degree of expectation. Only the two-steps relation can be considered as a cause-effect one, while each single step is weakly related in a causal way.

For instance, in problem 8, a causal discontinuity is detected:

P1: This morning Chiara lighted the fire.
P2: Chiara had to keep the windows open during the afternoon.
M3: The fire made a lot of smoke. (Subject 13)

3.5. Evaluating the plausibility of the model

This type of response is close to the process of comprehension of a coherent text. In fact, it occurs when no discontinuity is found by the tests described in 4.3.: in other words, the two premises may be considered by the subjects as close enough to constitute a single, complex state of affairs.

Model M12, the result of the function INTEGRATE, may now undergo the plausibility test (see Fig. 1).

The purpose of the test for plausibility is to check if all the tokens are linked among them by valid, meaningful relations. In particular, if a causal link between two events is suggested, subjects have to evaluate the link's degree of reliability (Bara, Carassa and Geminiani, 1984). If the plausibility has a negative outcome, M12 has to be transformed in a more plausible model. In the positive case, the model may be directly developed.

Moreover, a stabilized model could be followingly developed: this occurs quite frequently with the second responses of our subjects.

3.6. The integrated responses

DEVELOP: It takes as input the integrated model M12, once judged by the subjects as well connected. The model is temporally expanded along the line in the future (or sometimes in the past), that subjects think is the most probable. The output of this function is model M123, which is extended in the future respect to M12.

The new model presents the same tokens and relations of the integrated model, plus some novelties (different correlations or new tokens linked to the core) which furtherly enrich the state of affairs described.

For instance, in problem 11, we have:

P1: Anna has an important meeting in New York.
P2: Anna is afraid to fly.
M123: She will go by ship. (Subject 16)

STABILIZE: It takes as input the integrated model M12, if its plausibility is valued by the subjects as not sufficient. The model is enriched by expliciting new relations between tokens; these relations play the role of enabling conditions in the higher level model. The asterisk (*) marking model M12 in output signals that useful inferences have been explicited.

For instance, in problem 10, we have:

P1: Bruno invites Albert to a tennis game.
P2: Albert refuses Bruno's invitation.
M12*: Albert is not able to play tennis. (Subject 14)

4. THE EXPERIMENT

We conducted a preliminary experiment to verify our hypotheses. We predicted three types of possible responses (connected, stabilized, developed) depending on the output of the discontinuity and plausibility tests, and we confronted these predictions with the types of inference actually produced by the subjects.

4.1. Results

For each couple of sentences, the expected inference type has been confronted with the inference type experimentally obtained.

The number of problems predicted to have a connected response is low (8 on 54 problems). In fact, as a first stage of study of everyday inferences, we decided to concentrate on how people handle integrated models. As a matter of fact, it seems more difficult to analyze how two models, perceived as discontinuos, may be connected. In this case, a deeper analysis of the possible relations between models is requested. Moreover, the relations between models, among which the most important is the causal one (see Bower, Black and Turner, 1984), present problems quite different with respect to the relations among tokens within a model.

The results support the efficacy of the discontinuity test. Nevertheless, two (on 54) problems present unexpected conclusion; other kinds of discontinuity may have affected the subjects' performance.

The predictions made on the basis of the plausibility test were confirmed in 36 problems on 46 ones. The subjective interpretation of how good are the internal relations of the integrated model M12 plays a relevant role in the decisions between developed and stabilized responses. Again, it is necessary to furtherly analyze the testing procedures, to be able to explain the behavior of individual subjects, when different by the statistical predictions. Moreover, after stabilizing a model, subjects may develop it, as it has shown by the answers successive to the first one: in other words, a model may firstly be stabilized, and successively be developed.

5. DISCUSSION

Norman (1983) has introduced a useful distinction between "conceptual models" and "mental models". Conceptual models are intended as tools for the understanding or teaching of physical system. Mental models are what people really have in their heads and what guides their use of things.

Kieras and Bovair (1984) tried to specify conceptual models, named by them "device models", as some kind of understanding of how a device works in terms of its internal structure and processes. For Kieras and Bovair device models are a special case of mental models, specific for the examined physical system and domain dependent.

What we tried to do in this paper is to correspondingly investigate the use of mental models, considered as aspecific and domain indipendent.

As regard to the relation between formal and everyday reasoning, it is possible to reconduct syllogistic inferences to our "stabilized" responses. This supports our initial claim that formal and everyday reasoning constitute a unique domain, where the same structure and processes operate, even with different boundaries (access to general knowledge, existence of correct answers etc.). A further point is that the different types of inferences we analyzed, may correspond not only to objective features of the stories, but also to individual differencies in the reasoning style of our subjects.

In this sense, we are not satisfied of our statistical predictions, which are not enough detailed to account for the behavior of single subjects.

Informations about the generation of these inference processes are in our opinion indispensable to understand how mental models actually work. Conducting the same type of experiments on subjects in developmental age is our next step of research.

The long term goal of this strategy is also to elucidate notions like causality — its genesis and development — in the theoretical framework of mental models.

The homogeneous use of the same basic structure through different ages is in opposition to the theories (see Piaget and Inhelder, 1955) of the acquisition of an abstract correct logic via distinct stages of imperfect processes of thought. In our opinion, the investigation of the evolution of models appears to be of the same relevance of the investigation of different areas of inference, to stabilize the paradigm of mental models.

ACKNOWLEDGMENTS: This research has been supported by a grant of the Ministero della Pubblica Istruzione, for the year 1984.

6. REFERENCES

Bara B.G., Carassa A.G., Geminiani G.C., 1984. 'Inference processes in everyday reasoning'. In: Plander D., ed. Artificial Intelligence and Information-Control Systems of Robots. Elsevier, Amsterdam, 87-90.

Bara B.G., Carassa A.G., Geminiani G.C., 1985. 'Mental models in everyday reasoning'. <u>Proceedings of Cognitiva 85.</u> Paris.

Bower G.H., Black J.B., Turner T.J., 1979. 'Scripts in memory for text'. <u>Cognitive Psychology,</u> 1, 177–220.

Johnson-Laird P.N., 1983. <u>Mental Models.</u> Cambridge University Press, Cambridge.

Johnson-Laird P.N., Bara B.G., 1984. 'Syllogistic Inference'. <u>Cognition,</u> 16, 1–61.

Kieras D.E., Bovair S., 1984. 'The role of a mental model in learning to operate a device'. <u>Cognitive Science,</u> 8, 3, 255–273.

Norman D.A., 1983. 'Some observations on mental models'. In: Gentner D., Stevens A.L., eds. <u>Mental Models.</u> Lawrence Erlbaum Associates, Hillsdale, N.J., 7–14.

Piaget J., Inhelder B., 1955. <u>De la logique de l'enfant a' la logique de l'adolescent.</u> PUF, Paris.

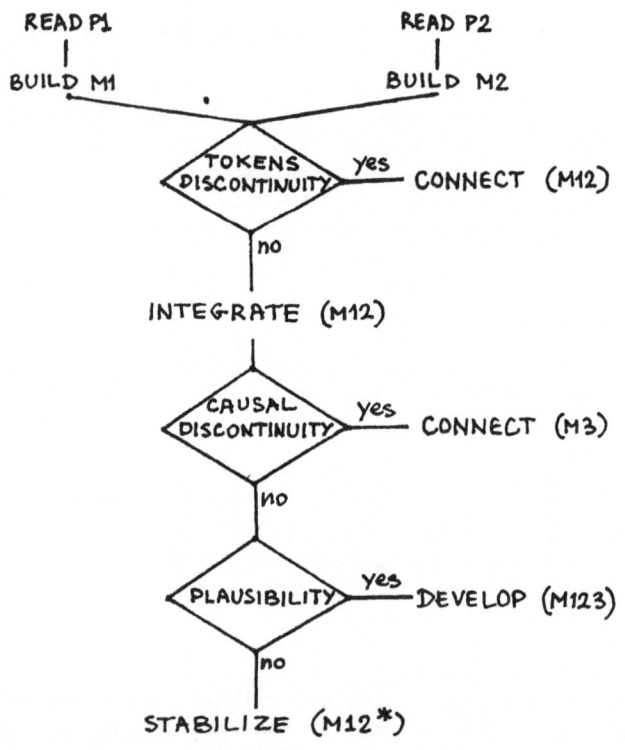

Figure 1.   The global scheme

LOGICAL STRATIFICATION OF ORGANIC INTELLIGENCE

J.J.Koenderink and A.J.van Doorn
Department of Medical and Physiological Physics
Physics Laboratory, State University Utrecht
Princetonplein 5
3584 CC Utrecht
The Netherlands

Computers are supervised signal processors: they perform syntactic transformations automatically whereas the semantics is supplied by the user. They are worthless as paradigmata for organic intelligences which are unsupervised agents. E.g. the cruise missile is an unsupervised automaton with a set goal. Agents are not amenable to scientific study except when we know their goals: The goal is given to the agent, it is not analysable within its own logical domain. This precludes difficulties associated with the notion of "final cause" and turns the agent into a possible object of study. Similarly organisms can be understood as automata with set goals, the so called drives (as hunger, thirst, satiation, pleasure, ...) which are served by fixed procedures known as releasers by biologists. Drives and releasers are irrational and ad hoc in the organism's own logical system. (A rat may drive itself to exhaustion or kill itself when we trigger one of its basic drives with certain pharmaca). Only when we are able to discern the basic drive system of an agent does it become a possible subject to scientific study. In order to begin such a study one has to pry apart the diverse disjunct logical strata involved, a process that often leads to conflicts and apparent paradoxes in the literature.

Organisms are automata that are coupled to the world through two interfaces (often intermingled hardware wise, but functionally distinct), a sensorium and a motorium. The main problem is in understanding the nature of this coupling. We first of all discriminate between structure (or spatiotemporal differentiation) in the physical world, signals in measuring apparatus and automatic guidance systems (AGS's; purely syntactic transformers) and the semantic domain. Relations between these disparate logical strata are usually avoided, but in this case essential.

R. Trappl (ed.), Cybernetics and Systems '86, 871–878.

We start with a few definitions:
--- In the physical world (both the environment and the organism's hardware) we discern structure and energy conversions. E.g. the structure of an ambient electromagnetic field gives rise to an electrochemical structure in the human cortical area 17. Nature provides no signals, still less meaning, but only structure and conversion.
--- Signals are defined relative to machine hardware (a physical system for which a deterministic theory exists). A physical state gives rise to a signal if it conforms to a certain physical format. (A floppy disc shows discernable physical structure, but it only carries signals with respect to certain disc drives that are configured to certain conventions). In machine hardware energy conversion can also be described (on another logical stratum) as signal processing. This is a purely syntactical matter, no concepts of meaning are involved at all.
--- Semantic processes are on quite another logical level. The term can be used in two distinct senses, i.e. the introspective analysis of soliloquy (which strictly falls outside the realm of scientific enquiry) and the modelling of agents. This latter sense can denote a scientific endeavour if the goals of the agent are assumed (axiomatically). In such cases meaning can be defined relative to these goals (in the sense of Gibson's "affordances") and one may speak of knowledge as semantic structure and transformation (also called "reasoning") which underly efficacious action. Again efficaciousness is relative to the goals. If one describes the behaviour (that is: the sequence of physical states of the agent and its environment) in terms of a semantic model one studies a conscious agent. If one studies (perhaps the same!) organism in terms of signal processing one studies an automaton. Again, studied in terms of physicochemical variables one studies a physical system. The terminology is technical and serves to distinguish the various disparate logical strata involved. There is no obvious relation to something like "meaning", "knowledge" or "consciousness" as applied to introspection, such are not amenable to scientific description at all (according to the common understanding of "science". Of course this does not mean that the latter are necessarily senseless).

The main aim of this paper is to clarify the logical stratification involved in the study of the sensori-motor interface. We attempt this by outlining a kind of "minimum model" of a complicated organism (like a vertebrate) both as a physical system, an automaton and as a conscious agent. The level on which one chooses to study an organism is often forced by pragmatics in view of sheer complexity. Thus the peripheral sensor and motor parts are usually amenable to physicochemical methods and one typically studies energy conversions of various kinds. The peripheral nervous system and local parts of the central nervous system (CNS) yield more easily to the signal processing approach. Thus one studies transduction or the physical formats involved in going from the physical to the syntactic domain.

(This is possible because we now understand nerve cells and nervous circuitry as deterministic machines). One studies signal processing, that is the functional relations between signals. Sheer complexity forbids numerical prediction in the physical domain. In the CNS the complexity even forbids a description in terms of automata, at least with a precision that allows numerical prediction. One thus devises a model of the agent on the semantic level. (This is what distinguishes a biological from a physiological approach). Such a model depends wholly on assumed goals, as entities that are unanalysable in the semantic system itself (true semantic "atoms"), but do define it (like Euclid's axioms of geometry).

The sensorium consists first of all of specialized tissue (often of the body surface) which has the property to change state reversibly when certain environmental forces act on it. In allied nerve fibers the occurrence of all-or-none events shows that one had better change from the physicochemical to the machine (syntactic) description there: thus one has occasion to study the physical formats of the sensory organs. (Mueller's doctrine). It is often possible to pursue the signal processing for quite a while, e.g. in mammals one describes a multitude of topologically ordered maps of (syntactic) structures with various selectivities to aspects of the "physical stimulation". We perceive a massively parallel, bottom-up signal processing leading up to this veritable "atlas of maps" and then more or less loose track in a confusion of detail. For the motorium the situation is similar: on the very periphery one discerns the conversion of physicochemical into mechanical forms of energy, one discerns "motor maps" (a kind of piano key-boards, with "synergies" under the keys) and one may study tranduction and physical formats. Of the structures central to the key-boards we know very little indeed.

Many mechanisms of sensorimotor control are known, from simple "reflex arcs" to complicated automatic guidance systems (AGS's). Many of them are just about simple enough to be studied as automata (or will be so studied in the foreseeable future). They appear to be largely autonomous, unsupervised (like "sub-agents") except that the CNS may "wake them up"or "put them to sleep" and sometimes may set their goals in an overall sort of way. Thus the CNS appears to deal with "logical device drivers" and is largely screened from what actually goes on. (The better known systems appear to be autonomous also in the sense that what goes on in them doesn't figure in introspection. E.g. the complicated system subserving the regulation of posture is largely an unconscious affair).

The atlas of the sensorium, the key-boards of the motorium, the AGS's of sensorimotor control and the basic drive system (BDS) with its releasers (which figure as concepts of the root language of the BDS) appear to be the "interfaces" and "basic operating system" of the agent viewed as a semantic processor. In building such a model we have to include the environment. This world model supplies a link between the motorium and the sensorium because of a complicated causal nexus (the "laws of physics", etc.). This turns the system of AGS's into a partly hierarchical, partly heterarchical nexus of informationally closed loops. (in the syntactic sense!). Together with the BDS this closure of the chain serves to define the semantics. The semantic structure has to include its own internal world model (or has to entertain "physical theories") in order to act efficaciously (relative to the goals set by the BDS) and these physical theories are the "logical formats" that define the concepts of the semantics (like meteorological theory may turn a set of measurements jotted down on a map into "a front"), whereas the goals define its values.

The semantic processor is a decision structure that continually issues forth a chain of decisions resulting in motor commands and perceptions (v.i.). As yet there appears to be no reason to pick anything more complicated than a Turing machine as a model for the semantic processor in organisms. (Note that the observable behaviour contains more than the results of motor commands: unsupervised AGS's may interfere and many epiphenomena of the hardware such as muscular tremor and spasms are physically indistinguishable from voluntary motor output. Such physiognomic behaviour may actually be meaningful to other agents).

Thus the model's structure is somewhat like this:
A (serial!) Turing machine is fitted with a basic structure that contains the releasers as root semantic units. This core forms the BDS and subserves a rudimentary "knowledge how". (No"knowledge why" at this point). The machine may address an "input tape" (the top layers of the sensorium), which is strictly read-only (no"top down processing"!) as follows: the machine sends a command word to an "atlas manager" (which merely selects from the simultaneous structure of signals in the sensorium) and gets a data word in return. (Not a small glimpse of an inner screen: whereas the maps may appear "iconic" to the external observer the data word has merely a logical, not a geometrical structure. It is a quality, not a glyph). The command word at the same time issues a logical format by which the data word is interpreted. This is a mechanism of "focal attention" (often likened to a "searchlight in the psychological literature) and it interpretes syntactic structure. Thus the same structure in the sensorium may lead to different meaning. Similarly the machine may use its "output tape" (the key-boards of the motorium and the AGS's). The machine issues command words to logical device drivers:from there on syntactic and physical descriptions have to be used. Only the "orchestration" is amenable to semantic description. Anything beyond the logical formats is "environment" to the semantic domain, even if it belongs to part of the neural system of the organism. In the sequel we denote the machine as "CNS", although we understand this term in an abstract, machine theoretical sense, not as a piece of hardware, nor as a spatially localized entity.

In order to act efficaciously the CNS entertains and develops world models (at the rock bottom these are just the releasers noted in very young or lower animals, at the highest levels they are our scientific theories). Apart from generally applicable "laws" the CNS develops stores of knowledge of more specific, but still rather general character (e.g. an "encyclopedia of "verba visibilia" containing ordered sets of generic views of more or less solid objects, etc.; and a library of "libretto's" of often encountered scenes and transactions, e.g. killing certain types of prey in certain ways,etc.), and it develops an "awareness" or "present whereabouts monitor" (the "four W's" of journalism: When, Where, What, Who). This mechanism may be thought of as a pointer to the libretto that is currently acted out, with pointers to data used as "actual parameters" and to present intentions (data structures that can be used to issue sequences of commands that "act out" the libretto in different ways).

Although this may sound rather vague, the fact is that such a view already supplies alternatives to several well known models of what perception is about. For instance, the peripheral visual system is a syntactic processor, it doesn't deal with meaning at all (sends no messages to the brain). Thus it can be massively parallel and the proliferation of maps presents no problem: there need be no convergence at the next step at all! The sensorium is merely an extension of – or mirror to – the physical world (as such completely objective although it is selective through its architecture; it "condenses" the available structure by throwing out what does not serve efficacious action), it does in no way "compute perceptions". Perception is a semantic construct that cannot be understood as a "transformation of sensory input", but only as a creative construct ("model" or "theory"; as in physics) used to guide action. Whether this construct is "true" is a matter of whether it is efficacious with respect to the goals, not whether it conforms to our view of what the world ought to look like. The model (perception) is checked by the CNS through taking selective, model guided, and model interpreted readings from the sensorium. Evidence may well exist in different maps, yet we should expect no pointers between the maps, rather all pointers go from a central registration of "corroborative evidence" to the maps. That this model (which differs from the usual views on sensory systems) is really quite reasonable may be gleaned from a simple paradigm:

A weather bureau's "sensorium" consists of a great many services which are rendered by personel without formal training in meteorology. One form of final output of this sensorium is a set of different "weather maps". These are purely syntactic structures. (They may be automatically drawn by machines fed with radiographically received data or plotted by unskilled personel). The perception or "present weather" is a semantic construct for which a (usually small) team of scientists is responsible. They use experience (the encyclopedia's; libretto's) to find e.g. fronts.

Fronts do not occur on the raw maps, they are creative constructs based on an awareness of the previous situation (four W's), of how fronts ought to behave (model) and on evidence such as can be traced on the maps. Several types of map are used simultaneously (wind field, pressure, temperature, humidity, topography 500mBar, etc.), other sensory data is also referred to (isolated soundings of the vertical structure, radar data, satelite data, etc.). "Multisensory" perception is the rule although no interactions between, e.g. the personel taking barometric readings and the radar unit are involved. Fronts are drawn boldly over oceanic regions where hardly any data exist (blind spots), and through regions where the maps show conflicting evidence, some of which has to be sensibly neglected. Note that there is no "top down processing" (no tampering with charts), nor a "final map". (Although several "final maps" may in fact be issued to specific users, e.g. agriculturists, sports events organizers, air traffic, etc., the percept "present weather" is on no final map). In their spare times (the forecasts had better be punctual!) the scientists use their experience and study of the data to refine and change the model (meteorological theories), which may change the future perception of similar data. Many other human endeavours (e.g. exploration geophysics, traffic control on air bases, etc.) offer equally good paradigmata.

We have left out the "early warning systems" (EWS's) in the discussion up till now. Such EWS's occur mainly in two types: those that interrupt the CNS and trigger usually defensive actions (e.g. reaction on a sudden sting) and those that seem to be monitored and compete for attention. The first type is protopathic, i.e. after the interrupt the CNS has to find out what happened, whereas the second are modal and serve to draw attention to structural changes in the input. (A kind of global attention, not unlike a global map with "alert lights" that is habitually glanced at shortly in control rooms). Such systems are also present in the paradigmata mentioned earlier and do in no way obviate the structure of the sensorium as discussed.

The process of "bootstrapping up" from the BDS to more general and complex models of the world is a creative process not unlike scientific praxis. Interestingly, it doesn't seem to matter whether the original models make much sense at all (the BDS provides only axiomatic, ad hoc knowledge): after all the sciences in their present state evolved from astrology and alchemy too!

Note that the CNS's input tape changes continually. It contains both present and past order, and also "future" order in the sense of kinematical extrapolations (conservative and safe "predictions" which causally depend on the past via well understood algorithms and contain no "guesses", like the numerical forecasts used by meteorologists which are computed via well understood dynamic theories). Hypothetical structures are necessary in perception as in science but they are restricted to the CNS whereas the measuring

876

systems should be objective and necessarily operate purely in the syntactic domain. Thus the "punctum temporum" is really expanded into a "specious present" already on the input tape. The span is limited,however. It defines a short time memory (STM) span, which has to be distinguished from the long time memory (LTM) due to the (both read and write) tape of the processor itself. Thus STM contains syntactic, LTM semantic units. In most cases LTM will be extended to a much larger virtual memory that cannot be addressed via the atlas manager but via a special set of motor commands used to aim the physical sensors. (E.g. head and eye-muscles). The world is really part of the sensorium in this way, although it has to be addressed in a roundabout way. (And, predictably, this appears to be a rather autonomous process, e.g. most people are not aware of their eyemovements at all. The CNS need only issue a different command word and will receive the data word with a certain delay. This is possible because the sensorium is - as a purely syntactic processor - merely an extension of the world anyway).

Since the Turing machine has to operate in real time and to issue efficacious commands at a sufficiently high rate, it very likely operates in cycles. (Such as one may observe in cats who show transitions from one type of behaviour to the next - e.g. caring for the fur, catching flies, rolling on the back, jumping, ... - at a rate of say 0.1 to 2 Hz). We may expect a typical cycle to be somewhat like this (note that the cycle is interruptable at all times through protopathic EWS's, although completion routines may have to be activated before the cycle can be ended):

- monitor present goals (of which higher order ones may have been set earlier, although the root ones are fixed).
- get present whereabouts (link to presently active libretto);
- monitor progress of active AGS's (not all of which may be counted on to send completion signals!);
- check alert signals;
- compute what to do next;
- wake up the necessary AGS's;
- set alert systems;
- compute present whereabouts, issue goals to AGS's;
- send final GO! or HOLD! commands to AGS's;
- initiate next cycle.

If sufficient time is left this can be put to good use to consider alternatives for long term behaviour patterns. The CNS simulates likely courses of events, short circuiting the environment through its world models. This prepares the CNS to eventualities (like the war games played by generals) and thus promotes efficacious action. One special kind of such behaviour even includes the world: these are the explorative actions in which the CNS issues output commands to influence its own input tape. Not only may the causal structure of the world be probed in this manner, and the sensorium mensurated, but the CNS may actively hunt for new structure. There is no essential difference with running simulation programs, except that the CNS may alter its world model but has to accept the world as it is ("External" to it, but not in the spatial sense).

It is important to note that the semantic description of any agent is necessarily in terms of semantics devised by the scientist studying it: apart from the model the agent is just another physical system. One observes merely physical structure, a breakdown into intended motor output (with semantic content), physiognomic output (epiphenomena of the hardware) and physical/physiological disturbance is a creative act of perception on the side of the scientist who employs a hypothetical model to effect this breakdown. Only diagnostic channels exist, no dialectical ones. All "communication" takes place through the shared interface which is the physical world for scientist and agent cannot "exchange signals" in the semantic domain. (Although the scientist may study agents that can be broken down into component agents: but then "dialogue" is really "soliloquy"!). The act of building a semantic model of an agent (which includes the decision to recognize an "agent" in the first place!) is an act of translation. (After all, all language even in exchanges between native speakers of a common natural language is ideosyncratic by necessity). Similarly the communication between disparate agents (which cannot be an exchange of semantic structure) can be understood as the coupling of two diagnostic channels in which the two agents build semantic models of each other, and thus "translate each others output" which is strictly equivalent to perceiving (in the active sense, including "probing") each other. They may synchronize their behaviour in this way without strictly possessing a common language: both semantic domains are in different logical strata except when we choose to treat them as a single, composite agent.

In this sense perception is equivalent to translating the world and the ancient maxim that likens it to "reading the Book of Nature" makes deeper sense than it is usually credited with. The present discussion also reveals that perception ought really be the central issue in AI. Apart from perception organic intelligence is merely a system of irrational values (BDS), not a semantic system in any useful sense. It is only relative to these irrational goals that the concepts of the semantic system can have an existence at all, however! The only way out appears to be to allow merely the study of automata and physical systems as true science. This would prohibit the study of intelligences as a scientific endeavour: intelligence and meaning would be irrational (scientifically unanalyzable) aspects of the scientist in his own introspection. If one considers this to be unacceptable, then one has to accept an axiomatic element (also an irrational element, but a controlled one in the sense of the mathematician's world) as a necessary part of the scientific theory of agents.

878

CM-system:
New Methodoloy for Automated Theorem Proving
and
Program Synthesis Systems

Marta Fraňová
L.R.I.
Bât. 490
91940 Orsay
France

Abstract: A new Automated Theorem Proving system methodology for theorems requiring a proof by induction principle is proposed. The key idea of our methodology is a **construction** of a given formula instead of its "decomposition" as it is done when using resolution, Beth's tableaux or rewriting systems.
In the present paper we give a description of our methodology from the general system methodology's point of view. Our emphasis will be on underlying ideas rather than technical details.
This work was partly supported by an ESPRIT (ALPES 363) project.

Introduction

Automated Theorem Proving (ATP) systems are one of the most important parts of Automated Reasoning (AR) systems, as is said in [wos01]. And, as is commonly accepted (see [bledsoe01]), the main goal of research in ATP is to build programs that are effective in finding, or helping to find proofs of theorems from mathematics, and other fields of application. It would be quite acceptable for such a program to be incapable of proving theorems in a specific area if it was effective at proving the theorems that most interested users (i.e. special-purpose program). The problem with attaining the goal is that some of the weaker systems operate without much "inteligent" guidance, often generating thousands of consequences of the axioms before finding a proof or giving up. Therefore, as it is not at all surprising, THE major research activity (see [bledsoe01]) is to devise methods (or strategies) for guiding the program (system) so that it makes enough of the right deductions, and not too many of the "wrong" ones.
It is known that various refinements or alternatives of already known methods (such as resolution, Beth's method of semantic tableaux, rewriting systems) have been designed and implemented. Therefore, the present tendency in ATP (see [bundy01]) is the augmentation of known logical deduction techniques with heuristic techniques to control the search for a proof.
Instead of following this tendency in ATP we propose, in this paper, a new ATP system methodology for theorems requiring a proof using the induction principle. We call such a system an Inductive Theorem Prover (ITP). Our ITP can be characterised as a special purpose ATP system, but there are no restrictions on acceptance of theorems with existenial quantifier. than existing ITP systems.
The key idea of our methodology is the **construction** of a given formula instead of its "decomposition" as it is done when using resolution, Beth's tableaux, or rewriting systems. The logical description of our system can be found in [franova10]. A comparison

879

R. Trappl (ed.), Cybernetics and Systems '86, 879–886.

with existing ATP systems is given in [franova03].

In the present paper we give a description of our methodology from the point of view of general system methodology. Our emphasis will be on the underlying ideas rather than on the technical details. We then illustrate how our system works on a simple example.

1. Motivation (Imitation of mathematical reasoning)

In [franova06] we compared our approach with that of a kind of student cheating during examinations. Because we had a possibility to see that such a comparaison helps understanding of our methodology, let us give it briefly.

Let us suppose that, during an examination, an intelligent student has to solve the integral

$$\int \sqrt{\frac{arccos\ x}{1-x^2}}\,dx\,, \tag{1}$$

and, that he does not know how to do it. Then, he glances at his neighbour's paper, and he sees that the result of the given integral is

$$-\frac{2}{3}(arccos\ x)^{\frac{3}{2}}.$$

So he knows that he **wants** to obtain this result.

As simply puting down this result is not sufficient, he must explain how this result was obtained (by giving the rules, substitutions, ... he used).

Therefore he tries to remember if he knows any integration rule giving something of the form

$$-\frac{1}{const}t^{const}.$$

Let us suppose that he finds the rule

$$\int t^n\ dt = \frac{1}{n+1} * t^{n+1}, \tag{R1}$$

and so he can conclude

$$-\int t^{\frac{1}{2}}\ dt = -\frac{2}{3}t^{\frac{3}{2}}. \tag{2}$$

Naturally, he remembers to replace t by (arccos x), therefore he finds dt for $t = arccos\ x$. *The result obtained*

$$dt = -\frac{1}{\sqrt{1-x^2}}\,dx$$

helps him to rewrite (2) into the form

$$-\int \sqrt{(arccos\ x)}\ \frac{1}{\sqrt{1-x^2}}\,dx\ =\ -\frac{2}{3}(arccos\ x)^{\frac{3}{2}}$$

The last problem is then to verify that

$$-\int \sqrt{(arccos\ x)}\ \frac{1}{\sqrt{1-x^2}}\,dx\quad can\ be\ transformed\ into\quad \int \sqrt{\frac{arccos\ x}{1-x^2}}\,dx.$$

He succeeds, and so he can write down the **solution** of integral (1): *We solve (1) by the substitution method. Let t be the substitution variable and let t = arccos x. Then*

$$dt = -\frac{1}{\sqrt{1-x^2}}\,dx.$$

and so we obtain

$$\int \sqrt{\frac{arccos\ x}{1-x^2}}\,dx = \int \sqrt{(arccos\ x)} * \frac{1}{\sqrt{1-x^2}}\,dx =$$

$$= -\int \sqrt{t}\ dt = -\frac{2}{3}t^{\frac{3}{2}} = -\frac{2}{3}(arccos\ x)^{\frac{3}{2}}.$$

The reader can see that the knowledge of the result helped in finding its explanation, i.e. helped to find a **solution** of the given problem.

When proving theorems using the induction principle we can proceed in the same way. In the following part we explain why this is possible. One should notice, first, that when we say that we know what we want to obtain it does not mean that we know **how** to obtain it. Therefore the reader is asked to accept this sense of knowing what has to be obtained.

2. What is proving theorems using the induction principle?

It is known that it is nothing but *an application of a valid form of a deductive inference called the induction principle (IP) in order to prove theorems about elements of a set for which such a valid form (of IP) exists.*

For instance, for natural numbers (NAT) we can consider two valid forms of the induction principle:

$$\frac{F(0) \quad F(a) \Rightarrow F(Suc(a))}{\forall x\ F(x)} \qquad \text{or} \qquad \frac{(\forall a\ [(a<t) \Rightarrow F(a)]) \Rightarrow F(t)}{\forall x. F(x)}$$

The knowledge this deduction-theoretic conception of the induction does not mean knowing how to prove theorems. (As in the case of the knowledge of integration rules one must not know how to solve integrals.) One quickly realizes that when one takes, for instance, the first scheme of IP, and one is supposed to prove F(Suc(a)) from F(a). There is no inference

$$\frac{F(a)}{F(Suc(a))}$$

so proving the implication $F(a) \Rightarrow F(Suc(a))$ becomes the main problem of ATP by induction. Now, let the reader notice that when using the first scheme of IP for proving a theorem $\forall x\ F(x)$, we know **what** we want to obtain. We want to obtain
- in the basic case: for a "concrete element" (here 0) the formula **F(0)** from axioms of our theory
- in the general case: for a "concrete element" (here Suc(a)) the formula **F(Suc(a))** from axioms of our theory, and the induction hypothesis F(a).

The variable x to which, in the basic case, we "associate" the value 0, and, in the general case, the value Suc(a), is called induction variable. We say also that x is represented by 0, and Suc(a), respectively. For a given theorem the corresponding basic, and general, cases are called also inductive subproblems.

Notice that in the general case it is not necessary to consider all the elements that are smaller than Suc(a). We have to consider just one element: the predecessor of Suc(a).

When using the second scheme of IP we also know what we want to obtain, but the problem is that in this case, for a "concrete" element t, we have to consider *explicitly all the elements that are smaller than t* (or, to invent a well-founded ordering for which this scheme can be applied, and that is far from being trivial for automatization). Therefore, the first scheme of IP seems to be more suitable for a really automated theorem prover.

In [franova10] we give a general formulation of the induction principle for well-founded types (called constructable domains - see [franova09]), the interested (details-seeking) reader is referred to these publications.

Example 1. Let us suppose that we want to prove $\forall x \, \forall y \{ (x>0) \implies (x-1 < x+y) \}$. Let x be the induction variable, let us denote by σ_1 the substitution $\{ x \leftarrow 1 \}$, by σ_a the substitution $\{ x \leftarrow a \}$, by $\sigma_{Suc(a)}$ the substitution $\{ x \leftarrow Suc(a) \}$, and let the formula $\forall u \, (a-1 < a+u)$ be the induction hypothesis. Then the proof of the given theorem requires:

in the basic case : for an arbitrary element y obtaining of the formula $\sigma_1 \{(x-1 < x+y)\}$.

in the general case : for an arbitrary element y obtaining of the formula $\sigma_{Suc(a)} \{(x-1 < x+y)\}$ supposing the validity of the induction hypothesis.

Notice that depending on the set of elements to which we want apply the induction principle the proof of a given theorem T is decomposed into several inductive sub-problems SP. The proof of T can require that further theorems T_1, T_2, ... are proven. In order to distinguish between these theorems we say that the theorem T is solved on the level 0, and the level of T_j depends on the success (resp. the failure) of proving T_{j-1}. If T_{j-1} requires that T_j be proven then we put level(T_j) = add1 (level (T_{j-1})), in the oposite case (i.e. T_{j-1} has been proved) level(T_j) = level(T_{j-1}). Then the base-scheme of an inductive theorem prover (ITP) can be represented in the following way:

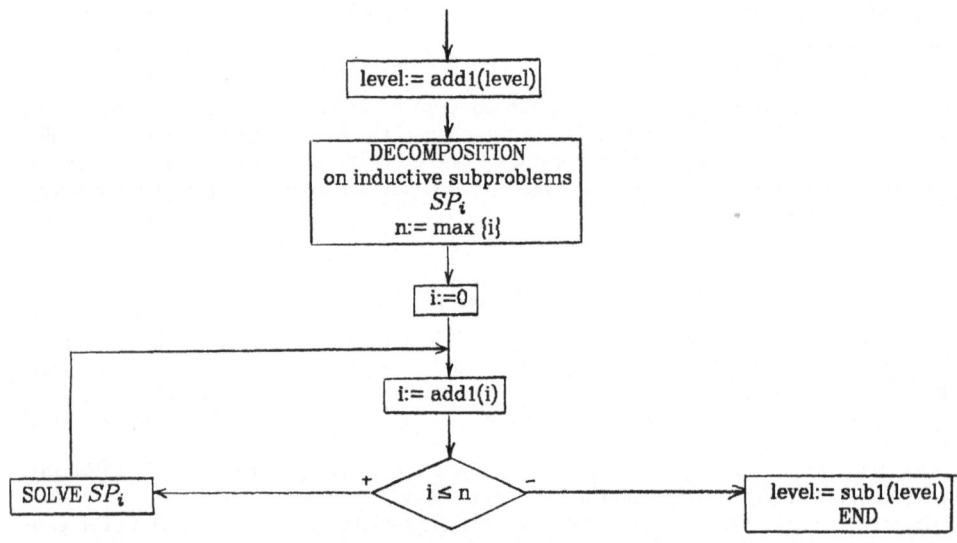

Figure 1. General flow diagram of ITP

It is clear that the base-scheme of any ITP is explicitly or implicitly the same. The originality of each ITP is then determined by the DECOMPOSITION and SOLVE units.

The decomposition on inductive subproblems is, in our approach, oriented towards obtaining (for any well-founded set) basic and general cases in a way analogous to that using the first scheme of IP for natural numbers. This is solved in [franova03].

As we mentioned above, our approach is characterised as being that of a construction of valid formulae, i.e. the SOLVE part of Figure 1. is based on a "constructor" of formulae. In the following section we give an informal explanation of this **construction.**

3. Construction of valid formulae

We shall first present some heuristic considerations.

In formal theories any formula is composed of formulae called primitive (or atomic) formulae. Let Q_n be an n-ary predicate, let $t_1, ..., t_n$ be terms. An atomic formula is $Q_n(t_1, t_2, ..., t_n)$. So, an atomic formula F is determined by the predicate-name, and its arguments. We say that an atomic formula is constructed from a predicate-name, and from its argument. Therefore, when we want to construct a formula F, given by a predicate-name Q_n, and the set (ordered with respect to the position of its element) of arguments $\{t_1, ..., t_n\}$, we can construct the formula $Q_n(t_1, t_2, ..., t_n)$ following the schemes:

$$
\begin{array}{llllllll}
Q_n & (\; - & , & - & , & - & , & \cdots & , & - & , & - &) \\
Q_n & (\; t_1 & , & - & , & - & , & \cdots & , & - & , & - &) \\
Q_n & (\; t_1 & , & t_2 & , & - & , & \cdots & , & - & , & - &) \\
\end{array}
$$

$$
\begin{array}{llllllll}
Q_n & (\; t_1 & , & t_2 & , & t_3 & , & \cdots & , & t_{n-1} & , & - &) \\
Q_n & (\; t_1 & , & t_2 & , & t_3 & , & \cdots & , & t_{n-1} & , & t_n &),
\end{array}
$$

where $-$ means that we do not consider that particular argument. Now, if we want to speak about a construction of a valid formula $Q_n(t_1, t_2, ..., t_n)$, we must during the above mentioned construction take into consideration a definition of the predicate Q_n. The above described "scheme-construction" is then changed to the following "valid-scheme-construction":

We construct a scheme $Q_n(\, -, -, ..., - \,)$ with empty places $-$ instead of arguments. Then we replace the first empty argument place by t_1 and the next ones by abstract arguments $\xi_2^1, ..., \xi_n^1$. We obtain a scheme

(1) $$Q_n(t_1, \xi_2^1, ..., \xi_n^2).$$

Because we want to speak about the "validity" of this scheme, the definition of the predicate Q_n will give us the class C_1 of all the $\xi_2^1, ..., \xi_n^1$ for which $Q_n(t_1, \xi_2^1, ..., \xi_n^1)$ is a valid formula. It is clear that if $Q_n(t_1, t_2, ..., t_n)$ is a valid formula then C_1 cannot be an empty class. Therefore with respect to condition c_1 characterising C_1 we try to replace ξ_2^1 by t_2. If it is possible, we obtain (we say that we construct) a new scheme

(2) $$Q_n(t_1, t_2, \xi_3^2, ..., \xi_n^2).$$

Now, the definition of Q_n allows us to speak about the validity of (2) and so we obtain the class C_2 of all $\xi_3^2, ..., \xi_n^2$ for which $Q_n(t_1, t_2, \xi_3^2, ..., \xi_n^2)$ is a valid formula. We continue for i=3, ..., n-1 and, if, in the last step, the abstract argument ξ_n^{n-1} can be, in the scheme $Q_n(t_1, t_2, ..., t_{n-1}, \xi_n^{n-1})$, replaced with respect to the condition c_{n-1} by t_n, we say that we have succeeded in constructing the valid formula $Q_n(t_1, t_2, ..., t_{n-1}, t_n)$.

In the following, a fact that some formula F is satisfied only if a condition C is satisfied (which is written in logical notation $C \Rightarrow F$) will be expressed by: F is satisfied *under validity* of C. Analogously, an operation is performed under validity of a condition C only if at each step of this operation C is a valid formula.

So, we have established a procedure which enables an atomic formula to be proved by its construction. This proof does not consist of explicit applications of deduction rules but of: (for i= 2, ..., n) *the construction of the scheme* $Q_n(t_1, ..., t_{i-1}, \xi_i^{i-1}, \xi_{i+1}^{i-1}, ..., \xi_n^{i-1})$ *together with the class* C_{i-1} *and the condition* c_{i-1}, *and transformation of the abstract argument* ξ_i^{i-1} *into* t_i *under validity of the condition* c_{i-1}.

Then the scheme of the unit CONSTRUCT for the construction of an atomic formula $Q_n(t_1, t_2, ..., t_n)$ can be represented as follows:

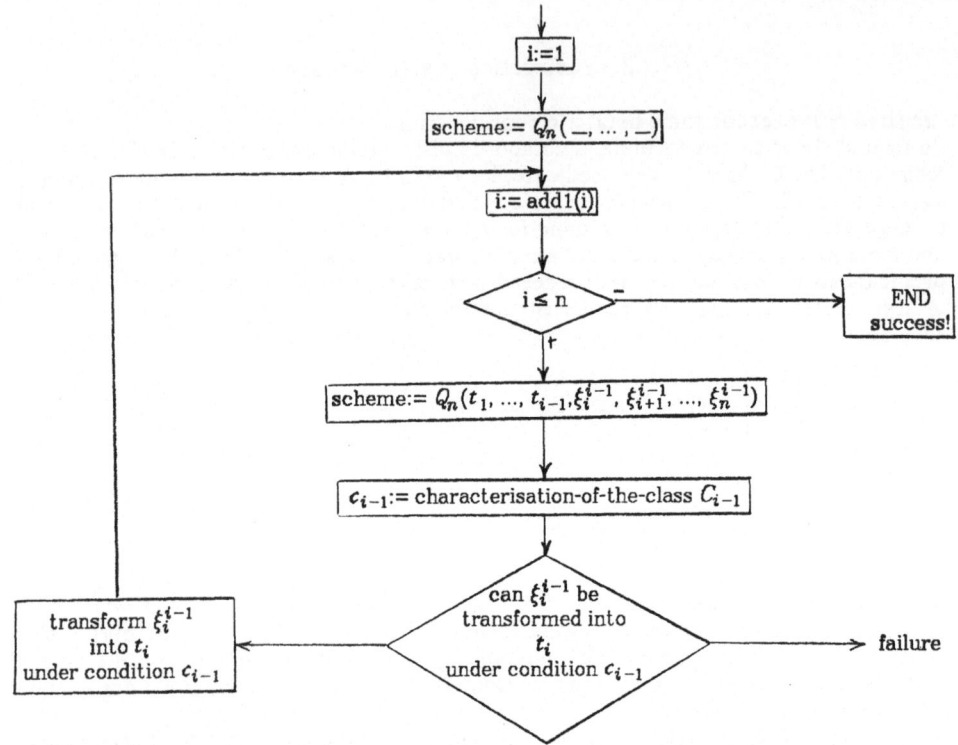

Figure 2. Flow diagram for the constructor of atomic formulae

Example 2. Let us suppose that we want to prove the theorem given in the preceding example. Let the definition of the predicate $<$ be the following:

$x_1 < x_2$ holds only if
$$\begin{cases} (x_1 = 0) \land (\neg (x_2 = 0)) \\ (x_1 = \text{Suc}(a)) \land (a < x_2) \land (\neg (x_2 = \text{Suc}(a))) \end{cases}$$

As it is shown in example 1. the formula $x\text{-}1 < x\text{+}y$ has to be constructed. In the first step of our construction we obtain the scheme $x\text{-}1 < \xi$. The class C_1 determined by definition of the predicate $<$ is

$\{\xi| (x\text{-}1 = 0) \land (\neg (\xi = 0))\} \cup \{\xi| (x\text{-}1 = \text{Suc}(a)) \land (a < \xi) \land (\neg (\xi = \text{Suc}(a)))\}$, i.e.

$\{\xi| (x\text{-}1 = 0) \land (\neg (\xi = 0))\} \cup \{\xi| (x\text{-}1 = \text{Suc}(a)) \land ((x\text{-}1)\text{-}1 < \xi) \land (\neg (\xi = x\text{-}1))\}$.

Let us denote by c_1' the condition $(x\text{-}1 = 0) \land (\neg (\xi = 0))$ and by c_1'' the condition $(x\text{-}1 = \text{Suc}(a)) \land ((x\text{-}1)\text{-}1 < \xi) \land (\neg (\xi = x\text{-}1))$. The transformation of ξ into $x\text{+}y$ is then reduced to two subproblems of the same kind: the transformation of ξ into $x\text{+}y$ under condition c_1', and the transformation of ξ into $x\text{+}y$ under condition c_1''. The solution of this example can be found in section 4.

We have shown in [franova09] that proving theorems by induction can be reduced to proving formulae of the form $\forall x\, A_1(x) \land ... \land A_k(x)$. Therefore, the scheme of the "formula-constructor" which is a part of the SOLVE unit in Figure 1. can be represented in the following way:

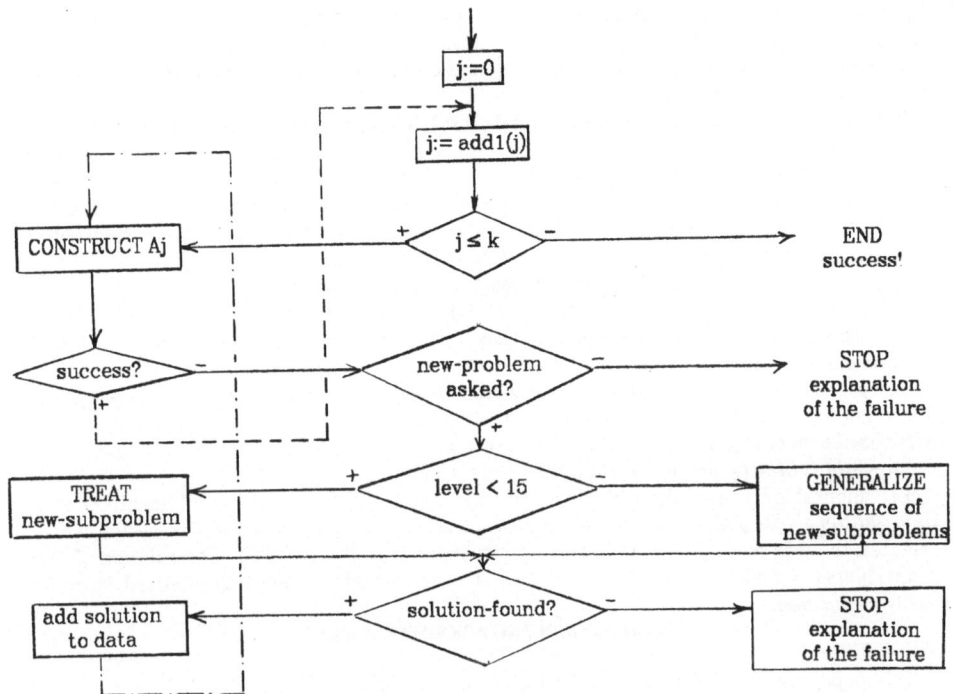

Figure 3. Flow diagram of the SOLVE unit

The interested reader can find explanations of Figure 3. in [franova10], and [franova06].

4. Example

In this part we give a solution of example 1. The choice of this example is not arbitrary; we had two reasons for taking this example: The predicate for which we perform construction is $<$, which will not allow the reader who is not totally familiar with existing ITP *to declare* our approach being the same as other approaches; and, this example is not solved by Boyer & Moore 's ATP using an induction hypothesis with a free variable, as is mentioned in [boyer-moore01], and confirmed in [boyer01].

So, our aim is to prove the theorem $\forall x \ \forall y \ \{ \ (x>0) \ \implies \ (\ x\text{-}1 < x+y \ ) \ \}$. The variable x will be chosen as the induction variable.

DECOMPOSITION on inductive subproblems: The condition x>0 reduces the domain NAT of the variable x to NAT-{0}, therefore the inductive proof of this theorem consists of the following basic (SP_1) and general (SP_2) cases:

SP_1: for x represented by 1 (i.e. the smallest element of NAT-{0}) prove $\forall y$ (x-1 < x+y).

SP_2: for x represented by Suc(a) together with the condition a>1 prove $\forall y$ (x-1 < x+y) supposing the validity of the (automatically) generated induction hypothesis $\forall u$ (a-1 < a+u).

For lack of space, the part SOLVE SP_1 is not explained here.

SOLVE SP_2 : In the general case x is represented by Suc(a), a>1. We have at our disposal the induction hypothesis $\forall u$ (a-1 < a+u), and we want to prove $\forall y$ (x-1 < x+y). Proving this theorem means taking an arbitrary element y_0, and constructing the formula x-1 < x+y_0.

CONSTRUCT (x-1 < x+y_0 ; for x=Suc(a), a>1 and a given y_0).

885

In the first step we construct the scheme $x\text{-}1 < \xi$. x occurs functionally in the term $x\text{-}1$. The evaluation of this term for the given representation of x by $\text{Suc}(a)$ gives $x\text{-}1 = a$. $a > 1$ gives the representation of a by $\text{Suc}(b)$, $b \geq 0$. The definition of the predicate $<$ allows us then to construct the valid scheme (S_2)

$$x\text{-}1 < \xi \text{ holds only if } b < \xi \wedge \neg (\xi = \text{Suc}(b)).$$

We know that the induction hypothesis should be applied. We therefore look if (and how) it can be done. From the definition of the predicate $<$ we have obtained in the scheme (S_2) recursive call $b < \xi$. The induction hypothesis is $a\text{-}1 < a+u$ for any u. We can see that b is $a\text{-}1$, and so we have $b < (b+1)+u$ for any u. This gives us a "concretization" of ξ in (S_2). ξ is transformed into $(b+1)+u$, and then by the immediate application of IH we obtain

$$x\text{-}1 < (b+1)+u \text{ holds only if } \neg ((b+1)+u = \text{Suc}(b)).$$

In the next step we would like to transform $(b+1)+u$ into the term $x+y_0$ only if $(b+1)+u$ can be written as $x+y_0$ for some y_0, and the condition $\neg ((b+1)+u = \text{Suc}(b))$ is satisfied. Therefore, for x represented by $\text{Suc}(a)$ we have the failure of the direct transformation, but two new problems (missing lemmas) are determined. We express these new subproblems using already introduced notation, i.e. $\text{Suc}(b)=a$, $b+1 = a$, $x = \text{Suc}(a)$, and so $\text{Suc}(b) = x\text{-}1$ and $b+1 = x\text{-}1$.

$new-subproblem_1$: prove $\forall x\ \forall u\ \neg ((x\text{-}1)+u = x\text{-}1)$

$new-subproblem_2$: prove $\forall x\ \forall u\ \exists y\ (x\text{-}1)+u = x+y$.

These subproblems are solved in the same way. Notice that the existential quantifier in the $new-subproblem_2$ does not cause any problem in our ATP, because our system is also oriented towards such (program synthesis) problems (see [franova03]). The solution of these subproblems is added to our data base and then the construction of the desired formula is easily performed.

CONCLUSION AND ACKNOWLEDGMENTS

In this paper we have attempted to present our approach to automated inductive theorem proving from the point of view of the general system methodology. Our system is based on classical logic, therefore our "constructive" approach should not be identified with that of intuitionists.

We claim that our formula construction is a new idea from the ATP research point of view but, as we have shown in the first section, many ordinary mathematical problems are solved in an analogous way, and as Professor Boyer noticed (see [boyer01]) every *mathematician* would prove theorems by induction in this way. Therefore, if the major goal of Artificial Intelligence (see [bundy01]) is to automate mathematical reasoning, why, in possible cases, could this automation not be only an imitation of mathematical reasoning?

I would like to express my warmest thanks to Yves Kodratoff. I am also grateful to Professors A. Bierman , W. W. Bledsoe, R. Boyer, A. Bundy, G. Kreisel, J.-L. Remy and R. Waldinger for the encouragement.

REFERENCES

[bledsoe01] Bledsoe W.W., Henschen L.J.: What is Automated Theorem Proving? Journal of Automated Reasoning, vol. 1, No. 1, 1985, pp. 23-28.

[boyer-moore01] R.S.Boyer, J.S.Moore: A Computational Logic; Academic Press, 1979.

[boyer01] R.S. Boyer: personal comunication during IJCAI-85, August 1985, Los Angeles.

[bundy01] A. Bundy: Discovery and Reasoning in Mathematics, in: Proceedings of the Ninth International Joint Conference on Artificial Intelligence, 1985, Los Angeles, pp. 1221-1231.

[franova03] M.Fraňová: CM - Strategy - A Formalization of "cheating" for Inductive Theorem Proving and Automatic Programming; Rapport de Recherche No.222, L.R.I., Orsay, Jully 1985.

[franova06] M.Fraňová: Inventing is Moderate Cheating or a Theory of Humble Invention; to appear: in Symposium Proceedings Cognitiva '85, CESTA - AFCET, June 1985, pp.535-540.

[franova09] M.Fraňová: Constructive Proofs in "Constructable Types"; in: Proceedings of Cinquième Congrès Reconnaissance des formes et Intelligence Artificielle; Grenoble, 27-29 Nov. 1985, pp. 345-360.

[franova10] M.Fraňová: CM-strategy : A Methodology for Inductive Theorem Proving or Constructive Well-Generalized Proofs, in: Proceedings of the Ninth International Joint Conference on Artificial Intelligence, August 1985, Los Angeles, pp. 1214-1220.

[wos01] L. Wos: What is Automated Reasoning; JAR, Vol.1, No.1, (1985), pp. 6-9.

STOCHASTIC LOGICAL EXPRESSIONS

István Ratkó
Computer and Automation Institute Hungarian
Academy of Sciences
Budapest, Victor Hugo u. 18-22, H-1132
Hungary

ABSTRACT. The problem was raised by a large data processing
task. Let be given a data file with fixed record length.
The users are often interested in data satisfying certain
conditions are given by logical expressions. How can we best
build the logical expressions into the program? On the last
meeting we presented a method of solving of the problem. In
this lecture we review the new results of the applied mathematical method.

1. INTRODUCTION

1.1. The mathematical background of the problem

Consider the logical expressions

$$L = L_1 \, or \, L_2 \, or \ldots or \, L_N, \text{ where}$$

$$L_i = L_{i1} \, and \, L_{i2} \, and \ldots and \, L.$$

$$(i = 1, 2, \ldots N)$$

Definition We call the number

$$r(L) = 1_1 + 1_2 + \ldots + 1_k + a_{k+1}$$

the evaluating number of L iff the 1_j-th conjunction of the
L_j disjunction is false, the 1-st, 2-nd, ..., (1_j-1)-th
conjunction are true $(j = 1, 2, \ldots, k)$, L_{k+1} is true and the
number of the conjunctions in L_{k+1} is a_{k+1}. If L_1 is true, let
$r(L)$ be a_1. It is obvious that $r(L)$ depends on the order
of the disjunctions and the order of conjunctions within
the particular disjunction. $r(L)$ is a random variable for
(assuming a given order) its value depends on random [2]
The minimization of the expected value of $r(L)$ i.e. $Er(L)$

887

R. Trappl (ed.), Cybernetics and Systems '86, 887–892.
© 1986 by D. Reidel Publishing Company.

dealt with.

1.2. Literary survey

In this section we try to survey the relation between the
optimization method suggested by us, specially our model and
the known models as well as methods.
    For this purpose we restrict ourselves to the examina-
tion of the connections with a) the decision tables b) the
minimization of Boole-function systems c) the analysis of
decisions.

1.2.1. *The decision tables*

Our problem can be formulated by a decision table: (the conditions are connected by AND, the rules by EXCLUSUVE OR .
It can be noticed that this special decision table as an
identical activity should be performed, except the rule
OTHER.
    Out of the three phases (reduction of rules, breakdown
of the table, rearrangement of the table) of the optimization of decision tables the third shows any affinity with
the our problem. This affinity covers its following points
of view: a required rule should be found with a minimal
number of decisions and the order of the rules in the table
should comply with the frequency of application of the particular rules. The attainment of this goal is promoted
among other by the various known optimization algorithms.
    It is obvious from the above that with the decision
tables optimize one thing and with our problem another.

1.2.2. *The minimization of Boole-function systems*

The disjunctive normal form is *minimal*, if it contains the
least letter of the disjunctive normal forms equivalent to
it; *shortest*, if its length is least of the disjunctive
normal forms equivalent to it. It is quite obvious that
these minimization tasks have *another* purpose so that results obtained there cannot be applied to our case.

1.2.3. *Decision analysis*

Assume that decider can choose among the strategies: S_1,
$S_2,\ldots,S_t$. Whichever he takes however, he must reckon with
one of the consequiencies: $K_1,K_2,\ldots,K_r$. We suppose that
the probabilities $p_{i,j}=P(K_j IS_i)$ as known, their meaning is
obvious. Of course

$$\sum_{i=1}^{r} p_{i,j}=1 \quad \text{for every j.}$$

888

There exists a real-valued function f defined on the set of consequencies for which $f(K_j) = f(K_1)$ iff the decider consider the consequence K_j of an importance greater, equal less than K_1. The function f is unique up to a positive linear transformation. Examine the next problem: which strategy results in the optimal decision in the following sentence: prefer the strategy S_i for which

$$\sum_{j=1}^{r} P_{i,j} f(K_j) \quad \text{is maximal. [1]}$$

Now look, how our enquiries can be put together with this model. The strategies $S_1, S_2, \ldots, S_t$ now correspond to the respective order of the disjunctions and within it to that of conjunctions. If the evaulating number of the logical expression is j then we say that the consequence K_j is realized.

Let $f(K_j) = -j$. The question: for which i the expression

$$-\sum_{j=1}^{r} P(K_j IS_j) j \quad \text{will be maximal?}$$

The question of this model is thus identical with our question raised in the introduction.

The difference resides in the structure of the starting data: the probabilities of the models do not coincide; the expression of one by the other and via versa causes serious difficulties in counting.

This, of course, does not exclude the possibility of the disclosure by further examinations of the muthual applicability of the results obtained in the two models.

2. RESULTS

Example 1   Let $L = L_{11}$ *or* $(L_{21}$ *and* $L_{22})$ and assume that

$$P(L_{21}.EQ.TRUE) \quad P(L_{22}.EQ.TRUE)$$

and the events $B_1 = L_{11}.EQ.TRUE$, $B_2 = L_{21}.EQ.TRUE$, $B_3 = L_{22}.EQ.TRUE$ are independent from each other. Let further be

$$L^+ = L_{11} \text{ } and \text{ } (L_{22} \text{ } and \text{ } L_{21}).$$

Is $Er(L)$ or $Er(L^+)$ greater?
It can be seen that $Er(L) < Er(L^+)$.

We can say that if we interchange the order of the elementary statement L_{21} and L_{22} then the evaluation of L come earlier to an end than of L^+.

This is generally not true. This is shown by

Example 2 Retaining the notations of the preceding example
we know the following:

$$P(B_1B_2B_3)=1/8-p \quad P(\bar{B}_1B_2B_3)=1/8-p \quad P(B_1\bar{B}_2B_3)=1/8+2p$$

$$P(B_1B_2\bar{B}_3)=1/8 \quad P(B_1\bar{B}_2\bar{B}_3)=1/8-p \quad P(\bar{B}_1B_2\bar{B}_3)=1/8+p$$

$$P(\bar{B}_1\bar{B}_2B_3)=1/8 \quad P(\bar{B}_1\bar{B}_2\bar{B}_3)=1/8$$

where $p<1/8$. What can we say about the relationship between
$Er(L)$ and $Er(L_+)$?
Now $Er(L) > Er(L^+)$.
     On the basis of the examples we can see that the
exchange of two elementary statements can both decrease and
increase the expected value of the evaluating number.
Examine now this problem generally. For this goes

Theorem 1 Let be

$$L=L_1 \, or L_2 \, or \ldots or L_j \, or(\ldots and L' \, and L'' \, and \ldots) or \ldots or L_N \text{ and}$$

$$L^+=L_1 \, or L_2 \, or \ldots or L_j \, and(\ldots and L'' \, and L' \, and \ldots) or \ldots or L_N$$

where L' and L'' are elementary statements. Then $Er(L) < Er(L^+)$
iff $P(L'=true|A) \, P(L''=true|A)$ where $A=(L_k$ is false
$(k=1,2,\ldots j)$, in L_{j+1} the elementary statements before L'
are true).

Definition Let us say that the elementary statements L'
and L'' are *independent* from each other if the $(L'=true)$ and
$(L''=true)$ events are independent.

Definition The disjunctions L_1 and L_2 are *independent*
from each other if every $L' \in L_1$ and $L'' \in L_2$ elementary sta-
tements(L' and L'') are independent from each other.
     In the following we shall examine some special cases.

Corollary 1 Assume that any two statements of expression
L are independent from each another. Then $Er(L) < Er(L^+)$ iff

$$P(L'=true) < P(L''=true).$$

     This is an immediate consequence of theorem 1.

Corollary 2 Assume that any two disjunctions are independent from each other. Let B the next event:
B=(In L_{j+1} the elementary statements preceding L' are true).
(c.f. the notations of theorem 1) In this case $Er(L) < Er(L^+)$
iff
$$P(L'=true|B) < P(L''=true|B).$$

890

Examine thereafter what we can say in the case of the exchange of two juxtaposed disjunctions about the evaluating number? Consider first an example.

Example 3 Let $L=L_{11}or(L_{21}andL_{22})$ $L^+=(L_{21}andL_{22})orL_{11}$

and assume that $B_1=(L_{11}=true)$, $B_2=(L_{21}=true)$, $B_3=(L_{22}=true)$ events are independent from each other.
Compare $Er(L)$ with $Er(L^+)$!
Because of independence it follows with elementary transformations that $Er(L)<Er(L^+)$ iff

$$\frac{1-2P(B_3)}{2-P(B_2)-P(B_3)} < P(B_1)$$

If $P(B_3)>1/2$ then this will obviously be fulfilled regardless of the order of magnitude of relation between the probabilities $P(B_1)$ and $P(B_2)$.
Without a detailed analysis of the latter inequality it can be seen that the exchange of two juxtaposed disjunctions presents even with a so simple assumption, a more diversified picture than the exchange of two juxtaposed conjunctions.
Consider the problem more generally.

Let $L=L_1orL_2or...orL_{j-1}orL_jorL_{j+1}orL_{j+2}or...orL_N$,

$L^+=L_1orL_2or...orL_{j-1}orL_{j+1}orL_jorL_{j+2}or...orL_N$ and

$A=(L_1=false, L_2=false,..., L_{j-1}=false)$.

Theorem 2 $Er(L)<Er(L^+)$ iff
$a_jP(L_j=true, L_{j+1}=true,A)+E[r(L_j)IL_j=false, L_{j+1}=true,A]\cdot$

$\cdot P(L_j=false, L_{j+1}=true)<$

$a_{j+1}P(L_j=true, L_{j+1}=true,A)+E[r(L_{j+1})IL_j=true, L_{j+1}=false,A]\cdot$

$\cdot P(L_j=true, L_{j+1}=false)$.

Consider a special case.

Corollary 3 Assume that any two disjunctions of L are independent of each other. Then $Er(L)<Er(L^+)$ iff

$$\frac{Er(L_j)}{P(L_j=false)} < \frac{Er(L_{j+1})}{P(L_{j+1}=false)}$$

Hereinafter we try to answer the question formulated at the end of introduction on the basis of theorems and corollaries.

Theorem 3   We set the logical expressions

$$L = L_1 \, or \, L_2 \, or \ldots or \, L_N, \text{ where}$$

$$L_j = L_{j1} \, and \, L_{j2} \, and \ldots and \, L_{jq} \quad (j = 1, 2, \ldots, N)$$

Assume that any two elementary statements of L are independent of each other.

For simplicity's sake assume the following: we have choosen the indicies so that

$$\frac{Er(L_1)}{P(L_1 = false)} < \frac{Er(L_2)}{P(L_2 = false)} < \ldots \frac{E(r(L_N))}{P(L_N = false)} \quad \text{(1a)}$$

$$P(L_{j1} = true) < P(L_{j2} = true) < \ldots < P(L_{jq_N} = true) \quad \text{(1b)}$$

Let L^+ be an arbitrary logical expression which originated from L by an exchange of conjunctions or disjunctions in the already mentioned way. Then $Er(L) < Er(L^+)$ i.e. $Er(L)$ will be minimal for such an order of disjunctions and conjunctions, respectively, for which (1a) and (1b) will be fulfilled.

References

[1] Fishburn.P.C.: Decision and value theory, John Wiley and sons, New York, 1964.
[2] István Ratkó: On evaulating of logical expression in programming languages, EMCS'84, Cybernetics and Systems Research 2., 1984, pp.611-613.
 3 Krámli A., Ruda M., Csukás M., Galambos M.: Large sample size statistical information system for HwB, EMCS'80, Data Analysis and Informatics, 1980, pp. 457-462.

A FORMALISM FOR SPECIFYING SOFTWARE GENERATION.

B.H.Rudall,
University College of North Wales, Bangor,
Gwynedd, LL57 1LD,
United Kingdom.

ABSTRACT. The use of computing machines involves the design, development and generation of software. Consideration is now given to the methods of formalizing these processes. In particular, methods of formalizing the process of generation, and the development of a mathematical notation to describe the production of software is outlined. It is shown that these notations allow for both the description and documentation of complex programming systems, and provide a mathematical basis for the extension of their properties. A formal notation is applied to describe software production applications, with particular attention to the problem of the transfer of software from one computing environment to another.

1. INTRODUCTION

Man's inter-relationship with the computer constitutes one of the most important studies in cybernetics. Current technology dictates that the computer user communicates with the machine through an interface which is largely controlled by the stored pre-assigned algorithms. The design development and the implementation of these algorithms is now a major concern in the race to produce new and more powerful computer systems.

Whilst computers are used to design and build these new machines, their use in preparing efficient algorithms, and the means of their representation in hardware, software or any other form has been very slow to develop.

The strategy of producing, for example, the machine software by automatic means is accepted, but the actual means of specification of the software and its exact means of generation are not sufficiently advanced to be generally used. Indeed, the principles and the techniques for generating software in this way, and the need to improve the man-machine interface by reducing 'program-writing', or 'software-programming' are accepted to be amoung the most ambitious research projects in computing and cybernetics.

Before software can be produced by conventional means or by some desirable methods which use automation, it has to be specified, and the

893

R. Trappl (ed.), Cybernetics and Systems '86, 893–900.

actual means of its production defined. This paper discusses a method
of describing in a formal way, the software to be produced and the
processes of generating it, using, where possible, the computing
machine itself.

2.0 METHODS OF SOFTWARE GENERATION.

It is now recognised that because the type of machine changes, the
facilities of existing high level computerlanguages are improved, and new
programming languages and software packages are introduced, software
has to be continually written or rewritten. The need, therefore, to
find ways of 'automating' the process is becoming of increasing
importance. Many software producers have developed 'software tools',
which are usually associated with particular software packages, to
enable their products to be specified and produced. Most of these
methods rely on the proven, 'cross-assembler technique'[1], the
'modelling or simulation technique' [2] or the use of a program
generator' which is simply a package developed to produce a program
of limited specification. [3]

3.0 SPECIFICATION OF SOFTWARE.

Although software is being produced by the conventional manual methods,
and in some instances by more automated means using the machines themselves, it is still badly defined and the means of its generation not
properly specified. Even the documentation describing how the computer
user can use the software is poor. The problems of producing a
complete specification of software packages, for example, would have to
contain not only the program text, but also the language compiler texts,
and   the machine's own 'hardware' specifications. Consequently it
is unlikely that the complete specifications of such a program, which
would necessarily be incomplete, would be required.

Many scientists have, however, produced techniques and notations
for incomplete specifications. Many of these specifications are
sufficiently precise and complete that other programs can be written to
interact with the specified software without additional information.

Similarly any notation that attempts to describe software production must necessarily be incomplete. But even the incomplete
specifications could be sufficiently precise to define a production
process in such a way that the new software could be produced automatically from existing software. Such a formalism has been designed
by the author[4] who has developed a formal notation to describe the
interactions of the pe-assigned algorithms of the computing machine
in the particular context of the program language processing system.

Although this has become a widely used, essentially graphical,
notation, an equivalent mathematical notation is being developed.

The system does, however, allow for the interactions between language compilers, interpreters, assemblers of a language processing system whether in a single or multi-computer environment to be described.

4. A NOTATION FOR DESCRIBING SOFTWARE PRODUCTION

Many of the major items used to describe software are ill defined. Compiler, translator, interpreter, processor, generator are only a few examples of the terms used to describe particular types of programs. Often the term 'transformation' is used to describe the action of a program. The program during its execution has a function which performs the transformation. A Pascal compiler could perhaps perform the function of transforming a program written in the language of Pascal to the machine language of a particular computer. Obviously each 'transform' must be properly defined. Similarly in the production of software by a given program the details of the production must be described.

In general the transform or production can be defined by the triple $(P, Q, F,)$ where P and Q are non-empty sets and to each element x in P there corresponds an element denoted by $f(x)$, in Q. A production defined by the function f of producing a program $P2$ from $P1$ would be denoted by $(P1, P2, f)$.

Much more information is, of course, required about the form and function of f. For example, the language in which f is described, the machine specified for its execution, the efficiency of the process, the method used for the production, the actual action of f during the execution by the computing machine. Such a specification is in fact better written in the form of n-tuples:

$$(P_1, P_2, P_3, \ldots . P_n)$$

where the n properties of the production are defined in the parameters $P_1, \ldots . P_n$.

4.1 Introduction to the P-Notation

It has been found that a more restricted form of the specification of a production is acceptable in describing a software production. The function form of P with its parameters has proved a convenient form. For the production of software required for the language processing systems the number of parameters P can be restricted to four.

This allows, for example, a language compiler T, written in a language 1 which compiles a program written in a language l_1, to another language l_2 on a machine to be described by:

$$T(l_1, l_2, l, M)$$

4.2 Definitions in P-notation

Several interesting and important features of software production can be exhibited using this notation, which in the case of software for language processing is restricted to the form for <u>production function</u> P:

P(L1,L2,L,M)

where L1 is the input language, L2 the output language and L is the language in which the production program P has been written. M is the machine specified for the execution.

A set of specifications S, which may of course, be another program, is defined as:

S(L,M)

where the specification is written in language L for execution on machine M.

An additional metalinguistic connective $\rightarrow$ is defined to mean 'input to or output from' a production.

For example, a Pascal compiler P, written in machine language ML for a machine M which is capable of compiling Pascal to ML would be described by:

P(Pascal,ML,ML,M)

and a Pascal program, which is a set of specifications written in Pascal, by:

S(Pascal,M)

The action of production would be described by:

S(Pascal,M)$\rightarrow$ P(Pascal,ML,ML,M)$\rightarrow$ S(ML,M)

In other words a piece of software specified as S is presented as input to the software production function P, which in turn automatically produces S specified in the language ML.

The specification S(ML,M) can, of course, be executed on machine M since it is now specified in the machine language ML of M. The metaconnective $\wedge$ can be used to indicate this execution.

4.3 Examples of software production

Many of the processes for software production which have a degree of automation, particularly language processing systems can be conveniently described in the P-notation. [5]

4.3.1 Production of a Pre-processor. A pre-processor W for a word processing system WORDTEXT, written and specified in Pascal (Pas) for a microcomputer QM, which has machine language QML, could be produced using the QM's Pascal compiler PQ. In P-notation it would be described by:

$$W(WT,Pas,Pas,QM) \rightarrow PQ(Pas,QML,QML,QM) \rightarrow W(WT,Pas,QML,QM)^\wedge$$

where WT is the command language of WORDTEXT.
The pre processor W is now available, in the language QML which can be directly executed on the microcomputer QM. Consequently any set S of commands for WORDTEXT can be executed:

$$S(WT,QM) \rightarrow W(WT,Pas,QML,QM) \rightarrow S(Pas,QM) \rightarrow PQ(Pas,QML,QML,QM) \rightarrow S(QML,QM)^\wedge$$

The final software production $S(QML,QM)$, the commands for a WORDTEXT program, are directly executed. This is a practical software production exercise, where Pascal was used as a specification language for WORDTEXT and the Pascal compiler for the microcomputer QM was used in a 'compiler-compiler' role.

4.3.2 Production of software using a Specification Language. If an acceptable specification language SL has been defined the process of preparing a software package Z, specified in SL for use on a machine M, which has ML as its language, is simply defined as:

$$Z(ZL,ML,SL,M) \rightarrow P(SL,ML,ML,M) \rightarrow Z(ZL,ML,ML,M)$$

where ZL is the command language of the package Z, and P is an established compiler that translates SL into ML on the machine M. Any set of specifications S written in ZL can now be executed on machine M:

$$S(ZL,M) \rightarrow Z(ZL,ML,ML,M) \rightarrow S(ML,M)^\wedge$$

4.3.3 Production of Software in a Multi-machine Environment. It is in a multi-machine environment that a describing notation must be regarded a essential. Many software production problems arise in such an environment when it is required to transfer one piece of software from one machine in a range to another. Often the well known methods of compiler conversion or bootstrapping are used.
    If for example, it is required to transfer a compiler CL for a language L which functions on a machine M1 which has machine language ML1, to another machine M2 with machine language ML2 a metalanguage of some form is required.

Using the P-notation the process can be described in three stages:

Stage 1

$$CL(L,ML2,L,M1) \rightarrow CL(L,ML1,ML1,M1) \rightarrow CL(L,ML2,ML1,M1)=Cl'(say)$$

Stage 2

$$CL(L,ML2,L,M1) \rightarrow CL' \rightarrow CL(L,ML2,ML2,M2)=CL''(say)$$

$$S(L,M2) \rightarrow CL'' \rightarrow S(ML2,M2)^{\wedge}$$

where CL'' is the compiler for L produced for execution on the machine M2. Any program specified by S, written in L can now be processed on another machine range.

This technique enables successively more advanced versions of CL to be produced for the language L, and transferred as required, automatically to other machine ranges.

5. Production of software using a Universal Compiling Language

If an acceptable universal compiling language UCL is available many of the specifications for the generation of new software can be simplified. If a machine called M1 has a compiler P for UCL then using one of the many 'compiler-compiler', or 'bootstrapping' techniques, new compilers, or software packages can be specified in UCL and generated. Let the machine language of M1 be ML1.

5.1 UCL in a single-machine environment.

To produce a new compiler for a language L on the machine M, the steps described in the P-notation would be:

$$C(L,ML1,UCL,M1) \longrightarrow P(UCL,ML1,ML1,M1) \longrightarrow C(L,ML1,ML1,M1)$$

$$\text{and, } S(L,M1) \longrightarrow C(L,ML1,ML1,M1) \longrightarrow S(ML1,M1)^{\wedge}$$

where C is the compiler required for the new language L and P is the established compiler for UCL on machine M1. S is any set of specifications for a program written in L

5.2 Extending UC1 in a single-machine environment

The compiler language UCL could be implemented on a machine M1 by writing, initially, a compiler P^1 for a simple version of UCL called UCL^1. A more sophisticated version of UCL, UCL^2 could be generated by writing a new compiler P^2 in UCL^1. Similarly new versions of UCL called UCL^3, UCL^4 .... UCL^{n+1} are produced using successively UCL^2, UCL^3 .... UCL^n.

This process of 'self-generation' would be specified as:

$$P^{i+1}(UCL^{i+1},ML1,UCL^i,M1) \longrightarrow P^i(UCL^i,ML1,ML1,M1)$$

$$\longrightarrow P^{i+1}(UCL^{i+1},ML1,ML1,M1)$$

for i = 1, 2, 3.......n.

The compiler P^{n+1} could now be used to produce compilers for other languages, or for extending the facilities of UCL. The work entailed updating P^{i+1} can be performed with the minimum of labour if the initial program is written in a systematic way, using a dictionary of terms and ML1 code translations.

5.3 Transfer of compilers in a Multimachine Environment

A recent application of the P-notation was to describe how a compiler for UCL could be transferred or converted to run on other machines in a multimachine environment. Using the techniques described in 5.2 more advanced versions of UCL were generated on M1 and transferred to machine M2. The i+1 th version of UCL, UCL^{i+1} produced on M1 is converted for M2 by the process:

$$P_2^{i+1} \; (UCL^{i+1}, ML2, UCL^{i+1}, M1) \longrightarrow Pi+1 \; (UCL^{i+1}, ML1, ML1, M1) \longrightarrow$$

$$P_2^{i+1} \; (UCL^{i+1}, ML2, ML1, M1)$$

which becomes P_2^{i+1} $(UCL^{i+1}, ML2, ML2, M2)$ the required compiler

when,

$$P_2^{i+1} \; (UCL^{i+1}, ML2, UCL^{i+1}, M1) \longrightarrow P_2^{i+1} (UCL^{i+1}, ML2, ML1, M1) \longrightarrow$$

$$P_2^{i+1} \; (UCL^{i+1}, ML2, ML2, M1)$$

is completed. P_2^{i+1} is the range of compilers for M2.

This specification allows for the generation of a variety of compliers with different facilities for both machines, whether only one or both machines are available.

6. Realization of the P-notation

The authors own extended T-notation has already provided a useful software tool and is used widely[4]. The development of a computerized version of the P-notation to provide a realistic production specification system is proceeding.

Obviously it is highly desirable that any metalanguage used to describe the production of software on a computing machine should itself be automated. A suite of procedures called SOFTEXT has been designed so that production processes can be described and executed using a computer system which preferably, has a graphics capability.

Currently the system consists of ten interlinked procedures which allow for the description of software production in the P-notation. The system is being developed to allow interaction between the user and the package, and graphical displays using the T-notation are to be provided. Already it has proved a most useful educational aid for teaching

899

computing.

7. CONCLUSIONS

The development of tools for the more efficient and cost effective
production of software is now becoming more prevalent. Unfortunately
most are confined to a particular software producer or system. The
notations and methodologies described in this paper are of more general
nature and allow for the software designer to interact with a machine
using these formal notions to describe the specifications of his designs,
and the proposed methods of generation. The next phase of this research
will concentrate on implementing these formal notations on current
machines.

8. REFERENCES

[1] Rudall,B.H 'Microprocessor in Cybernetics the Software Approach', In:
Computers & Cybernetics, Abacus Press, London, 1981, pp 142 - 152.

[2] Shepheard, N.T., Rudall, B.H., and Coates, R.F.W.,'Using the DEC-
System-10 to Model Multi-microprocessor Systems', In: Proceedings
of the DEC Symposium, Volume 7, Amsterdam, 1981, pp 91 - 98

[3] Naylor, C., Choosing and using a program generator, Sigma Technical
Press, London, 1984.

[4] Rudall, B.H., 'A Cybernetic Approach to Program Language Processing
Systems', In: Computers & Cybernetics, Abacus Press, London 1981,
pp 107 - 121.

[5] Rudall, B.H., 'Towards Automatic Software Generation', In: Robotica,
Cambridge University Press, Volume 3, Number 1, 1985, pp 31 - 34.

9. ACKNOWLEDGEMENT

This research is supported by Computer Science International,
United Kingdom. (0248) 712636.

MODULARISATION IN EDDA-S, A DATA FLOW DESIGN LANGUAGE
SUPPORTING INCREMENTAL SOFTWARE DEVELOPMENT

Renate Pitrik
Institut fuer Angewandte Informatik und Systemanalyse
Technische Universitaet Wien
Argentinierstrasse 8, A-1040 Wien, Austria

ABSTRACT. Current established software engineering methods suggest a
variety of specification and design techniques during the development
process. Novel functional or data flow methods, although employing a
unified approach by coherent decomposition of data flow diagrams, could
not be appreciated as a satisfactory solution to a wide range of problems. This paper suggests a hybrid approach integrating data flow with
established, classical design concepts. A pure design language, termed
EDDA-S, being independent of any specific programming language will be
introduced. The emphasis will be on the partitioning of a data flow
system model into modules, the description of the interconnections among
these modules and the role of a pure design language to support the
development process.

1 INTRODUCTION

The demand on computer applications with ever increasing complexity and
requirements on high quality let cost expenditures for software grow
rapidly. - Investigations into the means of raising software productivity show the importance of the early phases of software development and
strongly suggest to support them by formal approaches. Thereby inconsistencies and ambiguities shall be avoided which are most costly if
appearing in specification and design documents /Boeh 81/.
    Discomfort with the traditional software production which empha-
sizes the implementation phase and often leads to unsatisfactory
solutions regarding cost, time, the final system, etc., encourages
research into novel approaches /Rama 84/. Integrated environments
supporting the whole life cycle and providing formal means to be used
already at early phases are being developed.
    While modularisation is part of modern programming languages such
as Modula-2 /Wirt 82/ or ADA /ADA 80/, our goal with EDDA-S is to
provide a simple, graphical design language which on one hand is easily
derivable from a functional specification and on the other hand allows
for a straightforward transition to the implementation phase.
    The emphasis in this paper will be on the modularisation concept of

901

R. Trappl (ed.), Cybernetics and Systems '86, 901–908.
© *1986 by D. Reidel Publishing Company.*

EDDA-S which differs from current practices due to the *data flow* (DF) and pure *design* nature of EDDA-S. Furthermore it will be shown how EDDA-S modules support the transition to the implementation phase and contribute to a stepwise construction of software, called incremental development, whereby the design and implementation of modules may be interleaved.

Since EDDA-S is based on DF principles we first relate the DF approach to the conventional development process /Boeh 81/, /Zave 84/. In the third chapter EDDA-S with special emphasis on modularisation will be presented. Finally the role of EDDA-S in supporting incremental development will be discussed.

2 CONVENTIONAL SOFTWARE DEVELOPMENT AND THE DATA FLOW APPROACH

In *conventional* software development the specification phase is used to define the problem to be solved stating both functional and nonfunctional requirements on the system's external behaviour ("what") but not being explicit about the internal structure ("how"). During the design phase the internal structure of the system providing a decomposition into modules is determined. The modules are designed to produce the required behaviour, provide a program structure which is easy to understand, and meet the required constraints using the defined resources.

The DF approach differs from conventional software development in several aspects. Since DF graphs offer a graphical representation of DF languages /Hend 80/, /Acke 82/, /KePi 84/ which exposes the problem structure in a natural way and at the same time can be used to express function decomposition, DF languages are useful during the whole development process. During the specification phase the system is defined using DF graphs which serve as the formal functional specification. Stepwise refinement of DF graphs is employed up to the programming language level resulting in executable code. Since the resulting structure is problem oriented but not implementation oriented, transformations have to be performed to reconfigure the system to meet performance requirements /ViRa 84/. (The transformation step is not necessary if a DF computer providing nearly unlimited resources is available to execute the program.)

While in the conventional approach program code is to be written only at a very late stage, in the DF approach code is produced (no matter how inefficiently) almost immediately from the specification. The advantage of this proceeding is that a single language is used for the whole development process thus eliminating the errorprone transitions between different representations /TrKe 78/, /Kern 83/. On the other hand, if executable code shall be produced from the specification, the corresponding language has to be unforgiving in enforcing the formulation of every detail which results in complex and overloaded diagrams.

With EDDA-S we try to bridge this gap by *combining* the clear DF graph representation with a simple modularisation mechanism to design systems being implementable using conventional programming languages which are well supported by several programming environments.

3 THE DESIGN LANGUAGE EDDA-S

3.1 Design criteria

EDDA-S was designed under the following objectives:

- being a design language EDDA-S shall support the main
  activities of the design phase including the
  - description of the system and data structure
  - description of the interconnections of system parts
  - partitioning of the system into modules;

- EDDA-S shall be a pure *design* language in so far, as it gives a
  concise but (unlike its predescessor EDDA /TrKe 78/) programming
  language independent description of a system;

- support of *incremental* design and a simple, computer aided,
  structure preserving transition to the implementation phase so
  that implementation is limited to coding a module's *local* information.

3.2 The EDDA-S design model

An EDDA-S design model consists of four parts:

i)   The *activity* diagram part resulting from functional
     decomposition of activities and of data abstractions;
An EDDA-S activity diagram basically is a DF graph consisting of nodes
and arcs. The hierarchic organization of activity diagrams results in an
SADT-like structure /Ross 77/.
ii) The *type* diagram part which contains the logical
     descriptions of all data types appearing in activity diagrams;
The basic structured types in EDDA-S are identical with those used in
JSD /Jack 75/ but include selectors to allow for access to components of
structured data values.
iii) Specifications of *module interfaces* called EDDA-S windows;
iv) The so called *uses-graph* displaying the import relationship among
     modules.
More information on EDDA-S can be found in /Kern 85/, /Pitr 85a/.

3.3 Modularisation in EDDA-S

Unlike in a pure DF approach where DF graphs are refined up to the
program code level we proceed by using EDDA-S activity and data type
diagrams as starting points for the derivation of modules.
    There is no doubt that the partitioning of a problem into (mostly)
independent parts, generally called modules, offers several advantages.
These advantages are even more eminent if modules are not only used to
collect related subprograms and declarations (known for a long time as
procedural abstraction) but are also used to introduce some more modern
concepts like
    - all kinds of abstraction mechanisms
    - encapsulation of data

- separate compilation (with checking of interfaces)
- combined top down and bottom up design by seperating module definition from module implementation.

It can be seen from modular languages that the kernel of a modularisation concept can be designed almost *independently* of any specific high level language /Pitr 85b/. This is exactly the approach followed in EDDA-S. Being a pure design language based on data flow principles, the EDDA-S modularisation concept can be designed for great simplicity as will be argued in due course.

Some interesting discussions on modularisation can be found e.g. in /DeKr 76/,/Wirt 82/,/DoGo 82/.

3.3.1 Different kinds of modules
While conventional languages offer the module (or else called package, unit, ...) as such without explicitly considering different types, in EDDA-S we distinguish between *different* kinds of modules as shown in Tab. 1.

name	usage	comment
<u>activity</u> module	kernel of program;	imports subsidiary modules; an activity module corresponds to a part of the main program;
<u>collection</u> module	provides a collection of - type declarations - constant declarations - subprograms (with functional behaviour);	related declarations are defined in one place;
<u>adt</u> module (abstract data type)	definition of a data type with associated operations;	many instances of variables of adt may be defined in importing modules;
<u>database</u> module	encapsulation of data objects and procedures manipulating these objects;	for each object defined exactly one instance exists; provides history sensitivity;

Tab. 1: Categorization of EDDA-S modules

The explicit categorization of modules in EDDA-S enhances understandability in showing the role of a module at first glance.

904

3.3.2 Derivation of modules

While modular languages are not explicit about how to derive modules, the graphical representation of EDDA-S offers a good point to start with.

Activity modules can be derived directly from the nodes of the DF graph. It will depend on the size and structure of the problem and on the nonfunctional requirements, which nodes from what level of abstraction one should choose to be modules. The criteria for a good modularisation as proposed by the SD method presented e.g. in /JoCo 79/ are applicable as a good orientation in constructing modules. Especially the criterium of communication, which, according to SD should be as small as possible, is directly visible from the DF diagram representation: the number of data paths and their associated types explicitly determine the degree of communication. The criterium of maximal possible coherence should be fulfilled implicitly since functional decomposition is employed in constructing the EDDA-S model.

A type *collection* module can be taken to include the definitions of all data types used in more than one activity module. The individual type definitions are directly derived (possibly with refinements) from the type diagrams. Subprograms without history sensitivity not being local to one module are also defined in collection modules. An import clause in the "consumer" modules makes the appropriate subprograms accessible to those modules.

In *adt* (abstract data type) modules a data type together with its operations is defined. By importing an adt module any number of variables of the abstract data type may be defined in every importing module. In contrast, database modules are used to introduce global objects: for each variable defined within a database module there exists exactly one instance of the object defined. Additionally declarations of procedures to manipulate these objects are included. By using *database* modules, history sensitivity according to the objects encapsulated in a database module is provided.

3.3.3 Module and program structure in EDDA-S

Besides some well known advantages of modular languages (as mentioned before) EDDA-S modules are designed to fulfill some additional requirements:

i) all *interconnections* between modules should be specified on one module level and be visible by inspecting the specification part of a module (called window) only;

ii) visibility and scoping rules shall be very simple and straightforward;

iii) the module level shall offer a *transition* between the graphical DF graph representation and its textual coding and be independent of any specific implementation language.

In order to allow for separate compilation, top down and bottom up design, and to fulfill the requirements listed above, an EDDA-S model consists of a partitioning of the problem into modules in such a way that all identifiers which shall be accessible by more than one of these modules must be included in the window of some module. While this position implicitly makes these identifiers available for export, the name of the exporting module must explicitly be included in the importlists of all "consumer" modules.

As shown in Fig. 1, EDDA-S modules consist of two parts, a window and an implementation part which form a logical unit. While the *window* of a module includes the import list and forms an interface to the rest of the program, the *implementation* part contains the detailed coding which is hidden from the "outside". Since windows as well as implementation parts of modules may be compiled seperatly, it suffices to provide the windows of modules in order to check the importing modules for consistency of the interfaces. The implementation parts of the windows provided may be coded later and added to the system in a bottom up fashion.

| module identifier <u>window</u>
uses:importlist
export:
procedure headers
available for export | module identifier <u>implementation</u>

procedure headers plus bodies
and/or implementation of private
program parts |

Fig. 1: The overall structure of a module

In EDDA-S (unlike Modula-2 or ADA) modules may *not* be *nested*. This is because the same effect of establishing a scope within one module can be reached by defining a module at the same level and importing it to just one module. The single module level structure in EDDA-S has the advantage of allowing for very simple scoping rules. In combination with the fact that the imports of a module (i.e. those of the window as well as the implementation part) are listed in its window part, all the interconnections between modules can be seen by inspecting the single level of the window parts only.

4 TRANSITION TO THE IMPLEMENTATION PHASE

The window level of EDDA-S modules forms a link between the graphical design representation and its textual coding. We use a preprocessor to transform EDDA-S models directly into specification modules of some modular language (e.g. VAX-Pascal or ADA) and to generate skeletons of implementation modules. In our approach the structure of the design is directly used to create the structure of the program. In this way a clear transition, in which the usage of all identifiers can be traced, is achieved. Since the program structure is generated from the design, module implementation solely comprises the coding of information local to every module.

5 THE ROLE OF EDDA-S IN THE SOFTWARE DEVELOPMENT PROCESS

As mentioned before, the primary objective of EDDA-S is to support the construction of high quality software to run on conventional computer architectures.- Keeping in mind the problems with the data flow

approach, which are
- unforgiveness in respect to details and rigidity in the specification phase;
- lack of tool supported transformations leading to efficient code;

and its advantages being
- continuous support of the whole life cycle using a single language;
- provision of a problem oriented, implementation independent representation;

we suggest to combine the data flow with the conventional approach to compensate for the inadequacies of the former. Since the design and implementation of different modules may be interleaved an incremental construction of a system is possible, a great advantage for system extensions.

The price to be paid for providing a programming language independent design language is that just code *skeletons* but not complete programs can be generated automatically (to produce efficient code). If this were aimed at, a remarkably larger degree of detail information and rigidity would be necessary in the design phase which is nöt desirable.

6 CONCLUSION

In this paper we investigated the design phase and used it to integrate data flow and conventional concepts to suggest a design language to support an incremental approach to the development process. While at present data flow languages are used either with data flow architectures or to produce prototypes for von Neumann machines, the EDDA-S approach takes the data flow representation as the starting point for the introduction of a modular structure. In this way the advantages of a modular design (known from the conventional approach) can be complemented by the problem oriented representation using data flow principles.

Due to the mainly functional nature of the data flow representation the module structure of EDDA-S is especially simple and directly serves as the basis for the generation of a program code skeleton to be implemented in some programming language. - Thus a straightforward, structure preserving transition to the implementation phase is achieved.

With our research into EDDA-S we try to follow an evolutionary approach to contribute to the improvement of software development practice.

REFERENCES

/Acke 82/ Ackerman, W. B.: 'Data Flow Languages', in: IEEE-Computer, Feb. 1982, pp. 15-25.

/ADA 80/ *The Programming language ADA*, Reference Manual, Lecture Notes in Computer Science, Vol. 106, Springer Verlag, Berlin, 1981.

/Boeh 81/ Boehm, B. W., *Software Engineering Economics*, Prentice Hall Inc., 1981.

/Back 78/ Backus, J.: 'Can Programming Be Liberated from the von Neumann Style?, A Functional Style and Its Algebra of Programs', in: Communications of the ACM, Vol. 21, No. 8, Aug. 1978, pp. 613-641.

/DeKr 76/ DeRemer, F., Kron, H. H.: 'Programming-in-the-Large-Versus Programming-in-the-Small', Transactions on SE, Vol. SE-2, No. 2, p. 80-86, June 1976.

/DoGo 82/ Downes, V. A. and Goldsack, S. J.: *Programming Embedded Systems with ADA*, Prentice-Hall Inc., 1982.

/Hend 80/ Henderson, P.: *Functional Programming, Application and Implementation*, Prentice-Hall Int., 1980.

/Jack 75/ Jackson M. A.: *Principles of Program Design*, Academic Press, 1975.

/KePi 84/ Kerner, H., Pitrik R.: 'Functional Versus Imperative Programming - Complement or Contradiction?'; in: Cybernetics and Systems Research 2, R. Trappl (ed.), North Holland, 1984.

/Kern 83/ Kerner, H. et al.: 'EDDA, a Very High-Level Dataflow Specification Language', Proc. of the ESA/ESTEC Software Engineering Seminar, Oct. 11-14, 1983, ESTEC, Noordwijk, The Netherlands, 1983.

/Kern 85/ Kerner, H., Pitrik, R., Motschnig, H.: ' EDDA-S, eine graphische, strukturierte Datenflußsprache für den Software-Entwurf', GI/OCG/ÖGI-Jahrestagung 1985, 16.-20. Sept. 1985, Wien, Springer, 1985.

/Pitr 85a/ Pitrik, R.: 'Modularisierung in EDDA', TR 85/02/01, Inst. f. Angew. Informatik und Systemanalyse, TU-Wien, 1985.

/Pitr 85b/ Pitrik, R.: 'The Role of Modularisation in Functional and Conventional Languages', in: 3rd Internat. Workshop on Software Specification and Design, Aug. 26-27, 1985. London, IEEE, 1985.

/Rama 84/ Ramamoorthy, C. V. et al.: ' Software Engineering: Problems and Perspectives', IEEE Computer, Vil. 17, No. 10, Oct. 1984, pp. 191-210.

/Ross 77/ Ross, D. T.: 'Structured Analysis (SA): A Language for Communicating Ideas', in: IEEE Trans. on Software Engineering, Vol. 3, No. 1, 1977.

/TrKe 78/ Trattnig, W., Kerner, H.: 'EDDA, a Very High-Level Programming and Specification Language in the Style of SADT', in: IEEE-CS's Proc. of the 4th Int. Computer Software & Applications Conf., Chicago, Ill., USA, Oct. 29-31, 1980, pp. 436-443.

/ViRa 84/ Vick, C. R.: Ramamoorthy, C. V. (ed.): *Handbook of Software Engineering*, Van Nostrand Reinhold Electrical/Computer Science and Engineering Series, 1984.

/Wirt 82/ Wirth, N.: *Programming in Modula-2*, Springer-Verlag, 1982.

/YoCo 79/ Yourdon, E. and Constantine, L. L.: *Structured Design*, Prentice-Hall Inc., 1979.

A Fast Serial and Parallel Thinning Algorithm

P.S.P. Wang and Y.Y. Zhang
College of Computer Science
Northeastern University
Boston, MA 02115

ABSTRACT. A fast serial and parallel algorithm for thinning digital
patterns is presented. The processing speed is faster than the
algorithms in the literature [3],[4],[9],[12] in that it reads pixels
along the edge of the input pattern rather than all pixels in each
iteration. Using this algorithm an experiment is conducted and the
patterns such as "X","H","A", are tested. The results show that this
algorithm is faster, structure-preservative and more flexible in that
it can be done either sequentially or in parallel.

1. INTRODUCTION

     In dealing with image processing and pattern recognition problems,
it is well known that a binary digitized pattern is defined by a matrix
Q, where each element $q[i,j]$ is either 1 (dark point) or 0 (white point)
and these points are called pixels. "Thinning" is a process that
deletes the dark points and transforms the pattern into "thin" line
drawing known as a skeleton. The thinned pattern must preserve the
basic structure of the original pattern and the connectedness. It
plays a very important role in digital image processing and pattern
recognition since the outcome of thinning can largely determine the
effectiveness and efficiency of extracting the distinctive features
from the patterns. [10],[11]
     There are serial and parallel methods for thinning a digital
pattern. In serial method, the value of a pixel at the n th iteration
depends on the value of itself and the neighbours of the pixel at the
n th iteration. In a parallel processing the value of a pixel at the
n th iteration depends on the values of the pixel and its eight
neighbors at the (n-1) th iteration. Thus all the pixels of the
digital pattern can be thinned simultaneously.
     In the literature [12], a fast parallel algorithm for thinning
digital patterns is proposed. However there are some disadvantages,
such as erosion of diagonal patterns and they are overcome by the
literature [3],[4] and this paper. In the literature [4], the pixel
is flagged when it should be deleted at an iteration. So it is not a

909

R. Trappl (ed.), Cybernetics and Systems '86, 909–915.

parallel thinning algorithm. In this paper, a new serial and parallel algorithm is proposed, which is faster and structure-preservative.

2. BASIC DEFINITIONS AND NOTATIONS

In order to describe the algorithm in this paper, we give some definitions as follows.

Definition 1. The neighbors of a pixel, p:q[i,j], are identified by the eight directions, q[i-1,j], q[i-1,j+1], q[i,j+1], q[i+1,j-1], q[i,j-1], q[i-1,j-1] i.e. p[k],(k=0...8, p[8]=p[0]), shown in Figure 1.

p[7]:q[i-1,j-1]	p[0]:q[i-1,j]	p[1]:q[i-1,j+1]
p[6]: q[i,j-1]	p : q[i,j]	p[2]: q[i,j+1]
p[5]:q[i+1,j-1]	p[4]:q[i+1,j]	p[3]:q[i+1,j+1]

FIGURE 1. Pixel and its neighbors

Definition 2. The contour points of a digital pattern is defined as the set of pixels for which at least one of neighbors is white. In Figure 2. "a", "b",..,"s" are contour points, "t" is not contour point.

Definition 3. We called following (1) and (2) as S-condition
(1): A(p)=1 or C(p)=1;
(2): 1<B(p)<8;
Where A(p) is the number of white to dark transitions when the neighbors are taking a clockwise walk around p (i.e. along the neighbors of paxel p).

$$C(p)=\begin{cases} 1 & p[j-1]=1 \text{ and } p[j+1]=1 \text{ and } p[j]+p[k-1]+p[k]+p[k+1]=0 \\ & (k=1,3;\ j=(k+4) \bmod 8) \\ 0 & \text{otherwise} \end{cases}$$

B(p) is the number of neighbors of p which is not equal to zero. In Figure 2, for pixel "a", according to p[0],p[1],...,p[6], p[7], p[0] order, i.e., 001110000, so A(a)=1. B(a)=3. For pixel "h", according to p[2], p[3],..., p[7],p[0],p[1],p[2] order, i.e. 000110110. So A(h)=2. C(h)=1. B(h)=4.

Definition 4. The pattern of which contour points are connected into a loop is called single loop pattern, otherwise multi-loop pattern. In Appendix, digital pattern (b) is single loop while (a) is multi-loop.

```
        a b          e f
        s * c          * g
          * d      * h
          *    * i
             *
          r * j
          q * k
          p t l
          o n m
```

FIGURE 2. The digit pattern 'Y' and its thinning

910

3. SINGLE LOOP AND SERIAL THINNING

Single loop and serial thinning is the simplest method in our thinning algorithms. Such an algorithm is shown below. First we define the condition 1:
(1) S-condition, or
(2) B(p)=1 (at n_th iteration) and B(p[k])≠1 (before n_th iteration).

Algorithm 1.
Step
  1 : Determining the first contour point and its first neighbor:
      From up to down and left to right. It is called the first contour point if it meets a dark point and its p[0] is called the first neighbor of the first contour point.
  2 : if NOT condition 1 then go to 4 .
  3 : q[i,j]:=0.
  4 : Determining next contour point and its first neighbor:
      For the current contour from its first neighbor according to clockwise order to meet the first "1" of "01" is called the next contour point, and the "0" of "01" is called the first neighbor of next contour point, but if the next contour point is p[t] (t=1,3,5,7) of the current contour point and p[t+1] 0, then the next contour point should change to p[t+1].
  5 : if no contour point is deleted at a loop thinning then exit else go to 2 .
      In Figure 2, "a" is the first contour point for pattern "Y". p[0] of "a" is the first neighbor of the contour "a". The next contour point of "a" is "b". p[1] of "a" is the first neighbor of "b". The next contour point of "m" is "n". The p[5] of "m" is the first neighbor of "n". In Figure 2. "a", "b",...,"t" are deleted in order. The set of start "*" is the result of thinning digital pattern "Y".

4. MULTI-LOOP AND SERIAL THINNING.

It is assumed that m is the loop number of Multi-loop. L(k) (k=1..m) is the identified unit of k loop. If L(k)=1, then the k loop needs to continue thinning. L(k)=0 means that there is no contour point to be deleted. If L(1)=0,...,L(n)=0, then the whole thinning of pattern is terminated. In Algorithm 2, we first test L(k) (1≤k≤M) and see if it is either 1 or 0. If L(k)=0 then no pixel in the k loop can be thinned, jump to next loop. If L(k)=1 then thins k loop: first set L(k) to "0", then test every pixel of this loop to see whether or not it satisfies the condition 1. If it satisfies then delete the contour, set L(k) into "1" and continue thinning until finishing this loop. In Algorithm 2. A1(Q(k)) is a boolean procedure which is to test each contour point and to delete it which satisfies the condition 1 in the k loop. If at least one of the contour points satisfies condition 1 then A1(Q(k))='true', otherwise A1(Q(k))='false'.

Algorithm 2.

Step
```
1 : L(1)=1,...,L(m)=1.
2 : if L(1)+...+L(m)=0 then exit.
3 : for k=1 to m do if L(k)=1 then
    begin L(k):=0;
            if A1(Q(k)) then L(k):=1
    end;
    go to  2 ;
```

5. MULTI-LOOP AND PARALLEL THINNING.

In parallel processing, the value given to a point at n-th thinning depends on the values given to the point and its eight neighbors at the (n-1)-th thinning. The flowchart of algorithm 3 is the same as algorithm 2, except the condition 1 has to change to condition 2 as follows:

1 : odd loop: S-condition and $(p[0]+p[6])*p[2]*p[4]=0$.
2 : even loop: S-condition and $(p[2]+p[4])*p[0]*p[6]=0$.

We can also design single loop and parallel algorithm, by changing condition 1 to condition 2 in algorithm 1.

6. THE RESULTS OF EXPERIMENTS.

To compare the performances of several algorithms (algo.1,algo.2, algo.3 in this paper, algo.NS [4], algo.ZS [12], algo.SR [9]), all algorithms were coded in PASCAL version 2.00 and run on an IBM Personal Computer XT. These algorithms were tested on digital patterns "H" and "A". The units of time taken by these algorithms are shown in Table 1 (the unit is sec.). From Table 1, it is shown that the algorithm 1 is the fastest, but it is only for single loop and serial thinning. From these results, the speed is close when there are fewer pixels. If the number of pixels are increased, the algorithms 1_3 are faster than other algorithms. In Appendix, we show the results of thinning using algorithm 3. It is also shown that the connectedness and the original shape are kept quite well.

pattern	"H"	"A"
algo. 1	7.36	
algo. 2	7.80	8.57
algo. 3	9.56	10.43
algo.ZS	11.59	10.65
algo.NS	12.91	11.25
algo.SR	16.53	14.11

Table 1. The comparision of time
consumed by different thinning
              algorithms.

7. DISCUSSIONS AND CONCLUSIONS.

The algorithm SR is presented by Stefanelli and Rosenfeld as a "simplified version" of Hilditch approach, which is a parallel algorithm. Zhang and Suen presented the algorithm ZS, which is also a parallel algorithm. However, both of them have to overcome the disadvantage found by preserving structures. For example, using algorithm ZS and SR to thin the digital pattern "X", the results are as shown in Figure 3(d) and (e). (Figure 3(a) is the original pattern.) They lose the structures of original pattern. The algorithm NS can almost keep the shape of the original pattern for thinning as shown in Fig.3(c), but sometimes it can not exactly keep the basic structure as shown in Fig.4 and it is not a parallel algorithm as we defined above. In this paper the algorithm we presented can keep the structure of original pattern. It can be used for serial and parallel thinning and the speed is faster.

For future research, it would be interesting and worthwhile to explore thinning algorithms for high-dimensional patterns. Realizing the advantages of our approach, it would also be very interesting to polish, implement and apply this serial and parallel thinning algorithm to a variety of pattern recognition problems including: character recognition, fingerprint recognition, signature verification, medical diagnosis, business application, industrial parts inspection, computer vision and robotics.

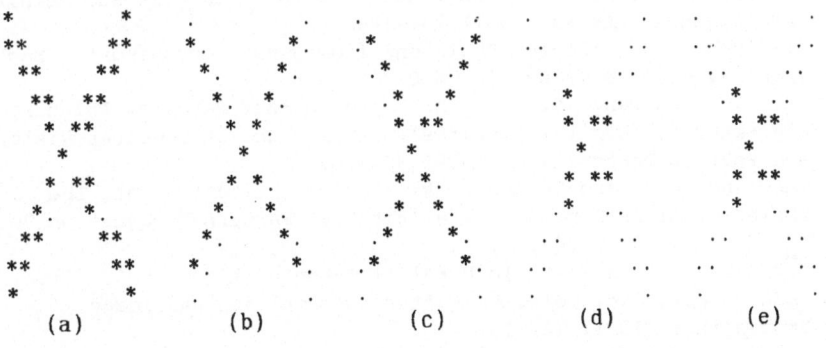

FIGURE 3.Comparing different algorithms for thinning pattern "X".

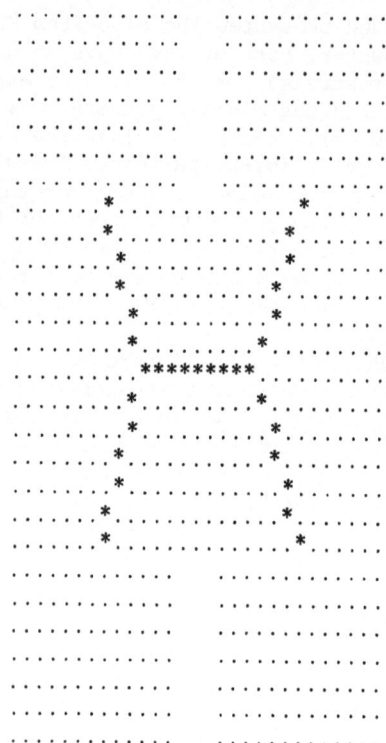

FIGURE 4.   Thinning of the character 'H' using the algorithm NS.

REFERENCES.

1. Arcelli C., Cordella, L.P. and Levialdi, S. 'From Local Maxima to Connected Skeletons'. IEEE Trans. Pattern Analysis and Machine Intelligence, PAMI-3 (1981) 134-143.
2. Hilditch, C.J. 'Linear Skeletons from Square Cupboards'. Machine Intelligence. 4 (1969) 403-420.
3. Lü, H.E. and Wang, P.S.P. 'An Improved Fast Parallel Thinning Algorithm for Digital Patterns'. IEEE Proc. on Computer Vision and Pattern Recognition (1985) 364-367.
4. Naccache, N.J. and Shinghal, R. 'An Investigation into The Skeletonization Approach of Hilditch'. Pattern Recognition Vol. 17. No. 3 (1984) 274-284.
5. Pavlidis, T. 'A Flexible Parallel Thinning Algorithm'. Proc. IEEE Compct. Soc. Conf. on Pattern Recognition and Image Processing. (1981) 162-167.
6. Rahier, M.C. and Jespers, P.G.A. 'Dedicated LSI for A Microprocessor Controlled Hand Carried OCR System'. IEEE Journal of Solid State Circults Vol. SC-15, No. 1 (1980) 15-24.
7. Rosenfeld, 'A Connectivity in Digital Picture' J.ACM 17 (1971) 146-160.

8. Rosenfeld, A. 'A Characterization of Parallel Thinning Algorithm'. Info. Contral 29 (1975) 286-291.

9. Stefanelli, S. and Rosenfeld, A. 'Some Parallel Thinning Algorithms for Digital Patterns'. J.ACM 18 (1971) 255-264.

10. Wang, P.S.P. 'An Application of Array Grammars to Clustering Analysis for Syntactic Patterns'. Pattern Recognition Vol 17, No. 4 (1984) 441-451.

11. Wang, P.S.P. (Ed). Intelligent Systems, Imaging Technology and Software Engineering. Sungkang Computer Book Co. (1984).

12. Zhang, T.Y. and Suen, C.Y. 'A Fast Parallel Algorithm for Thinning Digital Patterns'. CACM 27 (1984) 236-239.

Appendix: Thinning of different digital patterns using the algorithm 3.

(a). The letter "A"

(b). The letter "H"

HIERARCHICAL DYNAMIC DATA STRUCTURE FOR REPRESENTING OPTIMAL ADAPTIVE CONTROLLERS BY ASSEMBLIES

M. de la Sen
Dpto. de Fisica
Facultad de Ciencias
Universidad del País Vasco
Leioa (Vizcaya). Aptdo. 644 de Bilbao. Spain

ABSTRACT. A data structure representing assemblies for optimal adaptive controllers in a database is presented consisting of two parts. The first part is the data structure used to store topological information on each component of the assembly. The second part is the data structure used to store information on how all the components in the assembly are connected.

Optimal Adaptive Controllers for improving the transient performances in adaptive systems require, in general, more than one adaptation level¡ The usual adaptation level which yields as final result the generation of the input to the controlled object and at least, one supervisory level which acts on the free parameters of the adaptive controller (or modifies its standard equations) so as to improve the adaptation transients. Therefore, a tree structure using the concept of "virtual link" is created to represent the relationships between the components in an assembly structure.

INTRODUCTION AND BACKGROUND

Most of researchers in the area of CAD have devoted their work to study individual components. However, in practice, assemblies rather than individual components must be considered. Assemblies are a natural way of performing CAD for certain mechanical problems which have individual components. However, the associated informatic structures can be useful for other designs in which a hierarchical structuration of the actions must be used in a problem topological context. Requicha[1] has used the so-called CSG (constructive solid geometry) for modelling systems. In the CSG data structure, what is stored is the procedure by which an object was created, rather than the information on the final object; namely, the sequence of set operations such as union, difference, and intersection of the primitives is stored. Lieberman[2] and Wesley[3] described a geometric modelling system AUTOPASS, that generates a database in which components and assemblie blies are represented by nodes in a graph structure. The branches of the graph represent connections or relationships among components such as "part of", "attachment", "constraint" and "assembly". Also,

917

R. Trappl (ed.), Cybernetics and Systems '86, 917–923.
© *1986 by D. Reidel Publishing Company.*

for each branch, an associated homogeneous transformation matrix is stored to specify the relative orientation and location of one with respect to the other. The nodes also store physical or key identification properties of an algorithm. The data structure in AUTOPASS is very similar to the CSG representation for a component, i.e., the relationships correspond to the primitives. Lee[4] studies the problem of data structures which require more information such as mating features between components.

The concept of "virtual link" is created in Reference 4 and used to store an assembly composed of many subassemblies in a hierarchy. In this structure, any mating pair of two subassemblies or one subassembly and one component is connected by a virtual link. If more than two components are mutually related, several virtual links can be used so that every pair of mating components occupies one virtual link. This design seems to have some of the suitable properties of the two former ones since one subassembly can be composed of several ones where every pair is connected by a virtual link. In this way, the terminal nodes of an assembly graph will be the components of the assembly, and component data for each component are connected to these terminal nodes. If several identical components appear in an assembly, data for only one component is stored, by using the concept of instance. In this case, virtual links point to the instances rather than the components.

The objective of this work is to present a sistematically organized data structure as a set hierarchically ordered assemblies for the problem of optimal adaptive controllers[5] which improve the transients. The assemblies are related to the external representation of the two adaptation levels namely, that associated with usual adaptive algorithms (i.e., updating of the parameters of the adaptive controller generation of the input to the plant), and the supervisory one[5] which updates the free parameters of the algorithm, by means of iterative optimal techniques, within their stability domain in order to recalculate the adaptive controller parameters so as to improve the adaptation transients. The dynamic modification of the data structure by using the database is also described in the same context. Sequential dynamical lists are implemented related to the data modification of the main assemblies.

ALGORITHM, ARRAYS:THEIR CONTENTS

Let us denote by $<x,y>$ the inner product of x and y. Given the difference equation $x_{t+1} = A_t x_t + b_t u_t$, $t \geq 0$ and the Hamiltonian $H \hat{=} p_0 + <p_t, A_t x_k> + <p_t, b_t u_t>$, an iterative technique[7] to find the optimal input sequence $\{u_t\}$ on $[0,N]$ with $x_0 \neq 0$ is

0. Set $k=0$

1. Set $u_{tk}=0$, and solve for $x_{kN} = \prod_{t=0}^{N-1} [A_t] x_0$ (assumed $\neq 0$)

2. Find $\bar{x}_{kN} = \prod_{t=0}^{N-1} [A_t] x_0 + \sum_{t=0}^{N-1} \prod_{i=t}^{N-1} [A_{i+1}] b_t \bar{u}_{kt}$, where $\bar{u}_{kt}$ mini-

mizes $< c_{kt}, u_t > = < \prod_{t=0}^{N-1} [A_t]b_t \, u_t, \, x_0 N^{-z} >$

- <u>Define</u> $w_k(t) = \bar{x}_k(t) - x_k(t)$; $y_k(t) = x_k(t) - z$

3. <u>Choose</u> $\lambda_{kt} = sat \, (-< y_t, \, Q \, w_t > / < w_t, \, Q \, w_t >)$
   (where sat $(\gamma) = \gamma$ if $|\gamma| \leq 1$, and sgn (γ), otherwise)
4. <u>Compute</u> $x_{(k+1)} = (1 - \lambda_{kt}) \, x_{kt} + \lambda_{kt} \, \bar{x}_{kt}(t)$

5. <u>Do</u> $t \longleftarrow t+1$ and <u>go to</u> 2 <u>until</u> $t = N+1$
6. <u>Do</u> $k \longleftarrow k+1$ and <u>go to</u> 2 <u>until</u> $\lambda_{kN} = 0$

    The application to adaptive control is made by using two asemblies. The Assembly 1 is the basic adaptive algorithm and the Assembly 2 is the optimization of the free parameter at a second hierarchical level. The horizon size is time-varying and finite. It slide as time increases. For ezh sampling point k, one uses the horizon[5] $[k-N_{1k}, \, k+N_{2k}] = \underbrace{[k-N_{1k}, \, k)}_{\substack{\text{correction} \\ \text{horizon}}} \cup \underbrace{[k, \, k+N_{2k}]}_{\substack{\text{prediction} \\ \text{horizon}}}$

Level 1 (Assembly 1)
    A standard adaptive algorithm[5] is

$$\hat{\theta}(t) = \hat{\theta}(t-1) + \frac{a(t) \, \phi(t-d)[y(t) - < \phi(t-1) \, \phi(t-d) >]}{1 + < \phi(t-d), \, \phi(t-d) >} = \begin{bmatrix} \hat{b}_0(t) \\ \hat{\theta}_0(t) \end{bmatrix}$$

where $\hat{\theta}(.)$ is the adaptive controller parameter whose dimension depends with upperblunds of the controlled object, $\phi(t-d)$ is a finite sequence of inputs $u(.)$ and $y(.)$ which is called the measurement vector, and $a(t)$ is the free algorithm parameter which leads to convergence if $0 < a(t) < 2$, $\forall t \geq 0$.

Level 2 (Assembly 2)
    Its function is to select one free AP (algorithm parameter, i. e., $a(t)$) such as the adaptation transient performances. As intermediate step, one derives the equivalent system for the used adaptive algorithm which is quasilinear and which approximately describes the reflection of the local variations of the "a priori" AP on the tracking error sequence. Its optimal solution is translated in iterative AP "a posteriori" modifications.
$y^*(t)$ is the reference sequence, $\tilde{\theta}(t) = \theta$ (the true parameter vector) $- \hat{\theta}(t)$

1. Modeling of the ES; $x(t) \triangleq \epsilon(t+d) = y(t+d) - y^*(t+d) = x(t-1) + b(t-1)$
   $\tilde{u}(t-1) + w(t-1)$, $\forall t \in [j - N_{1j}, \, j + N_{2j}]$, $\forall j \geq N_{1j} \geq 0$

    1.a. $b(t-1) \triangleq - < \tilde{\theta}(t-1), \, b_0 \, \phi(t-d) > \triangle \alpha(t)$
    1.b. $w(t-1) \triangleq - < \tilde{\theta}(t-1), \, b_0 \, \phi(t-d) > \alpha_0(t) + < \tilde{\theta}(t-1), \, b_0 \, \phi(t) >$

    1.c. $\alpha(t) \triangleq a(t) \frac{< \phi(t-d), \, \phi(t) >}{1 + < \phi(t-d), \, \phi(t-d) >} = \alpha_0(t) + \triangle \alpha(t) \, \tilde{u}(t-1)$

    $\alpha_1(t)$ if $\tilde{u}(t-1) = -1$, $\alpha_2(t)$ if $\tilde{u}(t-1) = +1$, $\alpha \in (\alpha_1, \, \alpha_2)$ if $|\tilde{u}| < 1$

2. Compute $\tilde{u}_{(.)}(.)$ from the iterative procedure $\forall\ t\in[j-N_{1j},\ j+N_2]$;

$\forall\ j\geqslant N_1$

3. Compute $a^P(t)\longleftarrow 1+\dfrac{<\phi(t),\ \phi(t-d)>}{<\phi(t-d),\ \phi(t-d)>}(\alpha_o(t)+\Delta\alpha(t)\ \tilde{u}(t-1))$

4. Do $k\longleftarrow k+1$

5. Estimate interactively 5a, 5b below

5a: $y(t)$, $\forall\ t\in[j,\ j+N_2]$ from one prediction method[5] (For instance $y(t+1)\longleftarrow y(t)+\dfrac{y(t)-y(t-1)}{T}$ (T: sampling period. This is

the so-called heuristic prediction method which uses Taylor series expansions using finite differences).

5b. $u(t)\longleftarrow \hat{b}_o^{-1}(t)\ [y^*(t+d)-<\hat{\theta}_o(t),\ \phi_o(t)>]$; $\forall\ t\in[j,\ j+N_2]$

6. **While** $k\leq k_{max}$, **go to** step 1 (This corresponds from a realistic point of view in adaptive control to the requirement that $\lambda_k\rightarrow 0$ in the basic iterative scheme).

7. Generate the (really applied) input to the plant

$u(j)=\hat{b}_o^{-1}(j)\ [y^*(j+d)-<\hat{\theta}_o(j),\ \phi_o(j)>]$

8. Do $k\longleftarrow 0$ (iteration index), $j\longleftarrow j+1$ (action of sliding the horizon) and **go to** step 1.

The organization of the arrays and their contents is now described

ASSEMBLY

- Name of the assembly
    * Assembly 0 $\longleftrightarrow$ whole algorithm
    * Assembly 1 $\longleftrightarrow$ Level 1: adaptation algorithm
    * Assembly 2 $\longleftrightarrow$ Level 2: iterative optimization
- Pointer to the first virtual link of the inmediate lower level:
    * Pointers from Assembly i to Assembly j; i=0,1; j⩾i (Data from Assembly 0 to Assemblies 1-2, and results of the actual adaptation state to the optimization procedure). Data ≡ output measurements) generated input values.

VIRTUAL LINK

- Pointer to the next virtual link
    * In Assembly 0, ϕ
    * In Assembly 1. Pointer $j\longrightarrow j+1$ (the next optimization horizon)
    * In Assembly 2. Pointer to $j-N_{1j}$ (the bottom of the next optimization procedure once the horizon is slided).
- Pointer to an assembly or a subassembly of the inmediate upper level
    * Pointers to test subassemblies (adapting?, optimizing?, chan-

ging AP or iterative method?)
* Pointers from Assembly 2 to Assembly 1 (to reaply the iterative procedure by modifying the ES parameters) and from Assem
bly 1 to Assembly 0, to transfer results (input the plant, and
and evaluation of the system registered performances to the
human or automatic superviser).
* Number of records of Assembly 1 (length of the optimization
horizon) related to the virtual link.
* Number of records of Assembly 2 (number of iterative optimization pass) related to the virtual link.
- Pointer to the other components or subassemblies of the pair
   * Pointer from a virtual link Assembly 1 ⟶ Subassembly 11 (≙
   pointer to the current presiction method) and to subassembly
   14 (≙ receding the prediction horizon).
   * Pointer from a virtual link Assembly 1 ⟶ Subassembly 12 (=
   pointer to the current AP, if more than one).
   * Pointer from a virtual link of Assembly 1 ⟶ Subassembly 13
   (parameterization of the ES).
   * Pointer from Assembly 2 ⟶ Subassembly 21 (=pointer to tthe
   current iterative method if more than one).
   * Pointer from Assembly 2 ⟶ Subassembly 31 (= pointer to the
   translation optimal equivalent input ⟶ AP-modification).

Remark
      The subassembly of receding the horizon has forbbiden zones as
excessive lengths according to the order of the plant or the computing time / storage requirements. The same occurs for the AP values leading to instability contained in the AP value. This makes
some possible structures to be forbidden by sparse parts of the corresponding transformation matrices .

SUBASSEMBLY

- Name of Subassembly: (11);(12); (13); (14); (21); (11α = prediction methods; α =1,...; 12β = AP s; β =1,...). Test subassemblies
(adapt, optimize, etc., Bad performance results. slide the hori-
zon directly). Subassemblies for specific tasks receding the prediction horizon, computation of the predicted measurements, trans
lation optimal equivalent input ⟶ AP - modification).
- Pointer to subassembly of the inmediate upper-level from (i j_i)
to i; i=1,3; j_1=1,2 and 4; j_2=1, j_3=1
- Pointer to the first virtual link of the inmediate lower level.
From the prediction method Subassembly (11α) and parameterization of the ES Subassembly (13) to virtual link of Assembly 2
and to Subassembly (14) of receding the horizon).
- Store the derived transformation from the assembly or the subassembly of immediate upper level (Subassemblies (11), (12), (13),
(14), (2/31)) or the corresponding data (the remaining ones).

921

MATING-FEATURE

- Type of mating (1. adapting, 2. optimizing, 3. sliding, 4. changing the AP; 5. changing the iterative method).
- Mating feature (adapting or optimizing, adapting or sliding the horizon; changing or not the AP; changing or not the iterative method).
- Clearance between mating features is given by the order in the use of the virtual links.

Remarks

(1) Each assembly can be automatically updated for modifications in the size of any component in the assembly without modifuing explicity the transformation. For instance, the number of records of the Assemblies 1-2 together with the structural links between Assemblies ──➤ Assemblies, Subassemblies (leading to transformation matrices) automatically modifies the corresponding sizes.

(2) The structures presented only distinguish predictions from real measurements at the subassembly (11α) ≙ prediction method (i.e., either it predicts measurements on the corresponding subhorizon or it acquires real measurements and stores them in the corresponding memory addresses). The remaining structures manipulate predictions and real measurements in a similar way.

(3) Assemblies and subassemblies contain in this case the programmes and intermediate and final data corresponding to specific subrou‾tines or the coordination mechanism. That is, the associate data structure with sets of assemblies / subassemblies have been applied to dynamic informatic structures (i.e., execution of interconnected tasks within a hierarchical context).

(4) The lists associated with each problem (optimization, adaptation translation optimization ──➤ modification of the free parameters) are sequentially organized with links pointing to the next memory positions[+]

CONCLUSIONS

The data structure described in this paper for adaptive controllers with improved characteristics has the following characteristics. It derives transformation matrices between hierarchical structures from mating feature information between the topological sequen-

[+] Assembly 1 uses a circular list (pointer of the last position to the first position. Last position losses information when sliding the horizon and new information is put in this position) Assembly 2 and subassembly (31) are developed in usual linked which are destroyed when the horizon is slided. This structure is not expensive in storage requirements.

ce of actions in the real-time or simulation problem; Dynamic s-
tructures (execution of an algorithm) can be manipulated. The struc
tures stores only possible assemblies. Structures which are not compatible are delected and rejected.

REFERENCES

1. Requicha, A. A. G. "Representations for rigid solids: Theory, methods and systems" ACM Comput. Surv., Vol 12, No. A (December
   1980)

2. Lieberman, L.I, and Wesley, M. A. "AUTOPASS; an automatic program system for computer controlled mechanical assembly, IBM J.
   Res. Dev. (July 1977) pp. 321-333.

3. Wesley, M. A, Lozano-Perez, T, Lieberman, L.I., Lavin, M.A. and
   Grossman, C.D. "A geometric modelling system for automated mechanical assembly" IBM J. Res. Dev., Vol. 24 No.1 (January 1980)
   pp. 64-74 .

4. Lee, K and Gossard, D.C. "A hierarchical data structure for representing assemblies: part 1" Comput. Aided Des., Vol. 17,
   No. 1 (Jan, Feb. 1984), pp. 15-19.

5. De la Sen, M. "A simple method to improve the transients in adap
   tive systems" Proc. IEEE, Vol. 72, No. 1 (1984) pp . 131-134.

6. Wegner, P "Programming languages, information structures, and
   machine organization, McGraw-Hill, New York, USA (1968).

7. Plant, J. B. Some iterative solution in optimal control Research
   Monograph No. 44, M.I.T. Press, "assachusetts (1968).

AUTHOR INDEX